# COMPLETE PELICAN SHAKESPEARE

## THE HISTORIES AND THE NON-DRAMATIC POETRY

# COMPLETE PELICAN

# SHAKESPEARE

## THE HISTORIES AND
## THE NON-DRAMATIC
## POETRY

GENERAL EDITOR ALFRED HARBAGE

PENGUIN BOOKS

*Penguin Books Ltd, Harmondsworth, Middlesex, England*
*Penguin Books, 625 Madison Avenue, New York, New York 10022, U.S.A.*
*Penguin Books Australia Ltd, Ringwood, Victoria, Australia*
*Penguin Books Canada Ltd, 2801 John Street, Markham, Ontario, Canada L3R 1B4*
*Penguin Books ( N.Z.) Ltd, 182–190 Wairau Road, Auckland 10, New Zealand*

*The Pelican text published in thirty-eight volumes between 1956 and 1967*
*Revised edition first published in one volume by Penguin Books Inc. 1969*
*Reprinted 1969, 1970 (twice), 1972, 1974, 1975*
*This three-volume edition first published by Penguin Books 1981*

*Designed by Hans Schmoller, R.D.I.*

*Made and printed in Great Britain by Butler & Tanner Ltd,*
*Frome and London*

# TABLE OF CONTENTS

## THE HISTORIES

## THE NON-DRAMATIC POETRY

# THE HISTORIES

# FOREWORD

**A**lthough history has been dramatized at many times, the history play as a distinctive genre is uniquely Elizabethan. It was a purely popular type, never appearing in the select "private" theatres as distinct from the large arenas, and its life span was little more than fifteen years : only isolated examples fall outside the period 1589–1604. Entries in the *Stationers' Register* and the titles of plays issued in quarto let us trace the increasing awareness of its separate identity. At first the term "history" was most often applied to some comic or romantic stage fiction, while plays treating actual past events were issued under a variety of labels such as "Reign of," "Contention of," "Life and Death of," and, especially, "Tragedy of." Shakespeare's *3 Henry VI, Richard III,* and *Richard II* were all originally published as "tragedies." However, a few years later, his *1 Henry IV* and *Henry V* were published as "histories," and the term began to appear in the classifications mentioned above in the foreword to the comedies. Shakespeare not only excelled in this genre ; he, more than anyone else, created it. Although there had been earlier intimations of its appearance, the only actual examples that can be plausibly dated before Shakespeare's *Henry VI* plays are *The Troublesome Reign of King John* and *The Famous Victories of Henry V,* and there is some doubt even about these. It used to be thought that Marlowe's *Edward II* pointed Shakespeare the way, but it now appears likely that the indebtedness was the other way round.

The type emerged ca. 1587–90 amidst a theatrical brood which may be described in general as "documentaries." Biblical history had been dramatized for centuries, and when the commercial theatre burgeoned in London it was natural that the playwrights should exploit historical and biographical accounts, Roman, Persian, Turkish, ancient British, and so on. Why it was that only plays about native kings, and those since the Norman Conquest, should have come to be thought of as "histories" is an interesting question. The stories of Lear, Macbeth, and Cymbeline, as well as those of John, the Richards, and the Henrys appear in Holinshed's *Chronicles.* The stories of Caesar, Antony, and Coriolanus are just as "historical" as those of the English kings. Externally there is little distinction between Shakespeare's treatment of English and Roman history. There are the same broad canvases teeming with national figures, the same telescoping of actual events, the same interplay of personal and political forces, the same arbitrements upon the field of battle, and, at least in some of the plays on English history, the same tragic end for the titular characters. Nevertheless the editors of the folio made the separation as a matter of course. Plays previously published as "tragedies" like *Richard III* and *Richard II* were grouped with the histories while plays previously published as "histories" such as *Titus Andronicus, King Lear,* and *Troilus and Cressida* were grouped with the Roman plays and others as tragedies.

The critical consensus is that the distinction made was not a superficial one based merely upon subject matter. The history play is distinct because the inescapable relevance of its subject matter exerted a shaping influence. Nashe praised *1 Henry VI* as a "reproofe to these degenerate effeminate dayes of ours," and Heywood exclaimed, "What English blood, seeing the person of any bold Englishman presented, and doth not hugge his fame and hunnye at his valor . . . !" Authors and audience had a personal stake in such drama, which was bound to arouse emotions of pride and solicitude, and which inevitably attached to itself the function of providing inspiration and admonition. The characters alter from play to play but the protagonist remains the same : England. No corresponding entity appears in the Roman, Turkish, and other "historical" plays. This does not mean that, in the histories, Shakespeare sacrificed art to propaganda. There is more objectivity, subtlety, and suspension of issues than we have any right to expect, not to mention the rich vein of pure entertainment, but it does mean that he expressed in these plays certain attitudes and ideals born of the past national experience and the present national situation. What these attitudes and ideals were is explained elsewhere in this volume, in the General Introduction and in the introductions to the plays themselves.

In the folio the histories are arranged in the order of the reigns they treat. The eight from *Richard II* to *Richard III* provide a synoptic view of the crucial period from 1398 to 1485 when modern England was being born. We witness the dynastic struggle between the houses of York and Lancaster (the "Wars of the Roses"), stemming from the deposition of Richard Plantagenet by Henry Bolingbroke, and ending on Bosworth Field with the ascendance of the first Tudor monarch, Henry VII. The two additional plays have been called "prologue" and "epilogue" to the series, *King John* because it provides an early thirteenth-century preview of the evils of civil war, and *Henry VIII* because it provides an early sixteenth-century demonstration of the Tudor success in establishing national unity, symbolized in the birth of Princess Elizabeth. (A genealogical chart appended to *3 Henry VI* traces the lines of the leaders in the eight central plays.)

Although something is to be said for the folio arrangement, it has not been followed in the present edition. We are interested in the plays as literature rather than history, and an arrangement in order of composition suggests something about Shakespeare's development as a literary artist. The histories offer an especially good opportunity, because it so happens that we are pretty certain of their order and of the fact that each play as we have it represents the author's abilities in the year to which it is assigned. It is possible that *1 Henry VI* was written or revised a little later than *2 & 3 Henry VI*, but the possibility scarcely affects the above generalization. The Jack Cade scenes in *2 Henry VI* prove that Shakespeare's comic talents ripened early and that he was able to burlesque rebellion as well in 1592 as he was in 1611 (in *The Tempest*). As we proceed from *Richard III* to *Richard II,* both good but good in strikingly different ways, we see the poet-dramatist come into his own. It should be added that neither a chronological arrangement, nor our interest in the history play as a type, should mislead us into viewing the plays merely in terms of each other. Except possibly for the *Henry VI* group, each is radically different from the rest. As with the comedies, a variety of elements is successfully fused in a variety of ways. If we focus our attention upon Henry, Hal, and Falstaff in *1 Henry IV,* "historical-comical" seems an apt label, but Hotspur is in it too – and a strand of the "tragical." Most conspicuously absent from the histories is romantic love-interest, the "pastoral," but in *Henry V* there is even a trace of that.

A. H.

# THE FIRST PART OF
# KING HENRY THE SIXTH

## INTRODUCTION

*The First Part of King Henry the Sixth* is a play about the outbreak of civil war. As the first in a four-play series depicting the Wars of the Roses, it is naturally concerned with causes of that conflict. Its dominant note is helpless anxiety. The prevailing metaphors are of disharmony, in the cosmos, the kingdom, the family, and the individual. Foreboding comets and "bad revolting stars" signify the death of Henry V and the misrule of his son. Planetary omens threaten the English, seem to favor the French. Other pervasive metaphors of discord are drawn from fire, disease, and grim personifications of Death. The kingdom is portrayed as a rebellious family wherein uncle turns against nephew, wife against husband, cousin against cousin.

As the Duke of Exeter informs us in choral soliloquy, the meaning of the play is plain, didactic, and sobering:

> no simple man that sees
> This jarring discord of nobility,
> This shouldering of each other in the court,
> This factious bandying of their favorites,
> But that it doth presage some ill event.
> 'Tis much when sceptres are in children's hands,
> But more when envy breeds unkind division.
> There comes the ruin, there begins confusion.
>
> IV, i, 187–94

Shakespeare's theme, as in his later tetralogy from *Richard II* to *Henry V*, stresses the need for orthodox succession to the throne. The idea was a commonplace, readily apparent in Shakespeare's chief sources, the chronicles of Hall, Fabyan, and Holinshed. Nevertheless the dramatic treatment is characteristically Shakespearean even in this early play. Henry VI, like his predecessor Richard II, is presented as an immature king surrounded by ambitious kinsmen. Worse still in view of the Elizabethan concern for secure dynasty, Henry's claim to the throne is uncertain because of the usurpation of power by his grandfather, Henry IV (Bolingbroke). From this genealogical uncertainty arise the factions of Lancaster and York. The confrontation of these two houses gives unity and balance to a portrait of political chaos.

Scenes of confrontation abound, and characters usually appear in contrasting pairs. One such grouping pits the Bishop of Winchester against Humphrey, Duke of Gloucester. Winchester is the illegitimate great-uncle of the king, a man of thwarted ambition plotting against his legitimately born relatives who rule. As a priest he is wholly corrupt and hypocritical, neglecting pastoral duties, flaunting elegant robes, and buying political power with his exorbitant income derived in part from houses of prostitution. Humphrey is uncle to the king and Protector during Henry's minority, doing his best to uphold civil order. Shakespeare's sympathies are undisguised. The power of the Catholic Church opposes that of the state; the priest's tawny coats openly defy the authority of the Protector's blue coats. The good Humphrey is powerless in time of civil unrest to prevent continual ecclesiastical scheming.

The parallel confrontation of the Duke of Somerset and Richard Plantagenet gives rise to the dynastic names of Lancaster and York. Somerset, an ally of Winchester and the wily Earl of Suffolk, is head of the "Lancastrian" party not out of loyalty to King Henry VI (who inherited the title of Lancaster from his great-grandfather, John of Gaunt) but out of factious envy of Richard and a desire to rule the king and realm for his own benefit. Shakespeare does not wish to give the impression, however, that the Lancastrians alone are in the wrong. Richard Plantagenet is also an opportunist, albeit with an understandable motive. He claims a right of succession from Edward III superior to the claim of his kinsman Henry VI. He is a man of political sagacity, tact, bravery, and honor. His dying uncle Mortimer and his father the Earl of Cambridge appear to have been persecuted by the Lancastrian kings because of the Yorkist claim. The virtuous Humphrey supports Richard against the taunts of Somerset. Richard deserves at least to be restored to his lost title of York, like the wronged Bolingbroke in the first act of *Richard II*. But, again like Bolingbroke, how much greater power will Richard seek once his ambition is aroused? Shakespeare's fascination with this question produces the most subtle characterization in this early play. Richard has learned the art of silence while still seeking support, but he confides that his silences are deliberately deceptive. He almost flares into speech when King Henry chooses to wear the red rose of Lancaster at his coronation, but mutters instead: "An if I wist he did – But let it rest. / Other affairs must now be managèd." The choric Exeter in soliloquy interprets the ominously unfinished sentence:

> Well didst thou, Richard, to suppress thy voice;
> For, had the passions of thy heart burst out,
> I fear we should have seen deciphered there
> More rancorous spite, more furious raging broils,
> Than yet can be imagined or supposed.
>
> IV, i, 182–86

Shakespeare gives us a vivid premonition of his first fully developed villain: Richard Plantagenet's son and namesake, who was to become Richard III.

Civil conflict is imminent because unscrupulous men of both parties are taking advantage of a weak child king. The play does not, however, portray the wars at home. The actual military encounters take place in France rather than in England. The subject is not civil butchery, but the loss of England's greatness abroad owing to division at home:

> Amongst the soldiers this is mutterèd,
> That here you maintain several factions,
> And whilst a field should be dispatched and fought
> You are disputing of your generals.
>
> I, i, 70–73

Throughout the play the action alternates between the English court and the French campaign. Scenes in France are often comic, especially in portraying Joan of Arc and her lover the Dauphin. The depraved portrait of Joan, founded upon English conceptions current in Shakespeare's time, may be distasteful to modern sensibilities but it is dramatically useful. It suggests that France triumphs in England's weakness, not in her own strength. Shakespeare is able to have it both ways: to affirm the natural superiority of Englishmen to the effete and unprincipled French, and at the same time to explain the downfall of the English armies.

Moreover, Joan's devil-worship, profligacy, and brazen falsehood echo similar corruptions among the factious English at home. Even Humphrey's wife, Eleanor, is guilty of trafficking with evil spirits in the next play of the sequence, *2 Henry VI*. Suffolk's machinations with Margaret of Anjou or Winchester's exploitation of houses of prostitution are scarcely more defensible than Joan's wantonness. And even Joan cannot outface Winchester in hypocrisy. In any case Joan is captured and led to execution; Winchester prospers as a disloyal ambassador, concluding a peace with France at the very moment the English are winning and could take all. The infection at home is more disastrous than the exterior threat of French force.

Most significant is the parallel of the great leaders who are victimized on these two fronts: Humphrey the Protector, and Lord Talbot the English general. They are both in the right, urging political stability, an end to quarrelling, united action against the French. Such voices of moderation and national purpose are destined to be silenced by hysteria, self-serving, and vacillation. Other well-intentioned men join Talbot and Humphrey: the Duke of Bedford, the Earl of Salisbury, Lucy, Glansdale, Gargrave. They die bravely but for a lost cause, while Sir John Falstaff saves his life with dishonor and loss of a battle. Like his more famous namesake, this Falstaff counsels discretion as the better part of valor. In this early play, however, such advice lacks humorous awareness of the ironic complexities of "honor." This Falstaff is a simple coward and traitor. War against the French is sanctioned by divine right and national destiny as in *Henry V*. Talbot is a national hero betrayed, not a Hotspur or Troilus entrapped by an outmoded and idealistic code of chivalry. If this French war is absurd, it is so not for ambiguity of cause but for inadequacy of political leadership.

The victim who must bear the weight of political betrayal is Lord Talbot – "bought and sold Lord Talbot," "ringed about with bold adversity," who "Drops bloody sweat from his war-wearied limbs." He is indeed a soldier of Christ, radiant and cheerful in death, forgiving toward his enemies, more concerned for his son than for himself. He is above all triumphant over Death – not merely his own, but the personified figure who would reap a harvest of misery from man's fallen condition:

> Thou antic Death, which laugh'st us here to scorn,
> Anon, from thy insulting tyranny,
> Coupled in bonds of perpetuity,
> Two Talbots, wingèd through the lither sky,
> In thy despite shall scape mortality.
>
> IV, vii, 18–22

The image of Daedalus and Icarus escaping the Cretan labyrinth, and the explicitly Christian image of resurrection, combine to produce triumph at the moment of ultimate meaninglessness. Father and son are rejoined in everlasting harmony. The right relation of the family has been preserved.

Shakespeare may be forgiven if, in his effort to counterbalance his stark theme, he overstates the character of Talbot. The general is superhuman in life as in death. In his first appearance he tells Salisbury how he had held off a troop of armed French with his bare hands, "And with my nails digged stones out of the ground / To hurl at the beholders of my shame." He would like to take vengeance on Falstaff with "bare fists." He is reputed to twist bars of steel. He is Samson among the Philistines but without Samson's earlier weakness for women. In fact the light-hearted episode with the Countess of Auvergne reveals the temperate ideal in the relation of the sexes. Talbot is as Mars should be with Venus: witty, debonair, courteous yet wary, supremely masculine and rational, fair-minded in victory. As such he is implicitly contrasted with the frail, uxorious King Henry.

Indeed, Talbot is the standard of patriotic right reason by which Shakespeare measures the decline in other characters. Talbot is the embodiment of firmness and yet fair play toward the French. By his wit and friendly courtesy he wins the allegiance of the Countess of Auvergne, who had hoped to destroy him as an enemy. Anticipating Shakespeare's later portrait of Henry V, Talbot forbids his men to pillage the French countryside. His methods of siege are just though rigorous, publicized and infallible so that his enemies know what they can expect and how they can avoid it by timely surrender. Talbot demonstrates also the temperate ideal of man's quest for earthly fame – an underlying theme of major consequence in this didactic play. Neither unscrupulous in personal ambition like Winchester and York, nor timorous in commitment to the right cause like Henry VI, Talbot and his virtuous son are concerned that their name be remembered forever as a synonym for valor. This fame, along with their achieving heaven, compensates for the seeming injustice of their deaths. Yet Talbot is denied the sort of tragic experience in which a man discovers a causal relationship between his character and his fate. No flaw exists in Talbot to produce his fate. He is victimized rather than self-destroyed. *The First Part of King Henry the Sixth* is not even his play; it ends not tragically but anticlimactically.

The contrast between Talbot and Henry is instructive. Henry is in part a victim, too. He has been forced to accept leadership in a world he did not make, a leadership for which he is woefully unprepared. He starts with the finest intentions. He occupies the impartial ground of regal authority, aided by the wise Protector Humphrey. He attempts not to choose sides in the squabbles of Lancaster and York. Yet in his vacillation he becomes an appeaser rather than a moderator. Presumably in the interest of being "fair" to both sides, he gives Somerset and York equal but divided authority in France. This decision costs the life of Talbot. Henry lacks insight to fathom the motives of his peers, and so commissions the untrustworthy Winchester to make peace with France when the English could in fact have won.

Such a pathetic figure has no claim to tragic stature. Yet in many ways the play, as its title suggests, is his. He is the pivot of all the antagonisms, the pawn of destiny, the weakling Everyman unable to distinguish Good Counsel from Evil Counsel. He takes on broadly representative characteristics in England's secular soul struggle, becoming the human symbol of England divided against herself. The uninterrupted decline of such a generic figure is intentionally distressing. Inclined at first to follow the counsel of Humphrey, Henry is at last the tool of Somerset and Suffolk. His decisions are no longer ignorantly misdirected, but willful. Ultimately we see him afflicted with unreal passion for a domineering woman he has never seen (Margaret of Anjou), surrendering control of himself in a trite simile of mocking epic grandeur :

> And like as rigor of tempestuous gusts
> Provokes the mightiest hulk against the tide,
> So am I driven by breath of her renown
> Either to suffer shipwrack or arrive
> Where I may have fruition of her love.
>
> V, v, 5–9

Only such a tyranny of will over reason can explain Henry's refusal of a far more prudent match already contracted by Humphrey's means. Henry voids his solemn oath, refuses a dowry and a political alliance of great advantage, turns loose two of the best territories in France, and authorizes Suffolk to levy a ruinous tax on the English – all to satisfy a whim of the flesh.

Structural, thematic, and metaphoric unity argue for Shakespeare's authorship of the whole play. Until recently, however, scholars have been reluctant to accord the play firm status in the canon. Theories of multiple authorship have assigned portions of the text to Greene, Marlowe, Nashe, Peele, or Lodge, and have recognized Shakespeare's hand only in such scenes as the Temple garden quarrel (II, iv), the death of Mortimer (II, v), the death of Talbot (IV, ii–vii), and Suffolk's wooing of Margaret (V, iii). The unreliable criteria for such disintegration are chiefly those of "taste" and style. Nineteenth-century critics in particular found repellent the treatment of Joan of Arc and declared it unworthy of Shakespeare's genius. Although unable to concur as to which parts belong to whom, the disintegrators have pointed out verbal similarities to writings of Shakespeare's contemporaries as evidence of multiple authorship. Numerous irregularities of verse and contradictions in fact (e.g., in I, iii the Bishop of Winchester wears a "broad cardinal's hat" whereas in V, i he has just been "called unto a cardinal's degree") have been offered as signs of revision. The hypothesis alleges that young Shakespeare was employed as a journeyman mender of an old play, and that Heminge and Condell included it in the first folio because Shakespeare had made a slight contribution or because they needed it to fill out the Lancastrian cycle of plays. The theory is by no means dead but is now largely discredited. Shakespeare himself may have committed some errors in this early play ; other errors may be due to his reliance on chronicle sources or to transcription.

Equally vexed is the question of order of composition among the three parts of *Henry VI.* Part One was registered for printing in the first folio as "The thirde parte of Henry ye Sixt." This odd numbering seems to imply later composition, but may simply reflect the fact that Parts Two and Three had appeared in print years before (as pirated quartos) and so were already registered. Nevertheless, scholars have argued from internal evidence that Part One was adapted to conform with Parts Two and Three, and that the Suffolk–Margaret episode in particular is an afterthought intended as a transition to Part Two. Against this hypothesis evidence has been offered that the bad quartos of Parts Two and Three recollect important portions of Part One, including alleged alterations like the Margaret–Suffolk scenes. Furthermore, in theme the ending of the play is not an unconnected new episode but a melancholy fulfillment of Exeter's prophecies. It now seems possible that Shakespeare wrote all parts of *Henry VI* in normal chronological order. If this view prevails, scholarship will have returned full circle to the position of Dr Johnson in 1765, who gave all of *Henry VI* to Shakespeare and observed of Part Two, "It is apparent that this play begins where the former ends, and continues the series of transactions, of which it presupposes the first part already known. This is sufficient proof that the second and third parts were not written without dependence on the first."

If *The First Part of King Henry the Sixth* was written before Parts Two and Three, it was early indeed and of momentous importance in the history of the Elizabethan chronicle play. Unless there was a rival play on Talbot of which we know nothing – and this seems unlikely – Shakespeare's play was in existence by August, 1592, when Nashe's *Pierce Penilesse* eloquently praised the spectacle of Lord Talbot :

How would it have joyed brave Talbot (the terror of the French) to think that after he had lain two hundred years in his tomb he should triumph again on the stage, and have his bones new embalmed with the tears of ten thousand spectators at least (at several times) who, in the tragedian that represents his person, imagine they behold him fresh bleeding.

As a tremendous stage success capitalizing on feelings of national pride in the aftermath of the Armada (July, 1588), the play must have done much to set the vogue in a new genre only clumsily explored by the earlier anonymous *Famous Victories of Henry V.* Shakespeare was evidently a pioneer as well as perfector of the English chronicle play. His *Henry VI* plays almost certainly preceded and influenced Marlowe's *Edward II.*

The play, to be sure, is a work more of promise than perfection. Aside from Richard Plantagenet and Henry, its characters are simplified heroes or villains. The language is declamatory, the examination of character external and public, the political commentary overtly didactic. Patterns of structural balancing reveal the young artist questing for the certainties of controlling form. Verbal ingenuity, and such staging gymnastics as sieges or scaling operations, suggest intoxication with a new medium. Nevertheless, these extravagances are part of the play's appeal, like the vigor, the dramatic variety, the full panoply, the moral zeal investing Talbot's triumph and death. As Nashe testifies, Shakespeare's audience responded instinctively to a new genius of the stage.

*University of Chicago*      DAVID BEVINGTON

## NOTE ON THE TEXT

The play was first printed in the folio of 1623 as *The first Part of Henry the Sixt*. The nature of the copy used by the printers is still in dispute, but recent opinion favors the position that it was a manuscript in Shakespeare's own hand. The folio text is divided, erratically, into acts and scenes; the act–scene division employed marginally for reference in the present edition is the somewhat more rational one of later editors. Otherwise the folio text is followed closely except for the usual modernization of spelling and punctuation, and the normalization of the speech-prefixes. Proper names have been regularized: *Reignier* (for the common Reigneir and occasional Reynold or Reignard), *Dauphin* (for Dolphin), *Pucelle* (for Puzel), *Woodville* (for Wooduile), *Auvergne* (for Ouergne), *Pole* (for Poole), *Beaufort* (for Beauford), *Coeur-de-lion* (for Cordelion), *Burgundy* (for Burgonie), *Basset* (for Bassit), *Armagnac* (for Arminack). The only other substantive departures from the folio text (F) are listed below, with the adopted reading in italics followed by the folio reading in roman.

I, i, 176 *steal* (Mason conjecture; adopted by Singer) send (F)

I, ii, 30 *bred* (Rowe) breed (F)   76 *whilst* (Eds) whilest (F)   99 *five* (Steevens) fine (F)   113 *rites* (Pope) rights (F)   131 *halcyon* (F3) Halcyons (F)

I, iii, 29 *Humphrey* (Theobald) Vmpheir (F)

I, iv, 10 *Wont* (Tyrwhitt conj.; Steevens) Went (F)   27 *Duke* (Theobald) Earle (F)   69 s.d. *shoot* (Rowe) shot (F)

I, vi, 22 *of* (Capell conj.; Dyce) or (F)

II, i, 7 s.d. *Enter . . . ladders* (Cairncross) Enter . . . ladders: Their Drummes beating a Dead March (F)   29 *all together* (Rowe) altogether (F)   77 *them* (Capell) them. Exeunt (F)

II, ii, s.d. *their . . . dead march* (This ed.; placed at II, i, 7 s.d. in F)   20 *Arc* (Rowe) Acre (F)   59 s.d. *Whispers* (Johnson; placed at end of line in F)

II, iv, 117 *wiped* (F2) whipt (F)   132 *sir* (F2; omitted in F)

II, v, 3 *rack* (Pope) Wrack (F)   121 s.d. *Exeunt* (Eds) Exit (F)

III, i, 52 *Somerset* (Theobald; the line is part of preceding speech by Warwick in F)   53 *Warwick* (Theobald) Som. (F)   162 *that alone* (F2) that all alone (F)   198 *should lose* (F2) loose (F)

III, iv, 27 s.d. *Manent* (Eds) Manet (F)

IV, i, s.d. *Exeter, and Governor* (Pope) and Gouernor Exeter (F)   151 *umpire* (Eds) Vmper (F)   173 s.d. *Manent* (Eds) Manet (F)   180 *wist* (Capell) wish (F)

IV, ii, 3 *calls* (Eds) call (F)   15 *General* (Eds) Cap. (F)   34 *due* (Theobald) dew (F)   50 *moody-mad and* (Capell) moodie mad: And (F)

IV, iii, 5 *Talbot. As* (F2: Talbot; as) Talbot as (F)   17, 30, 34, 47 *Lucy* (Theobald) 2. Mes. (F)   20 *waist* (Eds) waste (F)

IV, iv, 16 *legions* (Rowe) Regions (F)

IV, vii, 89, 94 *'em* (Theobald) him (F)   96 s.d. *Exeunt* (Eds) Exit (F)

V, iii, 11 *legions* (Warburton conj.; Singer) Regions (F)   47 *reverent* (Eds) reuerend (F)   57 *her* (F3) his (F)   179 *modestly* (Eds) modestie (F)   192 *And* (Capell) Mad (F)

V, iv, 28 *suck'dst* (Eds) suck'st (F)   37 *one* (Malone) me (F)   49 *Arc* (Rowe) Aire (F)   93 s.d. *Enter Cardinal* (Capell; placed at line 91 in F)

V, v, 60 *It most* (Rowe) Most (F)   82 *love* (F2) Ioue (F)

# THE FIRST PART OF
# KING HENRY THE SIXTH

*

I, i   *Dead march. Enter the Funeral of King Henry the Fifth, attended on by the Duke of Bedford, Regent of France ; the Duke of Gloucester, Protector ; the Duke of Exeter, [the Earl of] Warwick, the Bishop of Winchester, and the Duke of Somerset [with Heralds, etc.].*

**BEDFORD**
Hung be the heavens with black, yield day to night !
Comets, importing change of times and states,
Brandish your crystal tresses in the sky
And with them scourge the bad revolting stars
That have consented unto Henry's death –
King Henry the Fifth, too famous to live long !
England ne'er lost a king of so much worth.

**GLOUCESTER**
England ne'er had a king until his time.
9   Virtue he had, deserving to command ;
10  His brandished sword did blind men with his beams ;

His arms spread wider than a dragon's wings ;
His sparkling eyes, replete with wrathful fire,
More dazzled and drove back his enemies
Than midday sun fierce bent against their faces.
What should I say ? His deeds exceed all speech.
He ne'er lift up his hand but conquerèd.           16

**EXETER**
We mourn in black. Why mourn we not in blood ?
Henry is dead and never shall revive.
Upon a wooden coffin we attend,
And death's dishonorable victory
We with our stately presence glorify,
Like captives bound to a triumphant car.
What ? Shall we curse the planets of mishap
That plotted thus our glory's overthrow ?
Or shall we think the subtile-witted French
Conjurers and sorcerers, that, afraid of him,
By magic verses have contrived his end ?

**WINCHESTER**
He was a king blessed of the King of Kings.
Unto the French the dreadful judgment day
So dreadful will not be as was his sight.

The battles of the Lord of Hosts he fought;
The church's prayers made him so prosperous.

GLOUCESTER

33 The church? Where is it? Had not churchmen prayed,
His thread of life had not so soon decayed.
None do you like but an effeminate prince
Whom like a schoolboy you may overawe.

WINCHESTER

Gloucester, whate'er we like, thou art Protector
And lookest to command the prince and realm.

39 Thy wife is proud. She holdeth thee in awe
More than God or religious churchmen may.

GLOUCESTER

Name not religion, for thou lov'st the flesh,
And ne'er throughout the year to church thou go'st,
Except it be to pray against thy foes.

BEDFORD

44 Cease, cease these jars, and rest your minds in peace!
Let's to the altar. Heralds, wait on us.

46 Instead of gold we'll offer up our arms,
Since arms avail not, now that Henry's dead.

48 Posterity, await for wretched years,
When at their mothers' moist'ned eyes babes shall suck,

50 Our isle be made a nourish of salt tears,
And none but women left to wail the dead.
Henry the Fifth, thy ghost I invocate:
Prosper this realm, keep it from civil broils!
Combat with adverse planets in the heavens!
A far more glorious star thy soul will make
Than Julius Caesar or bright –
*Enter a Messenger.*

MESSENGER

My honorable lords, health to you all.
Sad tidings bring I to you out of France,
Of loss, of slaughter, and discomfiture.
Guyenne, Champagne, Rheims, Orleans,
Paris, Guysors, Poictiers, are all quite lost.

BEDFORD

What say'st thou, man, before dead Henry's corse?
Speak softly, or the loss of those great towns

64 Will make him burst his lead and rise from death.

GLOUCESTER

65 Is Paris lost? Is Roan yielded up?
If Henry were recalled to life again,
These news would cause him once more yield the ghost.

EXETER

How were they lost? What treachery was used?

MESSENGER

No treachery, but want of men and money.
Amongst the soldiers this is mutterèd,
That here you maintain several factions,

72 And whilst a field should be dispatched and fought

73 You are disputing of your generals.
One would have ling'ring wars, with little cost;

75 Another would fly swift, but wanteth wings;
A third thinks, without expense at all,
By guileful fair words peace may be obtained.
Awake, awake, English nobility!
Let not sloth dim your honors new begot.

80 Cropped are the flower-de-luces in your arms;
Of England's coat one half is cut away.    *[Exit.]*

EXETER

82 Were our tears wanting to this funeral,
These tidings would call forth her flowing tides.

BEDFORD

Me they concern; regent I am of France.
Give me my steelèd coat, I'll fight for France.
Away with these disgraceful wailing robes!
Wounds will I lend the French, instead of eyes,    87
To weep their intermissive miseries.    88
*Enter to them another Messenger.*

MESSENGER

Lords, view these letters, full of bad mischance.
France is revolted from the English quite,
Except some petty towns of no import.
The Dauphin Charles is crownèd king in Rheims;
The Bastard of Orleans with him is joined;
Reignier, Duke of Anjou, doth take his part;
The Duke of Alençon flieth to his side.    *Exit.*

EXETER

The Dauphin crownèd king? All fly to him?
O, whither shall we fly from this reproach?

GLOUCESTER

We will not fly, but to our enemies' throats!
Bedford, if thou be slack, I'll fight it out.

BEDFORD

Gloucester, why doubt'st thou of my forwardness?
An army have I mustered in my thoughts,
Wherewith already France is overrun.
*Enter another Messenger.*

MESSENGER

My gracious lords, to add to your laments,
Wherewith you now bedew King Henry's hearse,
I must inform you of a dismal fight    105
Betwixt the stout Lord Talbot and the French.

WINCHESTER

What? Wherein Talbot overcame, is't so?

MESSENGER

O, no! wherein Lord Talbot was o'erthrown.
The circumstance I'll tell you more at large.    109
The tenth of August last this dreadful lord,    110
Retiring from the siege of Orleans,
Having full scarce six thousand in his troop,    112
By three and twenty thousand of the French
Was round encompassèd and set upon.
No leisure had he to enrank his men;
He wanted pikes to set before his archers;    116
Instead whereof, sharp stakes plucked out of hedges
They pitchèd in the ground confusedly
To keep the horsemen off from breaking in.
More than three hours the fight continuèd,
Where valiant Talbot above human thought
Enacted wonders with his sword and lance.

33 *prayed* (with pun on 'preyed')   39 *Thy wife* (Eleanor, guilty of ambition and witchcraft in *2 Henry VI*); *holdeth . . . awe* i.e. keeps you in subjection   44 *jars* discords   46 *arms* weapons   48–50 *Posterity . . . tears* i.e. later generations, look for evil times, when mothers shall feed their children with their tears, and Britain shall also nurse her children (i.e. inhabitants) with tears only   50 *nourish* nurse   64 *lead* leaden wrappings for corpse   65 *Roan* Rouen   72 *field* battle; *dispatched* settled   73 *of* about   75 *wanteth* lacks   80 *Cropped* plucked; *arms* coat of arms (Henry VI was supposed to be 'Heir of France,' since the French had yielded to his victorious father. Instead, Charles Dauphin was proclaimed king. Henry VI thus faced the loss of his right to wear the '*fleurs-de-lis,*' national emblem of France, in his coat of arms.)   82 *wanting* lacking   87 *Wounds . . . eyes* i.e. he will cause them to shed blood instead of tears   88 *intermissive* temporarily interrupted, now to be resumed   105 *dismal* dire   109 *at large* in detail   110 *dreadful* inspiring dread   112 *full scarce* i.e. scarce full, barely   116 *wanted pikes* lacked ironbound stakes (for defense against cavalry)

Hundreds he sent to hell, and none durst stand him;
Here, there, and everywhere enraged he slew.
The French exclaimed the devil was in arms;
126 All the whole army stood agazed on him.
His soldiers, spying his undaunted spirit,
128 'A Talbot! a Talbot!' cried out amain
And rushed into the bowels of the battle.
Here had the conquest fully been sealed up
131 If Sir John Falstaff had not played the coward.
132 He, being in the vaward, placed behind
With purpose to relieve and follow them,
Cowardly fled, not having struck one stroke.
Hence grew the general wrack and massacre.
136 Enclosèd were they with their enemies.
137 A base Walloon, to win the Dauphin's grace,
Thrust Talbot with a spear into the back,
Whom all France with their chief assembled strength
Durst not presume to look once in the face.

BEDFORD
Is Talbot slain? Then I will slay myself
For living idly here in pomp and ease
Whilst such a worthy leader, wanting aid,
Unto his dastard foemen is betrayed.

MESSENGER
O, no, he lives, but is took prisoner,
And Lord Scales with him, and Lord Hungerford;
Most of the rest slaughtered or took likewise.

BEDFORD
148 His ransom there is none but I shall pay.
I'll hale the Dauphin headlong from his throne;
His crown shall be the ransom of my friend.
151 Four of their lords I'll change for one of ours.
Farewell, my masters; to my task will I.
Bonfires in France forthwith I am to make
154 To keep our great Saint George's feast withal.
Ten thousand soldiers with me I will take,
Whose bloody deeds shall make all Europe quake.

MESSENGER
So you had need, for Orleans is beseiged;
The English army is grown weak and faint;
159 The Earl of Salisbury craveth supply
And hardly keeps his men from mutiny,
Since they, so few, watch such a multitude.     *[Exit.]*

EXETER
Remember, lords, your oaths to Henry sworn,

Either to quell the Dauphin utterly
Or bring him in obedience to your yoke.

BEDFORD
I do remember it, and here take my leave
To go about my preparation.     *Exit Bedford.*

GLOUCESTER
I'll to the Tower with all the haste I can     167
To view th' artillery and munition,
And then I will proclaim young Henry king.
    *Exit Gloucester.*

EXETER
To Eltham will I, where the young king is,     170
Being ordained his special governor,
And for his safety there I'll best devise.     *Exit.*

WINCHESTER
Each hath his place and function to attend.
I am left out; for me nothing remains.
But long I will not be Jack out of office.
The king from Eltham I intend to steal
And sit at chiefest stern of public weal.     *Exit.* 177

    *

*Sound a flourish. Enter Charles [the Dauphin],*     I, ii
*Alençon, and Reignier, marching with Drum and*
*Soldiers.*

CHARLES
Mars his true moving, even as in the heavens     1
So in the earth, to this day is not known.
Late did he shine upon the English side;     3
Now we are victors, upon us he smiles.
What towns of any moment but we have?     5
At pleasure here we lie, near Orleans;
Otherwhiles the famished English, like pale ghosts,     7
Faintly besiege us one hour in a month.

ALENÇON
They want their porridge and their fat bull-beeves.
Either they must be dieted like mules     10
And have their provender tied to their mouths,
Or piteous they will look, like drownèd mice.

REIGNIER
Let's raise the siege. Why live we idly here?     13
Talbot is taken, whom we wont to fear.     14
Remaineth none but mad-brained Salisbury,
And he may well in fretting spend his gall.     16
Nor men nor money hath he to make war.     17

CHARLES
Sound, sound alarum! We will rush on them.     18
Now for the honor of the forlorn French!
Him I forgive my death that killeth me
When he sees me go back one foot or fly.     *Exeunt.*
    *Here alarum. They are beaten back by the English with*
    *great loss. Enter Charles, Alençon, and Reignier.*

CHARLES
Who ever saw the like? What men have I!
Dogs! cowards! dastards! I would ne'er have fled
But that they left me 'midst my enemies.

REIGNIER
Salisbury is a desperate homicide;
He fighteth as one weary of his life.
The other lords, like lions wanting food,
Do rush upon us as their hungry prey.     28

ALENÇON
Froissart, a countryman of ours, records     29

126 *agazed on* astounded at    128 *amain* vehemently    131 *Falstaff* ('Fastolfe' in the chronicles; but Shakespeare wrote 'Falstaff' and later gave the same name, replacing 'Oldcastle' in the chronicles, to the more famous coward knight of *1 & 2 Henry IV* and *Merry Wives*)    132 *being . . . behind* bringing up the rear of the vanguard    136 *with* by    137 *Walloon* citizen of a province now in southern Belgium    148 *His . . . pay* i.e. my deeds of vengeance and rescue are all the ransom the French can expect from us    151 *change* exchange, i.e. kill in retaliation (since four Frenchmen are worth but one Englishman)    154 *Saint George's feast* (traditionally April 23; but England's patron saint might be celebrated with bonfires after any military victory)    159 *supply* reinforcements    167 *Tower* Tower of London    170 *Eltham* a royal residence, south of London    177 *at chiefest stern* supremely at the helm

I, ii *Before Orleans in France*    1 *Mars . . . moving* Mars' precise movement (the planet's seemingly eccentric orbit was a source of astronomical controversy)    3 *Late* lately    5 *of . . . have* i.e. of any importance that we do not possess    7 *Otherwhiles* at times    10 *dieted* fed    13 *raise* i.e. end by driving off the besieging armies    14 *wont* were accustomed    16 *spend his gall* expend his irritation    17 *Nor* neither    18 *alarum* call to arms    28 *hungry* arousing hunger    29 *Froissart* a fourteenth-century French chronicler

30 England all Olivers and Rowlands bred
   During the time Edward the Third did reign.
   More truly now may this be verified,
33 For none but Samsons and Goliases
   It sendeth forth to skirmish. One to ten?
35 Lean raw-boned rascals, who would e'er suppose
   They had such courage and audacity?

CHARLES
   Let's leave this town; for they are harebrained slaves,
38 And hunger will enforce them to be more eager.
   Of old I know them. Rather with their teeth
   The walls they'll tear down than forsake the siege.

REIGNIER
41 I think by some odd gimmors or device
42 Their arms are set, like clocks, still to strike on.
   Else ne'er could they hold out so as they do.
   By my consent, we'll even let them alone.

ALENÇON
   Be it so.
      *Enter the Bastard of Orleans.*

BASTARD
   Where's the Prince Dauphin? I have news for him.

CHARLES
   Bastard of Orleans, thrice welcome to us.

BASTARD
48 Methinks your looks are sad, your cheer appalled.
   Hath the late overthrow wrought this offense?
   Be not dismayed, for succor is at hand.
   A holy maid hither with me I bring
   Which by a vision sent to her from heaven
   Ordainèd is to raise this tedious siege
   And drive the English forth the bounds of France.
   The spirit of deep prophecy she hath,
56 Exceeding the nine sibyls of old Rome.
   What's past and what's to come she can descry.
   Speak, shall I call her in? Believe my words,
   For they are certain and unfallible.

CHARLES
   Go, call her in. *[Exit Bastard.]* But first, to try her skill,
   Reignier, stand thou as Dauphin in my place.
   Question her proudly, let thy looks be stern.
63 By this means shall we sound what skill she hath.
      *Enter Joan Pucelle [and Bastard].*

REIGNIER
   Fair maid, is't thou wilt do these wondrous feats?

PUCELLE
   Reignier, is't thou that thinkest to beguile me?
   Where is the Dauphin? Come, come from behind.
   I know thee well, though never seen before.
   Be not amazed, there's nothing hid from me.
   In private will I talk with thee apart.
   Stand back, you lords, and give us leave awhile.

REIGNIER
71 She takes upon her bravely at first dash.

PUCELLE
   Dauphin, I am by birth a shepherd's daughter,
   My wit untrained in any kind of art.
   Heaven and our Lady gracious hath it pleased
   To shine on my contemptible estate.
   Lo, whilst I waited on my tender lambs
   And to sun's parching heat displayed my cheeks,
   God's Mother deignèd to appear to me,
   And in a vision full of majesty
   Willed me to leave my base vocation

And free my country from calamity.
Her aid she promised and assured success.
In complete glory she revealed herself;
And whereas I was black and swart before,
With those clear rays which she infused on me     85
That beauty am I blessed with, which you may see.
Ask me what question thou canst possible,
And I will answer unpremeditated.
My courage try by combat, if thou dar'st,
And thou shalt find that I exceed my sex.
Resolve on this: thou shalt be fortunate     91
If thou receive me for thy warlike mate.     92

CHARLES
Thou hast astonished me with thy high terms.     93
Only this proof I'll of thy valor make:     94
In single combat thou shalt buckle with me,     95
And if thou vanquishest, thy words are true.
Otherwise I renounce all confidence.     97

PUCELLE
I am prepared. Here is my keen-edged sword,
Decked with five flower-de-luces on each side,
The which at Touraine in Saint Katherine's churchyard
Out of a great deal of old iron I chose forth.

CHARLES
Then come, a God's name! I fear no woman.

PUCELLE
And while I live, I'll ne'er fly from a man.
   *Here they fight, and Joan de Pucelle overcomes.*

CHARLES
Stay, stay thy hands! Thou art an Amazon
And fightest with the sword of Deborah.     105

PUCELLE
Christ's Mother helps me, else I were too weak.

CHARLES
Whoe'er helps thee, 'tis thou that must help me!
Impatiently I burn with thy desire;     108
My heart and hands thou hast at once subdued.
Excellent Pucelle, if thy name be so,
Let me thy servant and not sovereign be.
'Tis the French Dauphin sueth to thee thus.

PUCELLE
I must not yield to any rites of love,
For my profession's sacred from above.
When I have chasèd all thy foes from hence,
Then will I think upon a recompense.

CHARLES
Meantime, look gracious on thy prostrate thrall.

REIGNIER
My lord, methinks, is very long in talk.

ALENÇON
Doubtless he shrives this woman to her smock;     119
Else ne'er could he so long protract his speech.

---

30 *England . . . bred* i.e. England's knights were all as chivalrous as the best who followed Charlemagne   33 *Goliases* Goliaths   35 *rascals* wretches   38 *eager* (1) fierce, (2) hungry   41 *gimmors* gimmals, mechanical joints for transmitting motion as in clockwork   42 *still* continually   48 *cheer appalled* countenance made pale and downcast   56 *sibyls* prophetesses in the ancient world   63 s.d. *Pucelle* virgin   71 *takes . . . bravely* plays her part well   85 *With* by virtue of   91 *Resolve on* be sure of   92 *warlike mate* (throughout this scene the military terms have ribald double meanings)   93 *high terms* lofty language   94 *proof* trial   95 *buckle* join in close struggle (with erotic suggestion)   97 *confidence* (1) firm trust, (2) intimacy   105 *Deborah* Hebrew prophetess, judge over Israel, and successful commander of the army against Sisera (Judges iv)   108 *thy desire* i.e. desire for thee   119 *shrives* examines; *to her smock* i.e. completely (with double meaning)

REIGNIER
121 Shall we disturb him, since he keeps no mean?

ALENÇON
He may mean more than we poor men do know.
These women are shrewd tempters with their tongues.

REIGNIER
My lord, where are you? What devise you on?
Shall we give o'er Orleans, or no?

PUCELLE
Why, no, I say, distrustful recreants,
Fight till the last gasp. I'll be your guard.

CHARLES
What she says, I'll confirm. We'll fight it out.

PUCELLE
Assigned am I to be the English scourge.
This night the siege assuredly I'll raise.
131 Expect Saint Martin's summer, halcyon days,
Since I have enterèd into these wars.
Glory is like a circle in the water,
Which never ceaseth to enlarge itself
Till by broad spreading it disperse to naught.
With Henry's death the English circle ends;
Dispersèd are the glories it included.
138 Now am I like that proud insulting ship
Which Caesar and his fortune bare at once.

CHARLES
140 Was Mahomet inspirèd with a dove?
Thou with an eagle art inspirèd then!
142 Helen, the mother of great Constantine,
143 Nor yet Saint Philip's daughters, were like thee.
Bright star of Venus, fall'n down on the earth,
How may I reverently worship thee enough?

ALENÇON
Leave off delays and let us raise the siege.

REIGNIER
Woman, do what thou canst to save our honors.
Drive them from Orleans and be immortalized.

CHARLES
149 Presently we'll try. Come, let's away about it.
No prophet will I trust if she prove false.        *Exeunt.*

*

*Enter Gloucester, with his Servingmen*        I, iii
*[in blue coats].*

GLOUCESTER
I am come to survey the Tower this day.        1
Since Henry's death I fear there is conveyance.        2
Where be these warders that they wait not here?
Open the gates! 'Tis Gloucester that calls.
*[Servingmen knock.]*

1. WARDER *[within]*
Who's there that knocks so imperiously?

GLOUCESTER'S 1. MAN
It is the noble Duke of Gloucester.

2. WARDER *[within]*
Whoe'er he be, you may not be let in.

1. MAN
Villains, answer you so the Lord Protector?

1. WARDER *[within]*
The Lord protect him! So we answer him.
We do no otherwise than we are willed.        10

GLOUCESTER
Who willèd you? or whose will stands but mine?
There's none Protector of the realm but I.
Break up the gates, I'll be your warrantize.        13
Shall I be flouted thus by dunghill grooms?        14
*Gloucester's men rush at the Tower gates, and
Woodville the Lieutenant speaks within.*

WOODVILLE
What noise is this? What traitors have we here?

GLOUCESTER
Lieutenant, is it you whose voice I hear?
Open the gates. Here's Gloucester that would enter.

WOODVILLE
Have patience, noble Duke. I may not open;
The Cardinal of Winchester forbids.
From him I have express commandement
That thou nor none of thine shall be let in.

GLOUCESTER
Faint-hearted Woodville, prizest him 'fore me?
Arrogant Winchester, that haughty prelate,
Whom Henry our late sovereign ne'er could brook?        24
Thou art no friend to God or to the king.
Open the gates, or I'll shut thee out shortly.

SERVINGMEN
Open the gates unto the Lord Protector,
Or we'll burst them open if that you come not quickly.        28
*Enter to the Protector at the Tower gates Winchester
and his men in tawny coats.*

WINCHESTER
How now, ambitious Humphrey, what means this?

GLOUCESTER
Peeled priest, dost thou command me to be shut out?        30

WINCHESTER
I do, thou most usurping proditor,        31
And not Protector of the king or realm.

GLOUCESTER
Stand back, thou manifest conspirator,
Thou that contrivedst to murder our dead lord,        34
Thou that giv'st whores indulgences to sin,        35
I'll canvass thee in thy broad cardinal's hat        36
If thou proceed in this thy insolence.

WINCHESTER
Nay, stand thou back. I will not budge a foot.
This be Damascus, be thou cursèd Cain,        39
To slay thy brother Abel, if thou wilt.        40

---

121 *keeps no mean* is immoderate  131 *Saint Martin's summer* i.e. Indian summer (since St Martin's day is November 11), hence, success after a period of stormy fortune; *halcyon days* a period of calm around December when the kingfisher (halcyon) supposedly breeds in a nest on the sea 138–39 *Now . . . once* (according to Plutarch, Caesar, aboard a small vessel in a storm, calmed the mariners with the thought that Caesar and his fortune were proof against drowning)  140 *Mahomet . . . dove* (Mohammed reputedly taught a dove to take feed at his ears; he claimed that the dove was the Holy Ghost and that it brought him divine revelation)  142 *Helen* St Helena, purported discoverer of the true cross  143 *Saint Philip's daughters* i.e. prophesying virgins (Acts xxi, 9)  149 *Presently* immediately
I, iii *Before the Tower of London*  s.d. *blue coats* (customarily worn by servingmen)  1 *survey* inspect  2 *conveyance* sharp dealings, theft  10 *willed* commanded  13 *warrantize* authorization  14 s.d. *within* i.e. from the tiring house or actors' dressing area (the stage backdrop or façade is envisaged in this scene as the Tower, with occupants of the Tower behind the gates backstage)  24 *brook* endure  28 s.d. *tawny coats* (worn by summoners of an ecclesiastical court)  30 *Peeled* i.e. tonsured  31 *proditor* traitor  34 *dead lord* i.e. Henry V  35 *giv'st . . . sin* (Winchester historically received revenue from houses of prostitution in the London suburb of Southwark)  36 *canvass* buffet (literally, toss in a blanket)  39 *Damascus* (popular belief held that Cain slew Abel on the site of this later city)  40 *brother* (Winchester is actually Gloucester's half-uncle)

**GLOUCESTER**
I will not slay thee, but I'll drive thee back.
42   Thy scarlet robes as a child's bearing cloth
I'll use to carry thee out of this place.

**WINCHESTER**
44   Do what thou dar'st ! I beard thee to thy face.

**GLOUCESTER**
What ? Am I dared and bearded to my face ?
46   Draw, men, for all this privilegèd place,
Blue coats to tawny coats. Priest, beware your beard.
I mean to tug it and to cuff you soundly.
Under my feet I stamp thy cardinal's hat.
50   In spite of pope or dignities of church,
Here by the cheeks I'll drag thee up and down.

**WINCHESTER**
52   Gloucester, thou wilt answer this before the pope.

**GLOUCESTER**
53   Winchester goose ! I cry a rope, a rope !
Now beat them hence. Why do you let them stay ?
Thee I'll chase hence, thou wolf in sheep's array.
Out, tawny coats ! Out, scarlet hypocrite !
*Here Gloucester's men beat out the Cardinal's men,*
*and enter in the hurly-burly the Mayor of London*
*and his Officers.*

**MAYOR**
Fie, lords, that you, being supreme magistrates,
Thus contumeliously should break the peace !

**GLOUCESTER**
Peace, mayor, thou know'st little of my wrongs.
Here's Beaufort, that regards nor God nor king,
61   Hath here distrained the Tower to his use.

**WINCHESTER**
Here's Gloucester, a foe to citizens ;
63   One that still motions war and never peace,
O'ercharging your free purses with large fines,
That seeks to overthrow religion
Because he is Protector of the realm,
And would have armor here out of the Tower
68   To crown himself king and suppress the prince.

**GLOUCESTER**
I will not answer thee with words, but blows.
*Here they skirmish again.*

**MAYOR**
Naught rests for me in this tumultuous strife
But to make open proclamation.
Come, officer, as loud as e'er thou canst,
Cry.

**[OFFICER]** All manner of men assembled here in arms this
day against God's peace and the king's, we charge and
command you, in his highness' name, to repair to your
several dwelling places, and not to wear, handle, or use
any sword, weapon, or dagger henceforward, upon pain
of death.

**GLOUCESTER**
Cardinal, I'll be no breaker of the law ;
81   But we shall meet and break our minds at large.

**WINCHESTER**
Gloucester, we'll meet to thy cost, be sure.
Thy heart-blood I will have for this day's work.

**MAYOR**
84   I'll call for clubs if you will not away.
This cardinal's more haughty than the devil.

**GLOUCESTER**
Mayor, farewell. Thou dost but what thou mayst.

**WINCHESTER**
Abominable Gloucester, guard thy head ;
For I intend to have it ere long.
*Exeunt [severally, Gloucester and Winchester*
*with their Servingmen].*

**MAYOR**
See the coast cleared, and then we will depart.
Good God, these nobles should such stomachs bear !   90
I myself fight not once in forty year.    *Exeunt.*

\*

*Enter the Master Gunner of Orleans and his Boy.*   I, iv

**MASTER GUNNER**
Sirrah, thou know'st how Orleans is besieged    1
And how the English have the suburbs won.

**BOY**
Father, I know, and oft have shot at them,
Howe'er unfortunate I missed my aim.    4

**MASTER GUNNER**
But now thou shalt not. Be thou ruled by me.
Chief master gunner am I of this town ;
Something I must do to procure me grace.    7
The Prince's espials have informèd me    8
How the English, in the suburbs close intrenched,
Wont through a secret grate of iron bars
In yonder tower to overpeer the city,
And thence discover how with most advantage
They may vex us with shot or with assault.
To intercept this inconvenience    14
A piece of ordnance 'gainst it I have placed,    15
And even these three days have I watched,
If I could see them. Now do thou watch,
For I can stay no longer.
If thou spy'st any, run and bring me word,
And thou shalt find me at the governor's.    *Exit.*

**BOY**
Father, I warrant you ; take you no care.
I'll never trouble you if I may spy them.    *Exit.* 22
*Enter Salisbury and Talbot on the turrets with*
*[Sir William Glansdale, Sir Thomas Gargrave, and]*
*others.*

**SALISBURY**
Talbot, my life, my joy, again returned ?
How wert thou handled being prisoner,
Or by what means gots thou to be released ?    25
Discourse, I prithee, on this turret's top.

**TALBOT**
The Duke of Bedford had a prisoner
Called the brave Lord Ponton de Santrailles ;
For him was I exchanged and ransomèd.
But with a baser man-of-arms by far    30

---

42 *bearing cloth* christening robe   44 *beard* defy   46 *for . . . place* i.e.
despite ordinances forbidding drawing of weapons near a royal residence
50 *dignities* dignitaries   52 *answer* pay for   53 *Winchester goose* a venereal
disorder   61 *distrained* confiscated   63 *still motions* always advocates   68
*prince* king, i.e. Henry VI   81 *break our minds* (1) express our views, (2)
crack heads ; *at large* at length   84 *call for clubs* rallying cry for London
apprentices with their clubs   90 *stomachs* tempers
I, iv The fortifications of Orleans   1 *Sirrah* (form of address used to
inferiors)   4 *Howe'er* although   7 *grace* honor   8 *espials* spies   14 *inconvenience* mischief   15 *'gainst* directed toward   22 s.d. *turrets* i.e. rear
stage gallery or some higher vantage point in the theatre   25 *gots* gottest
30 *baser man-of-arms* soldier of lower birth or rank

Once in contempt they would have bartered me ;
Which I disdaining scorned, and cravèd death
33 Rather than I would be so pilled esteemed.
34 In fine, redeemed I was as I desired.
But, O, the treacherous Falstaff wounds my heart,
Whom with my bare fists I would execute
If I now had him brought into my power.
SALISBURY
38 Yet tell'st thou not how thou wert entertained.
TALBOT
With scoffs and scorns and contumelious taunts
In open market place produced they me
To be a public spectacle to all.
'Here,' said they, 'is the terror of the French,
The scarecrow that affrights our children so.'
Then broke I from the officers that led me
And with my nails digged stones out of the ground
To hurl at the beholders of my shame.
My grisly countenance made others fly ;
None durst come near for fear of sudden death.
In iron walls they deemed me not secure ;
So great fear of my name 'mongst them were spread
That they supposed I could rend bars of steel
52 And spurn in pieces posts of adamant.
53 Wherefore a guard of chosen shot I had
54 That walked about me every minute while ;
And if I did but stir out of my bed,
56 Ready they were to shoot me to the heart.
*Enter the Boy with a linstock.*
SALISBURY
I grieve to hear what torments you endured.
But we will be revenged sufficiently.
Now it is supper time in Orleans.
Here, through this grate, I count each one
And view the Frenchmen how they fortify.
Let us look in ; the sight will much delight thee.
Sir Thomas Gargrave and Sir William Glansdale,
64 Let me have your express opinions
65 Where is best place to make our batt'ry next.
GARGRAVE
I think at the north gate, for there stands lords.
GLANSDALE
67 And I here, at the bulwark of the bridge.
TALBOT
68 For aught I see, this city must be famished
69 Or with light skirmishes enfeeblèd.

---

33 *pilled* peeled, i.e. stripped of dignity 34 *In fine* in short; *redeemed*
ransomed 38 *entertained* treated 52 *spurn* kick 53 *chosen shot* outstand-
ing marksmen 54 *minute while* minute's space 56 s.d. *linstock* forked
stick holding gunner's match 64 *express* definite 65 *batt'ry* artillery
platform 67 *bulwark* fortification 68 *must be* will have to be 69 s.d.
*they* i.e. the French (implies that the cannon, not visible to the audience,
is fired behind the scenes) 72 *chance* mischance 74 *mirror* example
81 *leave* cease from 95 *Plantagenet* (Salisbury's family name was Mon-
tacute, but he was descended from Edward I) 96 *Play . . . burn* (Salisbury
is likened to Nero as a type of heartless destroyer of cities ; Talbot vows
to emulate them both) 97 *only in* at the mere sound of 100 *gathered
head* drawn their forces together 103 *power* army 107 *Pucelle* maid ;
*pussel* slut ; *Dolphin* (near homonym for *Dauphin* – the dolphin was often
thought to be highest in the chain of being among fish) ; *dogfish* a small
shark (contemptibly low form of fish) 110 *me* at my request (ethical
dative)
I, v 4 *bout* a round at fighting (cf. Charles' 'buckling' with Joan in I, ii)
5 *conjure* constrain by sacred oath (a supernatural good, similar in method
but opposite in intent to her supernatural evil)

---

*Here they shoot, and Salisbury falls down [together
with Gargrave].*
SALISBURY
O Lord have mercy on us, wretched sinners !
GARGRAVE
O Lord have mercy on me, woeful man !
TALBOT
What chance is this that suddenly hath crossed us ? 72
Speak, Salisbury ; at least if thou canst speak.
How far'st thou, mirror of all martial men ? 74
One of thy eyes and thy cheek's side struck off ?
Accursèd tower ! Accursèd fatal hand
That hath contrived this woeful tragedy !
In thirteen battles Salisbury o'ercame ;
Henry the Fifth he first trained to the wars.
Whilst any trump did sound or drum struck up
His sword did ne'er leave striking in the field. 81
Yet liv'st thou, Salisbury ? Though thy speech doth fail,
One eye thou hast to look to heaven for grace.
The sun with one eye vieweth all the world.
Heaven, be thou gracious to none alive
If Salisbury wants mercy at thy hands !
Bear hence his body ; I will help to bury it.
Sir Thomas Gargrave, hast thou any life ?
Speak unto Talbot. Nay, look up to him.
Salisbury, cheer thy spirit with this comfort,
Thou shalt not die whiles –
He beckons with his hand and smiles on me,
As who should say, 'When I am dead and gone,
Remember to avenge me on the French.'
Plantagenet, I will, and like thee, 95
Play on the lute, beholding the towns burn. 96
Wretched shall France be only in my name. 97
*Here an alarum, and it thunders and lightens.*
What stir is this ? What tumult 's in the heavens ?
Whence cometh this alarum and the noise ?
*Enter a Messenger.*
MESSENGER
My lord, my lord, the French have gathered head ! 100
The Dauphin, with one Joan de Pucelle joined,
A holy prophetess new risen up,
Is come with a great power to raise the siege. 103
*Here Salisbury lifteth himself up and groans.*
TALBOT
Hear, hear, how dying Salisbury doth groan !
It irks his heart he cannot be revenged.
Frenchmen, I'll be a Salisbury to you.
Pucelle or pussel, Dolphin or dogfish, 107
Your hearts I'll stamp out with my horse's heels
And make a quagmire of your mingled brains.
Convey me Salisbury into his tent, 110
And then we'll try what these dastard Frenchmen dare.
*Alarum. Exeunt [with the bodies].*
*Here an alarum again, and Talbot pursueth the* I, v
*Dauphin and driveth him. Then enter Joan de Pucelle
driving Englishmen before her [and exit]. Then
enter Talbot.*
TALBOT
Where is my strength, my valor, and my force ?
Our English troops retire, I cannot stay them ;
A woman clad in armor chaseth them.
*Enter Pucelle.*
Here, here she comes. I'll have a bout with thee. 4
Devil or devil's dam, I'll conjure thee. 5

6   Blood will I draw on thee, thou art a witch,
7   And straightway give thy soul to him thou serv'st.

PUCELLE
Come, come 'tis only I that must disgrace thee.
     *Here they fight.*

TALBOT
Heavens, can you suffer hell so to prevail?
My breast I'll burst with straining of my courage
And from my shoulders crack my arms asunder
12   But I will chastise this high-minded strumpet.
     *They fight again.*

PUCELLE
Talbot, farewell; thy hour is not yet come.
I must go victual Orleans forthwith.
     *A short alarum. Then enter the town with Soldiers.*
O'ertake me if thou canst! I scorn thy strength.
Go, go, cheer up thy hungry-starvèd men.
Help Salisbury to make his testament.
This day is ours, as many more shall be.      *Exit.*

TALBOT
My thoughts are whirlèd like a potter's wheel;
I know not where I am nor what I do.
21   A witch by fear, not force, like Hannibal,
22   Drives back our troops and conquers as she lists.
So bees with smoke and doves with noisome stench
Are from their hives and houses driven away.
They called us, for our fierceness, English dogs;
Now, like to whelps, we crying run away.
     *A short alarum.*
Hark, countrymen! Either renew the fight
28   Or tear the lions out of England's coat,
29   Renounce your soil, give sheep in lions' stead.
30   Sheep run not half so treacherous from the wolf,
Or horse or oxen from the leopard,
As you fly from your oft-subduèd slaves.
     *Alarum. Here another skirmish.*
It will not be. Retire into your trenches.
You all consented unto Salisbury's death,
35   For none would strike a stroke in his revenge.
Pucelle is ent'red into Orleans
In spite of us or aught that we could do.
O, would I were to die with Salisbury!
The shame hereof will make me hide my head.
     *Exit Talbot. Alarum. Retreat.*

I, vi      *Flourish. Enter, on the walls, Pucelle, Dauphin,*
     *Reignier, Alençon, and Soldiers.*

PUCELLE
1   Advance our waving colors on the walls;
Rescued is Orleans from the English.
Thus Joan de Pucelle hath performed her word.

CHARLES
4   Divinest creature, Astraea's daughter,
How shall I honor thee for this success?
6   Thy promises are like Adonis' garden,
That one day bloomed and fruitful were the next.
France, triumph in thy glorious prophetess!
Recovered is the town of Orleans.
More blessèd hap did ne'er befall our state.

REIGNIER
Why ring not out the bells aloud throughout the town?
Dauphin, command the citizens make bonfires
And feast and banquet in the open streets
To celebrate the joy that God hath given us.

ALENÇON
All France will be replete with mirth and joy
When they shall hear how we have played the men.

CHARLES
'Tis Joan, not we, by whom the day is won;
For which I will divide my crown with her,
And all the priests and friars in my realm
Shall in procession sing her endless praise.
A statelier pyramis to her I'll rear
Than Rhodope's of Memphis ever was.      22
In memory of her, when she is dead,
Her ashes, in an urn more precious
Than the rich-jewelled coffer of Darius,      25
Transported shall be at high festivals
Before the kings and queens of France.
No longer on Saint Denis will we cry,      28
But Joan de Pucelle shall be France's saint.
Come in, and let us banquet royally
After this golden day of victory.      *Flourish. Exeunt.*

\*

     *Enter a [French] Sergeant of a Band, with two*      II, i
     *Sentinels.*

SERGEANT
Sirs, take your places and be vigilant.
If any noise or soldier you perceive
Near to the walls, by some apparent sign      3
Let us have knowledge at the court of guard.      4

SENTINEL
Sergeant, you shall.      *[Exit Sergeant.]*
             Thus are poor servitors,      5
When others sleep upon their quiet beds,
Constrained to watch in darkness, rain, and cold.
     *Enter Talbot, Bedford, and Burgundy, [and Forces,]*
     *with scaling ladders.*

TALBOT
Lord regent, and redoubted Burgundy,      8
By whose approach the regions of Artois,
Wallon, and Picardy are friends to us,

6 *Blood . . . witch* (Talbot again proposes to fight black magic by virtuous magic, gaining power over her by obtaining a sample of her blood in honest combat)   7 *him* i.e. the Devil   12 *But I* if I do not; *high-minded* presumptuous   21 *Hannibal* Carthaginian general (who once rescued his army from encirclement by tying firebrands to the horns of 2,000 oxen and driving the oxen into the terrified Roman ranks)   22 *lists* pleases   28 *lions* (the English coat of arms displayed three lions passant)   29 *soil* country; *give . . . stead* i.e. display sheep on your coat of arms as symbols of cowardice   30 *treacherous* i.e. cowardly and treasonous   35 *his revenge* i.e. revenge of him
I, vi   s.d. *on the walls* (in scenes I, v through II, i the tiring-house façade becomes the defended walls of Orleans; the city is within the tiring house; the rear stage gallery is a walkway on the walls)   1 *Advance* raise aloft   4 *Astraea* goddess of Justice, who lived among men during the Golden Age but was forced to reascend to the heavens in the Iron Age; her return to earth would signal a new age of justice   6 *Adonis' garden* mythical garden of eternal profusion   22 *Rhodope* a Greek courtesan who became queen of Memphis and reputedly built the third pyramid   25 *coffer of Darius* (Alexander, vanquishing Darius in battle, took from him a priceless jewelled chest, in which Alexander is said to have placed the works of Homer as his worthiest possession deserving such a container)   28 *Saint Denis* patron saint of Paris
II, i The fortifications of Orleans   3 *apparent* plain   4 *court of guard* guard house   5 *servitors* common soldiers   8–10 *Burgundy . . . us* (Burgundy's alliance with the English in the time of Henry V had brought support not only from the important Duchy of Burgundy, southeast of Paris, but from territories friendly to him in the Low Countries)

11 This happy night the Frenchmen are secure,
Having all day caroused and banqueted.
Embrace we then this opportunity,
14 As fitting best to quittance their deceit,
15 Contrived by art and baleful sorcery.

BEDFORD
16 Coward of France! How much he wrongs his fame,
Despairing of his own arm's fortitude,
To join with witches and the help of hell!

BURGUNDY
Traitors have never other company.
But what's that Pucelle whom they term so pure?

TALBOT
A maid, they say.

BEDFORD                    A maid? and be so martial?

BURGUNDY
22 Pray God she prove not masculine ere long,
If underneath the standard of the French
She carry armor as she hath begun.

TALBOT
Well, let them practice and converse with spirits.
God is our fortress, in whose conquering name
Let us resolve to scale their flinty bulwarks.

BEDFORD
28 Ascend, brave Talbot. We will follow thee.

TALBOT
Not all together. Better far, I guess,
That we do make our entrance several ways;
That, if it chance the one of us do fail,
The other yet may rise against their force.

BEDFORD
Agreed. I'll to yond corner.

BURGUNDY                    And I to this.

TALBOT
And here will Talbot mount, or make his grave.
Now, Salisbury, for thee, and for the right
Of English Henry, shall this night appear
How much in duty I am bound to both.

SENTINEL
38 Arm, arm! the enemy doth make assault!
*[The English scale the walls.] Cry:* 'Saint George!
a Talbot!'
*The French leap o'er the walls in their shirts. Enter,
several ways, Bastard [of Orleans], Alençon,
Reignier, half ready and half unready.*

ALENÇON
How now, my lords? What, all unready so?

BASTARD
Unready? Ay, and glad we scaped so well.

REIGNIER
41 'Twas time, I trow, to wake and leave our beds,
Hearing alarums at our chamber doors.

ALENÇON
Of all exploits since first I followed arms
Ne'er heard I of a warlike enterprise
More venturous or desperate than this.

BASTARD
I think this Talbot be a fiend of hell.

REIGNIER
If not of hell, the heavens sure favor him.

ALENÇON
Here cometh Charles. I marvel how he sped.      48
*Enter Charles and Joan.*

BASTARD
Tut, holy Joan was his defensive guard.

CHARLES
Is this thy cunning, thou deceitful dame?       50
Didst thou at first, to flatter us withal,       51
Make us partakers of a little gain
That now our loss might be ten times so much?

PUCELLE
Wherefore is Charles impatient with his friend?
At all times will you have my power alike?
Sleeping or waking must I still prevail,
Or will you blame and lay the fault on me?
Improvident soldiers, had your watch been good,
This sudden mischief never could have fall'n!    59

CHARLES
Duke of Alençon, this was your default
That, being captain of the watch to-night,        61
Did look no better to that weighty charge.

ALENÇON
Had all your quarters been as safely kept         63
As that whereof I had the government,
We had not been thus shamefully surprised.

BASTARD
Mine was secure.

REIGNIER                    And so was mine, my lord.

CHARLES
And for myself, most part of all this night
Within her quarter and mine own precinct
I was employed in passing to and fro
About relieving of the sentinels.
Then how or which way should they first break in?

PUCELLE
Question, my lords, no further of the case,
How or which way. 'Tis sure they found some place
But weakly guarded, where the breach was made.    74
And now there rests no other shift but this—      75
To gather our soldiers, scattered and dispersed,
And lay new platforms to endamage them.           77
*Alarum. Enter a Soldier, crying* 'A Talbot!
a Talbot!' *They fly, leaving their clothes behind.*

SOLDIER
I'll be so bold to take what they have left.
The cry of 'Talbot' serves me for a sword;
For I have loaden me with many spoils,
Using no other weapon but his name.      *Exit.*
*Enter Talbot, Bedford, Burgundy, [a Captain, and     II, ii
others,] their drums beating a dead march.*

BEDFORD
The day begins to break and night is fled,
Whose pitchy mantle overveiled the earth.
Here sound retreat and cease our hot pursuit.
*Retreat [sounded].*

11 *secure* unsuspecting  14 *quittance* requite  15 *art* black magic  16
*Coward* i.e. Dauphin; *fame* reputation  22–25 *masculine, standard, carry
armor, practice, converse* (ribald double entendres)  28–34 *Ascend...grave*
(the three leaders actually ascend to the rear stage gallery on separate
scaling ladders brought on stage, Talbot in the center and one companion at
each side)  38 s.d. *o'er the walls* (some of the routed French, emerging from
the tiring house, leap from the rear stage gallery down to the main stage;
some use other entrances)  41 *trow* believe  48 *sped* fared  50 *cunning*
skill  51 *flatter* encourage with false hopes  59 *mischief* calamity  61 *to-
night* last night  63 *kept* guarded  74 *But* only  75 *rests* remains; *shift*
device  77 *platforms* schemes

**TALBOT**

    Bring forth the body of old Salisbury

5  And here advance it in the market place,

6  The middle center of this cursèd town.

    Now have I paid my vow unto his soul :

8  For every drop of blood was drawn from him

    There hath at least five Frenchmen died to-night.

    And that hereafter ages may behold

    What ruin happened in revenge of him,

    Within their chiefest temple I'll erect

    A tomb, wherein his corpse shall be interred ;

    Upon the which, that every one may read,

    Shall be engraved the sack of Orleans,

16  The treacherous manner of his mournful death,

    And what a terror he had been to France.

    But, lords, in all our bloody massacre,

19  I muse we met not with the Dauphin's grace,

20  His new-come champion, virtuous Joan of Arc,

    Nor any of his false confederates.

**BEDFORD**

    'Tis thought, Lord Talbot, when the fight began,

    Roused on the sudden from their drowsy beds,

    They did amongst the troops of armèd men

    Leap o'er the walls for refuge in the field.

**BURGUNDY**

    Myself, as far as I could well discern

    For smoke and dusky vapors of the night,

28  Am sure I scared the Dauphin and his trull,

    When arm in arm they both came swiftly running,

    Like to a pair of loving turtledoves

    That could not live asunder day or night.

    After that things are set in order here,

    We'll follow them with all the power we have.

       *Enter a Messenger.*

**MESSENGER**

    All hail, my lords ! Which of this princely train

    Call ye the warlike Talbot, for his acts

    So much applauded through the realm of France ?

**TALBOT**

    Here is the Talbot. Who would speak with him ?

**MESSENGER**

    The virtuous lady, Countess of Auvergne,

    With modesty admiring thy renown,

    By me entreats, great lord, thou wouldst vouchsafe

41  To visit her poor castle where she lies,

    That she may boast she hath beheld the man

43  Whose glory fills the world with loud report.

**BURGUNDY**

    Is it even so ? Nay, then I see our wars

    Will turn unto a peaceful comic sport,

46  When ladies crave to be encount'red with.

47  You may not, my lord, despise her gentle suit.

**TALBOT**

    Ne'er trust me then ; for when a world of men

    Could not prevail with all their oratory,

    Yet hath a woman's kindness overruled ;

    And therefore tell her I return great thanks

    And in submission will attend on her.

    Will not your honors bear me company ?

**BEDFORD**

54  No, truly, 'tis more than manners will ;

    And I have heard it said, unbidden guests

    Are often welcomest when they are gone.

**TALBOT**

    Well, then, alone (since there's no remedy)

    I mean to prove this lady's courtesy.      58

    Come hither, captain. *(Whispers).* You perceive my

      mind.      59

**CAPTAIN**

    I do, my lord, and mean accordingly.    *Exeunt.* 60

*

      *Enter Countess [and her Porter].*    II, iii

**COUNTESS**

    Porter, remember what I gave in charge,    1

    And when you have done so, bring the keys to me.

**PORTER**

    Madam, I will.      *Exit.*

**COUNTESS**

    The plot is laid. If all things fall out right,

    I shall as famous be by this exploit

    As Scythian Tomyris by Cyrus' death.    6

    Great is the rumor of this dreadful knight,    7

    And his achievements of no less account.

    Fain would mine eyes be witness with mine ears,

    To give their censure of these rare reports.    10

       *Enter Messenger and Talbot.*

**MESSENGER**

    Madam,

    According as your ladyship desired,

    By message craved, so is Lord Talbot come.

**COUNTESS**

    And he is welcome. What ? Is this the man ?

**MESSENGER**

    Madam, it is.

**COUNTESS**    Is this the scourge of France ?

    Is this the Talbot, so much feared abroad    16

    That with his name the mothers still their babes ?    17

    I see report is fabulous and false.

    I thought I should have seen some Hercules,    19

    A second Hector, for his grim aspect    20

    And large proportion of his strong-knit limbs.    21

    Alas, this is a child, a silly dwarf.    22

    It cannot be this weak and writhled shrimp    23

    Should strike such terror to his enemies.

**TALBOT**

    Madam, I have been bold to trouble you ;

    But since your ladyship is not at leisure,

    I'll sort some other time to visit you.    *[Going.]* 27

**COUNTESS**

    What means he now ? Go ask him whither he goes.

**MESSENGER**

    Stay, my Lord Talbot ; for my lady craves

**II, ii**  **5** *advance* raise aloft on bier  **6** *middle . . . town* (the stage is now the center of Orleans by a simple imaginative transfer of outside to inside) **8** *was* i.e. that was  **16** *mournful* causing sorrow  **19** *muse* wonder  **20** *virtuous* (ironic)  **28** *trull* strumpet  **41** *lies* dwells  **43** *report* (1) acclaim, (2) noise  **46** *encount'red* (1) met, (2) wooed  **47** *gentle* well-bred  **54** *will* require  **58** *prove* test  **59** *mind* intent  **60** *mean* intent to act
**II, iii** The castle of the Countess of Auvergne  **1** *gave in charge* ordered **6** *Tomyris* queen of Scythia who overcame Cyrus in battle, and in revenge for her son's death had Cyrus' head thrown into a wineskin of human blood **7** *dreadful* causing dread  **10** *censure* judgment (echoing the story of Solomon and the Queen of Sheba ; see II Chronicles ix, 6)  **16** *abroad* everywhere  **17** *still* quiet  **19, 20** *Hercules, Hector* (types of manly strength) **20** *for* on account of  **21** *proportion* size  **22** *silly* frail  **23** *writhled* shrivelled **27** *sort* choose

To know the cause of your abrupt departure.

TALBOT

31 Marry, for that she's in a wrong belief,
32 I go to certify her Talbot's here.

*Enter Porter with keys.*

COUNTESS

If thou be he, then art thou prisoner.

TALBOT

Prisoner? to whom?

COUNTESS      To me, bloodthirsty lord.

35 And for that cause I trained thee to my house.
36 Long time thy shadow hath been thrall to me,
For in my gallery thy picture hangs;
But now the substance shall endure the like,
And I will chain these legs and arms of thine
40 That hast by tyranny these many years
Wasted our country, slain our citizens,
42 And sent our sons and husbands captive.

TALBOT Ha, ha, ha!

COUNTESS

44 Laughest thou, wretch? Thy mirth shall turn to moan.

TALBOT

45 I laugh to see your ladyship so fond
To think that you have aught but Talbot's shadow
Whereon to practice your severity.

COUNTESS

Why, art not thou the man?

TALBOT      I am indeed.

COUNTESS

Then have I substance too.

TALBOT

No, no, I am but shadow of myself.
You are deceived, my substance is not here;
52 For what you see is but the smallest part
And least proportion of humanity.
54 I tell you, madam, were the whole frame here,
55 It is of such a spacious lofty pitch
Your roof were not sufficient to contain't.

COUNTESS

57 This is a riddling merchant for the nonce!
He will be here, and yet he is not here.
How can these contrarieties agree?

TALBOT

60 That will I show you presently.

*Winds his horn. Drums strike up. A peal of ordnance.
Enter Soldiers.*

How say you, madam? Are you now persuaded

That Talbot is but a shadow of himself?
These are his substance, sinews, arms, and strength,
With which he yoketh your rebellious necks,
Razeth your cities, and subverts your towns    65
And in a moment makes them desolate.

COUNTESS

Victorious Talbot, pardon my abuse.    67
I find thou art no less than fame hath bruited,    68
And more than may be gathered by thy shape.
Let my presumption not provoke thy wrath,
For I am sorry that with reverence
I did not entertain thee as thou art.    72

TALBOT

Be not dismayed, fair lady, nor misconster    73
The mind of Talbot as you did mistake
The outward composition of his body.
What you have done hath not offended me;
Nor other satisfaction do I crave
But only, with your patience, that we may    78
Taste of your wine and see what cates you have;    79
For soldiers' stomachs always serve them well.    80

COUNTESS

With all my heart, and think me honorèd
To feast so great a warrior in my house.      *Exeunt.*

\*

*Enter Richard Plantagenet, Warwick, Somerset,*    II, iv
*Pole [Earl of Suffolk, Vernon], and others.*

RICHARD

Great lords and gentlemen, what means this silence?
Dare no man answer in a case of truth?

SUFFOLK

Within the Temple hall we were too loud.    3
The garden here is more convenient.    4

RICHARD

Then say at once if I maintained the truth;    5
Or else was wrangling Somerset in th' error?

SUFFOLK

Faith, I have been a truant in the law    7
And never yet could frame my will to it,    8
And therefore frame the law unto my will.

SOMERSET

Judge you, my Lord of Warwick, then between us.

WARWICK

Between two hawks, which flies the higher pitch,    11
Between two dogs, which hath the deeper mouth,    12
Between two blades, which bears the better temper,
Between two horses, which doth bear him best,    14
Between two girls, which hath the merriest eye,
I have perhaps some shallow spirit of judgment;
But in these nice sharp quillets of the law,    17
Good faith, I am no wiser than a daw.    18

RICHARD

Tut, tut, here is a mannerly forbearance.
The truth appears so naked on my side
That any purblind eye may find it out.    21

SOMERSET

And on my side it is so well apparelled,
So clear, so shining, and so evident,
That it will glimmer through a blind man's eye.

RICHARD

Since you are tongue-tied and so loath to speak,

---

31 *Marry* (a mild interjection); *for that* because   32 *certify* inform   35 *trained* lured   36 *shadow* image, portrait; *thrall* slave   40 *tyranny* cruelty   42 *captivate* made prisoner   44 *moan* lamentation   45 *fond* foolish   52–53 *what . . . humanity* (1) the body is the least significant part of the whole of man, (2) I am a mere fraction of my army   54 *frame* (1) structure of man, (2) engine (i.e. his army)   55 *pitch* height   57 *riddling merchant* riddlemonger; *nonce* occasion   60 *presently* immediately; s.d. *Winds* blows   65 *subverts* overthrows   67 *abuse* (1) deceiving of you, (2) self-delusion   68 *fame* report; *bruited* announced   72 *entertain* receive   73 *misconster* misconstrue   78 *patience* permission   79 *cates* delicacies   80 *stomachs* (1) appetites, (2) courage
II, iv The Temple garden, London   3, 4 *Temple hall, garden* (the Wars of the Roses are imagined as beginning in a quarrel among young aristocrats studying law at the London Inns of Court)   3 *were* should have been   5–6 *Then . . . error* i.e. heads I win, tails you lose   7 *a truant* neglectful of study   8 *frame* adapt   11 *pitch* elevation   12 *mouth* bark   14 *bear him* carry himself   17 *nice sharp quillets* fine subtle distinctions   18 *daw* jackdaw (proverbially a stupid bird)   21 *purblind* partially blind

26 In dumb significants proclaim your thoughts.
Let him that is a true-born gentleman
28 And stands upon the honor of his birth,
29 If he suppose that I have pleaded truth,
From off this brier pluck a white rose with me.

SOMERSET
Let him that is no coward nor no flatterer,
32 But dare maintain the party of the truth,
Pluck a red rose from off this thorn with me.

WARWICK
34 I love no colors, and without all color
Of base insinuating flattery
I pluck this white rose with Plantagenet.

SUFFOLK
I pluck this red rose with young Somerset,
38 And say withal I think he held the right.

VERNON
Stay, lords and gentlemen, and pluck no more
Till you conclude that he upon whose side
The fewest roses are cropped from the tree
42 Shall yield the other in the right opinion.

SOMERSET
43 Good Master Vernon, it is well objected.
44 If I have fewest, I subscribe in silence.

RICHARD
And I.

VERNON
Then for the truth and plainness of the case
I pluck this pale and maiden blossom here,
Giving my verdict on the white rose side.

SOMERSET
Prick not your finger as you pluck it off,
Lest, bleeding, you do paint the white rose red
And fall on my side so against your will.

VERNON
If I, my lord, for my opinion bleed,
53 Opinion shall be surgeon to my hurt
And keep me on the side where still I am.

SOMERSET
Well, well, come on! Who else?

LAWYER [to Somerset]
Unless my study and my books be false,
The argument you held was wrong in you;
In sign whereof I pluck a white rose too.

RICHARD
Now, Somerset, where is your argument?

SOMERSET
60 Here in my scabbard, meditating that
Shall dye your white rose in a bloody red.

RICHARD
62 Meantime your cheeks do counterfeit our roses;
For pale they look with fear, as witnessing
The truth on our side.

SOMERSET                    No, Plantagenet,
'Tis not for fear, but anger, that thy cheeks
Blush for pure shame to counterfeit our roses,
And yet thy tongue will not confess thy error.

RICHARD
68 Hath not thy rose a canker, Somerset?

SOMERSET
Hath not thy rose a thorn, Plantagenet?

RICHARD
70 Ay, sharp and piercing, to maintain his truth,
Whiles thy consuming canker eats his falsehood.

SOMERSET
Well, I'll find friends to wear my bleeding roses,
That shall maintain what I have said is true
Where false Plantagenet dare not be seen.

RICHARD
Now by this maiden blossom in my hand,
I scorn thee and thy fashion, peevish boy.            76

SUFFOLK
Turn not thy scorns this way, Plantagenet.

RICHARD
Proud Pole, I will, and scorn both him and thee.            78

SUFFOLK
I'll turn my part thereof into thy throat.

SOMERSET
Away, away, good William de la Pole.
We grace the yeoman by conversing with him.            81

WARWICK
Now, by God's will, thou wrong'st him, Somerset.
His grandfather was Lionel Duke of Clarence,            83
Third son to the third Edward, King of England.
Spring crestless yeoman from so deep a root?            85

RICHARD
He bears him on the place's privilege,            86
Or durst not for his craven heart say thus.

SOMERSET
By him that made me, I'll maintain my words
On any plot of ground in Christendom.
Was not thy father, Richard Earl of Cambridge,
For treason executed in our late king's days?
And by his treason stand'st not thou attainted,            92
Corrupted, and exempt from ancient gentry?            93
His trespass yet lives guilty in thy blood,
And till thou be restored thou art a yeoman.            95

RICHARD
My father was attachèd, not attainted,            96
Condemned to die for treason, but no traitor;
And that I'll prove on better men than Somerset,
Were growing time once ripened to my will.
For your partaker Pole, and you yourself,            100
I'll note you in my book of memory
To scourge you for this apprehension.            102
Look to it well and say you are well warned.

SOMERSET
Ah, thou shalt find us ready for thee still;
And know us by these colors for thy foes,
For these my friends in spite of thee shall wear.

26 *dumb significants* silent symbols   28 *stands upon* insists on   29 *pleaded* argued (one of many legal terms in this scene)   32 *party* side in a legal case   34 *color* semblance   38 *withal* besides   42 *yield* concede (at law)   43 *objected* urged, brought forward (at law)   44 *subscribe* concur (literally, sign at bottom of a document)   53 *Opinion* reputation (punning on the sense of 'belief' in the line above)   60 *that* i.e. that which   62 *counterfeit* imitate   68 *canker* i.e. cankerworm, a caterpillar that feeds on buds and leaves   70 *his* its   76 *fashion* i.e. of wearing red roses   78 *Pole* Suffolk's family name (as in l. 80)   81 *grace* honor; *yeoman* freeholder below rank of gentleman (Plantagenet lost his lands and titles when his father was executed for treason by Henry V)   83 *grandfather* (actually great-great-grandfather)   85 *crestless* (1) lacking heraldic crest, (2) cowardly   86 *bears . . . privilege* i.e. presumes upon the legal asylum of the Inns of Court (granted them as ancient religious houses and as courts of law)   92–93 *attainted, Corrupted* (the legal effects of a bill of attainder were to deprive the culprit's descendants of title)   93 *exempt* excluded; *gentry* rank of gentlemen   95 *restored* given back lands and titles   96 *attachèd, not attainted* (as Plantagenet insists, his father was actually arrested and executed summarily for treason by order of Henry V, not by a full bill of attainder in Parliament; he implies that perfect justice was not done)   100 *partaker* part-taker, ally   102 *apprehension* notion

RICHARD

And, by my soul, this pale and angry rose,
108  As cognizance of my blood-drinking hate,
Will I for ever, and my faction, wear
Until it wither with me to my grave
111  Or flourish to the height of my degree.

SUFFOLK

Go forward, and be choked with thy ambition!
And so farewell until I meet thee next.          *Exit.*

SOMERSET

114  Have with thee, Pole. Farewell, ambitious Richard. *Exit.*

RICHARD

115  How I am braved and must perforce endure it!

WARWICK

116  This blot that they object against your house
Shall be wiped out in the next parliament,
Called for the truce of Winchester and Gloucester;
And if thou be not then created York,
I will not live to be accounted Warwick.
121  Meantime, in signal of my love to thee,
Against proud Somerset and William Pole
Will I upon thy party wear this rose;
And here I prophesy: this brawl to-day
Grown to this faction in the Temple garden
Shall send, between the red rose and the white,
A thousand souls to death and deadly night.

RICHARD

Good Master Vernon, I am bound to you
That you on my behalf would pluck a flower.

VERNON

In your behalf still will I wear the same.

LAWYER

And so will I.

RICHARD

Thanks, gentle sir.
Come, let us four to dinner. I dare say
This quarrel will drink blood another day.          *Exeunt.*

\*

II, v          *Enter Mortimer, brought in a chair, and Jailers.*

MORTIMER

Kind keepers of my weak decaying age,
Let dying Mortimer here rest himself.
Even like a man new halèd from the rack,
So fare my limbs with long imprisonment;
5  And these grey locks, the pursuivants of death,
6  Nestor-like agèd in an age of care,
7  Argue the end of Edmund Mortimer.
These eyes, like lamps whose wasting oil is spent,
9  Wax dim, as drawing to their exigent;

Weak shoulders, overborne with burdening grief,
And pithless arms, like to a withered vine
That droops his sapless branches to the ground.
Yet are these feet (whose strengthless stay is numb,          13
Unable to support this lump of clay)
Swift-wingèd with desire to get a grave,
As witting I no other comfort have.          16
But tell me, keeper, will my nephew come?

KEEPER

Richard Plantagenet, my lord, will come.
We sent unto the Temple, unto his chamber,
And answer was returned that he will come.

MORTIMER

Enough. My soul shall then be satisfied.
Poor gentleman, his wrong doth equal mine.          22
Since Henry Monmouth first began to reign          23
Before whose glory I was great in arms,
This loathsome sequestration have I had;          25
And even since then hath Richard been obscured,
Deprived of honor and inheritance.
But now the arbitrator of despairs,
Just Death, kind umpire of men's miseries,
With sweet enlargement doth dismiss me hence.          30
I would his troubles likewise were expired,          31
That so he might recover what was lost.
*Enter Richard.*

KEEPER

My lord, your loving nephew now is come.

MORTIMER

Richard Plantagenet, my friend, is he come?

RICHARD

Ay, noble uncle, thus ignobly used,
Your nephew, late despisèd Richard, comes.          36

MORTIMER

Direct mine arms I may embrace his neck
And in his bosom spend my latter gasp.          38
O, tell me when my lips do touch his cheeks,
That I may kindly give one fainting kiss!          40
And now declare, sweet stem from York's great stock,          41
Why didst thou say of late thou wert despised?

RICHARD

First lean thine agèd back against mine arm,
And in that ease I'll tell thee my disease.          44
This day in argument upon a case          45
Some words there grew 'twixt Somerset and me;
Among which terms he used his lavish tongue
And did upbraid me with my father's death;
Which obloquy set bars before my tongue,
Else with the like I had requited him.
Therefore, good uncle, for my father's sake,
In honor of a true Plantagenet,
And for alliance sake, declare the cause          53
My father, Earl of Cambridge, lost his head.

MORTIMER

That cause, fair nephew, that imprisoned me
And hath detained me all my flow'ring youth
Within a loathsome dungeon, there to pine,
Was cursèd instrument of his decease.

RICHARD

Discover more at large what cause that was,          59
For I am ignorant and cannot guess.

MORTIMER

I will, if that my fading breath permit
And death approach not ere my tale be done.

---

108 *cognizance* badge   111 *degree* noble rank   114 *Have with thee* let us go
115 *braved* defied   116 *object* urge   121 *signal* token
II, v The Tower of London   5 *pursuivants* heralds   6 *Nestor* aged leader
in the Trojan wars   7 *Argue* portend   9 *exigent* end   13 *stay is numb*
support is powerless   16 *As witting* as if they knew   22 *his wrong* i.e. the
wrong done him   23 *Henry Monmouth* Henry V   25 *sequestration* isola-
tion, loss of property and freedom (Shakespeare apparently confuses
Edmund Mortimer with his cousin Sir John, who was imprisoned)   30
*enlargement* freedom   31 *expired* ended   36 *late* lately   38 *latter* final
40 *kindly* (1) affectionately, (2) to a kinsman   41 *stem* (from the metaphor of
the genealogical tree)   44 *disease* grievance   45 *This day* (Plantagenet has
come to the Tower prison directly after his argument in Temple garden, to
find out more about his father's disgrace)   53 *alliance* kinship's   59
*Discover* expound; *at large* fully

Henry the Fourth, grandfather to this king,
64 Deposed his nephew Richard, Edward's son,
The first-begotten and the lawful heir
Of Edward king, the third of that descent;
67 During whose reign, the Percies of the north,
Finding his usurpation most unjust,
Endeavored my advancement to the throne.
The reason moved these warlike lords to this
Was for that (young Richard thus removed,
Leaving no heir begotten of his body)
I was the next by birth and parentage;
74 For by my mother I derivèd am
From Lionel Duke of Clarence, third son
To King Edward the Third; whereas he
From John of Gaunt doth bring his pedigree,
Being but fourth of that heroic line.
79 But mark. As in this haughty great attempt
They laborèd to plant the rightful heir,
I lost my liberty, and they their lives.
Long after this, when Henry the Fifth
(Succeeding his father Bolingbroke) did reign,
Thy father, Earl of Cambridge, then derived
From famous Edmund Langley, Duke of York,
Marrying my sister that thy mother was,
Again, in pity of my hard distress,
Levied an army, weening to redeem
And have installed me in the diadem;
90 But, as the rest, so fell that noble earl,
And was beheaded. Thus the Mortimers,
In whom the title rested, were suppressed.

RICHARD
Of which, my lord, your honor is the last.

MORTIMER
True, and thou seest that I no issue have,
95 And that my fainting words do warrant death.
96 Thou art my heir. The rest I wish thee gather;
But yet be wary in thy studious care.

RICHARD
Thy grave admonishments prevail with me.
But yet methinks my father's execution
Was nothing less than bloody tyranny.

MORTIMER
With silence, nephew, be thou politic.
Strong fixèd is the house of Lancaster
And like a mountain, not to be removed.
But now thy uncle is removing hence,
As princes do their courts when they are cloyed
With long continuance in a settled place.

RICHARD
O uncle, would some part of my young years
108 Might but redeem the passage of your age!

MORTIMER
Thou dost then wrong me, as that slaughterer doth
Which giveth many wounds when one will kill.
Mourn not, except thou sorrow for my good;
112 Only give order for my funeral.
And so farewell, and fair be all thy hopes,
And prosperous be thy life in peace and war!
*Dies.*

RICHARD
And peace, no war, befall thy parting soul!
In prison hast thou spent a pilgrimage
And like a hermit overpassed thy days.
Well, I will lock his counsel in my breast,

And what I do imagine, let that rest.    119
Keepers, convey him hence, and I myself
Will see his burial better than his life.
     *Exeunt [Jailers, with Mortimer's body].*
Here dies the dusky torch of Mortimer,
Choked with ambition of the meaner sort.    123
And for those wrongs, those bitter injuries,
Which Somerset hath offered to my house
I doubt not but with honor to redress;
And therefore haste I to the parliament,
Either to be restorèd to my blood    128
Or make my will th' advantage of my good.    *Exit.* 129

\*

*Flourish. Enter King, Exeter, Gloucester,*    III, i
*Winchester, Warwick, Somerset, Suffolk, Richard*
*Plantagenet [and others]. Gloucester offers to put up*
*a bill. Winchester snatches it, tears it.*

WINCHESTER
Com'st thou with deep premeditated lines,
With written pamphlets studiously devised,
Humphrey of Gloucester? If thou canst accuse
Or aught intend'st to lay unto my charge,
Do it without invention, suddenly,    5
As I with sudden and extemporal speech
Purpose to answer what thou canst object.    7

GLOUCESTER
Presumptuous priest, this place commands my patience,
Or thou shouldst find thou hast dishonored me.
Think not, although in writing I preferred    10
The manner of thy vile outrageous crimes,
That therefore I have forged, or am not able
Verbatim to rehearse the method of my pen.    13
No, prelate, such is thy audacious wickedness,
Thy lewd, pestiferous, and dissentious pranks,    15
As very infants prattle of thy pride.
Thou art a most pernicious usurer;
Froward by nature, enemy to peace,    18
Lascivious, wanton, more than well beseems
A man of thy profession and degree.
And for thy treachery, what's more manifest,
In that thou laids't a trap to take my life
As well at London Bridge as at the Tower?
Beside, I fear me, if thy thoughts were sifted,
The King thy sovereign is not quite exempt
From envious malice of thy swelling heart.

WINCHESTER
Gloucester, I do defy thee. Lords, vouchsafe
To give me hearing what I shall reply.
If I were covetous, ambitious, or perverse,
As he will have me, how am I so poor?

---

64 *nephew* blood relative (here, first cousin)   67 *whose* i.e. Henry IV's
74 *mother* (Shakespeare here confuses Edmund with his uncle Edmund)
79 *haughty* high-pitched   90 *noble earl* (treated unsympathetically in
*Henry V*)   95 *warrant* assure   96 *gather* (1) infer, (2) collect   108 *redeem*
buy back   112 *give order* make arrangements   119 *let that rest* leave that
alone   123 *the meaner sort* people of inferior rank (i.e. Bolingbroke and his
family)   128 *blood* hereditary rights   129 *make . . . good* make some
opportunity for advancement out of my sheer determination
**III, i** The Parliament house   s.d. *put up a bill* present an indictment   5
*invention* premeditation; *suddenly* extempore   7 *object* urge, argue   10 *preferred* set out   13 *rehearse . . . pen* recount the sum of what I have written
15 *lewd* wicked   18 *Froward* perverse

Or how haps it I seek not to advance
Or raise myself, but keep my wonted calling?
And for dissension, who preferreth peace
34 More than I do, except I be provoked?
35 No, my good lords, it is not that offends;
It is not that that hath incensed the duke.
It is because no one should sway but he,
No one but he should be about the king;
And that engenders thunder in his breast
And makes him roar these accusations forth.
But he shall know I am as good –

GLOUCESTER
42 As good? Thou bastard of my grandfather!

WINCHESTER
Ay, lordly sir! For what are you, I pray,
But one imperious in another's throne?

GLOUCESTER
Am I not Protector, saucy priest?

WINCHESTER
And am not I a prelate of the church?

GLOUCESTER
47 Yes, as an outlaw in a castle keeps
48 And useth it to patronage his theft.

WINCHESTER
Unreverent Gloucester.

GLOUCESTER                    Thou art reverent
50 Touching thy spiritual function, not thy life.

WINCHESTER
Rome shall remedy this.

WARWICK                    Roam thither then.

SOMERSET
My lord, it were your duty to forbear.

WARWICK
Ay, see the bishop be not overborne.

SOMERSET
Methinks my lord should be religious
And know the office that belongs to such.

WARWICK
Methinks his lordship should be humbler.
If fitteth not a prelate so to plead.

SOMERSET
58 Yes, when his holy state is touched so near.

WARWICK
State holy, or unhallowed, what of that?
Is not his grace Protector to the king?

RICHARD [aside]
Plantagenet, I see, must hold his tongue,
Lest it be said, 'Speak, sirrah, when you should;
Must your bold verdict enter talk with lords?'
Else would I have a fling at Winchester.

KING
Uncles of Gloucester and of Winchester,
The special watchmen of our English weal,
I would prevail, if prayers might prevail,
To join your hearts in love and amity.

34 *except* unless   35 *that* i.e. that which   42 *grandfather* John of Gaunt (who fathered the illegitimate Beauforts by his mistress, Catherine Swynford)   47 *keeps* dwells   48 *patronage* maintain   50 *Touching . . . function* i.e. in title only   58 *holy . . . near* high ecclesiastical status is so closely attacked   78 *bishop* i.e. bishop's   79 *late* lately   81 *contrary parts* opposing factions   92 *peevish* senseless   93 *unaccustomed* (1) unusual, (2) contrary to good custom   99 *inkhorn mate* low pedant   103 *pitch a field* drive in sharp stakes to protect against cavalry   110 *prefer* assist in bringing about   113 *Except* unless; *repulse* refusal

O, what a scandal is it to our crown
That two such noble peers as ye should jar!     70
Believe me, lords, my tender years can tell
Civil dissension is a viperous worm
That gnaws the bowels of the commonwealth.
    *A noise within*, 'Down with the tawny coats!'
What tumult's this?

WARWICK                    An uproar, I dare warrant,
Begun through malice of the bishop's men.
    *A noise again*, 'Stones! stones!'
    *Enter Mayor.*

MAYOR
O my good lords, and virtuous Henry,
Pity the city of London, pity us!
The bishop and the Duke of Gloucester's men,     78
Forbidden late to carry any weapon,     79
Have filled their pockets full of pebble stones
And, banding themselves in contrary parts,     81
Do pelt so fast at one another's pate
That many have their giddy brains knocked out.
Our windows are broke down in every street
And we, for fear, compelled to shut our shops.
    *Enter in skirmish [Servingmen of Gloucester and
    Winchester] with bloody pates.*

KING
We charge you, on allegiance to ourself,
To hold your slaught'ring hands and keep the peace.
Pray, uncle Gloucester, mitigate this strife.

1. SERVINGMAN Nay, if we be forbidden stones, we'll
fall to it with our teeth.

2. SERVINGMAN
Do what ye dare, we are as resolute.
    *Skirmish again.*

GLOUCESTER
You of my household, leave this peevish broil     92
And set this unaccustomed fight aside.     93

3. SERVINGMAN
My lord, we know your grace to be a man
Just and upright, and for your royal birth
Inferior to none but to his majesty;
And ere that we will suffer such a prince,
So kind a father of the commonweal,
To be disgraced by an inkhorn mate,     99
We and our wives and children all will fight
And have our bodies slaught'red by thy foes.

1. SERVINGMAN
Ay, and the very parings of our nails
Shall pitch a field when we are dead.     103
    *Begin again.*

GLOUCESTER                    Stay, stay, I say!
And if you love me, as you say you do,
Let me persuade you to forbear awhile.

KING
O, how this discord doth afflict my soul!
Can you, my Lord of Winchester, behold
My sighs and tears and will not once relent?
Who should be pitiful if you be not?
Or who should study to prefer a peace     110
If holy churchmen take delight in broils?

WARWICK
Yield, my Lord Protector, yield, Winchester,
Except you mean with obstinate repulse     113
To slay your sovereign and destroy the realm.
You see what mischief, and what murder too,

Hath been enacted through your enmity.
Then be at peace, except ye thirst for blood.

WINCHESTER
He shall submit, or I will never yield.

GLOUCESTER
Compassion on the king commands me stoop,
Or I would see his heart out ere the priest
121    Should ever get that privilege of me.

WARWICK
Behold, my Lord of Winchester, the duke
123    Hath banishèd moody discontented fury,
As by his smoothèd brows it doth appear.
Why look you still so stern and tragical?

GLOUCESTER
Here, Winchester, I offer thee my hand.

KING
Fie, uncle Beaufort, I have heard you preach
That malice was a great and grievous sin;
And will not you maintain the thing you teach,
But prove a chief offender in the same?

WARWICK
131    Sweet king! The bishop hath a kindly gird.
For shame, my Lord of Winchester, relent.
What, shall a child instruct you what to do?

WINCHESTER
Well, Duke of Gloucester, I will yield to thee.
Love for thy love and hand for hand I give.

GLOUCESTER [aside]
Ay, but I fear me with a hollow heart. –
See here, my friends and loving countrymen:
This token serveth for a flag of truce
Betwixt ourselves and all our followers.
So help me God as I dissemble not.

WINCHESTER [aside]
So help me God as I intend it not.

KING
O loving uncle, kind Duke of Gloucester,
How joyful am I made by this contract!
144    Away, my masters. Trouble us no more,
But join in friendship, as your lords have done.

1. SERVINGMAN
Content. I'll to the surgeon's.

2. SERVINGMAN                    And so will I.

3. SERVINGMAN
147    And I will see what physic the tavern affords.
                Exeunt [Servingmen, Mayor, etc.].

WARWICK
Accept this scroll, most gracious sovereign,
Which in the right of Richard Plantagenet
We do exhibit to your majesty.

GLOUCESTER
Well urged, my Lord of Warwick; for, sweet prince,
152    An if your grace mark every circumstance,
You have great reason to do Richard right,
154    Especially for those occasions
At Eltham Place I told your majesty.

KING
And those occasions, uncle, were of force.
Therefore, my loving lords, our pleasure is
158    That Richard be restorèd to his blood.

WARWICK
Let Richard be restorèd to his blood.
160    So shall his father's wrongs be recompensed.

WINCHESTER
As will the rest, so willeth Winchester.

KING
If Richard will be true, not that alone
But all the whole inheritance I give
That doth belong unto the house of York,
From whence you spring by lineal descent.

RICHARD
Thy humble servant vows obedience
And humble service till the point of death.

KING
Stoop then and set your knee against my foot,
And in reguerdon of that duty done                    169
I girt thee with the valiant sword of York.
Rise, Richard, like a true Plantagenet,
And rise created princely Duke of York.

RICHARD
And so thrive Richard as thy foes may fall;
And as my duty springs, so perish they
That grudge one thought against your majesty.

ALL
Welcome, high prince, the mighty Duke of York!

SOMERSET [aside]
Perish, base prince, ignoble Duke of York!

GLOUCESTER
Now will it best avail your majesty
To cross the seas and to be crowned in France.
The presence of a king engenders love
Amongst his subjects and his loyal friends,
As it disanimates his enemies.                    182

KING
When Gloucester says the word, King Henry goes,
For friendly counsel cuts off many foes.

GLOUCESTER
Your ships already are in readiness.
                Sennet. Flourish. Exeunt. Manet Exeter.

EXETER
Ay, we may march in England or in France,
Not seeing what is likely to ensue.
This late dissension grown betwixt the peers
Burns under feignèd ashes of forged love
And will at last break out into a flame.
As fest'red members rot but by degree
Till bones and flesh and sinews fall away,
So will this base and envious discord breed.
And now I fear that fatal prophecy
Which in the time of Henry named the Fifth
Was in the mouth of every sucking babe:
That Henry born at Monmouth should win all
And Henry born at Windsor should lose all;
Which is so plain that Exeter doth wish
His days may finish ere that hapless time.          Exit.

*

121 *privilege of* advantage yielded by   123 *moody* haughty   131 *kindly*
*gird* proper rebuke   144 *masters* (condescending term for servants)   147
*physic* remedy   152 *An if* if   154 *occasions* circumstances   158 *restorèd*
*. . . blood* i.e. reinstated in the inherited titles forfeited by his father   160
*recompensed* compensated   169 *reguerdon* requital   182 *disanimates* dis-
pirits

III, ii     *Enter Pucelle disguised, with four Soldiers [dressed like countrymen] with sacks upon their backs.*

PUCELLE
1   These are the city gates, the gates of Roan,
2   Through which our policy must make a breach.
3   Take heed, be wary how you place your words ;
4   Talk like the vulgar sort of marketmen
5   That come to gather money for their corn.
   If we have entrance, as I hope we shall,
7   And that we find the slothful watch but weak,
   I'll by a sign give notice to our friends,
   That Charles the Dauphin may encounter them.

SOLDIER
  Our sacks shall be a mean to sack the city,
  And we be lords and rulers over Roan.
  Therefore we'll knock.
    *Knock.*

13 WATCH *[within]* Che la ?

PUCELLE
  Peasauns, la pouvre gens de Fraunce,
  Poor market folks that come to sell their corn.

WATCH *[opening the gates]*
  Enter, go in ; the market bell is rung.

PUCELLE
  Now, Roan, I'll shake thy bulwarks to the ground.
                 *Exeunt [into the city].*
  *Enter Charles, Bastard, Alençon [, Reignier, and Soldiers].*

CHARLES
  Saint Denis bless this happy stratagem,
  And once again we'll sleep secure in Roan.

BASTARD
20   Here ent'red Pucelle and her practisants.
  Now she is there, how will she specify
  Here is the best and safest passage in ?

REIGNIER
  By thrusting out a torch from yonder tower,
  Which, once discerned, shows that her meaning is,
25   No way to that, for weakness, which she ent'red.
  *Enter Pucelle on the top, thrusting out a torch burning.*

PUCELLE
  Behold, this is the happy wedding torch
  That joineth Roan unto her countrymen,
  But burning fatal to the Talbonites.     *[Exit.]*

BASTARD
  See, noble Charles, the beacon of our friend.
  The burning torch in yonder turret stands.

CHARLES
31   Now shine it like a comet of revenge,
32   A prophet to the fall of all our foes !

REIGNIER
  Defer no time ; delays have dangerous ends.
  Enter and cry 'The Dauphin !' presently,     34
  And then do execution on the watch.
    *Alarum. [They storm the gates.]*
    *An alarum. Talbot in an excursion [from within].*

TALBOT
  France, thou shalt rue this treason with thy tears
  If Talbot but survive thy treachery.
  Pucelle, that witch, that damnèd sorceress,
  Hath wrought this hellish mischief unawares,     39
  That hardly we escaped the pride of France.     *Exit.* 40
  *An alarum. Excursions. Bedford brought in sick in a chair. Enter Talbot and Burgundy without ; within, Pucelle, Charles, Bastard, [Alençon,] and Reignier on the walls.*

PUCELLE
  Good morrow, gallants, want ye corn for bread ?
  I think the Duke of Burgundy will fast
  Before he'll buy again at such a rate.
  'Twas full of darnel. Do you like the taste ?     44

BURGUNDY
  Scoff on, vile fiend and shameless courtesan !
  I trust ere long to choke thee with thine own
  And make thee curse the harvest of that corn.

CHARLES
  Your grace may starve, perhaps, before that time.

BEDFORD
  O, let no words, but deeds, revenge this treason !

PUCELLE
  What will you do, good greybeard, break a lance
  And run a-tilt at death within a chair ?

TALBOT
  Foul fiend of France and hag of all despite,
  Encompassed with thy lustful paramours,
  Becomes it thee to taunt his valiant age
  And twit with cowardice a man half dead ?
  Damsel, I'll have a bout with you again,     56
  Or else let Talbot perish with this shame.

PUCELLE
  Are ye so hot, sir ? Yet, Pucelle, hold thy peace.     58
  If Talbot do but thunder, rain will follow.
    *They [the English] whisper together in counsel.*
  God speed the parliament ; who shall be the Speaker ?

TALBOT
  Dare ye come forth and meet us in the field ?

PUCELLE
  Belike your lordship takes us then for fools,
  To try if that our own be ours or no.

TALBOT
  I speak not to that railing Hecate,     64
  But unto thee, Alençon, and the rest.
  Will ye, like soldiers, come and fight it out ?

ALENÇON
  Signior, no.

TALBOT
  Signior, hang ! Base muleters of France !     68
  Like peasant footboys do they keep the walls
  And dare not take up arms like gentlemen.

PUCELLE
  Away, captains. Let's get us from the walls,
  For Talbot means no goodness by his looks.
  God b'uy, my lord. We came but to tell you     73

---

III, ii Before Rouen in France  1 *These . . . Roan* (the gates lead into the tiring house, representing Rouen in this scene ; appearances 'on the walls' are from the rear stage gallery as in I, vi)  2 *policy* stratagem  3 *place* arrange  4 *vulgar* common (not disparaging)  5 *corn* wheat  7 *that* if  13 *Che la ?* who is there ? (argot French)  20 *practisants* conspirators  25 *No . . . weakness* i.e. no way compares in weakness with that ;  s.d. *on the top* (an upper vantage point in the tiring-house façade ?)  31 *shine it* may it shine  32 *prophet* omen  34 *presently* immediately  39 *mischief unawares* harm unexpectedly  40 *hardly* with difficulty ; *pride* power  44 *darnel* weed  56, 58 *bout, hot* (sexual double entendres)  64 *Hecate* goddess identified with the moon and the underworld (hence guardian of witches)  68 *Base muleters* mule drivers of low birth  73 *b'uy* be with you

That we are here.                    *Exeunt from the walls.*

TALBOT
And there will we be too ere it be long,
Or else reproach be Talbot's greatest fame !
Vow, Burgundy, by honor of thy house,
78  Pricked on by public wrongs sustained in France,
Either to get the town again or die ;
And I, as sure as English Henry lives
81  And as his father here was conqueror,
As sure as in this late betrayèd town
83  Great Coeur-de-lion's heart was buried,
So sure I swear to get the town or die.

BURGUNDY
My vows are equal partners with thy vows.

TALBOT
86  But, ere we go, regard this dying prince,
The valiant Duke of Bedford. Come, my lord,
We will bestow you in some better place,
89  Fitter for sickness and for crazy age.

BEDFORD
Lord Talbot, do not so dishonor me.
Here will I sit, before the walls of Roan,
And will be partner of your weal or woe.

BURGUNDY
Courageous Bedford, let us now persuade you.

BEDFORD
Not to be gone from hence ; for once I read
95  That stout Pendragon in his litter sick
Came to the field and vanquishèd his foes.
97  Methinks I should revive the soldiers' hearts,
Because I ever found them as myself.

TALBOT
Undaunted spirit in a dying breast !
Then be it so. Heavens keep old Bedford safe !
And now no more ado, brave Burgundy,
102  But gather we our forces out of hand
And set upon our boasting enemy.
                    *Exit [Talbot with others to the assault.*
                    *Manent Bedford and Attendants].*
        *An alarum. Excursions. Enter Sir John Falstaff*
        *and a Captain.*

CAPTAIN
Whither away, Sir John Falstaff, in such haste ?

FALSTAFF
Whither away ? To save myself by flight.
We are like to have the overthrow again.

CAPTAIN
What ? will you fly and leave Lord Talbot ?

FALSTAFF                                        Ay,
All the Talbots in the world, to save my life.        *Exit.*

CAPTAIN
Cowardly knight, ill fortune follow thee !        *Exit.*
        *Retreat. Excursions. Pucelle, Alençon and Charles*
        *fly.*

BEDFORD
110  Now, quiet soul, depart when heaven please,
For I have seen our enemies' overthrow.
What is the trust or strength of foolish man ?
They that of late were daring with their scoffs
114  Are glad and fain by flight to save themselves.
        *Bedford dies and is carried in by two in his chair.*
        *An alarum. Enter Talbot, Burgundy, and the rest.*

TALBOT
Lost and recovered in a day again !

This is a double honor, Burgundy.
Yet heavens have glory for this victory !

BURGUNDY
Warlike and martial Talbot, Burgundy
Enshrines thee in his heart and there erects
Thy noble deeds as valor's monuments.

TALBOT
Thanks, gentle duke. But where is Pucelle now ?        121
I think her old familiar is asleep.                    122
Now where's the Bastard's braves and Charles his      123
   glikes ?
What, all amort ? Roan hangs her head for grief       124
That such a valiant company are fled.
Now will we take some order in the town,              126
Placing therein some expert officers,
And then depart to Paris to the king,
For there young Henry with his nobles lie.

BURGUNDY
What wills Lord Talbot pleaseth Burgundy.

TALBOT
But yet, before we go, let's not forget
The noble Duke of Bedford, late deceased,
But see his exequies fulfilled in Roan.               133
A braver soldier never couchèd lance,
A gentler heart did never sway in court.
But kings and mightiest potentates must die,
For that's the end of human misery.        *Exeunt.*

\*

        *Enter Charles, Bastard, Alençon, Pucelle [and*        III, ii
        *Soldiers].*

PUCELLE
Dismay not, princes, at this accident,                1
Nor grieve that Roan is so recoverèd.
Care is no cure, but rather corrosive,                3
For things that are not to be remedied.
Let frantic Talbot triumph for a while
And like a peacock sweep along his tail ;
We'll pull his plumes and take away his train,        7
If Dauphin and the rest will be but ruled.            8

CHARLES
We have been guided by thee hitherto
And of thy cunning had no diffidence.                 10
One sudden foil shall never breed distrust.           11

BASTARD
Search out thy wit for secret policies,
And we will make thee famous through the world.

ALENÇON
We'll set thy statue in some holy place
And have thee reverenced like a blessèd saint.
Employ thee then, sweet virgin, for our good.         16

78 *Pricked on* goaded   81 *father . . . conqueror* (Henry V captured Rouen in
1418)   83 *Great . . . burièd* (Richard I willed his heart to be buried in Rouen
as an expression of esteem for that city)   86 *regard* attend to   89 *crazy*
decrepit   95–96 *Pendragon . . . foes* (told of Uther Pendragon's brother in
his victory against the Saxons)   97 *Methinks* it seems to me   102 *out of*
*hand* at once   110–11 *Now . . . overthrow* (an echo of the *Nunc Dimittis* ;
see Luke ii, 29–32)   114 *fain* well pleased   121 *gentle* noble   122 *old*
*familiar* customary attendant spirit (i.e. the Devil)   123 *braves* bravado ;
*Charles his glikes* Charles' scoffs   124 *amort* sick to death   126 *take some*
*order* make arrangements   133 *exequies* funeral rites
III, iii *Fields* near Rouen   1 *accident* unforeseen event   3 *corrosive*
aggravating   7 *train* (1) army, (2) peacock's tail   8 *be but ruled* follow
instructions   10 *cunning* skill in magic ; *diffidence* distrust   11 *foil* repulse
16 *Employ thee* exert thyself

PUCELLE
Then thus it must be ; this doth Joan devise :
By fair persuasions, mixed with sug'red words,
We will entice the Duke of Burgundy
To leave the Talbot and to follow us.

CHARLES
Ay, marry, sweeting, if we could do that,
France were no place for Henry's warriors,
Nor should that nation boast it so with us,
24   But be extirpèd from our provinces.

ALENÇON
25   For ever should they be expulsed from France
And not have title of an earldom here.

PUCELLE
Your honors shall perceive how I will work
To bring this matter to the wishèd end.
       *Drum sounds afar off.*
Hark, by the sound of drum you may perceive
Their powers are marching unto Paris-ward.
       *Here sound an English march.*
There goes the Talbot, with his colors spread,
And all the troops of English after him.
       *[Here sound a] French march.*
Now in the rearward comes the duke and his.
34   Fortune in favor makes him lag behind.
Summon a parley ; we will talk with him.
       *Trumpets sound a parley.*

CHARLES
A parley with the Duke of Burgundy !
       *[Enter Burgundy and Troops.]*

BURGUNDY
Who craves a parley with the Burgundy ?

PUCELLE
The princely Charles of France, thy countryman.

BURGUNDY
What say'st thou, Charles ? for I am marching hence.

CHARLES
Speak, Pucelle, and enchant him with thy words.

PUCELLE
41   Brave Burgundy, undoubted hope of France,
Stay, let thy humble handmaid speak to thee.

BURGUNDY
Speak on ; but be not over-tedious.

PUCELLE
Look on thy country, look on fertile France,
And see the cities and the towns defaced
By wasting ruin of the cruel foe,
As looks the mother on her lowly babe
48   When death doth close his tender-dying eyes.
See, see the pining malady of France !
50   Behold the wounds, the most unnatural wounds,
Which thou thyself hast given her woeful breast.
O, turn thy edgèd sword another way ;
Strike those that hurt, and hurt not those that help !
One drop of blood drawn from thy country's bosom
Should grieve thee more than streams of foreign gore.
Return thee therefore with a flood of tears
And wash away thy country's stainèd spots.

24 *extirpèd* rooted out   25 *expulsed* expelled   34 *in favor* benevolently
41 *undoubted* fearless   48 *tender-dying* dying at a tender age   50 *unnatural*
against law of kinship   60 *exclaims on* accuses loudly   61 *progeny* ancestry
76 *wandering* erring   78 *haughty* lofty   88 *bravely* (1) courageously, (2)
splendidly   91 *prejudice* harm
III, iv The royal palace in Paris   4 *duty* feudal obeisance

BURGUNDY
Either she hath bewitched me with her words,
Or nature makes me suddenly relent.

PUCELLE
Besides, all French and France exclaims on thee,         60
Doubting thy birth and lawful progeny.                    61
Who join'st thou with but with a lordly nation
That will not trust thee but for profit's sake ?
When Talbot hath set footing once in France
And fashioned thee that instrument of ill,
Who then but English Henry will be lord,
And thou be thrust out like a fugitive ?
Call we to mind, and mark but this for proof:
Was not the Duke of Orleans thy foe?
And was he not in England prisoner ?
But when they heard he was thine enemy,
They set him free without his ransom paid,
In spite of Burgundy and all his friends.
See then, thou fight'st against thy countrymen
And join'st with them will be thy slaughtermen.
Come, come, return. Return, thou wandering lord.         76
Charles and the rest will take thee in their arms.

BURGUNDY
I am vanquishèd. These haughty words of hers             78
Have batt'red me like roaring cannon-shot
And made me almost yield upon my knees. –
Forgive me, country, and sweet countrymen !
And, lords, accept this hearty kind embrace.
My forces and my power of men are yours.
So farewell, Talbot. I'll no longer trust thee.

PUCELLE
Done like a Frenchman – *[aside]* turn and turn again.

CHARLES
Welcome, brave duke. Thy friendship makes us fresh.

BASTARD
And doth beget new courage in our breasts.

ALENÇON
Pucelle hath bravely played her part in this             88
And doth deserve a coronet of gold.

CHARLES
Now let us on, my lords, and join our powers,
And seek how we may prejudice the foe.      *Exeunt.*  91

*

*Enter the King, Gloucester, Winchester, [Richard*    III, iv
*Duke of] York, Suffolk, Somerset, Warwick,*
*Exeter [, Vernon, Basset, and others]. To them, with*
*his Soldiers, Talbot.*

TALBOT
My gracious prince, and honorable peers,
Hearing of your arrival in this realm,
I have awhile given truce unto my wars
To do my duty to my sovereign ;                          4
In sign whereof this arm that hath reclaimed
To your obedience fifty fortresses,
Twelve cities, and seven wallèd towns of strength,
Beside five hundred prisoners of esteem,
Lets fall his sword before your highness' feet
       *[Kneels.]*
And with submissive loyalty of heart
Ascribes the glory of his conquest got
First to my God and next unto your grace.

KING

  Is this the Lord Talbot, uncle Gloucester,
  That hath so long been resident in France?

GLOUCESTER

  Yes, if it please your majesty, my liege.

KING

  Welcome, brave captain and victorious lord!
  When I was young (as yet I am not old)
  I do remember how my father said
  A stouter champion never handled sword.
20  Long since we were resolvèd of your truth,
  Your faithful service, and your toil in war;
  Yet never have you tasted our reward
23  Or been reguerdoned with so much as thanks,
  Because till now we never saw your face.
  Therefore stand up, and for these good deserts
  We here create you Earl of Shrewsbury,
  And in our coronation take your place.
      *Sennet. Flourish. Exeunt. Manent Vernon and Basset.*

VERNON

28  Now, sir, to you, that were so hot at sea,
  Disgracing of these colors that I wear
  In honor of my noble Lord of York –
  Dar'st thou maintain the former words thou spak'st?

BASSET

32  Yes, sir, as well as you dare patronage
  The envious barking of your saucy tongue
  Against my lord the Duke of Somerset.

VERNON

  Sirrah, thy lord I honor as he is.

BASSET

  Why, what is he? As good a man as York.

VERNON

  Hark ye, not so. In witness take ye that.
      *Strikes him.*

BASSET

  Villain, thou knowest the law of arms is such
39  That whoso draws a sword, 'tis present death,
  Or else this blow should broach thy dearest blood.
  But I'll unto his majesty and crave
  I may have liberty to venge this wrong,
  When thou shalt see I'll meet thee to thy cost.

VERNON

  Well, miscreant, I'll be there as soon as you,
  And after meet you, sooner than you would.    *Exeunt.*

IV, i    *Enter King, Gloucester, Winchester, [Richard*
      *Duke of] York, Suffolk, Somerset, Warwick,*
      *Talbot, Exeter, and Governor [of Paris].*

GLOUCESTER

  Lord Bishop, set the crown upon his head.

WINCHESTER

  God save King Henry, of that name the sixth!

GLOUCESTER

  Now, governor of Paris, take your oath,
      *[Governor kneels.]*
4  That you elect no other king but him,
  Esteem none friends but such as are his friends,
6  And none your foes but such as shall pretend
  Malicious practices against his state.
  This shall ye do, so help you righteous God.
      *[Governor retires.]*

    *Enter Falstaff.*

FALSTAFF

  My gracious sovereign, as I rode from Calais

  To haste unto your coronation,
  A letter was delivered to my hands,
  Writ to your grace from th' Duke of Burgundy.

TALBOT

  Shame to the Duke of Burgundy and thee!
  I vowed, base knight, when I did meet thee next
  To tear the Garter from thy craven's leg,      15
    *[Plucks it off.]*
  Which I have done, because unworthily
  Thou wast installèd in that high degree.
  Pardon me, princely Henry, and the rest.
  This dastard, at the battle of Poictiers,      19
  When, but in all, I was six thousand strong
  And that the French were almost ten to one,
  Before we met or that a stroke was given,
  Like to a trusty squire did run away;      23
  In which assault we lost twelve hundred men.
  Myself and divers gentlemen beside
  Were there surprised and taken prisoners.
  Then judge, great lords, if I have done amiss,
  Or whether that such cowards ought to wear
  This ornament of knighthood, yea or no?

GLOUCESTER

  To say the truth, this fact was infamous,      30
  And ill beseeming any common man;      31
  Much more a knight, a captain, and a leader.

TALBOT

  When first this order was ordained, my lords,
  Knights of the Garter were of noble birth,
  Valiant and virtuous, full of haughty courage,    35
  Such as were grown to credit by the wars;    36
  Not fearing death nor shrinking for distress,    37
  But always resolute in most extremes.      38
  He then that is not furnished in this sort     39
  Doth but usurp the sacred name of knight,
  Profaning this most honorable order,
  And should (if I were worthy to be judge)
  Be quite degraded, like a hedge-born swain    43
  That doth presume to boast of gentle blood.

KING

  Stain to thy countrymen, thou hear'st thy doom.
  Be packing therefore, thou that wast a knight.    46
  Henceforth we banish thee on pain of death.
      *[Exit Falstaff.]*
  And now, Lord Protector, view the letter
  Sent from our uncle Duke of Burgundy.

GLOUCESTER

  What means his grace that he hath changed his style?   50
  No more but plain and bluntly 'To the king'?
  Hath he forgot he is his sovereign?
  Or doth this churlish superscription
  Pretend some alteration in good will?      54
  What's here? *[Reads]* 'I have, upon especial cause,
  Moved with compassion of my country's wrack

---

**20** *we* (the royal plural); *resolvèd* convinced  **23** *reguerdoned* rewarded **28** *hot* angry  **32** *patronage* defend  **39** *present* immediate (since duelling at court was punishable by death)
**IV, i 4** *elect* acknowledge  **6** *pretend* intend  **15** *Garter* badge of the Order of the Garter  **19** *Poictiers* (perhaps confused with Patay)  **23** *trusty squire* (contemptuous)  **30** *fact* misdeed  **31** *common* lacking noble rank  **35** *haughty* lofty  **36** *were . . . credit* had risen to renown  **37** *for distress* in face of hardship  **38** *most* greatest  **39** *furnished . . . sort* so endowed  **43** *hedge-born swain* low-born rustic  **46** *Be packing* be off  **50** *style* form of address  **54** *Pretend* import

Together with the pitiful complaints
Of such as your oppression feeds upon,
Forsaken your pernicious faction
And joined with Charles, the rightful King of France.'
O monstrous treachery ! Can this be so ?
That in alliance, amity, and oaths
There should be found such false dissembling guile ?

KING

64    What ? Doth my uncle Burgundy revolt ?

GLOUCESTER

He doth, my lord, and is become your foe.

KING

Is that the worst this letter doth contain ?

GLOUCESTER

It is the worst, and all, my lord, he writes.

KING

Why, then Lord Talbot there shall talk with him
And give him chastisement for this abuse.
How say you, my lord ? Are you not content ?

TALBOT

71    Content, my liege ? Yes. But that I am prevented,
I should have begged I might have been employed.

KING

73    Then gather strength and march unto him straight.
74    Let him perceive how ill we brook his treason
And what offense it is to flout his friends.

TALBOT

76    I go, my lord, in heart desiring still
You may behold confusion of your foes.     *[Exit.]*
     *Enter Vernon and Basset.*

VERNON

78    Grant me the combat, gracious sovereign.

BASSET

And me, my lord, grant me the combat too.

RICHARD

80    This is my servant. Hear him, noble prince.

SOMERSET

And this is mine. Sweet Henry, favor him.

KING

Be patient, lords, and give them leave to speak.
Say, gentlemen, what makes you thus exclaim ?
And wherefore crave you combat ? or with whom ?

VERNON

With him, my lord, for he hath done me wrong.

BASSET

And I with him, for he hath done me wrong.

KING

What is that wrong whereof you both complain ?
First let me know, and then I'll answer you.

BASSET

Crossing the sea from England into France,
This fellow here with envious carping tongue
Upbraided me about the rose I wear,
92    Saying the sanguine color of the leaves
Did represent my master's blushing cheeks

When stubbornly he did repugn the truth     94
About a certain question in the law
Argued betwixt the Duke of York and him ;
With other vile and ignominious terms.
In confutation of which rude reproach,
And in defense of my lord's worthiness,
I crave the benefit of law of arms.     100

VERNON

And that is my petition, noble lord.
For though he seem with forgèd quaint conceit     102
To set a gloss upon his bold intent,     103
Yet know, my lord, I was provoked by him,
And he first took exceptions at this badge,
Pronouncing that the paleness of this flower
Bewrayed the faintness of my master's heart.     107

RICHARD

Will not this malice, Somerset, be left ?

SOMERSET

Your private grudge, my Lord of York, will out,
Though ne'er so cunningly you smother it.

KING

Good Lord, what madness rules in brainsick men
When for so slight and frivolous a cause
Such factious emulations shall arise !     113
Good cousins both, of York and Somerset,
Quiet yourselves, I pray, and be at peace.

RICHARD

Let his dissension first be tried by fight,
And then your highness shall command a peace.

SOMERSET

The quarrel toucheth none but us alone.     118
Betwixt ourselves let us decide it then.

RICHARD

There is my pledge. Accept it, Somerset.     120

VERNON

Nay, let it rest where it began at first.

BASSET

Confirm it so, mine honorable lord.

GLOUCESTER

Confirm it so ? Confounded be your strife,
And perish ye with your audacious prate !
Presumptuous vassals, are you not ashamed
With this immodest clamorous outrage
To trouble and disturb the king and us ?
And you, my lords, methinks you do not well
To bear with their perverse objections :     129
Much less to take occasion from their mouths
To raise a mutiny betwixt yourselves.
Let me persuade you take a better course.

EXETER

It grieves his highness. Good my lords, be friends.

KING

Come hither you that would be combatants.
Henceforth I charge you, as you love our favor,
Quite to forget this quarrel and the cause.
And you, my lords : remember where we are,
In France, amongst a fickle wavering nation.
If they perceive dissension in our looks
And that within ourselves we disagree,
How will their grudging stomachs be provoked     141
To willfull disobedience, and rebel !
Beside, what infamy will there arise
When foreign princes shall be certified     144
That for a toy, a thing of no regard,     145

64 *uncle* (Henry's uncle the Duke of Bedford married Burgundy's sister Anne)   71 *am prevented* have been anticipated   73 *strength* forces; *straight* immediately   74 *brook* endure   76 *still* always   78 *the combat* a duel   80 *servant* retainer (not menial)   92 *sanguine* blood-red ; *leaves* petals   94 *repugn* oppose   100 *benefit* legal privilege   102 *quaint conceit* ingenious fancy   103 *set . . . upon* give fair outward appearance to   107 *Bewrayed* revealed   113 *emulations* rivalries   118 *toucheth* involves   120 *pledge* gage in a duel (usually a glove)   129 *objections* mutual accusations   141 *grudging stomachs* resentful tempers   144 *certified* informed   145 *toy* trifle ; *regard* consequence

King Henry's peers and chief nobility
Destroyed themselves and lost the realm of France!
O, think upon the conquest of my father,
My tender years, and let us not forgo
150 That for a trifle that was bought with blood!
Let me be umpire in this doubtful strife.
I see no reason, if I wear this rose,
    *[Puts on a red rose.]*
That any one should therefore be suspicious
I more incline to Somerset than York.
Both are my kinsmen, and I love them both.
As well they may upbraid me with my crown
Because forsooth the King of Scots is crowned.
But your discretions better can persuade
Than I am able to instruct or teach;
And therefore, as we hither came in peace,
So let us still continue peace and love.
Cousin of York, we institute your grace
To be our regent in these parts of France;
And, good my Lord of Somerset, unite
Your troops of horsemen with his bands of foot;
And like true subjects, sons of your progenitors,
167 Go cheerfully together and digest
Your angry choler on your enemies.
Ourself, my Lord Protector, and the rest,
After some respite will return to Calais;
From thence to England, where I hope ere long
To be presented, by your victories,
173 With Charles, Alençon, and that traitorous rout.
    *Exeunt. Manent [Richard Duke of] York,*
        *Warwick, Exeter, Vernon.*

WARWICK
My Lord of York, I promise you, the king
Prettily, methought, did play the orator.
RICHARD
And so he did; but yet I like it not,
In that he wears the badge of Somerset.
WARWICK
Tush, that was but his fancy. Blame him not.
I dare presume, sweet prince, he thought no harm.
RICHARD
180 An if I wist he did – But let it rest.
Other affairs must now be managèd.
    *Exeunt. Flourish. Manet Exeter.*
EXETER
Well didst thou, Richard, to suppress thy voice;
For, had the passions of thy heart burst out,
I fear we should have seen deciphered there
More rancorous spite, more furious raging broils,
Than yet can be imagined or supposed.
187 But howsoe'er, no simple man that sees
This jarring discord of nobility,
This shouldering of each other in the court,
190 This factious bandying of their favorites,
But that it doth presage some ill event.
192 'Tis much when sceptres are in children's hands,
193 But more when envy breeds unkind division.
There comes the ruin, there begins confusion.    *Exit.*

       *

*Enter Talbot, with Trump and Drum before*    IV, ii
*Bordeaux.*
TALBOT
Go to the gates of Bordeaux, trumpeter.
Summon their general unto the wall.
    *[Trumpet] sounds. Enter General, aloft [with his men].*
English John Talbot, captains, calls you forth,
Servant in arms to Harry King of England;
And thus he would: Open your city gates,     5
Be humble to us, call my sovereign yours
And do him homage as obedient subjects,
And I'll withdraw me and my bloody power;
But if you frown upon this proffered peace,
You tempt the fury of my three attendants,
Lean famine, quartering steel, and climbing fire,    11
Who in a moment even with the earth
Shall lay your stately and air-braving towers,
If you forsake the offer of their love.
GENERAL
Thou ominous and fearful owl of death,
Our nation's terror and their bloody scourge,
The period of thy tyranny approacheth.     17
On us thou canst not enter but by death;
For I protest we are well fortified
And strong enough to issue out and fight.
If thou retire, the Dauphin, well appointed,    21
Stands with the snares of war to tangle thee.
On either hand thee there are squadrons pitched    23
To wall thee from the liberty of flight;     24
And no way canst thou turn thee for redress
But death doth front thee with apparent spoil    26
And pale destruction meets thee in the face.
Ten thousand French have ta'en the sacrament    28
To rive their dangerous artillery     29
Upon no Christian soul but English Talbot.
Lo, there thou stand'st, a breathing valiant man
Of an invincible unconquered spirit.
This is the latest glory of thy praise
That I thy enemy due thee withal;     34
For ere the glass that now begins to run
Finish the process of his sandy hour,
These eyes that see thee now well-colorèd
Shall see thee withered, bloody, pale, and dead.
    *Drum afar off.*
Hark, hark! The Dauphin's drum, a warning bell,
Sings heavy music to thy timorous soul;
And mine shall ring thy dire departure out.
    *Exit [with his men].*
TALBOT
He fables not; I hear the enemy.
Out, some light horsemen, and peruse their wings.    43
O, negligent and heedless discipline!
How are we parked and bounded in a pale,     45
A little herd of England's timorous deer,

---

150 *That . . . that* for a trifle that which   167 *digest* dissipate   173 *rout*
rabble   180 *An . . . wist* if I knew for certain   187 *simple* common   190
*bandying* verbal contending; *favorites* followers   192 *much* serious   193
*unkind* intra-family
IV, ii Before the walls of Bordeaux   5 *would* wishes   11 *quartering* dismembering the slain enemy   17 *period* end   21 *appointed* equipped   23
*thee* of thee; *pitched* set in battle order   24 *wall* hem in   26 *front* face;
*spoil* slaughter (hunting metaphor, continued from *snares* in l. 22)   28 *ta'en
the sacrament* i.e. sworn a solemn oath   29 *rive* fire   34 *due* endue   43
*peruse* reconnoitre   45 *parked* enclosed; *pale* fenced-in area

47 Mazed with a yelping kennel of French curs!
48 If we be English deer, be then in blood:
49 Not rascal-like, to fall down with a pinch,
   But rather, moody-mad and desperate stags,
51 Turn on the bloody hounds with heads of steel
   And make the cowards stand aloof at bay.
   Sell every man his life as dear as mine,
   And they shall find dear deer of us, my friends.
   God and Saint George, Talbot and England's right,
   Prosper our colors in this dangerous fight!     [Exeunt.]

\*

IV, iii          Enter a Messenger that meets [Richard Duke of] York.
                 Enter York, with Trumpet and many Soldiers.
   RICHARD
   Are not the speedy scouts returned again
   That dogged the mighty army of the Dauphin?
   MESSENGER
3  They are returned, my lord, and give it out
   That he is marched to Bordeaux with his power
   To fight with Talbot. As he marched along,
   By your espials were discoverèd
   Two mightier troops than that the Dauphin led,
   Which joined with him and made their march for
     Bordeaux.
   RICHARD
   A plague upon that villain Somerset
   That thus delays my promisèd supply
   Of horsemen that were levied for this siege!
   Renownèd Talbot doth expect my aid,
13 And I am louted by a traitor villain
   And cannot help the noble chevalier.
   God comfort him in this necessity!
16 If he miscarry, farewell wars in France.
       Enter another Messenger [Sir William Lucy].
   LUCY
   Thou princely leader of our English strength,
   Never so needful on the earth of France,
   Spur to the rescue of the noble Talbot,
   Who now is girdled with a waist of iron
   And hemmed about with grim destruction.
   To Bordeaux, warlike duke! to Bordeaux, York!
   Else farewell Talbot, France, and England's honor.
   RICHARD
   O God, that Somerset, who in proud heart
25 Doth stop my cornets, were in Talbot's place!
   So should we save a valiant gentleman
   By forfeiting a traitor and a coward.
   Mad ire and wrathful fury makes me weep
   That thus we die while remiss traitors sleep.
   LUCY
30 O, send some succor to the distressed lord!

RICHARD
He dies, we lose; I break my warlike word;
We mourn, France smiles; we lose, they daily get;
All long of this vile traitor Somerset.                    33
LUCY
Then God take mercy on brave Talbot's soul
And on his son, young John, who two hours since
I met in travel toward his warlike father.
This seven years did not Talbot see his son,
And now they meet where both their lives are done.
RICHARD
Alas, what joy shall noble Talbot have
To bid his young son welcome to his grave?
Away! Vexation almost stops my breath
That sund'red friends greet in the hour of death.
Lucy, farewell. No more my fortune can                     43
But curse the cause I cannot aid the man.
Maine, Blois, Poictiers, and Tours are won away,
Long all of Somerset and his delay.
                              Exit [with Soldiers].
LUCY
Thus, while the vulture of sedition
Feeds in the bosom of such great commanders,
Sleeping neglection doth betray to loss
The conquest of our scarce-cold conqueror,
That ever-living man of memory,                            51
Henry the Fifth. Whiles they each other cross,
Lives, honors, lands, and all hurry to loss.
       Enter Somerset, with his Army [, a Captain of        IV, iv
       Talbot's with him].
SOMERSET
It is too late; I cannot send them now.
This expedition was by York and Talbot
Too rashly plotted. All our general force                   3
Might with a sally of the very town
Be buckled with. The over-daring Talbot
Hath sullied all his gloss of former honor
By this unheedful, desperate, wild adventure.
York set him on to fight, and die in shame,
That, Talbot dead, great York might bear the name.
CAPTAIN
Here is Sir William Lucy, who with me
Set from our o'ermatched forces forth for aid.
SOMERSET
How now, Sir William, whither were you sent?
LUCY
Whither, my lord? From bought and sold Lord Talbot,        13
Who, ringed about with bold adversity,
Cries out for noble York and Somerset
To beat assailing death from his weak legions;
And whiles the honorable captain there
Drops bloody sweat from his war-wearied limbs,
And, in advantage ling'ring, looks for rescue,             19
You, his false hopes, the trust of England's honor,        20
Keep off aloof with worthless emulation.                   21
Let not your private discord keep away
The levied succors that should lend him aid,
While he, renownèd noble gentleman,
Yields up his life unto a world of odds.
Orleans the Bastard, Charles, Burgundy,
Alençon, Reignier compass him about,
And Talbot perisheth by your default.
SOMERSET
York set him on; York should have sent him aid.

---

47 *Mazed* bewildered   48 *in blood* in prime vigor   49 *rascal* (1) lean or
inferior deer, (2) rabble; *pinch* nip of the hounds   51 *heads of steel* horns
like swords
IV, iii Fields in Gascony   3 *give it out* report   13 *louted* made a fool of
16 *miscarry* come to harm   25 *cornets* companies of cavalry   30 *distressed*
in difficulties (not 'upset')   33 *long of* on account of   43 *can* is able to do
51 *ever-living . . . memory* man of ever-living memory
IV, iv   3–5 *All . . . with* the mere town garrison, without other aid, might
safely come forth to engage our whole army   13 *bought and sold* i.e. betrayed as by Judas   19 *in advantage ling'ring* finding his best hope in delay-
ing action   20 *trust* trustee   21 *worthless emulation* senseless rivalry

LUCY
30   And York as fast upon your grace exclaims,
     Swearing that you withhold his levied host,
     Collected for this expedition.

SOMERSET
33   York lies. He might have sent and had the horse.
     I owe him little duty, and less love,
     And take foul scorn to fawn on him by sending.

LUCY
     The fraud of England, not the force of France,
     Hath now entrapped the noble-minded Talbot.
     Never to England shall he bear his life,
     But dies betrayed to fortune by your strife.

SOMERSET
     Come, go. I will dispatch the horsemen straight;
     Within six hours they will be at his aid.

LUCY
     Too late comes rescue. He is ta'en or slain;
     For fly he could not, if he would have fled;
     And fly would Talbot never, though he might.

SOMERSET
     If he be dead, brave Talbot, then adieu!

LUCY
     His fame lives in the world, his shame in you.     *Exeunt*.

*

IV, v     *Enter Talbot and his Son.*

TALBOT
     O young John Talbot, I did send for thee
     To tutor thee in stratagems of war,
     That Talbot's name might be in thee revived
     When sapless age and weak unable limbs
     Should bring thy father to his drooping chair.
     But O malignant and ill-boding stars!
     Now thou art come unto a feast of death,
8    A terrible and unavoided danger.
     Therefore, dear boy, mount on my swiftest horse,
     And I'll direct thee how thou shalt escape
     By sudden flight. Come, dally not, be gone.

JOHN
     Is my name Talbot? and am I your son?
     And shall I fly? O, if you love my mother,
     Dishonor not her honorable name
     To make a bastard and a slave of me.
     The world will say he is not Talbot's blood
     That basely fled when noble Talbot stood.

TALBOT
     Fly, to revenge my death if I be slain.

JOHN
     He that flies so will ne'er return again.

TALBOT
     If we both stay, we both are sure to die.

JOHN
     Then let me stay, and father, do you fly.
22   Your loss is great, so your regard should be:
     My worth unknown, no loss is known in me.
     Upon my death the French can little boast;
     In yours they will, in you all hopes are lost.
     Flight cannot stain the honor you have won;
     But mine it will, that no exploit have done.
28   You fled for vantage, every one will swear;
     But if I bow, they'll say it was for fear.
     There is no hope that ever I will stay

If the first hour I shrink and run away.
Here on my knee I beg mortality                              32
Rather than life preserved with infamy.

TALBOT
     Shall all thy mother's hopes lie in one tomb?

JOHN
     Ay, rather than I'll shame my mother's womb.

TALBOT
     Upon my blessing I command thee go.

JOHN
     To fight I will, but not to fly the foe.

TALBOT
     Part of thy father may be saved in thee.

JOHN
     No part of him but will be shame in me.

TALBOT
     Thou never hadst renown, nor canst not lose it.

JOHN
     Yes, your renownèd name. Shall flight abuse it?

TALBOT
     Thy father's charge shall clear thee from that stain.

JOHN
     You cannot witness for me, being slain.                43
     If death be so apparent, then both fly.               44

TALBOT
     And leave my followers here to fight and die?
     My age was never tainted with such shame.             46

JOHN
     And shall my youth be guilty of such blame?
     No more can I be severed from your side
     Than can yourself yourself in twain divide.
     Stay, go, do what you will – the like do I;
     For live I will not if my father die.

TALBOT
     Then here I take my leave of thee, fair son,
     Born to eclipse thy life this afternoon.
     Come, side by side together live and die,
     And soul with soul from France to heaven fly.
                              *Exit [with Son].*
     *Alarum. Excursions, wherein Talbot's Son is hemmed*   IV, vi
     *about and Talbot rescues him.*

TALBOT
     Saint George and victory! Fight, soldiers, fight!
     The regent hath with Talbot broke his word
     And left us to the rage of France his sword.          3
     Where is John Talbot? Pause, and take thy breath.
     I gave thee life and rescued thee from death.

JOHN
     O twice my father, twice am I thy son!
     The life thou gav'st me first was lost and done
     Till with thy warlike sword, despite of fate,
     To my determined time thou gav'st new date.           9

TALBOT
     When from the Dauphin's crest thy sword struck fire,
     It warmed thy father's heart with proud desire
     Of bold-faced victory. Then leaden age,
     Quickened with youthful spleen and warlike rage,      13

30 *upon . . . exclaims* accuses your grace   33 *might . . . had* i.e. had and might
have sent
IV, v *Fields near Bordeaux*   8 *unavoided* unavoidable   22 *regard* heed for
your safety   28 *vantage* military advantage   32 *mortality* death   43 *being
slain* if you are slain   44 *apparent* certain   46 *age* lifetime
IV, vi   3 *France his* France's   9 *determined* to which a limit has been set;
*date* limit   13 *Quickened* revived; *spleen* ardor

Beat down Alençon, Orleans, Burgundy,
And from the pride of Gallia rescued thee.
The ireful Bastard Orleans, that drew blood
From thee, my boy, and had the maidenhood
Of thy first fight, I soon encounterèd
20   And interchanging blows, I quickly shed
Some of his bastard blood; and in disgrace
Bespoke him thus: 'Contaminated, base,
And misbegotten blood I spill of thine,
23   Mean and right poor, for that pure blood of mine
Which thou didst force from Talbot, my brave boy.'
25   Here, purposing the Bastard to destroy,
Came in strong rescue. Speak, thy father's care.
Art thou not weary, John? How dost thou fare?
Wilt thou yet leave the battle, boy, and fly,
29   Now thou art sealed the son of chivalry?
Fly, to revenge my death when I am dead.
The help of one stands me in little stead.
32   O, too much folly is it, well I wot,
To hazard all our lives in one small boat.
If I to-day die not with Frenchmen's rage,
35   To-morrow I shall die with mickle age.
By me they nothing gain an if I stay;
'Tis but the short'ning of my life one day.
In thee thy mother dies, our household's name,
My death's revenge, thy youth, and England's fame.
All these, and more, we hazard by thy stay;
All these are saved if thou wilt fly away.

JOHN
42   The sword of Orleans hath not made me smart;
These words of yours draw lifeblood from my heart.
44   On that advantage, bought with such a shame,
To save a paltry life and slay bright fame,
Before young Talbot from old Talbot fly,
The coward horse that bears me fall and die!
48   And like me to the peasant boys of France,
To be shame's scorn and subject of mischance!
Surely, by all the glory you have won,
An if I fly, I am not Talbot's son.
52   Then talk no more of flight. It is no boot.
If son to Talbot, die at Talbot's foot.

TALBOT
54   Then follow thou thy desp'rate sire of Crete,
Thou Icarus. Thy life to me is sweet.
If thou wilt fight, fight by thy father's side;
And, commendable proved, let's die in pride.
                *Exit [with Son].*

IV, vii    *Alarum. Excursions. Enter old Talbot, led [by a
        Servant].*

TALBOT
Where is my other life? Mine own is gone.
O, where's young Talbot? Where is valiant John?
Triumphant Death, smeared with captivity,

Young Talbot's valor makes me smile at thee.
5   When he perceived me shrink and on my knee,
His bloody sword he brandished over me
And like a hungry lion did commence
Rough deeds of rage and stern impatience;
9   But when my angry guardant stood alone,
10   Tend'ring my ruin and assailed of none,
Dizzy-eyed fury and great rage of heart
Suddenly made him from my side to start
13   Into the clust'ring battle of the French;
And in that sea of blood my boy did drench
His over-mounting spirit; and there died
My Icarus, my blossom, in his pride.
     *Enter [Soldiers] with John Talbot, borne.*

SERVANT
O my dear lord, lo where your son is borne!

TALBOT
Thou antic Death, which laugh'st us here to scorn,
Anon, from thy insulting tyranny,
Coupled in bonds of perpetuity,
21   Two Talbots, wingèd through the lither sky,
In thy despite shall scape mortality.
23   O thou whose wounds become hard-favored Death,
Speak to thy father ere thou yield thy breath!
25   Brave Death by speaking, whether he will or no.
Imagine him a Frenchman, and thy foe.
27   Poor boy! he smiles, methinks, as who should say,
'Had Death been French, then Death had died to-day.'
Come, come, and lay him in his father's arms.
My spirit can no longer bear these harms.
Soldiers, adieu. I have what I would have,
Now my old arms are young John Talbot's grave.   *Dies.*
     *Enter Charles, Alençon, Burgundy, Bastard, and
     Pucelle.*

CHARLES
Had York and Somerset brought rescue in,
We should have found a bloody day of this.

BASTARD
35   How the young whelp of Talbot's, raging wood,
36   Did flesh his puny sword in Frenchmen's blood!

PUCELLE
Once I encount'red him and thus I said,
38   'Thou maiden youth, be vanquished by a maid.'
But with a proud majestical high scorn
He answered thus, 'Young Talbot was not born
41   To be the pillage of a giglot wench.'
So, rushing in the bowels of the French,
He left me proudly, as unworthy fight.

BURGUNDY
Doubtless he would have made a noble knight.
45   See where he lies inhearsèd in the arms
46   Of the most bloody nurser of his harms.

BASTARD
Hew them to pieces, hack their bones asunder
Whose life was England's glory, Gallia's wonder.

CHARLES
O, no, forbear! For that which we have fled
During the life, let us not wrong it dead.
     *Enter Lucy [attended, a French Herald preceding].*

LUCY
Herald, conduct me to the Dauphin's tent,
To know who hath obtained the glory of the day.

CHARLES
On what submissive message art thou sent?

---

20 *in disgrace* as an insult   23 *Mean* inferior   25 *purposing* as I purposed   29 *sealed* certified   32 *wot* know   35 *mickle* great   42 *smart* suffer   44 *On that advantage* to gain these benefits (i.e. safety, revenge)   48 *like* liken   52 *boot* use   54 *Crete* (site of labyrinth from which Daedalus and his son Icarus attempted to escape on wings)
IV, vii   5 *shrink* give way in battle   9 *guardant* protector   10 *Tend'ring* being concerned for   13 *clust'ring battle* swarming army   21 *lither* yielding   23 *become . . . Death* make beautiful even the hideous visage of death   25 *Brave* defy   27 *as who* as if one   35 *wood* mad   36 *puny* used for the first time in battle   38 *maiden* untried in battle   41 *giglot* wanton   45 *inhearsèd* as in a coffin   46 *nurser . . . harms* one who fostered his injurious power (toward the French)

LUCY
Submission, Dauphin? 'Tis a mere French word.
We English warriors wot not what it means.
I come to know what prisoners thou hast ta'en
And to survey the bodies of the dead.

CHARLES
58 For prisoners ask'st thou? Hell our prison is.
But tell me whom thou seek'st.

LUCY
60 But where's the great Alcides of the field,
Valiant Lord Talbot, Earl of Shrewsbury,
Created for his rare success in arms
Great Earl of Washford, Waterford, and Valence,
Lord Talbot of Goodrig and Urchinfield,
Lord Strange of Blackmere, Lord Verdun of Alton,
Lord Cromwell of Wingfield, Lord Furnival of Shef-
field,
The thrice-victorious Lord of Falconbridge,
Knight of the noble order of Saint George,
Worthy Saint Michael, and the Golden Fleece,
70 Great Marshal to Henry the Sixth
Of all his wars within the realm of France?

PUCELLE
Here's a silly stately style indeed!
The Turk, that two and fifty kingdoms hath,
Writes not so tedious a style as this.
Him that thou magnifi'st with all these titles,
Stinking and flyblown lies here at our feet.

LUCY
Is Talbot slain, the Frenchmen's only scourge,
Your kingdom's terror and black Nemesis?
O, were mine eyeballs into bullets turned,
80 That I in rage might shoot them at your faces!
O that I could but call these dead to life!
It were enough to fright the realm of France.
Were but his picture left amongst you here,
It would amaze the proudest of you all.
Give me their bodies, that I may bear them hence
And give them burial as beseems their worth.

PUCELLE
I think this upstart is old Talbot's ghost,
He speaks with such a proud commanding spirit.
For God's sake, let him have 'em! To keep them here,
They would but stink and putrefy the air.

CHARLES
Go take their bodies hence.

LUCY
I'll bear them hence; but from their ashes shall be
reared
93 A phoenix that shall make all France afeard.

CHARLES
So we be rid of them, do with 'em what thou wilt.
And now to Paris in this conquering vein.
All will be ours, now bloody Talbot's slain.     *Exeunt.*

\*

V, i     *Sennet. Enter King, Gloucester, and Exeter.*

KING
Have you perused the letters from the pope,
The emperor, and the Earl of Armagnac?

GLOUCESTER
I have, my lord, and their intent is this:
They humbly sue unto your excellence

To have a godly peace concluded of
Between the realms of England and of France.

KING
How doth your grace affect their motion?     7

GLOUCESTER
Well, my good lord, and as the only means
To stop effusion of our Christian blood
And stablish quietness on every side.

KING
Ay, marry, uncle; for I always thought
It was both impious and unnatural
That such immanity and bloody strife     13
Should reign among professors of one faith.

GLOUCESTER
Beside, my lord, the sooner to effect
And surer bind this knot of amity,
The Earl of Armagnac, near knit to Charles,     17
A man of great authority in France,
Proffers his only daughter to your grace
In marriage, with a large and sumptuous dowry.

KING
Marriage, uncle? Alas, my years are young,
And fitter is my study and my books
Than wanton dalliance with a paramour.
Yet, call th' ambassadors; and as you please,
So let them have their answers every one.
I shall be well content with any choice
Tends to God's glory and my country's weal.     27
*Enter Winchester [in cardinal's habit] and three
Ambassadors [one a Papal Legate].*

EXETER *[aside]*
What, is my Lord of Winchester installed,
And called unto a cardinal's degree?
Then I perceive that will be verified
Henry the Fifth did sometime prophesy:
'If once he come to be a cardinal,
He'll make his cap coequal with the crown.'

KING
My lords ambassadors, your several suits
Have been considered and debated on.
Your purpose is both good and reasonable,
And therefore are we certainly resolved
To draw conditions of a friendly peace,
Which by my Lord of Winchester we mean
Shall be transported presently to France.     40

GLOUCESTER
And for the proffer of my lord your master,
I have informed his highness so at large     42
As, liking of the lady's virtuous gifts,
Her beauty, and the value of her dower,
He doth intend she shall be England's queen.

KING
In argument and proof of which contract
Bear her this jewel, pledge of my affection.
And so, my Lord Protector, see them guarded
And safely brought to Dover, wherein shipped
Commit them to the fortune of the sea.
*Exeunt [all but Winchester and the Legate].*

58 *Hell . . . is* i.e. we dispatch our victims straight to hell   60 *Alcides*
Hercules, son of Alcaeus   93 *phoenix* mythical bird that arises regenerated
from its own ashes
V, i The royal palace in London   7 *affect* incline toward; *motion* proposal
13 *immanity* monstrous cruelty   17 *knit* related   27 *Tends* which tends
40 *presently* immediately   42 *at large* fully

**WINCHESTER**
Stay, my lord legate. You shall first receive
The sum of money which I promisèd
Should be delivered to his holiness
54 For clothing me in these grave ornaments.
**LEGATE**
I will attend upon your lordship's leisure.
　　　*[Steps aside.]*
**WINCHESTER**
Now Winchester will not submit, I trow,
Or be inferior to the proudest peer.
Humphrey of Gloucester, thou shalt well perceive
That neither in birth or for authority
The bishop will be overborne by thee.
I'll either make thee stoop and bend thy knee
Or sack this country with a mutiny. 　　*Exeunt.*

*

V, ii　　*Enter Charles, Burgundy, Alençon, Bastard,*
　　　　*Reignier, and Joan.*
**CHARLES**
These news, my lords, may cheer our drooping spirits :
2 'Tis said the stout Parisians do revolt
And turn again unto the warlike French.
**ALENÇON**
Then march to Paris, royal Charles of France,
And keep not back your powers in dalliance.
**PUCELLE**
Peace be amongst them if they turn to us ;
7 Else ruin combat with their palaces !
　　　*Enter Scout.*
**SCOUT**
Success unto our valiant general
9 And happiness to his accomplices !
**CHARLES**
What tidings send our scouts ? I prithee speak.
**SCOUT**
The English army, that divided was
Into two parties, is now conjoined in one
And means to give you battle presently.
**CHARLES**
Somewhat too sudden, sirs, the warning is,
But we will presently provide for them.
**BURGUNDY**
I trust the ghost of Talbot is not there.
Now he is gone, my lord, you need not fear.
**PUCELLE**
Of all base passions fear is most accursed.
Command the conquest, Charles, it shall be thine,
Let Henry fret and all the world repine.
**CHARLES**
Then on, my lords ; and France be fortunate ! 　*Exeunt.*

*Alarum. Excursions. Enter Joan de Pucelle.* 　　V, iii
**PUCELLE**
The regent conquers and the Frenchmen fly.
Now help, ye charming spells and periapts ; 　　　2
And ye choice spirits that admonish me, 　　　3
And give me signs of future accidents. 　　　4
　　　*Thunder.*
You speedy helpers that are substitutes 　　　5
Under the lordly monarch of the north,
Appear and aid me in this enterprise !
　　　*Enter Fiends.*
This speedy and quick appearance argues proof
Of your accustomed diligence to me.
Now, ye familiar spirits that are culled
Out of the powerful legions under earth,
Help me this once, that France may get the field. 　12
　　　*They walk, and speak not.*
O, hold me not with silence over-long !
Where I was wont to feed you with my blood,
I'll lop a member off and give it you
In earnest of a further benefit,
So you do condescend to help me now.
　　　*They hang their heads.*
No hope to have redress ? My body shall
Pay recompense if you will grant my suit.
　　　*They shake their heads.*
Cannot my body nor blood-sacrifice
Entreat you to your wonted furtherance ?
Then take my soul – my body, soul, and all,
Before that England give the French the foil. *They depart.*
See, they forsake me ! Now the time is come
That France must vail her lofty-plumèd crest 　　25
And let her head fall into England's lap.
My ancient incantations are too weak, 　　　27
And hell too strong for me to buckle with.
Now, France, thy glory droopeth to the dust. 　　*Exit.*
　　　*Excursions. Burgundy and [Richard Duke of] York*
　　　*fight hand to hand. French fly. [Pucelle is taken.]*
**RICHARD**
Damsel of France, I think I have you fast.
Unchain your spirits now with spelling charms 　　31
And try if they can gain your liberty.
A goodly prize, fit for the devil's grace ! 　　　33
See how the ugly witch doth bend her brows
As if, with Circe, she would change my shape. 　　35
**PUCELLE**
Changed to a worser shape thou canst not be.
**RICHARD**
O, Charles the Dauphin is a proper man ! 　　　37
No shape but his can please your dainty eye. 　　38
**PUCELLE**
A plaguing mischief light on Charles and thee.
And may ye both be suddenly surprised 　　　40
By bloody hands in sleeping on your beds !
**RICHARD**
Fell banning hag, enchantress, hold thy tongue. 　　42
**PUCELLE**
I prithee give me leave to curse awhile.
**RICHARD**
Curse, miscreant, when thou com'st to the stake. *Exeunt.*
　　　*Alarum. Enter Suffolk, with Margaret in his hand.*
**SUFFOLK**
Be what thou wilt, thou art my prisoner.
　　　*Gazes on her.*

---

54 *grave ornaments* robes of official dignity
V, ii Fields before Angiers 　2 *stout* brave 　7 *Else . . . palaces* otherwise let
ruin destroy their palaces 　9 *accomplices* associates
V, iii 　2 *charming* working by incantation ; *periapts* amulets 　3 *admonish*
forewarn 　4 *accidents* occurrences 　5 *substitutes* deputies 　12 *get the
field* win the battle 　25 *vail* lower 　27 *ancient* former 　31 *spelling charms*
charms that cast spells 　33 *devil's grace* his grace the devil (a mocking
title) 　35 *Circe* a fabled sorceress who turned men into swine 　37 *proper*
handsome 　38 *dainty* fastidious 　40 *surprised* captured 　42 *Fell banning*
fierce cursing

O fairest beauty, do not fear nor fly!
For I will touch thee but with reverent hands;
48  I kiss these fingers for eternal peace
And lay them gently on thy tender side.
Who art thou? Say, that I may honor thee.

MARGARET
Margaret my name, and daughter to a king,
The King of Naples, whosoe'er thou art.

SUFFOLK
An earl I am and Suffolk am I called.
Be not offended, nature's miracle,
Thou art allotted to be ta'en by me.
So doth the swan her downy cygnets save,
Keeping them prisoner underneath her wings.
Yet, if this servile usage once offend,
Go and be free again as Suffolk's friend.
          *She is going.*
O, stay! [*Aside*] I have no power to let her pass.
My hand would free her, but my heart says no.
62  As plays the sun upon the glassy streams,
Twinkling another counterfeited beam,
So seems this gorgeous beauty to mine eyes.
Fain would I woo her, yet I dare not speak.
I'll call for pen and ink and write my mind.
Fie, de la Pole, disable not thyself.
Hast not a tongue? Is she not here?
Wilt thou be daunted at a woman's sight?
Ay, beauty's princely majesty is such
71  Confounds the tongue and makes the senses rough.

MARGARET
Say, Earl of Suffolk, if thy name be so,
What ransom must I pay before I pass?
For I perceive I am thy prisoner.

SUFFOLK
How canst thou tell she will deny thy suit
Before thou make a trial of her love?

MARGARET
Why speak'st thou not? What ransom must I pay?

SUFFOLK
She's beautiful, and therefore to be wooed;
She is a woman, therefore to be won.

MARGARET
Will thou accept of ransom, yea or no?

SUFFOLK
81  Fond man, remember that thou hast a wife.
Then how can Margaret be thy paramour?

MARGARET
I were best to leave him, for he will not hear.

SUFFOLK
84  There all is marred; there lies a cooling card.

MARGARET
85  He talks at randon. Sure the man is mad.

SUFFOLK
And yet a dispensation may be had.

MARGARET
And yet I would that you would answer me.

SUFFOLK
I'll win this Lady Margaret. For whom?
89  Why, for my king. Tush, that's a wooden thing!

MARGARET
He talks of wood. It is some carpenter.

SUFFOLK
Yet so my fancy may be satisfied
And peace establishèd between these realms.

But there remains a scruple in that too;
For though her father be the King of Naples,
Duke of Anjou and Maine, yet is he poor,
And our nobility will scorn the match.

MARGARET
Hear ye, captain? Are you not at leisure?

SUFFOLK
It shall be so, disdain they ne'er so much.
Henry is youthful and will quickly yield. –
Madam, I have a secret to reveal.

MARGARET
What though I be enthralled? He seems a knight    101
And will not any way dishonor me.

SUFFOLK
Lady, vouchsafe to listen what I say.

MARGARET
Perhaps I shall be rescued by the French,
And then I need not crave his courtesy.

SUFFOLK
Sweet madam, give me hearing in a cause –

MARGARET
Tush, women have been captive ere now.

SUFFOLK
Lady, wherefore talk you so?

MARGARET
I cry you mercy, 'tis but quid for quo.    109

SUFFOLK
Say, gentle princess, would you not suppose
Your bondage happy, to be made a queen?

MARGARET
To be a queen in bondage is more vile
Than is a slave in base servility;
For princes should be free.

SUFFOLK                        And so shall you,
If happy England's royal king be free.

MARGARET
Why, what concerns his freedom unto me?

SUFFOLK
I'll undertake to make thee Henry's queen,
To put a golden sceptre in thy hand
And set a precious crown upon thy head,
If thou wilt condescend to be my –

MARGARET                                        What?

SUFFOLK
His love.

MARGARET
I am unworthy to be Henry's wife.

SUFFOLK
No, gentle madam. I unworthy am
To woo so fair a dame to be his wife
And have no portion in the choice myself.    125
How say you, madam? Are ye so content?

MARGARET
An if my father please, I am content.

SUFFOLK
Then call our captains and our colors forth.
And, madam, at your father's castle walls

48 *for* in token of    62–64 *As plays . . . eyes* i.e. she seems as gorgeous as
the sun's reflection twinkling upon the water's surface    71 *Confounds* that
it confounds    81 *Fond* foolish    84 *cooling card* opponent's card which
dashes one's hopes    85 *randon* random    89 *wooden* stupid (either the king,
or the plan itself)    101 *enthralled* captive    109 *cry you mercy* beg your
pardon; *quid for quo* tit for tat    125 *the choice* (1) the choosing, (2) the
thing chosen

We'll crave a parley to confer with him.
  *Sound [a parley]. Enter Reignier on the walls.*
See, Reignier, see, thy daughter prisoner.

REIGNIER
To whom?

SUFFOLK  To me.

REIGNIER    Suffolk, what remedy?
I am a soldier, and unapt to weep
Or to exclaim on fortune's fickleness.

SUFFOLK
Yes, there is remedy enough, my lord.
Consent, and for thy honor give consent,
Thy daughter shall be wedded to my king,
Whom I with pain have wooed and won thereto;
And this her easy-held imprisonment
Hath gained thy daughter princely liberty.

REIGNIER
Speaks Suffolk as he thinks?

SUFFOLK    Fair Margaret knows
142 That Suffolk doth not flatter, face, or feign.

REIGNIER
Upon thy princely warrant I descend
To give thee answer of thy just demand.
      *[Exit from the walls.]*

SUFFOLK
And here I will expect thy coming.
  *Trumpets sound. Enter Reignier [below].*

REIGNIER
Welcome, brave earl, into our territories.
Command in Anjou what your honor pleases.

SUFFOLK
Thanks, Reignier, happy for so sweet a child,
Fit to be made companion with a king.
What answer makes your grace unto my suit?

REIGNIER
Since thou dost deign to woo her little worth
To be the princely bride of such a lord,
Upon condition I may quietly
Enjoy mine own, the country Maine and Anjou,
Free from oppression or the stroke of war,
My daughter shall be Henry's, if he please.

SUFFOLK
That is her ransom. I deliver her,
And those two counties I will undertake
Your grace shall well and quietly enjoy.

REIGNIER
160 And I again, in Henry's royal name,
161 As deputy unto that gracious king,
Give thee her hand for sign of plighted faith.

SUFFOLK
Reignier of France, I give thee kingly thanks,
164 Because this is in traffic of a king.
  *[Aside]*
And yet methinks I could be well content
To be mine own attorney in this case. –

---

142 *face* deceive 160 *again* in return 161 *deputy* (refers to Suffolk)
164 *traffic* business 170 *as it becomes* as befits such a jewel 183 *taint*
tainted 184 *withal* moreover 186 *peevish* trifling 189 *Minotaurs* (there
was but one Minotaur, a monster part bull and part man, at the center of
the Cretan labyrinth built by Daedalus) 190 *her wondrous praise* praise of
this wondrous woman 192 *extinguish* eclipse 193 *Repeat their semblance*
rehearse the description of her virtues
V, iv The English camp in Anjou 5 *timeless* premature 7 *miser* wretch
9 *friend* kinsman

I'll over then to England with this news
And make this marriage to be solemnized.
So, farewell, Reignier. Set this diamond safe
In golden palaces, as it becomes.  170

REIGNIER
I do embrace thee as I would embrace
The Christian prince King Henry, were he here.

MARGARET
Farewell, my lord. Good wishes, praise and prayers
Shall Suffolk ever have of Margaret.
    *She is going.*

SUFFOLK
Farewell, sweet madam. But hark you, Margaret –
No princely commendations to my king?

MARGARET
Such commendations as becomes a maid,
A virgin, and his servant, say to him.

SUFFOLK
Words sweetly placed and modestly directed.
But, madam, I must trouble you again –
No loving token to his majesty?

MARGARET
Yes, my good lord: a pure unspotted heart,
Never yet taint with love, I send the king.  183

SUFFOLK
And this withal.  184
  *Kiss her.*

MARGARET
That for thyself. I will not so presume
To send such peevish tokens to a king.  186
    *[Exeunt Reignier and Margaret.]*

SUFFOLK
O wert thou for myself! But, Suffolk, stay.
Thou mayst not wander in that labyrinth;
There Minotaurs and ugly treasons lurk.  189
Solicit Henry with her wondrous praise.  190
Bethink thee on her virtues that surmount,
And natural graces that extinguish art;  192
Repeat their semblance often on the seas,  193
That, when thou com'st to kneel at Henry's feet,
Thou mayst bereave him of his wits with wonder. *Exit.*

        *

*Enter [Richard, Duke of] York, Warwick,*  V, iv
*Shepherd, Pucelle [guarded].*

RICHARD
Bring forth that sorceress condemned to burn.

SHEPHERD
Ah, Joan, this kills thy father's heart outright.
Have I sought every country far and near,
And, now it is my chance to find thee out,
Must I behold thy timeless cruel death?  5
Ah, Joan, sweet daughter Joan, I'll die with thee!

PUCELLE
Decrepit miser! base ignoble wretch!  7
I am descended of a gentler blood.
Thou art no father nor no friend of mine.  9

SHEPHERD
Out, out! My lords, an please you, 'tis not so.
I did beget her, all the parish knows.
Her mother liveth yet, can testify
She was the first fruit of my bach'lorship.

WARWICK
Graceless, wilt thou deny thy parentage?

RICHARD
This argues what her kind of life hath been,
16  Wicked and vile ; and so her death concludes.

SHEPHERD
17  Fie, Joan, that thou wilt be so obstacle !
18  God knows thou art a collop of my flesh,
And for thy sake have I shed many a tear.
Deny me not, I prithee, gentle Joan.

PUCELLE
Peasant, avaunt ! You have suborned this man,
Of purpose to obscure my noble birth.

SHEPHERD
23  'Tis true, I gave a noble to the priest
The morn that I was wedded to her mother.
Kneel down and take my blessing, good my girl.
Wilt thou not stoop ? Now cursèd be the time
Of thy nativity ! I would the milk
Thy mother gave thee when thou suck'dst her breast
Had been a little ratsbane for thy sake.
Or else, when thou didst keep my lambs afield,
I wish some ravenous wolf had eaten thee.
32  Dost thou deny thy father, cursèd drab ?
O, burn her, burn her ! Hanging is too good.          *Exit.*

RICHARD
Take her away ; for she hath lived too long,
To fill the world with vicious qualities.

PUCELLE
First let me tell you whom you have condemned :
Not one begotten of a shepherd swain,
But issued from the progeny of kings,
Virtuous and holy, chosen from above
By inspiration of celestial grace
To work exceeding miracles on earth.
I never had to do with wicked spirits.
But you, that are polluted with your lusts,
Stained with the guiltless blood of innocents,
Corrupt and tainted with a thousand vices –
Because you want the grace that others have,
You judge it straight a thing impossible
To compass wonders but by help of devils.
No, misconceivèd, Joan of Arc hath been
50  A virgin from her tender infancy,
Chaste and immaculate in very thought,
Whose maiden blood, thus rigorously effused,
Will cry for vengeance at the gates of heaven.

RICHARD
Ay, ay. Away with her to execution.

WARWICK
And hark ye, sirs. Because she is a maid,
Spare for no fagots, let there be enow.
Place barrels of pitch upon the fatal stake,
That so her torture may be shortenèd.

PUCELLE
Will nothing turn your unrelenting hearts ?
60  Then, Joan, discover thine infirmity,
That warranteth by law to be thy privilege.
I am with child, ye bloody homicides.
Murder not then the fruit within my womb,
Although ye hale me to a violent death.

RICHARD
65  Now heaven forfend ! The holy maid with child ?

WARWICK
The greatest miracle that e'er ye wrought.
Is all your strict preciseness come to this ?

RICHARD
She and the Dauphin have been juggling.
I did imagine what would be her refuge.

WARWICK
Well, go to. We'll have no bastards live,
Especially since Charles must father it.

PUCELLE
You are deceived. My child is none of his.
It was Alençon that enjoyed my love.

RICHARD
Alençon, that notorious Machiavel ?          74
It dies, an if it had a thousand lives.

PUCELLE
O, give me leave, I have deluded you.
'Twas neither Charles nor yet the duke I named,
But Reignier, King of Naples, that prevailed.

WARWICK
A married man ! That's most intolerable.

RICHARD
Why, here's a girl ! I think she knows not well,
There were so many, whom she may accuse.

WARWICK
It's sign she hath been liberal and free.

RICHARD
And yet, forsooth, she is a virgin pure !
Strumpet, thy words condemn thy brat and thee.
Use no entreaty, for it is in vain.

PUCELLE
Then lead me hence ; with whom I leave my curse.
May never glorious sun reflex his beams
Upon the country where you make abode ;
But darkness and the gloomy shade of death
Environ you, till mischief and despair          90
Drive you to break your necks or hang yourselves !
*Exit [guarded].*

RICHARD
Break thou in pieces and consume to ashes,
Thou foul accursèd minister of hell !
*Enter [Winchester, now] Cardinal [, attended].*

WINCHESTER
Lord regent, I do greet your excellence
With letters of commission from the king.
For know, my lords, the states of Christendom,
Moved with remorse of these outrageous broils,
Have earnestly implored a general peace
Betwixt our nation and the aspiring French ;
And here at hand the Dauphin and his train
Approacheth, to confer about some matter.

RICHARD
Is all our travail turned to this effect ?          102
After the slaughter of so many peers,
So many captains, gentlemen, and soldiers,
That in this quarrel have been overthrown
And sold their bodies for their country's benefit,
Shall we at last conclude effeminate peace ?
Have we not lost most part of all the towns
By treason, falsehood, and by treachery
Our great progenitors had conquerèd ?

---

16 *concludes* (1) verifies, (2) ends    17 *obstacle* (he means to say 'obstinate')
18 *collop* slice    23 *noble* coin worth 6s. 8d.    32 *drab* whore    60 *discover*
reveal    65 *forfend* forbid    74 *Machiavel* Italian whose doctrines Elizabethans regarded as the epitome of intrigue and immoral expediency
102 *travail* toil

O, Warwick, Warwick ! I foresee with grief
The utter loss of all the realm of France.

WARWICK

Be patient, York. If we conclude a peace,
114 It shall be with such strict and severe covenants
115 As little shall the Frenchmen gain thereby.

*Enter Charles, Alençon, Bastard, Reignier [and
others].*

CHARLES

Since, lords of England, it is thus agreed
That peaceful truce shall be proclaimed in France,
We come to be informèd by yourselves
What the conditions of that league must be.

RICHARD

120 Speak, Winchester ; for boiling choler chokes
The hollow passage of my poisoned voice
By sight of these our baleful enemies.

WINCHESTER

Charles, and the rest, it is enacted thus :
124 That, in regard King Henry gives consent,
125 Of mere compassion and of lenity,
To ease your country of distressful war
And suffer you to breathe in fruitful peace,
You shall become true liegemen to his crown ;
And, Charles, upon condition thou wilt swear
To pay him tribute and submit thyself,
Thou shalt be placed as viceroy under him
And still enjoy thy regal dignity.

ALENÇON

Must he be then as shadow of himself ?
Adorn his temples with a coronet,
And yet, in substance and authority,
Retain but privilege of a private man ?
This proffer is absurd and reasonless.

CHARLES

'Tis known already that I am possessed
With more than half the Gallian territories
140 And therein reverenced for their lawful king.
Shall I, for lucre of the rest unvanquished,
Detract so much from that prerogative
As to be called but viceroy of the whole ?
No, lord ambassador. I'll rather keep
That which I have than, coveting for more,
146 Be cast from possibility of all.

RICHARD

Insulting Charles, hast thou by secret means
Used intercession to obtain a league,
149 And, now the matter grows to compromise,
150 Stand'st thou aloof upon comparison ?
Either accept the title thou usurp'st,
152 Of benefit proceeding from our king
153 And not of any challenge of desert,
Or we will plague thee with incessant wars.

REIGNIER *[aside to Charles]*

My lord, you do not well in obstinacy
To cavil in the course of this contract.
If once it be neglected, ten to one
We shall not find like opportunity.

ALENÇON *[aside to Charles]*

To say the truth, it is your policy            159
To save your subjects from such massacre
And ruthless slaughters as are daily seen
By our proceeding in hostility ;
And therefore take this compact of a truce,
Although you break it when your pleasure serves.

WARWICK

How say'st thou, Charles ? Shall our condition stand ?   165

CHARLES

It shall ;
Only reserved, you claim no interest
In any of our towns of garrison.

RICHARD

Then swear allegiance to his majesty :
As thou art knight, never to disobey
Nor be rebellious to the crown of England,
Thou, nor thy nobles, to the crown of England.

*[Charles and the rest give tokens of fealty.]*

So, now dismiss your army when ye please,
Hang up your ensigns, let your drums be still,
For here we entertain a solemn peace.          *Exeunt.*

\*

*Enter Suffolk, in conference with the King,*    V, v
*Gloucester, and Exeter.*

KING

Your wondrous rare description, noble earl,
Of beauteous Margaret hath astonished me.
Her virtues, graced with external gifts,
Do breed love's settled passions in my heart ;   4
And like as rigor of tempestuous gusts
Provokes the mightiest hulk against the tide,    6
So am I driven by breath of her renown
Either to suffer shipwrack or arrive
Where I may have fruition of her love.

SUFFOLK

Tush, my good lord, this superficial tale        10
Is but a preface of her worthy praise.           11
The chief perfections of that lovely dame,
Had I sufficient skill to utter them,
Would make a volume of enticing lines
Able to ravish any dull conceit ;                15
And, which is more, she is not so divine,
So full replete with choice of all delights,
But with as humble lowliness of mind
She is content to be at your command –
Command, I mean, of virtuous chaste intents,
To love and honor Henry as her lord.

KING

And otherwise will Henry ne'er presume.
Therefore, my Lord Protector, give consent
That Marg'ret may be England's royal queen.

GLOUCESTER

So should I give consent to flatter sin.         25
You know, my lord, your highness is betrothed
Unto another lady of esteem.
How shall we then dispense with that contract

---

114 *covenants* articles of agreement   115 *As* that   120 *choler* anger   124
*in regard* inasmuch as   125 *mere* pure ; *lenity* mercifulness   146 *cast*
excluded   149 *grows to compromise* approaches a peaceful solution   150
*comparison* rhetorical quibbling   152 *Of benefit* as feudal beneficiary
153 *challenge of desert* claim of right to the title   159 *policy* politic course
165 *condition* treaty terms
V, v The royal palace in London   4 *settled* rooted   6 *Provokes* impels ;
*hulk* ship   10 *superficial* dealing merely with her most obvious virtues
11 *her worthy praise* praise of her full worth   15 *conceit* imagination
25 *flatter* extenuate

And not deface your honor with reproach?

SUFFOLK
As doth a ruler with unlawful oaths,
31 Or one that at a triumph, having vowed
32 To try his strength, forsaketh yet the lists
By reason of his adversary's odds.
A poor earl's daughter is unequal odds,
And therefore may be broke without offense.

GLOUCESTER
Why, what, I pray, is Margaret more than that?
Her father is no better than an earl,
Although in glorious titles he excel.

SUFFOLK
Yes, my lord, her father is a king,
The King of Naples and Jerusalem,
And of such great authority in France
As his alliance will confirm our peace
And keep the Frenchmen in allegiance.

GLOUCESTER
And so the Earl of Armagnac may do,
Because he is near kinsman unto Charles.

EXETER
46 Beside, his wealth doth warrant a liberal dower,
Where Reignier sooner will receive than give.

SUFFOLK
A dow'r, my lords? Disgrace not so your king
That he should be so abject, base, and poor
To choose for wealth and not for perfect love.
Henry is able to enrich his queen,
And not to seek a queen to make him rich.
So worthless peasants bargain for their wives,
As market men for oxen, sheep, or horse.
Marriage is a matter of more worth
Than to be dealt in by attorneyship.
57 Not whom we will, but whom his grace affects,
Must be companion of his nuptial bed.
And therefore, lords, since he affects her most,
It most of all these reasons bindeth us
In our opinions she should be preferred.
For what is wedlock forcèd but a hell,
An age of discord and continual strife?
Whereas the contrary bringeth bliss
And is a pattern of celestial peace.
Whom should we match with Henry, being a king,
But Margaret, that is daughter to a king?
Her peerless feature, joinèd with her birth,
Approves her fit for none but for a king.
70 Her valiant courage and undaunted spirit
(More than in women commonly is seen)

Will answer our hope in issue of a king.
For Henry, son unto a conqueror,
Is likely to beget more conquerors
If with a lady of so high resolve
As is fair Margaret he be linked in love.
Then yield, my lords, and here conclude with me
That Margaret shall be queen, and none but she.

KING
Whether it be through force of your report,
80 My noble Lord of Suffolk, or for that
81 My tender youth was never yet attaint
With any passion of inflaming love,
I cannot tell; but this I am assured,
I feel such sharp dissension in my breast,
Such fierce alarums both of hope and fear,
As I am sick with working of my thoughts.
87 Take therefore shipping; post, my lord, to France;
Agree to any covenants, and procure
That Lady Margaret do vouchsafe to come
To cross the seas to England and be crowned
King Henry's faithful and anointed queen.
92 For your expenses and sufficient charge,
93 Among the people gather up a tenth.
Be gone, I say; for till you do return
95 I rest perplexèd with a thousand cares.
And you, good uncle, banish all offense.
97 If you censure me by what you were,
Not what you are, I know it will excuse
This sudden execution of my will.
100 And so conduct me where, from company,
I may revolve and ruminate my grief.        *Exit.*

GLOUCESTER
Ay, grief, I fear me, both at first and last.
                    *Exit Gloucester [with Exeter].*

SUFFOLK
Thus Suffolk hath prevailed; and thus he goes,
As did the youthful Paris once to Greece,
105 With hope to find the like event in love
But prosper better than the Trojan did.
Margaret shall now be queen, and rule the king;
But I will rule both her, the king, and realm.        *Exit.*

31 *triumph* tournament   32 *lists* tilting area at a tournament   46 *warrant* guarantee   57 *affects* desires   80 *for that* because   81 *attaint* diseased   87 *post* hurry   92 *charge* money to spend   93 *tenth* percentage of value of personal property appropriated as tax   95 *rest* remain   97–98 *censure . . . are* i.e. measure my proposed extravagances by the libertinism of your own youth, not by the gravity of your present age   100 *from company* alone   105 *event* outcome (i.e. Paris' winning of Helen)

# THE SECOND AND THIRD PARTS OF
# KING HENRY THE SIXTH

## INTRODUCTION

During the fifteenth century the English won and lost France, fought a disastrous civil war at home, and brought Henry VII, the first of the Tudor monarchs, to the throne. This period had a special fascination for the Elizabethans. The times were near enough to be influential and well remembered, yet far enough away to be safely idealized. Readily available were extensive historical and legendary accounts devoted wholly or partially to fifteenth-century personages and happenings, among them John Foxe's *Acts and Monuments of Martyrs*, the *Mirror for Magistrates*, Fabyan's, Stowe's, Grafton's, and Holinshed's chronicles, and Edward Hall's *Union of the Two Noble and Illustre Families of Lancaster and York*. Very early in his career, Shakespeare sensed the poetic, dramatic, and patriotic possibilities in these materials and began to shape from them historical dramas designed to edify and delight. He thus became one of the first of the popular dramatists to turn to English history for source material, and it is just possible that he was the first to do so. He may, then, have been the originator, at least as far as the commercial theatre is concerned, of a kind of play that was to figure prominently in the development of the Elizabethan drama.

From Edward Hall particularly, Shakespeare derived not only information about the men, manners, and events of the preceding era but also a theory of history which imposed a unity on diverse and seemingly inexplicable phenomena, for it was Hall (and from him, Holinshed) who expressed most clearly for Renaissance England the doctrine that God's hand is present in human history, that events, while subject to the free will of the participants, are nonetheless overseen ultimately by a Providence through which order will eventually be restored to a world rendered chaotic by sin. In addition, the focus of Shakespeare's history plays was determined by the view taken by Hall and earlier writers of what was historically significant; history for them was chiefly political history, an account of the rise and fall of great men or those who aspired to be great, of statecraft and public affairs, of faction, sedition, rebellion, war and battle – in short, an account of the vicissitudes and triumphs of the state and its prince. In his sources, then, Shakespeare found a great wealth of detail pertaining to character and event preselected according to a well-defined concept of significance, and, underlying all the detail, a philosophy of history which allowed the actions of men to stand in the foreground but which saw behind these actions a logic proceeding from the irrevocable, although sometimes obscure, development of God's plan for England's good.

In the works of these chroniclers Shakespeare saw also an interpretation of fifteenth-century history which has been called the "Tudor myth"; he seems not only to have found this interpretation compatible with his own personal beliefs but also to have recognized in it a strong dramatic potential, particularly suited for didactic purposes. The Tudor myth sprang from the Elizabethans' strong sense of cosmic order, of which political order was a part, and their acute discomfort upon the emergence of symptoms construed to indicate a dislocation of order. The political disasters of the fifteenth century were obviously a kind of disorder, which, according to the concept of sin and retribution, could best be understood as a punishment visited by God upon the people of England for some grave wrong. Logic and a sense of justice required that a sin deserving this punishment be identified, and the chroniclers, looking back to 1399 and 1400, settled upon the deposition and murder of Richard II by Henry Bolingbroke as the crucial event. Richard had been a weak and irresponsible ruler but he had been a king, God's anointed, and the theory was developed that to rebel against a king, however bad a monarch he was, was to violate God's will and thus to commit the cardinal political crime. The troubles that attended Bolingbroke's reign as Henry IV were seen as ample proof of God's displeasure with him and with the realm. During the time of the hero-king Henry V there was a temporary respite, but, as justice remained unsatisfied, the subjects of his son Henry VI had to suffer the lawlessness and confusion that marked the Wars of the Roses and a culminating horror in the tyranny of the monstrous Richard III. But as suffering leads to penitence and finally to forgiveness, God at last relented, and in the person of Henry VII, the founder of the Tudor dynasty, He again blessed England with a strong and able leader who brought peace to the land and instituted an enlightened statecraft which was to lead eventually to the glorious reign of his granddaughter, Elizabeth I. So went the myth. It was fostered by the Tudors because in a general way it strengthened the position of the monarch at the same time that it specifically provided a divine sanction for the somewhat questionable legitimacy of Henry VII's claim to the crown. It was accepted by most Elizabethans because, as they looked at the cycle from the vantage point of their own time, it had a fitness and an appealing optimism. That it did not fully accord with historical data was a matter of no very great concern, for historical truth, while comprehending facts, was not regarded as being precisely correspondent to them but correspondent as well to doctrines acceptable to and significant for the present. This view permitted the chroniclers a certain latitude in their accounts of the past, and it also gave Shakespeare the license necessary for the transformation of history into drama.

Although Shakespeare tightened the narrative fabric somewhat by condensing, altering the chronology of events, and changing the age of some of the characters, the span of time covered by *2* and *3 Henry VI* is so large and so crowded with great affairs that the structure of the plays was almost bound to be loose. Such episodic structure had an authority derived from the medieval mystery cycles, and it had been given fresh sanction by Marlowe's *Tamburlaine*; it permitted the inclusion within a single dramatic framework of highly diversified materials which contributed to the effect of copiousness greatly admired in Elizabethan literature. Yet, evidently in an attempt to achieve some unity and to increase the significance of the episodes, Shakespeare also made use of a theme inherited from the morality play and previously employed in the morality-like interlude *Respublica* and in such courtly historical dramas as *King Johan* and *Gorboduc*. This theme worked allegorically to make the realm itself the center of the dramatic action; the plays, then, are not ultimately about Henry VI or York or Edward or the others but about England itself as it suffers through a retributive civil war immediately caused by the weakness of the king and the corruption of the nobility. They are, in addition, part of a series of essays in definition, as Shakespeare explores the attributes of kingship. What makes a strong and happy state? A good king. What makes a good king? This for Shakespeare seems to have been a complicated question to the many branches of which he gave no easy or final answers.

That it was Shakespeare's intention to convey this complex theme is suggested by certain parts of the action which he developed either entirely on his own or from meagre suggestions in his sources and which he rendered in the stylized, ritualistic manner of the morality play, such as the formal alignment of characters in the opening scene of *2 Henry VI*, the representation of the flatly virtuous Iden (*2 Henry VI*, IV, x), the scene depicting the king on the molehill (*3 Henry VI*, II, v), the abuse of Clifford's corpse by the Yorkists (*3 Henry VI, II, vi*), and Edward's wooing of Lady Grey to the accompaniment of Clarence's and Gloucester's mocking commentary (*3 Henry VI*, III, ii). Dramatic action of this kind serves as an articulation of theme rather than as a rendition of events supposed to be true; it directs our understanding toward the internal significance of the entire action rather than to its depiction alone. But his sense of theatre was too keen for Shakespeare to rest content with a rigidly allegorical representation of a doctrinaire political ideology. He entered imaginatively into the life of many of his characters; moreover, he seized whatever opportunity he could to create effects which would be striking in performance at the same time that they contributed to the general ideas upon which the plays were based. A good example is his handling in *2 Henry VI* of the conflict between Queen Margaret and the Duchess of Gloucester. According to history, Queen Margaret did not arrive in England until several years after the Duchess' fall, but Shakespeare departed from his sources to bring the two together, evidently because he thought that dramatic capital could thus be gained. Not only is the clash between the two ambitious and overbearing women intrinsically interesting, but it helps to define the divided loyalties of the nobility, to create the atmosphere of jealous strife which pervades the court, and to foreshadow the

ruin of the good Duke Humphrey. An equally good example of Shakespeare's manipulation of his sources for dramatic effect is his treatment of Jack Cade, whose thematic importance is discussed more fully below. We may note here, however, that many of the incidents represented as occurring during Cade's Rebellion Shakespeare found in the chronicle accounts of the Peasants' Revolt of 1381 and that he completely ignored certain favorable traits in Cade's character as it was described by Holinshed because they obviously ran counter to his purposes.

In spite of these efforts to achieve coherence, *2* and *3 Henry VI* remain rather sprawling plays which lack a strongly represented central character, either good or evil, about whom incidents within their complicated plots could have been arranged. The king, to be sure, is present throughout, but he, far from being a dynamic figure, is nearly the perfect symbol of inaction. That he has many private virtues is clear, but they express themselves publicly only as impotence, irresolution, and for all his conscientiousness, an extraordinary indifference to the preservation of England's power and dignity among nations. Duke Humphrey, whose fall from power provides the focal point of the first two acts and part of the third of *2 Henry VI*, has many of the public virtues wanting in the king – particularly a practical shrewdness combined with a vigorous and self-sacrificing dedication to an ideal of service to the realm – but his confidence in the power of his own innocence and good faith makes him a rather easy victim of the queen and the wolvish nobles, who see him as an obstacle to their own acquisition of power. As Duke Humphrey descends, York rises. His claim to the throne is better than Henry's, and, as he has courage, patriotism (self-interested though it may be), and force of character, he would undoubtedly make a better ruler, but his ambition is flagrant and his method of satisfying it Machiavellian. He is further guilty in ignoring the principle that all kings, regardless of the manner in which their crowns were obtained, are inviolate. As a part of his program, he has stimulated Jack Cade's Rebellion, the development and suppression of which occupies the fourth act. By the beginning of the fifth, York has an army in the field and, with the support of his sons and the Nevils, declares for the crown by open rebellion, against the opposition of Queen Margaret and the Cliffords. York's victory at the Battle of St Albans ensues, yet, as Henry still lives, *2 Henry VI* ends with York still short of achieving the crown.

The action of *3 Henry VI*, which begins immediately after the Battle of St Albans, is set in motion by Henry's proposal that he be allowed to reign during his lifetime at the price of disinheriting his son in favor of York, a compromise which York swears to respect but which causes Queen Margaret to seek military support from the northern barons. During the first act Margaret's army forces the surrender of the city of York; the act closes with York dead, his head impaled upon the battlements of the city. The Lancastrians are temporarily triumphant, but a Yorkist army under Edward and Richard has yet to be encountered. The second act is devoted chiefly to the Yorkists' defeat of Margaret's powers, with Warwick's help, and Edward's subsequent claiming of the crown; and the third to the capture of King Henry, Edward's proposal to Lady Grey and the consequent destruction of a possible French alliance, Margaret's appeal to Lewis of France for aid, and Warwick's shift of allegiance to the

Lancastrian cause. In the long and busy fourth act, Edward is overthrown and then regains his power. The fifth is given over to the campaign, replete with alarms and excursions, which culminates in the final Yorkist victory at Tewkesbury and the murder of the Prince of Wales and King Henry. At the end of the play it would seem that the Yorkist cause should be won and that King Edward should be secure upon the throne, but by this time a new contender has appeared in Richard of Gloucester, who vows to wade to majesty through the blood of his brothers and nephews. The plays, then, are of epic scope, and the tentative emergence of York as the central figure of the Second Part and of Edward as the central figure of the Third is obstructed by a shifting emphasis upon a bewildering number of minor characters who strut and fret for a scene or two, sell one another out, and then die their gory deaths at the base of Fortune's relentless wheel. The implication of the historical accounts becomes, in fact, something of an embarrassment to the plays themselves; the tragedy of the times was that no one man was both strong enough and good enough to lead the country, the king being deficient in public virtue and the house of York in private. As yet not even such a villain as Richard of Gloucester was later to prove had come forward with sufficient force to be dominant. Thus no well-defined protagonist was at hand, and the allegorical figure of England was too vague to serve as an agent of dramatic concentration.

Certain episodes, however, are brilliantly rendered and skillfully fitted into the framework of the whole drama. For example, Shakespeare apparently wanted to show that corruption at the top of the state was certain to penetrate to the bottom, that if the nobles were so criminally foolish as to abandon the ideal of loyalty to the king and commonwealth to serve themselves it was only to be expected that the people would behave in a similar way. His vehicle for conveying this important aspect of his theme was the sinister farce of Cade's Rebellion, which not only shows political chaos manifesting itself on a lower social level than that occupied by the nobles but also, in pointing toward the Wars of the Roses, characterizes them as a kind of universal folly that would be ridiculous were its consequences not so grave. In the world of Cade and his followers, ordinary values are completely inverted, manifest impossibility replaces fact, and right reason becomes a series of puns, defective syllogisms, and contradictions in terms. In Cade's England all is in order when most out of order – seven halfpenny loaves will be sold for a penny, the three-hooped pot will have ten hoops, the pissing conduit will run nothing but claret for a year; it is a capital crime to read and write English and high treason to speak Latin. The massive confusion of such a world is shown not only by the brutality of Cade's actions but also by the havoc wrought upon the arts of language when the rebels speak. The dialogue succeeds in being very funny while simultaneously serving sternly serious purposes, among them the reflection of such cruelty as Clifford's murder of Rutland and such false logic as Warwick's legalistic argument in support of York's claim to the throne (2 Henry VI, II, ii, 53–62).

What emerges most strongly from such scenes is a powerful irony. The characters in the plays are living, all unaware, within a web of significance which connects individual actions. The law of cause and effect is always operating, but the individual, having lost his hold upon

moral realities because of pride, selfishness, or weakness, cannot see beyond the moment. With morality gone, the old values which make for goodness in men and stability in the state become perverted. The keeping of oaths becomes a matter of expediency. Family loyalty breeds only revenge, which breeds only counter-revenge. Caught up in circumstances which are very imperfectly understood, fathers kill their sons and sons their fathers. Desire for the sweet fruition of an earthly crown leads only to a molehill like that upon which an actual king is to sit and wish that he were anything but a king. Justice becomes confused with self-interest, piety becomes cowardice, and good reasons replace right reason. The ultimate origin of this anarchy lies behind, in history; its ultimate outcome lies ahead, and no character can perceive it except dimly in very occasional moments of foreboding or prophesy. Within the plays certain incidents provide ironical commentaries on others (as, for instance, the mock-heroic combat of the drunken Horner and the frightened Peter casts an ironic light on the hollow chivalry of the nobles), but throughout both our perspective is modified by the discrepancy between our historical knowledge of the outcome of it all and the characters' more limited vision.

It is no doubt impossible to read or to see 2 and 3 Henry VI without thinking of the Shakespeare that was to come, for in them many things are attempted that were later to be better done. Their language is sometimes stilted and inflexible, adorned with elaborate conceits which are more ornamental than integral; their psychology does not often inquire very far beyond the self-love to which Renaissance moralists conventionally attributed man's corruption. It is a mistake, however, to underrate them. When they were written, there was only one other playwright, Marlowe, who just might have done the job more expertly, and there is no real assurance that he could have managed so well. The mature Shakespeare is noted, among many other things, for unsurpassed skill in dramatic design, for language so pregnant and beautiful that one can only wonder at it, for characters so admirably conceived that they never release their holds upon the imagination, and for as deep an insight into the mystery of things as any writer ever achieved. All these virtues are present, at least in embryonic form, in 2 and 3 Henry VI.

*University of Wisconsin*
*Milwaukee*      ROBERT K. TURNER, JR

*Duke University*      GEORGE WALTON WILLIAMS

## NOTE ON THE TEXTS

*The Second and Third Parts of King Henry the Sixth* were printed in the folio of 1623, evidently from a manuscript in Shakespeare's hand except for a few brief passages, and the folio text has been closely followed in the present edition. The version of Part Two printed in quarto in 1594 and the version of Part Three printed in octavo in 1595 are discussed in Appendix B, with an explanation of the use made of them in this edition. A list of all substantive departures from the folio text is included in this Appendix. Neither the quarto–octavo nor the folio versions are divided into acts and scenes. The act–scene division here supplied marginally is that of earlier editors. (The present editors have collaborated closely on all portions of this edition, with Professor Turner drafting the Introduction, Professor Williams collating the text, and both writing the glosses.)

# THE SECOND PART OF
# KING HENRY THE SIXTH

[NAMES OF THE ACTORS

King Henry the Sixth
Humphrey, Duke of Gloucester, his uncle
Henry, Cardinal Beaufort, Bishop of Winchester,
   great-uncle to the King
Richard Plantagenet, Duke of York
Edward and Richard, his sons
Edmund Beaufort, Duke of Somerset
William de la Pole, Duke of Suffolk
Humphrey Stafford, Duke of Buckingham
Thomas, Lord Clifford
Young Clifford, his son John
Richard Nevil, Earl of Salisbury
Richard Nevil, Earl of Warwick, his son
Thomas, Lord Scales
Sir James Fiennes, Lord Say
Sir Humphrey Stafford
William Stafford, his brother
Sir John Stanley
Vaux
Matthew Goffe
A Lieutenant, Master, Mate, and Walter Whitmore

Two Gentlemen, prisoners with Suffolk
Alexander Iden, a Kentish gentleman
John Hume and John Southwell, two priests
Roger Bolingbroke, a conjurer
Thomas Horner, an armorer
Peter Thump, his man
Clerk of Chartham
Mayor of Saint Albans
Saunder Simpcox, an impostor
Jack Cade, a rebel
John, Dick the butcher, Smith the weaver, and other Rebels
Two Murderers
A Spirit
Margaret, Queen to King Henry
Eleanor Cobham, Duchess of Gloucester
Margery Jourdain, a witch
Wife to Simpcox
Lords, Ladies, Attendants, Petitioners, Aldermen, Herald,
   Beadle, Sheriff, Officers, Citizens, Prentices, Falconers,
   Guards, Soldiers, Messengers, etc.

Scene : *England*]

\*

I, i    *Flourish of trumpets, then hautboys. Enter King,*
      *Duke Humphrey [of Gloucester], Salisbury,*
      *Warwick, and [Cardinal] Beaufort [of Winchester],*
      *on the one side ; the Queen, Suffolk, York,*
      *Somerset, and Buckingham on the other.*

SUFFOLK
  As by your high imperial majesty
  I had in charge at my depart for France,
3  As procurator to your excellence,
  To marry Princess Margaret for your grace,
  So, in the famous ancient city Tours,
6  In presence of the Kings of France and Sicil,
  The Dukes of Orleans, Calaber, Bretagne, and Alençon,
  Seven earls, twelve barons, and twenty reverend bishops,
  I have performed my task and was espoused ;
  And humbly now upon my bended knee
  In sight of England and her lordly peers
  Deliver up my title in the queen
  To your most gracious hands, that are the substance
  Of that great shadow I did represent :
  The happiest gift that ever marquess gave,
  The fairest queen that ever king received.

KING
  Suffolk, arise. Welcome, Queen Margaret.
18  I can express no kinder sign of love

Than this kind kiss. O Lord, that lends me life,
Lend me a heart replete with thankfulness.
For thou hast given me in this beauteous face
A world of earthly blessings to my soul,
If sympathy of love unite our thoughts.

QUEEN
Great King of England and my gracious lord,
The mutual conference that my mind hath had,    25
By day, by night, waking and in my dreams,
In courtly company or at my beads,
With you, mine alderliefest sovereign,    28
Makes me the bolder to salute my king    29
With ruder terms, such as my wit affords
And over-joy of heart doth minister.    31

KING
Her sight did ravish, but her grace in speech,
Her words yclad with wisdom's majesty,    33
Makes me from wond'ring fall to weeping joys,
Such is the fullness of my heart's content.
Lords, with one cheerful voice welcome my love.

I, i The royal palace in London   s.d. *Flourish* fanfare, more elaborate than
a sennet (see I, iii, 98 s.d., n.)  3 *procurator* legal agent, proxy  6 *Sicil* i.e.
Sicily ; Queen Margaret's father, Reignier  18–19 *kinder . . . kind* more
natural . . . loving  25 *mutual conference* intimate intercourse  28 *alderliefest* most dear  29 *salute* greet  31 *minister* suggest  33 *yclad* clad

ALL *(kneel)*
Long live Queen Margaret, England's happiness !
QUEEN
We thank you all.
*Flourish.*
SUFFOLK
My Lord Protector, so it please your grace,
Here are the articles of contracted peace
Between our sovereign and the French king Charles,
For eighteen months concluded by consent.
43 GLOUCESTER *(reads)* 'Inprimis, It is agreed between the
French king Charles and William de la Pole, Marquess
of Suffolk, ambassador for Henry King of England, that
the said Henry shall espouse the Lady Margaret,
daughter unto Reignier King of Naples, Sicilia, and
Jerusalem, and crown her Queen of England ere the
thirtieth of May next ensuing.
'*Item*, that the duchy of Anjou and the county of Maine
shall be released and delivered to the king her father' –
*[Gloucester lets it fall.]*
KING
Uncle, how now ?
GLOUCESTER     Pardon me, gracious lord,
Some sudden qualm hath struck me at the heart,
And dimmed mine eyes that I can read no further.
KING
55 Uncle of Winchester, I pray read on.
CARDINAL *[reads]* 'Item, It is further agreed between
them that the duchies of Anjou and Maine shall be
released and delivered over to the king her father, and
she sent over of the King of England's own proper cost
and charges, without having any dowry.'
KING
They please us well. Lord marquess, kneel down.
We here create thee the first Duke of Suffolk
And girt thee with the sword. Cousin of York,
We here discharge your grace from being regent
I' th' parts of France till term of eighteen months
Be full expired. Thanks, uncle Winchester,
Gloucester, York, Buckingham, Somerset,
Salisbury, and Warwick.
We thank you all for this great favor done
70 In entertainment to my princely queen.
Come, let us in, and with all speed provide
To see her coronation be performed.
    *Exit King, [with] Queen, and Suffolk.*
    *Manet [Gloucester, staying all] the rest.*
GLOUCESTER
Brave peers of England, pillars of the state,
To you Duke Humphrey must unload his grief –
Your grief, the common grief of all the land.
76 What ? Did my brother Henry spend his youth,
His valor, coin, and people in the wars ?
78 Did he so often lodge in open field,

In winter's cold and summer's parching heat,
To conquer France, his true inheritance ?    80
And did my brother Bedford toil his wits
To keep by policy what Henry got ?
Have you yourselves, Somerset, Buckingham,
Brave York, Salisbury, and victorious Warwick,
Received deep scars in France and Normandy ?
Or hath mine uncle Beaufort and myself,
With all the learned council of the realm,
Studied so long, sat in the Council House
Early and late, debating to and fro
How France and Frenchmen might be kept in awe,    90
And hath his highness in his infancy
Crownèd in Paris in despite of foes ?
And shall these labors and these honors die ?
Shall Henry's conquest, Bedford's vigilance,
Your deeds of war, and all our counsel die ?
O peers of England, shameful is this league.
Fatal this marriage, cancelling your fame,
Blotting your names from books of memory.
Rasing the characters of your renown,    99
Defacing monuments of conquered France,    100
Undoing all as all had never been !
CARDINAL
Nephew, what means this passionate discourse,
This peroration with such circumstance ?    103
For France, 'tis ours ; and we will keep it still.
GLOUCESTER
Ay, uncle, we will keep it if we can,
But now it is impossible we should.
Suffolk, the new-made duke that rules the roast,    107
Hath given the duchy of Anjou and Maine
Unto the poor King Reignier, whose large style    109
Agrees not with the leanness of his purse.
SALISBURY
Now, by the death of Him that died for all,
These counties were the keys of Normandy.
But wherefore weeps Warwick, my valiant son ?
WARWICK
For grief that they are past recovery ;
For were there hope to conquer them again,
My sword should shed hot blood, mine eyes no tears.
Anjou and Maine ? Myself did win them both ;
Those provinces these arms of mine did conquer ;
And are the cities that I got with wounds
Delivered up again with peaceful words ?
Mort Dieu !    121
YORK
For Suffolk's duke, may he be suffocate,
That dims the honor of this warlike isle.
France should have torn and rent my very heart
Before I would have yielded to this league.
I never read but England's kings have had
Large sums of gold and dowries with their wives,
And our King Henry gives away his own
To match with her that brings no vantages.
GLOUCESTER
A proper jest, and never heard before,
That Suffolk should demand a whole fifteenth    131
For costs and charges in transporting her.
She should have stayed in France, and starved in France,
Before –
CARDINAL
My Lord of Gloucester, now ye grow too hot.

---

43 *Inprimis* imprimis, first (marks the first point agreed upon in a contract ;
subsequent points are signalled by *item*, 'similarly,' as at l. 50)   55 *Uncle* i.e.
great-uncle (the cardinal was the half-brother of Henry VI's grandfather,
Henry IV)   76 *brother Henry* i.e. Henry V   78 *lodge* lie   80 *true inheritance*
(through Henry V's ancestor Isabella of France, wife of Edward II of
England ; see *Henry V*, I, i, 87–89)   90 *awe* reverential obedience   99
*Rasing . . . of* erasing the letters which record   100 *monuments* (1) stones,
(2) documents (preservers of memory)   103 *circumstance* detail   107 *rules
the roast* domineers   109 *large style* pompous title   121 *Mort Dieu* (an
oath ; literally, by God's death)   131 *fifteenth* i.e. the proceeds from a tax of
this amount on subjects' real property

It was the pleasure of my lord the king.

GLOUCESTER

My Lord of Winchester, I know your mind.
'Tis not my speeches that you do mislike,
But 'tis my presence that doth trouble ye.
Rancor will out. Proud prelate, in thy face
I see thy fury. If I longer stay,
We shall begin our ancient bickerings.
143 Lordings, farewell; and say, when I am gone,
I prophesied, France will be lost ere long.
      *Exit Humphrey [Duke of Gloucester].*

CARDINAL

So, there goes our Protector in a rage.
'Tis known to you he is mine enemy;
Nay more, an enemy unto you all,
And no great friend, I fear me, to the king.
149 Consider, lords, he is the next of blood
And heir apparent to the English crown.
Had Henry got an empire by his marriage
And all the wealthy kingdoms of the west,
There's reason he should be displeased at it.
Look to it, lords. Let not his smoothing words
Bewitch your hearts; be wise and circumspect.
What though the common people favor him,
Calling him 'Humphrey, the good Duke of Gloucester,'
Clapping their hands and crying with loud voice
'Jesu maintain your royal Excellence!'
With 'God preserve the good Duke Humphrey!'
161 I fear me, lords, for all this flattering gloss,
He will be found a dangerous Protector.

BUCKINGHAM

Why should he then protect our sovereign,
He being of age to govern of himself?
Cousin of Somerset, join you with me,
And all together with the Duke of Suffolk,
167 We'll quickly hoise Duke Humphrey from his seat.

CARDINAL

168 This weighty business will not brook delay;
169 I'll to the Duke of Suffolk presently.       *Exit Cardinal.*

SOMERSET

Cousin of Buckingham, though Humphrey's pride
And greatness of his place be grief to us,
Yet let us watch the haughty cardinal;
His insolence is more intolerable
Than all the princes' in the land beside.
If Gloucester be displaced, he'll be Protector.

BUCKINGHAM

Or thou or I, Somerset, will be Protector
Despite Duke Humphrey or the cardinal.
      *Exeunt Buckingham and Somerset.*

SALISBURY

178 Pride went before, ambition follows him.
While these do labor for their own preferment,
Behooves it us to labor for the realm.
I never saw but Humphrey Duke of Gloucester
Did bear him like a noble gentleman.
Oft have I seen the haughty cardinal,
More like a soldier than a man o' th' church,
As stout and proud as he were lord of all,
Swear like a ruffian and demean himself
Unlike the ruler of a commonweal.
Warwick my son, the comfort of my age,
189 Thy deeds, thy plainness, and thy housekeeping
Hath won the greatest favor of the commons,

Excepting none but good Duke Humphrey.
And, brother York, thy acts in Ireland    192
In bringing them to civil discipline,
Thy late exploits done in the heart of France
When thou wert regent for our sovereign,
Have made thee feared and honored of the people.
Join we together for the public good,
In what we can to bridle and suppress
The pride of Suffolk and the cardinal
With Somerset's and Buckingham's ambition;
And, as we may, cherish Duke Humphrey's deeds
While they do tend the profit of the land.

WARWICK

So God help Warwick, as he loves the land
And common profit of his country.

YORK

And so says York – [aside] for he hath greatest cause.

SALISBURY

Then let's make haste away, and look unto the main.    206

WARWICK

Unto the main? O father, Maine is lost.
That Maine which by main force Warwick did win,    208
And would have kept so long as breath did last.
Main chance, father, you meant, but I meant Maine,
Which I will win from France or else be slain.
      *Exeunt Warwick and Salisbury. Manet York.*

YORK

Anjou and Maine are given to the French,
Paris is lost; the state of Normandy
Stands on a tickle point now they are gone.    214
Suffolk concluded on the articles,
The peers agreed, and Henry was well pleased
To change two dukedoms for a duke's fair daughter.
I cannot blame them all. What is't to them?
'Tis thine they give away, and not their own.    219
Pirates may make cheap pennyworths of their pillage,    220
And purchase friends, and give to courtesans,
Still revelling like lords till all be gone,    222
While as the silly owner of the goods    223
Weeps over them and wrings his hapless hands    224
And shakes his head and trembling stands aloof
While all is shared and all is borne away,
Ready to starve and dare not touch his own.
So York must sit and fret and bite his tongue    228
While his own lands are bargained for and sold.
Methinks the realms of England, France, and Ireland
Bear that proportion to my flesh and blood
As did the fatal brand Althaea burnt    232
Unto the prince's heart of Calydon.
Anjou and Maine both given unto the French?
Cold news for me! for I had hope of France,

143 *Lordings* my lords· 149 *next of blood* (since Henry VI has no child as yet, the crown would pass, in the event of his death, to Gloucester, his uncle and nearest blood relative) 161 *flattering gloss* specious praise 167 *hoise* hoist 168 *brook* endure 169 *presently* immediately 178 *Pride . . . ambition* i.e. the cardinal . . . Buckingham and Somerset 189 *housekeeping* hospitality, management of personal affairs 192 *brother* i.e. brother-in-law 206 *main* most important stake (a term in hazard, a dice game, to which Warwick alludes further at l. 210) 208 *main* overpowering 214 *tickle* unstable 219 *thine* (York addresses himself in the second person) 220 *pennyworths* bargains 222 *Still* continually 223 *silly* helpless 224 *hapless* unlucky 228 *bite his tongue* hold his tongue 232 *fatal brand* (the prince of Calydon, Meleager, died when his mother, Althaea, in a rage burned a piece of wood [brand] upon which the Fates had said his life depended)

Even as I have of fertile England's soil.
A day will come when York shall claim his own;
238 And therefore I will take the Nevils' parts,
And make a show of love to proud Duke Humphrey,
And when I spy advantage, claim the crown,
For that's the golden mark I seek to hit.
242 Nor shall proud Lancaster usurp my right,
Nor hold the sceptre in his childish fist,
Nor wear the diadem upon his head,
Whose churchlike humors fits not for a crown.
Then, York, be still awhile, till time do serve.
Watch thou and wake when others be asleep,
To pry into the secrets of the state,
Till Henry, surfeiting in joys of love,
With his new bride and England's dear-bought queen,
251 And Humphrey with the peers be fallen at jars.
252 Then will I raise aloft the milk-white rose,
With whose sweet smell the air shall be perfumed,
And in my standard bear the arms of York
To grapple with the house of Lancaster;
256 And force perforce I'll make him yield the crown
Whose bookish rule hath pulled fair England down.
*Exit York.*

*

I, ii     *Enter Duke Humphrey [of Gloucester] and his wife
Eleanor.*

ELEANOR
Why droops my lord like over-ripened corn
2 Hanging the head at Ceres' plenteous load?
Why doth the great Duke Humphrey knit his brows,
As frowning at the favors of the world?
Why are thine eyes fixed to the sullen earth,
Gazing on that which seems to dim thy sight?
What seest thou there? King Henry's diadem,
8 Enchased with all the honors of the world?
9 If so, gaze on and grovel on thy face
Until thy head be circled with the same.
Put forth thy hand, reach at the glorious gold.
What, is't too short? I'll lengthen it with mine;
And having both together heaved it up,
We'll both together lift our heads to heaven
And never more abase our sight so low
As to vouchsafe one glance unto the ground.

GLOUCESTER
O Nell, sweet Nell, if thou dost love thy lord,
18 Banish the canker of ambitious thoughts.
And may that thought, when I imagine ill
Against my king and nephew, virtuous Henry,
Be my last breathing in this mortal world.
My troublous dreams this night doth make me sad.

ELEANOR
What dreamed my lord? Tell me, and I'll requite it
With sweet rehearsal of my morning's dream.

GLOUCESTER
Methought this staff, mine office-badge in court,

238 *Nevils'* i.e. Salisbury's and Warwick's    242 *Lancaster* (Henry VI was
also Duke of Lancaster)    251 *be . . . jars* quarrel    252 *milk-white rose* (the
symbol of the house of York)    256 *force perforce* by violent force
I, ii The Duke of Gloucester's house    2 *Ceres* goddess of agriculture
8 *Enchased* adorned    9 *grovel . . . face* i.e. in adoration    18 *canker* ulcer
32 *argument* proof    42 *ill-nurtured* ill-bred    47 *hammering* hammering out,
devising    54 *checked* rebuked    68 *Sir* (the title of respect given priests as
well as knights)    71 *grace* (only monarchs could be addressed as 'majesty';
'grace' was the proper appellation for a duke or duchess)

Was broke in twain, by whom I have forgot,
But as I think, it was by th' cardinal;
And on the pieces of the broken wand
Were placed the heads of Edmund Duke of Somerset
And William de la Pole, first Duke of Suffolk.
This was my dream; what it doth bode, God knows.

ELEANOR
Tut, this was nothing but an argument     32
That he that breaks a stick of Gloucester's grove
Shall lose his head for his presumption.
But list to me, my Humphrey, my sweet duke.
Methought I sat in seat of majesty
In the cathedral church of Westminster;
And in that chair where kings and queens were crowned,
Where Henry and Dame Margaret kneeled to me
And on my head did set the diadem –

GLOUCESTER
Nay, Eleanor, then must I chide outright.
Presumptuous dame, ill-nurtured Eleanor,     42
Art thou not second woman in the realm,
And the Protector's wife, beloved of him?
Hast thou not worldly pleasure at command
Above the reach or compass of thy thought?
And wilt thou still be hammering treachery     47
To tumble down thy husband and thyself
From top of honor to disgrace's feet?
Away from me, and let me hear no more.

ELEANOR
What, what, my lord? Are you so choleric
With Eleanor for telling but her dream?
Next time I'll keep my dreams unto myself
And not be checked.     54

GLOUCESTER
Nay, be not angry. I am pleased again.
*Enter Messenger.*

MESSENGER
My Lord Protector, 'tis his highness' pleasure
You do prepare to ride unto Saint Albans,
Where as the king and queen do mean to hawk.

GLOUCESTER
I go. Come, Nell, thou wilt ride with us?

ELEANOR
Yes, my good lord, I'll follow presently.
*Exit Humphrey [with Messenger].*
Follow I must; I cannot go before
While Gloucester bears this base and humble mind.
Were I a man, a duke, and next of blood,
I would remove these tedious stumbling blocks
And smooth my way upon their headless necks;
And being a woman, I will not be slack
To play my part in Fortune's pageant.
Where are you there? Sir John! Nay, fear not, man.     68
We are alone; here's none but thee, and I.
*Enter Hume.*

HUME
Jesus preserve your royal majesty.

ELEANOR
What say'st thou? Majesty? I am but grace.     71

HUME
But by the grace of God and Hume's advice
Your grace's title shall be multiplied.

ELEANOR
What say'st thou, man? Hast thou as yet conferred
With Margery Jourdain, the cunning witch,

With Roger Bolingbroke, the conjurer?
And will they undertake to do me good?

HUME
This they have promisèd, to show your highness
A spirit raised from depth of under ground
That shall make answer to such questions
As by your grace shall be propounded him.

ELEANOR
It is enough. I'll think upon the questions.
When from Saint Albans we do make return
We'll see these things effected to the full.
Here, Hume, take this reward; make merry, man,
With thy confederates in this weighty cause.
                              *Exit Eleanor.*

HUME
Hume must make merry with the duchess' gold.
88   Marry and shall! But how now, Sir John Hume?
Seal up your lips and give no words but mum;
The business asketh silent secrecy.
Dame Eleanor gives gold to bring the witch;
Gold cannot come amiss, were she a devil.
Yet have I gold flies from another coast:
I dare not say, from the rich cardinal
And from the great and new-made Duke of Suffolk;
Yet I do find it so; for, to be plain,
97   They (knowing Dame Eleanor's aspiring humor)
Have hirèd me to undermine the duchess
99   And buzz these conjurations in her brain.
100  They say, 'A crafty knave does need no broker';
Yet am I Suffolk and the cardinal's broker.
Hume, if you take not heed, you shall go near
To call them both a pair of crafty knaves.
Well, so it stands; and thus, I fear, at last
105  Hume's knavery will be the duchess' wrack
106  And her attainture will be Humphrey's fall.
107  Sort how it will, I shall have gold for all.    *Exit.*

*

I, iii    *Enter three or four Petitioners, the Armorer's Man*
          *[Peter] being one.*

1. PETITIONER  My masters, let's stand close. My Lord
Protector will come this way by and by, and then we
3   may deliver our supplications in the quill.
2. PETITIONER  Marry, the Lord protect him, for he's a
good man, Jesu bless him!
          *Enter Suffolk and Queen.*
1. PETITIONER  Here 'a comes, methinks, and the queen
with him. I'll be the first, sure.
2. PETITIONER  Come back, fool. This is the Duke of
Suffolk and not my Lord Protector.
SUFFOLK  How now, fellow? Wouldst anything with me?
1. PETITIONER  I pray, my lord, pardon me. I took ye
for my Lord Protector.
QUEEN  For my Lord Protector? Are your supplications
to his lordship? Let me see them. What is thine?
1. PETITIONER  Mine is, an't please your grace, against
John Goodman, my Lord Cardinal's man, for keeping
my house, and lands, and wife and all, from me.
SUFFOLK  Thy wife too? That's some wrong indeed.
What's yours? What's here? *[reads]* 'Against the Duke
20   of Suffolk, for enclosing the commons of Melford.'
How now, sir knave?

2. PETITIONER  Alas, sir, I am but a poor petitioner of
our whole township.
PETER *[presents his petition]*  Against my master, Thomas
Horner, for saying that the Duke of York was rightful
heir to the crown.
QUEEN  What say'st thou? Did the Duke of York say he
was rightful heir to the crown?
PETER  That my master was? No, forsooth! My master
said that he was, and that the king was an usurper.
SUFFOLK  Who is there?
          *Enter Servant.*
Take this fellow in and send for his master with a pur-   32
suivant presently. We'll hear more of your matter before
the king.                    *Exit [Servant with Peter].*
QUEEN
And as for you that love to be protected
Under the wings of our Protector's grace,
Begin your suits anew and sue to him.
          *Tear the supplication.*
Away, base cullions! Suffolk, let them go.      38
ALL  Come, let's be gone.              *Exeunt.*
QUEEN
My Lord of Suffolk, say, is this the guise,       40
Is this the fashions in the court of England?
Is this the government of Britain's isle,
And this the royalty of Albion's king?            43
What, shall King Henry be a pupil still,
Under the surly Gloucester's governance?
Am I a queen in title and in style
And must be made a subject to a duke?
I tell thee, Pole, when in the city Tours
Thou ran'st a-tilt in honor of my love            49
And stol'st away the ladies' hearts of France,
I thought King Henry had resembled thee
In courage, courtship, and proportion;            52
But all his mind is bent to holiness,
To number Ave-Maries on his beads;                54
His champions are the prophets and apostles,      55
His weapons holy saws of sacred writ;             56
His study is his tiltyard, and his loves
Are brazen images of canonized saints.
I would the college of the cardinals              59
Would choose him pope and carry him to Rome
And set the triple crown upon his head.           61
That were a state fit for his holiness.
SUFFOLK
Madam, be patient. As I was cause
Your highness came to England, so will I
In England work your grace's full content.
QUEEN
Beside the haughty Protector, have we Beaufort
The imperious churchman, Somerset, Buckingham,
And grumbling York; and not the least of these

88 *Marry and shall* indeed he will  97 *humor* inclination  99 *buzz* whisper
100 *broker* agent  105 *wrack* ruin  106 *attainture* conviction  107 *Sort . . .*
*will* no matter how it turns out
I, iii The palace  3 *in the quill* (1) in a body, (2) illiterate error for 'in
sequel' (?)  20 *enclosing the commons* fencing public ground for private
use  32 *pursuivant* officer  38 *cullions* rascals, scum  40 *guise* manner
43 *Albion's* England's  49 *ran'st a-tilt* jousted  52 *courtship* courtliness;
*proportion* physique  54 *Ave-Maries* Hail Maries (prayers to the Blessed
Virgin)  55 *champions* defenders (with reference to valiant fighting men
who defend the honor and title of the king)  56 *saws* sayings  59 *college . . .*
*cardinals* the pope's council  61 *triple crown* papal crown

But can do more in England than the king.

SUFFOLK

70 And he of these that can do most of all
Cannot do more in England than the Nevils;
Salisbury and Warwick are no simple peers.

QUEEN

Not all these lords do vex me half so much
As that proud dame, the Lord Protector's wife.
She sweeps it through the court with troops of ladies,
More like an empress than Duke Humphrey's wife.
Strangers in court do take her for the queen.
She bears a duke's revenues on her back,
And in her heart she scorns our poverty.
Shall I not live to be avenged on her?
81 Contemptuous base-born callet as she is,
She vaunted 'mongst her minions t' other day,
The very train of her worst wearing gown
Was better worth than all my father's lands
Till Suffolk gave two dukedoms for his daughter.

SUFFOLK

86 Madam, myself have limed a bush for her,
87 And placed a choir of such enticing birds
And she will light to listen to the lays
That never mount to trouble you again.
So let her rest. And, madam, list to me,
For I am bold to counsel you in this:
Although we fancy not the cardinal,
Yet must we join with him and with the lords
Till we have brought Duke Humphrey in disgrace.
As for the Duke of York, this late complaint
Will make but little for his benefit.
So one by one we'll weed them all at last.
98 And you yourself shall steer the happy helm.
      *Sound a sennet. Enter the King, [York and*
      *Somerset on both sides of the King, whispering with*
      *him,] Duke Humphrey [of Gloucester], Cardinal*
      *[Beaufort], Buckingham, Salisbury, Warwick,*
      *and [Eleanor] the Duchess [of Gloucester].*

KING

For my part, noble lords, I care not which:
Or Somerset or York, all's one to me.

YORK

If York have ill demeaned himself in France,
102 Then let him be denayed the regentship.

SOMERSET

If Somerset be unworthy of the place,
Let York be regent; I will yield to him.

WARWICK

Whether your grace be worthy, yea or no,
Dispute not that. York is the worthier.

CARDINAL

Ambitious Warwick, let thy betters speak!

WARWICK

The cardinal's not my better in the field.

BUCKINGHAM

All in this presence are thy betters, Warwick.

WARWICK

Warwick may live to be the best of all.

SALISBURY

Peace, son! and show some reason, Buckingham,
Why Somerset should be preferred in this.

QUEEN

Because the king forsooth will have it so.

GLOUCESTER

Madam, the king is old enough himself
To give his censure. These are no women's matters.   115

QUEEN

If he be old enough, what needs your grace
To be Protector of his excellence?

GLOUCESTER

Madam, I am Protector of the realm,
And at his pleasure will resign my place.

SUFFOLK

Resign it then and leave thine insolence.
Since thou wert king (as who is king but thou?)
The commonwealth hath daily run to wrack,
The Dauphin hath prevailed beyond the seas,   123
And all the peers and nobles of the realm
Have been as bondmen to thy sovereignty.

CARDINAL

The commons hast thou racked; the clergy's bags   126
Are lank and lean with thy extortions.

SOMERSET

Thy sumptuous buildings and thy wife's attire   128
Have cost a mass of public treasury.

BUCKINGHAM

Thy cruelty in execution
Upon offenders hath exceeded law,
And left thee to the mercy of the law.

QUEEN

Thy sale of offices and towns in France –
If they were known, as the suspect is great –   134
Would make thee quickly hop without thy head.
                              *Exit Humphrey.*
      *[The Queen drops her fan.]*
Give me my fan. What, minion, can ye not?
      *She gives the Duchess a box on the ear.*
I cry you mercy, madam. Was it you?   137

ELEANOR

Was't I? Yea, I it was, proud Frenchwoman.
Could I come near your beauty with my nails,
I would set my ten commandments in your face.   140

KING

Sweet aunt, be quiet. 'Twas against her will.   141

ELEANOR

Against her will, good king? Look to't in time.
She'll hamper thee and dandle thee like a baby.   143
Though in this place most master wear no breeches,   144
She shall not strike Dame Eleanor unrevenged.
                              *Exit Eleanor.*

BUCKINGHAM

Lord Cardinal, I will follow Eleanor,
And listen after Humphrey, how he proceeds.
She's tickled now; her fume needs no spurs,   148
She'll gallop far enough to her destruction.
                              *Exit Buckingham.*

81 *callet* strumpet   86 *limed a bush* put lime on twigs of a bush to catch birds, i.e. set a trap   87 *enticing birds* i.e. decoys   98 s.d. *sennet* trumpet call signalling a ceremonial entrance or exit   102 *denayed* denied   115 *censure* decision   123 *Dauphin* eldest son of the King of France; here, Charles VII (so called by the English because they consider Henry VI the true King of France)   126 *racked* taxed exorbitantly (literally, tortured on the rack)   128 *sumptuous buildings* (Somerset refers specifically to Greenwich Palace)   134 *suspect* suspicion   137 *cry you mercy* beg your pardon   140 *ten commandments* i.e. fingernails   141 *against her will* i.e. an accident   143 *hamper* (1) obstruct, (2) cradle   144 *most master* the greatest master (i.e. the queen, who wears no breeches)   148 *tickled* irritated; *fume* rage

*Enter [Duke] Humphrey.*

GLOUCESTER

Now, lords, my choler being overblown
With walking once about the quadrangle,
I come to talk of commonwealth affairs.
As for your spiteful false objections,
Prove them, and I lie open to the law;
But God in mercy so deal with my soul
As I in duty love my king and country.
But to the matter that we have in hand:
158  I say, my sovereign, York is meetest man
To be your regent in the realm of France.

SUFFOLK

Before we make election, give me leave
To show some reason, of no little force,
That York is most unmeet of any man.

YORK

I'll tell thee, Suffolk, why I am unmeet:
First, for I cannot flatter thee in pride;
Next, if I be appointed for the place,
My Lord of Somerset will keep me here
167  Without discharge, money, or furniture
Till France be won into the Dauphin's hands.
169  Last time I danced attendance on his will
Till Paris was besieged, famished, and lost.

WARWICK

171  That can I witness; and a fouler fact
Did never traitor in the land commit.

SUFFOLK

Peace, headstrong Warwick!

WARWICK

Image of pride, why should I hold my peace?
*Enter [Horner the] Armorer, and his Man
[Peter, guarded].*

SUFFOLK

Because here is a man accused of treason.
Pray God the Duke of York excuse himself.

YORK

Doth any one accuse York for a traitor?

KING

What mean'st thou, Suffolk? Tell me, what are these?

SUFFOLK

Please it your majesty, this is the man
That doth accuse his master of high treason.
His words were these: that Richard Duke of York
Was rightful heir unto the English crown
And that your majesty was an usurper.

KING

Say, man, were these thy words?

ARMORER  An't shall please your majesty, I never said
nor thought any such matter. God is my witness, I am
falsely accused by the villain.

188  PETER  By these ten bones, my lords, he did speak them
to me in the garret one night, as we were scouring my
Lord of York's armor.

YORK

191  Base dunghill villain and mechanical,
I'll have thy head for this thy traitor's speech.
I do beseech your royal majesty,
Let him have all the rigor of the law.

ARMORER  Alas, my lord, hang me if ever I spake the
words! My accuser is my prentice; and when I did correct him for his fault the other day, he did vow upon his
knees he would be even with me. I have good witness of

this. Therefore I beseech your majesty, do not cast
away an honest man for a villain's accusation.

KING

Uncle, what shall we say to this in law?

GLOUCESTER

This doom, my lord, if I may judge:          202
Let Somerset be regent o'er the French,
Because in York this breeds suspicion;
And let these have a day appointed them
For single combat in convenient place,
For he hath witness of his servant's malice.
This is the law, and this Duke Humphrey's doom.

SOMERSET

I humbly thank your royal majesty.

ARMORER

And I accept the combat willingly.

PETER  Alas, my lord, I cannot fight; for God's sake pity
my case. The spite of man prevaileth against me. O
Lord have mercy upon me; I shall never be able to fight
a blow. O Lord, my heart!

GLOUCESTER

Sirrah, or you must fight or else be hanged.

KING

Away with them to prison! and the day
Of combat shall be the last of the next month.
Come, Somerset, we'll see thee sent away.
*Flourish. Exeunt.*

\*

*Enter [Margery Jourdain] the Witch, the two Priests*  I, iv
*[Hume and Southwell], and Bolingbroke.*

HUME  Come, my masters. The duchess, I tell you, ex-
pects performance of your promises.

BOLINGBROKE  Master Hume, we are therefore provided. Will her ladyship behold and hear our exorcisms?  4

HUME  Ay, what else? Fear you not her courage.

BOLINGBROKE  I have heard her reported to be a woman
of an invincible spirit. But it shall be convenient, Master
Hume, that you be by her aloft while we be busy below;
and so I pray you go in God's name and leave us. (*Exit
Hume.*) Mother Jourdain, be you prostrate and grovel
on the earth. John Southwell, read you, and let us to our
work.

*Enter [Duchess] Eleanor aloft [, followed by Hume].*

ELEANOR  Well said, my masters, and welcome all. To
this gear, the sooner the better.          13

BOLINGBROKE

Patience, good lady; wizards know their times.
Deep night, dark night, the silence of the night,
The time of night when Troy was set on fire,
The time when screech owls cry and bandogs howl          17
And spirits walk and ghosts break up their graves—
That time best fits the work we have in hand.
Madam, sit you and fear not. Whom we raise
We will make fast within a hallowed verge.          21
*Here do the ceremonies belonging [to conjuring],
and make the circle. Bolingbroke or Southwell reads:*

158 *meetest* fittest   167 *furniture* furnishings   169 *Last time* (cf. *1 Henry VI*,
IV, iii, 9–11)   171 *fact* deed   188 *ten bones* i.e. fingers   191 *mechanical*
manual laborer, i.e. low person   202 *doom* judgment
I, iv Gloucester's house   4 *exorcisms* conjurations   13 *gear* business   17
*bandogs* leashed watch-dogs   21 *verge* circle; s.d. *Conjuro te* I conjure you
(the beginning of a typical conjuration; it would perhaps continue 'by the
infernal powers' and, after these were named, 'to appear')

56

'Conjuro te,' *etc. It thunders and lightens terribly ;*
*then the Spirit riseth.*
22 SPIRIT Adsum.
23 WITCH Asnath,
By the eternal God, whose name and power
Thou tremblest at, answer that I shall ask ;
For till thou speak thou shalt not pass from hence.
SPIRIT
27 Ask what thou wilt. That I had said and done !
BOLINGBROKE *[reads]*
'First of the king ; what shall of him become ?'
SPIRIT
29 The duke yet lives that Henry shall depose ;
But him outlive, and die a violent death.
*[As the Spirit speaks, Southwell writes the answer.]*
BOLINGBROKE
'What fates await the Duke of Suffolk ?'
SPIRIT
By water shall he die and take his end.
BOLINGBROKE
'What shall befall the Duke of Somerset ?'
SPIRIT
Let him shun castles.
Safer shall he be upon the sandy plains
Than where castles mounted stand.
37 Have done, for more I hardly can endure.
BOLINGBROKE
Descend to darkness and the burning lake.
39 False fiend, avoid !
*Thunder and lightning. Exit Spirit*
*[sinking down again].*
*Enter the Duke of York and the Duke of Buckingham,*
*with their Guard, and break in.*
YORK
Lay hands upon these traitors and their trash.
41 Beldam, I think we watched you at an inch.
What, madam, are you there ? The king and common-
weal
Are deeply indebted for this piece of pains.
My Lord Protector will, I doubt it not,
45 See you well guerdoned for these good deserts.
ELEANOR
Not half so bad as thine to England's king,
47 Injurious duke, that threatest where's no cause.

22 *Adsum* I am here   23 *Asnath* (anagram of 'Sat[h]an'; evil spirits were
frequently addressed in anagrams)   27 *That* would that   29–30 *The . . .
death* (deliberately ambiguous ; cf. ll. 60–61)   37 *Have done* finish quickly
39 *False* treacherous (without reference to the information he has given);
*avoid* begone - 41 *Beldam* witch ; *at an inch* closely   45 *guerdoned . . .
deserts* rewarded for these worthy actions (ironically)   47 *Injurious* insulting   49 *clapped up* imprisoned   51 *Stafford* (presumably the captain of
the guard and one of Buckingham's kinsmen)   52 *We'll . . . forthcoming*
we'll take charge of your magic gear until it is produced as evidence against
you   56 *devil's writ* devil's writing (as opposed to Holy Writ)   60 *just*
precisely   60–61 *Aio . . . posse* (1) I say that you, descendant of Aeacus,
can overcome the Romans, (2) I say that the Romans can overcome you,
descendant of Aeacus (the ambiguous answer given by the oracle to Pyrrhus,
king of Epirus, when he asked whether he could conquer Rome)   69
*hardly . . . hardly* with difficulty . . . barely
II, i St Albans   1 *at the brook* beside the brook, i.e. for water-fowl   2
*these . . . day* for the last seven years   4 *had . . . out* would not have flown
at the game (because of the wind)   5 *point* position of vantage to wind-
ward about which the hawk flies as she awaits her prey   6 *pitch* altitude ;
the peak of the hawk's flight, from which she swoops down   10 *hawks*
(Suffolk and later the cardinal allude not only to the hawks just flown
by Gloucester but also to his heraldic badge, a hawk with a maiden's
head)

BUCKINGHAM
True, madam, none at all. What call you this ?
*[Shows her the papers.]*
Away with them ! Let them be clapped up close                49
And kept asunder. You, madam, shall with us.
Stafford, take her to thee.                                  51
We'll see your trinkets here all forthcoming.               52
All away !    *Exit [Stafford, those above and those below*
*following, guarded].*
YORK
Lord Buckingham, methinks you watched her well.
A pretty plot, well chosen to build upon.
Now pray, my lord, let's see the devil's writ.              56
What have we here ?
*Reads.*
'The duke yet lives that Henry shall depose ;
But him outlive, and die a violent death.'
Why, this is just 'Aio te, Aeacida,                          60
Romanos vincere posse.' Well, to the rest :
'Tell me, what fate awaits the Duke of Suffolk ?'
'By water shall he die and take his end.'
'What shall betide the Duke of Somerset ?'
'Let him shun castles.
Safer shall he be upon the sandy plains
Than where castles mounted stand.'
Come, come, my lords ; these oracles
Are hardly attained and hardly understood.                  69
The king is now in progress towards Saint Albans,
With him the husband of this lovely lady.
Thither goes these news as fast as horse can carry them –
A sorry breakfast for my Lord Protector.
BUCKINGHAM
Your grace shall give me leave, my Lord of York,
To be the post, in hope of his reward.
YORK
At your pleasure, my good lord.    *[Exit Buckingham.]*
Who's within there, ho ?
*Enter a Servingman.*
Invite my lords of Salisbury and Warwick
To sup with me to-morrow night. Away !    *Exeunt.*

\*

*Enter the King, Queen, [with her hawk on her fist,]*    II, i
*Protector [Gloucester], Cardinal, and Suffolk, [as if*
*they came from hawking ;] with Falconers halloaing.*
QUEEN
Believe me, lords, for flying at the brook                   1
I saw not better sport these seven years' day.               2
Yet, by your leave, the wind was very high,
And ten to one old Joan had not gone out.                    4
KING *[to Gloucester]*
But what a point, my lord, your falcon made                  5
And what a pitch she flew above the rest.                    6
To see how God in all his creatures works :
Yea, man and birds are fain of climbing high.
SUFFOLK
No marvel, an it like your majesty,
My Lord Protector's hawks do tower so well ;                10
They know their master loves to be aloft
And bears his thoughts above his falcon's pitch.
GLOUCESTER
My lord, 'tis but a base ignoble mind
That mounts no higher than a bird can soar.

CARDINAL
I thought as much. He would be above the clouds.

GLOUCESTER
Ay, my Lord Cardinal, how think you by that?
Were it not good your grace could fly to heaven?

KING
The treasury of everlasting joy.

CARDINAL
Thy heaven is on earth, thine eyes and thoughts
Beat on a crown, the treasure of thy heart;
Pernicious Protector, dangerous peer,
22    That smooth'st it so with king and commonweal.

GLOUCESTER
What, cardinal, is your priesthood grown peremptory?
24    'Tantaene animis coelestibus irae?'
Churchmen so hot? Good uncle, hide such malice;
26    With such holiness can you do it.

SUFFOLK
No malice, sir, no more than well becomes
So good a quarrel and so bad a peer.

GLOUCESTER
As who, my lord?

SUFFOLK                Why, as you, my lord,
An't like your lordly Lord's Protectorship.

GLOUCESTER
Why, Suffolk, England knows thine insolence.

QUEEN
And thy ambition, Gloucester.

KING                                I prithee, peace,
Good queen, and whet not on these furious peers,
For blessed are the peacemakers on earth.

CARDINAL
Let me be blessed for the peace I make
Against this proud Protector with my sword.

GLOUCESTER [aside to Cardinal]
Faith, holy uncle, would 'twere come to that.

CARDINAL [aside to Gloucester]
Marry, when thou dar'st.

GLOUCESTER [aside to Cardinal]
39    Make up no factious numbers for the matter;
In thine own person answer thy abuse.

CARDINAL [aside to Gloucester]
Ay, where thou dar'st not peep; and if thou dar'st,
This evening on the east side of the grove.

KING
How now, my lords?

CARDINAL                Believe me, cousin Gloucester,
44    Had not your man put up the fowl so suddenly,
We had had more sport. – [Aside to Gloucester] Come
with thy two-hand sword.

GLOUCESTER
True uncle –
[Aside to Cardinal]
47    Are ye advised? The east side of the grove.

CARDINAL [aside to Gloucester]
I am with you.

KING                Why, how now, uncle Gloucester?

GLOUCESTER
Talking of hawking; nothing else, my lord.
[Aside to Cardinal]
Now, by God's Mother, priest, I'll shave your crown for
this,
51    Or all my fence shall fail.

CARDINAL [aside to Gloucester]
'Medice, teipsum.'                                                52
Protector, see to't well; protect yourself.

KING
The winds grow high; so do your stomachs, lords.        54
How irksome is this music to my heart!
When such strings jar, what hope of harmony?
I pray, my lords, let me compound this strife.            57
        Enter one [Townsman] crying 'A miracle!'

GLOUCESTER
What means this noise?
Fellow, what miracle dost thou proclaim?

TOWNSMAN
A miracle! a miracle!

SUFFOLK
Come to the king and tell him what miracle.

TOWNSMAN
Forsooth, a blind man at Saint Alban's shrine
Within this half hour hath received his sight –
A man that ne'er saw in his life before.

KING
Now God be praised, that to believing souls
Gives light in darkness, comfort in despair.
        Enter the Mayor of Saint Albans and his Brethren,
        [with music,] bearing the man [Simpcox] between
        two in a chair [, Simpcox's Wife and a crowd of
        Townsmen following].

CARDINAL
Here comes the townsmen on procession                    67
To present your highness with the man.

KING
Great is his comfort in this earthly vale,
Although by his sight his sin be multiplied.

GLOUCESTER
Stand by, my masters. Bring him near the king;
His highness' pleasure is to talk with him.

KING
Good fellow, tell us here the circumstance,
That we for thee may glorify the Lord.
What, hast thou been long blind, and now restored?

SIMPCOX
Born blind, an't please your grace.

WIFE Ay indeed was he.

SUFFOLK What woman is this?

WIFE His wife, an't like your worship.

GLOUCESTER
Hadst thou been his mother, thou couldst have better  80
told.

KING
Where wert thou born?

SIMPCOX
At Berwick in the North, an't like your grace.

KING
Poor soul, God's goodness hath been great to thee.
Let never day nor night unhallowed pass
But still remember what the Lord hath done.

---

22 smooth'st it flatters  24 Tantaene . . . irae? do heavenly minds nourish
such great wrath? (Aeneid, I, 11)  26 can you i.e. you can (but defective
metre suggests that the line is corrupt)  39 Make . . . numbers do not
make up a war-party  44 put . . . fowl startled the game into flight  47
advised agreed  51 fence skill in swordsmanship  52 Medice, teipsum
physician, [cure] thyself  54 stomachs passions  57 compound compose
67 on in

QUEEN
Tell me, good fellow, cam'st thou here by chance
Or of devotion to this holy shrine?

SIMPCOX
God knows, of pure devotion, being called
A hundred times and oft'ner in my sleep
90 By good Saint Alban, who said, 'Simon, come;
Come offer at my shrine and I will help thee.'

WIFE
Most true, forsooth, and many time and oft
Myself have heard a voice to call him so.

CARDINAL
What, art thou lame?

SIMPCOX                    Ay, God Almighty help me.

SUFFOLK
How cam'st thou so?

SIMPCOX                    A fall off of a tree.

WIFE
A plum tree, master.

GLOUCESTER                    How long hast thou been blind?

SIMPCOX
O, born so, master.

GLOUCESTER                    What, and wouldst climb a tree?

SIMPCOX
98 But that in all my life, when I was a youth.

WIFE
Too true, and bought his climbing very dear.

GLOUCESTER
Mass, thou lovedst plums well, that wouldst venture so.

SIMPCOX
101 Alas, good master, my wife desired some damsons
And made me climb, with danger of my life.

GLOUCESTER
A subtle knave. But yet it shall not serve.
Let me see thine eyes. Wink now. Now open them.
In my opinion yet thou seest not well.

SIMPCOX Yes, master, clear as day, I thank God and Saint
Alban.

GLOUCESTER
Say'st thou me so? What color is this cloak of?

SIMPCOX
Red, master; red as blood.

GLOUCESTER
110 Why, that's well said. What color is my gown of?

SIMPCOX
Black, forsooth; coal-black, as jet.

KING
Why then, thou know'st what color jet is of?

SUFFOLK
And yet, I think, jet did he never see.

GLOUCESTER
But cloaks and gowns before this day a many.

WIFE
Never before this day in all his life.

GLOUCESTER Tell me, sirrah, what's my name?

SIMPCOX Alas, master, I know not.

GLOUCESTER What's his name?

SIMPCOX I know not.

GLOUCESTER Nor his?

SIMPCOX No indeed, master.

GLOUCESTER What's thine own name?

SIMPCOX Saunder Simpcox, an if it please you, master.

GLOUCESTER Then, Saunder, sit there, the lying'st
knave in Christendom. If thou hadst been born blind,
thou mightst as well have known all our names as thus to
name the several colors we do wear. Sight may distinguish of colors; but suddenly to nominate them all, it    128
is impossible. My lords, Saint Alban here hath done a
miracle; and would ye not think his cunning to be great
that could restore this cripple to his legs again?

SIMPCOX O master, that you could!

GLOUCESTER My masters of Saint Albans, have you not
beadles in your town, and things called whips?    134

MAYOR Yes, my lord, if it please your grace.

GLOUCESTER Then send for one presently.

MAYOR Sirrah, go fetch the beadle hither straight.
                                        *Exit [a Townsman].*

GLOUCESTER Now fetch me a stool hither by and by. *[A
stool brought.]* Now, sirrah, if you mean to save yourself
from whipping, leap me over this stool and run away.    140

SIMPCOX
Alas, master, I am not able to stand alone;
You go about to torture me in vain.
                                        *Enter a Beadle with whips.*

GLOUCESTER Well, sir, we must have you find your legs.
Sirrah beadle, whip him till he leap over that same stool.

BEADLE I will, my lord. Come on, sirrah, off with your
doublet quickly.

SIMPCOX Alas, master, what shall I do? I am not able to
stand.
                *After the Beadle hath hit him once, he leaps over the
                stool and runs away; and they follow and cry
                'A miracle!'*

KING
O God, seest thou this, and bearest so long?

QUEEN
It made me laugh to see the villain run.

GLOUCESTER
Follow the knave, and take this drab away.    151

WIFE
Alas, sir, we did it for pure need.

GLOUCESTER Let them be whipped through every market town till they come to Berwick, from whence they
came.                    *Exit [Mayor with the Townsmen].*

CARDINAL
Duke Humphrey has done a miracle to-day.

SUFFOLK
True; made the lame to leap and fly away.

GLOUCESTER
But you have done more miracles than I;
You made in a day, my lord, whole towns to fly.    158
                        *Enter Buckingham.*

KING
What tidings with our cousin Buckingham?

BUCKINGHAM
Such as my heart doth tremble to unfold.
A sort of naughty persons, lewdly bent,    161
Under the countenance and confederacy
Of Lady Eleanor, the Protector's wife,

90 *Simon* (the name of which Simpcox [Simon-boy] is an informal variant)
98 *But . . . life* never in all my life except    101 *damsons* a kind of plum
128 *nominate* name    134 *beadles* constables    140 *me* for me (ethical dative)
151 *drab* low woman    158 *made . . . fly* i.e. by giving the French provinces
away in exchange for the queen    161 *sort* gang; *naughty* worthless (with
implications of wickedness); *lewdly* wickedly

164 The ringleader and head of all this rout,
Have practiced dangerously against your state,
Dealing with witches and with conjurers,
Whom we have apprehended in the fact,
Raising up wicked spirits from under ground,
169 Demanding of King Henry's life and death
And other of your highness' privy council,
171 As more at large your grace shall understand.

CARDINAL *[aside to Gloucester]*
And so, my Lord Protector, by this means
173 Your lady is forthcoming yet at London.
This news, I think, hath turned your weapon's edge.
'Tis like, my lord, you will not keep your hour.

GLOUCESTER *[aside to Cardinal]*
Ambitious churchman, leave to afflict my heart.
Sorrow and grief have vanquished all my powers ;
And, vanquished as I am, I yield to thee
Or to the meanest groom.

KING
O God, what mischiefs work the wicked ones,
Heaping confusion on their own heads thereby !

QUEEN
182 Gloucester, see here the tainccture of thy nest,
And look thyself be faultless, thou wert best.

GLOUCESTER
Madam, for myself, to heaven I do appeal,
How I have loved my king and commonweal ;
And for my wife, I know not how it stands.
Sorry I am to hear what I have heard.
Noble she is ; but if she have forgot
Honor and virtue and conversed with such
As, like to pitch, defile nobility,
I banish her my bed and company
And give her as a prey to law and shame
That hath dishonored Gloucester's honest name.

KING
Well, for this night we will repose us here.
To-morrow toward London back again
To look into this business thoroughly
And call these foul offenders to their answers
198 And poise the cause in justice' equal scales,
199 Whose beam stands sure, whose rightful cause prevails.
                                        *Flourish. Exeunt.*

*

II, ii     *Enter York, Salisbury, and Warwick.*
YORK
Now, my good Lords of Salisbury and Warwick,
Our simple supper ended, give me leave
3 In this close walk to satisfy myself
In craving your opinion of my title,
Which is infallible, to England's crown.

SALISBURY
My lord, I long to hear it at full.

WARWICK
Sweet York, begin ; and if thy claim be good,
The Nevils are thy subjects to command.

YORK
Then thus :
10 Edward the Third, my lords, had seven sons :
The first, Edward the Black Prince, Prince of Wales ;
The second, William of Hatfield ; and the third,
Lionel Duke of Clarence ; next to whom
Was John of Gaunt, the Duke of Lancaster ;

The fifth was Edmund Langley, Duke of York ;
The sixth was Thomas of Woodstock, Duke of Gloucester ;
William of Windsor was the seventh and last.
Edward the Black Prince died before his father
And left behind him Richard, his only son,
Who after Edward the Third's death reigned as king     20
Till Henry Bolingbroke, Duke of Lancaster,
The eldest son and heir of John of Gaunt,
Crowned by the name of Henry the Fourth,
Seized on the realm, deposed the rightful king,
Sent his poor queen to France from whence she came,
And him to Pomfret, where, as all you know,
Harmless Richard was murdered traitorously.

WARWICK
Father, the duke hath told the truth.
Thus got the house of Lancaster the crown.

YORK
Which now they hold by force, and not by right ;     30
For Richard, the first son's heir, being dead,
The issue of the next son should have reigned.

SALISBURY
But William of Hatfield died without an heir.

YORK
The third son, Duke of Clarence, from whose line
I claim the crown, had issue, Philippe, a daughter,
Who married Edmund Mortimer, Earl of March.
Edmund had issue, Roger Earl of March ;
Roger had issue, Edmund, Anne, and Eleanor.

SALISBURY
This Edmund in the reign of Bolingbroke,     39
As I have read, laid claim unto the crown ;
And, but for Owen Glendower, had been king,
Who kept him in captivity till he died.
But to the rest.

YORK          His eldest sister, Anne,
My mother, being heir unto the crown,
Married Richard Earl of Cambridge, who was son
To Edmund Langley, Edward the Third's fifth son.
By her I claim the kingdom. She was heir
To Roger Earl of March, who was the son
Of Edmund Mortimer, who married Philippe,
Sole daughter unto Lionel Duke of Clarence.
So, if the issue of the elder son
Succeed before the younger, I am king.

WARWICK
What plain proceedings is more plain than this ?     53
Henry doth claim the crown from John of Gaunt,
The fourth son ; York claims it from the third.

---

164 *rout* disorderly crowd   169 *Demanding* inquiring   171 *at large* in full
173 *forthcoming* to be tried (see I, iv, 52)   182 *tainccture* fouling (with
overtones of 'treason')   198 *poise* weigh   199 *stands sure* is perfectly level
(indicating no bias)
II, ii   The Duke of York's garden   3 *close* private, secluded   39 *Edmund*
(Shakespeare here follows the chroniclers in an error and adds some
confusion of his own. Edmund Mortimer, 3rd Earl of March, and son-in-
law of Lionel, Duke of Clarence, actually had two sons, Roger, 4th Earl of
March, and Sir Edmund. Sir Edmund was captured by Glendower and
married his daughter [see *1 Henry IV*]. It was Roger Mortimer's son
Edmund, 5th Earl of March and nephew of Sir Edmund, who was York's
mother's brother and had been named heir to the throne by Richard II.
These two are confused in *1 Henry IV* and *1 Henry VI* as well as here. But
the further detail, that Edmund was kept by Glendower captive until his
death [l. 42], seems to have been derived by Shakespeare incorrectly from
Hall, who mentions, in conjunction with his account of Edmund, that
Glendower kept Lord Grey of Ruthvin, another son-in-law, 'in captivitee
till he died.')   53 *proceedings* line of descent

56 Till Lionel's issue fails, his should not reign.
It fails not yet, but flourishes in thee
58 And in thy son, fair slips of such a stock.
Then, father Salisbury, kneel we together,
And in this private plot be we the first
That shall salute our rightful sovereign
With honor of his birthright to the crown.

BOTH
Long live our sovereign Richard, England's king.

YORK
We thank you, lords. But I am not your king
Till I be crowned and that my sword be stained
With heart-blood of the house of Lancaster.
And that's not suddenly to be performed,
68 But with advice and silent secrecy.
Do you as I do in these dangerous days:
70 Wink at the Duke of Suffolk's insolence,
At Beaufort's pride, at Somerset's ambition,
At Buckingham and all the crew of them,
Till they have snared the shepherd of the flock,
That virtuous prince, the good Duke Humphrey.
'Tis that they seek; and they in seeking that
Shall find their deaths, if York can prophesy.

SALISBURY
My lord, break we off. We know your mind at full.

WARWICK
My heart assures me that the Earl of Warwick
Shall one day make the Duke of York a king.

YORK
And, Nevil, this I do assure myself,
Richard shall live to make the Earl of Warwick
The greatest man in England but the king.　　*Exeunt.*

\*

I, iii
*Sound trumpets. Enter the King and State, [i.e. the
Queen, Gloucester, Suffolk, Buckingham, and the
Cardinal,] with Guard, to banish the Duchess.
[Enter, guarded, the Duchess of Gloucester, Margery
Jourdain, Hume, Southwell, and Bolingbroke. And
then enter to them York, Salisbury, and Warwick.]*

KING
Stand forth, Dame Eleanor Cobham, Gloucester's wife.
In sight of God and us your guilt is great.
Receive the sentence of the law for sins
Such as by God's book are adjudged to death.
　　*[To Jourdain and the others]*
You four, from hence to prison back again;
From thence unto the place of execution.
The witch in Smithfield shall be burned to ashes,
And you three shall be strangled on the gallows.
　　*[To the Duchess]*
You, madam, for you are more nobly born,
10 Despoilèd of your honor in your life,
Shall, after three days' open penance done,
Live in your country here in banishment
With Sir John Stanley in the Isle of Man.

ELEANOR
Welcome is banishment. Welcome were my death.

GLOUCESTER
Eleanor, the law, thou seest, hath judgèd thee.
I cannot justify whom the law condemns.
　　*[Exeunt the Duchess and the
　　　　other prisoners, guarded.]*
Mine eyes are full of tears, my heart of grief.
Ah, Humphrey, this dishonor in thine age
Will bring thy head with sorrow to the ground.
I beseech your majesty give me leave to go;
Sorrow would solace, and mine age would ease.　　21

KING
Stay, Humphrey Duke of Gloucester, ere thou go,
Give up thy staff. Henry will to himself
Protector be; and God shall be my hope,
My stay, my guide, and lantern to my feet.
And go in peace, Humphrey, no less beloved
Than when thou wert Protector to thy king.

QUEEN
I see no reason why a king of years
Should be to be protected like a child.
God and King Henry govern England's helm.　　30
Give up your staff, sir, and the king his realm.　　31

GLOUCESTER
My staff? Here, noble Henry, is my staff.
As willingly do I the same resign
As e'er thy father Henry made it mine;
And even as willingly at thy feet I leave it
As others would ambitiously receive it.
Farewell, good king. When I am dead and gone,
May honorable peace attend thy throne. *Exit Gloucester.*

QUEEN
Why, now is Henry king, and Margaret queen,
And Humphrey Duke of Gloucester scarce himself,
That bears so shrewd a maim; two pulls at once–　　41
His lady banished, and a limb lopped off.
This staff of honor raught, there let it stand　　43
Where it best fits to be, in Henry's hand.

SUFFOLK
Thus droops this lofty pine and hangs his sprays;
Thus Eleanor's pride dies in her youngest days.　　46

YORK
Lords, let him go. Please it your majesty,
This is the day appointed for the combat,
And ready are the appellant and defendant,
The armorer and his man, to enter the lists;　　50
So please your highness to behold the fight.

QUEEN
Ay, good my lord; for purposely therefore
Left I the court, to see this quarrel tried.

KING
A God's name see the lists and all things fit.　　54
Here let them end it, and God defend the right.

YORK
I never saw a fellow worse bestead　　56
Or more afraid to fight than is the appellant,
The servant of this armorer, my lords.
　　*Enter, at one door, the Armorer [Horner] and his
　　Neighbors, drinking to him so much that he is drunk;
　　and he enters with a Drum before him, and his staff
　　with a sandbag fastened to it; and, at the other door,
　　his Man [Peter], with a Drum and sandbag, and
　　Prentices drinking to him.*

---

56 *his* i.e. Gaunt's　58 *slips* cuttings　68 *advice* mature reflection　70 *Wink
at* ignore
II, iii The palace in London　21 *would* would have　30 *govern* (with the
Latin sense of 'steer')　31 *king his* king's　41 *bears . . . maim* suffers so
severe a loss; *pulls* pluckings　43 *raught* reached (by us)　46 *in . . . days*
at last (?)　50 *lists* the barriers defining an arena for fighting or tilting;
hence, the arena itself　54 *A* in　56 *bestead* prepared

1. NEIGHBOR Here, neighbor Horner, I drink to you in a
60 cup of sack; and fear not, neighbor, you shall do well
enough.

62 2. NEIGHBOR And here, neighbor, here's a cup of charneco.

64 3. NEIGHBOR And here's a pot of good double-beer,
neighbor. Drink, and fear not your man.

ARMORER Let it come, i' faith, and I'll pledge you all;
67 and a fig for Peter.

1. PRENTICE Here, Peter, I drink to thee; and be not
afraid.

2. PRENTICE Be merry, Peter, and fear not thy master.
Fight for credit of the prentices.

PETER I thank you all. Drink, and pray for me, I pray
you; for I think I have taken my last draught in this
world. Here, Robin, an if I die, I give thee my apron;
and, Will, thou shalt have my hammer; and here, Tom,
take all the money that I have. O Lord bless me, I pray
God, for I am never able to deal with my master, he
hath learnt so much fence already.

SALISBURY Come, leave your drinking and fall to blows.
Sirrah, what's thy name?

PETER Peter, forsooth.

SALISBURY Peter? What more?

PETER Thump.

SALISBURY Thump? Then see thou thump thy master
well.

ARMORER Masters, I am come hither, as it were, upon my
man's instigation, to prove him a knave and myself an
honest man; and touching the Duke of York, I will take
my death I never meant him any ill, nor the king, nor the
86 queen; and therefore, Peter, have at thee with a downright blow.

YORK Dispatch. This knave's tongue begins to double.
Sound, trumpets, alarum to the combatants!
*[Alarum.] They fight, and Peter strikes him down.*

ARMORER Hold, Peter, hold! I confess, I confess treason.
*[Dies.]*

YORK Take away his weapon. Fellow, thank God, and the
good wine in thy master's way.

PETER O God, have I overcome mine enemies in this
presence? O Peter, thou hast prevailed in right.

KING
Go, take hence that traitor from our sight,
For by his death we do perceive his guilt,
And God in justice hath revealed to us
The truth and innocence of this poor fellow,
Which he had thought to have murdered wrongfully.
Come, fellow, follow us for thy reward.
*Sound a flourish. Exeunt.*

\*

II, iv        *Enter Duke Humphrey [of Gloucester] and his
Men in mourning cloaks.*

GLOUCESTER
Thus sometimes hath the brightest day a cloud,
And after summer evermore succeeds
Barren winter with his wrathful nipping cold;
So cares and joys abound, as seasons fleet.
Sirs, what's o'clock?

SERVANT                Ten, my lord.

GLOUCESTER
Ten is the hour that was appointed me
To watch the coming of my punished duchess.

Uneath may she endure the flinty streets                8
To tread them with her tender-feeling feet.
Sweet Nell, ill can thy noble mind abrook
The abject people gazing on thy face,                   11
With envious looks laughing at thy shame,
That erst did follow thy proud chariot wheels           13
When thou didst ride in triumph through the streets.
But, soft, I think she comes, and I'll prepare
My tear-stained eyes to see her miseries.
    *Enter the Duchess [barefoot] in a white sheet, [with
    verses pinned upon her back] and a taper burning in
    her hand, with the Sheriff and Officers [and Sir John
    Stanley. A crowd following].*

SERVANT
So please your grace, we'll take her from the sheriff.

GLOUCESTER
No, stir not for your lives. Let her pass by.

ELEANOR
Come you, my lord, to see my open shame?
Now thou dost penance too. Look how they gaze.
See how the giddy multitude do point
And nod their heads and throw their eyes on thee.
Ah, Gloucester, hide thee from their hateful looks,
And in thy closet pent up, rue my shame              24
And ban thine enemies, both mine and thine.          25

GLOUCESTER
Be patient, gentle Nell; forget this grief.

ELEANOR
Ah, Gloucester, teach me to forget myself.
For, whilst I think I am thy married wife
And thou a prince, Protector of this land,
Methinks I should not thus be led along,
Mailed up in shame, with papers on my back,          31
And followed with a rabble that rejoice
To see my tears and hear my deep-fet groans.         33
The ruthless flint doth cut my tender feet;
And when I start, the envious people laugh
And bid me be advisèd how I tread.
Ah, Humphrey, can I bear this shameful yoke?
Trowest thou that e'er I'll look upon the world      38
Or count them happy that enjoys the sun?
No; dark shall be my light, and night my day;
To think upon my pomp shall be my hell.
Sometime I'll say, I am Duke Humphrey's wife,
And he a prince, and ruler of the land;
Yet so he ruled, and such a prince he was,
As he stood by whilst I, his forlorn duchess,
Was made a wonder and a pointing-stock              46
To every idle rascal follower.
But be thou mild and blush not at my shame,
Nor stir at nothing till the axe of death
Hang over thee, as sure it shortly will.
For Suffolk – he that can do all in all
With her that hateth thee and hates us all –
And York and impious Beaufort, that false priest,

---

60 *sack* a stong, dry wine   62 *charneco* a sweet wine   64 *double-beer* strong
beer   67 *a fig for Peter* I hold Peter in the utmost contempt (usually
accompanied with a gesture made by putting the thumb between the first
and second fingers)   86 *downright* straight down
II, iv *A street*   8 *Uneath* with difficulty, scarcely   11 *abject* common, low-
born   13 *erst* formerly   24 *closet* private room   25 *ban* curse   31 *Mailed
up* wrapped up (as a hawk is wrapped up to prevent her struggling)   33
*deep-fet* deeply fetched   38 *Trowest thou* do you believe   46 *pointing-stock*
a person pointed at in scorn

Have all limed bushes to betray thy wings,
And fly thou how thou canst, they'll tangle thee.
But fear not thou until thy foot be snared,
57 Nor never seek prevention of thy foes.

GLOUCESTER
Ah, Nell, forbear; thou aimest all awry.
59 I must offend before I be attainted;
And had I twenty times so many foes,
And each of them had twenty times their power,
62 All these could not procure me any scathe
So long as I am loyal, true, and crimeless.
Wouldst have me rescue thee from this reproach?
Why, yet thy scandal were not wiped away,
But I in danger for the breach of law.
Thy greatest help is quiet, gentle Nell.
68 I pray thee sort thy heart to patience;
These few days' wonder will be quickly worn.
*Enter a Herald.*

HERALD
I summon your grace to his majesty's parliament,
71 Holden at Bury the first of this next month.

GLOUCESTER
And my consent ne'er asked herein before?
73 This is close dealing. Well, I will be there.
*[Exit Herald.]*
My Nell, I take my leave. And, master sheriff,
Let not her penance exceed the king's commission.

SHERIFF
76 An't please your grace, here my commission stays,
And Sir John Stanley is appointed now
To take her with him to the Isle of Man.

GLOUCESTER
Must you, Sir John, protect my lady here?

STANLEY
So am I given in charge, may't please your grace.

GLOUCESTER
81 Entreat her not the worse in that I pray
You use her well. The world may laugh again,
And I may live to do you kindness if
You do it her; and so, Sir John, farewell.

ELEANOR
What, gone, my lord, and bid me not farewell?

GLOUCESTER
Witness my tears, I cannot stay to speak.
*Exit Gloucester [with his Men].*

ELEANOR
Art thou gone too? All comfort go with thee!
For none abides with me. My joy is death –
Death, at whose name I oft have been afeard,
90 Because I wished this world's eternity.
Stanley, I prithee go, and take me hence;
I care not whither, for I beg no favor.
Only convey me where thou art commanded.

STANLEY
Why, madam, that is to the Isle of Man,
There to be used according to your state. 95

ELEANOR
That's bad enough, for I am but reproach; 96
And shall I then be used reproachfully?

STANLEY
Like to a duchess and Duke Humphrey's lady –
According to that state you shall be used.

ELEANOR
Sheriff, farewell, and better than I fare,
Although thou hast been conduct of my shame. 101

SHERIFF
It is my office; and, madam, pardon me.

ELEANOR
Ay, ay, farewell; thy office is discharged.
Come, Stanley, shall we go?

STANLEY
Madam, your penance done, throw off this sheet,
And go we to attire you for our journey.

ELEANOR
My shame will not be shifted with my sheet. 107
No, it will hang upon my richest robes
And show itself, attire me how I can.
Go, lead the way; I long to see my prison. *Exeunt.*

\*

*Sound a sennet. Enter [two Heralds before, then]*   III, i
*Buckingham [and] Suffolk, [then] York [and the]*
*Cardinal, [then the] King [and the] Queen, [then]*
*Salisbury and Warwick [with their attendants]*
*to the Parliament.*

KING
I muse my Lord of Gloucester is not come. 1
'Tis not his wont to be the hindmost man,
Whate'er occasion keeps him from us now.

QUEEN
Can you not see? or will ye not observe
The strangeness of his altered countenance?
With what a majesty he bears himself,
How insolent of late he is become,
How proud, how peremptory, and unlike himself?
We know the time since he was mild and affable, 9
And if we did but glance a far-off look,
Immediately he was upon his knee,
That all the court admired him for submission;
But meet him now and, be it in the morn,
When every one will give the time of day, 14
He knits his brow and shows an angry eye
And passeth by with stiff unbowèd knee,
Disdaining duty that to us belongs.
Small curs are not regarded when they grin, 18
But great men tremble when the lion roars, 19
And Humphrey is no little man in England.
First note that he is near you in descent,
And should you fall, he is the next will mount.
Me seemeth then it is no policy, 23
Respecting what a rancorous mind he bears 24
And his advantage following your decease,
That he should come about your royal person
Or be admitted to your highness' council.
By flattery hath he won the commons' hearts;
And when he please to make commotion,

57 *prevention of* prior safeguards against   59 *attainted* condemned for treason   62 *scathe* harm   68 *sort* adapt   71 *Holden* to be held; *Bury* i.e. Bury St Edmunds   73 *close* secret   76 *commission stays* authority stops 81 *Entreat* treat   90 *this world's eternity* endless worldly pleasures   95 *state* social rank (but Eleanor at l. 96 shifts the meaning to 'condition') 96 *but reproach* entirely a thing to be reproached   101 *conduct* conductor 107 *shifted* changed (with a pun on 'shift,' a chemise)
III, i A hall for the session of Parliament (at Bury St Edmunds)   1 *muse* wonder   9 *We . . . since* we remember that once   14 *give . . . day* say good morning   18 *grin* show their teeth   19 *lion* i.e. Gloucester (who, as the prince, is symbolized by the kingly lion)   23 *Me . . . policy* it seems to me that it is not wise   24 *Respecting* considering

'Tis to be feared they all will follow him.
Now 'tis the spring, and weeds are shallow-rooted.
Suffer them now, and they'll o'ergrow the garden
33 And choke the herbs for want of husbandry.
The reverent care I bear unto my lord
35 Made me collect these dangers in the duke.
36 If it be fond, call it a woman's fear;
Which fear if better reasons can supplant,
38 I will subscribe and say I wronged the duke.
My Lord of Suffolk, Buckingham, and York,
Reprove my allegation if you can,
Or else conclude my words effectual.

SUFFOLK
Well hath your highness seen into this duke,
And had I first been put to speak my mind,
I think I should have told your grace's tale.
45 The duchess by his subornation,
46 Upon my life, began her devilish practices;
Or if he were not privy to those faults,
48 Yet by reputing of his high descent –
As next the king he was successive heir,
And such high vaunts of his nobility –
51 Did instigate the bedlam brainsick duchess
By wicked means to frame our sovereign's fall.
Smooth runs the water where the brook is deep,
And in his simple show he harbors treason.
The fox barks not when he would steal the lamb.
No, no, my sovereign; Gloucester is a man
57 Unsounded yet and full of deep deceit.

CARDINAL
Did he not, contrary to form of law,
59 Devise strange deaths for small offenses done?

YORK
And did he not in his protectorship
Levy great sums of money through the realm
For soldiers' pay in France, and never sent it?
By means whereof the towns each day revolted.

BUCKINGHAM
Tut, these are petty faults to faults unknown
Which time will bring to light in smooth Duke
    Humphrey.

KING
66 My lords at once, the care you have of us,
To mow down thorns that would annoy our foot,
Is worthy praise; but, shall I speak my conscience,
Our kinsman Gloucester is as innocent
From meaning treason to our royal person
As is the sucking lamb or harmless dove.
72 The duke is virtuous, mild, and too well-given
To dream on evil or to work my downfall.

QUEEN
74 Ah, what's more dangerous than this fond affiance?
Seems he a dove? His feathers are but borrowed,
For he's disposèd as the hateful raven.
Is he a lamb? His skin is surely lent him,
For he's inclined as is the ravenous wolves.
79 Who cannot steal a shape that means deceit?
Take heed, my lord. The welfare of us all
Hangs on the cutting short that fraudful man.
    *Enter Somerset.*

SOMERSET
All health unto my gracious sovereign.

KING
Welcome, Lord Somerset. What news from France?

SOMERSET
That all your interest in those territories
Is utterly bereft you; all is lost.

KING
Cold news, Lord Somerset; but God's will be done.

YORK [aside]
Cold news for me, for I had hope of France
As firmly as I hope for fertile England.
Thus are my blossoms blasted in the bud,
And caterpillars eat my leaves away;
But I will remedy this gear ere long                    91
Or sell my title for a glorious grave.
    *Enter Gloucester.*

GLOUCESTER
All happiness unto my lord the king.
Pardon, my liege, that I have stayed so long.          94

SUFFOLK
Nay, Gloucester, know that thou art come too soon
Unless thou wert more loyal than thou art.
I do arrest thee of high treason here.

GLOUCESTER
Well, Suffolk, thou shalt not see me blush
Nor change my countenance for this arrest.
A heart unspotted is not easily daunted.
The purest spring is not so free from mud
As I am clear from treason to my sovereign.
Who can accuse me? Wherein am I guilty?

YORK
'Tis thought, my lord, that you took bribes of France
And, being Protector, stayed the soldiers' pay,       105
By means whereof his highness hath lost France.

GLOUCESTER
Is it but thought so? What are they that think it?
I never robbed the soldiers of their pay
Nor ever had one penny bribe from France.
So help me God as I have watched the night –          110
Ay, night by night – in studying good for England!
That doit that e'er I wrested from the king,          112
Or any groat I hoarded to my use,                     113
Be brought against me at my trial day!
No! Many a pound of mine own proper store,            115
Because I would not tax the needy commons,
Have I dispersèd to the garrisons                      117
And never asked for restitution.

CARDINAL
It serves you well, my lord, to say so much.

GLOUCESTER
I say no more than truth, so help me God.

YORK
In your protectorship you did devise
Strange tortures for offenders, never heard of,
That England was defamed by tyranny.

GLOUCESTER
Why, 'tis well known that, whiles I was Protector,

33 *husbandry* cultivation  35 *collect* infer  36 *fond* foolish  38 *subscribe* acknowledge in writing  45 *subornation* instigation to crime  46 *Upon my life* (an oath: Eleanor was accused of practicing upon the king's life, not Suffolk's)  48 *reputing* thinking repeatedly  51 *bedlam* crazy  57 *Unsounded* unrevealed  59 *strange* exceptionally cruel, illegal  66 *at once* going to the heart of the matter (?), collectively (?)  72 *well-given* welldisposed  74 *fond affiance* foolish confidence  79 *Who . . . deceit* i.e. who that intends to deceive cannot assume a role  91 *gear* business  94 *stayed* delayed  105 *stayed* withheld  110 *watched* remained awake throughout  112, 113 *doit, groat* coins of little value  115 *proper* personal  117 *dispersèd* paid from the purse

Pity was all the fault that was in me;
For I should melt at an offender's tears
And lowly words were ransom for their fault.
Unless it were a bloody murderer,
Or foul felonious thief that fleeced poor passengers,
130   I never gave them condign punishment.
Murder indeed, that bloody sin, I tortured
132   Above the felon or what trespass else.

SUFFOLK
133   My lord, these faults are easy, quickly answered;
But mightier crimes are laid unto your charge,
Whereof you cannot easily purge yourself.
I do arrest you in his highness' name
And here commit you to my Lord Cardinal
To keep until your further time of trial.

KING
My Lord of Gloucester, 'tis my special hope
140   That you will clear yourself from all suspense.
My conscience tells me you are innocent.

GLOUCESTER
Ah, gracious lord, these days are dangerous.
Virtue is choked with foul ambition
And charity chased hence by rancor's hand;
Foul suboration is predominant
And equity exiled your highness' land.
147   I know their complot is to have my life,
And if my death might make this island happy
149   And prove the period of their tyranny,
I would expend it with all willingness.
But mine is made the prologue to their play,
For thousands more, that yet suspect no peril,
Will not conclude their plotted tragedy.
Beaufort's red sparkling eyes blab his heart's malice
And Suffolk's cloudy brow his stormy hate;
Sharp Buckingham unburdens with his tongue
The envious load that lies upon his heart;
And dogged York, that reaches at the moon,
Whose overweening arm I have plucked back,
160   By false accuse doth level at my life;
And you, my sovereign lady, with the rest,
Causeless have laid disgraces on my head
And with your best endeavor have stirred up
164   My liefest liege to be mine enemy.
Ay, all of you have laid your heads together –
166   Myself had notice of your conventicles –
And all to make away my guiltless life.
I shall not want false witness to condemn me
Nor store of treasons to augment my guilt.
The ancient proverb will be well effected:
'A staff is quickly found to beat a dog.'

CARDINAL
My liege, his railing is intolerable.
If those that care to keep your royal person
From treason's secret knife and traitor's rage
175   Be thus upbraided, chid, and rated at,
And the offender granted scope of speech,

'Twill make them cool in zeal unto your grace.

SUFFOLK
Hath he not twit our sovereign lady here     178
With ignominious words, though clerkly couched,     179
As if she had subornèd some to swear
False allegations to o'erthrow his state?

QUEEN
But I can give the loser leave to chide.

GLOUCESTER
Far truer spoke than meant; I lose indeed.
Beshrew the winners, for they played me false;     184
And well such losers may have leave to speak.

BUCKINGHAM
He'll wrest the sense and hold us here all day.     186
Lord Cardinal, he is your prisoner.

CARDINAL
Sirs, take away the duke and guard him sure.

GLOUCESTER
Ah, thus King Henry throws away his crutch
Before his legs be firm to bear his body.
Thus is the shepherd beaten from thy side,
And wolves are gnarling who shall gnaw thee first.     192
Ah that my fear were false, ah that it were!
For, good King Henry, thy decay I fear.
         *Exit Gloucester [with the Cardinal's men].*

KING
My lords, what to your wisdoms seemeth best
Do or undo, as if ourself were here.

QUEEN
What, will your highness leave the parliament?

KING
Ay, Margaret. My heart is drowned with grief,
Whose flood begins to flow within mine eyes:
My body round engirt with misery –     200
For what's more miserable than discontent?
Ah, uncle Humphrey, in thy face I see
The map of honor, truth, and loyalty;
And yet, good Humphrey, is the hour to come
That e'er I proved thee false or feared thy faith.
What low'ring star now envies thy estate
That these great lords and Margaret our queen
Do seek subversion of thy harmless life?
Thou never didst them wrong nor no man wrong.
And as the butcher takes away the calf
And binds the wretch and beats it when it strains,
Bearing it to the bloody slaughterhouse,
Even so remorseless have they borne him hence;
And as the dam runs lowing up and down,     214
Looking the way her harmless young one went,
And can do naught but wail her darling's loss,
Even so myself bewails good Gloucester's case
With sad unhelpful tears, and with dimmed eyes
Look after him and cannot do him good,
So mighty are his vowèd enemies.
His fortunes I will weep, and 'twixt each groan
Say 'Who's a traitor? Gloucester he is none.'
         *[Exit King with Buckingham, Salisbury,*
                         *and Warwick.]*

QUEEN
Free lords, cold snow melts with the sun's hot beams.     223
Henry my lord is cold in great affairs,
Too full of foolish pity; and Gloucester's show
Beguiles him as the mournful crocodile
With sorrow snares relenting passengers,

---

130 *condign* well-deserved   132 *Above . . . else* beyond felony or any other crime   133 *easy* unimportant   140 *suspense* doubt as to your character 147 *complot* conspiracy   149 *period* end   160 *accuse* accusation; *level* aim 164 *liefest liege* dearest sovereign   166 *conventicles* secret gatherings   175 *rated at* complained against   178 *twit* twitted   179 *clerkly couched* artfully, learnedly phrased   184 *Beshrew* bad luck to   186 *wrest the sense* distort the meaning   192 *gnarling* snarling   214 *dam* mother   223 *Free* noble, generous

Or as the snake, rolled in a flow'ring bank,
229  With shining checkered slough, doth sting a child
That for the beauty thinks it excellent.
Believe me, lords, were none more wise than I –
And yet herein I judge mine own wit good –
This Gloucester should be quickly rid the world,
To rid us from the fear we have of him.

CARDINAL
That he should die is worthy policy;
236  But yet we want a color for his death.
'Tis meet he be condemned by course of law.

SUFFOLK
But, in my mind, that were no policy.
The king will labor still to save his life,
240  The commons haply rise to save his life;
241  And yet we have but trivial argument,
More than mistrust, that shows him worthy death.

YORK
243  So that, by this, you would not have him die.

SUFFOLK
244  Ah, York, no man alive so fain as I.

YORK [aside]
'Tis York that hath more reason for his death. –
But, my Lord Cardinal, and you, my Lord of Suffolk,
Say as you think and speak it from your souls:
248  Were't not all one an empty eagle were set
To guard the chicken from a hungry kite
As place Duke Humphrey for the king's Protector?

QUEEN
So the poor chicken should be sure of death.

SUFFOLK
Madam, 'tis true; and were't not madness then
253  To make the fox surveyor of the fold?
Who being accused a crafty murderer,
255  His guilt should be but idly posted over
Because his purpose is not executed.
No, let him die in that he is a fox,
By nature proved an enemy to the flock,
259  Before his chaps be stained with crimson blood,
As Humphrey, proved by treasons, to my liege.
261  And do not stand on quillets how to slay him;
262  Be it by gins, by snares, by subtlety,
Sleeping or waking, 'tis no matter how,
So he be dead; for that is good deceit.
265  Which mates him first that first intends deceit.

QUEEN
Thrice-noble Suffolk, 'tis resolutely spoke.

SUFFOLK
Not resolute, except so much were done,
For things are often spoke and seldom meant;
But that my heart accordeth with my tongue,
Seeing the deed is meritorious,
And to preserve my sovereign from his foe,
272  Say but the word, and I will be his priest.

CARDINAL
But I would have him dead, my Lord of Suffolk,
274  Ere you can take due orders for a priest.
275  Say you consent and censure well the deed,
And I'll provide his executioner,
I tender so the safety of my liege.

SUFFOLK
Here is my hand, the deed is worthy doing.

QUEEN
And so say I.

YORK
And I. And now we three have spoke it,
It skills not greatly who impugns our doom.          281
        Enter a Post.

POST
Great lords, from Ireland am I come amain          282
To signify that rebels there are up          283
And put the Englishmen unto the sword.
Send succors, lords, and stop the rage betime,          285
Before the wound do grow uncurable;
For, being green, there is great hope of help.          287

CARDINAL
A breach that craves a quick expedient stop.
What counsel give you in this weighty cause?

YORK
That Somerset be sent as regent thither.
'Tis meet that lucky ruler be employed;          291
Witness the fortune he hath had in France.

SOMERSET
If York with all his far-fet policy          293
Had been the regent there instead of me,
He never would have stayed in France so long.

YORK
No, not to lose it all, as thou hast done.
I rather would have lost my life betimes          297
Than bring a burden of dishonor home
By staying there so long till all were lost.
Show me one scar charactered on thy skin.          300
Men's flesh preserved so whole do seldom win.

QUEEN
Nay then, this spark will prove a raging fire
If wind and fuel be brought to feed it with.
No more, good York; sweet Somerset, be still.
Thy fortune, York, hadst thou been regent there,
Might happily have proved far worse than his.          306

YORK
What, worse than naught? Nay, then a shame take all!

SOMERSET
And, in the number, thee that wishest shame!

CARDINAL
My Lord of York, try what your fortune is.
Th' uncivil kerns of Ireland are in arms          310
And temper clay with blood of Englishmen.          311
To Ireland will you lead a band of men,
Collected choicely, from each county some,
And try your hap against the Irishmen?

YORK
I will, my lord, so please his majesty.

SUFFOLK
Why, our authority is his consent,
And what we do establish he confirms.
Then, noble York, take thou this task in hand.

229 *slough* skin   236 *color* legal pretext (with a quibble arising from *die* / dye
in l. 235)   240 *haply* perhaps   241 *argument* proof   243 *by this* i.e. by your
reasoning   244 *fain* eager   248 *empty* i.e. hungry   253 *surveyor* overseer
255 *posted over* disregarded   259 *chaps* i.e. chops, jaws   261 *stand on
quillets* be scrupulous about details   262 *gins* engines, i.e. traps   265 *mates*
checkmates   272 *be his priest* i.e. give him the last rites (with obvious
irony)   274 *take . . . priest* prepare yourself for the priesthood   275
*censure well* approve   281 *doom* judgment   282 *amain* hastily   283 *signify*
announce   285 *betime* soon   287 *green* fresh   291 *meet* fitting   293 *far-
fet* far-fetched, artfully contrived   297 *betimes* forthwith   300 *charactered*
inscribed   306 *happily* haply, perhaps   310 *uncivil kerns* wild and irregular
foot-soldiers   311 *temper* soften

YORK

I am content. Provide me soldiers, lords,
320  Whiles I take order for mine own affairs.

SUFFOLK

A charge, Lord York, that I will see performed.
But now return we to the false Duke Humphrey.

CARDINAL

No more of him ; for I will deal with him
That henceforth he shall trouble us no more.
325  And so break off ; the day is almost spent.
326  Lord Suffolk, you and I must talk of that event.

YORK

My Lord of Suffolk, within fourteen days
328  At Bristow I expect my soldiers,
For there I'll ship them all for Ireland.

SUFFOLK

I'll see it truly done, my Lord of York.
                    *Exeunt. Manet York.*

YORK

Now, York, or never, steel thy fearful thoughts
332  And change misdoubt to resolution.
Be that thou hop'st to be ; or what thou art
Resign to death : it is not worth th' enjoying.
335  Let pale-faced fear keep with the mean-born man
And find no harbor in a royal heart.
Faster than springtime show'rs comes thought on
     thought,
338  And not a thought but thinks on dignity.
My brain, more busy than the laboring spider,
340  Weaves tedious snares to trap mine enemies.
Well, nobles, well, 'tis politicly done
To send me packing with an host of men.
343  I fear me you but warm the starvèd snake,
Who, cherished in your breasts, will sting your hearts.
'Twas men I lacked, and you will give them me ;
I take it kindly. Yet be well assured
You put sharp weapons in a madman's hands.
Whiles I in Ireland nourish a mighty band,
I will stir up in England some black storm
Shall blow ten thousand souls to heaven – or hell ;
And this fell tempest shall not cease to rage
Until the golden circuit on my head,
Like to the glorious sun's transparent beams,
354  Do calm the fury of this mad-bred flaw.
355  And for a minister of my intent
I have seduced a headstrong Kentishman,
John Cade of Ashford,
To make commotion, as full well he can,
359  Under the title of John Mortimer.
In Ireland have I seen this stubborn Cade
Oppose himself against a troop of kerns,
362  And fought so long till that his thighs with darts

Were almost like a sharp-quilled porpentine ;          363
And in the end being rescued, I have seen
Him caper upright like a wild Morisco,                 365
Shaking the bloody darts as he his bells.
Full often, like a shag-haired crafty kern,
Hath he conversèd with the enemy
And undiscovered come to me again
And given me notice of their villainies.
This devil here shall be my substitute ;
For that John Mortimer which now is dead
In face, in gait, in speech, he doth resemble.
By this I shall perceive the commons' mind,
How they affect the house and claim of York.           375
Say he be taken, racked, and torturèd ;
I know no pain they can inflict upon him
Will make him say I moved him to those arms.
Say that he thrive, as 'tis great like he will ;       379
Why, then from Ireland come I with my strength
And reap the harvest which that rascal sowed ;
For, Humphrey being dead, as he shall be,
And Henry put apart, the next for me.          *Exit.*

\*

*Enter two or three running over the stage, from the*    III, ii
*murder of Duke Humphrey.*

1. MURDERER

Run to my Lord of Suffolk ; let him know
We have dispatched the duke, as he commanded.

2. MURDERER

O that it were to do ! What have we done ?               3
Didst ever hear a man so penitent ?
          *Enter Suffolk.*

1. MURDERER

Here comes my lord.

SUFFOLK

Now, sirs, have you dispatched this thing ?

1. MURDERER

Ay, my good lord ; he's dead.

SUFFOLK

Why, that's well said. Go, get you to my house ;
I will reward you for this venturous deed.
The king and all the peers are here at hand.
Have you laid fair the bed ? Is all things well,
According as I gave directions ?

1. MURDERER

'Tis, my good lord.

SUFFOLK

Away ! be gone !                    *Exeunt [Murderers].*
          *Sound trumpets. Enter the King, the Queen,*
          *Cardinal, Somerset, with Attendants.*

KING

Go call our uncle to our presence straight.
Say we intend to try his grace to-day,
If he be guilty, as 'tis publishèd.                    17

SUFFOLK

I'll call him presently, my noble lord.          *Exit.*

KING

Lords, take your places ; and I pray you all
Proceed no straiter 'gainst our uncle Gloucester       20
Than from true evidence, of good esteem,
He be approved in practice culpable.                   22

QUEEN

God forbid any malice should prevail
That faultless may condemn a nobleman ;                24

320 *take order for* arrange   325 *break off* talk no more   326 *event* outcome
328 *Bristow* Bristol   332 *misdoubt* fear   335 *keep* live   338 *dignity* high
position   340 *tedious* complicated   343 *starvèd* frozen   354 *flaw* squall
355 *minister* agent   359 *Mortimer* (the family name of the descendants of
Philippe, daughter of Lionel, Duke of Clarence, third son of Edward III.
Cade would thus claim the crown through the same line as York himself,
cf. II, ii, 10 ff.)   362 *darts* light spears (with which kerns were usually
armed)   363 *porpentine* porcupine   365 *Morisco* morris-dancer   375 *affect*
like   379 *great like* very likely
III, ii A room adjoining Gloucester's bedchamber   3 *O . . . do* i.e. would
that it had not been done yet   17 *If* whether   20 *straiter* stricter   22
*approved* proved   24 *That . . . nobleman* i.e. that may condemn a nobleman
who is faultless

Pray God he may acquit him of suspicion.

KING

I thank thee, Meg. These words content me much.
    *Enter Suffolk.*
How now? Why look'st thou pale? Why tremblest thou?
Where is our uncle? What's the matter, Suffolk?

SUFFOLK

Dead in his bed, my lord; Gloucester is dead.

QUEEN

30   Marry, God forfend!

CARDINAL

God's secret judgment. I did dream to-night
32   The duke was dumb and could not speak a word.
    *King sounds.*

QUEEN

How fares my lord? Help, lords! The king is dead.

SOMERSET

34   Rear up his body; wring him by the nose.

QUEEN

Run, go! help, help! O Henry, ope thine eyes.

SUFFOLK

He doth revive again. Madam, be patient.

KING

O heavenly God.

QUEEN     How fares my gracious lord?

SUFFOLK

Comfort, my sovereign. Gracious Henry, comfort.

KING

What, doth my Lord of Suffolk comfort me?
40   Came he right now to sing a raven's note,
Whose dismal tune bereft my vital pow'rs,
And thinks he that the chirping of a wren
By crying comfort from a hollow breast
Can chase away the first-conceivèd sound?
Hide not thy poison with such sugared words.
Lay not thy hands on me. Forbear, I say!
Their touch affrights me as a serpent's sting.
Thou baleful messenger, out of my sight!
Upon thy eyeballs murderous tyranny
Sits in grim majesty to fright the world.
Look not upon me, for thine eyes are wounding.
52   Yet do not go away. Come, basilisk,
And kill the innocent gazer with thy sight;
For in the shade of death I shall find joy –
In life but double death, now Gloucester's dead.

QUEEN

56   Why do you rate my Lord of Suffolk thus?
Although the duke was enemy to him,
Yet he most Christianlike laments his death;
And for myself, foe as he was to me,
Might liquid tears or heart-offending groans
61   Or blood-consuming sighs recall his life,
I would be blind with weeping, sick with groans,
Look pale as primrose with blood-drinking sighs,
And all to have the noble duke alive.
What know I how the world may deem of me?
66   For it is known we were but hollow friends.
It may be judged I made the duke away;
So shall my name with slander's tongue be wounded
And princes' courts be filled with my reproach.
This get I by his death. Ay me unhappy,
To be a queen, and crowned with infamy!

KING

Ah, woe is me for Gloucester, wretched man.

QUEEN

Be woe for me, more wretched than he is.
What, dost thou turn away, and hide thy face?
I am no loathsome leper. Look on me.
What? Art thou like the adder waxen deaf?    76
Be poisonous too, and kill thy forlorn queen.
Is all thy comfort shut in Gloucester's tomb?
Why, then Dame Margaret was ne'er thy joy.
Erect his statue and worship it,    80
And make my image but an alehouse sign.
Was I for this nigh wracked upon the sea
And twice by awkward wind from England's bank    83
Drove back again unto my native clime?
What boded this but well-forewarning wind
Did seem to say, 'Seek not a scorpion's nest
Nor set no footing on this unkind shore'?
What did I then but cursed the gentle gusts
And he that loosed them forth their brazen caves,    89
And bid them blow toward England's blessèd shore
Or turn our stern upon a dreadful rock?
Yet Aeolus would not be a murderer,
But left that hateful office unto thee.
The pretty vaulting sea refused to drown me,
Knowing that thou wouldst have me drowned on shore
With tears as salt as sea through thy unkindness.
The splitting rocks cowered in the sinking sands
And would not dash me with their ragged sides,
Because thy flinty heart, more hard than they,    99
Might in thy palace perish Margaret.
As far as I could ken thy chalky cliffs,    101
When from thy shore the tempest beat us back,
I stood upon the hatches in the storm,
And when the dusky sky began to rob
My earnest-gaping sight of thy land's view,
I took a costly jewel from my neck,
A heart it was, bound in with diamonds,
And threw it toward thy land. The sea received it,
And so I wished thy body might my heart;
And even with this I lost fair England's view,
And bid mine eyes be packing with my heart,    111
And called them blind and dusky spectacles    112
For losing ken of Albion's wishèd coast.    113
How often have I tempted Suffolk's tongue
(The agent of thy foul inconstancy)
To sit and witch me as Ascanius did    116
When he to madding Dido would unfold    117
His father's acts commenced in burning Troy!
Am I not witched like her? or thou not false like him?
Ay me, I can no more. Die, Margaret!
For Henry weeps that thou dost live so long.
    *Noise within. Enter Warwick, [Salisbury,] and*
    *many Commons.*

30 *forfend* forbid   32 s.d. *sounds* swoons   34 *Rear up* raise; *wring . . . nose* (supposed to aid in restoring consciousness)   40 *raven's note* (a bad omen)   52 *basilisk* a fabulous serpent, said to kill by its look   56 *rate* complain against, berate   61 *blood-consuming* (because each sigh was thought to cost the heart a drop of blood)   66 *hollow friends* i.e. enemies   76 *waxen* grown   80 *statue* (trisyllabic: 'statuë')   83 *awkward* adverse   89 *he* i.e. Aeolus, god of the winds   99 *Because* so that   101 *ken* discern   111 *be packing* be gone   112 *spectacles* viewers (specifically telescopes)   113 *Albion's* England's   116 *witch* bewitch; *Ascanius* son of the Trojan hero Aeneas (in the *Aeneid* it is Cupid disguised as Ascanius who is on hand when Aeneas himself tells Dido, queen of Carthage, of his adventures)   117 *madding* going mad (in this case, with love)

**WARWICK**
It is reported, mighty sovereign,
That good Duke Humphrey traitorously is murdered
By Suffolk and the Cardinal Beaufort's means.
The commons, like an angry hive of bees
That want their leader, scatter up and down
And care not who they sting in his revenge.
128 Myself have calmed their spleenful mutiny
129 Until they hear the order of his death.

**KING**
That he is dead, good Warwick, 'tis too true;
But how he died God knows, not Henry.
Enter his chamber, view his breathless corpse,
133 And comment then upon his sudden death.

**WARWICK**
That shall I do, my liege. Stay, Salisbury,
With the rude multitude till I return.          *[Exit.]*
          *[Exit Salisbury with the Commons.]*

**KING**
O thou that judgest all things, stay my thoughts –
My thoughts, that labor to persuade my soul
Some violent hands were laid on Humphrey's life.
139 If my suspect be false, forgive me, God;
For judgment only doth belong to thee.
141 Fain would I go to chafe his paly lips
With twenty thousand kisses and to drain
Upon his face an ocean of salt tears,
To tell my love unto his dumb deaf trunk,
And with my fingers feel his hand unfeeling.
146 But all in vain are these mean obsequies;
          *Bed put forth [with the body. Enter Warwick].*
And to survey his dead and earthy image,
What were it but to make my sorrow greater?

**WARWICK**
Come hither, gracious sovereign, view this body.

**KING**
That is to see how deep my grave is made;
For with his soul fled all my worldly solace,
For seeing him, I see my life in death.

**WARWICK**
As surely as my soul intends to live
With that dread King that took our state upon him
To free us from his Father's wrathful curse,
I do believe that violent hands were laid
Upon the life of this thrice-famèd duke.

**SUFFOLK**
A dreadful oath, sworn with a solemn tongue.
159 What instance gives Lord Warwick for his vow?

**WARWICK**
See how the blood is settled in his face.
161 Oft have I seen a timely-parted ghost,
Of ashy semblance, meagre, pale, and bloodless,
Being all descended to the laboring heart,
Who, in the conflict that it holds with death,
Attracts the same for aidance 'gainst the enemy,
Which with the heart there cools, and ne'er returneth
To blush and beautify the cheek again.

But see, his face is black and full of blood;
His eyeballs further out than when he lived,
Staring full ghastly, like a strangled man;
His hair upreared, his nostrils stretched with struggling;
His hands abroad displayed, as one that grasped
And tugged for life and was by strength subdued.
Look, on the sheets his hair, you see, is sticking;
His well-proportioned beard made rough and rugged,
Like to the summer's corn by tempest lodged.          176
It cannot be but he was murdered here.
The least of all these signs were probable.

**SUFFOLK**
Why, Warwick, who should do the duke to death?
Myself and Beaufort had him in protection,
And we, I hope, sir, are no murderers.

**WARWICK**
But both of you were vowed Duke Humphrey's foes,
And you (forsooth) had the good duke to keep.
'Tis like you would not feast him like a friend,
And 'tis well seen he found an enemy.

**QUEEN**
Then you belike suspect these noblemen
As guilty of Duke Humphrey's timeless death.          187

**WARWICK**
Who finds the heifer dead and bleeding fresh
And sees fast-by a butcher with an axe,
But will suspect 'twas he that made the slaughter?
Who finds the partridge in the puttock's nest          191
But may imagine how the bird was dead,
Although the kite soar with unbloodied beak?
Even so suspicious is this tragedy.

**QUEEN**
Are you the butcher, Suffolk? Where's your knife?
Is Beaufort termed a kite? Where are his talons?

**SUFFOLK**
I wear no knife to slaughter sleeping men;
But here's a vengeful sword, rusted with ease,
That shall be scourèd in his rancorous heart
That slanders me with murder's crimson badge.
Say, if thou dar'st, proud Lord of Warwickshire,
That I am faulty in Duke Humphrey's death.
          *[Exeunt Cardinal, Somerset, and Attendants.*
                    *Bed drawn in.]*

**WARWICK**
What dares not Warwick, if false Suffolk dare him?

**QUEEN**
He dares not calm his contumelious spirit,          204
Nor cease to be an arrogant controller,          205
Though Suffolk dare him twenty thousand times.

**WARWICK**
Madam, be still – with reverence may I say,
For every word you speak in his behalf
Is slander to your royal dignity.

**SUFFOLK**
Blunt-witted lord, ignoble in demeanor!
If ever lady wronged her lord so much,
Thy mother took into her blameful bed
Some stern untutored churl, and noble stock
Was graft with crab-tree slip, whose fruit thou art,          214
And never of the Nevils' noble race.

**WARWICK**
But that the guilt of murder bucklers thee,          216
And I should rob the deathsman of his fee,
Quitting thee thereby of ten thousand shames,          218

128 *spleenful* angry   129 *order* manner   133 *comment . . . upon* explain
139 *suspect* suspicion   141 *chafe* warm; *paly* pale   146 *obsequies* funeral
rites   159 *instance* proof   161 *timely-parted* departed at a fitting time
176 *lodged* levelled   187 *timeless* untimely   191 *puttock's* kite's (cf. l. 196)
204 *contumelious* contentious   205 *controller* critic   214 *slip* cutting
(probably with punning reference to the sense 'moral lapse')   216 *bucklers*
shields   218 *Quitting* ridding

And that my sovereign's presence makes me mild,
I would, false murd'rous coward, on thy knee
221   Make thee beg pardon for thy passèd speech
And say it was thy mother that thou meant'st,
That thou thyself wast born in bastardy;
224   And after all this fearful homage done,
Give thee thy hire, and send thy soul to hell,
Pernicious bloodsucker of sleeping men!

SUFFOLK
Thou shalt be waking while I shed thy blood,
If from this presence thou dar'st go with me.

WARWICK
Away even now, or I will drag thee hence!
Unworthy though thou art, I'll cope with thee
And do some service to Duke Humphrey's ghost.
          Exeunt [Suffolk and Warwick, pulling him out].

KING
What stronger breastplate than a heart untainted?
Thrice is he armed that hath his quarrel just,
And he but naked, though locked up in steel,
Whose conscience with injustice is corrupted.
          A noise within [of Commons crying 'Down with
          Suffolk'].

QUEEN
What noise is this?
          Enter Suffolk and Warwick, with their weapons
          drawn.

KING
Why, how now, lords? your wrathful weapons drawn
Here in our presence? Dare you be so bold?
Why, what tumultuous clamor have we here?

SUFFOLK
The trait'rous Warwick, with the men of Bury,
Set all upon me, mighty sovereign.
          Enter Salisbury [from the Commons within, again
          crying 'Down with Suffolk'].

SALISBURY [to the Commons within]
242   Sirs, stand apart. The king shall know your mind. –
Dread lord, the commons send you word by me,
Unless Lord Suffolk straight be done to death
Or banishèd fair England's territories,
They will by violence tear him from your palace
And torture him with grievous ling'ring death.
They say, by him the good Duke Humphrey died;
They say, in him they fear your highness' death;
And mere instinct of love and loyalty –
251   Free from a stubborn opposite intent,
As being thought to contradict your liking –
253   Makes them thus forward in his banishment.
They say, in care of your most royal person,
That if your highness should intend to sleep
And charge that no man should disturb your rest
In pain of your dislike or pain of death,
Yet, notwithstanding such a strait edict,
Were there a serpent seen with forkèd tongue
That slily glided towards your majesty,
It were but necessary you were waked,
Lest, being suffered in that harmful slumber,
263   The mortal worm might make the sleep eternal.
And therefore do they cry, though you forbid,
That they will guard you, whe'r you will or no,
266   From such fell serpents as false Suffolk is;
With whose envenomèd and fatal sting
Your loving uncle, twenty times his worth,

They say is shamefully bereft of life.

COMMONS [within]
An answer from the king, my Lord of Salisbury!

SUFFOLK
'Tis like the commons, rude unpolished hinds,          271
Could send such message to their sovereign!
But you, my lord, were glad to be employed,
To show how quaint an orator you are.          274
But all the honor Salisbury hath won
Is that he was the lord ambassador
Sent from a sort of tinkers to the king.          277

COMMONS [within]
An answer from the king, or we will all break in!

KING
Go, Salisbury, and tell them all from me
I thank them for their tender loving care;
And had I not been cited so by them,          281
Yet did I purpose as they do entreat.
For sure my thoughts do hourly prophesy
Mischance unto my state by Suffolk's means;
And therefore by His Majesty I swear
Whose far unworthy deputy I am,
He shall not breathe infection in this air          287
But three days longer, on the pain of death.
          [Exit Salisbury.]

QUEEN
O Henry, let me plead for gentle Suffolk.

KING
Ungentle queen, to call him gentle Suffolk.
No more, I say. If thou dost plead for him,
Thou wilt but add increase unto my wrath.
Had I but said, I would have kept my word;
But when I swear, it is irrevocable. –
If after three days' space thou here be'st found
On any ground that I am ruler of,
The world shall not be ransom for thy life. –
Come, Warwick, come, good Warwick, go with me;
I have great matters to impart to thee.
          Exit [King with Warwick].

QUEEN
Mischance and sorrow go along with you;
Heart's discontent and sour affliction
Be playfellows to keep you company.
There's two of you; the devil make a third,
And threefold vengeance tend upon your steps.

SUFFOLK
Cease, gentle queen, these execrations
And let thy Suffolk take his heavy leave.          306

QUEEN
Fie, coward woman and soft-hearted wretch.
Hast thou not spirit to curse thine enemy?

SUFFOLK
A plague upon them! Wherefore should I curse them?
Would curses kill as doth the mandrake's groan,          310

221 *passèd* just spoken   224 *fearful homage* cowardly submission   242 *stand apart* separate, fall back   251-52 *Free . . . liking* i.e. innocent of any stubbornness in crossing your desire   253 *forward in* insistent upon   263 *mortal worm* deadly snake   266 *fell* savage, cruel   271 *'Tis like* it is likely (ironic); *hinds* boors   274 *quaint* clever   277 *sort* gang   281 *cited* incited   287 *breathe infection in* infect by breathing into   306 *heavy* mournful   310 *mandrake's groan* (the mandrake, a poisonous plant with a forked root that gave it a vague similarity to the human form, was supposed, when pulled from the ground, to utter a cry or groan which could kill the hearer or drive him mad)

I would invent as bitter searching terms,
312 As curst, as harsh, and horrible to hear,
Delivered strongly through my fixèd teeth,
With full as many signs of deadly hate,
As lean-faced Envy in her loathsome cave.
My tongue should stumble in mine earnest words,
Mine eyes should sparkle like the beaten flint,
318 Mine hair be fixed an end, as one distract;
319 Ay, every joint should seem to curse and ban;
And even now my burdened heart would break
Should I not curse them. Poison be their drink!
Gall, worse than gall, the daintiest that they taste;
323 Their sweetest shade a grove of cypress trees;
324 Their chiefest prospect murd'ring basilisks;
325 Their softest touch as smart as lizards' stings;
Their music frightful as the serpent's hiss,
327 And boding screech owls make the consort full!
All the foul terrors in dark-seated hell –

QUEEN
Enough, sweet Suffolk. Thou torment'st thyself;
And these dread curses, like the sun 'gainst glass,
Or like an overchargèd gun, recoil
And turn the force of them upon thyself.

SUFFOLK
333 You bade me ban, and will you bid me leave?
Now by the ground that I am banished from,
Well could I curse away a winter's night,
Though standing naked on a mountain top
Where biting cold would never let grass grow,
And think it but a minute spent in sport.

QUEEN
O, let me entreat thee cease! Give me thy hand,
That I may dew it with my mournful tears;
Nor let the rain of heaven wet this place
342 To wash away my woeful monuments.
O, could this kiss be printed in thy hand,
    [Kisses his hand.]
344 That thou mightst think upon these by the seal
Through whom a thousand sighs are breathed for thee!
346 So get thee gone, that I may know my grief.
347 'Tis but surmised whiles thou art standing by,
As one that surfeits, thinking on a want.
349 I will repeal thee or, be well assured,
350 Adventure to be banishèd myself;
And banishèd I am, if but from thee.
Go, speak not to me. Even now be gone.
O, go not yet! Even thus two friends condemned
Embrace, and kiss, and take ten thousand leaves,
Loather a hundred times to part than die.
Yet now farewell, and farewell life with thee.

SUFFOLK
Thus is poor Suffolk ten times banishèd,
Once by the king and three times thrice by thee.
'Tis not the land I care for, wert thou thence.
A wilderness is populous enough,
So Suffolk had thy heavenly company;
For where thou art, there is the world itself
With every several pleasure in the world; 363
And where thou art not, desolation.
I can no more. Live thou to joy thy life;
Myself no joy in naught, but that thou liv'st.
    Enter Vaux.

QUEEN
Whither goes Vaux so fast? What news, I prithee?

VAUX
To signify unto his majesty
That Cardinal Beaufort is at point of death,
For suddenly a grievous sickness took him
That makes him gasp and stare and catch the air,
Blaspheming God and cursing men on earth.
Sometime he talks as if Duke Humphrey's ghost
Were by his side; sometime he calls the king
And whispers to his pillow, as to him,
The secrets of his overchargèd soul;
And I am sent to tell his majesty
That even now he cries aloud for him.

QUEEN
Go tell this heavy message to the king.     Exit [Vaux]. 379
Ay me! What is this world? What news are these?
But wherefore grieve I at an hour's poor loss, 381
Omitting Suffolk's exile, my soul's treasure?
Why only, Suffolk, mourn I not for thee,
And with the southern clouds contend in tears – 384
Theirs for the earth's increase, mine for my sorrow's?
Now get thee hence. The king thou know'st is coming.
If thou be found by me, thou art but dead.

SUFFOLK
If I depart from thee, I cannot live;
And in thy sight to die, what were it else
But like a pleasant slumber in thy lap?
Here could I breathe my soul into the air,
As mild and gentle as the cradle-babe
Dying with mother's dug between its lips;
Where, from thy sight, I should be raging mad
And cry out for thee to close up mine eyes,
To have thee with thy lips to stop my mouth.
So shouldst thou either turn my flying soul,
Or I should breathe it so into thy body,
And then it lived in sweet Elysium. 399
To die by thee were but to die in jest;
From thee to die were torture more than death.
O, let me stay, befall what may befall!

QUEEN
Away! Though parting be a fretful corrosive, 403
It is applièd to a deathful wound. 404
To France, sweet Suffolk. Let me hear from thee;
For wheresoe'er thou art in this world's globe,
I'll have an Iris that shall find thee out. 407

SUFFOLK
I go.

QUEEN   And take my heart with thee.
    [She kisses him.]

SUFFOLK
A jewel, locked into the woefull'st cask 409

312 *curst* full of damnation   318 *an* on; *distract* distracted   319 *ban* chide bitterly   323 *cypress trees* (because often planted near cemeteries)   324 *basilisks* (see III, ii, 52n.)   325 *lizards'* serpents'   327 *consort* band of musicians   333 *leave* stop   342 *monuments* remembrances (i.e. the marks of my tears)   344 *That . . . seal* i.e. that by the impression (seal) my lips make upon your hand, you may think of them (*these* [lips] is the antecedent of *whom*)   346 *know* fully realize   347-48 *'Tis . . . want* i.e. while you remain here, I can only guess at the experience of hunger   349 *repeal thee* have your banishment repealed   350 *Adventure* risk   363 *several* different, distinct   379 *heavy* serious, sad   381 *hour's poor loss* (the cardinal, an old man, had only a short time to live; the loss of this 'hour' is not worth great grief)   384 *southern clouds* (conventional source of rain)   399 *Elysium* classical Paradise   403 *corrosive* painful medicine   404 *deathful* deadly   407 *Iris* messenger of Juno, queen of the gods   409 *cask* casket

That ever did contain a thing of worth.
Even as a splitted bark, so sunder we.
This way fall I to death.

QUEEN                    This way for me.
                         *Exeunt [severally].*

\*

III, iii        *Enter the King, Salisbury, and Warwick, to the*
                *Cardinal in bed [raving and staring as if mad].*

KING
How fares my lord ? Speak, Beaufort, to thy sovereign.

CARDINAL
If thou be'st Death, I'll give thee England's treasure,
Enough to purchase such another island,
So thou wilt let me live and feel no pain.

KING
Ah, what a sign it is of evil life
Where death's approach is seen so terrible.

WARWICK
Beaufort, it is thy sovereign speaks to thee.

CARDINAL
Bring me unto my trial when you will.
9 Died he not in his bed ? Where should he die ?
Can I make men live, whe'r they will or no ?
O, torture me no more ! I will confess.
Alive again ? Then show me where he is.
I'll give a thousand pound to look upon him.
He hath no eyes ; the dust hath blinded them.
Comb down his hair. Look, look ! it stands upright,
16 Like lime-twigs set to catch my wingèd soul.
Give me some drink, and bid the apothecary
Bring the strong poison that I bought of him.

KING
O thou eternal Mover of the heavens,
Look with a gentle eye upon this wretch.
O, beat away the busy meddling fiend
That lays strong siege unto this wretch's soul,
And from his bosom purge this black despair.

WARWICK
See how the pangs of death do make him grin.

SALISBURY
Disturb him not ; let him pass peaceably.

KING
Peace to his soul, if God's good pleasure be.
Lord Cardinal, if thou think'st on heaven's bliss,
Hold up thy hand, make signal of thy hope.
He dies and makes no sign. O God, forgive him.

WARWICK
30 So bad a death argues a monstrous life.

KING
Forbear to judge, for we are sinners all.
32 Close up his eyes and draw the curtain close,
And let us all to meditation.            *Exeunt.*

\*

IV, i          *Alarum. Fight at sea. Ordnance goes off. Enter*
               *Lieutenant, [Master, Mate, Walter Whitmore, and*
               *Soldiers, guarding] Suffolk [disguised, and*
               *Gentlemen].*

LIEUTENANT
1 The gaudy, blabbing, and remorseful day
Is crept into the bosom of the sea,

And now loud-howling wolves arouse the jades           3
That drag the tragic melancholy night,
Who with their drowsy, slow, and flagging wings
Clip dead men's graves, and from their misty jaws       6
Breathe foul contagious darkness in the air.
Therefore bring forth the soldiers of our prize ;       8
For, whilst our pinnace anchors in the Downs,           9
Here shall they make their ransom on the sand
Or with their blood stain this discolored shore.
Master, this prisoner freely give I thee ;
And thou that art his Mate, make boot of this ;        13
The other, Walter Whitmore, is thy share.

1. GENTLEMAN
What is my ransom, Master ? Let me know.

MASTER
A thousand crowns, or else lay down your head.

MATE
And so much shall you give, or off goes yours.

LIEUTENANT
What, think you much to pay two thousand crowns,
And bear the name and port of gentlemen ?              19
Cut both the villains' throats, for die you shall.
The lives of those which we have lost in fight
Be counterpoised with such a petty sum ?

1. GENTLEMAN
I'll give it, sir, and therefore spare my life.

2. GENTLEMAN
And so will I, and write home for it straight.

WHITMORE
I lost mine eye in laying the prize aboard,           25
          *[To Suffolk]*
And therefore to revenge it shalt thou die ;
And so should these, if I might have my will.

LIEUTENANT
Be not so rash ; take ransom, let him live.

SUFFOLK
Look on my George ; I am a gentleman.                 29
Rate me at what thou wilt, thou shalt be paid.        30

WHITMORE
And so am I. My name is Walter Whitmore.
How now ? Why starts thou ? What, doth death affright ?

SUFFOLK
Thy name affrights me, in whose sound is death.       33
A cunning man did calculate my birth                  34
And told me that by water I should die.
Yet let not this make thee be bloody-minded ;
Thy name is Gaultier, being rightly sounded.          37

WHITMORE
Gaultier or Walter, which it is I care not.
Never yet did base dishonor blur our name
But with our sword we wiped away the blot ;
Therefore, when merchantlike I sell revenge,

**III, iii** The Cardinal's bedchamber    **9** *he* i.e. Duke Humphrey    **16** *lime-twigs* (see I, iii, 86n.)    **30** *argues* gives proof of    **32** *curtain* i.e. of the bed
**IV, i** The coast of Kent, near the Downs    **1** *gaudy* bright ; *blabbing* garrulous, telltale ; *remorseful* full of pitiable events    **3** *jades* horses, i.e. the dragons of Hecate, which draw the night across the sky    **6** *Clip* embrace
**8** *soldiers . . . prize* i.e. the soldiers we have captured    **9** *Downs* anchorage off Kent    **13** *boot* profit    **19** *port* demeanor    **25** *laying . . . aboard* boarding the captured ship    **29** *George* badge representing Saint George and the dragon, an insigne of the Order of the Garter    **30** *Rate* value    **33** *sound* (*Walter* was pronounced 'Wa'ter')    **34** *cunning man* fortune-teller ; *calculate my birth* (astrologers required the moment of one's birth in order to cast a horoscope)    **37** *Gaultier* (*Walter* in French)

42  Broke be my sword, my arms torn and defaced,
    And I proclaimed a coward through the world.

SUFFOLK
    Stay, Whitmore, for thy prisoner is a prince,
    The Duke of Suffolk, William de la Pole.

WHITMORE
    The Duke of Suffolk muffled up in rags ?

SUFFOLK
    Ay, but these rags are no part of the duke.
    [Jove sometime went disguised, and why not I ?]

LIEUTENANT
    But Jove was never slain, as thou shalt be.

SUFFOLK
50  Obscure and lousy swain, King Henry's blood,
    The honorable blood of Lancaster,
52  Must not be shed by such a jaded groom.
    Hast thou not kissed thy hand and held my stirrup ?
54  Bare-headed plodded by my footcloth mule,
    And thought thee happy when I shook my head ?
    How often hast thou waited at my cup,
57  Fed from my trencher, kneeled down at the board,
    When I have feasted with Queen Margaret ?
59  Remember it, and let it make thee crestfall'n,
60  Ay, and allay this thy abortive pride.
61  How in our voiding lobby hast thou stood
    And duly waited for my coming forth !
    This hand of mine hath writ in thy behalf,
    And therefore shall it charm thy riotous tongue.

WHITMORE
65  Speak, captain, shall I stab the forlorn swain ?

LIEUTENANT
    First let my words stab him, as he hath me.

SUFFOLK
    Base slave, thy words are blunt, and so art thou.

LIEUTENANT
    Convey him hence, and on our long-boat's side
    Strike off his head.

SUFFOLK                        Thou dar'st not, for thy own.

70  LIEUTENANT  Pole –
    SUFFOLK  Pole ?

LIEUTENANT
72  Ay, kennel, puddle, sink ! whose filth and dirt
    Troubles the silver spring where England drinks.
    Now will I dam up this thy yawning mouth
    For swallowing the treasure of the realm.
    Thy lips that kissed the queen shall sweep the ground,
    And thou that smiledst at good Duke Humphrey's death

Against the senseless winds shall grin in vain,          78
Who in contempt shall hiss at thee again.
And wedded be thou to the hags of hell
For daring to affy a mighty lord                         81
Unto the daughter of a worthless king,
Having neither subject, wealth, nor diadem.
By devilish policy art thou grown great,
And, like ambitious Sulla, overgorged                    85
With gobbets of thy mother's bleeding heart.             86
By thee Anjou and Maine were sold to France ;
The false revolting Normans thorough thee                88
Disdain to call us lord, and Picardy
Hath slain their governors, surprised our forts,
And sent the ragged soldiers wounded home.
The princely Warwick and the Nevils all,
Whose dreadful swords were never drawn in vain,
As hating thee, are rising up in arms ;
And now the house of York, thrust from the crown
By shameful murder of a guiltless king
And lofty, proud, encroaching tyranny,
Burns with revenging fire, whose hopeful colors
Advance our half-faced sun, striving to shine,          99
Under the which is writ 'Invitis nubibus.'              100
The commons here in Kent are up in arms,
And to conclude, reproach and beggary
Is crept into the palace of our king,
And all by thee. Away ! convey him hence.

SUFFOLK
    O that I were a god, to shoot forth thunder
    Upon these paltry, servile, abject drudges.
    Small things make base men proud. This villain here,
    Being captain of a pinnace, threatens more
    Than Bargulus, the strong Illyrian pirate.          109
    Drones suck not eagles' blood but rob beehives.
    It is impossible that I should die
    By such a lowly vassal as thyself.
    Thy words move rage and not remorse in me.
    I go of message from the queen to France.
    I charge thee waft me safely 'cross the Channel.    115

LIEUTENANT  Walter !

WHITMORE
    Come, Suffolk, I must waft thee to thy death.

SUFFOLK  Paene gelidus timor occupat artus. It is thee   118
    I fear.

WHITMORE
    Thou shalt have cause to fear before I leave thee.
    What, are ye daunted now ? Now will ye stoop ?

1. GENTLEMAN
    My gracious lord, entreat him, speak him fair.

SUFFOLK
    Suffolk's imperial tongue is stern and rough,
    Used to command, untaught to plead for favor.
    Far be it we should honor such as these
    With humble suit. No, rather let my head
    Stoop to the block than these knees bow to any
    Save to the God of heaven and to my king ;
    And sooner dance upon a bloody pole
    Than stand uncovered to the vulgar groom.           129
    True nobility is exempt from fear.
    More can I bear than you dare execute.

LIEUTENANT
    Hale him away and let him talk no more.

SUFFOLK
    Come, soldiers, show what cruelty ye can,

---

42 *arms* coat of arms  50 *King Henry's blood* (Suffolk falsely claimed that his mother was a distant cousin of Henry VI)  52 *jaded* (1) lowly-bred, (2) having to do with horses  54 *footcloth mule* mule covered with an ornamented caparison  57 *trencher* platter  59 *crestfall'n* humble (with punning allusion to Whitmore's claim to gentility, the 'crest' being a part of the armorial bearings)  60 *abortive* monstrous  61 *voiding lobby* waiting room  65 *captain* (a courtesy title given – as customarily – to the lieutenant because he is the commander of a ship)  70–72 *Pole . . . kennel* (word-play on 'poll' [head], 'Pole' [Suffolk's family name, pronounced 'pool'], and 'pool' [of water]; a kennel is an open gutter)  72 *sink* cesspool  78 *senseless* unfeeling  81 *affy* affiance  85 *Sulla* Lucius Cornelius Sulla (138–78 B.C.), the first Roman dictator to issue proscriptions  86 *gobbets* chunks of flesh  88 *thorough* through  99 *half-faced sun* (a sun bursting through clouds was the device of Edward III and Richard II, the *guiltless king* of l. 96)  100 *Invitis nubibus* in spite of clouds (source unidentified)  109 *Bargulus* i.e. Bardylis (fl. 383 B.C.) a Balkan chieftain (Shakespeare's 'Bargulus' comes from Cicero, *De Officiis*, II, 11)  115 *waft* transport by water  118 *Paene . . . artus* cold fear seizes my limbs almost entirely  129 *uncovered* bareheaded

That this my death may never be forgot.
135　Great men oft die by vile bezonians.
A Roman sworder and banditto slave
137　Murdered sweet Tully; Brutus' bastard hand
138　Stabbed Julius Caesar; savage islanders
Pompey the Great; and Suffolk dies by pirates.
*Exit Walter [Whitmore] with Suffolk.*

LIEUTENANT
And as for these whose ransom we have set,
It is our pleasure one of them depart.
Therefore come you with us, and let him go.
*Exeunt Lieutenant and the rest.*
*Manet the First Gentleman.*
*Enter Walter [Whitmore] with the body [of Suffolk].*

WHITMORE
There let his head and lifeless body lie
Until the queen his mistress bury it.　　　*Exit Walter.*

1. GENTLEMAN
O barbarous and bloody spectacle!
His body will I bear unto the king.
If he revenge it not, yet will his friends;
148　So will the queen, that living held him dear.
*[Exit with the body.]*

*

IV, ii　　*Enter two Rebels [with long staves].*
1. REBEL Come and get thee a sword, though made of a
2　lath. They have been up these two days.
2. REBEL They have the more need to sleep now then.
1. REBEL I tell thee Jack Cade the clothier means to dress
5　the commonwealth and turn it and set a new nap upon it.
2. REBEL So he had need, for 'tis threadbare. Well, I say
it was never merry world in England since gentlemen
8　came up.
1. REBEL O miserable age! Virtue is not regarded in
handicraftsmen.
11　2. REBEL The nobility think scorn to go in leather aprons.
1. REBEL Nay, more, the king's council are no good
workmen.
2. REBEL True; and yet it is said, 'Labor in thy vocation'; which is as much to say as 'Let the magistrates be
laboring men'; and therefore should we be magistrates.
1. REBEL Thou hast hit it; for there's no better sign of a
brave mind than a hard hand.
2. REBEL I see them, I see them! There's Best's son, the
20　tanner of Wingham –
1. REBEL He shall have the skins of our enemies to make
22　dog's leather of.
2. REBEL And Dick the butcher –
1. REBEL Then is sin struck down like an ox and iniquity's throat cut like a calf.
2. REBEL And Smith the weaver.
27　1. REBEL Argo, their thread of life is spun.
2. REBEL Come, come, let's fall in with them.
*Drum. Enter Cade, Dick [the] Butcher, Smith the*
*Weaver, and a Sawyer, with infinite numbers*
*[bearing long staves].*
CADE We, John Cade, so termed of our supposed father –
30　BUTCHER *[aside]* Or rather, of stealing a cade of herrings.
31　CADE For our enemies shall fall before us, inspired with
the spirit of putting down kings and princes – Command silence!
BUTCHER Silence!
35　CADE My father was a Mortimer –

BUTCHER *[aside]* He was an honest man and a good brick-　36
layer.
CADE My mother a Plantagenet –
BUTCHER *[aside]* I knew her well. She was a midwife.
CADE My wife descended of the Lacies.　　　　　　　39
BUTCHER *[aside]* She was indeed a pedlar's daughter and
sold many laces.
WEAVER *[aside]* But now of late, not able to travel with
her furred pack, she washes bucks here at home.　　43
CADE Therefore am I of an honorable house.
BUTCHER *[aside]* Ay, by my faith, the field is honorable　45
and there was he born, under a hedge; for his father had
never a house but the cage.　　　　　　　　　　　47
CADE Valiant I am.
WEAVER *[aside]* 'A must needs, for beggary is valiant.　49
CADE I am able to endure much.
BUTCHER *[aside]* No question of that, for I have seen him
whipped three market days together.
CADE I fear neither sword nor fire.
WEAVER *[aside]* He need not fear the sword, for his coat
is of proof.　　　　　　　　　　　　　　　　　55
BUTCHER *[aside]* But methinks he should stand in fear of
fire, being burnt i' th' hand for stealing of sheep.　57
CADE Be brave then, for your captain is brave and vows
reformation. There shall be in England seven halfpenny
loaves sold for a penny; the three-hooped pot shall have　60
ten hoops, and I will make it felony to drink small beer.　61
All the realm shall be in common, and in Cheapside　62
shall my palfrey go to grass; and when I am king, as　63
king I will be –
ALL God save your majesty!
CADE I thank you, good people – there shall be no money;
all shall eat and drink on my score; and I will apparel　67
them all in one livery, that they may agree like brothers
and worship me their lord.
BUTCHER The first thing we do, let's kill all the lawyers.
CADE Nay, that I mean to do. Is not this a lamentable
thing, that of the skin of an innocent lamb should be
made parchment? that parchment, being scribbled o'er,

---

135 *bezonians* beggars　137 *Tully* i.e. Marcus Tullius Cicero; *Brutus'*
*bastard hand* (Brutus was reputed to be the bastard son of Julius Caesar)
138 *savage islanders* i.e. of Lesbos (according to one version of the story;
according to Plutarch, Pompey was killed in Egypt by his former officers
in Ptolemy's hire)　148 s.d. *body* (and the head, with which the queen
enters at IV, iv)
IV, ii A heath in Kent near London (Blackheath)　2 *lath* slight piece of
wood　5 *nap* the fuzz or down on the surface of a piece of cloth (with
allusion to Cade's occupation of shearman, mentioned at l. 121)　8 *came*
*up* rose into fashion　11 *leather aprons* (worn by workmen)　20 *Wingham* a
village near Canterbury　22 *dog's leather* (used for gloves)　27 *Argo* ergo,
therefore (mispronounced)　30 *cade* barrel　31 *fall* (punning on 'cado,' I
fall)　35 *Mortimer* (who could, like York, claim the crown through Lionel,
Duke of Clarence; see III, i, 359n.)　36 *bricklayer* (invited by a pun on
'Mortimer' / 'mortarer')　39 *Lacies* (Lacy was the surname of the Earls of
Lincoln)　43 *furred pack* pedlar's pack, made of skin with the hair outward;
*washes bucks* does laundry ('buck' is lye; 'bucks' are the clothes treated with
it. There is also a punning reference to 'furred pack' as a herd of deer.)　45
*field* (with punning allusion to a heraldic 'field,' the surface of an escutcheon)　47 *cage* a small portable prison for the exposure of minor criminals
in public places　49 *valiant* sturdy (the giving of alms to 'valiant beggars,'
those able to work, was illegal)　55 *proof* (1) of good quality, reliable (of a
coat of mail), (2) well-worn　57 *burnt i' th' hand* branded　60 *three-*
*hooped pot* (Wooden drinking pots were banded with metal, a quart pot
having three bands or hoops. Cade means that for the price of a quart
one will be able to buy more than three quarts.)　61 *small beer* weak beer
(everyone will drink stronger double-beer)　62 *Cheapside* the location
of many of the London markets　63 *palfrey* saddle horse　67 *score*
account

should undo a man? Some say the bee stings, but I say
'tis the bee's wax; for I did but seal once to a thing, and I
was never mine own man since. How now? Who's
there?

*Enter a Clerk [as prisoner].*

77 WEAVER The clerk of Chartham. He can write and read
78 and cast account.

CADE O monstrous!

80 WEAVER We took him setting of boys' copies.

CADE Here's a villain.

82 WEAVER Has a book in his pocket with red letters in't.

CADE Nay, then he is a conjurer.

84 BUTCHER Nay, he can make obligations and write court-
hand.

85 CADE I am sorry for't. The man is a proper man, of mine
honor. Unless I find him guilty, he shall not die. Come
hither, sirrah, I must examine thee. What is thy name?

CLERK Emmanuel.

89 BUTCHER They use to write it on the top of letters. 'Twill
go hard with you.

CADE Let me alone. Dost thou use to write thy name? or
hast thou a mark to thyself, like an honest plain-dealing
man?

CLERK Sir, I thank God, I have been so well brought up
that I can write my name.

ALL He hath confessed. Away with him! He's a villain
and a traitor.

CADE Away with him, I say. Hang him with his pen and
inkhorn about his neck. *Exit one with the Clerk.*

*Enter Messenger.*

MESSENGER Where's our general?

100 CADE Here I am, thou particular fellow.

MESSENGER Fly, fly, fly! Sir Humphrey Stafford and his
brother are hard by, with the king's forces.

CADE Stand, villain, stand, or I'll fell thee down. He shall
be encount'red with a man as good as himself. He is but
a knight, is 'a?

106 MESSENGER No.

CADE To equal him, I will make myself a knight presently.
*[Kneels.]* Rise up Sir John Mortimer. *[Rises.]* Now have
at him!

*Enter Sir Humphrey Stafford and his brother
[William], with Drum and Soldiers.*

STAFFORD
110 Rebellious hinds, the filth and scum of Kent,
Marked for the gallows, lay your weapons down;
Home to your cottages, forsake this groom.
113 The king is merciful, if you revolt.

WILLIAM
But angry, wrathful, and inclined to blood,
If you go forward. Therefore yield or die.

77 *Chartham* a village near Canterbury 78 *cast account* do arithmetic 80
*setting . . . copies* preparing handwriting exercises for boys 82 *book . . .
in't* (probably a primer) 84 *obligations* bonds; *court-hand* varieties of
handwriting, used for legal documents 85 *proper* decent looking 89
*They . . . letters* (Emmanuel, 'God with us,' was sometimes prefixed to letters
and documents) 100 *particular* (in answer to 'general') 106 *No* i.e. yes,
he is only a knight 110 *hinds* peasants 113 *revolt* turn back 116 *pass* care
121 *shearman* workman who cuts the nap from cloth during its manufacture
(cf. l. 5) 135 *too* very 139 *drudge's* workman's 145 *span-counter* a game
in which one player attempts to toss a counter to land less than a span's
distance from another's counter 146 *crowns* (1) coins stamped with a
crown, (2) kings or kingdoms, by synecdoche 148 *Lord Say* (James
Fiennes, Lord Say and Sele and Treasurer of England at the time of Cade's
rebellion, had been associated with Suffolk in the loss of Anjou and Maine.
He was hated for his harshness.) 150 *mained* maimed

CADE
As for these silken-coated slaves, I pass not. 116
It is to you, good people, that I speak,
Over whom (in time to come) I hope to reign,
For I am rightful heir unto the crown.

STAFFORD
Villain, thy father was a plasterer,
And thou thyself a shearman, art thou not? 121

CADE
And Adam was a gardener.

WILLIAM And what of that?

CADE
Marry, this: Edmund Mortimer, Earl of March,
Married the Duke of Clarence' daughter, did he not?

STAFFORD Ay, sir.

CADE
By her he had two children at one birth.

WILLIAM That's false.

CADE
Ay, there's the question. But I say 'tis true.
The elder of them, being put to nurse,
Was by a beggar woman stol'n away
And, ignorant of his birth and parentage,
Became a bricklayer when he came to age.
His son am I. Deny it if you can.

BUTCHER
Nay, 'tis too true. Therefore he shall be king. 135

WEAVER Sir, he made a chimney in my father's house,
and the bricks are alive at this day to testify it. Therefore
deny it not.

STAFFORD
And will you credit this base drudge's words 139
That speaks he knows not what?

ALL
Ay, marry, will we. Therefore get ye gone.

WILLIAM
Jack Cade, the Duke of York hath taught you this.

CADE *[aside]*
He lies, for I invented it myself. –
Go to, sirrah, tell the king from me that, for his father's
sake, Henry the Fifth (in whose time boys went to span- 145
counter for French crowns), I am content he shall reign, 146
but I'll be Protector over him.

BUTCHER And furthermore we'll have the Lord Say's 148
head for selling the dukedom of Maine.

CADE And good reason; for thereby is England mained 150
and fain to go with a staff, but that my puissance holds it
up. Fellow kings, I tell you that that Lord Say hath
gelded the commonwealth and made it an eunuch; and
more than that, he can speak French, and therefore he is
a traitor.

STAFFORD
O gross and miserable ignorance.

CADE Nay, answer, if you can. The Frenchmen are our
enemies. Go to then, I ask but this: Can he that speaks
with the tongue of an enemy be a good counsellor, or
no?

ALL No, no! and therefore we'll have his head.

WILLIAM
Well, seeing gentle words will not prevail, 160
Assail them with the army of the king.

STAFFORD
Herald, away; and throughout every town
Proclaim them traitors that are up with Cade,

That those which fly before the battle ends
May, even in their wives' and children's sight,
Be hanged up for example at their doors;
And you that be the king's friends, follow me.
                 *Exit [Stafford with his men].*

CADE
And you that love the commons, follow me.
Now show yourself men; 'tis for liberty!
We will not leave one lord, one gentleman;
171   Spare none but such as go in clouted shoon,
For they are thrifty honest men and such
As would (but that they dare not) take our parts.

BUTCHER They are all in order and march toward us.

CADE But then are we in order when we are most out of
order. Come, march forward!            *Exeunt.*

IV, iii      *Alarums to the fight, wherein both the Staffords are*
           *slain. Enter Cade and the rest.*

CADE Where's Dick, the butcher of Ashford?

BUTCHER Here, sir.

CADE They fell before thee like sheep and oxen, and thou
behavedst thyself as if thou hadst been in thine own
slaughterhouse. Therefore thus will I reward thee: the
6   Lent shall be as long again as it is, and thou shalt have a
license to kill for a hundred lacking one.

BUTCHER I desire no more.

CADE And, to speak truth, thou deserv'st no less. This
monument of the victory will I bear *[puts on Sir Hum-*
*phrey's helmet]*; and the bodies shall be dragged at my
horse heels till I do come to London, where we will have
the mayor's sword borne before us.

BUTCHER If we mean to thrive and do good, break open
the jails and let out the prisoners.

16 CADE Fear not that, I warrant thee. Come, let's march towards London.            *Exeunt.*

             *

IV, iv      *Enter the King, with a supplication, and the Queen*
           *with Suffolk's head; the Duke of Buckingham and*
           *the Lord Say.*

QUEEN *[apart]*
Oft have I heard that grief softens the mind
And makes it fearful and degenerate.
Think therefore on revenge and cease to weep.
But who can cease to weep, and look on this?
Here may his head lie on my throbbing breast,
But where's the body that I should embrace?

BUCKINGHAM What answer makes your grace to the
rebels' supplication?

KING
I'll send some holy bishop to entreat,
10   For God forbid so many simple souls
Should perish by the sword. And I myself,
Rather than bloody war shall cut them short,
Will parley with Jack Cade their general.
But stay, I'll read it over once again.

QUEEN *[apart]*
Ah, barbarous villains; hath this lovely face
Ruled like a wandering planet over me,
And could it not enforce them to relent
That were unworthy to behold the same?

KING
Lord Say, Jack Cade hath sworn to have thy head.

SAY
20   Ay, but I hope your highness shall have his.

KING
How now, madam?
Still lamenting and mourning for Suffolk's death?
I fear me, love, if that I had been dead,
Thou wouldest not have mourned so much for me.

QUEEN
No, my love, I should not mourn, but die for thee.
          *Enter a Messenger.*

KING
How now, what news? Why com'st thou in such haste?

MESSENGER
The rebels are in Southwark. Fly, my lord!     27
Jack Cade proclaims himself Lord Mortimer,
Descended from the Duke of Clarence' house,
And calls your grace usurper openly
And vows to crown himself in Westminster.
His army is a ragged multitude
Of hinds and peasants, rude and merciless.     33
Sir Humphrey Stafford and his brother's death
Hath given them heart and courage to proceed.
All scholars, lawyers, courtiers, gentlemen,
They call false caterpillars and intend their death.

KING
O graceless men! they know not what they do.

BUCKINGHAM
My gracious lord, retire to Killingworth     39
Until a power be raised to put them down.

QUEEN
Ah, were the Duke of Suffolk now alive,
These Kentish rebels would be soon appeased.

KING
Lord Say, the traitors hate thee;
Therefore away with us to Killingworth.

SAY
So might your grace's person be in danger.
The sight of me is odious in their eyes;
And therefore in this city will I stay
And live alone as secret as I may.
          *Enter another Messenger.*

MESSENGER
Jack Cade hath gotten London Bridge;
The citizens fly and forsake their houses;
The rascal people, thirsting after prey,
Join with the traitor, and they jointly swear
To spoil the city and your royal court.     53

BUCKINGHAM
Then linger not, my lord. Away, take horse!

KING
Come, Margaret. God, our hope, will succor us.

QUEEN *[aside]*
My hope is gone now Suffolk is deceased.

KING *[to Lord Say]*
Farewell, my lord. Trust not the Kentish rebels.

BUCKINGHAM
Trust nobody, for fear you be betrayed.

171 *clouted shoon* hobnailed shoes
IV, iii   6–7 *Lent . . . one* (In Queen Elizabeth's reign the slaughtering
of meat was forbidden during Lent except for the provision of the sick.
For Dick's benefit Cade will double the length of Lent and allow him to
supply meat to ninety-nine people a week or, possibly, to slaughter ninety-
nine animals a week.)   16 *Fear* doubt
IV, iv The royal palace in London    s.d. *Lord Say* (see IV, ii, 148n.)   27
*Southwark* a suburb south of London, in Surrey   33 *hinds* workers, peasants
39 *Killingworth* i.e. Kenilworth Castle in Warwickshire   53 *spoil* despoil

SAY
The trust I have is in mine innocence,
And therefore am I bold and resolute.          *Exeunt.*

\*

IV, v          *Enter [aloft] Lord Scales upon the Tower, walking.*
          *Then enters two or three Citizens below.*

SCALES
How now ? Is Jack Cade slain ?

1. CITIZEN No, my lord, nor likely to be slain ; for they
have won the Bridge, killing all those that withstand
them. The Lord Mayor craves aid of your honor from
the Tower to defend the city from the rebels.

SCALES
Such aid as I can spare you shall command,
But I am troubled here with them myself ;
The rebels have assayed to win the Tower.
9 But get you to Smithfield and gather head,
And thither I will send you Matthew Goffe.
Fight for your king, your country, and your lives ;
And so farewell, for I must hence again.          *Exeunt.*

\*

IV, vi          *Enter Jack Cade and the rest, and strikes his staff on*
          *London Stone.*

CADE Now is Mortimer lord of this city. And here, sitting
upon London Stone, I charge and command that, of the
3 city's cost, the pissing conduit run nothing but claret
wine this first year of our reign. And now henceforward
it shall be treason for any that calls me other than Lord
Mortimer.
          *Enter a Soldier, running.*

SOLDIER Jack Cade ! Jack Cade !

CADE Knock him down there.
          *They kill him.*

BUTCHER If this fellow be wise, he'll never call ye Jack
Cade more. I think he hath a very fair warning.
          *[Enter Messenger.]*

MESSENGER My lord, there's an army gathered together
in Smithfield.

CADE Come then, let's go fight with them. But first go and
set London Bridge on fire, and, if you can, burn down
the Tower too. Come, let's away.          *Exeunt omnes.*

IV, v Before the Tower of London   s.d. *Lord Scales* (Lord Thomas Scales,
who had fought with Talbot in France, was charged by the king with the
defense of the Tower)   9 *Smithfield* a section of London, in which there
were open fields
IV, vi The streets of London   s.d. *London Stone* an ancient landmark, in
Cannon Street   3 *pissing conduit* a fountain from which the poor drew water
IV, vii   1 *Savoy* the London residence of the Duke of Lancaster (an
anachronism, as the building was burned during Wat Tyler's rebellion and
not rebuilt until 1505)   2 *Inns of Court* the centre of legal training and
practice   7 *sore* (1) poor, (2) painful   19–20 *one-and-twenty . . . pound*
i.e. very high personal property taxes ('fifteens' were a levy of one-fifteenth
the value; 'one-and-twenty fifteens' is a deliberate exaggeration)   20 *the
last subsidy* at the time of the last general tax   22 *serge* (from 'say,' a silk
resembling serge; *buckram* a stiff, coarse linen (used in making props and
artificial figures for the stage; thus, 'false')   23 *within point-blank of*
i.e. directly before   25 *Basimecu* i.e. '*baise-mon-cul,*' kiss-my-arse   27
*besom* broom   31 *score . . . tally* (To furnish a record of a debt, a stick
would be scored or marked transversely and then split lengthwise, one
half being retained by the debtor and one by the creditor. The two halves
were called tallies.)   32 *king his* king's   39–40 *could not read* i.e. could not
read Latin and thus claim exemption from civil trial through 'benefit of
clergy'   42 *footcloth* (see IV, i, 54n.)   51 *bona . . . gens* a good country, a
wicked people

*Alarums. Matthew Goffe is slain, and all the rest*          IV, vii
*[of the loyal forces]. Then enter Jack Cade with his*
*company.*

CADE So, sirs. Now go some and pull down the Savoy ;   1
others to th' Inns of Court. Down with them all !          2

BUTCHER I have a suit unto your lordship.

CADE Be it a lordship, thou shalt have it for that word.

BUTCHER Only that the laws of England may come out of
your mouth.

2. REBEL *[aside]* Mass, 'twill be sore law then, for he was   7
thrust in the mouth with a spear, and 'tis not whole yet.

WEAVER *[aside]* Nay, John, it will be stinking law, for his
breath stinks with eating toasted cheese.

CADE I have thought upon it ; it shall be so. Away, burn
all the records of the realm ! My mouth shall be the
parliament of England.

2. REBEL *[aside]* Then we are like to have biting statutes,
unless his teeth be pulled out.

CADE And henceforward all things shall be in common.
          *Enter a Messenger.*

MESSENGER My lord, a prize, a prize ! Here's the Lord
Say, which sold the towns in France ; he that made us
pay one-and-twenty fifteens, and one shilling to the   19
pound, the last subsidy.          20
          *Enter First Rebel, with the Lord Say.*

CADE Well, he shall be beheaded for it ten times. Ah, thou
say, thou serge, nay, thou buckram lord : now art thou   22
within point-blank of our jurisdiction regal. What canst   23
thou answer to my majesty for giving up of Normandy
unto Mounsieur Basimecu, the Dauphin of France ? Be   25
it known unto thee by these presence, even the presence
of Lord Mortimer, that I am the besom that must sweep   27
the court clean of such filth as thou art. Thou hast most
traitorously corrupted the youth of the realm in erecting
a grammar school ; and whereas, before, our forefathers
had no other books but the score and the tally, thou hast   31
caused printing to be used, and, contrary to the king his   32
crown and dignity, thou hast built a paper mill. It will be
proved to thy face that thou hast men about thee that usually talk of a noun and a verb and such abominable words
as no Christian ear can endure to hear. Thou hast appointed justices of peace, to call poor men before them
about matters they were not able to answer. Moreover,
thou hast put them in prison, and because they could   39
not read, thou hast hanged them, when, indeed, only for
that cause they have been most worthy to live. Thou
dost ride in a footcloth, dost thou not ?          42

SAY What of that ?

CADE Marry, thou ought'st not to let thy horse wear a
cloak when honester men than thou go in their hose and
doublets.

BUTCHER And work in their shirt too ; as myself, for
example, that am a butcher.

SAY You men of Kent –

BUTCHER What say you of Kent ?

SAY Nothing but this – 'tis 'bona terra, mala gens.'          51

CADE Away with him, away with him ! He speaks Latin.

SAY
Hear me but speak, and bear me where'er you will.
Kent, in the Commentaries Caesar writ,
Is termed the civil'st place of all this isle.
Sweet is the country, because full of riches ;
The people liberal, valiant, active, wealthy,
Which makes me hope you are not void of pity.

I sold not Maine, I lost not Normandy;
Yet to recover them would lose my life.
61 Justice with favor have I always done;
Prayers and tears have moved me, gifts could never.
When have I aught exacted at your hands,
But to maintain the king, the realm, and you?
Large gifts have I bestowed on learnèd clerks,
66 Because my book preferred me to the king.
And, seeing ignorance is the curse of God,
Knowledge the wing wherewith we fly to heaven,
Unless you be possessed with devilish spirits,
You cannot but forbear to murder me.
This tongue hath parleyed unto foreign kings
72 For your behoof.
CADE  Tut! when struck'st thou one blow in the field?
SAY
Great men have reaching hands. Oft have I struck
Those that I never saw, and struck them dead.
1. REBEL  O monstrous coward! What, to come behind
folks?
SAY
These cheeks are pale for watching for your good.
CADE  Give him a box o' th' ear, and that will make 'em
red again.
SAY
80 Long sitting to determine poor men's causes
Hath made me full of sickness and diseases.
82 CADE  Ye shall have a hempen caudle then and pap with a
hatchet.
BUTCHER  Why dost thou quiver, man?
SAY
The palsy, and not fear, provokes me.
CADE  Nay, he nods at us, as who should say, 'I'll be even
with you.' I'll see if his head will stand steadier on a pole
or no. Take him away and behead him.
SAY
Tell me: wherein have I offended most?
Have I affected wealth or honor? Speak.
Are my chests filled up with extorted gold?
Is my apparel sumptuous to behold?
Whom have I injured, that ye seek my death?
These hands are free from guiltless blood-shedding,
This breast from harboring foul deceitful thoughts.
O, let me live!
CADE [aside]  I feel remorse in myself with his words, but
I'll bridle it. He shall die, an it be but for pleading so
99 well for his life. – Away with him! he has a familiar under
100 his tongue; he speaks not a God's name. Go, take him
away, I say, and strike off his head presently; and then
102 break into his son-in-law's house, Sir James Cromer,
and strike off his head, and bring them both upon two
poles hither.
ALL  It shall be done.
SAY
Ah, countrymen! If when you make your prayers,
God should be so obdurate as yourselves,
How would it fare with your departed souls?
And therefore yet relent, and save my life.
CADE  Away with him, and do as I command ye.
                              [Exeunt some with the Lord Say.]
The proudest peer in the realm shall not wear a head on
his shoulders unless he pay me tribute. There shall not a
maid be married but she shall pay to me her maidenhead
113 ere they have it. Men shall hold of me in capite; and we

charge and command that their wives be as free as heart
can wish or tongue can tell.
BUTCHER  My lord, when shall we go to Cheapside and
take up commodities upon our bills?          117
CADE  Marry, presently.          118
ALL  O brave!          119
         Enter two with the heads [of the Lord Say and
         Sir James Cromer upon two poles].
CADE  But is not this braver? Let them kiss one another, 120
for they loved well when they were alive. Now part them
again, lest they consult about the giving up of some
more towns in France. Soldiers, defer the spoil of the
city until night; for with these borne before us instead
of maces will we ride through the streets, and at every 125
corner have them kiss. Away!
                              Exit [Cade with his Company].
         Alarum and retreat. Enter again Cade and all his    IV,
         rabblement.
CADE  Up Fish Street! down Saint Magnus Corner! Kill 1
and knock down! Throw them into Thames!          2
         Sound a parley.
What noise is this I hear? Dare any be so bold to sound
retreat or parley when I command them kill?
         Enter Buckingham and Old Clifford.
BUCKINGHAM
Ay, here they be that dare and will disturb thee.
Know, Cade, we come ambassadors from the king
Unto the commons, whom thou hast misled,
And here pronounce free pardon to them all
That will forsake thee and go home in peace.
CLIFFORD
What say ye, countrymen? Will ye relent
And yield to mercy whilst 'tis offered you,
Or let a rebel lead you to your deaths?
Who loves the king, and will embrace his pardon,
Fling up his cap and say 'God save his majesty!'
Who hateth him and honors not his father,
Henry the Fifth, that made all France to quake,
Shake he his weapon at us and pass by.
ALL  God save the king! God save the king!
CADE  What, Buckingham and Clifford, are ye so brave?
And you, base peasants, do ye believe him? Will you
needs be hanged with your pardons about your necks? 21
Hath my sword therefore broke through London gates,
that you should leave me at the White Hart in South- 23
wark? I thought ye would never have given out these 24
arms till you had recovered your ancient freedom. But
you are all recreants and dastards and delight to live in
slavery to the nobility. Let them break your backs with

61 *favor* lenience  66 *book* learning  72 *behoof* behalf  80 *sitting* i.e. as a
judge  82 *caudle* warm gruel ('hempen caudle' was a euphemism for the
hangman's rope)  82–83 *pap . . . hatchet* (proverbial, meaning to punish –
children, usually – under the guise of kindness)  99 *familiar* attendant evil
spirit, for whose services one sold his soul to the Devil  100 *a* in  102 *Sir
James Cromer* (actually Sir William Cromer, who was sheriff of Kent in
1445 and perhaps in 1450. His widow, Lord Say's daughter, was later to
marry Sir Alexander Iden, who killed Cade.)  113 *in capite* by grant
directly from the king ('*capite*': head, permitting a punning allusion to
*maidenhead* l. 112)  117 *take . . . bills* buy goods on credit (with pun on
'bills': halberds)  118 *presently* immediately  119 *brave* splendid  120
*braver* worthier, better  125 *maces* staffs of office
IV, viii  1 *Fish Street* (just across London Bridge from Southwark);
*Saint Magnus Corner* (St Magnus' Church was at the end of Fish Street,
near London Bridge)  2 s.d. *parley* trumpet call indicating a temporary
truce  21 *hanged . . . necks* i.e. pardons will be worthless  23 *White Hart*
an inn, next to Chaucer's Tabard  24 *given out* abandoned

burdens, take your houses over your heads, ravish your
wives and daughters before your faces. For me, I will
make shift for one; and so God's curse light upon you
all!

ALL We'll follow Cade! We'll follow Cade!

CLIFFORD
Is Cade the son of Henry the Fifth
That thus you do exclaim you'll go with him?
Will he conduct you through the heart of France
And make the meanest of you earls and dukes?
Alas, he hath no home, no place to fly to;
Nor knows he how to live but by the spoil,
Unless by robbing of your friends and us.
39    Were't not a shame that whilst you live at jar
The fearful French, whom you late vanquishèd,
41    Should make a start o'er seas and vanquish you?
Methinks already in this civil broil
I see them lording it in London streets,
44    Crying 'Villiago!' unto all they meet.
Better ten thousand base-born Cades miscarry
Than you should stoop unto a Frenchman's mercy.
To France, to France, and get what you have lost;
Spare England, for it is your native coast.
Henry hath money, you are strong and manly;
God on our side, doubt not of victory.

ALL A Clifford! a Clifford! We'll follow the king and
Clifford.

CADE [aside] Was ever feather so lightly blown to and fro
as this multitude? The name of Henry the Fifth hales
them to an hundred mischiefs and makes them leave me
56    desolate. I see them lay their heads together to surprise
57    me. My sword make way for me, for here is no staying.
In despite of the devils and hell, have through the very
middest of you! and heavens and honor be witness that
no want of resolution in me, but only my followers' base
and ignominious treason, makes me betake me to my
heels.     Exit [Cade, running through them with his
                            sword, and flies away].

BUCKINGHAM
What, is he fled? Go some, and follow him;
And he that brings his head unto the king
Shall have a thousand crowns for his reward.
                         Exeunt some of them.
Follow me, soldiers. We'll devise a mean
To reconcile you all unto the king.     Exeunt omnes.

\*

IV, ix      Sound trumpets. Enter King, Queen, and [Edmund,
         Duke of] Somerset, on the terrace [aloft].

KING
1    Was ever king that joyed an earthly throne
And could command no more content than I?
No sooner was I crept out of my cradle
But I was made a king, at nine months old.

Was never subject longed to be a king
As I do long and wish to be a subject.
     Enter [below] Buckingham and [Old] Clifford.

BUCKINGHAM
Health and glad tidings to your majesty!

KING
Why, Buckingham, is the traitor Cade surprised?    8
Or is he but retired to make him strong?
     Enter [below] Multitudes with halters about their
     necks.

CLIFFORD
He is fled, my lord, and all his powers do yield,
And humbly thus, with halters on their necks,
Expect your highness' doom of life or death.    12

KING
Then, heaven, set ope thy everlasting gates
To entertain my vows of thanks and praise.    14
Soldiers, this day have you redeemed your lives
And showed how well you love your prince and country.
Continue still in this so good a mind,
And Henry, though he be infortunate,
Assure yourselves, will never be unkind.
And so, with thanks, and pardon to you all,
I do dismiss you to your several countries.    21

ALL
God save the king! God save the king!
     Enter a Messenger.

MESSENGER
Please it your grace to be advertisèd    23
The Duke of York is newly come from Ireland
And with a puissant and a mighty power
Of gallowglasses and stout kerns    26
Is marching hitherward in proud array,
And still proclaimeth, as he comes along,
His arms are only to remove from thee
The Duke of Somerset, whom he terms a traitor.

KING
Thus stands my state, 'twixt Cade and York distressed;
Like to a ship that, having 'scaped a tempest,
Is straightway calmed, and boarded with a pirate.    33
But now is Cade driven back, his men dispersed,    34
And now is York in arms to second him.    35
I pray thee, Buckingham, go and meet him,
And ask him what's the reason of these arms;
Tell him I'll send Duke Edmund to the Tower.
And, Somerset, we will commit thee thither
Until his army be dismissed from him.

SOMERSET
My lord,
I'll yield myself to prison willingly,
Or unto death, to do my country good.

KING
In any case, be not too rough in terms,
For he is fierce and cannot brook hard language.    45

BUCKINGHAM
I will, my lord, and doubt not so to deal
As all things shall redound unto your good.

KING
Come, wife, let's in, and learn to govern better;
For yet may England curse my wretched reign.    49
                      Flourish. Exeunt.

39 *jar* discord   41 *start* sudden attack   44 *Villiago* villain   56 *surprise*
capture   57 *staying* hesitating
IV, ix A royal palace (Kenilworth)   1 *joyed* enjoyed   8 *surprised* taken
12 *Expect* await; *doom* judgment   14 *entertain* receive   21 *countries*
regions   23 *advertisèd* informed   26 *gallowglasses* . . . *kerns* Irish clans-
men, foot soldiers usually armed with axe and sword or darts respectively
33 *calmed* becalmed   34 *But now* just now   35 *second* follow   45 *brook*
endure   49 *yet* up to now

\*

IV, x     *Enter Cade.*

CADE Fie on ambitions! Fie on myself, that have a sword
and yet am ready to famish. These five days have I hid me
in these woods and durst not peep out, for all the country
4 is laid for me; but now am I so hungry that, if I might
5 have a lease of my life for a thousand years, I could stay
no longer. Wherefore, on a brick wall have I climbed
7 into this garden, to see if I can eat grass, or pick a sallet
8 another while, which is not amiss to cool a man's stomach this hot weather. And I think this word 'sallet' was
10 born to do me good; for many a time, but for a sallet, my
11 brainpan had been cleft with a brown bill; and many a
time, when I have been dry, and bravely marching, it
hath served me instead of a quart pot to drink in; and
now the word 'sallet' must serve me to feed on.

    *Enter Iden [and his men].*

IDEN
Lord, who would live turmoilèd in the court
And may enjoy such quiet walks as these?
This small inheritance my father left me
Contenteth me, and worth a monarchy.
I seek not to wax great by others' waning,
Or gather wealth, I care not with what envy.
21 Sufficeth that I have maintains my state
And send the poor well pleasèd from my gate.

CADE Here's the lord of the soil come to seize me for a
24 stray, for entering his fee simple without leave. – Ah,
villain, thou wilt betray me and get a thousand crowns of
the king by carrying my head to him; but I'll make thee
27 eat iron like an ostrich and swallow my sword like a
great pin ere thou and I part.

IDEN
29 Why, rude companion, whatsoe'er thou be,
I know thee not. Why then should I betray thee?
Is't not enough to break into my garden
And like a thief to come to rob my grounds,
Climbing my walls in spite of me the owner,
34 But thou wilt brave me with these saucy terms?

CADE Brave thee? Ay, by the best blood that ever was
36 broached, and beard thee too. Look on me well. I have
37 eat no meat these five days; yet, come thou and thy five
men, and if I do not leave you all as dead as a doornail, I
pray God I may never eat grass more.

IDEN
Nay, it shall ne'er be said, while England stands,
That Alexander Iden, an esquire of Kent,
42 Took odds to combat a poor famished man.
Oppose thy steadfast-gazing eyes to mine;
See if thou canst outface me with thy looks.
Set limb to limb, and thou art far the lesser;
Thy hand is but a finger to my fist,
47 Thy leg a stick comparèd with this truncheon;
My foot shall fight with all the strength thou hast;
And if mine arm be heavèd in the air,
Thy grave is digged already in the earth.
As for words, whose greatness answers words,
Let this my sword report what speech forbears.

CADE By my valor, the most complete champion that ever
I heard. Steel, if thou turn the edge, or cut not out the
burly-boned clown in chines of beef ere thou sleep in
thy sheath, I beseech God on my knees thou mayst
be turned to hobnails.

    *Here they fight. [Cade falls.]*

O, I am slain! Famine and no other hath slain me. Let

ten thousand devils come against me, and give me but
the ten meals I have lost, and I'd defy them all. Wither, 60
garden, and be henceforth a burying place to all that do
dwell in this house, because the unconquered soul of
Cade is fled.

IDEN
Is't Cade that I have slain, that monstrous traitor?
Sword, I will hallow thee for this thy deed
And hang thee o'er my tomb when I am dead.
Ne'er shall this blood be wipèd from thy point,
But thou shalt wear it as a herald's coat,
To emblaze the honor that thy master got. 69

CADE Iden, farewell, and be proud of thy victory. Tell
Kent from me, she hath lost her best man, and exhort
all the world to be cowards; for I, that never feared any,
am vanquished by famine, not by valor.

    *Dies.*

IDEN
How much thou wrong'st me, heaven be my judge.
Die, damnèd wretch, the curse of her that bare thee!
And as I thrust thy body in with my sword, 76
So wish I, I might thrust thy soul to hell!
Hence will I drag thee headlong by the heels 78
Unto a dunghill, which shall be thy grave,
And there cut off thy most ungracious head,
Which I will bear in triumph to the king,
Leaving thy trunk for crows to feed upon.

    *Exit [with his men and Cade's body].*

\*

    *Enter York and his army of Irish, with Drum and*   V, i
    *Colors.*

YORK
From Ireland thus comes York to claim his right
And pluck the crown from feeble Henry's head.
Ring bells aloud, burn bonfires clear and bright,
To entertain great England's lawful king.
Ah, Sancta Majestas! who would not buy thee dear; 5
Let them obey that knows not how to rule.
This hand was made to handle naught but gold;
I cannot give due action to my words
Except a sword or sceptre balance it.
A sceptre shall it have, have I a soul, 10
On which I'll toss the fleur-de-luce of France. 11

    *Enter Buckingham.*
    *[Aside]*

Whom have we here? Buckingham, to disturb me?
The king hath sent him sure. I must dissemble.

BUCKINGHAM
York, if thou meanest well, I greet thee well.

IV, x Iden's garden (Kent) 4 *is laid for* is watching for (cf. 'They are
laying for him') 5 *stay* wait 7 *a sallet* salad greens 8 *while* time 10
*sallet* helmet (cf. IV, iii, 9–11) 11 *brown bill* halberd, varnished to prevent
rust 21 *that* that which 24 *fee simple* land held in unencumbered legal
possession (the holder of which had the right to seize stray animals found
on his property) 27 *eat . . . ostrich* (according to Elizabethan natural
history, the ostrich ate iron for his health) 29 *rude companion* base fellow
34 *brave* confront boldly; *saucy* insolent 36 *beard* defy 37 *eat* (pronounced 'et') 42 *odds* advantage 47 *truncheon* stout staff (i.e. Iden's
leg) 69 *emblaze* signify, set forth publicly 76 *thrust . . . sword* thrust my
sword into thy body 78 *headlong* at full length
V, i Fields (between London and St Albans) s.d. *Drum* i.e. drummer;
*Colors* flags 5 *Sancta Majestas* sacred majesty 10 *have I* as sure as I have
11 *toss* impale, as on a pike; *fleur-de-luce* (device on the arms of France)

YORK
Humphrey of Buckingham, I accept thy greeting.
Art thou a messenger or come of pleasure?

BUCKINGHAM
A messenger from Henry, our dread liege,
To know the reason of these arms in peace;
Or why thou, being a subject as I am,
Against thy oath and true allegiance sworn
Should raise so great a power without his leave,
Or dare to bring thy force so near the court.

YORK [aside]
Scarce can I speak, my choler is so great.
O, I could hew up rocks and fight with flint,
I am so angry at these abject terms;
26  And now, like Ajax Telamonius,
On sheep or oxen could I spend my fury.
I am far better born than is the king,
More like a king, more kingly in my thoughts.
30  But I must make fair weather yet a while,
Till Henry be more weak, and I more strong. –
Buckingham, I prithee pardon me
That I have given no answer all this while.
My mind was troubled with deep melancholy.
The cause why I have brought this army hither
Is to remove proud Somerset from the king,
Seditious to his grace and to the state.

BUCKINGHAM
That is too much presumption on thy part.
But if thy arms be to no other end,
The king hath yielded unto thy demand.
The Duke of Somerset is in the Tower.

YORK
Upon thine honor, is he prisoner?

BUCKINGHAM
Upon mine honor, he is prisoner.

YORK
Then, Buckingham, I do dismiss my powers.
Soldiers, I thank you all. Disperse yourselves;
46  Meet me to-morrow in Saint George's Field,
You shall have pay and everything you wish.
                 [Exeunt Soldiers.]
And let my sovereign, virtuous Henry,
49  Command my eldest son, nay, all my sons,
As pledges of my fealty and love.
I'll send them all as willing as I live.
Land, goods, horse, armor, anything I have
Is his to use, so Somerset may die.

BUCKINGHAM
York, I commend this kind submission.
We twain will go into his highness' tent.
    Enter King and Attendants.

KING
Buckingham, doth York intend no harm to us
That thus he marcheth with thee arm in arm?

YORK
In all submission and humility
York doth present himself unto your highness.

26 *Ajax Telamonius* (Ajax, son of Telamon, in a mad rage attacked a flock
of sheep, believing them to be his enemies)  30 *make fair weather* dissemble
46 *Saint George's Field* an open field between Southwark and Lambeth,
used as a parade ground  49 *Command* demand  63 *discomfited* routed
64 *rude* simple, uncultivated  73 *degree* social rank  86 *front* confront  92
*brook* endure (with pun on *broken*, l. 91)  97 *palmer's* pilgrim's  100
*Achilles' spear* (Telephus was cured by rust from the spear of Achilles, by
which he had been wounded)  103 *act* enact

KING
Then what intends these forces thou dost bring?

YORK
To heave the traitor Somerset from hence
And fight against that monstrous rebel Cade,
Who since I heard to be discomfited.     63
    Enter Iden, with Cade's head.

IDEN
If one so rude and of so mean condition    64
May pass into the presence of a king,
Lo, I present your grace a traitor's head,
The head of Cade, whom I in combat slew.

KING
The head of Cade? Great God, how just art thou!
O, let me view his visage, being dead,
That living wrought me such exceeding trouble.
Tell me my friend, art thou the man that slew him?

IDEN
I was, an't like your majesty.

KING
How art thou called, and what is thy degree?    73

IDEN
Alexander Iden, that's my name;
A poor esquire of Kent that loves his king.

BUCKINGHAM
So please it you, my lord, 'twere not amiss
He were created knight for his good service.

KING
Iden, kneel down. [He kneels.] Rise up a knight.
    [He rises.]
We give thee for reward a thousand marks,
And will that thou henceforth attend on us.

IDEN
May Iden live to merit such a bounty,
And never live but true unto his liege.
    Enter Queen and Somerset.

KING
See, Buckingham, Somerset comes with th' queen.
Go bid her hide him quickly from the duke.

QUEEN
For thousand Yorks he shall not hide his head,
But boldly stand and front him to his face.    86

YORK
How now? Is Somerset at liberty?
Then, York, unloose thy long-imprisoned thoughts
And let thy tongue be equal with thy heart.
Shall I endure the sight of Somerset?
False king, why hast thou broken faith with me,
Knowing how hardly I can brook abuse?    92
King did I call thee? No! thou art not king,
Not fit to govern and rule multitudes,
Which dar'st not, no, nor canst not rule a traitor.
That head of thine doth not become a crown;
Thy hand is made to grasp a palmer's staff    97
And not to grace an awful princely sceptre.
That gold must round engirt these brows of mine,
Whose smile and frown, like to Achilles' spear,    100
Is able with the change to kill and cure.
Here is a hand to hold a sceptre up
And with the same to act controlling laws.    103
Give place. By heaven, thou shalt rule no more
O'er him whom heaven created for thy ruler.

SOMERSET
O monstrous traitor! I arrest thee, York,

Of capital treason 'gainst the king and crown.
Obey, audacious traitor ; kneel for grace.

YORK

Wouldst have me kneel ? First let me ask of these
110 If they can brook I bow a knee to man.
Sirrah, call in my sons to be my bail. *[Exit an Attendant.]*
112 I know, ere they will have me go to ward,
113 They'll pawn their swords for my enfranchisement.

QUEEN

114 Call hither Clifford. Bid him come amain
To say if that the bastard boys of York
Shall be the surety for their traitor father.
*[Exit an Attendant.]*

YORK

117 O blood-bespotted Neapolitan,
Outcast of Naples, England's bloody scourge,
The sons of York, thy betters in their birth,
120 Shall be their father's bail ; and bane to those
That for my surety will refuse the boys !
*Enter Edward and Richard [with Drum and Soldiers
at one door].*
See where they come. I'll warrant they'll make it good.
*Enter Clifford [and his Son with Drum and Soldiers
at the other door. Clifford kneels to King Henry].*

QUEEN

And here comes Clifford to deny their bail.

CLIFFORD

Health and all happiness to my lord the king.

YORK

I thank thee, Clifford. Say, what news with thee ?
Nay, do not fright us with an angry look.
We are thy sovereign, Clifford ; kneel again.
For thy mistaking so, we pardon thee.

CLIFFORD

This is my king, York, I do not mistake ;
But thou mistakes me much to think I do.
131 To Bedlam with him ! Is the man grown mad ?

KING

132 Ay, Clifford. A bedlam and ambitious humor
Makes him oppose himself against his king.

CLIFFORD

He is a traitor ; let him to the Tower,
And chop away that factious pate of his.

QUEEN

He is arrested, but will not obey.
His sons, he says, shall give their words for him.

YORK

Will you not, sons ?

EDWARD

Ay, noble father, if our words will serve.

RICHARD

And if words will not, then our weapons shall.

CLIFFORD

Why, what a brood of traitors have we here.

YORK

Look in a glass and call thy image so.
I am thy king, and thou a false-heart traitor.
144 Call hither to the stake my two brave bears,
That with the very shaking of their chains
146 They may astonish these fell-lurking curs.
Bid Salisbury and Warwick come to me.
*[Exit an Attendant.]
Enter the Earls of Warwick and Salisbury [with
Drum and Soldiers].*

CLIFFORD

Are these thy bears ? We'll bait thy bears to death
And manacle the berard in their chains        149
If thou dar'st bring them to the baiting place.

RICHARD

Oft have I seen a hot o'erweening cur
Run back and bite because he was withheld,
Who, being suffered with the bear's fell paw,      153
Hath clapped his tail between his legs and cried ;
And such a piece of service will you do
If you oppose yourselves to match Lord Warwick.

CLIFFORD

Hence, heap of wrath, foul indigested lump,       157
As crooked in thy manners as thy shape.

YORK

Nay, we shall heat you thoroughly anon.

CLIFFORD

Take heed lest by your heat you burn yourselves.

KING

Why Warwick, hath thy knee forgot to bow ?
Old Salisbury, shame to thy silver hair,
Thou mad misleader of thy brainsick son.
What, wilt thou on thy deathbed play the ruffian
And seek for sorrow with thy spectacles ?       165
O, where is faith ? O, where is loyalty ?
If it be banished from the frosty head,
Where shall it find a harbor in the earth ?
Wilt thou go dig a grave to find our war,
And shame thine honorable age with blood ?
Why art thou old, and want'st experience ?
Or wherefore dost abuse it if thou hast it ?
For shame ! In duty bend thy knee to me,
That bows unto the grave with mickle age.       174

SALISBURY

My lord, I have considered with myself
The title of this most renownèd duke
And, in my conscience, do repute his grace       177
The rightful heir to England's royal seat.

KING

Hast thou not sworn allegiance unto me ?

SALISBURY I have.

KING

Canst thou dispense with heaven for such an oath ?  181

SALISBURY

It is great sin to swear unto a sin,
But greater sin to keep a sinful oath.
Who can be bound by any solemn vow
To do a murd'rous deed, to rob a man,
To force a spotless virgin's chastity,
To reave the orphan of his patrimony,         187
To wring the widow from her customed right,      188

110 *they* i.e. his hands (cf. l. 102) (?), his weapons (?) (perhaps a line has been lost) 112 *to ward* into custody 113 *pawn . . . enfranchisement* pledge (used ironically) their swords for my freedom 114 *amain* speedily 117 *Neapolitan* (because Margaret's father claimed the kingdom of Naples) 120 *bane* destruction 131 *Bedlam* Bethlehem Hospital, for the insane 132 *bedlam . . . humor* mad . . . disposition 144–46 *stake, bears, chains, curs* (allusions to bearbaiting, at which chained bears were attacked by dogs. Warwick's badge was a bear and a ragged staff.) 146 *fell-lurking* treacherous 149 *berard* i.e. bear-herd, keeper of the bears 153 *suffered* hurt; *fell* ruthless, dangerous 157–58 *heap . . . shape* (in reference to Richard's premature birth and his deformities. Bear cubs too were supposed to be born as lumps of matter which were licked into shape by their dam.) 165 *spectacles* eyes 174 *mickle* much 177 *repute* consider 181 *dispense* make terms 187 *reave* bereave 188 *customed right* traditional right to a portion of her husband's estate

And have no other reason for this wrong
But that he was bound by a solemn oath?

QUEEN

191   A subtle traitor needs no sophister.

KING

Call Buckingham and bid him arm himself.

YORK

Call Buckingham and all the friends thou hast,
I am resolved for death or dignity.

CLIFFORD

The first I warrant thee, if dreams prove true.

WARWICK

Thou were best to go to bed and dream again
To keep thee from the tempest of the field.

CLIFFORD

I am resolved to bear a greater storm
Than any thou canst conjure up to-day;

200   And that I'll write upon thy burgonet,
Might I but know thee by thy house's badge.

WARWICK

202   Now, by my father's badge, old Nevil's crest,
The rampant bear chained to the ragged staff,
This day I'll wear aloft my burgonet,

205   As on a mountain top the cedar shows,
That keeps his leaves in spite of any storm,
Even to affright thee with the view thereof.

CLIFFORD

And from thy burgonet I'll rend thy bear
And tread it under foot with all contempt,
Despite the berard that protects the bear.

YOUNG CLIFFORD

And so to arms, victorious father,
To quell the rebels and their complices.

RICHARD

Fie! charity, for shame! Speak not in spite,
For you shall sup with Jesu Christ to-night.

YOUNG CLIFFORD

215   Foul stigmatic, that's more than thou canst tell.

RICHARD

If not in heaven, you'll surely sup in hell.

                              *Exeunt [severally].*

V, ii     *[Alarums to the battle.] Enter Warwick.*

WARWICK

Clifford of Cumberland, 'tis Warwick calls!
And if thou dost not hide thee from the bear,
Now, when the angry trumpet sounds alarum
And dead men's cries do fill the empty air,
Clifford, I say, come forth and fight with me!
Proud Northern lord, Clifford of Cumberland,
Warwick is hoarse with calling thee to arms.

        *Enter York.*

191 *sophister* clever disputer   200 *burgonet* light helmet, upon which the wearer's device was usually mounted   202 *old Nevil's crest* (Warwick actually inherited his earldom and the bear device from his wife's family, the Beauchamps; the Nevils' device was a bull)   205 *cedar* (symbol of royalty) 215 *stigmatic* a criminal branded with the mark of his crime (as Richard is 'branded' by his deformities)
V, ii  14 *chase* game  20 *bearing* demeanor  21 *fast* firmly  27 *lay* wager; *Address thee* prepare yourself  28 *La fin . . . oeuvres* the end crowns every work  32 *frames* fashions  35 *part* party  37 *dedicate* dedicated  38–40 *nor he . . . valor* i.e. the man who loves himself may have the outward trappings of valor (*circumstance*: accident), but he lacks the essence of valor  41 *premisèd* foretold (?), being sent before their time (?)  44 *Particularities* details  48 *chair-days* days of comfort and ease enjoyed in old age  53 *dew to fire* (there was a common notion that fine droplets of water sprayed on fire would make it burn hotter by reducing the flames to coals)

How now, my noble lord? What, all afoot?

YORK

The deadly-handed Clifford slew my steed;
But match to match I have encount'red him
And made a prey for carrion kites and crows
Even of the bonny beast he loved so well.

        *Enter Clifford.*

WARWICK

Of one or both of us the time is come.

YORK

Hold, Warwick, seek thee out some other chase,   14
For I myself must hunt this deer to death.

WARWICK

Then nobly, York! 'Tis for a crown thou fight'st.
As I intend, Clifford, to thrive to-day,
It grieves my soul to leave thee unassailed.

                    *Exit Warwick.*

CLIFFORD

What seest thou in me, York? Why dost thou pause?

YORK

With thy brave bearing should I be in love   20
But that thou art so fast mine enemy.   21

CLIFFORD

Nor should thy prowess want praise and esteem
But that 'tis shown ignobly and in treason.

YORK

So let it help me now against thy sword
As I in justice and true right express it.

CLIFFORD

My soul and body on the action both.

YORK

A dreadful lay! Address thee instantly.   27
    *[Alarums. They fight, and York kills Clifford.]*

CLIFFORD   La fin couronne les oeuvres.   28
    *[Dies.]*

YORK

Thus war hath given thee peace, for thou art still.
Peace with his soul, heaven, if it be thy will.   *[Exit.]*
    *Enter Young Clifford.*

YOUNG CLIFFORD

Shame and confusion! All is on the rout.
Fear frames disorder, and disorder wounds   32
Where it should guard. O war, thou son of hell,
Whom angry heavens do make their minister,
Throw in the frozen bosoms of our part   35
Hot coals of vengeance. Let no soldier fly.
He that is truly dedicate to war   37
Hath no self-love; nor he that loves himself   38
Hath not essentially, but by circumstance,
The name of valor. *[Sees his father's body.]* O, let the vile world end
And the premisèd flames of the last day   41
Knit earth and heaven together.
Now let the general trumpet blow his blast,
Particularities and petty sounds   44
To cease. Wast thou ordained, dear father,
To lose thy youth in peace and to achieve
The silver livery of advisèd age,
And in thy reverence and thy chair-days thus   48
To die in ruffian battle? Even at this sight
My heart is turned to stone; and while 'tis mine,
It shall be stony. York not our old men spares;
No more will I their babes. Tears virginal
Shall be to me even as the dew to fire;   53

And beauty, that the tyrant oft reclaims,
Shall to my flaming wrath be oil and flax.
Henceforth I will not have to do with pity.
Meet I an infant of the house of York,
58  Into as many gobbets will I cut it
59  As wild Medea young Absyrtus did.
In cruelty will I seek out my fame.
61  Come, thou new ruin of old Clifford's house :
62  As did Aeneas old Anchises bear,
So bear I thee upon my manly shoulders ;
But then Aeneas bare a living load,
65  Nothing so heavy as these woes of mine.
                                    *[Exit with the body.]*
*[Alarums.] Enter Richard and Somerset to fight.*
*[Somerset is killed.]*

RICHARD
So lie thou there.
For underneath an alehouse' paltry sign,
The Castle in Saint Albans, Somerset
69  Hath made the wizard famous in his death.
Sword, hold thy temper ; heart, be wrathful still.
71  Priests pray for enemies, but princes kill.     *[Exit.]*
*[Alarums again.] Fight. Excursions. [And then
enter some bearing the Duke of Buckingham wounded
to his tent ; they pass over and go off.] Enter King,
Queen, and others.*

QUEEN
Away, my lord ! You are slow. For shame, away !
KING
73  Can we outrun the heavens ? Good Margaret, stay.
QUEEN
74  What are you made of ? You'll nor fight nor fly.
Now is it manhood, wisdom, and defense
76  To give the enemy way, and to secure us
By what we can, which can no more but fly.
            *Alarum afar off.*
If you be ta'en, we then should see the bottom
79  Of all our fortunes ; but if we haply 'scape
(As well we may, if not through your neglect),
We shall to London get, where you are loved,
And where this breach now in our fortunes made
May readily be stopped.
            *Enter [Young] Clifford.*

YOUNG CLIFFORD
But that my heart 's on future mischief set,
I would speak blasphemy ere bid you fly,
86  But fly you must. Uncurable discomfit
Reigns in the hearts of all our present parts.
Away, for your relief ! and we will live
89  To see their day and then our fortune give.
Away, my lord, away !                     *Exeunt.*
V, iii  *Alarum. Retreat. [Flourish.] Enter York, Richard,
Warwick, and Soldiers, with Drum and Colors.*

YORK
Old Salisbury, who can report of him,
2   That winter lion, who in rage forgets

Agèd contusions and all brush of time          3
And, like a gallant in the brow of youth,      4
Repairs him with occasion ? This happy day     5
Is not itself, nor have we won one foot,
If Salisbury be lost.
RICHARD                 My noble father,
Three times to-day I holp him to his horse,    8
Three times bestrid him ; thrice I led him off, 9
Persuaded him from any further act ;
But still where danger was, still there I met him ;  11
And like rich hangings in a homely house,      12
So was his will in his old feeble body.
But, noble as he is, look where he comes.
            *Enter Salisbury.*

SALISBURY
Now, by my sword, well hast thou fought to-day.
By th' mass, so did we all. I thank you, Richard ;
God knows how long it is I have to live,
And it hath pleased Him that three times to-day
You have defended me from imminent death.
Well, lords, we have not got that which we have.  20
'Tis not enough our foes are this time fled,
Being opposites of such repairing nature.       22
YORK
I know our safety is to follow them ;
For, as I hear, the king is fled to London
To call a present court of parliament.
Let us pursue him ere the writs go forth.        26
What says Lord Warwick ? Shall we after them ?
WARWICK
After them ? Nay, before them, if we can.
Now, by my faith, lords, 'twas a glorious day.
Saint Albans battle, won by famous York,
Shall be eternized in all age to come.           31
Sound drum and trumpets, and to London all ;
And more such days as these to us befall !     *Exeunt.*

58 *gobbets* lumps of flesh   59 *Medea . . . Absyrtus* (as she fled by ship with Jason, Medea murdered her brother Absyrtus and threw pieces of his body into the sea, so that her father, stopping to collect them, would be delayed in his pursuit)   61 *new . . . house* i.e. old Clifford's body   62 *Aeneas . . . Anchises* (as they escaped from fallen Troy, Aeneas carried his aged father, Anchises, on his shoulders)   65 *heavy* (1) weighty, (2) sorrowful   69 *Hath . . . death* (the spirit raised by Margery Jourdain had said that Somerset should shun castles; see I, iv, 34)   71 s.d. *Excursions* attacks and counter-attacks   73 *outrun the heavens* escape the decision of God   74 *nor . . . nor* neither . . . nor   76 *secure us* make us safe   79 *haply* perhaps   86 *Uncurable discomfit* hopeless defeat   89 *To see . . . give* i.e. to see their day of defeat and give them the bad luck we now suffer
V, iii  s.d. *Drum* i.e. drummer   2 *winter* i.e. ancient   3 *brush* collision   4 *gallant* young lover; *brow* front, top   5 *Repairs . . . occasion* revives himself with action   8 *holp* helped   9 *bestrid him* stood over him to protect him   11 *still . . . still* always . . . always   12 *homely* modest   20 *got . . . have* i.e. secured what we have won   22 *opposites . . . nature* enemies who can so quickly recover   26 *writs* (calling the parliament)   31 *eternized* immortalized

# THE THIRD PART OF
# KING HENRY THE SIXTH

\*

**I, i**    *Alarum. Enter [wearing white roses in their hats,*
*Richard] Plantagenet, [Duke of York,] Edward,*
*Richard, Norfolk, Montague, Warwick, [with*
*Drum] and Soldiers.*

WARWICK
I wonder how the king escaped our hands ?

YORK
While we pursued the horsemen of the North,
He slily stole away and left his men ;
Whereat the great Lord of Northumberland,
5   Whose warlike ears could never brook retreat,
Cheered up the drooping army ; and himself,
Lord Clifford, and Lord Stafford, all abreast,
Charged our main battle's front and, breaking in,
9   Were by the swords of common soldiers slain.

EDWARD
Lord Stafford's father, Duke of Buckingham,

Is either slain or wounded dangerous ;
I cleft his beaver with a downright blow.    12
That this is true, father, behold his blood.
*[Shows his bloody sword.]*

MONTAGUE
And, cousin, here's the Earl of Wiltshire's blood,
Whom I encount'red as the battles joined.

RICHARD
Speak thou for me and tell them what I did.
*[Throws down Somerset's head.]*

YORK
Richard hath best deserved of all my sons.
But is your grace dead, my Lord of Somerset ?

NORFOLK
Such hope have all the line of John of Gaunt.    19

RICHARD
Thus do I hope to shake King Henry's head.

WARWICK
And so do I. Victorious Prince of York,
Before I see thee seated in that throne
Which now the house of Lancaster usurps,
I vow by heaven these eyes shall never close.
This is the palace of the fearful king
And this the regal seat. Possess it, York ;
For this is thine, and not King Henry's heirs'.

---

I, i Parliament House in London   s.d. *Alarum* a trumpet call   5 *brook*
endure ; *retreat* i.e. the trumpet call signalling retreat   9 *Were . . . slain*
(in 2 *Henry VI*, V, ii, Clifford is killed by York)   12 *beaver* helmet (actually
the face-piece)   19 *Such . . . Gaunt* i.e. may all the descendants of John
of Gaunt look for the same fate (Edmund, 2nd Duke of Somerset, was
a grandson of John of Gaunt, Duke of Lancaster ; Henry VI was a great-
grandson)

YORK

Assist me then, sweet Warwick, and I will ;

For hither we have broken in by force.

NORFOLK

We'll all assist you. He that flies shall die.

YORK

Thanks, gentle Norfolk. Stay by me, my lords ;

32 And, soldiers, stay, and lodge by me this night.

*They go up.*

WARWICK

And when the king comes, offer him no violence

34 Unless he seek to thrust you out perforce.

*[The Soldiers conceal themselves.]*

YORK

The queen this day here holds her parliament,

But little thinks we shall be of her council.

By words or blows here let us win our right.

RICHARD

Armed as we are, let's stay within this house.

WARWICK

The bloody parliament shall this be called

Unless Plantagenet, Duke of York, be king

And bashful Henry deposed, whose cowardice

Hath made us bywords to our enemies.

YORK

Then leave me not, my lords. Be resolute.

I mean to take possession of my right.

WARWICK

Neither the king, nor he that loves him best,

The proudest he that holds up Lancaster,

47 Dares stir a wing if Warwick shake his bells.

I'll plant Plantagenet, root him up who dares.

49 Resolve thee, Richard ; claim the English crown.

*[York sits in the throne.]*

*Flourish. Enter King Henry, Clifford, Northumber-
land, Westmoreland, Exeter, and the rest [with red
roses in their hats].*

KING HENRY

My lords, look where the sturdy rebel sits,

51 Even in the chair of state ! Belike he means,

Backed by the power of Warwick, that false peer,

To aspire unto the crown and reign as king.

Earl of Northumberland, he slew thy father,

And thine, Lord Clifford, and you both have vowed
revenge

On him, his sons, his favorites, and his friends.

NORTHUMBERLAND

If I be not, heavens be revenged on me.

CLIFFORD

The hope thereof makes Clifford mourn in steel.

WESTMORELAND

What, shall we suffer this ? Let's pluck him down.

My heart for anger burns. I cannot brook it.

KING HENRY

Be patient, gentle Earl of Westmoreland.

CLIFFORD

62 Patience is for poltroons, such as he.

He durst not sit there, had your father lived.

My gracious lord, here in the parliament

Let us assail the family of York.

NORTHUMBERLAND

Well hast thou spoken, cousin. Be it so.

KING HENRY

67 Ah, know you not the city favors them

And they have troops of soldiers at their beck ?

EXETER

But when the duke is slain, they'll quickly fly.

KING HENRY

Far be the thought of this from Henry's heart,

To make a shambles of the parliament house.    71

Cousin of Exeter, frowns, words, and threats

Shall be the war that Henry means to use.

Thou factious Duke of York, descend my throne

And kneel for grace and mercy at my feet.

I am thy sovereign.

YORK             I am thine.

EXETER

For shame, come down. He made thee Duke of York.

YORK

It was my inheritance, as the earldom was.    78

EXETER

Thy father was a traitor to the crown.    79

WARWICK

Exeter, thou art a traitor to the crown

In following this usurping Henry.

CLIFFORD

Whom should he follow but his natural king ?

WARWICK

True, Clifford ; and that's Richard Duke of York.

KING HENRY

And shall I stand, and thou sit in my throne ?

YORK

It must and shall be so. Content thyself.

WARWICK

Be Duke of Lancaster ; let him be king.

WESTMORELAND

He is both king and Duke of Lancaster,

And that the Lord of Westmoreland shall maintain.

WARWICK

And Warwick shall disprove it. You forget

That we are those which chased you from the field

And slew your fathers and with colors spread    91

Marched through the city to the palace gates.

NORTHUMBERLAND

Yes, Warwick, I remember it to my grief ;

And, by his soul, thou and thy house shall rue it.

WESTMORELAND

Plantagenet, of thee and these thy sons,

Thy kinsmen, and thy friends, I'll have more lives

Than drops of blood were in my father's veins.

CLIFFORD

Urge it no more ; lest that instead of words

I send thee, Warwick, such a messenger

As shall revenge his death before I stir.

WARWICK

Poor Clifford, how I scorn his worthless threats.

YORK

Will you we show our title to the crown ?

---

32 s.d. *They go up* (the chair of state, which York occupies, is probably placed on a raised platform)   34 *perforce* by force   47 *if . . . bells* i.e. when his blood is up (bells were fastened to the legs of hawks ; their ringing supposedly increased the falcons' ferocity in attacking their prey)   49 *Resolve thee* decide firmly   51 *Belike* it is likely that   62 *poltroons* cowards   67 *the city* i.e. London (as distinct from the court)   71 *shambles* slaughterhouse   78 *earldom* i.e. the Earldom of March (a title inherited by York from his mother, Anne Mortimer ; it was through the Mortimers that he also claimed the crown – cf. II, i, 179)   79 *Thy father . . . crown* (York's father, Richard, Earl of Cambridge, was executed during the reign of Henry V)   91 *colors* flags

If not, our swords shall plead it in the field.

KING HENRY

What title hast thou, traitor, to the crown?

105 Thy father was, as thou art, Duke of York;
Thy grandfather, Roger Mortimer, Earl of March.
I am the son of Henry the Fifth,
Who made the Dauphin and the French to stoop
And seized upon their towns and provinces.

WARWICK

110 Talk not of France, sith thou hast lost it all.

KING HENRY

111 The Lord Protector lost it, and not I.
When I was crowned I was but nine months old.

RICHARD

You are old enough now, and yet methinks you lose.
Father, tear the crown from the usurper's head.

EDWARD

Sweet father, do so. Set it on your head.

MONTAGUE [to York]

Good brother, as thou lov'st and honorest arms,
Let's fight it out and not stand cavilling thus.

RICHARD

Sound drums and trumpets, and the king will fly.

YORK

Sons, peace!

KING HENRY

Peace thou! and give King Henry leave to speak.

WARWICK

Plantagenet shall speak first. Hear him, lords,
And be you silent and attentive too,
For he that interrupts him shall not live.

KING HENRY

Think'st thou that I will leave my kingly throne,
Wherein my grandsire and my father sat?
No! First shall war unpeople this my realm;
Ay, and their colors, often borne in France,
And now in England to our heart's great sorrow,
129 Shall be my winding sheet. Why faint you, lords?
My title 's good, and better far than his.

WARWICK

Prove it, Henry, and thou shalt be king.

KING HENRY

Henry the Fourth by conquest got the crown.

YORK

'Twas by rebellion against his king.

KING HENRY [aside]

I know not what to say; my title 's weak. —
Tell me, may not a king adopt an heir?

YORK

What then?

KING HENRY

137 An if he may, then am I lawful king,
For Richard, in the view of many lords,
Resigned the crown to Henry the Fourth,
Whose heir my father was, and I am his.

YORK

He rose against him, being his sovereign,
And make him to resign his crown perforce.

WARWICK

Suppose, my lords, he did it unconstrained,
Think you 'twere prejudicial to his crown?

EXETER

No; for he could not so resign his crown
But that the next heir should succeed and reign.

KING HENRY

Art thou against us, Duke of Exeter?

EXETER

His is the right, and therefore pardon me.

YORK

Why whisper you, my lords, and answer not?

EXETER

My conscience tells me he is lawful king.     150

KING HENRY [aside]

All will revolt from me and turn to him.

NORTHUMBERLAND

Plantagenet, for all the claim thou lay'st,
Think not that Henry shall be so deposed.

WARWICK

Deposed he shall be, in despite of all.

NORTHUMBERLAND

Thou art deceived. 'Tis not thy Southern power
Of Essex, Norfolk, Suffolk, nor of Kent,
Which makes thee thus presumptuous and proud,
Can set the Duke up in despite of me.

CLIFFORD

King Henry, be thy title right or wrong,
Lord Clifford vows to fight in thy defense.     160
May that ground gape and swallow me alive
Where I shall kneel to him that slew my father.

KING HENRY

O Clifford, how thy words revive my heart.

YORK

Henry of Lancaster, resign thy crown.
What mutter you or what conspire you, lords?

WARWICK

Do right unto this princely Duke of York,
Or I will fill the house with armèd men
And over the chair of state, where now he sits,
Write up his title with usurping blood.     169
    *He stamps with his foot, and the Soldiers show*
    *themselves.*

KING HENRY

My Lord of Warwick, hear but one word.
Let me for this my lifetime reign as king.

YORK

Confirm the crown to me and to mine heirs
And thou shalt reign in quiet while thou liv'st.

KING HENRY

I am content. Richard Plantagenet,
Enjoy the kingdom after my decease.

CLIFFORD

What wrong is this unto the prince your son!

WARWICK

What good is this to England and himself!

WESTMORELAND

Base, fearful, and despairing Henry.

CLIFFORD

How hast thou injured both thyself and us!

WESTMORELAND

I cannot stay to hear these articles.     180

NORTHUMBERLAND

Nor I.

CLIFFORD
Come, cousin, let us tell the queen these news.

WESTMORELAND
Farewell, faint-hearted and degenerate king,
In whose cold blood no spark of honor bides.
*[Exit Westmoreland with his men.]*

NORTHUMBERLAND
Be thou a prey unto the house of York
186 And die in bands for this unmanly deed.
*[Exit Northumberland with his men.]*

CLIFFORD
In dreadful war mayst thou be overcome
Or live in peace abandoned and despised!
*[Exit Clifford with his men.]*

WARWICK
Turn this way, Henry, and regard them not.

EXETER
They seek revenge and therefore will not yield.

KING HENRY
Ah, Exeter.

WARWICK     Why should you sigh, my lord?

KING HENRY
Not for myself, Lord Warwick, but my son,
Whom I unnaturally shall disinherit.
194 But be it as it may. *[To York.]* I here entail
The crown to thee and to thine heirs forever,
Conditionally that here thou take an oath
To cease this civil war, and whilst I live
To honor me as thy king and sovereign,
And neither by treason nor hostility
To seek to put me down and reign thyself.

YORK
This oath I willingly take, and will perform.
*Here they come down.*

WARWICK
Long live King Henry! Plantagenet, embrace him.

KING HENRY
203 And long live thou, and these thy forward sons.

YORK
Now York and Lancaster are reconciled.

EXETER
205 Accursed be he that seeks to make them foes!     *Sennet.*

YORK
206 Farewell, my gracious lord. I'll to my castle.
*[Exit York with his sons.]*

WARWICK
And I'll keep London with my soldiers.
*[Exit Warwick with his men.]*

NORFOLK
And I to Norfolk with my followers.
*[Exit Norfolk with his men.]*

MONTAGUE
209 And I unto the sea, from whence I came.
*[Exit Montague with his men.]*

KING HENRY
And I with grief and sorrow to the court.
*Enter the Queen [Margaret and Edward, Prince of Wales].*

EXETER
211 Here comes the queen, whose looks bewray her anger.
I'll steal away.

KING HENRY     Exeter, so will I.

QUEEN MARGARET
Nay, go not from me. I will follow thee.

KING HENRY
Be patient, gentle queen, and I will stay.

QUEEN MARGARET
Who can be patient in such extremes?
Ah, wretched man! Would I had died a maid
And never seen thee, never borne thee son,
Seeing thou hast proved so unnatural a father.
Hath he deserved to lose his birthright thus?
220 Hadst thou but loved him half so well as I,
Or felt that pain which I did for him once,
Or nourished him as I did with my blood,
Thou wouldst have left thy dearest heart-blood there
Rather than have made that savage duke thine heir
And disinherited thine only son.

PRINCE
Father, you cannot disinherit me.
If you be king, why should not I succeed?

KING HENRY
Pardon me, Margaret. Pardon me, sweet son.
The Earl of Warwick and the duke enforced me.

QUEEN MARGARET
Enforced thee? Art thou king, and wilt be forced?
I shame to hear thee speak. Ah, timorous wretch,
Thou hast undone thyself, thy son, and me,
233 And giv'n unto the house of York such head
As thou shalt reign but by their sufferance.
To entail him and his heirs unto the crown,
What is it but to make thy sepulchre
And creep into it far before thy time?
Warwick is chancellor and the lord of Calais;
239 Stern Falconbridge commands the narrow seas;
The duke is made Protector of the realm;
And yet shalt thou be safe? Such safety finds
242 The trembling lamb environèd with wolves.
243 Had I been there, which am a silly woman,
244 The soldiers should have tossed me on their pikes
245 Before I would have granted to that act.
But thou preferr'st thy life before thine honor;
And seeing thou dost, I here divorce myself
Both from thy table, Henry, and thy bed
Until that act of parliament be repealed
Whereby my son is disinherited.
The Northern lords, that have forsworn thy colors,
Will follow mine, if once they see them spread;
And spread they shall be, to thy foul disgrace
And utter ruin of the house of York.
Thus do I leave thee. Come, son, let's away.
Our army is ready. Come, we'll after them.

KING HENRY
Stay, gentle Margaret, and hear me speak.

QUEEN MARGARET
Thou hast spoke too much already. Get thee gone.

186 *bands* bonds    194 *entail* bequeath inalienably    203 *forward* spirited
205 s.d. *Sennet* a trumpet call indicating a ceremonial entrance or exit
206 *castle* i.e. Sandal, near Wakefield, Yorkshire    209 *I . . . came* (John
Nevil, Marquess of Montague, did not come from the sea, and in I, ii is at
Sandal Castle. It is possible that he has been confused with his uncle,
William Nevil. See l. 239n.)    211 *bewray* expose    233 *giv'n . . . head* i.e.
slackened the horse's reins so as to allow him to move his head more freely
and, hence, to run more rapidly    239 *Stern . . . seas* (William Nevil, Baron
Fauconberg and Warwick's uncle, served as Warwick's deputy at Calais
in 1459–60, whence he would have commanded the Straits of Dover – the
'narrow seas')    242 *environèd* surrounded    243 *silly* helpless    244 *pikes*
halberds    245 *granted* conceded

KING HENRY
Gentle son Edward, thou wilt stay with me?
QUEEN MARGARET
260 Ay, to be murdered by his enemies!
PRINCE
When I return with victory from the field
I'll see your grace. Till then I'll follow her.
QUEEN MARGARET
Come, son, away. We may not linger thus.
[Exeunt Queen Margaret and the Prince.]
KING HENRY
Poor queen! How love to me and to her son
Hath made her break out into terms of rage.
Revengèd may she be on that hateful duke,
Whose haughty spirit, wingèd with desire,
268 Will cost my crown and like an empty eagle
269 Tire on the flesh of me and of my son.
The loss of those three lords torments my heart.
I'll write unto them and entreat them fair.
Come, cousin, you shall be the messenger.
EXETER
273 And I hope, shall reconcile them all.
Exit [King Henry with Exeter]. Flourish.

*

I, ii      Enter Richard, Edward, and Montague.
RICHARD
1 Brother, though I be youngest, give me leave.
EDWARD
No, I can better play the orator.
MONTAGUE
But I have reasons strong and forcible.
Enter the Duke of York.
YORK
Why, how now, sons and cousin? at a strife?
What is your quarrel? How began it first?
EDWARD
No quarrel, but a slight contention.
YORK
About what?
RICHARD
About that which concerns your grace and us –
The crown of England, father, which is yours.
YORK
Mine, boy? Not till King Henry be dead.
RICHARD
Your right depends not on his life or death.
EDWARD
Now you are heir; therefore enjoy it now.
13 By giving the house of Lancaster leave to breathe,
It will outrun you, father, in the end.
YORK
I took an oath that he should quietly reign.
EDWARD
But for a kingdom any oath may be broken.
I would break a thousand oaths to reign one year.

RICHARD
No. God forbid your grace should be forsworn.
YORK
I shall be, if I claim by open war.
RICHARD
I'll prove the contrary if you'll hear me speak.
YORK
Thou canst not, son. It is impossible.
RICHARD
An oath is of no moment, being not took 22
Before a true and lawful magistrate
That hath authority over him that swears.
Henry had none, but did usurp the place.
Then, seeing 'twas he that made you to depose, 26
Your oath, my lord, is vain and frivolous.
Therefore, to arms! And, father, do but think
How sweet a thing it is to wear a crown,
Within whose circuit is Elysium 30
And all that poets feign of bliss and joy.
Why do we linger thus? I cannot rest
Until the white rose that I wear be dyed
Even in the lukewarm blood of Henry's heart.
YORK
Richard, enough. I will be king or die.
Cousin, thou shalt to London presently 36
And whet on Warwick to this enterprise.
Thou, Richard, shalt to the Duke of Norfolk
And tell him privily of our intent. 39
You, Edward, shall unto my Lord Cobham,
With whom the Kentishmen will willingly rise.
In them I trust; for they are soldiers,
Witty, courteous, liberal, full of spirit.
While you are thus employed, what resteth more 44
But that I seek occasion how to rise,
And yet the king not privy to my drift, 46
Nor any of the house of Lancaster?
Enter a Messenger.
But stay, what news? Why com'st thou in such post? 48
MESSENGER
The queen with all the Northern earls and lords
Intend here to besiege you in your castle.
She is hard by with twenty thousand men;
And therefore fortify your hold, my lord. 52
YORK
Ay, with my sword. What, think'st thou that we fear
them?
Edward and Richard, you shall stay with me;
My cousin Montague shall post to London.
Let noble Warwick, Cobham, and the rest,
Whom we have left protectors of the king,
With pow'rful policy strengthen themselves 58
And trust not simple Henry nor his oaths.
MONTAGUE
Cousin, I go. I'll win them; fear it not.
And thus most humbly I do take my leave.
Exit Montague.
Enter [Sir John] Mortimer, and [Sir Hugh,] his
brother.
YORK
Sir John and Sir Hugh Mortimer, mine uncles,
You are come to Sandal in a happy hour.
The army of the queen mean to besiege us.
JOHN
She shall not need; we'll meet her in the field.

268 *cost* accost, assail    269 *Tire* feed greedily    273 s.d. *Flourish* a trumpet fanfare
I, ii The Duke of York's castle, Sandal (Wakefield)    1 *give me leave* allow me (to speak)    13 *leave to breathe* i.e. a respite    22 *moment* importance    26 *depose* swear    30 *Elysium* classical Paradise    36 *presently* immediately    39 *privily* secretly    44 *what resteth more* what else remains    46 *privy to* aware of    48 *post* haste    52 *hold* stronghold    58 *policy* stratagem

YORK
What, with five thousand men?
RICHARD
Ay, with five hundred, father, for a need.
68 A woman's general. What should we fear?
*A march afar off.*
EDWARD
I hear their drums. Let's set our men in order
70 And issue forth and bid them battle straight.
YORK
Five men to twenty! Though the odds be great,
I doubt not, uncle, of our victory.
Many a battle have I won in France
74 When as the enemy hath been ten to one.
Why should I not now have the like success?
*Alarum. Exit [York with the rest].*

\*

I, iii          *Enter Rutland and his Tutor.*
RUTLAND
Ah, whither shall I fly to scape their hands?
Ah, tutor, look where bloody Clifford comes.
*Enter Clifford [and Soldiers].*
CLIFFORD
Chaplain, away! Thy priesthood saves thy life.
As for the brat of this accursèd duke,
Whose father slew my father, he shall die.
TUTOR
And I, my lord, will bear him company.
CLIFFORD
Soldiers, away with him!
TUTOR
Ah, Clifford, murder not this innocent child,
Lest thou be hated both of God and man.
*Exit [dragged off by Soldiers].*
CLIFFORD
How now? Is he dead already? Or is it fear
That makes him close his eyes? I'll open them.
RUTLAND
12 So looks the pent-up lion o'er the wretch
That trembles under his devouring paws;
14 And so he walks, insulting o'er his prey,
And so he comes, to rend his limbs asunder.
Ah, gentle Clifford, kill me with thy sword
And not with such a cruel threat'ning look.
Sweet Clifford, hear me speak before I die.
I am too mean a subject for thy wrath.
20 Be thou revenged on men and let me live.
CLIFFORD
In vain thou speak'st, poor boy. My father's blood
Hath stopped the passage where thy words should enter.
RUTLAND
Then let my father's blood open it again.
He is a man, and, Clifford, cope with him.
CLIFFORD
Had I thy brethren here, their lives and thine
Were not revenge sufficient for me.
No, if I digged up thy forefathers' graves
And hung their rotten coffins up in chains,
It could not slake mine ire nor ease my heart.
30 The sight of any of the house of York
Is as a Fury to torment my soul;
And till I root out their accursèd line

And leave not one alive, I live in hell.
Therefore –
RUTLAND
O, let me pray before I take my death!
To thee I pray. Sweet Clifford, pity me.
CLIFFORD
Such pity as my rapier's point affords.
RUTLAND
I never did thee harm. Why wilt thou slay me?
CLIFFORD
Thy father hath.
RUTLAND          But 'twas ere I was born.
Thou hast one son. For his sake pity me.
Lest in revenge thereof, sith God is just,          41
He be as miserably slain as I.
Ah, let me live in prison all my days;
And when I give occasion of offense,
Then let me die, for now thou hast no cause.
CLIFFORD
No cause?
Thy father slew my father. Therefore die.
*[Stabs him.]*
RUTLAND
Di faciant laudis summa sit ista tuae!          48
*[Dies.]*
CLIFFORD
Plantagenet, I come, Plantagenet!
And this thy son's blood cleaving to my blade
Shall rust upon my weapon till thy blood,
Congealed with this, do make me wipe off both.     *Exit.*
*Alarum. Enter Richard Duke of York.*          I, iv
YORK
The army of the queen hath got the field.
My uncles both are slain in rescuing me,
And all my followers to the eager foe
Turn back and fly, like ships before the wind          4
Or lambs pursued by hunger-starvèd wolves.
My sons – God knows what hath bechancèd them;
But this I know, they have demeaned themselves          7
Like men born to renown by life or death.
Three times did Richard make a lane to me
And thrice cried 'Courage, father! fight it out!'
And full as oft came Edward to my side
With purple falchion, painted to the hilt          12
In blood of those that had encount'red him.
And when the hardiest warriors did retire,
Richard cried 'Charge! and give no foot of ground!'
And cried 'A crown, or else a glorious tomb!
A sceptre, or an earthly sepulchre!'
With this we charged again; but out alas!
We bodged again, as I have seen a swan          19
With bootless labor swim against the tide          20
And spend her strength with overmatching waves.     21
*A short alarum within.*
Ah, hark! The fatal followers do pursue,
And I am faint and cannot fly their fury;
And were I strong, I would not shun their fury.

---

68 s.d. *A march* drum-beats  70 *straight* immediately  74 *When as* when
I, iii Fields near York's castle  12 *pent-up* caged, hence fierce  14 *insulting*
exulting  41 *sith* since  48 *Di . . . tuae* may the gods grant that this be the
height of your fame (Ovid, *Heroides*, II, 66)
I, iv  4 *Turn back* i.e. turn their backs  7 *demeaned* behaved  12 *falchion*
curved broadsword  19 *bodged* botched  20 *bootless* fruitless  21 *with*
against

25 The sands are numb'red that makes up my life.
Here must I stay and here my life must end.
    *Enter the Queen [Margaret], Clifford, Northumber-*
    *land, the young Prince, and Soldiers.*
Come, bloody Clifford, rough Northumberland,
I dare your quenchless fury to more rage.
29 I am your butt and I abide your shot.

NORTHUMBERLAND
Yield to our mercy, proud Plantagenet.

CLIFFFORD
Ay, to such mercy as his ruthless arm
With downright payment showed unto my father.
33 Now Phaeton hath tumbled from his car
34 And made an evening at the noontide prick.

YORK
35 My ashes, as the phoenix, may bring forth
A bird that will revenge upon you all;
And in that hope I throw mine eyes to heaven,
Scorning whate'er you can afflict me with.
Why come you not? What? multitudes, and fear?

CLIFFORD
So cowards fight when they can fly no further;
So doves do peck the falcon's piercing talons;
So desperate thieves, all hopeless of their lives,
Breathe out invectives 'gainst the officers.

YORK
O Clifford, but bethink thee once again,
45 And in thy thought o'errun my former time;
And, if thou canst for blushing, view this face,
And bite thy tongue that slanders him with cowardice
Whose frown hath made thee faint and fly ere this.

CLIFFORD
49 I will not bandy with thee word for word,
50 But buckle with thee blows, twice two for one.

QUEEN MARGARET
Hold, valiant Clifford! For a thousand causes
I would prolong awhile the traitor's life.
Wrath makes him deaf. Speak thou, Northumberland.

NORTHUMBERLAND
Hold, Clifford! Do not honor him so much
To prick thy finger, though to wound his heart.
56 What valor were it, when a cur doth grin,
For one to thrust his hand between his teeth
When he might spurn him with his foot away?
59 It is war's prize to take all vantages;
60 And ten to one is no impeach of valor.
    *[Fight and take him.]*

CLIFFORD
61 Ay, ay, so strives the woodcock with the gin.

---

25 *sands* i.e. in the hourglass   29 *butt* target for archery   33 *Phaeton* the son of Apollo, who took his father's sun-chariot and, unable to manage it, was dashed to pieces (a conventional symbol of presumption, appropriate here because the sun was a Yorkist device)   34 *noontide prick* mark on sundial indicating noon   35 *phoenix* a miraculous bird that died through spontaneous combustion and rose again from its own ashes   45 *o'errun* review   49 *bandy* exchange   50 *buckle* grapple, engage   56 *grin* show his teeth   59 *prize* reward   60 *impeach* calling in question   61 *woodcock* (proverbially stupid, as was the *cony*, l. 62); *gin* engine, trap   62 *cony* rabbit   64 *true* honest   67 *stand . . . here* (with allusion to the 'king of the molehill,' a term of contempt)   68 *raught* reached   69 *but* only   71 *revelled* enjoyed yourself   73 *mess* a group of four   75 *prodigy* monster   77 *mutinies* rebellions   79 *napkin* handkerchief   92 *fee'd* paid   96 *marry* by the Virgin Mary (with weakened force)   103 *pale* encircle   108 *breathe* rest   110 *orisons* prayers   114 *Amazonian* (the Amazons, who figure in classical story, were a legendary race of female warriors)   116 *vizard-like* mask-like

---

NORTHUMBERLAND
So doth the cony struggle in the net.    62

YORK
So triumph thieves upon their conquered booty;
So true men yield, with robbers so o'ermatched.    64

NORTHUMBERLAND
What would your grace have done unto him now?

QUEEN MARGARET
Brave warriors, Clifford and Northumberland,
Come, make him stand upon this molehill here    67
That raught at mountains with outstretchèd arms,    68
Yet parted but the shadow with his hand.    69
What, was it you that would be England's king?
Was't you that revelled in our parliament    71
And made a preachment of your high descent?
Where are your mess of sons to back you now?    73
The wanton Edward, and the lusty George?
And where's that valiant crookback prodigy,    75
Dicky your boy, that with his grumbling voice
Was wont to cheer his dad in mutinies?    77
Or, with the rest, where is your darling Rutland?
Look, York! I stained this napkin with the blood    79
That valiant Clifford with his rapier's point
Made issue from the bosom of the boy;
And if thine eyes can water for his death,
I give thee this to dry thy cheeks withal.
Alas, poor York! but that I hate thee deadly,
I should lament thy miserable state.
I prithee grieve, to make me merry, York.
What? hath thy fiery heart so parched thine entrails
That not a tear can fall for Rutland's death?
Why art thou patient, man? Thou shouldst be mad;
And I to make thee mad do mock thee thus.
Stamp, rave, and fret, that I may sing and dance.
Thou wouldst be fee'd, I see, to make me sport.    92
York cannot speak unless he wear a crown.
A crown for York! and, lords, bow low to him.
Hold you his hands whilst I do set it on.
    *[Puts a paper crown on his head.]*
Ay, marry, sir, now looks he like a king.    96
Ay, this is he that took King Henry's chair
And this is he was his adopted heir.
But how is it that great Plantagenet
Is crowned so soon, and broke his solemn oath?
As I bethink me, you should not be king
Till our King Henry had shook hands with death.
And will you pale your head in Henry's glory    103
And rob his temples of the diadem
Now in his life, against your holy oath?
O, 'tis a fault too too unpardonable.
Off with the crown, and with the crown his head.
And whilst we breathe, take time to do him dead.    108

CLIFFORD
That is my office, for my father's sake.

QUEEN MARGARET
Nay, stay. Let's hear the orisons he makes.    110

YORK
She-wolf of France, but worse than wolves of France,
Whose tongue more poisons than the adder's tooth,
How ill-beseeming is it in thy sex
To triumph like an Amazonian trull    114
Upon their woes whom fortune captivates.
But that thy face is vizard-like, unchanging,    116
Made impudent with use of evil deeds,

118  I would assay, proud queen, to make thee blush.
    To tell thee whence thou cam'st, of whom derived,
    Were shame enough to shame thee, wert thou not shame-
       less.
121  Thy father bears the type of King of Naples,
122  Of both the Sicils and Jerusalem,
123  Yet not so wealthy as an English yeoman.
    Hath that poor monarch taught thee to insult?
125  It needs not nor it boots thee not, proud queen,
126  Unless the adage must be verified,
    That beggars mounted run their horse to death.
    'Tis beauty that doth oft make women proud;
    But God he knows thy share thereof is small.
    'Tis virtue that doth make them most admired;
    The contrary doth make thee wond'red at.
132  'Tis government that makes them seem divine;
    The want thereof makes thee abominable.
    Thou art as opposite to every good
135  As the Antipodes are unto us
136  Or as the South to the Septentrion.
    O tiger's heart wrapped in a woman's hide!
    How couldst thou drain the lifeblood of the child,
    To bid the father wipe his eyes withal,
    And yet be seen to bear a woman's face?
    Women are soft, mild, pitiful, and flexible;
    Thou stern, obdurate, flinty, rough, remorseless.
    Bid'st thou me rage? Why, now thou hast thy wish.
    Wouldst have me weep? Why, now thou hast thy will.
    For raging wind blows up incessant showers,
    And when the rage allays the rain begins.
147  These tears are my sweet Rutland's obsequies,
    And every drop cries vengeance for his death
149  'Gainst thee, fell Clifford, and thee, false Frenchwoman.

NORTHUMBERLAND
150  Beshrew me but his passions moves me so
    That hardly can I check my eyes from tears.

YORK
    That face of his the hungry cannibals
    Would not have touched, would not have stained with
      blood;
    But you are more inhuman, more inexorable –
155  O, ten times more! – than tigers of Hyrcania.
156  See, ruthless queen, a hapless father's tears.
    This cloth thou dipp'dst in blood of my sweet boy,
    And I with tears do wash the blood away.
    Keep thou the napkin and go boast of this;
160  And if thou tell'st the heavy story right,
    Upon my soul, the hearers will shed tears.
    Yea, even my foes will shed fast-falling tears
    And say, 'Alas, it was a piteous deed!'
    There, take the crown, and with the crown my curse;
    And in thy need such comfort come to thee
    As now I reap at thy too cruel hand.
    Hard-hearted Clifford, take me from the world.
    My soul to heaven, my blood upon your heads.

NORTHUMBERLAND
    Had he been slaughterman to all my kin,
    I should not for my life but weep with him
171  To see how inly sorrow gripes his soul.

QUEEN MARGARET
172  What, weeping-ripe, my Lord Northumberland?
    Think but upon the wrong he did us all
174  And that will quickly dry thy melting tears.

CLIFFORD
    Here's for my oath, here's for my father's death.
    *[Stabs him.]*

QUEEN MARGARET
    And here's to right our gentle-hearted king.
    *[Stabs him.]*

YORK
    Open thy gate of mercy, gracious God,
    My soul flies through these wounds to seek out thee.
    *[Dies.]*

QUEEN MARGARET
    Off with his head and set it on York gates,
    So York may overlook the town of York.
    *Flourish. Exit [Queen Margaret with her followers].*

\*

    *A march. Enter Edward, Richard, and their Power.*   II, i

EDWARD
    I wonder how our princely father scaped,
    Or whether he be 'scaped away or no
    From Clifford's and Northumberland's pursuit.
    Had he been ta'en, we should have heard the news;
    Had he been slain, we should have heard the news;
    Or had he scaped, methinks we should have heard
    The happy tidings of his good escape.
    How fares my brother? Why is he so sad?

RICHARD
    I cannot joy until I be resolved
    Where our right valiant father is become.   10
    I saw him in the battle range about
    And watched him how he singled Clifford forth.   12
    Methought he bore him in the thickest troop
    As doth a lion in a herd of neat,   14
    Or as a bear encompassed round with dogs,
    Who having pinched a few and made them cry,   16
    The rest stand all aloof and bark at him.
    So fared our father with his enemies;
    So fled his enemies my warlike father.
    Methinks 'tis prize enough to be his son.   20
    See how the morning opes her golden gates
    And takes her farewell of the glorious sun.
    How well resembles it the prime of youth
    Trimmed like a younker prancing to his love.   24

EDWARD
    Dazzle mine eyes, or do I see three suns?   25

RICHARD
    Three glorious suns, each one a perfect sun,
    Not separated with the racking clouds,   27
    But severed in a pale clear-shining sky.
    See, see! They join, embrace, and seem to kiss,

---

118 *assay* try   121 *type* title   122 *both the Sicils* i.e. Sicily and Naples   123 *yeoman* landowner (below the rank of gentleman)   125 *boots* profits   126 *adage* proverb   132 *government* self-control   135 *Antipodes* the other side of the world   136 *Septentrion* the Big Dipper, i.e. the North   147 *obsequies* funeral rites   149 *fell* cruel   150 *Beshrew* curse   155 *Hyrcania* a region of ancient Persia (the reference to the fierceness of Hyrcanian tigers is ultimately from the *Aeneid*, IV, 366–67)   160 *heavy* sorrowful   171 *inly* heartfelt   172 *weeping-ripe* ready for weeping   174 *melting tears* tears arising from a softened heart
II, i Fields near the Welsh border (Marches)   10 *Where . . . is become* what has happened to . . .   12 *forth* out   14 *neat* cattle   16 *pinched* bitten   20 *prize* privilege   24 *Trimmed* dressed up; *younker* young man   25 *Dazzle mine eyes* do my eyes blur   27 *racking* passing

As if they vowed some league inviolable.
Now are they but one lamp, one light, one sun.
32  In this the heaven figures some event.

EDWARD

'Tis wondrous strange, the like yet never heard of.
34  I think it cites us, brother, to the field,
That we, the sons of brave Plantagenet,
36  Each one already blazing by our meeds,
Should notwithstanding join our lights together
38  And overshine the earth, as this the world.
Whate'er it bodes, henceforward will I bear
Upon my target three fair-shining suns.

RICHARD

41  Nay, bear three daughters. By your leave I speak it,
42  You love the breeder better than the male.
        *Enter one [Messenger] blowing [a horn].*
But what art thou whose heavy looks foretell
Some dreadful story hanging on thy tongue?

MESSENGER

Ah, one that was a woeful looker-on
46  When as the noble Duke of York was slain,
Your princely father and my loving lord.

EDWARD

O speak no more, for I have heard too much.

RICHARD

Say how he died, for I will hear it all.

MESSENGER

50  Environèd he was with many foes,
51  And stood against them as the hope of Troy
Against the Greeks that would have ent'red Troy.
But Hercules himself must yield to odds;
And many strokes, though with a little axe,
Hews down and fells the hardest-timbered oak.
By many hands your father was subdued,
But only slaught'red by the ireful arm
Of unrelenting Clifford and the queen,
59  Who crowned the gracious duke in high despite,
Laughed in his face, and when with grief he wept,
The ruthless queen gave him, to dry his cheeks,
A napkin steepèd in the harmless blood
Of sweet young Rutland, by rough Clifford slain;
And after many scorns, many foul taunts,
They took his head and on the gates of York
They set the same; and there it doth remain,
The saddest spectacle that e'er I viewed.

EDWARD

Sweet Duke of York, our prop to lean upon,
Now thou art gone, we have no staff, no stay.
70  O Clifford, boist'rous Clifford, thou hast slain
The flow'r of Europe for his chivalry;
And treacherously hast thou vanquished him,
For hand to hand he would have vanquished thee.

Now my soul's palace is become a prison.                     74
Ah, would she break from hence, that this my body
Might in the ground be closèd up in rest.
For never henceforth shall I joy again;
Never, O never, shall I see more joy.

RICHARD

I cannot weep, for all my body's moisture
Scarce serves to quench my furnace-burning heart;
Nor can my tongue unload my heart's great burden,
For selfsame wind that I should speak withal
Is kindling coals that fires all my breast
And burns me up with flames that tears would quench.
To weep is to make less the depth of grief.
Tears, then, for babes; blows and revenge for me!
Richard, I bear thy name; I'll venge thy death
Or die renownèd by attempting it.

EDWARD

His name that valiant duke hath left with thee;
His dukedom and his chair with me is left.

RICHARD

Nay, if thou be that princely eagle's bird,                   91
Show thy descent by gazing 'gainst the sun;                   92
For chair and dukedom, throne and kingdom say,               93
Either that is thine, or else thou wert not his.
        *March. Enter Warwick, Marquess Montague, and
        their Army.*

WARWICK

How now, fair lords, what fare? What news abroad?

RICHARD

Great Lord of Warwick, if we should recompt
Our baleful news and at each word's deliverance              97
Stab poniards in our flesh till all were told,
The words would add more anguish than the wounds.
O valiant lord, the Duke of York is slain.

EDWARD

O Warwick, Warwick, that Plantagenet
Which held thee dearly as his soul's redemption
Is by the stern Lord Clifford done to death.

WARWICK

Ten days ago I drowned these news in tears;
And now, to add more measure to your woes,
I come to tell you things sith then befallen.                106
After the bloody fray at Wakefield fought,
Where your brave father breathed his latest gasp,           108
Tidings, as swiftly as the posts could run,
Were brought me of your loss and his depart.                110
I, then in London, keeper of the king,
Mustered my soldiers, gathered flocks of friends,
[And very well appointed, as I thought,]                     113
Marched toward Saint Albans to intercept the queen,
Bearing the king in my behalf along;
For by my scouts I was advertisèd                            116
That she was coming with a full intent
To dash our late decree in parliament
Touching King Henry's oath and your succession.
Short tale to make, we at Saint Albans met,
Our battles joined, and both sides fiercely fought;
But whether 'twas the coldness of the king,
Who looked full gently on his warlike queen,
That robbed my soldiers of their heated spleen,             124
Or whether 'twas report of her success,
Or more than common fear of Clifford's rigor,
Who thunders to his captives blood and death,

32 *figures* prefigures, foretells   34 *cites* incites   36 *meeds* merits   38 *overshine* light up; *this* i.e. this phenomenon   41 *daughters* (with obvious pun on *suns*, l. 40)   42 *breeder* female; s.d. *blowing [a horn]* (indicating that the Messenger is a post-rider)   46 *When as* when   50 *Environèd* surrounded   51 *hope of Troy* i.e. Hector   59 *in high despite* with great contempt   70 *boist'rous* savage   74 *soul's palace* i.e. body   91 *bird* young   92 *gazing 'gainst the sun* (Eagles, according to Pliny and many later writers, could gaze at the sun without blinking. The sun here may symbolize the king; the eagle may be an allusion to a Yorkist badge.)   93 *chair* (symbol of a duke's authority, as *throne* is of a king's)   97 *baleful* deadly   106 *sith* since   108 *latest* last   110 *depart* death   113 *appointed* equipped   116 *advertisèd* informed   124 *spleen* spirit

I cannot judge ; but to conclude with truth,
Their weapons like to lightning came and went ;
Our soldiers', like the night owl's lazy flight
131 Or like an idle thresher with a flail,
Fell gently down, as if they struck their friends.
I cheered them up with justice of our cause,
With promise of high pay and great rewards ;
But all in vain ; they had no heart to fight,
And we (in them) no hope to win the day ;
So that we fled : the king unto the queen ;
Lord George your brother, Norfolk, and myself,
139 In haste, post-haste, are come to join with you ;
140 For in the Marches here we heard you were,
141 Making another head to fight again.

EDWARD
Where is the Duke of Norfolk, gentle Warwick ?
And when came George from Burgundy to England ?

WARWICK
Some six miles off the duke is with the soldiers,
And for your brother, he was lately sent
146 From your kind aunt, Duchess of Burgundy,
With aid of soldiers to this needful war.

RICHARD
148 'Twas odds belike when valiant Warwick fled.
Oft have I heard his praises in pursuit,
150 But ne'er till now his scandal of retire.

WARWICK
Nor now my scandal, Richard, dost thou hear ;
For thou shalt know this strong right hand of mine
Can pluck the diadem from faint Henry's head
154 And wring the awful sceptre from his fist,
Were he as famous and as bold in war
As he is famed for mildness, peace, and prayer.

RICHARD
I know it well, Lord Warwick. Blame me not.
'Tis love I bear thy glories make me speak.
But in this troublous time what's to be done ?
Shall we go throw away our coats of steel
And wrap our bodies in black mourning gowns,
162 Numb'ring our Ave-Maries with our beads ?
Or shall we on the helmets of our foes
164 Tell our devotion with revengeful arms ?
If for the last, say 'Ay,' and to it, lords.

WARWICK
Why, therefore Warwick came to seek you out,
And therefore comes my brother Montague.
Attend me, lords. The proud insulting queen
169 With Clifford and the haught Northumberland,
170 And of their feather many moe proud birds,
171 Have wrought the easy-melting king like wax.
He swore consent to your succession,
His oath enrollèd in the parliament ;
And now to London all the crew are gone,
To frustrate both his oath, and what beside
May make against the house of Lancaster.
Their power, I think, is thirty thousand strong.
Now if the help of Norfolk and myself
179 With all the friends that thou, brave Earl of March,
Amongst the loving Welshmen canst procure,
Will but amount to five-and-twenty thousand,
182 Why, via ! to London will we march
And once again bestride our foaming steeds,
And once again cry 'Charge !' upon our foes,
But never once again turn back and fly.

RICHARD
Ay, now methinks I hear great Warwick speak.
Ne'er may he live to see a sunshine day          187
That cries 'Retire !' if Warwick bid him stay.

EDWARD
Lord Warwick, on thy shoulder will I lean,
And when thou fail'st (as God forbid the hour)
Must Edward fall, which peril heaven forfend.    191

WARWICK
No longer Earl of March, but Duke of York,
The next degree is England's royal throne ;      193
For King of England shalt thou be proclaimed
In every borough as we pass along ;
And he that throws not up his cap for joy
Shall for the fault make forfeit of his head.
King Edward, valiant Richard, Montague,
Stay we no longer, dreaming of renown,
But sound the trumpets and about our task.

RICHARD
Then, Clifford, were thy heart as hard as steel,
As thou hast shown it flinty by thy deeds,
I come to pierce it or to give thee mine.

EDWARD
Then strike up drums. God and Saint George for us !
*Enter a Messenger.*

WARWICK
How now ? What news ?

MESSENGER
The Duke of Norfolk sends you word by me
The queen is coming with a puissant host,         207
And craves your company for speedy counsel.

WARWICK
Why, then it sorts. Brave warriors, let's away.   209
*Exeunt omnes.*

*

*Flourish. Enter the King [Henry], the Queen*     II,
*[Margaret], Clifford, Northumberland, and young*
*Prince, with Drum and Trumpets.*

QUEEN MARGARET
Welcome, my lord, to this brave town of York.
Yonder's the head of that arch-enemy
That sought to be encompassed with your crown.
Doth not the object cheer your heart, my lord ?

KING HENRY
Ay, as the rocks cheer them that fear their wrack.   5
To see this sight it irks my very soul.
Withhold revenge, dear God ! 'Tis not my fault,
Nor wittingly have I infringed my vow.              8

---

131 *flail* an instrument for threshing, a stout stick joined to a longer handle
by a leather thong   139 *post-haste* as speedily as post-riders   140 *marches*
borders (here, of Wales)   141 *Making another head* gathering another
force   146 *aunt . . . Burgundy* (Isabel, Duchess of Burgundy, was a granddaughter of John of Gaunt and a distant cousin to Edward. Holinshed says
that George and Richard were sent for protection to the Duke of Burgundy
after York's death and remained with him until Edward was crowned.)
148 *'Twas odds belike* no doubt the odds were heavily against him   150
*scandal of retire* disgrace because of retreating   154 *awful* awe-inspiring
162 *Ave-Maries* Hail Maries (prayers to the Blessed Virgin)   164 *Tell our
devotion* (1) count off our prayers, as on a rosary, (2) declare our love
(ironically)   169 *haught* haughty   170 *moe* more   171 *wrought* worked
on, persuaded ; *easy-melting* soft-hearted, easily swayed   179 *Earl of
March* i.e. Edward (his title before York's death ; see l. 192)   182 *via*
forward   187 *he* i.e. anyone   191 *forfend* forbid   193 *degree* rank   207
*puissant* powerful   209 *sorts* works out well
II, ii Before the walls of York   5 *wrack* ruin   8 *wittingly* knowingly

CLIFFORD
9  My gracious liege, this too much lenity
   And harmful pity must be laid aside.
   To whom do lions cast their gentle looks?
   Not to the beast that would usurp their den.
   Whose hand is that the forest bear doth lick?
14 Not his that spoils her young before her face.
   Who scapes the lurking serpent's mortal sting?
   Not he that sets his foot upon her back.
   The smallest worm will turn, being trodden on,
   And doves will peck in safeguard of their brood.
19 Ambitious York did level at thy crown,
   Thou smiling while he knit his angry brows.
   He, but a duke, would have his son a king
22 And raise his issue like a loving sire;
   Thou, being a king, blest with a goodly son,
   Didst yield consent to disinherit him,
   Which argued thee a most unloving father.
   Unreasonable creatures feed their young;
   And though man's face be fearful to their eyes,
   Yet, in protection of their tender ones,
   Who hath not seen them, even with those wings
   Which sometime they have used with fearful flight,
   Make war with him that climbed unto their nest,
   Offering their own lives in their young's defense?
   For shame, my liege. Make them your precedent.
   Were it not pity that this goodly boy
   Should lose his birthright by his father's fault
   And long hereafter say unto his child,
   'What my great-grandfather and grandsire got
38 My careless father fondly gave away'?
   Ah, what a shame were this. Look on the boy,
   And let his manly face, which promiseth
   Successful fortune, steel thy melting heart
   To hold thine own and leave thine own with him.
KING HENRY
   Full well hath Clifford played the orator,
44 Inferring arguments of mighty force.
   But, Clifford, tell me, didst thou never hear
   That things ill got had ever bad success?
47 And happy always was it for that son
48 Whose father for his hoarding went to hell?
   I'll leave my son my virtuous deeds behind,
   And would my father had left me no more.
51 For all the rest is held at such a rate
   As brings a thousandfold more care to keep
   Than in possession any jot of pleasure.
   Ah, cousin York, would thy best friends did know
   How it doth grieve me that thy head is here.
QUEEN MARGARET
   My lord, cheer up your spirits. Our foes are nigh,
57 And this soft courage makes your followers faint.
58 You promised knighthood to our forward son.
   Unsheathe your sword and dub him presently.

9 *lenity* gentleness  14 *spoils* destroys  19 *level* aim  22 *raise* promote
38 *fondly* foolishly  44 *Inferring* adducing  47 *happy . . . it* were things
always good  48 *for* because of  51 *rate* cost  57 *faint* faint-hearted
58 *forward* high-spirited, precocious  64 *apparent* heir apparent  66 *toward* promising  69 *backing of* in support of;  *Duke of York* i.e. Edward
72 *Darraign your battle* deploy your forces  80 s.d. *Clarence* i.e. George
(though George is not created Duke of Clarence until II, vi, 104, he is
consistently termed Clarence in stage directions and speech-prefixes
before then)  83 *bide* await  84 *rate thy minions* berate your favorites
97 *sort* gang

Edward, kneel down.
KING HENRY
   Edward Plantagenet, arise a knight,
   And learn this lesson: Draw thy sword in right.
PRINCE
   My gracious father, by your kingly leave,
   I'll draw it as apparent to the crown                    64
   And in that quarrel use it to the death.
CLIFFORD
   Why, that is spoken like a toward prince.                66
              *Enter a Messenger.*
MESSENGER
   Royal commanders, be in readiness;
   For with a band of thirty thousand men
   Comes Warwick, backing of the Duke of York,             69
   And in the towns, as they do march along,
   Proclaims him king, and many fly to him.
   Darraign your battle, for they are at hand.             72
CLIFFORD
   I would your highness would depart the field.
   The queen hath best success when you are absent.
QUEEN MARGARET
   Ay, good my lord, and leave us to our fortune.
KING HENRY
   Why, that's my fortune too. Therefore I'll stay.
NORTHUMBERLAND
   Be it with resolution, then, to fight.
PRINCE
   My royal father, cheer these noble lords
   And hearten those that fight in your defense.
   Unsheathe your sword, good father. Cry 'Saint George!'  80
       *March. Enter Edward, Warwick, Richard, Clarence,*
          *Norfolk, Montague, and Soldiers.*
EDWARD
   Now, perjured Henry, wilt thou kneel for grace
   And set thy diadem upon my head,
   Or bide the mortal fortune of the field?                83
QUEEN MARGARET
   Go rate thy minions, proud insulting boy                84
   Becomes it thee to be thus bold in terms
   Before thy sovereign and thy lawful king?
EDWARD
   I am his king, and he should bow his knee.
   I was adopted heir by his consent;
   Since when, his oath is broke; for, as I hear,
   You that are king, though he do wear the crown,
   Have caused him by new act of parliament
   To blot out me and put his own son in.
CLIFFORD
   And reason too;
   Who should succeed the father but the son?
RICHARD
   Are you there, butcher? O, I cannot speak.
CLIFFORD
   Ay, Crookback, here I stand to answer thee,
   Or any he, the proudest of thy sort.                    97
RICHARD
   'Twas you that killed young Rutland, was it not?
CLIFFORD
   Ay, and old York, and yet not satisfied.
RICHARD
   For God's sake, lords, give signal to the fight.
WARWICK
   What say'st thou, Henry? Wilt thou yield the crown?

QUEEN MARGARET
Why, how now, long-tongued Warwick?
Dare you speak?
When you and I met at Saint Albans last,
Your legs did better service than your hands.

WARWICK
Then 'twas my turn to fly, and now 'tis thine.

CLIFFORD
You said so much before, and yet you fled.

WARWICK
'Twas not your valor, Clifford, drove me thence.

NORTHUMBERLAND
No, nor your manhood that durst make you stay.

RICHARD
109   Northumberland, I hold thee reverently.
Break off the parley, for scarce I can refrain
The execution of my big-swol'n heart
Upon that Clifford, that cruel child-killer.

CLIFFORD
I slew thy father. Call'st thou him a child?

RICHARD
Ay, like a dastard and a treacherous coward,
As thou didst kill our tender brother Rutland.
But ere sun set I'll make thee curse the deed.

KING HENRY
Have done with words, my lords, and hear me speak.

QUEEN MARGARET
Defy them then, or else hold close thy lips.

KING HENRY
I prithee give no limits to my tongue.
I am a king, and privileged to speak.

CLIFFORD
My liege, the wound that bred this meeting here
Cannot be cured by words. Therefore be still.

RICHARD
Then, executioner, unsheathe thy sword.
124   By Him that made us all, I am resolved
125   That Clifford's manhood lies upon his tongue.

EDWARD
Say, Henry, shall I have my right, or no?
A thousand men have broke their fasts to-day
That ne'er shall dine unless thou yield the crown.

WARWICK
129   If thou deny, their blood upon thy head.
For York in justice puts his armor on.

PRINCE
If that be right which Warwick says is right,
There is no wrong, but everything is right.

RICHARD
133   Whoever got thee, there thy mother stands;
134   For well I wot thou hast thy mother's tongue.

QUEEN MARGARET
But thou art neither like thy sire nor dam,
136   But like a foul misshapen stigmatic,
Marked by the Destinies to be avoided,
138   As venom toads or lizards' dreadful stings.

RICHARD
139   Iron of Naples, hid with English gilt,
Whose father bears the title of a king
141   (As if a channel should be called the sea),
142   Sham'st thou not, knowing whence thou art extraught,
To let thy tongue detect thy base-born heart?

EDWARD
144   A wisp of straw were worth a thousand crowns,

To make this shameless callet know herself.   145
Helen of Greece was fairer far than thou,   146
Although thy husband may be Menelaus;
And ne'er was Agamemnon's brother wronged
By that false woman as this king by thee.
His father revelled in the heart of France,   150
And tamed the king, and made the Dauphin stoop;
And had he matched according to his state,   152
He might have kept that glory to this day;
But when he took a beggar to his bed
And graced thy poor sire with his bridal day,   155
Even then that sunshine brewed a show'r for him
That washed his father's fortunes forth of France   157
And heaped sedition on his crown at home.
For what hath broached this tumult but thy pride?   159
Hadst thou been meek, our title still had slept,   160
And we, in pity of the gentle king,
Had slipped our claim until another age.   162

CLARENCE
But when we saw our sunshine made thy spring
And that thy summer bred us no increase,   164
We set the axe to thy usurping root;   165
And though the edge hath something hit ourselves,   166
Yet know thou, since we have begun to strike,
We'll never leave till we have hewn thee down
Or bathed thy growing with our heated bloods.   169

EDWARD
And in this resolution I defy thee,
Not willing any longer conference,
Since thou denied'st the gentle king to speak.   172
Sound trumpets! Let our bloody colors wave,
And either victory, or else a grave!

QUEEN MARGARET
Stay, Edward.

EDWARD
No, wrangling woman, we'll no longer stay.
These words will cost ten thousand lives this day.

                 *Exeunt omnes.*

\*

*Alarum. Excursions. Enter Warwick.*    II, iii

WARWICK
Forspent with toil, as runners with a race,   1
I lay me down a little while to breathe;   2
For strokes received and many blows repaid

109 *reverently* in respect   124 *resolved* convinced   125 *Clifford's . . . tongue* i.e. he talks better than he fights   129 *deny* refuse   133 *got* begot   134 *wot* know   136 *stigmatic* one branded (stigmatized) by deformity   138 *venom* venomous   139 *Iron . . . gilt* i.e. you cheap Neapolitan, whose worthlessness is concealed by English gold (probably with punning allusion to Suffolk's 'guilt' in paying so high a price for her)   141 *channel* gutter   142 *Sham'st thou not* are you not ashamed; *extraught* extracted   144 *wisp of straw* (traditional mark of a scold)   145 *callet* lewd woman   146-48 *Helen . . . Menelaus . . . Agamemnon* (Paris of Troy abducted Helen, wife of Menelaus, King of Sparta, who was brother to Agamemnon, King of Mycenae; here Helen is the typical false woman and Menelaus the typical cuckold. There is an allusion to the belief that Prince Edward was not the son of Henry VI.)   150 *His father* i.e. Henry V   152 *he* i.e. Henry VI; *matched* wedded; *state* worth, dignity   155 *graced . . . day* i.e. did honor (grace) to him by marrying his daughter   157 *of* from   159 *broached* started (literally, set flowing)   160 *title* claim to the throne   162 *slipped* forgone   164 *increase* harvest   165 *usurping* (because she is wife to Henry, regarded by the Yorkists as a usurper)   166 *something* somewhat   169 *bathed* watered   172 *denied'st* forbade
II, iii Fields near York (Towton)   s.d. *Alarum* trumpet call – 'to arms'; *Excursions* attacks and counter-attacks   1 *Forspent* utterly wearied   2 *breathe* rest

Have robbed my strong-knit sinews of their strength,
5  And spite of spite needs must I rest awhile.
   *Enter Edward, running.*

EDWARD
Smile, gentle heaven, or strike, ungentle death,
7  For this world frowns, and Edward's sun is clouded.

WARWICK
8  How now, my lord ? What hap ? What hope of good ?
   *Enter Clarence.*

CLARENCE
Our hap is loss, our hope but sad despair,
Our ranks are broke and ruin follows us.
What counsel give you ? Whither shall we fly ?

EDWARD
12  Bootless is flight. They follow us with wings,
13  And weak we are and cannot shun pursuit.
   *Enter Richard.*

RICHARD
Ah, Warwick, why hast thou withdrawn thyself ?
15  Thy brother's blood the thirsty earth hath drunk,
16  Broached with the steely point of Clifford's lance ;
And in the very pangs of death he cried,
Like to a dismal clangor heard from far,
'Warwick, revenge ! Brother, revenge my death !'
So, underneath the belly of their steeds,
That stained their fetlocks in his smoking blood,
The noble gentleman gave up the ghost.

WARWICK
Then let the earth be drunken with our blood !
I'll kill my horse, because I will not fly.
Why stand we like soft-hearted women here,
26  Wailing our losses, whiles the foe doth rage,
27  And look upon, as if the tragedy
Were played in jest by counterfeiting actors ?
Here on my knee I vow to God above
I'll never pause again, never stand still,
Till either death hath closed these eyes of mine
Or fortune given me measure of revenge.

EDWARD
O Warwick, I do bend my knee with thine
And in this vow do chain my soul to thine.
And ere my knee rise from the earth's cold face,
I throw my hands, mine eyes, my heart to thee,
Thou setter up and plucker down of kings,
38  Beseeching thee (if with thy will it stands)
That to my foes this body must be prey,
Yet that thy brazen gates of heaven may ope
And give sweet passage to my sinful soul.
Now, lords, take leave until we meet again,
Where'er it be, in heaven or in earth.

RICHARD
Brother, give me thy hand ; and, gentle Warwick,
Let me embrace thee in my weary arms.
I, that did never weep, now melt with woe

---

5 *spite of spite* come what may   7 *sun* i.e. good fortune (with allusion
to the Yorkist sun device)   8 *hap* fortune   12 *Bootless* worthless, hopeless   13 *shun* avoid   15 *Thy brother's blood* (a reference to the 'Bastard
of Salisbury,' Warwick's half-brother, killed at Ferrybridge)   16 *Broached*
set flowing   26 *whiles* while   27 *upon* on   38 *stands* agrees   56 *Forslow* delay
II, iv   1 *singled* chosen one from the herd (a hunting term)   4 *environed*
surrounded   12 *chase* prey
II, v   3 *of* on (for warmth)   13 *fell* cruel   14 *on this molehill* (see I, iv,
67n.)   22 *swain* countryman   24 *dials quaintly* sundials artfully (perhaps
alluding to the shepherds' practise of cutting sundials in the turf of hill-
sides)

---

That winter should cut off our springtime so.

WARWICK
Away, away ! Once more, sweet lords, farewell.

CLARENCE
Yet let us all together to our troops,
And give them leave to fly that will not stay,
And call them pillars that will stand to us ;
And, if we thrive, promise them such rewards
As victors wear at the Olympian games.
This may plant courage in their quailing breasts ;
For yet is hope of life and victory.
Forslow no longer ! Make we hence amain !      56
   *Exeunt.*

   *Excursions. Enter Richard [at one door] and*      II, iv
   *Clifford [at the other].*

RICHARD
Now, Clifford, I have singled thee alone.      1
Suppose this arm is for the Duke of York,
And this for Rutland – both bound to revenge,
Wert thou environed with a brazen wall.      4

CLIFFORD
Now, Richard, I am with thee here alone.
This is the hand that stabbed thy father York,
And this the hand that slew thy brother Rutland !
And here's the heart that triumphs in their death
And cheers these hands that slew thy sire and brother
To execute the like upon thyself.
And so have at thee !
   *They fight. Warwick comes. Clifford flies.*

RICHARD
Nay, Warwick, single out some other chase,      12
For I myself will hunt this wolf to death.      *Exeunt.*

   *Alarum. Enter King Henry alone.*      II, v

KING HENRY
This battle fares like to the morning's war,
When dying clouds contend with growing light,
What time the shepherd, blowing of his nails,      3
Can neither call it perfect day nor night.
Now sways it this way, like a mighty sea
Forced by the tide to combat with the wind ;
Now sways it that way, like the selfsame sea
Forced to retire by fury of the wind.
Sometime the flood prevails, and then the wind ;
Now one the better, then another best ;
Both tugging to be victors, breast to breast,
Yet neither conqueror nor conquerèd.
So is the equal poise of this fell war.      13
Here on this molehill will I sit me down.      14
To whom God will, there be the victory.
For Margaret my queen, and Clifford too,
Have chid me from the battle, swearing both
They prosper best of all when I am thence.
Would I were dead, if God's good will were so,
For what is in this world but grief and woe ?
O God ! methinks it were a happy life
To be no better than a homely swain ;      22
To sit upon a hill, as I do now,
To carve out dials quaintly, point by point,      24
Thereby to see the minutes how they run –
How many makes the hour full complete,
How many hours brings about the day,
How many days will finish up the year,
How many years a mortal man may live ;
When this is known, then to divide the times –

So many hours must I tend my flock,
So many hours must I take my rest,
33 So many hours must I contemplate,
34 So many hours must I sport myself;
So many days my ewes have been with young,
36 So many weeks ere the poor fools will ean,
So many months ere I shall shear the fleece.
So minutes, hours, days, weeks, months, and years,
39 Passed over to the end they were created,
Would bring white hairs unto a quiet grave.
Ah, what a life were this! how sweet, how lovely!
Gives not the hawthorn bush a sweeter shade
43 To shepherds looking on their silly sheep
Than doth a rich embroidered canopy
To kings that fear their subjects' treachery?
O yes, it doth, a thousandfold it doth.
And to conclude, the shepherd's homely curds,
His cold thin drink out of his leather bottle,
49 His wonted sleep under a fresh tree's shade,
All which secure and sweetly he enjoys,
51 Is far beyond a prince's delicates,
His viands sparkling in a golden cup,
53 His body couchèd in a curious bed,
When care, mistrust, and treason waits on him.

     *Alarum. Enter a Son that hath killed his father,*
     *at one door [bearing the body in his arms].*

   SON
Ill blows the wind that profits nobody.
This man whom hand to hand I slew in fight
57 May be possessèd with some store of crowns;
58 And I that, haply, take them from him now
May yet, ere night, yield both my life and them
To some man else, as this dead man doth me.
Who's this? O God! It is my father's face,
62 Whom in this conflict I, unwares, have killed.
63 O heavy times, begetting such events.
64 From London by the king was I pressed forth;
My father, being the Earl of Warwick's man,
Came on the part of York, pressed by his master;
And I, who at his hands received my life,
Have by my hands of life bereavèd him.
Pardon me, God, I knew not what I did.
And pardon, father, for I knew not thee.
My tears shall wipe away these bloody marks;
And no more words till they have flowed their fill.

   KING HENRY
O piteous spectacle, O bloody times!
Whiles lions war and battle for their dens,
75 Poor harmless lambs abide their enmity.
Weep, wretched man, I'll aid thee tear for tear;
And let our hearts and eyes, like civil war,
78 Be blind with tears and break o'ercharged with grief.

     *Enter, at another door, a Father that hath killed*
     *his son, bearing of his son.*

   FATHER
Thou that so stoutly hast resisted me,
Give me thy gold, if thou hast any gold;
For I have bought it with an hundred blows.
But let me see. Is this our foeman's face?
Ah, no, no, no! It is mine only son!
Ah, boy, if any life be left in thee,
Throw up thine eye. See, see what show'rs arise,
Blown with the windy tempest of my heart
Upon thy wounds, that kills mine eye and heart.

O, pity, God, this miserable age.
What stratagems, how fell, how butcherly,    89
Erroneous, mutinous, and unnatural,    90
This deadly quarrel daily doth beget.
O boy! thy father gave thee life too soon,
And hath bereft thee of thy life too late.    93

   KING HENRY
Woe above woe, grief more than common grief;
O that my death would stay these ruthful deeds!    95
O, pity, pity, gentle heaven, pity!
The red rose and the white are on his face,
The fatal colors of our striving houses.
The one his purple blood right well resembles;
The other his pale cheeks, methinks, presenteth.    100
Wither one rose, and let the other flourish.
If you contend, a thousand lives must wither.

   SON
How will my mother for a father's death
Take on with me, and ne'er be satisfied.    104

   FATHER
How will my wife for slaughter of my son
Shed seas of tears, and ne'er be satisfied.

   KING HENRY
How will the country for these woeful chances
Misthink the king, and not be satisfied.    108

   SON
Was ever son so rued a father's death?

   FATHER
Was ever father so bemoaned his son?

   KING HENRY
Was ever king so grieved for subject's woe?
Much is your sorrow; mine ten times so much.

   SON
I'll bear thee hence, where I may weep my fill.
               *[Exit with the body.]*

   FATHER
These arms of mine shall be thy winding sheet;
My heart, sweet boy, shall be thy sepulchre,
For from my heart thine image ne'er shall go.
My sighing breast shall be thy funeral bell;
And so obsequious will thy father be,    118
Even for the loss of thee, having no more,
As Priam was for all his valiant sons.    120
I'll bear thee hence, and let them fight that will,
For I have murdered where I should not kill.
               *Exit [with the body].*

   KING HENRY
Sad-hearted men, much overgone with care,    123
Here sits a king more woeful than you are.
     *Alarums. Excursions. Enter the Queen [Margaret],*
     *the Prince, and Exeter.*

   PRINCE
Fly, father, fly! for all your friends are fled
And Warwick rages like a chafèd bull.    126

33 *contemplate* meditate, pray   34 *sport* amuse   36 *ean* give birth   39 *end they* end for which they   43 *silly* innocent   49 *wonted* accustomed   51 *delicates* dainty foods   53 *curious* (1) elaborately wrought, (2) full of cares   57 *crowns* money   58 *haply* by chance   62 *unwares* unknowingly   63 *heavy* miserable   64 *pressed* impressed, drafted   75 *abide* endure   78 *o'ercharged* overfilled   89 *stratagems* bloody acts; *fell* cruel   90 *Erroneous* criminal   93 *late* recently   95 *ruthful* pitiful   100 *presenteth* symbolizes   104 *Take on* be profoundly distressed; *satisfied* comforted   108 *Misthink* misunderstand, blame   118 *obsequious* dutiful in mourning   120 *Priam* king of Troy (whose fifty sons were killed defending the city)   123 *overgone* overcome   126 *chafèd* angry

Away! for death doth hold us in pursuit.

QUEEN MARGARET

128 Mount you, my lord. Toward Berwick post amain.
Edward and Richard, like a brace of greyhounds
Having the fearful flying hare in sight,
With fiery eyes, sparkling for very wrath,
And bloody steel grasped in their ireful hands,
Are at our backs; and therefore hence amain.

EXETER

Away! for vengeance comes along with them.
Nay, stay not to expostulate; make speed!
Or else come after. I'll away before.

KING HENRY

Nay, take me with thee, good sweet Exeter.
Not that I fear to stay, but love to go
Whither the queen intends. Forward, away!          *Exeunt.*

I, vi    *A loud alarum. Enter Clifford, wounded [with an
arrow in his neck].*

CLIFFORD

Here burns my candle out; ay, here it dies,
2 Which, whiles it lasted, gave King Henry light.
3 O Lancaster! I fear thy overthrow
More than my body's parting with my soul.
5 My love and fear glued many friends to thee,
6 And now I fall, thy tough commixture melts,
7 Impairing Henry, strength'ning misproud York.
[The common people swarm like summer flies;]
9 And whither fly the gnats but to the sun?
And who shines now but Henry's enemies?
11 O Phoebus, hadst thou never given consent
12 That Phaeton should check thy fiery steeds,
13 Thy burning car never had scorched the earth!
14 And, Henry, hadst thou swayed as kings should do,
Or as thy father and his father did,
Giving no ground unto the house of York,
17 They never then had sprung like summer flies;
I and ten thousand in this luckless realm
Had left no mourning widows for our death,
20 And thou this day hadst kept thy chair in peace.
21 For what doth cherish weeds but gentle air?
And what makes robbers bold but too much lenity?
23 Bootless are plaints and cureless are my wounds;
No way to fly, nor strength to hold out flight;
The foe is merciless and will not pity,
For at their hands I have deserved no pity.
The air hath got into my deadly wounds
And much effuse of blood doth make me faint.
Come, York and Richard, Warwick and the rest.
30 I stabbed your fathers' bosoms; split my breast.
*[Faints.]*
*Alarum and retreat. Enter Edward, Warwick,
Richard, and Soldiers, Montague, and Clarence.*

EDWARD

Now breathe we, lords. Good fortune bids us pause
And smooth the frowns of war with peaceful looks.
Some troops pursue the bloody-minded queen
That led calm Henry, though he were a king,
As doth a sail, filled with a fretting gust,          35
Command an argosy to stem the waves.          36
But thinks you, lords, the Clifford fled with them?

WARWICK

No, 'tis impossible he should escape;
For, though before his face I speak the words,
Your brother Richard marked him for the grave;
And wheresoe'er he is, he's surely dead.
*Clifford groans [and dies].*

EDWARD

Whose soul is that which takes her heavy leave?

RICHARD

A deadly groan, like life and death's departing.

EDWARD

See who it is, and now the battle's ended,
If friend or foe, let him be gently used.

RICHARD

Revoke that doom of mercy, for 'tis Clifford,          46
Who not contented that he lopped the branch
In hewing Rutland when his leaves put forth,
But set his murd'ring knife unto the root
From whence that tender spray did sweetly spring:
I mean our princely father, Duke of York.

WARWICK

From off the gates of York fetch down the head,
Your father's head, which Clifford placed there;
Instead whereof let this supply the room.          54
Measure for measure must be answerèd.

EDWARD

Bring forth that fatal screech owl to our house,          56
That nothing sung but death to us and ours.
Now death shall stop his dismal threat'ning sound
And his ill-boding tongue no more shall speak.          59

WARWICK

I think his understanding is bereft.          60
Speak, Clifford, dost thou know who speaks to thee?
Dark cloudy death o'ershades his beams of life,
And he nor sees, nor hears us what we say.          63

RICHARD

O, would he did! and so, perhaps, he doth.
'Tis but his policy to counterfeit,          65
Because he would avoid such bitter taunts
Which in the time of death he gave our father.

CLARENCE

If so thou think'st, vex him with eager words.          68

RICHARD

Clifford, ask mercy, and obtain no grace.

EDWARD

Clifford, repent in bootless penitence.

WARWICK

Clifford, devise excuses for thy faults.

CLARENCE

While we devise fell tortures for thy faults.          72

RICHARD

Thou didst love York, and I am son to York.

EDWARD

Thou pitied'st Rutland; I will pity thee.

CLARENCE

Where's Captain Margaret, to fence you now?          75

128 *Berwick* Berwick-on-Tweed, Northumberland; *post amain* ride speedily
II, vi    2 *whiles* while    3 *Lancaster* i.e. the house of Lancaster    5 *My . . .
fear* the love and respect I commanded    6 *commixture* compound    7 *Impairing* weakening; *misproud* unjustly proud    9 *sun* (another allusion to the
Yorkist sun device)    11 *Phoebus* Phoebus Apollo, the sun    12 *Phaeton* (see
I, iv, 33n.); *check* manage    13 *car* chariot    14 *swayed* ruled    17 *sprung*
multiplied    20 *chair* i.e. of state, throne    21 *cherish* foster    23 *Bootless*
useless    30 s.d. *retreat* a trumpet call – 'recall'    35 *fretting* (1) blowing in
gusts, (2) nagging    36 *argosy* large merchant ship    46 *doom* judgment    54
*this* i.e. Clifford's head; *supply the room* take the place    56 *screech owl* (a
bird of ill omen)    59 *ill-boding* foretelling ill    60 *understanding* consciousness    63 *nor . . . nor* neither . . . nor    65 *policy* stratagem    68 *eager* biting,
bitter    72 *fell* cruel    75 *fence* protect

WARWICK

76  They mock thee, Clifford. Swear as thou wast wont.

RICHARD

What, not an oath ? Nay, then the world goes hard
When Clifford cannot spare his friends an oath.
I know by that he's dead ; and, by my soul,
If this right hand would buy two hours' life,
That I (in all despite) might rail at him,
This hand should chop it off, and with the issuing blood
83  Stifle the villain whose unstanchèd thirst
York and young Rutland could not satisfy.

WARWICK

Ay, but he's dead. Off with the traitor's head
And rear it in the place your father's stands.
And now to London with triumphant march,
There to be crownèd England's royal king ;
From whence shall Warwick cut the sea to France
And ask the Lady Bona for thy queen.
91  So shalt thou sinew both these lands together ;
And, having France thy friend, thou shalt not dread
The scattered foe that hopes to rise again ;
For though they cannot greatly sting to hurt,
95  Yet look to have them buzz to offend thine ears.
First will I see the coronation,
And then to Brittany I'll cross the sea
To effect this marriage, so it please my lord.

EDWARD

Even as thou wilt, sweet Warwick, let it be ;
For in thy shoulder do I build my seat,
And never will I undertake the thing
Wherein thy counsel and consent is wanting.
Richard, I will create thee Duke of Gloucester ;
And George, of Clarence. Warwick, as ourself,
Shall do and undo as him pleaseth best.

RICHARD

Let me be Duke of Clarence, George of Gloucester ;
107  For Gloucester's dukedom is too ominous.

WARWICK

108  Tut, that's a foolish observation ;
Richard, be Duke of Gloucester. Now to London
To see these honors in possession.                    Exeunt.

*

III, i          Enter two Keepers with crossbows in their hands.

1. KEEPER

1   Under this thick-grown brake we'll shroud ourselves,
2   For through this laund anon the deer will come,
And in this covert will we make our stand,
4   Culling the principal of all the deer.

2. KEEPER

I'll stay above the hill, so both may shoot.

1. KEEPER

That cannot be ; the noise of thy crossbow
Will scare the herd, and so my shoot is lost.
8   Here stand we both and aim we at the best ;
9   And, for the time shall not seem tedious,
I'll tell thee what befell me on a day
11   In this self-place where now we mean to stand.

2. KEEPER

Here comes a man. Let's stay till he be past.
          Enter the King [Henry, disguised,] with a prayer
          book.

KING HENRY

From Scotland am I stol'n, even of pure love,          13
To greet mine own land with my wishful sight.          14
No, Harry, Harry, 'tis no land of thine ;
Thy place is filled, thy sceptre wrung from thee,
Thy balm washed off wherewith thou was anointed.
No bending knee will call thee Caesar now,
No humble suitors press to speak for right :          19
No, not a man comes for redress of thee ;          20
For how can I help them, and not myself ?

1. KEEPER

Ay, here's a deer whose skin 's a keeper's fee.          22
This is the quondam king. Let's seize upon him.          23

KING HENRY

Let me embrace thee, sour adversity,
For wise men say it is the wisest course.          25

2. KEEPER

Why linger we ? Let us lay hands upon him.

1. KEEPER

Forbear awhile. We'll hear a little more.

KING HENRY

My queen and son are gone to France for aid ;
And, as I hear, the great commanding Warwick
Is thither gone to crave the French king's sister
To wife for Edward. If this news be true,
Poor queen and son, your labor is but lost ;
For Warwick is a subtle orator
And Lewis a prince soon won with moving words.
By this account, then, Margaret may win him ;
For she's a woman to be pitied much.
Her sighs will make a batt'ry in his breast ;          37
Her tears will pierce into a marble heart ;
The tiger will be mild whiles she doth mourn,
And Nero will be tainted with remorse          40
To hear and see her plaints, her brinish tears.          41
Ay, but she's come to beg ; Warwick, to give ;
She on his left side, craving aid for Henry ;
He on his right, asking a wife for Edward.
She weeps, and says her Henry is deposed ;
He smiles, and says his Edward is installed ;
That she, poor wretch, for grief can speak no more,          47
While Warwick tells his title, smooths the wrong,          48
Inferreth arguments of mighty strength,          49
And in conclusion wins the king from her
With promise of his sister, and what else,          51
To strengthen and support King Edward's place.
O Margaret, thus 'twill be ; and thou, poor soul,
Art then forsaken, as thou went'st forlorn.

2. KEEPER

Say, what art thou that talk'st of kings and queens ?

76 wont accustomed  83 unstanchèd unquenchable  91 sinew join (as if
tied with sinew)  95 buzz circulate scandal  107 too ominous (because
the three immediately preceding Dukes of Gloucester had died violent
deaths. These were Humphrey, in 2 Henry VI ; Thomas of Woodstock,
often referred to in Richard II ; and Hugh Spenser, a favorite of Edward II.)
108 observation comment
III, i A forest glade near Scottish border  s.d. Keepers gamekeepers  1 brake
thicket  2 laund glade  4 Culling selecting  8 at the best as well as we can
9 for so that  11 self-place same place  13 even of precisely because of  14
wishful longing  19 speak for right beg for justice  20 of from  22 fee
perquisite  23 quondam former  25 it i.e. accepting adversity  37 batt'ry
breach  40 Nero (traditionally hard-hearted and cruel) ; tainted affected
41 brinish salty  47 That so that  48 tells his title explains Edward's claim
to the throne ; smooths glosses over  49 Inferreth adduces  51 and what
else i.e. and who knows what other promises

KING HENRY
More than I seem, and less than I was born to :
A man at least, for less I should not be ;
And men may talk of kings, and why not I ?
2. KEEPER
Ay, but thou talk'st as if thou wert a king.
KING HENRY
Why, so I am in mind, and that's enough.
2. KEEPER
But if thou be a king, where is thy crown ?
KING HENRY
My crown is in my heart, not on my head ;
63   Not decked with diamonds and Indian stones,
Nor to be seen. My crown is called content ;
A crown it is that seldom kings enjoy.
2. KEEPER
Well, if you be a king crowned with content,
Your crown content and you must be contented
To go along with us ; for, as we think,
You are the king King Edward hath deposed ;
And we his subjects, sworn in all allegiance,
Will apprehend you as his enemy.
KING HENRY
But did you never swear, and break an oath ?
2. KEEPER
No, never such an oath ; nor will not now.
KING HENRY
Where did you dwell when I was King of England ?
2. KEEPER
Here in this country where we now remain.
KING HENRY
I was anointed king at nine months old ;
My father and my grandfather were kings ;
And you were sworn true subjects unto me ;
And tell me then, have you not broke your oaths ?
1. KEEPER
No ;
81   For we were subjects but while you were king.
KING HENRY
Why, am I dead ? Do I not breathe a man ?
Ah, simple men, you know not what you swear.
Look, as I blow this feather from my face
And as the air blows it to me again,
Obeying with my wind when I do blow
And yielding to another when it blows,
Commanded always by the greater gust –
Such is the lightness of you common men.
90   But do not break your oaths ; for of that sin
My mild entreaty shall not make you guilty.
Go where you will, the king shall be commanded ;
And be you kings. Command, and I'll obey.
1. KEEPER
We are true subjects to the king, King Edward.

KING HENRY
So would you be again to Henry
If he were seated as King Edward is.
1. KEEPER
We charge you, in God's name and the king's,
To go with us unto the officers.
KING HENRY
In God's name, lead. Your king's name be obeyed ;
And what God will, that let your king perform ;    100
And what he will, I humbly yield unto.    *Exeunt.*

\*

*Enter King Edward, [Richard of] Gloucester,*   III, ii
*Clarence, Lady Grey [a widow].*
KING EDWARD
Brother of Gloucester, at Saint Albans field
This lady's husband, Sir Richard Grey, was slain,    2
His lands then seized on by the conqueror.
Her suit is now to repossess those lands ;
Which we in justice cannot well deny,
Because in quarrel of the house of York
The worthy gentleman did lose his life.
RICHARD
Your highness shall do well to grant her suit.
It were dishonor to deny it her.
KING EDWARD
It were no less ; but yet I'll make a pause.
RICHARD *[aside to Clarence]*
Yea, is it so ?
I see the lady hath a thing to grant
Before the king will grant her humble suit.
CLARENCE *[aside to Richard]*
He knows the game. How true he keeps the wind.    14
RICHARD *[aside to Clarence]*
Silence.
KING EDWARD
Widow, we will consider of your suit ;
And come some other time to know our mind.
WIDOW
Right gracious lord, I cannot brook delay.    18
May it please your highness to resolve me now,    19
And what your pleasure is shall satisfy me.
RICHARD *[aside]*
Ay, widow ? Then I'll warrant you all your lands    21
An if what pleases him shall pleasure you.
Fight closer or, good faith, you'll catch a blow.    23
CLARENCE *[aside to Richard]*
I fear her not, unless she chance to fall.
RICHARD *[aside to Clarence]*
God forbid that, for he'll take vantages.
KING EDWARD
How many children hast thou, widow ? Tell me.
CLARENCE *[aside to Richard]*
I think he means to beg a child of her.    27
RICHARD *[aside to Clarence]*
Nay, then, whip me ; he'll rather give her two.    28
WIDOW
Three, my most gracious lord.
RICHARD *[aside]*
You shall have four if you'll be ruled by him.
KING EDWARD
'Twere pity they should lose their father's lands.

63 *Indian stones* gems (probably pearls)  81 *but* only
III, ii The royal palace in London  2 *Sir Richard Grey* (Lady Grey's
husband, actually Sir John, was killed at the second battle of St Albans,
where he fought for the Lancastrians. The facts are given correctly in
*Richard III*, I, iii, 126–29.)  14 *keeps the wind* hunts downwind, so as not to
alarm the game  18 *brook* endure  19 *resolve me* free me from uncertainty
21 *warrant* guarantee  23–25 *Fight closer . . . catch a blow . . . fall . . .
vantages* (all duelling terms, here used with obvious double meaning)  27
*beg . . . her* apply to her for a wardship, a source of profit if the child were
high-born (with bawdy overtones)  28 *whip me* (a mild imprecation ; or
perhaps, literally, for being so childish as to think so)

**WIDOW**
Be pitiful, dread lord, and grant it then.

**KING EDWARD**
33   Lords, give us leave. I'll try this widow's wit.

**RICHARD** *[aside]*
34   Ay, good leave have you; for you will have leave
Till youth take leave and leave you to the crutch.
*[Retires with Clarence.]*

**KING EDWARD**
Now tell me, madam, do you love your children?

**WIDOW**
Ay, full as dearly as I love myself.

**KING EDWARD**
And would you not do much to do them good?

**WIDOW**
To do them good I would sustain some harm.

**KING EDWARD**
Then get your husband's lands, to do them good.

**WIDOW**
Therefore I came unto your majesty.

**KING EDWARD**
I'll tell you how these lands are to be got.

**WIDOW**
So shall you bind me to your highness' service.

**KING EDWARD**
44   What service wilt thou do me if I give them?

**WIDOW**
What you command that rests in me to do.

**KING EDWARD**
46   But you will take exceptions to my boon.

**WIDOW**
47   No, gracious lord, except I cannot do it.

**KING EDWARD**
Ay, but thou canst do what I mean to ask.

**WIDOW**
Why, then I will do what your grace commands.

**RICHARD** *[aside to Clarence]*
50   He plies her hard, and much rain wears the marble.

**CLARENCE** *[aside to Richard]*
As red as fire? Nay then, her wax must melt.

**WIDOW**
Why stops my lord? Shall I not hear my task?

**KING EDWARD**
An easy task. 'Tis but to love a king.

**WIDOW**
That's soon performed, because I am a subject.

**KING EDWARD**
Why then, thy husband's lands I freely give thee.

**WIDOW**
I take my leave with many thousand thanks.

**RICHARD** *[aside to Clarence]*
The match is made. She seals it with a curtsy.

**KING EDWARD**
But stay thee. 'Tis the fruits of love I mean.

**WIDOW**
The fruits of love I mean, my loving liege.

**KING EDWARD**
Ay, but, I fear me, in another sense.
What love, think'st thou, I sue so much to get?

**WIDOW**
My love till death, my humble thanks, my prayers;
That love which virtue begs and virtue grants.

**KING EDWARD**
No, by my troth, I did not mean such love.

**WIDOW**
Why, then you mean not as I thought you did.

**KING EDWARD**
But now you partly may perceive my mind.

**WIDOW**
My mind will never grant what I perceive
Your highness aims at, if I aim aright.    68

**KING EDWARD**
To tell thee plain, I aim to lie with thee.

**WIDOW**
To tell you plain, I had rather lie in prison.

**KING EDWARD**
Why, then thou shalt not have thy husband's lands.

**WIDOW**
Why, then mine honesty shall be my dower;    72
For by that loss I will not purchase them.

**KING EDWARD**
Therein thou wrong'st thy children mightily.

**WIDOW**
Herein your highness wrongs both them and me.
But, mighty lord, this merry inclination
Accords not with the sadness of my suit.    77
Please you dismiss me, either with ay or no.

**KING EDWARD**
Ay, if thou wilt say ay to my request;
No, if thou dost say no to my demand.

**WIDOW**
Then, no, my lord. My suit is at an end.

**RICHARD** *[aside to Clarence]*
The widow likes him not; she knits her brows.

**CLARENCE** *[aside to Richard]*
He is the bluntest wooer in Christendom.

**KING EDWARD** *[aside]*
Her looks doth argue her replete with modesty;
Her words doth show her wit incomparable;
All her perfections challenge sovereignty.
One way or other, she is for a king;
And she shall be my love, or else my queen. –
Say that King Edward take thee for his queen?

**WIDOW**
'Tis better said than done, my gracious lord.
I am a subject fit to jest withal,
But far unfit to be a sovereign.

**KING EDWARD**
Sweet widow, by my state I swear to thee    93
I speak no more than what my soul intends;
And that is, to enjoy thee for my love.

**WIDOW**
And that is more than I will yield unto.
I know I am too mean to be your queen,
And yet too good to be your concubine.

**KING EDWARD**
You cavil, widow. I did mean my queen.    99

**WIDOW**
'Twill grieve your grace my sons should call you father.

**KING EDWARD**
No more than when my daughters call thee mother.

---

33 *give us leave* pardon us (i.e. please go away)   34–35 *good leave . . . have leave . . . take leave . . . leave you to* willing pardon . . . take liberties . . . bid farewell . . . pass you on to (because you will be too old to be amorous)   44 *service* (1) duty, (2) sexual attention   46 *boon* request   47 *except* unless   50 *plies* urges   68 *aim* guess   72 *honesty* virtue   77 *sadness* seriousness   93 *state* kingship   99 *cavil* make frivolous objections

Thou art a widow, and thou hast some children;
And, by God's Mother, I, being but a bachelor,
104 Have other some. Why, 'tis a happy thing
To be the father unto many sons.
Answer no more, for thou shalt be my queen.

RICHARD *[aside to Clarence]*
107 The ghostly father now hath done his shrift.

CLARENCE *[aside to Richard]*
108 When he was made a shriver, 'twas for shift.

KING EDWARD
109 Brothers, you muse what chat we two have had.

RICHARD
110 The widow likes it not, for she looks very sad.

KING EDWARD
You'ld think it strange if I should marry her.

CLARENCE
To who, my lord?

KING EDWARD      Why, Clarence, to myself.

RICHARD
113 That would be ten days' wonder at the least.

CLARENCE
That's a day longer than a wonder lasts.

RICHARD
By so much is the wonder in extremes.

KING EDWARD
Well, jest on, brothers. I can tell you both
Her suit is granted for her husband's lands.
      *Enter a Nobleman.*

NOBLEMAN
My gracious lord, Henry your foe is taken
And brought your prisoner to your palace gate.

KING EDWARD
See that he be conveyed unto the Tower.
And go we, brothers, to the man that took him
122 To question of his apprehension.
Widow, go you along. Lords, use her honorably.
      *Exeunt. Manet Richard.*

RICHARD
Ay, Edward will use women honorably.
Would he were wasted, marrow, bones, and all,
That from his loins no hopeful branch may spring
127 To cross me from the golden time I look for.
And yet, between my soul's desire and me –
The lustful Edward's title buried –

Is Clarence, Henry, and his son young Edward,
And all the unlooked-for issue of their bodies,    131
To take their rooms ere I can place myself.    132
A cold premeditation for my purpose.    133
Why, then I do but dream on sovereignty,
Like one that stands upon a promontory
And spies a far-off shore where he would tread,
Wishing his foot were equal with his eye,
And chides the sea that sunders him from thence,    137
Saying he'll lade it dry to have his way:    139
So do I wish the crown, being so far off;
And so I chide the means that keeps me from it,    141
And so, I say, I'll cut the causes off,
Flattering me with impossibilities.    143
My eye 's too quick, my heart o'erweens too much,    144
Unless my hand and strength could equal them.
Well, say there is no kingdom then for Richard:
What other pleasure can the world afford?
I'll make my heaven in a lady's lap
And deck my body in gay ornaments
And witch sweet ladies with my words and looks.    150
O miserable thought, and more unlikely
Than to accomplish twenty golden crowns.
Why, love forswore me in my mother's womb;
And, for I should not deal in her soft laws,    154
She did corrupt frail nature with some bribe
To shrink mine arm up like a withered shrub;
To make an envious mountain on my back,    157
Where sits deformity to mock my body;
To shape my legs of an unequal size;
To disproportion me in every part,
Like to a chaos, or an unlicked bear-whelp,    161
That carries no impression like the dam.    162
And am I then a man to be beloved?
O monstrous fault to harbor such a thought.
Then, since this earth affords no joy to me
But to command, to check, to o'erbear such    166
As are of better person than myself,    167
I'll make my heaven to dream upon the crown
And, whiles I live, t' account this world but hell
Until my misshaped trunk that bears this head
Be round impalèd with a glorious crown.    171
And yet I know not how to get the crown,
For many lives stand between me and home;    173
And I – like one lost in a thorny wood,
That rents the thorns and is rent with the thorns,
Seeking a way and straying from the way,
Not knowing how to find the open air
But toiling desperately to find it out –
Torment myself to catch the English crown;
And from that torment I will free myself
Or hew my way out with a bloody axe.
Why, I can smile, and murder whiles I smile,
And cry 'Content!' to that which grieves my heart,
And wet my cheeks with artificial tears,
And frame my face to all occasions.
I'll drown more sailors than the mermaid shall;    186
I'll slay more gazers than the basilisk;    187
I'll play the orator as well as Nestor,    188
Deceive more slily than Ulysses could    189
And, like a Sinon, take another Troy.    190
I can add colors to the chameleon,
Change shapes with Proteus for advantages,    192
And set the murderous Machiavel to school.    193

104 *other some* some others   107 *ghostly father* i.e. confessor ('ghostly': spiritual); *done his shrift* finished hearing confession   108 *for shift* (1) as a trick to serve some purpose, (2) for the sake of a chemise (to say that a woman was 'shriven to her shift' was a common off-color joke meaning that she had been seduced)   109 *muse* wonder   110 *sad* serious   113 *ten days' wonder* i.e. a most marvellous thing (proverbially, a novelty attracts for only nine days)   122 *question ... apprehension* inquire about his capture   127 *cross me from* interfere with my attaining   131 *unlooked-for* unanticipated   132 *rooms* places   133 *cold premeditation* discouraging forecast   137 *equal with* as capable as   139 *lade* ladle, scoop   141 *means* obstacles   143 *me* myself   144 *o'erweens* presumes   150 *witch* bewitch   154 *for* so that   157 *envious* detested   161 *chaos* unformed mass; *unlicked bear-whelp* (bear cubs were supposedly born as lumps of matter and licked into shape by their dams)   162 *impression* shape   166 *check* rebuke; *o'erbear* dominate   167 *of better person* more personable   171 *impalèd* encircled   173 *home* i.e. my goal   186 *mermaid* siren   187 *basilisk* a fabulous serpent whose look killed   188 *Nestor* aged Greek warrior at the siege of Troy, noted for his wisdom   189 *Ulysses* Greek warrior, subject of the *Odyssey*, noted for his craft   190 *Sinon* the Greek who persuaded the Trojans to bring the Wooden Horse into the city   192 *Proteus* a sea-deity who, when captured, changed his shape; *for advantages* as my purpose dictates   193 *Machiavel* Machiavelli, Italian political philosopher, known in England as an advocate of guile and ruthlessness in the attainment of political objectives

Can I do this, and cannot get a crown?
Tut, were it farther off, I'll pluck it down.                    *Exit.*

\*

III, iii          *Flourish. Enter Lewis the French King, his sister*
                 *Bona, his Admiral, called Bourbon; Prince Edward,*
                 *Queen Margaret, and the Earl of Oxford. Lewis*
                 *sits, and riseth up again.*

LEWIS
Fair Queen of England, worthy Margaret,
2    Sit down with us. It ill befits thy state
And birth that thou shouldst stand while Lewis doth sit.
QUEEN MARGARET
No, mighty King of France. Now Margaret
5    Must strike her sail, and learn awhile to serve
Where kings command. I was, I must confess,
7    Great Albion's queen in former golden days;
But now mischance hath trod my title down
And with dishonor laid me on the ground,
Where I must take like seat unto my fortune
And to my humble seat conform myself.
LEWIS
Why, say, fair queen, whence springs this deep despair?
QUEEN MARGARET
From such a cause as fills mine eyes with tears
And stops my tongue, while heart is drowned in cares.
LEWIS
15   Whate'er it be, be thou still like thyself,
And sit thee by our side. *Seats her by him.* Yield not thy
     neck
To fortune's yoke – but let thy dauntless mind
Still ride in triumph over all mischance.
Be plain, Queen Margaret, and tell thy grief.
20   It shall be eased if France can yield relief.
QUEEN MARGARET
Those gracious words revive my drooping thoughts
And give my tongue-tied sorrows leave to speak.
Now therefore be it known to noble Lewis
That Henry, sole possessor of my love,
25   Is, of a king, become a banished man
26   And forced to live in Scotland a forlorn;
While proud ambitious Edward Duke of York
Usurps the regal title and the seat
Of England's true anointed lawful king.
This is the cause that I, poor Margaret,
With this my son, Prince Edward, Henry's heir,
Am come to crave thy just and lawful aid;
And if thou fail us, all our hope is done.
Scotland hath will to help, but cannot help;
Our people and our peers are both misled,
Our treasure seized, our soldiers put to flight,
And (as thou seest) ourselves in heavy plight.
LEWIS
Renowned queen, with patience calm the storm
39   While we bethink a means to break it off.
QUEEN MARGARET
40   The more we stay, the stronger grows our foe.
LEWIS
The more I stay, the more I'll succor thee.
QUEEN MARGARET
42   O, but impatience waiteth on true sorrow.
And see where comes the breeder of my sorrow.
                    *Enter Warwick.*

LEWIS
What's he approacheth boldly to our presence?
QUEEN MARGARET
Our Earl of Warwick, Edward's greatest friend.
LEWIS
Welcome, brave Warwick, what brings thee to France?
               *He descends. She ariseth.*
QUEEN MARGARET [*aside*]
Ay, now begins a second storm to rise;
For this is he that moves both wind and tide.
WARWICK
From worthy Edward, King of Albion,
My lord and sovereign and thy vowèd friend,
I come, in kindness and unfeignèd love,
First to do greetings to thy royal person,
And then to crave a league of amity,
And lastly to confirm that amity
With nuptial knot, if thou vouchsafe to grant
That virtuous Lady Bona, thy fair sister,                    56
To England's king in lawful marriage.
QUEEN MARGARET [*aside*]
If that go forward, Henry's hope is done.
WARWICK [*speaking to Bona*]
And, gracious madam, in our king's behalf,
I am commanded, with your leave and favor,
Humbly to kiss your hand, and with my tongue
To tell the passion of my sovereign's heart;
Where fame, late ent'ring at his heedful ears,
Hath placed thy beauty's image and thy virtue.
QUEEN MARGARET
King Lewis, and Lady Bona, hear me speak
Before you answer Warwick. His demand
Springs not from Edward's well-meant honest love,
But from deceit, bred by necessity;
For how can tyrants safely govern home
Unless abroad they purchase great alliance?                    70
To prove him tyrant this reason may suffice,
That Henry liveth still; but were he dead,
Yet here Prince Edward stands, King Henry's son.
Look, therefore, Lewis, that by this league and marriage
Thou draw not on thy danger and dishonor;
For though usurpers sway the rule awhile,                    76
Yet heav'ns are just and time suppresseth wrongs.
WARWICK
Injurious Margaret!                    78
PRINCE                    And why not queen?
WARWICK
Because thy father Henry did usurp,
And thou no more art prince than she is queen.
OXFORD
Then Warwick disannuls great John of Gaunt,                    81
Which did subdue the greatest part of Spain;                    82
And after John of Gaunt, Henry the Fourth,
Whose wisdom was a mirror to the wisest;
And after that wise prince, Henry the Fifth,
Who by his prowess conquerèd all France.

III, iii The royal palace in France   2 *state* status   5 *strike her sail* lower
her sail (a mark of deference rendered at sea to a senior)   7 *Albion's*
England's   15 *be thou . . . thyself* i.e. behave always in a way appropriate
to your greatness   20 *France* the King of France   25 *of* instead of   26
*forlorn* outcast   39 *break it off* stop it   40 *stay* delay   42 *waiteth on* attends
56 *sister* i.e. sister-in-law   76 *sway* exercise   78 *Injurious* insulting   81
*disannuls* cancels out   82 *Which . . . Spain* (Gaunt did campaign in Spain,
but his successes were minor)

From these our Henry lineally descends.

WARWICK
Oxford, how haps it in this smooth discourse
You told not how Henry the Sixth hath lost
All that which Henry the Fifth had gotten?
Methinks these peers of France should smile at that.
92 But for the rest : you tell a pedigree
Of threescore and two years – a silly time
To make prescription for a kingdom's worth.

OXFORD
Why, Warwick, canst thou speak against thy liege,
Whom thou obeyèd'st thirty and six years,
And not bewray thy treason with a blush?

WARWICK
Can Oxford, that did ever fence the right,
99 Now buckler falsehood with a pedigree?
For shame! Leave Henry and call Edward king.

OXFORD
101 Call him my king by whose injurious doom
102 My elder brother, the Lord Aubrey Vere,
103 Was done to death? and more than so, my father,
Even in the downfall of his mellowed years,
When nature brought him to the door of death?
No, Warwick, no! While life upholds this arm,
This arm upholds the house of Lancaster.

WARWICK
And I the house of York.

LEWIS
Queen Margaret, Prince Edward, and Oxford,
Vouchsafe at our request to stand aside
While I use further conference with Warwick.
*They stand aloof.*

QUEEN MARGARET
Heavens grant that Warwick's words bewitch him not.

LEWIS
Now, Warwick, tell me, even upon thy conscience,
Is Edward your true king? For I were loath
To link with him that were not lawful chosen.

WARWICK
Thereon I pawn my credit and mine honor.

LEWIS
But is he gracious in the people's eye?

WARWICK
The more that Henry was unfortunate.

LEWIS
Then further : all dissembling set aside,
Tell me for truth the measure of his love
Unto our sister Bona.

WARWICK                    Such it seems
122 As may beseem a monarch like himself.
Myself have often heard him say and swear
124 That this his love was an eternal plant,

Whereof the root was fixed in virtue's ground,
The leaves and fruit maintained with beauty's sun,
Exempt from envy, but not from disdain,          127
Unless the Lady Bona quit his pain.

LEWIS
Now, sister, let us hear your firm resolve.

BONA
Your grant, or your denial, shall be mine.        130
*(Speaks to Warwick)*
Yet I confess that often ere this day,
When I have heard your king's desert recounted,   132
Mine ear hath tempted judgment to desire.

LEWIS
Then, Warwick, thus : our sister shall be Edward's,
And now forthwith shall articles be drawn
Touching the jointure that your king must make,   136
Which with her dowry shall be counterpoised.      137
Draw near, Queen Margaret, and be a witness
That Bona shall be wife to the English king.

PRINCE
To Edward, but not to the English king.

QUEEN MARGARET
Deceitful Warwick, it was thy device
By this alliance to make void my suit.
Before thy coming Lewis was Henry's friend.

LEWIS
And still is friend to him, and Margaret.
But if your title to the crown be weak,
As may appear by Edward's good success,
Then 'tis but reason that I be released
From giving aid which late I promisèd.
Yet shall you have all kindness at my hand
That your estate requires and mine can yield.

WARWICK
Henry now lives in Scotland at his ease,
Where having nothing, nothing can he lose.
And as for you yourself, our quondam queen,       153
You have a father able to maintain you,
And better 'twere you troubled him than France.

QUEEN MARGARET
Peace, impudent and shameless Warwick, peace,
Proud setter up and puller down of kings,
I will not hence till with my talk and tears
(Both full of truth) I make King Lewis behold
Thy sly conveyance and thy lord's false love ;    160
For both of you are birds of selfsame feather.    161
*Post blowing a horn within.*

LEWIS
Warwick, this is some post to us or thee.
*Enter the Post.*

POST [speaks to Warwick]
My lord ambassador, these letters are for you,
Sent from your brother, Marquess Montague ;
[To Lewis]
These from our king unto your majesty ;
[To Margaret]
And, madam, these for you : from whom I know not.
*They all read their letters.*

OXFORD
I like it well that our fair queen and mistress
Smiles at her news, while Warwick frowns at his.

PRINCE
Nay, mark how Lewis stamps as he were nettled.
I hope all's for the best.

---

92–94 *you . . . worth* i.e. the line you describe runs for sixty-two years, a ridiculously short time upon which to base a claim sanctioned by custom (*prescription*) to the wealth and honor of kingship  99 *buckler* shield  101 *injurious doom* unjust judgment  102 *Lord Aubrey Vere* (Holinshed reports that in 1462 the 12th Earl of Oxford and Lord Aubrey Vere, his eldest son, were accused of treason and executed)  103 *more than so* yet more  122 *beseem* befit  124 *eternal* i.e. heavenly  127–28 *Exempt . . . pain* i.e. Edward's love will be free from the effects of sharp criticism (*envy*) of Lady Bona (because of her coldness to his suit), but it will suffer from rejection (*disdain*) unless she reward his passion for her (*quit his pain*)  130 *grant* concurrence  132 *desert* merit  136 *jointure* marriage settlement  137 *counterpoised* matched  153 *quondam* former  160 *conveyance* trickery  161 s.d. *Post* dispatch-rider

**LEWIS**
Warwick, what are thy news? and yours, fair queen?

**QUEEN MARGARET**
Mine such as fill my heart with unhoped joys.

**WARWICK**
Mine full of sorrow and heart's discontent.

**LEWIS**
What? Has your king married the Lady Grey?
175   And now, to soothe your forgery and his,
Sends me a paper to persuade me patience?
Is this th' alliance that he seeks with France?
Dare he presume to scorn us in this manner?

**QUEEN MARGARET**
I told your majesty as much before.
This proveth Edward's love and Warwick's honesty.

**WARWICK**
King Lewis, I here protest in sight of heaven
And by the hope I have of heavenly bliss
That I am clear from this misdeed of Edward's —
No more my king, for he dishonors me,
But most himself, if he could see his shame.
Did I forget that by the House of York
187   My father came untimely to his death?
188   Did I let pass th' abuse done to my niece?
189   Did I impale him with the regal crown?
Did I put Henry from his native right?
191   And am I guerdoned at the last with shame?
Shame on himself, for my desert is honor;
And to repair my honor, lost for him,
I here renounce him and return to Henry.
My noble queen, let former grudges pass,
And henceforth I am thy true servitor.
I will revenge his wrong to Lady Bona
And replant Henry in his former state.

**QUEEN MARGARET**
Warwick, these words have turned my hate to love,
And I forgive and quite forget old faults
And joy that thou becom'st King Henry's friend.

**WARWICK**
So much his friend, ay, his unfeignèd friend,
That, if King Lewis vouchsafe to furnish us
With some few bands of chosen soldiers,
I'll undertake to land them on our coast
And force the tyrant from his seat by war.
'Tis not his new-made bride shall succor him.
And as for Clarence, as my letters tell me,
He's very likely now to fall from him
210   For matching more for wanton lust than honor
Or than for strength and safety of our country.

**BONA**
Dear brother, how shall Bona be revenged
But by thy help to this distressèd queen?

**QUEEN MARGARET**
Renownèd prince, how shall poor Henry live
Unless thou rescue him from foul despair?

**BONA**
My quarrel and this English queen's are one.

**WARWICK**
And mine, fair Lady Bona, joins with yours.

**LEWIS**
And mine with hers and thine and Margaret's.
Therefore, at last, I firmly am resolved
You shall have aid.

**QUEEN MARGARET**
Let me give humble thanks for all at once.

**LEWIS**
Then, England's messenger, return in post
And tell false Edward, thy supposèd king,
That Lewis of France is sending over masquers   224
To revel it with him and his new bride.
Thou seest what's passed. Go fear thy king withal.   226

**BONA**
Tell him, in hope he'll prove a widower shortly,
I'll wear the willow garland for his sake.   228

**QUEEN MARGARET**
Tell him my mourning weeds are laid aside
And I am ready to put armor on.

**WARWICK**
Tell him from me that he hath done me wrong
And therefore I'll uncrown him ere't be long.
There's thy reward. Be gone.     *Exit Post.*

**LEWIS**     But, Warwick,
Thou and Oxford, with five thousand men,
Shall cross the seas and bid false Edward battle;
And as occasion serves, this noble queen
And prince shall follow with a fresh supply.
Yet, ere thou go, but answer me one doubt:
What pledge have we of thy firm loyalty?

**WARWICK**
This shall assure my constant loyalty,
That if our queen and this young prince agree,
I'll join mine eldest daughter, and my joy,   242
To him forthwith in holy wedlock bands.

**QUEEN MARGARET**
Yes, I agree, and thank you for your motion.   244
Son Edward, she is fair and virtuous.
Therefore delay not; give thy hand to Warwick
And, with thy hand, thy faith irrevocable
That only Warwick's daughter shall be thine.

**PRINCE**
Yes, I accept her, for she well deserves it,
And here to pledge my vow I give my hand.
*He gives his hand to Warwick.*

**LEWIS**
Why stay we now? Those soldiers shall be levied,
And thou, Lord Bourbon, our High Admiral,
Shall waft them over with our royal fleet.   253
I long till Edward fall by war's mischance
For mocking marriage with a dame of France.
*Exeunt. Manet Warwick.*

**WARWICK**
I came from Edward as ambassador,
But I return his sworn and mortal foe.
Matter of marriage was the charge he gave me,
But dreadful war shall answer his demand.
Had he none else to make a stale but me?   260

---

175 *forgery* deceit   187 *My . . . death* (according to the chronicles, Salisbury, Warwick's father, was captured by the Lancastrians at Wakefield and beheaded, as was York)   188 *Did . . . niece* (Holinshed reports that Edward 'would have defloured' Warwick's 'daughter or his neece')   189 *impale him* encircle his brow   191 *guerdoned* rewarded   210 *matching* marrying   224 *masquers* participants in a courtly dramatic performance or revel (ironically)   226 *fear* frighten; *withal* with it   228 *willow garland* (symbol of rejected love)   242 *eldest daughter* (actually his younger daughter, Anne, as his elder daughter, Isabella, is to marry Clarence. In the chronicles, Isabella and Clarence are already married at this time.)   244 *motion* offer   253 *waft* transport by water   260 *stale* dupe

Then none but I shall turn his jest to sorrow.
I was the chief that raised him to the crown
And I'll be chief to bring him down again ;
Not that I pity Henry's misery,
But seek revenge on Edward's mockery.                    *Exit.*

\*

**V, i**          *Enter Richard, Clarence, Somerset, and Montague.*

RICHARD
Now tell me, brother Clarence, what think you
Of this new marriage with the Lady Grey ?
Hath not our brother made a worthy choice ?

CLARENCE
Alas, you know 'tis far from hence to France,
5    How could he stay till Warwick made return ?

SOMERSET
My lords, forbear this talk. Here comes the king.
        *Flourish. Enter King Edward, Lady Grey [as*
        *Queen Elizabeth], Pembroke, Stafford, Hastings.*
        *Four stand on one side and four on the other.*

RICHARD
And his well-chosen bride.

CLARENCE
8    I mind to tell him plainly what I think.

KING EDWARD
Now, brother of Clarence, how like you our choice,
10    That you stand pensive, as half malcontent ?

CLARENCE
As well as Lewis of France or the Earl of Warwick,
Which are so weak of courage and in judgment
13    That they'll take no offense at our abuse.

KING EDWARD
Suppose they take offense without a cause :
They are but Lewis and Warwick ; I am Edward,
Your king and Warwick's, and must have my will.

RICHARD
And shall have your will, because our king.
Yet hasty marriage seldom proveth well.

KING EDWARD
Yea, brother Richard, are you offended too ?

RICHARD
Not I.
No, God forbid that I should wish them severed
Whom God hath joined together. Ay, and 'twere pity
To sunder them that yoke so well together.

KING EDWARD
24    Setting your scorns and your mislike aside,
Tell me some reason why the Lady Grey
Should not become my wife and England's queen.
And you too, Somerset, and Montague,
Speak freely what you think.

CLARENCE
Then this is mine opinion, that King Lewis
Becomes your enemy for mocking him
About the marriage of the Lady Bona.

RICHARD
And Warwick, doing what you gave in charge,
Is now dishonorèd by this new marriage.

KING EDWARD
What if both Lewis and Warwick be appeased
By such invention as I can devise ?                      35

MONTAGUE
Yet, to have joined with France in such alliance
Would more have strengthened this our commonwealth
'Gainst foreign storms than any home-bred marriage.

HASTINGS
Why, knows not Montague that of itself
England is safe, if true within itself ?

MONTAGUE
But the safer when 'tis backed with France.

HASTINGS
'Tis better using France than trusting France.
Let us be backed with God, and with the seas,
Which he hath giv'n for fence impregnable,
And with their helps only defend ourselves.
In them and in ourselves our safety lies.

CLARENCE
For this one speech Lord Hastings well deserves
To have the heir of the Lord Hungerford.

KING EDWARD
Ay, what of that ? It was my will and grant.
And for this once my will shall stand for law.

RICHARD
And yet methinks your grace hath not done well
To give the heir and daughter of Lord Scales
Unto the brother of your loving bride.                   53
She better would have fitted me or Clarence ;
But in your bride you bury brotherhood.

CLARENCE
Or else you would not have bestowed the heir
Of the Lord Bonville on your new wife's son              57
And leave your brothers to go speed elsewhere.           58

KING EDWARD
Alas, poor Clarence ! Is it for a wife
That thou art malcontent ? I will provide thee.

CLARENCE
In choosing for yourself you showed your judgment,
Which being shallow, you shall give me leave
To play the broker in mine own behalf ;                  63
And to that end I shortly mind to leave you.

KING EDWARD
Leave me or tarry, Edward will be king
And not be tied unto his brother's will.

QUEEN ELIZABETH
My lords, before it pleased his majesty
To raise my state to title of a queen,
Do me but right, and you must all confess
That I was not ignoble of descent,
And meaner than myself have had like fortune.
But as this title honors me and mine,
So your dislikes, to whom I would be pleasing,           73
Doth cloud my joys with danger and with sorrow.         74

KING EDWARD
My love, forbear to fawn upon their frowns.
What danger or what sorrow can befall thee
So long as Edward is thy constant friend
And their true sovereign, whom they must obey ?
Nay, whom they shall obey, and love thee too,

---

IV, i The royal palace in London   5 *stay* wait   8 *mind* intend   10 *malcontent* one disgusted with the world   13 *abuse* insult   24 *mislike* displeasure   35 *invention* plan   53 *brother . . . bride* i.e. Lord Rivers   57 *son*
i.e. Sir Thomas Grey, Marquess Dorset   58 *go speed* prosper (for themselves)   63 *broker* agent   73 *dislikes* disapproval   74 *danger* apprehension

Unless they seek for hatred at my hands ;
Which if they do, yet will I keep thee safe,
And they shall feel the vengeance of my wrath.

RICHARD *[aside]*
I hear ; yet say not much, but think the more.
    *Enter a Post.*

KING EDWARD
Now, messenger, what letters or what news
From France ?

POST
My sovereign liege, no letters, and few words,
But such as I, without your special pardon,
Dare not relate.

KING EDWARD
89   Go to, we pardon thee. Therefore, in brief,
90   Tell me their words as near as thou canst guess them.
What answer makes King Lewis unto our letters ?

POST
92   At my depart these were his very words :
'Go tell false Edward, thy supposèd king,
That Lewis of France is sending over masquers
To revel it with him and his new bride.'

KING EDWARD
96   Is Lewis so brave ? Belike he thinks me Henry.
But what said Lady Bona to my marriage ?

POST
These were her words, uttered with mild disdain :
'Tell him, in hope he'll prove a widower shortly,
I'll wear the willow garland for his sake.'

KING EDWARD
I blame not her. She could say little less.
She had the wrong. But what said Henry's queen ?
103   For I have heard that she was there in place.

POST
'Tell him,' quoth she, 'my mourning weeds are done
And I am ready to put armor on.'

KING EDWARD
Belike she minds to play the Amazon.
But what said Warwick to these injuries ?

POST
He, more incensed against your majesty
Than all the rest, discharged me with these words :
'Tell him from me that he hath done me wrong,
And therefore I'll uncrown him ere't be long.'

KING EDWARD
Ha ! durst the traitor breathe out so proud words ?
Well, I will arm me, being thus forewarned.
They shall have wars and pay for their presumption.
But say, is Warwick friends with Margaret ?

POST
Ay, gracious sovereign. They are so linked in friendship
That young Prince Edward marries Warwick's daughter.

CLARENCE *[aside]*
118   Belike the elder ; Clarence will have the younger. –
Now, brother king, farewell, and sit you fast ;
For I will hence to Warwick's other daughter,
121   That, though I want a kingdom, yet in marriage
I may not prove inferior to yourself.
You that love me and Warwick, follow me.
    *Exit Clarence, and Somerset follows.*

RICHARD *[aside]*
Not I.
My thoughts aim at a further matter. I
Stay not for the love of Edward but the crown.

KING EDWARD
Clarence and Somerset both gone to Warwick ?
Yet am I armed against the worst can happen ;
And haste is needful in this desp'rate case.
Pembroke and Stafford, you in our behalf
Go levy men and make prepare for war.     131
They are already, or quickly will be landed.
Myself in person will straight follow you.
    *Exeunt Pembroke and Stafford.*
But ere I go, Hastings and Montague,
Resolve my doubt. You twain, of all the rest,
Are near to Warwick by blood and by alliance.
Tell me if you love Warwick more than me.
If it be so, then both depart to him ;
I rather wish you foes than hollow friends.     139
But if you mind to hold your true obedience,
Give me assurance with some friendly vow,
That I may never have you in suspect.     142

MONTAGUE
So God help Montague as he proves true.

HASTINGS
And Hastings as he favors Edward's cause.

KING EDWARD
Now, brother Richard, will you stand by us ?

RICHARD
Ay, in despite of all that shall withstand you.

KING EDWARD
Why, so ! then am I sure of victory.
Now therefore let us hence, and lose no hour
Till we meet Warwick with his foreign power.     *Exeunt.*

*

*Enter Warwick and Oxford in England with French*   IV,
*Soldiers.*

WARWICK
Trust me, my lord, all hitherto goes well.
The common people by numbers swarm to us.
    *Enter Clarence and Somerset.*
But see where Somerset and Clarence comes.
Speak suddenly, my lords, are we all friends ?

CLARENCE
Fear not that, my lord.

WARWICK
Then, gentle Clarence, welcome unto Warwick ;
And welcome, Somerset. I hold it cowardice
To rest mistrustful where a noble heart
Hath pawned an open hand in sign of love.     9
Else might I think that Clarence, Edward's brother,
Were but a feignèd friend to our proceedings.
But welcome, sweet Clarence. My daughter shall be
  thine.
And now what rests but, in night's coverture,     13
Thy brother being carelessly encamped,
His soldiers lurking in the towns about,     15
And but attended by a simple guard,
We may surprise and take him at our pleasure ?

89 *Go to* all right, don't worry   90 *guess* approximate   92 *depart* departure   96 *Belike* perhaps   103 *in place* present   118 *Belike . . . younger* (see III, iii, 242n.)   121 *want* lack   131 *prepare* preparation   139 *hollow* empty, i.e. untrustworthy   142 *suspect* suspicion

IV, ii Fields near Warwick   9 *pawned* pledged   13 *rests* remains ; *in night's coverture* under cover of night   15 *lurking* idling

Our scouts have found the adventure very easy;

19 That as Ulysses and stout Diomede

With sleight and manhood stole to Rhesus' tents
And brought from thence the Thracian fatal steeds,
So we, well covered with the night's black mantle,
At unawares may beat down Edward's guard
And seize himself. I say not, slaughter him,

25 For I intend but only to surprise him.
You that will follow me to this attempt,
Applaud the name of Henry with your leader.
     *They all cry* 'Henry!'

28 Why then, let's on our way in silent sort.
For Warwick and his friends, God and Saint George!
         *Exeunt.*

             *

, iii      *Enter three Watchmen, to guard King Edward's tent.*

1. WATCHMAN
Come on, my masters. Each man take his stand.

2 The king by this is set him down to sleep.

2. WATCHMAN
What, will he not to bed?

1. WATCHMAN
Why, no; for he hath made a solemn vow
Never to lie and take his natural rest
Till Warwick or himself be quite suppressed.

2. WATCHMAN
To-morrow then belike shall be the day,
If Warwick be so near as men report.

3. WATCHMAN
But say, I pray, what nobleman is that
That with the king here resteth in his tent?

1. WATCHMAN
'Tis the Lord Hastings, the king's chiefest friend.

3. WATCHMAN
O, is it so? But why commands the king
That his chief followers lodge in towns about him,
While he himself keeps in the cold field?

2. WATCHMAN
'Tis the more honor, because more dangerous.

3. WATCHMAN

16 Ay, but give me worship and quietness.
I like it better than a dangerous honor.

18 If Warwick knew in what estate he stands,

19 'Tis to be doubted he would waken him.

1. WATCHMAN
Unless our halberds did shut up his passage.

2. WATCHMAN
Ay! wherefore else guard we his royal tent
But to defend his person from night-foes?
     *Enter Warwick, Clarence, Oxford, Somerset, and*
     *French Soldiers, silent all.*

WARWICK
This is his tent; and see where stand his guard.
Courage, my masters, honor now or never!
But follow me, and Edward shall be ours.

1. WATCHMAN Who goes there?

2. WATCHMAN Stay, or thou diest!
     *Warwick and the rest cry all* 'Warwick! Warwick!'
     *and set upon the Guard, who fly, crying* 'Arm! arm!',
     *Warwick and the rest following them.*
     *The Drum playing and Trumpet sounding, enter*
     *Warwick, Somerset, and the rest, bringing [Edward]*
     *the King out in his gown, sitting in a chair.*
     *Richard and Hastings flies over the stage.*

SOMERSET
What are they that fly there?

WARWICK
Richard and Hastings. Let them go. Here is the duke.

KING EDWARD
The duke? Why, Warwick, when we parted
Thou called'st me king.

WARWICK      Ay, but the case is altered.   31

When you disgraced me in my embassade,   32
Then I degraded you from being king,
And come now to create you Duke of York.
Alas, how should you govern any kingdom
That know not how to use ambassadors,
Nor how to be contented with one wife,
Nor how to use your brothers brotherly,
Nor how to study for the people's welfare,
Nor how to shroud yourself from enemies?   40

KING EDWARD
Yea, brother of Clarence, art thou here too?
Nay, then I see that Edward needs must down.   42
Yet, Warwick, in despite of all mischance,
Of thee thyself, and all thy complices,   44
Edward will always bear himself as king.
Though Fortune's malice overthrow my state,
My mind exceeds the compass of her wheel.   47

WARWICK
Then, for his mind, be Edward England's king,
     *Takes off his crown.*
But Henry now shall wear the English crown
And be true king indeed, thou but the shadow.
My Lord of Somerset, at my request
See that forthwith Duke Edward be conveyed
Unto my brother, Archbishop of York.   53
When I have fought with Pembroke and his fellows,
I'll follow you and tell what answer
Lewis and the Lady Bona send to him.
Now for a while farewell, good Duke of York.

KING EDWARD
What fates impose, that men must needs abide;
It boots not to resist both wind and tide.   59
     *They lead him out forcibly. Exeunt.*

OXFORD
What now remains, my lords, for us to do
But march to London with our soldiers?

WARWICK
Ay, that's the first thing that we have to do,
To free King Henry from imprisonment
And see him seated in the regal throne.
     *Exit [Warwick with the rest].*

             *

---

19–21 *That . . . steeds* (The oracle predicted that Troy would not fall if the
horses of Rhesus, king of Thrace, grazed on the Trojan plain. To prevent
their doing so, Ulysses and Diomedes captured them on a night raid.)
25 *surprise* capture   28 *sort* manner
IV, iii Edward's camp near Warwick   2 *this* i.e. this time   16 *worship* a
place of dignity   18 *estate* condition   19 *doubted* feared   31 *the case is
altered* things have changed (a proverbial expression)   32 *embassade*
embassy   40 *shroud* conceal, protect   42 *needs must down* must necessarily
be put down   44 *complices* accomplices   47 *compass* circumference   53
*Archbishop of York* i.e. George Nevil   59 *boots not* is no use

IV, iv        *Enter Rivers and Lady Grey [as Queen Elizabeth].*

RIVERS
Madam, what makes you in this sudden change?

QUEEN ELIZABETH
Why, brother Rivers, are you yet to learn
What late misfortune is befall'n King Edward?

RIVERS
What? Loss of some pitched battle against Warwick?

QUEEN ELIZABETH
No, but the loss of his own royal person.

RIVERS
Then is my sovereign slain?

QUEEN ELIZABETH
Ay, almost slain, for he is taken prisoner,
Either betrayed by falsehood of his guard
Or by his foe surprised at unawares;
And, as I further have to understand,
11  Is new committed to the Bishop of York,
12  Fell Warwick's brother, and by that our foe.

RIVERS
These news, I must confess, are full of grief.
Yet, gracious madam, bear it as you may;
Warwick may lose, that now hath won the day.

QUEEN ELIZABETH
Till then fair hope must hinder life's decay.
And I the rather wean me from despair
For love of Edward's offspring in my womb.
This is it that makes me bridle passion
And bear with mildness my misfortune's cross.
Ay, ay, for this I draw in many a tear
22  And stop the rising of bloodsucking sighs,
Lest with my sighs or tears I blast or drown
King Edward's fruit, true heir to th' English crown.

RIVERS
25  But, madam, where is Warwick then become?

QUEEN ELIZABETH
I am informèd that he comes toward London
To set the crown once more on Henry's head.
Guess thou the rest. King Edward's friends must down.
29  But, to prevent the tyrant's violence
(For trust not him that hath once broken faith),
I'll hence forthwith unto the sanctuary,
To save, at least, the heir of Edward's right.
There shall I rest secure from force and fraud.
Come, therefore, let us fly while we may fly.
If Warwick take us, we are sure to die.        *Exeunt.*

*

IV, v        *Enter Richard, Lord Hastings, and Sir William
Stanley.*

RICHARD
Now, my Lord Hastings and Sir William Stanley,
Leave off to wonder why I drew you hither
3  Into this chiefest thicket of the park.
Thus stands the case: you know our king, my brother,
Is prisoner to the bishop here, at whose hands
He hath good usage and great liberty;
And often, but attended with weak guard,
8  Comes hunting this way to disport himself.
9  I have advertised him by secret means
That if about this hour he make this way
11  Under the color of his usual game,
He shall here find his friends with horse and men
To set him free from his captivity.

*Enter King Edward and a Huntsman with him.*

HUNTSMAN
This way, my lord, for this way lies the game.

KING EDWARD
Nay, this way, man, see where the huntsmen stand.
Now, brother of Gloucester, Lord Hastings, and the rest,
Stand you thus close to steal the bishop's deer?        17

RICHARD
Brother, the time and case requireth haste.
Your horse stands ready at the park corner.

KING EDWARD
But whither shall we then?

HASTINGS
To Lynn, my lord.        21

KING EDWARD        And ship from thence to Flanders?

RICHARD
Well guessed, believe me; for that was my meaning.

KING EDWARD
Stanley, I will requite thy forwardness.        23

RICHARD
But wherefore stay we? 'Tis no time to talk.

KING EDWARD
Huntsman, what say'st thou? Wilt thou go along?

HUNTSMAN
Better do so than tarry and be hanged.

RICHARD
Come then, away. Let's ha' no more ado.

KING EDWARD
Bishop, farewell. Shield thee from Warwick's frown
And pray that I may repossess the crown.        *Exeunt.*

*

*Flourish. Enter King Henry the Sixth, Clarence,
Warwick, Somerset, young Henry [Earl of
Richmond], Oxford, Montague, and Lieutenant
[of the Tower].*        IV

KING HENRY
Master lieutenant, now that God and friends
Have shaken Edward from the regal seat
And turned my captive state to liberty,
My fear to hope, my sorrows unto joys,
At our enlargement what are thy due fees?        5

LIEUTENANT
Subjects may challenge nothing of their sovereigns;
But if an humble prayer may prevail,
I then crave pardon of your majesty.

KING HENRY
For what, lieutenant? for well using me?
Nay, be thou sure I'll well requite thy kindness
For that it made my imprisonment a pleasure;
Ay, such a pleasure as incagèd birds
Conceive when, after many moody thoughts,
At last by notes of household harmony

IV, iv The royal palace in London  11 *new* recently; *Bishop* i.e. archbishop  12 *Fell* cruel; *by that* i.e. because of that relationship  22 *bloodsucking sighs* (sighing was supposed to waste the heart's blood, which
explains why *hope* can *hinder life's decay* [l. 16])  25 *become* gone  29
*prevent* forestall
IV, v The Archbishop of York's park  3 *chiefest* largest  8 *disport* amuse
9 *advertised* notified  11 *Under . . . game* i.e. as though he were merely
hunting  17 *close* hidden  21 *Lynn* i.e. King's Lynn, on the Norfolk coast
23 *forwardness* zeal
IV, vi The Tower of London  s.d. *Lieutenant* Deputy Warden  5 *enlargement* release; *fees* (due because prisoners who could afford it were
charged for special quarters and food)

They quite forget their loss of liberty.
But, Warwick, after God, thou set'st me free,
And chiefly therefore I thank God and thee;
He was the author, thou the instrument.
Therefore, that I may conquer fortune's spite
By living low, where fortune cannot hurt me,
And that the people of this blessèd land
22  May not be punished with my thwarting stars,
Warwick, although my head still wear the crown,
I here resign my government to thee,
For thou art fortunate in all thy deeds.

WARWICK
26  Your grace hath still been famed for virtuous,
And now may seem as wise as virtuous
By spying and avoiding fortune's malice,
29  For few men rightly temper with the stars.
Yet in this one thing let me blame your grace,
31  For choosing me when Clarence is in place.

CLARENCE
32  No, Warwick, thou art worthy of the sway,
To whom the heavens in thy nativity
Adjudged an olive branch and laurel crown,
As likely to be blest in peace and war;
And therefore I yield thee my free consent.

WARWICK
37  And I choose Clarence only for Protector.

KING HENRY
Warwick and Clarence, give me both your hands.
Now join your hands, and with your hands your hearts,
That no dissension hinder government.
I make you both Protectors of this land,
While I myself will lead a private life
And in devotion spend my latter days,
To sin's rebuke and my Creator's praise.

WARWICK
What answers Clarence to his sovereign's will?

CLARENCE
That he consents, if Warwick yield consent,
For on thy fortune I repose myself.

WARWICK
Why then, though loath, yet must I be content.
We'll yoke together, like a double shadow
50  To Henry's body, and supply his place;
I mean, in bearing weight of government,
While he enjoys the honor and his ease.
And, Clarence, now then it is more than needful
Forthwith that Edward be pronounced a traitor
And all his lands and goods be confiscate.

CLARENCE
What else? And that succession be determined.

WARWICK
Ay, therein Clarence shall not want his part.

KING HENRY
But with the first of all your chief affairs,
Let me entreat (for I command no more)
60  That Margaret your queen and my son Edward

Be sent for, to return from France with speed;
For till I see them here, by doubtful fear
My joy of liberty is half eclipsed.

CLARENCE
It shall be done, my sovereign, with all speed.

KING HENRY
My Lord of Somerset, what youth is that
Of whom you seem to have so tender care?

SOMERSET
My liege, it is young Henry, Earl of Richmond.      67

KING HENRY
Come hither, England's hope. *Lays his hand on his head.*
   If secret powers
Suggest but truth to my divining thoughts,          69
This pretty lad will prove our country's bliss.
His looks are full of peaceful majesty,
His head by nature framed to wear a crown,
His hand to wield a sceptre, and himself
Likely in time to bless a regal throne.
Make much of him, my lords; for this is he
Must help you more than you are hurt by me.
   *Enter a Post.*

WARWICK
What news, my friend?

POST
That Edward is escapèd from your brother
And fled, as he hears since, to Burgundy.           79

WARWICK
Unsavory news! But how made he escape?

POST
He was conveyed by Richard Duke of Gloucester      81
And the Lord Hastings, who attended him             82
In secret ambush on the forest side
And from the bishop's huntsmen rescued him;
For hunting was his daily exercise.

WARWICK
My brother was too careless of his charge.
But let us hence, my sovereign, to provide
A salve for any sore that may betide.              88
   *Exeunt. Manent Somerset, Richmond, and Oxford.*

SOMERSET
My lord, I like not of this flight of Edward's,
For doubtless Burgundy will yield him help
And we shall have more wars before't be long.
As Henry's late presaging prophecy
Did glad my heart with hope of this young Richmond,
So doth my heart misgive me, in these conflicts
What may befall him, to his harm and ours.
Therefore, Lord Oxford, to prevent the worst,
Forthwith we'll send him hence to Brittany
Till storms be past of civil enmity.

OXFORD
Ay, for if Edward repossess the crown,
'Tis like that Richmond with the rest shall down.

SOMERSET
It shall be so; he shall to Brittany.
Come therefore, let's about it speedily.      *Exeunt.*

\*

*Flourish. Enter [King] Edward, Richard, Hastings,*   IV, vii
*and Soldiers [a troop of Hollanders].*

KING EDWARD
Now, brother Richard, Lord Hastings, and the rest,
Yet thus far Fortune maketh us amends

---

22 *thwarting stars* stars (instruments of fortune) whose influence impedes
happiness and success   26 *still* always   29 *temper . . . stars* i.e. come to
terms with their fate   31 *in place* here   32 *sway* rule   37 *only* alone   67
*Henry* (the future Henry VII; at his accession to the throne the Wars of
the Roses finally ceased)   69 *divining* foretelling the future   79 *he* i.e.
your brother, the Archbishop of York   81 *conveyed* secretly carried away
82 *attended* waited for   88 *betide* develop
IV, vii Before the walls of York

And says that once more I shall interchange
4 My wanèd state for Henry's regal crown.
Well have we passed and now repassed the seas
And brought desirèd help from Burgundy.
What then remains, we being thus arrived
8 From Ravenspurgh haven before the gates of York,
But that we enter, as into our dukedom?

RICHARD
The gates made fast! Brother, I like not this.
11 For many men that stumble at the threshold
Are well foretold that danger lurks within.

KING EDWARD
13 Tush, man, abodements must not now affright us;
By fair or foul means we must enter in,
For hither will our friends repair to us.

HASTINGS
My liege, I'll knock once more to summon them.
*Enter [aloft], on the walls, the Mayor of York and his*
*Brethren [the Aldermen].*

MAYOR
My lords, we were forewarnèd of your coming
And shut the gates for safety of ourselves;
For now we owe allegiance unto Henry.

KING EDWARD
But, Master Mayor, if Henry be your king,
Yet Edward at the least is Duke of York.

MAYOR
True, my good lord. I know you for no less.

KING EDWARD
23 Why, and I challenge nothing but my dukedom,
As being well content with that alone.

RICHARD *[aside]*
But when the fox hath once got in his nose,
He'll soon find means to make the body follow.

HASTINGS
Why, Master Mayor, why stand you in a doubt?
Open the gates. We are King Henry's friends.

MAYOR
Ay, say you so? The gates shall then be opened.
*He descends [with the Aldermen].*

RICHARD
A wise stout captain, and soon persuaded.

HASTINGS
31 The good old man would fain that all were well,
32 So 'twere not long of him; but being entered,
I doubt not, I, but we shall soon persuade
Both him and all his brothers unto reason.
*Enter [below] the Mayor, [bringing the keys in*
*his hand,] and two Aldermen.*

KING EDWARD
So, Master Mayor. These gates must not be shut
But in the night or in the time of war.
What, fear not, man, but yield me up the keys;
*Takes his keys.*
For Edward will defend the town and thee
39 And all those friends that deign to follow me.
*March. Enter Montgomery with Drum and Soldiers.*

RICHARD
40 Brother, this is Sir John Montgomery,
Our trusty friend, unless I be deceived.

KING EDWARD
Welcome, Sir John; but why come you in arms?

MONTGOMERY
To help King Edward in his time of storm,
As every loyal subject ought to do.

KING EDWARD
Thanks, good Montgomery. But we now forget
Our title to the crown and only claim
Our dukedom till God please to send the rest.

MONTGOMERY
Then fare you well, for I will hence again.
I came to serve a king and not a duke.
Drummer, strike up, and let us march away. 50
*The Drum begins to march.*

KING EDWARD
Nay, stay, Sir John, awhile, and we'll debate
By what safe means the crown may be recovered.

MONTGOMERY
What talk you of debating? In few words,
If you'll not here proclaim yourself our king,
I'll leave you to your fortune and be gone
To keep them back that come to succor you.
Why shall we fight, if you pretend no title? 57

RICHARD
Why, brother, wherefore stand you on nice points? 58

KING EDWARD
When we grow stronger, then we'll make our claim;
Till then 'tis wisdom to conceal our meaning.

HASTINGS
Away with scrupulous wit! Now arms must rule. 61

RICHARD
And fearless minds climb soonest unto crowns.
Brother, we will proclaim you out of hand; 63
The bruit thereof will bring you many friends. 64

KING EDWARD
Then be it as you will; for 'tis my right,
And Henry but usurps the diadem.

MONTGOMERY
Ay, now my sovereign speaketh like himself
And now will I be Edward's champion. 68

HASTINGS
Sound trumpet. Edward shall be here proclaimed.
Come, fellow soldier, make thou proclamation.
*Flourish. Sound.*

SOLDIER 'Edward the Fourth, by the grace of God, King
of England and France, and Lord of Ireland, etc.' 72

MONTGOMERY
And whosoe'er gainsays King Edward's right,
By this I challenge him to single fight.
*Throws down his gauntlet.*

ALL Long live Edward the Fourth!

KING EDWARD
Thanks, brave Montgomery, and thanks unto you all.
If fortune serve me I'll requite this kindness.
Now for this night let's harbor here in York,
And when the morning sun shall raise his car 79
Above the border of this horizon,
We'll forward towards Warwick and his mates;

---

4 *wanèd* faded, declined   8 *Ravenspurgh* (on the Yorkshire coast, at the mouth of the River Humber)   11 *stumble at the threshold* (a sign of bad luck)   13 *abodements* omens   23 *challenge* claim   31 *would fain* desires   32 *So . . . him* as long as he bears no responsibility   39 *deign* are willing   40 *Sir John Montgomery* (called Sir Thomas in the Chronicles, which report that he met Edward at Nottingham after the securing of York)   50 s.d. *march* i.e. commence beating a march   57 *pretend* claim   58 *nice points* minor details   61 *wit* reasoning   63 *out of hand* immediately   64 *bruit* news   68 *champion* defender   72 *etc.* (the soldier adds the conventional titles of the monarch)   79 *car* chariot

82   For well I wot that Henry is no soldier.
83   Ah, froward Clarence, how evil it beseems thee
     To flatter Henry and forsake thy brother.
     Yet, as we may, we'll meet both thee and Warwick.
     Come on, brave soldiers. Doubt not of the day,
     And that once gotten, doubt not of large pay.
                        *Exeunt [as into the city].*

\*

**V, viii**       *Flourish. Enter the King [Henry], Warwick,*
             *Montague, Clarence, Oxford, and Exeter.*

WARWICK
1   What counsel, lords ? Edward from Belgia,
2   With hasty Germans and blunt Hollanders,
     Hath passed in safety through the narrow seas
4   And with his troops doth march amain to London,
     And many giddy people flock to him.
OXFORD
     Let's levy men and beat him back again.
CLARENCE
     A little fire is quickly trodden out,
8   Which, being suffered, rivers cannot quench.
WARWICK
     In Warwickshire I have true-hearted friends,
     Not mutinous in peace, yet bold in war.
11   Those will I muster up ; and thou, son Clarence,
     Shalt stir up in Suffolk, Norfolk, and in Kent
     The knights and gentlemen to come with thee.
     Thou, brother Montague, in Buckingham,
     Northampton, and in Leicestershire shalt find
     Men well inclined to hear what thou command'st.
     And thou, brave Oxford, wondrous well beloved,
     In Oxfordshire shalt muster up thy friends.
     My sovereign, with the loving citizens,
     Like to his island girt in with the ocean
     Or modest Dian circled with her nymphs,
     Shall rest in London till we come to him.
     Fair lords, take leave and stand not to reply.
     Farewell, my sovereign.
KING HENRY
25   Farewell, my Hector and my Troy's true hope.
CLARENCE
     In sign of truth I kiss your highness' hand.
KING HENRY
     Well-minded Clarence, be thou fortunate.
MONTAGUE
     Comfort, my lord, and so I take my leave.
OXFORD *[kisses Henry's hand]*
     And thus I seal my truth and bid adieu.
KING HENRY
     Sweet Oxford, and my loving Montague,
31   And all at once, once more a happy farewell.

WARWICK
     Farewell, sweet lords. Let's meet at Coventry.
             *Exeunt [all but King Henry and Exeter].*
KING HENRY
     Here at the palace will I rest awhile.
     Cousin of Exeter, what thinks your lordship ?
     Methinks the power that Edward hath in field
     Should not be able to encounter mine.
EXETER
     The doubt is that he will seduce the rest.      37
KING HENRY
     That's not my fear. My meed hath got me fame.    38
     I have not stopped mine ears to their demands
     Nor posted off their suits with slow delays.      40
     My pity hath been balm to heal their wounds,
     My mildness hath allayed their swelling griefs,
     My mercy dried their water-flowing tears.
     I have not been desirous of their wealth
     Nor much oppressed them with great subsidies,    45
     Nor forward of revenge, though they much erred.    46
     Then why should they love Edward more than me ?
     No, Exeter, these graces challenge grace ;
     And when the lion fawns upon the lamb,
     The lamb will never cease to follow him.
        *Shout within, 'A Lancaster ! A Lancaster !'*
EXETER
     Hark, hark, my lord ! what shouts are these ?
        *Enter [King] Edward and his Soldiers [, with*
        *Richard].*
KING EDWARD
     Seize on the shamefaced Henry, bear him hence,    52
     And once again proclaim us King of England.
     You are the fount that makes small brooks to flow.
     Now stops thy spring ; my sea shall suck them dry
     And swell so much the higher by their ebb.
     Hence with him to the Tower. Let him not speak.
        *Exit [Guard] with King Henry [and Exeter].*
     And, lords, toward Coventry bend we our course,
     Where peremptory Warwick now remains.      59
     The sun shines hot, and if we use delay,      60
     Cold biting winter mars our hoped-for hay.
RICHARD
     Away betimes, before his forces join,      62
     And take the great-grown traitor unawares.
     Brave warriors, march amain toward Coventry. *Exeunt.*

\*

        *Enter [aloft] Warwick, the Mayor of Coventry,*    **V, i**
        *two Messengers, and others, upon the walls.*
WARWICK
     Where is the post that came from valiant Oxford ?
     How far hence is thy lord, mine honest fellow ?
1 . MESSENGER
     By this at Dunsmore, marching hitherward.      3
WARWICK
     How far off is our brother Montague ?
     Where is the post that came from Montague ?
2 . MESSENGER
     By this at Daintry, with a puissant troop.      6
        *Enter Somervile [aloft].*
WARWICK
     Say, Somervile, what says my loving son ?
     And by thy guess how nigh is Clarence now ?

---

82 *wot* know   83 *froward* perverse, refractory
IV, viii The Bishop of London's palace   1 *Belgia* the Netherlands   2
*hasty* rash, quick-tempered ; *blunt* merciless   4 *amain* speedily   8 *suffered*
tolerated   11 *son* i.e. son-in-law   25 *my Troy's* (because London [New
Troy] was supposedly founded by Brutus, legendary grandson of the
Trojan hero Aeneas)   31 *at once* together   37 *doubt* fear   38 *meed* rewards
given for merit, generosity   40 *posted off* treated lightly, postponed   45
*subsidies* taxes   46 *forward of* eager for   52 *shamefaced* shamefast, modest
59 *peremptory* overbearing   60–61 *The sun . . . hay* i.e. we should make hay
while the sun shines   62 *betimes* at once
V, i Before the walls of Coventry   3 *Dunsmore* Dunsmore Heath, between
Coventry and Daventry   6 *Daintry* i.e. Daventry, about twenty miles
south-east of Coventry ; *puissant* strong

SOMERVILE

9  At Southam I did leave him with his forces
And do expect him here some two hours hence.

WARWICK

Then Clarence is at hand. I hear his drum.

SOMERVILE

12  It is not his, my lord. Here Southam lies.
The drum your honor hears marcheth from Warwick.

WARWICK

14  Who should that be ? Belike unlooked-for friends.

SOMERVILE

They are at hand, and you shall quickly know.
    *March. Flourish. Enter [below, King] Edward,*
    *Richard, and Soldiers.*

KING EDWARD

16  Go, trumpet, to the walls, and sound a parle.

RICHARD

See how the surly Warwick mans the wall.

WARWICK

18  O unbid spite ! Is sportful Edward come ?
Where slept our scouts or how are they seduced

20  That we could hear no news of his repair ?

KING EDWARD

Now, Warwick, wilt thou ope the city gates,
Speak gentle words, and humbly bend thy knee.
Call Edward king and at his hands beg mercy,
And he shall pardon thee these outrages.

WARWICK

Nay, rather, wilt thou draw thy forces hence,
Confess who set thee up and plucked thee down,
Call Warwick patron, and be penitent ?
And thou shalt still remain the Duke of York.

RICHARD

I thought at least he would have said 'the king' ;
Or did he make the jest against his will ?

WARWICK

Is not a dukedom, sir, a goodly gift ?

RICHARD

Ay, by my faith, for a poor earl to give ;

33  I'll do thee service for so good a gift.

WARWICK

'Twas I that gave the kingdom to thy brother.

KING EDWARD

Why, then 'tis mine, if but by Warwick's gift.

WARWICK

36  Thou art no Atlas for so great a weight ;
And, weakling, Warwick takes his gift again,
And Henry is my king, Warwick his subject.

KING EDWARD

But Warwick's king is Edward's prisoner ;
And, gallant Warwick, do but answer this :
What is the body when the head is off ?

RICHARD

42  Alas that Warwick had no more forecast,

43  But, whiles he thought to steal the single ten,
The king was slily fingered from the deck.
You left poor Henry at the bishop's palace
And ten to one you'll meet him in the Tower.

KING EDWARD

'Tis even so. Yet you are Warwick still.

RICHARD

48  Come, Warwick, take the time. Kneel down, kneel
    down.

49  Nay, when ? Strike now, or else the iron cools.

WARWICK

I had rather chop this hand off at a blow
And with the other fling it at thy face
Than bear so low a sail to strike to thee.    52

KING EDWARD

Sail how thou canst, have wind and tide thy friend,
This hand, fast wound about thy coal-black hair,
Shall, whiles thy head is warm and new cut off,
Write in the dust this sentence with thy blood :
'Wind-changing Warwick now can change no more.'  57
    *Enter Oxford, with Drum and Colors.*

WARWICK

O cheerful colors, see where Oxford comes.

OXFORD

Oxford, Oxford, for Lancaster !
    *[Exeunt Oxford and his men as into the city.]*

RICHARD

The gates are open ; let us enter too.

KING EDWARD

So other foes may set upon our backs.    61
Stand we in good array, for they no doubt
Will issue out again and bid us battle.    63
If not, the city being but of small defense,
We'll quickly rouse the traitors in the same.    65
    *[Enter Oxford aloft.]*

WARWICK

O, welcome, Oxford, for we want thy help.
    *Enter Montague, with Drum and Colors.*

MONTAGUE

Montague, Montague, for Lancaster !
    *[Exeunt Montague and his men as into the city.]*

RICHARD

Thou and thy brother both shall buy this treason
Even with the dearest blood your bodies bear.

KING EDWARD

The harder matched, the greater victory.
My mind presageth happy gain and conquest.
    *Enter Somerset, with Drum and Colors.*

SOMERSET

Somerset, Somerset, for Lancaster !
    *[Exeunt Somerset and his men as into the city.]*

RICHARD

Two of thy name, both Dukes of Somerset,    73
Have sold their lives unto the house of York ;
And thou shalt be the third, if this sword hold.
    *Enter Clarence, with Drum and Colors.*

WARWICK

And lo where George of Clarence sweeps along,

---

9 *Southam* (about ten miles southeast of Coventry) 12–13 *It . . . Warwick* (the city of Warwick lies southwest of Coventry ; the earl has slightly mistaken his directions, as Somervile points out) 14 *Belike* no doubt 16 *parle* parley, a trumpet call requesting a truce for conference 18 *unbid* uninvited, unwelcome ; *sportful* lascivious 20 *repair* approach 33 *do thee service* accept you as my feudal overlord (ironically) 36 *Thou . . . Atlas* i.e. you cannot bear (Atlas, a Titan, supported the world on his shoulders) 42 *forecast* forethought 43 *single ten* mere ten (the ten, highest of the plain cards, is worth having, but not in comparison with the king) 48 *take the time* seize the opportunity 49 *Nay, when* (an exclamation indicating impatience) 52 *bear . . . thee* (see III, iii, 5n.) 57 *Wind-changing* i.e. fickle, inconstant 61 *So* if so 63 *bid* offer 65 *rouse . . . in* drive . . . from (a hunting term) 73 *Two . . . name* (The Somerset being addressed is Edmund, the 4th duke. His elder brother, Henry Beaufort, 3rd duke, was executed after the Battle of Hexham, 1464, though his defection from Edward is described in IV, i and ii as taking place in 1470. Their father, Edmund, 2nd duke, was killed at St Albans, 1445 ; it is his head that Richard flings down at I, i, 16.)

Of force enough to bid his brother battle ;
With whom an upright zeal to right prevails
More than the nature of a brother's love.
Come, Clarence, come ; thou wilt, if Warwick call.
*[Sound a parle and Richard and Clarence whisper*
*together.]*

CLARENCE

Father of Warwick, know you what this means ?
*[Takes his red rose out of his hat.]*
Look here, I throw my infamy at thee.
I will not ruinate my father's house,

84 Who gave his blood to lime the stones together,
85 And set up Lancaster. Why, trowest thou, Warwick,
86 That Clarence is so harsh, so blunt, unnatural,
To bend the fatal instruments of war
Against his brother and his lawful king ?
89 Perhaps thou wilt object my holy oath.
To keep that oath were more impiety
91 Than Jephtha when he sacrificed his daughter.
I am so sorry for my trespass made
That, to deserve well at my brother's hands,
I here proclaim myself thy mortal foe,
With resolution, wheresoe'er I meet thee
(As I will meet thee if thou stir abroad),
To plague thee for thy foul misleading me.
And so, proud-hearted Warwick, I defy thee
And to my brother turn my blushing cheeks.
Pardon me, Edward, I will make amends ;
And, Richard, do not frown upon my faults,
102 For I will henceforth be no more unconstant.

KING EDWARD

Now welcome more, and ten times more beloved,
Than if thou never hadst deserved our hate.

RICHARD

Welcome, good Clarence. This is brotherlike.

WARWICK

106 O passing traitor, perjured and unjust.

KING EDWARD

What, Warwick, wilt thou leave the town and fight ?
Or shall we beat the stones about thine ears ?

WARWICK

Alas, I am not cooped here for defense.
110 I will away towards Barnet presently
And bid thee battle, Edward, if thou dar'st.

---

84 *lime* cement   85 *trowest thou* do you believe   86 *blunt* unfeeling   89
*object* raise as an objection   91 *Jephtha* (see Judges xi, 30–40)   102 *un-*
*constant* fickle, disloyal   106 *passing* surpassing   110 *Barnet* (about ten miles
north of London and seventy-five miles southeast of Coventry. At IV, viii
the dramatist had departed from the historical order of events : in mid-
March, 1471, from York [IV, vii] Edward had moved south to Coventry,
to which Warwick had withdrawn. Here the Yorkist army invited battle.
When Warwick declined, Edward continued south, occupying the town
of Warwick, whence he doubled back to Coventry to challenge the Lancastrian forces once more. When Warwick again refused, Edward marched
south, capturing London and Henry VI on April 11, this time with the
Lancastrians following. By April 13 Warwick had reached Barnet, where
early the next day he encountered the Yorkist army, which had marched
north from London. Because he put Henry's capture [IV, viii] out of its
historical sequence, the dramatist is here forced to treat Barnet as though it
lay adjacent to Coventry.)
V, ii Fields near Coventry (Barnet)   2 *bug* goblin ; *feared* frightened
11 *cedar* (symbol of pre-eminence)   12–13 *eagle . . . lion* (the allusion may
be general, i.e. 'royal creatures'; or it may be intended specifically, through
the identification of the men with their emblems : i.e. 'eagle': Richard of
York, as perhaps at II, i, 92, and 'lion': Henry VI, three rampant lions
being represented on his royal arms)   13 *ramping* rampant   14 *overpeered*
overlooked ; *Jove's . . . tree* i.e. the oak   31 *puissant* strong   41 *latest* final
45 *mought* might

---

KING EDWARD

Yes, Warwick, Edward dares and leads the way.
Lords, to the field. Saint George and victory !
*Exeunt [King Edward and his company below,*
*Warwick and his company aloft]. March.*
*[Enter below as out of the city] Warwick and*
*his company [and] follows [King Edward].*

\*

*Alarum and excursions. Enter [King] Edward,*    V, ii
*bringing forth Warwick wounded.*

KING EDWARD

So, lie thou there ! Die thou, and die our fear !
For Warwick was a bug that feared us all.    2
Now, Montague, sit fast. I seek for thee,
That Warwick's bones may keep thine company.    *Exit.*

WARWICK

Ah, who is nigh ? Come to me, friend or foe,
And tell me who is victor, York or Warwick.
Why ask I that ? My mangled body shows,
My blood, my want of strength, my sick heart shows,
That I must yield my body to the earth
And, by my fall, the conquest to my foe.
Thus yields the cedar to the axe's edge,    11
Whose arms gave shelter to the princely eagle,    12
Under whose shade the ramping lion slept,    13
Whose top-branch overpeered Jove's spreading tree    14
And kept low shrubs from winter's powerful wind.
These eyes, that now are dimmed with death's black veil,
Have been as piercing as the midday sun
To search the secret treasons of the world.
The wrinkles in my brows, now filled with blood,
Were likened oft to kingly sepulchres ;
For who lived king but I could dig his grave ?
And who durst smile when Warwick bent his brow ?
Lo now my glory smeared in dust and blood ;
My parks, my walks, my manors that I had,
Even now forsake me ; and of all my lands
Is nothing left me but my body's length.
Why, what is pomp, rule, reign, but earth and dust ?
And, live we how we can, yet die we must.
*Enter Oxford and Somerset.*

SOMERSET

Ah, Warwick, Warwick, wert thou as we are,
We might recover all our loss again.
The queen from France hath brought a puissant power.    31
Even now we heard the news. Ah, couldst thou fly !

WARWICK

Why, then I would not fly. Ah, Montague,
If thou be there, sweet brother, take my hand
And with thy lips keep in my soul awhile.
Thou lov'st me not ; for, brother, if thou didst,
Thy tears would wash this cold congealèd blood
That glues my lips and will not let me speak.
Come quickly, Montague, or I am dead.

SOMERSET

Ah, Warwick, Montague hath breathed his last,
And to the latest gasp cried out for Warwick    41
And said, 'Commend me to my valiant brother.'
And more he would have said, and more he spoke,
Which sounded like a cannon in a vault,
That mought not be distinguished ; but at last    45
I well might hear, delivered with a groan,
'O, farewell, Warwick !'

WARWICK

Sweet rest his soul. Fly, lords, and save yourselves ;
For Warwick bids you all farewell, to meet in heaven.
                    [Dies.]

OXFORD

Away, away, to meet the queen's great power.
                    Here they bear away his body. Exeunt.

V, iii          Flourish. Enter King Edward in triumph ;
                with Richard, Clarence, and the rest.

KING EDWARD

Thus far our fortune keeps an upward course
And we are graced with wreaths of victory ;
But in the midst of this bright-shining day
I spy a black, suspicious, threat'ning cloud
That will encounter with our glorious sun
Ere he attain his easeful western bed.
I mean, my lords, those powers that the queen
8   Hath raised in Gallia have arrived our coast
And, as we hear, march on to fight with us.

CLARENCE

A little gale will soon disperse that cloud
And blow it to the source from whence it came.
Thy very beams will dry those vapors up,
13  For every cloud engenders not a storm.

RICHARD

The queen is valued thirty thousand strong,
And Somerset, with Oxford, fled to her.
16  If she have time to breathe, be well assured
Her faction will be full as strong as ours.

KING EDWARD

18  We are advertised by our loving friends
That they do hold their course toward Tewkesbury.
20  We, having now the best at Barnet field,
21  Will thither straight, for willingness rids way ;
And as we march our strength will be augmented
In every county as we go along.
Strike up the drum. Cry 'Courage !' and away.   Exeunt.

                    *

V, iv           Flourish. March. Enter the Queen [Margaret],
                young [Prince] Edward, Somerset, Oxford, and
                Soldiers.

QUEEN MARGARET

Great lords, wise men ne'er sit and wail their loss
2   But cheerly seek how to redress their harms.
What though the mast be now blown overboard,
The cable broke, the holding anchor lost,
And half our sailors swallowed in the flood ?
Yet lives our pilot still. Is't meet that he
Should leave the helm and, like a fearful lad,
With tearful eyes add water to the sea
And give more strength to that which hath too much,
10  Whiles, in his moan, the ship splits on the rock,
Which industry and courage might have saved ?
Ah, what a shame, ah, what a fault were this.
Say Warwick was our anchor. What of that ?
And Montague our topmast. What of him ?
15  Our slaught'red friends the tackles. What of these ?
Why, is not Oxford here, another anchor ?
And Somerset, another goodly mast ?
18  The friends of France our shrouds and tacklings ?
And, though unskillful, why not Ned and I
20  For once allowed the skillful pilot's charge ?
We will not from the helm, to sit and weep,

But keep our course (though the rough wind say no)
From shelves and rocks that threaten us with wrack.      23
As good to chide the waves as speak them fair.
And what is Edward but a ruthless sea ?
What Clarence but a quicksand of deceit ?
And Richard but a ragged fatal rock ?
All these the enemies to our poor bark.
Say you can swim – alas, 'tis but a while,
Tread on the sand – why there you quickly sink,
Bestride the rock – the tide will wash you off
Or else you famish : that's a threefold death.
This speak I, lords, to let you understand,
If case some one of you would fly from us,                34
That there's no hoped-for mercy with the brothers
More than with ruthless waves, with sands and rocks.
Why, courage then, what cannot be avoided
'Twere childish weakness to lament or fear.

PRINCE

Methinks a woman of this valiant spirit
Should, if a coward heard her speak these words,
Infuse his breast with magnanimity
And make him, naked, foil a man-at-arms.                  42
I speak not this as doubting any here ;
For did I but suspect a fearful man,
He should have leave to go away betimes,                  45
Lest in our need he might infect another
And make him of like spirit to himself.
If any such be here (as God forbid !)
Let him depart before we need his help.

OXFORD

Women and children of so high a courage,
And warriors faint ? Why, 'twere perpetual shame.
O brave young prince, thy famous grandfather            52
Doth live again in thee. Long mayst thou live
To bear his image and renew his glories.

SOMERSET

And he that will not fight for such a hope,
Go home to bed, and, like the owl by day,
If he arise, be mocked and wondered at.

QUEEN MARGARET

Thanks, gentle Somerset ; sweet Oxford, thanks.

PRINCE

And take his thanks that yet hath nothing else.
                    Enter a Messenger.

MESSENGER

Prepare you, lords ; for Edward is at hand,
Ready to fight. Therefore be resolute.

OXFORD

I thought no less. It is his policy
To haste thus fast, to find us unprovided.                63

SOMERSET

But he's deceived ; we are in readiness.

QUEEN MARGARET

This cheers my heart, to see your forwardness.            65

V, iii  8 *Gallia* France   13 *engenders* begets   16 *breathe* i.e. gather her
strength   18 *advertised* notified   20 *having . . . best* having now overcome
21 *rids way* i.e. decreases the distance
V, iv Fields near Tewkesbury   2 *cheerly* cheerfully   10 *in* at   15 *tackles*
lines and pulleys for raising sail (running rigging)   18 *shrouds* lines bracing
the mast (standing rigging); *tacklings* fittings and similar equipment
20 *charge* responsibility (i.e. to guide the ship)   23 *shelves* sandbanks;
*wrack* wreck, ruin   34 *If* in   42 *foil a man-at-arms* defeat an armed man
45 *betimes* immediately   52 *grandfather* i.e. Henry V   63 *unprovided* unprepared   65 *forwardness* zeal

OXFORD

66   Here pitch our battle; hence we will not budge.
> *Flourish and march. Enter [King] Edward, Richard,*
> *Clarence, and Soldiers.*

KING EDWARD

Brave followers, yonder stands the thorny wood
Which, by the heavens' assistance and your strength,
Must by the roots be hewn up yet ere night.
I need not add more fuel to your fire,
71   For well I wot ye blaze to burn them out.
Give signal to the fight, and to it, lords!

QUEEN MARGARET

Lords, knights and gentlemen, what I should say
74   My tears gainsay; for every word I speak,
Ye see I drink the water of my eye.
Therefore, no more but this: Henry, your sovereign,
Is prisoner to the foe, his state usurped,
His realm a slaughterhouse, his subjects slain,
His statutes cancelled, and his treasure spent;
And yonder is the wolf that makes this spoil.
You fight in justice. Then, in God's name, lords,
82   Be valiant and give signal to the fight.
> *Alarum [to the battle: they fight]; retreat [and King*
> *Edward and his company fly, driven out by Queen*
> *Margaret and her company]. Excursions [and the*
> *chambers be discharged, and re-enter King Edward*
> *and his company, making a great shout and cry*
> *'A York, a York'; and then the Queen Margaret,*
> *Prince, Oxford, and Somerset are taken].*    *Exeunt.*

V, v   *Flourish. Enter [King] Edward, Richard, [with*
> *Soldiers guarding] Queen [Margaret as prisoner],*
> *Clarence, [with Soldiers guarding] Oxford,*
> *Somerset [as prisoners].*

KING EDWARD

1   Now here a period of tumultuous broils.
2   Away with Oxford to Hames Castle straight.
For Somerset, off with his guilty head!
Go bear them hence. I will not hear them speak.

OXFORD

For my part, I'll not trouble thee with words.

SOMERSET

Nor I, but stoop with patience to my fortune.
> *Exeunt [Oxford and Somerset, guarded].*

QUEEN MARGARET

So part we sadly in this troublous world
8   To meet with joy in sweet Jerusalem.

KING EDWARD

Is proclamation made that who finds Edward
Shall have a high reward, and he his life?

RICHARD

It is. And lo where youthful Edward comes.
> *Enter [Soldiers, with] the Prince.*

KING EDWARD

Bring forth the gallant; let us hear him speak.
What? Can so young a thorn begin to prick?
Edward, what satisfaction canst thou make   14
For bearing arms, for stirring up my subjects,
And all the trouble thou hast turned me too?

PRINCE

Speak like a subject, proud ambitious York!
Suppose that I am now my father's mouth;
Resign thy chair, and where I stand kneel thou,
Whilst I propose the selfsame words to thee
Which, traitor, thou wouldst have me answer to.

QUEEN MARGARET

Ah, that thy father had been so resolved.

RICHARD

That you might still have worn the petticoat   23
And ne'er have stol'n the breech from Lancaster.   24

PRINCE

Let Aesop fable in a winter's night.   25
His currish riddles sorts not with this place.   26

RICHARD

By heaven, brat, I'll plague ye for that word.

QUEEN MARGARET

Ay, thou wast born to be a plague to men.

RICHARD

For God's sake take away this captive scold.

PRINCE

Nay, take away this scolding crook-back rather.

KING EDWARD

Peace, willful boy, or I will charm your tongue.   31

CLARENCE

Untutored lad, thou art too malapert.   32

PRINCE

I know my duty; you are all undutiful.
Lascivious Edward, and thou perjured George,
And thou misshapen Dick, I tell ye all
I am your better, traitors as ye are,
And thou usurp'st my father's right and mine.

KING EDWARD

Take that, the likeness of this railer here.   38
> *Stabs him.*

RICHARD

Sprawl'st thou? Take that, to end thy agony.   39
> *Richard stabs him.*

CLARENCE

And there's for twitting me with perjury.
> *Clarence stabs him.*

QUEEN MARGARET

O, kill me too!

RICHARD

Marry, and shall.   42
> *Offers to kill her.*

KING EDWARD

Hold, Richard, hold; for we have done too much.

RICHARD

Why should she live to fill the world with words?

KING EDWARD

What? Doth she swoon? Use means for her recovery.

RICHARD

Clarence, excuse me to the king my brother.
I'll hence to London on a serious matter;
Ere ye come there, be sure to hear some news.   48

CLARENCE   What? what?

RICHARD   The Tower, the Tower.     *Exit.*

---

66 *pitch our battle* deploy our forces   71 *wot* know   74 *gainsay* forbid
82 s.d. *chambers* saluting cannon (to simulate ordnance)
V, v   1 *period* full stop   2 *Hames Castle* i.e. Hanmes Castle, near Calais
(where Oxford was confined after his capture in 1474, three years later than
Tewkesbury)   8 *Jerusalem* i.e. Heaven, the New Jerusalem   14 *satisfac-*
*tion* recompense   23 *still* always   24 *breech* breeches   25–26 *Let . . . place*
i.e. you lie about the relationship between my mother and father (with a
gibe at Richard, for Aesop was supposedly stunted and deformed)   26
*currish* mean, cynical; *sorts not* are not appropriate   31 *charm your tongue*
i.e. silence you ('charm': cast a spell upon)   32 *malapert* impertinent
38 *this railer* i.e. Queen Margaret   39 *Sprawl'st thou* do you struggle in
your death-throes   42 *Marry, and shall* I will indeed ('marry': by the
Virgin Mary)   48 *be sure to* be confident that you will

QUEEN MARGARET
O Ned, sweet Ned, speak to thy mother, boy.
Canst thou not speak? O traitors! murderers!
They that stabbed Caesar shed no blood at all,
Did not offend, nor were not worthy blame,
55 If this foul deed were by, to equal it.
56 He was a man; this (in respect) a child,
And men ne'er spend their fury on a child.
What's worse than murderer, that I may name it?
No, no, my heart will burst an if I speak.
And I will speak, that so my heart may burst.
Butchers and villains, bloody cannibals,
How sweet a plant have you untimely cropped.
You have no children, butchers; if you had,
The thought of them would have stirred up remorse;
But if you ever chance to have a child,
Look in his youth to have him so cut off
67 As, deathsmen, you have rid this sweet young prince.

KING EDWARD
Away with her! Go bear her hence perforce!

QUEEN MARGARET
Nay, never bear me hence, dispatch me here.
Here sheathe thy sword, I'll pardon thee my death.
What, wilt thou not? Then, Clarence, do it thou.

CLARENCE
By heaven, I will not do thee so much ease.

QUEEN MARGARET
Good Clarence, do! Sweet Clarence, do thou do it!

CLARENCE
Didst thou not hear me swear I would not do it?

QUEEN MARGARET
75 Ay, but thou usest to forswear thyself.
'Twas sin before, but now 'tis charity.
What, wilt thou not? Where is that devil's butcher,
78 Hard-favored Richard? Richard, where art thou?
79 Thou art not here. Murder is thy almsdeed.
80 Petitioners for blood thou ne'er put'st back.

KING EDWARD
Away, I say. I charge ye bear her hence.

QUEEN MARGARET
So come to you and yours as to this prince.
                    *Exit Queen [Margaret, guarded].*

KING EDWARD
Where's Richard gone?

CLARENCE
84 To London, all in post; and, as I guess,
To make a bloody supper in the Tower.

KING EDWARD
He's sudden if a thing comes in his head.
87 Now march we hence, discharge the common sort
With pay and thanks, and let's away to London
And see our gentle queen how well she fares.
90 By this, I hope, she hath a son for me.
                    *Exit [King Edward with his company].*

*

V, vi          *Enter [King] Henry the Sixth and Richard, with the*
               *Lieutenant in the Tower.*

RICHARD
1 Good day, my lord. What, at your book so hard?

KING HENRY
Ay, my good lord – 'my lord' I should say rather.
'Tis sin to flatter. 'Good' was little better.
'Good Gloucester' and 'good devil' were alike,

And both preposterous. Therefore, not 'good lord.'   5

RICHARD
Sirrah, leave us to ourselves; we must confer.
                    *[Exit Lieutenant.]*

KING HENRY
So flies the reckless shepherd from the wolf;        7
So first the harmless sheep doth yield his fleece,
And next his throat unto the butcher's knife.
What scene of death hath Roscius now to act?         10

RICHARD
Suspicion always haunts the guilty mind;
The thief doth fear each bush an officer.

KING HENRY
The bird that hath been limèd in a bush              13
With trembling wings misdoubteth every bush;         14
And I, the hapless male to one sweet bird,           15
Have now the fatal object in my eye
Where my poor young was limed, was caught, and killed.

RICHARD
Why, what a peevish fool was that of Crete           18
That taught his son the office of a fowl.
And yet, for all his wings, the fool was drowned.

KING HENRY
I, Daedalus; my poor boy, Icarus;
Thy father, Minos, that denied our course;
The sun that seared the wings of my sweet boy,
Thy brother Edward; and thyself, the sea
Whose envious gulf did swallow up his life.          25
Ah, kill me with thy weapon, not with words.
My breast can better brook thy dagger's point        27
Than can my ears that tragic history.
But wherefore dost thou come? Is't for my life?

RICHARD
Think'st thou I am an executioner?

KING HENRY
A persecutor I am sure thou art.
If murdering innocents be executing,
Why, then thou art an executioner.

RICHARD
Thy son I killed for his presumption.

KING HENRY
Hadst thou been killed when first thou didst presume,
Thou hadst not lived to kill a son of mine.
And thus I prophesy, that many a thousand
Which now mistrust no parcel of my fear,             38
And many an old man's sigh and many a widow's,
And many an orphan's water-standing eye –            40
Men for their sons, wives for their husbands,
Orphans for their parents' timeless death –          42
Shall rue the hour that ever thou wast born.
The owl shrieked at thy birth, an evil sign;

55 *equal* compare with   56 *in respect* by comparison   67 *rid* killed   75
*thou . . . to forswear* you have the habit of forswearing   78 *Hard-favored*
grim in appearance   79 *almsdeed* charity   80 *Petitioners . . . back* you never
turn away those who ask for blood   84 *post* haste   87 *common sort* ordinary
soldiers   90 *this* this time
V, vi The Tower of London   1 *book* (of devotions)   5 *preposterous* unnatural   7 *reckless* heedless   10 *Roscius* famous Roman actor (died 62 B.C.),
supposed by the Elizabethans to be a tragedian   13 *limèd* caught with birdlime   14 *misdoubteth* suspects   15 *male* father; *bird* chick   18–25 *fool . . .
life* (Daedalus wished to escape from Crete, having been imprisoned there by
King Minos. He devised wings for himself and his son Icarus, fastening
them on with wax. The father flew to safety, but Icarus rose too near the sun;
the heat melted the wax, and Icarus fell into the sea and drowned.)   25 *envious gulf* hateful gullet   27 *brook* tolerate   38 *mistrust no parcel* do not suspect any part   40 *water-standing* full of tears   42 *timeless* untimely

45 The night crow cried, aboding luckless time;
     Dogs howled and hideous tempest shook down trees;
47 The raven rooked her on the chimney's top,
48 And chattering pies in dismal discords sung.
     Thy mother felt more than a mother's pain,
     And yet brought forth less than a mother's hope,
     To wit, an indigested and deformèd lump,
     Not like the fruit of such a goodly tree.
     Teeth hadst thou in thy head when thou wast born,
     To signify thou cam'st to bite the world;
     And, if the rest be true which I have heard,
     Thou cam'st –

RICHARD
     I'll hear no more. Die, prophet, in thy speech.
         *Stabs him.*
     For this (amongst the rest) was I ordained.

KING HENRY
     Ay, and for much more slaughter after this.
     O, God forgive my sins and pardon thee.
     *Dies.*

RICHARD
     What? Will the aspiring blood of Lancaster
     Sink in the ground? I thought it would have mounted.
     See how my sword weeps for the poor king's death.
64 O may such purple tears be always shed
     From those that wish the downfall of our house.
     If any spark of life be yet remaining,
     Down, down to hell, and say I sent thee thither,
         *Stabs him again.*
     I, that have neither pity, love, nor fear.
     Indeed 'tis true that Henry told me of;
     For I have often heard my mother say
     I came into the world with my legs forward.
     Had I not reason, think ye, to make haste
     And seek their ruin that usurped our right?
     The midwife wondered, and the women cried,
     'O, Jesus bless us! He is born with teeth!'
     And so I was; which plainly signified
     That I should snarl and bite and play the dog.
     Then, since the heavens have shaped my body so,
79 Let hell make crook'd my mind to answer it.
     I have no brother, I am like no brother;
     And this word 'love,' which greybeards call divine,
     Be resident in men like one another,
     And not in me. I am myself alone.
     Clarence, beware. Thou keep'st me from the light;
85 But I will sort a pitchy day for thee;
86 For I will buzz abroad such prophecies
     That Edward shall be fearful of his life;
     And then, to purge his fear, I'll be thy death.
     King Henry and the prince his son are gone.
     Clarence, thy turn is next, and then the rest,
     Counting myself but bad till I be best.
     I'll throw thy body in another room

     And triumph, Henry, in thy day of doom.
         *Exit [with the body].*

\*

*Flourish. Enter King [Edward], Queen [Elizabeth],*   V, vii
*Clarence, Richard, Hastings, Nurse [with the young
Prince], and Attendants.*

KING EDWARD
     Once more we sit in England's royal throne,
     Repurchased with the blood of enemies.
     What valiant foemen, like to autumn's corn,    3
     Have we mowed down in tops of all their pride.
     Three Dukes of Somerset, threefold renowned
     For hardy and undoubted champions;    6
     Two Cliffords, as the father and the son;    7
     And two Northumberlands – two braver men
     Ne'er spurred their coursers at the trumpet's sound;    9
     With them, the two brave bears, Warwick and    10
        Montague,
     That in their chains fettered the kingly lion
     And made the forest tremble when they roared.
     Thus have we swept suspicion from our seat    13
     And made our footstool of security.
     Come hither, Bess, and let me kiss my boy.
     Young Ned, for thee thine uncles and myself
     Have in our armors watched the winter's night,    17
     Went all afoot in summer's scalding heat,
     That thou mightst repossess the crown in peace;
     And of our labors thou shalt reap the gain.

RICHARD *[aside]*
     I'll blast his harvest, if your head were laid;    21
     For yet I am not looked on in the world.    22
     This shoulder was ordained so thick to heave,
     And heave it shall some weight or break my back.
     Work thou the way, and thou shalt execute.    25

KING EDWARD
     Clarence and Gloucester, love my lovely queen,
     And kiss your princely nephew, brothers both.

CLARENCE
     The duty that I owe unto your majesty
     I seal upon the lips of this sweet babe.    29

QUEEN ELIZABETH
     Thanks, noble Clarence; worthy brother, thanks.

RICHARD
     And that I love the tree from whence thou sprang'st
     Witness the loving kiss I give the fruit.
         *[Aside]*
     To say the truth, so Judas kissed his master
     And cried 'All hail!' when as he meant all harm.

KING EDWARD
     Now am I seated as my soul delights,
     Having my country's peace and brothers' loves.

CLARENCE
     What will your grace have done with Margaret?
     Reignier, her father, to the King of France
     Hath pawned the Sicils and Jerusalem,
     And hither have they sent it for her ransom.

KING EDWARD
     Away with her, and waft her hence to France.    41
     And now what rests but that we spend the time
     With stately triumphs, mirthful comic shows,    43
     Such as befits the pleasure of the court?
     Sound drums and trumpets! Farewell sour annoy!
     For here I hope begins our lasting joy.    *Exeunt omnes.*

---

45 *night crow* nightjar or owl; *aboding* foreboding · 47 *rooked her* squatted
48 *pies* magpies   64 *purple* i.e. bloody   79 *answer* accord with   85 *sort*
seek out (as being befitting); *pitchy* black   86 *buzz* whisper (scandal)
V, vii The royal palace in London   3 *corn* wheat   6 *undoubted* fearless
7 *as* to wit   9 *coursers* war horses   10 *bears* (the bear was the emblem of
the Nevils)   13 *suspicion* apprehension   17 *watched* stayed awake during
21 *laid* laid down (dead)   22 *looked on* respected   25 *thou . . . thou* (he
indicates his head and his arm or shoulder)   29 *seal* pledge   41 *waft* convoy
43 *triumphs* festivities

# APPENDIX A: GENEALOGICAL CHARTS

These charts do not attempt to be complete records of the families included, but they cite all the descendants of Edward III who are of consequence (by presence or parenthood) in these two plays and they mention every person of quality in the two lists of dramatis personae with the exception of the following:

PART TWO

*William de la Pole, Duke of Suffolk.* Not of royal blood, despite his claim in Part II, IV, i, 50–51.
*Lord Say.* Sir James Fiennes, Lord Say and Sele, Treasurer of England (d. 1450).
*Sir Humphrey Stafford* and *William Stafford.* These brothers appear to have been kinsmen of the Earls of Stafford.
*Vaux.* Presumably Sir William Vaux (d. 1471).
*Sir Matthew Gough.* A military man, friend of the Lord Scales.

PART THREE

*Earl of Pembroke.* Sir William Herbert (d. 1469).
*Lord Stafford.* Sir Humphrey Stafford, Earl of Devon (d. 1469).
*Sir John* and *Sir Hugh Mortimer.* These brothers are thought to be illegitimate sons of an unidentified Mortimer.
*Sir John Montgomery.* Called Sir Thomas in Holinshed (d. 1495).
*Somervile.* Not identified.

In the charts the names of persons in the plays of the two tetralogies are printed in italics. The order of the names does not necessarily indicate the order of birth.

THE LINE OF EDWARD III

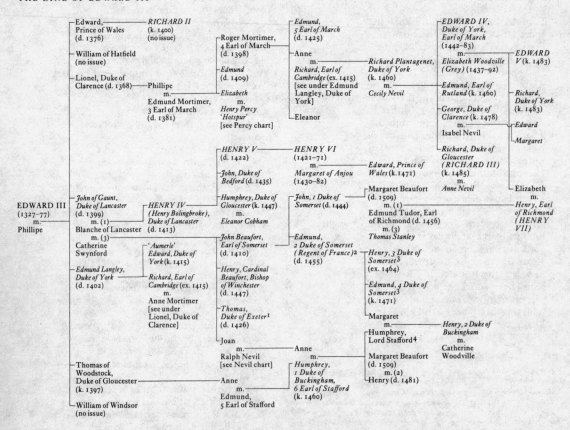

1. Though Thomas died in 1426, Shakespeare has evidently retained him for Part Three.
2. Part Two; Part Three, I, i, 16.

3. Part Three; these have been combined: Henry is in Act IV, Edmund in Act V.
4. Part Three, I, i, 7.

## PERCY–NEVIL

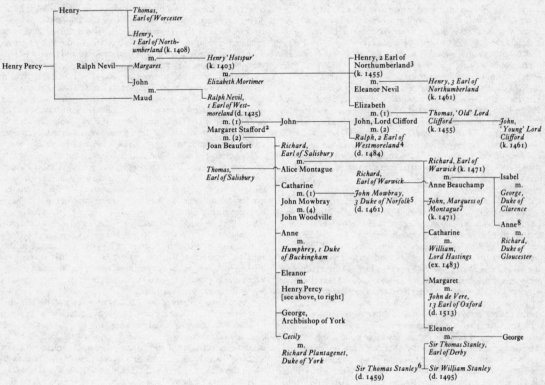

```
Henry ──── Thomas,
              Earl of Worcester

           Henry,
           1 Earl of North-
           umberland (k. 1408)
           m. ──── Henry 'Hotspur'        Henry, 2 Earl of
Henry Percy ── Ralph Nevil ── Margaret    (k. 1403)                Northumberland3
                                          m. ──────────────────    (k. 1455)
                              John        Elizabeth Mortimer       m. ──── Henry, 3 Earl of
                              m.                                    Eleanor Nevil    Northumberland
                              Maud                                                   (k. 1461)
                                          Ralph Nevil,
                                          1 Earl of West-          Elizabeth
                                          moreland (d. 1425)       m. (1) ──── Thomas, 'Old' Lord
                                          m. (1)                   John, Lord Clifford    Clifford    John,
                                          Margaret Stafford2 ── John    m. (2)         (k. 1455)   'Young' Lord
                                          m. (2)                   Ralph, 2 Earl of              Clifford
                                          Joan Beaufort            Westmoreland4                 (k. 1461)
                                          Richard,                 (d. 1484)
                                          Earl of Salisbury
                                          m.                       Richard, Earl of
                           Thomas,        Alice Montague           Warwick (k. 1471)
                           Earl of Salisbury                       m. ──── Isabel
                                          Catharine    Richard,    Anne Beauchamp   m.
                                          m. (1)       Earl of Warwick              George,
                                          John Mowbray ── John Mowbray,   John, Marquess of   Duke of
                                          m. (4)       3 Duke of Norfolk5   Montague7         Clarence
                                          John Woodville  (d. 1461)       (k. 1471)
                                                                                              Anne8
                                          Anne                            Catharine    m.
                                          m.                              m.           Richard,
                                          Humphrey, 1 Duke                William,     Duke of
                                          of Buckingham                   Lord Hastings Gloucester
                                                                          (ex. 1483)
                                          Eleanor
                                          m.                              Margaret
                                          Henry Percy                     m.
                                          [see above, to right]           John de Vere,
                                                                          13 Earl of Oxford
                                          George,                         (d. 1513)
                                          Archbishop of York
                                                                          Eleanor
                                          Cecily                          m. ──── George
                                          m.                              Sir Thomas Stanley,
                                          Richard Plantagenet,            Earl of Derby
                                          Duke of York
                                              Sir Thomas Stanley6   Sir William Stanley
                                              (d. 1459)            (d. 1495)
```

## WOODVILLE

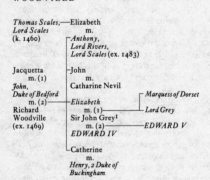

```
Thomas Scales, ── Elizabeth
Lord Scales       m.
(k. 1460)         Anthony,
                  Lord Rivers,
                  Lord Scales (ex. 1483)

Jacquetta         John
m. (1)            m.
John,             Catharine Nevil
Duke of Bedford
m. (2)            Elizabeth          Marquess of Dorset
Richard           m. (1)             Lord Grey
Woodville         Sir John Grey1
(ex. 1469)        m. (2)             EDWARD V
                  EDWARD IV

                  Catharine
                  m.
                  Henry, 2 Duke of
                  Buckingham
```

1. Called Sir Richard at Part Three, III, ii, 2.
2. Sister of Edmund, 5th Earl of Stafford.
3. Mentioned Part Three, I, i, 4.
4. The personality depicted is historically that of his brother John.
5. Died 1461; it is possible, but unlikely, that his son is intended.

6. The guardian of Eleanor Cobham, called John in Part Two.
7. And from 1464 to 1470, Earl of Northumberland.
8. Betrothed to Edward, son of Henry VI, but not married. Shakespeare has reversed the ages of Isabel and Anne.

Among scholars the question of the authorship of *2 and 3 Henry VI* has long been a vexing one. The inclusion of the plays in the folio of 1623 indicates that Heminge and Condell, Shakespeare's friends and fellow-actors who compiled the volume, considered him to have been their author. However, as these same compilers also included at least one play, *Henry VIII*, which is generally admitted to have been written jointly by Shakespeare and John Fletcher, the degree of Shakespeare's involvement in the Henry VI plays is left open. The problem is further complicated by the existence of two different versions of both Part Two and Part Three. Part Two first appeared in quarto in 1594 as *The First part of the Contention betwixt the two famous Houses of York and Lancaster, with the death of the good Duke Humphrey : And the banishment and death of the Duke of Suffolke, and the Tragicall end of the proud Cardinall of Winchester, with the notable Rebellion of Iacke Cade : And the Duke of Yorkes first claime unto the Crowne*; Part Three was published in octavo in 1595 as *The true Tragedie of Richard Duke of Yorke, and the death of good King Henrie the Sixt, with the whole contention betweene the two Houses Lancaster and Yorke*. Both plays were reprinted separately in 1600, and in 1619 they were combined under the general title *The Whole Contention betweene the two Famous Houses, Lancaster and Yorke. With the Tragicall ends of the good Duke Humfrey, Richard Duke of Yorke, and King Henrie the sixt*. In the folio of 1623 these two early versions were superseded by new texts, considerably fuller than their predecessors, under the titles *The second Part of Henry the Sixt, with the death of the Good Duke Humfrey* and *The third Part of Henry the Sixt, with the death of the Duke of Yorke*.

The first critic to take a position on the authorship problem was Lewis Theobald, who in 1734 suggested that the plays were not entirely by Shakespeare. Dr Johnson disputed Theobald's position, claiming the plays to be wholly Shakespearean. A more extensive early analysis was that of Edmond Malone in *A Dissertation on the Three Parts of Henry VI* (1787). Here Malone (who had previously supported the opposite view) argued (1) that the plays were originally the work of other dramatists, revised or rewritten by Shakespeare because their "inferior parts are not merely unequal to the rest . . . but of quite a different complexion from the inferior parts" of Shakespeare's recognized work; (2) that the quarto and octavo editions of the plays represented the original versions and the folio editions the Shakespearean revisions; and (3) that a complaint by Robert Greene in 1592 pointed clearly to the fact that Shakespeare had plagiarized from Greene in writing the plays. The complaint appeared in Greene's *Groats-worth of Wit*, addressed to three of Greene's literary associates – presumably Marlowe, Nashe, and Peele – warning them against relying on the good faith of actors :

Base minded men, all three of you, if by my miserie you be not warnd : for unto none of you (like mee) sought those burres [the actors] to cleave : those Puppets (I meane) that spake from our mouths, those Anticks garnisht in our colours. Is it not strange, that I, to whom they all have beene beholding : is it not like that you, to whome they all have beene beholding, shall (were yee in that case as I am now) bee both at once of them forsaken : Yes trust them not : for there is an upstart Crow, beautified with our feathers, that with his *Tygers hart wrapt in a Players hyde*, supposes he is as well able to bombast out a blanke verse as the best of you : and beeing an absolute *Johannes fac totum*, is in his owne conceit the onely Shake-scene in a countrey . . . whilest you may, seeke you better Maisters.

Malone interpreted this complaint as Greene's retaliation for the hard treatment that he – an educated man – had received from ignorant and callous players who had made their fortunes by parroting his lines while he lay dying in penury. Greene singled out one player who was so presumptuous as to attempt to write plays and, specifically, to rewrite a play on Henry VI written by Greene himself. This "Shake-scene" was Shakespeare : the "Tygers hart wrapt in a Players hyde" was Greene's parody of Shakespeare's "tiger's heart wrapped in a woman's hide" (*3 Henry VI*, I, iv, 137), a phrase, according to Malone, stolen from Greene.

Malone's view of the evidence, though often questioned, was not supplanted until in 1929 Professor Peter Alexander and in 1930 Miss Madeleine Doran, working independently in Great Britain and America, reached the conclusion that the quarto and octavo editions were not early plays by Greene or others but were versions of the folio texts which had been derived chiefly by actors writing down (or dictating to a scribe) what they could remember of parts they had learned for performances of Shakespeare's plays. The two scholars demonstrated that the 1594 and 1595 editions bore marks regularly accepted as denoting texts memorially reconstructed for sale to a printer or for use in the provinces by an acting company that did not have access to the official prompt-book. The 1594 and 1595 texts thus, though earlier in date of publication than those of 1623, were later in the line of transmission; so far from being early drafts revised and improved into the folio versions, they were versions derived from the folio texts and mutilated in the process. Professor Alexander explained Greene's charge against "Shake-scene" not as one of plagiarism but as one of presumptuous conceit; Greene indicated by the quotation of the line no more than that Shakespeare was the author of *Henry VI*, Part Three (and hence of Part Two). Thus it was argued that the existence of the differing versions could no longer be used as evidence bearing on the question of authorship.

This interpretation of the evidence was accepted in the 1930's and 1940's by one after another of the leading Shakespearean critics. Malone's belief that the 1594 and 1595 editions represented the work of Greene and others while the folio represented the Shakespearean revisions is now conceded by most critics to have been erroneous. On the other hand, the repudiation of Malone's other points on authorship and plagiarism has not received complete assent.

This fact is effectively represented by the appearance in the 1950's of editions of the plays in the two chief British series of Shakespeare, one editor supporting Greene, Nashe, and Peele as joint authors of work revised by Shakespeare, the other supporting Shakespeare as sole author.

John Dover Wilson in his editions of 1951 and 1952 in the Cambridge New Shakespeare supports Malone's belief that Greene was charging Shakespeare with misappropriation of Greene's material. Wilson does so by pointing to Greene's other uses of Aesop's fable of the "upstart Crow, beautified with our feathers," which all refer to literary plagiarism, the vice with which the allusion was conventionally associated. Working solely with the folio versions, Wilson analyzes the two plays and the writings of Greene, Nashe, and Peele. On the basis of "common verbal parallels, . . . syntactical peculiarities, little mannerisms and tricks of style, proverbial phrases, . . . classical or other allusions, and clichés of various types," Wilson concludes that Greene was responsible for the plotting of the two Parts and for the verse (with perhaps a little help from Peele in Part Three) and that Nashe was responsible for the prose of the Jack Cade scenes. Shakespeare revised throughout with varying degrees of thoroughness.

Andrew S. Cairncross in his edition of 1957 in the New Arden series rejects this position by arguing that the offensive plagiarism was not wholesale but only the re-use of particular allusions or occasional bits and pieces of material. He sees the verbal and stylistic parallels as an inconclusive demonstration of joint authorship; they can be explained as the work of a young author deliberately copying the devices and mannerisms of men who have practiced the craft before him. Cairncross argues for sole Shakespearean authorship and derives the difficulties and inconsistencies in the plays from two causes. The first of these is external to transmission – the requirement of the official censor that many passages be rewritten so as not to give offense to authority. The second is textual – the use of the early version in the printing of the late. These two explanations are both fresh suggestions in the argument; their evaluation will follow in the years to come.

Both Wilson and Cairncross took for granted Alexander's and Miss Doran's demonstrations of memorial reconstruction as the method of origin of *The Contention* and *The True Tragedy*, but this matter has been recently re-opened by C. T. Prouty, who, in a study of *The Contention and Shakespeare's 2 Henry VI* (1954), argues for a return to Malone's theory of revision. While Prouty's thesis has received little support from other scholars, its very existence proves the continuing uncertainty over the textual history of the plays. And, as if the authorship question were not sufficiently troublesome, there is also disagreement about the date of composition of the two Parts, a matter linked not only with authorship but also with the date of composition of the plays which adjoin them, *1 Henry VI* and *Richard III*.

The Diary of Philip Henslowe, who had financial interests in the Elizabethan theatre, records that in March, 1592, Lord Strange's Men performed a play called *Harey the vj*, and beside the entry is the notation "ne," which presumably means that the play was new and being presented for the first time. Because in the same year Thomas Nashe in *Pierce Pennilesse* referred to a current play featuring the exploits of Talbot, the hero of the wars in France, and because Talbot has a significant role in Shakespeare's *1 Henry VI*, it is tempting to identify *1 Henry VI* with the play mentioned by Nashe as well as with *Harey the vj*. One difficulty with this interpretation of the evidence is that *Harey the vj* definitely belonged to Strange's Men while the other plays in the series belonged to Pembroke's Men, at least at some period in their history. *Harey the vj* may thus have no direct bearing on the problems related to Shakespeare's Henry VI plays, and Nashe's allusion may have been either to a lost *Harey the vj* or to *1 Henry VI*.

The anterior date of the Henry VI plays, it has recently been argued, can be fixed by the registering for publication in December, 1589, of Books I–III of Spenser's *The Faerie Queene*, for *1 Henry VI* shows the influence of this work in several places, and their posterior date by the publication in 1591 of a play called *The Troublesome Raigne of King John*, which seems to draw some of its language from other dramatic works, including *Richard III*, generally agreed to be the last in Shakespeare's series to be written. As Greene died on September 3, 1592, his parody of the line from *3 Henry VI* proves the existence of the play by that date. Within these limits, 1590 has been assigned as the approximate date of composition of both *2* and *3 Henry VI*. There are some, however, who, while willing to accept a date of 1589, 1590, or 1591 for *2* and *3 Henry VI*, feel that *Harey the vj* was probably *1 Henry VI*; if Henslowe's "ne" means "new" in 1592, then it would follow that the plays were not written sequentially but *1 Henry VI* after *2* and *3 Henry VI*, although it may later have been revised to make it fit into the first place in the series. Supporting this line of reasoning is the fact that Talbot, who looms large in *1 Henry VI*, is ignored in *2* and *3*, even being omitted from Gloucester's list of those who suffered in France (*2 Henry VI*, I, i, 78–87).

Although scholars cannot as yet agree on precise dates for *2* and *3 Henry VI*, there is no question of the fact that Shakespeare had a hand in them very early in his career, about the same time as his writing of *Titus Andronicus* and *The Comedy of Errors* and possibly before. There is, moreover, general agreement that even if he was not the sole author of the two history plays, Shakespeare exercised the dominant force in shaping them into their present form, and that he worked on them sequentially and meant them to be considered as related, even though both plays are sufficiently self-contained to be performed separately. Thus we are probably not far off the mark in speaking of them as though their conception and execution were altogether his while silently acknowledging the possibility that he worked from earlier plays.

The present edition is based on the assumption that *The First Part of the Contention* and *The True Tragedie* are versions of the two Parts memorially reconstructed by actors. Hence they possess little authority for the text of the dialogue, but in disclosing details of performance they solve some theatrical problems which seem to have been left by Shakespeare to the discretion of the dramatic company. Their stage directions have therefore been generously incorporated in square brackets into this text, but where these directions offer a staging clearly not intended by the folio text, they have been ignored.

The folio versions give indications of having been printed from authorial manuscript, and on them the present editions are based. Two brief passages in the folio (Part Two, IV, v, 1–IV, vi, 6; Part Three, IV, ii, 1–18) would seem to have been printed directly from the quarto versions of 1619, perhaps because the manuscript was illegible. For the present editions, the folio versions have been corrected and emended by reference to the quarto and octavo, and the following lines have been admitted to supply omissions in the folio: Part Two, IV, i, 48; Part Three, II, i, 113; II, vi, 8. The collation of the folio by Mr Charlton Hinman has disclosed three substantive press variants, all in Part Three, V, vii, 25–42; these have been printed in the corrected readings.

The folio preserves in stage directions and speech-prefixes the names of five or six "bit" actors: Part Two, IV, ii, 1–28, the two Rebels are named Bevis and John Holland; IV, vii, 7, 14, the Rebel is named John (see l. 9); IV, vii, 20, the Rebel with the Lord Say is named George (presumably Bevis' Christian name); IV, ii, 99–106, the Messenger is named Michael (possibly an actor's name); Part Three, I, ii, 47 s.d. and 49, the Messenger is named Gabriel (Gabriel Spencer); III, i, the two Keepers are named Sinklo and Humfrey (John Sinklo and Humfrey Jeffes). The present edition substitutes dramatic designations for each of the above in both stage directions and speech-prefixes as indicated in the following list of emendations, which includes all substantive departures from the copy text. The adopted reading in italics is followed by the folio reading in roman.

### 2 HENRY VI

I, i, 176 *Protector* (Q) Protectors    177, 211 s.d. *Exeunt* (Eds) Exit    254 *in* (F2) in in

I, ii, 37 *Westminster*; (This ed.) Westminster,    40 *diadem* – (This ed.) Diadem.

I, iii, 6 *1. Petitioner* (F4) Peter    13 *For* (Wordsworth) To    29 *master was* (Warburton) Mistresse was    39 s.d. *Exeunt* (Eds) Exit    98 *helm.* (Eds) Helme. Exit.    140 *would* (Q) could

I, iv, 15 *silence* (Q) silent    23 *Asnath* (Cairncross) Asmath    60 *te* (Warburton) Omitted    61 *posse* (Eds) posso

II, i, 48 *Cardinal* (Theobald) Cardinall,    106 *Alban* (F3) Albones    130 *his* (Q) it,

II, ii, 45 *son* (Rowe) Omitted    46 *son* (Theobald) Sonnes Sonne

II, iii, 3 *sins* (Theobald) sinne    30 *helm* (Steevens) Realme

III, i, s.d. (order of entrance in procession is from Q; the order in F is King, Queen, Cardinal, Suffolk, York, Buckingham, Salisbury, Warwick)    211 *strains* (Vaughan) strayes    260 *treasons* (Hudson) Reasons

III, ii, 14 s.d. *Somerset* (Eds) Suffolke, Somerset    26 *Meg* (Capell) Nell    79, 100, 120 *Margaret* (Rowe) Elianor    116 *witch* (Theobald) watch    332 *turn* (Rowe) turnes    385 *sorrow's* (This ed.) sorrowes

IV, i, s.d. (characters other than Lieutenant and Suffolk listed from Q; F reads 'and others')    48 *Jove . . . I?* (Q) Omitted    50 *Suffolk* (before l. 51 in F)    71 *Suffolk* (Alexander) Sir    72 *Lieutenant* (Alexander) Lord    86 mother's bleeding (Rowe) Mother-bleeding    94 *are* (Rowe) and    118 *Paene* (Malone) Pine    133 *Suffolk* (before l. 134 in F)    142 s.d. *Exeunt* (Eds) Exit

IV, ii, s.d. *two Rebels* (This ed.) Bevis, and Iohn Holland    1–28 *1. Rebel, 2. Rebel* (This ed.) Bevis, Hol.    31 *fall* (F4) faile    92 *an* (F2) a    98 s.d., 99, 101, 106 *Messenger* (This ed.) Michael    124 *this :* (Eds) this

IV, iv, 43 *hate* (F2) hateth    58 *be* (F2) Omitted    59 *Say* (Q) Omitted

IV, vi, 11 *Messenger* (This ed.) Dicke

IV, vii, 7, 14 *2. Rebel* (This ed.) Iohn    9 *Weaver* (Cairncross) Smith    20 s.d. *First Rebel* (This ed.) George    63–64 *hands, / But* (Johnson conj.; Rann) hands? / Kent    76 *1. Rebel* (This

ed.) George   82 *caudle* (F4) Candle   *pap with a* (Farmer conj.;
Cairncross) the help of   119 s.d. *two* (Q) one
IV, viii, 12 *rebel* (Singer) rabble
IV, ix, 33 *calmed* (F4) calme
IV, x, 19 *waning* (Rowe) warning   56 *God* (Q) Iove
V, i, 109 *these* (Theobald) thee   111 *sons* (Q) sonne   113 *for* (F2)
of   194 *or* (Rowe) and   196 *Thou* (Cairncross) You   201
*house's* (F2) housed
V, ii, 28 *oeuvres* (Eds) eumenes
V, iii, 1 *Old* (Q) Of   29 *faith* (Q) hand

### 3 HENRY VI

I, i, 14 *cousin* (as in O at I, ii, 1, 36, 55) Brother   69 *Exeter* (O)
Westm   83 *and* (F2) Omitted   105 *Thy* (O) My   201 s.d.
(after l. 205 in F)   205 s.d. *Sennet* (followed by 'Here they come
down' in F)   259 *with* (F2) Omitted   261 *from* (O) to
I, ii, 4 *cousin* (as in O at I, ii, 1, 36, 55) Brother   36 *Cousin* (O)
Brother   47 s.d. *a Messenger* (O) Gabriel   49 *Messenger* (O)
Gabriel   55 *cousin* (O) Brother   60 *Cousin* (O) Brother
I, iv, 50 *buckle* (O) buckler
II, i, 113 *And . . . thought* (O) Omitted   131 *an idle* (O) a lazie
II, ii, 89 *Since* (Eds) Cla. Since   116 *sun set* (O) Sunset   133
*Richard* (O) War
II, iii, 49 *all together* (Rowe) altogether
II, v, 37 *months* (Rowe) yeares   54 s.d. *door* (followed by 'and a
Father that hath kill'd his Sonne at another doore' in F)   78 s.d.
*Enter . . . son* (replaces 'Enter Father, bearing of his Sonne' in
F)   79 *hast* (F3) hath   119 *Even* (Capell) Men
II, vi, 6 *commixture* (O) Commixtures   8 *The . . . flies* (O) Omitted
42 *Edward* (O) Rich   43 *Richard* (O) Omitted   44 *Edward. See
who it is , and* (Capell) See who it is. / Ed. And   60 *his* (F2) is

III, i, s.d. *two Keepers* (O) Sinklo, and Humfrey   1–97 *1. Keeper,
2. Keeper* (Malone) Sink., Hum.   24 *thee . . . adversity* (Dyce)
the . . . Adversaries   55 *that* (O) Omitted
III, ii, 3 *lands* (O) Land   123 *honorably* (O) honourable
III, iii, 124 *eternal* (O) externall   156 *peace* (F2) Omitted   161 s.d.
(after l. 160 in F)   228 *I'll* (O) I
IV, i, 93 *thy* (O) the
IV, ii, 15 *towns* (Theobald) Towne
IV, iii, s.d. *King Edward's* (Eds) the Kings   59 s.d. (after l. 57 in F)
IV, v, 4 *stands* (F2) stand   8 *Comes* (F2) Come   21 *King Edward*
(Wilson) Omitted   *ship* (F2) shipt
IV, vi, 55 *be* (Malone) Omitted   88 s.d. *Manent* (Eds) Manet
IV, viii, s.d. *Exeter* (Capell) Somerset   6 *Oxford* (O) King
V, i, 78 *an* (Rowe) in
V, iv, 27 *ragged* (Rowe) raged
V, v, 50 *The* (O) Omitted   77 *butcher* (O) butcher Richard
V, vi, s.d. *in the Tower* (O) on the Walles*
V, vii, 5 *renowned* (Rowe) Renowne   25 *and* (corrected F) add
(uncorrected F)   *and thou* (O) and that   27 *kiss* (corrected F)
'tis (uncorrected F)   30 *Queen Elizabeth* (O) Cla   *Thanks* (F3)
Thanke   38 *Reignier* (Rowe) Reynard   42 *rests* (corrected F)
tests (uncorrected F)

* Stage directions throughout have indicated the use of the usual facilities
of an Elizabethan stage with the exception of a "discovery" recess. The rear
stage gallery has several times been used to represent the walls of a city, or an
elevated gallery. Only in the present instance does the folio direction locate
the action "on the Walles" when there is no simultaneous and related action
on the stage proper. The location given in the octavo "in the Tower" suggests that this scene, too, was played on the stage proper, with the locale
given in the author's script regarded as literary and not theatrical.

# THE TRAGEDY OF
# KING RICHARD THE THIRD

## INTRODUCTION

From the earliest times *The Tragedy of King Richard the Third* has proved one of Shakespeare's most successful plays in the theatre, but the enthusiasms it arouses are of a different order from, let us say, the enthusiasms we feel for a *Macbeth*. It is in fact Shakespeare's most whole-hearted excursion into melodrama, and a brief comparison with a tragedy like *Macbeth*, in certain surface appearances so similar, in so many vital respects so different, can be revealing. Both Richard and Macbeth fascinate us, but our concern for Richard moves only (with the exception of one brief moment in Act V) on the level of admiration for a kind of virtuoso in evil who satisfies us by being so utterly competent, a creation which wins us, partly in spite of ourselves, by his sheer audacity and enormity. Macbeth, however, wins us simply because he is first of all a man, with the glories, failures, and complexities which that proud title carries with it – "What a piece of work is a man!" Of this feeling there is essentially nothing in *Richard III*. Where then lies the secret of the perennial popularity of the play, next to *Hamlet* the most frequently produced of Shakespeare's plays?

In part the answer lies in the uncomplicated, even obvious nature of the play and its principal characters. They wear their hearts upon their sleeves, and no mystery of the unresolved teases an audience into taking thought. An easy virtue perhaps, but one to be reckoned with, especially when it is combined with immense energy, an energy which pervades not only the central character but the play as a whole. From the Marlowe-like opening soliloquy in which Richard with engaging frankness invites us to watch him play the villain to the famous closing cry – "A horse! a horse! my kingdom for a horse!" – Shakespeare rarely allows the pace to slacken or tensions to relax. In one way this effect of pace is achieved through the ruthless handling of historical time, creating always a sense of the pressure both of the moment and of the threatening future. The pattern or formal structure of the play also furthers the effect of pace. As a structural device, Shakespeare, in defiance of history, has introduced the commanding and ominous old Queen Margaret, who, in her choric role (she is nothing but a voice), evokes the past, lashes the present, and forebodes the future, setting up in her memorable curse scene (I, iii) the pattern through which we watch, with a growing sense of the inevitable, the seemingly inexorable march of events. Other devices, similar in effect to the curse pattern – foreshadowing dreams, oaths sworn only to be broken, continual flashes of rather obvious dramatic irony – serve to give form to the play, as, at the same time, they accelerate and regulate its pace. In this connection, Shakespeare's use of the "dramatic moment" deserves particular attention. Little

episodes or sudden turns are skillfully exploited to bring out the full theatrical potentiality of the larger and dominating pattern of the scene. For example: the brilliant trick by which Richard turns Margaret's curse upon herself (I, iii); the clever device for announcing Clarence's death (II, i); the strawberry scene heralding the fall of Hastings (III, iv); the clock scene (IV, ii); Richard's abortive attempt to drown out the curses of his mother and Queen Elizabeth with trumpet and drum (IV, iv).

As the center of energy in the play stands Richard himself. Professor E. M. W. Tillyard has well remarked that he is Shakespeare's first character to impress himself upon us as being "larger than life." Shakespeare spares him and us nothing, even heightening the already "monstrous" portrait left for us by his political enemies, and leaving us in no doubt about Richard's ultimate responsibility for all the evil in the play. Such focussing and concentration justifies itself in terms of sheer theatrical effectiveness, and Richard pursues evil with a whole-souled quality which almost achieves a kind of inverted moral significance – he works so hard at being the very best kind of villain. In projecting this character Shakespeare was influenced, of course, by the extreme Elizabethan conception of Machiavellian policy. Already in *3 Henry VI* Richard had promised to "set the murderous Machiavel to school" (III, ii, 193) and had flaunted his rejection of all such human weaknesses as "pity, love, nor fear" – "I am myself alone" (V, vi, 68, 83):

> Why, I can smile, and murder whiles I smile,
> And cry 'Content!' to that which grieves my heart,
> And wet my cheeks with artificial tears,
> And frame my face to all occasions....
> I'll play the orator as well as Nestor,
> Deceive more slily than Ulysses could
> And, like a Sinon, take another Troy.
> I can add colors to the chameleon.... (III, ii, 182–91)

Here already is the essential Richard whom Shakespeare presents in the opening lines of *Richard III*: his hypocrisy, his play-acting (cf. *Richard III*, III, v, 1–11), his powers of persuasion, his fox-like slyness (a special attribute of the Machiavellian), above all his virtuosity as a villain. Richard's only virtue is his courage (also granted to him by Shakespeare's sources), though one is tempted to admit his gruesome sense of humor as another. Once only does the audience suffer any real emotional involvement with Richard. When he awakes after the ghostly visitation of his eleven victims, he momentarily exposes himself as a mere man; in place of the brilliant artifact we see a terrified human creature unable to find pity or love in himself even for himself – nothing but fear. It is a moving moment, but to speak of development in Richard's character would be, I think, to set the emphasis in the wrong place and to confuse this play with Shakespearean tragedy. Richard is a static character; he emerges complete at the very beginning and never undergoes any basic change. "I am determinèd to prove a villain," he says, and the play consists largely in our watching breathlessly as he moves from crime to crime keeping his promise to us. Such singleness and simplicity of purpose has, of course, both structural and dramatic value, but we never really allow ourselves to be blinded to the limitations which, like other aspects of this play, it imposes ultimately on the kind of play Shakespeare is writing.

*The Tragedy of King Richard the Third*, or, as it is perhaps better described in the running titles of the first folio, *The Life and Death of Richard the Third*, may safely be dated between 1591 and 1594. For historical materials Shakespeare turned, as in his other English history plays, to the second edition of Holinshed's *Chronicles* (1587), a compilation drawing heavily, through Hall's *Chronicle* (1550), on the celebrated *Life of Richard the Third* usually attributed to Sir Thomas More and on Polydore Vergil's *Historia Anglica* (1534). A few details may be traced directly to Hall. Both More's *Life* (if indeed More and not Cardinal Morton was the author) and Polydore Vergil's account are savagely anti-Yorkist, and the portrait of Richard which emerges is darkly colored and almost wholly unfavorable. Curiously different is the verdict of many modern historians who tend to equal extremes in rehabilitating Richard. For the average reader, however, Shakespeare has once and for all settled Richard's character – as well try, in the words of a favorite Elizabethan proverb, to wash the Ethiop! In addition to his use of the chronicles, Shakespeare probably owes a few suggestions to an anonymous play, *The True Tragedie of Richard the Third* (printed 1594), and possibly even to the early three-part Latin play *Richardus Tertius* (1579) by Thomas Legge.

An extreme, but not uncharacteristic, example of Shakespeare's dramatic treatment of history may be found in the two opening scenes. In the first, Shakespeare combines events of 1477 (the arrest of Clarence), of 1483 (the reported final sickness of Edward IV), and of 1471 (the projected marriage of Richard with Lady Anne), the last date being underscored by Richard's opening soliloquy which implies the beginning of Edward's reign. This preparation leads directly into the second scene: the funeral procession of the recently dead Henry VI (1471), a situation which is made to serve for the occasion of Richard's triumphantly outrageous wooing of Lady Anne, daughter-in-law of Henry VI and widow of his son, Edward, Prince of Wales, both his victims. Thus with a few bold strokes Shakespeare highhandedly telescopes and confuses the events of thirteen years, reducing them, as it were, to a single moment. With what justification, we may ask. The answer: art and the theatre. With Richard as the center of his play, Shakespeare is most vitally concerned to concentrate on him any situation which can be made to exploit the immediate dramatic potentialities of his character; for this he needs the Clarence affair and the Anne wooing, both nicely calculated to play up different facets of Richard's personality. For the same reason, Edward IV must be relegated to a subordinate role and dismissed from the play with a quick hand. Even as he recognizes all

this and arranges for it, Shakespeare also senses the dramatic advantage of preserving an immediate continuity with *3 Henry VI* by picking up the story where that play had left it – with Richard's murder of Henry VI and the accession of Edward IV. In the place of history, time, and logic Shakespeare gives us a dramatic fiction, a play.

Paradoxically, however, *Richard III* remains very much a "history" play, for Shakespeare is here deeply concerned with political themes: the role of the king, good (Henry) and bad (Richard), with an intermediate type in Edward IV; Richard both as the type of the Scourge of God, working out England's crime in the deposition and murder of Richard II, and as the "unsuccessive" tyrant whom, even under Tudor doctrine, it was righteous to depose; the emergence of the great Tudor dynasty under the newly crowned Lancastrian Henry VII, who by his marriage to the Yorkist Princess Elizabeth was to heal the long-festering wounds of the Wars of the Roses. One must always remember, too, that *Richard III* is the last in a series of eight closely interrelated plays (though at this time only the three parts of *Henry VI* had been written) and that throughout it Shakespeare is careful by reference and allusion (particularly through the figure of old Queen Margaret) to preserve a sense of a larger historical continuity – of the flow of events seen in terms of cause and effect, of a past and a future, as well as of a bare present.

In style and diction *Richard III* belongs markedly to Shakespeare's early serious manner, a manner much influenced by the University playwrights, Marlowe and Greene, sometimes to such a degree that it is difficult to recognize Shakespeare's special idiom. In general the style is more rhetorical than poetic, depending for its effect upon a variety of artificial and cleverly manipulated figures or "flowers of rhetoric." In many ways, of course, it is the perfect instrument for a Richard – witty, hard, and brilliantly efficient, always glancing, parrying, thrusting. This effect comes out most obviously in the rapier-like exchanges (a development of Senecan stichomythia, one of a great many Senecan traces in the play) between Richard and Lady Anne (I, ii) or Richard and Queen Elizabeth (IV, iv). Like so many of the other rhetorical devices in the play, this device depends for its effect on some variety of verbal or structural "repetition": of words within the line to give a turn of thought or play on words, of words or phrases linking line to line, of phrase balanced against phrase, of line against line, of speech against speech. But it must be noticed that although this wrought and over-wrought kind of verse sets the dominant stylistic tone and is admirably effective in realizing for us the peculiarly hard-edged, amoral world on the surface of which the characters move, it does not exclude a great deal of stylistic variety even within itself. Moreover, in contrast are the moments of sudden racy colloquialism – like a breath of fresh air – most of which occur in Richard's speeches and lend him a personal turn of speech which we quickly come to recognize as peculiarly a part of him. In this respect, as critics have noticed, he is Shakespeare's first character to possess a "voice" of his own. To this may be added some occasional touches of effective pathos in lines like those at IV, i, 97–103 and the grimly humorous prose of the First and Second Murderers, an early example of Shakespeare's use of comedy to intensify the horror of the moment, here set against a background of what are almost the only imaginatively poetic speeches in the whole play – those in which Clarence relates his dream (I, iv). These and some later speeches of Clarence in the same scene look forward to the kind of poetry with which, a year or two later, Shakespeare endows Richard II and which, in its turn, becomes the perfect medium for expressing the weak, indeterminate, word-drunk king – one, so unlike Richard III, with no capacity for a "world . . . to bustle in."

The Restoration and earlier eighteenth century were temperamentally given to "improving" Shakespeare's plays, and in 1700 Colley Cibber produced his version of *Richard III*. Briefly, Cibber omits Edward IV, Clarence, and Queen Margaret and begins the play just before Richard's murder of Henry VI. The result is a generally tightened-up play which is even more theatrical than Shakespeare's. For roughly a hundred and fifty years Cibber's version, with slight changes, held the stage unchallenged, and Cibber's lines "Off with his head – so much for Buckingham!" and "Conscience avaunt! Richard's himself again!" are often understandably attributed to Shakespeare. Even today Cibber is still very much alive. Witness Sir Lawrence Olivier's motion picture version which drew heavily not only on Cibber but on Cibber's "improver," David Garrick! There is perhaps a moral worth pondering here, for Cibber's longevity is unique among the many "improvers" of Shakespearean plays, and *Richard III* is the only Shakespearean play in which we can still tolerate an alien hand.

*Harvard University*                    G. BLAKEMORE EVANS

## NOTE ON THE TEXT

*Richard III* was first printed in quarto form in 1597 from copy evidently representing the communal effort of the acting company to reconstruct the play when deprived of their regular prompt-book. There were seven additional quarto editions, Quarto 6 (1622), after correction against an independent manuscript, presumably serving as copy for the first folio text (1623), except for two sections (III, i, 1–158, and V, iii, 48 to end) which appear to have been set up from an uncorrected copy of Quarto 3 (1602). The textual problem involved is one of the most complex in Shakespeare, and is further discussed in the appendix. The present edition is based on the folio text, with the addition, in square brackets, of about thirty-three lines from the first quarto, the most important group being IV, ii, 97–115. The quartos are undivided into acts and scenes. The folio text is divided, and this division received editorial elaboration: III, iv became III, iv, v, vi, vii; IV, ii became IV, ii, iii; and V, ii became V, ii, iii, iv, v. In the present edition the editorial divisions are indicated marginally, but the points where the action is continuous are treated as explained in the general foreword. Stage directions not in the folio are bracketed even though they may appear in the quartos.

# THE TRAGEDY OF
# KING RICHARD THE THIRD

[NAMES OF THE ACTORS

King Edward the Fourth
Edward, Prince of Wales, afterwards Edward V } sons to
Richard, Duke of York } the King
George, Duke of Clarence } brothers
Richard, Duke of Gloucester, afterwards } to the
    Richard III } King
A young Son of Clarence (Edward Plantagenet,
    Earl of Warwick)
Henry, Earl of Richmond, afterwards Henry VII
Cardinal Bourchier, Archbishop of Canterbury
Thomas Rotherham, Archbishop of York
John Morton, Bishop of Ely
Duke of Buckingham
Duke of Norfolk
Earl of Surrey, his son
Anthony Woodeville, Earl Rivers, brother to Queen
    Elizabeth
Marquess of Dorset and Lord Grey, her sons
Earl of Oxford
Lord Hastings
Lord Stanley (also called Earl of Derby)
Lord Lovel
Sir Thomas Vaughan
Sir Richard Ratcliffe
Sir William Catesby

Sir James Tyrrel
Sir James Blunt
Sir Walter Herbert
Sir Robert Brakenbury, Lieutenant of the Tower
Keeper in the Tower
Sir William Brandon
Christopher Urswick, a priest
Lord Mayor of London
Sheriff of Wiltshire
Tressel and Berkeley, gentlemen attending on Lady Anne
Ghosts of Henry VI; Edward, Prince of Wales, his son; and
    other victims of Richard
Elizabeth, Queen to Edward IV
Margaret, widow of Henry VI
Duchess of York, mother to Edward IV, Gloucester, and
    Clarence
Lady Anne, widow of Edward, Prince of Wales, son to
    Henry VI; afterwards married to Richard, Duke of
    Gloucester
A young Daughter of Clarence (Lady Margaret
    Plantagenet)
Lords, Gentlemen, and other Attendants; a Pursuivant
    (Hastings), a Page, a Scrivener, a Priest, Bishops,
    Citizens, Aldermen, Councillors, Murderers,
    Messengers, Soldiers, &c.

Scene : *London and other parts of England*]

\*

I, i    *Enter Richard, Duke of Gloucester, solus.*
RICHARD
    Now is the winter of our discontent
2  Made glorious summer by this son of York;
    And all the clouds that lowered upon our house
    In the deep bosom of the ocean buried.
    Now are our brows bound with victorious wreaths,
6  Our bruisèd arms hung up for monuments,
7  Our stern alarums changed to merry meetings,
8  Our dreadful marches to delightful measures.
9  Grim-visaged war hath smoothed his wrinklèd front,
10  And now, instead of mounting barbèd steeds
11  To fright the souls of fearful adversaries,
    He capers nimbly in a lady's chamber
13  To the lascivious pleasing of a lute.
    But I, that am not shaped for sportive tricks
    Nor made to court an amorous looking-glass;
    I, that am rudely stamped, and want love's majesty
17  To strut before a wanton ambling nymph;
    I, that am curtailed of this fair proportion,
19  Cheated of feature by dissembling Nature,

Deformed, unfinished, sent before my time
Into this breathing world, scarce half made up,   21
And that so lamely and unfashionable   22
That dogs bark at me as I halt by them –
Why I, in this weak piping time of peace,   24
Have no delight to pass away the time,
Unless to see my shadow in the sun
And descant on mine own deformity.   27
And therefore, since I cannot prove a lover
To entertain these fair well-spoken days,
I am determinèd to prove a villain
And hate the idle pleasures of these days.

**I, i** A London street   **2** *son* (with play on 'sun')   **6** *arms* armor; *monuments* memorials   **7** *alarums* calls to arms   **8** *measures* stately dances   **9** *front* forehead   **10** *barbèd* armed with protective covering, studded or spiked, on breast and flanks   **11** *fearful* timid   **13** *lascivious pleasing* seductive charm   **17** *ambling* walking affectedly   **19** *feature* form of body; *dissembling* deceiving (because my greatness is cloaked by a false appearance)   **21** *breathing* living   **22** *unfashionable* misshapen (cf. I, ii, 250)   **24** *piping* (the pipe or recorder was associated with peace, as the fife with war)   **27** *descant* compose variations on a simple theme (the speech illustrates this line: the theme, Richard's deformity)

128

32 Plots have I laid, inductions dangerous,
33 By drunken prophecies, libels, and dreams,
To set my brother Clarence and the king
In deadly hate the one against the other;
And if King Edward be as true and just
As I am subtle, false, and treacherous,
38 This day should Clarence closely be mewed up
About a prophecy which says that G
Of Edward's heirs the murderer shall be.
Dive, thoughts, down to my soul – here Clarence comes!
    *Enter Clarence guarded, and Brakenbury*
    *[Lieutenant of the Tower].*
Brother, good day. What means this armèd guard
That waits upon your grace?

CLARENCE           His majesty,
44 Tend'ring my person's safety, hath appointed
45 This conduct to convey me to the Tower.

RICHARD
Upon what cause?

CLARENCE         Because my name is George.

RICHARD
Alack, my lord, that fault is none of yours:
He should for that commit your godfathers.
49 O, belike his majesty hath some intent
50 That you should be new christ'ned in the Tower.
But what's the matter, Clarence, may I know?

CLARENCE
Yea, Richard, when I know; for I protest
As yet I do not. But, as I can learn,
He hearkens after prophecies and dreams,
55 And from the cross-row plucks the letter G,
56 And says a wizard told him that by G
His issue disinherited should be.
And, for my name of George begins with G,
It follows in his thought that I am he.
60 These (as I learn) and suchlike toys as these
Hath moved his highness to commit me now.

RICHARD
Why this it is, when men are ruled by women:
'Tis not the king that sends you to the Tower;
My Lady Grey his wife, Clarence, 'tis she
65 That tempers him to this extremity.
Was it not she, and that good man of worship,
67 Anthony Woodeville, her brother there,
That made him send Lord Hastings to the Tower,
From whence this present day he is deliverèd?
We are not safe, Clarence – we are not safe.

32 *inductions* initial plans  33 *drunken prophecies* prophecies uttered under the influence of drink  38 *mewed up* imprisoned (cf. l. 132)  44 *Tend'ring* being concerned for (irony)  45 *conduct* escort; *convey* conduct (with play on 'steal'); *Tower* the Tower of London (frequently used as a prison)  49 *belike* probably  50 *new christ'ned* (anticipates, ironically, Clarence's drowning in I, iv)  55 *cross-row* alphabet  56 *wizard* wise man or male witch  60 *toys* trifles, fancies  65 *tempers* moulds  67 *Woodeville* i.e. Earl Rivers (trisyllabic)  72 *night-walking heralds* i.e. secret messengers (agents of assignation)  73 *Mistress Shore* i.e. Jane Shore, mistress of Edward IV ('mistress,' however, was regularly applied to any woman, married or unmarried, as a title of respect)  81 *widow* i.e. Queen Elizabeth (cf. l. 109)  82 *dubbed* knighted (a malicious pairing of Queen Elizabeth and Mistress Shore entirely without basis)  83 *gossips* (people, traditionally, with a lot to say)  85 *straitly* strictly  88 *An* if  92 *Well struck in years* (a politic way of saying 'old')  97 *nought* nothing  99 *naught* i.e. the sexual act  103 *withal* at the same time  106 *abjects* most servile subjects (with play on 'outcasts')  110 *enfranchise* release from confinement  111–12 *disgrace . . . imagine* (with an obvious double meaning)  115 *lie for* go to prison in place of (with play on 'tell lies about')  116 *perforce* of necessity

CLARENCE
By heaven, I think there is no man is secure
But the queen's kindred, and night-walking heralds  72
That trudge betwixt the king and Mistress Shore.  73
Heard you not what an humble suppliant
Lord Hastings was for his delivery?

RICHARD
Humbly complaining to her deity
Got my Lord Chamberlain his liberty.
I'll tell you what, I think it is our way,
If we will keep in favor with the king,
To be her men and wear her livery.
The jealous o'erworn widow and herself,  81
Since that our brother dubbed them gentlewomen,  82
Are mighty gossips in our monarchy.  83

BRAKENBURY
I beseech your graces both to pardon me:
His majesty hath straitly given in charge  85
That no man shall have private conference
(Of what degree soever) with your brother.

RICHARD
Even so? An please your worship, Brakenbury,  88
You may partake of anything we say.
We speak no treason, man. We say the king
Is wise and virtuous, and his noble queen
Well struck in years, fair, and not jealous.  92
We say that Shore's wife hath a pretty foot,
A cherry lip, a bonny eye, a passing pleasing tongue;
And that the queen's kindred are made gentlefolks.
How say you, sir? Can you deny all this?

BRAKENBURY
With this, my lord, myself have nought to do.  97

RICHARD
Naught to do with Mistress Shore? I tell thee, fellow,
He that doth naught with her (excepting one)  99
Were best to do it secretly alone.

BRAKENBURY
What one, my lord?

RICHARD
Her husband, knave. Wouldst thou betray me?

BRAKENBURY
I do beseech your grace to pardon me, and withal  103
Forbear your conference with the noble duke.

CLARENCE
We know thy charge, Brakenbury, and will obey.

RICHARD
We are the queen's abjects, and must obey.  106
Brother, farewell. I will unto the king;
And whatsoe'er you will employ me in,
Were it to call King Edward's widow sister,
I will perform it to enfranchise you.  110
Meantime, this deep disgrace in brotherhood  111
Touches me deeper than you can imagine.

CLARENCE
I know it pleaseth neither of us well.

RICHARD
Well, your imprisonment shall not be long:
I will deliver you, or else lie for you.  115
Meantime, have patience.

CLARENCE          I must perforce. Farewell.  116
    *Exit Clarence [with Brakenbury and Guard].*

RICHARD
Go, tread the path that thou shalt ne'er return:
Simple plain Clarence, I do love thee so

That I will shortly send thy soul to heaven,
If heaven will take the present at our hands.
But who comes here ? The new-deliverèd Hastings ?
*Enter Lord Hastings.*

HASTINGS
Good time of day unto my gracious lord.

RICHARD
As much unto my good Lord Chamberlain.
Well are you welcome to the open air.
125  How hath your lordship brooked imprisonment ?

HASTINGS
With patience, noble lord, as prisoners must ;
But I shall live, my lord, to give them thanks
That were the cause of my imprisonment.

RICHARD
No doubt, no doubt ; and so shall Clarence too,
For they that were your enemies are his
And have prevailed as much on him as you.

HASTINGS
More pity that the eagles should be mewed,
Whiles kites and buzzards prey at liberty.

RICHARD
What news abroad ?

HASTINGS
No news so bad abroad as this at home :
The king is sickly, weak, and melancholy,
And his physicians fear him mightily.

RICHARD
Now, by Saint John, that news is bad indeed !
O, he hath kept an evil diet long
140  And overmuch consumed his royal person :
'Tis very grievous to be thought upon.
Where is he ? In his bed ?

HASTINGS  He is.

RICHARD
Go you before, and I will follow you.       *Exit Hastings.*
He cannot live, I hope, and must not die
146  Till George be packed with posthorse up to heaven.
147  I'll in, to urge his hatred more to Clarence
148  With lies well steeled with weighty arguments ;
And, if I fail not in my deep intent,
Clarence hath not another day to live :
Which done, God take King Edward to his mercy
And leave the world for me to bustle in !
153  For then I'll marry Warwick's youngest daughter.
What though I killed her husband and her father ?
The readiest way to make the wench amends
Is to become her husband and her father :
The which will I – not all so much for love
158  As for another secret close intent
By marrying her which I must reach unto.
But yet I run before my horse to market :
Clarence still breathes ; Edward still lives and reigns ;
When they are gone, then must I count my gains.     *Exit.*

\*

I, ii       *Enter the corse of Henry the Sixth, with Halberds to*
            *guard it ; Lady Anne being the mourner [attended*
            *by Tressel and Berkeley].*

ANNE
Set down, set down your honorable load –
If honor may be shrouded in a hearse –
3  Whilst I awhile obsequiously lament

Th' untimely fall of virtuous Lancaster.
*[The Bearers set down the hearse.]*
Poor key-cold figure of a holy king,                     5
Pale ashes of the house of Lancaster,
Thou bloodless remnant of that royal blood,
Be it lawful that I invocate thy ghost
To hear the lamentations of poor Anne,
Wife to thy Edward, to thy slaught'red son
Stabbed by the selfsame hand that made these wounds !
Lo, in these windows that let forth thy life
I pour the helpless balm of my poor eyes.                13
O, cursèd be the hand that made these holes !
Cursèd the heart that had the heart to do it !
Cursèd the blood that let this blood from hence !
More direful hap betide that hated wretch               17
That makes us wretched by the death of thee
Than I can wish to wolves – to spiders, toads,
Or any creeping venomed thing that lives !
If ever he have child, abortive be it,
Prodigious, and untimely brought to light,               22
Whose ugly and unnatural aspect
May fright the hopeful mother at the view,
And that be heir to his unhappiness !                    25
If ever he have wife, let her be made
More miserable by the life of him
Than I am made by my young lord and thee !
Come, now towards Chertsey with your holy load,          29
Taken from Paul's to be interrèd there.                  30
*[The Bearers take up the hearse.]*
And still, as you are weary of this weight,              31
Rest you, whiles I lament King Henry's corse.            32
*Enter Richard, Duke of Gloucester.*

RICHARD
Stay, you that bear the corse, and set it down.

ANNE
What black magician conjures up this fiend
To stop devoted charitable deeds ?                       35

RICHARD
Villains, set down the corse, or, by Saint Paul,
I'll make a corse of him that disobeys !

GENTLEMAN
My lord, stand back, and let the coffin pass.

RICHARD
Unmannered dog ! Stand thou, when I command !            39
Advance thy halberd higher than my breast,               40
Or, by Saint Paul, I'll strike thee to my foot
And spurn upon thee, beggar, for thy boldness.           42
*[The Bearers set down the hearse.]*

ANNE
What, do you tremble ? Are you all afraid ?
Alas, I blame you not, for you are mortal,

125 *brooked* tolerated   146 *with posthorse* (figuratively, the quickest way)
147 *urge . . . to* incite his anger more against   148 *steeled* strengthened
as with iron   153 *Warwick's youngest daughter* i.e. Lady Anne, widow of
Prince Edward   158 *secret close intent* (Richard, aiming at the throne,
schemes to ally himself with the line of Lancaster as a useful preliminary
move)
I, ii The same   s.d. *corse* corpse ; *Halberds* halberdiers (guards, carrying
halberds ; see l. 40 below)   3 *obsequiously* in a manner fitting a funeral   5
*key-cold* very cold (as a metal key)   13 *helpless* affording no help   17 *hap*
*betide* fortune befall   22 *Prodigious* unnatural, monstrous   25 *unhappiness*
innate evil   29 *Chertsey* the monastery of Chertsey near London   30
*Paul's* St Paul's Cathedral, London   31 *still, as* whenever   32 *whiles I*
*lament* during which time I will lament   35 *devoted* sacred   39 *Stand* halt
40 *Advance . . . breast* raise your halberd (a long-handled poleaxe with a pike
attached) to upright position   42 *spurn upon* stamp under foot

And mortal eyes cannot endure the devil.
Avaunt, thou dreadful minister of hell!
Thou hadst but power over his mortal body;
His soul thou canst not have. Therefore, be gone.

RICHARD

49 Sweet saint, for charity, be not so curst.

ANNE

Foul devil, for God's sake hence, and trouble us not,
51 For thou hast made the happy earth thy hell,
Filled it with cursing cries and deep exclaims.
If thou delight to view thy heinous deeds,
54 Behold this pattern of thy butcheries.
O gentlemen, see! See dead Henry's wounds
56 Open their congealed mouths and bleed afresh!
Blush, blush, thou lump of foul deformity;
58 For 'tis thy presence that exhales this blood
From cold and empty veins where no blood dwells.
Thy deeds inhuman and unnatural
Provokes this deluge most unnatural.
O God, which this blood mad'st, revenge his death!
O earth, which this blood drink'st, revenge his death!
Either heav'n with lightning strike the murd'rer dead;
65 Or earth gape open wide and eat him quick,
As thou dost swallow up this good king's blood
Which his hell-governed arm hath butcherèd!

RICHARD

Lady, you know no rules of charity,
Which renders good for bad, blessings for curses.

ANNE

Villain, thou know'st nor law of God nor man:
No beast so fierce but knows some touch of pity.

RICHARD

But I know none, and therefore am no beast.

ANNE

O wonderful, when devils tell the truth!

RICHARD

More wonderful, when angels are so angry.
Vouchsafe, divine perfection of a woman,
Of these supposèd crimes to give me leave
By circumstance but to acquit myself.

ANNE

78 Vouchsafe, diffused infection of a man,
Of these known evils, but to give me leave
By circumstance t' accuse thy cursèd self.

RICHARD

Fairer than tongue can name thee, let me have
Some patient leisure to excuse myself.

ANNE

Fouler than heart can think thee, thou canst make
84 No excuse current but to hang thyself.

RICHARD

By such despair I should accuse myself.

ANNE

And by despairing shalt thou stand excusèd
For doing worthy vengeance on thyself
That didst unworthy slaughter upon others.

RICHARD

Say that I slew them not?

ANNE            Then say they were not slain.
But dead they are, and, devilish slave, by thee.

RICHARD

I did not kill your husband.

ANNE            Why, then he is alive.

RICHARD

Nay, he is dead, and slain by Edward's hands.

ANNE

In thy foul throat thou li'st! Queen Margaret saw
Thy murd'rous falchion smoking in his blood;    94
The which thou once didst bend against her breast,
But that thy brothers beat aside the point.

RICHARD

I was provokèd by her sland'rous tongue
That laid their guilt upon my guiltless shoulders.

ANNE

Thou wast provokèd by thy bloody mind
That never dream'st on aught but butcheries.
Didst thou not kill this king?

RICHARD            I grant ye.

ANNE

Dost grant me, hedgehog? Then God grant me too
Thou mayst be damnèd for that wicked deed!
O, he was gentle, mild, and virtuous!

RICHARD

The better for the King of Heaven that hath him.

ANNE

He is in heaven, where thou shalt never come.

RICHARD

Let him thank me that holp to send him thither;    107
For he was fitter for that place than earth.

ANNE

And thou unfit for any place, but hell.

RICHARD

Yes, one place else, if you will hear me name it.

ANNE

Some dungeon.

RICHARD          Your bedchamber.

ANNE

Ill rest betide the chamber where thou liest!

RICHARD

So will it, madam, till I lie with you.

ANNE

I hope so.

RICHARD    I know so. But, gentle Lady Anne,
To leave this keen encounter of our wits
And fall something into a slower method –
Is not the causer of the timeless deaths    117
Of these Plantagenets, Henry and Edward,
As blameful as the executioner?

ANNE

Thou wast the cause and most accursed effect.    120

RICHARD

Your beauty was the cause of that effect –
Your beauty, that did haunt me in my sleep
To undertake the death of all the world,
So I might live one hour in your sweet bosom.

ANNE

If I thought that, I tell thee, homicide,    125
These nails should rent that beauty from my cheeks.

RICHARD

These eyes could not endure that beauty's wrack;    127

---

49 *curst* shrewish   51 *happy* naturally pleasant   54 *pattern* example   56
*bleed afresh* (in popular belief the wounds of a murdered man bled in the
presence of the murderer)   58 *exhales* draws out   65 *quick* alive   78
*diffused infection* shapeless plague (more for sound than sense; cf. l. 75)   84
*current* authentic or acceptable   94 *falchion* slightly hooked sword   107 *holp*
helped   117 *timeless* untimely   120 *effect* i.e. executioner (l. 119) or efficient
agent   125 *homicide* murderer   127 *wrack* ruin

You should not blemish it, if I stood by :
As all the world is cheerèd by the sun,
So I by that. It is my day, my life.

ANNE
Black night o'ershade thy day, and death thy life !

RICHARD
Curse not thyself, fair creature – thou art both.

ANNE
I would I were, to be revenged on thee.

RICHARD
It is a quarrel most unnatural,
To be revenged on him that loveth thee.

ANNE
It is a quarrel just and reasonable,
To be revenged on him that killed my husband.

RICHARD
He that bereft thee, lady, of thy husband,
Did it to help thee to a better husband.

ANNE
140 His better doth not breathe upon the earth.

RICHARD
He lives, that loves thee better than he could.

ANNE
Name him.

RICHARD            Plantagenet.

ANNE                        Why that was he.

RICHARD
The selfsame name, but one of better nature.

ANNE
Where is he ?

RICHARD            Here.
            [She] spits at him.  Why dost thou spit at me ?

ANNE
Would it were mortal poison for thy sake !

RICHARD
Never came poison from so sweet a place.

ANNE
147 Never hung poison on a fouler toad.
Out of my sight ! Thou dost infect mine eyes.

RICHARD
149 Thine eyes, sweet lady, have infected mine.

ANNE
150 Would they were basilisks to strike thee dead !

RICHARD
151 I would they were, that I might die at once ;
For now they kill me with a living death.
Those eyes of thine from mine have drawn salt tears,
154 Shamed their aspects with store of childish drops :
These eyes, which never shed remorseful tear –
No, when my father York and Edward wept
To hear the piteous moan that Rutland made
158 When black-faced Clifford shook his sword at him ;
159 Nor when thy warlike father, like a child,
Told the sad story of my father's death
And twenty times made pause to sob and weep,
That all the standers-by had wet their cheeks
Like trees bedashed with rain – in that sad time
My manly eyes did scorn an humble tear ;
And what these sorrows could not thence exhale,
Thy beauty hath, and made them blind with weeping.
I never sued to friend nor enemy ;
168 My tongue could never learn sweet smoothing word ;
But, now thy beauty is proposed my fee,
My proud heart sues, and prompts my tongue to speak.

*She looks scornfully at him.*
Teach not thy lip such scorn ; for it was made
For kissing, lady, not for such contempt.
If thy revengeful heart cannot forgive,
Lo, here I lend thee this sharp-pointed sword,
Which if thou please to hide in this true breast
And let the soul forth that adoreth thee,
I lay it naked to the deadly stroke                        177
And humbly beg the death upon my knee.
            *He lays his breast open. She offers at [it] with his
            sword.*
Nay, do not pause : for I did kill King Henry –
But 'twas thy beauty that provokèd me.
Nay, now dispatch : 'twas I that stabbed young Edward –
But 'twas thy heavenly face that set me on.            182
            *She falls the sword.*
Take up the sword again, or take up me.

ANNE
Arise, dissembler : though I wish thy death,
I will not be thy executioner.

RICHARD
Then bid me kill myself, and I will do it.

ANNE
I have already.

RICHARD            That was in thy rage :
Speak it again, and even with the word
This hand, which for thy love did kill thy love,
Shall for thy love kill a far truer love ;
To both their deaths shalt thou be accessary.            191

ANNE
I would I knew thy heart.

RICHARD
'Tis figured in my tongue.

ANNE
I fear me both are false.

RICHARD
Then never was man true.

ANNE
Well, well, put up your sword.

RICHARD
Say then my peace is made.

ANNE
That shalt thou know hereafter.

RICHARD
But shall I live in hope ?

ANNE
All men, I hope, live so.

[RICHARD]
Vouchsafe to wear this ring.

[ANNE
To take is not to give.]
            *[Richard slips the ring on her finger.]*

RICHARD
Look how my ring encompasseth thy finger,
Even so thy breast encloseth my poor heart :
Wear both of them, for both of them are thine.

147 *poison . . . toad* (toads were considered venomous)  149 *eyes . . . mine*
(the eyes were believed to be the entry-ports of love)  150 *basilisks* fabulous
reptiles capable of killing with a look  151 *at once* once and for all  154
*aspects* glances  158 *black-faced* gloomy, evilly portentous  159 *thy . . . father*
i.e. Richard Nevil, Earl of Warwick, known as the 'King-maker'  168
*smoothing* flattering  177 *naked* (1) bare, (2) unarmed  182 s.d. *falls* drops
191 *accessary* acceding

206  And if thy poor devoted servant may
     But beg one favor at thy gracious hand,
     Thou dost confirm his happiness for ever.
ANNE  What is it?
RICHARD
     That it may please you leave these sad designs
     To him that hath most cause to be a mourner,
212  And presently repair to Crosby House;
     Where – after I have solemnly interred
     At Chertsey monast'ry this noble king
     And wet his grave with my repentant tears –
216  I will with all expedient duty see you.
217  For divers unknown reasons I beseech you,
     Grant me this boon.
ANNE
     With all my heart; and much it joys me too
     To see you are become so penitent.
     Tressel and Berkeley, go along with me.
RICHARD
     Bid me farewell.
222  ANNE            'Tis more than you deserve;
     But since you teach me how to flatter you,
     Imagine I have said farewell already.
          *Exeunt two [Tressel and Berkeley], with Anne.*
[RICHARD
     Sirs, take up the corse.]
GENTLEMAN            Towards Chertsey, noble lord?
RICHARD
226  No, to Whitefriars – there attend my coming.
               *Exit [Guard with Bearers and] corse.*
     Was ever woman in this humor wooed?
     Was ever woman in this humor won?
     I'll have her, but I will not keep her long.
     What? I that killed her husband and his father
     To take her in her heart's extremest hate,
     With curses in her mouth, tears in her eyes,
     The bleeding witness of my hatred by,
     Having God, her conscience, and these bars against me,
     And I no friends to back my suit at all
     But the plain devil and dissembling looks?
237  And yet to win her! All the world to nothing!
     Ha!
     Hath she forgot already that brave prince,
     Edward, her lord, whom I, some three months since,
241  Stabbed in my angry mood at Tewkesbury?
     A sweeter and a lovelier gentleman,
243  Framed in the prodigality of nature –
     Young, valiant, wise, and (no doubt) right royal –
     The spacious world cannot again afford;
246  And will she yet abase her eyes on me,

That cropped the golden prime of this sweet prince        247
And made her widow to a woeful bed?
On me, whose all not equals Edward's moi'ty?              249
On me, that halts and am misshapen thus?
My dukedom to a beggarly denier,                          251
I do mistake my person all this while!
Upon my life, she finds (although I cannot)
Myself to be a marv'llous proper man.                     254
I'll be at charges for a looking-glass                    255
And entertain a score or two of tailors
To study fashions to adorn my body:
Since I am crept in favor with myself,
I will maintain it with some little cost.
But first I'll turn yon fellow in his grave,              260
And then return lamenting to my love.
Shine out, fair sun, till I have bought a glass,
That I may see my shadow as I pass.            *Exit.*

                         *

          *Enter the Queen Mother [Elizabeth], Lord Rivers,*      I, iii
          *[Marquess of Dorset,] and Lord Grey.*
RIVERS
     Have patience, madam; there's no doubt his majesty
     Will soon recover his accustomed health.
GREY
     In that you brook it ill, it makes him worse:            3
     Therefore for God's sake entertain good comfort
     And cheer his grace with quick and merry eyes.
QUEEN ELIZABETH
     If he were dead, what would betide on me?                6
GREY
     No other harm but loss of such a lord.
QUEEN ELIZABETH
     The loss of such a lord includes all harms.
GREY
     The heavens have blessed you with a goodly son
     To be your comforter when he is gone.
QUEEN ELIZABETH
     Ah, he is young; and his minority
     Is put unto the trust of Richard Gloucester,
     A man that loves not me, nor none of you.
RIVERS
     Is it concluded he shall be Protector?
QUEEN ELIZABETH
     It is determined, not concluded yet:                     15
     But so it must be, if the king miscarry.
               *Enter Buckingham and [Stanley, Earl of] Derby.*
GREY
     Here come the lords of Buckingham and Derby.
BUCKINGHAM
     Good time of day unto your royal grace!
DERBY
     God make your majesty joyful, as you have been!
QUEEN ELIZABETH
     The Countess Richmond, good my Lord of Derby,            20
     To your good prayer will scarcely say 'Amen.'
     Yet, Derby, notwithstanding she's your wife
     And loves not me, be you, good lord, assured
     I hate not you for her proud arrogance.
DERBY
     I do beseech you, either not believe
     The envious slanders of her false accusers;

---

206 *servant* (1) one in subjection, (2) lover   212 *presently* at once; *Crosby House* (Richard's center of operations)   216 *expedient* speedy   217 *unknown* secret   222 *'Tis . . . deserve* i.e. to fare well is more than you deserve   226 *Whitefriars* a Carmelite priory, south of Fleet Street, London   237 *All . . . nothing* all odds against me   241 *Tewkesbury* (scene of the battle in which the Lancastrians were finally defeated and Prince Edward killed)   243 *prodigality* profuseness   246 *abase* cast down or make base   247 *cropped . . . prince* i.e. cut him off in the flower of youth   249 *moi'ty* half   251 *denier* copper coin, twelfth of a sou (dissyllabic)   254 *marv'llous proper* wonderfully handsome   255 *at charges for* at the expense of   260 *in* into
I, iii The royal palace   3 *brook* endure   6 *betide on* happen to   15 *determined, not concluded* resolved, not officially decreed   20 *Countess Richmond* mother of the Earl of Richmond (later Henry VII), now wife of Lord Stanley, Earl of Derby

Or, if she be accused on true report,
Bear with her weakness, which I think proceeds
29 From wayward sickness, and no grounded malice.

QUEEN ELIZABETH
Saw you the king to-day, my Lord of Derby?

DERBY
31 But now the Duke of Buckingham and I
Are come from visiting his majesty.

QUEEN ELIZABETH
What likelihood of his amendment, lords?

BUCKINGHAM
Madam, good hope; his grace speaks cheerfully.

QUEEN ELIZABETH
God grant him health! Did you confer with him?

BUCKINGHAM
36 Ay, madam: he desires to make atonement
Between the Duke of Gloucester and your brothers,
And between them and my Lord Chamberlain,
And sent to warn them to his royal presence.

QUEEN ELIZABETH
Would all were well! but that will never be:
41 I fear our happiness is at the height.
    *Enter Richard [and Lord Hastings].*

RICHARD
They do me wrong, and I will not endure it!
Who is it that complains unto the king
That I (forsooth) am stern, and love them not?
By holy Paul, they love his grace but lightly
That fill his ears with such dissentious rumors.
Because I cannot flatter and look fair,
48 Smile in men's faces, smooth, deceive, and cog,
49 Duck with French nods and apish courtesy,
I must be held a rancorous enemy.
Cannot a plain man live and think no harm,
But thus his simple truth must be abused
53 With silken, sly, insinuating Jacks?

GREY
To who in all this presence speaks your grace?

RICHARD
55 To thee, that hast nor honesty nor grace:
When have I injured thee? when done thee wrong?
Or thee? or thee? or any of your faction?
A plague upon you all! His royal grace
(Whom God preserve better than you would wish!)
60 Cannot be quiet scarce a breathing while
61 But you must trouble him with lewd complaints.

QUEEN ELIZABETH
Brother of Gloucester, you mistake the matter:
63 The king, on his own royal disposition,
And not provoked by any suitor else,
Aiming (belike) at your interior hatred,
That in your outward action shows itself
Against my children, brothers, and myself,
Makes him to send, that he may learn the ground.

RICHARD
I cannot tell: the world is grown so bad
That wrens make prey where eagles dare not perch.
Since every Jack became a gentleman,
There's many a gentle person made a Jack.

QUEEN ELIZABETH
Come, come, we know your meaning, brother
    Gloucester:
You envy my advancement and my friends'.
God grant we never may have need of you!

RICHARD
Meantime, God grants that I have need of you.
Our brother is imprisoned by your means,
Myself disgraced, and the nobility
Held in contempt, while great promotions
Are daily given to ennoble those
That scarce, some two days since, were worth a noble. 81

QUEEN ELIZABETH
By Him that raised me to this careful height 82
From that contented hap which I enjoyed, 83
I never did incense his majesty
Against the Duke of Clarence, but have been
An earnest advocate to plead for him.
My lord, you do me shameful injury
Falsely to draw me in these vile suspects. 88

RICHARD
You may deny that you were not the mean
Of my Lord Hastings' late imprisonment.

RIVERS
She may, my lord, for –

RICHARD
She may, Lord Rivers! why, who knows not so?
She may do more, sir, than denying that:
She may help you to many fair preferments,
And then deny her aiding hand therein
And lay those honors on your high desert.
What may she not? She may – ay, marry, may she – 97

RIVERS
What, marry, may she?

RICHARD
What, marry, may she? Marry with a king,
A bachelor and a handsome stripling too:
Iwis your grandam had a worser match. 101

QUEEN ELIZABETH
My Lord of Gloucester, I have too long borne
Your blunt upbraidings and your bitter scoffs:
By heaven, I will acquaint his majesty
Of those gross taunts that oft I have endured.
I had rather be a country servant maid
Than a great queen with this condition,
To be so baited, scorned, and stormèd at: 108
    *Enter old Queen Margaret [behind].*
Small joy have I in being England's queen.

QUEEN MARGARET *[aside]*
And less'ned be that small, God I beseech him!
Thy honor, state, and seat is due to me. 111

RICHARD
What? Threat you me with telling of the king?
[Tell him, and spare not. Look, what I have said]
I will avouch't in presence of the king:
I dare adventure to be sent to th' Tow'r.
'Tis time to speak: my pains are quite forgot. 116

---

29 *wayward sickness* illness not yielding readily to treatment   31 *But now* just now   36 *atonement* reconciliation   41 *happiness . . . height* good fortune has reached its peak (any further movement of the wheel of fortune will be down)   48 *smooth* flatter; *cog* cheat   49 *French nods* affected salutations   53 *Jacks* low-bred, worthless fellows (with play on French *Jacques*)   55 *grace* sense of duty or virtue (with play on the title *your grace*, l. 54)   60 *breathing while* i.e. long enough to catch his breath   61 *lewd* wicked   63–68 *The king . . . send* (syntax confused; for 'Makes him to send' understand 'sends')   63 *disposition* inclination   81 *noble* (1) gold coin, worth 6s. 8d., (2) nobleman   82 *careful* full of anxiety   83 *hap* fortune   88 *in* into; *suspects* suspicions   97 *marry* indeed (with play on 'wed')   101 *Iwis* certainly   108 *baited* harassed   111 *state* high rank (as queen); *seat* throne   116 *pains* efforts on his behalf

QUEEN MARGARET [aside]
Out, devil! I do remember them too well:
Thou kill'dst my husband Henry in the Tower,
And Edward, my poor son, at Tewkesbury.

RICHARD
Ere you were queen, ay, or your husband king,
121 I was a packhorse in his great affairs;
A weeder-out of his proud adversaries,
A liberal rewarder of his friends:
To royalize his blood I spent mine own.

QUEEN MARGARET [aside]
Ay, and much better blood than his or thine.

RICHARD
126 In all which time you and your husband Grey
Were factious for the house of Lancaster;
And, Rivers, so were you. Was not your husband
In Margaret's battle at Saint Albans slain?
Let me put in your minds, if you forget,
What you have been ere this, and what you are;
Withal, what I have been, and what I am.

QUEEN MARGARET [aside]
A murd'rous villain, and so still thou art.

RICHARD
134 Poor Clarence did forsake his father, Warwick;
Ay, and forswore himself (which Jesu pardon!) –

QUEEN MARGARET [aside]
Which God revenge!

RICHARD
To fight on Edward's party for the crown;
138 And for his meed, poor lord, he is mewèd up.
I would to God my heart were flint like Edward's,
Or Edward's soft and pitiful like mine:
I am too childish-foolish for this world.

QUEEN MARGARET [aside]
Hie thee to hell for shame, and leave this world,
143 Thou cacodemon! there thy kingdom is.

RIVERS
My Lord of Gloucester, in those busy days
Which here you urge to prove us enemies,
We followed then our lord, our sovereign king.
So should we you, if you should be our king.

RICHARD
If I should be? I had rather be a pedlar:
Far be it from my heart, the thought thereof!

QUEEN ELIZABETH
As little joy, my lord, as you suppose
You should enjoy, were you this country's king –
As little joy you may suppose in me
That I enjoy, being the queen thereof.

QUEEN MARGARET [aside]
A little joy enjoys the queen thereof;
For I am she, and altogether joyless.
I can no longer hold me patient.
[Comes forward.]

Hear me, you wrangling pirates, that fall out
In sharing that which you have pilled from me!          158
Which of you trembles not that looks on me?
If not, that I am queen, you bow like subjects,          160
Yet that, by you deposed, you quake like rebels?
Ah, gentle villain, do not turn away!

RICHARD
Foul wrinklèd witch, what mak'st thou in my sight?          163

QUEEN MARGARET
But repetition of what thou hast marred:
That will I make before I let thee go.

RICHARD
Wert thou not banishèd on pain of death?

QUEEN MARGARET
I was; but I do find more pain in banishment
Than death can yield me here by my abode.
A husband and a son thou ow'st to me –
And thou a kingdom – all of you allegiance.
This sorrow that I have, by right is yours,
And all the pleasures you usurp are mine.

RICHARD
The curse my noble father laid on thee          173
When thou didst crown his warlike brows with paper
And with thy scorns drew'st rivers from his eyes
And then, to dry them, gav'st the duke a clout          176
Steeped in the faultless blood of pretty Rutland –
His curses then, from bitterness of soul
Denounced against thee, are all fall'n upon thee;
And God, not we, hath plagued thy bloody deed.

QUEEN ELIZABETH
So just is God, to right the innocent.

HASTINGS
O, 'twas the foulest deed to slay that babe,
And the most merciless, that e'er was heard of!

RIVERS
Tyrants themselves wept when it was reported.

DORSET
No man but prophesied revenge for it.

BUCKINGHAM
Northumberland, then present, wept to see it.

QUEEN MARGARET
What? were you snarling all before I came,
Ready to catch each other by the throat,
And turn you all your hatred now on me?
Did York's dread curse prevail so much with heaven
That Henry's death, my lovely Edward's death,
Their kingdom's loss, my woeful banishment,
Should all but answer for that peevish brat?          193
Can curses pierce the clouds and enter heaven?
Why then, give way, dull clouds, to my quick curses!          195
Though not by war, by surfeit die your king,
As ours by murder, to make him a king!
Edward thy son, that now is Prince of Wales,
For Edward our son, that was Prince of Wales,
Die in his youth by like untimely violence!
Thyself a queen, for me that was a queen,
Outlive thy glory, like my wretched self!
Long mayst thou live to wail thy children's death
And see another, as I see thee now,
Decked in thy rights as thou art stalled in mine!          205
Long die thy happy days before thy death,
And, after many length'ned hours of grief,
Die neither mother, wife, nor England's queen!
Rivers and Dorset, you were standers-by,          209

121 *packhorse* beast of burden, drudge   126–29 *husband . . . Saint Albans*
(the queen's first husband, Sir John Grey, was killed at the battle of Saint
Albans fighting against the Yorkists)   134 *father, Warwick* (Clarence
temporarily went over to the Lancastrians to marry Warwick's daughter,
Isabel Nevil)   138 *meed* reward; *mewèd up* imprisoned   143 *cacodemon* evil
spirit   158 *pilled* plundered   160–61 *that . . . that* because . . . because   163
*mak'st thou* are you doing (but Margaret replies as if Richard had meant
'What are you making?')   173–80 *The curse . . . deed* (see *3 Henry VI, I, iv*)
176 *clout* handkerchief   193 *but answer for* merely be equal to   195 *quick*
full of life   205 *stalled* installed   209–11 *Rivers . . . daggers* (none of them
was present in the scene as shown in *3 Henry VI, V, v*)

And so wast thou, Lord Hastings, when my son
Was stabbed with bloody daggers : God, I pray him
That none of you may live his natural age,
But by some unlooked accident cut off !

RICHARD

214 Have done thy charm, thou hateful with'red hag !

QUEEN MARGARET

And leave out thee ? stay, dog, for thou shalt hear me.
If heaven have any grievous plague in store
Exceeding those that I can wish upon thee,
O, let them keep it till thy sins be ripe,
And then hurl down their indignation
On thee, the troubler of the poor world's peace !
The worm of conscience still begnaw thy soul !
Thy friends suspect for traitors while thou liv'st,
And take deep traitors for thy dearest friends !
224 No sleep close up that deadly eye of thine,
Unless it be while some tormenting dream
Affrights thee with a hell of ugly devils !
227 Thou elvish-marked, abortive, rooting hog !
Thou that wast sealed in thy nativity
229 The slave of nature and the son of hell !
230 Thou slander of thy heavy mother's womb !
Thou loathèd issue of thy father's loins !
Thou rag of honor ! thou detested –

RICHARD

Margaret.

QUEEN MARGARET Richard !

RICHARD                         Ha !

QUEEN MARGARET         I call thee not.

RICHARD

234 I cry thee mercy then ; for I did think
That thou hadst called me all these bitter names.

QUEEN MARGARET

Why, so I did, but looked for no reply.
237 O, let me make the period to my curse !

RICHARD

'Tis done by me, and ends in 'Margaret.'

QUEEN ELIZABETH

Thus have you breathed your curse against yourself.

QUEEN MARGARET

240 Poor painted queen, vain flourish of my fortune !
Why strew'st thou sugar on that bottled spider
Whose deadly web ensnareth thee about ?
Fool, fool ! thou whet'st a knife to kill thyself.
The day will come that thou shalt wish for me
To help thee curse this poisonous bunch-backed toad.

HASTINGS

246 False-boding woman, end thy frantic curse,
247 Lest to thy harm thou move our patience.

QUEEN MARGARET

Foul shame upon you ! you have all moved mine.

RIVERS

Were you well served, you would be taught your duty.

QUEEN MARGARET

To serve me well, you all should do me duty,
Teach me to be your queen, and you my subjects :
O, serve me well, and teach yourselves that duty !

DORSET

Dispute not with her ; she is lunatic.

QUEEN MARGARET

254 Peace, Master Marquess, you are malapert :
255 Your fire-new stamp of honor is scarce current.
256 O, that your young nobility could judge

What 'twere to lose it and be miserable !
They that stand high have many blasts to shake them,
And if they fall, they dash themselves to pieces.

RICHARD

Good counsel, marry ! Learn it, learn it, Marquess.

DORSET

It touches you, my lord, as much as me.

RICHARD

Ay, and much more ; but I was born so high :
Our aery buildeth in the cedar's top                  263
And dallies with the wind and scorns the sun.        264

QUEEN MARGARET

And turns the sun to shade – alas ! alas !
Witness my son, now in the shade of death,
Whose bright outshining beams thy cloudy wrath
Hath in eternal darkness folded up.
Your aery buildeth in our aery's nest :
O God, that seest it, do not suffer it !
As it is won with blood, lost be it so !

BUCKINGHAM

Peace, peace, for shame ! if not, for charity.

QUEEN MARGARET

Urge neither charity nor shame to me :
    [Turning to the others]
Uncharitably with me have you dealt,
And shamefully my hopes by you are butchered.
My charity is outrage, life my shame,
And in that shame still live my sorrow's rage !

BUCKINGHAM

Have done, have done.

QUEEN MARGARET

O princely Buckingham, I'll kiss thy hand
In sign of league and amity with thee :              280
Now fair befall thee and thy noble house !
Thy garments are not spotted with our blood,
Nor thou within the compass of my curse.

BUCKINGHAM

Nor no one here ; for curses never pass
The lips of those that breathe them in the air.

QUEEN MARGARET

I will not think but they ascend the sky             286
And there awake God's gentle-sleeping peace.
O Buckingham, take heed of yonder dog !
Look when he fawns he bites ; and when he bites,     28
His venom tooth will rankle to the death.
Have not to do with him, beware of him :
Sin, death, and hell have set their marks on him,
And all their ministers attend on him.

RICHARD

What doth she say, my Lord of Buckingham ?

BUCKINGHAM

Nothing that I respect, my gracious lord.

214 *charm* magic spell (Richard addresses Margaret as a witch; cf. l. 163 above)   224 *deadly* killing (like the eye of a basilisk; cf. I, ii, 150)   227 *elvish-marked* marked at birth by evil fairies; *hog* (Richard's badge was a white boar)   229 *slave of nature* naturally slavish or base-minded   230 *heavy mother's womb* mother's heavy womb, or sad mother's womb   234 *cry thee mercy* beg your pardon (sarcasm)   237 *period* end (as of a sentence; cf. II, i, 44)   240 *painted queen* queen in outward show; *flourish* meaningless decoration   246 *False-boding* prophesying falsely   247 *patience* (trisyllabic)   254 *malapert* impudent   255 *Your . . . current* your title is so new-coined that it is scarcely legal tender   256 *young nobility* new state of honor   263 *aery* brood of young eagles   264-65 *sun . . . sun* (double play on 'sun,' (1) as king symbol and (2) as son)   286 *not think but* believe   289 *Look when* whenever

QUEEN MARGARET
What, dost thou scorn me for my gentle counsel?
And soothe the devil that I warn thee from?
O, but remember this another day,
When he shall split thy very heart with sorrow,
300 And say poor Margaret was a prophetess!
Live each of you the subjects to his hate,
And he to yours, and all of you to God's!       *Exit.*

BUCKINGHAM
My hair doth stand an end to hear her curses.

RIVERS
And so doth mine. I muse why she's at liberty.

RICHARD
I cannot blame her. By God's holy Mother,
She hath had too much wrong, and I repent
My part thereof that I have done to her.

QUEEN ELIZABETH
I never did her any to my knowledge.

RICHARD
Yet you have all the vantage of her wrong:
310 I was too hot to do somebody good
That is too cold in thinking of it now.
Marry, as for Clarence, he is well repaid;
313 He is franked up to fatting for his pains—
God pardon them that are the cause thereof!

RIVERS
A virtuous and a Christianlike conclusion—
316 To pray for them that have done scathe to us.

RICHARD
So do I ever—*(speaks to himself)* being well advised;
For had I cursed now, I had cursed myself.
*Enter Catesby.*

CATESBY
Madam, his majesty doth call for you;
And for your grace; and yours, my gracious lord.

QUEEN ELIZABETH
Catesby, I come. Lords, will you go with me?

RIVERS
We wait upon your grace.
      *Exeunt all but [Richard of] Gloucester.*

RICHARD
I do the wrong, and first begin to brawl.
The secret mischiefs that I set abroach
325 I lay unto the grievous charge of others.
Clarence, who I indeed have cast in darkness,
327 I do beweep to many simple gulls—
Namely, to Derby, Hastings, Buckingham—
And tell them 'tis the queen and her allies
That stir the king against the duke my brother.
Now they believe it, and withal whet me
To be revenged on Rivers, Dorset, Grey.
But then I sigh, and, with a piece of Scripture,
Tell them that God bids us do good for evil:
And thus I clothe my naked villainy
With odd old ends stol'n forth of holy writ,
And seem a saint, when most I play the devil.

310 *too hot . . . good* i.e. too eager in helping Edward to the crown  313
*franked . . . fatting* shut in a sty for fattening (i.e. slaughter)  316 *scathe*
injury  325 *lay . . . of* impute as a severe accusation against  327 *gulls* fools
349 *prate* talk idly, chatter  352 *fall* let fall
I, iv The Tower of London  4 *faithful* believing in religion  13 *hatches*
moveable planks forming a kind of deck  17 *giddy footing* foothold producing dizziness  27 *Inestimable . . . jewels* i.e. precious stones without
number and costly ornaments (jewels) beyond price

*Enter two Murderers.*
But soft! Here come my executioners.
How now, my hardy, stout, resolvèd mates!
Are you now going to dispatch this thing?   340

1. MURDERER
We are, my lord, and come to have the warrant,
That we may be admitted where he is.

RICHARD
Well thought upon; I have it here about me:
    *[Gives the warrant.]*
When you have done, repair to Crosby Place.
But, sirs, be sudden in the execution,
Withal obdurate, do not hear him plead;
For Clarence is well-spoken, and perhaps
May move your hearts to pity if you mark him.

1. MURDERER
Tut, tut, my lord! we will not stand to prate;   349
Talkers are no good doers. Be assured:
We go to use our hands, and not our tongues.

RICHARD
Your eyes drop millstones when fools' eyes fall tears.   352
I like you, lads: about your business straight.
Go, go, dispatch.

1. MURDERER     We will, my noble lord.     *[Exeunt.]*

          *

*Enter Clarence and Keeper.*       I, iv

KEEPER
Why looks your grace so heavily to-day?

CLARENCE
O, I have passed a miserable night,
So full of fearful dreams, of ugly sights,
That, as I am a Christian faithful man,   4
I would not spend another such a night
Though 'twere to buy a world of happy days—
So full of dismal terror was the time.

KEEPER
What was your dream, my lord? I pray you tell me.

CLARENCE
Methoughts that I had broken from the Tower
And was embarked to cross to Burgundy,
And in my company my brother Gloucester,
Who from my cabin tempted me to walk
Upon the hatches: thence we looked toward England   13
And cited up a thousand heavy times,
During the wars of York and Lancaster,
That had befall'n us. As we paced along
Upon the giddy footing of the hatches,   17
Methought that Gloucester stumblèd, and in falling
Struck me (that thought to stay him) overboard
Into the tumbling billows of the main.
O Lord! methought what pain it was to drown!
What dreadful noise of waters in mine ears!
What sights of ugly death within mine eyes!
Methoughts I saw a thousand fearful wracks;
A thousand men that fishes gnawed upon;
Wedges of gold, great anchors, heaps of pearl,
Inestimable stones, unvaluèd jewels,   27
All scatt'red in the bottom of the sea:
Some lay in dead men's skulls, and in the holes
Where eyes did once inhabit, there were crept
(As 'twere in scorn of eyes) reflecting gems,

That wooed the slimy bottom of the deep
And mocked the dead bones that lay scatt'red by.

**KEEPER**
Had you such leisure in the time of death
To gaze upon these secrets of the deep?

**CLARENCE**
Methought I had; and often did I strive
37 To yield the ghost; but still the envious flood
Stopped in my soul, and would not let it forth
To find the empty, vast, and wand'ring air,
40 But smothered it within my panting bulk,
Who almost burst to belch it in the sea.

**KEEPER**
Awaked you not in this sore agony?

**CLARENCE**
No, no, my dream was lengthened after life.
O, then, began the tempest to my soul!
I passed (methought) the melancholy flood,
46 With that sour ferryman which poets write of,
Unto the kingdom of perpetual night.
48 The first that there did greet my stranger soul
Was my great father-in-law, renownèd Warwick,
Who spake aloud, 'What scourge for perjury
Can this dark monarchy afford false Clarence?'
And so he vanished. Then came wand'ring by
53 A shadow like an angel, with bright hair
Dabbled in blood, and he shrieked out aloud,
55 'Clarence is come – false, fleeting, perjured Clarence,
That stabbed me in the field by Tewkesbury:
Seize on him, Furies, take him ùnto torment!'
With that (methoughts) a legion of foul fiends
Environed me, and howlèd in mine ears
Such hideous cries that with the very noise
I, trembling, waked, and for a season after
Could not believe but that I was in hell,
Such terrible impression made my dream.

**KEEPER**
No marvel, lord, though it affrighted you;
I am afraid (methinks) to hear you tell it.

**CLARENCE**
Ah, keeper, keeper, I have done these things
(That now give evidence against my soul)
For Edward's sake, and see how he requites me!
O God! if my deep pray'rs cannot appease thee,
But thou wilt be avenged on my misdeeds,
Yet execute thy wrath in me alone:
O, spare my guiltless wife and my poor children!
Keeper, I prithee sit by me awhile.
74 My soul is heavy, and I fain would sleep.

**KEEPER**
I will, my lord. God give your grace good rest!
*[Clarence sleeps.]*
*Enter Brakenbury, the Lieutenant.*

**BRAKENBURY**
76 Sorrow breaks seasons and reposing hours,
Makes the night morning and the noontide night:
Princes have but their titles for their glories,
An outward honor for an inward toil;
80 And for unfelt imaginations
They often feel a world of restless cares;
So that between their titles and low name
There's nothing differs but the outward fame.
*Enter two Murderers.*

1. **MURDERER** Ho! who's here?

**BRAKENBURY**
What wouldst thou, fellow? and how cam'st thou hither?

1. **MURDERER** I would speak with Clarence, and I came hither on my legs.

**BRAKENBURY** What, so brief?

2. **MURDERER** 'Tis better, sir, than to be tedious. Let him see our commission, and talk no more.
*[Brakenbury] reads [it].*

**BRAKENBURY**
I am, in this, commanded to deliver
The noble Duke of Clarence to your hands.
I will not reason what is meant hereby,
Because I will be guiltless from the meaning. 94
There lies the duke asleep, and there the keys.
I'll to the king and signify to him
That thus I have resigned to you my charge.

1. **MURDERER** You may, sir; 'tis a point of wisdom. Fare you well.  *Exit [Brakenbury with Keeper].*

2. **MURDERER** What? Shall I stab him as he sleeps?

1. **MURDERER** No. He'll say 'twas done cowardly when he wakes.

2. **MURDERER** Why, he shall never wake until the great Judgment Day.

1. **MURDERER** Why, then he'll say we stabbed him sleeping.

2. **MURDERER** The urging of that word 'judgment' hath bred a kind of remorse in me.

1. **MURDERER** What? Art thou afraid?

2. **MURDERER** Not to kill him, having a warrant; but to be damned for killing him, from the which no warrant 11(
can defend me.

1. **MURDERER** I thought thou hadst been resolute.

2. **MURDERER** So I am – to let him live.

1. **MURDERER** I'll back to the Duke of Gloucester and tell him so.

2. **MURDERER** Nay, I prithee stay a little. I hope this pas- 11(
sionate humor of mine will change. It was wont to hold me but while one tells twenty.

1. **MURDERER** How dost thou feel thyself now?

2. **MURDERER** Faith, some certain dregs of conscience are yet within me.

1. **MURDERER** Remember our reward when the deed 's done.

2. **MURDERER** Zounds, he dies! I had forgot the reward.

1. **MURDERER** Where's thy conscience now?

2. **MURDERER** O, in the Duke of Gloucester's purse.

1. **MURDERER** When he opens his purse to give us our reward, thy conscience flies out.

2. **MURDERER** 'Tis no matter; let it go. There's few or none will entertain it.

1. **MURDERER** What if it come to thee again? 13(

2. **MURDERER** I'll not meddle with it; it makes a man a coward. A man cannot steal, but it accuseth him; a man cannot swear, but it checks him; a man cannot lie with his neighbor's wife, but it detects him. 'Tis a blushing shame-faced spirit that mutinies in a man's bosom. It fills a man full of obstacles. It made me once restore a

---

37 *yield the ghost* i.e. die; *still* always   40 *bulk* body   46 *ferryman* Charon
48 *stranger* newly arrived   53 *A shadow* i.e. Edward, Prince of Wales, son
of Henry VI   55 *fleeting* unstable   74 *My soul . . . sleep* (an omen of
disaster)   76 *reposing hours* i.e. hours proper to sleep   80 *for unfelt imaginations* for the sake of imaginary and unreal gratifications (Dr Johnson)   94
*will be* wish to be   116 *passionate* compassionate

purse of gold that (by chance) I found. It beggars any
man that keeps it. It is turned out of towns and cities for
a dangerous thing, and every man that means to live
well endeavors to trust to himself and live without it.

1. MURDERER Zounds, 'tis even now at my elbow, persuading me not to kill the duke.

43 2. MURDERER Take the devil in thy mind, and believe
44 him not. He would insinuate with thee but to make thee
sigh.

1. MURDERER I am strong-framed; he cannot prevail
with me.

47 2. MURDERER Spoke like a tall man that respects thy
reputation. Come, shall we fall to work?

49 1. MURDERER Take him on the costard with the hilts of
thy sword, and then throw him into the malmsey butt in
the next room.

52 2. MURDERER O excellent device! and make a sop of him.

1. MURDERER Soft! he wakes.

2. MURDERER Strike!

1. MURDERER No, we'll reason with him.

CLARENCE
Where art thou, keeper? Give me a cup of wine.

2. MURDERER
You shall have wine enough, my lord, anon.

CLARENCE
In God's name, what art thou?

1. MURDERER
A man, as you are.

CLARENCE
But not as I am, royal.

1. MURDERER
Nor you as we are, loyal.

CLARENCE
Thy voice is thunder, but thy looks are humble.

1. MURDERER
My voice is now the king's, my looks mine own.

CLARENCE
164 How darkly and how deadly dost thou speak!
Your eyes do menace me. Why look you pale?
Who sent you hither? Wherefore do you come?

BOTH To, to, to —

CLARENCE
To murder me?

BOTH Ay, ay.

CLARENCE
You scarcely have the hearts to tell me so,
And therefore cannot have the hearts to do it.
Wherein, my friends, have I offended you?

1. MURDERER
Offended us you have not, but the king.

CLARENCE
I shall be reconciled to him again.

2. MURDERER
Never, my lord; therefore prepare to die.

CLARENCE
176 Are you drawn forth among a world of men

---

To slay the innocent? What is my offense?
Where is the evidence that doth accuse me?
What lawful quest have given their verdict up    179
Unto the frowning judge? or who pronounced
The bitter sentence of poor Clarence' death
Before I be convict by course of law?
To threaten me with death is most unlawful:
I charge you, as you hope [to have redemption
By Christ's dear blood shed for our grievous sins,]
That you depart, and lay no hands on me.
The deed you undertake is damnable.    187

1. MURDERER
What we will do, we do upon command.

2. MURDERER
And he that hath commanded is our king.

CLARENCE
Erroneous vassals! the great King of Kings
Hath in the table of his law commanded
That thou shalt do no murder. Will you then
Spurn at his edict, and fulfil a man's?
Take heed; for he holds vengeance in his hand
To hurl upon their heads that break his law.

2. MURDERER
And that same vengeance doth he hurl on thee
For false forswearing and for murder too:
Thou didst receive the sacrament to fight
In quarrel of the house of Lancaster.

1. MURDERER
And like a traitor to the name of God
Didst break that vow, and with thy treacherous blade
Unrip'st the bowels of thy sov'reign's son.

2. MURDERER
Whom thou wast sworn to cherish and defend.

1. MURDERER
How canst thou urge God's dreadful law to us
When thou hast broke it in such dear degree?    205

CLARENCE
Alas! for whose sake did I that ill deed?
For Edward, for my brother, for his sake.
He sends you not to murder me for this,
For in that sin he is as deep as I.
If God will be avengèd for the deed,
O, know you yet he doth it publicly!
Take not the quarrel from his pow'rful arm.
He needs no indirect or lawless course
To cut off those that have offended him.

1. MURDERER
Who made thee then a bloody minister
When gallant-springing brave Plantagenet,
That princely novice, was struck dead by thee?    217

CLARENCE
My brother's love, the devil, and my rage.

1. MURDERER
Thy brother's love, our duty, and thy faults
Provoke us hither now to slaughter thee.

CLARENCE
O, if you love my brother, hate not me:
I am his brother, and I love him well.
If you are hired for meed, go back again,    223
And I will send you to my brother Gloucester,
Who shall reward you better for my life
Than Edward will for tidings of my death.

2. MURDERER
You are deceived. Your brother Gloucester hates you.

---

143-44 *Take . . . not* call on the devil's aid and pay no heed to conscience (?)
or, trap the devil conscience in your reason and pay no heed to him (?)   **144**
*insinuate* ingratiate himself   **147** *tall* valiant   **149** *costard* head   **152** *sop*
wafer floated in a cup of wine   **164** *deadly* threatening death   **176** *drawn
. . . men* i.e. specially chosen among all mankind   **179** *quest* jury   **187**
*damnable* leading to damnation (for you)   **205** *dear degree* serious measure
**217** *novice* one just beginning his duties   **223** *meed* reward

**CLARENCE**
O, no, he loves me and he holds me dear :
Go you to him from me.

**1. MURDERER** Ay, so we will.

**CLARENCE**
Tell him, when that our princely father York
Blessed his three sons with his victorious arm
[And charged us from his soul to love each other,]
He little thought of this divided friendship :
Bid Gloucester think of this, and he will weep.

**1. MURDERER**
Ay, millstones, as he lessoned us to weep.

**CLARENCE**
236 O, do not slander him, for he is kind.

**1. MURDERER**
237 Right as snow in harvest. Come, you deceive yourself ;
'Tis he that sends us to destroy you here.

**CLARENCE**
It cannot be, for he bewept my fortune,
And hugged me in his arms, and swore with sobs
That he would labor my delivery.

**1. MURDERER**
Why so he doth, when he delivers you
From this earth's thraldom to the joys of heaven.

**2. MURDERER**
Make peace with God, for you must die, my lord.

**CLARENCE**
Have you that holy feeling in your souls
To counsel me to make my peace with God,
And are you yet to your own souls so blind
That you will war with God by murd'ring me ?
O, sirs, consider, they that set you on
250 To do this deed will hate you for the deed.

**2. MURDERER**
What shall we do ?

**CLARENCE** Relent, and save your souls.
Which of you, if you were a prince's son,
Being pent from liberty, as I am now,
If two such murderers as yourselves came to you,
Would not entreat for life ?

**1. MURDERER**
Relent ? No : 'tis cowardly and womanish.

**CLARENCE**
Not to relent is beastly, savage, devilish.
My friend [to Second Murderer], I spy some pity in thy
looks.
O, if thine eye be not a flatterer,
260 Come thou on my side, and entreat for me
As you would beg, were you in my distress.
A begging prince what beggar pities not ?

**2. MURDERER**
Look behind you, my lord !

**1. MURDERER**
Take that ! and that ! (Stabs him.) If all this will not do,
I'll drown you in the malmsey butt within.
*Exit [with the body].*

**2. MURDERER**
A bloody deed, and desperately dispatched !
How fain (like Pilate) would I wash my hands
Of this most grievous murder !
*Enter First Murderer.*

**1. MURDERER**
How now ? What mean'st thou that thou help'st me not ?
270 By heavens, the duke shall know how slack you have been.

**2. MURDERER**
I would he knew that I had saved his brother !
Take thou the fee and tell him what I say,
For I repent me that the duke is slain. *Exit.*

**1. MURDERER**
So do not I. Go, coward as thou art.
Well, I'll go hide the body in some hole
Till that the duke give order for his burial ;
And when I have my meed, I will away,
For this will out, and then I must not stay. *Exit.* 27

\*

*Flourish. Enter the King [Edward], sick, the* I
*Queen, Lord Marquess Dorset, [Grey,] Rivers,*
*Hastings, Catesby, [and] Buckingham.*

**KING EDWARD**
Why, so : now have I done a good day's work.
You peers, continue this united league.
I every day expect an embassage
From my Redeemer to redeem me hence ;
And more in peace my soul shall part to heaven,
Since I have made my friends at peace on earth.
Hastings and Rivers, take each other's hand ;
Dissemble not your hatred, swear your love. 8

**RIVERS**
By heaven, my soul is purged from grudging hate,
And with my hand I seal my true heart's love.

**HASTINGS**
So thrive I as I truly swear the like !

**KING EDWARD**
Take heed you dally not before your king, 12
Lest he that is the supreme King of Kings
Confound your hidden falsehood and award
Either of you to be the other's end.

**HASTINGS**
So prosper I as I swear perfect love !

**RIVERS**
And I as I love Hastings with my heart !

**KING EDWARD**
Madam, yourself is not exempt from this ;
Nor you, son Dorset ; Buckingham, nor you :
You have been factious one against the other. 20
Wife, love Lord Hastings, let him kiss your hand,
And what you do, do it unfeignedly.

**QUEEN ELIZABETH**
There, Hastings. I will never more remember
Our former hatred, so thrive I and mine !

**KING EDWARD**
Dorset, embrace him ; Hastings, love Lord Marquess.

**DORSET**
This interchange of love, I here protest,
Upon my part shall be inviolable.

**HASTINGS**
And so swear I.

**KING EDWARD**
Now, princely Buckingham, seal thou this league
With thy embracements to my wife's allies,
And make me happy in your unity.

---

236 *kind* (1) with feelings natural to a brother, (2) good   237 *Right as* just as
much as   278 *this will out* i.e. murder will out (proverbial)
II, i The royal palace   8 *Dissemble . . . hatred* do not hide hatred under a
false appearance (of love)   12 *dally* trifle

BUCKINGHAM *[to the Queen]*

32 Whenever Buckingham doth turn his hate
Upon your grace, but with all duteous love
Doth cherish you and yours, God punish me
With hate in those where I expect most love!
When I have most need to employ a friend,
And most assurèd that he is a friend,
Deep, hollow, treacherous, and full of guilè
Be he unto me! This do I beg of God,
When I am cold in love to you or yours.
    *Embrace.*

KING EDWARD

A pleasing cordial, princely Buckingham,
Is this thy vow unto my sickly heart.
There wanteth now our brother Gloucester here
44 To make the blessèd period of this peace.

BUCKINGHAM

And in good time,
Here comes Sir Richard Ratcliffe and the duke.
    *Enter [Sir Richard] Ratcliffe and [Richard, Duke of]*
    *Gloucester.*

RICHARD

Good morrow to my sovereign king and queen;
And, princely peers, a happy time of day!

KING EDWARD

Happy indeed, as we have spent the day:
Gloucester, we have done deeds of charity,
Made peace of enmity, fair love of hate,
Between these swelling wrong-incensèd peers.

RICHARD

A blessèd labor, my most sovereign lord:
Among this princely heap, if any here
By false intelligence or wrong surmise
Hold me a foe –
If I unwittingly, or in my rage,
Have aught committed that is hardly borne
By any in this presence, I desire
60 To reconcile me to his friendly peace.
'Tis death to me to be at enmity:
I hate it, and desire all good men's love.
First, madam, I entreat true peace of you,
Which I will purchase with my duteous service;
Of you, my noble cousin Buckingham,
If ever any grudge were lodged between us;
67 Of you, and you, Lord Rivers, and of Dorset,
68 That, all without desert, have frowned on me;
Dukes, earls, lords, gentlemen – indeed, of all.
I do not know that Englishman alive
With whom my soul is any jot at odds
72 More than the infant that is born to-night.
I thank my God for my humility.

QUEEN ELIZABETH

A holy day shall this be kept hereafter:

I would to God all strifes were well compounded.
My sovereign lord, I do beseech your highness
To take our brother Clarence to your grace.

RICHARD

Why, madam, have I off'red love for this,
To be so flouted in this royal presence?     79
Who knows not that the gentle duke is dead?
    *They all start.*
You do him injury to scorn his corse.     81

KING EDWARD

Who knows not he is dead? Who knows he is?

QUEEN ELIZABETH

All-seeing heaven, what a world is this!

BUCKINGHAM

Look I so pale, Lord Dorset, as the rest?

DORSET

Ay, my good lord; and no man in the presence     85
But his red color hath forsook his cheeks.

KING EDWARD

Is Clarence dead? The order was reversed.

RICHARD

But he (poor man) by your first order died,
And that a wingèd Mercury did bear:
Some tardy cripple bare the countermand,
That came too lag to see him buirèd.     91
God grant that some, less noble and less loyal,
Nearer in bloody thoughts, but not in blood,
Deserve not worse than wretched Clarence did,
And yet go current from suspicion!     95
    *Enter [Lord Stanley,] Earl of Derby.*

DERBY

A boon, my sovereign, for my service done!     96

KING EDWARD

I prithee peace. My soul is full of sorrow.

DERBY

I will not rise unless your highness hear me.

KING EDWARD

Then say at once what is it thou requests.

DERBY

The forfeit, sovereign, of my servant's life,     100
Who slew to-day a riotous gentleman
Lately attendant on the Duke of Norfolk.

KING EDWARD

Have I a tongue to doom my brother's death,
And shall that tongue give pardon to a slave?
My brother killed no man – his fault was thought –
And yet his punishment was bitter death.
Who sued to me for him? Who (in my wrath)
Kneeled at my feet and bid me be advised?
Who spoke of brotherhood? Who spoke of love?
Who told me how the poor soul did forsake
The mighty Warwick and did fight for me?     111
Who told me, in the field at Tewkesbury,
When Oxford had me down, he rescuèd me     113
And said, 'Dear brother, live, and be a king'?
Who told me, when we both lay in the field
Frozen (almost) to death, how he did lap me
Even in his garments, and did give himself
(All thin and naked) to the numb-cold night?
All this from my remembrance brutish wrath
Sinfully plucked, and not a man of you     120
Had so much grace to put it in my mind.
But when your carters or your waiting vassals
Have done a drunken slaughter and defaced

---

32–35 *Whenever . . . love* (construction incoherent; for 'but,' l. 33, understand 'nor')   44 *period* conclusion (cf. I, iii, 237)   60 *reconcile . . . peace* i.e. bring myself into friendly relations with him   67 *of Dorset* ('Lord' understood)   68 *all without desert* entirely without my having deserved it   72 *More . . . infant* i.e. more than that infant's soul is   79 *flouted* mocked at   81 *scorn his corse* i.e. joke about the dead   85 *presence* i.e. king's presence   91 *lag* late   95 *go . . . suspicion* are accepted (as legal tender at face value) without question   96 *boon* favor   100 *forfeit . . . life* (the remission of the forfeit is the boon)   111 *Warwick* (Clarence returned to the Yorkist side after marrying Warwick's daughter, thus perjuring himself)   113 *Oxford* (an incident neither historical nor in *3 Henry VI*)

The precious image of our dear Redeemer,
You straight are on your knees for pardon, pardon ;
And I (unjustly too) must grant it you.
            *[Derby rises.]*
But for my brother not a man would speak,
Nor I (ungracious) speak unto myself
For him, poor soul ! The proudest of you all
130 Have been beholding to him in his life ;
Yet none of you would once beg for his life.
O God ! I fear thy justice will take hold
On me and you, and mine and yours, for this.
Come, Hastings, help me to my closet. Ah, poor Clar-
ence !                 *Exeunt some with King and Queen.*

RICHARD
This is the fruits of rashness ! Marked you not
How that the guilty kindred of the queen
Looked pale when they did hear of Clarence' death ?
O, they did urge it still unto the king !
God will revenge it. Come, lords, will you go
140 To comfort Edward with our company ?

BUCKINGHAM
We wait upon your grace.                 *Exeunt.*

*

II, ii     *Enter the old Duchess of York, with the two*
           *Children of Clarence [Edward and Margaret*
           *Plantagenet].*

BOY
    Good grandam, tell us, is our father dead ?

DUCHESS OF YORK No, boy.

GIRL
    Why do you weep so oft, and beat your breast,
    And cry 'O Clarence, my unhappy son' ?

BOY
    Why do you look on us, and shake your head,
    And call us orphans, wretches, castaways,
    If that our noble father were alive ?

DUCHESS OF YORK
8   My pretty cousins, you mistake me both.
    I do lament the sickness of the king,
    As loath to lose him, not your father's death :
    It were lost sorrow to wail one that's lost.

BOY
    Then you conclude, my grandam, he is dead.

13  The king mine uncle is too blame for it :
    God will revenge it, whom I will importune
    With earnest prayers all to that effect.

GIRL
    And so will I.

DUCHESS OF YORK
    Peace, children, peace ! The king doth love you well.
18  Incapable and shallow innocents,
    You cannot guess who caused your father's death.

BOY
    Grandam, we can ; for my good uncle Gloucester
    Told me the king, provoked to it by the queen,
22  Devised impeachments to imprison him ;
    And when my uncle told me so, he wept,
    And pitied me, and kindly kissed my cheek ;
    Bade me rely on him as on my father,
    And he would love me dearly as a child.

DUCHESS OF YORK
27  Ah, that deceit should steal such gentle shape

And with a virtuous visor hide deep vice !              28
He is my son – ay, and therein my shame ;
Yet from my dugs he drew not this deceit.

BOY
Think you my uncle did dissemble, grandam ?

DUCHESS OF YORK Ay, boy.

BOY
I cannot think it. Hark ! What noise is this ?
            *Enter the Queen [Elizabeth], with her hair about*
            *her ears, Rivers and Dorset after her.*

QUEEN ELIZABETH
Ah, who shall hinder me to wail and weep,
To chide my fortune, and torment myself ?
I'll join with black despair against my soul
And to myself become an enemy.

DUCHESS OF YORK
What means this scene of rude impatience ?         38

QUEEN ELIZABETH
To make an act of tragic violence.
Edward, my lord, thy son, our king, is dead !
Why grow the branches when the root is gone ?
Why wither not the leaves that want their sap ?
If you will live, lament ; if die, be brief,
That our swift-wingèd souls may catch the king's,
Or like obedient subjects follow him
To his new kingdom of ne'er-changing night.

DUCHESS OF YORK
Ah, so much interest have I in thy sorrow
As I had title in thy noble husband.                    48
I have bewept a worthy husband's death,
And lived with looking on his images ;                 50
But now two mirrors of his princely semblance         51
Are cracked in pieces by malignant death,
And I for comfort have but one false glass
That grieves me when I see my shame in him.
Thou art a widow ; yet thou art a mother,
And hast the comfort of thy children left ;
But death hath snatched my husband from mine arms
And plucked two crutches from my feeble hands,
Clarence and Edward. O, what cause have I            59
(Thine being but a moi'ty of my moan)                 60
To overgo thy woes and drown thy cries !

BOY
Ah, aunt ! you wept not for our father's death.
How can we aid you with our kindred tears ?           63

GIRL
Our fatherless distress was left unmoaned :
Your widow-dolor likewise be unwept !

QUEEN ELIZABETH
Give me no help in lamentation ;
I am not barren to bring forth complaints.            67
All springs reduce their currents to mine eyes,       68
That I, being governed by the watery moon,

II, ii The same  8 *you . . . both* you both misunderstand me  13 *too blame*
blameworthy ('blame' felt as adjectival)  18 *Incapable* without power of
understanding  22 *impeachments* accusations  27 *shape* disguise  28 *visor*
mask  38–39 *scene . . . violence* (note the playhouse imagery ; cf. ll. 27–28
and III, v, 1–11)  48 *title* legal right  50 *lived with* i.e. kept myself alive
by ; *images* i.e. children  51 *mirrors* i.e. Clarence and King Edward  59
*what . . . I* what a cause I have  60 *moi'ty of my moan* half (the cause) of my
grief  63 *kindred tears* i.e. tears belonging to relatives  67 *I . . . complaints*
I have a full capacity for uttering complaints  68 *reduce* bring (as to a
reservoir)

May send forth plenteous tears to drown the world.
Ah for my husband, for my dear lord Edward!

CHILDREN
Ah for our father, for our dear lord Clarence!

DUCHESS OF YORK
Alas for both, both mine, Edward and Clarence!

QUEEN ELIZABETH
What stay had I but Edward? and he's gone.

CHILDREN
What stay had we but Clarence? and he's gone.

DUCHESS OF YORK
What stays had I but they? and they are gone.

QUEEN ELIZABETH
Was never widow had so dear a loss.

CHILDREN
Were never orphans had so dear a loss.

DUCHESS OF YORK
Was never mother had so dear a loss.
Alas! I am the mother of these griefs:
81  Their woes are parcelled, mine is general.
She for an Edward weeps, and so do I;
I for a Clarence weep, so doth not she:
These babes for Clarence weep, [and so do I;
I for an Edward weep,] so do not they.
Alas, you three on me, threefold distressed,
Pour all your tears! I am your sorrow's nurse,
88  And I will pamper it with lamentation.

DORSET
Comfort, dear mother; God is much displeased
That you take with unthankfulness his doing.
In common worldly things 'tis called ungrateful
With dull unwillingness to repay a debt
Which with a bounteous hand was kindly lent;
94  Much more to be thus opposite with heaven
95  For it requires the royal debt it lent you.

RIVERS
Madam, bethink you like a careful mother
Of the young prince your son. Send straight for him;
Let him be crowned; in him your comfort lives.
Drown desperate sorrow in dead Edward's grave
And plant your joys in living Edward's throne.
    *Enter Richard, Buckingham, [Stanley Earl of]*
    *Derby, Hastings, and Ratcliffe.*

RICHARD
Sister, have comfort. All of us have cause
To wail the dimming of our shining star;
But none can help our harms by wailing them.
Madam, my mother, I do cry you mercy;
I did not see your grace. Humbly on my knee
I crave your blessing.

DUCHESS OF YORK
God bless thee, and put meekness in thy breast,
Love, charity, obedience, and true duty!

RICHARD
Amen!—*[aside]* and make me die a good old man!

That is the butt-end of a mother's blessing;
I marvel that her grace did leave it out.

BUCKINGHAM
You cloudy princes and heart-sorrowing peers
That bear this heavy mutual load of moan,          113
Now cheer each other in each other's love.
Though we have spent our harvest of this king,
We are to reap the harvest of his son.
The broken rancor of your high-swol'n hates,       117
But lately splintered, knit, and joined together,  118
Must gently be preserved, cherished, and kept.
Me seemeth good that with some little train        120
Forthwith from Ludlow the young prince be fet      121
Hither to London, to be crowned our king.

RIVERS
Why with some little train, my Lord of Buckingham?

BUCKINGHAM
Marry, my lord, lest by a multitude                124
The new-healed wound of malice should break out,
Which would be so much the more dangerous
By how much the estate is green and yet ungoverned. 127
Where every horse bears his commanding rein
And may direct his course as please himself,
As well the fear of harm as harm apparent,
In my opinion, ought to be prevented.

RICHARD
I hope the king made peace with all of us;
And the compact is firm and true in me.

RIVERS
And so in me; and so (I think) in all.
Yet, since it is but green, it should be put
To no apparent likelihood of breach,
Which haply by much company might be urged.
Therefore I say with noble Buckingham
That it is meet so few should fetch the prince.

HASTINGS
And so say I.

RICHARD
Then be it so; and go we to determine
Who they shall be that straight shall post to Ludlow.
Madam, and you, my sister, will you go
To give your censures in this business?            144
[BOTH
With all our hearts.]
        *Exeunt. Manent Buckingham and Richard.*

BUCKINGHAM
My lord, whoever journeys to the prince,
For God sake let not us two stay at home;
For by the way I'll sort occasion,                 148
As index to the story we late talked of,           149
To part the queen's proud kindred from the prince.

RICHARD
My other self, my counsel's consistory,            151
My oracle, my prophet, my dear cousin,
I, as a child, will go by thy direction.
Toward Ludlow then, for we'll not stay behind. *Exeunt.*

*

---

*Enter one Citizen at one door and another at the other.* II, iii

1. CITIZEN
Good morrow, neighbor. Whither away so fast?

2. CITIZEN
I promise you, I scarcely know myself.

81 *parcelled* particular to each one  88 *pamper . . . lamentation* i.e. feed
sorrow with sorrow  94 *opposite with* opposed to  95 *For* because  113
*load of moan* i.e. weight or cause of lamentation  117–19 *The broken . . .
kept* (meaning confused; understand 'broken rancor' as implying 'new-
found amity')  118 *splintered* set in splints  120 *Me seemeth* it seems to
me  121 *Ludlow* town in south Shropshire; *fet* fetched  124 *multitude*
large train or following  127 *estate is green* administration of government is
untried  144 *censures* judgments  148 *sort occasion* make an opportunity
149 *index* prologue  151 *consistory* council chamber
II, iii A London street

Hear you the news abroad ?

1 . CITIZEN                    Yes, that the king is dead.

2 . CITIZEN

4   Ill news, by'r Lady – seldom comes the better :

5   I fear, I fear 'twill prove a giddy world.

*Enter another Citizen.*

3 . CITIZEN

Neighbors, God speed !

1 . CITIZEN                    Give you good morrow, sir.

3 . CITIZEN

Doth the news hold of good King Edward's death ?

2 . CITIZEN

Ay, sir, it is too true. God help the while !

3 . CITIZEN

Then, masters, look to see a troublous world.

1 . CITIZEN

No, no ! By God's good grace his son shall reign.

3 . CITIZEN

Woe to that land that's governed by a child !

2 . CITIZEN

12  In him there is a hope of government,
Which, in his nonage, council under him,
And, in his full and ripenèd years, himself,
No doubt shall then, and till then, govern well.

1 . CITIZEN

So stood the state when Henry the Sixth
Was crowned in Paris but at nine months old.

3 . CITIZEN

18  Stood the state so ? No, no, good friends, God wot !
For then this land was famously enriched
20  With politic grave counsel ; then the king
Had virtuous uncles to protect his grace.

1 . CITIZEN

Why, so hath this, both by his father and mother.

3 . CITIZEN

Better it were they all came by his father,
Or by his father there were none at all ;
For emulation who shall now be nearest
Will touch us all too near, if God prevent not.
O, full of danger is the Duke of Gloucester,
28  And the queen's sons and brothers haught and proud ;
And were they to be ruled, and not to rule,
30  This sickly land might solace as before.

1 . CITIZEN

Come, come, we fear the worst. All will be well.

3 . CITIZEN

32  When clouds are seen, wise men put on their cloaks ;
When great leaves fall, then winter is at hand ;
When the sun sets, who doth not look for night ?
Untimely storms makes men expect a dearth.
36  All may be well ; but if God sort it so,
'Tis more than we deserve or I expect.

2 . CITIZEN

Truly, the hearts of men are full of fear :
39  You cannot reason (almost) with a man
That looks not heavily and full of dread.

3 . CITIZEN

Before the days of change, still is it so.
By a divine instinct men's minds mistrust
Ensuing danger ; as by proof we see
The water swell before a boist'rous storm.
But leave it all to God. Whither away ?

2 . CITIZEN

Marry, we were sent for to the justices.

3 . CITIZEN

And so was I. I'll bear you company.          *Exeunt.*

*

*Enter [the] Archbishop [of York], [the] young*          II,
*[Duke of] York, the Queen [Elizabeth], and the*
*Duchess [of York].*

ARCHBISHOP

Last night, I hear, they lay at Stony Stratford ;          1
And at Northampton they do rest to-night ;          2
To-morrow, or next day, they will be here.

DUCHESS OF YORK

I long with all my heart to see the prince :
I hope he is much grown since last I saw him.

QUEEN ELIZABETH

But I hear no. They say my son of York
Has almost overta'en him in his growth.

YORK

Ay, mother ; but I would not have it so.

DUCHESS OF YORK

Why, my good cousin ? it is good to grow.

YORK

Grandam, one night as we did sit at supper,
My uncle Rivers talked how I did grow
More than my brother. 'Ay,' quoth my uncle
    Gloucester,
'Small herbs have grace ; great weeds do grow apace.'          13
And since, methinks, I would not grow so fast,
Because sweet flow'rs are slow and weeds make haste.

DUCHESS OF YORK

Good faith, good faith, the saying did not hold
In him that did object the same to thee :          17
He was the wretched'st thing when he was young,
So long a-growing and so leisurely
That, if his rule were true, he should be gracious.          20

ARCHBISHOP

And so no doubt he is, my gracious madam.

DUCHESS OF YORK

I hope he is ; but yet let mothers doubt.

YORK

Now, by my troth, if I had been rememb'red,          23
I could have given my uncle's grace a flout          24
To touch his growth nearer than he touched mine.

DUCHESS OF YORK

How, my young York ? I prithee let me hear it.

YORK

Marry (they say) my uncle grew so fast
That he could gnaw a crust at two hours old :
'Twas full two years ere I could get a tooth.

4 *seldom . . . better* (times are bad) but are likely to be worse (proverbial) 5 *giddy* inconstant or mad  12–15 *In him . . . well* (confused construction : there is hope for the land ; for one who in his minority governs wisely with the aid of counsel will in his maturity govern well in his own person)  18 *wot* knows  20 *counsel* professional advisers  28 *haught* haughty  30 *solace* be happy  32–35 *When . . . dearth* (a series of 'moral sentences' in the manner of Senecan tragedy)  36 *sort* dispose  39 *You . . . man* i.e. there is almost no man with whom you can reason
II, iv The royal palace  1 *Stony Stratford* town in Buckinghamshire  2 *Northampton* town in Northamptonshire (Historically the order of these two towns is correct, though dramatically the order is difficult since Stony Stratford is closer to London than Northampton is – see l. 3. The quartos reverse the order.)  13 *grace* beneficent virtue  17 *object* urge  20 *gracious* (playing on *grace*, l. 13)  23 *troth* faith ; *been rememb'red* considered  24 *flout* scoff

30 Grandam, this would have been a biting jest.

**DUCHESS OF YORK**
I prithee, pretty York, who told thee this?

**YORK**
Grandam, his nurse.

**DUCHESS OF YORK**
His nurse? Why, she was dead ere thou wast born.

**YORK**
If 'twere not she, I cannot tell who told me.

**QUEEN ELIZABETH**
35 A parlous boy! Go to, you are too shrewd.

**DUCHESS OF YORK**
Good madam, be not angry with the child.

**QUEEN ELIZABETH**
37 Pitchers have ears.
*Enter a Messenger.*

**ARCHBISHOP**
Here comes a messenger. What news?

**MESSENGER**
Such news, my lord, as grieves me to report.

**QUEEN ELIZABETH**
How doth the prince?

**MESSENGER**               Well, madam, and in health.

**DUCHESS OF YORK**
What is thy news?

**MESSENGER**
42 Lord Rivers and Lord Grey are sent to Pomfret,
43 And with them Sir Thomas Vaughan, prisoners.

**DUCHESS OF YORK**
Who hath committed them?

**MESSENGER**               The mighty dukes,
Gloucester and Buckingham.

**ARCHBISHOP**               For what offense?

**MESSENGER**
46 The sum of all I can I have disclosed.
Why or for what the nobles were committed
Is all unknown to me, my gracious lord.

**QUEEN ELIZABETH**
Ay me! I see the ruin of my house.
The tiger now hath seized the gentle hind;
51 Insulting tyranny begins to jut
52 Upon the innocent and aweless throne:
Welcome destruction, blood, and massacre!
54 I see (as in a map) the end of all.

**DUCHESS OF YORK**
Accursèd and unquiet wrangling days,
How many of you have mine eyes beheld!
57 My husband lost his life to get the crown,
And often up and down my sons were tossed
For me to joy and weep their gain and loss;
And being seated, and domestic broils
Clean overblown, themselves the conquerors

Make war upon themselves, brother to brother,
Blood to blood, self against self. O preposterous    63
And frantic outrage, end thy damnèd spleen,    64
Or let me die, to look on death no more!

**QUEEN ELIZABETH**
Come, come, my boy; we will to sanctuary.    66
Madam, farewell.

**DUCHESS OF YORK** Stay, I will go with you.

**QUEEN ELIZABETH**
You have no cause.

**ARCHBISHOP** *[to the Queen]* My gracious lady, go,
And thither bear your treasure and your goods.
For my part, I'll resign unto your grace
The seal I keep; and so betide to me
As well I tender you and all of yours!    72
Go, I'll conduct you to the sanctuary.            *Exeunt.*

\*

*The trumpets sound. Enter young Prince*    III, i
*[Edward of Wales], the Dukes of Gloucester and*
*Buckingham, Lord Cardinal [Bourchier, Catesby,]*
*with others.*

**BUCKINGHAM**
Welcome, sweet prince, to London, to your chamber.    1

**RICHARD**
Welcome, dear cousin, my thoughts' sovereign:
The weary way hath made you melancholy.

**PRINCE EDWARD**
No, uncle; but our crosses on the way    4
Have made it tedious, wearisome, and heavy.
I want more uncles here to welcome me.    6

**RICHARD**
Sweet prince, the untainted virtue of your years
Hath not yet dived into the world's deceit:
Nor more can you distinguish of a man
Than of his outward show, which, God he knows,
Seldom or never jumpeth with the heart.    11
Those uncles which you want were dangerous;
Your grace attended to their sug'red words
But looked not on the poison of their hearts:
God keep you from them, and from such false friends!

**PRINCE EDWARD**
God keep me from false friends! – but they were none.

**RICHARD**
My lord, the Mayor of London comes to greet you.
*Enter Lord Mayor [and his Train].*

**LORD MAYOR**
God bless your grace with health and happy days!

**PRINCE EDWARD**
I thank you, good my lord, and thank you all.
*[Mayor and his Train stand aside.]*
I thought my mother and my brother York
Would long ere this have met us on the way.
Fie, what a slug is Hastings that he comes not    22
To tell us whether they will come or no!
*Enter Lord Hastings.*

**BUCKINGHAM**
And, in good time, here comes the sweating lord.

**PRINCE EDWARD**
Welcome, my lord. What, will our mother come?

**HASTINGS**
On what occasion God he knows, not I,    26
The queen your mother and your brother York

---

30 *biting* (note play on 'teeth' in ll. 28–29)   35 *parlous* cunning   37
*Pitchers have ears* (proverbial: little pitchers have wide ears – said of
children)   42 *Pomfret* castle in Yorkshire   43 *Vaughan* (dissyllabic throughout)   46 *can* know   51 *jut* encroach upon   52 *aweless* inspiring no awe
54 *map* (figuratively) something representing (future) events in epitome
57–63 *My husband . . . self* (note the 'wheel of fortune' theme underlying
these lines)   63 *preposterous* inverting the natural order   64 *spleen* malice
66 *sanctuary* the cathedral precincts in which civil law was powerless   72
*tender* care for
III, i A London street   1 *chamber* (London was known as *camera regis* or
king's chamber)   4 *crosses* annoyances (play on *melancholy*, l. 3)   6 *want*
(1) am lacking in, (2) desire (cf. l. 12)   11 *jumpeth* accords   22 *slug* lazy
fellow (sluggard)   26 *On what occasion* for what reason

Have taken sanctuary. The tender prince
Would fain have come with me to meet your grace,
30   But by his mother was perforce withheld.

BUCKINGHAM
31   Fie, what an indirect and peevish course
Is this of hers! Lord Cardinal, will your grace
Persuade the queen to send the Duke of York
34   Unto his princely brother presently?
If she deny, Lord Hastings, go with him
And from her jealous arms pluck him perforce.

CARDINAL BOURCHIER
My Lord of Buckingham, if my weak oratory
Can from his mother win the Duke of York,
Anon expect him here; but if she be obdurate
To mild entreaties, God in heaven forbid
We should infringe the holy privilege
Of blessèd sanctuary! Not for all this land
Would I be guilty of so deep a sin.

BUCKINGHAM
You are too senseless-obstinate, my lord,
45   Too ceremonious and traditional.
46   Weigh it but with the grossness of this age,
You break not sanctuary in seizing him:
The benefit thereof is always granted
To those whose dealings have deserved the place
And those who have the wit to claim the place.
This prince hath neither claimed it nor deserved it,
And therefore, in mine opinion, cannot have it.
Then, taking him from thence that is not there,
You break no privilege nor charter there.
Oft have I heard of sanctuary men,
But sanctuary children never till now.

CARDINAL BOURCHIER
My lord, you shall overrule my mind for once.
Come on, Lord Hastings, will you go with me?

HASTINGS
I go, my lord.

PRINCE EDWARD
Good lords, make all the speedy haste you may.
             *Exeunt Cardinal and Hastings.*
Say, uncle Gloucester, if our brother come,
Where shall we sojourn till our coronation?

RICHARD
Where it seems best unto your royal self.
If I may counsel you, some day or two
65   Your highness shall repose you at the Tower;
Then where you please, and shall be thought most fit
For your best health and recreation.

PRINCE EDWARD
68   I do not like the Tower, of any place.
Did Julius Caesar build that place, my lord?

BUCKINGHAM
He did, my gracious lord, begin that place,
Which, since, succeeding ages have re-edified.

PRINCE EDWARD
Is it upon record, or else reported
Successively from age to age, he built it?

BUCKINGHAM
Upon record, my gracious lord.

PRINCE EDWARD
But say, my lord, it were not regist'red,
Methinks the truth should live from age to age,
As 'twere retailed to all posterity,

Even to the general all-ending day.

RICHARD *[aside]*
So wise so young, they say, do never live long.

PRINCE EDWARD
What say you, uncle?

RICHARD
I say, without characters fame lives long.     81
     *[Aside]*
Thus, like the formal Vice, Iniquity,     82
I moralize two meanings in one word.     83

PRINCE EDWARD
That Julius Caesar was a famous man:
With what his valor did enrich his wit,     85
His wit set down to make his valor live.
Death makes no conquest of this conqueror,
For now he lives in fame, though not in life.
I'll tell you what, my cousin Buckingham –

BUCKINGHAM
What, my gracious lord?

PRINCE EDWARD
An if I live until I be a man,     91
I'll win our ancient right in France again
Or die a soldier as I lived a king.

RICHARD *[aside]*
Short summers lightly have a forward spring.     94
     *Enter [the] young [Duke of] York, Hastings, and*
     *Cardinal [Bourchier].*

BUCKINGHAM
Now in good time, here comes the Duke of York.

PRINCE EDWARD
Richard of York, how fares our loving brother?

YORK
Well, my dread lord – so must I call you now.     97

PRINCE EDWARD
Ay, brother – to our grief, as it is yours:
Too late he died that might have kept that title,     99
Which by his death hath lost much majesty.

RICHARD
How fares our cousin, noble Lord of York?

YORK
I thank you, gentle uncle. O, my lord,
You said that idle weeds are fast in growth:
The prince my brother hath outgrown me far.

RICHARD
He hath, my lord.

YORK            And therefore is he idle?

RICHARD
O my fair cousin, I must not say so.

YORK
Then he is more beholding to you than I.     107

RICHARD
He may command me as my sovereign,

---

30 *perforce* forcibly   31 *indirect and peevish* devious and perverse   34 *presently* at once   45 *ceremonious* tied by formalities   46 *grossness* coarseness or lack of refinement (in a moral sense)   65 *Tower* the Tower of London (associated in the prince's mind with imprisonment; cf. I, i, 45) 68 *of any place* of all places   81 *characters* written records   82 *formal Vice, Iniquity* i.e. the conventional Vice figure called Iniquity (the Vice in sixteenth-century morality plays symbolized in one character all the vices) 83 *moralize . . . word* play on a double meaning (as the Vice did) in a single phrase (i.e. *live long,* l. 79)   85 *what* that with which   91 *An if* if   94 *Short . . . spring* i.e. those who die young are usually (*lightly*) precocious (proverbial; cf. l. 79)   97 *dread* to be feared (as king)   99 *late* recently 107 *beholding* indebted

But you have power in me as in a kinsman.

YORK
I pray you, uncle, give me this dagger.

RICHARD
111   My dagger, little cousin ? With all my heart.

PRINCE EDWARD
A beggar, brother ?

YORK
Of my kind uncle, that I know will give,
And being but a toy, which is no grief to give.

RICHARD
A greater gift than that I'll give my cousin.

YORK
A greater gift ? O, that's the sword to it.

RICHARD
Ay, gentle cousin, were it light enough.

YORK
118   O, then I see you will part but with light gifts !
In weightier things you'll say a beggar nay.

RICHARD
It is too heavy for your grace to wear.

YORK
121   I weigh it lightly, were it heavier.

RICHARD
What, would you have my weapon, little lord ?

YORK
I would, that I might thank you as you call me.

RICHARD How ?
YORK Little.

PRINCE EDWARD
126   My Lord of York will still be cross in talk.
Uncle, your grace knows how to bear with him.

YORK
You mean, to bear me, not to bear with me.
Uncle, my brother mocks both you and me :
Because that I am little, like an ape,
He thinks that you should bear me on your shoulders.

BUCKINGHAM [aside to Hastings]
132   With what a sharp-provided wit he reasons !
To mitigate the scorn he gives his uncle,
He prettily and aptly taunts himself :
So cunning, and so young, is wonderful.

RICHARD
My lord, will't please you pass along ?
Myself and my good cousin Buckingham
Will to your mother, to entreat of her
To meet you at the Tower and welcome you.

YORK
What, will you go unto the Tower, my lord ?

PRINCE EDWARD
My Lord Protector needs will have it so.

YORK
I shall not sleep in quiet at the Tower.

RICHARD
Why, what should you fear ?

YORK
Marry, my uncle Clarence' angry ghost :
My grandam told me he was murd'red there.

PRINCE EDWARD
I fear no uncles dead.

RICHARD
Nor none that live, I hope.

PRINCE EDWARD
An if they live, I hope I need not fear.     148
But come, my lord ; with a heavy heart,
Thinking on them, go I unto the Tower.
    *A sennet. Exeunt Prince [Edward], York, Hastings*
    *[, Cardinal Bourchier, and others]. Manent Richard,*
    *Buckingham, and Catesby.*

BUCKINGHAM
Think you, my lord, this little prating York     151
Was not incensèd by his subtle mother     152
To taunt and scorn you thus opprobriously ?

RICHARD
No doubt, no doubt. O, 'tis a perilous boy,     154
Bold, quick, ingenious, forward, capable :
He is all the mother's, from the top to toe.     156

BUCKINGHAM
Well, let them rest. Come hither, Catesby.     157
Thou art sworn as deeply to effect what we intend
As closely to conceal what we impart.
Thou know'st our reasons urged upon the way.
What think'st thou ? Is it not an easy matter
To make William Lord Hastings of our mind
For the instalment of this noble duke     163
In the seat royal of this famous isle ?

CATESBY
He for his father's sake so loves the prince
That he will not be won to aught against him.

BUCKINGHAM
What think'st thou then of Stanley ? Will not he ?     167

CATESBY
He will do all in all as Hastings doth.

BUCKINGHAM
Well then, no more but this : go, gentle Catesby,
And, as it were far off, sound thou Lord Hastings
How he doth stand affected to our purpose,     171
And summon him to-morrow to the Tower
To sit about the coronation.     173
If thou dost find him tractable to us,     174
Encourage him, and tell him all our reasons :
If he be leaden, icy, cold, unwilling,
Be thou so too, and so break off the talk,
And give us notice of his inclination ;
For we to-morrow hold divided councils,     179
Wherein thyself shalt highly be employed.

RICHARD
Commend me to Lord William. Tell him, Catesby,     181
His ancient knot of dangerous adversaries
To-morrow are let blood at Pomfret Castle,
And bid my lord, for joy of this good news,
Give Mistress Shore one gentle kiss the more.

---

111 *My . . . heart* (Richard would, with all his heart, like to give York his
dagger in his heart)   118 *light* slight or trivial   121 *weigh it lightly* consider it of little value   126 *still be cross* i.e. always be twisting words   132
*sharp-provided* keenly thought out   148 *they* i.e. Rivers and Grey (Grey
was actually Prince Edward's stepbrother)   151 *prating* overtalkative
152 *incensèd* incited   154 *perilous* shrewd or dangerously cunning (cf.
*parlous*, II, iv, 35, the more usual form, but Richard's use of the stronger
form may here be intentional)   156 *He . . . mother's* i.e. he takes after his
mother   157 *let them rest* i.e. leave them (for the moment)   163 *instalment*
formal installation   167 *Stanley* i.e. the Earl of Derby, Lord Stanley   171
*How . . . affected* how he is disposed   173 *sit* i.e. hold consultation   174
*tractable* compliant   179 *divided councils* i.e. two separate council meetings
(cf. III, ii, 12–14), one a private consultation unknown to the public council
181 *Lord William* i.e. Hastings

BUCKINGHAM
Good Catesby, go effect this business soundly.
CATESBY
My good lords both, with all the heed I can.
RICHARD
Shall we hear from you, Catesby, ere we sleep?
CATESBY
You shall, my lord.
RICHARD
At Crosby House, there shall you find us both.
                                        *Exit Catesby.*
BUCKINGHAM
Now, my lord, what shall we do if we perceive
192  Lord Hastings will not yield to our complots?
RICHARD
Chop off his head! Something we will determine.
194  And look when I am king, claim thou of me
195  The earldom of Hereford and all the moveables
Whereof the king my brother was possessed.
BUCKINGHAM
I'll claim that promise at your grace's hand.
RICHARD
And look to have it yielded with all kindness.
199  Come, let us sup betimes, that afterwards
We may digest our complots in some form.   *Exeunt.*

*

III, ii          *Enter a Messenger to the door of Hastings.*
MESSENGER
My lord! my lord!
HASTINGS [*within*]
Who knocks?
MESSENGER
One from the Lord Stanley.
                    *Enter Lord Hastings.*
HASTINGS
What is't a clock?
MESSENGER
Upon the stroke of four.
HASTINGS
6  Cannot my Lord Stanley sleep these tedious nights?
MESSENGER
So it appears by that I have to say:
First, he commends him to your noble self.
HASTINGS
What then?
MESSENGER
Then certifies your lordship that this night
11  He dreamt the boar had rasèd off his helm:
Besides, he says there are two councils kept;
And that may be determined at the one
14  Which may make you and him to rue at th' other.
Therefore he sends to know your lordship's pleasure,
16  If you will presently take horse with him
And with all speed post with him toward the North
To shun the danger that his soul divines.
HASTINGS
Go, fellow, go, return unto thy lord;
Bid him not fear the separated council.
His honor and myself are at the one,
And at the other is my good friend Catesby;
Where nothing can proceed that toucheth us
Whereof I shall not have intelligence.

Tell him his fears are shallow, without instance;   25
And for his dreams, I wonder he's so simple
To trust the mock'ry of unquiet slumbers.
To fly the boar before the boar pursues
Were to incense the boar to follow us,
And make pursuit where he did mean no chase.
Go, bid thy master rise and come to me,
And we will both together to the Tower,
Where he shall see the boar will use us kindly.
MESSENGER
I'll go, my lord, and tell him what you say.   *Exit.*
            *Enter Catesby.*
CATESBY
Many good morrows to my noble lord!
HASTINGS
Good morrow, Catesby; you are early stirring.
What news, what news, in this our tott'ring state?
CATESBY
It is a reeling world indeed, my lord,   38
And I believe will never stand upright
Till Richard wear the garland of the realm.
HASTINGS
How! wear the garland! Dost thou mean the crown?
CATESBY
Ay, my good lord.
HASTINGS
I'll have this crown of mine cut from my shoulders   43
Before I'll see the crown so foul misplaced.
But canst thou guess that he doth aim at it?
CATESBY
Ay, on my life, and hopes to find you forward   46
Upon his party for the gain thereof;
And thereupon he sends you this good news,
That this same very day your enemies,
The kindred of the queen, must die at Pomfret.
HASTINGS
Indeed I am no mourner for that news,
Because they have been still my adversaries;   52
But that I'll give my voice on Richard's side
To bar my master's heirs in true descent –
God knows I will not do it, to the death!
CATESBY
God keep your lordship in that gracious mind!
HASTINGS
But I shall laugh at this a twelvemonth hence,   57
That they which brought me in my master's hate,
I live to look upon their tragedy.
Well, Catesby, ere a fortnight make me older,
I'll send some packing that yet think not on't.
CATESBY
'Tis a vile thing to die, my gracious lord,
When men are unprepared and look not for it.
HASTINGS
O monstrous, monstrous! and so falls it out

192 *complots* conspiracies  194 *look when* as soon as  195 *moveables* (cf. Holinshed: 'a great quantitie of the kings treasure, and of his household stuffe')  199 *betimes* soon
III, ii Before Lord Hastings' house  6 *tedious* (this word seems to suggest that Hastings cannot sleep either)  11 *boar* (see I, iii, 227); *rasèd . . . helm* figuratively, cut off his head  14 *rue* grieve (at what was decided)  16 *presently* at once  25 *instance* evidence  38 *reeling* (cf. II, iii, 5)  43 *crown . . . shoulders* (foreshadows Hastings' death and looks back to l. 11)  46–47 *forward Upon* lending strong support to  52 *still* always  57–59 *But . . . tragedy* (construction difficult; for the sense, omit *they* in l. 58 and insert l. 59 after *That* in l. 58)

With Rivers, Vaughan, Grey ; and so 'twill do
With some men else, that think themselves as safe
As thou and I, who (as thou know'st) are dear
To princely Richard and to Buckingham.

CATESBY
The princes both make high account of you –
    [Aside]
70  For they account his head upon the Bridge.
HASTINGS
I know they do, and I have well deserved it.
    Enter Lord Stanley [Earl of Derby].
Come on, come on ! Where is your boar-spear, man ?
Fear you the boar, and go so unprovided ?
DERBY
My lord, good morrow. Good morrow, Catesby.
75  You may jest on, but, by the Holy Rood,
I do not like these several councils, I.
HASTINGS
My lord,
I hold my life as dear as you do yours,
And never in my days, I do protest,
Was it so precious to me as 'tis now.
Think you, but that I know our state secure,
82  I would be so triumphant as I am ?
DERBY
The lords at Pomfret, when they rode from London,
84  Were jocund and supposed their states were sure,
And they indeed had no cause to mistrust ;
But yet you see how soon the day o'ercast.
87  This sudden stab of rancor I misdoubt :
Pray God, I say, I prove a needless coward !
89  What, shall we toward the Tower ? The day is spent.
HASTINGS
Come, come, have with you. Wot you what, my lord ?
To-day the lords you talked of are beheaded.
DERBY
They, for their truth, might better wear their heads
93  Than some that have accused them wear their hats.
94  But come, my lord, let's away.
    Enter a Pursuivant [also named Hastings].
HASTINGS
Go on before. I'll talk with this good fellow.
    Exeunt Lord Stanley [Earl of Derby],
            and Catesby.
How now, sirrah ? How goes the world with thee ?
PURSUIVANT
The better that your lordship please to ask.
HASTINGS
I tell thee, man, 'tis better with me now
Than when thou met'st me last where now we meet.

Then was I going prisoner to the Tower
By the suggestion of the queen's allies ;
But now I tell thee (keep it to thyself)
This day those enemies are put to death,
And I in better state than e'er I was.
PURSUIVANT
God hold it, to your honor's good content !          105
HASTINGS
Gramercy, fellow. There, drink that for me.          106
    Throws him his purse.
PURSUIVANT  I thank your honor.        Exit Pursuivant.
    Enter a Priest.
PRIEST
Well met, my lord. I am glad to see your honor.
HASTINGS
I thank thee, good Sir John, with all my heart.      109
I am in your debt for your last exercise ;           110
Come the next Sabbath, and I will content you.
    [He whispers in his ear.]
PRIEST
I'll wait upon your lordship.
    Enter Buckingham.
BUCKINGHAM
What, talking with a priest, Lord Chamberlain ?
Your friends at Pomfret, they do need the priest ;
Your honor hath no shriving work in hand.            115
HASTINGS
Good faith, and when I met this holy man,
The men you talk of came into my mind.
What, go you toward the Tower ?
BUCKINGHAM
I do, my lord, but long I cannot stay there.
I shall return before your lordship thence.
HASTINGS
Nay, like enough, for I stay dinner there.
BUCKINGHAM [aside]
And supper too, although thou know'st it not. –
Come, will you go ?
HASTINGS              I'll wait upon your lordship. Exeunt.

                        *

    Enter Sir Richard Ratcliffe, with Halberds, carrying   III, iii
    the Nobles [Rivers, Grey, and Vaughan] to death at
    Pomfret.
[RATCLIFFE  Come, bring forth the prisoners.]
RIVERS
Sir Richard Ratcliffe, let me tell thee this :
To-day shalt thou behold a subject die
For truth, for duty, and for loyalty.
GREY
God bless the prince from all the pack of you !
A knot you are of damnèd bloodsuckers.
VAUGHAN
You live that shall cry woe for this hereafter.
RATCLIFFE
Dispatch ! The limit of your lives is out.
RIVERS
O Pomfret, Pomfret ! O thou bloody prison,
Fatal and ominous to noble peers !
Within the guilty closure of thy walls
Richard the Second here was hacked to death ;
And, for more slander to thy dismal seat,            13
We give to thee our guiltless blood to drink.

70 *Bridge* London Bridge (traitors' heads were displayed on poles on the
gateway entrances to it) 75 *Holy Rood* Christ's cross 82 *triumphant*
exultant 84 *jocund* merry 87 *This . . . misdoubt* i.e. I fear this sudden
blow (the capture of Rivers, Vaughan, and Grey) arising out of hatred
89 *day is spent* (the folio reading is questionable since it is just after 4 a.m.;
the quartos omit the time reference) 93 *some . . . hats* (probably a veiled
reference to Richard and Buckingham, whose rank as dukes gave them the
privilege of wearing the so-called ducal cap in the royal presence, no head-
covering resembling a hat being allowed below the rank of duke) 94 *s.d.*
*Pursuivant* state messenger with authority to execute warrants 105 *God
hold it* i.e. may God continue this state of affairs 106 *Gramercy* much
thanks 109 *Sir John* ('sir' was a title of respect applied to the clergy; no
reference here to knighthood) 110 *exercise* sermon 115 *shriving work* i.e.
'deathbed' confessions
III, iii Pomfret Castle 13 *for . . . seat* i.e. in order to bring greater shame
upon Pomfret, a place which already bodes disaster

GREY

Now Margaret's curse is fall'n upon our heads,
When she exclaimed on Hastings, you, and I,
For standing by when Richard stabbed her son.

RIVERS

Then cursed she Richard, then cursed she Buckingham,
Then cursed she Hastings. O, remember, God,
To hear her prayer for them, as now for us!
And for my sister and her princely sons,
Be satisfied, dear God, with our true blood,
Which, as thou know'st, unjustly must be spilt.

RATCLIFFE

24    Make haste. The hour of death is expiate.

RIVERS

Come, Grey; come, Vaughan; let us here embrace.
Farewell, until we meet again in heaven.    *Exeunt.*

\*

III, iv        *Enter Buckingham, [Lord Stanley Earl of] Derby,
                Hastings, Bishop of Ely, Norfolk, Ratcliffe, Lovel,
                with others, at a table.*

HASTINGS

Now, noble peers, the cause why we are met
2    Is to determine of the coronation.
In God's name, speak. When is the royal day?

BUCKINGHAM

Is all things ready for the royal time?

DERBY

5    It is, and wants but nomination.

BISHOP OF ELY

To-morrow then I judge a happy day.

BUCKINGHAM

Who knows the Lord Protector's mind herein?
8    Who is most inward with the noble duke?

BISHOP OF ELY

Your grace, we think, should soonest know his mind.

BUCKINGHAM

We know each other's faces; for our hearts,
He knows no more of mine than I of yours;
Or I of his, my lord, than you of mine.
Lord Hastings, you and he are near in love.

HASTINGS

I thank his grace, I know he loves me well;
But, for his purpose in the coronation,
16    I have not sounded him, nor he delivered
His gracious pleasure any way therein;
But you, my honorable lords, may name the time,
And in the duke's behalf I'll give my voice,
Which, I presume, he'll take in gentle part.
        *Enter [Richard, Duke of] Gloucester.*

BISHOP OF ELY

In happy time, here comes the duke himself.

RICHARD

My noble lords and cousins all, good morrow.
I have been long a sleeper; but I trust
24    My absence doth neglect no great design
Which by my presence might have been concluded.

BUCKINGHAM

Had you not come upon your cue, my lord,
William Lord Hastings had pronounced your part—
I mean, your voice for crowning of the king.

RICHARD

Than my Lord Hastings no man might be bolder.

His lordship knows me well, and loves me well.
My Lord of Ely, when I was last in Holborn
I saw good strawberries in your garden there.
I do beseech you send for some of them.

BISHOP OF ELY

Marry and will, my lord, with all my heart.   *Exit Bishop.*

RICHARD

Cousin of Buckingham, a word with you.
        *[Takes him aside.]*
Catesby hath sounded Hastings in our business
And finds the testy gentleman so hot                        37
That he will lose his head ere give consent
His master's child, as worshipfully he terms it,            39
Shall lose the royalty of England's throne.                 40

BUCKINGHAM

Withdraw yourself awhile. I'll go with you.
        *Exeunt [Richard and Buckingham].*

DERBY

We have not yet set down this day of triumph:
To-morrow, in my judgment, is too sudden;
For I myself am not so well provided
As else I would be, were the day prolonged.                 45
        *Enter the Bishop of Ely.*

BISHOP OF ELY

Where is my lord the Duke of Gloucester?
I have sent for these strawberries.

HASTINGS

His grace looks cheerfully and smooth this morning;
There's some conceit or other likes him well               49
When that he bids good morrow with such spirit.
I think there's never a man in Christendom
Can lesser hide his love or hate than he,
For by his face straight shall you know his heart.

DERBY

What of his heart perceive you in his face
By any livelihood he showed to-day?                         55

HASTINGS

Marry, that with no man here he is offended;
For were he, he had shown it in his looks.

[DERBY

I pray God he be not, I say.]
        *Enter Richard and Buckingham.*

RICHARD

I pray you all, tell me what they deserve
That do conspire my death with devilish plots
Of damnèd witchcraft, and that have prevailed              61
Upon my body with their hellish charms.

HASTINGS

The tender love I bear your grace, my lord,
Makes me most forward in this princely presence
To doom th' offenders, whosoe'er they be:
I say, my lord, they have deservèd death.

RICHARD

Then be your eyes the witness of their evil.
Look how I am bewitched. Behold, mine arm

24 *expiate* fully come (cf. l. 8)
III, iv Within the Tower of London   2 *determine of* come to a decision
concerning   5 *nomination* the fixing   8 *inward* intimate   16 *I... him* (but
Richard had in fact sounded Hastings; cf. l. 36)   24 *neglect ... design* i.e.
cause no great design to be neglected   37 *testy* quick-tempered; *hot* burning (with his resolve)   39 *worshipfully* i.e. using words expressing honor or
regard   40 *royalty* sovereignty   45 *the day prolonged* i.e. a later day set
49 *conceit* (happy) idea or device   55 *livelihood* vivacity   61–62 *prevailed
Upon* got the better of

Is like a blasted sapling, withered up ;
And this is Edward's wife, that monstrous witch,
71    Consorted with that harlot, strumpet Shore,
That by their witchcraft thus have markèd me.

HASTINGS
If they have done this deed, my noble lord –

RICHARD
If ? Thou protector of this damnèd strumpet,
Talk'st thou to me of ifs ? Thou art a traitor.
Off with his head ! Now by Saint Paul I swear
I will not dine until I see the same.
Lovel and Ratcliffe, look that it be done :
The rest that love me, rise and follow me.
        *Exeunt. Manent Lovel and Ratcliffe,*
                *with the Lord Hastings.*

HASTINGS
80    Woe, woe for England, not a whit for me !
81    For I, too fond, might have prevented this.
Stanley did dream the boar did rase our helms ;
But I did scorn it and disdain to fly.
84    Three times to-day my footcloth horse did stumble,
And started when he looked upon the Tower,
As loath to bear me to the slaughterhouse.
O, now I need the priest that spake to me !
I now repent I told the pursuivant,
89    As too triumphing, how mine enemies
To-day at Pomfret bloodily were butchered,
91    And I myself secure, in grace and favor.
O Margaret, Margaret, now thy heavy curse
Is lighted on poor Hastings' wretched head !

RATCLIFFE
Come, come, dispatch ! The duke would be at dinner.
Make a short shrift ; he longs to see your head.

HASTINGS
96    O momentary grace of mortal men,
Which we more hunt for than the grace of God !
98    Who builds his hope in air of your good looks
Lives like a drunken sailor on a mast,
Ready with every nod to tumble down
Into the fatal bowels of the deep.

LOVEL
102    Come, come, dispatch ! 'Tis bootless to exclaim.

HASTINGS
O bloody Richard ! Miserable England !
I prophesy the fearfull'st time to thee
That ever wretched age hath looked upon.
Come, lead me to the block ; bear him my head.
They smile at me who shortly shall be dead.    *Exeunt.*

*

71 *Consorted* associated  80 *whit* bit  81 *fond* foolish  84 *footcloth horse*
horse caparisoned with a richly wrought covering reaching almost to the
ground  89 *triumphing* exulting  91 *secure* (1) safe, (2) careless  96 *grace*
favor  98 *of . . . looks* out of your kind glances (suggesting approval)
102 *bootless* useless
**III, v** The walls of the Tower  s.d. *rotten* rusty; *ill-favored* ugly  8 *Intending* pretending  10 *offices* particular functions  17 *o'erlook* inspect
25 *harmless* (supply 'most'; cf. l. 33)  27 *book* i.e. table book or 'diary'
31 *conversation* sexual intimacy  32 *attainder of suspects* stain of suspicions
33 *shelt'red* hidden (supply 'most')  36 *great preservation* i.e. the fortunate
forestalling of an evil that might have happened

*Enter Richard [Duke of Gloucester], and*        III, v
*Buckingham, in rotten armor, marvellous ill-favored.*

RICHARD
Come, cousin, canst thou quake and change thy color,
Murder thy breath in middle of a word,
And then again begin, and stop again,
As if thou were distraught and mad with terror ?

BUCKINGHAM
Tut, I can counterfeit the deep tragedian,
Speak and look back, and pry on every side,
Tremble and start at wagging of a straw :
Intending deep suspicion, ghastly looks        8
Are at my service, like enforcèd smiles ;
And both are ready in their offices,        10
At any time to grace my stratagems.
But what, is Catesby gone ?

RICHARD
He is ; and see, he brings the Mayor along.
        *Enter the Mayor and Catesby.*

BUCKINGHAM
Lord Mayor –

RICHARD
Look to the drawbridge there !

BUCKINGHAM
Hark ! a drum.

RICHARD
Catesby, o'erlook the walls.        17

BUCKINGHAM
Lord Mayor, the reason we have sent –

RICHARD
Look back ! defend thee ! Here are enemies !

BUCKINGHAM
God and our innocence defend and guard us !
        *Enter Lovel and Ratcliffe, with Hastings' head.*

RICHARD
Be patient, they are friends – Ratcliffe and Lovel.

LOVEL
Here is the head of that ignoble traitor,
The dangerous and unsuspected Hastings.

RICHARD
So dear I loved the man that I must weep :
I took him for the plainest harmless creature        25
That breathed upon the earth a Christian ;
Made him my book, wherein my soul recorded        27
The history of all her secret thoughts.
So smooth he daubed his vice with show of virtue
That, his apparent open guilt omitted –
I mean, his conversation with Shore's wife –        31
He lived from all attainder of suspects.        32

BUCKINGHAM
Well, well, he was the covert'st shelt'red traitor        33
That ever lived. [Look ye, my Lord Mayor.]
Would you imagine, or almost believe,
Were't not that by great preservation        36
We live to tell it, that the subtle traitor
This day had plotted, in the Council House,
To murder me and my good Lord of Gloucester ?

MAYOR
Had he done so ?

RICHARD
What ? Think you we are Turks or infidels ?
Or that we would, against the form of law,
Proceed thus rashly in the villain's death
But that the extreme peril of the case,

The peace of England, and our persons' safety
Enforced us to this execution?

MAYOR

Now fair befall you! He deserved his death,
48 And your good graces both have well proceeded
To warn false traitors from the like attempts.

BUCKINGHAM

I never looked for better at his hands
After he once fell in with Mistress Shore:
Yet had we not determined he should die
Until your lordship came to see his end,
Which now the loving haste of these our friends,
55 Something against our meanings, have prevented;
Because, my lord, I would have had you heard
57 The traitor speak, and timorously confess
The manner and the purpose of his treasons,
That you might well have signified the same
60 Unto the citizens, who haply may
61 Misconster us in him and wail his death.

MAYOR

But, my good lord, your grace's words shall serve,
As well as I had seen, and heard him speak;
And do not doubt, right noble princes both,
But I'll acquaint our duteous citizens
66 With all your just proceedings in this cause.

RICHARD

And to that end we wished your lordship here,
68 T' avoid the censures of the carping world.

BUCKINGHAM

69 But since you come too late of our intent,
70 Yet witness what you hear we did intend:
And so, my good Lord Mayor, we bid farewell.
                                        Exit Mayor.

RICHARD

Go after, after, cousin Buckingham.
73 The Mayor towards Guildhall hies him in all post:
74 There, at your meet'st advantage of the time,
Infer the bastardy of Edward's children.
Tell them how Edward put to death a citizen
Only for saying he would make his son
78 Heir to the Crown, meaning indeed his house,
Which by the sign thereof was termèd so.
80 Moreover, urge his hateful luxury
81 And bestial appetite in change of lust,
Which stretched unto their servants, daughters, wives,
Even where his raging eye or savage heart,
Without control, lusted to make a prey.
Nay, for a need, thus far come near my person:
Tell them, when that my mother went with child
Of that insatiate Edward, noble York,
My princely father, then had wars in France,
And by true computation of the time
Found that the issue was not his begot;
Which well appearèd in his lineaments,
Being nothing like the noble duke my father.
Yet touch this sparingly, as 'twere far off,
Because, my lord, you know my mother lives.

BUCKINGHAM

Doubt not, my lord, I'll play the orator
96 As if the golden fee for which I plead
Were for myself – and so, my lord, adieu.

RICHARD

98 If you thrive well, bring them to Baynard's Castle,
Where you shall find me well accompanied

With reverend fathers and well-learnèd bishops.

BUCKINGHAM

I go; and towards three or four a clock
Look for the news that the Guildhall affords.
                                *Exit Buckingham.*

RICHARD

Go, Lovel, with all speed to Doctor Shaw –    103
[To Catesby]
Go thou to Friar Penker. – Bid them both    104
Meet me within this hour at Baynard's Castle.
                *Exeunt [Lovel, Catesby, and Ratcliffe].*
Now will I go to take some privy order    106
To draw the brats of Clarence out of sight,
And to give order that no manner person    108
Have any time recourse unto the princes.    *Exit.*

*

*Enter a Scrivener [with a paper in his hand].*    III,

SCRIVENER

Here is the indictment of the good Lord Hastings,
Which in a set hand fairly is engrossed    2
That it may be to-day read o'er in Paul's.    3
And mark how well the sequel hangs together:
Eleven hours I have spent to write it over,
For yesternight by Catesby was it sent me;
The precedent was full as long a-doing;    7
And yet within these five hours Hastings lived,
Untainted, unexamined, free, at liberty.
Here's a good world the while! Who is so gross    10
That cannot see this palpable device?
Yet who's so bold but says he sees it not?
Bad is the world, and all will come to nought
When such ill dealing must be seen in thought.    14
                                        *Exit.*

*Enter Richard [Duke of Gloucester] and*    III,
*Buckingham at several doors.*

RICHARD

How now, how now? What say the citizens?

BUCKINGHAM

Now, by the holy Mother of our Lord,
The citizens are mum, say not a word.

RICHARD

Touched you the bastardy of Edward's children?

BUCKINGHAM

I did, with his contract with Lady Lucy    5
And his contract by deputy in France;    6
Th' unsatiate greediness of his desire

48 *proceeded* done   55 *prevented* anticipated   57 *timorously* full of fear
60 *haply* perhaps   61 *Misconster . . . him* i.e. misunderstand our manner of
dealing with him   66 *cause* affair or action (perhaps with legal overtones)
68 *carping* overcritical   69 *of* i.e. in terms of   70 *witness* i.e. bear witness to
73 *Guildhall* the 'town hall' of London; *post haste*   74 *meet'st . . . time* i.e.
the psychological moment   78 *Crown . . . house* i.e. a tavern called 'The
Crown'   80 *luxury* lasciviousness   81 *change of lust* i.e. alteration in the
object of his lust   96 *golden fee* i.e. the crown (play on 'lawyer's fee')   98
*Baynard's Castle* Richard's stronghold between Blackfriars and London
Bridge   103, 104 *Shaw, Penker* well-known preachers   106 *take . . . order*
make some secret arrangement   108–09 *no . . . unto* i.e. no person of any sort
should have, at any time, admittance to
III, vi Before Baynard's Castle   2 *in . . . engrossed* is written neatly in a
formal legal hand   3 *Paul's* i.e. St Paul's Cathedral   7 *precedent* exemplar
(i.e. the prepared indictment)   10 *the while* just now; *gross* stupid   14 *seen
in thought* expressed only in thinking
III, vii   5 *Lady Lucy* Elizabeth Lucy (to whom Edward IV was not actually
contracted, although she bore him a child)   6 *contract . . . France* (reference
to Edward IV's overtures for marriage with Bona, sister-in-law of Lewis IX
of France; cf. *3 Henry VI*, III, iii, and below, ll. 181–82)

And his enforcement of the city wives ;
His tyranny for trifles ; his own bastardy,
As being got, your father then in France,
And his resemblance, being not like the duke.
Withal I did infer your lineaments,
13 Being the right idea of your father
Both in your form and nobleness of mind ;
Laid open all your victories in Scotland,
Your discipline in war, wisdom in peace,
Your bounty, virtue, fair humility ;
Indeed, left nothing fitting for your purpose
Untouched, or slightly handlèd in discourse ;
And when mine oratory drew to an end,
I bid them that did love their country's good
Cry, 'God save Richard, England's royal king !'

RICHARD
And did they so ?

BUCKINGHAM
No, so God help me, they spake not a word,
But, like dumb statuës or breathing stones,
Stared each on other, and looked deadly pale.
Which when I saw, I reprehended them
And asked the Mayor what meant this wilful silence.
His answer was, the people were not usèd
30 To be spoke to but by the Recorder.
Then he was urged to tell my tale again :
'Thus saith the duke, thus hath the duke inferred,' –
But nothing spake in warrant from himself.
When he had done, some followers of mine own,
At lower end of the hall, hurled up their caps,
And some ten voices cried, 'God save King Richard !'
And thus I took the vantage of those few :
'Thanks, gentle citizens and friends,' quoth I.
'This general applause and cheerful shout
Argues your wisdoms and your love to Richard' –
And even here brake off and came away.

RICHARD
What tongueless blocks were they ! Would they not
    speak ?

[BUCKINGHAM
No, by my troth, my lord.]

RICHARD
Will not the Mayor then and his brethren come ?

BUCKINGHAM
45 The Mayor is here at hand. Intend some fear ;
46 Be not you spoke with but by mighty suit ;
And look you get a prayer book in your hand
And stand between two churchmen, good my lord,
49 For on that ground I'll make a holy descant ;
And be not easily won to our requests.
51 Play the maid's part : still answer nay, and take it.

RICHARD
I go ; and if you plead as well for them

As I can say nay to thee for myself,
No doubt we bring it to a happy issue.

BUCKINGHAM
Go, go, up to the leads ! The Lord Mayor knocks.    55
                        [Exit Richard.]
        Enter the Mayor [, Aldermen,] and Citizens.
Welcome, my lord. I dance attendance here ;
I think the duke will not be spoke withal.    57
        Enter Catesby.
Now, Catesby, what says your lord to my request ?

CATESBY
He doth entreat your grace, my noble lord,
To visit him to-morrow or next day :
He is within, with two right reverend fathers,
Divinely bent to meditation,    62
And in no worldly suits would he be moved
To draw him from his holy exercise.

BUCKINGHAM
Return, good Catesby, to the gracious duke :
Tell him, myself, the Mayor and Aldermen,
In deep designs, in matter of great moment,
No less importing than our general good,    68
Are come to have some conference with his grace.

CATESBY
I'll signify so much unto him straight.    Exit.

BUCKINGHAM
Ah ha, my lord ! this prince is not an Edward.
He is not lulling on a lewd love-bed,    72
But on his knees at meditation ;
Not dallying with a brace of courtesans,
But meditating with two deep divines ;    75
Not sleeping, to engross his idle body,    76
But praying, to enrich his watchful soul.
Happy were England, would this virtuous prince
Take on his grace the sovereignty thereof ;
But sure I fear we shall not win him to it.

MAYOR
Marry, God defend his grace should say us nay !    81

BUCKINGHAM
I fear he will. Here Catesby comes again.
        Enter Catesby.
Now, Catesby, what says his grace ?

CATESBY                                    My lord,
He wonders to what end you have assemblèd
Such troops of citizens to come to him,
His grace not being warned thereof before :
He fears, my lord, you mean no good to him.

BUCKINGHAM
Sorry I am my noble cousin should
Suspect me that I mean no good to him :
By heaven, we come to him in perfit love ;    90
And so once more return and tell his grace.
                        Exit [Catesby].
When holy and devout religious men
Are at their beads, 'tis much to draw them thence,    93
So sweet is zealous contemplation.
        Enter Richard aloft, between two Bishops. [Catesby
        returns.]

MAYOR
See where his grace stands, 'tween two clergymen.

BUCKINGHAM
Two props of virtue for a Christian prince,
To stay him from the fall of vanity ;    97
And see, a book of prayer in his hand –

13 *right idea* true image    30 *Recorder* (a magistrate appointed by the mayor and aldermen to serve as an 'oral record' of proceedings in city law courts and government)    45 *Intend* pretend    46 *by mighty suit* by great solicitation    49 *descant* (see I, i, 27)    51 *maid's* girl's ; *answer . . . it* i.e. keep saying no, but at the same time accept whatever is being offered (proverbial)    55 *leads* sheets of metal used to cover a (flat) roof    57 *withal* with    62 *Divinely bent* (1) spiritually inclined, (2) kneeling like a divine (cf. l. 73)    68 *No . . . than* i.e. of no less significance than one concerned with    72 *lulling* lolling, lounging    75 *deep* i.e. spiritually and academically learned    76 *engross* fatten    81 *defend* forbid    90 *perfit* perfect    93 *'tis much* i.e. it takes a great deal    97 *fall of vanity* downfall caused by vanity

99    True ornaments to know a holy man.
Famous Plantagenet, most gracious prince,
Lend favorable ear to our requests,
And pardon us the interruption
Of thy devotion and right Christian zeal.

RICHARD
My lord, there needs no such apology:
I do beseech your grace to pardon me,
Who, earnest in the service of my God,
Deferred the visitation of my friends.
But, leaving this, what is your grace's pleasure?

BUCKINGHAM
Even that (I hope) which pleaseth God above
And all good men of this ungoverned isle.

RICHARD
I do suspect I have done some offense
112   That seems disgracious in the city's eye,
And that you come to reprehend my ignorance.

BUCKINGHAM
You have, my lord. Would it might please your grace,
On our entreaties, to amend your fault!

RICHARD
Else wherefore breathe I in a Christian land?

BUCKINGHAM
Know then it is your fault that you resign
The supreme seat, the throne majestical,
The scept'red office of your ancestors,
120   Your state of fortune and your due of birth,
The lineal glory of your royal house,
To the corruption of a blemished stock;
123   Whiles, in the mildness of your sleepy thoughts,
Which here we waken to our country's good,
125   The noble isle doth want her proper limbs;
Her face defaced with scars of infamy,
Her royal stock graft with ignoble plants,
128   And almost should'red in the swallowing gulf
Of dark forgetfulness and deep oblivion.
130   Which to recure, we heartily solicit
Your gracious self to take on you the charge
And kingly government of this your land;
Not as Protector, steward, substitute,
134   Or lowly factor for another's gain;
135   But as successively, from blood to blood,
136   Your right of birth, your empery, your own.
For this, consorted with the citizens,
Your very worshipful and loving friends,
And by their vehement instigation,
In this just cause come I to move your grace.

RICHARD
I cannot tell if to depart in silence,
Or bitterly to speak in your reproof,
143   Best fitteth my degree or your condition.
If not to answer, you might haply think
145   Tongue-tied ambition, not replying, yielded
To bear the golden yoke of sovereignty
147   Which fondly you would here impose on me.
If to reprove you for this suit of yours,
149   So seasoned with your faithful love to me,
Then, on the other side, I checked my friends.
Therefore – to speak, and to avoid the first,
And then, in speaking, not to incur the last –
153   Definitively thus I answer you.
Your love deserves my thanks, but my desert
Unmeritable shuns your high request.

First, if all obstacles were cut away,
And that my path were even to the crown,              157
As the ripe revenue and due of birth,
Yet so much is my poverty of spirit,                 159
So mighty and so many my defects,
That I would rather hide me from my greatness,
Being a bark to brook no mighty sea,                 162
Than in my greatness covet to be hid                 163
And in the vapor of my glory smothered.
But, God be thanked, there is no need of me,
And much I need to help you, were there need:
The royal tree hath left us royal fruit,
Which, mellowed by the stealing hours of time,
Will well become the seat of majesty
And make (no doubt) us happy by his reign.
On him I lay that you would lay on me,
The right and fortune of his happy stars,            172
Which God defend that I should wring from him!

BUCKINGHAM
My lord, this argues conscience in your grace,
But the respects thereof are nice and trivial,       175
All circumstances well considerèd.
You say that Edward is your brother's son:
So say we too, but not by Edward's wife;
For first was he contract to Lady Lucy –
Your mother lives a witness to his vow –
And afterward by substitute betrothed                181
To Bona, sister to the King of France.
These both put off, a poor petitioner,
A care-crazed mother to a many sons,
A beauty-waning and distressèd widow,
Even in the afternoon of her best days,
Made prize and purchase of his wanton eye,           187
Seduced the pitch and height of his degree           188
To base declension and loathed bigamy.               189
By her, in his unlawful bed, he got
This Edward, whom our manners call the prince.
More bitterly could I expostulate,
Save that, for reverence to some alive,
I give a sparing limit to my tongue.
Then, good my lord, take to your royal self          195
This proffered benefit of dignity;
If not to bless us and the land withal,
Yet to draw forth your noble ancestry
From the corruption of abusing times
Unto a lineal true-derivèd course.

MAYOR
Do, good my lord; your citizens entreat you.

---

99 *ornaments* (referring to the clergymen and prayer book)   112 *disgracious* disliked   120 *state of fortune* position of greatness   123 *sleepy* reposeful   125 *proper* own   128 *should'red in* violently jostled into   130 *recure* restore to health   134 *factor* agent   135 *successively* in order of succession   136 *empery* empire or sole rule   143 *fitteth . . . condition* accords with my rank (as duke) or your social position (as commoners)   145 *Tongue-tied . . . yielded* i.e. silence yields consent (proverbial)   147 *fondly* foolishly   149 *seasoned* made agreeable (given a pleasant taste)   153 *Definitively* once and for all   157 *even* without impediment   159 *poverty of spirit* lack of self-assertion (perhaps meant also as an indirect compliment to himself, since 'Blessed are the poor in spirit' [Matthew v, 3])   162 *bark* small sailing vessel   163 *Than . . . hid* than desire to be enveloped by my greatness   172 *happy* auspicious   175 *respects . . . nice* i.e. the considerations on which you argue are overscrupulous   181 *substitute* proxy   187 *purchase* booty   188 *Seduced . . . degree* i.e. led away (or down from) the eminence and greatness associated with his noble rank   189 *declension* falling away from a high standard   195 *good my lord* my good lord

**BUCKINGHAM**
Refuse not, mighty lord, this proffered love.
**CATESBY**
O, make them joyful, grant their lawful suit!
**RICHARD**
Alas, why would you heap this care on me?
I am unfit for state and majesty:
I do beseech you take it not amiss,
I cannot nor I will not yield to you.
**BUCKINGHAM**
208   If you refuse it – as, in love and zeal,
Loath to depose the child, your brother's son;
As well we know your tenderness of heart
211   And gentle, kind, effeminate remorse,
Which we have noted in you to your kindred
213   And egally indeed to all estates –
214   Yet know, whe'er you accept our suit or no,
Your brother's son shall never reign our king,
But we will plant some other in.the throne
To the disgrace and downfall of your house;
And in this resolution here we leave you.
Come, citizens. Zounds, I'll entreat no more!
[RICHARD]
O, do not swear, my lord of Buckingham.]
    *Exeunt [Buckingham, Mayor, Aldermen,*
    *and Citizens].*
**CATESBY**
Call him again, sweet prince, accept their suit:
222   If you deny them, all the land will rue it.
**RICHARD**
Will you enforce me to a world of cares?
Call them again. I am not made of stones,
But penetrable to your kind entreaties,
Albeit against my conscience and my soul.
    *Enter Buckingham and the rest.*
Cousin of Buckingham, and sage grave men,
Since you will buckle fortune on my back,
229   To bear her burden, whe'er I will or no,
I must have patience to endure the load;
But if black scandal or foul-faced reproach
232   Attend the sequel of your imposition,
233   Your mere enforcement shall acquittance me
From all the impure blots and stains thereof;
For God doth know, and you may partly see,
How far I am from the desire of this.
**MAYOR**
God bless your grace! We see it and will say it.
**RICHARD**
In saying so you shall but say the truth.
**BUCKINGHAM**
Then I salute you with this royal title –
Long live King Richard, England's worthy king!
**ALL**
Amen.

208 *as* i.e. as the result of being   211 *kind, effeminate remorse* natural, tender pity   213 *egally* equally   214 *whe'er* whether   222 *rue* suffer for   229 *To* i.e. in order to make me   232 *your imposition* i.e. the fortune (kingship) which you lay upon me   233 *mere* absolute; *acquittance* acquit   IV, i Before the Tower   3 *for my life* i.e. staking my life upon it   10 *gratulate* congratulate   19 *The Lord . . . title* i.e. may God in his capacity as Richard's legal guardian exercise his authority to prevent Richard from getting the title of king   20 *bounds* barriers   25 *take . . . thee* i.e. take your office upon myself   26 *leave it* i.e. give up my office   30 *looker-on* beholder (or here perhaps 'guardian')

**BUCKINGHAM**
To-morrow may it please you to be crowned?
**RICHARD**
Even when you please, for you will have it so.
**BUCKINGHAM**
To-morrow then we will attend your grace,
And so most joyfully we take our leave.
**RICHARD** *[to the Bishops]*
Come, let us to our holy work again. –
Farewell, my cousin; farewell, gentle friends.    *Exeunt.*

         \*

    *Enter the Queen [Elizabeth], the Duchess of*    IV, i
    *York, and Marquess [of] Dorset [at one door];*
    *Anne Duchess of Gloucester [, Lady Margaret*
    *Plantagenet, Clarence's young daughter, at*
    *another door].*
**DUCHESS OF YORK**
Who meets us here? My niece Plantagenet,
Led in the hand of her kind aunt of Gloucester?
Now, for my life, she's wand'ring to the Tower    3
On pure heart's love, to greet the tender prince.
Daughter, well met.
**ANNE**         God give your graces both
A happy and a joyful time of day!
**QUEEN ELIZABETH**
As much to you, good sister. Whither away?
**ANNE**
No farther than the Tower, and, as I guess,
Upon the like devotion as yourselves,
To gratulate the gentle princes there.    10
**QUEEN ELIZABETH**
Kind sister, thanks. We'll enter all together.
    *Enter the Lieutenant [Brakenbury].*
And in good time, here the Lieutenant comes.
Master Lieutenant, pray you, by your leave,
How doth the prince, and my young son of York?
**LIEUTENANT**
Right well, dear madam. By your patience,
I may not suffer you to visit them;
The king hath strictly charged the contrary.
**QUEEN ELIZABETH**
The king? Who's that?
**LIEUTENANT**       I mean the Lord Protector.
**QUEEN ELIZABETH**
The Lord protect him from that kingly title!    19
Hath he set bounds between their love and me?    20
I am their mother; who shall bar me from them?
**DUCHESS OF YORK**
I am their father's mother; I will see them.
**ANNE**
Their aunt I am in law, in love their mother;
Then bring me to their sights. I'll bear thy blame
And take thy office from thee on my peril.    25
**LIEUTENANT**
No, madam, no! I may not leave it so:    26
I am bound by oath, and therefore pardon me.
        *Exit Lieutenant.*
    *Enter Stanley [Earl of Derby].*
**DERBY**
Let me but meet you, ladies, an hour hence,
And I'll salute your grace of York as mother
And reverend looker-on of two fair queens.    30

*[To Anne]*
Come, madam, you must straight to Westminster,
There to be crownèd Richard's royal queen.

QUEEN ELIZABETH

33 Ah, cut my lace asunder,
That my pent heart may have some scope to beat,
Or else I swoon with this dead-killing news!

ANNE

Despiteful tidings! O unpleasing news!

DORSET

Be of good cheer. Mother, how fares your grace?

QUEEN ELIZABETH

O Dorset, speak not to me, get thee gone!
Death and destruction dogs thee at thy heels;
40 Thy mother's name is ominous to children.
If thou wilt outstrip death, go cross the seas,
And live with Richmond, from the reach of hell.
Go hie thee, hie thee from this slaughterhouse,
Lest thou increase the number of the dead
And make me die the thrall of Margaret's curse,
46 Nor mother, wife, nor England's counted queen.

DERBY

Full of wise care is this your counsel, madam:
48 Take all the swift advantage of the hours.
49 You shall have letters from me to my son
50 In your behalf, to meet you on the way:
51 Be not ta'en tardy by unwise delay.

DUCHESS OF YORK

52 O ill-dispersing wind of misery!
O my accursèd womb, the bed of death!
54 A cockatrice hast thou hatched to the world,
Whose unavoided eye is murderous.

DERBY

Come, madam, come! I in all haste was sent.

ANNE

And I with all unwillingness will go.
58 O, would to God that the inclusive verge
Of golden metal that must round my brow
Were red-hot steel, to sear me to the brains!
61 Anointed let me be with deadly venom
And die ere men can say, 'God save the queen!'

QUEEN ELIZABETH

Go, go, poor soul! I envy not thy glory.
To feed my humor wish thyself no harm.

ANNE

No? Why! when he that is my husband now
Came to me as I followed Henry's corse,
When scarce the blood was well washed from his hands
Which issuèd from my other angel husband
And that dear saint which then I weeping followed –
O, when, I say, I looked on Richard's face,
This was my wish: 'Be thou,' quoth I, 'accursed
72 For making me, so young, so old a widow!
And when thou wed'st, let sorrow haunt thy bed;
And be thy wife, if any be so mad,
More miserable by the life of thee
Than thou hast made me by my dear lord's death!'
Lo, ere I can repeat this curse again,
Within so small a time, my woman's heart
Grossly grew captive to his honey words
And proved the subject of mine own soul's curse,
Which hitherto hath held mine eyes from rest;
For never yet one hour in his bed
83 Did I enjoy the golden dew of sleep,

But with his timorous dreams was still awaked. 84
Besides, he hates me for my father Warwick.
And will (no doubt) shortly be rid of me.

QUEEN ELIZABETH

Poor heart, adieu! I pity thy complaining. 87

ANNE

No more than with my soul I mourn for yours.

DORSET

Farewell, thou woeful welcomer of glory.

ANNE

Adieu, poor soul, that tak'st thy leave of it.

DUCHESS OF YORK *[to Dorset]*

Go thou to Richmond, and good fortune guide thee!
*[To Anne]*
Go thou to Richard, and good angels tend thee!
*[To Queen Elizabeth]*
Go thou to sanctuary, and good thoughts possess thee!
I to my grave, where peace and rest lie with me!
Eighty odd years of sorrow have I seen,
And each hour's joy wracked with a week of teen. 96

QUEEN ELIZABETH

Stay, yet look back with me unto the Tower.
Pity, you ancient stones, those tender babes
Whom envy hath immured within your walls –
Rough cradle for such little pretty ones!
Rude ragged nurse, old sullen playfellow
For tender princes – use my babies well!
So foolish sorrows bids your stones farewell.   *Exeunt.*

\*

*Sound a sennet. Enter Richard [as King], in pomp,*    IV
*Buckingham, Catesby, Ratcliffe, Lovel [, a Page,*
*and others].*

KING RICHARD

Stand all apart. Cousin of Buckingham –

BUCKINGHAM

My gracious sovereign?

KING RICHARD

Give me thy hand.
  *Sound. [Here he ascendeth the throne.]*
             Thus high, by thy advice
And thy assistance, is King Richard seated:
But shall we wear these glories for a day?
Or shall they last, and we rejoice in them?

BUCKINGHAM

Still live they, and for ever let them last!

KING RICHARD

Ah, Buckingham, now do I play the touch, 8
To try if thou be current gold indeed:
Young Edward lives. Think now what I would speak.

33 *cut my lace* (Elizabethan women wore tightly laced bodices)   40 *ominous*
portending evil   46 *counted* esteemed   48 *Take . . . hours* i.e. make full use
of your head start   49 *You . . . me* i.e. I will have letters written   50 *to
. . . way* (supply 'telling him' before 'to')   51 *ta'en* taken, caught   52 *ill-
dispersing* misfortune-scattering   54 *cockatrice* basilisk (see I, ii, 150)
58 *inclusive verge* surrounding circle (i.e. the crown, with reference to the
band of red-hot steel sometimes placed as punishment on the heads of
traitors)   61 *Anointed* (anointing with holy oil was part of the ceremony
of coronation)   72 *so young . . . widow* (being so young she will be a widow
for a long time before she too dies)   83 *golden dew* i.e. precious refreshment
84 *timorous* full of fear; *still* continuously   87 *complaining* cause for complaint   96 *wracked* destroyed; *teen* grief
IV, ii The royal palace   s.d. *sennet* a special set of notes on the trumpet
used for entrance and exit of processions   8 *touch* touchstone (a means of
testing gold)

BUCKINGHAM
Say on, my loving lord.
KING RICHARD
Why, Buckingham, I say I would be king.
BUCKINGHAM
Why, so you are, my thrice-renownèd liege.
KING RICHARD
Ha! Am I king? 'Tis so. But Edward lives.
BUCKINGHAM
True, noble prince.
15 KING RICHARD          O bitter consequence,
That Edward still should live true noble prince!
Cousin, thou wast not wont to be so dull.
Shall I be plain? I wish the bastards dead,
And I would have it suddenly performed.
What say'st thou now? Speak suddenly, be brief.
BUCKINGHAM
Your grace may do your pleasure.
KING RICHARD
Tut, tut, thou art all ice; thy kindness freezes.
Say, have I thy consent that they shall die?
BUCKINGHAM
Give me some little breath, some pause, dear lord,
Before I positively speak in this:
26 I will resolve you herein presently.    Exit Buck[ingham].
CATESBY [aside to another]
The king is angry. See, he gnaws his lip.
KING RICHARD
28 I will converse with iron-witted fools
And unrespective boys. None are for me
30 That look into me with considerate eyes.
High-reaching Buckingham grows circumspect.
Boy!
PAGE
My lord?
KING RICHARD
Know'st thou not any whom corrupting gold
Will tempt unto a close exploit of death?
PAGE
I know a discontented gentleman
Whose humble means match not his haughty spirit:
Gold were as good as twenty orators,
And will, no doubt, tempt him to anything.
KING RICHARD
What is his name?
PAGE                    His name, my lord, is Tyrrel.
KING RICHARD
I partly know the man. Go call him hither, boy.
                              Exit [Page].
42 The deep-revolving witty Buckingham
No more shall be the neighbor to my counsels.
44 Hath he so long held out with me, untired,
And stops he now for breath? Well, be it so.
          Enter Stanley [Earl of Derby].
How now, Lord Stanley? What's the news?
DERBY                    Know, my loving lord,

The Marquess Dorset, as I hear, is fled
To Richmond in the parts where he abides.
          [Stands aside.]
KING RICHARD
Come hither, Catesby. Rumor it abroad
That Anne my wife is very grievous sick:
I will take order for her keeping close.            51
Inquire me out some mean poor gentleman,
Whom I will marry straight to Clarence' daughter.
The boy is foolish, and I fear not him.            54
Look how thou dream'st! I say again, give out
That Anne, my queen, is sick and like to die.
About it! for it stands me much upon            57
To stop all hopes whose growth may damage me.
                              [Exit Catesby.]
I must be married to my brother's daughter,
Or else my kingdom stands on brittle glass:
Murder her brothers, and then marry her—
Uncertain way of gain! But I am in
So far in blood that sin will pluck on sin.
Tear-falling pity dwells not in this eye.            64
          Enter [Page, with] Tyrrel.
Is thy name Tyrrel?
TYRREL
James Tyrrel, and your most obedient subject.
KING RICHARD
Art thou indeed?
TYRREL                    Prove me, my gracious lord.
KING RICHARD
Dar'st thou resolve to kill a friend of mine?
TYRREL
Please you;                                        69
But I had rather kill two enemies.
KING RICHARD
Why, there thou hast it! Two deep enemies,
Foes to my rest and my sweet sleep's disturbers,
Are they that I would have thee deal upon:
Tyrrel, I mean those bastards in the Tower.
TYRREL
Let me have open means to come to them,            75
And soon I'll rid you from the fear of them.
KING RICHARD
Thou sing'st sweet music. Hark, come hither, Tyrrel.
Go, by this token. Rise, and lend thine ear.
          Whispers.
There is no more but so: say it is done,
And I will love thee and prefer thee for it.
TYRREL
I will dispatch it straight.                    Exit.
          Enter Buckingham.
BUCKINGHAM
My lord, I have considered in my mind
The late request that you did sound me in.
KING RICHARD
Well, let that rest. Dorset is fled to Richmond.
BUCKINGHAM
I hear the news, my lord.
KING RICHARD
Stanley, he is your wife's son. Well, look unto it.
BUCKINGHAM
My lord, I claim the gift, my due by promise,
For which your honor and your faith is pawned:
Th' earldom of Hereford and the moveables
Which you have promisèd I shall possess.            90

---

15 *consequence* conclusion  26 *presently* at once  28–29 *iron-witted* . . .
*unrespective* unfeeling . . . thoughtless  30 *considerate* (eyes) which weigh
my motives, thoughtful  42 *deep-revolving* profoundly politic  44 *held
out* i.e. lasted the course  51 *take* . . . *close* make arrangements for her
imprisonment  54 *foolish* i.e. an idiot  57 *stands* . . . *upon* is of great
importance to me  64 *Tear-falling* i.e. weeping  69 *Please you* if it pleases
you  75 *open* free

**KING RICHARD**
Stanley, look to your wife : if she convey
Letters to Richmond, you shall answer it.

**BUCKINGHAM**
What says your highness to my just request ?

**KING RICHARD**
I do remember me Henry the Sixth
Did prophesy that Richmond should be king
96 When Richmond was a little peevish boy.
A king ! – perhaps – [perhaps –

**BUCKINGHAM**
My lord –

**KING RICHARD**
How chance the prophet could not at that time
Have told me, I being by, that I should kill him ?

**BUCKINGHAM**
My lord, your promise for the earldom !

**KING RICHARD**
Richmond ! When last I was at Exeter,
The Mayor in courtesy showed me the castle,
104 And called it Rouge-mount ; at which name I started,
105 Because a bard of Ireland told me once
I should not live long after I saw Richmond.

**BUCKINGHAM**
My lord –

**KING RICHARD**
Ay, what's a clock ?

**BUCKINGHAM**
I am thus bold to put your grace in mind
Of what you promised me.

**KING RICHARD**                          Well, but what's a clock ?

**BUCKINGHAM**
Upon the stroke of ten.

**KING RICHARD**                          Well, let it strike.

**BUCKINGHAM**
Why let it strike ?

**KING RICHARD**
113 Because that like a Jack thou keep'st the stroke
Betwixt thy begging and my meditation.
I am not in the giving vein to-day.]

**BUCKINGHAM**
116 May it please you to resolve me in my suit.

**KING RICHARD**
Thou troublest me ; I am not in the vein.
                          *Exeunt [all but Buckingham].*

**BUCKINGHAM**
And is it thus ? Repays he my deep service
With such contempt ? Made I him king for this ?
O, let me think on Hastings, and be gone
121 To Brecknock while my fearful head is on !          *Exit.*

\*

IV, iii          *Enter Tyrrel.*

**TYRREL**
The tyrannous and bloody act is done,
2 The most arch deed of piteous massacre
That ever yet this land was guilty of.
Dighton and Forrest, who I did suborn
To do this piece of ruthless butchery,
Albeit they were fleshed villains, bloody dogs,
7 Melted with tenderness and kind compassion,
Wept like to children in their death's sad story.
'O, thus,' quoth Dighton, 'lay the gentle babes.'
'Thus, thus,' quoth Forrest, 'girdling one another

Within their alablaster innocent arms.          11
Their lips were four red roses on a stalk,
Which in their summer beauty kissed each other.
A book of prayers on their pillow lay,
Which once,' quoth Forrest, 'almost changed my mind ;
But O ! the devil' – there the villain stopped ;
When Dighton thus told on – 'We smotherèd
The most replenishèd sweet work of nature          18
That from the prime creation e'er she framèd.'          19
Hence both are gone with conscience and remorse :
They could not speak ; and so I left them both,
To bear this tidings to the bloody king.
          *Enter [King] Richard.*
And here he comes. All health, my sovereign lord !

**KING RICHARD**
Kind Tyrrel, am I happy in thy news ?

**TYRREL**
If to have done the thing you gave in charge          25
Beget your happiness, be happy then,
For it is done.

**KING RICHARD** But didst thou see them dead ?

**TYRREL**
I did, my lord.

**KING RICHARD** And buried, gentle Tyrrel ?

**TYRREL**
The chaplain of the Tower hath buried them ;
But where (to say the truth) I do not know.

**KING RICHARD**
Come to me, Tyrrel, soon at after supper,
When thou shalt tell the process of their death.          32
Meantime, but think how I may do thee good,
And be inheritor of thy desire.
Farewell till then.

**TYRREL**                          I humbly take my leave.          *[Exit.]*

**KING RICHARD**
The son of Clarence have I pent up close,
His daughter meanly have I matched in marriage,
The sons of Edward sleep in Abraham's bosom,
And Anne my wife hath bid this world good night.
Now, for I know the Britain Richmond aims          40
At young Elizabeth, my brother's daughter,
And by that knot looks proudly on the crown,          42
To her go I, a jolly thriving wooer.
          *Enter Ratcliffe.*

**RATCLIFFE**
My lord –

**KING RICHARD**
Good or bad news, that thou com'st in so bluntly ?

**RATCLIFFE**
Bad news, my lord. Morton is fled to Richmond,
And Buckingham, backed with the hardy Welshmen,
Is in the field, and still his power increaseth.

96 *peevish* foolish   104 *Rouge-mount* i.e. Redhill (the incident is historical, but the play on 'Richmond' is forced)   105 *bard* (the Celtic bards or poets were also considered prophets)   113 *Jack* a metal figure of a man which appeared to strike the hours in early clocks (play on 'lowbred fellow'; cf. *begging*, l. 114)   113–14 *keep'st . . . meditation* (like a Jack you) suspend the moment of striking (i.e. coming to the point in your begging suit) and thus disturb my train of thought (so *let it strike*, l. 111)   116 *resolve* i.e. give a final answer   121 *Brecknock* a manor house in Wales ; *fearful* full of fears
IV, iii The same   2 *most arch* chiefest   7 *kind* natural   11 *alablaster* white (same as 'alabaster')   18 *replenishèd* complete (in the sense of being full of virtues and beauty)   19 *prime* first   25 *done* i.e. had done   32 *process* story   40 *for* because ; *Britain* Breton   42 *knot* i.e. marriage

KING RICHARD

     Ely with Richmond troubles me more near
     Than Buckingham and his rash-levied strength.
51   Come ! I have learned that fearful commenting
     Is leaden servitor to dull delay ;
53   Delay leads impotent and snail-paced beggary.
54   Then fiery expedition be my wing,
55   Jove's Mercury, and herald for a king !
     Go, muster men. My counsel is my shield ;
     We must be brief when traitors brave the field.    *Exeunt.*

\*

, iv     *Enter old Queen Margaret.*

QUEEN MARGARET

1   So now prosperity begins to mellow
     And drop into the rotten mouth of death.
     Here in these confines slily have I lurked
     To watch the waning of mine enemies.
5   A dire induction am I witness to,
6   And will to France, hoping the consequence
     Will prove as bitter, black, and tragical.
     Withdraw thee, wretched Margaret ! Who comes here ?
         *[Retires.]*
     *Enter Duchess [of York] and Queen [Elizabeth].*

QUEEN ELIZABETH

     Ah, my poor princes ! ah, my tender babes !
10   My unblown flowers, new-appearing sweets !
     If yet your gentle souls fly in the air
12   And be not fixed in doom perpetual,
     Hover about me with your airy wings
     And hear your mother's lamentation !

QUEEN MARGARET *[aside]*

     Hover about her. Say that right for right
     Hath dimmed your infant morn to agèd night.

DUCHESS OF YORK

17   So many miseries have crazed my voice
     That my woe-wearied tongue is still and mute.
     Edward Plantagenet, why art thou dead ?

QUEEN MARGARET *[aside]*

20   Plantagenet doth quit Plantagenet ;
21   Edward for Edward pays a dying debt.

QUEEN ELIZABETH

     Wilt thou, O God, fly from such gentle lambs
     And throw them in the entrails of the wolf ?
24   When didst thou sleep when such a deed was done ?

51–52 *fearful . . . servitor* timorous talk is the sluggish attendant   53 *beggary* ruin   54 *expedition* speed   55 *Mercury* messenger of the gods (note Richard's neat equation of himself with Jove, king of the gods) IV, iv Before the royal palace   1–2 *So . . . death* (image taken from ripe fruit falling and rotting on the ground)   5 *induction* beginning (as of a play)   6 *consequence* conclusion (as the catastrophe of a play)   10 *sweets* fragrant flowers   12 *fixed . . . perpetual* i.e. assigned by God's judgment to their final place of punishment or reward   17 *crazed* cracked   20 *quit* make up for   21 *dying debt* i.e. a debt for which the payment is death   24 *When* when ever (before this time)   26 *mortal-living* dead-alive   27 *grave's . . . usurped* i.e. a dead body tyrannized over by life   28 *Brief abstract* epitome ('brief' may also be intended to limit 'record')   36 *seniory* seniority   37 *frown . . . hand* i.e. have the mastery in looking grim or dismal   39 *Tell over* count   45 *holp'st* helpedest   52 *excellent* pre-eminently   53 *reigns . . . souls* i.e. flourishes (as a ruler) upon the tears wept from sore eyes of those individuals (whom he has injured)   56 *carnal* carnivorous   58 *pew-fellow* companion   64 *quit* redeem   65 *but boot* i.e. thrown in as an extra   69 *adulterate* guilty of adultery   71 *intelligencer* secret agent   72 *Only . . . factor* above all others chosen as their agent   75–77 *Earth . . . pray* (Shakespeare seems to be thinking of the conclusion of Marlowe's *Doctor Faustus*)

QUEEN MARGARET *[aside]*

     When holy Harry died, and my sweet son.

DUCHESS OF YORK

     Dead life, blind sight, poor mortal-living ghost,    26
     Woe's scene, world's shame, grave's due by life usurped,   27
     Brief abstract and record of tedious days,    28
     Rest thy unrest on England's lawful earth,
        *[Sits down.]*
     Unlawfully made drunk with innocent blood !

QUEEN ELIZABETH

     Ah that thou wouldst as soon afford a grave
     As thou canst yield a melancholy seat !
     Then would I hide my bones, not rest them here.
     Ah, who hath any cause to mourn but we ?
        *[Sits down by her.]*

QUEEN MARGARET *[comes forward]*

     If ancient sorrow be most reverent,
     Give mine the benefit of seniory    36
     And let my griefs frown on the upper hand.    37
     If sorrow can admit society,
        *[Sits down with them.]*
     [Tell over your woes again by viewing mine].    39
     I had an Edward, till a Richard killed him ;
     I had a Harry, till a Richard killed him :
     Thou hadst an Edward, till a Richard killed him ;
     Thou hadst a Richard, till a Richard killed him.

DUCHESS OF YORK

     I had a Richard too, and thou didst kill him ;
     I had a Rutland too, thou holp'st to kill him.    45

QUEEN MARGARET

     Thou hadst a Clarence too, and Richard killed him.
     From forth the kennel of thy womb hath crept
     A hellhound that doth hunt us all to death :
     That dog, that had his teeth before his eyes,
     To worry lambs and lap their gentle blood,
     That foul defacer of God's handiwork,
     That excellent grand tyrant of the earth    52
     That reigns in gallèd eyes of weeping souls,    53
     Thy womb let loose to chase us to our graves.
     O upright, just, and true-disposing God,
     How do I thank thee that this carnal cur    56
     Preys on the issue of his mother's body
     And makes her pew-fellow with others' moan !    58

DUCHESS OF YORK

     O Harry's wife, triumph not in my woes !
     God witness with me, I have wept for thine.

QUEEN MARGARET

     Bear with me ! I am hungry for revenge,
     And now I cloy me with beholding it.
     Thy Edward he is dead, that killed my Edward ;
     Thy other Edward dead, to quit my Edward ;    64
     Young York he is but boot, because both they    65
     Matched not the high perfection of my loss.
     Thy Clarence he is dead that stabbed my Edward,
     And the beholders of this frantic play,
     Th' adulterate Hastings, Rivers, Vaughan, Grey,
     Untimely smoth'red in their dusky graves.    69
     Richard yet lives, hell's black intelligencer ;    71
     Only reserved their factor to buy souls    72
     And send them thither. But at hand, at hand,
     Ensues his piteous and unpitied end.
     Earth gapes, hell burns, fiends roar, saints pray,    75
     To have him suddenly conveyed from hence.
     Cancel his bond of life, dear God, I pray,

That I may live and say, 'The dog is dead.'

**QUEEN ELIZABETH**
O, thou didst prophesy the time would come
That I should wish for thee to help me curse
That bottled spider, that foul bunch-backed toad !

**QUEEN MARGARET**
I called thee then vain flourish of my fortune ;
I called thee then poor shadow, painted queen,
The presentation of but what I was,

85      The flattering index of a direful pageant,
One heaved a-high to be hurled down below,
A mother only mocked with two fair babes,

88      A dream of what thou wast, a garish flag,
To be the aim of every dangerous shot ;
A sign of dignity, a breath, a bubble,

91      A queen in jest, only to fill the scene.
Where is thy husband now ? Where be thy brothers ?
Where be thy two sons ? Wherein dost thou joy ?
Who sues and kneels and says, 'God save the queen' ?
Where be the bending peers that flattered thee ?
Where be the thronging troops that followed thee ?

97      Decline all this, and see what now thou art :
For happy wife, a most distressèd widow ;
For joyful mother, one that wails the name ;
For one being sued to, one that humbly sues ;

101     For queen, a very caitiff crowned with care ;
For she that scorned at me, now scorned of me ;
For she being feared of all, now fearing one ;
For she commanding all, obeyed of none.
Thus hath the course of justice whirled about
And left thee but a very prey to time,
Having no more but thought of what thou wast,
To torture thee the more, being what thou art.
Thou didst usurp my place, and dost thou not
Usurp the just proportion of my sorrow ?

111     Now thy proud neck bears half my burdened yoke,
From which even here I slip my weary head
And leave the burden of it all on thee.
Farewell, York's wife, and queen of sad mischance !
These English woes shall make me smile in France.

**QUEEN ELIZABETH**
O thou well skilled in curses, stay awhile
And teach me how to curse mine enemies !

**QUEEN MARGARET**
Forbear to sleep the nights, and fast the days ;
Compare dead happiness with living woe ;
Think that thy babes were sweeter than they were
And he that slew them fouler than he is :

122     Bett'ring thy loss makes the bad causer worse ;
Revolving this will teach thee how to curse.

**QUEEN ELIZABETH**
124     My words are dull. O, quicken them with thine !

**QUEEN MARGARET**
Thy woes will make them sharp and pierce like mine.
         *Exit [Queen] Margaret.*

**DUCHESS OF YORK**
Why should calamity be full of words ?

**QUEEN ELIZABETH**
127     Windy attorneys to their client's woes,
128     Airy succeeders of intestate joys,
Poor breathing orators of miseries,
Let them have scope ! Though what they will impart
Help nothing else, yet do they ease the heart.

**DUCHESS OF YORK**
If so, then be not tongue-tied : go with me,
And in the breath of bitter words let's smother
My damnèd son that thy two sweet sons smothered.
The trumpet sounds. Be copious in exclaims.
        *Enter King Richard and his Train [marching, with*
        *Drums and Trumpets].*

**KING RICHARD**
Who intercepts me in my expedition ?       136

**DUCHESS OF YORK**
O, she that might have intercepted thee,
By strangling thee in her accursèd womb,
From all the slaughters (wretch !) that thou hast done !

**QUEEN ELIZABETH**
Hid'st thou that forehead with a golden crown
Where should be branded, if that right were right,
The slaughter of the prince that owed that crown    142
And the dire death of my poor sons and brothers ?
Tell me, thou villain-slave, where are my children ?   144

**DUCHESS OF YORK**
Thou toad, thou toad, where is thy brother Clarence ?
And little Ned Plantagenet, his son ?

**QUEEN ELIZABETH**
Where is the gentle Rivers, Vaughan, Grey ?

**DUCHESS OF YORK**
Where is kind Hastings ?

**KING RICHARD**
A flourish, trumpets ! Strike alarum, drums !
Let not the heavens hear these telltale women
Rail on the Lord's anointed. Strike, I say !
        *Flourish. Alarums.*
Either be patient and entreat me fair,
Or with the clamorous report of war
Thus will I drown your exclamations.

**DUCHESS OF YORK**
Art thou my son ?

**KING RICHARD**
Ay, I thank God, my father, and yourself.

**DUCHESS OF YORK**
Then patiently hear my impatience.

**KING RICHARD**
Madam, I have a touch of your condition       158
That cannot brook the accent of reproof.        159

**DUCHESS OF YORK**
O, let me speak !

**KING RICHARD**    Do then, but I'll not hear.

**DUCHESS OF YORK**
I will be mild and gentle in my words.

**KING RICHARD**
And brief, good mother, for I am in haste.

---

85 *index* prologue; *pageant* play or show   88–89 *garish . . . shot* brightly colored standard-bearer (an appearance only, thus picking up *painted queen*, l. 83) who draws the fire of all enemies   91 *queen . . . scene* i.e. a mute player-queen   97 *Decline* run through in order (as in a paradigm)   101 *caitiff* wretch   111 *burdened* burdensome   122 *Bett'ring . . . worse* i.e. magnifying thy loss makes the perpetrator of the evil appear even worse than he is   124 *quicken* put life into   127 *Windy . . . woes* (words are) airy pleaders for the woes of their client (i.e. the one suffering)   128 *succeeders . . . joys* heirs of joys which died without issue (folio reading 'intestine' [inward] may possibly be right; 'intestate' from quartos)   136 *expedition* (1) military undertaking, (2) haste   142 *owed* possessed by right   144 *villain-slave* lowest criminal (with suggestions of 'lowbred' in 'villain' [serf] and 'slave')   158 *condition* temperament   159 *accent* language

DUCHESS OF YORK

163 Art thou so hasty ? I have stayed for thee
(God knows) in torment and in agony.

KING RICHARD

And came I not at last to comfort you ?

DUCHESS OF YORK

166 No, by the Holy Rood, thou know'st it well,
Thou cam'st on earth to make the earth my hell.
A grievous burden was thy birth to me ;

169 Tetchy and wayward was thy infancy ;

170 Thy schooldays frightful, desp'rate, wild, and furious ;
Thy prime of manhood daring, bold, and venturous ;

172 Thy age confirmed, proud, subtle, sly, and bloody,
More mild, but yet more harmful – kind in hatred.
What comfortable hour canst thou name
That ever graced me with thy company ?

KING RICHARD

176 Faith, none, but Humphrey Hour, that called your grace
To breakfast once, forth of my company.

178 If I be so disgracious in your eye,
Let me march on and not offend you, madam.
Strike up the drum.

DUCHESS OF YORK    I prithee hear me speak.

KING RICHARD

You speak too bitterly.

DUCHESS OF YORK      Hear me a word ;
For I shall never speak to thee again.

KING RICHARD

So.

DUCHESS OF YORK

Either thou wilt die by God's just ordinance
Ere from this war thou turn a conqueror,
Or I with grief and extreme age shall perish
And never more behold thy face again.
Therefore take with thee my most grievous curse,
Which in the day of battle tire thee more

190 Than all the complete armor that thou wear'st !
My prayers on the adverse party fight,
And there the little souls of Edward's children
Whisper the spirits of thine enemies
And promise them success and victory !
Bloody thou art, bloody will be thy end ;
Shame serves thy life and doth thy death attend.    *Exit*.

QUEEN ELIZABETH

Though far more cause, yet much less spirit to curse
Abides in me. I say amen to her.

KING RICHARD

Stay, madam ; I must talk a word with you.

QUEEN ELIZABETH

I have no moe sons of the royal blood 200
For thee to slaughter. For my daughters, Richard,
They shall be praying nuns, not weeping queens ;
And therefore level not to hit their lives. 203

KING RICHARD

You have a daughter called Elizabeth,
Virtuous and fair, royal and gracious.

QUEEN ELIZABETH

And must she die for this ? O, let her live,
And I'll corrupt her manners, stain her beauty, 207
Slander myself as false to Edward's bed,
Throw over her the veil of infamy :
So she may live unscarred of bleeding slaughter,
I will confess she was not Edward's daughter.

KING RICHARD

Wrong not her birth ; she is a royal princess.

QUEEN ELIZABETH

To save her life, I'll say she is not so.

KING RICHARD

Her life is safest only in her birth. 214

QUEEN ELIZABETH

And only in that safety died her brothers.

KING RICHARD

Lo, at their birth good stars were opposite.

QUEEN ELIZABETH

No, to their lives ill friends were contrary. 217

KING RICHARD

All unavoided is the doom of destiny. 218

QUEEN ELIZABETH

True, when avoided grace makes destiny : 219
My babes were destined to a fairer death
If grace had blessed thee with a fairer life.

KING RICHARD

You speak as if that I had slain my cousins !

QUEEN ELIZABETH

Cousins indeed, and by their uncle cozened 223
Of comfort, kingdom, kindred, freedom, life :
Whose hand soever lanched their tender hearts, 225
Thy head (all indirectly) gave direction. 226
No doubt the murd'rous knife was dull and blunt
Till it was whetted on thy stone-hard heart
To revel in the entrails of my lambs.
But that still use of grief makes wild grief tame, 230
My tongue should to thy ears not name my boys
Till that my nails were anchored in thine eyes ;
And I, in such a desp'rate bay of death, 233
Like a poor bark of sails and tackling reft,
Rush all to pieces on thy rocky bosom.

KING RICHARD

Madam, so thrive I in my enterprise
And dangerous success of bloody wars
As I intend more good to you and yours
Than ever you or yours by me were harmed !

QUEEN ELIZABETH

What good is covered with the face of heaven, 240
To be discovered, that can do me good ?

KING RICHARD

Th' advancement of your children, gentle lady.

QUEEN ELIZABETH

Up to some scaffold, there to lose their heads↲

KING RICHARD

Unto the dignity and height of fortune,

163 *stayed* waited   166 *Holy Rood* Christ's cross   169 *Tetchy and way-ward* fretful and willful   170 *frightful* full of fears   172 *age confirmed* i.e. having reached full maturity   176 *Humphrey Hour* (meaning un-certain ; perhaps 'that hour when you were paradoxically without food' [cf. 'dining with Duke Humphrey': going hungry])   178 *disgracious* un-pleasing   190 *complete armor* i.e. a full suit of armor, from head to foot   200 *moe* more (in number)   203 *level . . . lives* i.e. do not take aim to kill them   207 *manners* moral character   214 *only* above all else   217 *con-trary* opposed   218 *unavoided* unavoidable ; *doom* lot   219 *avoided grace* one who has rejected God's prevenient grace (i.e. Richard)   223 *cozened* cheated or betrayed   225 *lanched* pierced   226 *all indirectly* i.e. even if not in express terms   230 *But that still* except that continual   233 *bay* inlet (with play on the hunting term 'at bay': driven to a last stand)   240 *What . . . heaven* i.e. what good is yet to be found in this world (not already discovered)

245 The high imperial type of this earth's glory.
QUEEN ELIZABETH
Flatter my sorrow with report of it :
Tell me, what state, what dignity, what honor
248 Canst thou demise to any child of mine ?
KING RICHARD
Even all I have – ay, and myself and all –
250 Will I withal endow a child of thine,
251 So in the Lethe of thy angry soul
Thou drown the sad remembrance of those wrongs
Which thou supposest I have done to thee.
QUEEN ELIZABETH
Be brief, lest that the process of thy kindness
Last longer telling than thy kindness' date.
KING RICHARD
256 Then know that from my soul I love thy daughter.
QUEEN ELIZABETH
My daughter's mother thinks it with her soul.
KING RICHARD
What do you think ?
QUEEN ELIZABETH
That thou dost love my daughter from thy soul.
So from thy soul's love didst thou love her brothers,
And from my heart's love I do thank thee for it.
KING RICHARD
Be not so hasty to confound my meaning :
I mean that with my soul I love thy daughter
And do intend to make her Queen of England.
QUEEN ELIZABETH
Well then, who dost thou mean shall be her king ?
KING RICHARD
Even he that makes her queen. Who should be else ?
QUEEN ELIZABETH
What, thou ?
KING RICHARD Even so. How think you of it ?
QUEEN ELIZABETH
How canst thou woo her ?
KING RICHARD               That would I learn of you,
269 As one being best acquainted with her humor.
QUEEN ELIZABETH
And wilt thou learn of me ?
KING RICHARD               Madam, with all my heart.
QUEEN ELIZABETH
Send to her by the man that slew her brothers
A pair of bleeding hearts ; thereon engrave
'Edward' and 'York' ; then haply will she weep :
Therefore present to her – as sometimes Margaret
Did to thy father, steeped in Rutland's blood –
A handkercher, which say to her did drain
The purple sap from her sweet brother's body,
278 And bid her wipe her weeping eyes withal.
If this inducement move her not to love,
Send her a letter of thy noble deeds :
Tell her thou mad'st away her uncle Clarence,
Her uncle Rivers ; ay (and for her sake !),
283 Mad'st quick conveyance with her good aunt Anne.
KING RICHARD
You mock me, madam ; this is not the way
To win your daughter.
QUEEN ELIZABETH               There is no other way,
Unless thou couldst put on some other shape,
And not be Richard that hath done all this.
KING RICHARD
Say that I did all this for love of her.

QUEEN ELIZABETH
Nay, then indeed she cannot choose but hate thee,
Having bought love with such a bloody spoil.            290
KING RICHARD
Look what is done cannot be now amended :               291
Men shall deal unadvisedly sometimes,
Which after-hours gives leisure to repent.
If I did take the kingdom from your sons,
To make amends I'll give it to your daughter ;
If I have killed the issue of your womb,
To quicken your increase I will beget                   297
Mine issue of your blood upon your daughter.
A grandam's name is little less in love
Than is the doting title of a mother ;
They are as children but one step below,
Even of your metal, of your very blood,                 302
Of all one pain, save for a night of groans
Endured of her for whom you bid like sorrow :           304
Your children were vexation to your youth,
But mine shall be a comfort to your age.
The loss you have is but a son being king,
And by that loss your daughter is made queen.
I cannot make you what amends I would ;
Therefore accept such kindness as I can.                310
Dorset your son, that with a fearful soul               311
Leads discontented steps in foreign soil,
This fair alliance quickly shall call home
To high promotions and great dignity.
The king, that calls your beauteous daughter wife,
Familiarly shall call thy Dorset brother :
Again shall you be mother to a king,
And all the ruins of distressful times
Repaired with double riches of content.
What ! we have many goodly days to see :
The liquid drops of tears that you have shed
Shall come again, transformed to orient pearl,          322
Advantaging their love with interest                    323
Of ten times double gain of happiness.
Go then, my mother ; to thy daughter go ;
Make bold her bashful years with your experience ;
Prepare her ears to hear a wooer's tale ;
Put in her tender heart th' aspiring flame
Of golden sovereignty ; acquaint the princess
With the sweet silent hours of marriage joys ;
And when this arm of mine hath chastisèd
The petty rebel, dull-brained Buckingham,
Bound with triumphant garlands will I come              333
And lead thy daughter to a conqueror's bed ;
To whom I will retail my conquest won,                  335
And she shall be sole victoress, Caesar's Caesar.
QUEEN ELIZABETH
What were I best to say ? Her father's brother

245 *imperial type* symbol of rule   248 *demise* transmit   250 *withal* with
251 *Lethe* a river in Hell (to drink of which induced forgetfulness)   256
*from my soul* with my very soul (but Queen Elizabeth takes Richard to
mean that his love is 'from' [i.e. separated from] his inmost feelings)   269
*humor* temperament   278 *withal* with (it)   283 *quick conveyance* with
speedy removal of   290 *spoil* slaughter (hunting term : the breaking up of
the quarry after the kill)   291 *Look what* whatever   297 *quicken your
increase* i.e. give new life to your (dead) offspring   302 *metal* substance
304 *of* by ; *bid* underwent, suffered   310 *can* i.e. am able to give   311 *fearful* full of fears   322 *orient* shining   323 *love* i.e. the love which gave rise
to the tears   333 *triumphant garlands* i.e. garlands befitting a military
triumph (in the Roman sense)   335 *retail* recount (though Shakespeare
would seem to mean 'transmit')

Would be her lord? Or shall I say her uncle?
Or he that slew her brothers and her uncles?
Under what title shall I woo for thee
That God, the law, my honor, and her love
Can make seem pleasing to her tender years?

KING RICHARD
343  Infer fair England's peace by this alliance.

QUEEN ELIZABETH
Which she shall purchase with still-lasting war.

KING RICHARD
Tell her the king, that may command, entreats.

QUEEN ELIZABETH
That at her hands which the king's King forbids.

KING RICHARD
Say she shall be a high and mighty queen.

QUEEN ELIZABETH
348  To vail the title, as her mother doth.

KING RICHARD
Say I will love her everlastingly.

QUEEN ELIZABETH
But how long shall that title 'ever' last?

KING RICHARD
Sweetly in force unto her fair life's end.

QUEEN ELIZABETH
But how long fairly shall her sweet life last?

KING RICHARD
As long as heaven and nature lengthens it.

QUEEN ELIZABETH
As long as hell and Richard likes of it.

KING RICHARD
Say I, her sovereign, am her subject low.

QUEEN ELIZABETH
356  But she, your subject, loathes such sovereignty.

KING RICHARD
Be eloquent in my behalf to her.

QUEEN ELIZABETH
An honest tale speeds best being plainly told.

KING RICHARD
Then plainly to her tell my loving tale.

QUEEN ELIZABETH
360  Plain and not honest is too harsh a style.

KING RICHARD
Your reasons are too shallow and too quick.

QUEEN ELIZABETH
O no, my reasons are too deep and dead –
Too deep and dead (poor infants) in their graves.

KING RICHARD
Harp not on that string, madam; that is past.

QUEEN ELIZABETH
Harp on it still shall I till heartstrings break.

KING RICHARD
366  Now, by my George, my garter, and my crown –

QUEEN ELIZABETH
Profaned, dishonored, and the third usurped.

KING RICHARD
I swear –

QUEEN ELIZABETH  By nothing, for this is no oath:
Thy George, profaned, hath lost his lordly honor;
Thy garter, blemished, pawned his knightly virtue;
Thy crown, usurped, disgraced his kingly glory.
If something thou wouldst swear to be believed,
Swear then by something that thou hast not wronged.

KING RICHARD
Then by myself –

QUEEN ELIZABETH  Thyself is self-misused.

KING RICHARD
Now by the world –

QUEEN ELIZABETH  'Tis full of thy foul wrongs.

KING RICHARD
My father's death –

QUEEN ELIZABETH  Thy life hath it dishonored.

KING RICHARD
Why then, by God –

QUEEN ELIZABETH  God's wrong is most of all:
If thou didst fear to break an oath with him,
The unity the king my husband made          379
Thou hadst not broken, nor my brothers died.
If thou hadst feared to break an oath by him,
Th' imperial metal, circling now thy head,          382
Had graced the tender temples of my child,
And both the princes had been breathing here,
Which now, two tender bedfellows for dust,
Thy broken faith hath made the prey for worms.
What canst thou swear by now?

KING RICHARD                    The time to come.

QUEEN ELIZABETH
That thou hast wrongèd in the time o'erpast;
For I myself have many tears to wash
Hereafter time, for time past wronged by thee.          390
The children live whose fathers thou hast slaughtered,
Ungoverned youth, to wail it in their age;          392
The parents live whose children thou hast butchered,
Old barren plants, to wail it with their age.
Swear not by time to come, for that thou hast
Misused ere used, by times ill-used o'erpast.

KING RICHARD
As I intend to prosper and repent,          397
So thrive I in my dangerous affairs
Of hostile arms! Myself myself confound!
Heaven and fortune bar me happy hours!
Day, yield me not thy light, nor, night, thy rest!
Be opposite all planets of good luck
To my proceeding if, with dear heart's love,
Immaculate devotion, holy thoughts,
I tender not thy beauteous princely daughter!
In her consists my happiness and thine;
Without her, follows to myself and thee,
Herself, the land, and many a Christian soul,
Death, desolation, ruin, and decay.
It cannot be avoided but by this;          410
It will not be avoided but by this.
Therefore, dear mother (I must call you so),
Be the attorney of my love to her:
Plead what I will be, not what I have been –
Not my deserts, but what I will deserve;
Urge the necessity and state of times,

343 *Infer* imply  348 *vail* abase, lower (quarto reading 'wail' is perhaps preferable)  356 *sovereignty* (1) rule, (2) ruler (i.e. Richard)  360 *Plain . . . style* i.e. plain style (cf. the proverb 'Truth is plain') unless it is sincere will be too harsh; lies (i.e. things not honest) need the decorated style  366 *George . . . garter* (a jewelled pendant with the figure of St George and the gold collar from which it hung were parts of the insignia of the Order of the Garter)  379 *unity* (the 'reconciliation' in II, i)  382 *imperial metal* i.e. royal crown  390 *Hereafter* future  392 *Ungoverned* i.e. without parents  397-98 *As . . . So* to the degree I mean to do well and repent, to such a degree  397-405 *As . . . daughter* (note that Richard here in effect curses himself, bringing the curses in this scene to a final focus)

417   And be not peevish-fond in great designs.

QUEEN ELIZABETH
Shall I be tempted of the devil thus?

KING RICHARD
Ay, if the devil tempt you to do good.

QUEEN ELIZABETH
420   Shall I forget myself to be myself?

KING RICHARD
Ay, if yourself's remembrance wrong yourself.

QUEEN ELIZABETH
Yet thou didst kill my children.

KING RICHARD
But in your daughter's womb I bury them,
Where, in that nest of spicery, they will breed
425   Selves of themselves, to your recomforture.

QUEEN ELIZABETH
Shall I go win my daughter to thy will?

KING RICHARD
And be a happy mother by the deed.

QUEEN ELIZABETH
I go. Write to me very shortly,
And you shall understand from me her mind.

KING RICHARD
Bear her my true love's kiss; and so farewell—
                *Exit Q[ueen Elizabeth].*
431   Relenting fool, and shallow, changing woman!
       *Enter Ratcliffe [, Catesby following].*
How now? What news?

RATCLIFFE
Most mighty sovereign, on the western coast
Rideth a puissant navy; to our shores
Throng many doubtful hollow-hearted friends,
436   Unarmed, and unresolved to beat them back.
437   'Tis thought that Richmond is their admiral;
438   And there they hull, expecting but the aid
Of Buckingham to welcome them ashore.

KING RICHARD
Some light-foot friend post to the Duke of Norfolk:
Ratcliffe, thyself—or Catesby—where is he?

CATESBY
Here, my good lord.

KING RICHARD       Catesby, fly to the duke.

CATESBY
I will, my lord, with all convenient haste.

KING RICHARD
Ratcliffe, come hither. Post to Salisbury.
When thou com'st thither—
     *[To Catesby]*       Dull unmindful villain,
Why stay'st thou here and go'st not to the duke?

CATESBY
First, mighty liege, tell me your highness' pleasure,
What from your grace I shall deliver to him.

KING RICHARD
O, true, good Catesby: bid him levy straight
The greatest strength and power that he can make
And meet me suddenly at Salisbury.

CATESBY
I go.                         *Exit.*

RATCLIFFE
What, may it please you, shall I do at Salisbury?

KING RICHARD
Why, what wouldst thou do there before I go?

RATCLIFFE
455   Your highness told me I should post before.

KING RICHARD
My mind is changed.
      *Enter Lord Stanley [Earl of Derby].*
                Stanley, what news with you?

DERBY
None good, my liege, to please you with the hearing,
Nor none so bad but well may be reported.

KING RICHARD
Hoyday, a riddle! Neither good nor bad!
What need'st thou run so many miles about,
When thou mayest tell thy tale the nearest way?
Once more, what news?

DERBY          Richmond is on the seas.

KING RICHARD
There let him sink, and be the seas on him!
White-livered runagate, what doth he there?     464

DERBY
I know not, mighty sovereign, but by guess.

KING RICHARD
Well, as you guess?

DERBY
Stirred up by Dorset, Buckingham, and Morton,
He makes for England, here to claim the crown.

KING RICHARD
Is the chair empty? is the sword unswayed?     469
Is the king dead? the empire unpossessed?     470
What heir of York is there alive but we?
And who is England's king but great York's heir?
Then tell me, what makes he upon the seas?     473

DERBY
Unless for that, my liege, I cannot guess.

KING RICHARD
Unless for that he comes to be your liege,
You cannot guess wherefore the Welshman comes.
Thou wilt revolt and fly to him, I fear.

DERBY
No, my good lord; therefore mistrust me not.

KING RICHARD
Where is thy power then to beat him back?
Where be thy tenants and thy followers?
Are they not now upon the western shore,
Safe-conducting the rebels from their ships?

DERBY
No, my good lord, my friends are in the North.

KING RICHARD
Cold friends to me! What do they in the North     484
When they should serve their sovereign in the West?

DERBY
They have not been commanded, mighty king:
Pleaseth your majesty to give me leave,
I'll muster up my friends and meet your grace
Where and what time your majesty shall please.

KING RICHARD
Ay, thou wouldst be gone to join with Richmond:

417 *peevish-fond* foolishly self-willed (folio reading 'peevish found' may possibly be correct; Q1 reads 'peevish, fond')   420 *Shall . . . be myself* i.e. shall I forget who I am   425 *recomforture* consolation   431 *shallow* superficial   436 *unresolved* undetermined how to act   437 *their admiral* i.e. of the *navy* of l. 434   438 *hull* drift with the winds   455 *post* hasten   464 *runagate* vagabond or, perhaps, deserter (cf. V, iii, 317)   469 *sword* i.e. the sword of state, part of the king's regalia symbolic of power   470 *empire* kingdom (i.e. the thing requiring rule)   473 *makes he* is he doing   484 *Cold* chilling (with play on Derby's friends being in the North)

But I'll not trust thee.

DERBY                              Most mighty sovereign,
You have no cause to hold my friendship doubtful.
I never was nor never will be false.

KING RICHARD
Go then and muster men. But leave behind
Your son, George Stanley. Look your heart be firm,
Or else his head's assurance is but frail.

DERBY
So deal with him as I prove true to you.           *Exit.*
    *Enter a Messenger.*

1. MESSENGER
My gracious sovereign, now in Devonshire,
As I by friends am well advertisèd,
Sir Edward Courtney and the haughty prelate,
Bishop of Exeter, his elder brother,
With many moe confederates, are in arms.
    *Enter another Messenger.*

2. MESSENGER
In Kent, my liege, the Guildfords are in arms,
And every hour more competitors
Flock to the rebels, and their power grows strong.
    *Enter another Messenger.*

3. MESSENGER
My lord, the army of great Buckingham —

KING RICHARD
Out on you, owls! Nothing but songs of death?
    *He striketh him.*
There, take thou that, till thou bring better news.

3. MESSENGER
The news I have to tell your majesty
Is that by sudden floods and fall of waters
Buckingham's army is dispersed and scattered,
And he himself wand'red away alone,
No man knows whither.

KING RICHARD            I cry thee mercy :
There is my purse to cure that blow of thine.
Hath any well-advisèd friend proclaimed
Reward to him that brings the traitor in ?

3. MESSENGER
Such proclamation hath been made, my lord.
    *Enter another Messenger.*

4. MESSENGER
Sir Thomas Lovel and Lord Marquess Dorset,
'Tis said, my liege, in Yorkshire are in arms.
But this good comfort bring I to your highness :
The Britain navy is dispersed by tempest ;
Richmond in Dorsetshire sent out a boat
Unto the shore to ask those on the banks
If they were his assistants, yea or no ;

Who answered him they came from Buckingham
Upon his party. He, mistrusting them,
Hoised sail, and made his course again for Britain.   527

KING RICHARD
March on, march on, since we are up in arms ;
If not to fight with foreign enemies,
Yet to beat down these rebels here at home.
    *Enter Catesby.*

CATESBY
My liege, the Duke of Buckingham is taken.
That is the best news. That the Earl of Richmond
Is with a mighty power landed at Milford
Is colder tidings, but yet they must be told.

KING RICHARD
Away towards Salisbury ! While we reason here,
A royal battle might be won and lost.
Some one take order Buckingham be brought
To Salisbury ; the rest march on with me.
    *Flourish. Exeunt.*

*

    *Enter [Lord Stanley Earl of] Derby, and*       IV, v
    *Sir Christopher [Urswick, a priest].*

DERBY
Sir Christopher, tell Richmond this from me :
That in the sty of the most deadly boar
My son George Stanley is franked up in hold ;       3
If I revolt, off goes young George's head ;
The fear of that holds off my present aid.
So get thee gone ; commend me to thy lord.
Withal say that the queen hath heartily consented
He should espouse Elizabeth her daughter.          8
But tell me, where is princely Richmond now ?

CHRISTOPHER
At Pembroke, or at Ha'rford-West in Wales.          10

DERBY
What men of name resort to him ?

CHRISTOPHER
Sir Walter Herbert, a renownèd soldier,
Sir Gilbert Talbot, Sir William Stanley,
Oxford, redoubted Pembroke, Sir James Blunt,       14
And Rice ap Thomas, with a valiant crew,
And many other of great name and worth ;
And towards London do they bend their power,
If by the way they be not fought withal.

DERBY
Well, hie thee to thy lord. I kiss his hand :
My letter will resolve him of my mind.
    *[Gives letter.]*
Farewell.                                      *Exeunt.*

*

    *Enter Buckingham with Halberds [and the Sheriff],*   V, i
    *led to execution.*

BUCKINGHAM
Will not King Richard let me speak with him ?

SHERIFF
No, my good lord ; therefore be patient.

BUCKINGHAM
Hastings, and Edward's children, Grey and Rivers,
Holy King Henry and thy fair son Edward,
Vaughan and all that have miscarrièd
By underhand corrupted foul injustice,

---

496 *head's assurance* i.e. that his head will not be cut off   499 *advertisèd*
informed   500, 503 *Courtney, Guildfords* (supporters of Buckingham)
502 *moe* more (in number)   507 *owls* (the hoot or song of the owl was
frequently believed to portend evil)   513 *cry thee mercy* beg your pardon
515 *well-advisèd* foresighted   518 *Lovel* (supporter of Buckingham)   521
*Britain* Breton   527 *Hoised* hoisted ; *Britain* Brittany
IV, v Lord Stanley's house   s.d. *Sir* (see III, ii, 109)   3 *franked up in
hold* shut up (as in a *sty*, l. 2) in custody (the *boar* in l. 2 being, of course,
Richard)   8 *He . . . daughter* (Shakespeare's reference here to Richmond's
projected marriage with Princess Elizabeth makes it fairly certain that
we should interpret Queen Elizabeth's apparent capitulation to Richard in
IV, iv, 426–29 as a ruse to trick him)   10 *Pembroke* county in southwestern
Wales (see reference to the Pembroke family, l. 14) ; *Ha'rford-West* town
in Pembroke   14 *redoubted* dreaded ; *Pembroke* i.e. Jasper Tudor, Richmond's uncle
V, i An open place in Salisbury

7    If that your moody discontented souls
     Do through the clouds behold this present hour,
9    Even for revenge mock my destruction !
10   This is All Souls' day, fellow, is it not ?
     SHERIFF
     It is, my lord.
     BUCKINGHAM
12   Why, then All Souls' day is my body's doomsday.
     This is the day which in King Edward's time
     I wished might fall on me when I was found
     False to his children and his wife's allies ;
     This is the day wherein I wished to fall
     By the false faith of him whom most I trusted ;
18   This, this All Souls' day to my fearful soul
19   Is the determined respite of my wrongs :
     That high All-seer which I dallied with
     Hath turned my feignèd prayer on my head
     And given in earnest what I begged in jest.
     Thus doth He force the swords of wicked men
     To turn their own points in their masters' bosoms ;
     Thus Margaret's curse falls heavy on my neck :
     'When he,' quoth she, 'shall split thy heart with sorrow,
     Remember Margaret was a prophetess.' –
     Come lead me, officers, to the block of shame.
     Wrong hath but wrong, and blame the due of blame.
                              *Exeunt Buckingham with Officers.*

*

V, ii     *Enter Richmond, Oxford, [Sir James] Blunt, [Sir
           Walter] Herbert, and others, with Drum and Colors.*
     RICHMOND
     Fellows in arms, and my most loving friends,
     Bruised underneath the yoke of tyranny,
3    Thus far into the bowels of the land
     Have we marched on without impediment ;
5    And here receive we from our father Stanley
     Lines of fair comfort and encouragement.
     The wretched, bloody, and usurping boar,
     That spoiled your summer fields and fruitful vines,
     Swills your warm blood like wash, and makes his trough
10   In your embowelled bosoms – this foul swine
11   Is now even in the centry of this isle,
     Near to the town of Leicester, as we learn :
     From Tamworth thither is but one day's march.
     In God's name cheerly on, courageous friends,
     To reap the harvest of perpetual peace
     By this one bloody trial of sharp war.
     OXFORD
17   Every man's conscience is a thousand men,
     To fight against this guilty homicide.
     HERBERT
     I doubt not but his friends will turn to us.
     BLUNT
     He hath no friends but what are friends for fear,
     Which in his dearest need will fly from him.
     RICHMOND
     All for our vantage. Then in God's name march !
     True hope is swift and flies with swallow's wings ;
     Kings it makes gods, and meaner creatures kings.
                              *Exeunt omnes.*

*

          *Enter King Richard in arms, with Norfolk, Ratcliffe,*   V
          *and the Earl of Surrey [, and Soldiers].*
     KING RICHARD
     Here pitch our tent, even here in Bosworth field.
     My Lord of Surrey, why look you so sad ?                       2
     SURREY
     My heart is ten times lighter than my looks.
     KING RICHARD
     My Lord of Norfolk –
     NORFOLK                   Here, most gracious liege.
     KING RICHARD
     Norfolk, we must have knocks. Ha ! must we not ?
     NORFOLK
     We must both give and take, my loving lord.
     KING RICHARD
     Up with my tent ! Here will I lie to-night ;
          *[Soldiers begin to set up the King's tent.]*
     But where to-morrow ? Well, all's one for that.               8
     Who hath descried the number of the traitors ?
     NORFOLK
     Six or seven thousand is their utmost power.
     KING RICHARD
     Why, our battalia trebles that account :                      11
     Besides, the king's name is a tower of strength,
     Which they upon the adverse faction want.                     13
     Up with the tent ! Come, noble gentlemen,
     Let us survey the vantage of the ground.                      15
     Call for some men of sound direction :                        16
     Let's lack no discipline, make no delay,
     For, lords, to-morrow is a busy day.          *Exeunt.*
          *Enter Richmond, Sir William Brandon, Oxford, and*
          *Dorset [, Herbert, and Blunt. Some of the Soldiers*
          *pitch Richmond's tent].*
     RICHMOND
     The weary sun hath made a golden set
     And by the bright tract of his fiery car                      20
     Gives token of a goodly day to-morrow.
     Sir William Brandon, you shall bear my standard.
     Give me some ink and paper in my tent :
     I'll draw the form and model of our battle,
     Limit each leader to his several charge,
     And part in just proportion our small power.
     My Lord of Oxford, – you, Sir William Brandon, –
     And you, Sir Walter Herbert – stay with me.
     The Earl of Pembroke keeps his regiment ;
     Good Captain Blunt, bear my good-night to him,                30

7 *discontented souls* i.e. souls which could not rest in peace until their
violent deaths had been revenged  9 *Even for* i.e. impelled by  10 *All
Souls' day* November 2, the day on which the Roman Catholic Church
intercedes for all Christian souls  12 *doomsday* day of final judgment
(death being the sentence)  18 *fearful* terrified  19 *determined . . . wrongs*
i.e. the foreordained moment past which no cessation (of punishment) will
be granted for all the wrongs I have committed
V, ii A camp near Tamworth  3 *bowels* heart or center (Richmond's army
is at Tamworth, Staffordshire, on its way to the scene of the final battle
with Richard at Bosworth Field, Leicestershire ; cf. ll. 12–13)  5 *our*
(royal plural) ; *father Stanley* (Richmond was the son of Edmund Tudor
and Margaret Beaufort ; Lord Stanley, Earl of Derby, was his mother's
third husband)  10 *embowelled* disembowelled  11 *centry* center  17 *conscience* i.e. his conscience tells him that he is on the 'right' side
V, iii Bosworth Field  2 *sad* heavy-spirited  8 *all's . . . that* i.e. it makes
no difference  11 *battalia* armed forces  13 *want* lack  15 *the vantage
. . . ground* i.e. the military advantages offered by the spot chosen for the
battle  16 *of sound direction* capable of giving sound orders  20 *tract*
track ; *car* chariot (with reference to the chariot of Phoebus, god of the
sun)

And by the second hour in the morning
Desire the earl to see me in my tent:
Yet one thing more, good captain, do for me –
Where is Lord Stanley quartered, do you know?

BLUNT
Unless I have mista'en his colors much
(Which well I am assured I have not done),
His regiment lies half a mile at least
South from the mighty power of the king.

RICHMOND
If without peril it be possible,
40 Sweet Blunt, make some good means to speak with him
And give him from me this most needful note.

BLUNT
Upon my life, my lord, I'll undertake it;
And so God give you quiet rest to-night!

RICHMOND
Good night, good Captain Blunt.        [Exit Blunt.]
                              Come, gentlemen,
Let us consult upon to-morrow's business.
In to my tent; the dew is raw and cold.
                    They withdraw into the tent.
Enter [, to his tent, King] Richard, Ratcliffe,
Norfolk, and Catesby.

KING RICHARD
What is't a clock?

CATESBY                It's supper time, my lord;
48 It's nine a clock.

KING RICHARD I will not sup to-night.
Give me some ink and paper.
50 What? is my beaver easier than it was?
And all my armor laid into my tent?

CATESBY
It is, my liege; and all things are in readiness.

KING RICHARD
Good Norfolk, hie thee to thy charge;
54 Use careful watch, choose trusty sentinels.

NORFOLK
I go, my lord.

KING RICHARD
Stir with the lark to-morrow, gentle Norfolk.

NORFOLK
I warrant you, my lord.              Exit.

KING RICHARD
Catesby!

CATESBY
My lord?

59 KING RICHARD Send out a pursuivant-at-arms
To Stanley's regiment; bid him bring his power
Before sunrising, lest his son George fall

Into the blind cave of eternal night.      [Exit Catesby.]
Fill me a bowl of wine. Give me a watch.            63
Saddle white Surrey for the field to-morrow.       64
Look that my staves be sound and not too heavy.    65
Ratcliffe!

RATCLIFFE
My lord?

KING RICHARD
Saw'st thou the melancholy Lord Northumberland?

RATCLIFFE
Thomas the Earl of Surrey and himself,
Much about cockshut time, from troop to troop     70
Went through the army, cheering up the soldiers.

KING RICHARD
So, I am satisfied. Give me a bowl of wine.
I have not that alacrity of spirit
Nor cheer of mind that I was wont to have.
     [Wine brought.]
Set it down. Is ink and paper ready?

RATCLIFFE
It is, my lord.

KING RICHARD
Bid my guard watch. Leave me. Ratcliffe,
About the mid of night come to my tent
And help to arm me. Leave me, I say.      Exit Ratcliffe.
                    [King Richard withdraws
                        into his tent, and sleeps.]
Enter [Lord Stanley Earl of] Derby, to Richmond
in his tent [, Lords and others attending].

DERBY
Fortune and victory sit on thy helm!

RICHMOND
All comfort that the dark night can afford
Be to thy person, noble father-in-law!
Tell me, how fares our loving mother?

DERBY
I, by attorney, bless thee from thy mother,        84
Who prays continually for Richmond's good:
So much for that. The silent hours steal on
And flaky darkness breaks within the east.         87
In brief, for so the season bids us be,
Prepare thy battle early in the morning            89
And put thy fortune to the arbitrement
Of bloody strokes and mortal-staring war.          91
I, as I may – that which I would I cannot –
With best advantage will deceive the time          93
And aid thee in this doubtful shock of arms.
But on thy side I may not be too forward,
Lest, being seen, thy brother, tender George,
Be executed in his father's sight.
Farewell. The leisure and the fearful time         98
Cuts off the ceremonious vows of love
And ample interchange of sweet discourse
Which so long sund'red friends should dwell upon.
God give us leisure for these rites of love!
Once more adieu: be valiant, and speed well!

RICHMOND
Good lords, conduct him to his regiment.
I'll strive with troublèd thoughts, to take a nap, 105
Lest leaden slumber peise me down to-morrow,       106
When I should mount with wings of victory:
Once more, good night, kind lords and gentlemen.
                    Exeunt. Manet Richmond.
O Thou, whose captain I account myself,

---

48 *nine a clock* (too late for an Elizabethan supper; the 'six of clocke' of Quarto 1 fits this context better, but is obviously too early for the time indications in scene ii and later)  50 *beaver* face-guard of a helmet  54 *Use careful watch* i.e. see that a thorough alert is observed  59 *pursuivant-at-arms* junior officer, attending on a herald  63 *a watch* a special guard (cf. l. 77) or a timepiece  64 *white Surrey* (Richard entered Leicester on a 'great white courser' [Holinshed], but the name is Shakespeare's and must not be confused with Surrey in l. 69)  65 *staves* lance shafts  70 *cockshut time* evening twilight  84 *attorney* proxy  87 *flaky darkness* i.e. darkness still flaked with light  89 *battle* armed forces (see *battalia*, l. 11 above)  91 *mortal-staring* killing (like the basilisk) with a glance of the eye  93 *With . . . time* i.e. will make the greatest profit of the moment without giving the appearance of doing so  98 *leisure . . . time* (lack of) time and the threat of the moment  105 *with troublèd thoughts* i.e. in spite of my disturbing thoughts  106 *peise* weigh

Look on my forces with a gracious eye ;
111 Put in their hands thy bruising irons of wrath,
That they may crush down with a heavy fall
The usurping helmets of our adversaries ;
Make us thy ministers of chastisement,
That we may praise thee in the victory.
To thee I do commend my watchful soul
117 Ere I let fall the windows of mine eyes :
Sleeping and waking. O, defend me still !
  *Sleeps.*
  *Enter the Ghost of Prince Edward, son to Henry the*
  *Sixth.*
 GHOST *(to Richard)*
Let me sit heavy on thy soul to-morrow !
Think how thou stab'st me in my prime of youth
At Tewkesbury : despair therefore, and die !
 *(To Richmond)*
122 Be cheerful, Richmond ; for the wrongèd souls
Of butcherèd princes fight in thy behalf.
King Henry's issue, Richmond, comforts thee.
  *Enter the Ghost of Henry the Sixth.*
 GHOST *(to Richard)*
125 When I was mortal, my anointed body
By thee was punchèd full of deadly holes.
Think on the Tower, and me : despair, and die !
Harry the Sixth bids thee despair, and die !
 *(To Richmond)*
Virtuous and holy, be thou conqueror !
Harry, that prophesied thou shouldst be king,
Doth comfort thee in thy sleep : live, and flourish !
  *Enter the Ghost of Clarence.*
 GHOST *[to Richard]*
Let me sit heavy in thy soul to-morrow –
133 I that was washed to death with fulsome wine,
Poor Clarence by thy guile betrayed to death !
To-morrow in the battle think on me,
136 And fall thy edgeless sword : despair, and die !
 *(To Richmond)*
137 Thou offspring of the house of Lancaster,
The wrongèd heirs of York do pray for thee ;
Good angels guard thy battle ! live, and flourish !
  *Enter the Ghosts of Rivers, Grey, and Vaughan.*
 RIVERS *[to Richard]*
Let me sit heavy in thy soul to-morrow,
Rivers, that died at Pomfret ! despair, and die !
 GREY
Think upon Grey, and let thy soul despair !
 VAUGHAN
Think upon Vaughan, and with guilty fear
Let fall thy lance : despair, and die !
 ALL *(to Richmond)*
Awake, and think our wrongs in Richard's bosom
Will conquer him ! Awake, and win the day !
  *Enter the Ghost of Lord Hastings.*
 GHOST *[to Richard]*
Bloody and guilty, guiltily awake
And in a bloody battle end thy days !
Think on Lord Hastings : despair, and die !
 *(To Richmond)*
150 Quiet untroublèd soul, awake, awake !
Arm, fight, and conquer, for fair England's sake !
  *Enter the Ghosts of the two young Princes.*
 GHOSTS *[to Richard]*
Dream on thy cousins smotherèd in the Tower.

Let us be lead within thy bosom, Richard,
And weigh thee down to ruin, shame, and death !
Thy nephews' souls bid thee despair, and die !
 *(To Richmond)*
Sleep, Richmond, sleep in peace and wake in joy.
Good angels guard thee from the boar's annoy ! 157
Live, and beget a happy race of kings !
Edward's unhappy sons do bid thee flourish.
  *Enter the Ghost of Anne, his wife.*
 GHOST *(to Richard)*
Richard, thy wife, that wretched Anne thy wife,
That never slept a quiet hour with thee,
Now fills thy sleep with perturbations :
To-morrow in the battle think on me,
And fall thy edgeless sword : despair, and die !
 *(To Richmond)*
Thou quiet soul, sleep thou a quiet sleep.
Dream of success and happy victory !
Thy adversary's wife doth pray for thee.
  *Enter the Ghost of Buckingham.*
 GHOST *(to Richard)*
The first was I that helped thee to the crown ;
The last was I that felt thy tyranny.
O, in the battle think on Buckingham,
And die in terror of thy guiltiness !
Dream on, dream on, of bloody deeds and death :
Fainting, despair ; despairing, yield thy breath !
 *(To Richmond)*
I died for hope ere I could lend thee aid ; 174
But cheer thy heart and be thou not dismayed :
God and good angels fight on Richmond's side,
And Richard falls in height of all his pride !
  *[The Ghosts vanish.] Richard starts out of his dream.*
 KING RICHARD
Give me another horse ! Bind up my wounds !
Have mercy, Jesu ! Soft ! I did but dream.
O coward conscience, how dost thou afflict me !
The lights burn blue. It is now dead midnight.
Cold fearful drops stand on my trembling flesh.
What do I fear ? Myself ? There's none else by.
Richard loves Richard : that is, I am I. 184
Is there a murderer here ? No. Yes, I am :
Then fly. What, from myself ? Great reason why –
Lest I revenge. What, myself upon myself ?
Alack, I love myself. Wherefore ? For any good
That I myself have done unto myself ?
O no ! Alas, I rather hate myself
For hateful deeds committed by myself.
I am a villain. Yet I lie, I am not.
Fool, of thyself speak well. Fool, do not flatter.
My conscience hath a thousand several tongues, 194
And every tongue brings in a several tale,
And every tale condemns me for a villain.

111 *irons* swords 117 *windows* eyelids 122 *cheerful* full of joy 125 *anointed* (see IV, i, 61n.) 133 *fulsome* sickening or satiating 136 *fall . . . sword* i.e. let thy sword, figuratively blunted by thinking about Clarence's murder, drop (1) out of your hand, or (2) down, so that it is no longer a means of defense 137 *offspring . . . Lancaster* (Richmond's mother was a Beaufort and the Beaufort line traced back to John of Gaunt, Duke of Lancaster, the father of Bolingbroke, who became Henry IV) 157 *annoy* molestation 174 *for hope* for the intent (of helping) (?) 184 *I am I* (this reading, that of all texts except Quarto 1, has the sanction of all later editors, but the reading 'I and I' of Quarto 1, here admittedly the basic text, makes equally good sense) 194 *several* separate

Perjury, perjury, in the highest degree,
Murder, stern murder, in the direst degree,
99 All several sins, all used in each degree,
Throng to the bar, crying all, 'Guilty! guilty!'
I shall despair. There is no creature loves me;
And if I die, no soul will pity me.
And, wherefore should they, since that I myself
Find in myself no pity to myself?
Methought the souls of all that I had murdered
Came to my tent, and every one did threat
To-morrow's vengeance on the head of Richard.
     *Enter Ratcliffe.*
RATCLIFFE
  My lord!
KING RICHARD
  Zounds, who is there?
RATCLIFFE
10 Ratcliffe, my lord, 'tis I. The early village cock
  Hath twice done salutation to the morn:
  Your friends are up and buckle on their armor.
[KING RICHARD
  O Ratcliffe, I have dreamed a fearful dream!
  What think'st thou? Will our friends prove all true?
RATCLIFFE
  No doubt, my lord.]
KING RICHARD          O Ratcliffe, I fear, I fear!
RATCLIFFE
  Nay, good my lord, be not afraid of shadows.
KING RICHARD
  By the apostle Paul, shadows to-night
  Have struck more terror to the soul of Richard
  Than can the substance of ten thousand soldiers
  Armèd in proof and led by shallow Richmond.
  'Tis not yet near day. Come, go with me.
22 Under our tents I'll play the easedropper,
  To see if any mean to shrink from me.
          *Exeunt Richard and Ratcliffe.*
     *Enter the Lords to Richmond sitting in his tent.*
LORDS
  Good morrow, Richmond.
RICHMOND
25 Cry mercy, lords and watchful gentlemen,
  That you have ta'en a tardy sluggard here.
LORDS
  How have you slept, my lord?
RICHMOND
28 The sweetest sleep, and fairest-boding dreams
  That ever ent'red in a drowsy head
  Have I since your departure had, my lords.
  Methought their souls whose bodies Richard murdered
32 Came to my tent and cried on victory.
33 I promise you my soul is very jocund

In the remembrance of so fair a dream.
How far into the morning is it, lords?
LORDS
  Upon the stroke of four.
RICHMOND
  Why, then 'tis time to arm and give direction.
     *His Oration to his Soldiers.*
  More than I have said, loving countrymen,
  The leisure and enforcement of the time          239
  Forbids to dwell upon. Yet remember this:
  God and our good cause fight upon our side;
  The prayers of holy saints and wrongèd souls,
  Like high-reared bulwarks, stand before our faces.  243
  Richard except, those whom we fight against
  Had rather have us win than him they follow.
  For what is he they follow? Truly, gentlemen,
  A bloody tyrant and a homicide;
  One raised in blood and one in blood established;   248
  One that made means to come by what he hath,       249
  And slaughterèd those that were the means to help him;
  A base foul stone, made precious by the foil       251
  Of England's chair, where he is falsely set;
  One that hath ever been God's enemy.
  Then if you fight against God's enemy,
  God will in justice ward you as his soldiers;      255
  If you do sweat to put a tyrant down,
  You sleep in peace, the tyrant being slain;
  If you do fight against your country's foes,
  Your country's fat shall pay your pains the hire;  259
  If you do fight in safeguard of your wives,
  Your wives shall welcome home the conquerors;
  If you do free your children from the sword,
  Your children's children quits it in your age:     263
  Then in the name of God and all these rights,
  Advance your standards, draw your willing swords.
  For me, the ransom of my bold attempt             266
  Shall be this cold corpse on the earth's cold face;
  But if I thrive, the gain of my attempt
  The least of you shall share his part thereof.
  Sound drums and trumpets boldly and cheerfully:
  God and Saint George! Richmond and victory!
                              *[Exeunt.]*
     *Enter King Richard, Ratcliffe [and Soldiers].*
KING RICHARD
  What said Northumberland as touching Richmond?
RATCLIFFE
  That he was never trainèd up in arms.
KING RICHARD
  He said the truth. And what said Surrey then?
RATCLIFFE
  He smiled and said, 'The better for our purpose.'
KING RICHARD
  He was in the right, and so indeed it is.
          *Clock strikes.*
  Tell the clock there. Give me a calendar.          277
  Who saw the sun to-day?
RATCLIFFE                      Not I, my lord.
KING RICHARD
  Then he disdains to shine; for by the book
  He should have braved the East an hour ago.
  A black day will it be to somebody.
  Ratcliffe!
RATCLIFFE
  My lord?

199 *All ... degree* all kinds of sins, each one practised in all its comparative
stages (e.g. bad, worse, worst; cf. ll. 197–98)  222 *easedropper* eaves-
dropper  225 *Cry mercy* beg pardon  228 *fairest-boding* most propitious
232 *cried on* urged (me) on to  233 *jocund* joyful  239 *leisure* (see l. 98)
243 *bulwarks* defensive ramparts  248 *One ... established* i.e. one who
came to the throne through bloodshed and has held it through further
bloodshed (this is the theme of Richmond's justification for deposing
Richard)  249 *One ... means* i.e. one who did not let events take their
natural course but engineered them to his advantage  251 *foil* metal leaf
(*England's chair* or throne) placed under a jewel (Richard) to make it
appear more brilliant than it is  255 *ward* protect  259 *fat* abundant
fertility  263 *quits* requites  266–67 *the ransom ... face* i.e. (if we fail)
my only ransom (freeing from captivity) will be by death  277 *calendar*
almanac

KING RICHARD  The sun will not be seen to-day;
The sky doth frown and low'r upon our army.
285  I would these dewy tears were from the ground.
Not shine to-day? Why, what is that to me
More than to Richmond? For the selfsame heaven
That frowns on me looks sadly upon him.
    *Enter Norfolk.*

NORFOLK
Arm, arm, my lord; the foe vaunts in the field.

KING RICHARD
290  Come, bustle, bustle! Caparison my horse!
Call up Lord Stanley, bid him bring his power.
I will lead forth my soldiers to the plain,
And thus my battle shall be orderèd:
My foreward shall be drawn out all in length,
Consisting equally of horse and foot;
Our archers shall be placèd in the midst;
John Duke of Norfolk, Thomas Earl of Surrey,
Shall have the leading of this foot and horse.
299  They thus directed, we will follow
300  In the main battle, whose puissance on either side
301  Shall be well wingèd with our chiefest horse.
302  This, and Saint George to boot! What think'st thou,
    Norfolk?

NORFOLK
A good direction, warlike sovereign.
This found I on my tent this morning.
    *[He showeth him a paper.]*
305  'Jockey of Norfolk, be not so bold,
306  For Dickon thy master is bought and sold.'

KING RICHARD
A thing devisèd by the enemy.
308  Go, gentlemen, every man unto his charge.
Let not our babbling dreams affright our souls;
Conscience is but a word that cowards use,
Devised at first to keep the strong in awe:
312  Our strong arms be our conscience, swords our law!
March on, join bravely, let us to it pell-mell,
If not to heaven, then hand in hand to hell.
    *[His Oration to his Army.]*
315  What shall I say more than I have inferred?
316  Remember whom you are to cope withal—
317  A sort of vagabonds, rascals, and runaways,
318  A scum of Britains and base lackey peasants,
Whom their o'ercloyèd country vomits forth
To desperate adventures and assured destruction.
You sleeping safe, they bring to you unrest;
You having lands, and blessed with beauteous wives,
323  They would restrain the one, distain the other.
And who doth lead them but a paltry fellow,
325  Long kept in Britain at our mother's cost,
A milksop, one that never in his life
327  Felt so much cold as over shoes in snow?
Let's whip these stragglers o'er the seas again,
Lash hence these overweening rags of France,
These famished beggars, weary of their lives,
331  Who (but for dreaming on this fond exploit)
332  For want of means (poor rats) had hanged themselves.
If we be conquerèd, let men conquer us,
And not these bastard Britains, whom our fathers
Have in their own land beaten, bobbed, and thumped,
And, in record, left them the heirs of shame.
Shall these enjoy our lands? lie with our wives?
Ravish our daughters?

    *Drum afar off.*      Hark! I hear their drum.
Fight, gentlemen of England! Fight, bold yeomen!
Draw, archers, draw your arrows to the head!
Spur your proud horses hard, and ride in blood!          341
Amaze the welkin with your broken staves!                342
    *Enter a Messenger.*
What says Lord Stanley? Will he bring his power?

MESSENGER
My lord, he doth deny to come.

KING RICHARD
Off with his son George's head!

NORFOLK
My lord, the enemy is past the marsh:
After the battle let George Stanley die.

KING RICHARD
A thousand hearts are great within my bosom!
Advance our standards, set upon our foes.
Our ancient word of courage, fair Saint George,      350
Inspire us with the spleen of fiery dragons!          35▪
Upon them! Victory sits on our helms.    *[Exeunt.]*

*

    *Alarum; excursions. Enter [Norfolk and Forces;*    V,
    *to him] Catesby.*

CATESBY
Rescue, my Lord of Norfolk, rescue, rescue!
The king enacts more wonders than a man,
Daring an opposite to every danger:                      3
His horse is slain, and all on foot he fights,
Seeking for Richmond in the throat of death.
Rescue, fair lord, or else the day is lost!
    *Alarums. Enter [King] Richard.*

KING RICHARD
A horse! a horse! my kingdom for a horse!               7

CATESBY
Withdraw, my lord; I'll help you to a horse.

KING RICHARD
Slave, I have set my life upon a cast,                  9
And I will stand the hazard of the die.               10
I think there be six Richmonds in the field;          11
Five have I slain to-day instead of him.
A horse! a horse! my kingdom for a horse!  *[Exeunt.]*

285 *dewy tears* i.e. morning dew ('tears' because the sky frowns, l. 284)
290 *Caparison* cover with a rich horse-cloth  299 *directed* placed tactically
300 *puissance* force or power  301 *well wingèd . . . horse* i.e. the best horsemen will be well deployed as wings (on either side of the main body of
troops; cf. *main battle*, l. 300)  302 *to boot* as a helper  305 *Jockey*
John or Jack (familiar form)  306 *Dickon* i.e. Richard or Dick (familiar
form)  308–42 *Go . . . staves* (note how Shakespeare is moved imaginatively
by Richard in these lines; cf. the comparative flatness of Richmond's
oration, ll. 238–71)  312 *strong . . . conscience* i.e. might makes right  315
*inferred* reported  316 *cope withal* meet with  317 *sort* band  318 *Britains*
Bretons; *lackey* camp-following  323 *restrain* deprive you of; *distain*
dishonor, sully  325 *Britain* Brittany  327 *over . . . snow* i.e. snow deeper
than shoe level  331 *but for* if it were not for; *fond* foolish  332 *means* the
wherewithal to live  341 *in blood* (1) in full vigor (a hunting term), (2)
smeared with blood from spurring  342 *welkin* sky; *staves* lance shafts
350 *word* battle cry  351 *spleen* fiery temper
V, iv The same  3 *Daring an opposite* offering himself as an opponent
7 *A horse . . . horse* (cf. *The True Tragedie of Richard III:* 'A horse, a
horse, a fresh horse.' It seems likely that Shakespeare derived his famous
line from this rather flat hint.)  9 *cast* throw (of the dice)  10 *die* (singular
of dice)  11 *six Richmonds* i.e. in addition to Richmond, five other men
dressed and armed to resemble Richmond (a common safety measure)

**, v**

*Alarum. Enter [King] Richard and Richmond ; they*
*fight ; Richard is slain. Retreat and flourish.*
*Enter Richmond, [Lord Stanley Earl of] Derby,*
*bearing the crown, with divers other Lords.*

RICHMOND
God and your arms be praised, victorious friends !
The day is ours ; the bloody dog is dead.

DERBY
Courageous Richmond, well hast thou acquit thee.
Lo, here this long usurpèd royalty
From the dead temples of this bloody wretch
Have I plucked off, to grace thy brows withal.
Wear it, enjoy it, and make much of it.

RICHMOND
Great God of heaven, say amen to all !
But tell me, is young George Stanley living ?

DERBY
He is, my lord, and safe in Leicester town,
Whither, if it please you, we may now withdraw us.

RICHMOND
What men of name are slain on either side ?

DERBY
John Duke of Norfolk, Walter Lord Ferrers,
Sir Robert Brakenbury, and Sir William Brandon.

RICHMOND
Inter their bodies as become their births.
Proclaim a pardon to the soldiers fled
That in submission will return to us ;
And then, as we have ta'en the sacrament,          18
We will unite the White Rose and the Red.          19
Smile heaven upon this fair conjunction,          20
That long have frowned upon their enmity !
What traitor hears me, and says not amen ?
England hath long been mad and scarred herself ;
The brother blindly shed the brother's blood ;
The father rashly slaughtered his own son ;          25
The son, compelled, been butcher to the sire :
All this divided York and Lancaster,
Divided in their dire division,
O, now let Richmond and Elizabeth,
The true succeeders of each royal house,
By God's fair ordinance conjoin together !
And let their heirs (God, if thy will be so)
Enrich the time to come with smooth-faced peace,
With smiling plenty, and fair prosperous days !
Abate the edge of traitors, gracious Lord,          35
That would reduce these bloody days again          36
And make poor England weep in streams of blood !
Let them not live to taste this land's increase
That would with treason wound this fair land's peace !
Now civil wounds are stopped, peace lives again :
That she may long live here, God say amen !

                                        *Exeunt.*

V, v  **s.d.** *Retreat* a trumpet signal for Richard's men to retire  18 *as
. . . sacrament* (referring to the oath, taken by Richmond in the cathedral
at Rheims, that he would marry Princess Elizabeth as soon as he was
possessed of the crown)  19 *White Rose . . . Red* i.e. the badges of the
Yorkist and Lancastrian factions respectively ; the marriage of Richmond
(Lancastrian) and Princess Elizabeth (Yorkist) will bring an end to the
so-called Wars of the Roses (see ll. 27–31)  20 *conjunction* marriage union
(with play on the astrological meaning : the Sun [the king symbol : Rich-
mond] and Venus [Elizabeth] will be 'in conjunction,' i.e. in the same sign of
the zodiac at the same time)  25–26 *The father . . . sire* (Shakespeare
seems to be recalling *3 Henry VI*, II, v)  35 *Abate the edge* i.e. blunt the
sharpness (of traitors' swords)  36 *reduce* bring back

## APPENDIX : THE QUARTO AND FOLIO TEXTS

As pointed out in the "Note on the text," the textual problems
involved in *Richard III* are extremely complex and no completely
satisfactory agreement among textual critics has yet been reached.
The fact that the greater part of the first folio (1623) text is probably printed from a copy of Quarto 6 (1622) which had been corrected against a manuscript (possibly Shakespeare's autograph or
a "fair copy" of Shakespeare's autograph) opens the way to many
possibilities of corruption. First, the person (or persons) responsible for collating the manuscript with Quarto 6 seems to have
been erratic in the care with which he executed his task. Second,
two substantial stretches of text (III, i, 1–158, and V, iii, 48 to
end), in all about 500 lines, appear to have been printed directly
from an uncorrected copy of Quarto 3 (1602). Third, Quarto 1
(1597), from which the succeeding seven quartos derive in a
mounting spiral of compositorial error and unauthoritative emendation, is generally accepted as a memorially reported text and
hence of uncertain authority in all its readings. It will thus be seen
that the first folio text may be considered open to question at
almost every point ; nevertheless, because it shows evidence of
authoritative correction from a manuscript source and because it
contains a substantial number of unique lines, it remains the best
extant text of the play and has been used as the basis of the present
edition.

In the passages unique to the first folio we come closer perhaps
to Shakespeare's original and unadulterated text than in any other
parts of the play. They have, therefore, a special interest. The
following is a complete list of these passages (single words and
phrases not included) :

I, ii, 16, 25, 155–66  I, iii, 115, 166–68, 353–54 ('straight . . .

lord')  I, iv, 28, 36–37 ('and . . . ghost'), 69–72, 84, 98–99
('Fare you well'), 112–13, 129 ("Tis no matter'), 165, 211,
252–55, 261, 263
II, i, 25, 141  II, ii, 16, 89–100, 123–40  II, iii, 6 ('Give . . . sir')
II, iv, 67
III, i, 172–73  III, ii, 112, 123 ('I'll . . . lordship')  III, iii, 7–8,
16  III, iv, 102–05  III, v, 7, 97 ('and . . . adieu'), 103–05
III, vii, 5–6, 8, 11, 24 ('they . . . word'), 37, 82 ('Here . . .
again'), 98–99, 120, 127, 144–53, 202, 245
IV, i, 2–6, 14 ('and . . . York'), 36, 97–103  IV, ii, 2, 41 ('I . . .
man'), 45 ('Well, be it so')  IV, iii, 35 ('I . . . leave')  IV, iv,
20–21, 28, 52–53, 103, 160, 173, 180 ('Strike . . . drum'),
222–35, 276–77 ('which . . . body'), 288–342, 387 ('What . . .
now'), 400, 429, 432, 443–44 ('I will . . . hither'), 452
V, iii, 27–28, 43

Stated generally, the theory on which the present text has been
constructed is as follows. Taking the first folio text as a basis,
the readings of the folio text have been preferred to those of the
quarto texts (in most cases only Quarto 1 is concerned) except
(1) where the folio text follows readings of Quartos 2–6 in prefer-
ence to the reading of Quarto 1 (the inference is that, since the
readings of the later quartos are without authority, the corrector
of the copy for the first folio, working probably for the most part
with a copy of Quarto 6, has failed to correct his text at these
points and that we, therefore, approach more nearly to Shakespeare's original by reverting to Quarto 1) ; (2) where the folio
text (at III, i, 1–158, and V, iii, 48 to end) is apparently printed
directly from an uncorrected copy of Quarto 3, since in these passages Quarto 1, equivocal though it may be, must be considered

as the basic text (the folio readings for these two sections of the text are recorded in the textual notes); (3) where the folio text omits passages or words in Quarto 1 which are so excellent that they stand on their own merits (e.g. IV, ii, 97–115) or are necessary for the meaning (the additional passages supplied from Quarto 1 have been placed in square brackets and are not otherwise recorded in the textual notes, whereas additions of one or two words are unbracketed but are recorded); (4) where the folio text is manifestly in error (e.g. see the textual note at II, i, 68). This is the theory, but in practice some editorial judgment in the choice of readings has still to be admitted.

In the following textual notes all significant variations from the first folio text (1623) have been recorded, but no attempt has been made to set up a complete textual apparatus in terms of the eight quarto and four folio editions. The student will find such an apparatus in either the "Cambridge Shakespeare" (1892) or the New Variorum *Richard III* (1909). The abbreviations here used are : F = the folios of 1623, 1632, 1664, 1685. Where the folios do not agree among themselves the reading of F1 (= the first folio) has been given; the readings of the later folios, whether one or more may agree with F1, have not been recorded. Q = the six quartos of 1597, 1598, 1602, 1605, 1612, 1622 (the last two quartos of 1629 and 1634 are of no concern here). Where there is disagreement among the quartos the reading of Q1 (= Quarto 1) has been given, but this distinction is not intended to exclude the possible agreement of some of the remaining five quartos with Q1. In a majority of cases where a Q1 reading has been preferred to a F1 reading, the F1 reading represents a reading inherited from Quartos 2–6. QF = agreement of the first six quartos and the four folios. Eds = emendation by editors of Shakespeare from Nicholas Rowe (1709) to the present day. Significant readings in the quartos for which there is no general equivalent in the folio text and which have not otherwise been included as part of the present edition are also recorded in the textual notes.

Stage directions or parts of stage directions enclosed in square brackets have been added either from Q1 or from Rowe and later editors and are not recorded in the textual notes. In III, i, 1–158, and V, iii, 48 to end, where the copy-text is basically Q1, the stage directions of F1 have still been preferred to those of Q1, and Q1 stage directions bracketed as elsewhere. The usage of *u* and *v* has been modernized in the QF readings, and a grave accent has been added in some QF readings to clarify the pronunciation of the final -*èd*. Throughout the adopted reading is in italics.

I, i, 38 *up* (Q.subs.) up : (F)   41 s.d. *Clarence guarded* (Eds) Clarence with a gard of men (Q) Clarence, and Brakenbury, guarded (F)   45 *the* (Q) th' (F)   52 *for* (Q) but (F)   64 *she* (Q subs.) shee. (F1)   65 *tempers . . . extremity* (Q1) tempts him to this harsh Extremity (F)   71 *is secure* (Eds) is securde (Q1) secure (F)   75 *Lord . . . delivery* (Q adds 'to her' after *was*)   his (Q) her (F1)   88 *so?* (Eds) so (Q) so, (F)   95 *gentlefolks* (Q1) gentle Folkes (F1)   101–02 *Brakenbury. What . . . betray me?* (first appears in Q2, 1598)   124 *the* (Q1) this (F)   133 *prey* (Q) play (F)

I, ii, 27 *life* (Eds ; cf. IV, i, 75) death (QF)   39 *Stand* (Q) Stand'st (F1)   78 *a* (Q) Omitted (F)   80 *t'accuse* (Eds) to curse (QF)   102 *hedgehog?* (Eds) hedgehogge (Q) Hedgehogge, (F)   138 *thee* (Q) the (F)   141 *He lives . . . could* (Q adds 'Go to,' before *He*)   195 *was man* (Q1) man was (F)   201 *Vouchsafe . . . ring* (given to Anne in F ; here assigned as in Q)   235 *at all* (Q1) withall (F)

I, iii, 17 *come the lords* (Q1) comes the Lord (F)   68 *he . . . ground* (F) thereby he may gather / The ground of your ill will and to remove it (Q1)   101 *Iwis* (Q1) I wis (F)   141 *childish-foolish* (Eds) childish, foolish (Q1) childish foolish (F)   159 *of* (Q) off (F1)   214 *with'red* (Q1) wither'd (F)   246 *False-boding* (Eds) false boading (QF)   287 *gentle-sleeping* (Eds) gentle sleeping (QF)   303 *Buckingham* (F) Hast. (Q)   308 *Queen Elizabeth* (Eds) Qu. (Q1) Hast. (Q6) Mar. (F1)   341, 349 *1. Murderer* (Eds) Execu. (Q) Vil. (F)   343 *Well . . . about me* (Q precedes *Well* with 'It was')   350 *doers. Be* (F4) doers be (Q1) dooers, be (F1)   354 *1. Murderer* (Eds) Vil. (F) Speech omitted (Q)

I, iv, s.d. *Keeper* (Keeper's role is given to Brakenbury in Q)   13 *thence* (Q1) there (F)   22 *waters* (Q1) water (F)   48 *stranger soul* (Q) Stranger-soule (F)   58 *methoughts* (Q1) me thought (F)   68 *requites* (Q) requits (F1)   86 *1. Murderer* (Eds) Execu. (Q)   2. Mur. (F)   89 *2. Murderer* (Eds) 2 Exe. (Q) 1. (F)   100 *I* (Q1) we (F)   103 *Why, he* (Q reads 'When he wakes, / Why foole he')   110–11 *warrant can* (Q adds 'for it' after *warrant*)   120 *Faith* (Q) Omitted (F)   124 *Zounds* (Q) Come (F)   131 *I'll not . . . with it* (Q adds 'it is a dangerous thing' after *it*)   138 *It is turned . . . towns* (Q adds 'all' before *towns*)   141 *Zounds* (Q) Omitted (F)   146 *I am strong-framed* (Q adds 'Tut' before *I am*)   *strong-framed* (Eds) strong in fraud (Q) strong fram'd (F)   146 *he cannot prevail . . . me* (Q adds 'I warrant thee' after *me*)   153–54 *Soft! . . . Strike!* (Q reads '1 Harke he stirs, shall I strike.')   166 *Who . . . come* (Q reads 'Tell me who are you, wherefore come you thither)   167 *Both* (Eds) Am. (Q) 2 (F)   184–85 *to have . . . sins* (Q) for any goodnesse (F)   208 *He sends . . . this* (Q adds 'Why sirs' before *He*)   216 *gallant-springing* (Eds) gallant springing (QF)   221 *O, if you* (Q) If you do (F)   234 *of* (Q) on (F)   235 *lessoned* (Q1) lessonèd (F)   261 *As . . . distress* (after l. 255 in F ; omitted in Q)   265 *drown . . . within* (Q reads 'chop thee in the malmesey But, in the next roome')   270 *heavens* (Q1) Heaven (F)

II, i, s.d. (F adds 'Woodvill' in repetition of *Rivers*)   5 *in* (Q) to (F)   7 *Hastings and Rivers* (Eds) Rivers and Hastings (Q) Dorset and Rivers (F)   28 *And so swear I* (Q adds 'my Lord' after *I*)   39 *God* (Q) heaven (F)   46 *comes . . . duke* (Q reads 'comes the noble Duke')   52 *wrong-incensèd* (Eds) wrong insencèd (QF)   57 *unwittingly* (Q) unwillingly (F ; i.e. unintentionally, possibly the true reading)   59 *By* (Q) To (F)   68 *That, all . . . frowned on me* (F follows this line with 'Of you Lord Woodvill, and Lord Scales of you' ; both names are titles of Rivers, already referred to in l. 67)   82 *King Edward* (F) Ryv. (Q)   93 *but* (Q) and (F)   108 *at* (Q) and (F1)   117 *Even . . . give himself* (Q1 adds 'owne' before *garments*)

II, ii, 1 *Boy* (Q) Edw. (F)   3 *Girl* (Eds) Daugh. (F ; throughout) Boy (Q)   47 *I* (Q) Omitted (F)   83 *weep* (Q) weepes (F1)   86 *distressed,* (Q1) distrest: (F1)   112 *cloudy princes* (Q) clowdy-Princes (F)   *heart-sorrowing peers* (Q1) hart-sorrowing-Peeres (F)   142, 154 *Ludlow* (Q) London (F)   144 *To give . . . business* (Q adds 'waighty' before *business*)   145 *Both* (Eds) Ans. (Q ; speech omitted in F)

II, iii, 8 *Ay, sir . . . true* (Q reads '1 It doth.')   32 *wise men* (Q) wisemen (F1)   43 *Ensuing* (Q) Pursuing (F ; catchword 'Ensuing' in F1)

II, iv, 1 *hear* (Q1) heard (F)   21 *Archbishop* (Eds) Car. (Q) Yor. (F)   38 *Here . . . news?* (Q reads 'Here comes your sonne, Lo : M. Dorset. / What newes Lo : Marques ?)   65 *death* (Q) earth (F)

III, i, 8 *dived* (F) divèd (Q)   9 *Nor* (Q) No (F)   40 *God in heaven* (Q1) God (F)   43 *deep* (Q1) great (F)   44 *senseless-obstinate* (Eds) sencelesse obstinate (QF)   51 *claimed . . . deserved* (F) claimèd . . . deservèd (Q)   56 *never* (Q) ne're (F)   57 *overrule* (Q) o're-rule (F)   60 s.d. *Exeunt* (Eds) Exit (Q3, F)   63 *seems* (Q1) thinkst (F)   71 *since, succeeding* (F) since succeeding (Q)   78 *all-ending* (Q1) ending (F)   82 *Vice, Iniquity* (F) vice iniquity (Q1)   86 *valor* (Q) valure (Q1)   87 *this* (Q1) his (F)   96 *loving* (Q1) noble (F)   97 *dread* (Q1) deare (F)   98 *brother – to* (Eds) brother to (Q1) brother, to (F)   111 *With all* (F) withall (Q1)   120 *heavy* (Q1) weightie (F)   123 *as* (Q1) as, as (F1)   132 *sharp-provided* (Eds) sharpe provided (QF)   133–34 *uncle, . . . himself :* (F) Unckle : . . . himselfe, (Q1)   141 *needs* (Q1) Omitted (F)   145 *grandam* (Eds) Granam (Q)   *murd'red* (Q) murther'd (F)   149 *with* (Q) and with (F)   150 s.d. *Hastings* (Eds) Hast. Dors. (Q) Hastings, and Dorset (F ; Dorset has not been present in the scene)   s.d. *Manent* (F2) manet (Q, F1)   171–74 *purpose . . . us* (Q reads 'purpose, if he be willing')

III, ii, 2 *Who knocks* (Q adds 'at the dore' after *knocks*)   3 s.d. *Enter Lord Hastings* (after l. 5 in F)   41 *How! . . . garland!* (Eds) Howe? . . . garland? (Q1) How . . . Garland? (F)   *Dost* (F3) Doest (Q, F1)   60 *Well . . . older* (Q reads 'I tell thee Catesby. Cat. What my Lord? / Hast. Ere a fortnight make me elder') 78 *you do* (Q) Omitted (F) 89–91 *What . . . lords* (Q reads 'But come my Lo: shall we to the tower? *Hast.* I go: but stay, heare you not the newes, / This day those men') 91 *talked* (Q1) talke (F) 95 *Go . . . fellow* (Q reads 'Go you before, Ile follow presently') s.d. *Exeunt* (Eds) Exit (Q3, F) 96 *How now, sirrah* (Q reads 'Well met Hastings') 108–09 *Priest. Well . . . heart* (Q reads '*Hast.* What Sir Iohn, you are wel met')

III, iv, 10 *We know . . . hearts* (In Q Buckingham precedes this line with 'Who I my Lo?') 31 *My . . . when* (Q reads '*Hast.* I thanke your Grace. / *Glo.* My Lo: of Elie, *Bish.* My Lo: / *Glo.* When) 34 *Marry . . . heart* (Q reads 'I go my Lord') 79 s.d. *Manent* (F2) manet (Q, F1) 82 *rase* (Q) rowse (F) *our helms* (F) his helme (Q; perhaps correctly) 83 *But* (Q) And (F)

III, v, 5 *Tut . . . tragedian* (Q adds 'feare not me' after *Tut*) 12–14 *But . . . Mayor* – (Q reads '*Glo.* Here comes the Maior. / *Buc.* Let me alone to entertaine him. Lo: Maior,') 20 *innocence* (Q1) Innocencie (F) 21 *Be . . . Lovel.* (Q reads 'O, O, be quiet, it is Catesby.' with Lovel's following speech given to Catesby) 34 *Look . . . Mayor* (from Q, where it follows l. 26) 50–51 *I never . . . Shore* (assigned to Mayor in Q) 66 *cause* (Q1) case (F) 74 *meet'st advantage* (Q1) meetest vantage (F) 102 *Look for . . . affords* (Q adds 'and so my Lord farewell' after *affords*) 104 *Penker* (Eds) Peuker (F1) Omitted (Q) 105 s.d. *Exeunt* (Eds) Exit (F, Omitted Q) 109 s.d. *Exit* (Q) Exeunt (F1)

III, vi, 12 *who's* (Q1) who (F)

III, vii, 20 *mine* (Q1) my (F) *to an* (Q1) toward (F) 33 *spake* (Q1) spoke (F) 40 *wisdoms* (Q1) wisdome (F) 52 *I . . . plead* (Q reads 'Feare not me, if thou canst pleade') 55–56 *Go . . . lord* (Q reads 'You shal see what I can do, get you up to the leads. Exit. / Now my L. Maior,') 58 *Now . . . request?* (Q reads 'Here coms his servant: how now Catesby what saies he.') 83 *My lord* (Q) Omitted (F) 125 *her* (Q1) his (F) 126 *Her* (Q) His (F) 127 *Her* (Eds) His (F; line omitted in Q) 131–32 *charge . . . land* (Q reads 'soveraingtie thereof') 219 *Zounds, I'll* (Q) we will (F) 222 *If . . . it* (Q reads '*Ano.* Doe, good my lord, least all the land do rew it) 247 *cousin* (Q) Cousins (F)

IV, i, 2–7 *Led . . . away* (Q reads 'Sister well met, whether awaie so fast') 14 *How . . . York* (Q reads 'How fares the Prince') 16 *them* (F) him (Q) 18 *The king . . . Protector* (Q adds 'I crie you mercie' before *mean*) 28 *an* (Q1) one (F) 30 *looker-on* (Eds) looker on (QF)

IV, ii, 13 *liege* (Q) Lord (F) 36 *I know . . . gentleman* (Q precedes this line with 'My lord') 42 *deep-revolving* (Eds) deepe revolving (QF) 48 *To Richmond . . . abides* (Q adds 'beyond the seas' after *parts*) 49 *Come hither, Catesby.* (Q reads 'Catesby. Cat.* My lord.') 71 *there* (Q) then (F) 81 *I . . . straight* (Q1 reads 'Tis done my gracious lord. / *King* Shal we heare from thee Tirrel ere we sleep? / *Tir.* Ye shall my lord' – apparently a memorial slip repeating III, i, 188–89) 89 *Hereford* (F2) Herford (Q) Hertford (F1) 104 *called* (Eds) callèd (Q) 116–17 *May . . . Thou* (Q reads 'Whie then resolve me whether you wil or no? / *King.* Tut, tut, thou') 117 s.d. *Exeunt* (Eds) Exit (QF)

IV, iii, 5 *ruthless* (Q1) ruthfull (F) 7 *kind* (Q1) milde (F) 8 *to* (F) two (Q) 13 *Which* (Q1) And (F) 15 *once* (Q) one (F) 27 *For it is done* (Q adds 'my Lord' after *done*) 31 *at* (Q) and (F) 33 *thee* (Q) the (F1) 50 *rash-levied* (Eds) rash levied (QF) 53 *leads* (Q) leds (F1)

IV, iv, 10 *unblown* (Q) unblowed (F1) *new-appearing* (Eds) new appearing (QF) 17–19 *Duchess of York. So . . . dead?* (after l. 34 in Q) 26 *mortal-living* (Eds) mortal living (QF) 41 *Harry* (Eds) Richard (Q) Husband (F) 45 *holp'st* (Q3) hopst (Q1, F1) 52 *That excellent . . . earth* (follows l. 53 in F; both lines omitted in Q) 64 *Thy* (Q) The (F) 70 *smoth'red* (Q1) smother'd (F) 86 *a-high* (Eds) a high (QF) 100–01 *For one . . . with care* (Q reverses order of lines) 103 *feared* (Eds) fearèd (F) 112 *weary* (Q1) wearied (F) 118 *nights . . . days* (Q1) night . . . day (F) 128 *intestate* (Q) intestine (F) 132 *so, then* (Q) so then, (F1) 141 *Where* (Q) Where't (F) 147–48 *Where . . . Hastings* (Q reads 'Where is kind Hastings, Rivers, Vaughan, Gray') 180–81 *I prithee . . . bitterly* (Q reads 'O heare me speake for I shal never see thee more. / *King.* Come, come, you are too

bitter') 200 *moe* (Q1) more (F) 239 *or* (Q1) and (F) 241 *discovered* (Q1) discoverèd (F) 266 *should be else* (Q1) else should bee (F) 268 *would I* (Q1) I would (F) 274 *sometimes* (Q1) sometime (F) 276 *handkercher* (Q1) hand-kercheefe (F) 284 *is* (Q) Omitted (F1) 324 *Of ten times* (Eds) Of ten-times (F1) Often-times (F2) 344 *still-lasting* (Eds) still lasting (QF) 365 *Harp . . . break* (follows l. 363 in F; order here from Q1) 368 *swear* – (Eds) sweare by nothing. (Q) sweare. (F) 377 *God – / God's* (Q) Heaven. / Heanens (F) 392 *in* (Q1) with (F) 396 *o'erpast* (Q) repast (F) 417 *peevish-fond* (Eds) peevish, fond (Q1) peevish found (F) 431 *shallow, changing* (Eds) shallow changing (Q) shallow-changing (F) s.d. *Enter Ratcliffe* (as in Q, which omits l. 432; comes after l. 432 in F) 444 *Ratcliffe* (Eds) Catesby (F) Omitted (Q) 457 *None good,* (F4) None good (Q) None, good (F1) 494 *Go then . . . behind* (Q adds 'heare you' after *But*) 507 *you* (Q1) ye (F) 509–10 *The news . . . waters* (Q reads 'Your grace mistakes, the newes I bring is good, / My newes is that by sudden floud, and fall of water') 513–14 *I cry . . . thine* (Q reads 'O I crie you mercie, I did mistake, / Ratcliffe reward him, for the blow I gave him') 534 *tidings* (Q1) Newes (F)

IV, v, 10 *Ha'rford-West* (Q) Hertford West (F)

V, i, 11 *my lord* (Q) Omitted (F)

V, iii, 2 *My Lord of Surrey* (Q reads 'Whie, how now Catesbie' with next speech-prefix '*Cat*,') 4 *My . . . liege* (Q reads 'Norffolke, come hether') 28 *you* (F2) your (F1) 46 *In to* (Q1) Into (F) 48 *nine* (F) sixe (Q) 54 *sentinels* (F) centinell (Q) 58 *Catesby* (Q) Ratcliffe (F) 59 *Catesby* (Eds) Rat. (QF) 61 *sun-rising* (F) sun rising (Q1) 65–66 *heavy. / Ratcliffe* (F) heavy Ratcliffe (Q1) 68 *thou* (Q) Omitted (F) 80 *sit* (F) set (Q1) 83 *loving* (Q1) Noble (F)· 86 *that. The* (F) that the (Q1) 90 *the* (Q) th' (F) 91 *mortal-staring* (Eds) mortal staring (QF) 101 *sund'red* (Q) sundried (Q1) 102 *rites* (F) rights (Q) 105 *thoughts* (Q) noise (F) 113 *The* (Q) Th' (F) 115 *the* (Q1) thy (F) 123 *butcherèd* (Q1) butcher'd (F) 126 *deadly* (Q1) Omitted (F) 127 *me: despair* (F) me despaire (Q1) 131 *thy* (Q) Omitted (F) *sleep: live* (F) sleepe live (Q1) 132 *sit* (F) set (Q1) 146 *Will* (F) Wel (Q1) 151 s.d. *Enter . . . young Princes* (in Q1 the ghosts of the two young princes precede the ghost of Hastings; the F order is that of the time of their deaths, as in Q3) 155 *souls bid* (Q) soule bids (F1) 162 *perturbations* (F) preturbations (Q1) 177 *falls* (Q) fall (F) 181 *now* (Q1) not (F) 183 *What . . . fear? Myself?* (Q1) What? . . . feare my Selfe? (F) 184 *am* (F) and (Q1) 186 *reason why* – (Eds) reason whie (Q1) reason: why? (F) 197 *perjury* (Q1) Omitted (F) *highest* (Q) high'st (F) 198 *direst* (Q) dyr'st (F) 200 *Throng* (Q1) Throng all (F) *the* (Q) th' (F) 202 *will* (Q1) shall (F) 203 *And* (Q) Nay (F) 209 *Zounds, who is* (Q) Who's (F) 223 *see* (Q1) heare (F) 228 *fairest-boding* (Eds) fairest boding (Q) 233 *soul* (F) Heart (F) 243 *high-reared* (Eds) high reard (QF) 244 *Richard except,* (Q3) Richard, except (Q1) (Richard except) (F) 248 *established* (F) establishèd (Q) 250 *slaughterèd* (Q) slaughter'd (F) 251 *foil* (Q1) soile (F) 256 *sweat* (Q1) sweare (F) 271 s.d. *Ratcliffe [and Soldiers]* (Eds) Rat, &c. (Q) Ratcliffe, and Catesby (F) 275 *smiled* (F) smilèd (Q) 281–82 *somebody. / Ratcliffe!* (F1) some bodie Rat. (Q) 293 *orderèd* (Q) ordred (F) 294 *out all* (Q1) Omitted (F) 298 *this* (Q1) the (F) 301 *well wingèd* (Q) well-wingèd (F1) 302 *boot* (F) bootes (Q1) 308 *unto* (Q) to (F) 310 *Conscience is but* (Q1) For Conscience is (F) 312 *conscience, swords* (F) conscience swords, (Q1) 313 *to it* (Q) too't (F) 321 *to you* (Q1) you to (F) 322 *wives* (Q1) wifes (Q1) 326 *milksop* (F) milkesopt (Q1) 336 *in* (Q1) on (F) 339 *Fight* (Q1) Right (F) *bold* (Q1) boldly (F) 352 *them! Victory* (Eds) them victorie (Q1) them, Victorie (F) *helms* (Q1) helpes (F1)

V, v, 4 *this . . . royalty* (Q1) these long usurped Royalties (F) 7 *enjoy it* (Q1) Omitted (F) 11 *if it please . . . now* (Q) (if you please) we may (F) 13 *Derby* (F; speech printed as s.d. in Q) *Walter Lord Ferrers* (Eds) Water Lord Ferris (Q1) Walter Lord Ferris (F) 25 *slaughtered* (Q1) slaughterèd (F1) 28 *division,* (Eds) devision. (QF) 32 *their* (Q1) thy (F) 33 *smooth-faced* (F1) smooth-faste (Q1)

# THE LIFE AND DEATH OF KING JOHN

## INTRODUCTION

*King John* is not only a powerful and moving drama in its own right, but it is particularly interesting for the insight it affords into Shakespeare's development as a dramatic artist, since it occupies a pivotal position in relation to his history plays as well as his tragedies. As a history play, it reveals Shakespeare's mastery of techniques he had employed in the looser, more episodic *Henry VI* plays and *Richard III*, and his experimentation with techniques he was to master in *Richard II* and the *Henry IV* plays. As a tragedy, it is interesting for its conception of a hero frustrated by a sin which he repents but cannot cancel, doomed to destruction by his commitment to evil means in striving for great ends. With such a view of man Shakespeare had dealt in the earlier *Titus Andronicus*, and he was to return to it with greater power in such plays as *Julius Caesar* and *Coriolanus*. As Shakespeare's revision of *The Troublesome Reign of John*, an anonymous two-part play printed in 1591, *King John* enables us to see how Shakespeare could shape the crude matter of an unpalatable source play into a sophisticated and original work of art.

History and tragedy are closely fused in *King John*, for the hero is destroyed by complicity in the death of Arthur, son of his elder brother Geoffrey, and thus with a better claim to the throne than his own. The king's sin is dictated by political necessity, for Arthur's claim can lead only to perpetual civil war; and Arthur stands, moreover, for the power of Rome, supported by France and Austria. The opposing political forces are clearly aligned at the beginning of the play : John and the Bastard stand for English nationalism and royal supremacy, while Arthur stands for a divided England, prey to invading foreign forces and subject to the power of the papacy. John represents principles dear to Tudor Englishmen, and his cause must triumph, but Shakespeare, in his usual manner, tempers the emotional commitment of his audience to the Tudor political position by his portrait of the cruel Queen Elinor and by causing this position to demand the death of a child, as he similarly heightens sympathy for Arthur by his portrait of the pathetic Constance. The tragedy of King John is that to attain political victory he must sacrifice his own humanity. He is destroyed by a cleavage between his public and private morality, just as a similar division in a somewhat later play is to destroy the noble Brutus of *Julius Caesar*.

Unfortunately there is no external evidence of any kind as to the date of *King John*, but its stylistic relation to the plays which clearly preceded it and to those which seem to have followed it would suggest that it was written sometime between 1592 and 1596, with 1594 perhaps most likely. It follows *The Troublesome Reign* closely, although it tempers the virulent anti-Catholicism of the source, omitting the most offensive scenes, perhaps – as has been suggested – out of deference to the Catholic Earl of Southampton whose patronage Shakespeare was seeking. It has been suggested in recent years that the play may have been written as early as 1590, based directly on Holinshed's *Chronicles*, Foxe's *Book of Martyrs*, the *Historia Maior* of Matthew Paris, and several Latin chronicles which could have been available to Shakespeare only in manuscript. This theory would hold further that *The Troublesome Reign*, printed in 1591, is not Shakespeare's source, but rather a corrupt version (bad quarto) of a play written in imitation of Shakespeare's some months later in the same year of 1590. Were this theory sustained, we would have to reconsider many of our views of *King John*, but it has won little acceptance among scholars, since it is based upon very tenuous "evidence" involving hypotheses more difficult to entertain than the simpler one that *The Troublesome Reign* was the earlier of the two plays and Shakespeare's source.

*King John* would have been "timely" whatever its date, since it deals with political issues which had come to be associated by Tudor historians with the reign of its titular character ; we must remember that a very important value of history in Shakespeare's day was its power to teach political lessons, and that Shakespeare was, to some extent, bound in this play by the view of King John which had been shaped before him by Protestant chroniclers and by the political issues which they had found inherent in his story. We must note that a central issue of the play (as of its source) – the relation of England to the church of Rome – was also the most pressing political problem of Shakespeare's England, and that many Elizabethan writers were particularly interested in King John because they saw his reign as parallel in many respects to that of their own queen.

Although the early British historians, right through the humanist Polydore Vergil, had been fairly harsh in their treatment of King John, with the Reformation we note a change. William Tyndale in 1528 accused the chronicles of distortion and praised John for his opposition to the papacy. Tyndale was followed in this by John Bale, a fiery Reformation polemicist, who in the following decade wrote a two-part morality play called *Kynge Johan* in which he used John's career to champion the cause of the Reformation. King John was similarly eulogized by the reformer John Foxe in his *Book of Martyrs*, and this Protestant view was adopted by chroniclers such as Richard Grafton and Raphael Holinshed, upon whose works *The Troublesome Reign* was based ; and they were works Shakespeare undoubtedly read also before revising the old play. These writers, with little regard for historical fact, had made King John into a pre-Reformation hero, a king before Henry VIII who had dared oppose the papacy. He was not the tyrannical signer of *Magna Carta* whom we know. Indeed, *Magna Carta* receives no mention in this play, for it was regarded by Shakespeare's contemporaries not as a triumph for liberty, but rather as a shameful attempt to weaken the central monarchy in which most Elizabethans firmly believed, and whose virtues they saw reflected in the absolute rule of Queen Elizabeth. John to them was rather the symbol of English nationalism who had rallied the dissident barons against France and Austria, as well as the champion of royal supremacy who had defied the papal legate and died a martyr, poisoned by a treacherous monk, although historically King John appears to have died of overeating.

Shakespeare's play is informed by this view of King John, and like its source it asserts the doctrines which John's career commonly was called upon to illustrate: nationalism, royal supremacy, the evils of rebellion, and the right of a king to be answerable for his sins to God alone. But more than anything else – and here Shakespeare goes beyond his sources and reveals his own particular bent – the play affirms the inseparability of public and private virtue, that only a good man can be a good king. It asserts also that a nation can be united only when a king has learned to subordinate his personal desires to the good of his country. These themes are carried in the parallel progressions of King John and the Bastard, Faulconbridge, two characters created as foils to one another: the Bastard strong where John is weak, and learning to rise and reestablish the glory of England as John declines and lets it fall. By their relation to one another the play is unified. When the Bastard surrenders his power to the new king in the final act, the audience sees that the goal of national unity which John had vainly sought has in fact been realized. John the man has been destroyed, but England, through the Bastard, is nevertheless triumphant.

Shakespeare makes clear that John is a usurper, but he establishes also that until the death of Arthur, John is a good, even a great, king, and that as the *de facto* ruler he merits the support of the nobility, a political point to be made again in the *Henry IV* plays. Arthur's inadequacy is emphasized by his own weakness and by the forces with whom he is associated. He stands also for the kind of child king which Tudor Englishmen conventionally mirrored in the unfortunate Henry VI, and such as they feared most among the possible successors to the now old and ailing Queen Elizabeth. John's greatness appears in his defiance of the French ambassador and the papal legate, in his victory before Angiers, and in the love and loyalty with which he is served by Faulconbridge, one of the most remarkable creations of Shakespeare's early career, a character so dear to audiences that some critics have been tempted to see him as the hero of the play, although to do so is to distort *King John* and destroy its unity.

John is the hero, and his greatness is emphasized up to the middle of the third act. He begins to degenerate both as man and as king when in III, iii he calls for the murder of Arthur. The Bastard, conversely, wins little triumph until the beginning of John's decline. At the beginning of the play he is fairly low on Fortune's wheel, a landless bastard, albeit the son of Coeur-de-lion, bearing the moral stigma of his illegitimacy, which he affirms proudly in spite of his mother's shame. He has a straightforward heartiness and charm which immediately win us to him, but he has little initial claim to virtue. Only as John declines does the Bastard's moral stature begin to be evident, becoming more and more clear until he is ready to assume the leadership of England which John, because of his own sin, can no longer bear.

The role of Constance is relatively brief, but historically it has been prized by actresses and has been performed by some of the greatest, although her savage interchange with Queen Elinor usually has been omitted on the stage. She is the last of Shakespeare's wailing women, bridging the gap between the weeping queens of *Richard III* and the queen of *Richard II*, with her gentle, more controlled, and finally more moving sorrow. The lamentations of Constance may disturb modern audiences by their excess, but they are Shakespeare's dramatic means of swaying the sympathies of his audience away from King John in the third act, and when this has been accomplished Constance drops out of the play. The alienation of the audience from John is completed in the scene, almost too painful to be staged, in which Arthur pleads with Hubert for his eyes. We now behold the fall of John and the collapse of his power as Hubert shows his inability to execute his commission and as England's enemies prepare their forces for a new onslaught. The fourth act shows us not a triumphant King John but a fearful one, vainly trusting in a new coronation to consolidate the power which the audience knows he has lost already. He is now struck repeated blows: he learns that his mother is dead, that his nobles have deserted him, and that the French army is prepared to invade England. He sees at once that his troubles all stem from his order to Hubert. He is torn by remorse – there is no pretense in his joy when he hears that Arthur has not been killed after all – but his remorse is of no avail, and even though he has had no hand in the actual death of Arthur he must bear the guilt for it. How abject and powerless he has now become appears in his ignominious capitulation to the papal legate he had once so proudly defied.

When the Bastard castigates Hubert for the death of Arthur, Shakespeare is placing Faulconbridge in opposition to what John has become, aligning him clearly on the side of virtue. He has every reason to desert John, but in spite of Arthur's death he decides to remain with his king rather than join the rebelling nobles, and in this decision he attains his full stature, for he masters his own personal passion and places the good of England above all other considerations. He now becomes the symbol of English strength and unity, and it is only fitting that John should relinquish his power to him. Before this symbol the French army is powerless; John's capitulation to Pandulph is undone, the rebellious lords are won back to the crown, and the Bastard closes the play with his great apostrophe to England. He might at the end become king himself, but he recognizes the primacy of legitimate succession, and in surrendering his power to the young Henry III he sets the welfare of England above his personal glory, assuring to his country a continuance of orderly government, with a lawful king upon the throne. Under the new regime England will enjoy a greater degree of felicity than it had ever known under King John, and in assuring this the triumph of Faulconbridge is both an ethical and a political one, for while serving his country he has learned also to master himself.

In Shakespeare's English history plays the kingdom itself is conceived of as a kind of dramatic entity, for in its welfare dramatic interest is always centered. In this play England is finally victorious in spite of the sins of her king, and she is able to achieve victory through the rise of Faulconbridge, who comes to occupy John's forfeited role and to stand for the political and ethical ideals which John was incapable of attaining. The king himself dies ignobly, but Shakespeare suggests (V, vii, 70–73) that he is able at last to save his soul. His sincere remorse for the death of Arthur, and the victory of England in spite of all, win for him the possibility of expiation. Faulconbridge and Prince Henry indicate Shakespeare's final judgment as they sing the dead king's praises. King John dies not a treacherous villain but the royal martyr he had been made into before Shakespeare approached the subject.

Although there is no evidence of a specific performance of *King John* earlier than the revival at Covent Garden by John Rich in 1737, the play has been fairly popular ever since. In early performances the part of Arthur was played usually by a girl, and even more unfortunate, during the eighteenth and nineteenth centuries the play was often adapted and distorted for purposes of political propaganda, the most notable instance being Colley Cibber's *Papal Tyranny in the Reign of King John*, produced at Covent Garden in 1745, after many years of preparation, with Cibber making his final stage appearance as Pandulph. Five days after this opening David Garrick launched a rival version – presumably going back to Shakespeare – at Drury Lane, playing the part of John himself. In later years he played the Bastard as well, but he always preferred the titular role. The play had its first American production in Philadelphia in 1768.

*King John* owes much of its stage popularity to the appeal for actors of three great roles: King John, the Bastard, and Constance. These parts have been played by the greatest figures in both the British and American theatre. The play was a favorite in the repertory of John Philip Kemble and Sarah Siddons from 1783 until their retirement, Mrs Siddons playing Constance for the last time in 1812 and Kemble appearing as John just a few days before he left the stage in 1817. Edmund and Charles Kean, William Macready, and Sir Herbert Beerbohm Tree were all responsible for memorable productions, as were Edwin Booth and Robert Mantell in the United States. In more recent years the play has had a new burst of popularity, and scarcely a year goes by without at least one important production. *King John* has all the ingredients of great drama: action, character, poetry, and a presiding moral vision.

*State University of New York*      IRVING RIBNER
*at Stony Brook*

## NOTE ON THE TEXT

This edition follows closely the only substantive text of *King John*, that of the first folio (1623). The folio text seems to have been set up from Shakespeare's own draft, possibly corrected before printing, particularly in the two final acts, by reference to the theatre prompt-copy. It is a fairly good text, but it shows some confusion and inconsistency in the names of characters in speech headings and stage directions. These have been corrected and regularized in the present edition, and a few additional emendations have been made, as listed below. The folio text is divided, somewhat haphazardly, into acts and scenes. In the act–scene division here supplied marginally II, i corresponds to folio I, ii; III, i to folio II and III, i; III, ii and iii to folio III, ii; III, iv to folio III, iii.

The following substantive departures in italics have been made from the folio text. Some are readings from the second (1632), third (1663), or fourth (1683) folios; others are emendations made early in the history of Shakespearean scholarship and accepted by most modern editors. The authority for each is indicated parenthetically, followed by the first folio reading in roman.

I, i, 147 *I would* (F2) It would   237 *Could he get me* (Vaughan) Could get me   257 *Thou art* (F4) That art

II, i, 1 *King Philip* (Theobald) Lewis   63 *Ate* (Rowe) Ace   113 *breast* (F2) beast   144 *shows* (Theobald) shooes   149 *King Philip* (Theobald) King Lewis   150 *King Philip* (Theobald) Lewis   215 *Confront* (Rowe) Comfort   259 *roundure* (Capell) rounder   325 *Citizen* (Rowe) Hubert   335 *run* (F2) room   368 *Citizen* (Rowe) Fra.   371 *Kinged* (Tyrwhitt) Kings   416 *Citizen* (Rowe) Hubert

III, i, 110 *day* (Theobald) daies   148 *task* (Theobald) tast

III, iii, 39 *ear* (Collier) race

III, iv, 44 *not holy* (F4) holy   64 *friends* (Rowe) fiends   110 *world's* (Pope) words

IV, i, 92 *mote* (Wilson) moth

IV, ii, 1 *again* (F3) against   42 *when* (Tyrwhitt) then   73 *Does* (F4) Do

IV, iii, 33 *man* (F2) mans   41 *Have you* (F3) you have   155 *ceinture* (Moore Smith) center

V, ii, 26 *Were* (F2) Was   36 *grapple* (Pope) cripple   43 *hast thou* (F4) hast   135 *these* (Rowe) this

V, vi, 12 *eyeless* (Theobald) endless

V, vii, 17 *mind* (Rowe) winde   21 *cygnet* (Rowe) Symet   42 *strait* (Pope) straight   108 *give you thanks* (Rowe) giue thankes

# THE LIFE AND DEATH OF KING JOHN

[NAMES OF THE ACTORS

| | |
|---|---|
| *King John* | *Philip, King of France* |
| *Prince Henry, son to the King* | *Lewis, the Dauphin* |
| *Arthur, Duke of Britain, nephew to the King* | *Lymoges, Duke of Austria* |
| *The Earl of Pembroke* | *Cardinal Pandulph, the Pope's legate* |
| *The Earl of Essex* | *Melun, a French lord* |
| *The Earl of Salisbury* | *Chatillion, ambassador from France* |
| *The Lord Bigot* | *Queen Elinor, mother to King John* |
| *Hubert de Burgh* | *Constance, mother to Arthur* |
| *Robert Faulconbridge, son to Sir Robert Faulconbridge* | *Blanch of Spain, niece to King John* |
| *Philip the Bastard, his half-brother* | *Lady Faulconbridge* |
| *James Gurney, servant to Lady Faulconbridge* | *Lords, Ladies, Citizens of Angiers, Sheriff, Heralds, Officers,* |
| *Peter of Pomfret, a prophet* | *Soldiers, Executioners, Messengers, and other Attendants* |

Scene : *England and France*]

\*

I, i     *Enter King John, Queen Elinor, Pembroke, Essex,*
      *and Salisbury, with the Chatillion of France.*

KING JOHN
    Now, say, Chatillion, what would France with us ?

CHATILLION
3   Thus, after greeting, speaks the King of France
    In my behavior to the majesty,
4   The borrowed majesty, of England here.

ELINOR
    A strange beginning : 'borrowed majesty' !

KING JOHN
6   Silence, good mother ; hear the embassy.

CHATILLION
7   Philip of France, in right and true behalf
    Of thy deceasèd brother Geoffrey's son,
    Arthur Plantagenet, lays most lawful claim
    To this fair island and the territories,
    To Ireland, Poitiers, Anjou, Touraine, Maine,
    Desiring thee to lay aside the sword
    Which sways usurpingly these several titles,
    And put the same into young Arthur's hand,
    Thy nephew and right royal sovereign.

KING JOHN
16   What follows if we disallow of this ?

CHATILLION
17   The proud control of fierce and bloody war,

---

I, i The court of King John   3 *In my behavior* through my person   4 *borrowed* stolen   6 *embassy* message   7 *in right and true behalf* in support of the lawful claim   16 *disallow of* refuse   17 *proud control* overbearing compulsion   20 *Controlment* compulsion   25 *report* deliver your message (with secondary meaning of thunder)   26 *cannon* (an anachronism, since gunpowder had not yet been invented)   27 *trumpet* (as a herald)   28 *decay* destruction   29 *conduct* escort   36 *arguments of love* (1) expressions of affection, (2) friendly discussions   37 *manage* government

    To enforce these rights so forcibly withheld.

KING JOHN
    Here have we war for war and blood for blood,
    Controlment for controlment ; so answer France.    20

CHATILLION
    Then take my king's defiance from my mouth,
    The farthest limit of my embassy.

KING JOHN
    Bear mine to him, and so depart in peace.
    Be thou as lightning in the eyes of France,
    For, ere thou canst report, I will be there.    25
    The thunder of my cannon shall be heard.    26
    So, hence ! Be thou the trumpet of our wrath    27
    And sullen presage of your own decay.    28
    An honorable conduct let him have ;    29
    Pembroke, look to't. Farewell, Chatillion.
                  *Exit Chatillion and Pembroke.*

ELINOR
    What now, my son ! Have I not ever said
    How that ambitious Constance would not cease
    Till she had kindled France and all the world
    Upon the right and party of her son ?
    This might have been prevented and made whole
    With very easy arguments of love,    36
    Which now the manage of two kingdoms must    37
    With fearful bloody issue arbitrate.

KING JOHN
    Our strong possession and our right for us.

ELINOR
    Your strong possession much more than your right,
    Or else it must go wrong with you and me –
    So much my conscience whispers in your ear,
    Which none but heaven, and you, and I, shall hear.
      *Enter a Sheriff [who speaks aside to Essex].*

ESSEX

My liege, here is the strangest controversy,
Come from the country to be judged by you,
That e'er I heard. Shall I produce the men?

KING JOHN

Let them approach.
Our abbeys and our priories shall pay
49   This expeditious charge.
      *Enter Robert Faulconbridge, and Philip [his bastard
      brother].*
                     What men are you?

BASTARD

Your faithful subject, I, a gentleman,
Born in Northamptonshire, and eldest son,
As I suppose, to Robert Faulconbridge,
A soldier, by the honor-giving hand
54   Of Cordelion knighted in the field.

KING JOHN

What art thou?

ROBERT

The son and heir to that same Faulconbridge.

KING JOHN

Is that the elder, and art thou the heir?
You came not of one mother then, it seems.

BASTARD

Most certain of one mother, mighty king;
That is well known; and, as I think, one father.
But for the certain knowledge of that truth
62   I put you o'er to heaven and to my mother.
Of that I doubt, as all men's children may.

ELINOR

Out on thee, rude man! Thou dost shame thy mother
65   And wound her honor with this diffidence.

BASTARD

I, madam? No, I have no reason for it;
That is my brother's plea and none of mine;
68   The which if he can prove, 'a pops me out
At least from fair five hundred pound a year.
Heaven guard my mother's honor and my land!

KING JOHN

A good blunt fellow. Why, being younger born,
Doth he lay claim to thine inheritance?

BASTARD

I know not why, except to get the land.
74   But once he slandered me with bastardy.
75   But whe'r I be as true begot or no,
76   That still I lay upon my mother's head;
But that I am as well begot, my liege –
78   Fair fall the bones that took the pains for me –
Compare our faces and be judge yourself.
If old Sir Robert did beget us both,
And were our father, and this son like him,
O old Sir Robert, father, on my knee
I give heaven thanks I was not like to thee!

KING JOHN

Why, what a madcap hath heaven lent us here!

ELINOR

85   He hath a trick of Cordelion's face;
86   The accent of his tongue affecteth him.
Do you not read some tokens of my son
In the large composition of this man?

KING JOHN

Mine eye hath well examinèd his parts,
And finds them perfect Richard. Sirrah, speak.

What doth move you to claim your brother's land?

BASTARD

Because he hath a half-face like my father.     92
With half that face would he have all my land –
A half-faced groat five hundred pound a year!     94

ROBERT

My gracious liege, when that my father lived,
Your brother did employ my father much –

BASTARD

Well sir, by this you cannot get my land.
Your tale must be how he employed my mother.

ROBERT

And once dispatched him in an embassy     99
To Germany, there with the emperor
To treat of high affairs touching that time.
Th' advantage of his absence took the king,
And in the mean time sojourned at my father's;
Where how he did prevail I shame to speak,     104
But truth is truth; large lengths of seas and shores
Between my father and my mother lay,
As I have heard my father speak himself,
When this same lusty gentleman was got.     108
Upon his death-bed he by will bequeathed
His lands to me, and took it on his death     110
That this my mother's son was none of his;
And if he were, he came into the world
Full fourteen weeks before the course of time.
Then, good my liege, let me have what is mine,
My father's land, as was my father's will.

KING JOHN

Sirrah, your brother is legitimate.
Your father's wife did after wedlock bear him,
And if she did play false, the fault was hers,
Which fault lies on the hazards of all husbands     119
That marry wives. Tell me, how if my brother,
Who, as you say, took pains to get this son,
Had of your father claimed this son for his?
In sooth, good friend, your father might have kept
This calf, bred from his cow, from all the world.
In sooth he might; then, if he were my brother's,
My brother might not claim him, nor your father,
Being none of his, refuse him. This concludes;     127
My mother's son did get your father's heir;
Your father's heir must have your father's land.

ROBERT

Shall then my father's will be of no force
To dispossess that child which is not his?

BASTARD

Of no more force to dispossess me, sir,
Than was his will to get me, as I think.

ELINOR

Whether hadst thou rather be a Faulconbridge,
And like thy brother, to enjoy thy land,     135

49 *expeditious* speedy, sudden   54 *Cordelion* Coeur-de-lion, i.e. King Richard I   62 *put you o'er* refer you   65 *diffidence* distrust   68 *'a* he   74 *once* on a single occasion which he dare not repeat   75 *whe'r* whether   76 *lay . . . head* let my mother account for   78 *fall* befall   85 *trick* characteristic expression   86 *affecteth* resembles   92 *half-face* profile (with secondary meaning of imperfect)   94 *half-faced groat* a thin silver coin with a profile stamped upon it, also an imperfect or inferior coin   99 *dispatched* sent   104 *shame* am ashamed   108 *lusty* merry; *got* conceived   110 *took it on his death* swore on his deathbed (the most solemn kind of oath)   119 *lies on the hazards* is one of the risks   127 *refuse* disclaim; *concludes* settles the question decisively   135 *like thy brother* i.e. in physical appearance (being of the same father), and therefore not a bastard, and entitled to his land

Or the reputed son of Cordelion,

137 Lord of thy presence and no land beside?

BASTARD

Madam, and if my brother had my shape
And I had his, Sir Robert's his, like him,

140 And if my legs were two such riding-rods,
My arms such eel-skins stuffed, my face so thin

142 That in mine ear I durst not stick a rose
Lest men should say, 'Look where three-farthings
    goes!'
And, to his shape, were heir to all this land,
Would I might never stir from off this place,
I would give it every foot to have this face;
I would not be Sir Nob in any case.

ELINOR

I like thee well. Wilt thou forsake thy fortune,
Bequeath thy land to him, and follow me?
I am a soldier and now bound to France.

BASTARD

Brother, take you my land, I'll take my chance.
Your face hath got five hundred pound a year,
Yet sell your face for five pence and 'tis dear.
Madam, I'll follow you unto the death.

ELINOR

Nay, I would have you go before me thither.

BASTARD

Our country manners give our betters way.

KING JOHN

What is thy name?

BASTARD

Philip, my liege, so is my name begun;
Philip, good old Sir Robert's wife's eldest son.

KING JOHN

160 From henceforth bear his name whose form thou
    bearest.
Kneel thou down Philip, but rise more great;
Arise Sir Richard, and Plantagenet.

BASTARD

Brother by th' mother's side, give me your hand.
My father gave me honor, yours gave land.

165 Now blessèd be the hour, by night or day,
When I was got, Sir Robert was away!

ELINOR

The very spirit of Plantagenet!

I am thy grandam, Richard; call me so.

BASTARD

Madam, by chance but not by truth; what though?   169
Something about, a little from the right,
In at the window, or else o'er the hatch:   171
Who dares not stir by day must walk by night,
And have is have, however men do catch.
Near or far off, well won is still well shot,
And I am I, howe'er I was begot.

KING JOHN

Go, Faulconbridge. Now hast thou thy desire;
A landless knight makes thee a landed squire.   177
Come, madam, and come, Richard, we must speed
For France, for France, for it is more than need.

BASTARD

Brother, adieu; good fortune come to thee!
For thou wast got i' th' way of honesty.

                      *Exeunt all but Bastard.*

A foot of honor better than I was,
But many a many foot of land the worse.
Well, now can I make any Joan a lady.   184
'Good den, Sir Richard!' – 'God-a-mercy, fellow' –   185
And if his name be George, I'll call him Peter,
For new-made honor doth forget men's names;
'Tis too respective and too sociable   188
For your conversion. Now your traveller,   189
He and his toothpick at my worship's mess,   190
And when my knightly stomach is sufficed,
Why then I suck my teeth and catechize
My pickèd man of countries: 'My dear sir' –   193
Thus, leaning on mine elbow, I begin –
'I shall beseech you' – that is question now;
And then comes answer like an Absey-book;   196
'O, sir,' says answer, 'at your best command,
At your employment, at your service, sir';
'No, sir,' says question, 'I, sweet sir, at yours';
And so, ere answer knows what question would,
Saving in dialogue of compliment,   201
And talking of the Alps and Apennines,
The Pyrenean and the river Po,
It draws toward supper in conclusion so.
But this is worshipful society,
And fits the mounting spirit like myself,
For he is but a bastard to the time   207
That doth not smack of observation.   208
And so am I, whether I smack or no,
And not alone in habit and device,   210
Exterior form, outward accoutrement,
But from the inward motion to deliver   212
Sweet, sweet, sweet poison for the age's tooth,   213
Which, though I will not practise to deceive,
Yet, to avoid deceit, I mean to learn;   215
For it shall strew the footsteps of my rising.   216
But who comes in such haste in riding-robes?
What woman-post is this? Hath she no husband   218
That will take pains to blow a horn before her?   219

       *Enter Lady Faulconbridge and James Gurney.*

O me! 'Tis my mother. How now, good lady!
What brings you here to court so hastily?

LADY FAULCONBRIDGE

Where is that slave, thy brother? Where is he,
That holds in chase mine honor up and down?   223

BASTARD

My brother Robert? Old Sir Robert's son?

---

137 *presence* person   140 *riding-rods* switches used by riders   142–43 *ear . . . goes* (certain coins were distinguished from others by a rose behind Queen Elizabeth's head; he is saying that his brother dare not place a rose behind his ear, as a lover might, lest he be taken for a three-farthing piece, his face being so thin)   160 *form* physical characteristics   165 *hour* (with a possible pun on 'whore,' since both words were pronounced identically)   169 *truth* honesty, chaste conduct   171 *In . . . hatch* (proverbial expressions referring to illegitimate birth)   177 *landless knight* i.e. the Bastard (who has just renounced his land in favor of his brother)   184 *Joan* (name used for any girl of lowly station)   185 *Good den* God give you good even; *God-a-mercy* God reward you   188 *respective* respectful, courteous   189 *conversion* change of status   190 *toothpick* (a sign of affectation, associated particularly with the foreign traveller); *mess* dinner table   193 *pickèd* (1) refined, rarefied, (2) whose teeth have been picked   196 *Absey-book* ABC book, primer for instruction of children (the Bastard is mimicking the kind of question-and-answer exercise found in such books)   201 *dialogue of compliment* formal, elegant address   207 *but a bastard to the time* no true son of the age   208 *observation* obsequiousness   210 *habit* dress   212 *motion* impulse   213 *Sweet . . . poison* flattery   215 *deceit* being deceived   216 *it . . . rising* i.e. flattery will accompany his rise to greatness as rushes are strewn upon a great man's floor   218 *woman-post* female courier   219 *blow a horn* i.e. announce his cuckoldry and her infidelity   223 *holds in chase* pursues to destroy

225 Colbrand the giant, that same mighty man?
Is it Sir Robert's son that you seek so?

LADY FAULCONBRIDGE
Sir Robert's son! Ay, thou unreverend boy,
Sir Robert's son! Why scorn'st thou at Sir Robert?
He is Sir Robert's son, and so art thou.

BASTARD
James Gurney, wilt thou give us leave awhile?

GURNEY
Good leave, good Philip.

231 BASTARD          Philip sparrow! James,
232 There's toys abroad; anon I'll tell thee more. *Exit James.*
Madam, I was not old Sir Robert's son.
Sir Robert might have eat his part in me
Upon Good Friday and ne'er broke his fast.

236 Sir Robert could do well – marry, to confess –
Could he get me! Sir Robert could not do it.
We know his handiwork. Therefore, good mother,
239 To whom am I beholding for these limbs?
240 Sir Robert never holp to make this leg.

LADY FAULCONBRIDGE
Hast thou conspirèd with thy brother too,
That for thine own gain shouldst defend mine honor?
243 What means this scorn, thou most untoward knave?

BASTARD
244 Knight, knight, good mother, Basilisco-like.
245 What! I am dubbed; I have it on my shoulder.
But, mother, I am not Sir Robert's son;
I have disclaimed Sir Robert and my land;
Legitimation, name, and all is gone.
Then, good my mother, let me know my father;
250 Some proper man I hope; who was it, mother?

LADY FAULCONBRIDGE
Hast thou denied thyself a Faulconbridge?

BASTARD
As faithfully as I deny the devil.

LADY FAULCONBRIDGE
King Richard Cordelion was thy father.
By long and vehement suit I was seduced
To make room for him in my husband's bed.
Heaven lay not my transgression to my charge!
Thou art the issue of my dear offense,
258 Which was so strongly urged past my defense.

BASTARD
259 Now, by this light, were I to get again,
Madam, I would not wish a better father.
261 Some sins do bear their privilege on earth,
And so doth yours; your fault was not your folly.
263 Needs must you lay your heart at his dispose,
Subjected tribute to commanding love,
Against whose fury and unmatchèd force
266 The aweless lion could not wage the fight,
Nor keep his princely heart from Richard's hand.
He that perforce robs lions of their hearts
May easily win a woman's. Ay, my mother,
With all my heart I thank thee for my father!
Who lives and dares but say thou didst not well
When I was got, I'll send his soul to hell.
Come, lady, I will show thee to my kin,
And they shall say, when Richard me begot,
If thou hadst said him nay, it had been sin.
Who says it was, he lies; I say 'twas not.     *Exeunt.*

\*

Enter before Angiers, Philip, King of France, Lewis,   II, i
[the] Dauphin, Austria, Constance, Arthur
[and Attendants].

KING PHILIP
Before Angiers well met, brave Austria.
Arthur, that great forerunner of thy blood,     2
Richard, that robbed the lion of his heart
And fought the holy wars in Palestine,
By this brave duke came early to his grave;     5
And for amends to his posterity,
At our importance hither is he come     7
To spread his colors, boy, in thy behalf,
And to rebuke the usurpation
Of thy unnatural uncle, English John.
Embrace him, love him, give him welcome hither.

ARTHUR
God shall forgive you Cordelion's death
The rather that you give his offspring life,
Shadowing their right under your wings of war.     14
I give you welcome with a powerless hand,
But with a heart full of unstainèd love.
Welcome before the gates of Angiers, duke.

LEWIS
A noble boy! Who would not do thee right?

AUSTRIA
Upon thy cheek lay I this zealous kiss,
As seal to this indenture of my love,     20
That to my home I will no more return
Till Angiers and the right thou hast in France,
Together with that pale, that white-faced shore,
Whose foot spurns back the ocean's roaring tides
And coops from other lands her islanders,     25
Even till that England, hedged in with the main,
That water-wallèd bulwark, still secure     27
And confident from foreign purposes,
Even till that utmost corner of the west
Salute thee for her king. Till then, fair boy,
Will I not think of home, but follow arms.

CONSTANCE
O, take his mother's thanks, a widow's thanks,
Till your strong hand shall help to give him strength
To make a more requital to your love.     34

AUSTRIA
The peace of heaven is theirs that lift their swords
In such a just and charitable war.

225 *Colbrand* a Danish giant killed by Guy of Warwick in the old romance 231 *Philip sparrow* (since he has just been knighted, he objects to being called merely Philip, the common name for a sparrow) 232 *toys* rumors 236–37 *Sir Robert . . . get me* (he is incredulous at the suggestion that one like Sir Robert might be his father) 239 *beholding* indebted 240 *holp* helped 243 *untoward* ill-mannered 244 *Basilisco-like* (the Bastard mocks himself by comparing himself to Basilisco, the cowardly, braggart knight in *Soliman and Perseda*, an old play probably by Thomas Kyd) 245 *dubbed* made a knight 250 *proper* handsome 258 *urged . . . defense* forced in spite of my protests 259 *get* be conceived 261 *do bear . . . earth* are allowed on earth but not in heaven 263 *dispose* disposal 266 *aweless lion* (King Richard, according to legend, had slain a lion by thrusting his hand down its throat and tearing out its heart, which he then ate; hence his nickname)
II, i Before the gates of Angiers 2 *forerunner of thy blood* ancestor (Arthur was actually the nephew of Richard, son of his brother Geoffrey) 5 *brave duke* Austria (although Richard actually was killed before the castle of the Viscount Limoges; Shakespeare, following his source, combines the two characters) 7 *importance* request 14 *Shadowing* sheltering 20 *indenture* sealed contract 25 *coops* encloses for protection 27 *still* forever 34 *more* greater

KING PHILIP

37 Well then, to work ; our cannon shall be bent
Against the brows of this resisting town.
39 Call for our chiefest men of discipline,
40 To cull the plots of best advantages.
We'll lay before this town our royal bones,
Wade to the market-place in Frenchmen's blood,
But we will make it subject to this boy.

CONSTANCE

Stay for an answer to your embassy,
45 Lest unadvised you stain your swords with blood.
My Lord Chatillion may from England bring
That right in peace which here we urge in war,
And then we shall repent each drop of blood
49 That hot rash haste so indirectly shed.
*Enter Chatillion.*

KING PHILIP

A wonder, lady ! Lo, upon thy wish,
Our messenger, Chatillion, is arrived !
What England says, say briefly, gentle lord ;
53 We coldly pause for thee ; Chatillion, speak.

CHATILLION

Then turn your forces from this paltry siege
And stir them up against a mightier task.
England, impatient of your just demands,
Hath put himself in arms. The adverse winds,
58 Whose leisure I have stayed, have given him time
To land his legions all as soon as I.
60 His marches are expedient to this town,
His forces strong, his soldiers confident.
With him along is come the mother-queen,
63 An Ate ; stirring him to blood and strife ;
With her her niece, the Lady Blanch of Spain ;
With them a bastard of the king's deceased ;
66 And all th' unsettled humors of the land,
67 Rash, inconsiderate, fiery voluntaries,
68 With ladies' faces and fierce dragons' spleens,
Have sold their fortunes at their native homes,
70 Bearing their birthrights proudly on their backs,
To make a hazard of new fortunes here.
In brief, a braver choice of dauntless spirits
73 Than now the English bottoms have waft o'er
Did never float upon the swelling tide,
75 To do offense and scathe in Christendom.

37 *bent* directed   39 *discipline* military training or experience   40 *cull . . . advantages* select the most suitable locations for placing cannons   45 *unadvised* unwisely, without adequate consideration   49 *indirectly* unjustly   53 *coldly* calmly   58 *stayed* waited for   60 *expedient to* hastening towards   63 *Ate* the Greek goddess of mischief and vengeance   66 *unsettled humors* restless disgruntled men   67 *voluntaries* volunteers   68 *dragons' spleens* hot tempers (since the spleen was regarded as the seat of the passions)   70 *Bearing . . . backs* having sold their estates to purchase armor   73 *bottoms* ships   75 *scathe* harm   76 *churlish* lowly, inferior   77 *circumstance* details   79 *expedition* haste   82 *occasion* emergency   85 *lineal* due by right of descent   87 *correct* punish   91 *England's* i.e. Arthur's (since Philip takes him to be the lawful king of England)   93 *This toil . . . thine* i.e. John should be fighting for Arthur's cause rather than against him   95 *under-wrought* undermined   96 *sequence of posterity* hereditary succession to the throne   97 *Outfacèd infant state* intimidated a child king   101-03 *little abstract . . . volume* i.e. Arthur as a child is like a shortened edition of his father, Geoffrey, but in time he will grow to be as complete a volume (of virtues) as his father was   106 *this* (a famous crux ; may refer to Arthur, John's crown, or the city of Angiers, depending upon what the actor indicates by his arm)   109 *owe* own ; *o'ermasterest* usurpest   111 *draw . . . articles* demand that I answer your charges   112 *supernal* heavenly   116 *impeach* accuse   123 *queen* (with play on 'quean,' whore) ; *check* control (with possible allusion to game of chess)

The interruption of their churlish drums   76
Cuts off more circumstance ; they are at hand.   77
*Drum beats.*
To parley or to fight, therefore prepare.

KING PHILIP

How much unlooked for is this expedition !   79

AUSTRIA

By how much unexpected, by so much
We must awake endeavor for defense,
For courage mounteth with occasion.   82
Let them be welcome then ; we are prepared.
*Enter King [John] of England, Bastard,*
*Queen [Elinor], Blanch, Pembroke, and others.*

KING JOHN

Peace be to France, if France in peace permit
Our just and lineal entrance to our own.   85
If not, bleed France, and peace ascend to heaven,
Whiles we, God's wrathful agent, do correct   87
Their proud contempt that beats His peace to heaven.

KING PHILIP

Peace be to England, if that war return
From France to England, there to live in peace.
England we love, and for that England's sake   91
With burden of our armor here we sweat.
This toil of ours should be a work of thine,   93
But thou from loving England art so far
That thou hast under-wrought his lawful king,   95
Cut off the sequence of posterity,   96
Outfacèd infant state, and done a rape   97
Upon the maiden virtue of the crown.
Look here upon thy brother Geoffrey's face.
These eyes, these brows, were molded out of his ;
This little abstract doth contain that large   101
Which died in Geoffrey, and the hand of time
Shall draw this brief into as huge a volume.
That Geoffrey was thy elder brother born,
And this his son. England was Geoffrey's right
And this is Geoffrey's in the name of God.   106
How comes it then that thou art called a king,
When living blood doth in these temples beat,
Which owe the crown that thou o'ermasterest ?   109

KING JOHN

From whom hast thou this great commission, France,
To draw my answer from thy articles ?   111

KING PHILIP

From that supernal judge that stirs good thoughts   112
In any breast of strong authority,
To look into the blots and stains of right.
That judge hath made me guardian to this boy,
Under whose warrant I impeach thy wrong   116
And by whose help I mean to chastise it.

KING JOHN

Alack, thou dost usurp authority.

KING PHILIP

Excuse it is to beat usurping down.

ELINOR

Who is it thou dost call usurper, France ?

CONSTANCE

Let me make answer : thy usurping son.

ELINOR

Out, insolent ! Thy bastard shall be king
That thou mayst be a queen and check the world !   123

CONSTANCE

My bed was ever to thy son as true

As thine was to thy husband, and this boy
Liker in feature to his father Geoffrey
Than thou and John in manners, being as like

128 As rain to water, or devil to his dam.
My boy a bastard ! By my soul I think
His father never was so true begot.
It cannot be and if thou wert his mother.

ELINOR
132 There's a good mother, boy, that blots thy father.

CONSTANCE
133 There's a good grandam, boy, that would blot thee.

AUSTRIA
Peace !

134 BASTARD   Hear the crier.

AUSTRIA        What the devil art thou ?

BASTARD
One that will play the devil, sir, with you,
136 An 'a may catch your hide and you alone.
137 You are the hare of whom the proverb goes,
Whose valor plucks dead lions by the beard.
139 I'll smoke your skin-coat, an I catch you right.
Sirrah, look to 't ; i' faith, I will, i' faith.

BLANCH
O well did he become that lion's robe,
That did disrobe the lion of that robe !

BASTARD
143 It lies as sightly on the back of him
144 As great Alcides' shows upon an ass.
But, ass, I'll take that burden from your back,
Or lay on that shall make your shoulders crack.

AUSTRIA
147 What cracker is this same that deafs our ears
With this abundance of superfluous breath ?
149 King Philip, determine what we shall do straight.

KING PHILIP
150 Women and fools, break off your conference.
King John, this is the very sum of all :
152 England and Ireland, Angiers, Touraine, Maine,
In right of Arthur do I claim of thee.
Wilt thou resign them and lay down thy arms ?

KING JOHN
My life as soon ! I do defy thee, France.
Arthur of Britain, yield thee to my hand,
And out of my dear love I'll give thee more
Than e'er the coward hand of France can win.
Submit thee, boy.

ELINOR        Come to thy grandam, child.

CONSTANCE
160 Do, child, go to it grandam, child ;
Give grandam kingdom, and it grandam will
Give it a plum, a cherry, and a fig.
There's a good grandam.

ARTHUR        Good my mother, peace !
I would that I were low laid in my grave.
165 I am not worth this coil that's made for me.

ELINOR
His mother shames him so, poor boy, he weeps.

CONSTANCE
167 Now shame upon you, whe'r she does or no !
His grandam's wrongs, and not his mother's shames,
169 Draws those heaven-moving pearls from his poor eyes,
Which heaven shall take in nature of a fee.
Ay, with these crystal beads heaven shall be bribed
To do him justice and revenge on you.

ELINOR
Thou monstrous slanderer of heaven and earth !

CONSTANCE
Thou monstrous injurer of heaven and earth !
Call not me slanderer ; thou and thine usurp
The dominations, royalties, and rights   176
Of this oppressèd boy. This is thy eldest son's son,   177
Infortunate in nothing but in thee.   178
Thy sins are visited in this poor child ;   179
The canon of the law is laid on him,   180
Being but the second generation
Removèd from thy sin-conceiving womb.

KING JOHN
Bedlam, have done.   183

CONSTANCE      I have but this to say,
That he is not only plaguèd for her sin,   184
But God hath made her sin and her the plague
On this removèd issue, plagued for her   186
And with her plague ; her sin his injury,
Her injury the beadle to her sin,   188
All punished in the person of this child,
And all for her ; a plague upon her.

ELINOR
Thou unadvisèd scold, I can produce   191
A will that bars the title of thy son.   192

CONSTANCE
Ay, who doubts that ? A will ! A wicked will ;
A woman's will ; a cankered grandam's will !   194

KING PHILIP
Peace, lady ! Pause, or be more temperate.
It ill beseems this presence to cry aim   196
To these ill-tunèd repetitions.
Some trumpet summon hither to the walls   198
These men of Angiers. Let us hear them speak
Whose title they admit, Arthur's or John's.
      *Trumpet sounds. Enter a Citizen upon the walls.*

CITIZEN
Who is it that hath warned us to the walls ?   201

KING PHILIP
'Tis France, for England.

KING JOHN       England for itself.
You men of Angiers, and my loving subjects—

---

128 *dam* mother   132 *blots* slanders   133 *grandam* grandmother   134 *Hear the crier* (the Bastard mocks Austria by likening him to the town crier who called for silence in the courts)   136 *An 'a* if he   137 *the proverb* i.e. 'hares may pull dead lions by the beard' (it occurs in the *Adagia* of Erasmus)   139 *smoke your skin-coat* thrash you (alluding also to King Richard's lion skin, which Austria is wearing)   143 *sightly* appropriately   144 *Alcides* Hercules, who wore the skin of the Nemean lion he had slain   147 *cracker* boaster   149 *straight* immediately   150 *fools* children   152 *Angiers* (here confused with Anjou)   160–63 *Do . . . grandam* (Constance uses baby talk to ridicule Elinor's invitation)   165 *coil* fuss   167 *whe'r* whether   169 *Draws* draw; *pearls* tears   176 *dominations* sovereignties   177 *eldest son's son* oldest grandson, a biblical form (not son of your oldest son, which Arthur was not)   178 *Infortunate* unfortunate   179 *visited* punished   180 *canon of the law* i.e. that the sins of parents be visited upon their children to the third and fourth generation   183 *Bedlam* lunatic   184–90 *That . . . upon her* (a perhaps intentionally obscure passage, the sense being that Arthur is being punished for the sin of Elinor – her giving birth to John, whom Constance is calling a bastard – by the very presence of Elinor and John, that they are laying the scourge upon him which should be laid upon Elinor)   186 *removèd issue* distant descendant   188 *beadle* a parish official who meted out corporal punishment, to prostitutes in particular   191 *unadvisèd* rash   192 *A will* (the last testament of King Richard I, which named his brother John heir to the throne)   194 *cankered* malignant   196 *cry aim* give encouragement   198 *trumpet* trumpeter   201 *warned* summoned

KING PHILIP
    You loving men of Angiers, Arthur's subjects,
205    Our trumpet called you to this gentle parle –
KING JOHN
    For our advantage ; therefore hear us first.
207    These flags of France, that are advancèd here
208    Before the eye and prospect of your town,
209    Have hither marched to your endamagement.
    The cannons have their bowels full of wrath,
    And ready mounted are they to spit forth
    Their iron indignation 'gainst your walls.
    All preparation for a bloody seige
    And merciless proceeding by these French
215    Confront your city's eyes, your winking gates,
    And but for our approach those sleeping stones,
217    That as a waist doth girdle you about,
218    By the compulsion of their ordinance
    By this time from their fixèd beds of lime
220    Had been dishabited, and wide havoc made
    For bloody power to rush upon your peace.
    But on the sight of us your lawful king,
223    Who painfully with much expedient march
    Have brought a countercheck before your gates,
    To save unscratched your city's threat'ned cheeks,
    Behold, the French amazed vouchsafe a parle ;
    And now, instead of bullets wrapped in fire,
    To make a shaking fever in your walls,
    They shoot but calm words folded up in smoke,
230    To make a faithless error in your ears.
    Which trust accordingly, kind citizens,
232    And let us in, your king, whose labored spirits,
233    Forwearied in this action of swift speed,
234    Craves harborage within your city walls.
KING PHILIP
236    When I have said, make answer to us both.
    Lo ! In this right hand, whose protection
    Is most divinely vowed upon the right
238    Of him it holds, stands young Plantagenet,
    Son to the elder brother of this man,
240    And king o'er him and all that he enjoys.
    For this downtrodden equity we tread
242    In warlike march these greens before your town,
    Being no further enemy to you
    Than the constraint of hospitable zeal,
    In the relief of this oppressèd child,
    Religiously provokes. Be pleasèd then
    To pay that duty which you truly owe
248    To him that owes it, namely this young prince ;
    And then our arms, like to a muzzled bear,
250    Save in aspect, hath all offense sealed up.

205 *parle* conference 207 *advancèd* raised 208 *prospect* view 209
*endamagement* injury 215 *winking* closed as in sleep 217 *waist* belt;
*doth* do 218 *ordinance* artillery 220 *dishabited* dislodged 223 *painfully*
laboriously; *expedient* speedy 230 *faithless* perfidious, disloyal; *error*
falsehood 232 *labored* oppressed by labor 233 *Forwearied* tired out;
*action* campaign 234 *harborage* shelter, acceptance 236 *In this right
hand* led by my right hand 238 *holds* supports 240 *enjoys* possesses
242 *greens* grassy ground outside the city gates 248 *owes* owns 250 *Save
in aspect* except for appearance 253 *retire* withdrawal 258 *fondly pass*
foolishly ignore 259 *roundure* circumference 260 *messengers of war*
cannon balls 261 *discipline* military skill 264 *which* in which 270
*proves* is proved 276 *and else* and otherwise 278 *bloods* men of mettle,
and of good family 280 *in his face* opposing him 281 *compound* agree
285 *fleet* pass away 288 *swinged* thrashed 290 *fence* swordsmanship,
defense 291 *lioness* (a slang expression for whore) 292–93 *set . . . you*
cause you to grow the horns of a cuckold (a common joke of the time)

    Our cannons' malice vainly shall be spent
    Against th' invulnerable clouds of heaven,
    And with a blessèd and unvexed retire,                253
    With unhacked swords and helmets all unbruised,
    We will bear home that lusty blood again
    Which here we came to spout against your town,
    And leave your children, wives, and you, in peace.
    But if you fondly pass our proffered offer,            258
    'Tis not the roundure of your old-faced walls          259
    Can hide you from our messengers of war.               260
    Though all these English and their discipline          261
    Were harbored in their rude circumference.
    Then tell us, shall your city call us lord,
    In that behalf which we have challenged it ?           264
    Or shall we give the signal to our rage
    And stalk in blood to our possession ?
CITIZEN
    In brief, we are the King of England's subjects.
    For him, and in his right, we hold this town.
KING JOHN
    Acknowledge then the king, and let me in.
CITIZEN
    That can we not ; but he that proves the king,         270
    To him will we prove loyal. Till that time
    Have we rammed up our gates against the world.
KING JOHN
    Doth not the crown of England prove the king ?
    And if not that, I bring you witnesses,
    Twice fifteen thousand hearts of England's breed –
BASTARD
    Bastards, and else.                                    276
KING JOHN
    To verify our title with their lives.
KING PHILIP
    As many and as well-born bloods as those –            278
BASTARD
    Some bastards, too.
KING PHILIP
    Stand in his face to contradict his claim.            280
CITIZEN
    Till you compound whose right is worthiest,           281
    We for the worthiest hold the right from both.
KING JOHN
    Then God forgive the sins of all those souls
    That to their everlasting residence,
    Before the dew of evening fall, shall fleet,           285
    In dreadful trial of our kingdom's king !
KING PHILIP
    Amen, amen ! Mount, chevaliers ! To arms !
BASTARD
    Saint George, that swinged the dragon, and e'er since  288
    Sits on's horseback at mine hostess' door,
    Teach us some fence ! *[to Austria]* Sirrah, were I at home  290
    At your den, sirrah, with your lioness,                291
    I would set an ox head to your lion's hide,            292
    And make a monster of you.
AUSTRIA                              Peace ! No more.
BASTARD
    O tremble, for you hear the lion roar.
KING JOHN
    Up higher to the plain, where we'll set forth
    In best appointment all our regiments.
BASTARD
    Speed then, to take advantage of the field.

**KING PHILIP**
It shall be so ; and at the other hill
Command the rest to stand. God, and our right ! *Exeunt.*
*Here after excursions, enter the Herald of France*
*with Trumpets, to the gates.*

**FRENCH HERALD**
You men of Angiers, open wide your gates,
And let young Arthur, Duke of Britain, in,
Who by the hand of France this day hath made
Much work for tears in many an English mother,
Whose sons lie scattered on the bleeding ground.
305 Many a widow's husband grovelling lies,
Coldly embracing the discolored earth,
And victory with little loss doth play
Upon the dancing banners of the French,
309 Who are at hand, triumphantly displayed,
To enter conquerors and to proclaim
Arthur of Britain England's king and yours.
*Enter English Herald, with Trumpet.*

**ENGLISH HERALD**
Rejoice, you men of Angiers, ring your bells.
King John, your king and England's, doth approach,
314 Commander of this hot malicious day.
Their armors, that marched hence so silver-bright,
316 Hither return all gilt with Frenchmen's blood.
There stuck no plume in any English crest
318 That is removèd by a staff of France.
Our colors do return in those same hands
That did display them when we first marched forth,
And like a jolly troop of huntsmen come
322 Our lusty English, all with purpled hands
323 Dyed in the dying slaughter of their foes.
Open your gates and give the victors way.

**CITIZEN**
325 Heralds, from off our towers we might behold,
326 From first to last, the onset and retire
Of both your armies, whose equality
328 By our best eyes cannot be censurèd.
Blood hath bought blood, and blows have answered
blows,
Strength matched with strength, and power confronted
power.
Both are alike, and both alike we like.
One must prove greatest. While they weigh so even,
We hold our town for neither, yet for both.
*Enter the two Kings, with their powers, at several*
*doors.*

**KING JOHN**
France, hast thou yet more blood to cast away ?
Say, shall the current of our right run on ?
Whose passage, vexed with thy impediment,
Shall leave his native channel and o'erswell
With course disturbed even thy confining shores,
Unless thou let his silver water keep
A peaceful progress to the ocean.

**KING PHILIP**
England, thou hast not saved one drop of blood
In this hot trial more than we of France ;
Rather, lost more. And by this hand I swear,
344 That sways the earth this climate overlooks,
Before we will lay down our just-borne arms,
We'll put thee down, 'gainst whom these arms we bear,
347 Or add a royal number to the dead,
Gracing the scroll that tells of this war's loss

With slaughter couplèd to the name of kings.

**BASTARD**
Ha, majesty ! How high thy glory towers
When the rich blood of kings is set on fire !
O now doth death line his dead chaps with steel !      352
The swords of soldiers are his teeth, his fangs ;
And now he feasts, mousing the flesh of men            354
In undetermined differences of kings.                  355
Why stand these royal fronts amazèd thus ?             356
Cry 'havoc !', kings ; back to the stainèd field,      357
You equal potents, fiery kindled spirits !             358
Then let confusion of one part confirm                 359
The other's peace ; till then, blows, blood, and death !

**KING JOHN**
Whose party do the townsmen yet admit ?                361

**KING PHILIP**
Speak, citizens, for England ; who's your king ?

**CITIZEN**
The King of England, when we know the king.

**KING PHILIP**
Know him in us, that here hold up his right.

**KING JOHN**
In us, that are our own great deputy,
And bear possession of our person here,
Lord of our presence, Angiers, and of you.

**CITIZEN**
A greater power than we denies all this,
And till it be undoubted, we do lock
Our former scruple in our strong-barred gates,
Kinged of our fear, until our fears, resolved,          371
Be by some certain king purged and deposed.

**BASTARD**
By heaven, these scroyles of Angiers flout you, kings,  373
And stand securely on their battlements
As in a theatre, whence they gape and point
At your industrious scenes and acts of death.
Your royal presences be ruled by me.
Do like the mutines of Jerusalem,                       378
Be friends awhile and both conjointly bend              379
Your sharpest deeds of malice on this town.
By east and west let France and England mount
Their battering cannon chargèd to the mouths,
Till their soul-fearing clamors have brawled down       383
The flinty ribs of this contemptuous city.
I'd play incessantly upon these jades,                  385
Even till unfencèd desolation                           386
Leave them as naked as the vulgar air.                  387
That done, dissever your united strengths,

305 *grovelling* prone, on his belly   309 *displayed* deployed, spread out
314 *hot malicious* hotly and violently fought   316 *gilt* made red   318
*staff* shaft of a spear   322 *purpled* bloody   323 *Dyed . . . foes* (it was a
custom for hunters to dip their hands in the blood of the slain deer)   325
*Citizen* (in the folio this speech is given to Hubert, identifying him with
the citizen of Angiers)   326 *retire* retreat   328 *censurèd* estimated   344
*climate* portion of the sky   347 *royal number* a royal item (on the scroll
bearing the official list of the dead)   352 *chaps* jaws   354 *mousing* tearing
355 *undetermined differences* unsettled quarrels   356 *fronts* faces (literally,
foreheads)   357 *havoc* (this cry was a traditional signal for indiscriminate
slaughter with no taking of prisoners)   358 *potents* powers   359 *confusion*
defeat; *part* party   361 *yet* now   371 *Kinged of* ruled by   373 *scroyles*
scoundrels   378 *mutines of Jerusalem* (when Jerusalem was besieged by
the Emperor Titus, warring factions within the city united in common
struggle against the Romans)   379 *bend* direct   383 *brawled down* beaten
down with noise   385 *play . . . jades* fire repeatedly upon these wretches
386 *unfencèd* defenseless   387 *naked* unarmed ; *vulgar* common to all

And part your mingled colors once again;
Turn face to face and bloody point to point.
91 Then in a moment fortune shall cull forth
92 Out of one side her happy minion,
To whom in favor she shall give the day,
And kiss him with a glorious victory.
95 How like you this wild counsel, mighty states?
96 Smacks it not something of the policy?

KING JOHN
Now, by the sky that hangs above our heads,
I like it well. France, shall we knit our powers
And lay this Angiers even with the ground,
Then after fight who shall be king of it?

BASTARD
And if thou hast the mettle of a king,
402 Being wronged as we are by this peevish town,
Turn thou the mouth of thy artillery,
As we will ours, against these saucy walls;
And when that we have dashed them to the ground,
406 Why then defy each other, and pell-mell
Make work upon ourselves, for heaven or hell.

KING PHILIP
Let it be so. Say, where will you assault?

KING JOHN
We from the west will send destruction
Into this city's bosom.

AUSTRIA
I from the north.

411 KING PHILIP      Our thunder from the south
412 Shall rain their drift of bullets on this town.

BASTARD [aside]
413 O prudent discipline! From north to south
Austria and France shoot in each other's mouth.
I'll stir them to it. Come, away, away!

CITIZEN
Hear us, great kings; vouchsafe a while to stay,
And I shall show you peace and fair-faced league,
Win you this city without stroke or wound,
Rescue those breathing lives to die in beds,
That here come sacrifices for the field.
Persever not, but hear me, mighty kings.

KING JOHN
422 Speak on with favor; we are bent to hear.

CITIZEN
That daughter there of Spain, the Lady Blanch,

391 *fortune* chance (commonly personified in medieval and Renaissance literature as a fickle goddess)   392 *minion* sweetheart, favorite   395 *states* kings   396 *policy* art of politics in pejorative sense, involving trickery and deceit (the Bastard is rather naively boasting of his ability as a politician)   402 *peevish* obstinate   406 *pell-mell* in confusion   411 *thunder* cannon   412 *drift* rain   413 *discipline* military skill   422 *favor* permission; *bent* inclined   424 *near to England* a close relative of King John   428 *zealous love* holy love, as opposed to lust   431 *bound* contain   433 *complete* perfect   434–36 *If . . . not he* (a type of word play in which Elizabethans delighted, the sense being that each requires the other to make his own perfection even more perfect)   441 *silver currents* (marriage was often celebrated in Elizabethan love poetry as a joining of two streams of water)   447 *match* (1) marriage, (2) the match which fires the cannon   448 *spleen* violent energy   454 *peremptory* determined   455 *stay* obstacle   457 *rags* (death was often portrayed in medieval art as a skeleton clad in rags)   462 *bounce* bang   463 *bastinado* a beating with a stick   466 *Zounds* by God's wounds   468 *list* pay close heed   471 *unsured* insecure   476 *capable of* susceptible to; *ambition* desire to come to terms   477–79 *Lest . . . what it was* lest the French king's desire to help Arthur, now melted by the pleas of the citizen of Angiers, become as firm as it was before   478 *remorse* compassion   481 *treaty* proposal

Is near to England. Look upon the years
424
Of Lewis the Dauphin and that lovely maid.
If lusty love should go in quest of beauty,
Where should he find it fairer than in Blanch?
If zealous love should go in search of virtue,
428
Where should he find it purer than in Blanch?
If love ambitious sought a match of birth,
Whose veins bound richer blood than Lady Blanch?
431
Such as she is, in beauty, virtue, birth,
Is the young Dauphin every way complete.
433
If not complete of, say he is not she,
434
And she again wants nothing, to name want,
If want it be not that she is not he.
He is the half part of a blessèd man,
Left to be finishèd by such as she,
And she a fair divided excellence,
Whose fulness of perfection lies in him.
O, two such silver currents when they join
441
Do glorify the banks that bound them in;
And two such shores to two such streams made one,
Two such controlling bounds shall you be, kings,
To these two princes, if you marry them.
This union shall do more than battery can
To our fast-closèd gates; for at this match,
447
With swifter spleen than powder can enforce,
448
The mouth of passage shall we fling wide ope,
And give you entrance; but without this match,
The sea enragèd is not half so deaf,
Lions more confident, mountains and rocks
More free from motion, no, not death himself
In mortal fury half so peremptory,
454
As we to keep this city.

BASTARD         Here's a stay,
455
That shakes the rotten carcass of old death
Out of his rags! Here's a large mouth, indeed,
457
That spits forth death and mountains, rocks and seas,
Talks as familiarly of roaring lions
As maids of thirteen do of puppy-dogs.
What cannoneer begot this lusty blood?
He speaks plain cannon fire and smoke and bounce.
462
He gives the bastinado with his tongue.
463
Our ears are cudgelled; not a word of his
But buffets better than a fist of France.
Zounds! I was never so bethumped with words
466
Since I first called my brother's father dad.

ELINOR
Son, list to this conjunction, make this match.
468
Give with our niece a dowry large enough,
For by this knot thou shalt so surely tie
Thy now unsured assurance to the crown
471
That yon green boy shall have no sun to ripe
The bloom that promiseth a mighty fruit.
I see a yielding in the looks of France.
Mark how they whisper. Urge them while their souls
Are capable of this ambition,
476
Lest zeal, now melted by the windy breath
477
Of soft petitions, pity, and remorse,
478
Cool and congeal again to what it was.

CITIZEN
Why answer not the double majesties
This friendly treaty of our threat'ned town?
481

KING PHILIP
Speak England first, that hath been forward first
To speak unto this city. What say you?

KING JOHN

    If that the Dauphin there, thy princely son,
    Can in this book of beauty read 'I love,'
    Her dowry shall weigh equal with a queen ;
487  For Angiers and fair Touraine, Maine, Poitiers,
    And all that we upon this side the sea,
    Except this city now by us besieged,
490  Find liable to our crown and dignity,
    Shall gild her bridal bed and make her rich
    In titles, honors, and promotions,
    As she in beauty, education, blood,
494  Holds hand with any princess of the world.

KING PHILIP

    What sayst thou, boy ? Look in the lady's face.

LEWIS

    I do, my lord, and in her eye I find
    A wonder or a wondrous miracle,
498  The shadow of myself formed in her eye,
    Which, being but the shadow of your son,
    Becomes a sun, and makes your son a shadow.
    I do protest I never loved myself
    Till now infixèd I beheld myself,
503  Drawn in the flattering table of her eye.
         *Whispers with Blanch.*

BASTARD

504  Drawn in the flattering table of her eye !
    Hanged in the frowning wrinkle of her brow !
506  And quartered in her heart ! He doth espy
    Himself love's traitor ; this is pity now,
    That hanged and drawn and quartered, there should be
    In such a love so vile a lout as he.

BLANCH

    My uncle's will in this respect is mine.
    If he see aught in you that makes him like,
    That anything he sees which moves his liking,
513  I can with ease translate it to my will ;
    Or if you will, to speak more properly,
    I will enforce it easily to my love.
    Further I will not flatter you, my lord,
    That all I see in you is worthy love,
    Than this : that nothing do I see in you,
519  Though churlish thoughts themselves should be your
       judge,
    That I can find should merit any hate.

KING JOHN

    What say these young ones ? What say you, my niece ?

BLANCH

522  That she is bound in honor still to do
523  What you in wisdom still vouchsafe to say.

KING JOHN

    Speak then, Prince Dauphin. Can you love this lady ?

LEWIS

    Nay, ask me if I can refrain from love,
    For I do love her most unfeignèdly.

KING JOHN

    Then do I give Volquessen, Touraine, Maine,
    Poitiers, and Anjou, these five provinces,
    With her to thee ; and this addition more,
    Full thirty thousand marks of English coin.
    Philip of France, if thou be pleased withal,
    Command thy son and daughter to join hands.

KING PHILIP

533  It likes us well. Young princes, close your hands.

AUSTRIA

    And your lips too, for I am well assured
    That I did so when I was first assured.    53

KING PHILIP

    Now, citizens of Angiers, ope your gates,
    Let in that amity which you have made,    53
    For at Saint Mary's chapel presently
    The rites of marriage shall be solemnized.
    Is not the Lady Constance in this troop ?
    I know she is not, for this match made up
    Her presence would have interrupted much.
    Where is she and her son ? Tell me, who knows.

LEWIS

    She is sad and passionate at your highness' tent.    54

KING PHILIP

    And, by my faith, this league that we have made
    Will give her sadness very little cure.
    Brother of England, how may we content
    This widow lady ? In her right we came,
    Which we, God knows, have turned another way,
    To our own vantage.

KING JOHN          We will heal up all,
    For we'll create young Arthur Duke of Britain
    And Earl of Richmond, and this rich fair town
    We make him lord of. Call the Lady Constance.
    Some speedy messenger bid her repair
    To our solemnity. I trust we shall,    55
    If not fill up the measure of her will,
    Yet in some measure satisfy her so,
    That we shall stop her exclamation.    55
    Go we, as well as haste will suffer us,    55
    To this unlooked for, unpreparèd pomp.
         *Exeunt [all but the Bastard].*

BASTARD

    Mad world ! Mad kings ! Mad composition !    56
    John, to stop Arthur's title in the whole,
    Hath willingly departed with a part,    56
    And France, whose armor conscience buckled on,
    Whom zeal and charity brought to the field
    As God's own soldier, rounded in the ear    56
    With that same purpose-changer, that sly devil,    56
    That broker, that still breaks the pate of faith,    56
    That daily break-vow, he that wins of all,
    Of kings, of beggars, old men, young men, maids,
    Who, having no external thing to lose
    But the word 'maid,' cheats the poor maid of that,    57
    That smooth-faced gentleman, tickling commodity,    57
    Commodity, the bias of the world ;    57
    The world, who of itself is peisèd well,    57

---

487 *Angiers* i.e. Anjou  490 *liable* subject  494 *Holds hand with* equals
498 *shadow* reflection (the elaborate sun-mistress conceit, very common
in Shakespeare's day, emphasizes the artificiality of the wooing)  503
*Drawn* pictured ; *table* flat surface on which a picture is painted  504
*Drawn* (with a quibble on the sense of disembowelled)  506 *quartered*
lodged (with quibble ; Elizabethan traitors were hanged, drawn, and
quartered)  513 *translate it to my will* cause it to suit my own desires
519 *churlish* miserly (of praise)  522, 523 *still* always  533 *likes* pleases
535 *assured* betrothed  537 *that amity* those friends  544 *passionate*
angry  555 *our solemnity* the wedding ceremony  558 *stop her exclamation*
silence her loud complaints  559 *suffer* permit  561 *composition* agreement  563 *departed with* relinquished  566 *rounded* whispered  567 *With*
by  568 *broker* go-between (in a pejorative sense, as a pander)  571 *Who*
i.e. the maids  573 *tickling* flattering ; *commodity* self-interest  574 *bias*
the weight in a bowling ball which causes it to curve  575 *peisèd* balanced,
weighted

Made to run even upon even ground,
577 Till this advantage, this vile-drawing bias,
This sway of motion, this commodity,
579 Makes it take head from all indifference,
And this same bias, this commodity,
This bawd, this broker, this all-changing word,
583 Clapped on the outward eye of fickle France,
Hath drawn him from his own determined aid,
585 From a resolved and honorable war,
To a most base and vile-concluded peace.
And why rail I on this commodity?
588 But for because he hath not wooed me yet.
Not that I have the power to clutch my hand
590 When his fair angels would salute my palm,
591 But for my hand, as unattempted yet,
Like a poor beggar, raileth on the rich.
Well, whiles I am a beggar, I will rail
And say there is no sin but to be rich;
And being rich, my virtue then shall be
To say there is no vice but beggary.
597 Since kings break faith upon commodity,
Gain, be my lord, for I will worship thee!      *Exit.*

\*

II, i      *Enter Constance, Arthur, and Salisbury.*

CONSTANCE

Gone to be married! Gone to swear a peace!
False blood to false blood joined! Gone to be friends!
Shall Lewis have Blanch, and Blanch those provinces?
It is not so; thou hast misspoke, misheard.
Be well advised, tell o'er thy tale again.
It cannot be; thou dost but say 'tis so.
I trust I may not trust thee, for thy word
Is but the vain breath of a common man.
Believe me, I do not believe thee, man;
I have a king's oath to the contrary.
Thou shalt be punished for thus frighting me,
For I am sick and capable of fears,
Oppressed with wrongs, and therefore full of fears,
A widow, husbandless, subject to fears,
A woman, naturally born to fears;
And though thou now confess thou didst but jest,
17 With my vexed spirits I cannot take a truce,
But they will quake and tremble all this day.
What dost thou mean by shaking of thy head?
Why dost thou look so sadly on my son?

---

577 *vile-drawing* leading into evil   579 *take . . . indifference* rush away from all moderation   583 *eye* (1) vision, (2) that part of the bowl where the bias was placed; *France* (Philip is now the bowl drawn aside by the bias in his eye; the outward eye is distinguished from the inner, or conscience) 585 *resolved* already decided upon   588 *But for because* merely because 590 *angels* Elizabethan coins bearing the relief of an angel   591 *unattempted* untempted   597 *upon* because of
III, i The quarters of the French King   17 *take a truce* make peace   22 *rheum* moisture, tears   23 *peering o'er* overflowing   27 *them* i.e. the French king and his advisers   42 *content* calm, quiet   44 *slanderous* a disgrace 45 *blots* blemishes; *sightless* unsightly   46 *swart* of dark complexion; *prodigious* deformed, bearing the mark of the Devil   56 *adulterates* (1) commits adultery, (2) changes, shows her fickleness   57 *with her golden hand* by bribery; *plucked on* incited   63 *Envenom* vituperate   65 *underbear* endure   69 *grief . . . stoop* (Constance sees herself as the slave of the grief which she possesses but which masters her)   70 *state* royal court

---

What means that hand upon that breast of thine?
22 Why holds thine eye that lamentable rheum,
23 Like a proud river peering o'er his bounds?
Be these sad signs confirmers of thy words?
Then speak again, not all thy former tale,
But this one word, whether thy tale be true.

SALISBURY

As true as I believe you think them false
27 That give you cause to prove my saying true.

CONSTANCE

O if thou teach me to believe this sorrow,
Teach thou this sorrow how to make me die!
And let belief and life encounter so
As doth the fury of two desperate men
Which in the very meeting fall and die.
Lewis marry Blanch! O boy, then where art thou?
France friend with England, what becomes of me?
Fellow, be gone! I cannot brook thy sight.
This news hath made thee a most ugly man.

SALISBURY

What other harm have I, good lady, done,
But spoke the harm that is by others done?

CONSTANCE

Which harm within itself so heinous is
As it makes harmful all that speak of it.

ARTHUR

42 I do beseech you, madam, be content.

CONSTANCE

If thou that bid'st me be content wert grim,
44 Ugly and slanderous to thy mother's womb,
45 Full of unpleasing blots and sightless stains,
46 Lame, foolish, crooked, swart, prodigious,
Patched with foul moles and eye-offending marks,
I would not care, I then would be content,
For then I should not love thee; no, nor thou
Become thy great birth, nor deserve a crown.
But thou art fair, and at thy birth, dear boy,
Nature and fortune joined to make thee great.
Of nature's gifts thou mayst with lilies boast
And with the half-blown rose. But fortune, O!
She is corrupted, changed, and won from thee.
56 Sh' adulterates hourly with thine uncle John,
57 And with her golden hand hath plucked on France
To tread down fair respect of sovereignty,
And made his majesty the bawd to theirs.
France is a bawd to fortune and King John,
That strumpet fortune, that usurping John!
Tell me, thou fellow, is not France forsworn?
63 Envenom him with words, or get thee gone
And leave those woes alone which I alone
65 Am bound to underbear.

SALISBURY      Pardon me, madam,
I may not go without you to the kings.

CONSTANCE

Thou mayst, thou shalt; I will not go with thee.
I will instruct my sorrows to be proud,
69 For grief is proud and makes his owner stoop.
70 To me and to the state of my great grief
Let kings assemble, for my grief 's so great
That no supporter but the huge firm earth
Can hold it up. Here I and sorrows sit.
Here is my throne; bid kings come bow to it.
     *[Seats herself on the ground.]*

*Enter King John, [King Philip of] France,*
*[Lewis, the] Dauphin, Blanch, Elinor, Philip [the*
*Bastard], Austria, Constance [and Attendants].*

KING PHILIP
'Tis true, fair daughter, and this blessèd day
76 Ever in France shall be kept festival.
To solemnize this day the glorious sun
Stays in his course and plays the alchemist,
Turning with splendor of his precious eye
80 The meagre cloddy earth to glittering gold.
The yearly course that brings this day about
Shall never see it but a holy day.

CONSTANCE *[rising]*
A wicked day, and not a holy day!
What hath this day deserved? What hath it done
That it in golden letters should be set
86 Among the high tides in the calendar?
Nay, rather turn this day out of the week,
This day of shame, oppression, perjury.
89 Or, if it must stand still, let wives with child
Pray that their burdens may not fall this day,
91 Lest that their hopes prodigiously be crossed.
92 But on this day let seamen fear no wrack;
No bargains break that are not this day made;
This day all things begun come to ill end;
Yea, faith itself to hollow falsehood change!

KING PHILIP
By heaven, lady, you shall have no cause
To curse the fair proceedings of this day.
98 Have I not pawned to you my majesty?

CONSTANCE
99 You have beguiled me with a counterfeit
100 Resembling majesty, which, being touched and tried,
Proves valueless. You are forsworn, forsworn.
102 You came in arms to spill mine enemies' blood,
103 But now in arms you strengthen it with yours.
The grappling vigor and rough frown of war
105 Is cold in amity and painted peace,
106 And our oppression hath made up this league.
Arm, arm, you heavens, against these perjured kings!
A widow cries; be husband to me, heavens!
Let not the hours of this ungodly day
Wear out the day in peace; but, ere sunset,
Set armèd discord 'twixt these perjured kings!
Hear me! O, hear me!

AUSTRIA                    Lady Constance, peace!

CONSTANCE
War! War! No peace! Peace is to me a war.
O, Lymoges! O, Austria! Thou dost shame
115 That bloody spoil. Thou slave, thou wretch, thou coward!
Thou little valiant, great in villainy!
Thou ever strong upon the stronger side!
Thou fortune's champion, that dost never fight
119 But when her humorous ladyship is by
To teach thee safety! Thou art perjured too,
121 And sooth'st up greatness. What a fool art thou,
122 A ramping fool, to brag and stamp and swear
123 Upon my party! Thou cold-blooded slave,
Hast thou not spoke like thunder on my side,
Been sworn my soldier, bidding me depend
Upon thy stars, thy fortune, and thy strength,
127 And dost thou now fall over to my foes?
Thou wear a lion's hide! Doff it for shame,

And hang a calfskin on those recreant limbs.    129

AUSTRIA
O that a man should speak those words to me!

BASTARD
And hang a calfskin on those recreant limbs.

AUSTRIA
Thou dar'st not say so, villain, for thy life.

BASTARD
And hang a calfskin on those recreant limbs.

KING JOHN
We like not this; thou dost forget thyself.
*Enter Pandulph.*

KING PHILIP
Here comes the holy legate of the Pope.

PANDULPH
Hail, you anointed deputies of heaven!
To thee, King John, my holy errand is.
I Pandulph, of fair Milan cardinal,
And from Pope Innocent the legate here,
Do in his name religiously demand
Why thou against the church, our holy mother,
So wilfully dost spurn; and force perforce    142
Keep Stephen Langton, chosen Archbishop
Of Canterbury, from that holy see.
This, in our foresaid holy father's name,
Pope Innocent, I do demand of thee.

KING JOHN
What earthy name to interrogatories    147
Can task the free breath of a sacred king?
Thou canst not, cardinal, devise a name
So slight, unworthy and ridiculous,
To charge me to an answer, as the Pope.    151
Tell him this tale, and from the mouth of England
Add thus much more, that no Italian priest
Shall tithe or toll in our dominions;    154
But as we under heaven are supreme head,
So under Him that great supremacy,
Where we do reign, we will alone uphold,
Without th' assistance of a mortal hand.
So tell the Pope, all reverence set apart    159
To him and his usurped authority.

KING PHILIP
Brother of England, you blaspheme in this.

KING JOHN
Though you and all the kings of Christendom
Are led so grossly by this meddling priest,    163
Dreading the curse that money may buy out,
And by the merit of vile gold, dross, dust,
Purchase corrupted pardon of a man,

---

76 *festival* as a holiday   80 *meagre* barren   86 *high tides* great festivals
89 *stand still* remain   91 *prodigiously be crossed* be disappointed by the
birth of a monster   92 *But* except; *wrack* shipwreck   98 *pawned* pledged
99 *counterfeit* false coin   100 *touched and tried* tested by being rubbed on
a touchstone   102 *in arms* wearing armor   103 *in arms* embracing one
another; *yours* your blood relative, Lewis   105 *Is . . . peace* lies dead in a
new friendship and pretended peace   106 *oppression* distress   115 *bloody
spoil* i.e. the lion skin he wears   119 *humorous* fickle, capricious   121
*sooth'st up* flatterest   122 *ramping* rushing wildly about like a lion   123
*Upon my party* on my side   127 *fall over* desert   129 *calfskin* (material
of which coats for household fools traditionally were made; alluding also
to the cowardice of Austria); *recreant* cowardly   142 *spurn* oppose with
contempt; *force perforce* by forcible means   147–48 *What . . . king* what
mortal man can compel a king to answer questions   147 *interrogatories*
formal questions put to a witness in a court of law   151 *charge* command
154 *tithe or toll* collect church revenues   159 *set apart* discarded   163
*grossly* stupidly

167 Who in that sale sells pardon from himself,
Though you and all the rest, so grossly led,
This juggling witchcraft with revenue cherish,
Yet I alone, alone do me oppose
Against the Pope, and count his friends my foes.

PANDULPH
Then, by the lawful power that I have,
Thou shalt stand cursed and excommunicate;
And blessèd shall he be that doth revolt
From his allegiance to an heretic;
And meritorious shall that hand be called,
Canonized and worshipped as a saint,
That takes away by any secret course
Thy hateful life.

CONSTANCE     O lawful let it be
That I have room with Rome to curse awhile!
Good father cardinal, cry thou amen
182 To my keen curses, for without my wrong
There is no tongue hath power to curse him right.

PANDULPH
There's law and warrant, lady, for my curse.

CONSTANCE
And for mine too. When law can do no right,
Let it be lawful that law bar no wrong.
Law cannot give my child his kingdom here,
For he that holds his kingdom holds the law;
Therefore, since law itself is perfect wrong,
How can the law forbid my tongue to curse?

PANDULPH
Philip of France, on peril of a curse,
Let go the hand of that arch-heretic,
193 And raise the power of France upon his head,
Unless he do submit himself to Rome.

ELINOR
Look'st thou pale, France? Do not let go thy hand.

CONSTANCE
196 Look to that, devil, lest that France repent,
And by disjoining hands, hell lose a soul.

AUSTRIA
King Philip, listen to the cardinal.

BASTARD
And hang a calfskin on his recreant limbs.

AUSTRIA
200 Well, ruffian, I must pocket up these wrongs,
Because –

BASTARD     Your breeches best may carry them.

KING JOHN
Philip, what sayst thou to the cardinal?

CONSTANCE
What should he say, but as the cardinal?

LEWIS
Bethink you, father, for the difference
Is purchase of a heavy curse from Rome,
Or the light loss of England for a friend.

---

167 *Who . . . himself* i.e. the seller of indulgences damns his own soul
182–83 *without . . . right* he cannot be adequately cursed without recognition of his wrong against me    193 *upon* against    196 *devil* i.e. Elinor
200 *pocket up* put up with    207 *Forgo the easier* relinquish the less important
209 *new untrimmèd* having just removed her bridal gown, still a virgin
213 *needs* of necessity    224 *make my person yours* put yourself in my
position    225 *bestow yourself* behave    230 *latest breath* most recent speech
235 *clap* strike hands together to seal a bargain    238 *difference* quarrel
241 *Unyoke this seizure* separate the hands clasped in friendship; *regreet*
return of the salutation of friendship    242 *Play fast and loose* cheat    243
*unconstant* fickle

Forgo the easier.     207

BLANCH     That's the curse of Rome.

CONSTANCE
O Lewis, stand fast! The devil tempts thee here
In likeness of a new untrimmèd bride.     209

BLANCH
The Lady Constance speaks not from her faith,
But from her need.

CONSTANCE     O, if thou grant my need,
Which only lives but by the death of faith,
That need must needs infer this principle,     213
That faith would live again by death of need.
O then, tread down my need, and faith mounts up;
Keep my need up, and faith is trodden down!

KING JOHN
The king is moved and answers not to this.

CONSTANCE
O be removed from him, and answer well!

AUSTRIA
Do so, King Philip; hang no more in doubt.

BASTARD
Hang nothing but a calfskin, most sweet lout.

KING PHILIP
I am perplexed, and know not what to say.

PANDULPH
What canst thou say but will perplex thee more,
If thou stand excommunicate and cursed?

KING PHILIP
Good reverend father, make my person yours,     224
And tell me how you would bestow yourself.     225
This royal hand and mine are newly knit,
And the conjunction of our inward souls
Married in league, coupled and linked together
With all religious strength of sacred vows.
The latest breath that gave the sound of words     230
Was deep-sworn faith, peace, amity, true love
Between our kingdoms and our royal selves,
And even before this truce, but new before,
No longer than we well could wash our hands
To clap this royal bargain up of peace,     235
Heaven knows, they were besmeared and overstained
With slaughter's pencil, where revenge did paint
The fearful difference of incensèd kings.     238
And shall these hands, so lately purged of blood,
So newly joined in love, so strong in both,
Unyoke this seizure and this kind regreet?     241
Play fast and loose with faith? So jest with heaven,     242
Make such unconstant children of ourselves,     243
As now again to snatch our palm from palm,
Unswear faith sworn, and on the marriage-bed
Of smiling peace to march a bloody host,
And make a riot on the gentle brow
Of true sincerity? O holy sir,
My reverend father, let it not be so!
Out of your grace, devise, ordain, impose
Some gentle order, and then we shall be blessed
To do your pleasure and continue friends.

PANDULPH
All form is formless, order orderless,
Save what is opposite to England's love.
Therefore to arms! Be champion of our church,
Or let the church, our mother, breathe her curse,
A mother's curse, on her revolting son.
France, thou mayst hold a serpent by the tongue,

259 A casèd lion by the mortal paw,
A fasting tiger safer by the tooth,
Than keep in peace that hand which thou dost hold.

**KING PHILIP**
I may disjoin my hand, but not my faith.

**PANDULPH**
263 So mak'st thou faith an enemy to faith,
And like a civil war set'st oath to oath,
Thy tongue against thy tongue. O, let thy vow
First made to heaven, first be to heaven performed,
That is, to be the champion of our church.
What since thou swor'st is sworn against thyself
And may not be performèd by thyself,
270 For that which thou hast sworn to do amiss
Is not amiss when it is truly done;
And being not done, where doing tends to ill,
The truth is then most done not doing it.
The better act of purposes mistook
Is to mistake again; though indirect,
Yet indirection thereby grows direct,
And falsehood falsehood cures, as fire cools fire
Within the scorchèd veins of one new burned.
It is religion that doth make vows kept,
280 But thou hast sworn against religion,
By what thou swear'st, against the thing thou swear'st,
And mak'st an oath the surety for thy truth
Against an oath; the truth thou art unsure
To swear swears only not to be forsworn;
Else what a mockery should it be to swear!
But thou dost swear only to be forsworn;
And most forsworn to keep what thou dost swear.
Therefore thy later vows against thy first
Is in thyself rebellion to thyself,
And better conquest never canst thou make
291 Than arm thy constant and thy nobler parts
292 Against these giddy loose suggestions;
Upon which better part our prayers come in,
If thou vouchsafe them. But, if not, then know
The peril of our curses light on thee
296 So heavy as thou shalt not shake them off,
But in despair die under their black weight.

**AUSTRIA**
Rebellion, flat rebellion!

298 **BASTARD**                    Will't not be?
Will not a calfskin stop that mouth of thine?

**LEWIS**
Father, to arms!

**BLANCH**          Upon thy wedding-day?
301 Against the blood that thou hast marrièd?
What, shall our feast be kept with slaughtered men?
303 Shall braying trumpets and loud churlish drums,
304 Clamors of hell, be measures to our pomp?
O husband, hear me! Ay, alack, how new
Is 'husband' in my mouth! Even for that name,
Which till this time my tongue did ne'er pronounce,
Upon my knee I beg, go not to arms
Against mine uncle.

**CONSTANCE**          O, upon my knee,
Made hard with kneeling, I do pray to thee,
311 Thou virtuous Dauphin, alter not the doom
312 Forethought by heaven.

**BLANCH**
Now shall I see thy love. What motive may
Be stronger with thee than the name of wife?

**CONSTANCE**
That which upholdeth him that thee upholds,
His honor. O thine honor, Lewis, thine honor!

**LEWIS**
I muse your majesty doth seem so cold,
When such profound respects do pull you on.          318

**PANDULPH**
I will denounce a curse upon his head.          319

**KING PHILIP**
Thou shalt not need. England, I will fall from thee.          320

**CONSTANCE**
O fair return of banished majesty!

**ELINOR**
O foul revolt of French inconstancy!

**KING JOHN**
France, thou shalt rue this hour within this hour.

**BASTARD**
Old time the clock-setter, that bald sexton time,          324
Is it as he will? Well then, France shall rue.

**BLANCH**
The sun's o'ercast with blood. Fair day, adieu!
Which is the side that I must go withal?
I am with both. Each army hath a hand,
And in their rage, I having hold of both,
They whirl asunder and dismember me.
Husband, I cannot pray that thou mayst win.
Uncle, I needs must pray that thou mayst lose.
Father, I may not wish the fortune thine.
Grandam, I will not wish thy wishes thrive.
Whoever wins, on that side shall I lose;
Assurèd loss before the match be played.

**LEWIS**
Lady, with me, with me thy fortune lies.

**BLANCH**
There where my fortune lives, there my life dies.

**KING JOHN**
Cousin, go draw our puissance together. [Exit Bastard.]          339
France, I am burned up with inflaming wrath,
A rage whose heat hath this condition,          341
That nothing can allay, nothing but blood,
The blood, and dearest-valued blood, of France.

**KING PHILIP**
Thy rage shall burn thee up, and thou shalt turn
To ashes, ere our blood shall quench that fire.
Look to thyself, thou art in jeopardy.

**KING JOHN**
No more than he that threats. To arms let's hie! Exeunt.

*

259 casèd caged; mortal deadly   263–65 So . . . tongue you are swearing against the religious faith to which you already are pledged   270–78 For . . . burned i.e. Philip by not performing what he has just vowed may turn his wrong to right; when one has done wrong it is often easier to return to the true path by another wrong than to retrace one's steps (this doctrine of equivocation was particularly hated by Elizabethan Protestants)   280–87 But . . . swear since you have sworn by your faith against your faith (true religion), you make a mockery of swearing; you commit the greatest breach of faith by keeping the oath you have just sworn   291 arm by arming   292 giddy unsafe, insecure; suggestions temptations   296 as that   298 Will't not be is nothing of any use   301 blood blood-relationship   303 churlish rude   304 measures melodies   311 doom decision   312 Forethought predestined   318 profound respects weighty considerations   319 denounce proclaim   320 fall from forsake   324 Old time the clock-setter (the sexton's job included setting the church clock as well as digging graves; he is thus easily identified with time, the destroyer of life)   339 Cousin kinsman; draw our puissance muster our army   341 condition quality

ii *Alarums, excursions. Enter Bastard, with Austria's*
*head.*

BASTARD
Now, by my life, this day grows wondrous hot.
2 Some airy devil hovers in the sky
And pours down mischief. Austria's head lie there,
4 While Philip breathes.
*Enter [King] John, Arthur, Hubert.*
KING JOHN
5 Hubert, keep this boy. Philip, make up;
My mother is assailèd in our tent,
And ta'en, I fear.
BASTARD My lord, I rescued her;
Her highness is in safety, fear you not.
But on, my liege, for very little pains
Will bring this labor to a happy end.
*Exit [with the others].*
iii *Alarums, excursions, retreat. Enter [King] John,*
*Elinor, Arthur, Bastard, Hubert, Lords.*
KING JOHN *[to Elinor]*
So shall it be ; your grace shall stay behind
So strongly guarded. *[to Arthur]* Cousin, look not sad.
Thy grandam loves thee, and thy uncle will
As dear be to thee as thy father was.
ARTHUR
O this will make my mother die with grief !
KING JOHN *[to the Bastard]*
6 Cousin, away for England ! Haste before,
And ere our coming see thou shake the bags
8 Of hoarding abbots ; imprisoned angels
Set at liberty. The fat ribs of peace
Must by the hungry now be fed upon.
Use our commission in his utmost force.
BASTARD
12 Bell, book, and candle shall not drive me back
13 When gold and silver becks me to come on.
I leave your highness. Grandam, I will pray –
If ever I remember to be holy –
For your fair safety ; so I kiss your hand.
ELINOR
Farewell, gentle cousin.
17 KING JOHN Coz, farewell. *[Exit Bastard.]*
ELINOR
Come hither, little kinsman. Hark, a word.
*[She takes Arthur aside.]*
KING JOHN
Come hither, Hubert. O my gentle Hubert,
We owe thee much ! Within this wall of flesh
There is a soul counts thee her creditor,
22 And with advantage means to pay thy love ;
And, my good friend, thy voluntary oath
Lives in this bosom, dearly cherishèd.
Give me thy hand. I had a thing to say,
But I will fit it with some better tune.
By heaven, Hubert, I am almost ashamed
28 To say what good respect I have of thee.

HUBERT
I am much bounden to your majesty. 29
KING JOHN
Good friend, thou hast no cause to say so yet,
But thou shalt have ; and creep time ne'er so slow,
Yet it shall come for me to do thee good.
I had a thing to say, but let it go.
The sun is in the heaven, and the proud day,
Attended with the pleasures of the world,
Is all too wanton and too full of gawds 36
To give me audience. If the midnight bell
Did with his iron tongue and brazen mouth
Sound on into the drowsy ear of night ;
If this same were a churchyard where we stand,
And thou possessèd with a thousand wrongs ;
Or if that surly spirit, melancholy,
Had baked thy blood and made it heavy, thick,
Which else runs tickling up and down the veins,
Making that idiot, laughter, keep men's eyes
And strain their cheeks to idle merriment,
A passion hateful to my purposes ;
Or if that thou couldst see me without eyes,
Hear me without thine ears, and make reply
Without a tongue, using conceit alone, 50
Without eyes, ears, and harmful sound of words ;
Then, in despite of brooded watchful day, 52
I would into thy bosom pour my thoughts.
But ah, I will not. Yet I love thee well,
And, by my troth, I think thou lov'st me well.
HUBERT
So well, that what you bid me undertake,
Though that my death were adjunct to my act, 57
By heaven, I would do it.
KING JOHN Do not I know thou wouldst ?
Good Hubert ! Hubert, Hubert, throw thine eye
On yon young boy. I'll tell thee what, my friend,
He is a very serpent in my way,
And wheresoe'er this foot of mine doth tread
He lies before me. Dost thou understand me ?
Thou art his keeper.
HUBERT And I'll keep him so
That he shall not offend your majesty.
KING JOHN
Death.
HUBERT My lord ?
KING JOHN A grave.
HUBERT He shall not live.
KING JOHN Enough.
I could be merry now. Hubert, I love thee.
Well, I'll not say what I intend for thee.
Remember. Madam, fare you well.
I'll send those powers o'er to your majesty. 70
ELINOR
My blessing go with thee !
KING JOHN For England, cousin, go.
Hubert shall be your man, attend on you 72
With all true duty. On toward Calais, ho ! *Exeunt.*

III, ii A field of battle near Angiers 2 *Some . . . sky* a thunderstorm
threatens 4 *breathes* rests 5 *make up* advance to the front line
III, iii 6 *before* ahead of us 8 *angels* coins (with the usual pun) 12 *Bell,
book, and candle* (instruments used in the ritual of excommunication) 13
*becks* beckons 17 *Coz* kinsman 22 *advantage* interest ; *pay* repay 28
*respect* opinion 29 *bounden* obliged 36 *gawds* showy ornaments, such as
the flowers in springtime 50 *conceit* understanding 52 *brooded* brooding
57 *adjunct to* the result of 70 *powers* troops 72 *man* servant

III, iv    *Enter [King Philip of] France, [Lewis, the]*
           *Dauphin, Pandulph, Attendants.*

KING PHILIP

1   So, by a roaring tempest on the flood,
2   A whole armado of convicted sail
    Is scattered and disjoined from fellowship.

PANDULPH

    Courage and comfort! All shall yet go well.

KING PHILIP

    What can go well when we have run so ill?
    Are we not beaten? Is not Angiers lost?
    Arthur ta'en prisoner? Divers dear friends slain?
    And bloody England into England gone,
9   O'erbearing interruption, spite of France?

LEWIS

    What he hath won, that hath he fortified.
11  So hot a speed with such advice disposed,
    Such temperate order in so fierce a cause,
13  Doth want example. Who hath read or heard
    Of any kindred action like to this?

KING PHILIP

    Well could I bear that England had this praise,
16  So we could find some pattern of our shame.
           *Enter Constance.*
    Look, who comes here! A grave unto a soul,
    Holding th' eternal spirit, against her will,
19  In the vile prison of afflicted breath.
    I prithee, lady, go away with me.

CONSTANCE

    Lo, now! Now see the issue of your peace!

KING PHILIP

    Patience, good lady! Comfort, gentle Constance!

CONSTANCE

23  No, I defy all counsel, all redress,
    But that which ends all counsel, true redress,
    Death, death. O, amiable, lovely death!
    Thou odoriferous stench! Sound rottenness!
27  Arise forth from the couch of lasting night,
    Thou hate and terror to prosperity,
    And I will kiss thy detestable bones,
30  And put my eyeballs in thy vaulty brows,
    And ring these fingers with thy household worms,
32  And stop this gap of breath with fulsome dust,
    And be a carrion monster like thyself.
    Come, grin on me, and I will think thou smil'st
35  And buss thee as thy wife! Misery's love,
    O, come to me!

KING PHILIP    O fair affliction, peace!

CONSTANCE

    No, no, I will not, having breath to cry.
    O that my tongue were in the thunder's mouth!
    Then with a passion would I shake the world,
40  And rouse from sleep that fell anatomy
    Which cannot hear a lady's feeble voice,
42  Which scorns a modern invocation.

PANDULPH

    Lady, you utter madness and not sorrow.

CONSTANCE

    Thou art not holy to belie me so.
    I am not mad; this hair I tear is mine.
    My name is Constance; I was Geoffrey's wife.
    Young Arthur is my son, and he is lost!
    I am not mad. I would to heaven I were,
49  For then 'tis like I should forget myself.

    O, if I could, what grief should I forget!
    Preach some philosophy to make me mad,
    And thou shalt be canonized, cardinal.
    For, being not mad but sensible of grief,                    53
    My reasonable part produces reason
    How I may be delivered of these woes,                        55
    And teaches me to kill or hang myself.
    If I were mad, I should forget my son,
    Or madly think a babe of clouts were he.                     58
    I am not mad. Too well, too well I feel
    The different plague of each calamity.

KING PHILIP

    Bind up those tresses. O, what love I note
    In the fair multitude of those her hairs!
    Where but by chance a silver drop hath fallen,              63
    Even to that drop ten thousand wiry friends                 64
    Do glue themselves in sociable grief,                       65
    Like true, inseparable, faithful loves,
    Sticking together in calamity.

CONSTANCE

    To England, if you will.                                    68

KING PHILIP         Bind up your hairs.

CONSTANCE

    Yes, that I will; and wherefore will I do it?
    I tore them from their bonds and cried aloud:
    'O that these hands could so redeem my son,
    As they have given these hairs their liberty!'
    But now I envy at their liberty,
    And will again commit them to their bonds,
    Because my poor child is a prisoner.
    And, Father Cardinal, I have heard you say
    That we shall see and know our friends in heaven.
    If that be true, I shall see my boy again,
    For since the birth of Cain, the first male child,
    To him that did but yesterday suspire,
    There was not such a gracious creature born.                81
    But now will canker sorrow eat my bud                       82
    And chase the native beauty from his cheek,
    And he will look as hollow as a ghost,
    As dim and meagre as an ague's fit,                         85
    And so he'll die; and rising so again,
    When I shall meet him in the court of heaven
    I shall not know him. Therefore never, never
    Must I behold my pretty Arthur more.

PANDULPH

    You hold too heinous a respect of grief.                    90

CONSTANCE

    He talks to me that never had a son.

III, iv The quarters of the French King   1 *flood* ocean   2 *armado* fleet
of warships; *convicted* doomed to destruction   9 *interruption* resistance;
*spite of* despite   11 *with such advice disposed* controlled with such good
judgment   13 *Doth want example* is without precedent   16 *So* if; *pattern*
example in the past   19 *breath* life   23 *defy* reject   27 *lasting* everlasting
30 *vaulty* arched   32 *stop . . . breath* stop up this mouth; *fulsome* physically
disgusting   35 *buss* kiss   40 *fell anatomy* cruel skeleton (as death traditionally was personified)   42 *modern invocation* ordinary supplication   49
*like* probable   53 *sensible* capable   55 *be delivered of* give birth to, separate
myself from (Constance sees death as her lover, grief as her child)   58
*babe of clouts* rag doll   63 *silver drop* tear   64 *wiry friends* hairs (wire was a
common metaphor for hair)   65 *sociable* sympathetic   68 *To England*
. . . *will* (a line which is usually taken as evidence of some revision in this
scene, since it bears no relation to its immediate context, but which may
be an answer to King Philip's invitation at l. 20)   81 *gracious* meriting
divine grace, destined for heaven   82 *canker* like a canker worm (which
destroys plants)   85 *dim* pale   90 *heinous a respect* terrible an opinion

**KING PHILIP**

92   You are as fond of grief as of your child.

**CONSTANCE**

Grief fills the room up of my absent child,
Lies in his bed, walks up and down with me,
Puts on his pretty looks, repeats his words,
96   Remembers me of all his gracious parts,
Stuffs out his vacant garments with his form.
Then have I reason to be fond of grief.
Fare you well. Had you such a loss as I,
I could give better comfort than you do.
01   I will not keep this form upon my head,
02   When there is such disorder in my wit.
O Lord! My boy, my Arthur, my fair son!
My life, my joy, my food, my all the world!
My widow-comfort, and my sorrows' cure!          *Exit.*

**KING PHILIP**

I fear some outrage, and I'll follow her.          *Exit.*

**LEWIS**

There's nothing in this world can make me joy.
Life is as tedious as a twice-told tale,
Vexing the dull ear of a drowsy man,
And bitter shame hath spoiled the sweet world's taste,
That it yields nought but shame and bitterness.

**PANDULPH**

Before the curing of a strong disease,
13   Even in the instant of repair and health,
The fit is strongest. Evils that take leave,
On their departure most of all show evil.
16   What have you lost by losing of this day?

**LEWIS**

All days of glory, joy, and happiness.

**PANDULPH**

If you had won it, certainly you had.
No, no; when fortune means to men most good,
She looks upon them with a threat'ning eye.
'Tis strange to think how much King John hath lost
In this which he accounts so clearly won.
Are not you grieved that Arthur is his prisoner?

**LEWIS**

As heartily as he is glad he hath him.

**PANDULPH**

Your mind is all as youthful as your blood.
Now hear me speak with a prophetic spirit,
For even the breath of what I mean to speak
28   Shall blow each dust, each straw, each little rub,
Out of the path which shall directly lead

Thy foot to England's throne. And therefore mark:
John hath seized Arthur, and it cannot be
That, whiles warm life plays in that infant's veins,
The misplaced John should entertain an hour,          133
One minute, nay, one quiet breath of rest.
A sceptre snatched with an unruly hand
Must be as boisterously maintained as gained,          136
And he that stands upon a slippery place
Makes nice of no vile hold to stay him up.          138
That John may stand, then Arthur needs must fall;
So be it, for it cannot be but so.

**LEWIS**

But what shall I gain by young Arthur's fall?

**PANDULPH**

You, in the right of Lady Blanch your wife,
May then make all the claim that Arthur did.

**LEWIS**

And lose it, life and all, as Arthur did.

**PANDULPH**

How green you are and fresh in this old world!          145
John lays you plots; the times conspire with you,          146
For he that steeps his safety in true blood          147
Shall find but bloody safety and untrue.
This act so evilly borne shall cool the hearts          149
Of all his people and freeze up their zeal,
That none so small advantage shall step forth          151
To check his reign, but they will cherish it;
No natural exhalation in the sky,          153
No scope of nature, no distempered day,          154
No common wind, no customèd event,          155
But they will pluck away his natural cause          156
And call them meteors, prodigies, and signs,
Abortives, presages, and tongues of heaven,          158
Plainly denouncing vengeance upon John.

**LEWIS**

May be he will not touch young Arthur's life,
But hold himself safe in his prisonment.

**PANDULPH**

O, sir, when he shall hear of your approach,
If that young Arthur be not gone already,
Even at that news he dies; and then the hearts
Of all his people shall revolt from him
And kiss the lips of unacquainted change,          166
And pick strong matter of revolt and wrath          167
Out of the bloody fingers' ends of John.
Methinks I see this hurly all on foot;          169
And, O, what better matter breeds for you          170
Than I have named! The bastard Faulconbridge
Is now in England ransacking the church,
Offending charity. If but a dozen French          173
Were there in arms, they would be as a call          174
To train ten thousand English to their side,          175
Or as a little snow, tumbled about,
Anon becomes a mountain. O noble Dauphin,          177
Go with me to the king. 'Tis wonderful
What may be wrought out of their discontent,
Now that their souls are topful of offense.          180
For England go; I will whet on the king.          181

**LEWIS**

Strong reasons make strange actions. Let us go.
If you say ay, the king will not say no.          *Exeunt.*

---

92 *fond of* foolishly infatuated with   96 *Remembers* reminds   101 *form* orderly arrangement of hair   102 *wit* mind   113 *repair* recovery   116 *day* day of battle   128 *dust* grain of dust; *rub* obstacle (in the game of bowls)   133 *misplaced* usurping   136 *boisterously* violently   138 *Makes . . . up* is not scrupulous about what evil means he uses to support himself   145 *green* inexperienced   146 *lays you plots* makes plans for your advantage   147-48 *he . . . untrue* he who bases his safety on his killing of the true king (Arthur) will find his safety bloody and false   149 *so evilly borne* carried out so wickedly   151 *advantage* opportunity   153 *exhalation* meteor   154 *scope of nature* a seemingly impossible event which is nevertheless within the possibility of nature; *distempered* full of bad weather   155 *customèd* ordinary   156 *his* its   158 *Abortives* corruptions of nature by untimely birth   166 *kiss . . . change* be enamored of any new change   167-68 *pick . . . John* find cause for revolt and anger in John's bloody deeds   169 *hurly* commotion; *on foot* started   170 *breeds* is ripening   173 *charity* good will   174 *call* decoy (as a bird call)   175 *train* attract   177 *Anon* soon   180 *topful of offense* filled to the brim with grievances   181 *whet on* incite

*

IV, i        *Enter Hubert and Executioners.*

HUBERT

Heat me these irons hot, and look thou stand
2    Within the arras. When I strike my foot
3    Upon the bosom of the ground, rush forth
And bind the boy which you shall find with me
Fast to the chair. Be heedful. Hence, and watch.

[1.] EXECUTIONER
6    I hope your warrant will bear out the deed.

HUBERT
7    Uncleanly scruples! Fear not you. Look to't.
                    *[Exeunt Executioners.]*
8    Young lad, come forth; I have to say with you.
        *Enter Arthur.*

ARTHUR

Good morrow, Hubert.

HUBERT                        Good morrow, little prince.

ARTHUR
10    As little prince, having so great a title
To be more prince, as may be. You are sad.

HUBERT

Indeed, I have been merrier.

ARTHUR                        Mercy on me!
Methinks nobody should be sad but I.
Yet I remember, when I was in France
15    Young gentlemen would be as sad as night,
16    Only for wantonness. By my christendom,
17    So I were out of prison and kept sheep,
I should be as merry as the day is long;
19    And so I would be here, but that I doubt
20    My uncle practises more harm to me.
He is afraid of me and I of him.
Is it my fault that I was Geoffrey's son?
No, indeed, is't not, and I would to heaven
I were your son, so you would love me, Hubert.

HUBERT *[aside]*
25    If I talk to him, with his innocent prate
He will awake my mercy which lies dead;
27    Therefore I will be sudden and dispatch.

ARTHUR

Are you sick, Hubert? You look pale to-day.
29    In sooth, I would you were a little sick,
That I might sit all night and watch with you.
I warrant I love you more than you do me.

HUBERT *[aside]*
His words do take possession of my bosom.
Read here, young Arthur. *[Shows a paper.]*
        *[Aside]*                How now, foolish rheum,
34    Turning dispiteous torture out of door!
I must be brief, lest resolution drop
Out at mine eyes in tender womanish tears.
37    Can you not read it? Is it not fair writ?

ARTHUR
38    Too fairly, Hubert, for so foul effect.
Must you with hot irons burn out both mine eyes?

HUBERT

Young boy, I must.

ARTHUR                        And will you?

HUBERT                                        And I will.

ARTHUR

Have you the heart? When your head did but ache,
I knit my handkercher about your brows—
43    The best I had, a princess wrought it me—
And I did never ask it you again;

And with my hand at midnight held your head,
And like the watchful minutes to the hour,        46
Still and anon cheered up the heavy time,        47
Saying, 'What lack you?' and 'Where lies your grief?'
Or 'What good love may I perform for you?'        49
Many a poor man's son would have lien still,        50
And ne'er have spoke a loving word to you,
But you at your sick service had a prince.        52
Nay, you may think my love was crafty love,        53
And call it cunning; do and if you will.
If heaven be pleased that you must use me ill,
Why then you must. Will you put out mine eyes?
These eyes that never did nor never shall
So much as frown on you?

HUBERT                        I have sworn to do it,
And with hot irons must I burn them out.

ARTHUR

Ah, none but in this iron age would do it!        60
The iron of itself, though heat red-hot,        61
Approaching near these eyes, would drink my tears
And quench this fiery indignation
Even in the matter of mine innocence,        64
Nay, after that, consume away in rust,
But for containing fire to harm mine eye.        66
Are you more stubborn-hard than hammered iron?
And if an angel should have come to me
And told me Hubert should put out mine eyes,
I would not have believed him—no tongue but Hubert's.

HUBERT *[stamps]*

Come forth.
        *[Enter Executioners, with a cord, irons, etc.]*
Do as I bid you do.

ARTHUR

O! save me, Hubert, save me! My eyes are out
Even with the fierce looks of these bloody men.

HUBERT

Give me the iron, I say, and bind him here.

ARTHUR

Alas, what need you be so boist'rous rough?        76
I will not struggle, I will stand stone still.
For heaven sake, Hubert, let me not be bound!
Nay, hear me, Hubert! Drive these men away,
And I will sit as quiet as a lamb.
I will not stir, nor wince, nor speak a word,
Nor look upon the iron angerly.        82
Thrust but these men away, and I'll forgive you,
Whatever torment you do put me to.

IV, i Within an English castle  2 *Within the arras* behind the curtains
3 *bosom* surface  6 *bear out* be sufficient to justify  7 *Uncleanly* improper,
unbecoming; *Fear not you* don't you worry  8 *to say with* something to say
to  10–11 *As . . . may be* as little of a prince (since I am in captivity) as one
with my great title possibly could be  15–16 *as sad . . . wantonness* melancholy merely as a whimsical affectation (a common pose among gentlemen
of Shakespeare's day)  16 *christendom* baptism, hence faith as a Christian
17 *So* if  19 *doubt* fear  20 *practises* plots  25 *prate* prattle  27 *dispatch*
do the job quickly  29 *sooth* truth  34 *dispiteous* merciless  37 *fair writ*
clearly written  38 *effect* purpose  43 *wrought it me* embroidered it for me
46 *watchful . . . hour* minutes which mark the progress of the hour  47 *Still
and anon* continually from time to time (Arthur compares his questions to
the ticking of the minutes, which makes the hour go by more quickly);
*heavy* dreary  49 *love* loving deed  50 *lien* lain (an archaic form preserved
for the metre)  52 *at your sick service* at your service (as a nurse) when you
were sick  53 *crafty* pretended  60 *iron age* cruel, degenerate present (as
opposed to the heroic golden age of antiquity)  61 *heat* heated  64 *matter
of mine innocence* tears, the signs of innocence  66 *But* merely  76 *what*
why  82 *angerly* angrily

HUBERT
85 Go, stand within. Let me alone with him.
   [1.] EXECUTIONER
86 I am best pleased to be from such a deed.
                   *[Exeunt Executioners.]*
ARTHUR
87 Alas! I then have chid away my friend!
   He hath a stern look but a gentle heart.
   Let him come back, that his compassion may
   Give life to yours.
HUBERT          Come, boy, prepare yourself.
ARTHUR
   Is there no remedy?
HUBERT         None, but to lose your eyes.
ARTHUR
92 O heaven, that there were but a mote in yours,
   A grain, a dust, a gnat, a wandering hair,
   Any annoyance in that precious sense.
95 Then feeling what small things are boisterous there,
   Your vile intent must needs seem horrible.
HUBERT
   Is this your promise? Go to, hold your tongue.
ARTHUR
98 Hubert, the utterance of a brace of tongues
   Must needs want pleading for a pair of eyes.
   Let me not hold my tongue, let me not, Hubert;
   Or, Hubert, if you will, cut out my tongue,
   So I may keep mine eyes. O, spare mine eyes,
   Though to no use but still to look on you!
104 Lo, by my troth, the instrument is cold
   And would not harm me.
HUBERT          I can heat it, boy.
ARTHUR
   No, in good sooth. The fire is dead with grief,
107 Being create for comfort, to be used
108 In undeserved extremes. See else yourself.
   There is no malice in this burning coal.
   The breath of heaven hath blown his spirit out
   And strewed repentant ashes on his head.
HUBERT
   But with my breath I can revive it, boy.
ARTHUR
   And if you do, you will but make it blush
   And glow with shame of your proceedings, Hubert.
115 Nay, it perchance will sparkle in your eyes,

And like a dog that is compelled to fight,
Snatch at his master that doth tarre him on.    117
All things that you should use to do me wrong
Deny their office. Only you do lack    119
That mercy which fierce fire and iron extends,    120
Creatures of note for mercy-lacking uses.    121
HUBERT
   Well, see to live; I will not touch thine eye
   For all the treasure that thine uncle owes.    123
   Yet am I sworn and I did purpose, boy,
   With this same very iron to burn them out.
ARTHUR
   O, now you look like Hubert! All this while
   You were disguisèd.
HUBERT         Peace! No more. Adieu.
   Your uncle must not know but you are dead.    128
   I'll fill these doggèd spies with false reports.    129
   And, pretty child, sleep doubtless and secure    130
   That Hubert for the wealth of all the world
   Will not offend thee.
ARTHUR       O heaven! I thank you, Hubert.
HUBERT
   Silence! No more! Go closely in with me.    133
   Much danger do I undergo for thee.        *Exeunt.*

*

   *Enter [King] John, Pembroke, Salisbury, and other*    IV, ii
   *Lords.*
KING JOHN
   Here once again we sit, once again crowned,    1
   And looked upon, I hope, with cheerful eyes.
PEMBROKE
   This 'once again,' but that your highness pleased,
   Was once superfluous. You were crowned before,
   And that high royalty was ne'er plucked off,
   The faiths of men ne'er stainèd with revolt.    6
   Fresh expectation troubled not the land    7
   With any longed for change or better state.    8
SALISBURY
   Therefore, to be possessed with double pomp,    9
   To guard a title that was rich before,    10
   To gild refinèd gold, to paint the lily,
   To throw a perfume on the violet,
   To smooth the ice, or add another hue
   Unto the rainbow, or with taper-light    14
   To seek the beauteous eye of heaven to garnish,
   Is wasteful and ridiculous excess.
PEMBROKE
   But that your royal pleasure must be done,
   This act is as an ancient tale new told,
   And in the last repeating troublesome,
   Being urgèd at a time unseasonable.
SALISBURY
   In this the antique and well noted face
   Of plain old form is much disfigurèd,    22
   And like a shifted wind unto a sail,    23
   It makes the course of thoughts to fetch about,    24
   Startles and frights consideration,    25
   Makes sound opinion sick and truth suspected,
   For putting on so new a fashioned robe.
PEMBROKE
   When workmen strive to do better than well,
   They do confound their skill in covetousness,    29

85 *Let . . . him* leave me to deal with him alone   86 *from* away from   87 *my friend* i.e. the executioner   92 *mote* speck of dust   95 *boisterous* irritating   98–99 *the utterance . . . pleading* even two tongues could not plead adequately   104 *troth* faith   107 *create* created   108 *In undeserved extremes* to inflict acts of cruelty which have not been deserved   115 *sparkle* throw out sparks   117 *tarre* provoke to fight   119 *Deny their office* refuse to perform their proper function   120 *extends* exhibit   121 *Creatures* i.e. fire and iron; *of note . . . uses* noted for their customary use in cruel affairs   123 *owes* owns   128 *but* other than that   129 *doggèd* malicious   130 *doubtless* without fear; *secure* assured   133 *closely* secretly
IV, ii The court of King John   1 *once again* (John has just had himself recrowned to mark the end of his domination by the church of Rome)   6 *stainèd* corrupted   7 *expectation* excited anticipation of change   8 *state* government   9 *pomp* solemn ceremony (coronation)   10 *guard* ornament a garment with trimmings   14–15 *with taper-light . . . garnish* to try to add to the sun's beauty by means of candlelight   22 *plain old form* simple customary behavior   23 *shifted wind* change of wind   24 *fetch about* change their direction   25 *consideration* thought (about the succession; by a second coronation John is causing others to question the validity of his title)   29 *confound . . . covetousness* destroy what they have done well by their desire to do even better

And oftentimes excusing of a fault
Doth make the fault the worse by the excuse,
32 As patches set upon a little breach
33 Discredit more in hiding of the fault
Than did the fault before it was so patched.

SALISBURY
To this effect, before you were new crowned,
36 We breathed our counsel, but it pleased your highness
37 To overbear it, and we are all well pleased,
38 Since all and every part of what we would
Doth make a stand at what your highness will.

KING JOHN
Some reasons of this double coronation
41 I have possessed you with and think them strong;
And more, more strong, when lesser is my fear,
43 I shall indue you with. Meantime but ask
What you would have reformed that is not well,
And well shall you perceive how willingly
I will both hear and grant you your requests.

PEMBROKE
Then I, as one that am the tongue of these
48 To sound the purposes of all their hearts,
Both for myself and them – but, chief of all,
50 Your safety, for the which myself and them
51 Bend their best studies – heartily request
52 Th' enfranchisement of Arthur, whose restraint
Doth move the murmuring lips of discontent
To break into this dangerous argument:
55 If what in rest you have in right you hold,
Why then your fears, which, as they say, attend
57 The steps of wrong, should move you to mew up
Your tender kinsman, and to choke his days
With barbarous ignorance and deny his youth
60 The rich advantage of good exercise.
61 That the time's enemies may not have this
62 To grace occasions, let it be our suit
That you have bid us ask, his liberty,
64 Which for our goods we do no further ask
65 Than whèreupon our weal, on you depending,
Counts it your weal he have his liberty.
*Enter Hubert.*

KING JOHN
Let it be so. I do commit his youth
To your direction. Hubert, what news with you?
*[Takes him apart.]*

PEMBROKE
This is the man should do the bloody deed;
He showed his warrant to a friend of mine.
71 The image of a wicked heinous fault
72 Lives in his eye. That close aspect of his
Does show the mood of a much troubled breast,
And I do fearfully believe 'tis done,
75 What we so feared he had a charge to do.

SALISBURY
The color of the king doth come and go
Between his purpose and his conscience,
78 Like heralds 'twixt two dreadful battles set.
79 His passion is so ripe it needs must break.

PEMBROKE
And when it breaks, I fear will issue thence
81 The foul corruption of a sweet child's death.

KING JOHN
We cannot hold mortality's strong hand.
Good lords, although my will to give is living,

The suit which you demand is gone and dead.
He tells us Arthur is deceased to-night.

SALISBURY
Indeed we feared his sickness was past cure.

PEMBROKE
Indeed we heard how near his death he was,
Before the child himself felt he was sick.
This must be answered either here or hence. 89

KING JOHN
Why do you bend such solemn brows on me? 90
Think you I bear the shears of destiny? 91
Have I commandment on the pulse of life?

SALISBURY
It is apparent foul play, and 'tis shame
That greatness should so grossly offer it. 94
So thrive it in your game! And so, farewell. 95

PEMBROKE
Stay yet, Lord Salisbury. I'll go with thee
And find th' inheritance of this poor child,
His little kingdom of a forcèd grave. 98
That blood which owed the breadth of all this isle, 99
Three foot of it doth hold – bad world the while! 100
This must not be thus borne. This will break out 101
To all our sorrows, and ere long, I doubt. 102
         *Exeunt [Lords].*

KING JOHN
They burn in indignation. I repent.
    *Enter Messenger.*
There is no sure foundation set on blood,
No certain life achieved by others' death.
A fearful eye thou hast. Where is that blood 106
That I have seen inhabit in those cheeks?
So foul a sky clears not without a storm.
Pour down thy weather. How goes all in France? 109

MESSENGER
From France to England. Never such a power
For any foreign preparation 111
Was levied in the body of a land.
The copy of your speed is learned by them, 113
For when you should be told they do prepare,
The tidings comes that they are all arrived. 115

KING JOHN
O, where hath our intelligence been drunk? 116
Where hath it slept? Where is my mother's care,
That such an army could be drawn in France, 118

32 *breach* hole in a garment 33 *fault* defect 36 *breathed* spoke 37 *overbear* veto by superior power 38–39 *Since . . . will* since our wishes can never run counter to your desires 41 *possessed you with* informed you of 43 *indue* furnish 48 *sound the purposes* express the proposals 50 *them* they 51 *Bend their best studies* direct their most diligent efforts 52 *enfranchisement* release from prison 55 *If . . . hold* if you hold rightfully what you possess peaceably 57 *mew up* shut up 60 *exercise* education of a gentleman 61 *time's enemies* those opposed to the present state of affairs 62 *grace occasions* make proper and acceptable their opportunities to attack 64 *our goods* our own good 65 *whereupon* to the extent that; *weal* welfare 71 *image* reflection 72 *close aspect* secret expression 75 *charge* order 78 *battles* armies arranged for battle; *set* assigned to perform duties 79 *break* burst open (like a boil) 81 *corruption* pus 89 *answered* accounted or atoned for; *here or hence* in this world or the next 90 *bend . . . brows* frown 91 *shears of destiny* instrument with which Atropos, one of the three Fates, cuts the thread of life 94 *That . . . offer it* that a king should act so outrageously 95 *So . . . game* may you suffer accordingly 98 *forcèd* imposed by violence 99 *blood* life; *owed* owned 100 *the while* where such things can happen 101 *borne* tolerated 102 *doubt* fear 106 *fearful* full of fear 109 *weather* tempest 111 *preparation* expedition 113 *copy* example; *learned* imitated 115 *arrived* landed 116 *intelligence* spy system 118 *drawn* mustered

And she not hear of it?

119 MESSENGER                  My liege, her ear
Is stopped with dust. The first of April died
Your noble mother; and, as I hear, my lord,
The Lady Constance in a frenzy died
Three days before. But this from rumor's tongue
124 I idly heard; if true or false I know not.

KING JOHN
125 Withhold thy speed, dreadful occasion!
O, make a league with me, till I have pleased
My discontented peers. What! Mother dead!
128 How wildly then walks my estate in France!
129 Under whose conduct came those powers of France
That thou for truth giv'st out are landed here?

MESSENGER
Under the Dauphin.

KING JOHN                  Thou hast made me giddy
With these ill tidings.
            *Enter Bastard and Peter of Pomfret.*
                        Now, what says the world
To your proceedings? Do not seek to stuff
My head with more ill news, for it is full.

BASTARD
But if you be afeard to hear the worst,
Then let the worst unheard fall on your head.

KING JOHN
137 Bear with me, cousin, for I was amazed
Under the tide; but now I breathe again
139 Aloft the flood and can give audience
To any tongue, speak it of what it will.

BASTARD
141 How I have sped among the clergymen
The sums I have collected shall express.
But as I travelled hither through the land,
144 I find the people strangely fantasied,
Possessed with rumors, full of idle dreams,
Not knowing what they fear, but full of fear.
And here's a prophet that I brought with me
148 From forth the streets of Pomfret, whom I found
With many hundreds treading on his heels,
To whom he sung, in rude harsh-sounding rimes,
That ere the next Ascension-day at noon,
Your highness should deliver up your crown.

KING JOHN
153 Thou idle dreamer, wherefore didst thou so?

PETER
Foreknowing that the truth will fall out so.

KING JOHN
Hubert, away with him; imprison him,
And on that day at noon, whereon he says

119–23 *her ear . . . before* (Queen Elinor actually died on April 1, 1204, but how Shakespeare could have gotten the day and month exactly right remains a mystery, for this was not recorded in any Elizabethan chronicle. Constance had died three years before, in 1201. Shakespeare compresses time.) 124 *idly* without paying full attention 125 *occasion* course of events 128 *walks* proceeds; *estate* power 129 *conduct* leadership 137 *amazed* bewildered 139 *Aloft* above 141 *sped* succeeded 144 *strangely fantasied* full of strange notions 148 *Pomfret* Pontefract in Yorkshire 153 *idle* foolish 158 *safety* safekeeping 159 *gentle* noble 167 *thrust . . . companies* associate with them 172 *adverse* hostile 173 *stout* bold 174 *Mercury* the messenger of the gods, who wore winged sandals 177 *sprightful* full of spirit 182 *five moons* (a type of unnatural phenomenon believed to herald disaster to a kingdom) 185 *beldams* hags 186 *prophesy upon it* attempt to explain the unnatural phenomenon 191 *action* gesticulation 198 *contrary* wrong 200 *embattailèd and ranked* ready for battle and arrayed in proper order

I shall yield up my crown, let him be hanged.
Deliver him to safety and return,                  158
For I must use thee.        *[Exit Hubert, with Peter.]*
                  O my gentle cousin,                  159
Hear'st thou the news abroad, who are arrived?

BASTARD
The French, my lord. Men's mouths are full of it.
Besides, I met Lord Bigot and Lord Salisbury,
With eyes as red as new-enkindled fire,
And others more, going to seek the grave
Of Arthur, whom they say is killed to-night
On your suggestion.

KING JOHN                  Gentle kinsman, go,
And thrust thyself into their companies.                  167
I have a way to win their loves again.
Bring them before me.

BASTARD                  I will seek them out.

KING JOHN
Nay, but make haste, the better foot before.
O, let me have no subject enemies,
When adverse foreigners affright my towns                  172
With dreadful pomp of stout invasion.                  173
Be Mercury, set feathers to thy heels,                  174
And fly like thought from them to me again.

BASTARD
The spirit of the time shall teach me speed.        *Exit.*

KING JOHN
Spoke like a sprightful noble gentleman.                  177
Go after him, for he perhaps shall need
Some messenger betwixt me and the peers;
And be thou he.

MESSENGER        With all my heart, my liege.        *[Exit.]*

KING JOHN
My mother dead!
            *Enter Hubert.*

HUBERT
My lord, they say five moons were seen to-night –                  182
Four fixèd, and the fifth did whirl about
The other four in wondrous motion.

KING JOHN
Five moons!

HUBERT        Old men and beldams in the streets                  185
Do prophesy upon it dangerously.                  186
Young Arthur's death is common in their mouths,
And when they talk of him, they shake their heads
And whisper one another in the ear;
And he that speaks doth gripe the hearer's wrist,
Whilst he that hears makes fearful action,                  191
With wrinkled brows, with nods, with rolling eyes.·
I saw a smith stand with his hammer, thus,
The whilst his iron did on the anvil cool,
With open mouth swallowing a tailor's news;
Who, with his shears and measure in his hand,
Standing on slippers, which his nimble haste
Had falsely thrust upon contrary feet,                  198
Told of a many thousand warlike French,
That were embattailèd and ranked in Kent.                  200
Another lean unwashed artificer
Cuts off his tale and talks of Arthur's death.

KING JOHN
Why seek'st thou to possess me with these fears?
Why urgest thou so oft young Arthur's death?
Thy hand hath murdered him. I had a mighty cause
To wish him dead, but thou hadst none to kill him.

HUBERT

207    No had, my lord ? Why, did you not provoke me ?

KING JOHN

208    It is the curse of kings to be attended
209    By slaves that take their humors for a warrant
210    To break within the bloody house of life,
211    And on the winking of authority
212    To understand a law, to know the meaning
       Of dangerous majesty, when, perchance, it frowns
214    More upon humor than advised respect.

HUBERT

       Here is your hand and seal for what I did.

KING JOHN

216    O, when the last accompt 'twixt heaven and earth
       Is to be made, then shall this hand and seal
       Witness against us to damnation !
       How oft the sight of means to do ill deeds
       Makes deeds ill done ! Hadst not thou been by,
       A fellow by the hand of nature marked,
222    Quoted and signed to do a deed of shame,
       This murder had not come into my mind ;
224    But taking note of thy abhorred aspect,
       Finding thee fit for bloody villainy,
226    Apt, liable to be employed in danger,
227    I faintly broke with thee of Arthur's death ;
       And thou, to be endearèd to a king,
229    Made it no conscience to destroy a prince.

HUBERT

       My lord –

KING JOHN

       Hadst thou but shook thy head or made a pause
232    When I spake darkly what I purposèd,
       Or turned an eye of doubt upon my face,
234    As bid me tell my tale in express words,
       Deep shame had struck me dumb, made me break off,
       And those thy fears might have wrought fears in me.
       But thou didst understand me by my signs
       And didst in signs again parley with sin ;
       Yea, without stop, didst let thy heart consent,
       And consequently thy rude hand to act
       The deed which both our tongues held vile to name.
       Out of my sight, and never see me more !
243    My nobles leave me, and my state is braved,
       Even at my gates, with ranks of foreign powers.
245    Nay, in the body of this fleshly land,
246    This kingdom, this confine of blood and breath,
247    Hostility and civil tumult reigns
       Between my conscience and my cousin's death.

HUBERT

       Arm you against your other enemies ;
       I'll make a peace between your soul and you.
       Young Arthur is alive. This hand of mine
252    Is yet a maiden and an innocent hand,
       Not painted with the crimson spots of blood.
       Within this bosom never entered yet
255    The dreadful motion of a murderous thought,
256    And you have slandered nature in my form,
       Which, howsoever rude exteriorly,
       Is yet the cover of a fairer mind
       Than to be butcher of an innocent child.

KING JOHN

       Doth Arthur live ? O, haste thee to the peers !
261    Throw this report on their incensèd rage,
       And make them tame to their obedience.

Forgive the comment that my passion made
Upon thy feature, for my rage was blind,          264
And foul imaginary eyes of blood                  265
Presented thee more hideous than thou art.
O, answer not, but to my closet bring             267
The angry lords with all expedient haste.
I conjure thee but slowly ; run more fast.    *Exeunt.* 269

                            *

ARTHUR

       The wall is high, and yet will I leap down.
       Good ground, be pitiful and hurt me not !
       There's few or none do know me ; if they did,
       This ship-boy's semblance hath disguised me quite.   4
       I am afraid, and yet I'll venture it.
       If I get down, and do not break my limbs,
       I'll find a thousand shifts to get away.              7
       As good to die and go, as die and stay.
               [*Leaps down.*]
       O me ! My uncle's spirit is in these stones !
       Heaven take my soul, and England keep my bones !  *Dies.*
               *Enter Pembroke, Salisbury, and Bigot.*

SALISBURY

       Lords, I will meet him at Saint Edmundsbury.         11
       It is our safety, and we must embrace                12
       This gentle offer of the perilous time.

PEMBROKE

       Who brought that letter from the cardinal ?

SALISBURY

       The Count Melun, a noble lord of France,
       Whose private with me of the Dauphin's love          16
       Is much more general than these lines import.        17

BIGOT

       To-morrow morning let us meet him then.

SALISBURY

       Or rather then set forward, for 'twill be
       Two long days' journey, lords, or ere we meet.       20
               *Enter Bastard.*

BASTARD

       Once more to-day well met, distempered lords !       21
       The king by me requests your presence straight.      22

SALISBURY

       The king hath dispossessed himself of us.
       We will not line his thin bestainèd cloak

207 *No had* had I not; *provoke* incite    208 *attended* served    209 *humors*
whims    210 *bloody house of life* human body, containing blood    211
*winking of authority* failure of the king to enforce the law    212 *understand*
infer    214 *upon humor* because of a whim ; *advised respect* carefully considered decision    216 *accompt* account, judgment    222 *Quoted and signed*
especially noted and marked out    224 *abhorred aspect* horrible appearance
226 *liable* suitable    227 *faintly broke with* hesitatingly confided in    229
*conscience* matter of conscience    232 *darkly* vaguely    234 *As* as if to ; *in
express words* clearly    243 *braved* defied    245 *fleshly land* his human body
(conceived of as a little world paralleling the physical universe in its composition)    246 *confine* territory bound by frontiers    247 *civil tumult*
internal war    252 *maiden* bloodless    255 *motion* impulse    256 *form* outward appearance    261 *Throw* i.e. as water, to quench the fire of rage
264 *feature* appearance    265 *imaginary eyes of blood* i.e. Hubert's eyes,
which in John's imagination seemed full of blood    267 *closet* private room
269 *conjure* solemnly urge
IV, iii Outside the wall of an English castle    4 *semblance* disguise    7 *shifts*
stratagems    11 *him* i.e. the Dauphin    12 *embrace* welcome    16 *private*
private communication ; *love* friendship    17 *general* comprehensive    20 *or
ere* before    21 *distempered* disgruntled    22 *straight* at once

With our pure honors, nor attend the foot
That leaves the print of blood where'er it walks.
Return and tell him so. We know the worst.

BASTARD
Whate'er you think, good words, I think, were best.

SALISBURY
29  Our griefs, and not our manners, reason now.

BASTARD
But there is little reason in your grief;
Therefore 'twere reason you had manners now.

PEMBROKE
Sir, sir, impatience hath his privilege.

BASTARD
'Tis true, to hurt his master, no man else.

SALISBURY
This is the prison. *[Sees Arthur.]* What is he lies here?

PEMBROKE
O death, made proud with pure and princely beauty!
The earth had not a hole to hide this deed.

SALISBURY
Murder, as hating what himself hath done,
Doth lay it open to urge on revenge.

BIGOT
Or when he doomed this beauty to a grave,
40  Found it too precious princely for a grave.

SALISBURY
Sir Richard, what think you? Have you beheld,
Or have you read or heard, or could you think,
Or do you almost think, although you see,
44  That you do see? Could thought, without this object,
Form such another? This is the very top,
The height, the crest, or crest unto the crest,
Of murder's arms. This is the bloodiest shame,
The wildest savagery, the vilest stroke,
49  That ever wall-eyed wrath or staring rage
50  Presented to the tears of soft remorse.

PEMBROKE
All murders past do stand excused in this.
52  And this, so sole and so unmatchable,
Shall give a holiness, a purity,
54  To the yet unbegotten sin of times,
And prove a deadly bloodshed but a jest,
56  Exampled by this heinous spectacle.

BASTARD
It is a damnèd and a bloody work,
58  The graceless action of a heavy hand,
If that it be the work of any hand.

SALISBURY
If that it be the work of any hand!
61  We had a kind of light what would ensue.
It is the shameful work of Hubert's hand,
63  The practice and the purpose of the king,

From whose obedience I forbid my soul,
Kneeling before this ruin of sweet life,
And breathing to his breathless excellence
The incense of a vow, a holy vow,
Never to taste the pleasures of the world,
Never to be infected with delight,                69
Nor conversant with ease and idleness,
Till I have set a glory to this hand,              71
By giving it the worship of revenge.               72

PEMBROKE, BIGOT
Our souls religiously confirm thy words.
    *Enter Hubert.*

HUBERT
Lords, I am hot with haste in seeking you.
Arthur doth live; the king hath sent for you.

SALISBURY
O, he is bold and blushes not at death.
Avaunt, thou hateful villain! Get thee gone!       77

HUBERT
I am no villain.

SALISBURY *[drawing his sword]* Must I rob the law?

BASTARD
Your sword is bright, sir; put it up again.

SALISBURY
Not till I sheathe it in a murderer's skin.

HUBERT
Stand back, Lord Salisbury, stand back, I say!
By heaven, I think my sword's as sharp as yours.
I would not have you, lord, forget yourself,
Nor tempt the danger of my true defense,           84
Lest I, by marking of your rage, forget            85
Your worth, your greatness, and nobility.

BIGOT
Out, dunghill! Dar'st thou brave a nobleman?       87

HUBERT
Not for my life, but yet I dare defend
My innocent life against an emperor.

SALISBURY
Thou art a murderer.

HUBERT                 Do not prove me so.           90
Yet I am none. Whose tongue soe'er speaks false,
Not truly speaks; who speaks not truly, lies.

PEMBROKE
Cut him to pieces.

BASTARD                 Keep the peace, I say.

SALISBURY
Stand by, or I shall gall you, Faulconbridge.      94

BASTARD
Thou wert better gall the devil, Salisbury.
If thou but frown on me, or stir thy foot,
Or teach thy hasty spleen to do me shame,          97
I'll strike thee dead. Put up thy sword betime,    98
Or I'll so maul you and your toasting-iron         99
That you shall think the devil is come from hell.

BIGOT
What wilt thou do, renownèd Faulconbridge?
Second a villain and a murderer?                   102

HUBERT
Lord Bigot, I am none.

BIGOT                 Who killed this prince?

HUBERT
'Tis not an hour since I left him well.
I honored him, I loved him, and will weep
My date of life out for his sweet life's loss.     106

29 *griefs* grievances; *reason* talk   40 *too . . . grave* (bodies of princes were entombed above ground)   44 *That* that which   49 *wall-eyed* with glaring eyes; *rage* madness   50 *remorse* pity   52 *sole* unique   54 *times* future ages   56 *Exampled by* compared with   58 *graceless* unholy; *heavy* wicked   61 *light* inkling   63 *practice* machination   69 *infected* diseased (delight under such circumstances is conceived of as a disease)   71 *this hand* i.e. either the dead Arthur's hand which Salisbury kisses, or his own hand raised in celebration of his vow   72 *worship* honor, dignity   77 *Avaunt* be gone   84 *true defense* (1) honest defense of my cause, (2) skilful use of my sword   85 *marking of* (1) observing, (2) striking a blow at   87 *brave* insult   90 *Do . . . so* i.e. by compelling me to kill you   94 *by* aside; *gall* injure   97 *spleen* wrath   98 *betime* at once   99 *toasting-iron* sword (a term of contempt)   102 *Second* support   106 *date* duration

SALISBURY
Trust not those cunning waters of his eyes,
For villainy is not without such rheum,
109 And he, long traded in it, makes it seem
Like rivers of remorse and innocency.
Away with me, all you whose souls abhor
112 Th' uncleanly savors of a slaughter-house,
For I am stifled with this smell of sin.

BIGOT
Away toward Bury, to the Dauphin there!

PEMBROKE
There tell the king he may inquire us out. *Exeunt Lords.*

BASTARD
Here's a good world! Knew you of this fair work?
Beyond the infinite and boundless reach
Of mercy, if thou didst this deed of death,
Art thou damned, Hubert.

HUBERT          Do but hear me, sir.

BASTARD
Ha! I'll tell thee what.
121 Thou'rt damned as black – nay, nothing is so black.
Thou art more deep damned than Prince Lucifer.
There is not yet so ugly a fiend of hell
As thou shalt be, if thou didst kill this child.

HUBERT
Upon my soul –

BASTARD       If thou didst but consent
To this most cruel act, do but despair,
And if thou want'st a cord, the smallest thread
That ever spider twisted from her womb
129 Will serve to strangle thee; a rush will be a beam
To hang thee on. Or wouldst thou drown thyself,
Put but a little water in a spoon,
And it shall be as all the ocean,
Enough to stifle such a villain up.
I do suspect thee very grievously.

HUBERT
If I in act, consent, or sin of thought,
Be guilty of the stealing that sweet breath
137 Which was embounded in this beauteous clay,
Let hell want pains enough to torture me.
I left him well.

BASTARD       Go, bear him in thine arms.
140 I am amazed, methinks, and lose my way
Among the thorns and dangers of this world.
How easy dost thou take all England up!
From forth this morsel of dead royalty
The life, the right and truth of all this realm
Is fled to heaven, and England now is left
146 To tug and scamble and to part by th' teeth
147 The unowed interest of proud swelling state.
Now for the bare-picked bone of majesty
149 Doth doggèd war bristle his angry crest
And snarleth in the gentle eyes of peace.
151 Now powers from home and discontents at home
152 Meet in one line, and vast confusion waits,
As doth a raven on a sick-fallen beast,
154 The imminent decay of wrested pomp.
155 Now happy he whose cloak and ceinture can
Hold out this tempest. Bear away that child,
And follow me with speed. I'll to the king.
158 A thousand businesses are brief in hand,
And heaven itself doth frown upon the land.    *Exit.*

*

*Enter King John and Pandulph, [with] Attendants.*    V,

KING JOHN
Thus have I yielded up into your hand
The circle of my glory.                 2

PANDULPH [*giving King John the crown*] Take again
From this my hand, as holding of the Pope,
Your sovereign greatness and authority.

KING JOHN
Now keep your holy word. Go meet the French,
And from his holiness use all your power
To stop their marches 'fore we are enflamed.
Our discontented counties do revolt.         8
Our people quarrel with obedience,
Swearing allegiance and the love of soul     10
To stranger blood, to foreign royalty.
This inundation of mistempered humor     12
Rests by you only to be qualified.         13
Then pause not, for the present time's so sick,
That present med'cine must be ministered,    15
Or overthrow incurable ensues.           16

PANDULPH
It was my breath that blew this tempest up,
Upon your stubborn usage of the Pope,      18
But since you are a gentle convertite,       19
My tongue shall hush again this storm of war
And make fair weather in your blust'ring land.
On this Ascension-day, remember well,
Upon your oath of service to the Pope,
Go I to make the French lay down their arms.    *Exit.*

KING JOHN
Is this Ascension-day? Did not the prophet
Say that before Ascension-day at noon
My crown I should give off? Even so I have.    27
I did suppose it should be on constraint,
But, heaven be thanked, it is but voluntary.
         *Enter Bastard.*

BASTARD
All Kent hath yielded; nothing there holds out
But Dover Castle. London hath received,
Like a kind host, the Dauphin and his powers.
Your nobles will not hear you, but are gone
To offer service to your enemy,
And wild amazement hurries up and down     35
The little number of your doubtful friends.    36

KING JOHN
Would not my lords return to me again
After they heard young Arthur was alive?

BASTARD
They found him dead and cast into the streets,
An empty casket, where the jewel of life
By some damned hand was robbed and ta'en away.

109 *long traded* experienced   112 *savors* odors   121 *black* (the traditional color of the devil and of all damned souls)   129 *rush* slender reed   137 *embounded . . . clay* enclosed within this beautiful body   140 *amazed* bewildered   146 *scamble* scramble   147 *unowed interest* disputed ownership   149 *doggèd* (1) fierce, (2) like a dog   151 *from home* foreign; *discontents* rebels   152 *in one line* together   154 *wrested pomp* usurped kingship   155 *ceinture* belt   158 *brief in hand* calling for immediate attention   V, i The court of King John   2 *circle* crown   8 *counties* shires, or noblemen   10 *love of soul* deepest love, loyalty   12 *inundation* . . . *humor* overgrowth, because of disorder, of one of the four elements of the body (John is drawing his metaphor from current medical terminology)   13 *Rests . . . qualified* can be reduced to proper proportions only by you   15 *ministered* administered   16 *overthrow* destruction   18 *Upon* because of   19 *convertite* convert   27 *give off* relinquish   35 *amazement* bewilderment   36 *doubtful* (1) frightened, (2) of questionable loyalty

**KING JOHN**
That villain Hubert told me he did live.

**BASTARD**
So, on my soul, he did, for aught he knew.
But wherefore do you droop? Why look you sad?
Be great in act, as you have been in thought.
Let not the world see fear and sad distrust
Govern the motion of a kingly eye.
48 Be stirring as the time; be fire with fire.
49 Threaten the threat'ner, and outface the brow
Of bragging horror. So shall inferior eyes,
That borrow their behaviors from the great,
Grow great by your example and put on
The dauntless spirit of resolution.
54 Away, and glister like the god of war
55 When he intendeth to become the field.
Show boldness and aspiring confidence.
What, shall they seek the lion in his den
And fright him there? And make him tremble there?
59 O, let it not be said! Forage, and run
To meet displeasure farther from the doors,
And grapple with him ere he come so nigh.

**KING JOHN**
The legate of the Pope hath been with me,
63 And I have made a happy peace with him,
And he hath promised to dismiss the powers
Led by the Dauphin.

**BASTARD**                    O inglorious league!
66 Shall we, upon the footing of our land,
67 Send fair-play orders and make compromise,
68 Insinuation, parley, and base truce
69 To arms invasive? Shall a beardless boy,
70 A cockered silken wanton, brave our fields
71 And flesh his spirit in a warlike soil,
72 Mocking the air with colors idly spread,
73 And find no check? Let us, my liege, to arms!
Perchance the cardinal cannot make your peace;
Or if he do, let it at least be said
They saw we had a purpose of defense.

**KING JOHN**
Have thou the ordering of this present time.

**BASTARD**
Away then, with good courage! Yet, I know,
79 Our party may well meet a prouder foe.        *Exeunt.*

*

48 *stirring* energetic   49 *outface* stare down   54 *glister* shine in armor   55
*become* adorn   59 *Forage* seek out the enemy   63 *happy* favorable   66 *upon*
. . . *land* standing on our native ground   67 *fair-play orders* chivalric stipulations   68 *Insinuation* self-ingratiation   69 *invasive* invading   70 *cockered*
pampered; *wanton* spoilt child; *brave* (1) insult, (2) display his finery in
71 *flesh* initiate in bloodshed   72 *idly* carelessly   73 *check* resistance   79
*prouder* more powerful
V, ii The Dauphin's quarters at St Edmundsbury   3 *precedent* first draft
of the treaty   4 *fair order* equitable conditions   10 *unurged* uncompelled
13 *plaster* dressing for a wound; *contemned* despised   14 *inveterate canker*
chronic sore   16 *metal* sword   19 *Cries out upon* appeals to   21 *physic*
cure   22 *deal* act   30 *spot* disgrace; *enforcèd* forced upon us   31 *grace*
pay homage to   32 *unacquainted colors* foreign banners   33 *remove* move
yourself, depart   34 *clippeth* embraces   35 *knowledge* awareness   38 *vein*
(1) blood vessel, (2) mood   40 *temper* state of mind   41 *affections* emotions
44 *compulsion* what you were forced to do; *brave respect* courageous consideration of your true duty   45 *dew* i.e. tears   46 *progress* move slowly
(like a king or queen in state; the metaphor emphasizes the nobility of
Salisbury's tears)   53 *Figured* decorated   56 *Commend* leave   59 *Full* . . .
*blood* full of human feeling

---

*Enter (in arms) [Lewis, the] Dauphin, Salisbury,*         V, ii
*Melun, Pembroke, Bigot, Soldiers.*

**LEWIS**
My Lord Melun, let this be copied out,
And keep it safe for our remembrance.
Return the precedent to those lords again,        3
That, having our fair order written down,        4
Both they and we, perusing o'er these notes,
May know wherefore we took the sacrament,
And keep our faiths firm and inviolable.

**SALISBURY**
Upon our sides it never shall be broken.
And, noble Dauphin, albeit we swear
A voluntary zeal and an unurgèd faith        10
To your proceedings, yet believe me, prince,
I am not glad that such a sore of time
Should seek a plaster by contemnèd revolt,        13
And heal the inveterate canker of one wound        14
By making many. O, it grieves my soul
That I must draw this metal from my side        16
To be a widow-maker! O, and there
Where honorable rescue and defense
Cries out upon the name of Salisbury.        19
But such is the infection of the time
That, for the health and physic of our right,        21
We cannot deal but with the very hand        22
Of stern injustice and confusèd wrong.
And is't not pity, O my grievèd friends,
That we, the sons and children of this isle,
Were born to see so sad an hour as this,
Wherein we step after a stranger, march
Upon her gentle bosom, and fill up
Her enemies' ranks – I must withdraw and weep
Upon the spot of this enforcèd cause –        30
To grace the gentry of a land remote,        31
And follow unacquainted colors here?        32
What, here? O nation, that thou couldst remove!        33
That Neptune's arms, who clippeth thee about,        34
Would bear thee from the knowledge of thyself,        35
And grapple thee unto a pagan shore,
Where these two Christian armies might combine
The blood of malice in a vein of league,        38
And not to spend it so unneighborly!

**LEWIS**
A noble temper dost thou show in this,        40
And great affections wrestling in thy bosom        41
Doth make an earthquake of nobility.
O, what a noble combat hast thou fought
Between compulsion and a brave respect!        44
Let me wipe off this honorable dew,        45
That silverly doth progress on thy cheeks.        46
My heart hath melted at a lady's tears,
Being an ordinary inundation,
But this effusion of such manly drops,
This shower, blown up by tempest of the soul,
Startles mine eyes, and makes me more amazed
Than had I seen the vaulty top of heaven
Figured quite o'er with burning meteors.        53
Lift up thy brow, renownèd Salisbury,
And with a great heart heave away this storm.
Commend these waters to those baby eyes        56
That never saw the giant world enraged,
Nor met with fortune other than at feasts,
Full warm of blood, of mirth, of gossiping.        59

Come, come; for thou shalt thrust thy hand as deep
Into the purse of rich prosperity
As Lewis himself. So, nobles, shall you all,
That knit your sinews to the strength of mine.
*Enter Pandulph.*

64 And even there, methinks, an angel spake.
Look, where the holy legate comes apace,
To give us warrant from the hand of heaven,

67 And on our actions set the name of right
With holy breath.

PANDULPH        Hail, noble prince of France!
The next is this: King John hath reconciled

70 Himself to Rome; his spirit is come in
That so stood out against the holy church,
The great metropolis and see of Rome.
Therefore thy threat'ning colors now wind up,
And tame the savage spirit of wild war,
That, like a lion fostered up at hand,
It may lie gently at the foot of peace,
And be no further harmful than in show.

LEWIS

78 Your grace shall pardon me; I will not back.
79 I am too high-born to be propertied,
80 To be a secondary at control,
Or useful serving-man and instrument
To any sovereign state throughout the world.
Your breath first kindled the dead coal of wars
Between this chastised kingdom and myself,
85 And brought in matter that should feed this fire;
And now 'tis far too huge to be blown out
With that same weak wind which enkindled it.
You taught me how to know the face of right,
89 Acquainted me with interest to this land,
Yea, thrust this enterprise into my heart;
And come ye now to tell me John hath made
His peace with Rome? What is that peace to me?
I, by the honor of my marriage-bed,
After young Arthur, claim this land for mine,
And, now it is half-conquered, must I back
Because that John hath made his peace with Rome?
Am I Rome's slave? What penny hath Rome borne,
What men provided, what munition sent,
99 To underprop this action? Is't not I
100 That undergo this charge? Who else but I,
101 And such as to my claim are liable,
Sweat in this business and maintain this war?
Have I not heard these islanders shout out,
104 *Vive le roi!* as I have banked their towns?
Have I not here the best cards for the game
To win this easy match played for a crown?
107 And shall I now give o'er the yielded set?
No, no, on my soul, it never shall be said.

PANDULPH
You look but on the outside of this work.

LEWIS
Outside or inside, I will not return
Till my attempt so much be glorified
As to my ample hope was promisèd
113 Before I drew this gallant head of war,
114 And culled these fiery spirits from the world,
115 To outlook conquest and to win renown
Even in the jaws of danger and of death.
*[Trumpet sounds.]*

117 What lusty trumpet thus doth summon us?

*Enter Bastard.*

BASTARD
According to the fair play of the world,    118
Let me have audience; I am sent to speak.    119
My holy Lord of Milan, from the king
I come, to learn how you have dealt for him,
And, as you answer, I do know the scope    122
And warrant limited unto my tongue.    123

PANDULPH
The Dauphin is too wilful-opposite,    124
And will not temporize with my entreaties.    125
He flatly says he'll not lay down his arms.

BASTARD
By all the blood that ever fury breathed,
The youth says well. Now hear our English king,
For thus his royalty doth speak in me.
He is prepared, and reason too he should.
This apish and unmannerly approach,    131
This harnessed masque and unadvisèd revel,    132
This unhaired sauciness and boyish troops,    133
The king doth smile at, and is well prepared
To whip this dwarfish war, these pigmy arms,
From out the circle of his territories.    136
That hand which had the strength, even at your door,
To cudgel you and make you take the hatch,    138
To dive, like buckets, in concealèd wells,
To crouch in litter of your stable planks,    140
To lie like pawns locked up in chests and trunks,    141
To hug with swine, to seek sweet safety out
In vaults and prisons, and to thrill and shake
Even at the crying of your nation's crow,    144
Thinking this voice an armèd Englishman –
Shall that victorious hand be feebled here
That in your chambers gave you chastisement?
No! Know the gallant monarch is in arms,
And like an eagle o'er his aery towers,    149
To souse annoyance that comes near his nest.    150
And you degenerate, you ingrate revolts,    151
You bloody Neroes, ripping up the womb    152
Of your dear mother England, blush for shame;
For your own ladies and pale-visaged maids
Like Amazons come tripping after drums,    155
Their thimbles into armèd gauntlets change,

64 *an angel spake* (has been variously explained: (1) a trumpet, like that of the angel announcing the last judgment, has just sounded, (2) Pandulph, the angel since he bears heaven's warrant, has just entered, (3) a pun on angel, a coin, with contemptuous reference to the Dauphin's mercenary motives) 67 *set* i.e. like a seal upon a warrant 70 *is come in* has submitted 78 *shall* must; *back* retreat 79 *propertied* treated like property, made a tool of 80 *secondary at control* agent controlled by another 85 *matter* fuel 89 *interest to* claim in 99 *underprop* support 100 *charge* expense 101 *liable* subject 104 *banked* sailed by 107 *give o'er* abandon; *yielded set* game already forfeited to me 113 *head* army 114 *culled* carefully selected 115 *outlook* stare down 117 *lusty* vigorous 118 *fair play* rules of chivalry 119 *to speak* i.e. rather than to fight 122 *as* according as; *scope* latitude 123 *limited* appointed 124 *wilful-opposite* stubbornly hostile 125 *temporize* come to terms 131 *apish* fantastic 132 *harnessed* in armor; *unadvisèd revel* thoughtless entertainment 133 *unhaired* beardless 136 *circle* compass 138 *take the hatch* leap over a half door or stile (like beaten dogs fleeing their masters) 140 *litter* bedding (for animals); *planks* floors 141 *pawns* articles in pawn 144 *your nation's crow* sound of the rooster, traditional symbol of France 149 *aery* eagle's nest; *towers* soars 150 *souse* swoop down on (like a bird of prey); *annoyance* threat of danger 151 *ingrate revolts* ungrateful rebels 152 *Neroes* (the Roman emperor Nero was said to have ripped open his mother's womb after murdering her) 155 *Amazons* female warriors of Greek mythology

157 Their needles to lances, and their gentle hearts
158 To fierce and bloody inclination.

LEWIS
159 There end thy brave, and turn thy face in peace.
We grant thou canst outscold us. Fare thee well.
We hold our time too precious to be spent
162 With such a brabbler.

PANDULPH          Give me leave to speak.

BASTARD
No, I will speak.

163 LEWIS          We will attend to neither.
Strike up the drums, and let the tongue of war
Plead for our interest and our being here.

BASTARD
Indeed, your drums, being beaten, will cry out,
And so shall you, being beaten. Do but start
An echo with the clamor of thy drum,
169 And even at hand a drum is ready braced
That shall reverberate all as loud as thine.
Sound but another, and another shall
172 As loud as thine rattle the welkin's ear
And mock the deep-mouthed thunder. For at hand –
174 Not trusting to this halting legate here,
Whom he hath used rather for sport than need –
Is warlike John; and in his forehead sits
177 A bare-ribbed death, whose office is this day
To feast upon whole thousands of the French.

LEWIS
Strike up our drums to find this danger out.

BASTARD
And thou shalt find it, Dauphin, do not doubt.     *Exeunt.*

*

iii     *Alarums. Enter [King] John and Hubert.*

KING JOHN
How goes the day with us ? O, tell me, Hubert.

HUBERT
Badly, I fear. How fares your majesty ?

KING JOHN
This fever that hath troubled me so long
Lies heavy on me. O, my heart is sick !
*Enter a Messenger.*

MESSENGER
My lord, your valiant kinsman, Faulconbridge,
Desires your majesty to leave the field
And send him word by me which way you go.

KING JOHN
Tell him, toward Swinstead, to the abbey there.

MESSENGER
Be of good comfort, for the great supply          9
That was expected by the Dauphin here,
Are wracked three nights ago on Goodwin sands.    11
This news was brought to Richard but even now.
The French fight coldly and retire themselves.    13

KING JOHN
Ay me ! This tyrant fever burns me up,            14
And will not let me welcome this good news.
Set on toward Swinstead. To my litter straight ;
Weakness possesseth me, and I am faint.     *Exeunt.*

*

*Enter Salisbury, Pembroke, and Bigot.*     V, iv

SALISBURY
I did not think the king so stored with friends.  1

PEMBROKE
Up once again ; put spirit in the French.
If they miscarry we miscarry too.

SALISBURY
That misbegotten devil, Faulconbridge,
In spite of spite, alone upholds the day.         5

PEMBROKE
They say King John, sore sick, hath left the field.
*Enter Melun wounded.*

MELUN
Lead me to the revolts of England here.           7

SALISBURY
When we were happy we had other names.

PEMBROKE
It is the Count Melun.

SALISBURY          Wounded to death.

MELUN
Fly, noble English ; you are bought and sold.     10
Unthread the rude eye of rebellion,               11
And welcome home again discarded faith.
Seek out King John and fall before his feet,
For if the French be lords of this loud day,
He means to recompense the pains you take         15
By cutting off your heads. Thus hath he sworn,
And I with him, and many moe with me,             17
Upon the altar at Saint Edmundsbury,
Even on that altar where we swore to you
Dear amity and everlasting love.

SALISBURY
May this be possible ? May this be true ?

MELUN
Have I not hideous death within my view,
Retaining but a quantity of life,                 23
Which bleeds away, even as a form of wax          24
Resolveth from his figure 'gainst the fire ?      25
What in the world should make me now deceive,
Since I must lose the use of all deceit ?         27
Why should I then be false, since it is true
That I must die here and live hence by truth ?    29
I say again, if Lewis do win the day,
He is forsworn if e'er those eyes of yours        31
Behold another day break in the east.
But even this night, whose black contagious breath 33
Already smokes about the burning crest            34
Of the old, feeble, and day-wearied sun,

157 *needles* (monosyllable ; in folio, 'Needl's') 158 *inclination* (1) disposition, (2) the slanting position of a knight charging with a lance (a quibble) 159 *brave* defiant boast 162 *brabbler* braggart 163 *attend* listen 169 *braced* with tightened skin (ready for playing) 172 *welkin's* sky's 174 *halting* wavering, ineffectual 177 *bare-ribbed death* i.e. death conceived of as a skeleton ; *office* function
V, iii The field of battle 9 *supply* reinforcements 11 *wracked* shipwrecked 13 *coldly* without enthusiasm 14 *tyrant* merciless
V, iv Open place near the field of battle 1 *stored* provided 5 *In spite of spite* despite anything we can do 7 *revolts* rebels 10 *bought and sold* betrayed 11 *Unthread . . . eye* retrace your steps (as a thread is withdrawn from the needle's eye) 15 *He* i.e. the Dauphin 17 *moe* more 23 *quantity* small amount 24–25 *as a form . . . fire* (witches were said to destroy their enemies by melting waxen images of them before a fire) 25 *Resolveth* dissolves ; *his figure* its shape 27 *use* profit, advantage 29 *live hence by truth* i.e. he will live in heaven to the extent that he has been truthful on earth 31 *forsworn* perjured 33 *contagious* bearing disease 34 *smokes* grows misty (as evening approaches)

Even this ill night, your breathing shall expire,
37 Paying the fine of rated treachery
38 Even with a treacherous fine of all your lives,
If Lewis by your assistance win the day.
Commend me to one Hubert with your king.
41 The love of him, and this respect besides,
42 For that my grandsire was an Englishman,
Awakes my conscience to confess all this.
44 In lieu whereof, I pray you, bear me hence
45 From forth the noise and rumor of the field,
Where I may think the remnant of my thoughts
In peace, and part this body and my soul
With contemplation and devout desires.

SALISBURY
49 We do believe thee, and beshrew my soul
50 But I do love the favor and the form
Of this most fair occasion, by the which
52 We will untread the steps of damnèd flight,
53 And like a bated and retirèd flood,
54 Leaving our rankness and irregular course,
55 Stoop low within those bounds we have o'erlooked,
And calmly run on in obedience
Even to our ocean, to our great King John.
My arm shall give thee help to bear thee hence,
For I do see the cruel pangs of death
60 Right in thine eye. Away, my friends! New flight,
61 And happy newness, that intends old right.

*Exeunt [leading off Melun].*

*

V, v          *Enter [Lewis, the] Dauphin, and his train.*

LEWIS
The sun of heaven methought was loath to set,
2 But stayed and made the western welkin blush,
When English measure backward their own ground
4 In faint retire. O, bravely came we off,
When with a volley of our needless shot,
After such bloody toil, we bid good night
7 And wound our tott'ring colors clearly up,
Last in the field, and almost lords of it!

*Enter a Messenger.*

MESSENGER
Where is my prince, the Dauphin?
LEWIS                     Here. What news?
MESSENGER
The Count Melun is slain. The English lords,
11 By his persuasion, are again fall'n off,
12 And your supply, which you have wished so long,
Are cast away and sunk on Goodwin sands.
LEWIS
14 Ah, foul, shrewd news! Beshrew thy very heart!
I did not think to be so sad to-night
As this hath made me. Who was he that said
King John did fly an hour or two before
18 The stumbling night did part our weary powers?
MESSENGER
Whoever spoke it, it is true, my lord.
LEWIS
20 Well, keep good quarter and good care to-night.
The day shall not be up so soon as I
22 To try the fair adventure of to-morrow.          *Exeunt.*

*

*Enter Bastard and Hubert, severally.*          V,

HUBERT
Who's there? Speak, ho! Speak quickly, or I shoot.
BASTARD
A friend. What art thou?
HUBERT                     Of the part of England.          2
BASTARD
Whither dost thou go?
HUBERT
What's that to thee? Why may not I demand
Of thine affairs as well as thou of mine?
BASTARD
Hubert, I think?
HUBERT          Thou hast a perfect thought.          6
I will upon all hazards well believe
Thou art my friend, that know'st my tongue so well.
Who art thou?
BASTARD          Who thou wilt; and if thou please,
Thou mayst befriend me so much as to think
I come one way of the Plantagenets.
HUBERT
Unkind remembrance! Thou and eyeless night          12
Have done me shame. Brave soldier, pardon me,          13
That any accent breaking from thy tongue          14
Should scape the true acquaintance of mine ear.
BASTARD
Come, come! Sans compliment, what news abroad?          16
HUBERT
Why, here walk I in the black brow of night
To find you out.
BASTARD          Brief, then; and what's the news?
HUBERT
O, my sweet sir, news fitting to the night,
Black, fearful, comfortless, and horrible.
BASTARD
Show me the very wound of this ill news.
I am no woman; I'll not swound at it.          22
HUBERT
The king, I fear, is poisoned by a monk.
I left him almost speechless and broke out          24
To acquaint you with this evil, that you might
The better arm you to the sudden time          26
Than if you had at leisure known of this.          27
BASTARD
How did he take it? Who did taste to him?          28
HUBERT
A monk, I tell you, a resolvèd villain,          29

37 *fine* penalty; *rated* (1) exposed at its true value, (2) rebuked, punished 38 *fine* end (note quibble) 41 *respect* consideration 42 *For that* because 44 *In lieu whereof* in payment for which 45 *rumor* noise 49 *beshrew* a curse upon 50 *favor and the form* outward appearance 52 *untread* retrace 53 *bated* abated 54 *rankness* overgrowth 55 *o'erlooked* overflowed 60 *Right* clearly 61 *happy newness* propitious change
V, v The Dauphin's quarters 2 *welkin* sky 4 *faint retire* timid retreat; *bravely* excellently; *came we off* we retired from battle 7 *tott'ring* (1) wavering, (2) in tatters (rags); *colors* banners; *clearly* neatly, without interference from the enemy 11 *are again fall'n off* have again broken faith 12 *supply* reinforcements 14 *shrewd* grievous, bitter; *Beshrew* curse 18 *stumbling* causing to stumble 20 *quarter* watch 22 *fair adventure* good fortune
V, vi An open place near Swinstead Abbey 2 *Of the part* on the side 6 *perfect* correct 12 *remembrance* memory; *eyeless* i.e. black 13 *done me shame* disgraced me (by causing my discourteous failure to recognize a friend) 14 *accent* speech 16 *Sans compliment* without formal speech 22 *swound* faint 24 *broke out* rushed away 26 *arm . . . time* prepare yourself for the emergency 27 *at leisure* after delay 28 *taste to* serve as food taster for 29 *resolvèd* determined

Whose bowels suddenly burst out. The king
31　Yet speaks and peradventure may recover.

BASTARD
Whom didst thou leave to tend his majesty?

HUBERT
Why, know you not? The lords are all come back,
And brought Prince Henry in their company,
At whose request the king hath pardoned them,
And they are all about his majesty.

BASTARD
Withhold thine indignation, mighty heaven,
38　And tempt us not to bear above our power!
39　I'll tell thee, Hubert, half my power this night,
40　Passing these flats, are taken by the tide.
These Lincoln Washes have devourèd them.
42　Myself, well mounted, hardly have escaped.
Away before! Conduct me to the king;
44　I doubt he will be dead or ere I come.　　　　*Exeunt.*

\*

vii　　　*Enter Prince Henry, Salisbury, and Bigot.*
PRINCE HENRY
It is too late. The life of all his blood
2　Is touched corruptibly, and his pure brain,
Which some suppose the soul's frail dwelling-house,
4　Doth, by the idle comments that it makes,
5　Foretell the ending of mortality.
　　　*Enter Pembroke.*
PEMBROKE
6　His highness yet doth speak, and holds belief
That, being brought into the open air,
It would allay the burning quality
9　Of that fell poison which assaileth him.
PRINCE HENRY
Let him be brought into the orchard here.
11　Doth he still rage?　　　　　*[Exit Bigot.]*
PEMBROKE　　　　He is more patient
Than when you left him; even now he sung.
PRINCE HENRY
13　O, vanity of sickness! Fierce extremes
14　In their continuance will not feel themselves.
Death, having preyed upon the outward parts,
16　Leaves them invisible, and his siege is now

Against the mind, the which he pricks and wounds
With many legions of strange fantasies,　　　　18
Which, in their throng and press to that last hold,　　　19
Confound themselves. 'Tis strange that death should　　20
　sing.
I am the cygnet to this pale faint swan,　　　　21
Who chants a doleful hymn to his own death,
And from the organ-pipe of frailty sings
His soul and body to their lasting rest.

SALISBURY
Be of good comfort, prince, for you are born
To set a form upon that indigest　　　　26
Which he hath left so shapeless and so rude.
　　　*[King] John brought in.*

KING JOHN
Ay, marry, now my soul hath elbow-room.
It would not out at windows, nor at doors.
There is so hot a summer in my bosom
That all my bowels crumble up to dust.
I am a scribbled form, drawn with a pen
Upon a parchment, and against this fire
Do I shrink up.

PRINCE HENRY　How fares your majesty?

KING JOHN
Poisoned – ill fare! Dead, forsook, cast off,　　　35
And none of you will bid the winter come
To thrust his icy fingers in my maw,　　　　37
Nor let my kingdom's rivers take their course
Through my burned bosom, nor entreat the north
To make his bleak winds kiss my parchèd lips
And comfort me with cold. I do not ask you much.
I beg cold comfort; and you are so strait　　　42
And so ingrateful, you deny me that.

PRINCE HENRY
O, that there were some virtue in my tears　　　44
That might relieve you.

KING JOHN　　　　　　The salt in them is hot.
Within me is a hell, and there the poison
Is as a fiend confined to tyrannize
On unreprievable condemnèd blood.　　　48
　　　*Enter Bastard.*

BASTARD
O, I am scalded with my violent motion　　　49
And spleen of speed to see your majesty.　　　50

KING JOHN
O cousin, thou art come to set mine eye!　　　51
The tackle of my heart is cracked and burnt,　　　52
And all the shrouds wherewith my life should sail　　53
Are turnèd to one thread, one little hair.
My heart hath one poor string to stay it by,
Which holds but till thy news be utterèd,
And then all this thou seest is but a clod
And module of confounded royalty.　　　58

BASTARD
The Dauphin is preparing hitherward,
Where heaven he knows how we shall answer him,　　60
For in a night the best part of my power,
As I upon advantage did remove,　　　62
Were in the Washes all unwarily　　　63
Devourèd by the unexpected flood.　　　64
　　　*[The King dies.]*

SALISBURY
You breathe these dead news in as dead an ear.　　　65
My liege! My lord! But now a king, now thus!

31 *peradventure* perhaps　38 *tempt . . . power* do not test us by making us endure more than we are able to　39 *power* army　40 *flats* low lands near the sea　42 *hardly* barely　44 *doubt* fear
V, vii The orchard of Swinstead Abbey　2 *touched corruptibly* infected so as to cause corruption　4 *idle* foolish　5 *mortality* life　6 *yet* still　9 *fell* cruel　11 *rage* rave　13 *extremes* extremities　14 *In . . . themselves* as they continue cease to be felt　16 *invisible* (modifies *Death*)　18 *fantasies* hallucinations　19 *throng and press* disordered rush; *hold* stronghold (the mind)　20 *Confound themselves* destroy one another (i.e. his delirious thoughts negate one another so that he is totally incoherent)　21 *cygnet* young swan (the swan was said to sing only one song during his life, just before his death)　26 *indigest* shapeless mass, state of confusion　35 *ill fare* (1) ill lot, (2) bad food　37 *maw* throat　42 *strait* niggardly　44 *virtue* healing power　48 *unreprievable* beyond reprieve　49 *scalded* heated　50 *spleen* eagerness　51 *set mine eye* i.e. close my eyes in death　52 *tackle* rigging of a ship　53 *shrouds* ropes supporting the mast of a ship　58 *module* mere image; *confounded* destroyed　60 *heaven he knows* only God knows　62 *upon advantage* to take advantage of a favorable opportunity; *remove* change position　63 *unwarily* unexpectedly　64 *unexpected flood* sudden flowing in of the tide　65 *dead news* (1) deadly news, (2) news of death

PRINCE HENRY

Even so must I run on, and even so stop.

68   What surety of the world, what hope, what stay,
When this was now a king, and now is clay?

BASTARD

Art thou gone so? I do but stay behind
To do the office for thee of revenge,
And then my soul shall wait on thee to heaven,

73   As it on earth hath been thy servant still.

74   Now, now, you stars that move in your right spheres,

75   Where be your powers? Show now your mended faiths,
And instantly return with me again,
To push destruction and perpetual shame
Out of the weak door of our fainting land.

79   Straight let us seek, or straight we shall be sought.
The Dauphin rages at our very heels.

SALISBURY

It seems you know not, then, so much as we.
The Cardinal Pandulph is within at rest,
Who half an hour since came from the Dauphin,
And brings from him such offers of our peace

85   As we with honor and respect may take,
With purpose presently to leave this war.

BASTARD

He will the rather do it when he sees

88   Ourselves well sinewèd to our defense.

SALISBURY

Nay, 'tis in a manner done already;

90   For many carriages he hath dispatched
To the seaside, and put his cause and quarrel
To the disposing of the cardinal;
With whom yourself, myself, and other lords,
If you think meet, this afternoon will post
To consummate this business happily.

BASTARD

Let it be so. And you, my noble prince,
With other princes that may best be spared,

Shall wait upon your father's funeral.

PRINCE HENRY

At Worcester must his body be interred,
For so he willed it.

BASTARD                     Thither shall it then.

And happily may your sweet self put on          101
The lineal state and glory of the land!          102
To whom, with all submission, on my knee,
I do bequeath my faithful services
And true subjection everlastingly.

SALISBURY

And the like tender of our love we make,          106
To rest without a spot for evermore.             107

PRINCE HENRY

I have a kind soul that would give you thanks,
And knows not how to do it but with tears.

BASTARD

O, let us pay the time but needful woe,          110
Since it hath been beforehand with our griefs.
This England never did, nor never shall,
Lie at the proud foot of a conqueror
But when it first did help to wound itself.
Now these her princes are come home again,
Come the three corners of the world in arms,      116
And we shall shock them. Nought shall make us rue  117
If England to itself do rest but true.        *Exeunt.*

68 *surety* certainty; *stay* support   73 *still* always   74 *stars . . . spheres* i.e. noblemen who have returned to their proper allegiance (revolving around the throne, as stars were believed in a harmonious cosmos to revolve around the earth)   75 *powers* armies; *mended faiths* restored loyalties   79 *Straight* immediately   85 *respect* self-respect   88 *sinewèd* strengthened   90 *carriages* vehicles   101 *happily* propitiously   102 *lineal state* kingship by right of birth   106 *tender* offer   107 *spot* blemish (of disloyalty)   110–11 *let . . . griefs* i.e. let us not weep more than necessary, since we have already paid the sad occasion enough of the grief due to it   116 *three corners* i.e. the rest of the world, England being the fourth corner   117 *shock* meet them with force

# THE TRAGEDY OF
# KING RICHARD THE SECOND

## INTRODUCTION

The increasing interest of thoughtful modern readers in *The Tragedy of King Richard the Second* is probably due in part to its unique position in Shakespeare's artistic development. Symbolic of this position is the fact that it is the only one of his better plays to be written entirely in verse. It would, perhaps, be fanciful to conclude that this is because poetry here plays a more functional role than in any of his other dramas. Yet the coincidence is striking, for *Richard II* is the first play in which Shakespeare makes his central figure an introspective, imaginative, and eloquent man – in short, a poet. This is the first of his characters into which he could freely have poured certain aspects of his own character and experience.

Richard is a lover of music, of pageantry, of luxurious hospitality; he is mercurial; he is highly self-conscious; he has the feeling for situations, the instinct for self-dramatization, of a born actor. It has indeed been supposed that Shakespeare the actor wrote the part for himself. We can at least agree that Richard is a person with whom Shakespeare as fact and tradition reveal him could eagerly have identified in these respects. If so, this may account for the unusual length of the part, and for the impression recorded by critics as diverse in temper as Coleridge and Sir Edmund Chambers that Richard is drawn with a skill unequalled except perhaps in *King Lear*, "a work of art and of love." It is worth remembering also that when some five years later Shakespeare next turned to a story in which the central figure was a self-conscious, sensitive, imaginative, and eloquent young prince, the result was the longest of all Shakespearean roles and the most popular, Hamlet.

At all events, the king's poetic nature is all-important in the total effect of *Richard II*. The story is that of a youthful, thoughtless, extravagant, and willfully unjust king who is responsible for the murder of his good uncle, Thomas, Duke of Gloucester, and the confiscation of his cousin Bolingbroke's estates, but whose dethronement leads eventually to the long and bloody Wars of the Roses,* and who in his fall becomes a sympathetic figure – in the eyes of his French biographers, indeed, a martyr. This seemingly impossible transformation is effected by exhibiting in the first two acts Richard's weakness as a king, and progressively thereafter his charm as a man. And the essence of that charm is that he is a poet, a minor poet, to be sure, a self-conscious, artificial poet, overfond of words and of rhetorical devices, but enough of a poet to win our hearts and make us forget how richly he deserves to be deposed.

But Richard's is one of the kinds of poetry with which

his creator was experimenting toward the end of 1595, when *Richard II* was written, and therein lies the significance of the play in Shakespeare's progress as an artist. No thoughtful reader of Shakespeare's early work can resist the impression that his natural bent was toward poetry, and that he learned the dramatist's trade, the constructing of a theatrically effective plot, slowly and with conscious effort. Pegasus was never allowed to run away with the team, for that would have courted failure in the theatre, but his irresponsibility is evident in the unconvincing lyricism of Tyrrel's report of the murderers in *Richard III*, IV, iii, or of Mercutio's speech about Queen Mab in *Romeo and Juliet*, I, iv, some forty lines of delightful fantasy which merely retard the plot. In the other plays of the so-called "lyrical group" written between 1593 and 1596, Shakespeare finds other important and legitimate uses for poetry in drama. But only Richard II, both protagonist and poet, allows his creator's winged horse full rein.

Thus with the economy of genius Shakespeare here solves two problems, one professional and the other personal, with a single stroke. Some of the satisfaction he must have felt is apparent in the profusion and splendor of the imagery in the play, in the intricate interweaving of image-patterns, and in the symmetry with which the images point up every stage in what Holinshed called God's "advancing" of Bolingbroke and "dejecting" of Richard. A good example is the emblematic transference of the sun from Richard (II, iv, 21; III, ii, 36 ff.; III, iii, 62 ff., 178 ff.) to Bolingbroke (IV, i, 260–62). Many other skeins of imagery may be traced through the play, such as the rise and fall of Fortune's buckets, the "theatre-like state," and the neglected or well-tended garden. But nothing is more delusory than the supposition that the poet deliberately planned these patterns; they illustrate the instinctive workings of his poetic imagination.

As implied above, *Richard II* is artistically akin to a cluster of plays which can be assigned with some confidence to the years 1593–96. It has much in common also (though less than the other plays of the "lyrical group" because of its paucity of love scenes) with his sonnets, many of which presumably belong to the same period, since we hear of them circulating "among his private friends" as early as 1598. These relationships, together with an admittedly equivocal reference to the private presentation of a "King Richard" in 1595, impel the majority of recent editors to assign the composition of the piece to the latter year. It came at a time when the aged Elizabeth I and her councillors were extremely sensitive to the possible political repercussions of stage plays. Consequently when it appeared in print in 1597 the actual dethronement (IV, i, 154–318) had been excised. It had

---

* The subject of Shakespeare's earlier tetralogy, *1, 2,* and *3 Henry VI* and *Richard III*.

almost certainly been included in the stage performances and may well have been banned by the censor of books for that very reason. It was not printed until 1608, when Elizabeth's successor, James I, was firmly seated on the English throne.

As for the queen's anxiety, the perspective of three and a half centuries makes clear that while, like every re-enactment of history, the play had political meaning, it can have had no political purpose, and that, in supposing it could be useful as propaganda, both her majesty's government and the opposition were deceived. It is a vivid, impartial re-creation of a political impasse which brought death to a tyrant, but to a usurper a troublesome reign, and to the realm eventually some thirty years of civil war. It *is* full of conflicting political ideas: the divine right of kings, the subject's duty of passive obedience, the dangers of irresponsible despotism, the complex qualities of an ideal ruler. But which of these ideas were Shakespeare's own is impossible to discern. On politics as on religion he preserves as always "the taciturnity of nature." What can be said of this aspect of *Richard II* is that here, as in all the histories, Shakespeare wrote as a true patriot and that England was the heroine. The continuing power of the play to interest audiences in England and elsewhere can come only from its universal human appeal as drama.

That *Richard II* was also planned as the first part of a great tetralogy completed in *1* and *2 Henry IV* and *Henry V*, is far from certain, although this view has been brilliantly maintained by recent scholars. Carlisle's prophecy (IV, i, 114–49, 322–23) does indeed foretell the woes to come in Henry VI and Richard III's time, while Richard himself (V, i, 57–65) predicts to one of the actual rebels the treacherous rebellion of the Percies in *1 Henry IV*:

> The time shall not be many hours of age
> More than it is, ere foul sin gathering head
> Shall break into corruption. Thou shalt think,
> Though he divide the realm and give thee half,
> It is too little, helping him to all.
> And he shall think that thou, which knowest the way
> To plant unrightful kings, wilt know again,
> Being ne'er so little urged another way,
> To pluck him headlong from the usurped throne.

Henry at the beginning of V, iii does foreshadow the character of Prince Hal in the next two histories as well as his transformation into the hero of *Henry V*. Many passages in the later three "parts" link them *retrospectively* with *Richard II*. But in the Hotspur of *Richard II* there is hardly any trace of the "gunpowder Percy" of *1 Henry IV*, and there is no hint anywhere of Falstaff. Highly qualified critics of the consecutive performance of the four pieces at Stratford in 1951 have commented that when played as a prologue to the tetralogy, *Richard II* becomes rather the rise of Bolingbroke than the tragedy of Richard, and such a reading is difficult to reconcile with the impression of Richard dwelt upon above. Perhaps the safest guess is that before writing *Richard II* the dramatist had in mind the whole framework of events as it was presented to him in his chronicle sources, but not the details of his characters and scenes. The four plays, though intricately and strongly connected, fall short of complete artistic unity.

The principal source of *Richard II* is the second edition (1587) of a popular compilation called *The Chronicles of England* by Raphael Holinshed, which provides the outlines of the events and characters. But there is evidence in both the plot and the dialogue that Shakespeare knew, and remembered striking details from, practically all the different versions of Richard's story available to him: the chronicles of Froissart and of Edward Hall; two or three French accounts of the deposition, favorable to Richard; the *Mirror for Magistrates*; the first four books of Samuel Daniel's poetical history of *The Civil Wars*; an earlier play, *Woodstock*, which deals with the murder of the Duke of Gloucester; and just possibly another earlier play on Richard II, of which however no record remains. It would be an obvious exaggeration to say that Shakespeare "did the research" on his subject with the thoroughness of a historian. He may, for example, have known *Woodstock* simply through having acted in it. But it is no less misleading to suppose that he was content with Holinshed's rather pedestrian narrative.

As usual, too, he altered history for dramatic effect, though in this instance without damage to the enduring truth of his picture. He also added brilliant improvisations not found in any of his sources: the conversation between Gaunt and the widowed Duchess of Gloucester (I, ii); Gaunt's deathbed speech and the conference of Northumberland, Ross, and Willoughby (II, i); the several appearances of the queen, especially in the Duke of York's garden at Langley (III, iv); the conception of Isabella as having the maturity and vitality of Richard's first queen, Anne of Bohemia, whereas she was in fact a child of eight when he married her; the deposition scene; the appearance of the Duchess of York to plead for her "son," Aumerle (he was actually her stepson); the presentation of Richard's coffin to Henry in the final scene. Unless the "old play" on Richard II should somewhere miraculously turn up, and prove to contain hints for all these alterations and additions, we must describe at least a quarter of the play as Shakespeare's invention.

The early stage history of *Richard II* is of unusual interest. Elizabeth herself exclaimed against it: "I am Richard II, know ye not that?... This tragedy was played forty times in open streets and houses." Even if we discount "forty" as a common round number, an angry exaggeration, or both, Dover Wilson's statement that the play "took London by storm" seems amply justified. Two new editions came out in a single year, 1598. In a poetical miscellany of 1600, more excerpts were included from *Richard II* than from any other drama. On Saturday, February 7, 1601, a performance by Shakespeare's company at the Globe was paid for by supporters of the Earl of Essex to stir up popular feeling in favor of his ill-starred attempt to seize the throne, and although the gentlemen who bespoke the performance were tried and punished, Shakespeare and his company apparently were not. On September 30, 1607, the piece was played by the crew of a ship en route to the West Indies. New editions were printed in 1608, 1615, 1623 (in the first folio), and 1634. In the summer of 1631 the Master of the Revels had £5 6s. 6d. from a benefit production at the Globe.

During the Restoration, the eighteenth, and the early nineteenth century at least six different stage adaptations of it were put on with some success in England and America. The chief Shakespearean actors of their respective centuries, Garrick (whose friend Dr Johnson disliked the play) and Irving (who planned a production but never put it on), are absent from the list of stars who have essayed the title role since 1700. But it has attracted such famous names as Macready, Edmund Kean, Wallack, Charles Kean, Junius Brutus Booth the elder, Edwin Booth, Benson, Granville-Barker, Beerbohm Tree, John Gielgud, Maurice Evans, Alec Guinness, and Michael Redgrave. In the twentieth-century American revival of 1937–38, directed by Miss Margaret Webster, Evans played it over three hundred times, and seemingly won for it some measure of continuing popularity on the stage and in television.

Curiously enough, considering its earlier and later success, until the third decade of the present century *Richard II* ranked well below several of Shakespeare's other histories – notably *1 Henry IV*, *Henry V*, and *Richard III* – in popularity on the stage. Critics have found it wanting in dramatic action, arresting characters (except Richard himself), and comic relief. But producers have been able to counterbalance these defects by spectacular staging of the pageantry of the tournament (I, iii) and – in an interpolated "episode" – of Richard's entry into London (V, ii); by expert playing of such scenes as the tearful interview of Gaunt and the Duchess of Gloucester (I, ii), the garden scene (III, iv), and Richard's farewell to his queen (V, i), which certainly lend variety of effect; and sometimes – though with questionable propriety – by portraying York throughout, and his duchess in V, ii, iii, as mildly humorous.

But on the stage, and even more surely for the reader, the play has its great moments. It is, in the words of Henry Morley, "full of passages that have floated out of their place in the drama to live in the minds of the people." Chief among these is John of Gaunt's apostrophe to England (II, i, 40 ff.), which even in American performances usually evokes a solid round of applause. And there are others: Saintsbury calls York's description of "our two cousins coming into London" (especially V, ii, 23–36) the most famous passage in the play; the pathos of Richard's soliloquy in prison (V, v, 1–66) has been highly praised, as have his monody on the divine right of kings (III, ii, 36–62) and that on the irony of kingship (III, ii, 144–70), the Bishop of Carlisle's prophecy (IV, i, 114–49), and Bolingbroke's forthright, vividly human rejection of the consolations of philosophy (I, iii, 294–303).

It would be a feeble actor who could not hold his audience, and an unimaginative reader who felt no thrill in the great moments of Richard's story: his passionate outbursts of hope and despair when he returns from Ireland, as Salisbury and then Scroop reluctantly tell of the disbanding of his Welsh army, the flocking of his subjects to Bolingbroke, and the deaths of his favorites; his cry as he descends to parley with the usurper, "Down, down I come, like glist'ring Phaethon"; above all, his tragic eloquence as he dramatizes his abdication before the Parliament which had so recently been his, and under the inscrutable eye of the "silent king."

*University of Pennsylvania*        MATTHEW W. BLACK

## NOTE ON THE TEXT

The present edition follows the text of the first quarto, 1597, which appears to have been printed from the author's draft. The abdication speeches, IV, i, 154–318, have been added from the text in the folio, 1623, which, though printed in the main from one of the later quartos of the play, was evidently corrected – especially in these speeches – by means of a playhouse prompt-copy. The speeches had first been printed in the fourth quarto, 1608, but with mislinings and omissions indicative of faulty copy. Nonetheless, many modern editions, including the present one, prefer some thirteen fourth-quarto readings. The quartos are not divided into acts and scenes. The act–scene division here supplied marginally follows the division in the folio except that V, iii is split into V, iii and iv, thus giving six scenes for this act instead of the five in the folio.

Below is a list of the substantive departures from the copy-texts, i.e. the folio of 1623 (F) for IV, i, 154–318, and the quarto of 1597 as press-corrected in all extant copies (Q). The adopted reading in italics with an indication of its source – usually the quartos of 1598 (Q2) and (Q3), of 1608 (Q4), of 1615 (Q5), and of 1634 (Q6), or the folios and early editors – is followed by the reading of the copy-texts in roman. Expansions of unmistakable abbreviations and corrections of obvious printing errors are not listed.

I, i, 118 *by my* (F) by (Q)    162 *Harry, when?* (Pope) Harry? when (Q)    178 *reputation. That* (F) Reputation that (Q)

I, ii, 47 *sit* (F) set (Q)    58 *it* (Q2) is (Q)    60 *begun* (Q2) begone (Q)

I, iii, 15 *thee* (Q2) the (Q)    33 *comest* (Q5) comes (Q)    43 *daring-hardy* (Theobald) daring, hardy, (Q)    58 *thee* (Q3) the (Q)    172 *then but* (F) but (Q)    180 *you owe* (F) y'owe (Q)    193 *far* (F2) fare (Q)    222 *night* (Q4) nightes (Q)    239 *had it* (Theobald) had't (Q)    289 *strewed* (Malone) strowd (Q)    308 *Where'er* (Q2) Where eare (Q)

I, iv, 20 *cousin,* (F) Coosens (Q)    52 s.d. *Enter Bushy* (F) Enter Bushy with newes (Q)    53 *Bushy, what news* (F) omitted (Q)

II, i, 15 *life's* (Rowe) liues (Q)    18 *fond* (Collier conj.; Camb.) found (Q)    19 *metres* (Steevens conj.; Malone) meeters (Q)    48 *a moat* (Q4) moat (Q)    85 *No, misery* (Q3) No misery (Q)    102 *incagèd* (Dyce) inraged (Q)    113 *now, not* (Theobald) now not, not (Q)    124 *brother* (Q2) brothers (Q)    130 *precedent* (Pope) president (Q)    168 *my own* (all but Petworth copy of Q) his own (Petworth copy)    177 *the* (F) a (Q)    229 *Ere't* (F) Eart (Q)    257 *king's* (Q3) King (Q)    277 *Blanc* (Camb. ii) Blan (Q)    280 *The son and heir of the Earl of Arundel* (supplied by Halliwell; not in early texts)    284 *Coint* (Halliwell) Coines (Q)    294 *gilt* (F) guilt (Q)

II, ii, 16 *eye* (F) eyes (Q)    25 *More's* (F) more is (Q)    31 *though in* (Collier) though on (Q2) thought on (Q)    39 *known – what* (Capell) knowen what (Q)    53 *Henry* (Var. 1821) H. (Q)    112 *Th' one* (F) T one (Q)    129 *that's* (F) that is (Q)    148 *Bagot* (White) omitted (Q)

II, iii, 9 *Cotswold* (Hanmer) Cotshall (Q)    25 *Why,* (Q3) Why (Q)    30 *lordship* (Q2) Lo : (Q)    36 *Hereford, boy?* (Q3) Herefords boy. (Q)

II, iv, 8 *all are* (Q2) are al (Q)

III, ii, 31 *offer* (Pope) offer, (Q)    32 *succor* (Pope) succors (Q)    40 *boldly* (Collier conj.; Hudson) bouldy (Q)    72 *O'erthrows* (F) Ouerthrowes (Q)    130 *won* (Q3) woon (Q)    134 *this offense* (F) this (Q)    170 *through* (Q2) thorough (Q)

III, iii, 13 *brief with you to* (F) brief to (Q)    59 *rain* (F) raigne (Q)    119 *a prince and just* (Sisson) princesse iust (Q)    202 *hand* (F) handes (Q)

III, iv, 11 *joy?* (Var. 1773) griefe (Q)    26 *pins* (F) pines (Q)    28 *change :* (F) change (Q)    29 *yon* (Q2) yong (Q)    55 *seized* (Q3) ceasde (Q)    57 *garden! We at* (Capell) garden at (Q)    80 *Cam'st* (Q2) Canst (Q)    85 *lord's* (F) Lo : (Q)

IV, i, 22 *him* (Q3) them (Q)    43 *Fitzwater* (F) Fitzwaters (Q)    54 *As* (Johnson) As it (Q)    55 *sun . . . sun* (Capell) sinne . . . sinne (Q)    *is my* (Q3) is (Q)    109 *thee* (Q2) the (Q)    114 *Marry* (F3) Mary (Q)    145 *you* (Q2) yon (Q)    165 *limbs* (Q4) knee (F)    183 *and on* (Q4) on (F)    *yours* (Q4) thine (F)    199 *tend* (Q4) 'tend (F)    210. *duty's* (Var. 1821) duties (Q4) dutious (F)    *rites* (Q4) Oathes (F)    215 *that swear* (Q4) are made (F)    229 *folly* (Q4) follyes (F)    237 *upon* (Q4) upon me (F)    250 *To undeck* (Q4) T'vndeck (F)    251 *and* (Q4) a (F)    255 *Nor* (Q4) No, nor (F)    260 *mockery king* (Q4) Mockerie, King (F)    267 *bankrout* (Q4) Bankrupt (F)    276 *the* (Q4) that (F)    285 *Was* (Q4) Is (F)    *that* (Q4) which (F)    286 *And* (Q4) That (F)    289 *a* (Q4) an (F)    296 *manners* (Q4) manner (F)    319 *On Wednesday next* (Q4) Let it be so, and loe on Wednesday next (Q)    333 *I will lay* (Pope) Ile lay (Q)

V, i, 32 *correction mildly* (Neilson) correction, mildly (Q)    41 *thee* (Q2) the (Q)    62 *And he* (Keightly conj.; Wilson) He (Q)

V, ii, 2 *off* (F) of (Q)    11 *thee* (F) the (Q)    17 *thee! Welcome* (Theobald) the Welcome (Q)    65 *bond* (Q2) band (Q)    94 *thee* (Q2) the (Q)    116 *And* (Q2) An (Q)

V, iii, 36 *that I may* (Q2) that May (Q)    43 *foolhardy* (Rolfe) foole, hardie (Q)    51 *passed* (Dyce) past (Q)    68 *And* (Q2) An (Q)    75 *voiced* (Q3) voice (Q)    111 *King Henry* (Q2) Yorke (Q)    135–36 *With all my heart I pardon him* (Pope) I pardon him with all my heart (Q)

V, v, 20 *through* (F) thorow (Q)    27 *sit* (Q3) set (Q)    79 *bestrid* (F) bestride (Q)

V, vi, 12 s.d. *Fitzwater* (Q6) Fitzwaters (Q)    25 *reverend* (Q3) reuerent (Q)    43 *thorough* (Camb.) through (Q)

# THE TRAGEDY OF
# KING RICHARD THE SECOND

\*

**I, i**     *Enter King Richard, John of Gaunt, with other*
    *Nobles and Attendants.*

KING
1   Old John of Gaunt, time-honored Lancaster,
2   Hast thou, according to thy oath and band,
    Brought hither Henry Hereford, thy bold son,
4   Here to make good the boist'rous late appeal,
5   Which then our leisure would not let us hear,
    Against the Duke of Norfolk, Thomas Mowbray?

GAUNT
    I have, my liege.

KING
    Tell me, moreover, hast thou sounded him
9   If he appeal the duke on ancient malice,
10  Or worthily, as a good subject should,
    On some known ground of treachery in him?

GAUNT
    As near as I could sift him on that argument,
13  On some apparent danger seen in him

---

I, i A room of state (Holinshed's *Chronicles*, Shakespeare's principal source
for *Richard II*, locates this scene 'within the castle of Windsor,' where the
king and his nobles sat on 'a great scaffold,' and gives the time as the latter
part of April, 1398) s.d. *Gaunt* Ghent (his birthplace) 1 *time-honored*
venerable (he was actually fifty-eight) 2 *band* bond (Gaunt was a pledge
for Bolingbroke's appearance) 4 *appeal* accusation (here of treason) made
by one who undertook under penalty to prove it 5 *our . . . us* (the royal
plural); *leisure* i.e. lack of leisure 9 *appeal* accuse; *malice* enmity 10
*worthily* justly 13 *apparent* obvious 18 *High-stomached* haughty 23
*hap* luck 24 *immortal title* i.e. angel or saint 26 *cause you come* matter you
come about 28 *what . . . object* what accusation do you make 32 *Tend'ring*
being lovingly mindful of 33 *misbegotten* of any other kind than that
begotten of love for the king 34 *appellant* as accuser

Aimed at your highness, no inveterate malice.

KING
    Then call them to our presence.    *[Exit Attendant.]*
                    Face to face,
    And frowning brow to brow, ourselves will hear
    The accuser and the accusèd freely speak.
    High-stomached are they both and full of ire,     18
    In rage deaf as the sea, hasty as fire.
    *Enter Bolingbroke and Mowbray.*

BOLINGBROKE
    Many years of happy days befall
    My gracious sovereign, my most loving liege!

MOWBRAY
    Each day still better other's happiness
    Until the heavens, envying earth's good hap,     23
    Add an immortal title to your crown!     24

KING
    We thank you both. Yet one but flatters us,
    As well appeareth by the cause you come–     26
    Namely, to appeal each other of high treason.
    Cousin of Hereford, what dost thou object     28
    Against the Duke of Norfolk, Thomas Mowbray?

BOLINGBROKE
    First – heaven be the record to my speech! –
    In the devotion of a subject's love,
    Tend'ring the precious safety of my prince     32
    And free from other, misbegotten hate,     33
    Come I appellant to this princely presence.     34
    Now, Thomas Mowbray, do I turn to thee,
    And mark my greeting well; for what I speak
    My body shall make good upon this earth

Or my divine soul answer it in heaven.
39 Thou art a traitor and a miscreant,
Too good to be so, and too bad to live,
Since the more fair and crystal is the sky,
The uglier seem the clouds that in it fly.
43 Once more, the more to aggravate the note,
With a foul traitor's name stuff I thy throat
And wish, so please my sovereign, ere I move,
46 What my tongue speaks my right-drawn sword may
   prove.

MOWBRAY
47 Let not my cold words here accuse my zeal.
48 'Tis not the trial of a woman's war,
49 The bitter clamor of two eager tongues,
Can arbitrate this cause betwixt us twain;
The blood is hot that must be cooled for this.
Yet can I not of such tame patience boast
As to be hushed and naught at all to say.
First, the fair reverence of your highness curbs me
From giving reins and spurs to my free speech,
56 Which else would post until it had returned
These terms of treason doubled down his throat.
Setting aside his high blood's royalty,
And let him be no kinsman to my liege,
I do defy him and I spit at him,
Call him a slanderous coward and a villain;
Which to maintain, I would allow him odds
63 And meet him, were I tied to run afoot
Even to the frozen ridges of the Alps,
65 Or any other ground inhabitable
Where ever Englishman durst set his foot.
Meantime let this defend my loyalty:
By all my hopes, most falsely doth he lie.

BOLINGBROKE
69 Pale trembling coward, there I throw my gage,
70 Disclaiming here the kinred of the king,
And lay aside my high blood's royalty,
72 Which fear, not reverence, makes thee to except.
If guilty dread have left thee so much strength
74 As to take up mine honor's pawn, then stoop.
By that and all the rites of knighthood else,
Will I make good against thee, arm to arm,
77 What I have spoke or thou canst worse devise.

MOWBRAY
I take it up; and by that sword I swear
Which gently laid my knighthood on my shoulder,
I'll answer thee in any fair degree
Or chivalrous design of knightly trial;
82 And when I mount, alive may I not light,
If I be traitor or unjustly fight!

KING
What doth our cousin lay to Mowbray's charge?
85 It must be great that can inherit us
So much as of a thought of ill in him.

BOLINGBROKE
87 Look what I speak, my life shall prove it true –
88 That Mowbray hath received eight thousand nobles
89 In name of lendings for your highness' soldiers,
90 The which he hath detained for lewd employments,
Like a false traitor and injurious villain.
Besides I say, and will in battle prove –
93 Or here, or elsewhere to the furthest verge
That ever was surveyed by English eye –
95 That all the treasons for these eighteen years

Complotted and contrivèd in this land
Fetch from false Mowbray their first head and spring. 97
Further I say, and further will maintain, 98
Upon his bad life to make all this good,
That he did plot the Duke of Gloucester's death, 100
Suggest his soon-believing adversaries, 101
And consequently, like a traitor coward, 102
Sluiced out his innocent soul through streams of blood;
Which blood, like sacrificing Abel's, cries,
Even from the tongueless caverns of the earth,
To me for justice and rough chastisement; 106
And, by the glorious worth of my descent,
This arm shall do it, or this life be spent.

KING
How high a pitch his resolution soars! 109
Thomas of Norfolk, what say'st thou to this?

MOWBRAY
O, let my sovereign turn away his face
And bid his ears a little while be deaf,
Till I have told this slander of his blood 113
How God and good men hate so foul a liar!

KING
Mowbray, impartial are our eyes and ears.
Were he my brother, nay, my kingdom's heir,
As he is but my father's brother's son,
Now by my sceptre's awe I make a vow, 118
Such neighbor nearness to our sacred blood
Should nothing privilege him nor partialize 120
The unstooping firmness of my upright soul.
He is our subject, Mowbray; so art thou:
Free speech and fearless I to thee allow.

MOWBRAY
Then, Bolingbroke, as low as to thy heart
Through the false passage of thy throat, thou liest!
Three parts of that receipt I had for Calais 126
Disbursed I duly to his highness' soldiers.
The other part reserved I by consent,
For that my sovereign liege was in my debt 129
Upon remainder of a dear account 130
Since last I went to France to fetch his queen. 131
Now swallow down that lie! For Gloucester's death,
I slew him not, but, to my own disgrace, 133
Neglected my sworn duty in that case.

39 *miscreant* un-Christian villain   43 *note* charge (of treason)   46 *right-drawn* drawn in a just cause   47 *accuse my zeal* cast doubt upon my ardor or loyalty   48 *woman's war* war of words   49 *eager* sharp   56 *post* ride at high speed   65 *inhabitable* uninhabitable   69 *gage* glove in token of defiance   70 *kinred* kinship   72 *except* use as an exception   74 *mine honor's pawn* i.e. the gage   77 *or . . . devise* or anything worse you can imagine I have said   82 *light* dismount   85–86 *inherit us . . . of* make us have   87 *Look what* whatever   88 *nobles* gold coins worth 6s. 8d. each   89 *lendings* pay advanced when regular pay cannot be given   90 *lewd* base   93 *Or* either   95 *eighteen years* (since the commons' revolt of 1381)   97 *head* source   98–99 *maintain . . . good* undertake to prove, by ending his wicked life   100 *Duke of Gloucester's death* (at Calais, while Mowbray was in command there; Gloucester was Richard's uncle and severest critic, and it is probable that the king ordered his execution)   101 *Suggest . . . adversaries* put his easily persuaded enemies up to it   102 *consequently* subsequently and as a result   106 *To me* (spoken with menacing emphasis, aimed at Richard)   109 *pitch* peak of a falcon's flight   113 *slander of* disgrace to   118 *my . . . awe* the reverence due my sceptre   120 *partialize* make partial, bias   126 *that receipt I had* the money I received   129 *For that* because   130 *dear account* heavy debt   131 *Since . . . queen* since my latest voyage in furtherance of Richard's marriage to Isabella of France   133–34 *I . . . case* (Mowbray speaks ambiguously; there is some evidence that he postponed the execution, and he probably did not actually perform it)

For you, my noble Lord of Lancaster,
The honorable father to my foe,
Once did I lay an ambush for your life –
A trespass that doth vex my grievèd soul ;
But ere I last received the sacrament,
140 I did confess it and exactly begged
Your grace's pardon, and I hope I had it.
142 This is my fault. As for the rest appealed,
It issues from the rancor of a villain,
144 A recreant and most degenerate traitor ;
145 Which in myself I boldly will defend,
146 And interchangeably hurl down my gage
Upon this overweening traitor's foot
To prove myself a loyal gentleman
Even in the best blood chambered in his bosom.
150 In haste whereof most heartily I pray
Your highness to assign our trial day.

KING
Wrath-kindled gentlemen, be ruled by me ;
153 Let's purge this choler without letting blood.
This we prescribe, though no physician ;
Deep malice makes too deep incision.
156 Forget, forgive ; conclude and be agreed ;
157 Our doctors say this is no month to bleed.
Good uncle, let this end where it begun ;
We'll calm the Duke of Norfolk, you your son.

GAUNT
160 To be a make-peace shall become my age.
Throw down, my son, the Duke of Norfolk's gage.

KING
And, Norfolk, throw down his.

GAUNT                    When, Harry, when ?
Obedience bids I should not bid again.

KING
164 Norfolk, throw down, we bid. There is no boot.

MOWBRAY
Myself I throw, dread sovereign, at thy foot.
My life thou shalt command, but not my shame.
The one my duty owes ; but my fair name,
168 Despite of death that lives upon my grave,
To dark dishonor's use thou shalt not have.
170 I am disgraced, impeached, and baffled here ;
Pierced to the soul with slander's venomed spear,
172 The which no balm can cure but his heart-blood
173 Which breathed this poison.

KING                    Rage must be withstood.

Give me his gage. Lions make leopards tame.                    174

MOWBRAY
Yea, but not change his spots ! Take but my shame,
And I resign my gage. My dear dear lord,
The purest treasure mortal times afford
Is spotless reputation. That away,
Men are but gilded loam or painted clay.
A jewel in a ten-times-barred-up chest
Is a bold spirit in a loyal breast.
Mine honor is my life, both grow in one ;
Take honor from me, and my life is done.
Then, dear my liege, mine honor let me try ;                    184
In that I live, and for that will I die.

KING
Cousin, throw up your gage. Do you begin.                    186

BOLINGBROKE
O, God defend my soul from such deep sin !
Shall I seem crestfallen in my father's sight ?
Or with pale beggar-fear impeach my height                    189
Before this outdared dastard ? Ere my tongue                    190
Shall wound my honor with such feeble wrong                    191
Or sound so base a parle, my teeth shall tear                    192
The slavish motive of recanting fear                    193
And spit it bleeding in his high disgrace,                    194
Where shame doth harbor, even in Mowbray's face.
                    [Exit Gaunt.]

KING
We were not born to sue, but to command ;
Which since we cannot do to make you friends,
Be ready, as your lives shall answer it,
At Coventry upon Saint Lambert's day.                    199
There shall your swords and lances arbitrate
The swelling difference of your settled hate.
Since we cannot atone you, we shall see                    202
Justice design the victor's chivalry.                    203
Lord Marshal, command our officers-at-arms
Be ready to direct these home alarms.                    205
                    Exit [with others].

*

*Enter John of Gaunt with the Duchess of Gloucester.*    I, ii

GAUNT
Alas, the part I had in Woodstock's blood                    1
Doth more solicit me than your exclaims
To stir against the butchers of his life !
But since correction lieth in those hands                    4
Which made the fault that we cannot correct,
Put we our quarrel to the will of heaven,
Who, when they see the hours ripe on earth,
Will rain hot vengeance on offenders' heads.

DUCHESS
Finds brotherhood in thee no sharper spur ?
Hath love in thy old blood no living fire ?
Edward's seven sons, whereof thyself art one,                    11
Were as seven vials of his sacred blood,
Or seven fair branches springing from one root.
Some of those seven are dried by nature's course,
Some of those branches by the Destinies cut ;
But Thomas, my dear lord, my life, my Gloucester,
One vial full of Edward's sacred blood,
One flourishing branch of his most royal root,
Is cracked, and all the precious liquor spilt,
Is hacked down, and his summer leaves all faded,

140 *exactly* completely and expressly   142 *rest appealed* remainder of the charge   144 *recreant* cowardly   145 *Which* which assertion   146 *interchangeably* in turn   150 *In haste whereof* to speed which   153 *choler* anger ; *letting blood* bleeding medicinally, with a quibble on bloodshed in combat   156 *conclude* make terms   157 *no month to bleed* (the almanacs prescribed certain seasons as favorable for bleeding)   160 *shall* will certainly   164 *boot* help for it   168 *Despite . . . lives* that will live, in spite of death   170 *impeached* accused ; *baffled* publicly disgraced   172–73 *his heart-blood Which* the heart-blood of that man who   173 *breathed* uttered   174 *Lions . . . leopards* i.e. kings . . . nobles   184 *try* put to trial   186 *throw up* (possibly to the king on his high seat)   189 *impeach my height* dishonor my high rank   190 *outdared* intimidated ; *dastard* coward   191 *feeble wrong* injury only a weak man would submit to   192 *parle* parley, truce   193 *motive* moving part, here his tongue   194 *in* to   199 *Saint Lambert's day* September 17   202 *atone* reconcile   203 *Justice . . . chivalry* justice point out the true knight by giving him the victory   205 *home alarms* troubles in England as distinct from the Irish war
I, ii Within a residence of the Duke of Lancaster   1 *the part . . . blood* my being his brother ; *Woodstock* (the Duke of Gloucester's name was Thomas of Woodstock)   4 *those hands* i.e. Richard's   11 *Edward* Edward III

21 By envy's hand and murder's bloody axe.
   Ah, Gaunt, his blood was thine! That bed, that womb,
23 That metal, that self mould that fashioned thee,
   Made him a man; and though thou livest and breathest,
   Yet art thou slain in him. Thou dost consent
   In some large measure to thy father's death
   In that thou seest thy wretched brother die,
28 Who was the model of thy father's life.
   Call it not patience, Gaunt; it is despair.
30 In suff'ring thus thy brother to be slaught'red
31 Thou showest the naked pathway to thy life,
   Teaching stern murder how to butcher thee.
   That which in mean men we entitle patience
   Is pale cold cowardice in noble breasts.
   What shall I say? To safeguard thine own life
   The best way is to venge my Gloucester's death.

GAUNT
37 God's is the quarrel; for God's substitute,
   His deputy anointed in his sight,
   Hath caused his death; the which if wrongfully,
   Let heaven revenge; for I may never lift
   An angry arm against his minister.

DUCHESS
   Where then, alas, may I complain myself?

GAUNT
   To God, the widow's champion and defense.

DUCHESS
   Why then, I will. Farewell, old Gaunt.
   Thou goest to Coventry, there to behold
46 Our cousin Hereford and fell Mowbray fight.
   O, sit my husband's wrongs on Hereford's spear,
   That it may enter butcher Mowbray's breast!
49 Or, if misfortune miss the first career,
   Be Mowbray's sins so heavy in his bosom
   That they may break his foaming courser's back
   And throw the rider headlong in the lists,
53 A caitiff recreant to my cousin Hereford!
54 Farewell, old Gaunt. Thy sometimes brother's wife
   With her companion, Grief, must end her life.

GAUNT
   Sister, farewell; I must to Coventry.
   As much good stay with thee as go with me!

DUCHESS
   Yet one word more! Grief boundeth where it falls,
   Not with the empty hollowness, but weight.
   I take my leave before I have begun,
   For sorrow ends not when it seemeth done.
   Commend me to thy brother, Edmund York.
   Lo, this is all. Nay, yet depart not so!
   Though this be all, do not so quickly go.
   I shall remember more. Bid him – ah, what? –
66 With all good speed at Plashy visit me.
   Alack, and what shall good old York there see
68 But empty lodgings and unfurnished walls,
69 Unpeopled offices, untrodden stones?
   And what hear there for welcome but my groans?
   Therefore commend me – let him not come there
   To seek out sorrow that dwells everywhere.
   Desolate, desolate will I hence and die!
   The last leave of thee takes my weeping eye.     Exeunt.

                                    *

*Enter Lord Marshal and the Duke Aumerle.*     I,

MARSHAL
   My Lord Aumerle, is Harry Hereford armed?

AUMERLE
   Yea, at all points, and longs to enter in.

MARSHAL
   The Duke of Norfolk, sprightfully and bold,     3
   Stays but the summons of the appellant's trumpet.

AUMERLE
   Why, then the champions are prepared, and stay
   For nothing but his majesty's approach.     6
      *The trumpets sound and the King enters with his*
      *Nobles [, Gaunt, Bushy, Bagot, Green, and others].*
      *When they are set, enter [Mowbray,] the Duke of*
      *Norfolk, in arms, defendant [, and Herald].*

KING
   Marshal, demand of yonder champion
   The cause of his arrival here in arms.
   Ask him his name and orderly proceed
   To swear him in the justice of his cause.

MARSHAL
   In God's name and the king's, say who thou art,
   And why thou comest thus knightly clad in arms;
   Against what man thou com'st, and what thy quarrel.
   Speak truly on thy knighthood and thy oath,
   As so defend thee heaven and thy valor!

MOWBRAY
   My name is Thomas Mowbray, Duke of Norfolk,
   Who hither come engagèd by my oath
   (Which God defend a knight should violate!)     18
   Both to defend my loyalty and truth
   To God, my king, and my succeeding issue
   Against the Duke of Hereford that appeals me;
   And, by the grace of God and this mine arm,
   To prove him, in defending of myself,
   A traitor to my God, my king, and me;
   And as I truly fight, defend me heaven!
      *The trumpets sound. Enter [Bolingbroke,] Duke of*
      *Hereford, appellant, in armor [and Herald].*

KING
   Marshal, ask yonder knight in arms
   Both who he is and why he cometh hither
   Thus plated in habiliments of war;     28
   And formally, according to our law,
   Depose him in the justice of his cause.     30

MARSHAL
   What is thy name? and wherefore com'st thou hither,
   Before King Richard in his royal lists?
   Against whom comest thou? and what's thy quarrel?
   Speak like a true knight, so defend thee heaven!

BOLINGBROKE
   Harry of Hereford, Lancaster, and Derby
   Am I, who ready here do stand in arms
   To prove, by God's grace and my body's valor
   In lists on Thomas Mowbray, Duke of Norfolk,

21 *envy* malicious enmity   23 *self* selfsame   28 *model* image   30 *suff'ring* permitting   31 *the naked pathway* the path to be open   37 *God's substitute* the king by divine right   46 *cousin* kinsman   49 *career* charge   53 *caitiff* captive   54 *sometimes* 'late'   66 *Plashy* Gloucester's country seat, in Essex   68 *unfurnished walls* rooms bare of furniture and hangings   69 *offices* workrooms
I, iii The lists at Coventry   s.d. *Aumerle* (as High Constable of England)   3 *sprightfully and bold* with spirit and boldly   6 s.d. *defendant* the challenged   18 *defend* forbid   28 *plated* armored   30 *Depose him* take his sworn deposition

That he is a traitor foul and dangerous
To God of heaven, King Richard, and to me;
And as I truly fight, defend me heaven!

MARSHAL
On pain of death, no person be so bold
Or daring-hardy as to touch the lists,
Except the Marshal and such officers
45 Appointed to direct these fair designs.

BOLINGBROKE
Lord Marshal, let me kiss my sovereign's hand
And bow my knee before his majesty;
For Mowbray and myself are like two men
That vow a long and weary pilgrimage.
Then let us take a ceremonious leave
And loving farewell of our several friends.

MARSHAL
The appellant in all duty greets your highness
And craves to kiss your hand and take his leave.

KING
We will descend and fold him in our arms.
Cousin of Hereford, as thy cause is right,
So be thy fortune in this royal fight!
Farewell, my blood; which if to-day thou shed,
Lament we may, but not revenge thee dead.

BOLINGBROKE
59 O, let no noble eye profane a tear
For me, if I be gored with Mowbray's spear.
As confident as is the falcon's flight
Against a bird, do I with Mowbray fight.
My loving lord, I take my leave of you;
Of you, my noble cousin, Lord Aumerle;
Not sick, although I have to do with death,
66 But lusty, young, and cheerly drawing breath.
67 Lo, as at English feasts, so I regreet
The daintiest last, to make the end most sweet.
O thou, the earthly author of my blood,
Whose youthful spirit, in me regenerate,
Doth with a twofold vigor lift me up
To reach at victory above my head,
73 Add proof unto mine armor with thy prayers,
And with thy blessings steel my lance's point,
75 That it may enter Mowbray's waxen coat
76 And furbish new the name of John a Gaunt
Even in the lusty havior of his son.

GAUNT
God in thy good cause make thee prosperous!
Be swift like lightning in the execution
And let thy blows, doubly redoublèd,
81 Fall like amazing thunder on the casque
Of thy adverse pernicious enemy.
Rouse up thy youthful blood; be valiant and live.

BOLINGBROKE
84 Mine innocence and Saint George to thrive!

MOWBRAY
However God or fortune cast my lot,

There lives or dies, true to King Richard's throne,
A loyal, just, and upright gentleman.
Never did captive with a freer heart                88
Cast off his chains of bondage and embrace
His golden uncontrolled enfranchisement,
More than my dancing soul doth celebrate
This feast of battle with mine adversary.
Most mighty liege, and my companion peers,
Take from my mouth the wish of happy years.
As gentle and as jocund as to jest                95
Go I to fight. Truth hath a quiet breast.

KING
Farewell, my lord. Securely I espy                97
Virtue with valor couchèd in thine eye.           98
Order the trial, Marshal, and begin.

MARSHAL
Harry of Hereford, Lancaster, and Derby,
Receive thy lance, and God defend the right!

BOLINGBROKE
Strong as a tower in hope, I cry amen.

MARSHAL [to an Officer]
Go bear this lance to Thomas, Duke of Norfolk.

[1.] HERALD
Harry of Hereford, Lancaster, and Derby
Stands here for God, his sovereign, and himself,
On pain to be found false and recreant,
To prove the Duke of Norfolk, Thomas Mowbray,
A traitor to his God, his king, and him,
And dares him to set forward to the fight.

2. HERALD
Here standeth Thomas Mowbray, Duke of Norfolk,
On pain to be found false and recreant,
Both to defend himself and to approve            112
Henry of Hereford, Lancaster, and Derby
To God, his sovereign, and to him disloyal,
Courageously and with a free desire
Attending but the signal to begin.               116

MARSHAL
Sound trumpets, and set forward combatants.
    [A charge sounded.]
Stay! The king hath thrown his warder down.      118

KING
Let them lay by their helmets and their spears
And both return back to their chairs again.
Withdraw with us; and let the trumpets sound
While we return these dukes what we decree.      122
    [A long flourish.]
Draw near,
And list what with our council we have done.     124
For that our kingdom's earth should not be soiled
With that dear blood which it hath fosterèd;
And for our eyes do hate the dire aspect
Of civil wounds ploughed up with neighbors' sword;
And for we think the eagle-wingèd pride
Of sky-aspiring and ambitious thoughts
With rival-hating envy set on you                131
To wake our peace, which in our country's cradle
Draws the sweet infant breath of gentle sleep;
Which so roused up with boist'rous untuned drums,
With harsh-resounding trumpets' dreadful bray
And grating shock of wrathful iron arms,
Might from our quiet confines fright fair peace
And make us wade even in our kinred's blood:
Therefore we banish you our territories.

45 *direct . . . designs* conduct this combat fairly  59 *profane* (because Bolingbroke's defeat would mean that he was a traitor)  66 *cheerly* cheerily  67 *regreet* greet  73 *proof* invulnerability  75 *enter . . . coat* pierce his armor as though it were wax  76 *a* of  81 *amazing* stupefying; *casque* helmet  84 *to thrive* I rely for success on  88 *freer* more willing  95 *gentle* tranquil; *jest* mock-fight  97 *Securely I espy* I am confident that I see  98 *couchèd* expressed  112 *approve* prove  116 *Attending* awaiting  118 *warder* gilded wand (held by Richard as commander of the trial)  122 *While* until; *s.d. flourish* trumpet-call  124 *list* listen to  131 *set on you* set you on

You, cousin Hereford, upon pain of life,
Till twice five summers have enriched our fields
142 Shall not regreet our fair dominions
143 But tread the stranger paths of banishment.

BOLINGBROKE
Your will be done. This must my comfort be –
That sun that warms you here shall shine on me,
And those his golden beams to you here lent
Shall point on me and gild my banishment.

KING
Norfolk, for thee remains a heavier doom,
Which I with some unwillingness pronounce :
150 The sly slow hours shall not determinate
151 The dateless limit of thy dear exile.
The hopeless word of 'never to return'
Breathe I against thee, upon pain of life.

MOWBRAY
A heavy sentence, my most sovereign liege,
And all unlooked for from your highness' mouth.
156 A dearer merit, not so deep a maim
As to be cast forth in the common air,
Have I deservèd at your highness' hands.
The language I have learnt these forty years,
My native English, now I must forgo ;
And now my tongue's use is to me no more
Than an unstringèd viol or a harp,
163 Or like a cunning instrument cased up
164 Or, being open, put into his hands
That knows no touch to tune the harmony.
Within my mouth you have enjailed my tongue,
167 Doubly portcullised with my teeth and lips ;
And dull, unfeeling, barren ignorance
Is made my jailer to attend on me.
I am too old to fawn upon a nurse,
Too far in years to be a pupil now.
What is thy sentence then but speechless death,
173 Which robs my tongue from breathing native breath ?

KING
174 It boots thee not to be compassionate.
175 After our sentence plaining comes too late.

MOWBRAY
Then thus I turn me from my country's light
To dwell in solemn shades of endless night.

KING
Return again and take an oath with thee.
179 Lay on our royal sword your banished hands ;
Swear by the duty that you owe to God
(Our part therein we banish with yourselves)
To keep the oath that we administer :
You never shall, so help you truth and God,
Embrace each other's love in banishment ;
Nor never look upon each other's face ;
Nor never write, regreet, nor reconcile
187 This low'ring tempest of your home-bred hate ;
188 Nor never by advisèd purpose meet
To plot, contrive, or complot any ill
'Gainst us, our state, our subjects, or our land.

BOLINGBROKE
I swear.

MOWBRAY
And I, to keep all this.

BOLINGBROKE
193 Norfolk, so far as to mine enemy :
By this time, had the king permitted us,

One of our souls had wand'red in the air,
Banished this frail sepulchre of our flesh,
As now our flesh is banished from this land.
Confess thy treasons ere thou fly the realm.
Since thou hast far to go, bear not along
The clogging burden of a guilty soul.

MOWBRAY
No, Bolingbroke. If ever I were traitor,
My name be blotted from the book of life
And I from heaven banished as from hence !
But what thou art, God, thou, and I do know ;
And all too soon, I fear, the king shall rue.
Farewell, my liege. Now no way can I stray.
Save back to England, all the world's my way.    Exit.

KING
Uncle, even in the glasses of thine eyes    20
I see thy grievèd heart. Thy sad aspect
Hath from the number of his banished years
Plucked four away.
    [To Bolingbroke]
                Six frozen winters spent,
Return with welcome home from banishment.

BOLINGBROKE
How long a time lies in one little word !
Four lagging winters and four wanton springs    21
End in a word, such is the breath of kings.

GAUNT
I thank my liege that in regard of me
He shortens four years of my son's exile.
But little vantage shall I reap thereby ;
For ere the six years that he hath to spend
Can change their moons and bring their times about,
My oil-dried lamp and time-bewasted light
Shall be extinct with age and endless night,
My inch of taper will be burnt and done,
And blindfold death not let me see my son.    22

KING
Why, uncle, thou hast many years to live.

GAUNT
But not a minute, king, that thou canst give.
Shorten my days thou canst with sullen sorrow
And pluck nights from me, but not lend a morrow.
Thou canst help time to furrow me with age,
But stop no wrinkle in his pilgrimage.    23
Thy word is current with him for my death,    23
But dead, thy kingdom cannot buy my breath.

KING
Thy son is banished upon good advice,
Whereto thy tongue a party-verdict gave.    23
Why at our justice seem'st thou then to low'r ?

GAUNT
Things sweet to taste prove in digestion sour.
You urged me as a judge ; but I had rather

142 *regreet* greet again  143 *stranger* alien  150 *determinate* end  151
*dateless* unlimited ; *limit* term ; *dear* bitter  156 *dearer* more welcome ;
*merit* reward ; *maim* crippling injury  163 *cunning* skillfully made  164
*open* out of its case  167 *portcullised* enclosed by a movable grating  173
*Which* thy sentence, which ; *breath* speech  174 *boots* helps ; *compassionate*
sorrowfuly lamenting  175 *plaining* complaining  179 *Lay . . . hands* (he
addresses both combatants)  187 *low'ring* threatening  188 *advisèd* con-
certed  193 *so . . . enemy* so far as I may speak to my sworn enemy  208
*glasses . . . eyes* your eyes as mirrors  214 *wanton* luxuriant  224 *blindfold
death* death, like a blindfold  230 *stop . . . pilgrimage* prevent no wrinkle
that time's course brings  231 *current* valid  234 *party-verdict* part of the
verdict

You would have bid me argue like a father.
O, had it been a stranger, not my child,
240 To smooth his fault I should have been more mild.
241 A partial slander sought I to avoid,
And in the sentence my own life destroyed.
Alas, I looked when some of you should say
I was too strict to make mine own away ;
But you gave leave to my unwilling tongue
246 Against my will to do myself this wrong.

KING
Cousin, farewell ; and, uncle, bid him so.
Six years we banish him, and he shall go.
　　　　　[Flourish.] Exit [King with his Train].

AUMERLE
249 Cousin, farewell. What presence must not know,
From where you do remain let paper show.

MARSHAL
My lord, no leave take I ; for I will ride,
As far as land will let me, by your side.

GAUNT
O, to what purpose dost thou hoard thy words
That thou returnest no greeting to thy friends ?

BOLINGBROKE
I have too few to take my leave of you,
When the tongue's office should be prodigal
To breathe the abundant dolor of the heart.

GAUNT
Thy grief is but thy absence for a time.

BOLINGBROKE
Joy absent, grief is present for that time.

GAUNT
What is six winters ? They are quickly gone.

BOLINGBROKE
To men in joy ; but grief makes one hour ten.

GAUNT
Call it a travel that thou tak'st for pleasure.

BOLINGBROKE
My heart will sigh when I miscall it so,
Which finds it an enforcèd pilgrimage.

GAUNT
The sullen passage of thy weary steps
266 Esteem as foil wherein thou art to set
The precious jewel of thy home return.

BOLINGBROKE
Nay, rather every tedious stride I make
269 Will but remember me what a deal of world
I wander from the jewels that I love.
Must I not serve a long apprenticehood
272 To foreign passages and, in the end,
Having my freedom, boast of nothing else
274 But that I was a journeyman to grief ?

GAUNT
All places that the eye of heaven visits

Are to a wise man ports and happy havens.
Teach thy necessity to reason thus :
There is no virtue like necessity.　　　　　278
Think not the king did banish thee,
But thou the king. Woe doth the heavier sit
Where it perceives it is but faintly borne.　　281
Go, say I sent thee forth to purchase honor,
And not, the king exiled thee ; or suppose
Devouring pestilence hangs in our air
And thou art flying to a fresher clime.
Look what thy soul holds dear, imagine it　　286
To lie that way thou goest, not whence thou com'st.
Suppose the singing birds musicians,
The grass whereon thou tread'st the presence strewed,　289
The flowers fair ladies, and thy steps no more
Than a delightful measure or a dance ;　　　291
For gnarling sorrow hath less power to bite　292
The man that mocks at it and sets it light.

BOLINGBROKE
O, who can hold a fire in his hand
By thinking on the frosty Caucasus ?
Or cloy the hungry edge of appetite
By bare imagination of a feast ?
Or wallow naked in December snow
By thinking on fantastic summer's heat ?　　299
O, no ! The apprehension of the good
Gives but the greater feeling to the worse.
Fell sorrow's tooth doth never rankle more　302
Than when he bites, but lanceth not the sore.

GAUNT
Come, come, my son, I'll bring thee on thy way.
Had I thy youth and cause, I would not stay.

BOLINGBROKE
Then, England's ground, farewell ; sweet soil, adieu,
My mother, and my nurse, that bears me yet !
Where'er I wander, boast of this I can,
Though banished, yet a true-born English man.
　　　　　　　　　　　　　　　　　Exeunt.

＊

　Enter the King, with Green, &c. [Bagot], at one　I, iv
　　door, and the Lord Aumerle at another.

KING
We did observe. Cousin Aumerle,
How far brought you high Hereford on his way ?

AUMERLE
I brought high Hereford, if you call him so,
But to the next high way, and there I left him.

KING
And say, what store of parting tears were shed ?

AUMERLE
Faith, none for me ; except the northeast wind,　　6
Which then blew bitterly against our faces,
Awaked the sleeping rheum, and so by chance　　8
Did grace our hollow parting with a tear.　　　9

KING
What said our cousin when you parted with him ?

AUMERLE
'Farewell !'
And, for my heart disdainèd that my tongue
Should so profane the word, that taught me craft
To counterfeit oppression of such grief
That words seemed buried in my sorrow's grave.
Marry, would the word 'farewell' have length'ned hours　16

240 *smooth* gloss over　241 *partial slander* slander of partiality to my
own son　246 *wrong* injury　249 *What . . . know* what you can't say here
266 *foil* thin, bright metal leaf placed under a gem to give it additional
brilliance　269 *remember* remind　272 *foreign passages* experiences abroad
274 *journeyman* worker for a daily wage, often itinerant　278 *necessity*
patiently enduring the inevitable　281 *faintly* faint-heartedly　286 *Look
what* whatever　289 *presence* royal audience chamber ; *strewed* i.e. the floor
covered with rushes　291 *measure* slow, formal dance　292 *gnarling*
snarling　299 *fantastic* imaginary　302 *rankle* inflict a painful, festering
wound
I, iv The court of King Richard　6 *for me* for my part　8 *rheum* moisture,
tears　9 *hollow* insincere　16 *Marry* indeed

And added years to his short banishment,
He should have had a volume of farewells;
But since it would not, he had none of me.

KING

20   He is our cousin, cousin; but 'tis doubt,
When time shall call him home from banishment,
22   Whether our kinsman come to see his friends.
Ourself and Bushy, Bagot here, and Green
Observed his courtship to the common people;
How he did seem to dive into their hearts
With humble and familiar courtesy;
What reverence he did throw away on slaves,
Wooing poor craftsmen with the craft of smiles
29   And patient underbearing of his fortune,
30   As 'twere to banish their affects with him.
Off goes his bonnet to an oyster-wench;
A brace of draymen bid God speed him well
And had the tribute of his supple knee,
With 'Thanks, my countrymen, my loving friends';
35   As were our England in reversion his,
And he our subjects' next degree in hope.

GREEN

Well, he is gone, and with him go these thoughts!
38   Now for the rebels which stand out in Ireland,
39   Expedient manage must be made, my liege,
Ere further leisure yield them further means
For their advantage and your highness' loss.

KING

We will ourself in person to this war;
43   And, for our coffers, with too great a court
44   And liberal largess, are grown somewhat light,
45   We are enforced to farm our royal realm,
The revenue whereof shall furnish us
For our affairs in hand. If that come short,
48   Our substitutes at home shall have blank charters,
Whereto, when they shall know what men are rich,
50   They shall subscribe them for large sums of gold
And send them after to supply our wants,
52   For we will make for Ireland presently.
*Enter Bushy.*
Bushy, what news?

BUSHY

Old John of Gaunt is grievous sick, my lord,
Suddenly taken, and hath sent posthaste
To entreat your majesty to visit him.

KING

Where lies he?

BUSHY

58   At Ely House.

KING

Now put it, God, in the physician's mind
To help him to his grave immediately!
61   The lining of his coffers shall make coats
To deck our soldiers for these Irish wars.
Come, gentlemen, let's all go visit him.
Pray God we may make haste, and come too late!

[ALL]

Amen.      *      *Exeunt.*

II, i     *Enter John of Gaunt, sick, with the Duke of York, &c.*

GAUNT

Will the king come, that I may breathe my last
In wholesome counsel to his unstaid youth?

YORK

Vex not yourself nor strive not with your breath,
For all in vain comes counsel to his ear.

GAUNT

O, but they say the tongues of dying men
Enforce attention like deep harmony.
Where words are scarce, they are seldom spent in vain,
For they breathe truth that breathe their words in pain.
He that no more court must say is listened more
    Than they whom youth and ease have taught to glose.   10
More are men's ends marked than their lives before.   11
    The setting sun, and music at the close,
As the last taste of sweets, is sweetest last,   13
Writ in remembrance more than things long past.
Though Richard my life's counsel would not hear,   15
My death's sad tale may yet undeaf his ear.   16

YORK

No; it is stopped with other, flattering sounds,
As praises, of whose taste the wise are fond,   18
Lascivious metres, to whose venom sound   19
The open ear of youth doth always listen;
Report of fashions in proud Italy,
Whose manners still our tardy apish nation   22
Limps after in base imitation.
Where doth the world thrust forth a vanity
(So it be new, there's no respect how vile)   25
That is not quickly buzzed into his ears?
Then all too late comes counsel to be heard
Where will doth mutiny with wit's regard.   28
Direct not him whose way himself will choose.
'Tis breath thou lack'st, and that breath wilt thou lose.

GAUNT

Methinks I am a prophet new inspired
And thus, expiring, do foretell of him:
His rash fierce blaze of riot cannot last,
For violent fires soon burn out themselves;
Small show'rs last long, but sudden storms are short;
He tires betimes that spurs too fast betimes;   36
With eager feeding food doth choke the feeder;
Light vanity, insatiate cormorant,   38
Consuming means, soon preys upon itself.
This royal throne of kings, this scept'red isle,
This earth of majesty, this seat of Mars,
This other Eden, demi-paradise,
This fortress built by Nature for herself
Against infection and the hand of war,   44
This happy breed of men, this little world,
This precious stone set in the silver sea,

---

20 *'tis* there is   22 *his friends* us of his own rank   29 *underbearing* enduring
30 *affects* affections   35 *in reversion* by right of legal succession   38
*stand out* resist   39 *Expedient* speedy; *manage* plans for controlling   43
*for* because; *too . . . court* too many courtiers (Richard's extravagance was
notorious)   44 *largess* gifts   45 *farm* lease (the authority to collect taxes
was deputed in exchange for cash in hand)   48 *blank charters* in effect,
loans to the crown on which the amount was filled in by the king's agents
50 *subscribe* put them down   52 *presently* at once   58 *Ely House* the
Bishop of Ely's palace in London   61 *coats* coats of mail
II, i Within Ely House   10 *glose* speak empty words in flattery   11 *marked*
heeded   13 *is sweetest last* lingers longest in memory   15 *life's* lifelong
16 *My . . . tale* my serious dying words   18 *of . . . fond* which even the
wise are too fond of   19 *venom* poisonous   22 *still* always; *tardy apish*
aping foreign fashions after they have become stale   25 *there's no respect*
no one considers   28 *will* natural inclination; *wit's regard* what reason
esteems   36 *betimes* early   38 *cormorant* glutton   44 *infection* plague and
moral contamination

Which serves it in the office of a wall,
Or as a moat defensive to a house,
Against the envy of less happier lands;
This blessed plot, this earth, this realm, this England,
This nurse, this teeming womb of royal kings,
52 Feared by their breed and famous by their birth,
Renownèd for their deeds as far from home,
For Christian service and true chivalry,
55 As is the sepulchre in stubborn Jewry
Of the world's ransom, blessed Mary's son;
This land of such dear souls, this dear dear land,
Dear for her reputation through the world,
Is now leased out (I die pronouncing it)
60 Like to a tenement or pelting farm.
England, bound in with the triumphant sea,
Whose rocky shore beats back the envious siege
Of wat'ry Neptune, is now bound in with shame,
64 With inky blots and rotten parchment bonds.
That England that was wont to conquer others
Hath made a shameful conquest of itself.
Ah, would the scandal vanish with my life,
How happy then were my ensuing death!

YORK
The king is come. Deal mildly with his youth;
70 For young hot colts, being raged, do rage the more.
    *Enter King and Queen, & c.[Aumerle, Bushy, Green,*
    *Bagot, Ross, and Willoughby].*

QUEEN
How fares our noble uncle Lancaster?

KING
What comfort, man? How is't with aged Gaunt?

GAUNT
73 O, how that name befits my composition!
Old Gaunt indeed, and gaunt in being old.
Within me grief hath kept a tedious fast;
And who abstains from meat that is not gaunt?
77 For sleeping England long time have I watched;
Watching breeds leanness, leanness is all gaunt.
The pleasure that some fathers feed upon
Is my strict fast – I mean my children's looks –
And therein fasting hast thou made me gaunt.
Gaunt am I for the grave, gaunt as a grave,
83 Whose hollow womb inherits naught but bones.

KING
84 Can sick men play so nicely with their names?

GAUNT
85 No, misery makes sport to mock itself.
Since thou dost seek to kill my name in me,
I mock my name, great king, to flatter thee.

KING
88 Should dying men flatter with those that live?

GAUNT
No, no! men living flatter those that die.

KING
Thou, now a-dying, sayest thou flatterest me.

GAUNT
O, no! thou diest, though I the sicker be.

KING
I am in health, I breathe, and see thee ill.

GAUNT
Now, he that made me knows I see thee ill;
Ill in myself to see, and in thee seeing ill.
Thy deathbed is no lesser than thy land,
Wherein thou liest in reputation sick;
And thou, too careless patient as thou art,
Committ'st thy anointed body to the cure
Of those physicians that first wounded thee.
A thousand flatterers sit within thy crown,
Whose compass is no bigger than thy head;
102 And yet, incagèd in so small a verge,
The waste is no whit lesser than thy land.
O, had thy grandsire, with a prophet's eye,
Seen how his son's son should destroy his sons,
From forth thy reach he would have laid thy shame,
107 Deposing thee before thou wert possessed,
Which art possessed now to depose thyself.
Why, cousin, wert thou regent of the world,
It were a shame to let this land by lease;
But, for thy world enjoying but this land,
Is it not more than shame to shame it so?
113 Landlord of England art thou now, not king.
114 Thy state of law is bondslave to the law,
And thou—

KING                A lunatic lean-witted fool,
116 Presuming on an ague's privilege,
117 Darest with thy frozen admonition
Make pale our cheek, chasing the royal blood
119 With fury from his native residence.
Now, by my seat's right royal majesty,
Wert thou not brother to great Edward's son,
122 This tongue that runs so roundly in thy head
Should run thy head from thy unreverent shoulders.

GAUNT
O, spare me not, my brother Edward's son,
For that I was his father Edward's son!
126 That blood already, like the pelican,
Hast thou tapped out and drunkenly caroused.
My brother Gloucester, plain well-meaning soul –
129 Whom fair befall in heaven 'mongst happy souls! –
130 May be a precedent and witness good
That thou respect'st not spilling Edward's blood.
Join with the present sickness that I have,
133 And thy unkindness be like crooked age,
To crop at once a too-long-withered flower.
Live in thy shame, but die not shame with thee!
These words hereafter thy tormenters be!
Convey me to my bed, then to my grave.
Love they to live that love and honor have.
    *Exit [borne off by Attendants].*

KING
And let them die that age and sullens have;
139 For both hast thou, and both become the grave.

YORK
I do beseech your majesty impute his words
To wayward sickliness and age in him.

---

52 *breed* ancestral reputation for valor   55 *stubborn* obstinate in rejecting
Christ and resisting the Crusaders   60 *tenement* rented land or building;
*pelting* paltry   64 *blots* i.e. the blank charters   70 *raged* enraged   73 *com-position* body and mind   77 *watched* stayed awake at night   83 *inherits*
will get   84 *so nicely* making such fine puns (Richard is ironical)   85 *to
mock* of mocking   88 *flatter with* seek to please   102 *verge* compass
107–08 *possessed . . . possessed* put in possession . . . possessed of a devil   113
*Landlord* one who leases out a property   114 *Thy . . . to the law* your legal
status is that of subject, not king   116 *ague's privilege* a not-too-ill man's
privilege to be cross   117 *frozen* chilly – cold and caused by a chill   119 *his*
its   122 *roundly* freely and bluntly   126 *pelican* (believed to feed its young
with its own blood)   129 *fair befall* may good befall   130 *precedent* token
133 *crooked* bent like a sickle   139 *sullens* sulks

He loves you, on my life, and holds you dear
As Harry Duke of Hereford, were he here.

KING

145 Right, you say true ! As Hereford's love, so his ;
As theirs, so mine ; and all be as it is !
*[Enter Northumberland.]*

NORTHUMBERLAND

My liege, old Gaunt commends him to your majesty.

KING

What says he ?

NORTHUMBERLAND  Nay, nothing ; all is said.
His tongue is now a stringless instrument ;
Words, life, and all, old Lancaster hath spent.

YORK

151 Be York the next that must be bankrout so !
Though death be poor, it ends a mortal woe.

KING

The ripest fruit first falls, and so doth he ;
154 His time is spent, our pilgrimage must be.
So much for that. Now for our Irish wars.
156 We must supplant those rough rug-headed kerns,
157 Which live like venom where no venom else
But only they have privilege to live.
159 And, for these great affairs do ask some charge,
Towards our assistance we do seize to us
The plate, coin, revenues, and moveables
Whereof our uncle Gaunt did stand possessed.

YORK

How long shall I be patient ? Ah, how long
Shall tender duty make me suffer wrong ?
Not Gloucester's death, nor Hereford's banishment,
166 Nor Gaunt's rebukes, nor England's private wrongs,
167 Nor the prevention of poor Bolingbroke
About his marriage, nor my own disgrace,
Have ever made me sour my patient cheek
Or bend one wrinkle on my sovereign's face.
I am the last of noble Edward's sons,
Of whom thy father, Prince of Wales, was first.
In war was never lion raged more fierce,
In peace was never gentle lamb more mild,
Than was that young and princely gentleman.
His face thou hast, for even so looked he,
177 Accomplished with the number of thy hours ;
But when he frowned, it was against the French
And not against his friends. His noble hand
Did win what he did spend, and spent not that
Which his triumphant father's hand had won.
His hands were guilty of no kinred blood,
But bloody with the enemies of his kin.
O Richard ! York is too far gone with grief,
185 Or else he never would compare between.

KING

Why, uncle, what's the matter ?

YORK                    O my liege,
Pardon me, if you please ; if not, I, pleased
188 Not to be pardoned, am content withal.
Seek you to seize and gripe into your hands
190 The royalties and rights of banished Hereford ?
Is not Gaunt dead ? and doth not Hereford live ?
Was not Gaunt just ? and is not Harry true ?
Did not the one deserve to have an heir ?
Is not his heir a well-deserving son ?
Take Hereford's rights away, and take from Time
196 His charters and his customary rights ;

Let not to-morrow then ensue to-day ;
Be not thyself – for how art thou a king
But by fair sequence and succession ?
Now, afore God (God forbid I say true !)
If you do wrongfully seize Hereford's rights,
Call in the letters patents that he hath
By his attorneys general to sue
His livery, and deny his off'red homage,
You pluck a thousand dangers on your head,
You lose a thousand well-disposèd hearts,
And prick my tender patience to those thoughts
Which honor and allegiance cannot think.

KING

Think what you will, we seize into our hands
His plate, his goods, his money, and his lands.

YORK

I'll not be by the while. My liege, farewell.
What will ensue hereof there's none can tell ;
But by bad courses may be understood
That their events can never fall out good.          *Exit.*

KING

Go, Bushy, to the Earl of Wiltshire straight.
Bid him repair to us to Ely House
To see this business. To-morrow next
We will for Ireland ; and 'tis time, I trow.
And we create, in absence of ourself,
Our uncle York Lord Governor of England ;
For he is just and always loved us well.
Come on, our queen. To-morrow must we part.
Be merry, for our time of stay is short.
          *[Flourish.] Exeunt King and Queen.*
          *Manet Northumberland [with Willoughby and Ross].*

NORTHUMBERLAND

Well, lords, the Duke of Lancaster is dead.

ROSS

And living too ; for now his son is duke.

WILLOUGHBY

Barely in title, not in revenues.

NORTHUMBERLAND

Richly in both, if justice had her right.

ROSS

My heart is great ; but it must break with silence,
Ere 't be disburdened with a liberal tongue.

NORTHUMBERLAND

Nay, speak thy mind ; and let him ne'er speak more
That speaks thy words again to do thee harm !

WILLOUGHBY

Tends that thou wouldst speak to the Duke of
          Hereford ?
If it be so, out with it boldly, man !
Quick is mine ear to hear of good towards him.

145 *Right . . . his* (the king purposely takes the opposite of York's meaning)
151 *bankrout* bankrupt  154 *must be* is yet to be finished  156 *rug-headed*
shaggy-haired ; *kerns* light-armed footsoldiers  157 *venom* poisonous
snakes  159 *charge* outlay  166 *Gaunt's rebukes* reprimands to Gaunt
167–68 *prevention . . . marriage* (Richard forestalled Bolingbroke's match
with the Duc du Berri's daughter)  177 *Accomplished . . . hours* at your
age  185 *compare between* make comparisons  188 *withal* nonetheless
190 *royalties* rights as a member of the royal family  196 *his customary
rights* (one of Time's rights was to bring the heir his inheritance)  197
*ensue* follow  202–04 *letters patents . . . livery* royal grants through legal
representatives to sue for possession of his inheritance  204 *homage*
avowal of allegiance  213 *by* with respect to  214 *events* outcomes  215
*Earl of Wiltshire* Richard's Lord Treasurer ; *straight* at once  217 *see*
see to ; *To-morrow next* to-morrow  218 *trow* believe  228 *great* swollen,
heavy  232 *Tends . . . to* does . . . concern

**ROSS**
No good at all that I can do for him;
Unless you call it good to pity him,
Bereft and gelded of his patrimony.

**NORTHUMBERLAND**
Now, afore God, 'tis shame such wrongs are borne
In him a royal prince and many moe
Of noble blood in this declining land.
The king is not himself, but basely led
By flatterers; and what they will inform,
Merely in hate, 'gainst any of us all,
That will the king severely prosecute
'Gainst us, our lives, our children, and our heirs.

**ROSS**
The commons hath he pilled with grievous taxes
And quite lost their hearts; the nobles hath he fined
For ancient quarrels and quite lost their hearts.

**WILLOUGHBY**
And daily new exactions are devised,
As blanks, benevolences, and I wot not what;
But what, a God's name, doth become of this?

**NORTHUMBERLAND**
Wars hath not wasted it, for warred he hath not,
But basely yielded upon compromise
That which his noble ancestors achieved with blows.
More hath he spent in peace than they in wars.

**ROSS**
The Earl of Wiltshire hath the realm in farm.

**WILLOUGHBY**
The king's grown bankrout, like a broken man.

**NORTHUMBERLAND**
Reproach and dissolution hangeth over him.

**ROSS**
He hath not money for these Irish wars,
His burdenous taxations notwithstanding,
But by the robbing of the banished duke.

**NORTHUMBERLAND**
His noble kinsman. Most degenerate king!
But, lords, we hear this fearful tempest sing,
Yet seek no shelter to avoid the storm.
We see the wind sit sore upon our sails,
And yet we strike not, but securely perish.

**ROSS**
We see the very wrack that we must suffer,
And unavoided is the danger now
For suffering so the causes of our wrack.

**NORTHUMBERLAND**
Not so. Even through the hollow eyes of death
I spy life peering; but I dare not say

How near the tidings of our comfort is.

**WILLOUGHBY**
Nay, let us share thy thoughts as thou dost ours.

**ROSS**
Be confident to speak, Northumberland.
We three are but thyself, and speaking so,
Thy words are but as thoughts. Therefore be bold.

**NORTHUMBERLAND**
Then thus: I have from Le Port Blanc, a bay
In Brittaine, received intelligence                          278
That Harry Duke of Hereford, Rainold Lord Cobham,
[The son and heir of the Earl of Arundel,]                   280
That late broke from the Duke of Exeter,                     281
His brother, Archbishop late of Canterbury,                  282
Sir Thomas Erpingham, Sir John Ramston,
Sir John Norbery, Sir Robert Waterton, and Francis
  Coint,
All these well furnished by the Duke of Brittaine
With eight tall ships, three thousand men of war,            286
Are making hither with all due expedience                    287
And shortly mean to touch our northern shore.
Perhaps they had ere this, but that they stay
The first departing of the king for Ireland.                 290
If then we shall shake off our slavish yoke,
Imp out our drooping country's broken wing,                  292
Redeem from broking pawn the blemished crown,                293
Wipe off the dust that hides our sceptre's gilt,             294
And make high majesty look like itself,
Away with me in post to Ravenspurgh;                         296
But if you faint, as fearing to do so,                       297
Stay and be secret, and myself will go.

**ROSS**
To horse, to horse! Urge doubts to them that fear.

**WILLOUGHBY**
Hold out my horse, and I will first be there.    *Exeunt.*  300

*

*Enter the Queen, Bushy, Bagot.*                    II, ii

**BUSHY**
Madam, your majesty is too much sad.
You promised, when you parted with the king,
To lay aside life-harming heaviness
And entertain a cheerful disposition.

**QUEEN**
To please the king, I did; to please myself,
I cannot do it. Yet I know no cause
Why I should welcome such a guest as grief
Save bidding farewell to so sweet a guest
As my sweet Richard. Yet again, methinks,
Some unborn sorrow, ripe in fortune's womb,
Is coming towards me, and my inward soul
With nothing trembles. At something it grieves              12
More than with parting from my lord the king.

**BUSHY**
Each substance of a grief hath twenty shadows,
Which shows like grief itself, but is not so;
For sorrow's eye, glazèd with blinding tears,
Divides one thing entire to many objects,
Like perspectives, which rightly gazed upon,                18
Show nothing but confusion – eyed awry,
Distinguish form. So your sweet majesty,
Looking awry upon your lord's departure,
Find shapes of grief more than himself to wail,

239 *moe* more    243 *Merely* purely    244 *prosecute* follow up    246 *pilled*
skinned    250 *blanks* blank charters (see I, iv, 48n.); *benevolences* 'voluntary'
loans to the crown; *wot* know    251 *a* in    265 *sit sore* press grievously
266 *strike* lower sail or strike back; *securely* overconfidently    268 *unavoided* unavoidable    278 *Brittaine* Brittany; *intelligence* information
280 (this line or a similarly worded one was deleted for political reasons;
Elizabeth had imprisoned the son of the then Earl of Arundel)    281 *broke*
escaped    282 *late* until recently (he had been deprived of the office by the
Pope at Richard's request)    286 *tall* fine; *men of war* fighting men    287
*expedience* speed    290 *The first departing* until after the departure    292
*Imp out* graft new feathers on    293 *broking pawn* the possession of the
king's moneylenders    294 *gilt* golden lustre    296 *post* haste; *Ravenspurgh*
a port on the River Humber, now submerged by the sea    297 *faint* are
faint-hearted    300 *Hold . . . and* if my horse holds out
II, ii Within Windsor Castle    12 *With* at    18 *perspectives* raised pictures or
designs which appear only when looked at from the side (*awry*)

Which, looked on as it is, is naught but shadows
Of what it is not. Then, thrice-gracious queen,
More than your lord's departure weep not. More's not
  seen;
Or if it be, 'tis with false sorrow's eye,
Which for things true weeps things imaginary.

QUEEN
It may be so; but yet my inward soul
Persuades me it is otherwise. Howe'er it be,
I cannot but be sad – so heavy sad
As, though in thinking on no thought I think,
Makes me with heavy nothing faint and shrink.

BUSHY
33 'Tis nothing but conceit, my gracious lady.

QUEEN
34 'Tis nothing less. Conceit is still derived
From some forefather grief. Mine is not so,
For nothing hath begot my something grief,
37 Or something hath the nothing that I grieve.
38 'Tis in reversion that I do possess;
But what it is, that is not yet known – what,
I cannot name. 'Tis nameless woe, I wot.
    *[Enter Green.]*

GREEN
God save your majesty! and well met, gentlemen.
I hope the king is not yet shipped for Ireland.

QUEEN
Why hopest thou so? 'Tis better hope he is;
For his designs crave haste, his haste good hope.
Then wherefore dost thou hope he is not shipped?

GREEN
46 That he, our hope, might have retired his power
And driven into despair an enemy's hope
48 Who strongly hath set footing in this land.
49 The banished Bolingbroke repeals himself
50 And with uplifted arms is safe arrived
At Ravenspurgh.

QUEEN            Now God in heaven forbid!

GREEN
52 Ah, madam, 'tis too true; and that is worse,
The Lord Northumberland, his son young Henry Percy,
The Lords of Ross, Beaumond, and Willoughby,
With all their powerful friends, are fled to him.

BUSHY
Why have you not proclaimed Northumberland
57 And all the rest revolted faction traitors?

GREEN
We have; whereupon the Earl of Worcester
59 Hath broken his staff, resigned his stewardship,
And all the household servants fled with him
To Bolingbroke.

QUEEN
So, Green, thou art the midwife to my woe,
63 And Bolingbroke my sorrow's dismal heir.
64 Now hath my soul brought forth her prodigy;
And I, a gasping new-delivered mother,
Have woe to woe, sorrow to sorrow joined.

BUSHY
Despair not, madam.

QUEEN          Who shall hinder me?
I will despair, and be at enmity
69 With cozening Hope. He is a flatterer,
A parasite, a keeper-back of Death,
71 Who gently would dissolve the bands of life,

Which false Hope lingers in extremity.
    *[Enter York.]*

GREEN
Here comes the Duke of York.

QUEEN
With signs of war about his aged neck.
O, full of careful business are his looks.
Uncle, for God's sake, speak comfortable words!

YORK
Should I do so, I should belie my thoughts.
Comfort's in heaven, and we are on the earth,
Where nothing lives but crosses, cares, and grief.
Your husband, he is gone to save far off,
Whilst others come to make him lose at home.
Here am I left to underprop his land,
Who, weak with age, cannot support myself.
Now comes the sick hour that his surfeit made;
Now shall he try his friends that flattered him.
    *[Enter a Servingman.]*

SERVINGMAN
My lord, your son was gone before I came.

YORK
He was? Why, so! Go all which way it will!
The nobles they are fled, the commons they are cold
And will, I fear, revolt on Hereford's side.
Sirrah, get thee to Plashy to my sister Gloucester;
Bid her send me presently a thousand pound.
Hold, take my ring.

SERVINGMAN
My lord, I had forgot to tell your lordship
To-day, as I came by, I callèd there –
But I shall grieve you to report the rest.

YORK
What is't, knave?

SERVINGMAN
An hour before I came the duchess died.

YORK
God for his mercy! what a tide of woes
Comes rushing on this woeful land at once!
I know not what to do. I would to God
(So my untruth had not provoked him to it)
The king had cut off my head with my brother's.
What, are there no posts dispatched for Ireland?
How shall we do for money for these wars?
Come, sister – cousin I would say – pray pardon me.
Go, fellow, get thee home, provide some carts
And bring away the armor that is there.
    *[Exit Servingman.]*
Gentlemen, will you go muster men?
If I know how or which way to order these affairs,
Thus disorderly thrust into my hands,
Never believe me. Both are my kinsmen.
Th' one is my sovereign, whom both my oath
And duty bids defend; t' other again

---

33 *conceit* fancy   34 *nothing less* anything but that   37 *something . . . grieve*
my causeless grief has something in it   38 *'Tis . . . possess* what I feel is
like a property which will devolve upon me later; I can't describe it yet
(see I, iv, 35n.)   46 *retired* drawn back   48 *strongly* with strong support
49 *repeals* recalls   50 *uplifted arms* brandished weapons   52 *that* what
57 *revolted . . . traitors* a rebellious clique of traitors   59 *staff* (the sign
of his office)   63 *dismal* ill-omened   64 *prodigy* monster   69 *cozening*
deceitful   71 *bands* bonds   72 *lingers* causes to linger   74 *With . . . neck*
in armor   75 *careful business* anxious preoccupation   79 *crosses* thwartings
84 *surfeit* excess   101 *untruth* disloyalty

Is my kinsman, whom the king hath wronged,
Whom conscience and my kinred bids to right.
Well, somewhat we must do. Come, cousin, I'll
117 Dispose of you.
Gentlemen, go muster up your men,
And meet me presently at Berkeley.
I should to Plashy too,
But time will not permit. All is uneven,
22 And everything is left at six and seven.
                                    *Exeunt Duke, Queen.*
                          *Manent Bushy, [Bagot,] Green.*

BUSHY
The wind sits fair for news to go for Ireland,
But none returns. For us to levy power
Proportionable to the enemy
Is all unpossible.
GREEN
Besides, our nearness to the king in love
28 Is near the hate of those love not the king.
BAGOT
And that's the wavering commons; for their love
Lies in their purses, and whoso empties them,
By so much fills their hearts with deadly hate.
BUSHY
32 Wherein the king stands generally condemned.
BAGOT
33 If judgment lie in them, then so do we,
Because we ever have been near the king.
GREEN
Well, I will for refuge straight to Bristol Castle.
The Earl of Wiltshire is already there.
BUSHY
37 Thither will I with you; for little office
38 Will the hateful commons perform for us,
Except like curs to tear us all to pieces.
Will you go along with us?
BAGOT
No; I will to Ireland to his majesty.
Farewell. If heart's presages be not vain,
We three here part that ne'er shall meet again.
BUSHY
That's as York thrives to beat back Bolingbroke.
GREEN
Alas, poor duke! The task he undertakes
Is numb'ring sands and drinking oceans dry.
Where one on his side fights, thousands will fly.
BAGOT
Farewell at once – for once, for all, and ever.
BUSHY
Well, we may meet again.
BAGOT                     I fear me, never. *[Exeunt.]*

                              *

iii    Enter [Bolingbroke the Duke of] Hereford, [and]
       Northumberland.
BOLINGBROKE
How far is it, my lord, to Berkeley now?

117 *Dispose of* make arrangements for   122 *at six and seven* in confusion
128 *those love* those who love   132 *Wherein* on which grounds   133 *If . . .
them* if our doom depends on them   137 *office* service   138 *hateful* angry
II, iii An open place in Gloucestershire   10 *In* by   12 *tediousness and
process* tedious process   16 *this* this expectation   22 *whencesoever* wherever
he may be   42 *raw* inexperienced   44 *approvèd* demonstrated

NORTHUMBERLAND
Believe me, noble lord,
I am a stranger here in Gloucestershire.
These high wild hills and rough uneven ways
Draws out our miles and makes them wearisome;
And yet your fair discourse hath been as sugar,
Making the hard way sweet and delectable.
But I bethink me what a weary way
From Ravenspurgh to Cotswold will be found
In Ross and Willoughby, wanting your company,      10
Which, I protest, hath very much beguiled
The tediousness and process of my travel;          12
But theirs is sweet'ned with the hope to have
The present benefit which I possess;
And hope to joy is little less in joy
Than hope enjoyed. By this the weary lords         16
Shall make their way seem short, as mine hath done
By sight of what I have, your noble company.
BOLINGBROKE
Of much less value is my company
Than your good words. But who comes here?
        *Enter Harry Percy.*
NORTHUMBERLAND
It is my son, young Harry Percy,
Sent from my brother Worcester, whencesoever.      22
Harry, how fares your uncle?
PERCY
I had thought, my lord, to have learned his health of
    you.
NORTHUMBERLAND
Why, is he not with the queen?
PERCY
No, my good lord; he hath forsook the court,
Broken his staff of office, and dispersed
The household of the king.
NORTHUMBERLAND          What was his reason?
He was not so resolved when last we spake together.
PERCY
Because your lordship was proclaimèd traitor.      30
But he, my lord, is gone to Ravenspurgh
To offer service to the Duke of Hereford;
And sent me over by Berkeley to discover
What power the Duke of York had levied there;
Then with directions to repair to Ravenspurgh.
NORTHUMBERLAND
Have you forgot the Duke of Hereford, boy?
PERCY
No, my good lord, for that is not forgot
Which ne'er I did remember. To my knowledge,
I never in my life did look on him.
NORTHUMBERLAND
Then learn to know him now. This is the duke.
PERCY
My gracious lord, I tender you my service,
Such as it is, being tender, raw, and young;       42
Which elder days shall ripen and confirm
To more approvèd service and desert.               44
BOLINGBROKE
I thank thee, gentle Percy; and be sure
I count myself in nothing else so happy
As in a soul rememb'ring my good friends;
And, as my fortune ripens with thy love,
It shall be still thy true love's recompense.
My heart this covenant makes, my hand thus seals it.

**NORTHUMBERLAND**

How far is it to Berkeley? and what stir
Keeps good old York there with his men of war?

**PERCY**

There stands the castle by yon tuft of trees,
Manned with three hundred men, as I have heard;
And in it are the Lords of York, Berkeley, and Seymour,
None else of name and noble estimate.

*[Enter Ross and Willoughby.]*

**NORTHUMBERLAND**

Here come the Lords of Ross and Willoughby,
Bloody with spurring, fiery red with haste.

**BOLINGBROKE**

Welcome, my lords. I wot your love pursues
A banished traitor. All my treasury
61 Is yet but unfelt thanks, which, more enriched,
Shall be your love and labor's recompense.

**ROSS**

Your presence makes us rich, most noble lord.

**WILLOUGHBY**

And far surmounts our labor to attain it.

**BOLINGBROKE**

Evermore thanks, the exchequer of the poor,
Which, till my infant fortune comes to years,
Stands for my bounty. But who comes here?

*[Enter Berkeley.]*

**NORTHUMBERLAND**

It is my Lord of Berkeley, as I guess.

**BERKELEY**

My Lord of Hereford, my message is to you.

**BOLINGBROKE**

My lord, my answer is – 'to Lancaster';
And I am come to seek that name in England;
And I must find that title in your tongue
Before I make reply to aught you say.

**BERKELEY**

Mistake me not, my lord. 'Tis not my meaning
75 To rase one title of your honor out.
To you, my lord, I come (what lord you will)
From the most gracious regent of this land,
The Duke of York, to know what pricks you on
79 To take advantage of the absent time
80 And fright our native peace with self-borne arms.

*[Enter York attended.]*

**BOLINGBROKE**

I shall not need transport my words by you;
Here comes his grace in person. My noble uncle!

*[Kneels.]*

**YORK**

Show me thy humble heart, and not thy knee,
84 Whose duty is deceivable and false.

**BOLINGBROKE**

My gracious uncle!

**YORK**

Tut, tut!
Grace me no grace, nor uncle me no uncle.
I am no traitor's uncle, and that word 'grace'
In an ungracious mouth is but profane.
Why have those banished and forbidden legs
91 Dared once to touch a dust of England's ground?
But then more why? – why have they dared to march
So many miles upon her peaceful bosom,
Frighting her pale-faced villages with war
95 And ostentation of despisèd arms?

Com'st thou because the anointed king is hence?
Why, foolish boy, the king is left behind,
And in my loyal bosom lies his power.
Were I but now lord of such hot youth
As when brave Gaunt thy father and myself
Rescued the Black Prince, that young Mars of men,
From forth the ranks of many thousand French,
O, then how quickly should this arm of mine,
Now prisoner to the palsy, chastise thee
And minister correction to thy fault!

**BOLINGBROKE**

My gracious uncle, let me know my fault;
On what condition stands it and wherein? 10

**YORK**

Even in condition of the worst degree,
In gross rebellion and detested treason.
Thou art a banished man; and here art come,
Before the expiration of thy time,
In braving arms against thy sovereign. 11

**BOLINGBROKE**

As I was banished, I was banished Hereford;
But as I come, I come for Lancaster. 11
And, noble uncle, I beseech your grace
Look on my wrongs with an indifferent eye. 11
You are my father, for methinks in you
I see old Gaunt alive. O, then, my father,
Will you permit that I shall stand condemned
A wandering vagabond, my rights and royalties
Plucked from my arms perforce, and given away
To upstart unthrifts? Wherefore was I born? 12
If that my cousin king be King in England,
It must be granted I am Duke of Lancaster.
You have a son, Aumerle, my noble cousin.
Had you first died, and he been thus trod down, 12
He should have found his uncle Gaunt a father
To rouse his wrongs and chase them to the bay. 12
I am denied to sue my livery here,
And yet my letters patents give me leave.
My father's goods are all distrained and sold; 13
And these, and all, are all amiss employed.
What would you have me do? I am a subject,
And I challenge law. Attorneys are denied me, 13
And therefore personally I lay my claim
To my inheritance of free descent. 13

**NORTHUMBERLAND**

The noble duke hath been too much abused.

**ROSS**

It stands your grace upon to do him right. 13

**WILLOUGHBY**

Base men by his endowments are made great. 13

**YORK**

My lords of England, let me tell you this:
I have had feeling of my cousin's wrongs,
And labored all I could to do him right;
But in this kind to come, in braving arms, 14

61 *unfelt* intangible  75 *rase* erase  79 *absent time* time of the king's absence  80 *self-borne* begotten and carried by you  84 *duty* i.e. act of kneeling; *deceivable* deceitful  91 *dust* speck  95 *ostentation* display; *despisèd* despicable  107 *On . . . it* on what defect in me is it based; *wherein* of what does it consist  112 *braving* defiant  114 *for* as  116 *indifferent* impartial  122 *unthrifts* spendthrifts  126 *first* i.e. before Gaunt  128 *rouse* rout from cover; *chase . . . bay* hunt them to the death  131 *distrained* seized  134 *challenge law* demand my rights  136 *my inheritance of* that which I inherit by  138 *It . . . upon* it's up to you  139 *his endowments* what they got from him  143 *kind* fashion

Be his own carver and cut out his way,
To find out right with wrong – it may not be ;
And you that do abet him in this kind
Cherish rebellion and are rebels all.

NORTHUMBERLAND

The noble duke hath sworn his coming is
But for his own ; and for the right of that
We all have strongly sworn to give him aid ;
And let him never see joy that breaks that oath !

YORK

Well, well, I see the issue of these arms.
I cannot mend it, I must needs confess,
54 Because my power is weak and all ill left ;
But if I could, by him that gave me life,
56 I would attach you all and make you stoop
Unto the sovereign mercy of the king ;
But since I cannot, be it known unto you
59 I do remain as neuter. So fare you well –
Unless you please to enter in the castle
And there repose you for this night.

BOLINGBROKE

An offer, uncle, that we will accept ;
But we must win your grace to go with us
To Bristol Castle, which they say is held
By Bushy, Bagot, and their complices,
56 The caterpillars of the commonwealth,
57 Which I have sworn to weed and pluck away.

YORK

It may be I will go with you ; but yet I'll pause,
For I am loath to break our country's laws.
70 Nor friends nor foes, to me welcome you are.
Things past redress are now with me past care. *Exeunt.*

\*

V     *Enter Earl of Salisbury and a Welsh Captain.*

WELSH CAPTAIN

My Lord of Salisbury, we have stayed ten days
2 And hardly kept our countrymen together,
And yet we hear no tidings from the king.
Therefore we will disperse ourselves. Farewell.

SALISBURY

Stay yet another day, thou trusty Welshman.
The king reposeth all his confidence in thee.

WELSH CAPTAIN

'Tis thought the king is dead. We will not stay.
8 The bay trees in our country all are withered,
And meteors fright the fixèd stars of heaven ;
The pale-faced moon looks bloody on the earth,
11 And lean-looked prophets whisper fearful change ;
Rich men look sad, and ruffians dance and leap –
The one in fear to lose what they enjoy,

154 *all ill left* everything left in disorder  156 *attach* arrest  159 *neuter*
neutral  166 *caterpillars* i.e. devourers  167 *weed* get rid of  170 *Nor . . .
are* as a neutral I welcome you
II, iv A Welsh camp  s.d. *Welsh Captain* (perhaps the famous Owen
Glendower who is mentioned in III, i, 43 and appears in *1 Henry IV*)  2
*hardly* with difficulty  8–10 *The . . . earth* i.e. earth and the heavens show
omens of disaster  11 *change* political upheaval  14 *to enjoy* in hope to
enjoy ; *rage* violence  17 *As* as being  22 *Witnessing* betokening  23 *wait
upon* offer allegiance to  24 *crossly* adversely
III, i Before Bristol Castle  3 *part* leave  4 *urging* stressing  10 *clean*
completely  11–12 *You have in manner . . . Made a divorce you have . . .*
made a kind of divorce  20 *foreign clouds* clouds of breath exhaled in a
foreign land  22 *signories* domains  23 *Disparked* thrown open to other
uses  24 *torn* broken ; *coat* coat of arms  25 *Rased out* erased ; *imprese*
heraldic emblem  37 *entreated* treated  38 *commends* remembrances

The other to enjoy by rage and war.                    14
These signs forerun the death or fall of kings.
Farewell. Our countrymen are gone and fled,
As well assured Richard their king is dead.    [*Exit.*] 17

SALISBURY

Ah, Richard ! with the eyes of heavy mind,
I see thy glory, like a shooting star,
Fall to the base earth from the firmament.
Thy sun sets weeping in the lowly west,
Witnessing storms to come, woe, and unrest ;     22
Thy friends are fled to wait upon thy foes,       23
And crossly to thy good all fortune goes.    [*Exit.*] 24

\*

*Enter [Bolingbroke] Duke of Hereford, York,*     III, i
*Northumberland, [Ross, Percy, Willoughby, with]*
*Bushy and Green prisoners.*

BOLINGBROKE

Bring forth these men.
Bushy and Green, I will not vex your souls
(Since presently your souls must part your bodies)   3
With too much urging your pernicious lives,         4
For 'twere no charity ; yet, to wash your blood
From off my hands, here in the view of men
I will unfold some causes of your deaths.
You have misled a prince, a royal king,
A happy gentleman in blood and lineaments,
By you unhappied and disfigured clean.               10
You have in manner with your sinful hours           11
Made a divorce betwixt his queen and him,
Broke the possession of a royal bed,
And stained the beauty of a fair queen's cheeks
With tears drawn from her eyes by your foul wrongs.
Myself – a prince by fortune of my birth,
Near to the king in blood, and near in love
Till you did make him misinterpret me –
Have stooped my neck under your injuries
And sighed my English breath in foreign clouds,     20
Eating the bitter bread of banishment,
Whilst you have fed upon my signories,               22
Disparked my parks and felled my forest woods,      23
From my own windows torn my household coat,          24
Rased out my imprese, leaving me no sign,            25
Save men's opinions and my living blood,
To show the world I am a gentleman.
This and much more, much more than twice all this,
Condemns you to the death. See them delivered over
To execution and the hand of death.

BUSHY

More welcome is the stroke of death to me
Than Bolingbroke to England. Lords, farewell.

GREEN

My comfort is that heaven will take our souls
And plague injustice with the pains of hell.

BOLINGBROKE

My Lord Northumberland, see them dispatched.
                    [*Exeunt Northumberland and others,*
                                *with the prisoners.*]
Uncle, you say the queen is at your house.
For God's sake, fairly let her be entreated.         37
Tell her I send to her my kind commends ;            38
Take special care my greetings be delivered.

YORK

A gentleman of mine I have dispatched

41 With letters of your love to her at large.
**BOLINGBROKE**
Thanks, gentle uncle. Come, lords, away,
43 To fight with Glendower and his complices.
44 A while to work, and after holiday.    *Exeunt.*

*

III, ii    *[Drums. Flourish and Colors.] Enter the King,*
*Aumerle, [the Bishop of] Carlisle, &c. [Soldiers and*
*Attendants].*

KING
Barkloughly Castle call they this at hand?
AUMERLE
2 Yea, my lord. How brooks your grace the air
After your late tossing on the breaking seas?
KING
Needs must I like it well. I weep for joy
To stand upon my kingdom once again.
Dear earth, I do salute thee with my hand,
Though rebels wound thee with their horses' hoofs.
8 As a long-parted mother with her child
9 Plays fondly with her tears and smiles in meeting,
So weeping, smiling, greet I thee, my earth,
11 And do thee favors with my royal hands.
Feed not thy sovereign's foe, my gentle earth,
Nor with thy sweets comfort his ravenous sense;
But let thy spiders that suck up thy venom,
And heavy-gaited toads, lie in their way,
Doing annoyance to the treacherous feet
Which with usurping steps do trample thee.
Yield stinging nettles to mine enemies;
And when they from thy bosom pluck a flower,
Guard it, I pray thee, with a lurking adder
21 Whose double tongue may with a mortal touch
Throw death upon thy sovereign's enemies.
23 Mock not my senseless conjuration, lords.
This earth shall have a feeling, and these stones
25 Prove armèd soldiers ere her native king
Shall falter under foul rebellion's arms.
CARLISLE
Fear not, my lord. That Power that made you king
Hath power to keep you king in spite of all.
The means that heavens yield must be embraced
And not neglected. Else heaven would,
And we will not. Heaven's offer we refuse,
The proffered means of succor and redress.
AUMERLE
He means, my lord, that we are too remiss,
34 Whilst Bolingbroke, through our security,
Grows strong and great in substance and in power.
KING
36 Discomfortable cousin! know'st thou not
37 That when the searching eye of heaven is hid
Behind the globe, that lights the lower world,
Then thieves and robbers range abroad unseen
In murders and in outrage boldly here;
But when from under this terrestrial ball
He fires the proud tops of the eastern pines
And darts his light through every guilty hole,
Then murders, treasons, and detested sins,
The cloak of night being plucked from off their backs,
Stand bare and naked, trembling at themselves?

So when this thief, this traitor Bolingbroke,
Who all this while hath revelled in the night
Whilst we were wand'ring with the Antipodes,    49
Shall see us rising in our throne, the east,
His treasons will sit blushing in his face,
Not able to endure the sight of day,
But self-affrighted tremble at his sin.
Not all the water in the rough rude sea
Can wash the balm off from an anointed king.    55
The breath of worldly men cannot depose    56
The deputy elected by the Lord.
For every man that Bolingbroke hath pressed    58
To lift shrewd steel against our golden crown,    59
God for his Richard hath in heavenly pay
A glorious angel. Then, if angels fight,
Weak men must fall; for heaven still guards the right.
    *Enter Salisbury.*
Welcome, my lord. How far off lies your power?    63
SALISBURY
Nor near nor farther off, my gracious lord,    64
Than this weak arm. Discomfort guides my tongue
And bids me speak of nothing but despair.
One day too late, I fear me, noble lord,
Hath clouded all thy happy days on earth.
O, call back yesterday, bid time return,
And thou shalt have twelve thousand fighting men!
To-day, to-day, unhappy day too late,
O'erthrows thy joys, friends, fortune, and thy state;
For all the Welshmen, hearing thou wert dead,
Are gone to Bolingbroke, dispersed, and fled.
AUMERLE
Comfort, my liege. Why looks your grace so pale?
KING
But now the blood of twenty thousand men    76
Did triumph in my face, and they are fled;
And, till so much blood thither come again,
Have I not reason to look pale and dead?
All souls that will be safe, fly from my side;
For time hath set a blot upon my pride.
AUMERLE
Comfort, my liege. Remember who you are.
KING
I had forgot myself. Am I not king?
Awake, thou coward majesty! thou sleepest.
Is not the king's name twenty thousand names?
Arm, arm, my name! A puny subject strikes
At thy great glory. Look not to the ground,
Ye favorites of a king. Are we not high?
High be our thoughts. I know my uncle York
Hath power enough to serve our turn. But who comes
here?

41 *at large* conveyed in full   43 *Glendower* (see II, iv, s.d.n.)   44 *after*
afterwards
III, ii Before Barkloughly Castle (Harlech in Wales)   2 *brooks* enjoys
8 *long-parted mother with* mother long parted from   9 *fondly* dotingly
11 *do . . . hands* salute thee by touching   21 *double* forked; *touch* wound
23 *senseless conjuration* solemn entreaty to things which cannot understand
it   25 *native* legitimate (Richard was born at Bordeaux)   34 *security*
overconfidence   36 *Discomfortable* discouraging   37–38 *when . . . world*
when the sun, lighting the other side of the world, is hidden from view
49 *Antipodes* the people on the other side of the world   55 *balm* consecrated
oil used in the coronation   56 *worldly* earthly   58 *pressed* drafted   59
*shrewd* keen   63 *power* army   64 *near* nearer   76 *twenty* (Richard exag-
gerates Salisbury's *twelve*)

*Enter Scroop.*

**SCROOP**

More health and happiness betide my liege
Than can my care-tuned tongue deliver him!

**KING**

Mine ear is open and my heart prepared.
94 The worst is worldly loss thou canst unfold.
Say, is my kingdom lost? Why, 'twas my care;
And what loss is it to be rid of care?
Strives Bolingbroke to be as great as we?
Greater he shall not be; if he serve God,
We'll serve him too, and be his fellow so.
Revolt our subjects? That we cannot mend;
They break their faith to God as well as us.
Cry woe, destruction, ruin, and decay:
The worst is death, and death will have his day.

**SCROOP**

Glad am I that your highness is so armed
To bear the tidings of calamity.
Like an unseasonable stormy day
Which makes the silver rivers drown their shores
As if the world were all dissolved to tears,
'09 So high above his limits swells the rage
Of Bolingbroke, covering your fearful land
With hard bright steel, and hearts harder than steel.
12 White-beards have armed their thin and hairless scalps
Against thy majesty. Boys with women's voices
14 Strive to speak big, and clap their female joints
In stiff unwieldy arms against thy crown.
16 Thy very beadsmen learn to bend their bows
17 Of double-fatal yew against thy state.
18 Yea, distaff-women manage rusty bills
19 Against thy seat. Both young and old rebel,
And all goes worse than I have power to tell.

**KING**

Too well, too well thou tell'st a tale so ill.
Where is the Earl of Wiltshire? Where is Bagot?
What is become of Bushy? Where is Green?
That they have let the dangerous enemy
25 Measure our confines with such peaceful steps?
If we prevail, their heads shall pay for it.
I warrant they have made peace with Bolingbroke.

**SCROOP**

Peace have they made with him indeed, my lord.

**KING**

O villains, vipers, damned without redemption!
Dogs easily won to fawn on any man!
Snakes in my heart-blood warmed that sting my heart!
Three Judases, each one thrice worse than Judas!
Would they make peace? Terrible hell make war

Upon their spotted souls for this offense!    134

**SCROOP**

Sweet love, I see, changing his property,    135
Turns to the sourest and most deadly hate.
Again uncurse their souls. Their peace is made
With heads, and not with hands. Those whom you curse   138
Have felt the worst of death's destroying wound
And lie full low, graved in the hollow ground.

**AUMERLE**

Is Bushy, Green, and the Earl of Wiltshire dead?

**SCROOP**

Ay, all of them at Bristol lost their heads.

**AUMERLE**

Where is the duke my father with his power?

**KING**

No matter where. Of comfort no man speak!
Let's talk of graves, of worms, and epitaphs,
Make dust our paper, and with rainy eyes
Write sorrow on the bosom of the earth.
Let's choose executors and talk of wills.
And yet not so – for what can we bequeath,
Save our deposèd bodies to the ground?
Our lands, our lives, and all are Bolingbroke's,
And nothing can we call our own but death
And that small model of the barren earth    153
Which serves as paste and cover to our bones.
For God's sake let us sit upon the ground
And tell sad stories of the death of kings!
How some have been deposed, some slain in war,
Some haunted by the ghosts they have deposed,    158
Some poisoned by their wives, some sleeping killed –
All murdered; for within the hollow crown
That rounds the mortal temples of a king
Keeps Death his court; and there the antic sits,    162
Scoffing his state and grinning at his pomp;
Allowing him a breath, a little scene,    164
To monarchize, be feared, and kill with looks;
Infusing him with self and vain conceit,    166
As if this flesh which walls about our life
Were brass impregnable; and humored thus,    168
Comes at the last, and with a little pin    169
Bores through his castle wall, and farewell king!
Cover your heads, and mock not flesh and blood
With solemn reverence. Throw away respect,
Tradition, form, and ceremonious duty;
For you have but mistook me all this while.
I live with bread like you, feel want, taste grief,
Need friends. Subjected thus,    176
How can you say to me I am a king?

**CARLISLE**

My lord, wise men ne'er sit and wail their woes,
But presently prevent the ways to wail.    179
To fear the foe, since fear oppresseth strength,
Gives, in your weakness, strength unto your foe,
And so your follies fight against yourself.
Fear, and be slain – no worse can come to fight;    183
And fight and die is death destroying death,
Where fearing dying pays death servile breath.    185

**AUMERLE**

My father hath a power. Inquire of him,    186
And learn to make a body of a limb.

**KING**

Thou chid'st me well. Proud Bolingbroke, I come

---

94 *The worst . . . unfold* the worst thou canst unfold is worldly loss  109
*his limits* its banks  112 *thin* sparsely haired  114 *clap* thrust; *female* i.e.
weak  116 *beadsmen* old pensioners who pray for their benefactor  117
*double-fatal* poisonous and used to make war-bows  118 *distaff-women*
spinning women; *manage* wield; *bills* halberds  119 *seat* throne  125
*Measure* travel over  134 *spotted* stained with treason  135 *property* distinctive quality  138 *with hands* by lifting their hands in surrender  153–54
*that . . . bones* that mould of earth that covers our bones – the body  158 *the
ghosts . . . deposed* the ghosts of the kings they have murdered  162 *antic*
clown  164–65 *scene, To monarchize* time on life's stage to play the monarch
166 *self . . . conceit* vain conceit of himself  168 *humored thus* while the king
is thus puffed up  169 *Comes* Death comes  176 *Subjected thus* subject as I
am – to these universal human needs  179 *prevent . . . wail* block the paths
to grief  183 *to fight* by fighting  185 *Where* whereas; *fearing dying* to be
afraid to die  186 *of* about

To change blows with thee for our day of doom.
This ague fit of fear is overblown.
An easy task it is to win our own.
Say, Scroop, where lies our uncle with his power?
Speak sweetly, man, although thy looks be sour.

SCROOP
Men judge by the complexion of the sky
195   The state and inclination of the day;
So may you by my dull and heavy eye:
  My tongue hath but a heavier tale to say.
198 I play the torturer, by small and small
To lengthen out the worst that must be spoken.
Your uncle York is joined with Bolingbroke,
And all your northern castles yielded up,
And all your southern gentlemen in arms
Upon his party.

KING     Thou hast said enough.
  [To Aumerle]
204 Beshrew thee, cousin, which didst lead me forth
Of that sweet way I was in to despair!
What say you now? What comfort have we now?
By heaven, I'll hate him everlastingly
That bids me be of comfort any more.
Go to Flint Castle. There I'll pine away;
A king, woe's slave, shall kingly woe obey.
That power I have, discharge; and let them go
212 To ear the land that hath some hope to grow,
For I have none. Let no man speak again
To alter this, for counsel is but vain.

AUMERLE
My liege, one word.

KING     He does me double wrong
That wounds me with the flatteries of his tongue.
Discharge my followers. Let them hence away,
From Richard's night to Bolingbroke's fair day.
         [Exeunt.]

      *

III, iii   Enter [with Drum and Colors] Bolingbroke, York,
     Northumberland [, Attendants, and Soldiers].

BOLINGBROKE
1 So that by this intelligence we learn
The Welshmen are dispersed, and Salisbury
Is gone to meet the king, who lately landed
With some few private friends upon this coast.

NORTHUMBERLAND
5 The news is very fair and good, my lord,
Richard not far from hence hath hid his head.

YORK
It would beseem the Lord Northumberland
To say 'King Richard.' Alack the heavy day
When such a sacred king should hide his head!

NORTHUMBERLAND
Your grace mistakes. Only to be brief,
Left I his title out.

YORK     The time hath been,
Would you have been so brief with him, he would
13 Have been so brief with you to shorten you,
14 For taking so the head, your whole head's length.

BOLINGBROKE
Mistake not, uncle, further than you should.

YORK
Take not, good cousin, further than you should,
17 Lest you mistake the heavens are over our heads.

BOLINGBROKE
I know it, uncle, and oppose not myself
Against their will. But who comes here?
  Enter Percy.
Welcome, Harry. What, will not this castle yield?

PERCY
The castle royally is manned, my lord,
Against thy entrance.

BOLINGBROKE
Royally?
Why, it contains no king?

PERCY      Yes, my good lord,
It doth contain a king. King Richard lies
Within the limits of yon lime and stone;
And with him are the Lord Aumerle, Lord Salisbury,
Sir Stephen Scroop, besides a clergyman
Of holy reverence – who, I cannot learn.

NORTHUMBERLAND
O, belike it is the Bishop of Carlisle.     30

BOLINGBROKE
Noble lords,
Go to the rude ribs of that ancient castle;
Through brazen trumpet send the breath of parley
Into his ruined ears, and thus deliver:
Henry Bolingbroke
On both his knees doth kiss King Richard's hand
And sends allegiance and true faith of heart
To his most royal person; hither come
Even at his feet to lay my arms and power,
Provided that my banishment repealed     40
And lands restored again be freely granted.
If not, I'll use the advantage of my power,
And lay the summer's dust with show'rs of blood
Rained from the wounds of slaughtered Englishmen;
The which, how far off from the mind of Bolingbroke
It is, such crimson tempest should bedrench
The fresh green lap of fair King Richard's land,
My stooping duty tenderly shall show.     48
Go signify as much, while here we march
Upon the grassy carpet of this plain.
Let's march without the noise of threat'ning drum,
That from this castle's tottered battlements    52
Our fair appointments may be well perused.    53
Methinks King Richard and myself should meet
With no less terror than the elements
Of fire and water when their thund'ring shock   56
At meeting tears the cloudy cheeks of heaven.
Be he the fire, I'll be the yielding water;
The rage be his, whilst on the earth I rain.    59
My water's on the earth, and not on him.     60
March on, and mark King Richard how he looks.
   The trumpets sound [a parle without and within, then
   a flourish. King] Richard appeareth on the walls
   [with the Bishop of Carlisle, Aumerle, Scroop, and
   Salisbury].

195 *inclination . . . day* trend of the weather   198–99 *by . . . spoken* in
breaking the worst news little by little   204 *Beshrew thee* confound you;
*forth* out   212 *ear* plough
III, iii Before Flint Castle in Wales   1 *intelligence* news   5–6 *The . . . head*
the news that Richard is in hiding not far away is auspicious and good   13
*to* as to   14 *taking . . . head* thus omitting his title   17 *mistake* ignore the
fact that   40 *repealed* revoked   48 *stooping duty* submissive kneeling;
*tenderly* considerately   52 *tottered* tattered, saw-toothed, crenellated   53
*appointments* equipment   56 *fire and water* lightning and clouds   59 *rain*
'reign'   60 *My . . . him* I fall upon the land, not upon him

See, see, King Richard doth himself appear,
As doth the blushing discontented sun
From out the fiery portal of the east
65  When he perceives the envious clouds are bent
To dim his glory and to stain the track
Of his bright passage to the occident.

YORK

68  Yet looks he like a king. Behold, his eye,
69  As bright as is the eagle's, lightens forth
Controlling majesty. Alack, alack, for woe,
That any harm should stain so fair a show!

KING [to Northumberland]

72  We are amazed; and thus long have we stood
To watch the fearful bending of thy knee,
Because we thought ourself thy lawful king,
And if we be, how dare thy joints forget
76  To pay their awful duty to our presence?
If we be not, show us the hand of God
That hath dismissed us from our stewardship;
For well we know no hand of blood and bone
Can gripe the sacred handle of our sceptre,
Unless he do profane, steal, or usurp.
And though you think that all, as you have done,
83  Have torn their souls by turning them from us
And we are barren and bereft of friends,
Yet know, my master, God omnipotent,
Is mustering in his clouds on our behalf
Armies of pestilence, and they shall strike
88  Your children yet unborn and unbegot
89  That lift your vassal hands against my head
And threat the glory of my precious crown.
Tell Bolingbroke, for yon methinks he stands,
That every stride he makes upon my land
93  Is dangerous treason. He is come to open
The purple testament of bleeding war.
But ere the crown he looks for live in peace,
Ten thousand bloody crowns of mothers' sons
97  Shall ill become the flower of England's face,
Change the complexion of her maid-pale peace
To scarlet indignation, and bedew
00  Her pastor's grass with faithful English blood.

NORTHUMBERLAND

The King of Heaven forbid our lord the king
02  Should so with civil and uncivil arms
Be rushed upon! Thy thrice-noble cousin
Harry Bolingbroke doth humbly kiss thy hand;
And by the honorable tomb he swears
That stands upon your royal grandsire's bones,
And by the royalties of both your bloods
(Currents that spring from one most gracious head),
And by the buried hand of warlike Gaunt,

And by the worth and honor of himself,
Comprising all that may be sworn or said,
His coming hither hath no further scope
Than for his lineal royalties, and to beg                    113
Enfranchisement immediate on his knees;                      114
Which on thy royal party granted once,                       115
His glittering arms he will commend to rust,                 116
His barbèd steeds to stables, and his heart                  117
To faithful service of your majesty.
This swears he, as he is a prince and just;
And as I am a gentleman, I credit him.

KING

Northumberland, say thus. The king returns:                  121
His noble cousin is right welcome hither;
And all the number of his fair demands
Shall be accomplished without contradiction.
With all the gracious utterance thou hast
Speak to his gentle hearing kind commends.                   126
    [To Aumerle]
We do debase ourselves, cousin, do we not,
To look so poorly and to speak so fair?
Shall we call back Northumberland and send
Defiance to the traitor, and so die?

AUMERLE

No, good my lord. Let's fight with gentle words
Till time lend friends, and friends their helpful swords.

KING

O God, O God! that e'er this tongue of mine
That laid the sentence of dread banishment
On yon proud man, should take it off again
With words of sooth! O that I were as great                  136
As is my grief, or lesser than my name!                      137
Or that I could forget what I have been!
Or not remember what I must be now!
Swell'st thou, proud heart? I'll give thee scope to beat,    140
Since foes have scope to beat both thee and me.              141

AUMERLE

Northumberland comes back from Bolingbroke.

KING

What must the king do now? Must he submit?
The king shall do it. Must he be deposed?
The king shall be contented. Must he lose
The name of king? A God's name, let it go!                   146
I'll give my jewels for a set of beads,                       147
My gorgeous palace for a hermitage,
My gay apparel for an almsman's gown,                        149
My figured goblets for a dish of wood,                       150
My sceptre for a palmer's walking staff,                     151
My subjects for a pair of carvèd saints,
And my large kingdom for a little grave,
A little little grave, an obscure grave;
Or I'll be buried in the king's high way,
Some way of common trade, where subjects' feet              156
May hourly trample on their sovereign's head;
For on my heart they tread now whilst I live,
And buried once, why not upon my head?
Aumerle, thou weep'st, my tender-hearted cousin!
We'll make foul weather with despisèd tears;
Our sighs and they shall lodge the summer corn              162
And make a dearth in this revolting land.                    163
Or shall we play the wantons with our woes                   164
And make some pretty match with shedding tears?
As thus – to drop them still upon one place
Till they have fretted us a pair of graves                   167

65 *he* the sun   68 *he* King Richard   69 *lightens forth* flashes out   72
*amazed* in a maze, utterly confused   76 *awful duty* awed obeisance   83
*torn* torn asunder   88–89 *Your . . . That* of you . . . who   89 *vassal* subject
93–94 *open . . . war* carry out the terms of war's bloody will   97 *flower . . .
face* blooming surface of the land   100 *Her pastor's* her shepherd's, i.e.
Richard's   102 *civil* borne by Englishmen against Englishmen; *uncivil*
rude   113 *lineal royalties* royal birthrights   114 *Enfranchisement* freedom
from banishment   115 *on . . . party* on your majesty's part   116 *commend*
hand over   117 *barbèd* armored   121 *returns* replies as follows   126 *commends* regards   136 *sooth* flattery   137 *name* title of king   140 *scope* room,
permission   141 *have scope* aim   146 *A* in   147 *set of beads* rosary   149
*almsman* one living on charity   150 *figured* embossed   151 *palmer* pilgrim
156 *trade* passage   162 *lodge* beat down   163 *revolting* rebelling   164 *play
the wantons* sport   167 *fretted* us washed out for us

Within the earth ; and therein laid – there lies
Two kinsmen digged their graves with weeping eyes.
Would not this ill do well ? Well, well, I see
I talk but idly, and you laugh at me.
Most mighty prince, my Lord Northumberland,
What says King Bolingbroke ? Will his majesty
Give Richard leave to live till Richard die ?

175 You make a leg, and Bolingbroke says ay.

NORTHUMBERLAND

176 My lord, in the base court he doth attend
To speak with you, may it please you to come down.

KING

178 Down, down I come, like glist'ring Phaeton,
179 Wanting the manage of unruly jades.
In the base court ? Base court, where kings grow base,
To come at traitors' calls and do them grace !
In the base court come down ? Down court ! down king !
For night owls shriek where mounting larks should sing.
*[Exeunt from above.]*

BOLINGBROKE

What says his majesty ?

NORTHUMBERLAND      Sorrow and grief of heart
185 Makes him speak fondly, like a frantic man.
Yet he is come.
*[Enter King Richard attended, below.]*

BOLINGBROKE

Stand all apart
And show fair duty to his majesty.
*He kneels down.*
My gracious lord –

KING

Fair cousin, you debase your princely knee
To make the base earth proud with kissing it.
192 Me rather had my heart might feel your love
Than my unpleased eye see your courtesy.
Up, cousin, up ! Your heart is up, I know,
Thus high at least *[touches his own head]*, although your
knee be low.

BOLINGBROKE *[rises]*

My gracious lord, I come but for mine own.

KING

Your own is yours, and I am yours, and all.

BOLINGBROKE

198 So far be mine, my most redoubted lord,
As my true service shall deserve your love.

KING

Well you deserve. They well deserve to have
That know the strong'st and surest way to get.
Uncle, give me your hand. Nay, dry your eyes.
203 Tears show their love, but want their remedies.
Cousin, I am too young to be your father,
Though you are old enough to be my heir.
What you will have, I'll give, and willing too ;
For do we must what force will have us do.
Set on towards London. Cousin, is it so ?

BOLINGBROKE

Yea, my good lord.

KING      Then I must not say no. *[Flourish. Exeunt.]*

\*

III, iv      *Enter the Queen with [two Ladies,] her Attendants.*

QUEEN

What sport shall we devise here in this garden
To drive away the heavy thought of care ?

LADY

Madam, we'll play at bowls.

QUEEN

'Twill make me think the world is full of rubs    4
And that my fortune runs against the bias.    5

LADY

Madam, we'll dance.

QUEEN

My legs can keep no measure in delight    7
When my poor heart no measure keeps in grief.
Therefore no dancing, girl ; some other sport.

LADY

Madam, we'll tell tales.

QUEEN

Of sorrow or of joy ?

LADY      Of either, madam.

QUEEN

Of neither, girl ;
For if of joy, being altogether wanting,
It doth remember me the more of sorrow ;
Or if of grief, being altogether had,    15
It adds more sorrow to my want of joy ;
For what I have I need not to repeat,
And what I want it boots not to complain.    18

LADY

Madam, I'll sing.

QUEEN      'Tis well that thou hast cause ;
But thou shouldst please me better, wouldst thou weep.

LADY

I could weep, madam, would it do you good.

QUEEN

And I could sing, would weeping do me good,
And never borrow any tear of thee.
*Enter Gardeners [one the Master, the other two his
Men].*
But stay, here come the gardeners.
Let's step into the shadow of these trees.
My wretchedness unto a row of pins,    26
They will talk of state, for every one doth so    27
Against a change : woe is forerun with woe.    28
*[Queen and Ladies step aside.]*

GARDENER

Go bind thou up yon dangling apricocks,    29
Which, like unruly children, make their sire
Stoop with oppression of their prodigal weight.    31
Give some supportance to the bending twigs.
Go thou and, like an executioner,
Cut off the heads of too-fast-growing sprays
That look too lofty in our commonwealth.
All must be even in our government.    36
You thus employed, I will go root away
The noisome weeds which without profit suck
The soil's fertility from wholesome flowers.

175 *You . . . ay* if you curtsy to him, Bolingbroke will say yes   176 *base court* lower or outer courtyard; *attend* wait   178 *Phaeton* (he borrowed the chariot of his father, the sun god, drove it unskillfully, nearly set the world on fire)   179 *Wanting . . . of* lacking control over ; *jades* poor horses   185 *fondly* foolishly ; *frantic* mad   192 *Me rather had* I would rather   198 *redoubted* dread   203 *want their remedies* cannot cure what causes them
III, iv The garden of the Duke of York's seat at Langley   4 *rubs* impediments (in the game of bowls)   5 *bias* curving course (of a bowl)   7–8 *measure . . . measure* stately dance . . . moderation   15 *had* had by me   18 *boots* helps   26 *My . . . pins* my grief against a trifle   27 *state* politics   28 *Against* expecting   29 *apricocks* apricots   31 *prodigal* excessive   36 *even* equal

[1.] MAN
40 Why should we, in the compass of a pale,
Keep law and form and due proportion,
Showing, as in a model, our firm estate,
When our sea-wallèd garden, the whole land,
Is full of weeds, her fairest flowers choked up,
Her fruit trees all unpruned, her hedges ruined,
46 Her knots disordered, and her wholesome herbs
Swarming with caterpillars?

GARDENER                 Hold thy peace.
He that hath suffered this disordered spring
Hath now himself met with the fall of leaf.
The weeds which his broad-spreading leaves did
    shelter,
51 That seemed in eating him to hold him up,
Are plucked up root and all by Bolingbroke –
I mean the Earl of Wiltshire, Bushy, Green.

[2.] MAN
What, are they dead?

GARDENER         They are; and Bolingbroke
Hath seized the wasteful king. O, what pity is it
That he had not so trimmed and dressed his land
57 As we this garden! We at time of year
Do wound the bark, the skin of our fruit trees,
59 Lest, being overproud in sap and blood,
60 With too much riches it confound itself.
Had he done so to great and growing men,
They might have lived to bear, and he to taste
Their fruits of duty. Superfluous branches
We lop away, that bearing boughs may live.
Had he done so, himself had borne the crown,
Which waste of idle hours hath quite thrown down.

[2.] MAN
What, think you the king shall be deposed?

GARDENER
68 Depressed he is already, and deposed
69 'Tis doubt he will be. Letters came last night
To a dear friend of the good Duke of York's
That tell black tidings.

QUEEN
72 O, I am pressed to death through want of speaking!
    [Comes forward.]
73 Thou old Adam's likeness, set to dress this garden,
How dares thy harsh rude tongue sound this unpleasing
    news?
75 What Eve, what serpent, hath suggested thee
To make a second fall of cursèd man?
Why dost thou say King Richard is deposed?
Dar'st thou, thou little better thing than earth,
79 Divine his downfall? Say, where, when, and how
Cam'st thou by this ill tidings? Speak, thou wretch!

GARDENER
Pardon me, madam. Little joy have I
To breathe this news; yet what I say is true.    82
King Richard, he is in the mighty hold
Of Bolingbroke. Their fortunes both are weighed.
In your lord's scale is nothing but himself,
And some few vanities that make him light;
But in the balance of great Bolingbroke,
Besides himself, are all the English peers,
And with that odds he weighs King Richard down.
Post you to London, and you will find it so.
I speak no more than every one doth know.

QUEEN
Nimble mischance, that art so light of foot,
Doth not thy embassage belong to me,    93
And am I last that knows it? O, thou thinkest
To serve me last, that I may longest keep
Thy sorrow in my breast. Come, ladies, go    96
To meet at London London's king in woe.
What, was I born to this, that my sad look
Should grace the triumph of great Bolingbroke?    99
Gard'ner, for telling me these news of woe,
Pray God the plants thou graft'st may never grow.
                  Exit [with Ladies].

GARDNER
Poor queen, so that thy state might be no worse,
I would my skill were subject to thy curse!
Here did she fall a tear; here in this place    104
I'll set a bank of rue, sour herb of grace.    105
Rue, even for ruth, here shortly shall be seen,    106
In the remembrance of a weeping queen.    Exeunt.

＊

*Enter Bolingbroke, with the Lords [Aumerle,*    IV, i
*Northumberland, Percy, Fitzwater, Surrey, and*
*another, with Bishop of Carlisle, Abbot of*
*Westminster, Attendants, and Herald] to*
*Parliament.*

BOLINGBROKE
Call forth Bagot.
    *Enter [Officers with] Bagot.*
Now, Bagot, freely speak thy mind,
What thou dost know of noble Gloucester's death;
Who wrought it with the king, and who performed    4
The bloody office of his timeless end.    5

BAGOT
Then set before my face the Lord Aumerle.

BOLINGBROKE
Cousin, stand forth, and look upon that man.

BAGOT
My Lord Aumerle, I know your daring tongue
Scorns to unsay what once it hath delivered.
In that dead time when Gloucester's death was plotted,    10
I heard you say, 'Is not my arm of length,    11
That reacheth from the restful English court    12
As far as Calais to mine uncle's head?'
Amongst much other talk that very time
I heard you say that you had rather refuse
The offer of an hundred thousand crowns
Than Bolingbroke's return to England;    17
Adding withal, how blest this land would be    18
In this your cousin's death.

AUMERLE                  Princes and noble lords,
What answer shall I make to this base man?

40 *pale* enclosed garden  46 *knots* flower-beds laid out in patterns  51 *in* while  57 *at . . . year* in season  59 *overproud in* swollen with  60 *confound* destroy  68 *Depressed* brought low  69 *'Tis doubt* there is fear  72 *pressed to death* tortured as by a heavy weight crushing me  73 *old Adam* the first gardener  75 *suggested* tempted  79 *Divine* prophesy by occult means  82 *To breathe* in speaking  93 *embassage* message  96 *Thy sorrow* the sorrow you report  99 *triumph* triumphal procession; *Bolingbroke* (in the original spelling, 'Bullingbrooke,' the name rimes with *look* in l. 98)  104 *fall* drop  105 *grace* repentance  106 *ruth* pity
IV, i Westminster Hall (September-October, 1399)  4 *wrought . . . king* worked on the king's mind to bring it about  5 *timeless* untimely  10 *dead* dark, silent  11 *of length* long  12 *restful* calm, untroubled by Gloucester  17 *Than . . . return* than have Bolingbroke return  18 *withal* besides

21 Shall I so much dishonor my fair stars
22 On equal terms to give him chastisement?
Either I must, or have mine honor soiled
24 With the attainder of his slanderous lips.
25 There is my gage, the manual seal of death
That marks thee out for hell. I say thou liest,
And will maintain what thou hast said is false
28 In thy heart-blood, though being all too base
29 To stain the temper of my knightly sword.

BOLINGBROKE
Bagot, forbear; thou shalt not take it up.

AUMERLE
31 Excepting one, I would he were the best
32 In all this presence that hath moved me so.

FITZWATER
33 If that thy valor stand on sympathy,
There is my gage, Aumerle, in gage to thine.
By that fair sun which shows me where thou stand'st,
I heard thee say, and vauntingly thou spak'st it,
That thou wert cause of noble Gloucester's death.
If thou deniest it twenty times, thou liest,
And I will turn thy falsehood to thy heart,
Where it was forgèd, with my rapier's point.

AUMERLE
Thou dar'st not, coward, live to see that day.

FITZWATER
Now, by my soul, I would it were this hour.

AUMERLE
Fitzwater, thou art damned to hell for this.

PERCY
Aumerle, thou liest. His honor is as true
45 In this appeal as thou art all unjust;
And that thou art so, there I throw my gage
To prove it on thee to the extremest point
Of mortal breathing. Seize it if thou dar'st.

AUMERLE
And if I do not, may my hands rot off
And never brandish more revengeful steel
Over the glittering helmet of my foe!

ANOTHER LORD
52 I task the earth to the like, forsworn Aumerle;
53 And spur thee on with full as many lies
As may be holloed in thy treacherous ear
55 From sun to sun. There is my honor's pawn.
56 Engage it to the trial, if thou darest.

AUMERLE
57 Who sets me else? By heaven, I'll throw at all!
I have a thousand spirits in one breast
To answer twenty thousand such as you.

SURREY
My Lord Fitzwater, I do remember well
The very time Aumerle and you did talk.

FITZWATER
62 'Tis very true. You were in presence then,
And you can witness with me this is true.

SURREY
As false, by heaven, as heaven itself is true!

FITZWATER
Surrey, thou liest.

SURREY                 Dishonorable boy!
That lie shall lie so heavy on my sword
That it shall render vengeance and revenge
Till thou the lie-giver and that lie do lie
In earth as quiet as thy father's skull.

In proof whereof there is my honor's pawn.
Engage it to the trial if thou dar'st.

FITZWATER
How fondly dost thou spur a forward horse!    72
If I dare eat, or drink, or breathe, or live,
I dare meet Surrey in a wilderness,    74
And spit upon him whilst I say he lies,
And lies, and lies. There is my bond of faith
To tie thee to my strong correction.
As I intend to thrive in this new world,    78
Aumerle is guilty of my true appeal.
Besides, I heard the banished Norfolk say
That thou, Aumerle, didst send two of thy men
To execute the noble duke at Calais.

AUMERLE
Some honest Christian trust me with a gage
That Norfolk lies. Here do I throw down this,
If he may be repealed to try his honor.    85

BOLINGBROKE
These differences shall all rest under gage    86
Till Norfolk be repealed. Repealed he shall be
And, though mine enemy, restored again
To all his lands and signories. When he is returned,
Against Aumerle we will enforce his trial.

CARLISLE
That honorable day shall never be seen.
Many a time hath banished Norfolk fought
For Jesu Christ in glorious Christian field,
Streaming the ensign of the Christian cross    94
Against black pagans, Turks, and Saracens;
And, toiled with works of war, retired himself    96
To Italy; and there, at Venice, gave
His body to that pleasant country's earth
And his pure soul unto his captain, Christ,
Under whose colors he had fought so long.

BOLINGBROKE
Why, Bishop, is Norfolk dead?

CARLISLE
As surely as I live, my lord.

BOLINGBROKE
Sweet peace conduct his sweet soul to the bosom    10
Of good old Abraham! Lords appellants,
Your differences shall all rest under gage
Till we assign you to your days of trial.
               *Enter York [attended].*

YORK
Great Duke of Lancaster, I come to thee
From plume-plucked Richard, who with willing soul    10
Adopts thee heir and his high sceptre yields
To the possession of thy royal hand.
Ascend his throne, descending now from him,
And long live Henry, fourth of that name!

21 *fair stars* high rank and fortune   22 *On . . . chastisement* as to fight him
as my equal in rank   24 *attainder* disgraceful accusation   25 *manual . . .*
*death* your death warrant sealed by my hand   28 *being* it is   29 *temper*
honorable quality   31 *one* i.e. Bolingbroke   32 *moved* angered   33 *If . . .*
*sympathy* if your valor can show itself only on those who are your equals in
blood   45 *all unjust* completely false   52 *task . . . like* burden the ground
with another gage   53 *lies* accusations of lying   55 *pawn* pledge   56
*Engage . . . trial* take it as a challenge to fight   57 *sets me* puts up stakes
against me; *throw at all* throw down gloves, like wagers at dice, against you
all   62 *in presence* present at court   72 *forward* willing   74 *in a wilderness*
i.e. where there would be no help and no escape   78 *in . . . world* under
the new king   85 *repealed* called back   86 *under gage* as challenges   94
*Streaming* flying   96 *toiled* worn out   103-04 *bosom . . . Abraham* heavenly
rest   108 *plume-plucked* sorry-looking, denuded

BOLINGBROKE
In God's name I'll ascend the regal throne.
CARLISLE
14    Marry, God forbid!
115    Worst in this royal presence may I speak,
116    Yet, best beseeming me to speak the truth :
Would God that any in this noble presence
Were enough noble to be upright judge
Of noble Richard! then true noblesse would
Learn him forbearance from so foul a wrong.
What subject can give sentence on his king?
And who sits here that is not Richard's subject?
Thieves are not judged but they are by to hear,
Although apparent guilt be seen in them;
And shall the figure of God's majesty,
His captain, steward, deputy elect,
Anointed, crownèd, planted many years,
Be judged by subject and inferior breath,
29    And he himself not present? O, forfend it God
30    That, in a Christian climate, souls refined
31    Should show so heinous, black, obscene a deed!
I speak to subjects, and a subject speaks,
Stirred up by God, thus boldly for his king.
My Lord of Hereford here, whom you call king,
Is a foul traitor to proud Hereford's king;
And if you crown him, let me prophesy,
The blood of English shall manure the ground
And future ages groan for this foul act;
Peace shall go sleep with Turks and infidels,
And in this seat of peace tumultuous wars
41    Shall kin with kin and kind with kind confound;
Disorder, horror, fear, and mutiny
Shall here inhabit, and this land be called
44    The field of Golgotha and dead men's skulls.
O, if you raise this house against this house,
It will the woefullest division prove
That ever fell upon this cursèd earth.
Prevent it, resist it, let it not be so,
Lest child, child's children cry against you woe.
NORTHUMBERLAND
Well have you argued, sir; and for your pains
51    Of capital treason we arrest you here.
My Lord of Westminster, be it your charge
To keep him safely till his day of trial.
54    [May it please you, lords, to grant the commons' suit.
BOLINGBROKE
Fetch hither Richard, that in common view
He may surrender. So we shall proceed
Without suspicion.
57    YORK                         I will be his conduct.    Exit.

114 *Marry* by the Virgin Mary    115 *Worst . . . speak* I may be by birth and
position the most unfit to speak    116 *best . . . truth* since it best beseems
me, a clergyman, to speak the truth, I say    129 *forfend* forbid    130 *souls
refined* civilized people    131 *obscene* ill-omened    141 *kin . . . kind* kinsmen
. . . fellow-countrymen    144 *Golgotha* 'the place of a skull,' Calvary    151
*Of* on the charge of; *capital* carrying the death penalty    154–318 *May . . .
fall* (see 'Note on the Text,' p. 636)    154 *suit* request that the causes of
Richard's deposition be published    157 *conduct* escort    159 *sureties* men
who will be responsible for your appearance    168 *favors* faces and friendly
acts    173 *Am . . . clerk* must I pray like the priest and say amen like the
clerk    178 *tired majesty* weariness of kingship    185 *owes* owns, has    196
*care . . . care . . . old care* grief . . . responsibility . . . failing diligence    197
*care . . . care . . . new care* anxiety . . . responsibility . . . fresh zeal    199 *tend*
go with    201 *Ay . . . ay* 'yes, no; no, yes,' but also 'I, no; no I'    203 *undo*
strip and ruin

BOLINGBROKE
Lords, you that here are under our arrest,
Procure your sureties for your days of answer.    159
Little are we beholding to your love,
And little looked for at your helping hands.
    *Enter Richard and York [with Officers bearing the
    crown, &c.].*
RICHARD
Alack, why am I sent for to a king
Before I have shook off the regal thoughts
Wherewith I reigned? I hardly yet have learned
To insinuate, flatter, bow, and bend my limbs.
Give sorrow leave a while to tutor me
To this submission. Yet I well remember
The favors of these men. Were they not mine?    168
Did they not sometime cry 'All hail!' to me?
So Judas did to Christ; but he, in twelve,
Found truth in all but one; I, in twelve thousand none.
God save the king! Will no man say amen?
Am I both priest and clerk? Well then, amen!    173
God save the king! although I be not he;
And yet amen, if heaven do think him me.
To do what service am I sent for hither?
YORK
To do that office of thine own good will
Which tired majesty did make thee offer –    178
The resignation of thy state and crown
To Henry Bolingbroke.
RICHARD
Give me the crown. Here, cousin, seize the crown.
Here, cousin,
On this side my hand, and on that side yours.
Now is this golden crown like a deep well
That owes two buckets, filling one another,    185
The emptier ever dancing in the air,
The other down, unseen, and full of water.
That bucket down and full of tears am I,
Drinking my griefs whilst you mount up on high.
BOLINGBROKE
I thought you had been willing to resign.
RICHARD
My crown I am, but still my griefs are mine.
You may my glories and my state depose,
But not my griefs. Still am I king of those.
BOLINGBROKE
Part of your cares you give me with your crown.
RICHARD
Your cares set up do not pluck my cares down.
My care is loss of care, by old care done;    196
Your care is gain of care, by new care won.    197
The cares I give I have, though given away;
They tend the crown, yet still with me they stay.    199
BOLINGBROKE
Are you contented to resign the crown?
RICHARD
Ay, no; no, ay; for I must nothing be;    201
Therefore no no, for I resign to thee.
Now mark me how I will undo myself.    203
I give this heavy weight from off my head
And this unwieldy sceptre from my hand,
The pride of kingly sway from out my heart.
With mine own tears I wash away my balm,
With mine own hands I give away my crown,
With mine own tongue deny my sacred state,

210 With mine own breath release all duty's rites.
     All pomp and majesty I do forswear;
     My manors, rents, revenues I forgo;
     My acts, decrees, and statutes I deny.
     God pardon all oaths that are broke to me!
215 God keep all vows unbroke that swear to thee!
     Make me, that nothing have, with nothing grieved,
     And thou with all pleased, that hast all achieved!
     Long mayst thou live in Richard's seat to sit,
     And soon lie Richard in an earthy pit!
     God save King Harry, unkinged Richard says,
     And send him many years of sunshine days!
     What more remains?

       NORTHUMBERLAND   No more, but that you read
     These accusations and these grievous crimes
     Committed by your person and your followers
225 Against the state and profit of this land,
     That, by confessing them, the souls of men
227 May deem that you are worthily deposed.

       RICHARD
228 Must I do so? and must I ravel out
     My weaved-up folly? Gentle Northumberland,
     If thy offenses were upon record,
     Would it not shame thee in so fair a troop
232 To read a lecture of them? If thou wouldst,
     There shouldst thou find one heinous article,
     Containing the deposing of a king
235 And cracking the strong warrant of an oath,
     Marked with a blot, damned in the book of heaven.
     Nay, all of you that stand and look upon
238 Whilst that my wretchedness doth bait myself,
     Though some of you, with Pilate, wash your hands,
     Showing an outward pity, yet you Pilates
241 Have here delivered me to my sour cross,
     And water cannot wash away your sin.

       NORTHUMBERLAND
243 My lord, dispatch. Read o'er these articles.

       RICHARD
     Mine eyes are full of tears; I cannot see.
     And yet salt water blinds them not so much
246 But they can see a sort of traitors here.
     Nay, if I turn mine eyes upon myself,
     I find myself a traitor with the rest;
     For I have given here my soul's consent
250 To undeck the pompous body of a king;
     Made glory base, and sovereignty a slave,
     Proud majesty a subject, state a peasant.

       NORTHUMBERLAND
     My lord –

       RICHARD
254 No lord of thine, thou haught, insulting man,
     Nor no man's lord. I have no name, no title –
256 No, not that name was given me at the font –
     But 'tis usurped. Alack the heavy day,
     That I have worn so many winters out
     And know not now what name to call myself!
     O that I were a mockery king of snow,
     Standing before the sun of Bolingbroke
     To melt myself away in water drops!
     Good king, great king, and yet not greatly good,
264 An if my word be sterling yet in England,
     Let it command a mirror hither straight,
     That it may show me what a face I have
     Since it is bankrout of his majesty.

       BOLINGBROKE
     Go some of you and fetch a looking glass.
                         *[Exit an Attendant.]*

       NORTHUMBERLAND
     Read o'er this paper while the glass doth come.

       RICHARD
     Fiend, thou torments me ere I come to hell!     27

       BOLINGBROKE
     Urge it no more, my Lord Northumberland.

       NORTHUMBERLAND
     The commons will not then be satisfied.

       RICHARD
     They shall be satisfied. I'll read enough
     When I do see the very book indeed
     Where all my sins are writ, and that's myself.
            *Enter one with a glass.*
     Give me the glass, and therein will I read.
     No deeper wrinkles yet? Hath sorrow struck
     So many blows upon this face of mine
     And made no deeper wounds? O flattering glass,
     Like to my followers in prosperity,
     Thou dost beguile me! Was this face the face
     That every day under his household roof
     Did keep ten thousand men? Was this the face
     That like the sun did make beholders wink?    28
     Was this the face that faced so many follies    28
     And was at last outfaced by Bolingbroke?
     A brittle glory shineth in this face.
     As brittle as the glory is the face,
       *[Dashes the glass to the floor.]*
     For there it is, cracked in a hundred shivers.
     Mark, silent king, the moral of this sport –
     How soon my sorrow hath destroyed my face.

       BOLINGBROKE
     The shadow of your sorrow hath destroyed    29
     The shadow of your face.

       RICHARD               Say that again.
     The shadow of my sorrow? Ha! let's see!
     'Tis very true: my grief lies all within;
     And these external manners of laments
     Are merely shadows to the unseen grief
     That swells with silence in the tortured soul.
     There lies the substance; and I thank thee, king,
     For thy great bounty that not only giv'st    30
     Me cause to wail, but teachest me the way
     How to lament the cause. I'll beg one boon,    30
     And then be gone and trouble you no more.
     Shall I obtain it?

       BOLINGBROKE    Name it, fair cousin.

       RICHARD
     Fair cousin? I am greater than a king;
     For when I was a king, my flatterers
     Were then but subjects; being now a subject,
     I have a king here to my flatterer.    30
     Being so great, I have no need to beg.

---

210 *duty's rites* ceremonies of respect   215 *swear* are sworn   225 *state and profit* ordered prosperity   227 *worthily* justly   228 *ravel out* unravel   232 *read . . . them* read them out like the lesson in church   235 *oath* i.e. your oath of allegiance to me   238 *bait* torment   241 *sour* bitter   243 *dispatch* make haste   246 *sort* gang   250 *pompous* stately   254 *haught* arrogant   256–57 *No . . . usurped* (Richard's enemies spread a rumor that he was illegitimate)   264 *An if* if; *sterling* valid currency   284 *wink* close their eyes   285 *faced* countenanced   292–93 *shadow . . . shadow* outward show...reflection   300 *that* who   302 *boon* favor   308 *to* as

BOLINGBROKE
Yet ask.

RICHARD
And shall I have?

BOLINGBROKE
You shall.

RICHARD
Then give me leave to go.

BOLINGBROKE
Whither?

RICHARD
Whither you will, so I were from your sights.

BOLINGBROKE
16    Go some of you, convey him to the Tower.

RICHARD
17    O, good! Convey? Conveyers are you all,
That rise thus nimbly by a true king's fall.]
            [Exit Richard, with some Lords and a Guard.]

BOLINGBROKE
On Wednesday next we solemnly proclaim
Our coronation. Lords, be ready all.
            Exeunt. Manent [the Abbot of] Westminster,
                [the Bishop of] Carlisle, Aumerle.

ABBOT
A woeful pageant have we here beheld.

CARLISLE
The woe's to come. The children yet unborn
Shall feel this day as sharp to them as thorn.

AUMERLE
You holy clergymen, is there no plot
To rid the realm of this pernicious blot?

ABBOT
My lord,
Before I freely speak my mind herein,
You shall not only take the sacrament
29    To bury mine intents, but also to effect
Whatever I shall happen to devise.
I see your brows are full of discontent,
Your hearts of sorrow, and your eyes of tears.
Come home with me to supper. I will lay
A plot shall show us all a merry day.        Exeunt.

                        *

*,i    Enter the Queen with [Ladies,] her Attendants.

QUEEN
This way the king will come. This is the way
2    To Julius Caesar's ill-erected tower,
To whose flint bosom my condemnèd lord
Is doomed a prisoner by proud Bolingbroke.
Here let us rest, if this rebellious earth
Have any resting for her true king's queen.
            Enter Richard [and Guard].
But soft, but see, or rather do not see,

My fair rose wither. Yet look up, behold,
That you in pity may dissolve to dew
And wash him fresh again with true-love tears.
Ah, thou the model where old Troy did stand,      11
Thou map of honor, thou King Richard's tomb,      12
And not King Richard! Thou most beauteous inn,    13
Why should hard-favored grief be lodged in thee
When triumph is become an alehouse guest?

RICHARD
Join not with grief, fair woman, do not so,
To make my end too sudden. Learn, good soul,
To think our former state a happy dream;
From which awaked, the truth of what we are
Shows us but this. I am sworn brother, sweet,
To grim Necessity, and he and I
Will keep a league till death. Hie thee to France
And cloister thee in some religious house.
Our holy lives must win a new world's crown,       24
Which our profane hours here have thrown down.     25

QUEEN
What, is my Richard both in shape and mind
Transformed and weak'ned? Hath Bolingbroke deposed
Thine intellect? Hath he been in thy heart?
The lion dying thrusteth forth his paw
And wounds the earth, if nothing else, with rage
To be o'erpow'red; and wilt thou pupil-like        31
Take the correction mildly, kiss the rod,
And fawn on rage with base humility,
Which art a lion and the king of beasts?

RICHARD
A king of beasts indeed! If aught but beasts,
I had been still a happy king of men.
Good sometimes queen, prepare thee hence for France.
Think I am dead, and that even here thou takest,
As from my deathbed, thy last living leave.
In winter's tedious nights sit by the fire
With good old folks, and let them tell thee tales   41
Of woeful ages long ago betid;
And ere thou bid good night, to quite their griefs  43
Tell thou the lamentable tale of me,
And send the hearers weeping to their beds.
For why, the senseless brands will sympathize       46
The heavy accent of thy moving tongue
And in compassion weep the fire out;
And some will mourn in ashes, some coal-black,
For the deposing of a rightful king.
            Enter Northumberland [attended].

NORTHUMBERLAND
My lord, the mind of Bolingbroke is changed.
You must to Pomfret, not unto the Tower.            52
And, madam, there is order ta'en for you:
With all swift speed you must away to France.

RICHARD
Northumberland, thou ladder wherewithal            55
The mounting Bolingbroke ascends my throne,
The time shall not be many hours of age
More than it is, ere foul sin gathering head       58
Shall break into corruption. Thou shalt think,
Though he divide the realm and give thee half,
It is too little, helping him to all.
And he shall think that thou, which knowest the way
To plant unrightful kings, wilt know again,
Being ne'er so little urged another way,
To pluck him headlong from the usurped throne.     65

316 *convey* escort    317 *Convey* slang for 'steal'    329 *bury mine intents* hide
what I intend
V, i A London street    2 *ill-erected* erected with evil results    11 *model*
. . . *stand* ground plan of ruin, like that of Troy after its fall    12 *map*
pattern    13–15 *inn . . . alehouse* mansion (Richard) . . . tavern (Bolingbroke)
24 *new world's* heavenly    25 *thrown* (two syllables)    31 *To be* at being
41–42 *tales . . . betid* tales of woe which happened in ages long past    43
*quite* requite; *griefs* tales of woe    46 *For why* because; *sympathize* respond
to    52 *Pomfret* Pontefract, or Pomfret, Castle in Yorkshire (the scene of
V, v)    55 *wherewithal* by means of which    58 *gathering head* coming to a
head, like a boil    65 *To* how to

66 The love of wicked men converts to fear;
That fear to hate, and hate turns one or both
68 To worthy danger and deservèd death.

NORTHUMBERLAND
My guilt be on my head, and there an end!
70 Take leave and part, for you must part forthwith.

RICHARD
Doubly divorced! Bad men, you violate
A twofold marriage – 'twixt my crown and me,
And then betwixt me and my married wife.
Let me unkiss the oath 'twixt thee and me;
And yet not so, for with a kiss 'twas made.
Part us, Northumberland – I towards the north,
77 Where shivering cold and sickness pines the clime;
My wife to France, from whence, set forth in pomp,
She came adornèd hither like sweet May,
80 Sent back like Hallowmas or short'st of day.

QUEEN
And must we be divided? Must we part?

RICHARD
Ay, hand from hand, my love, and heart from heart.

QUEEN
Banish us both, and send the king with me.

NORTHUMBERLAND
84 That were some love, but little policy.

QUEEN
Then whither he goes, thither let me go.

RICHARD
86 So two, together weeping, make one woe.
Weep thou for me in France, I for thee here.
88 Better far off than near, be ne'er the near.
Go, count thy way with sighs; I mine with groans.

QUEEN
So longest way shall have the longest moans.

RICHARD
Twice for one step I'll groan, the way being short,
And piece the way out with a heavy heart.
Come, come, in wooing sorrow let's be brief,
Since, wedding it, there is such length in grief.
One kiss shall stop our mouths, and dumbly part.
Thus give I mine, and thus take I thy heart.

QUEEN
Give me mine own again. 'Twere no good part
To take on me to keep and kill thy heart.
So, now I have mine own again, be gone,
That I may strive to kill it with a groan.

RICHARD
101 We make woe wanton with this fond delay.
Once more adieu! The rest let sorrow say.          *Exeunt.*

*

V, ii      *Enter Duke of York and the Duchess.*

DUCHESS
My lord, you told me you would tell the rest,
When weeping made you break the story off
Of our two cousins coming into London.

YORK
4 Where did I leave?

DUCHESS                    At that sad stop, my lord,
5 Where rude misgoverned hands from windows' tops
Threw dust and rubbish on King Richard's head.

YORK
Then, as I said, the duke, great Bolingbroke,

Mounted upon a hot and fiery steed
Which his aspiring rider seemed to know,          9
With slow but stately pace kept on his course,
Whilst all tongues cried, 'God save thee, Bolingbroke!'
You would have thought the very windows spake,
So many greedy looks of young and old
Through casements darted their desiring eyes
Upon his visage; and that all the walls
With painted imagery had said at once,            16
'Jesu preserve thee! Welcome, Bolingbroke!'
Whilst he, from the one side to the other turning,
Bareheaded, lower than his proud steed's neck,
Bespake them thus, 'I thank you, countrymen.'
And thus still doing, thus he passed along.

DUCHESS
Alack, poor Richard! Where rode he the whilst?

YORK
As in a theatre the eyes of men,
After a well-graced actor leaves the stage,       24
Are idly bent on him that enters next,            25
Thinking his prattle to be tedious,
Even so, or with much more contempt, men's eyes
Did scowl on gentle Richard. No man cried, 'God save
    him!'
No joyful tongue gave him his welcome home,
But dust was thrown upon his sacred head;
Which with such gentle sorrow he shook off,
His face still combating with tears and smiles,
The badges of his grief and patience,             33
That, had not God for some strong purpose steeled
The hearts of men, they must perforce have melted
And barbarism itself have pitied him.             36
But heaven hath a hand in these events,
To whose high will we bound our calm contents.    38
To Bolingbroke are we sworn subjects now,
Whose state and honor I for aye allow.            40
        *[Enter Aumerle.]*

DUCHESS
Here comes my son Aumerle.

YORK                            Aumerle that was;
But that is lost for being Richard's friend,      42
And, madam, you must call him Rutland now.
I am in parliament pledge for his truth
And lasting fealty to the new-made king.          45

DUCHESS
Welcome, my son. Who are the violets now          46
That strew the green lap of the new-come spring?

AUMERLE
Madam, I know not, nor I greatly care not.
God knows I had as lief be none as one.

YORK
Well, bear you well in this new spring of time,

66 *converts* changes  68 *worthy* merited  70 *part . . . part* separate . . .
depart  77 *pines the clime* make the climate an enfeebling one  80 *Hallowmas* All Saint's Day, November 1; *short'st of day* the winter solstice  84
*policy* political wisdom  86 *So* no, for thus  88 *near . . . near* being near,
never be nearer  101 *We . . . wanton* we play with our grief; *fond* foolishly
affectionate
V, ii The palace of the Duke of York  4 *leave* leave off  5 *misgoverned*
unruly; *windows' tops* upper windows  9 *Which . . . know* which seemed to
know its ambitious rider  16 *With . . . imagery* painted with figures like
a tapestry  24 *well-graced* graceful and well received  25 *idly* listlessly
33 *badges* tokens  36 *barbarism itself* even savages  38 *To . . . contents* we
limit our wishes to calm content with heaven's high will  40 *state* high
rank  42 *that* that title  45 *fealty* loyalty  46–47 *Who . . . spring* who are
the new king's favorites

Lest you be cropped before you come to prime.
52 What news from Oxford? Do these justs and triumphs
hold?
AUMERLE
For aught I know, my lord, they do.
YORK
You will be there, I know.
AUMERLE
If God prevent not, I purpose so.
YORK
What seal is that that hangs without thy bosom?
Yea, look'st thou pale? Let me see the writing.
AUMERLE
My lord, 'tis nothing.
YORK                        No matter then who see it.
I will be satisfied; let me see the writing.
AUMERLE
I do beseech your grace to pardon me.
It is a matter of small consequence
Which for some reasons I would not have seen.
YORK
Which for some reasons, sir, I mean to see.
I fear, I fear –
DUCHESS            What should you fear?
65 'Tis nothing but some bond that he is ent'red into
66 For gay apparel 'gainst the triumph day.
YORK
Bound to himself? What doth he with a bond
That he is bound to? Wife, thou art a fool.
Boy, let me see the writing.
AUMERLE
I do beseech you pardon me. I may not show it.
YORK
I will be satisfied. Let me see it, I say.
            *He plucks it out of his bosom and reads it.*
Treason, foul treason! Villain! traitor! slave!
DUCHESS
What is the matter, my lord?
YORK
Ho! who is within there?
            *[Enter a Servant.]*    Saddle my horse.
75 God for his mercy, what treachery is here!
DUCHESS
Why, what is it, my lord?
YORK
Give me my boots, I say. Saddle my horse.
                                *[Exit Servant.]*
Now, by mine honor, by my life, by my troth,
79 I will appeach the villain.
DUCHESS            What is the matter?
YORK
Peace, foolish woman.
DUCHESS
I will not peace. What is the matter, Aumerle?

AUMERLE
Good mother, be content. It is no more
Than my poor life must answer.
DUCHESS                        Thy life answer?
YORK
Bring me my boots! I will unto the king.
            *His Man enters with his boots.*
DUCHESS
Strike him, Aumerle. Poor boy, thou art amazed. –      85
            *[To York's Man]*
Hence, villain! Never more come in my sight.
YORK
Give me my boots, I say!        *[Servant does so and exit.]*
DUCHESS
Why, York, what wilt thou do?
Wilt thou not hide the trespass of thine own?
Have we more sons? or are we like to have?
Is not my teeming date drunk up with time?      91
And wilt thou pluck my fair son from mine age
And rob me of a happy mother's name?
Is he not like thee? Is he not thine own?
YORK
Thou fond mad woman,
Wilt thou conceal this dark conspiracy?
A dozen of them here have ta'en the sacrament,
And interchangeably set down their hands,      98
To kill the king at Oxford.
DUCHESS                        He shall be none;
We'll keep him here. Then what is that to him?      100
YORK
Away, fond woman! Were he twenty times
My son, I would appeach him.
DUCHESS                        Hadst thou groaned for him
As I have done, thou wouldst be more pitiful.      103
But now I know thy mind. Thou dost suspect
That I have been disloyal to thy bed
And that he is a bastard, not thy son.
Sweet York, sweet husband, be not of that mind!
He is as like thee as a man may be,
Not like to me, or any of my kin,
And yet I love him.
YORK                        Make way, unruly woman!        *Exit.*
DUCHESS
After, Aumerle! Mount thee upon his horse,      111
Spur post and get before him to the king,      112
And beg thy pardon ere he do accuse thee.
I'll not be long behind. Though I be old,
I doubt not but to ride as fast as York;
And never will I rise up from the ground
Till Bolingbroke have pardoned thee. Away, be gone!
                                *[Exeunt.]*

                            *

*Enter the King [Henry IV] with his Nobles [Percy*      V, iii
*and others].*

KING HENRY
Can no man tell me of my unthrifty son?      1
'Tis full three months since I did see him last.
If any plague hang over us, 'tis he.      3
I would to God, my lords, he might be found.
Inquire at London, 'mongst the taverns there,
For there, they say, he daily doth frequent,
With unrestrainèd loose companions,      7
Even such, they say, as stand in narrow lanes

52 *Do . . . hold* will these tourneys and victory celebrations be held  65 *is
ent'red into* has signed  66 *'gainst* in anticipation of  75 *God . . . mercy*
I pray God for his mercy  79 *appeach* accuse publicly  85 *him* i.e. the
servant  91 *teeming date* period of childbearing  98 *interchangeably . . .
hands* signed reciprocally, so that each had an indenture signed by all
100 *that* what they do  103 *pitiful* full of pity  111 *his horse* one of his
horses  112 *Spur post* ride fast
V, iii Windsor Castle  1 *unthrifty* prodigal  3 *plague* calamity (as prophesied by Carlisle)  7 *loose* wild

9 And beat our watch and rob our passengers,
10 Which he, young wanton and effeminate boy,
11 Takes on the point of honor to support
So dissolute a crew.

PERCY
My lord, some two days since I saw the prince
And told him of those triumphs held at Oxford.

KING HENRY
And what said the gallant?

PERCY
16 His answer was, he would unto the stews,
And from the common'st creature pluck a glove
And wear it as a favor, and with that
He would unhorse the lustiest challenger.

KING HENRY
As dissolute as desperate! Yet through both
I see some sparks of better hope, which elder years
May happily bring forth. But who comes here?
*Enter Aumerle, amazed.*

AUMERLE
Where is the king?

KING HENRY
What means our cousin, that he stares and looks
So wildly?

AUMERLE
God save your grace! I do beseech your majesty
To have some conference with your grace alone.

KING HENRY
Withdraw yourselves and leave us here alone.
*[Exeunt Percy and Lords.]*
What is the matter with our cousin now?

AUMERLE
For ever may my knees grow to the earth,
*[Kneels.]*
My tongue cleave to my roof within my mouth,
Unless a pardon ere I rise or speak.

KING HENRY
Intended, or committed, was this fault?
34 If on the first, how heinous e'er it be,
To win thy after-love I pardon thee.

AUMERLE
Then give me leave that I may turn the key,
That no man enter till my tale be done.

KING HENRY
Have thy desire.
*[Aumerle locks the door.] The Duke of York knocks
at the door and crieth.*

YORK *[within]*
My liege, beware! look to thyself!
Thou hast a traitor in thy presence there.

KING HENRY
Villain, I'll make thee safe.
*[Draws.]*

AUMERLE
Stay thy revengeful hand; thou hast no cause to fear.

YORK *[within]*
43 Open the door, secure foolhardy king!
44 Shall I for love speak treason to thy face?
Open the door, or I will break it open!
*[Enter York.]*

KING HENRY
What is the matter, uncle? Speak.
Recover breath; tell us how near is danger,
That we may arm us to encounter it.

YORK
Peruse this writing here, and thou shalt know
The treason that my haste forbids me show.    50

AUMERLE
Remember, as thou read'st, thy promise passed.
I do repent me. Read not my name there.
My heart is not confederate with my hand.

YORK
It was, villain, ere thy hand did set it down.
I tore it from the traitor's bosom, king.
Fear, and not love, begets his penitence.
Forget to pity him, lest thy pity prove    57
A serpent that will sting thee to the heart.

KING HENRY
O heinous, strong, and bold conspiracy!    59
O loyal father of a treacherous son!
Thou sheer, immaculate, and silver fountain,    61
From whence this stream through muddy passages
Hath held his current and defiled himself!
Thy overflow of good converts to bad,    64
And thy abundant goodness shall excuse
This deadly blot in thy digressing son.    66

YORK
So shall my virtue be his vice's bawd,
And he shall spend mine honor with his shame,
As thriftless sons their scraping fathers' gold.
Mine honor lives when his dishonor dies,
Or my shamed life in his dishonor lies.
Thou kill'st me in his life; giving him breath,
The traitor lives, the true man's put to death.

DUCHESS *[within]*
What ho, my liege! For God's sake let me in!

KING HENRY
What shrill-voiced suppliant makes this eager cry?

DUCHESS *[within]*
A woman, and thy aunt, great king. 'Tis I.
Speak with me, pity me, open the door!
A beggar begs that never begged before.

KING HENRY
Our scene is alt'red from a serious thing,
And now changed to 'The Beggar and the King.'    80
My dangerous cousin, let your mother in.
I know she is come to pray for your foul sin.

YORK
If thou do pardon, whosoever pray,
More sins for this forgiveness prosper may.
This fest'red joint cut off, the rest rest sound;
This let alone will all the rest confound.
*[Enter Duchess.]*

DUCHESS
O king, believe not this hardhearted man!
Love loving not itself, none other can.    88

YORK
Thou frantic woman, what dost thou make here?    89
Shall thy old dugs once more a traitor rear?

9 *watch* night patrolmen; *passengers* wayfarers   10 *Which* as to which; *wanton* 'sport'; *effeminate* self-indulgent   11 *Takes on the* takes it as a   16 *stews* brothels   34 *on the first* in the first category, intended   43 *secure* overconfident   44 *speak treason* call you a fool   50 *haste* breathlessness from hurrying   57 *Forget* forget your promise   59 *strong* flagrant   61 *sheer* pure   64 *converts* changes   66 *digressing* transgressing   80 'The . . . King' acting out the ballad of King Cophetua and the beggar-maid   88 *Love . . . can* if he does not love his own son, he cannot love anyone else   89 *make* do

**DUCHESS**
Sweet York, be patient. Hear me, gentle liege.
*[Kneels.]*

**KING HENRY**
Rise up, good aunt.

**DUCHESS**          Not yet, I thee beseech.
For ever will I walk upon my knees,
And never see day that the happy sees,
Till thou give joy, until thou bid me joy
By pardoning Rutland, my transgressing boy.

**AUMERLE**
Unto my mother's prayers I bend my knee.
*[Kneels.]*

**YORK**
Against them both my true joints bended be.
*[Kneels.]*
Ill mayst thou thrive if thou grant any grace!

**DUCHESS**
Pleads he in earnest? Look upon his face.
His eyes do drop no tears, his prayers are in jest;
His words come from his mouth, ours from our breast.
He prays but faintly and would be denied;
We pray with heart and soul and all beside.
His weary joints would gladly rise, I know;
106 Our knees still kneel till to the ground they grow.
His prayers are full of false hypocrisy;
Ours of true zeal and deep integrity.
Our prayers do outpray his; then let them have
That mercy which true prayer ought to have.

**KING HENRY**
Good aunt, stand up.

**DUCHESS**          Nay, do not say 'stand up.'
Say 'pardon' first, and afterwards 'stand up.'
An if I were thy nurse, thy tongue to teach,
'Pardon' should be the first word of thy speech.
I never longed to hear a word till now.
Say 'pardon' king; let pity teach thee how.
The word is short, but not so short as sweet;
No word like 'pardon' for kings' mouths so meet.

**YORK**
119 Speak it in French, king. Say 'Pardonne moi.'

**DUCHESS**
Dost thou teach pardon pardon to destroy?
Ah, my sour husband, my hardhearted lord,
That sets the word itself against the word!
123 Speak 'pardon' as 'tis current in our land;
124 The chopping French we do not understand.
Thine eye begins to speak, set thy tongue there;
Or in thy piteous heart plant thou thine ear,
127 That hearing how our plaints and prayers do pierce,
128 Pity may move thee 'pardon' to rehearse.

**KING HENRY**
Good aunt, stand up.

106 *still kneel* (will) kneel continually   119 *'Pardonne moi'* 'excuse me' – a
polite 'no'   123 *as . . . land* as customarily used in English   124 *The
chopping French* the French phrase, in which the words change their
meaning   127 *pierce* (then pronounced to rhyme with *rehearse*)   128
*rehearse* repeat   137 *brother-in-law* the Duke of Exeter; *the abbot* of
Westminster   138 *consorted crew* conniving gang
V, iv   5 *urged . . . together* emphasized it by repeating it   7 *wishtly* intently
11 *rid* get rid of
V, v   The keep in Pomfret Castle   8 *still-breeding* constantly breeding
10 *In . . . world* the creatures of fancy have their peculiar dispositions as
real people do   13 *scruples* doubts   13–14 *set . . . word* find one passage of
Scripture which contradicts another   17 *postern* narrow gate

**DUCHESS**          I do not sue to stand.
Pardon is all the suit I have in hand.

**KING HENRY**
I pardon him as God shall pardon me.

**DUCHESS**
O happy vantage of a kneeling knee!
Yet am I sick for fear. Speak it again.
Twice saying 'pardon' doth not pardon twain,
But makes one pardon strong.

**KING HENRY**          With all my heart
I pardon him.

**DUCHESS**          A god on earth thou art.
*[Rises.]*

**KING HENRY**
But for our trusty brother-in-law and the abbot,    137
With all the rest of that consorted crew,    138
Destruction straight shall dog them at the heels.
Good uncle, help to order several powers,
To Oxford, or where'er these traitors are.
They shall not live within this world, I swear,
But I will have them, if I once know where.
Uncle, farewell; and, cousin, adieu.
Your mother well hath prayed, and prove you true.

**DUCHESS**
Come, my old son. I pray God make thee new.
      *Exeunt [as Exton and Servant enter].*
    *Manet Sir Pierce Exton, & c.[Servant].*   **V, iv**

**EXTON**
Didst thou not mark the king, what words he spake?
'Have I no friend will rid me of this living fear?'
Was it not so?

**MAN**          These were his very words.

**EXTON**
'Have I no friend?' quoth he. He spake it twice
And urged it twice together, did he not?    5

**MAN**
He did.

**EXTON**
And speaking it, he wishtly looked on me,    7
As who should say, 'I would thou wert the man
That would divorce this terror from my heart!'
Meaning the king at Pomfret. Come, let's go.
I am the king's friend, and will rid his foe.    *[Exeunt.]*   11

\*

*Enter Richard, alone.*     **V, v**

**RICHARD**
I have been studying how I may compare
This prison where I live unto the world;
And, for because the world is populous,
And here is not a creature but myself,
I cannot do it. Yet I'll hammer it out.
My brain I'll prove the female to my soul,
My soul the father; and these two beget
A generation of still-breeding thoughts;    8
And these same thoughts people this little world,
In humors like the people of this world,    10
For no thought is contented. The better sort,
As thoughts of things divine, are intermixed
With scruples, and do set the word itself    13
Against the word:
As thus, 'Come, little ones,' and then again,
'It is as hard to come as for a camel
To thread the postern of a small needle's eye.'    17

Thoughts tending to ambition, they do plot
Unlikely wonders – how these vain weak nails
May tear a passage through the flinty ribs
21 Of this hard world, my ragged prison walls;
22 And, for they cannot, die in their own pride.
Thoughts tending to content flatter themselves
That they are not the first of fortune's slaves,
25 Nor shall not be the last; like seely beggars
26 Who, sitting in the stocks, refuge their shame,
That many have, and others must sit there.
And in this thought they find a kind of ease,
Bearing their own misfortunes on the back
Of such as have before endured the like.
Thus play I in one person many people,
And none contented. Sometimes am I king:
Then treasons make me wish myself a beggar,
And so I am. Then crushing penury
Persuades me I was better when a king;
Then am I kinged again; and by and by
Think that I am unkinged by Bolingbroke,
And straight am nothing. But whate'er I be,
Nor I, nor any man that but man is,
With nothing shall be pleased till he be eased
41 With being nothing. *(The music plays.)* Music do I hear?
Ha – ha – keep time! How sour sweet music is
When time is broke and no proportion kept!
So is it in the music of men's lives.
And here have I the daintiness of ear
46 To check time broke in a disordered string;
But, for the concord of my state and time,
Had not an ear to hear my true time broke.
I wasted time, and now doth time waste me;
50 For now hath time made me his numb'ring clock:
51 My thoughts are minutes; and with sighs they jar
52 Their watches on unto mine eyes, the outward watch,
53 Whereto my finger, like a dial's point,
Is pointing still, in cleansing them from tears.
Now, sir, the sound that tells what hour it is
Are clamorous groans, which strike upon my heart,
Which is the bell. So sighs and tears and groans
58 Show minutes, times, and hours. But my time
Runs posting on in Bolingbroke's proud joy,
60 While I stand fooling here, his Jack of the clock.
This music mads me. Let it sound no more;
62 For though it have holp madmen to their wits,
63 In me it seems it will make wise men mad.
Yet blessing on his heart that gives it me!
For 'tis a sign of love, and love to Richard
66 Is a strange brooch in this all-hating world.
    *Enter a Groom of the stable.*

GROOM
67 Hail, royal prince!
RICHARD             Thanks, noble peer.
The cheapest of us is ten groats too dear.
What art thou? and how comest thou hither,
70 Where no man never comes but that sad dog
That brings me food to make misfortune live?
GROOM
I was a poor groom of thy stable, king,
When thou wert king; who, travelling towards York,
With much ado, at length, have gotten leave
To look upon my sometimes royal master's face.
76 O, how it erned my heart when I beheld,
In London streets, that coronation day,

When Bolingbroke rode on roan Barbary,
That horse that thou so often hast bestrid,
80 That horse that I so carefully have dressed!
RICHARD
Rode he on Barbary? Tell me, gentle friend,
How went he under him?
GROOM
So proudly as if he disdained the ground.
RICHARD
So proud that Bolingbroke was on his back!
85 That jade hath eat bread from my royal hand;
86 This hand hath made him proud with clapping him.
Would he not stumble? would he not fall down,
Since pride must have a fall, and break the neck
Of that proud man that did usurp his back?
Forgiveness, horse! Why do I rail on thee,
Since thou, created to be awed by man,
Wast born to bear? I was not made a horse;
And yet I bear a burden like an ass,
94 Spurred, galled, and tired by jauncing Bolingbroke.
    *Enter one [Keeper] to Richard with meat.*
KEEPER
Fellow, give place. Here is no longer stay.
RICHARD
If thou love me, 'tis time thou wert away.
GROOM
What my tongue dares not, that my heart shall say.
                         *Exit Groom.*
KEEPER
My lord, will't please you to fall to?
RICHARD
Taste of it first, as thou art wont to do.      99
KEEPER
My lord, I dare not. Sir Pierce of Exton,
Who lately came from the king, commands the contrary.
RICHARD
The devil take Henry of Lancaster, and thee!
Patience is stale, and I am weary of it.
    *[Beats the Keeper.]*
KEEPER
Help, help, help!
    *The Murderers [Exton and Servants] rush in.*
RICHARD
How now! What means Death in this rude assault?
Villain, thy own hand yields thy death's instrument.
    *[Snatches a weapon from a Servant and kills him.]*
Go thou and fill another room in hell.      107
    *[Kills another.] Here Exton strikes him down.*
That hand shall burn in never-quenching fire
That staggers thus my person. Exton, thy fierce hand
Hath with the king's blood stained the king's own land.

21 *ragged* rugged   22 *pride* prime   25 *seely* simple-minded   26–27 *refuge . . . That* find refuge for their shame in the thought that   41 *being nothing* death   46 *check* rebuke; *disordered* playing ahead of or behind the beat   50 *numb'ring clock* clock showing hours and minutes (not an hourglass)   51 *jar* tick   52 *watches* periods; *outward watch* clock face, with a play on Richard's eyes, sleepless, peering outward   53 *dial's point* clock hand   58 *times* quarters and halves   60 *Jack of the clock* mannikin which strikes the hours   62 *holp* helped   63 *wise* sane   66 *strange brooch* rare jewel; *all-hating world* world where I am universally hated   67–68 *royal . . . dear* (a royal was a coin worth 10s., a noble 6s. 8d.; the difference was ten groats, a groat being fourpence)   70 *no . . . never* (an emphatic double negative); *sad dog* dismal fellow   76 *erned my heart* caused my heart to mourn   80 *dressed* groomed   85 *eat* eaten   86 *with clapping* by petting   94 *jauncing* making the horse prance, riding showily   99 *Taste . . . first* (a taster to insure that food was not poisoned was a royal prerogative)   107 *room* place

Mount, mount, my soul! thy seat is up on high;
Whilst my gross flesh sinks downward, here to die.
          *[Dies.]*

EXTON
As full of valor as of royal blood!
Both have I spilled. O, would the deed were good!
For now the devil, that told me I did well,
Says that this deed is chronicled in hell.
This dead king to the living king I'll bear.
Take hence the rest, and give them burial here.
                    *[Exeunt.]*

                    *

vi          *[Flourish.] Enter Bolingbroke [as King], with the*
            *Duke of York [, other Lords, and Attendants].*

    KING
    Kind uncle York, the latest news we hear
    Is that the rebels have consumed with fire
3   Our town of Ciceter in Gloucestershire;
    But whether they be ta'en or slain we hear not.
            *Enter Northumberland.*
    Welcome, my lord. What is the news?
    NORTHUMBERLAND
    First, to thy sacred state wish I all happiness.
    The next news is, I have to London sent
    The heads of Oxford, Salisbury, Blunt, and Kent.
9   The manner of their taking may appear
    At large discoursèd in this paper here.
    KING
    We thank thee, gentle Percy, for thy pains
    And to thy worth will add right worthy gains.
            *Enter Lord Fitzwater.*
    FITZWATER
    My lord, I have from Oxford sent to London
    The heads of Brocas and Sir Bennet Seely,
    Two of the dangerous consorted traitors
    That sought at Oxford thy dire overthrow.

V, vi Windsor Castle   3 *Ciceter* i.e. Cirencester   9 *taking* capture   20 *With clog* under the crippling weight   22 *abide* await   25 *reverend room* place of religious retirement   26 *joy* gladden   35 *deed of slander* deed to rouse slanderous talk against the crown   43 *thorough* through   48 *incontinent* immediately   51 *Grace* dignify with your presence

KING
Thy pains, Fitzwater, shall not be forgot.
Right noble is thy merit, well I wot.
          *Enter Henry Percy [and the Bishop of Carlisle].*
PERCY
The grand conspirator, Abbot of Westminster,
With clog of conscience and sour melancholy          20
Hath yielded up his body to the grave;
But here is Carlisle living, to abide          22
Thy kingly doom and sentence of his pride.
KING
Carlisle, this is your doom:
Choose out some secret place, some reverend room,          25
More than thou hast, and with it joy thy life.          26
So, as thou liv'st in peace, die free from strife;
For though mine enemy thou hast ever been,
High sparks of honor in thee have I seen.
          *Enter Exton, with [Attendants bearing] the coffin.*
EXTON
Great king, within this coffin I present
Thy buried fear. Herein all breathless lies
The mightiest of thy greatest enemies,
Richard of Bordeaux, by me hither brought.
KING
Exton, I thank thee not; for thou hast wrought
A deed of slander, with thy fatal hand,          35
Upon my head and all this famous land.
EXTON
From your own mouth, my lord, did I this deed.
KING
They love not poison that do poison need,
Nor do I thee. Though I did wish him dead,
I hate the murderer, love him murderèd.
The guilt of conscience take thou for thy labor,
But neither my good word nor princely favor.
With Cain go wander thorough shades of night,          43
And never show thy head by day nor light.
Lords, I protest my soul is full of woe
That blood should sprinkle me to make me grow.
Come, mourn with me for what I do lament,
And put on sullen black incontinent.          48
I'll make a voyage to the Holy Land
To wash this blood off from my guilty hand.
March sadly after. Grace my mournings here          51
In weeping after this untimely bier.          *[Exeunt.]*

# THE FIRST PART OF
# KING HENRY THE FOURTH

## INTRODUCTION

Shakespeare wrote *1 Henry IV* soon after *Richard II*. The plays are closely linked: *1 Henry IV* begins very soon after the end of *Richard II* and often refers to the events of that play; anticipations of *1 Henry IV* are planted in *Richard II*. As *Richard II* was written by 1596, the likely date for *1 Henry IV* is 1597.

Although the play was called *The History of Henry IV* in all the early printings beginning with the quarto of 1598 (it was differentiated from the second part only when the two were first printed together in the folio of 1623), it is not chiefly concerned with King Henry IV, and when he wrote it Shakespeare evidently had other interests in mind. As he followed it up with *2 Henry IV* and *Henry V*, it may seem that his idea was to write a series of plays on the ultimate origins of the Wars of the Roses similar to the series on these wars – the three parts of *Henry VI* and *Richard III* – which he had written more than five years earlier. But though the ultimate origins of the rivalry of Lancaster and York are to be found in the deposition of Richard II, the dire effects prophesied by the Bishop of Carlisle (*Richard II*, IV, i) were long postponed and fighting did not break out for almost half a century. Over this interval loomed the heroic figure of Henry of Monmouth, the savior of his country (or at least his father's reign) as Prince of Wales, the conqueror of France as King Henry V, who while he lived averted the consequences of disaffection. He is the theme of the two *Henry IV* plays and of *Henry V*. Moreover, it is a story with a triumphant, not a tragic, outcome, and it required a different mode of treatment from *Richard II*.

The real center of *1 Henry IV*, the only character active in all the elements of the plot, is Prince Hal. Shakespeare's decision to present him in two plays* rather than one must have grown out of the curious legend of the prince's wild youth that he found in the histories. These credited the victor of Agincourt, the most Christian of the medieval kings of England, with an unruly and profligate youth, spent in dissolute company, which, however, he shed like a coat the moment he was called upon to rule. The first phase of this astonishing development is the subject of this play; it is the prelude to the revelation of Henry V in all his glory.

Though the contrast between the truant prince and the glorious king is kept before us in this play, just as it is in *Henry V*, it is a contrast of appearances rather than realities. To Shakespeare the prince is the same man potentially as the king. The discrepancy is not between a bad prince and a good king but between the prince's true

nature and his reputation, between what he will be when called upon to assert himself and what he seems to be while idly, even basely, biding his time. There is no real reformation: the prince always knows what is right and prefers it; only appearances are against him. To reconcile this discrepancy Shakespeare resorted to a most unpsychological explanation, that the prince was deliberately waiting for the best opportunity to show the stuff he was made of, but evidently he thought it sufficient. Actually the play, by implication, gives a much better reason – that the prince was enjoying Falstaff – and this reason spectators at the play cordially accept.

The play, then, is a true story expanded and given additional dramatic force by the playwright's art. Much of it is based on the chronicler Holinshed's account of the reigns of Henry IV and Henry V. Shakespeare had also read the earlier chronicle of Hall (with whose story Holinshed's for the most part coincides) and Samuel Daniel's poem, *The Civil Wars* (1595), which magnifies the part of the prince in the battle of Shrewsbury and suggests his combat with Hotspur. An old play called *The Famous Victories of Henry V* had already covered the ground, beginning with the robbery on Gad's Hill and ending with the French marriage. As it is known to us only from an abbreviated and garbled version printed in 1598, it is hard to say how much Shakespeare, who presumably knew the authentic version of it, drew from it. But Shakespeare was not a historian but a playwright and his task was not to reproduce history but to transform it into drama. When good drama and history happened to coincide, he would give a faithful enough account of history as his informants had recorded it; when history proved recalcitrant to dramatization, he would ignore it or remold it to serve his purpose. As a result the play combines details perfectly true with others wholly imaginary. In a manner of speaking, the former warrant the latter. Shakespeare remembers that Bolingbroke landed at Ravenspurgh, swore an oath at Doncaster, and met Hotspur at Berkeley Castle; when he makes the king older than he really was and Hotspur younger it is not out of ignorance but out of a sense of what will make his play more effective. With the playwright's instinct for compressed and continuous action, he suppresses all indications of intervals of time between the successive episodes of the story, so that everything seems to happen in a few weeks, though actually a year elapsed between the defeat of Mortimer (June 22, 1402) and the battle of Shrewsbury (July 21, 1403). When history is silent, failing to explain why the prince played the madcap, what form his pranks took, what kind of man Hotspur really was, Shakespeare falls back on his invention. Occasionally history misled him: Holinshed confused the Sir Edmund

---

\* *1 Henry IV* and *Henry V*: to the present editor it seems more likely than not that *2 Henry IV* is an unpremeditated sequel to the first part, supplying the demand for more Falstaff.

Mortimer who married Glendower's daughter with his nephew Edmund Mortimer, fifth earl of March, who was proclaimed heir to the throne by Richard II in 1398, and Shakespeare followed.

The structure of the play is simple and the plot moves somewhat slowly. In the early scenes three oppositions are lined up: that of the rebels and the king and the loyal party, that of Hotspur and the prince, that of the prince's bad reputation and truant disposition and his actual sterling worth. All these are to be resolved on the battlefield of Shrewsbury and the play has little to do but march undeviatingly toward that final arbitrement. Successive scenes showing one or another of these opposed forces advancing towards the day of decision sharpen the oppositions. As the battle approaches, the alternating scenes become shorter and the various oppositions tend to merge. The events of the battle answer all questions: loyalty triumphs over disaffection, Hal over Hotspur, and the prince's valor and fidelity over all suspicions.

This simple plot (lacking the fresh complications and changes of alignment which make the plot of *Richard III* more exciting) is, however, greatly enlivened by the skill with which individual scenes are developed. The story of the robbery on Gad's Hill, a series of scenes which might be called a subplot if it did not come to an end before the play is half over, obviously gathers momentum as it develops and reaches its own peculiar climax. Some scenes are planned like miniature dramas. A good example is the scene at Glendower's house. It is useful to the plot only so far as it shows the rebels forging ahead with their preparations and wickedly planning to divide England. Shakespeare imposes dramatic form upon it by working up a temperamental antagonism between Hotspur and Glendower which reaches a high pitch a moment before Glendower backs down. The advantage which Hotspur gains thereby – it is not very great, for it lets him in for a dressing-down by Mortimer and Worcester – is short-lived, for presently Glendower takes the wind out of his sails by producing the supernatural music he had promised. The occasion of this music is brought about by the development of a contrast between the sentimental Mortimers, those odd victims of the barrier of language, and the unsentimental Percies. The scene is full of dramatic tension peculiar to itself and attains something like a dramatic resolution before it is over. The second tavern scene and the scene between the king and the prince also contain complete reversals of the situation presented at the outset.

The opposition of the Percies to the king, the historical backbone of the play, is no doubt a simple struggle for power, but dramatically at least it is a little more than that, for the whole is tinged with irony because of the king's equivocal claim to the throne and his consciousness of the instability of his position. The picture of him – old, shaken, and wan with care – is dramatic, not historical; he was actually a vigorous man in his middle thirties. He hankers after going on a crusade to expiate the wrong he did King Richard; he looks upon the prince's recalcitrance as a "rod of heaven" to punish his "mistreadings." The ambiguousness of his conduct – his determination to hold on to the prize he has gained and his twinges of conscience – is never resolved; he is more impressive and sounds deeper notes because he is never unequivocally presented as either the "vile politician" that Hotspur thinks he is or as something else.

The rivalry of the prince and Hotspur is the dramatic mainspring of the play: the stroke that kills the latter awards the palm of supremacy to the prince, checks rebellion, and confirms the prince's loyalty to his father. This antagonism is announced in the first scene of the play and kept alive, in one way or another, in almost every other. It is pure invention. Far from being a "northern youth," Hotspur was older than the prince's father, and, though he was certainly killed at Shrewsbury, nobody knows who killed him. Shakespeare undoubtedly strove to make the prince seem the better man. Hotspur's uncertain temper is emphasized in every scene in which he appears. His intractability is deplored by his father and his uncle (I, iii) and by his wife (II, iii); the prince's travesty of his daily routine of killing some six or seven dozen of Scots at a breakfast is a shrewd stroke. Worcester and Vernon question his leadership (IV, iii). His impatience of any praise of his adversary is twice underscored. His valedictory on the eve of the battle is a curious combination of bravado and fatalism. The crowning touch is added to his infatuation in the scene in which he partitions England and cavils at the details of the partition: obviously there is no sympathy for one who would dismember his native country. On the other hand, the prince is justified at every point. We are assured of his essential sobriety and dependability in the soliloquy he speaks at the end of the first scene in which he appears. The odium of his wild oats is transferred to Falstaff and dissolves in laughter. At the midpoint of the play he assures his father that he is true blue in spite of appearances, and though promise is not performance, performance follows in due course. He does full justice to Hotspur's prowess and reputation. His enemies testify to his valor and modesty (IV, i, 97 ff.; V, ii, 51 ff.). And on the day of decision he redeems his lost opinion triumphantly.

Yet all this careful weighting of the scales has often gone for nothing. Readers and spectators in the theatre become partisans of Hotspur and wish to reverse the verdict. Hotspur's disloyalty to the country he would divide out of selfish ambition is overlooked: we have a sneaking sympathy for rebels, especially in fiction. The prince is put down as a hypocrite because his cloaking of his right royal nature is the result of calculation – as if calculation were not the duty of a reasonable man and impulsive conduct a form of disorder. His later offenses, his rejection of Falstaff in *2 Henry IV* and his sanctimoniousness in *Henry V*, are made retroactive and added to the indictment. The real cause of this reversal of the verdict is, however, dramatic: Hotspur's part is aggressive and dynamic throughout while the prince must be kept under wraps till almost the end. The advantage to the actor who plays Hotspur, and the disadvantage to the actor who plays the prince, is enormous. Hotspur is by far the best acting part in the historical action of the play; he dazzles us so thoroughly as to disarm criticism. Since this is so, Shakespeare cannot escape responsibility, but in his defense it may be said that he has put up plenty of signposts to show which way our sympathies should take.

But even Hotspur is overshadowed by Falstaff, who is indeed the great triumph of this play. Otherwise a superior battle-piece, it is transfigured by his presence into something unique and transcendent. Falstaff was made out of whole cloth. There is a character corresponding to him in

*The Famous Victories,* but even if his part in that play as Shakespeare knew it was much more amusing than it is in the version we know, it hardly seems likely that he afforded Shakespeare more than a start. Nothing that history tells about either the Lollard martyr Sir John Oldcastle (as Falstaff was called in the earliest performances, before the name was changed out of deference to the displeasure of his living descendants) or Sir John Fastolfe (*1 Henry VI,* III, ii; IV, i) accounts for the immortal character that Shakespeare made. Falstaff is fitted to the role designed for him with the greatest adroitness. He becomes the embodiment of the prince's wild oats. The prince really does little or nothing reprehensible: he takes part in the robbery, but his character is carefully safeguarded from the start and he restores the money with advantage; otherwise he only gets a little tipsy, plays a poor practical joke on the drawer, and exchanges vituperation with Falstaff. It is Falstaff who creates the atmosphere of depravity, the prince sharing in it but not responsible for it and always standing somewhat apart from it. Falstaff is a kind of scapegoat: he takes upon him the vices which legend imputed to the prince. Further to exculpate the prince, the sting is extracted from these vices by presenting them only in the element of laughter, the infallible solvent of morality. Only the sternest self-control enables us to remember, as we laugh at Falstaff's drollery, that he is really a liar, a sponger, a glutton, a drunkard, a thief, and much more that we must disapprove of. As insulation for the prince's character, Falstaff is a superb dramatic invention.

Traditionally a comic character is the butt of ridicule, a simpleton, a monomaniac, or an impostor who, like that other Falstaff who swaggers through *The Merry Wives of Windsor,* overreaches himself in the end and is exposed to the derisive laughter of men of better judgment. But the Falstaff of this play, for all the verbal derision hurled at him by the prince and others, which he always parries skillfully enough, is never completely exposed, discomfited, or humiliated by the turn of events; he always manages to earn at least a draw and often something like a triumph. At the end of the play he is even left in dubious possession of the claim of victory over Hotspur. For success like this we have no derision; indeed, at least in fiction, it excites something much more like sympathy, and Falstaff carries away our admiration, or at least our astonishment, by his overwhelming effrontery. When we laugh with him we forfeit all chance of sitting in judgment upon him. The utter disabling of our normal censoriousness, the assigning to Falstaff of a role that is sympathetic as well as depraved, is indeed a triumph of the comic imagination.

Moreover, the equivocal Falstaff is the essential Falstaff. He is never twice quite the same; he is a series of impersonations. He is an inveterate comic actor and every man is a stooge who must play up to him. His parts are without number and every one is followed by its opposite: the old man and the frisky youth, the fat man and the active man (or at least a simulacrum thereof), the sponger and the lordly patron (of Bardolph and the likes of him), the libertine and the critic of manners (whose ruminations on the ways of the world are heavily flavored with biblical phraseology), the soldier and the coward – or at least the propounder of the axiom that the better part of valor is discretion. Of all his parts the most famous is that of the artful dodger: at least three times he is backed into a corner, only to wriggle out by a triumphant equivocation (he was a coward on instinct, the prince owes him his love and his love is worth a million, he gave Hotspur a wound in the thigh). Of all his parts the most surprising is that of debunker of honor: the soliloquy in which he proves it only a word might seem to undermine the whole basis of the serious parts of the play, but by that time we are so used to Falstaff's "wrenching the true cause the false way" that we take it as another piece of pseudo-logic like his argument that robbery is no sin if it is a man's vocation. His protean character makes the wrangle over his cowardice, which literary critics have been carrying on for a hundred and fifty years now, seem irrelevant. Of course Falstaff is a coward when he runs away or shams death; a brave man running away or playing dead would not be funny. But at the same time the complete aplomb with which he carries off these pieces of "discretion," utterly different from the teeth-chattering and knee-knocking of the craven coward, makes him a coward different from all others and much funnier. The laughter that greets Falstaff's sallies, so far as it is more than merely a tribute to his wit, is a delighted recognition of the adroitness with which he is always pretending to be something that we know he is not or at least was not a minute, an hour, or a day ago. His bright eye, his rum-soaked voice, and his unwieldy bulk dominate every situation in which he finds himself and he turns them all into mirth by assuming whatever part one would least expect of him. He blows through the play like a great gust of laughter and comes within an ace of turning Shakespeare's history of Henry IV into the comedy of Falstaff.

*University of Pennsylvania*                    M. A. Shaaber

The present text follows, with only a few emendations, that of the first quarto (1598), which is believed to have been printed from the author's draft. In the folio text of 1623, printed from the fifth quarto (1613), the play was first divided into acts and scenes. The act–scene division supplied marginally in the present text is that of the folio except that V, ii of the folio is divided into two scenes. Below are listed all substantive departures from the quarto text, with the adopted reading in italics followed by the quarto reading in roman. The letters Q0 represent a quarto of which only four leaves survive. It was probably published in 1598 and served as copy for Q1.

I, i, 30 *Therefor* (ed.) Therefore   62 *a dear* (Q5) deere   69 *blood* (Q5) bloud.

I, ii, 30–31 *moon. . . . proof now :* (Rowe) moone, . . . proofe. Now   74 *similes* (Q5) smiles   106 *Sugar? Jack,* (Capell) Sugar Iacke?   117 *Gad's Hill* (Wilson) Gadshill   148 *thou* (Pope) the   152 *Bardolph* (Theobald) Haruey   *Peto* (Dering) Rossill

I, iii, 96 *tongue* (Hanmer) tongue:   139 *struck* (Malone) strooke   201 *Hotspur* (Q5) Omitted (Q1)   254 *for I* (F) I   262 *granted. . . . lord,* (Thirlby) granted . . . Lord.   290 *course.* (Johnson) course

II, i, 32 *1. Carrier* (Hanmer) Car.   71 *foot land-rakers* (Hanmer) footlande rakers

II, ii, 16 *two-and-twenty* (F) xxii   20 (and throughout the play) *Bardolph* (F) Bardoll (or Bardol)   40 *Go hang* (Q3) Hang   48 *Bardolph. What* (Johnson) Bardoll, what   49 *Gadshill* (Johnson) Bar.   78 *Ah* (Rowe) a   102 *fat rogue* (Q0) rogue

II, iii, 4 *In respect* (Q6) in the respect   45 *thee* (Q2) the   66 *A roan* (Q3) Roane

II, iv, 31 *precedent* (President F) present   114 *(pitiful-hearted Titan!)* (Warburton) pittiful harted titan   164 *Prince* (Dering) Gads.   165, 167, 171 *Gadshill* (F) Ross.   232 *eel-skin* (Hanmer) elsskin   288 *Tell* (F) Faith tell   324 *Owen* (Dering) O   375 *tristful* (Dering) trustfull   431 *reverend* (F) reverent   450 *lean* (Q2) lane   468 *mad* (F3) made   510 *Peto* (F) Omitted (Q)   514 *Prince* (F) Omitted (Q)

III, i, 100 *cantle* (F) scantle   116 *I will* (Pope) I'le   128 *metre* (F) miter   131 *on* (Q3) an   261 *hot* (F) Hot.

III, ii, 110 *capital* (Q2) capitall.

III, iii, 32 *that's* (Q3) that   35 *Gad's Hill* (Wilson) Gadshill   54 *tithe* (Theobald) tight   71 *four-and-twenty* (F) xxiiii.   113 *no thing* (Q3) nothing   165 *guests* (Q2) ghesse   168 *court.* (Keightley) court   181 *two-and-twenty* (F) xxii.   191 *o'clock* (Q2) of clocke

IV, i, 20 *lord* (Capell) mind   55 *Is* (F) tis   108 *dropped* (Q2) drop   116 *altar* (Q4) altars   126 *cannot* (Q5) can   127 *yet* (Q5) it

IV, ii, 3 *Sutton Co'fil'* (Cambridge eds) Sutton cophill

IV, iii, 21 *horse* (Q5) horses   28 *ours* (Q6) our   72 *heirs as pages,* (Singer) heires, as Pages   82 *country's* (Q5) Countrey

V, i, 25 *I do* (F) I   131 *then?* (Q2) then   137 *will it* (Q2) wil

V, ii, 3 *undone* (Q5) vnder one   10 *ne'er* (F) neuer   70 *Upon* (Pope) On

V, iii, 22 *A* (Capell) Ah   39 *stand'st* (Q2) stands   50 *get'st* (Q2) gets

V, iv, 33 *So* (F) and   67 *Nor* (F) Now   91 *thee* (Q7) the   155 *ours* (Q2) our   156 *let's* (Q4) let us

V, v, 36 *bend you* (Q4) bend, you

# THE FIRST PART OF
# KING HENRY THE FOURTH

[NAMES OF THE ACTORS

| | |
|---|---|
| King Henry the Fourth | Gadshill |
| Henry, Prince of Wales ⎫ | Peto |
| Prince John of Lancaster ⎬ the King's sons | Bardolph |
| Earl of Westmoreland | Vintner of an Eastcheap Tavern |
| Sir Walter Blunt | Francis, a waiter |
| Thomas Percy, Earl of Worcester | Chamberlain of an inn at Rochester |
| Henry Percy, Earl of Northumberland | Ostler |
| Henry Percy ('Hotspur'), his son | Mugs and another Carrier |
| Edmund Mortimer, Earl of March | Travellers on the road from Rochester to London |
| Richard Scroop, Archbishop of York | Sheriff |
| Archibald, Earl of Douglas | Hotspur's Servant |
| Owen Glendower | Messenger from Northumberland |
| Sir Richard Vernon | Two Messengers (soldiers in Hotspur's army) |
| Sir John Falstaff | Lady Percy, Hotspur's wife and Mortimer's sister |
| Sir Michael, a friend of the Archbishop of York | Lady Mortimer, Glendower's daughter |
| Poins | Mistress Quickly, hostess of an Eastcheap Tavern |

Scene : *England and Wales*]

＊

I, i     *Enter the King, Lord John of Lancaster, Earl of*
*Westmoreland, [Sir Walter Blunt,] with others.*

KING

    So shaken as we are, so wan with care,
2  Find we a time for frighted peace to pant
3  And breathe short-winded accents of new broils
4  To be commenced in stronds afar remote.
5  No more the thirsty entrance of this soil
    Shall daub her lips with her own children's blood :
7  No more shall trenching war channel her fields,
    Nor bruise her flow'rets with the armèd hoofs
    Of hostile paces. Those opposèd eyes
10  Which, like the meteors of a troubled heaven,
    All of one nature, of one substance bred,
    Did lately meet in the intestine shock
13  And furious close of civil butchery,
    Shall now in mutual well-beseeming ranks
    March all one way and be no more opposed
    Against acquaintance, kindred, and allies.
    The edge of war, like an ill-sheathèd knife,
18  No more shall cut his master. Therefore, friends,
    As far as to the sepulchre of Christ –
    Whose soldier now, under whose blessed cross
    We are impressèd and engaged to fight –
22  Forthwith a power of English shall we levy,
    Whose arms were moulded in their mother's womb
    To chase these pagans in those holy fields
    Over whose acres walked those blessed feet
    Which fourteen hundred years ago were nailed
    For our advantage on the bitter cross.

    But this our purpose now is twelve month old,
    And bootless 'tis to tell you we will go.    29
    Therefor we meet not now. Then let me hear
    Of you, my gentle cousin Westmoreland,    31
    What yesternight our council did decree
    In forwarding this dear expedience.    33

WESTMORELAND

    My liege, this haste was hot in question    34
    And many limits of the charge set down    35
    But yesternight; when all athwart there came    36
    A post from Wales, loaden with heavy news,    37
    Whose worst was that the noble Mortimer,
    Leading the men of Herefordshire to fight
    Against the irregular and wild Glendower,
    Was by the rude hands of that Welshman taken,
    A thousand of his people butcherèd;
    Upon whose dead corpse there was such misuse,    43
    Such beastly shameless transformation,    44
    By those Welshwomen done as may not be
    Without much shame retold or spoken of.

I, i The Court of King Henry IV   2 *Find we* let us find   3 *accents* words
4 *stronds* strands, shores   5 *entrance* fissures (through which moisture
is absorbed)   7 *trenching* cutting; *channel* cut furrows in   10 *meteors*
atmospheric disturbances (perhaps a thunderstorm)   13 *close* hand-to-
hand fighting   18 *his* its   22 *power* army   29 *bootless* useless   31 *cousin*
form of address (no kinship implied)   33 *dear expedience* important expedition   34 *liege* feudal superior; *hot in question* warmly debated   35
*limits . . . charge* assignments of responsibility   36 *athwart* contrarily   37
*post* messenger; *heavy* depressing   43 *corpse* corpses   44 *transformation*
i.e. mutilation

246

KING
> It seems then that the tidings of this broil
> Brake off our business for the Holy Land.

WESTMORELAND
49 This, matched with other, did, my gracious lord;
50 For more uneven and unwelcome news
> Came from the north, and thus it did import:
> On Holy-rood Day the gallant Hotspur there,
> Young Harry Percy, and brave Archibald,
54 That ever-valiant and approvèd Scot,
55 At Holmedon met,
> Where they did spend a sad and bloody hour;
57 As by discharge of their artillery
> And shape of likelihood the news was told;
59 For he that brought them, in the very heat
60 And pride of their contention did take horse,
> Uncertain of the issue any way.

KING
> Here is a dear, a true-industrious friend,
> Sir Walter Blunt, new lighted from his horse,
> Stained with the variation of each soil
> Betwixt that Holmedon and this seat of ours,
> And he hath brought us smooth and welcome news.
> The Earl of Douglas is discomfited;
> Ten thousand bold Scots, two-and-twenty knights,
69 Balked in their own blood did Sir Walter see
> On Holmedon's plains. Of prisoners, Hotspur took
71 Mordake Earl of Fife and eldest son
> To beaten Douglas, and the Earl of Athol,
> Of Murray, Angus, and Menteith.
> And is not this an honourable spoil?
> A gallant prize? Ha, cousin, is it not?

WESTMORELAND
> In faith,
> It is a conquest for a prince to boast of.

KING
> Yea, there thou mak'st me sad, and mak'st me sin
> In envy that my Lord Northumberland
> Should be the father to so blest a son –
> A son who is the theme of honor's tongue,
> Amongst a grove the very straightest plant;
83 Who is sweet fortune's minion and her pride;
> Whilst I, by looking on the praise of him,
> See riot and dishonor stain the brow

> Of my young Harry. O that it could be proved
> That some night-tripping fairy had exchanged
> In cradle clothes our children where they lay,
> And called mine Percy, his Plantagenet!    89
> Then would I have his Harry, and he mine.    90
> But let him from my thoughts. What think you, coz,    91
> Of this young Percy's pride? The prisoners
> Which he in this adventure hath surprised
> To his own use he keeps, and sends me word    94
> I shall have none but Mordake Earl of Fife.

WESTMORELAND
> This is his uncle's teaching, this is Worcester,
> Malevolent to you in all aspects,    97
> Which makes him prune himself and bristle up    98
> The crest of youth against your dignity.

KING
> But I have sent for him to answer this;
> And for this cause awhile we must neglect
> Our holy purpose to Jerusalem.
> Cousin, on Wednesday next our council we
> Will hold at Windsor. So inform the lords;
> But come yourself with speed to us again;
> For more is to be said and to be done
> Than out of anger can be utterèd.

WESTMORELAND
> I will, my liege.                 *Exeunt.*

\*

*Enter Prince of Wales and Sir John Falstaff.*    I, ii

FALSTAFF Now, Hal, what time of day is it, lad?    1
PRINCE Thou art so fat-witted with drinking of old sack,    2
and unbuttoning thee after supper, and sleeping upon
benches after noon, that thou hast forgotten to demand    4
that truly which thou wouldest truly know. What a devil    5
hast thou to do with the time of the day? Unless hours
were cups of sack, and minutes capons, and clocks the
tongues of bawds, and dials the signs of leaping houses,    8
and the blessed sun himself a fair hot wench in flame-
colored taffeta, I see no reason why thou shouldst be so    10
superfluous to demand the time of the day.
FALSTAFF Indeed you come near me now, Hal; for we that    12
take purses go by the moon and the seven stars, and not by    13
Phoebus, he, that wand'ring knight so fair. And I    14
prithee, sweet wag, when thou art a king, as, God save
thy grace – majesty I should say, for grace thou wilt    16
have none –
PRINCE What, none?
FALSTAFF No, by my troth; not so much as will serve to    18
be prologue to an egg and butter.    19
PRINCE Well, how then? Come, roundly, roundly.    20
FALSTAFF Marry, then, sweet wag, when thou art king,    21
let not us that are squires of the night's body be called    22
thieves of the day's beauty. Let us be Diana's foresters,    23
gentlemen of the shade, minions of the moon; and let
men say we be men of good government, being    25
governed as the sea is, by our noble and chaste mistress
the moon, under whose countenance we steal.    27
PRINCE Thou sayest well, and it holds well too; for the    28
fortune of us that are the moon's men doth ebb and flow
like the sea, being governed, as the sea is, by the moon.
As, for proof now: a purse of gold most resolutely
snatched on Monday night and most dissolutely spent
on Tuesday morning; got with swearing 'Lay by,' and    33
spent with crying 'Bring in'; now in as low an ebb as the

---

49 *other* others, other tidings   50 *uneven* disconcerting   54 *approvèd* of proved valor   55 *Holmedon* Humbleton in Northumberland   57–58 *by . . . shape of likelihood* according to . . . probability   59 *them* news   60 *pride* height   69 *Balked* (1) heaped up, (2) defeated   71 *Mordake* i.e. Murdoch (actually son of the Duke of Albany)   83 *minion* favorite   89 *Plantagenet* family name of the kings descended from Henry II   90 *would I have* I would demand   91 *let him* let him go; *coz* cousin   94 *To . . . use* i.e. to collect their ransoms   97 *aspects* (literally) positions of a star   98 *prune* preen
I, ii An apartment of the Prince?   1 *what . . . it* (implies doubt that the person addressed is bright enough to know what time it is)   2 *sack* Spanish white wine   4 *benches* privy-seats   5 *truly* correctly   8 *dials* clocks   10–11 *be . . . demand* allow yourself the luxury of demanding   12 *you . . . now* i.e. you have me there   13 *go* (1) count time, (2) walk; *seven stars* Big Dipper   14 *Phoebus* the sun; *wand'ring knight* knight errant (suggested by the Knight of the Sun, the hero of a romance called *The Mirror of Knighthood*)   16 *thy grace* used, like 'your majesty,' in addressing royalty; *grace* virtuous motives   18 *troth* faith   19 *egg and butter* a mere snack, requiring only a short grace   20 *roundly* without beating about the bush.   21 *Marry* well, indeed   22 *squires* body-servants   23 *thieves . . . beauty* idlers by day; *Diana's foresters* i.e. a better-sounding name than 'thieves'   25 *government* conduct   27 *countenance* (1) face, (2) patronage; *steal* (1) rob, (2) walk stealthily   28 *it holds well* the comparison is appropriate   33 *Lay by* put down your weapons

35 foot of the ladder, and by-and-by in as high a flow as the
ridge of the gallows.

FALSTAFF By the Lord, thou say'st true, lad – and is not
my hostess of the tavern a most sweet wench?

39 PRINCE As the honey of Hybla, my old lad of the castle –
40 and is not a buff jerkin a most sweet robe of durance?

FALSTAFF How now, how now, mad wag? What, in thy
42 quips and thy quiddities? What a plague have I to do
with a buff jerkin?

44 PRINCE Why, what a pox have I to do with my hostess of
the tavern?

46 FALSTAFF Well, thou hast called her to a reckoning many
a time and oft.

PRINCE Did I ever call for thee to pay thy part?

FALSTAFF No; I'll give thee thy due, thou hast paid all
there.

PRINCE Yea, and elsewhere, so far as my coin would
stretch; and where it would not, I have used my credit.

FALSTAFF Yea, and so used it that, were it not here
apparent that thou art heir apparent – But I prithee,
sweet wag, shall there be gallows standing in England
55 when thou art king? and resolution thus fubbed as it is
56 with the rusty curb of old father antic the law? Do not
thou, when thou art king, hang a thief.

PRINCE No; thou shalt.

59 FALSTAFF Shall I? O rare! By the Lord, I'll be a brave
judge.

PRINCE Thou judgest false already. I mean, thou shalt
have the hanging of the thieves and so become a rare
hangman.

64 FALSTAFF Well, Hal, well; and in some sort it jumps with
65 my humor as well as waiting in the court, I can tell you.

66 PRINCE For obtaining of suits?

FALSTAFF Yea, for obtaining of suits, whereof the hang-
68 man hath no lean wardrobe. 'Sblood, I am as melan-
69 choly as a gib-cat or a lugged bear.

PRINCE Or an old lion, or a lover's lute.

71 FALSTAFF Yea, or the drone of a Lincolnshire bagpipe.

72 PRINCE What sayest thou to a hare, or the melancholy of
73 Moor Ditch?

FALSTAFF Thou hast the most unsavory similes, and art
75 indeed the most comparative, rascalliest, sweet young
prince. But, Hal, I prithee trouble me no more with
77 vanity. I would to God thou and I knew where a
78 commodity of good names were to be bought. An old
79 lord of the council rated me the other day in the street
about you, sir, but I marked him not; and yet he talked
very wisely, but I regarded him not; and yet he talked
wisely, and in the street too.

83 PRINCE Thou didst well, for wisdom cries out in the
streets, and no man regards it.

85 FALSTAF O, thou hast damnable iteration, and art indeed
able to corrupt a saint. Thou hast done much harm
upon me, Hal – God forgive thee for it! Before I knew
88 thee, Hal, I knew nothing; and now am I, if a man
should speak truly, little better than one of the wicked. I
must give over this life, and I will give it over! By the
91 Lord, an I do not, I am a villain! I'll be damned for
never a king's son in Christendom.

PRINCE Where shall we take a purse to-morrow, Jack?

94 FALSTAFF Zounds, where thou wilt, lad! I'll make one.
95 An I do not, call me villain and baffle me.

PRINCE I see a good amendment of life in thee – from
praying to purse-taking.

FALSTAFF Why, Hal, 'tis my vocation, Hal. 'Tis no sin
for a man to labor in his vocation.

*Enter Poins.*

Poins! Now shall we know if Gadshill have set a match. 100
O, if men were to be saved by merit, what hole in hell 101
were hot enough for him? This is the most omnipotent 102
villain that ever cried 'stand!' to a true man. 103

PRINCE Good morrow, Ned. 104

POINS Good morrow, sweet Hal. What says Monsieur
Remorse? What says Sir John Sack and Sugar? Jack,
how agrees the devil and thee about thy soul, that thou
soldest him on Good Friday last for a cup of Madeira
and a cold capon's leg?

PRINCE Sir John stands to his word, the devil shall have 110
his bargain; for he was never yet a breaker of proverbs.
He will give the devil his due. 112

POINS Then art thou damned for keeping thy word with
the devil.

PRINCE Else he had been damned for cozening the devil. 115

POINS But, my lads, my lads, to-morrow morning, by
four o'clock early, at Gad's Hill! There are pilgrims 117
going to Canterbury with rich offerings, and traders
riding to London with fat purses. I have vizards for you 119
all; you have horses for yourselves. Gadshill lies to- 120
night in Rochester. I have bespoke supper to-morrow
night in Eastcheap. We may do it as secure as sleep. If
you will go, I will stuff your purses full of crowns; if you
will not, tarry at home and be hanged!

FALSTAFF Hear ye, Yedward: if I tarry at home and go
not, I'll hang you for going.

POINS You will, chops? 127

FALSTAFF Hal, wilt thou make one?

PRINCE Who, I rob? I a thief? Not I, by my faith.

FALSTAFF There's neither honesty, manhood, nor good
fellowship in thee, nor thou cam'st not of the blood
royal if thou darest not stand for ten shillings. 132

PRINCE Well then, once in my days I'll be a madcap.

FALSTAFF Why, that's well said.

PRINCE Well, come what will, I'll tarry at home.

FALSTAFF By the Lord, I'll be a traitor then, when thou
art king.

PRINCE I care not.

POINS Sir John, I prithee, leave the prince and me alone.

35 *ladder* that from the platform to the ridge of the gallows, climbed by
the culprit   39 *Hybla* place in Sicily famous for honey; *old . . . castle*
(1) roisterer, (2) Oldcastle   40 *buff jerkin* leather jacket; *durance* (1) kind of
durable cloth, (2) imprisonment   42 *quiddities* hair-splittings   44 *pox*
syphilis   46 *reckoning* settlement (of the bill)   55 *resolution* courage;
*fubbed* thwarted   56 *antic* buffoon   59 *brave* splendid   64 *jumps with*
suits   65 *waiting* being in attendance; *court* i.e. the royal court   66 *suits*
petitions   68 *wardrobe* the clothes of those he hangs are the hangman's
perquisite; *'Sblood* by God's blood   69 *gib-cat* tomcat; *lugged* baited   71
*drone* bass pipe   72 *hare* proverbially melancholy   73 *Moor Ditch* an
open sewer   75 *comparative* abusive   77 *vanity* worldliness   78 *commodity* lot   79 *rated* rebuked   83–84 *wisdom . . . regards it* 'Wisdom crieth
without; she uttereth her voice in the streets. She crieth . . . saying, " . . . I
have stretched out my hand, and no man regarded" ' (Proverbs i, 20–24)
85 *iteration* repetition (of scriptural texts)   88 *knew nothing* was innocent
91 *an* if; *villain* the opposite of a gentleman   94 *Zounds* by God's wounds;
*make one* be one of the party   95 *baffle* degrade   100 *set a match* made
arrangements (for a holdup)   101 *saved by merit* i.e. as they are not: they
are saved by grace   102 *omnipotent* complete   103 *stand* i.e. hands up;
*true* honest   104 *morrow* morning   110 *stands to* i.e. is as good as   112
*his due* i.e. Falstaff's soul   115 *cozening* cheating   117 *Gad's Hill* on the
road from Canterbury to London   119 *vizards* masks   120 *lies* lodges
126 *chops* fat-cheeks   132 *stand* (1) make a fight, (2) pass current (*royal*:
10-shilling piece)

I will lay him down such reasons for this adventure that
he shall go.

FALSTAFF Well, God give thee the spirit of persuasion
and him the ears of profiting, that what thou speakest
may move and what he hears may be believed, that the
true prince may (for recreation sake) prove a false thief;
46 for the poor abuses of the time want countenance. Farewell; you shall find me in Eastcheap.

48 PRINCE Farewell, thou latter spring! farewell, All-
hallown summer!                          *[Exit Falstaff.]*

POINS Now, my good sweet honey lord, ride with us to-
morrow. I have a jest to execute that I cannot manage
alone. Falstaff, Bardolph, Peto, and Gadshill shall rob
53 those men that we have already waylaid; yourself and I
will not be there; and when they have the booty, if you
and I do not rob them, cut this head off from my
shoulders.

PRINCE How shall we part with them in setting forth?

POINS Why, we will set forth before or after them and appoint them a place of meeting, wherein it is at our
pleasure to fail; and then will they adventure upon the
exploit themselves, which they shall have no sooner
achieved, but we'll set upon them.

PRINCE Yea, but 'tis like that they will know us by our
64 horses, by our habits, and by every other appointment,
to be ourselves.

POINS Tut! our horses they shall not see – I'll tie them in
the wood; our vizards we will change after we leave
68 them; and, sirrah, I have cases of buckram for the
69 nonce, to immask our noted outward garments.

70 PRINCE Yea, but I doubt they will be too hard for us.

POINS Well, for two of them, I know them to be as true-
bred cowards as ever turned back; and for the third, if
he fight longer than he sees reason, I'll forswear arms.
74 The virtue of this jest will be the incomprehensible lies
that this same fat rogue will tell us when we meet at
76 supper: how thirty, at least, he fought with; what wards,
77 what blows, what extremities he endured; and in the reproof of this lives the jest.

PRINCE Well, I'll go with thee. Provide us all things
necessary and meet me to-morrow night in Eastcheap.
There I'll sup. Farewell.

POINS Farewell, my lord.                          *Exit.*

PRINCE
I know you all, and will awhile uphold
84 The unyoked humor of your idleness.
Yet herein will I imitate the sun,
86 Who doth permit the base contagious clouds
To smother up his beauty from the world,
88 That, when he please again to be himself,
Being wanted, he may be more wond'red at

146 *countenance* encouragement   148–49 *All-hallown summer* Indian summer   153 *waylaid* set an ambush for   164 *appointment* accoutrement   168
*sirrah* sir (as a rule addressed to inferiors; here it implies familiarity); *cases*
suits   168–69 *for the nonce* for this purpose   169 *noted* well-known   170
*doubt* fear; *too hard* too much   174 *incomprehensible* unlimited   176 *wards*
parries   177 *extremities* extreme hazards; *reproof* disproof   184 *idleness*
frivolity   186 *contagious* noxious   188 *That* so that   195 *accidents* events
199 *hopes* expectations   203 *foil* contrast   204 *to* as to; *skill* piece of good
policy   205 *Redeeming time* saving time from being lost
I, iii The Court of King Henry IV   3 *found me* found me out   5 *myself*
i.e. every inch a king   6 *condition* (mild) natural disposition   13 *holp*
helped; *portly* majestic   16 *Danger* defiance   19 *frontier* (literally) earth-
works (alluding to 'front': forehead)   26 *delivered* reported   27 *envy* ill
will; *misprision* misunderstanding   36 *milliner* (who sells scented gloves
and other haberdashery)

By breaking through the foul and ugly mists
Of vapors that did seem to strangle him.
If all the year were playing holidays,
To sport would be as tedious as to work;
But when they seldom come, they wished-for come,
And nothing pleaseth but rare accidents.                195
So, when this loose behavior I throw off
And pay the debt I never promised,
By how much better than my word I am,
By so much shall I falsify men's hopes;                199
And, like bright metal on a sullen ground,
My reformation, glitt'ring o'er my fault,
Shall show more goodly and attract more eyes
Than that which hath no foil to set it off.                203
I'll so offend to make offense a skill,                204
Redeeming time when men think least I will.     *Exit.* 205

                              *

KING
My blood hath been too cold and temperate,
Unapt to stir at these indignities,
And you have found me, for accordingly                3
You tread upon my patience; but be sure
I will from henceforth rather be myself,                5
Mighty and to be feared, than my condition,                6
Which hath been smooth as oil, soft as young down,
And therefore lost that title of respect
Which the proud soul ne'er pays but to the proud.

WORCESTER
Our house, my sovereign liege, little deserves
The scourge of greatness to be used on it –
And that same greatness too which our own hands
Have holp to make so portly.                13

NORTHUMBERLAND
My lord –

KING
Worcester, get thee gone, for I do see
Danger and disobedience in thine eye.                16
O, sir, your presence is too bold and peremptory,
And majesty might never yet endure
The moody frontier of a servant brow.                19
You have good leave to leave us: when we need
Your use and counsel, we shall send for you.
                              *Exit Worcester.*
You were about to speak.

NORTHUMBERLAND     Yea, my good lord.
Those prisoners in your highness' name demanded
Which Harry Percy here at Holmedon took,
Were, as he says, not with such strength denied
As is delivered to your majesty.                26
Either envy, therefore, or misprision                27
Is guilty of this fault, and not my son.

HOTSPUR
My liege, I did deny no prisoners.
But I remember, when the fight was done,
When I was dry with rage and extreme toil,
Breathless and faint, leaning upon my sword,
Came there a certain lord, neat and trimly dressed,
Fresh as a bridegroom, and his chin new reaped
Showed like a stubble land at harvest home.
He was perfumèd like a milliner,                36

And 'twixt his finger and his thumb he held
38 A pouncet box, which ever and anon
He gave his nose, and took't away again;
40 Who therewith angry, when it next came there,
41 Took it in snuff; and still he smiled and talked;
And as the soldiers bore dead bodies by,
He called them untaught knaves, unmannerly,
44 To bring a slovenly unhandsome corse
Betwixt the wind and his nobility.
46 With many holiday and lady terms
47 He questioned me, amongst the rest demanded
My prisoners in your majesty's behalf.
I then, all smarting with my wounds being cold,
To be so pestered with a popingay,
51 Out of my grief and my impatience
Answered neglectingly, I know not what —
He should, or he should not; for he made me mad
To see him shine so brisk, and smell so sweet,
And talk so like a waiting gentlewoman
56 Of guns and drums and wounds — God save the mark! —
57 And telling me the sovereignest thing on earth
58 Was parmacity for an inward bruise,
And that it was great pity, so it was,
This villainous saltpetre should be digged
Out of the bowels of the harmless earth,
62 Which many a good tall fellow had destroyed
So cowardly, and but for these vile guns,
He would himself have been a soldier.
65 This bald unjointed chat of his, my lord,
66 I answered indirectly, as I said,
And I beseech you, let not his report
68 Come current for an accusation
Betwixt my love and your high majesty.

BLUNT
The circumstance considered, good my lord,
Whate'er Lord Harry Percy then had said
To such a person, and in such a place,
At such a time, with all the rest retold,
May reasonably die, and never rise
75 To do him wrong, or any way impeach
What then he said, so he unsay it now.

KING
Why, yet he doth deny his prisoners,
But with proviso and exception,
79 That we at our own charge shall ransom straight
His brother-in-law, the foolish Mortimer;
Who, on my soul, hath willfully betrayed
The lives of those that he did lead to fight
Against that great magician, damned Glendower,
Whose daughter, as we hear, that Earl of March
Hath lately married. Shall our coffers, then,
Be emptied to redeem a traitor home?
87 Shall we buy treason? and indent with fears
When they have lost and forfeited themselves?
No, on the barren mountains let him starve!
For I shall never hold that man my friend
Whose tongue shall ask me for one penny cost
To ransom home revolted Mortimer.

HOTSPUR
Revolted Mortimer?
94 He never did fall off, my sovereign liege,
But by the chance of war. To prove that true
Needs no more but one tongue for all those wounds,
97 Those mouthèd wounds, which valiantly he took

When on the gentle Severn's sedgy bank,
In single opposition hand to hand,
He did confound the best part of an hour 100
In changing hardiment with great Glendower.
Three times they breathed, and three times did they 102
 drink,
Upon agreement, of swift Severn's flood;
Who then, affrighted with their bloody looks,
Ran fearfully among the trembling reeds
And hid his crisp head in the hollow bank, 106
Bloodstainèd with these valiant combatants.
Never did bare and rotten policy 108
Color her working with such deadly wounds; 109
Nor never could the noble Mortimer
Receive so many, and all willingly.
Then let not him be slandered with revolt.

KING
Thou dost belie him, Percy, thou dost belie him! 113
He never did encounter with Glendower.
I tell thee
He durst as well have met the devil alone
As Owen Glendower for an enemy.
Art thou not ashamed? But, sirrah, henceforth
Let me not hear you speak of Mortimer.
Send me your prisoners with the speediest means,
Or you shall hear in such a kind from me
As will displease you. My Lord Northumberland,
We license your departure with your son. —
Send us your prisoners, or you will hear of it.
         *Exeunt King [, Blunt, and train].*

HOTSPUR
An if the devil come and roar for them,
I will not send them. I will after straight 120
And tell him so; for I will ease my heart,
Albeit I make a hazard of my head.

NORTHUMBERLAND
What, drunk with choler? Stay, and pause awhile. 12
Here comes your uncle.
     *Enter Worcester.*

HOTSPUR          Speak of Mortimer?
Zounds, I will speak of him, and let my soul
Want mercy if I do not join with him!
Yea, on his part I'll empty all these veins,
And shed my dear blood drop by drop in the dust,
But I will lift the downtrod Mortimer
As high in the air as this unthankful king,
As this ingrate and cankered Bolingbroke. 13

NORTHUMBERLAND
Brother, the king hath made your nephew mad.

WORCESTER
Who struck this heat up after I was gone?

---

38 *pouncet box* perfume-box; *ever and anon* now and then    40 *Who* i.e. his
nose    41 *Took . . . snuff* (1) inhaled it, (2) resented (its being taken away);
*still* continually    44 *slovenly* nasty    46 *holiday and lady* affected and
effeminate    47 *questioned* kept on talking to    51 *grief* pain (from wounds)
56 *save the mark* avert anything so ridiculous    57 *sovereignest* most powerful
(to cure)    58 *parmacity* spermaçeti ointment    62 *tall* stout    65 *bald*
trivial    66 *indirectly* offhand    68 *Come current* be accepted    75 *do him
wrong* put him in the wrong; *impeach* discredit    79 *straight* at once    87
*indent* make terms; *fears* what we fear    94 *fall off* break his allegiance
97 *mouthèd* gaping    100 *confound* spend    101 *changing hardiment* trading
blows    102 *breathed* stopped to catch their breath    106 *crisp* curly    108
*policy* craft    109 *Color* disguise    113 *belie* tell lies about    126 *will after*
will go after    129 *choler* anger    137 *cankered* corrupt

HOTSPUR

40 He will (forsooth) have all my prisoners;
And when I urged the ransom once again
Of my wive's brother, then his cheek looked pale,
43 And on my face he turned an eye of death,
Trembling even at the name of Mortimer.

WORCESTER

I cannot blame him. Was not he proclaimed
By Richard that dead is, the next of blood?

NORTHUMBERLAND

He was; I heard the proclamation.
And then it was when the unhappy king
49 (Whose wrongs in us God pardon!) did set forth
Upon his Irish expedition;
From whence he intercepted did return
To be deposed, and shortly murderèd.

WORCESTER

And for whose death we in the world's wide mouth
Live scandalized and foully spoken of.

HOTSPUR

55 But soft, I pray you. Did King Richard then
56 Proclaim my brother Edmund Mortimer
Heir to the crown?

NORTHUMBERLAND He did; myself did hear it.

HOTSPUR

Nay, then I cannot blame his cousin king,
That wished him on the barren mountains starve.
But shall it be that you, that set the crown
Upon the head of this forgetful man,
And for his sake wear the detested blot
63 Of murderous subornation – shall it be
That you a world of curses undergo,
Being the agents or base second means,
The cords, the ladder, or the hangman rather?
O, pardon me that I descend so low
68 To show the line and the predicament
Wherein you range under this subtle king!
Shall it for shame be spoken in these days,
Or fill up chronicles in time to come,
That men of your nobility and power
73 Did gage them both in an unjust behalf
(As both of you, God pardon it! have done)
To put down Richard, that sweet lovely rose,
76 And plant this thorn, this canker, Bolingbroke?
And shall it in more shame be further spoken
That you are fooled, discarded, and shook off
By him for whom these shames ye underwent?
No! yet time serves wherein you may redeem
81 Your banished honors and restore yourselves
Into the good thoughts of the world again;
83 Revenge the jeering and disdained contempt

Of this proud king, who studies day and night
To answer all the debt he owes to you      185
Even with the bloody payment of your deaths.
Therefore I say –

WORCESTER      Peace, cousin, say no more;      187
And now I will unclasp a secret book,
And to your quick-conceiving discontents      189
I'll read you matter deep and dangerous,
As full of peril and adventurous spirit
As to o'erwalk a current roaring loud
On the unsteadfast footing of a spear.

HOTSPUR

If he fall in, good night, or sink or swim!      194
Send danger from the east unto the west,
So honor cross it from the north to south,      196
And let them grapple. O, the blood more stirs
To rouse a lion than to start a hare!

NORTHUMBERLAND

Imagination of some great exploit
Drives him beyond the bounds of patience.      200

HOTSPUR

By heaven, methinks it were an easy leap
To pluck bright honor from the pale-faced moon,
Or dive into the bottom of the deep,
Where fathom line could never touch the ground,
And pluck up drownèd honor by the locks,
So he that doth redeem her thence might wear      206
Without corrival all her dignities;      207
But out upon this half-faced fellowship!      208

WORCESTER

He apprehends a world of figures here,      209
But not the form of what he should attend.      210
Good cousin, give me audience for a while.

HOTSPUR

I cry you mercy.      212

WORCESTER      Those same noble Scots
That are your prisoners –

HOTSPUR      I'll keep them all.
By God, he shall not have a Scot of them!
No, if a Scot would save his soul, he shall not.
I'll keep them, by this hand!

WORCESTER      You start away
And lend no ear unto my purposes.
Those prisoners you shall keep.

HOTSPUR      Nay, I will! That's flat!
He said he would not ransom Mortimer,
Forbade my tongue to speak of Mortimer,
But I will find him when he lies asleep,
And in his ear I'll hollo 'Mortimer.'
Nay, I'll have a starling shall be taught to speak
Nothing but 'Mortimer,' and give it him
To keep his anger still in motion.      225

WORCESTER

Hear you, cousin, a word.

HOTSPUR

All studies here I solemnly defy      227
Save how to gall and pinch this Bolingbroke;
And that same sword-and-buckler Prince of Wales:      229
But that I think his father loves him not
And would be glad he met with some mischance,
I would have him poisoned with a pot of ale.

WORCESTER

Farewell, kinsman. I will talk to you
When you are better tempered to attend.

140 forsooth indeed, in truth   143 death deadly fear   149 wrongs in us
wrongs suffered because of us   155 soft hold on, wait a minute   156
brother i.e. brother-in-law   163 murderous subornation prompting of murder   168 line station; predicament category   173 gage bind; in . . . behalf
for the benefit of injustice   176 canker (1) wild rose, (2) ulcer   181
banished forfeited   183 disdained disdainful   185 answer satisfy   187
Peace be quiet, hold your tongue   189 quick-conceiving understanding
quickly   194 he i.e. the man on the spear; or . . . swim whether he sinks or
swims   196 So so that   200 patience self-control   206 So provided that
207 corrival partner   208 out upon away with; half-faced fellowship sharing
honor fifty-fifty   209 figures figments of the imagination   210 form
essence; attend give his attention to   212 cry you mercy beg your pardon
225 still ever   227 studies interests; defy renounce   229 sword-and-
buckler ruffianly

**NORTHUMBERLAND**

Why, what a wasp-stung and impatient fool
Art thou to break into this woman's mood,
Tying thine ear to no tongue but thine own!

**HOTSPUR**

Why, look you, I am whipped and scourged with rods,

239 Nettled, and stung with pismires when I hear
240 Of this vile politician, Bolingbroke.
In Richard's time – what do you call the place?
A plague upon it! it is in Gloucestershire;
243 'Twas where the madcap duke his uncle kept,
244 His uncle York – where I first bowed my knee
Unto this king of smiles, this Bolingbroke –
'Sblood! – when you and he came back from Ravens-
        purgh –

**NORTHUMBERLAND**

At Berkeley Castle.

**HOTSPUR**

You say true.

249 Why, what a candy deal of courtesy
This fawning greyhound then did proffer me!
'Look when his infant fortune came to age,'
252 And 'gentle Harry Percy,' and 'kind cousin' –
253 O, the devil take such cozeners! – God forgive me!
Good uncle, tell your tale, for I have done.

**WORCESTER**

Nay, if you have not, to it again.
256 We will stay your leisure.

**HOTSPUR**                          I have done, i' faith.

**WORCESTER**

Then once more to your Scottish prisoners.
Deliver them up without their ransom straight,
And make the Douglas' son your only mean
For powers in Scotland – which, for divers reasons
Which I shall send you written, be assured
Will easily be granted.
        [To Northumberland] You, my lord,
Your son in Scotland being thus employed,
Shall secretly into the bosom creep
Of that same noble prelate well-beloved,
The archbishop.

**HOTSPUR**                          Of York, is it not?

**WORCESTER**

267 True; who bears hard
268 His brother's death at Bristow, the Lord Scroop.
269 I speak not this in estimation,
As what I think might be, but what I know
Is ruminated, plotted, and set down,
And only stays but to behold the face
Of that occasion that shall bring it on.

**HOTSPUR**

I smell it. Upon my life, it will do well.

**NORTHUMBERLAND**

275 Before the game is afoot thou still let'st slip.

**HOTSPUR**

Why, it cannot choose but be a noble plot.
And then the power of Scotland and of York
To join with Mortimer, ha?

**WORCESTER**                          And so they shall.

**HOTSPUR**

In faith, it is exceedingly well aimed.

**WORCESTER**

And 'tis no little reason bids us speed
281 To save our heads by raising of a head;

For, bear ourselves as even as we can,
The king will always think him in our debt,
And think we think ourselves unsatisfied,
Till he hath found a time to pay us home.
And see already how he doth begin
To make us strangers to his looks of love.

**HOTSPUR**

He does, he does! We'll be revenged on him.

**WORCESTER**

Cousin, farewell. No further go in this
Than I by letters shall direct your course.
When time is ripe, which will be suddenly,
I'll steal to Glendower and Lord Mortimer,
Where you and Douglas, and our pow'rs at once,
As I will fashion it, shall happily meet,
To bear our fortunes in our own strong arms,
Which now we hold at much uncertainty.

**NORTHUMBERLAND**

Farewell, good brother. We shall thrive, I trust.

**HOTSPUR**

Uncle, adieu. O, let the hours be short
Till fields and blows and groans applaud our sport!
                                        *Exeunt.*

*

*Enter a Carrier with a lantern in his hand.*

1. CARRIER  Heigh-ho! an it be not four by the day, I'll be
hanged. Charles' wain is over the new chimney, and yet
our horse not packed. – What, ostler!

OSTLER [within]  Anon, anon.

1. CARRIER  I prithee, Tom, beat Cut's saddle, put a few
flocks in the point. Poor jade is wrung in the withers out
of all cess.

        *Enter another Carrier.*

2. CARRIER  Peas and beans are as dank here as a dog, and
that is the next way to give poor jades the bots. This
house is turned upside down since Robin Ostler died.

1. CARRIER  Poor fellow never joyed since the price of oats
rose. It was the death of him.

2. CARRIER  I think this be the most villainous house in all
London road for fleas. I am stung like a tench.

1. CARRIER  Like a tench? By the mass, there is ne'er a
king christen could be better bit than I have been since
the first cock.

2. CARRIER  Why, they will allow us ne'er a jordan, and
then we leak in your chimney, and your chamber-lye
breeds fleas like a loach.

1. CARRIER  What, ostler! come away and be hanged!
come away!

239 *pismires* ants  240 *politician* ignoble schemer  243 *kept* dwelt  244
*bowed* (see *Richard II*, II, iii)  249 *candy* sugary  252 *gentle* of gentle birth
253 *cozeners* cheaters  256 *stay* await  267 *bears hard* resents  268 *Scroop*
Earl of Wiltshire (*Richard II*, III, ii)  269 *in estimation* conjecturally  275
*still* always; *slip* loose the dogs  281 *head* army  282 *even* carefully
285 *home* fully  291 *suddenly* at once
II, i An inn yard at Rochester  1 *four . . . day* four in the morning  2
*Charles' wain* the Great Bear  3 *horse* horses  4 *Anon* right away  6 *flocks*
tufts of wool; *point* pommel; *jade* (contemptuous name for) horse; *wrung*
chafed  6–7 *out . . . cess* beyond estimation  8 *Peas and beans* fodder for
horses; *as dank . . . dog* i.e. very soggy  9 *next* quickest; *bots* maggots in
the intestines  14 *tench* a fish whose red spots may be likened to flea-
bites  16 *king christen* Christian king  17 *first cock* i.e. midnight  18
*jordan* chamberpot  19 *chimney* fireplace; *chamber-lye* urine  20 *like a
loach* as a loach (a prolific fish) breeds loaches  21 *come away* come here

2. CARRIER I have a gammon of bacon and two razes of ginger, to be delivered as far as Charing Cross.

1. CARRIER God's body! the turkeys in my pannier are quite starved. What, ostler! A plague on thee! hast thou never an eye in thy head? Canst not hear? An 'twere not as good deed as drink to break the pate on thee, I am a very villain. Come, and be hanged! Hast no faith in thee?

*Enter Gadshill.*

GADSHILL Good morrow, carriers. What's o'clock?

1. CARRIER I think it be two o'clock.

GADSHILL I prithee lend me thy lantern to see my gelding in the stable.

1. CARRIER Nay, by God, soft! I know a trick worth two of that, i' faith.

GADSHILL I pray thee lend me thine.

2. CARRIER Ay, when? canst tell? Lend me thy lantern, quoth he? Marry, I'll see thee hanged first!

GADSHILL Sirrah carrier, what time do you mean to come to London?

2. CARRIER Time enough to go to bed with a candle, I warrant thee. Come, neighbor Mugs, we'll call up the gentlemen. They will along with company, for they have great charge.          *Exeunt [Carriers].*

GADSHILL What, ho! chamberlain!

*Enter Chamberlain.*

CHAMBERLAIN At hand, quoth pickpurse.

GADSHILL That's even as fair as 'at hand, quoth the chamberlain'; for thou variest no more from picking of purses than giving direction doth from laboring: thou layest the plot how.

CHAMBERLAIN Good morrow, Master Gadshill. It holds current that I told you yesternight. There's a franklin in the Wild of Kent hath brought three hundred marks with him in gold. I heard him tell it to one of his company last night at supper – a kind of auditor, one that hath abundance of charge too, God knows what. They are up already and call for eggs and butter. They will away presently.

GADSHILL Sirrah, if they meet not with Saint Nicholas' clerks, I'll give thee this neck.

CHAMBERLAIN No, I'll none of it. I pray thee keep that for the hangman; for I know thou worshippest Saint Nicholas as truly as a man of falsehood may.

GADSHILL What talkest thou to me of the hangman? If I hang, I'll make a fat pair of gallows; for if I hang, old Sir John hangs with me, and thou knowest he is no starveling. Tut! there are other Troyans that thou dream'st not of, the which for sport sake are content to do the profession some grace; that would (if matters should be looked into) for their own credit sake make all whole. I am joined with no foot land-rakers, no long-staff sixpenny strikers, none of these mad mustachio purple-hued maltworms; but with nobility and tranquillity, burgomasters and great oneyers, such as can hold in, such as will strike sooner than speak, and speak sooner than drink, and drink sooner than pray; and yet, zounds, I lie, for they pray continually to their saint, the commonwealth, or rather, not pray to her, but prey on her, for they ride up and down on her and make her their boots.

CHAMBERLAIN What, the commonwealth their boots? Will she hold out water in foul way?

GADSHILL She will, she will! Justice hath liquored her. We steal as in a castle, cocksure. We have the receipt of fernseed, we walk invisible.

CHAMBERLAIN Nay, by my faith, I think you are more beholding to the night than to fernseed for your walking invisible.

GADSHILL Give me thy hand. Thou shalt have a share in our purchase, as I am a true man.

CHAMBERLAIN Nay, rather let me have it, as you are a false thief.

GADSHILL Go to; 'homo' is a common name to all men. Bid the ostler bring my gelding out of the stable. Farewell, you muddy knave.          *[Exeunt.]*

＊

*Enter Prince, Poins, Peto [and Bardolph].*          II, ii

POINS Come, shelter, shelter! I have removed Falstaff's horse, and he frets like a gummed velvet.

PRINCE Stand close.          *[They step aside.]*

*Enter Falstaff.*

FALSTAFF Poins! Poins, and be hanged! Poins!

PRINCE *[comes forward]* Peace, ye fat-kidneyed rascal! What a brawling dost thou keep!

FALSTAFF Where's Poins, Hal?

PRINCE He is walked up to the top of the hill; I'll go seek him.          *[Steps aside.]*

FALSTAFF I am accursed to rob in that thieve's company. The rascal hath removed my horse and tied him I know not where. If I travel but four foot by the squire further afoot, I shall break my wind. Well, I doubt not but to die a fair death for all this, if I scape hanging for killing that rogue. I have forsworn his company hourly any time this two-and-twenty years, and yet I am bewitched with the rogue's company. If the rascal have not given me medicines to make me love him, I'll be hanged. It could not be else: I have drunk medicines. Poins! Hal! A plague upon you both! Bardolph! Peto! I'll starve ere I'll rob a foot further. An 'twere not as good a deed as drink to turn true man and to leave these rogues, I am the veriest varlet that ever chewed with a tooth. Eight yards of uneven ground is threescore and ten miles afoot with me, and the stony-hearted villains know it well enough. A plague upon it when thieves cannot be true one to another! *(They whistle.)* Whew! A plague upon you all! Give me my horse, you rogues! give me my horse and be hanged!

23 *gammon of bacon* ham; *razes* roots    28 *the pate on thee* your head    29 *faith* trustworthiness    37 *Ay . . . tell* i.e. never    43 *will along* wish to go along    44 *charge* baggage    45 *chamberlain* male servant corresponding to chambermaid    46 *At . . . pickpurse* (proverbial)    47 *fair* apt    51-52 *holds current* is still true    52 *franklin* small landowner    53 *Wild* forest; *three hundred marks* £200    58 *presently* at once    59-60 *Saint Nicholas' clerks* highwaymen    61 *I'll none* I want none    67 *Troyans* sports    69 *profession* i.e. robbery; *grace* credit    71 *foot land-rakers* footpads    72 *strikers* holdup men    72-73 *mustachio . . . maltworms* topers with mustaches stained with beer    73 *tranquillity* those who live an easy life    74 *oneyers* officers; *hold in* keep their mouths shut    75 *speak* i.e. say 'hands up'    79 *boots* booty    81 *foul way* muddy road, i.e. tight place    82 *liquored* (1) greased, (2) bribed    83 *as . . . castle* with impunity    84 *fernseed* reputed to be invisible and to confer invisibility    89 *purchase* loot; *true* honest    92 *Go to* 'nuts'; *'homo' . . . men* i.e. they're all the same    94 *muddy* stupid    II, ii The highway at Gad's Hill    2 *frets* (1) fumes, (2) wears away; *gummed velvet* velvet stiffened with gum (and therefore liable to wear)    3 *close* where you won't be seen    5 *rascal* (literally) lean deer    6 *keep* keep up    12 *squire* foot-rule    18 *medicines* love potions    22 *true* honest    23 *varlet* scamp

PRINCE *[comes forward]* Peace, ye fat-guts! Lie down, lay thine ear close to the ground, and list if thou canst hear the tread of travellers.

FALSTAFF Have you any levers to lift me up again, being down? 'Sblood, I'll not bear mine own flesh so far afoot again for all the coin in thy father's exchequer. What a

35 plague mean ye to colt me thus?

PRINCE Thou liest; thou art not colted, thou art uncolted.

FALSTAFF I prithee, good Prince Hal, help me to my horse, good king's son.

39 PRINCE Out, ye rogue! Shall I be your ostler?

FALSTAFF Go hang thyself in thine own heir-apparent

41 garters! If I be ta'en, I'll peach for this. An I have not

42 ballads made on you all, and sung to filthy tunes, let a cup of sack be my poison. When a jest is so forward – and afoot too – I hate it.

*Enter Gadshill.*

GADSHILL Stand!

FALSTAFF So I do, against my will.

47 POINS *[comes forward]* O, 'tis our setter; I know his voice.

BARDOLPH What news?

49 GADSHILL Case ye, case ye! On with your vizards! There's money of the king's coming down the hill; 'tis going to the king's exchequer.

FALSTAFF You lie, ye rogue! 'Tis going to the king's tavern.

53 GADSHILL There's enough to make us all.

FALSTAFF To be hanged.

PRINCE Sirs, you four shall front them in the narrow lane; Ned Poins and I will walk lower. If they scape from your encounter, then they light on us.

PETO How many be there of them?

GADSHILL Some eight or ten.

FALSTAFF Zounds, will they not rob us?

PRINCE What, a coward, Sir John Paunch?

FALSTAFF Indeed, I am not John of Gaunt, your grandfather, but yet no coward, Hal.

64 PRINCE Well, we leave that to the proof.

POINS Sirrah Jack, thy horse stands behind the hedge. When thou need'st him, there thou shalt find him. Farewell and stand fast.

FALSTAFF Now cannot I strike him, if I should be hanged.

PRINCE *[aside to Poins]* Ned, where are our disguises?

POINS *[aside to Prince]* Here, hard by. Stand close.

*[Exeunt Prince and Poins.]*

71 FALSTAFF Now, my masters, happy man be his dole, say I. Every man to his business.

*Enter the Travellers.*

TRAVELLER Come, neighbor. The boy shall lead our horses down the hill; we'll walk afoot awhile and ease our legs.

THIEVES Stand!

TRAVELLER Jesus bless us!

FALSTAFF Strike! down with them! cut the villains'

78 throats! Ah, whoreson caterpillars! bacon-fed knaves! they hate us youth. Down with them! fleece them!

80 TRAVELLER O, we are undone, both we and ours for ever!

81 FALSTAFF Hang ye, gorbellied knaves, are ye undone?

82 No, ye fat chuffs; I would your store were here! On,

83 bacons, on! What, ye knaves! young men must live.

84 You are grandjurors, are ye? We'll jure ye, faith!

*Here they rob them and bind them. Exeunt.*

*Enter the Prince and Poins [in buckram suits].*

PRINCE The thieves have bound the true men. Now 8 could thou and I rob the thieves and go merrily to London, it would be argument for a week, laughter for a 8 month, and a good jest for ever.

POINS Stand close! I hear them coming.

*[They stand aside.]*

*Enter the Thieves again.*

FALSTAFF Come, my masters, let us share, and then to horse before day. An the prince and Poins be not two arrant cowards, there's no equity stirring. There's no 9 more valor in that Poins than in a wild duck. 9

PRINCE      ⎰ *As they are sharing, the prince and Poins*
Your money! ⎱ *set upon them. They all run away, and*
POINS        ⎰ *Falstaff, after a blow or two, runs away*
Villains!    ⎱ *too, leaving the booty behind them.*

PRINCE Got with much ease. Now merrily to horse. The thieves are all scattered, and possessed with fear so strongly that they dare not meet each other: each takes his fellow for an officer. Anyway, good Ned. Falstaff sweats to death and lards the lean earth as he walks along. Were't not for laughing, I should pity him.

POINS How the fat rogue roared!       *Exeunt.*

           \*

*Enter Hotspur solus, reading a letter.*    I

HOTSPUR 'But, for mine own part, my lord, I could be well contented to be there, in respect of the love I bear 2 your house.' He could be contented – why is he not 3 then? In respect of the love he bears our house! He shows in this he loves his own barn better than he loves our house. Let me see some more. 'The purpose you undertake is dangerous' – why, that's certain! 'Tis dangerous to take a cold, to sleep, to drink; but I tell you, my lord fool, out of this nettle, danger, we pluck this flower, safety. 'The purpose you undertake is dangerous, the friends you have named uncertain, the time itself unsorted, and your whole plot too light for 1 the counterpoise of so great an opposition.' Say you so, say you so? I say unto you again, you are a shallow, cowardly hind, and you lie. What a lackbrain is this! By 1 the Lord, our plot is a good plot as ever was laid; our friends true and constant: a good plot, good friends, and full of expectation; an excellent plot, very good friends. 1 What a frosty-spirited rogue is this! Why, my Lord of York commends the plot and the general course of the action. Zounds, an I were now by this rascal, I could brain him with his lady's fan. Is there not my father, my uncle, and myself; Lord Edmund Mortimer, my Lord of York, and Owen Glendower? Is there not, besides, the Douglas? Have I not all their letters to meet me in arms by the ninth of the next month, and are they not

35 *colt* befool   39 *Out* get out   41 *ta'en* arrested   42 *ballads* (scurrilous) songs   47 *setter* one who sets a match (I, ii, 100)   49 *Case ye* put on your masks   53 *make us all* make our fortunes   64 *proof* test   71 *dole* lot 78 *caterpillars* parasites   80 *ours* our families   81 *gorbellied* fat-paunched 82 *chuffs* misers; *your store* all your possessions   83 *bacons* fat men   84 *grandjurors* i.e. well-to-do citizens   85 *true* honest   87 *argument* something to talk about   92 *arrant* out-and-out; *equity* judicial discernment   93 *wild duck* notoriously timid

II, iii Hotspur's castle (at Warkworth)   2 *in respect of* on account of   3 *house* family   12 *unsorted* ill-chosen   12–13 *for the counterpoise of* to counterbalance   14 *hind* peasant   17 *expectation* promise

26 some of them set forward already? What a pagan rascal
27 is this! an infidel! Ha! you shall see now, in very sincerity of fear and cold heart will he to the king and lay
open all our proceedings. O, I could divide myself and
30 go to buffets for moving such a dish of skim milk with so
honorable an action! Hang him, let him tell the king!
we are prepared. I will set forward to-night.

    *Enter his Lady.*

How now, Kate? I must leave you within these two
hours.

LADY
O my good lord, why are you thus alone?
For what offense have I this fortnight been
A banished woman from my Harry's bed?
Tell me, sweet lord, what is't that takes from thee
38 Thy stomach, pleasure, and thy golden sleep?
Why dost thou bend thine eyes upon the earth,
And start so often when thou sit'st alone?
Why hast thou lost the fresh blood in thy cheeks
And given my treasures and my rights of thee
43 To thick-eyed musing and cursed melancholy?
In thy faint slumbers I by thee have watched,
And heard thee murmur tales of iron wars,
46 Speak terms of manage to thy bounding steed,
Cry 'Courage! to the field!' And thou hast talked
Of sallies and retires, of trenches, tents,
49 Of palisadoes, frontiers, parapets,
50 Of basilisks, of cannon, culverin,
Of prisoners' ransom, and of soldiers slain,
52 And all the currents of a heady fight.
Thy spirit within thee hath been so at war,
And thus hath so bestirred thee in thy sleep,
That beads of sweat have stood upon thy brow
Like bubbles in a late-disturbèd stream,
And in thy face strange motions have appeared,
Such as we see when men restrain their breath
59 On some great sudden hest. O, what portents are these?
60 Some heavy business hath my lord in hand,
And I must know it, else he loves me not.
HOTSPUR
What, ho!
    *[Enter a Servant.]*
    Is Gilliams with the packet gone?
SERVANT
He is, my lord, an hour ago.
HOTSPUR
Hath Butler brought those horses from the sheriff?
SERVANT
One horse, my lord, he brought even now.
HOTSPUR
What horse? A roan, a crop-ear, is it not?
SERVANT
It is, my lord.

HOTSPUR     That roan shall be my throne.
Well, I will back him straight. O esperancè!    68
Bid Butler lead him forth into the park.   *[Exit Servant.]*
LADY
But hear you, my lord.
HOTSPUR
What say'st thou, my lady?
LADY
What is it carries you away?
HOTSPUR
Why, my horse, my love – my horse!
LADY
Out, you mad-headed ape!
A weasel hath not such a deal of spleen    75
As you are tossed with. In faith,
I'll know your business, Harry; that I will!
I fear my brother Mortimer doth stir
About his title and hath sent for you    79
To line his enterprise; but if you go –    80
HOTSPUR
So far afoot, I shall be weary, love.
LADY
Come, come, you paraquito, answer me    82
Directly unto this question that I ask.
In faith, I'll break thy little finger, Harry,
An if thou wilt not tell me all things true.
HOTSPUR
Away, away, you trifler! Love? I love thee not;
I care not for thee, Kate. This is no world
To play with mammets and to tilt with lips.    88
We must have bloody noses and cracked crowns,
And pass them current too. Gods me, my horse!    90
What say'st thou, Kate? What wouldst thou have
  with me?
LADY
Do you not love me? do you not indeed?
Well, do not then; for since you love me not,
I will not love myself. Do you not love me?
Nay, tell me if you speak in jest or no.
HOTSPUR
Come, wilt thou see me ride?
And when I am a-horseback, I will swear
I love thee infinitely. But hark you, Kate:
I must not have you henceforth question me
Whither I go, nor reason whereabout.    100
Whither I must, I must, and to conclude,
This evening must I leave you, gentle Kate.
I know you wise, but yet no farther wise
Than Harry Percy's wife; constant you are,
But yet a woman; and for secrecy,
No lady closer, for I well believe
Thou wilt not utter what thou dost not know,
And so far will I trust thee, gentle Kate.
LADY
How? so far?
HOTSPUR
Not an inch further. But hark you, Kate:
Whither I go, thither shall you go too;
To-day will I set forth, to-morrow you.
Will this content you, Kate?
LADY             It must of force.   *Exeunt.* 113

26 *pagan* unbelieving  27 *very* veritable  30 *go to buffets* fall to blows  38
*stomach* appetite  43 *thick-eyed* dim-sighted  46 *manage* horsemanship
49 *palisadoes* stakes set in the ground to stop a charge; *frontiers* outworks
50 *basilisks, culverin* kinds of cannon  52 *heady* headlong  59 *hest* command, i.e. when making a special effort  60 *heavy* (1) weighty, (2) woeful
68 *esperancè* hope (the Percy battle-cry)  75 *weasel* proverbially quarrel-
some; *spleen* irascibility  79 *title* claim to the throne  80 *line* reinforce  82
*paraquito* parrot  88 *mammets* dolls  90 *pass them current* (1) deal them out,
(2) circulate (*crowns*: 5-shilling pieces); *Gods me* God save me  100 *reason
whereabout* discuss what for  113 *of force* of necessity

    *

II, iv          *Enter Prince and Poins.*

1 PRINCE Ned, prithee come out of that fat room and lend me thy hand to laugh a little.

POINS Where hast been, Hal?

4 PRINCE With three or four loggerheads amongst three or fourscore hogsheads. I have sounded the very bass-string of humility. Sirrah, I am sworn brother to a leash of drawers and can call them all by their christen names, as Tom, Dick, and Francis. They take it already upon their salvation that, though I be but Prince of Wales, yet I am the king of courtesy, and tell me flatly I am no proud Jack like Falstaff, but a Corinthian, a lad of mettle, a good boy (by the Lord, so they call me!), and when I am king of England I shall command all the good lads in Eastcheap. They call drinking deep, dye-ing scarlet; and when you breathe in your watering, they cry 'hem!' and bid you play it off. To conclude, I am so good a proficient in one quarter of an hour that I can drink with any tinker in his own language during my life. I tell thee, Ned, thou hast lost much honor that thou wert not with me in this action. But, sweet Ned – to sweeten which name of Ned, I give thee this penny-worth of sugar, clapped even now into my hand by an under-skinker, one that never spake other English in his life than 'Eight shillings and sixpence,' and 'You are welcome,' with this shrill addition, 'Anon, anon, sir! Score a pint of bastard in the Half-moon,' or so – but, Ned, to drive away the time till Falstaff come, I prithee do thou stand in some by-room while I question my puny drawer to what end he gave me the sugar; and do thou never leave calling 'Francis!' that his tale to me may be nothing but 'Anon!' Step aside, and I'll show thee a precedent.

POINS Francis!

33 PRINCE Thou art perfect.

POINS Francis!                                    [*Exit Poins.*]

*Enter [Francis, a] Drawer.*

35 FRANCIS Anon, anon, sir. – Look down into the Pom-garnet, Ralph.

PRINCE Come hither, Francis.

FRANCIS My lord?

39 PRINCE How long hast thou to serve, Francis?

FRANCIS Forsooth, five years, and as much as to –

POINS [*within*] Francis!

FRANCIS Anon, anon, sir.

PRINCE Five year! by'r Lady, a long lease for the clinking of pewter. But, Francis, darest thou be so valiant as to play the coward with thy indenture and show it a fair pair of heels and run from it?

47 FRANCIS O Lord, sir, I'll be sworn upon all the books in England I could find in my heart –

POINS [*within*] Francis!

FRANCIS Anon, sir.

PRINCE How old art thou, Francis?

52 FRANCIS Let me see: about Michaelmas next I shall be –

POINS [*within*] Francis!

FRANCIS Anon, sir. Pray stay a little, my lord.

PRINCE Nay, but hark you, Francis. For the sugar thou gavest me – 'twas a pennyworth, was't not?

FRANCIS O Lord! I would it had been two!

PRINCE I will give thee for it a thousand pound. Ask me when thou wilt, and thou shalt have it.

POINS [*within*] Francis!

FRANCIS Anon, anon.

PRINCE Anon, Francis? No, Francis; but to-morrow, Francis; or, Francis, a Thursday; or indeed, Francis, when thou wilt. But, Francis –

FRANCIS My lord?

PRINCE Wilt thou rob this leathern-jerkin, crystal-button, not-pated, agate-ring, puke-stocking, caddis-garter, smooth-tongue, Spanish-pouch –

FRANCIS O Lord, sir, who do you mean?

PRINCE Why then, your brown bastard is your only drink; for look you, Francis, your white canvas doublet will sully. In Barbary, sir, it cannot come to so much.

FRANCIS What, sir?

POINS [*within*] Francis!

PRINCE Away, you rogue! Dost thou not hear them call?

*Here they both call him. The Drawer stands amazed, not knowing which way to go.*
*Enter Vintner.*

VINTNER What, stand'st thou still, and hear'st such a calling? Look to the guests within. [*Exit Francis.*] My lord, old Sir John, with half-a-dozen more, are at the door. Shall I let them in?

PRINCE Let them alone awhile, and then open the door. [*Exit Vintner.*] Poins!

POINS [*within*] Anon, anon, sir.

*Enter Poins.*

PRINCE Sirrah, Falstaff and the rest of the thieves are at the door. Shall we be merry?

POINS As merry as crickets, my lad. But hark ye; what cunning match have you made with this jest of the drawer? Come, what's the issue?

PRINCE I am now of all humors that have showed themselves humors since the old days of goodman Adam to the pupil age of this present twelve o'clock at midnight.

[*Enter Francis.*]

What's o'clock, Francis?

FRANCIS Anon, anon, sir.                              [*Exit.*]

PRINCE That ever this fellow should have fewer words than a parrot, and yet the son of a woman! His industry is upstairs and downstairs, his eloquence the parcel of a reckoning. I am not yet of Percy's mind, the Hotspur of the North; he that kills me some six or seven dozen of Scots at a breakfast, washes his hands, and says to his wife, 'Fie upon this quiet life! I want work.' 'O my sweet Harry,' says she, 'how many hast thou killed to-day?' 'Give my roan horse a drench,' says he, and answers 'Some fourteen,' an hour after, 'a trifle, a trifle.' I prithee call in Falstaff. I'll play Percy, and that damned brawn shall play Dame Mortimer his wife.

---

II, iv Within an Eastcheap tavern  1 *fat* stuffy  4 *loggerheads* blockheads  6 *leash* i.e. three  7 *drawers* waiters  11 *Corinthian* good sport  12 *a good boy* one of the boys  15 *scarlet* the best scarlet dyes were made with topers' urine; *breathe* pause; *watering* drinking  16 *play* i.e. toss  19 *action* encounter, (literally) battle  21 *sugar* used to sweeten wine  22 *under-skinker* bartender's assistant  24 *Anon* i.e. coming  25 *bastard* sweet Spanish wine; *Half-moon* a room in the tavern  31 *precedent* something worth following  33 *Thou art perfect* you have learned your part  35 *Pomgarnet* Pomegranate (a room in the tavern)  39 *serve* i.e. as an apprentice  47 *books* i.e. Bibles  52 *Michaelmas* September 29  63 *a* on  66 *rob* i.e. by running away  67 *not-pated* short-haired; *agate-ring* seal ring; *puke-stocking* woolen-stocking; *caddis-garter* garter of worsted tape  71-72 *your . . . sully* i.e. you'll have to put up with a drawer's life  72 *it* i.e. sugar, imported from Barbary  76 s.d. *amazed* dumbfounded  87 *cunning match* sly game  88 *issue* outcome  91 *pupil age* youth  96 *parcel* details  98 *me* (redundant: ethical dative)  102 *drench* dose of medicine; *says he* (i.e. to a servant)  105 *brawn* fat pig

56 'Rivo!' says the drunkard. Call in ribs, call in tallow.

*Enter Falstaff [, Gadshill, Bardolph, and Peto ; Francis follows with wine].*

POINS Welcome, Jack. Where hast thou been?

108 FALSTAFF A plague of all cowards, I say, and a vengeance too! Marry and amen! Give me a cup of sack,
110 boy. Ere I lead this life long, I'll sew netherstocks, and
mend them and foot them too. A plague of all cowards!
112 Give me a cup of sack, rogue. Is there no virtue extant?
*He drinketh.*

113 PRINCE Didst thou never see Titan kiss a dish of butter
(pitiful-hearted Titan!) that melted at the sweet tale of
115 the sun's? If thou didst, then behold that compound.

116 FALSTAFF You rogue, here's lime in this sack too! There
is nothing but roguery to be found in villainous man.
Yet a coward is worse than a cup of sack with lime in it –
a villainous coward! Go thy ways, old Jack, die when
120 thou wilt; if manhood, good manhood, be not forgot
121 upon the face of the earth, then am I a shotten herring.
There lives not three good men unhanged in England;
and one of them is fat, and grows old. God help the
124 while! A bad world, I say. I would I were a weaver; I
125 could sing psalms or anything. A plague of all cowards, I
say still!

PRINCE How now, woolsack? What mutter you?

FALSTAFF A king's son! If I do not beat thee out of thy
kingdom with a dagger of lath and drive all thy subjects
afore thee like a flock of wild geese, I'll never wear hair
on my face more. You Prince of Wales?

PRINCE Why, you whoreson round man, what's the
matter?

FALSTAFF Are not you a coward? Answer me to that –
and Poins there?

POINS Zounds, ye fat paunch, an ye call me coward, by
the Lord, I'll stab thee.

FALSTAFF I call thee coward? I'll see thee damned ere I
call thee coward, but I would give a thousand pound I
could run as fast as thou canst. You are straight enough
140 in the shoulders; you care not who sees your back. Call
you that backing of your friends? A plague upon such
backing! Give me them that will face me. Give me a
cup of sack. I am a rogue if I drunk to-day.

PRINCE O villain! thy lips are scarce wiped since thou
drunk'st last.

146 FALSTAFF All is one for that. *(He drinketh.)* A plague of
all cowards, still say I.

PRINCE What's the matter?

FALSTAFF What's the matter? There be four of us here
have ta'en a thousand pound this day morning.

PRINCE Where is it, Jack? where is it?

FALSTAFF Where is it? Taken from us it is. A hundred
upon poor four of us!

PRINCE What, a hundred, man?

FALSTAFF I am a rogue if I were not at half-sword with a 155
dozen of them two hours together. I have scaped by
miracle. I am eight times thrust through the doublet,
four through the hose; my buckler cut through and
through; my sword hacked like a handsaw – ecce sig- 159
num! I never dealt better since I was a man. All would 160
not do. A plague of all cowards! Let them speak. If they
speak more or less than truth, they are villains and the
sons of darkness.

PRINCE Speak, sirs. How was it?

GADSHILL We four set upon some dozen –

FALSTAFF Sixteen at least, my lord.

GADSHILL And bound them.

PETO No, no, they were not bound.

FALSTAFF You rogue, they were bound, every man of
them, or I am a Jew else – an Ebrew Jew.

GADSHILL As we were sharing, some six or seven fresh
men set upon us –

FALSTAFF And unbound the rest, and then come in the
other. 173

PRINCE What, fought you with them all?

FALSTAFF All? I know not what you call all, but if I
fought not with fifty of them, I am a bunch of radish! If
there were not two or three and fifty upon poor old 177
Jack, then am I no two-legged creature.

PRINCE Pray God you have not murd'red some of
them.

FALSTAFF Nay, that's past praying for. I have peppered 180
two of them. Two I am sure I have paid, two rogues in 181
buckram suits. I tell thee what, Hal – if I tell thee a lie,
spit in my face, call me horse. Thou knowest my old
ward. Here I lay, and thus I bore my point. Four 184
rogues in buckram let drive at me.

PRINCE What, four? Thou saidst but two even now.

FALSTAFF Four, Hal. I told thee four.

POINS Ay, ay, he said four.

FALSTAFF These four came all afront and mainly thrust 189
at me. I made me no more ado but took all their seven 190
points in my target, thus. 191

PRINCE Seven? Why, there were but four even now.

FALSTAFF In buckram?

POINS Ay, four, in buckram suits.

FALSTAFF Seven, by these hilts, or I am a villain else. 195

PRINCE *[aside to Poins]* Prithee let him alone. We shall
have more anon.

FALSTAFF Dost thou hear me, Hal?

PRINCE Ay, and mark thee too, Jack.

FALSTAFF Do so, for it is worth the list'ning to. These
nine in buckram that I told thee of –

PRINCE So, two more already.

FALSTAFF Their points being broken – 203

POINS Down fell their hose.

FALSTAFF Began to give me ground; but I followed me
close, came in, foot and hand, and with a thought seven 206
of the eleven I paid.

PRINCE O monstrous! Eleven buckram men grown out of 208
two!

FALSTAFF But, as the devil would have it, three misbegotten knaves in Kendal green came at my back and
let drive at me; for it was so dark, Hal, that thou couldst
not see thy hand.

PRINCE These lies are like their father that begets them –
gross as a mountain, open, palpable. Why, thou clay-

---

106 *Rivo* (perhaps) bottoms up   108 *of* on   110 *sew netherstocks* a menial
occupation   112 *virtue* valor   113 *Titan* the sun   115 *compound* (sweating)
lump of butter   116 *lime* added surreptitiously to wine to make it sparkle
120 *manhood* valor   121 *shotten herring* a herring that has deposited its roe
124 *while* present time   125 *sing psalms* a habit for which the weavers
were notorious   146 *All . . . that* it makes no difference   155 *at half-
sword* at close quarters   159 *ecce signum* look at the evidence   160 *dealt*
dealt blows   173 *other* others   177 *three and fifty* the number of Spanish
ships engaged by Sir Richard Grenville in the *Revenge* (1591)   180 *peppered* made it hot for   181 *paid* i.e. killed   184 *ward* defensive stance; *lay*
stood   189 *afront* abreast; *mainly* violently   190 *me* (ethical dative)   191
*target* shield   195 *villain* no gentleman   203 *points* (1) sword-points, (2)
laces which hold up the clothes   206 *came in* advanced; *with a thought* as
quick as thought   208 *monstrous* astounding

216 brained guts, thou knotty-pated fool, thou whoreson
217 obscene greasy tallow-catch –

FALSTAFF What, art thou mad? art thou mad? Is not the
truth the truth?

PRINCE Why, how couldst thou know these men in
Kendal green when it was so dark thou couldst not see
thy hand? Come, tell us your reason. What sayest thou
to this?

POINS Come, your reason, Jack, your reason.

FALSTAFF What, upon compulsion? Zounds, an I were
225 at the strappado or all the racks in the world, I would not
tell you on compulsion. Give you a reason on compul-
227 sion? If reasons were as plentiful as blackberries, I
would give no man a reason upon compulsion, I.

229 PRINCE I'll be no longer guilty of this sin; this sanguine
coward, this bed-presser, this horseback-breaker, this
huge hill of flesh –

FALSTAFF 'Sblood, you starveling, you eel-skin, you
233 dried neat's-tongue, you bull's pizzle, you stockfish – O
for breath to utter what is like thee! – you tailor's yard,
235 you sheath, you bowcase, you vile standing tuck!

236 PRINCE Well, breathe awhile, and then to it again; and
when thou hast tired thyself in base comparisons, hear
me speak but this.

POINS Mark, Jack.

PRINCE We two saw you four set on four, and bound
them and were masters of their wealth. Mark now how a
plain tale shall put you down. Then did we two set on
243 you four and, with a word, outfaced you from your
prize, and have it; yea, and can show it you here in the
house. And, Falstaff, you carried your guts away as
nimbly, with as quick dexterity, and roared for mercy,
and still run and roared, as ever I heard bullcalf. What a
slave art thou to hack thy sword as thou hast done, and
then say it was in fight! What trick, what device, what
250 starting hole canst thou now find out to hide thee from
this open and apparent shame?

POINS Come, let's hear, Jack. What trick hast thou now?

FALSTAFF By the Lord, I knew ye as well as he that made
ye. Why, hear you, my masters. Was it for me to kill the
heir apparent? Should I turn upon the true prince?
Why, thou knowest I am as valiant as Hercules, but
257 beware instinct. The lion will not touch the true prince.
Instinct is a great matter. I was now a coward on instinct.
I shall think the better of myself, and thee, during my
life – I for a valiant lion, and thou for a true prince. But,
by the Lord, lads, I am glad you have the money. Host-
262 ess, clap to the doors. Watch to-night, pray to-morrow.
Gallants, lads, boys, hearts of gold, all the titles of good
fellowship come to you! What, shall we be merry? Shall
we have a play extempore?

266 PRINCE Content – and the argument shall be thy running
away.

FALSTAFF Ah, no more of that, Hal, an thou lovest me!
*Enter Hostess.*

HOSTESS O Jesu, my lord the Prince!

PRINCE How now, my lady the hostess? What say'st
thou to me?

HOSTESS Marry, my lord, there is a noble man of the
court at door would speak with you. He says he comes
from your father.

275 PRINCE Give him as much as will make him a royal man,
and send him back again to my mother.

FALSTAFF What manner of man is he?

HOSTESS An old man.

FALSTAFF What doth gravity out of his bed at midnight?
Shall I give him his answer?

PRINCE Prithee do, Jack.

FALSTAFF Faith, and I'll send him packing. *Exit.*

PRINCE Now, sirs. By'r Lady, you fought fair; so did you, 28
Peto; so did you, Bardolph. You are lions too, you ran
away upon instinct, you will not touch the true prince;
no – fie!

BARDOLPH Faith, I ran when I saw others run.

PRINCE Tell me now in earnest, how came Falstaff's
sword so hacked?

PETO Why, he hacked it with his dagger, and said he
would swear truth out of England but he would make 29
you believe it was done in fight, and persuaded us to do
the like.

BARDOLPH Yea, and to tickle our noses with speargrass to
make them bleed, and then to beslubber our garments
with it and swear it was the blood of true men. I did that 29
I did not this seven year before – I blushed to hear his
monstrous devices.

PRINCE O villain! thou stolest a cup of sack eighteen years
ago and wert taken with the manner, and ever since thou 29
hast blushed extempore. Thou hadst fire and sword on 30
thy side, and yet thou ran'st away. What instinct hadst
thou for it?

BARDOLPH My lord, do you see these meteors? Do you 30
behold these exhalations?

PRINCE I do.

BARDOLPH What think you they portend?

PRINCE Hot livers and cold purses.

BARDOLPH Choler, my lord, if rightly taken. 30

PRINCE No, if rightly taken, halter. 30

*Enter Falstaff.*

Here comes lean Jack; here comes bare-bone. How now,
my sweet creature of bombast? How long is't ago, Jack, 31
since thou sawest thine own knee?

FALSTAFF My own knee? When I was about thy years,
Hal, I was not an eagle's talent in the waist; I could have 31
crept into any alderman's thumb-ring. A plague of
sighing and grief! It blows a man up like a bladder. 31
There's villainous news abroad. Here was Sir John
Bracy from your father. You must to the court in the
morning. That same mad fellow of the north, Percy, and
he of Wales that gave Amamon the bastinado, and 32
made Lucifer cuckold, and swore the devil his true 32

216 *knotty-pated* thick-headed   217 *tallow-catch* tub or lump of tallow
225 *strappado* kind of torture   227 *reasons* (pronounced like 'raisins')
229 *sanguine* daring   233 *stockfish* dried cod   235 *standing tuck* unpliant
rapier   236 *breathe* catch your breath; *to it* go to it   243 *with a word* in
short; *outfaced* frightened away   250 *starting hole* subterfuge, (literally)
refuge for hunted animals   257 *beware* take heed of   262 *Watch . . . to-
morrow* cf. 'Watch and pray, that ye enter not into temptation' (Matthew
xxvi, 41)   266 *argument* subject   275 *a royal man* i.e. worth 10 shillings
(3s. 4d. more than a noble)   283 *fair* well   291 *but he would* if he did not
295 *true* law-abiding; *that* what   299 *taken . . . manner* caught with the
goods   300 *fire* i.e. a red nose and cheeks   303 *meteors* i.e. the red blotches
on his face   307 *Hot livers* the effect of drinking   308 *Choler* a choleric
(aggressive) disposition; *rightly taken* rightly understood   309 *rightly
taken* well captured; *halter* i.e. collar   311 *bombast* cotton padding   314
*talent* talon   316 *blows . . . up* (actually it was supposed to make him waste
away)   320 *Amamon* a devil; *bastinado* beating on the soles of the feet
321 *made . . . cuckold* i.e. gave him his horns

liegeman upon the cross of a Welsh hook – what a plague call you him?

POINS Owen Glendower.

FALSTAFF Owen, Owen – the same; and his son-in-law Mortimer, and old Northumberland, and that sprightly Scot of Scots, Douglas, that runs a-horseback up a hill perpendicular –

PRINCE He that rides at high speed and with his pistol kills a sparrow flying.

FALSTAFF You have hit it.

PRINCE So did he never the sparrow.

**332** FALSTAFF Well, that rascal hath good metal in him; he **333** will not run.

PRINCE Why, what a rascal art thou then, to praise him so for running!

FALSTAFF A-horseback, ye cuckoo! but afoot he will not budge a foot.

PRINCE Yes, Jack, upon instinct.

FALSTAFF I grant ye, upon instinct. Well, he is there too, **340** and one Mordake, and a thousand bluecaps more. Worcester is stol'n away to-night; thy father's beard is turned white with the news; you may buy land now as cheap as stinking mack'rel.

PRINCE Why then, it is like, if there come a hot June, and this civil buffeting hold, we shall buy maidenheads as they buy hobnails, by the hundreds.

FALSTAFF By the mass, lad, thou sayest true; it is like we shall have good trading that way. But tell me, Hal, art not thou horrible afeard? Thou being heir apparent, could the world pick thee out three such enemies again **351** as that fiend Douglas, that spirit Percy, and that devil Glendower? Art thou not horribly afraid? Doth not thy **353** blood thrill at it?

PRINCE Not a whit, i' faith. I lack some of thy instinct.

FALSTAFF Well, thou wilt be horribly chid to-morrow when thou comest to thy father. If thou love me, practise an answer.

PRINCE Do thou stand for my father and examine me upon the particulars of my life.

**360** FALSTAFF Shall I? Content. This chair shall be my state, this dagger my sceptre, and this cushion my crown.

**362** PRINCE Thy state is taken for a joined-stool, thy golden sceptre for a leaden dagger, and thy precious rich crown for a pitiful bald crown.

FALSTAFF Well, an the fire of grace be not quite out of thee, now shalt thou be moved. Give me a cup of sack to make my eyes look red, that it may be thought I have wept; for I must speak in passion, and I will do it in **369** King Cambyses' vein.

**370** PRINCE Well, here is my leg.

FALSTAFF And here is my speech. Stand aside, nobility.

HOSTESS O Jesu, this is excellent sport, i' faith!

FALSTAFF Weep not, sweet queen, for trickling tears are vain.

HOSTESS O, the Father, how he holds his countenance! **374**

FALSTAFF For God's sake, lords, convey my tristful queen! **375** For tears do stop the floodgates of her eyes.

HOSTESS O Jesu, he doth it as like one of these harlotry **377** players as ever I see!

FALSTAFF Peace, good pintpot. Peace, good tickle-brain. – Harry, I do not only marvel where thou spendest thy time, but also how thou art accompanied. For though the camomile, the more it is trodden on, the faster it grows, yet youth, the more it is wasted, the sooner it wears. That thou art my son I have partly thy mother's word, partly my own opinion, but chiefly a villainous trick of thine eye and a foolish hanging of thy **386** nether lip that doth warrant me. If then thou be son to **387** me, here lies the point: why, being son to me, art thou so pointed at? Shall the blessed sun of heaven prove a micher and eat blackberries? A question not to be **390** asked. Shall the son of England prove a thief and take purses? A question to be asked. There is a thing, Harry, which thou hast often heard of, and it is known to many in our land by the name of pitch. This pitch, as ancient **394** writers do report, doth defile; so doth the company thou keepest. For, Harry, now I do not speak to thee in drink, but in tears; not in pleasure, but in passion; not in words only, but in woes also: and yet there is a virtu-ous man whom I have often noted in thy company, but I know not his name.

PRINCE What manner of man, an it like your majesty?

FALSTAFF A goodly portly man, i' faith, and a corpulent; **401** of a cheerful look, a pleasing eye, and a most noble carriage; and, as I think, his age some fifty, or, by'r Lady, inclining to threescore; and now I remember me, his name is Falstaff. If that man should be lewdly given, **405** he deceiveth me; for, Harry, I see virtue in his looks. If then the tree may be known by the fruit, as the fruit by **407** the tree, then, peremptorily I speak it, there is virtue in **408** that Falstaff. Him keep with, the rest banish. And tell me now, thou naughty varlet, tell me where hast thou **410** been this month?

PRINCE Dost thou speak like a king? Do thou stand for me, and I'll play my father.

FALSTAFF Depose me? If thou dost it half so gravely, so majestically, both in word and matter, hang me up by the heels for a rabbit-sucker or a poulter's hare. **415**

PRINCE Well, here I am set.

FALSTAFF And here I stand. Judge, my masters.

PRINCE Now, Harry, whence come you?

FALSTAFF My noble lord, from Eastcheap.

PRINCE The complaints I hear of thee are grievous.

FALSTAFF 'Sblood, my lord, they are false! Nay, I'll tickle ye for a young prince, i' faith. **422**

PRINCE Swearest thou, ungracious boy? Henceforth **423** ne'er look on me. Thou art violently carried away from grace. There is a devil haunts thee in the likeness of an old fat man; a tun of man is thy companion. Why dost thou converse with that trunk of humors, that bolting **427** hutch of beastliness, that swoll'n parcel of dropsies, that huge bombard of sack, that stuffed cloakbag of guts, **429** that roasted Manningtree ox with the pudding in his **430**

---

332 *metal* material   333 *run* (1) run away, (2) melt   340 *bluecaps* Scots 351 *spirit* evil spirit   353 *thrill* run cold   360 *state* chair of state   362 *taken for* understood to be   369 *King Cambyses' vein* that of an early ranting tragedy   370 *leg* bow   374 *holds his countenance* keeps a straight face   375 *convey* escort hence; *tristful* sorrowful   377 *harlotry* scurvy   386 *trick* peculiarity   387 *warrant* assure   390 *micher* truant   394–95 *ancient writers* i.e. Ecclesiasticus xiii, 1   401 *goodly* handsome; *portly* dignified 405 *lewdly* wickedly   407 *tree . . . by the fruit* cf. Matthew xii, 33   408 *peremptorily* positively   410 *varlet* rascal   415 *rabbit-sucker* very young rabbit   422 *tickle . . . prince* divert you in the role of a young prince   423 *ungracious* graceless   427 *converse* associate; *humors* fluids of the body 427–28 *bolting hutch* large flour bin   429 *bombard* leather vessel   430 *Manningtree* ox famous for size; *pudding* stuffing

431 belly, that reverend vice, that grey iniquity, that father
432 ruffian, that vanity in years? Wherein is he good, but to
433 taste sack and drink it? wherein neat and cleanly, but to
434 carve a capon and eat it? wherein cunning, but in craft?
wherein crafty, but in villainy? wherein villainous, but
in all things? wherein worthy, but in nothing?
437 FALSTAFF I would your grace would take me with you.
Whom means your grace?
PRINCE That villainous abominable misleader of youth,
Falstaff, that old white-bearded Satan.
FALSTAFF My lord, the man I know.
PRINCE I know thou dost.
FALSTAFF But to say I know more harm in him than in
myself were to say more than I know. That he is old (the
more the pity), his white hairs do witness it; but that he
446 is (saving your reverence) a whoremaster, that I utterly
deny. If sack and sugar be a fault, God help the wicked!
If to be old and merry be a sin, then many an old host
that I know is damned. If to be fat be to be hated, then
450 Pharaoh's lean kine are to be loved. No, my good lord:
banish Peto, banish Bardolph, banish Poins; but for
sweet Jack Falstaff, kind Jack Falstaff, true Jack Falstaff,
valiant Jack Falstaff, and therefore more valiant being,
as he is, old Jack Falstaff, banish not him thy Harry's
company, banish not him thy Harry's company. Banish
plump Jack, and banish all the world!
PRINCE I do, I will.
*[A knocking heard.]*
*[Exeunt Hostess, Francis, and Bardolph.]*
*Enter Bardolph, running.*
BARDOLPH O, my lord, my lord! the sheriff with a most
459 monstrous watch is at the door.
FALSTAFF Out, ye rogue! Play out the play. I have much
to say in the behalf of that Falstaff.
*Enter the Hostess.*
HOSTESS O Jesu, my lord, my lord!
463 PRINCE Heigh, heigh, the devil rides upon a fiddlestick!
What's the matter?
HOSTESS The sheriff and all the watch are at the door.
They are come to search the house. Shall I let them in?
467 FALSTAFF Dost thou hear, Hal? Never call a true piece of
gold a counterfeit. Thou art essentially mad without
seeming so.
PRINCE And thou a natural coward without instinct.
471 FALSTAFF I deny your major. If you will deny the sheriff,
472 so; if not, let him enter. If I become not a cart as well as
another man, a plague on my bringing up! I hope I shall
474 as soon be strangled with a halter as another.
475 PRINCE Go hide thee behind the arras. The rest walk up
476 above. Now, my masters, for a true face and good con-
science.
478 FALSTAFF Both which I have had; but their date is out,
and therefore I'll hide me.                              *Exit.*
PRINCE Call in the sheriff.
*[Exeunt. Manent the Prince and Peto.]*
*Enter Sheriff and the Carrier.*
Now, master sheriff, what is your will with me?
SHERIFF
First, pardon me, my lord. A hue and cry
Hath followed certain men unto this house.
PRINCE
What men?
SHERIFF
One of them is well known, my gracious lord –

A gross fat man.
CARRIER          As fat as butter.
PRINCE
The man, I do assure you, is not here,
For I myself at this time have employed him.
And, sheriff, I will engage my word to thee                48
That I will by to-morrow dinner time
Send him to answer thee, or any man,
For anything he shall be charged withal;
And so let me entreat you leave the house.
SHERIFF
I will, my lord. There are two gentlemen
Have in this robbery lost three hundred marks.
PRINCE
It may be so. If he have robbed these men,
He shall be answerable; and so farewell.
SHERIFF
Good night, my noble lord.
PRINCE
I think it is good morrow, is it not?                       49
SHERIFF
Indeed, my lord, I think it be two o'clock.
                              *Exit [with Carrier].*
PRINCE This oily rascal is known as well as Paul's. Go      50
call him forth.
PETO Falstaff! Fast asleep behind the arras, and snorting
like a horse.
PRINCE Hark how hard he fetches breath. Search his
pockets.
*He searcheth his pockets and findeth certain papers.*
What hast thou found?
PETO Nothing but papers, my lord.
PRINCE Let's see what they be. Read them.
PETO *[reads]* 'Item, A capon    .    .    .    ii s. ii d.
              Item, Sauce    .    .    .    iiii d.
              Item, Sack two gallons    .    v s. viii d.
              Item, Anchovies and sack after
                  supper    .    .    .    ii s. vi d.
              Item, Bread    .    .    .    ob.'            51
PRINCE O monstrous! but one halfpennyworth of bread     51
to this intolerable deal of sack! What there is else, keep
close; we'll read it at more advantage. There let him     51
sleep till day. I'll to the court in the morning. We must
all to the wars, and thy place shall be honorable. I'll
procure this fat rogue a charge of foot, and I know his    51
death will be a march of twelve score. The money shall be  52
paid back again with advantage. Be with me betimes in      52
the morning, and so good morrow, Peto.
PETO Good morrow, good my lord.                *Exeunt.*

\*

431 *vice* chief comic character and mischief-maker of the moral plays  432 *vanity* (incarnation of) worldliness  433 *cleanly* deft  434 *cunning* skillful  437 *take . . . you* make yourself clear  446 *saving your reverence* excuse my speaking plainly  450 *kine* cf. Genesis xli, 18–21  459 *watch* posse of watchmen (constables)  463 *the devil . . . fiddlestick* much ado about nothing  467–69 *Never . . . so* (perhaps) you are crazy to banish such a sterling fellow as plump Jack  471 *major* (1) major premise, (2) mayor  472 *cart* (in which criminals were carried to execution)  474 *soon* quickly  475 *arras* tapestry which screened the walls  476 *true* honest  478 *date is out* term has expired  489 *engage* pledge  499 *morrow* morning  501 *Paul's* St Paul's Cathedral, the center of London life  513 *ob.* obolus, halfpenny  514 *monstrous* astounding  516 *close* to yourself; *advantage* favorable opportunity  519 *a charge of foot* command of a company of infantry  520 *twelve score* i.e. yards  521 *advantage* interest

, i   *Enter Hotspur, Worcester, Lord Mortimer, Owen*
      *Glendower.*

MORTIMER
  These promises are fair, the parties sure,
2   And our induction full of prosperous hope.

HOTSPUR Lord Mortimer, and cousin Glendower, will
  you sit down? And uncle Worcester. A plague upon it! I
  have forgot the map.

GLENDOWER
  No, here it is. Sit, cousin Percy;
  Sit, good cousin Hotspur, for by that name
8   As oft as Lancaster doth speak of you,
  His cheek looks pale, and with a rising sigh
  He wisheth you in heaven.

HOTSPUR And you in hell, as oft as he hears Owen
  Glendower spoke of.

GLENDOWER
  I cannot blame him. At my nativity
14  The front of heaven was full of fiery shapes
15  Of burning cressets, and at my birth
  The frame and huge foundation of the earth
  Shaked like a coward.

HOTSPUR Why, so it would have done at the same season
  if your mother's cat had but kittened, though yourself
  had never been born.

GLENDOWER
  I say the earth did shake when I was born.

HOTSPUR
  And I say the earth was not of my mind,
  If you suppose as fearing you it shook.

GLENDOWER
  The heavens were all on fire, the earth did tremble.

HOTSPUR
  O, then the earth shook to see the heavens on fire,
  And not in fear of your nativity.
  Diseasèd nature oftentimes breaks forth
  In strange eruptions; oft the teeming earth
  Is with a kind of colic pinched and vexed
  By the imprisoning of unruly wind
31  Within her womb, which, for enlargement striving,
32  Shakes the old beldame earth and topples down
  Steeples and mossgrown towers. At your birth
34  Our grandam earth, having this distemp'rature,
35  In passion shook.

GLENDOWER          Cousin, of many men
36  I do not bear these crossings. Give me leave
  To tell you once again that at my birth
  The front of heaven was full of fiery shapes,
  The goats ran from the mountains, and the herds
  Were strangely clamorous to the frighted fields.
  These signs have marked me extraordinary,
  And all the courses of my life do show

III, i Within Glendower's castle in Wales (Holinshed names as the meeting-
place the Archdeacon's house at Bangor, but in the play Glendower is
acting as host)  2 *induction* first step; *prosperous hope* hope of prospering
8 *Lancaster* i.e. the king  14 *front* forehead  15 *cressets* lights burning in
baskets mounted on poles  31 *enlargement* release  32 *beldame* grandmother  34 *distemp'rature* ailment  35 *passion* pain  36 *crossings* contradictions  44 *clipped in with* enclosed by  45 *chides* lashes  46 *read to*
instructed  48 *trace* follow; *tedious* laborious; *art* i.e. magic  49 *hold me*
*pace* keep pace with me; *deep* occult  50 *Welsh* i.e. bragging  53 *vasty*
*deep* abyss of the lower world  64 *made head* raised troops  67 *Booteless*
without advantage  69 *agues* malaria  70 *right* rightful possessions  71
*order* arrangement  73 *limits* territories  74 *hitherto* to this spot  79 *lying*
*off* starting  80 *tripartite* i.e. in triplicate; *drawn* drawn up  87 *father* i.e.
father-in-law  89 *may* will be able to

  I am not in the roll of common men.
  Where is he living, clipped in with the sea      44
  That chides the banks of England, Scotland, Wales,   45
  Which calls me pupil or hath read to me?        46
  And bring him out that is but woman's son
  Can trace me in the tedious ways of art          48
  And hold me pace in deep experiments.           49

HOTSPUR I think there's no man speaks better Welsh.  50
  I'll to dinner.

MORTIMER
  Peace, cousin Percy; you will make him mad.

GLENDOWER
  I can call spirits from the vasty deep.           53

HOTSPUR
  Why, so can I, or so can any man;
  But will they come when you do call for them?

GLENDOWER Why, I can teach you, cousin, to command
  the devil.

HOTSPUR
  And I can teach thee, coz, to shame the devil –
  By telling truth. Tell truth and shame the devil.
  If thou have power to raise him, bring him hither,
  And I'll be sworn I have power to shame him hence.
  O, while you live, tell truth and shame the devil!

MORTIMER
  Come, come, no more of this unprofitable chat.

GLENDOWER
  Three times hath Henry Bolingbroke made head    64
  Against my power; thrice from the banks of Wye
  And sandy-bottomed Severn have I sent him
  Booteless home and weather-beaten back.         67

HOTSPUR
  Home without boots, and in foul weather too?
  How scapes he agues, in the devil's name?        69

GLENDOWER
  Come, here is the map. Shall we divide our right    70
  According to our threefold order ta'en?           71

MORTIMER
  The archdeacon hath divided it
  Into three limits very equally.                   73
  England, from Trent and Severn hitherto,          74
  By south and east is to my part assigned;
  All westward, Wales beyond the Severn shore,
  And all the fertile land within that bound,
  To Owen Glendower; and, dear coz, to you
  The remnant northward lying off from Trent.       79
  And our indentures tripartite are drawn,          80
  Which being sealèd interchangeably
  (A business that this night may execute),
  To-morrow, cousin Percy, you and I
  And my good Lord of Worcester will set forth
  To meet your father and the Scottish power,
  As is appointed us, at Shrewsbury.
  My father Glendower is not ready yet,             87
  Nor shall we need his help these fourteen days.
    *[To Glendower]*
  Within that space you may have drawn together     89
  Your tenants, friends, and neighboring gentlemen.

GLENDOWER
  A shorter time shall send me to you, lords;
  And in my conduct shall your ladies come,
  From whom you now must steal and take no leave,
  For there will be a world of water shed
  Upon the parting of your wives and you.

HOTSPUR
96 Methinks my moiety, north from Burton here,
In quantity equals not one of yours.
98 See how this river comes me cranking in
And cuts me from the best of all my land
100 A huge half-moon, a monstrous cantle out.
I'll have the current in this place dammed up,
102 And here the smug and silver Trent shall run
103 In a new channel fair and evenly.
It shall not wind with such a deep indent
105 To rob me of so rich a bottom here.
GLENDOWER
Not wind? It shall, it must! You see it doth.
MORTIMER
Yea, but
Mark how he bears his course, and runs me up
With like advantage on the other side,
110 Gelding the opposèd continent as much
As on the other side it takes from you.
WORCESTER
112 Yea, but a little charge will trench him here
And on this north side win this cape of land;
And then he runs straight and even.
HOTSPUR
I'll have it so. A little charge will do it.
GLENDOWER
I will not have it alt'red.
HOTSPUR                    Will not you?
GLENDOWER
No, nor you shall not.
HOTSPUR                    Who shall say me nay?
GLENDOWER
Why, that will I.
HOTSPUR
Let me not understand you then; speak it in Welsh.
GLENDOWER
I can speak English, lord, as well as you;
For I was trained up in the English court,
Where, being but young, I framèd to the harp
Many an English ditty lovely well,
124 And gave the tongue a helpful ornament –
125 A virtue that was never seen in you.
HOTSPUR
Marry, and I am glad of it with all my heart!
I had rather be a kitten and cry mew
128 Than one of these same metre ballet-mongers.
129 I had rather hear a brazen canstick turned
Or a dry wheel grate on the axletree,
And that would set my teeth nothing on edge,
Nothing so much as mincing poetry.
133 'Tis like the forced gait of a shuffling nag.
GLENDOWER
Come, you shall have Trent turned.
HOTSPUR
I do not care. I'll give thrice so much land
To any well-deserving friend;
But in the way of bargain, mark ye me,
I'll cavil on the ninth part of a hair.
Are the indentures drawn? Shall we be gone?
GLENDOWER
The moon shines fair; you may away by night.
I'll haste the writer, and withal
142 Break with your wives of your departure hence.
I am afraid my daughter will run mad,

So much she doteth on her Mortimer.     *Exit.*
MORTIMER
Fie, cousin Percy! how you cross my father!
HOTSPUR
I cannot choose. Sometimes he angers me
With telling me of the moldwarp and the ant,     14
Of the dreamer Merlin and his prophecies,
And of a dragon and a finless fish,
A clip-winged griffin and a moulten raven,     15
A couching lion and a ramping cat,     15
And such a deal of skimble-skamble stuff     15
As puts me from my faith. I tell you what –     15.
He held me last night at least nine hours
In reckoning up the several devils' names     155
That were his lackeys. I cried 'hum,' and 'well, go to!'     156
But marked him not a word. O, he is as tedious
As a tired horse, a railing wife;
Worse than a smoky house. I had rather live
With cheese and garlic in a windmill far
Than feed on cates and have him talk to me     16
In any summer house in Christendom.
MORTIMER
In faith, he is a worthy gentleman,
Exceedingly well read, and profited     16.
In strange concealments, valiant as a lion,     16
And wondrous affable, and as bountiful
As mines of India. Shall I tell you, cousin?
He holds your temper in a high respect
And curbs himself even of his natural scope     16
When you come 'cross his humor. Faith, he does.
I warrant you that man is not alive
Might so have tempted him as you have done     17
Without the taste of danger and reproof.
But do not use it oft, let me entreat you.     174
WORCESTER
In faith, my lord, you are too willful-blame,     175
And since your coming hither have done enough
To put him quite besides his patience.     177
You must needs learn, lord, to amend this fault.
Though sometimes it show greatness, courage, blood –     17
And that's the dearest grace it renders you –     180
Yet oftentimes it doth present harsh rage,     18
Defect of manners, want of government,
Pride, haughtiness, opinion, and disdain;     18
The least of which haunting a nobleman
Loseth men's hearts, and leaves behind a stain
Upon the beauty of all parts besides,     186
Beguiling them of commendation.     18
HOTSPUR
Well, I am schooled. Good manners be your speed!     188
Here come our wives, and let us take our leave.

96 *moiety* share  98 *cranking* winding  100 *cantle* hunk  102 *smug* smooth
103 *fair* gently  105 *bottom* valley  110 *continent* land which it bounds
112 *charge* expenditure; *trench* dig a new channel  124 *tongue* i.e. words;
*ornament* i.e. music  125 *virtue* accomplishment  128 *ballet-mongers* ballad-
makers  129 *canstick* candlestick  133 *shuffling* hobbled  142 *Break with*
inform  147 *moldwarp* mole  150 *griffin* half lion, half eagle  151 *couching* crouching; *ramping* rearing on hind legs  152 *skimble-skamble* non-
sensical  153 *puts* forces  155 *several* different  156 *go to* 'you don't
say'  161 *cates* delicacies  164 *profited* proficient  165 *concealments*
secrets  169 *scope* freedom of speech  172 *tempted* provoked  174 *use* do
175 *willful-blame* willfully blamable  177 *besides* out of  179 *blood* spirit
180 *dearest grace* best credit  181 *present* represent  183 *opinion* arrogance
186 *parts* abilities  187 *Beguiling* robbing  188 *be your speed* give you good
fortune

*Enter Glendower with the Ladies.*

MORTIMER
90  This is the deadly spite that angers me –
    My wife can speak no English, I no Welsh.

GLENDOWER
    My daughter weeps; she will not part with you;
    She'll be a soldier too, she'll to the wars.

MORTIMER
94  Good father, tell her that she and my aunt Percy
    Shall follow in your conduct speedily.
        *Glendower speaks to her in Welsh, and she answers*
        *him in the same.*

GLENDOWER
96  She is desperate here. A peevish self-willed harlotry,
    One that no persuasion can do good upon.
        *The Lady speaks in Welsh.*

MORTIMER
    I understand thy looks. That pretty Welsh
99  Which thou pourest down from these swelling heavens
200  I am too perfect in; and, but for shame,
201  In such a parley should I answer thee.
        *The Lady again in Welsh.*
    I understand thy kisses, and thou mine,
203  And that's a feeling disputation.
    But I will never be a truant, love,
    Till I have learnt thy language; for thy tongue
206  Makes Welsh as sweet as ditties highly penned,
    Sung by a fair queen in a summer's bow'r,
208  With ravishing division, to her lute.

GLENDOWER
    Nay, if you melt, then will she run mad.
        *The Lady speaks again in Welsh.*

MORTIMER
    O, I am ignorance itself in this!

GLENDOWER
211  She bids you on the wanton rushes lay you down
    And rest your gentle head upon her lap,
    And she will sing the song that pleaseth you
    And on your eyelids crown the god of sleep,
215  Charming your blood with pleasing heaviness,
    Making such difference 'twixt wake and sleep
    As is the difference betwixt day and night
    The hour before the heavenly-harnessed team
    Begins his golden progress in the east.

MORTIMER
    With all my heart I'll sit and hear her sing.
221  By that time will our book, I think, be drawn.

GLENDOWER
    Do so, and those musicians that shall play to you
    Hang in the air a thousand leagues from hence,
    And straight they shall be here. Sit, and attend.

HOTSPUR  Come, Kate, thou art perfect in lying down. 225
    Come, quick, quick, that I may lay my head in thy lap.

LADY PERCY  Go, ye giddy goose.
        *The music plays.*

HOTSPUR
    Now I perceive the devil understands Welsh.
    And 'tis no marvel he is so humorous,          229
    By'r Lady, he is a good musician.

LADY PERCY  Then should you be nothing but musical,
    for you are altogether governed by humors. Lie still, ye 232
    thief, and hear the lady sing in Welsh.

HOTSPUR  I had rather hear Lady, my brach, howl in 234
    Irish.

LADY PERCY  Wouldst thou have thy head broken?

HOTSPUR  No.

LADY PERCY  Then be still.

HOTSPUR  Neither! 'Tis a woman's fault.

LADY PERCY  Now God help thee!

HOTSPUR  To the Welsh lady's bed.

LADY PERCY  What's that?

HOTSPUR  Peace! she sings.
        *Here the Lady sings a Welsh song.*
    Come, Kate, I'll have your song too.

LADY PERCY  Not mine, in good sooth.            244

HOTSPUR  Not yours, in good sooth? Heart! you swear
    like a comfit-maker's wife. 'Not you, in good sooth!' and 246
    'as true as I live!' and 'as God shall mend me!' and 'as
    sure as day!'
    And givest such sarcenet surety for thy oaths     249
    As if thou never walk'st further than Finsbury.   250
    Swear me, Kate, like a lady as thou art,          251
    A good mouth-filling oath, and leave 'in sooth'
    And such protest of pepper gingerbread            253
    To velvet guards and Sunday citizens.             254
    Come, sing.

LADY PERCY  I will not sing.

HOTSPUR  'Tis the next way to turn tailor or be red- 257
    breast-teacher. An the indentures be drawn, I'll away
    within these two hours; and so come in when ye will.
                                            *Exit.*

GLENDOWER
    Come, come, Lord Mortimer. You are as slow
    As hot Lord Percy is on fire to go.
    By this our book is drawn; we'll but seal,
    And then to horse immediately.

MORTIMER                      With all my heart.  *Exeunt.*

                        *

        *Enter the King, Prince of Wales, and others.*    III, ii
KING
    Lords, give us leave: the Prince of Wales and I
    Must have some private conference; but be near at
        hand,
    For we shall presently have need of you.  *Exeunt Lords.*
    I know not whether God will have it so
    For some displeasing service I have done,
    That, in his secret doom, out of my blood          6
    He'll breed revengement and a scourge for me;
    But thou dost in thy passages of life              8
    Make me believe that thou art only marked          9
    For the hot vengeance and the rod of heaven
    To punish my misreadings. Tell me else,

190 *spite* vexation  194 *aunt* (to Edmund Mortimer, Earl of March, but sister-in-law to Glendower's son-in-law)  196 *here* on this point; *peevish* childish; *harlotry* silly wench  199 *heavens* i.e. eyes  200 *perfect* proficient  201 *such a parley* the same language  203 *disputation* conversation  206 *highly* nobly  208 *division* melody  211 *wanton* luxurious  215 *blood* mood  221 *book* the indenture  225 *perfect* well-trained  229 *humorous* emotional  232 *humors* whims  234 *brach* bitch-hound  244 *sooth* truth  246 *comfit-maker's* confectioner's  249 *sarcenet* surety flimsy confirmation  250 *Finsbury* field near London frequented by citizens on Sundays  251 *me* (ethical dative)  253 *protest . . . gingerbread* mealy-mouthed swearing  254 *velvet guards* (middle-class women dressed up in clothes with) velvet trimmings  257 *next* easiest; *tailor* proverbially a singer  257-58 *be redbreast-teacher* teach birds to sing
III, ii Within the palace of King Henry IV  6 *doom* judgment  8 *thy . . . life* the actions of your life  9-10 *marked For* destined to be

263

12 Could such inordinate and low desires,
13 Such poor, such bare, such lewd, such mean attempts,
Such barren pleasures, rude society,
As thou art matched withal and grafted to,
Accompany the greatness of thy blood
17 And hold their level with thy princely heart?

PRINCE
So please your majesty, I would I could
19 Quit all offenses with as clear excuse
20 As well as I am doubtless I can purge
Myself of many I am charged withal.
22 Yet such extenuation let me beg
23 As, in reproof of many tales devised,
Which oft the ear of greatness needs must hear
25 By smiling pickthanks and base newsmongers,
I may, for some things true wherein my youth
Hath faulty wand'red and irregular,
28 Find pardon on my true submission.

KING
God pardon thee! Yet let me wonder, Harry,
30 At thy affections, which do hold a wing
31 Quite from the flight of all thy ancestors.
32 Thy place in council thou hast rudely lost,
Which by thy younger brother is supplied,
And art almost an alien to the hearts
Of all the court and princes of my blood.
36 The hope and expectation of thy time
Is ruined, and the soul of every man
Prophetically do forethink thy fall.
Had I so lavish of my presence been,
40 So common-hackneyed in the eyes of men,
So stale and cheap to vulgar company,
42 Opinion, that did help me to the crown,
43 Had still kept loyal to possession
And left me in reputeless banishment,
A fellow of no mark nor likelihood.
By being seldom seen, I could not stir
But, like a comet, I was wond'red at;
That men would tell their children, 'This is he!'
Others would say, 'Where? Which is Bolingbroke?'
50 And then I stole all courtesy from heaven,
And dressed myself in such humility
That I did pluck allegiance from men's hearts,
Loud shouts and salutations from their mouths
Even in the presence of the crownèd king.
Thus did I keep my person fresh and new,
My presence, like a robe pontifical,
57 Ne'er seen but wond'red at; and so my state,
Seldom but sumptuous, showed like a feast
59 And wan by rareness such solemnity.
60 The skipping king, he ambled up and down
61 With shallow jesters and rash bavin wits,
62 Soon kindled and soon burnt; carded his state;
Mingled his royalty with cap'ring fools;
64 Had his great name profanèd with their scorns
65 And gave his countenance, against his name,
66 To laugh at gibing boys and stand the push
67 Of every beardless vain comparative;
Grew a companion to the common streets,
69 Enfeoffed himself to popularity;
That, being daily swallowed by men's eyes,
They surfeited with honey and began
To loathe the taste of sweetness, whereof a little
More than a little is by much too much.

So, when he had occasion to be seen,
He was but as the cuckoo is in June,
Heard, not regarded – seen, but with such eyes
As, sick and blunted with community,   77
Afford no extraordinary gaze,
Such as is bent on sunlike majesty
When it shines seldom in admiring eyes;
But rather drowsed and hung their eyelids down,
Slept in his face, and rend'red such aspect   82
As cloudy men use to their adversaries,   83
Being with his presence glutted, gorged, and full.
And in that very line, Harry, standest thou;   85
For thou hast lost thy princely privilege
With vile participation. Not an eye   87
But is aweary of thy common sight,
Save mine, which hath desired to see thee more;
Which now doth that I would not have it do –
Make blind itself with foolish tenderness.

PRINCE
I shall hereafter, my thrice-gracious lord,
Be more myself.

KING           For all the world,
As thou art to this hour was Richard then
When I from France set foot at Ravenspurgh;
And even as I was then is Percy now.
Now, by my sceptre, and my soul to boot,
He hath more worthy interest to the state   98
Than thou, the shadow of succession;   99
For of no right, nor color like to right,   100
He doth fill fields with harness in the realm,   101
Turns head against the lion's armèd jaws,   102
And, being no more in debt to years than thou,
Leads ancient lords and reverend bishops on
To bloody battles and to bruising arms.
What never-dying honor hath he got
Against renownèd Douglas! whose high deeds,
Whose hot incursions and great name in arms
Holds from all soldiers chief majority   109
And military title capital   110
Through all the kingdoms that acknowledge Christ.
Thrice hath this Hotspur, Mars in swathling clothes,
This infant warrior, in his enterprises
Discomfited great Douglas; ta'en him once,
Enlargèd him, and made a friend of him,   115
To fill the mouth of deep defiance up   116
And shake the peace and safety of our throne.

---

12 *inordinate* beneath your position   13 *lewd* low; *attempts* undertakings   17 *hold . . . with* be on an equality with   19 *Quit* acquit myself of   20 *am doubtless* have no doubt; *purge* acquit   22 *extenuation* mitigation   23 *in reproof* upon disproof   25 *pickthanks* flatterers; *newsmongers* talebearers   28 *submission* admission of fault   30 *affections* inclinations; *hold a wing* take a course   31 *from* contrary to   32 *rudely* by violence   36 *time* i.e. youth   40 *common-hackneyed* vulgarized   42 *Opinion* i.e. public opinion   43 *Had* would have; *possession* i.e. the possessor   50 *courtesy* humility   57 *state* i.e. appearances in state   59 *wan* won; *such solemnity* i.e. that of a festival   60 *skipping* flighty   61 *rash* quick to burn; *bavin* (literally) brushwood   62 *carded* mixed with baseness   64 *their scorns* the scorn felt for them   65 *name* reputation   66 *stand the push* serve as the butt   67 *comparative* wise-cracker   69 *Enfeoffed* surrendered; *popularity* the populace   77 *community* commonness   82 *Slept in* disregarded; *aspect* look   83 *cloudy* sullen   85 *line* station   87 *vile participation* association with the mean   98 *interest* title   99 *the shadow of succession* a successor with a poor claim   100 *color* pretext   101 *harness* (men in) armor   102 *Turns head* marches with an army; *lion's* i.e. king's   109 *majority* preeminence   110 *capital* principal   115 *Enlargèd* set free   116 *fill . . . up* make defiance roar all the more loudly

And what say you to this? Percy, Northumberland,
The Archbishop's grace of York, Douglas, Mortimer
Capitulate against us and are up.
But wherefore do I tell these news to thee?
Why, Harry, do I tell thee of my foes,
Which art my nearest and dearest enemy?
Thou that art like enough, through vassal fear,
Base inclination, and the start of spleen,
To fight against me under Percy's pay,
To dog his heels and curtsy at his frowns,
To show how much thou art degenerate.

PRINCE
Do not think so. You shall not find it so.
And God forgive them that so much have swayed
Your majesty's good thoughts away from me.
I will redeem all this on Percy's head
And, in the closing of some glorious day,
Be bold to tell you that I am your son,
When I will wear a garment all of blood,
And stain my favors in a bloody mask,
Which, washed away, shall scour my shame with it.
And that shall be the day, whene'er it lights,
That this same child of honor and renown,
This gallant Hotspur, this all-praisèd knight,
And your unthought-of Harry chance to meet.
For every honor sitting on his helm,
Would they were multitudes, and on my head
My shames redoubled! For the time will come
That I shall make this northern youth exchange
His glorious deeds for my indignities.
Percy is but my factor, good my lord,
To engross up glorious deeds on my behalf;
And I will call him to so strict account
That he shall render every glory up,
Yea, even the slightest worship of his time,
Or I will tear the reckoning from his heart.
This in the name of God I promise here;
The which if he be pleased I shall perform,
I do beseech your majesty may salve
The long-grown wounds of my intemperance.
If not, the end of life cancels all bands,
And I will die a hundred thousand deaths
Ere break the smallest parcel of this vow.

KING
A hundred thousand rebels die in this!

Thou shalt have charge and sovereign trust herein.    161
    *Enter Blunt.*
How now, good Blunt? Thy looks are full of speed.

BLUNT
So hath the business that I come to speak of.    163
Lord Mortimer of Scotland hath sent word    164
That Douglas and the English rebels met
The eleventh of this month at Shrewsbury.
A mighty and a fearful head they are,    167
If promises be kept on every hand,
As ever off'red foul play in a state.

KING
The Earl of Westmoreland set forth to-day;
With him my son, Lord John of Lancaster;
For this advertisement is five days old.    172
On Wednesday next, Harry, you shall set forward;
On Thursday we ourselves will march. Our meeting    174
Is Bridgenorth; and, Harry, you shall march
Through Gloucestershire; by which account,
Our business valuèd, some twelve days hence    177
Our general forces at Bridgenorth shall meet.
Our hands are full of business. Let's away:
Advantage feeds him fat while men delay.    *Exeunt.*  180

*

*Enter Falstaff and Bardolph.*    III, iii

FALSTAFF Bardolph, am I not fall'n away vilely since
    this last action? Do I not bate? Do I not dwindle? Why,    2
    my skin hangs about me like an old lady's loose gown! I
    am withered like an old apple-john. Well, I'll repent,    4
    and that suddenly, while I am in some liking. I shall be    5
    out of heart shortly, and then I shall have no strength to    6
    repent. An I have not forgotten what the inside of a
    church is made of, I am a peppercorn, a brewer's horse.    8
    The inside of a church! Company, villainous company,
    hath been the spoil of me.

BARDOLPH Sir John, you are so fretful you cannot live
    long.

FALSTAFF Why, there is it! Come, sing me a bawdy song;
    make me merry. I was as virtuously given as a gentle-
    man need to be, virtuous enough: swore little, diced not
    above seven times a week, went to a bawdy house not
    above once in a quarter of an hour, paid money that I
    borrowed three or four times, lived well, and in good
    compass; and now I live out of all order, out of all    17
    compass.

BARDOLPH Why, you are so fat, Sir John, that you must
    needs be out of all compass – out of all reasonable com-
    pass, Sir John.

FALSTAFF Do thou amend thy face, and I'll amend my    22
    life. Thou art our admiral, thou bearest the lantern in    23
    the poop – but 'tis in the nose of thee. Thou art the
    Knight of the Burning Lamp.    25

BARDOLPH Why, Sir John, my face does you no harm.

FALSTAFF No, I'll be sworn. I make as good use of it as
    many a man doth of a death's-head or a memento mori.    28
    I never see thy face but I think upon hellfire and Dives    29
    that lived in purple; for there he is in his robes, burning,
    burning. If thou wert any way given to virtue, I would
    swear by thy face; my oath should be 'By this fire, that's    32
    God's angel.' But thou art altogether given over, and    33
    wert indeed, but for the light in thy face, the son of utter
    darkness. When thou ran'st up Gad's Hill in the night

120 *Capitulate* draw up articles of agreement; *up* in arms  124 *vassal*
slavish  125 *Base inclination* inclination towards baseness; *start of spleen*
perversity  132 *redeem* make up for  136 *favors* features  137 *shame*
disgrace  138 *lights* dawns  146 *indignities* unworthy traits  147 *factor*
agent  148 *engross up* buy up  151 *worship* honor; *time* lifetime  156
*intemperance* dissolute behavior  157 *bands* bonds  161 *charge* command
163 *hath* i.e. hath speed, is urgent  164 *Lord Mortimer of Scotland* a
Scottish nobleman, no relative of Edmund Mortimer  167 *head* force
172 *advertisement* information  174 *meeting* meeting-place  177 *Our business valuèd* considering how long our business will take  180 *Advantage*
opportunity; *fat* i.e. lazy
III, iii *Within an Eastcheap tavern*  2 *action* battle, i.e. the robbery; *bate*
grow thin  4 *apple-john* an apple eaten when the skin has shrivelled  5
*suddenly* immediately; *liking* (1) inclination, (2) good fettle  6 *out of heart*
depressed  8 *peppercorn* berry of pepper; *brewer's horse* i.e. lean and worn
out  17 *compass* (1) limit, (2) girth  22 *face* (which is violently inflamed
and pimpled)  23 *admiral* flagship; *lantern* (which the fleet follows)  25
*Knight . . . Lamp* i.e. if you were a knight the lamp would be your emblem
28 *death's-head* skull and crossbones (a pious reminder of mortality)  29
*Dives* the rich man of the parable in Luke xvi, 19–31  32–33 *By . . . angel*
cf. 'Who [God] maketh his angels spirits, his ministers a flaming fire'
(Psalms civ, 4)  33 *given over* abandoned as a reprobate

to catch my horse, if I did not think thou hadst been an
37   ignis fatuus or a ball of wildfire, there's no purchase in
38   money. O, thou art a perpetual triumph, an everlasting
    bonfire-light! Thou hast saved me a thousand marks in
40   links and torches, walking with thee in the night betwixt
    tavern and tavern; but the sack that thou hast drunk me
42   would have bought me lights as good cheap at the
    dearest chandler's in Europe. I have maintained that
44   salamander of yours with fire any time this two-and-
    thirty years. God reward me for it!
46 BARDOLPH 'Sblood, I would my face were in your belly!
    FALSTAFF God-a-mercy! so should I be sure to be heart-
    burnt.

    *Enter Hostess.*

49   How now, Dame Partlet the hen? Have you enquired
    yet who picked my pocket?
    HOSTESS Why, Sir John, what do you think, Sir John?
    Do you think I keep thieves in my house? I have
    searched, I have enquired, so has my husband, man by
54   man, boy by boy, servant by servant. The tithe of a hair
    was never lost in my house before.
    FALSTAFF Ye lie, hostess. Bardolph was shaved and lost
    many a hair, and I'll be sworn my pocket was picked.
58   Go to, you are a woman, go!
    HOSTESS Who, I? No; I defy thee! God's light, I was
    never called so in mine own house before!
    FALSTAFF Go to, I know you well enough.
    HOSTESS No, Sir John; you do not know me, Sir John. I
    know you, Sir John. You owe me money, Sir John, and
    now you pick a quarrel to beguile me of it. I bought you
    a dozen of shirts to your back.
66 FALSTAFF Dowlas, filthy dowlas! I have given them away
67   to bakers' wives; they have made bolters of them.
68 HOSTESS Now, as I am a true woman, holland of eight
69   shillings an ell. You owe money here besides, Sir John,
    for your diet and by-drinkings, and money lent you,
    four-and-twenty pound.
    FALSTAFF He had his part of it; let him pay.
    HOSTESS He? Alas, he is poor; he hath nothing.
    FALSTAFF How? Poor? Look upon his face. What call
    you rich? Let them coin his nose, let them coin his
76   cheeks. I'll not pay a denier. What, will you make a
77   younker of me? Shall I not take mine ease in mine inn
    but I shall have my pocket picked? I have lost a seal-
    ring of my grandfather's worth forty mark.
    HOSTESS O Jesu, I have heard the prince tell him, I know
    not how oft, that that ring was copper!
82 FALSTAFF How? the prince is a Jack, a sneak-up.
    'Sblood, an he were here, I would cudgel him like a dog
84   if he would say so.

    *Enter the Prince [and Peto], marching, and Falstaff*
    *meets them, playing upon his truncheon like a fife.*

85   How now, lad? Is the wind in that door, i' faith? Must
    we all march?
87 BARDOLPH Yea, two and two, Newgate fashion.
    HOSTESS My lord, I pray you hear me.
    PRINCE What say'st thou, Mistress Quickly? How doth
    thy husband? I love him well; he is an honest man.
    HOSTESS Good my lord, hear me.
    FALSTAFF Prithee let her alone and list to me.
    PRINCE What say'st thou, Jack?
    FALSTAFF The other night I fell asleep here behind the
    arras and had my pocket picked. This house is turned
    bawdy house; they pick pockets.

PRINCE What didst thou lose, Jack?
FALSTAFF Wilt thou believe me, Hal, three or four bonds
    of forty pound apiece and a seal-ring of my grand-
    father's.
PRINCE A trifle, some eightpenny matter.     10
HOSTESS So I told him, my lord, and I said I heard your
    grace say so; and, my lord, he speaks most vilely of you,
    like a foulmouthed man as he is, and said he would
    cudgel you.
PRINCE What! he did not?
HOSTESS There's neither faith, truth, nor womanhood
    in me else.
FALSTAFF There's no more faith in thee than in a
    stewed prune, nor no more truth in thee than in a drawn   10
    fox; and for womanhood, Maid Marian may be the   10
    deputy's wife of the ward to thee. Go, you thing, go!   11
HOSTESS Say, what thing? what thing?
FALSTAFF What thing? Why, a thing to thank God on.
HOSTESS I am no thing to thank God on, I would thou
    shouldst know it! I am an honest man's wife, and,
    setting thy knighthood aside, thou art a knave to call me
    so.
FALSTAFF Setting thy womanhood aside, thou art a
    beast to say otherwise.
HOSTESS Say, what beast, thou knave, thou?
FALSTAFF What beast? Why, an otter.
PRINCE An otter, Sir John? Why an otter?
FALSTAFF Why? She's neither fish nor flesh; a man
    knows not where to have her.     12
HOSTESS Thou art an unjust man in saying so. Thou or
    any man knows where to have me, thou knave, thou!
PRINCE Thou say'st true, hostess, and he slanders thee
    most grossly.
HOSTESS So he doth you, my lord, and said this other
    day you ought him a thousand pound.     12
PRINCE Sirrah, do I owe you a thousand pound?
FALSTAFF A thousand pound, Hal? A million! Thy love
    is worth a million; thou owest me thy love.
HOSTESS Nay, my lord, he called you Jack and said he
    would cudgel you.
FALSTAFF Did I, Bardolph?
BARDOLPH Indeed, Sir John, you said so.
FALSTAFF Yea, if he said my ring was copper.
PRINCE I say 'tis copper. Darest thou be as good as thy
    word now?
FALSTAFF Why, Hal, thou knowest, as thou art but man,
    I dare; but as thou art prince, I fear thee as I fear the   14
    roaring of the lion's whelp.
PRINCE And why not as the lion?
FALSTAFF The king himself is to be feared as the lion.
    Dost thou think I'll fear thee as I fear thy father? Nay,
    an I do, I pray God my girdle break.

37 *ignis fatuus* will-o'-the-wisp; *wildfire* fireworks   38 *triumph* torchlight
parade   40 *links* torches   42 *as good cheap* as cheap   44 *salamander* lizard
reputed to live in fire   46 *in your belly* i.e. rather than on your tongue   49
*Dame Partlet* hen in animal stories   54 *tithe* tenth part   58 *Go to* go on
66 *Dowlas* coarse linen   67 *bolters* flour-sifters   68 *holland* fine linen   69
*ell* measure of forty-five inches   76 *denier* one-twelfth of a sou   77 *younker*
greenhorn, victim   82 *Jack* knave; *sneak-up* sneak   84 s.d. *truncheon*
officer's stick   85 *in that door* in that quarter   87 *Newgate fashion* chained
together (like inmates of Newgate prison)   108–09 *drawn fox* driven from
cover (therefore tricky)   109 *womanhood* womanly respectability; *Maid
Marian* (disreputable) woman in morris dances   110 *deputy's wife* i.e.
eminently respectable woman; *to* compared to   122 *where . . . her* what to
make of her   128 *ought* owed

PRINCE O, if it should, how would thy guts fall about thy knees! But, sirrah, there's no room for faith, truth, nor honesty in this bosom of thine. It is all filled up with guts and midriff. Charge an honest woman with picking thy pocket? Why, thou whoreson, impudent, embossed rascal, if there were anything in thy pocket but tavern reckonings, memorandums of bawdy houses, and one poor pennyworth of sugar candy to make thee long-winded – if thy pocket were enriched with any other injuries but these, I am a villain. And yet you will stand to it; you will not pocket up wrong. Art thou not ashamed?

FALSTAFF Dost thou hear, Hal? Thou knowest in the state of innocency Adam fell, and what should poor Jack Falstaff do in the days of villainy? Thou seest I have more flesh than another man, and therefore more frailty. You confess then, you picked my pocket?

PRINCE It appears so by the story.

FALSTAFF Hostess, I forgive thee. Go make ready breakfast. Love thy husband, look to thy servants, cherish thy guests. Thou shalt find me tractable to any honest reason. Thou seest I am pacified still. Nay, prithee be gone. *Exit Hostess.*
Now, Hal, to the news at court. For the robbery, lad – how is that answered?

PRINCE O my sweet beef, I must still be good angel to thee. The money is paid back again.

FALSTAFF O, I do not like that paying back! 'Tis a double labor.

PRINCE I am good friends with my father, and may do anything.

FALSTAFF Rob me the exchequer the first thing thou doest, and do it with unwashed hands too.

BARDOLPH Do, my lord.

PRINCE I have procured thee, Jack, a charge of foot.

FALSTAFF I would it had been of horse. Where shall I find one that can steal well? O for a fine thief of the age of two-and-twenty or thereabouts! I am heinously unprovided. Well, God be thanked for these rebels. They offend none but the virtuous. I laud them, I praise them.

PRINCE Bardolph!

BARDOLPH My lord?

PRINCE
Go bear this letter to Lord John of Lancaster,
To my brother John; this to my Lord of Westmoreland.
*[Exit Bardolph.]*
Go, Peto, to horse, to horse; for thou and I
Have thirty miles to ride yet ere dinner time.
*[Exit Peto.]*
Jack, meet me to-morrow in the Temple Hall
At two o'clock in the afternoon.
There shalt thou know thy charge, and there receive

Money and order for their furniture.                                    193
The land is burning; Percy stands on high;
And either we or they must lower lie.              *[Exit.]*

FALSTAFF
Rare words! brave world! Hostess, my breakfast, come.    196
O, I could wish this tavern were my drum!        *Exit.*   197

\*

*[Enter Hotspur, Worcester, and Douglas.]*          IV, i

HOTSPUR
Well said, my noble Scot. If speaking truth
In this fine age were not thought flattery,
Such attribution should the Douglas have                        3
As not a soldier of this season's stamp
Should go so general current through the world.              5
By God, I cannot flatter, I do defy                                      6
The tongues of soothers! but a braver place                     7
In my heart's love hath no man than yourself.
Nay, task me to my word; approve me, lord.                    9

DOUGLAS
Thou art the king of honor.
No man so potent breathes upon the ground
But I will beard him.                                                           12
    *Enter one with letters.*

HOTSPUR                     Do so, and 'tis well. –
What letters hast thou there? – I can but thank you.

MESSENGER
These letters come from your father.

HOTSPUR
Letters from him? Why comes he not himself?

MESSENGER
He cannot come, my lord; he is grievous sick.

HOTSPUR
Zounds! how has he the leisure to be sick
In such a justling time? Who leads his power?                18
Under whose government come they along?

MESSENGER
His letters bears his mind, not I, my lord.

WORCESTER
I prithee tell me, doth he keep his bed?

MESSENGER
He did, my lord, four days ere I set forth,
And at the time of my departure thence
He was much feared by his physicians.                           24

WORCESTER
I would the state of time had first been whole             25
Ere he by sickness had been visited.
His health was never better worth than now.

HOTSPUR
Sick now? droop now? This sickness doth infect
The very lifeblood of our enterprise.
'Tis catching hither, even to our camp.
He writes me here that inward sickness –
And that his friends by deputation could not               32
So soon be drawn; nor did he think it meet                  33
To lay so dangerous and dear a trust
On any soul removed but on his own.                            35
Yet doth he give us bold advertisement,                       36
That with our small conjunction we should on,          37
To see how fortune is disposed to us;
For, as he writes, there is no quailing now,
Because the king is certainly possessed                         40
Of all our purposes. What say you to it?

---

150 *embossed* swollen  151 *rascal* (literally) lean deer  155 *injuries* things the loss of which would injure you  156 *stand to it* make a stand; *pocket up* endure  166 *still* always  176 *with unwashed hands* i.e. without delay  178 *charge of foot* infantry command  181 *unprovided* unprepared  193 *furniture* equipment  196 *brave* splendid  197 *tavern* (1) inn, (2) drum called 'tabor' or 'taborn'; *drum* (which leads soldiers into battle)
IV, i The rebel camp at Shrewsbury  3 *attribution* tribute  5 *go . . . current* be so universally honored  6 *defy* despise  7 *soothers* flatterers; *braver* better  9 *task* challenge; *approve* put to the test  12 *But* but that; *beard* defy  18 *justling* turbulent  24 *feared* feared for  25 *time* the times  32 *deputation* deputies  33 *drawn* assembled  35 *removed* but i.e. other than  36 *advertisement* advice  37 *conjunction* united force; *on* go on  40 *possessed* informed

**WORCESTER**
Your father's sickness is a maim to us.

**HOTSPUR**
A perilous gash, a very limb lopped off.
And yet, in faith, it is not! His present want
Seems more than we shall find it. Were it good
46 To set the exact wealth of all our states
47 All at one cast? to set so rich a main
48 On the nice hazard of one doubtful hour?
49 It were not good; for therein should we read
50 The very bottom and the soul of hope,
51 The very list, the very utmost bound
Of all our fortunes.

**DOUGLAS**     Faith, and so we should.
53 Where now remains a sweet reversion,
We may boldly spend upon the hope of what
Is to come in.
A comfort of retirement lives in this.

**HOTSPUR**
A rendezvous, a home to fly unto,
58 If that the devil and mischance look big
59 Upon the maidenhead of our affairs.

**WORCESTER**
But yet I would your father had been here.
61 The quality and hair of our attempt
62 Brooks no division. It will be thought
By some that know not why he is away,
64 That wisdom, loyalty, and mere dislike
Of our proceedings kept the earl from hence.
And think how such an apprehension
67 May turn the tide of fearful faction
And breed a kind of question in our cause.
For well you know we of the off'ring side
70 Must keep aloof from strict arbitrement,
71 And stop all sight-holes, every loop from whence
The eye of reason may pry in upon us.
73 This absence of your father's draws a curtain
That-shows the ignorant a kind of fear
Before not dreamt of.

75 **HOTSPUR**     You strain too far.
I rather of his absence make this use:
77 It lends a lustre and more great opinion,
A larger dare to our great enterprise,
Than if the earl were here; for men must think,
80 If we, without his help, can make a head
To push against a kingdom, with his help
We shall o'erturn it topsy-turvy down.
Yet all goes well; yet all our joints are whole.

**DOUGLAS**
As heart can think. There is not such a word
Spoke of in Scotland as this term of fear.
*Enter Sir Richard Vernon.*

**HOTSPUR**
My cousin Vernon! welcome, by my soul.

**VERNON**
Pray God my news be worth a welcome, lord.
The Earl of Westmoreland, seven thousand strong,
Is marching hitherwards; with him Prince John.

**HOTSPUR**
No harm. What more?

**VERNON**     And further, I have learned
The king himself in person is set forth,
92 Or hitherwards intended speedily,
With strong and mighty preparation.

**HOTSPUR**
He shall be welcome too. Where is his son,
The nimble-footed madcap Prince of Wales,
And his comrades, that daffed the world aside 96
And bid it pass? 97

**VERNON**     All furnished, all in arms;
All plumed like estridges that with the wind 98
Bated like eagles having lately bathed; 99
Glittering in golden coats like images;
As full of spirit as the month of May
And gorgeous as the sun at midsummer;
Wanton as youthful goats, wild as young bulls. 10
I saw young Harry with his beaver on, 10
His cushes on his thighs, gallantly armed, 10
Rise from the ground like feathered Mercury,
And vaulted with such ease into his seat
As if an angel dropped down from the clouds
To turn and wind a fiery Pegasus 10
And witch the world with noble horsemanship. 11

**HOTSPUR**
No more, no more! Worse than the sun in March,
This praise doth nourish agues. Let them come. 11
They come like sacrifices in their trim, 11
And to the fire-eyed maid of smoky war 11
All hot and bleeding will we offer them.
The mailèd Mars shall on his altar sit
Up to the ears in blood. I am on fire
To hear this rich reprisal is so nigh, 11
And yet not ours. Come, let me taste my horse, 11
Who is to bear me like a thunderbolt
Against the bosom of the Prince of Wales.
Harry to Harry shall, hot horse to horse,
Meet, and ne'er part till one drop down a corse.
O that Glendower were come!

**VERNON**     There is more news.
I learned in Worcester, as I rode along,
He cannot draw his power this fourteen days. 12

**DOUGLAS**
That's the worst tidings that I hear of yet.

**WORCESTER**
Ay, by my faith, that bears a frosty sound.

**HOTSPUR**
What may the king's whole battle reach unto? 12

**VERNON**
To thirty thousand.

**HOTSPUR**     Forty let it be.
My father and Glendower being both away,
The powers of us may serve so great a day.
Come, let us take a muster speedily.
Doomsday is near. Die all, die merrily.

---

46 *states* estates   47 *main* stake   48 *hazard* (1) peril, (2) dice game   49 *read* learn   50 *soul* (1) essence, (2) sole   51 *list* limit   53 *reversion* future prospects   58 *big* threatening   59 *maidenhead* early phase   61 *hair* nature   62 *Brooks* tolerates   64 *mere* utter   67 *fearful* timid; *faction* conspiracy   70 *arbitrement* scrutiny   71 *loop* loophole   73 *draws* opens   75 *strain* exaggerate   77 *opinion* prestige   80 *make a head* raise a force   92 *intended* intended to come   96 *daffed* thrust   97 *bid it pass* refused to take it seriously; *furnished* fitted out   98 *estridges* ostriches   99 *Bated* fluttered their wings   103 *Wanton* sportive   104 *beaver* i.e. helmet   105 *cushes* armor for the thighs   109 *wind* wheel; *Pegasus* i.e. mettlesome horse (literally, the winged horse of Greek mythology)   110 *witch* charm   112 *agues* (attributed to vapors drawn up by the sun)   113 *trim* decorations   114 *maid* the goddess Bellona   118 *reprisal* prize   119 *taste* feel   126 *draw* muster   129 *battle* army

DOUGLAS

5    Talk not of dying. I am out of fear
     Of death or death's hand for this one half-year.    *Exeunt.*

*

ii        *Enter Falstaff and Bardolph.*

FALSTAFF  Bardolph, get thee before to Coventry; fill me
     a bottle of sack. Our soldiers shall march through. We'll
     to Sutton Co'fil' to-night.

BARDOLPH  Will you give me money, captain?

5  FALSTAFF  Lay out, lay out.

6  BARDOLPH  This bottle makes an angel.

7  FALSTAFF  An if it do, take it for thy labor; an if it make

8    twenty, take them all; I'll answer the coinage. Bid my
     lieutenant Peto meet me at town's end.

BARDOLPH  I will, captain. Farewell.          *Exit.*

FALSTAFF  If I be not ashamed of my soldiers, I am a

12   soused gurnet. I have misused the king's press dam-

13   nably. I have got, in exchange of a hundred and fifty

14   soldiers, three hundred and odd pounds. I press me
     none but good householders, yeomen's sons; inquire
     me out contracted bachelors, such as had been asked

17   twice on the banes – such a commodity of warm slaves
     as had as lieve hear the devil as a drum, such as fear the

19   report of a caliver worse than a struck fowl or a hurt
     wild duck. I pressed me none but such toasts-and-
     butter, with hearts in their bellies no bigger than pins'

22   heads, and they have bought out their services; and

23   now my whole charge consists of ancients, corporals,

24   lieutenants, gentlemen of companies – slaves as ragged

25   as Lazarus in the painted cloth, where the glutton's
     dogs licked his sores; and such as indeed were never

27   soldiers, but discarded unjust servingmen, younger

28   sons to younger brothers, revolted tapsters, and

29   ostlers trade-fall'n; the cankers of a calm world and a
     long peace; ten times more dishonorable ragged than an

30   old fazed ancient; and such have I to fill up the rooms of
     them as have bought out their services that you would
     think that I had a hundred and fifty tattered prodigals

33   lately come from swine-keeping, from eating draff and
     husks. A mad fellow met me on the way, and told me I
     had unloaded all the gibbets and pressed the dead
     bodies. No eye hath seen such scarecrows. I'll not
     march through Coventry with them, that's flat. Nay,
     and the villains march wide betwixt the legs, as if they
     had gyves on, for indeed I had the most of them out of
     prison. There's not a shirt and a half in all my company,

and the half-shirt is two napkins tacked together and
thrown over the shoulders like a herald's coat without
sleeves; and the shirt, to say the truth, stol'n from my
host at Saint Alban's, or the red-nose innkeeper of
Daventry. But that's all one; they'll find linen enough
on every hedge.

*Enter the Prince and the Lord of Westmoreland.*

PRINCE  How now, blown Jack? How now, quilt?

FALSTAFF  What, Hal? How now, mad wag? What a devil
     dost thou in Warwickshire? My good Lord of West-
     moreland, I cry you mercy. I thought your honor had  49
     already been at Shrewsbury.

WESTMORELAND  Faith, Sir John, 'tis more than time
     that I were there, and you too, but my powers are there
     already. The king, I can tell you, looks for us all. We
     must away all night.          54

FALSTAFF  Tut, never fear me: I am as vigilant as a cat to  55
     steal cream.

PRINCE  I think, to steal cream indeed, for thy theft hath
     already made thee butter. But tell me, Jack, whose
     fellows are these that come after?

FALSTAFF  Mine, Hal, mine.

PRINCE  I did never see such pitiful rascals.

FALSTAFF  Tut, tut! good enough to toss; food for  62
     powder, food for powder. They'll fill a pit as well as
     better. Tush, man, mortal men, mortal men.

WESTMORELAND  Ay, but, Sir John, methinks they are
     exceeding poor and bare – too beggarly.

FALSTAFF  Faith, for their poverty, I know not where
     they had that, and for their bareness, I am sure they
     never learned that of me.

PRINCE  No, I'll be sworn, unless you call three fingers in
     the ribs bare. But, sirrah, make haste. Percy is already
     in the field.          *Exit.*

FALSTAFF  What, is the king encamped?

WESTMORELAND  He is, Sir John. I fear we shall stay
     too long.          *[Exit.]*

FALSTAFF  Well, to the latter end of a fray and the be-
     ginning of a feast fits a dull fighter and a keen guest.
                         *Exit.*

*

*Enter Hotspur, Worcester, Douglas, Vernon.*          IV, iii

HOTSPUR
     We'll fight with him to-night.

WORCESTER                    It may not be.

DOUGLAS
     You give him then advantage.

VERNON                    Not a whit.

HOTSPUR
     Why say you so? Looks he not for supply?          3

VERNON
     So do we.

HOTSPUR  His is certain, ours is doubtful.

WORCESTER
     Good cousin, be advised; stir not to-night.          5

VERNON
     Do not, my lord.

DOUGLAS          You do not counsel well.
     You speak it out of fear and cold heart.

VERNON
     Do me no slander, Douglas. By my life –
     And I dare well maintain it with my life –
     If well-respected honor bid me on,          10

135 *out of* free from
IV, ii The road to Coventry  5 *Lay out* put up the money yourself  6
*angel* 10 shillings  7 *An . . . do* (Falstaff pretends that Bardolph speaks of
coining angels)  8 *answer* be responsible for  12 *soused gurnet* pickled fish;
*press* right of conscription  13 *in exchange of* i.e. for letting off (150 con-
scripts)  14 *press* draft  17 *banes* banns (public announcement of intent
to marry, made three times); *warm* well-to-do  19 *caliver* musket  22
*bought . . . services* i.e. bribed me to let them stay at home  23 *charge* company; *ancients* ensigns (Falstaff has signed on a disproportionate number of
his recruits as officers in order to collect, and appropriate, their higher pay)
24 *gentlemen of companies* gentlemen volunteers  25 *Lazarus* the beggar in
the parable (Luke xvi, 19–31); *painted cloth* wall-hangings  27 *unjust*
dishonest  28 *revolted* runaway  29 *trade-fall'n* out of work; *cankers*
cankerworms  30 *fazed ancient* frayed flag  33 *draff* garbage  49 *cry you*
*mercy* beg your pardon  54 *must away* must march  55 *fear* worry about;
*vigilant* wakeful  62 *toss* i.e. on a pike
IV, iii The rebel camp  3 *supply* reinforcements  5 *be advised* listen to
reason  10 *well-respected* well-considered

I hold as little counsel with weak fear
As you, my lord, or any Scot that this day lives.
Let it be seen to-morrow in the battle
Which of us fears.

DOUGLAS     Yea, or to-night.

VERNON     Content.

HOTSPUR
To-night, say I.

VERNON
Come, come, it may not be. I wonder much,
17 Being men of such great leading as you are,
That you foresee not what impediments
19 Drag back our expedition. Certain horse
Of my cousin Vernon's are not yet come up.
Your uncle Worcester's horse came but to-day;
22 And now their pride and mettle is asleep,
Their courage with hard labor tame and dull,
That not a horse is half the half of himself.

HOTSPUR
So are the horses of the enemy
26 In general journey-bated and brought low.
The better part of ours are full of rest.

WORCESTER
The number of the king exceedeth ours.
For God's sake, cousin, stay till all come in.
*The trumpet sounds a parley.*
*Enter Sir Walter Blunt.*

BLUNT
I come with gracious offers from the king,
31 If you vouchsafe me hearing and respect.

HOTSPUR
Welcome, Sir Walter Blunt, and would to God
33 You were of our determination.
Some of us love you well; and even those some
Envy your great deservings and good name,
36 Because you are not of our quality,
But stand against us like an enemy.

BLUNT
38 And God defend but still I should stand so,
39 So long as out of limit and true rule
You stand against anointed majesty.
But to my charge. The king hath sent to know
The nature of your griefs, and whereupon
43 You conjure from the breast of civil peace
Such bold hostility, teaching his duteous land
Audacious cruelty. If that the king
Have any way your good deserts forgot,
Which he confesseth to be manifold,
He bids you name your griefs, and with all speed
You shall have your desires with interest,
And pardon absolute for yourself and these
51 Herein misled by your suggestion.

HOTSPUR
The king is kind, and well we know the king
Knows at what time to promise, when to pay.
My father and my uncle and myself
Did give him that same royalty he wears;
And when he was not six-and-twenty strong,
Sick in the world's regard, wretched and low,
A poor unminded outlaw sneaking home,
My father gave him welcome to the shore;
And when he heard him swear and vow to God
He came but to be Duke of Lancaster,
62 To sue his livery and beg his peace,

With tears of innocency and terms of zeal,
My father, in kind heart and pity moved,
Swore him assistance, and performed it too.
Now when the lords and barons of the realm
Perceived Northumberland did lean to him,
The more and less came in with cap and knee; 68
Met him in boroughs, cities, villages,
Attended him on bridges, stood in lanes, 70
Laid gifts before him, proffered him their oaths,
Gave him their heirs as pages, followed him
Even at the heels in golden multitudes. 73
He presently, as greatness knows itself, 74
Steps me a little higher than his vow
Made to my father, while his blood was poor, 76
Upon the naked shore at Ravenspurgh;
And now, forsooth, takes on him to reform 78
Some certain edicts and some strait decrees 79
That lie too heavy on the commonwealth;
Cries out upon abuses, seems to weep 81
Over his country's wrongs; and by this face, 82
This seeming brow of justice, did he win
The hearts of all that he did angle for;
Proceeded further—cut me off the heads 85
Of all the favorites that the absent king
In deputation left behind him here 87
When he was personal in the Irish war.

BLUNT
Tut! I came not to hear this.

HOTSPUR     Then to the point.
In short time after, he deposed the king;
Soon after that deprived him of his life;
And in the neck of that tasked the whole state; 92
To make that worse, suff'red his kinsman March
(Who is, if every owner were well placed,
Indeed his king) to be engaged in Wales, 95
There without ransom to lie forfeited;
Disgraced me in my happy victories, 97
Sought to entrap me by intelligence; 98
Rated mine uncle from the council board; 99
In rage dismissed my father from the court;
Broke oath on oath, committed wrong on wrong;
And in conclusion drove us to seek out
This head of safety, and withal to pry 10
Into his title, the which we find
Too indirect for long continuance.

BLUNT
Shall I return this answer to the king?

HOTSPUR
Not so, Sir Walter. We'll withdraw awhile.
Go to the king; and let there be impawned 10
Some surety for a safe return again,
And in the morning early shall mine uncle
Bring him our purposes; and so farewell.

17 *leading* leadership    19 *expedition* progress    22 *pride* mettle    26 *journey-bated* wearied    31 *respect* attention    33 *determination* mind    36 *quality* party    38 *defend* forbid    39 *rule* conduct    43 *civil* orderly    51 *suggestion* instigation    62 *sue his livery* sue as heir for his inheritance    68 *more and less* great and small    70 *stood in lanes* lined the roads    73 *golden* richly dressed    74 *knows itself* feels its own strength    76 *blood* spirit    78 *forsooth* (ironical)    79 *strait* strict    81 *Cries out upon* denounces    82 *face* pretext    85 *cut . . . heads* (see *Richard II*, III, i); *me* (ethical dative)    87 *In deputation* as deputies    92 *in the neck of* immediately after; *tasked* taxed    95 *engaged* held as hostage    97 *happy* fortunate    98 *intelligence* espionage    99 *Rated* scolded    103 *head* army; *withal* at the same time    108 *impawned* pledged

BLUNT
I would you would accept of grace and love.
HOTSPUR
And may be so we shall.
BLUNT                    Pray God you do.    *Exeunt.*

\*

iv        *Enter the Archbishop of York and Sir Michael.*
ARCHBISHOP
1  Hie, good Sir Michael; bear this sealèd brief
2  With wingèd haste to the lord marshal;
3  This to my cousin Scroop; and all the rest
To whom they are directed. If you knew
How much they do import, you would make haste.
SIR MICHAEL
My good lord,
I guess their tenor.
ARCHBISHOP        Like enough you do.
To-morrow, good Sir Michael, is a day
Wherein the fortune of ten thousand men
10  Must bide the touch; for, sir, at Shrewsbury,
As I am truly given to understand,
The king with mighty and quick-raisèd power
Meets with Lord Harry; and I fear, Sir Michael,
What with the sickness of Northumberland,
15  Whose power was in the first proportion,
And what with Owen Glendower's absence thence,
17  Who with them was a rated sinew too
And comes not in, overruled by prophecies –
I fear the power of Percy is too weak
20  To wage an instant trial with the king.
SIR MICHAEL
Why, my good lord, you need not fear;
There is Douglas and Lord Mortimer.
ARCHBISHOP
No, Mortimer is not there.
SIR MICHAEL
But there is Mordake, Vernon, Lord Harry Percy,
25  And there is my Lord of Worcester, and a head
Of gallant warriors, noble gentlemen.
ARCHBISHOP
And so there is; but yet the king hath drawn
The special head of all the land together –
The Prince of Wales, Lord John of Lancaster,
The noble Westmoreland and warlike Blunt,
31  And many moe corrivals and dear men
Of estimation and command in arms.
SIR MICHAEL
Doubt not, my lord, they shall be well opposed.
ARCHBISHOP
I hope no less, yet needful 'tis to fear;

IV, iv The palace of the Archbishop of York  1 *brief* letter  2 *lord marshal*
Thomas Mowbray, son of the Duke of Norfolk (*Richard II*, I, i, iii), an
inveterate enemy of the king  3 *Scroop* possibly Lord Scroop of Masham,
the archbishop's nephew, later executed for treason (*Henry V*, II, ii)  10
*bide the touch* withstand the test (touchstone)  15 *proportion* magnitude
17 *rated sinew* mainstay they counted on  20 *wage* risk; *instant* immediate
25 *head* force  31 *moe* more; *corrivals* partners, allies  36 *thrive* succeed
38 *confederacy* conspiracy
V, i The royal camp at Shrewsbury  3 *distemp'rature* unhealthy appearance
4 *trumpet* trumpeter  7 *sympathize* accord  8 *foul* i.e. foul weather  17
*obedient orb* orb of obedience  19 *exhaled meteor* vapor drawn up by the
sun (visible as streaks of light), regarded as an omen (*prodigy*)  24 *entertain* occupy, while away  26 *dislike* discord  29 *chewet* chatterer  32
*remember* remind  35 *posted* rode at top speed  40 *outdare* defy

And, to prevent the worst, Sir Michael, speed.
For if Lord Percy thrive not, ere the king    36
Dismiss his power, he means to visit us,
For he hath heard of our confederacy,         38
And 'tis but wisdom to make strong against him.
Therefore make haste. I must go write again
To other friends; and so farewell, Sir Michael.  *Exeunt.*

\*

*Enter the King, Prince of Wales, Lord John of*    V, i
*Lancaster, Sir Walter Blunt, Falstaff.*
KING
How bloodily the sun begins to peer
Above yon bulky hill! The day looks pale
At his distemp'rature.                         3
PRINCE              The southern wind
Doth play the trumpet to his purposes          4
And by his hollow whistling in the leaves
Foretells a tempest and a blust'ring day.
KING
Then with the losers let it sympathize,        7
For nothing can seem foul to those that win.   8
    *The trumpet sounds. Enter Worcester [and Vernon].*
How now, my Lord of Worcester? 'Tis not well
That you and I should meet upon such terms
As now we meet. You have deceived our trust
And made us doff our easy robes of peace
To crush our old limbs in ungentle steel.
This is not well, my lord; this is not well.
What say you to it? Will you again unknit
This churlish knot of all-abhorrèd war,
And move in that obedient orb again            17
Where you did give a fair and natural light,
And be no more an exhaled meteor,              19
A prodigy of fear, and a portent
Of broachèd mischief to the unborn times?
WORCESTER
Hear me, my liege.
For mine own part, I could be well content
To entertain the lag-end of my life            24
With quiet hours, for I do protest
I have not sought the day of this dislike.     26
KING
You have not sought it! How comes it then?
FALSTAFF
Rebellion lay in his way, and he found it.
PRINCE
Peace, chewet, peace!                          29
WORCESTER
It pleased your majesty to turn your looks
Of favor from myself and all our house;
And yet I must remember you, my lord,          32
We were the first and dearest of your friends.
For you my staff of office did I break
In Richard's time, and posted day and night    35
To meet you on the way and kiss your hand
When yet you were in place and in account
Nothing so strong and fortunate as I.
It was myself, my brother, and his son
That brought you home and boldly did outdare    40
The dangers of the time. You swore to us,
And you did swear that oath at Doncaster,
That you did nothing purpose 'gainst the state,

44 Nor claim no further than your new-fall'n right,
The seat of Gaunt, dukedom of Lancaster.
To this we swore our aid. But in short space
It rained down fortune show'ring on your head,
And such a flood of greatness fell on you –
What with our help, what with the absent king,
50 What with the injuries of a wanton time,
51 The seeming sufferances that you had borne,
And the contrarious winds that held the king
So long in his unlucky Irish wars
That all in England did repute him dead –
And from this swarm of fair advantages
You took occasion to be quickly wooed
57 To gripe the general sway into your hand;
Forgot your oath to us at Doncaster;
And, being fed by us, you used us so
60 As that ungentle gull, the cuckoo's bird,
Useth the sparrow – did oppress our nest;
Grew by our feeding to so great a bulk
That even our love durst not come near your sight
For fear of swallowing; but with nimble wing
We were enforced for safety sake to fly
66 Out of your sight and raise this present head;
Whereby we stand opposèd by such means
As you yourself have forged against yourself
69 By unkind usage, dangerous countenance,
70 And violation of all faith and troth
Sworn to us in your younger enterprise.

KING

72 These things, indeed, you have articulate,
Proclaimed at market crosses, read in churches,
74 To face the garment of rebellion
75 With some fine color that may please the eye
76 Of fickle changelings and poor discontents,
Which gape and rub the elbow at the news
Of hurlyburly innovation.
And never yet did insurrection want
80 Such water colors to impaint his cause,
Nor moody beggars, starving for a time
Of pell-mell havoc and confusion.

PRINCE

In both your armies there is many a soul
Shall pay full dearly for this encounter,
If once they join in trial. Tell your nephew
The Prince of Wales doth join with all the world
87 In praise of Henry Percy. By my hopes,
88 This present enterprise set off his head,
I do not think a braver gentleman,
More active-valiant or more valiant-young,
More daring or more bold, is now alive
To grace this latter age with noble deeds.
For my part, I may speak it to my shame,
I have a truant been to chivalry;
And so I hear he doth account me too.
Yet this before my father's majesty –
I am content that he shall take the odds
98 Of his great name and estimation,
And will, to save the blood on either side,
Try fortune with him in a single fight.

KING

101 And, Prince of Wales, so dare we venture thee,
102 Albeit considerations infinite
Do make against it. No, good Worcester, no!
We love our people well; even those we love

That are misled upon your cousin's part;
And, will they take the offer of our grace,
Both he, and they, and you, yea, every man
Shall be my friend again, and I'll be his.
So tell your cousin, and bring me word
What he will do. But if he will not yield,
Rebuke and dread correction wait on us, 111
And they shall do their office. So be gone.
We will not now be troubled with reply.
We offer fair; take it advisedly.

*Exit Worcester [with Vernon].*

PRINCE

It will not be accepted, on my life.
The Douglas and the Hotspur both together
Are confident against the world in arms.

KING

Hence, therefore, every leader to his charge;
For, on their answer, will we set on them,
And God befriend us as our cause is just!

*Exeunt. Manent Prince, Falstaff.*

FALSTAFF Hal, if thou see me down in the battle and
bestride me, so! 'Tis a point of friendship. 122

PRINCE Nothing but a colossus can do thee that friendship. Say thy prayers, and farewell. 124

FALSTAFF I would 'twere bedtime, Hal, and all well.

PRINCE Why, thou owest God a death. *[Exit.]*

FALSTAFF 'Tis not due yet: I would be loath to pay him
before his day. What need I be so forward with him that
calls not on me? Well, 'tis no matter; honor pricks me 129
on. Yea, but how if honor prick me off when I come on? 130
How then? Can honor set to a leg? No. Or an arm? No. 131
Or take away the grief of a wound? No. Honor hath no
skill in surgery then? No. What is honor? A word. What
is that word honor? Air – a trim reckoning! Who hath
it? He that died a Wednesday. Doth he feel it? No. Doth
he hear it? No. 'Tis insensible then? Yea, to the dead. 136
But will it not live with the living? No. Why? Detrac-
tion will not suffer it. Therefore I'll none of it. Honor is
a mere scutcheon – and so ends my catechism. *Exit.* 139

*

*Enter Worcester and Sir Richard Vernon.* V,

WORCESTER

O no, my nephew must not know, Sir Richard,
The liberal and kind offer of the king.

VERNON

'Twere best he did.

WORCESTER Then are we all undone.
It is not possible, it cannot be,
The king should keep his word in loving us.
He will suspect us still and find a time 6

44 *new-fall'n* lately inherited  50 *injuries* evils; *wanton* disordered  51
*sufferances* sufferings  57 *gripe* seize  60 *ungentle* rude; *gull* unfledged
bird  66 *head* armed force  69 *dangerous* threatening  70 *troth* truth
72 *articulate* specified  74 *face* trim  75 *color* i.e. excuse  76 *changelings*
turncoats  80 *water colors* i.e. thin pretexts  87 *hopes* i.e. of salvation
88 *set . . . head* not charged to his account  98 *estimation* reputation  101
*dare* would dare  102 *Albeit* were it not that  111 *wait* attend  122 *so
good*  124 *Say thy prayers* prepare for death  129 *calls . . . me* doesn't
demand payment  130 *prick me off* check me off  131 *set to* graft on  136
*insensible* imperceptible to the senses  139 *scutcheon* coat of arms borne at a
funeral
V, ii The battlefield at Shrewsbury  6 *still* constantly

To punish this offense in other faults.

8  Supposition all our lives shall be stuck full of eyes;
For treason is but trusted like the fox,
Who, ne'er so tame, so cherished and locked up,

11  Will have a wild trick of his ancestors.
Look how we can, or sad or merrily,
Interpretation will misquote our looks,
And we shall feed like oxen at a stall,

15  The better cherished still the nearer death.
My nephew's trespass may be well forgot;
It hath the excuse of youth and heat of blood,
And an adopted name of privilege –

19  A hare-brained Hotspur, governed by a spleen.
All his offenses live upon my head

21  And on his father's. We did train him on;

22  And, his corruption being ta'en from us,
We, as the spring of all, shall pay for all.
Therefore, good cousin, let not Harry know,
In any case, the offer of the king.

     *Enter Hotspur [and Douglas].*

VERNON

26  Deliver what you will, I'll say 'tis so.
Here comes your cousin.

HOTSPUR           My uncle is returned.
Deliver up my Lord of Westmoreland.
Uncle, what news?

WORCESTER

The king will bid you battle presently.

DOUGLAS

Defy him by the Lord of Westmoreland.

HOTSPUR

Lord Douglas, go you and tell him so.

DOUGLAS

Marry, and shall, and very willingly.      *Exit.*

WORCESTER

There is no seeming mercy in the king.

HOTSPUR

Did you beg any? God forbid!

WORCESTER

I told him gently of our grievances,

37  Of his oath-breaking, which he mended thus,

38  By now forswearing that he is forsworn.
He calls us rebels, traitors, and will scourge
With haughty arms this hateful name in us.

     *Enter Douglas.*

DOUGLAS

Arm, gentlemen! to arms! for I have thrown

42  A brave defiance in King Henry's teeth,

43  And Westmoreland, that was engaged, did bear it;
Which cannot choose but bring him quickly on.

WORCESTER

The Prince of Wales stepped forth before the king
And, nephew, challenged you to single fight.

HOTSPUR

O, would the quarrel lay upon our heads,
And that no man might draw short breath to-day
But I and Harry Monmouth! Tell me, tell me,
How showed his tasking? Seemed it in contempt?    50

VERNON

No, by my soul. I never in my life
Did hear a challenge urged more modestly,
Unless a brother should a brother dare
To gentle exercise and proof of arms.
He gave you all the duties of a man;       55
Trimmed up your praises with a princely tongue;   56
Spoke your deservings like a chronicle;
Making you ever better than his praise
By still dispraising praise valued with you;     59
And, which became him like a prince indeed,
He made a blushing cital of himself,       61
And chid his truant youth with such a grace
As if he mast'red there a double spirit
Of teaching and of learning instantly.       64
There did he pause; but let me tell the world,
If he outlive the envy of this day,       66
England did never owe so sweet a hope,     67
So much misconstrued in his wantonness.    68

HOTSPUR

Cousin, I think thou art enamorèd
Upon his follies. Never did I hear
Of any prince so wild a liberty.        71
But be he as he will, yet once ere night
I will embrace him with a soldier's arm,
That he shall shrink under my courtesy.
Arm, arm with speed! and, fellows, soldiers, friends,
Better consider what you have to do
Than I, that have not well the gift of tongue,
Can lift your blood up with persuasion.

     *Enter a Messenger.*

MESSENGER

My lord, here are letters for you.

HOTSPUR

I cannot read them now. –
O gentlemen, the time of life is short!
To spend that shortness basely were too long
If life did ride upon a dial's point,       83
Still ending at the arrival of an hour.      84
An if we live, we live to tread on kings;
If die, brave death, when princes die with us!    86
Now for our consciences, the arms are fair,
When the intent of bearing them is just.

     *Enter another Messenger.*

MESSENGER

My lord, prepare. The king comes on apace.

HOTSPUR

I thank him that he cuts me from my tale,
For I profess not talking. Only this –
Let each man do his best; and here draw I
A sword whose temper I intend to stain
With the best blood that I can meet withal
In the adventure of this perilous day.
Now, Esperancè! Percy! and set on.      95
Sound all the lofty instruments of war,     96
And by that music let us all embrace;
For, heaven to earth, some of us never shall
A second time do such a courtesy.

     *Here they embrace. The trumpets sound.*    [*Exeunt.*]

---

8 *Supposition* suspicious conjecture   11 *wild trick* trait of wildness   15 *cherished* fed   19 *spleen* fiery temper   21 *train* lure   22 *corruption* guilt; *ta'en* contracted   26 *Deliver* report   37 *mended* made up for   38 *forswearing* denying; *is forsworn* has repudiated (his oath)   42 *brave* haughty   43 *engaged* held as hostage   50 *tasking* challenge   55 *duties* due merits   56 *Trimmed up* adorned   59 *valued* compared   61 *cital* (1) citation, (2) impeachment   64 *instantly* simultaneously   66 *envy* malice   67 *owe* own   68 *wantonness* sportiveness   71 *liberty* licentiousness   83 *If* even if; *dial's* clock's   84 *Still . . . hour* i.e. if life were only an hour long; *Still* inevitably   86 *brave* glorious   95 *adventure* hazard   96 *Esperancè* hope (the Percy battle-cry)

V, iii        *The King enters with his power. Alarum to the battle.*
*[Exeunt.] Then enter Douglas and Sir Walter Blunt.*

BLUNT
What is thy name, that in battle thus
Thou crossest me? What honor dost thou seek
Upon my head?
DOUGLAS            Know then my name is Douglas,
And I do haunt thee in the battle thus
Because some tell me that thou art a king.
BLUNT
They tell thee true.
DOUGLAS
The Lord of Stafford dear to-day hath bought
Thy likeness, for instead of thee, King Harry,
This sword hath ended him. So shall it thee,
10   Unless thou yield thee as my prisoner.
BLUNT
I was not born a yielder, thou proud Scot;
And thou shalt find a king that will revenge
Lord Stafford's death.
      *They fight. Douglas kills Blunt. Then enter Hotspur.*
HOTSPUR O Douglas, hadst thou fought at Holmedon
thus, I never had triumphed upon a Scot.
DOUGLAS
All's done, all's won. Here breathless lies the king.
HOTSPUR Where?
DOUGLAS Here.
HOTSPUR
This, Douglas? No. I know this face full well.
A gallant knight he was, his name was Blunt;
21   Semblably furnished like the king himself.
DOUGLAS
22   A fool go with thy soul, whither it goes!
A borrowed title hast thou bought too dear:
Why didst thou tell me that thou wert a king?
HOTSPUR
The king hath many marching in his coats.
DOUGLAS
Now, by my sword, I will kill all his coats;
I'll murder all his wardrobe, piece by piece,
Until I meet the king.
HOTSPUR            Up and away!
29   Our soldiers stand full fairly for the day.      *Exeunt.*
      *Alarum. Enter Falstaff solus.*
30 FALSTAFF Though I could scape shot-free at London, I
31   fear the shot here. Here's no scoring but upon the pate.
Soft! who are you? Sir Walter Blunt. There's honor for
33   you! Here's no vanity! I am as hot as molten lead, and as
heavy too. God keep lead out of me. I need no more
weight than mine own bowels. I have led my rag-of-
36   muffins where they are peppered. There's not three of
my hundred and fifty left alive, and they are for the
town's end, to beg during life. But who comes here?
      *Enter the Prince.*
PRINCE
What, stand'st thou idle here? Lend me thy sword.
Many a nobleman lies stark and stiff
Under the hoofs of vaunting enemies,
Whose deaths are yet unrevenged. I prithee
Lend me thy sword.
FALSTAFF O Hal, I prithee give me leave to breathe
45   awhile. Turk Gregory never did such deeds in arms as I
46   have done this day. I have paid Percy; I have made him
sure.

PRINCE
He is indeed, and living to kill thee.                        47
I prithee lend me thy sword.
FALSTAFF Nay, before God, Hal, if Percy be alive, thou
get'st not my sword; but take my pistol, if thou wilt.
PRINCE Give it me. What, is it in the case?
FALSTAFF Ay, Hal. 'Tis hot, 'tis hot. There's that will
sack a city.
      *The Prince draws it out and finds it to be a bottle of*
      *sack.*
PRINCE
What, is it a time to jest and dally now?
      *He throws the bottle at him.*            *Exit.*
FALSTAFF Well, if Percy be alive, I'll pierce him. If he do 55
come in my way, so; if he do not, if I come in his will-
ingly, let him make a carbonado of me. I like not such 57
grinning honor as Sir Walter hath. Give me life; which
if I can save, so; if not, honor comes unlooked for, and
there's an end.                                              *Exit.*
      *Alarum. Excursions. Enter the King, the Prince, Lord* V,
      *John of Lancaster, Earl of Westmoreland.*
KING
I prithee, Harry, withdraw thyself; thou bleedest too
much.
Lord John of Lancaster, go you with him.
JOHN
Not I, my lord, unless I did bleed too.
PRINCE
I do beseech your majesty make up,                          4
Lest your retirement do amaze your friends.                 5
KING
I will do so.
My Lord of Westmoreland, lead him to his tent.
WESTMORELAND
Come, my lord, I'll lead you to your tent.
PRINCE
Lead me, my lord? I do not need your help;
And God forbid a shallow scratch should drive
The Prince of Wales from such a field as this,
Where stained nobility lies trodden on,
And rebels' arms triumph in massacres!
JOHN
We breathe too long. Come, cousin Westmoreland,
Our duty this way lies. For God's sake, come.
      *[Exeunt Prince John and Westmoreland.]*
PRINCE
By God, thou hast deceived me, Lancaster!
I did not think thee lord of such a spirit.
Before, I loved thee as a brother, John;
But now, I do respect thee as my soul.                      19
KING
I saw him hold Lord Percy at the point
With lustier maintenance than I did look for                21
Of such an ungrown warrior.
PRINCE            O, this boy
Lends mettle to us all!                                     *Exit.*

V, iii  s.d. *Alarum* signal to advance  21 *Semblably furnished* similarly
equipped  22 *A . . . soul* i.e. you are a fool  29 *fairly* auspiciously; *day*
victory  30 *shot-free* without paying bills  31 *scoring* (1) cutting, (2)
chalking up a debt  33 *Here's no vanity* (ironical) here's no empty honor
36 *peppered* done for  45 *Turk Gregory* a ferocious tyrant (invented by
Falstaff)  46 *made him sure* destroyed him  47 *indeed* i.e. sure (safe)  55
*pierce* pronounced 'perce'  57 *carbonado* broiled steak
V, iv  s.d. *Excursions* sorties  4 *make up* advance  5 *amaze* bewilder  19
*respect* regard  21 *lustier maintenance* more vigorous bearing

*[Enter Douglas.]*

DOUGLAS

24   Another king? They grow like Hydra's heads.
I am the Douglas, fatal to all those
That wear those colors on them. What art thou
That counterfeit'st the person of a king?

KING

The king himself, who, Douglas, grieves at heart
29   So many of his shadows thou hast met,
And not the very king. I have two boys
Seek Percy and thyself about the field;
But, seeing thou fall'st on me so luckily,
33   I will assay thee. So defend thyself.

DOUGLAS

I fear thou art another counterfeit;
And yet, in faith, thou bearest thee like a king.
But mine I am sure thou art, whoe'er thou be,
And thus I win thee.

*They fight. The King being in danger, enter Prince of
Wales.*

PRINCE

Hold up thy head, vile Scot, or thou art like
Never to hold it up again. The spirits
Of valiant Shirley, Stafford, Blunt are in my arms.
It is the Prince of Wales that threatens thee,
Who never promiseth but he means to pay.

*They fight. Douglas flieth.*

43   Cheerly, my lord. How fares your grace?
Sir Nicholas Gawsey hath for succor sent,
And so hath Clifton. I'll to Clifton straight.

KING

Stay and breathe awhile.
47   Thou hast redeemed thy lost opinion,
48   And showed thou mak'st some tender of my life,
In this fair rescue thou hast brought to me.

PRINCE

O God, they did me too much injury
51   That ever said I heark'ned for your death.
If it were so, I might have let alone
53   The insulting hand of Douglas over you,
Which would have been as speedy in your end
As all the poisonous potions in the world,
And saved the treacherous labor of your son.

KING

Make up to Clifton; I'll to Sir Nicholas Gawsey.   *Exit.*
*Enter Hotspur.*

HOTSPUR

If I mistake not, thou art Harry Monmouth.

PRINCE

Thou speak'st as if I would deny my name.

HOTSPUR

My name is Harry Percy.

PRINCE                         Why, then I see
A very valiant rebel of the name.

I am the Prince of Wales, and think not, Percy,
To share with me in glory any more.
Two stars keep not their motion in one sphere,          64
Nor can one England brook a double reign          65
Of Harry Percy and the Prince of Wales.

HOTSPUR

Nor shall it, Harry, for the hour is come
To end the one of us; and would to God
Thy name in arms were now as great as mine!

PRINCE

I'll make it greater ere I part from thee,
And all the budding honors on thy crest          71
I'll crop to make a garland for my head.

HOTSPUR

I can no longer brook thy vanities.          73
*They fight. Enter Falstaff.*

FALSTAFF   Well said, Hal! to it, Hal! Nay, you shall find   74
no boy's play here, I can tell you.
*Enter Douglas. He fighteth with Falstaff, who falls
down as if he were dead. [Exit Douglas.] The Prince
killeth Percy.*

HOTSPUR

O Harry, thou hast robbed me of my youth!
I better brook the loss of brittle life
Than those proud titles thou hast won of me.
They wound my thoughts worse than thy sword my
flesh.
But thoughts the slaves of life, and life time's fool,          80
And time, that takes survey of all the world,          81
Must have a stop. O, I could prophesy,
But that the earthy and cold hand of death
Lies on my tongue. No, Percy, thou art dust,
And food for –
*[Dies.]*

PRINCE

For worms, brave Percy. Fare thee well, great heart.
Ill-weaved ambition, how much art thou shrunk!
When that this body did contain a spirit,
A kingdom for it was too small a bound;
But now two paces of the vilest earth
Is room enough. This earth that bears thee dead
Bears not alive so stout a gentleman.
If thou wert sensible of courtesy,          93
I should not make so dear a show of zeal.          94
But let my favors hide thy mangled face;          95
And, even in thy behalf, I'll thank myself
For doing these fair rites of tenderness.
Adieu, and take thy praise with thee to heaven.
Thy ignominy sleep with thee in the grave,
But not rememb'red in thy epitaph.
*He spieth Falstaff on the ground.*
What, old acquaintance? Could not all this flesh
Keep in a little life? Poor Jack, farewell!
I could have better spared a better man.
O, I should have a heavy miss of thee          104
If I were much in love with vanity.          105
Death hath not struck so fat a deer to-day,
Though many dearer, in this bloody fray.
Embowelled will I see thee by-and-by;          108
Till then in blood by noble Percy lie.          *Exit.*
*Falstaff riseth up.*

FALSTAFF   Embowelled? If thou embowel me to-day, I'll
give you leave to powder me and eat me too to-morrow.   111
'Sblood, 'twas time to counterfeit, or that hot termagant   112

---

24 *Hydra's heads* (as soon as one was cut off, two others grew in its place)
29 *shadows* likenesses   33 *assay* challenge to trial   43 *Cheerly* cheer up
47 *redeemed* regained; *opinion* good name   48 *mak'st some tender of* have
some regard for   51 *heark'ned* waited   53 *insulting* exulting   64 *sphere*
orbit   65 *brook* endure   71 *crest* helmet   73 *vanities* boasts   74 *Well said*
well done   80 *fool* dupe, plaything   81 *takes survey of* oversees   93
*sensible* able to feel   94 *dear* heartfelt; *zeal* admiration   95 *favors* plumes
(of his helmet)   104 *have . . . thee* (1) miss you sadly, (2) miss something
heavy   105 *vanity* frivolity   108 *Embowelled* eviscerated (the first step in
embalming)   111 *powder* pickle in brine   112 *termagant* violent

113 Scot had paid me scot and lot too. Counterfeit? I lie; I am no counterfeit. To die is to be a counterfeit, for he is but the counterfeit of a man who hath not the life of a man; but to counterfeit dying when a man thereby liveth, is to be no counterfeit, but the true and perfect

118 image of life indeed. The better part of valor is discretion, in the which better part I have saved my life. Zounds, I am afraid of this gunpowder Percy, though he be dead. How if he should counterfeit too, and rise? By my faith, I am afraid he would prove the better counterfeit. Therefore I'll make him sure; yea, and I'll swear I killed him. Why may not he rise as well as I? Nothing confutes me but eyes, and nobody sees me. Therefore, sirrah [stabs him], with a new wound in your thigh, come you along with me.

> *He takes up Hotspur on his back. Enter Prince, and John of Lancaster.*

PRINCE
128 Come, brother John; full bravely hast thou fleshed
Thy maiden sword.

JOHN                     But, soft! whom have we here?
Did you not tell me this fat man was dead?

PRINCE
I did; I saw him dead,
Breathless and bleeding on the ground. Art thou alive,
133 Or is it fantasy that plays upon our eyesight?
I prithee speak. We will not trust our eyes
Without our ears. Thou art not what thou seem'st.

136 FALSTAFF No, that's certain, I am not a double man; but
137 if I be not Jack Falstaff, then am I a Jack. There is Percy. If your father will do me any honor, so; if not, let him kill the next Percy himself. I look to be either earl or duke, I can assure you.

PRINCE Why, Percy I killed myself, and saw thee dead!

FALSTAFF Didst thou? Lord, Lord, how this world is given to lying. I grant you I was down, and out of breath, and so was he; but we rose both at an instant and fought a long hour by Shrewsbury clock. If I may be believed, so; if not, let them that should reward valor bear the sin upon their own heads. I'll take it upon my death, I gave him this wound in the thigh. If the man were alive and would deny it, zounds! I would make him eat a piece of my sword.

JOHN
This is the strangest tale that ever I heard.

PRINCE
This is the strangest fellow, brother John.
Come, bring your luggage nobly on your back.
153 For my part, if a lie may do thee grace,
I'll gild it with the happiest terms I have.

> *A retreat is sounded.*

The trumpet sounds retreat; the day is ours.
Come, brother, let's to the highest of the field,
To see what friends are living, who are dead.

> *Exeunt [Prince Henry and Prince John].*

FALSTAFF I'll follow, as they say, for reward. He that rewards me, God reward him. If I do grow great, I'll grow
160 less; for I'll purge, and leave sack, and live cleanly, as a nobleman should do.          *Exit [bearing off the body].*

\*

> *The trumpets sound. Enter the King, Prince of Wales,* V, v
> *Lord John of Lancaster, Earl of Westmoreland, with Worcester and Vernon prisoners.*

KING
Thus ever did rebellion find rebuke.
Ill-spirited Worcester, did not we send grace,   2
Pardon, and terms of love to all of you?
And wouldst thou turn our offers contrary?
Misuse the tenor of thy kinsman's trust?
Three knights upon our party slain to-day,
A noble earl, and many a creature else
Had been alive this hour,
If like a Christian thou hadst truly borne
Betwixt our armies true intelligence.

WORCESTER
What I have done my safety urged me to;
And I embrace this fortune patiently,           12
Since not to be avoided it falls on me.

KING
Bear Worcester to the death, and Vernon too;
Other offenders we will pause upon.
> *[Exeunt Worcester and Vernon, guarded.]*
How goes the field?

PRINCE
The noble Scot, Lord Douglas, when he saw
The fortune of the day quite turned from him,
The noble Percy slain, and all his men
Upon the foot of fear, fled with the rest;       20
And falling from a hill, he was so bruised
That the pursuers took him. At my tent
The Douglas is, and I beseech your grace
I may dispose of him.

KING                        With all my heart.

PRINCE
Then, brother John of Lancaster, to you
This honorable bounty shall belong.             26
Go to the Douglas and deliver him
Up to his pleasure, ransomless and free.
His valors shown upon our crests to-day
Have taught us how to cherish such high deeds,
Even in the bosom of our adversaries.

JOHN
I thank your grace for this high courtesy,
Which I shall give away immediately.

KING
Then this remains, that we divide our power.
You, son John, and my cousin Westmoreland,
Towards York shall bend you with your dearest speed   36
To meet Northumberland and the prelate Scroop,
Who, as we hear, are busily in arms.
Myself and you, son Harry, will towards Wales
To fight with Glendower and the Earl of March.
Rebellion in this land shall lose his sway,
Meeting the check of such another day;
And since this business so fair is done,
Let us not leave till all our own be won.   *Exeunt.* 44

113 *scot and lot* i.e. thoroughly   118 *part* quality   128 *fleshed* initiated
133 *fantasy* hallucination   136 *double man* (1) spectre, (2) two men   137
*Jack* knave   153 *grace* credit   160 *purge* (1) repent, (2) 'grow less'
V, v The command post of the King   2 *grace* mercy   12 *patiently* with
fortitude   20 *Upon . . . fear* in flight for fear   26 *bounty* benevolence   36
*bend you* direct yourselves   44 *leave* cease

# THE SECOND PART OF
# KING HENRY THE FOURTH

## INTRODUCTION

To Shakespeare and his contemporaries, the history of their country between the accession of Richard II in 1377 and the Battle of Bosworth Field in 1485 provided a double fascination. It was a period of stirring events – of rebellion and counter-rebellion, and of victories over enemies abroad. Shrewsbury and Agincourt were names as familiar and evocative to Shakespeare's audience as are Antietam and Gettysburg to Americans of our own day. Owen Glendower and Harry Hotspur and Henry Bolingbroke were as well-remembered as John Brown and Stonewall Jackson and Ulysses Grant. As with us, the events and the men had been misted over with the passage of time, and the facts of history had been transmuted into tradition and even legend. But to the Elizabethans this period meant something more than romantic history. It served also as a "mirror," as they themselves put it, wherein Elizabeth's England might perceive important truths having to do with theories of government, the responsibility of the monarch, the duty of the subject, and the evil consequences of rebellion.

In the light of this interest, and of the consequent vogue for dramatized history which flourished in the theatres of the 1590's, it is not surprising that Shakespeare wrote no fewer than eight plays dealing with this period of English history. Four of these – the three Henry VI plays and *Richard III* – were written early in his career, but the other four – *Richard II*, the two parts of *Henry IV*, and *Henry V* – belong to the period when his craft as a dramatist and his lordship of language were approaching their full powers. *Richard II* portrayed the weakness and folly of Richard, his forced abdication, the succession of his cousin Henry Bolingbroke as King Henry IV, and finally the murder of Richard at Pomfret Castle. *1 Henry IV* told of the rebellion of those who had aided Henry to the throne and subsequently repented having done so, and of the defeat of the rebels at Shrewsbury; *2 Henry IV* told of the later rebellions, of the death of Henry IV, and of the succession of his son, Prince Hal, as Henry V. *Henry V*, treating of the English victories in France, brought the tetralogy to a close.

The present play, third in the tetralogy, was probably written in the spring of 1598 and produced on the stage immediately thereafter. It was printed in quarto in 1600, with a title page reading as follows: *The Second part of Henrie the fourth, continuing to his death, and coronation of Henrie the fift. With the humours of sir Iohn Falstaffe, and swaggering Pistoll. As it hath been sundrie times publikely acted by the right honourable, the Lord Chamberlaine his seruants. Written by William Shakespeare. London. Printed by V. S. for Andrew Wise, and William Aspley. 1600.* Unlike *1 Henry IV*, which went through six quarto

editions between 1598 and 1622, *2 Henry IV* was not reprinted until it appeared in the First Folio of 1623. Whether it was originally conceived as an afterthought, designed to capitalize upon the great success of its predecessor, or whether Shakespeare had planned from the start two plays on the reign of Henry IV is a point on which authorities differ. In either case the two plays constitute a dramatic entity. When read consecutively, they tell a unified and dramatically satisfying story.

For the principal events and the broad character outlines of the historical personages in the Henry IV plays, Shakespeare drew chiefly upon one of his favorite books – Raphael Holinshed's *Chronicles of the History of England*. He also levied to a certain extent upon other sources. He may have taken a hint or two from the chronicles of Edward Hall and John Stow. Some details of the exploits of the unregenerate Prince Hal he derived from Sir Thomas Elyot's *The Book Named the Governor* and from the old play called *The Famous Victories of Henry V*. In dealing with his source material, Shakespeare worked, here as always in his chronicle plays, as an artist, not as an historian. He telescoped chronology in the interest of compression – the historical period covered in *2 Henry IV* was ten years (1403–13), but the play conveys no impression of this lapse of time. He discarded historical details which were dramatically irrelevant, altered the ages of some of his characters, expanded or suppressed character traits. The result is imperfect history; the modern reader or playgoer derives from the plays only a vague or confused notion of chronology and the order of events. But Shakespeare was not exclusively concerned with what John Drinkwater has called "that vast mutability which is event"; he was concerned also with the wonder of personality and the dramatic interplay of one character with another. And of course with poetry.

In dramatizing the reign of Henry IV, Shakespeare was confronted with the difficulty that the character of the monarch himself was neither winsome nor essentially dramatic. In Richard II, the poet discovered a pathetic, perhaps a tragic figure; Henry IV, despite his grief for the conduct of a wayward son, was neither pathetic nor tragic. Henry V was a military hero; Bolingbroke, despite the victories which won and kept his throne, was not. Moreover, the historical Henry IV did not participate directly in some of the most significant events of the reign. Hence Shakespeare did not attempt to make the king the pivotal figure of the action. He wisely chose to focus much of our attention upon other characters. In *1 Henry IV* his problem was the less by reason of the presence in his sources of certain historical personages of indubitable dramatic value. Prince Hal, the rhapsodic Glendower, the madcap

Harry Percy and his charming wife Kate – these could be developed on the stage as vital figures. Especially Hotspur, whose reckless dedication to his cause made him an admirable foil to the apparently dissolute Hal. The contrast and conflict between the two Harry's becomes the most dramatic element in the play, overshadowing the father-son situation between king and prince, and the audience feels that the play has reached a suitable climax with the death of Hotspur at Shrewsbury Field.

Even so, however, Shakespeare chose not to rely solely upon the historical personages supplied him by the chroniclers. He invented the character of Falstaff, perhaps the most memorable comic character in the whole range of English fiction. The literary historians have taught us that Shakespeare's Falstaff is the culmination of a long tradition of the braggart soldier in Renaissance drama. No doubt Shakespeare was in some measure indebted to the tradition. But into this *miles gloriosus* he breathed the breath of individual life, and with a stroke of dramatic genius made him the center of a rowdy crew which included the Prince of Wales. Falstaff is a braggart, a liar, a lecher, a drunkard, a scrounger, a thief. But he is more – much more. His triumphant gift for extricating himself from the consequences of his misdoings has understandably endeared him to generations of theatre-goers. It is not surprising that a statue of the gargantuan knight stands among the figures in the grounds of the Memorial Theatre at Stratford, the symbol of Shakespeare's genius for comedy.

In *2 Henry IV*, dealing with events of the last years of Henry's reign, Shakespeare found the historical material less tractable than in *1 Henry IV*. Hotspur and Glendower were gone, the former slain by Prince Hal at Shrewsbury, the latter historically unavailable for the central action. Kate Percy indeed survives to make a fine speech lamenting her mate that's lost and denouncing the pusillanimity of her father-in-law Northumberland. Among the historical personages there remained the king, Prince Hal, the three other sons of the king, and the principal noblemen of the rival factions. With these Shakespeare does the best that he can. He also builds up, with moderate success, the characters of Richard Scroop, Archbishop of York, and the Lord Chief Justice. The former, who played but a minor role in *1 Henry IV*, is here the central figure in the rebellion in the north. He becomes the symbol of one of the political ideas of the play, the dilemma of the subject who, though acknowledging the principle of the divine right of kings, is yet galled by the abuse of power and feels compelled to take action against it. The Chief Justice, too, emerges as a lively personality, wise, humorous, realistic, who serves also as the voice of private decency and public authority to denounce the excesses of Falstaff and the profligacy of the Prince of Wales.

As with the characters, so with the principal dramatic narrative. In *1 Henry IV* there was the heroic action at Shrewsbury, where Prince Hal could speak a valedictory for the dead Hotspur:

> Fare thee well, great heart.
> Ill-weaved ambition, how much art thou shrunk!
> When that this body did contain a spirit,
> A kingdom for it was too small a bound;
> But now two paces of the vilest earth
> Is room enough. This earth that bears thee dead
> Bears not alive so stout a gentleman.

The later years of Henry's reign saw no such gallantry as this. Instead there was the bloodless, treacherous betrayal of the rebels at Gaultree Forest, which can end with nothing more heroic than Prince John of Lancaster's

> Strike up our drums, pursue the scattered stray.
> God, and not we, hath safely fought to-day.
> Some guard these traitors to the block of death,
> Treason's true bed and yielder up of breath.

Apart from this, Shakespeare's historical sources provided him with little material more dramatic than reports on the progress of the wars, debates concerning policy and strategy, and the like. On the historical side, the high moments of the play come at the end of Act IV and in Act V, with the portrayal of the old king on his deathbed, his final unscrupulous advice to the Prince of Wales concerning foreign wars, his death, and the coronation and transformation of the new king.

It is not surprising that Shakespeare, thus confronted with a paucity of truly dramatic history, develops his non-historical personages and situations to the extent that they dominate the play. It has often been pointed out that in *1 Henry IV* the proportion of the historical plot to the Falstaff story is 1649 lines to 1305, or roughly 5 to 4. In *2 Henry IV* the proportion has become 1422 lines to 1760, almost the precise reverse. Even without such statistics to guide him, the reader or playgoer is well aware that in this play Falstaff is the central figure. He overshadows the king and Hal, and his cronies overshadow the noble personages in the play. The Falstaff of most of the action of *2 Henry IV* is quite the equal of the Falstaff of *1 Henry IV*. We may say of him, as he says of himself, "The brain of this foolish compounded clay-man is not able to invent anything that intends to laughter more than I invent or is invented on me. I am not only witty in myself, but the cause that wit is in other men."

But Shakespeare has here done more than sustain and enlarge the Falstaff of the earlier play. He has also developed and individualized the characters of Falstaff's boon companions, and from a mere sketch in one scene in *1 Henry IV* he has created the memorable comic figure of Mistress Quickly, hostess of a tavern which tradition (but not Shakespeare, save for the merest hint – "Doth the old boar feed in the old frank?") identifies with the Boar's Head, which in Shakespeare's time (but not in Henry's) stood hard by the parish church of St Michael in Eastcheap. Mistress Quickly, a forebear of Mrs Malaprop, has been guilty of most of the amiable sins, but she is redeemed by simplicity and kindness of heart.

Apart from these, Shakespeare in this play invents four comic personages who had no existence in the earlier play – swaggering Pistol, Doll Tearsheet, a lady of joy, and the country justices Shallow and Silence. Modern audiences may find the rantings of Pistol tiresome and the love passages between Doll and Falstaff tasteless. But the two justices remain as entertaining to-day as they were on Shakespeare's stage – Shallow garrulous and gullible, Silence with his weakness for wine and his snatches of old songs. Generations of scholars have seen in the comic figure of Shallow a lampoon on some justice of the peace of Shakespeare's acquaintance. Identifications have ranged from Sir Thomas Lucy of Charlecote, near Stratford, on whose preserves, according to unsupported tradition, the youthful Shakespeare was involved in a poaching escapade, to William Gardiner, justice of the peace in the county of Surrey, with whom Shakespeare quarrelled in 1596. None of the identifications convinces a judicious mind. But the richness of the Gloucestershire local color against which Shallow is portrayed and the particularity of his fictitious recollections of his student days at Clement's Inn go far to explain the persistent belief that Shakespeare drew Shallow from the life.

In assigning to Falstaff a dominant role in the Henry IV plays and bringing him into close association with Prince Hal, Shakespeare created for himself the problem of disposing of Falstaff after the prince had become king. In the end, Shakespeare causes the new king to reject Falstaff summarily:

> I know thee not, old man. Fall to thy prayers.
> How ill white hairs become a fool and jester!
> I have long dreamed of such a kind of man,
> So surfeit-swelled, so old, and so profane,
> But, being awaked, I do despise my dream.

Our sympathy goes out to Falstaff; his "Master Shallow, I owe you a thousand pound" has for us a poignancy which Shakespeare did not intend. Yet we cannot deny the necessity for the rejection. A play portraying the victories of Henry V was in the offing. Obviously the hero of Agincourt could not continue to consort with Falstaff and his crew. As a concession to Fat Jack's popularity with the audience, the Epilogue to the present play promises that Sir John will appear in the sequel. But he does not appear. We hear only the Hostess's account of his passage to "Arthur's bosom," and Pistol's muted epitaph, "Falstaff he is dead, / And we must earn [grieve] therefore."

No element in 2 Henry IV has provoked more critical comment than the rejection of Falstaff. Most commentators have found it in their hearts to wish that the playwright had been able to dispose of old Jack in some way which would have permitted us to feel a greater admiration for the regenerate Hal. But an attentive reading will disclose the fact that Shakespeare has prepared us for the rejection. Nowhere in this play do we see Falstaff and the prince in the same kind of intimacy which marked their relationship in 1 Henry IV. Indeed, except for the rejection scene they are together just once, in the tavern scene in which Falstaff, as in the famous Gad's Hill episode of 1 Henry IV, is the victim of a princely joke. But the Gad's Hill episode ended on a note of friendly banter; here there is no banter. The prince's last words are

> By heaven, Poins, I feel me much to blame,
> So idly to profane the precious time. . . .
> Give me my sword and cloak. Falstaff, good night.

We have been warned of what is to follow. We need not condemn Hal too severely. Good judgment would have taught Falstaff that the laws of England would *not* be at his commandment after the death of the old king, and delicacy would have forbidden him to obtrude himself so abruptly into Hal's new situation. But good judgment and delicacy were not among Falstaff's qualities. It is Falstaff, not the prince, who compels the rejection.

Falstaff has provoked roars of laughter from the theatregoers of almost four centuries. Usually it is the Falstaff of 1 Henry IV who is presented on the stage. Occasionally, from Betterton's time to our own, actors and producers have ventured to condense both parts into a single play of manageable proportions. 2 Henry IV is less frequently presented as a separate play and in its entirety. However, on those occasions when it is, audiences find the experience delightful, and critics are impressed anew with Shakespeare's skill in mounting history upon the stage.

*University of Pennsylvania*          ALLAN G. CHESTER

## NOTE ON THE TEXT

The present edition is based on the quarto of 1600, which is believed to have been printed from Shakespeare's own manuscript and to supply a better text than the folio, although that of the latter is fuller. The list of characters has been added from the folio text, as well as certain passages evidently omitted from the quarto because they dwell at length upon the censorable subject of civil rebellion. (These are the bracketed lines, I, i, 166–79, 189–209; I, iii, 21–24, 36–55, 85–108; II, iii, 23–45; IV, i, 55–79, 103–39.) The quarto is not divided into acts and scenes, and the division here indicated marginally is that of the folio text, except that in the latter the first act contains five scenes owing to the Induction's being counted as a separate scene, and the fourth act contains only two scenes. The wording of the stage directions of the quarto has been retained, but the names of four characters who neither speak nor are referred to in the dialogue have been eliminated: "Fauconbridge" in the opening stage direction at I, iii; "Sir John Russell" in that at II, ii; "Bardolph" in that at IV, i; and "Kent" in that at IV, iv. In V, iv, "Sincklo" (presumably the actor taking the part) has been emended to "Beadle." Listed below are substantive departures from the quarto text, including additions from the folio other than those mentioned above. The adopted reading is given in italics followed by the quarto reading in roman.

*The Actors' Names* (printed at the end of the play in F)
Ind. *Induction* (i.e. the heading, F; omitted in Q)   35 *hold* (Theobald) *hole* (F; passage not in Q)
I, i, 126 *Too* (F) so   161 *Travers* (Capell) Umfr.   164 *Lean on your* (F) leaue on you   178 *brought* (F2) bring (F; passage not in Q)   183 *ventured, . . . proposed* (Capell) ventured . . . proposde,
I, ii, 19 *fledged* (F) fledge   35 *rascally* (F) rascal!   46 *Where's Bardolph?* (F; follows 'through it' in line above in Q)   47 *into* (F) in   92 *age* (F) an ague   114 *Falstaff* (F) Old.   161 *bear-herd* (F) Berod   165 *them, are* (F) the one   192–93 *and Prince Harry* (F; omitted in Q)
I, iii, 28 *on* (F) and   66 *a* (F) so,   79 *He . . . Welsh* (F) French and Welch he leaues his back vnarmde, they   109 *Mowbray* (F) Bish.
II, i, 14 *and that* (F; omitted in Q)   21 *vice* (F) view   25 *continuantly* (F) continually   76 *Fie!* (F; omitted in Q)   158 s.d. (follows line 155 in Q)   162 *Basingstoke* (F) Billingsgate

II, ii, 15 *viz.* (F) with   21 *thy* (F) the   *made a shift to* (F; omitted in Q)   77 *new* (F; omitted in Q)   80 *rabbit* (F) rabble   107 *borrower's* (Warburton) borrowed   122 *familiars* (F) family
II, iii, 11 *endeared* (F) endeere
II, iv, 12–13 *Dispatch . . . straight* (F; assigned to 'Dra.' in Q)   13 s.d. (follows line 17 in Q)   14 *3. Drawer* (Alexander) 2 Drawer (F) Francis (Q)   20 *2. Drawer* (F) Francis   106 *shall* (F) shall not   159 *Die* (F; omitted in Q)   202 *Ah* (F) a   205 *Ah,* (F) a   300 *him* (F) thee
III, ii, 25 *This . . . cousin* (F) Coosin, this sir Iohn   53 *[Shallow] . . . gentlemen* (F; assigned to 'Silence' in Q)   107 *Falstaff. Prick him* (F; printed as s.d. 'Iohn prickes him' after line 106 in Q)   131 *to* (F; omitted in Q)   186–87 *no more of that* (F; omitted in Q)   198 *Clement's Inn* (F) Clemham   216 *old* (F; omitted in Q)   277 *Master Shallow* (F; omitted in Q)
IV, i, 30 *Then, my lord,* (F; omitted in Q)   34 *rags* (F) rage   139 *indeed* (Theobald) and did (F; passage not in Q)
IV, ii, s.d. (follows IV, i, 226 in Q)   8 *man* (F) man talking   24 *Employ* (F) Imply   97 s.d. (follows line 96 in Q)   117 *and . . . yours* (F; omitted in Q)   122 *these traitors* (F) this traitour
IV, iii, 2 *I pray* (F; omitted in Q)   40 *their* (Q catchword) there   41 *Caesar* (Theobald) cosin   77–82 (printed as prose in Q)   80 *pray,* (F; omitted in Q)
IV, iv, 32 *meting* (F) meeting   52 *Canst . . . that?* (F; omitted in Q)   94 *heaven* (F) heavens   104 *write* (F) wet   *letters* (F) termes   132 *Softly, pray* (F; omitted in Q)
IV, v, 13 *altered* (F) uttred   49 *How . . . grace?* (F; omitted in Q)   75 *The virtuous sweets* (F; omitted in Q)   81 *hath* (F) hands   107 *Which* (F) Whom   160 *worst of* (F) worse then   177 *O my son,* (F; omitted in Q)
V, i, 21 *the other day* (F; omitted in Q)   *Hinckley* (F) Hunkley   43 *but a very* (F; omitted in Q)
V, ii, s.d. ('duke Humphrey, Thomas Clarence, Prince John, Westmerland' also listed in Q)
V, iii, 17–22, 32–36, 44–46, 51–52, 71–73, 90–94, 97–104, 113–17, 124–25, 137–38 (printed as prose in Q)
V, iv, 5 *enough* (F; omitted in Q)   6 *lately* (F; omitted in Q)   11 *He* (F) I
V, v, 5 *Robert* (F; omitted in Q)   15 *Shallow* (F) Pist.   17, 19 *Shallow* (Hanmer) Pist.   29 *all* (F; omitted in Q)   31–38 (printed as prose in Q)
Epi. 29–30 *and . . . queen* (F; follows line 14 in Q)

# THE SECOND PART OF
# KING HENRY THE FOURTH

## THE ACTORS' NAMES

Rumor, the Presenter
King Henry the Fourth
Prince Henry, afterwards crowned King Henry the Fifth
Prince John of Lancaster ⎫
Humphrey of Gloucester ⎬ sons to Henry IV and brethren to Henry V
Thomas of Clarence ⎭
[Earl of] Northumberland
[Richard Scroop] the Archbishop of York
[Lord] Mowbray
[Lord] Hastings ⎫
Lord Bardolph ⎬ opposites against King Henry IV
Travers
Morton
[Sir John] Coleville
[Earl of] Warwick
[Earl of] Westmoreland
[Earl of] Surrey
[Sir John Blunt] ⎫
Gower ⎬ of the King's party
Harcourt
Lord Chief Justice
[His Servant]

[Robert] Shallow ⎫ both country justices
Silence ⎭
Davy, servant to Shallow
Fang and Snare, two sergeants
[Ralph] Mouldy ⎫
[Simon] Shadow
[Thomas] Wart ⎬ country soldiers
[Francis] Feeble
[Peter] Bullcalf ⎭
Poins
[Sir John] Falstaff ⎫
Bardolph
Pistol ⎬ irregular humorists
Peto
[Falstaff's] Page ⎭
Northumberland's Wife
Percy's Widow [Lady Percy]
Hostess Quickly
Doll Tearsheet
[A Dancer as] Epilogue
[Francis and other] Drawers, Beadle [and other Officers], Grooms [, Porter, Messenger, Soldiers, Lords, Attendants]

[Scene : England]

\*

## INDUCTION

*Enter Rumor, painted full of tongues.*

RUMOR
Open your ears, for which of you will stop
The vent of hearing when loud Rumor speaks?
I, from the orient to the drooping west,
4 Making the wind my post-horse, still unfold
The acts commencèd on this ball of earth.
Upon my tongues continual slanders ride,
The which in every language I pronounce,
Stuffing the ears of men with false reports.
I speak of peace while covert enmity
Under the smile of safety wounds the world.
And who but Rumor, who but only I,
Make fearful musters and prepared defense
Whiles the big year, swoln with some other grief,
Is thought with child by the stern tyrant war,
And no such matter? Rumor is a pipe                      15
Blown by surmises, jealousies, conjectures,              16
And of so easy and so plain a stop                       17
That the blunt monster with uncounted heads,            18
The still-discordant wavering multitude,
Can play upon it. But what need I thus
My well-known body to anatomize
Among my household? Why is Rumor here?                   22
I run before King Harry's victory,
Who in a bloody field by Shrewsbury
Hath beaten down young Hotspur and his troops,          25
Quenching the flame of bold rebellion
Even with the rebels' blood. But what mean I
To speak so true at first? My office is                  28
To noise about that Harry Monmouth fell                  29
Under the wrath of noble Hotspur's sword,
And that the king before the Douglas' rage
Stooped his anointed head as low as death.               32
This have I rumored through the peasant towns            33
Between that royal field of Shrewsbury
And this worm-eaten hold of ragged stone,                35
Where Hotspur's father, old Northumberland,

Ind. **4** *still* ever **15** *pipe* wind instrument **16** *jealousies* suspicions **17** *of . . . stop* whose stops are so easily played upon **18** *blunt* stupid **22** *my household* i.e. the audience **25** *Hotspur* Harry Percy, killed by the Prince of Wales at Shrewsbury **28** *office* function **29** *Harry Monmouth* the Prince of Wales (Prince Hal) **32** *Stooped . . . death* was mortally wounded **33** *peasant towns* villages **35** *hold* stronghold (Warkworth Castle, seat of the Earl of Northumberland, where the action of the next scene occurs)

37    Lies crafty-sick. The posts come tiring on,
And not a man of them brings other news
Than they have learned of me. From Rumor's tongues
They bring smooth comforts false, worse than true
    wrongs.                                    *Exit Rumor.*

I, i        *Enter the Lord Bardolph at one door.*
LORD BARDOLPH
Who keeps the gate here, ho?
    *[Enter the Porter.]*        Where is the earl?
PORTER
What shall I say you are?
LORD BARDOLPH        Tell thou the earl
That the Lord Bardolph doth attend him here.
PORTER
His lordship is walked forth into the orchard.
Please it your honor, knock but at the gate,
And he himself will answer.
        *Enter the Earl of Northumberland.*
LORD BARDOLPH        Here comes the earl.
                    *[Exit Porter.]*
NORTHUMBERLAND
What news, Lord Bardolph? Every minute now
Should be the father of some stratagem.
The times are wild. Contention, like a horse
Full of high feeding, madly hath broke loose
And bears down all before him.
LORD BARDOLPH        Noble earl,
I bring you certain news from Shrewsbury.
NORTHUMBERLAND
13    Good, an God will!
LORD BARDOLPH    As good as heart can wish.
The king is almost wounded to the death;
And, in the fortune of my lord your son,
Prince Harry slain outright; and both the Blunts
Killed by the hand of Douglas. Young Prince John
And Westmoreland and Stafford fled the field;
19    And Harry Monmouth's brawn, the hulk Sir John,
Is prisoner to your son. O, such a day,
So fought, so followed, and so fairly won,
Came not till now to dignify the times
23    Since Caesar's fortunes!
NORTHUMBERLAND        How is this derived?
Saw you the field? Came you from Shrewsbury?
LORD BARDOLPH
I spake with one, my lord, that came from thence,
A gentleman well bred and of good name,
That freely rendered me these news for true.
NORTHUMBERLAND
Here comes my servant Travers, whom I sent
On Tuesday last to listen after news.
        *Enter Travers.*
LORD BARDOLPH
30    My lord, I overrode him on the way,
And he is furnished with no certainties
32    More than he haply may retail from me.
NORTHUMBERLAND
Now, Travers, what good tidings comes with you?
TRAVERS
My lord, Sir John Umfrevile turned me back
With joyful tidings and, being better horsed,
Outrode me. After him came spurring hard
37    A gentleman, almost forspent with speed,

That stopped by me to breathe his bloodied horse.
He asked the way to Chester, and of him
I did demand what news from Shrewsbury.
He told me that rebellion had bad luck
And that young Harry Percy's spur was cold.
With that, he gave his able horse the head,
And bending forward struck his armèd heels
Against the panting sides of his poor jade
Up to the rowel-head, and starting so
He seemed in running to devour the way,
Staying no longer question.
NORTHUMBERLAND        Ha! Again.
Said he young Harry Percy's spur was cold?
Of Hotspur Coldspur? That rebellion
Had met ill luck?
LORD BARDOLPH    My lord, I'll tell you what.
If my young lord your son have not the day,
Upon mine honor, for a silken point
I'll give my barony. Never talk of it.
NORTHUMBERLAND
Why should that gentleman that rode by Travers
Give then such instances of loss?
LORD BARDOLPH            Who, he?
He was some hilding fellow that had stolen
The horse he rode on, and, upon my life,
Spoke at a venture. Look, here comes more news.
        *Enter Morton.*
NORTHUMBERLAND
Yea, this man's brow, like to a title-leaf,
Foretells the nature of a tragic volume.
So looks the strand whereon the imperious flood
Hath left a witnessed usurpation.
Say, Morton, didst thou come from Shrewsbury?
MORTON
I ran from Shrewsbury, my noble lord,
Where hateful death put on his ugliest mask
To fright our party.
NORTHUMBERLAND    How doth my son and brother?
Thou tremblest, and the whiteness in thy cheek
Is apter than thy tongue to tell thy errand.
Even such a man, so faint, so spiritless,
So dull, so dead in look, so woebegone,
Drew Priam's curtain in the dead of night,
And would have told him half his Troy was burnt.
But Priam found the fire ere he his tongue,
And I my Percy's death ere thou report'st it.
This thou wouldst say, 'Your son did thus and thus;
Your brother thus. So fought the noble Douglas' –
Stopping my greedy ear with their bold deeds.
But in the end, to stop my ear indeed,
Thou hast a sigh to blow away this praise,
Ending with 'Brother, son, and all are dead.'
MORTON
Douglas is living, and your brother, yet;
But, for my lord your son –
NORTHUMBERLAND        Why, he is dead.
See what a ready tongue suspicion hath!

---

37 *crafty-sick* feigning sickness; *tiring on* riding until exhausted
I, i Before Northumberland's castle (at Warkworth)  13 *an* if  19 *brawn*
swine (referring to Falstaff's size and habits)  23 *fortunes* successes  30
*overrode* overtook  32 *haply* perhaps  37 *forspent* exhausted  48 *Staying*
waiting for  53 *point* lace for tying the breeches  57 *hilding* worthless
60 *title-leaf* title page  63 *a witnessed usurpation* evidences of its destruction
72 *Priam* king of Troy  78 *Stopping* filling

He that but fears the thing he would not know
Hath by instinct knowledge from others' eyes
That what he feared is chancèd. Yet speak, Morton.
Tell thou an earl his divination lies,
And I will take it as a sweet disgrace
And make thee rich for doing me such wrong.

MORTON
You are too great to be by me gainsaid.
Your spirit is too true, your fears too certain.

NORTHUMBERLAND
93 Yet, for all this, say not that Percy 's dead.
I see a strange confession in thine eye.
Thou shakest thy head and hold'st it fear or sin
To speak a truth. If he be slain, say so.
The tongue offends not that reports his death;
And he doth sin that doth belie the dead,
Not he which says the dead is not alive.
Yet the first bringer of unwelcome news
1 Hath but a losing office, and his tongue
Sounds ever after as a sullen bell,
Rememb'red tolling a departing friend.

LORD BARDOLPH
I cannot think, my lord, your son is dead.

MORTON
I am sorry I should force you to believe
That which I would to God I had not seen.
But these mine eyes saw him in bloody state,
8 Rendering faint quittance, wearied and outbreathed,
To Harry Monmouth, whose swift wrath beat down
The never-daunted Percy to the earth,
From whence with life he never more sprung up.
2 In few, his death, whose spirit lent a fire
Even to the dullest peasant in his camp,
4 Being bruited once, took fire and heat away
From the best-tempered courage in his troops.
For from his metal was his party steeled,
Which once in him abated, all the rest
Turned on themselves, like dull and heavy lead.
And as the thing that's heavy in itself,
Upon enforcement flies with greatest speed,
So did our men, heavy in Hotspur's loss,
Lend to this weight such lightness with their fear
That arrows fled not swifter toward their aim
Than did our soldiers, aiming at their safety,
Fly from the field. Then was that noble Worcester
Too soon ta'en prisoner; and that furious Scot,
The bloody Douglas, whose well-laboring sword
28 Had three times slain the appearance of the king,
29 'Gan vail his stomach and did grace the shame
Of those that turned their backs, and in his flight,
Stumbling in fear, was took. The sum of all
Is that the king hath won, and hath sent out
A speedy power to encounter you, my lord,

Under the conduct of young Lancaster
And Westmoreland. This is the news at full.

NORTHUMBERLAND
For this I shall have time enough to mourn.
In poison there is physic; and these news,
Having been well, that would have made me sick,
Being sick, have in some measure made me well.
And as the wretch whose fever-weakened joints,
Like strengthless hinges, buckle under life,
Impatient of his fit, breaks like a fire
Out of his keeper's arms, even so my limbs,
Weakened with grief, being now enraged with grief,          144
Are thrice themselves. Hence, therefore, thou nice          145
    crutch!
A scaly gauntlet now with joints of steel
Must glove this hand. And hence, thou sickly quoif!          147
Thou art a guard too wanton for the head          148
Which princes, fleshed with conquest, aim to hit.          149
Now bind my brows with iron, and approach
The ragged'st hour that time and spite dare bring          151
To frown upon the enraged Northumberland!
Let heaven kiss earth! Now let not Nature's hand
Keep the wild flood confined! Let order die!
And let this world no longer be a stage
To feed contention in a lingering act.
But let one spirit of the first-born Cain          157
Reign in all bosoms, that, each heart being set
On bloody courses, the rude scene may end,
And darkness be the burier of the dead!

[TRAVERS]
This strainèd passion doth you wrong, my lord.          161

LORD BARDOLPH
Sweet earl, divorce not wisdom from your honor.

MORTON
The lives of all your loving complices
Lean on your health, the which, if you give o'er
To stormy passion, must perforce decay.
[You cast the event of war, my noble lord,          166
And summed the account of chance, before you said,
'Let us make head.' It was your presurmise          168
That, in the dole of blows, your son might drop.          169
You knew he walked o'er perils, on an edge,
More likely to fall in than to get o'er.
You were advised his flesh was capable          172
Of wounds and scars and that his forward spirit
Would lift him where most trade of danger ranged.
Yet did you say, 'Go forth.' And none of this,
Though strongly apprehended, could restrain
The stiff-borne action. What hath then befallen,          177
Or what hath this bold enterprise brought forth,
More than that being which was like to be?]          179

LORD BARDOLPH
We all that are engagèd to this loss          180
Knew that we ventured on such dangerous seas
That if we wrought out life 'twas ten to one.
And yet we ventured, for the gain proposed
Choked the respect of likely peril feared.          184
And since we are o'erset, venture again.
Come, we will all put forth, body and goods.

MORTON
'Tis more than time. And, my most noble lord,
I hear for certain, and dare speak the truth,
[The gentle Archbishop of York is up          189
With well-appointed powers. He is a man

93 *for* in spite of   101 *losing office* thankless task   108 *faint quittance* weak
return of blows   112 *In few* in few words   114 *bruited* reported   128 *the
appearance . . . king* noblemen disguised as the king   129 *'Gan . . . stomach*
began to let his courage fail; *grace* excuse   144 *grief . . . grief* pain . . . sorrow
145 *nice* effeminate   147 *quoif* nightcap (or bandage)   148 *wanton* trifling
149 *fleshed* aroused, as a dog is aroused from feeding on raw meat   151
*ragged'st* roughest   157 *spirit . . . Cain* i.e. spirit of murder   161 *strainèd
passion* outburst of feeling   166 *cast the event* calculated the consequences
168 *make head* raise an army   169 *dole* chance distribution   172 *advised*
aware   177 *stiff-borne* obstinately carried out   179 *More . . . be* more than
the event which you knew was a possibility   180 *engagèd to* involved in
184 *respect* consideration   189–90 *is up . . . powers* has taken the field with a
well-equipped army

Who with a double surety binds his followers.
192  My lord your son had only but the corpse,
But shadows and the shows of men, to fight.
For that same word 'rebellion' did divide
The action of their bodies from their souls,
And they did fight with queasiness, constrained,
As men drink potions, that their weapons only
Seemed on our side. But for their spirits and souls,
This word 'rebellion,' it had froze them up,
As fish are in a pond. But now the bishop
Turns insurrection to religion.
Supposed sincere and holy in his thoughts,
He's followed both with body and with mind,
204  And doth enlarge his rising with the blood
205  Of fair King Richard, scraped from Pomfret stones;
206  Derives from heaven his quarrel and his cause;
Tells them he doth bestride a bleeding land,
208  Gasping for life under great Bolingbroke;
209  And more and less do flock to follow him.]
NORTHUMBERLAND
I knew of this before; but, to speak truth,
This present grief had wiped it from my mind.
Go in with me, and counsel every man
The aptest way for safety and revenge.
214  Get posts and letters, and make friends with speed.
Never so few, and never yet more need.    *Exeunt.*

\*

I, ii    *Enter Sir John [Falstaff] alone, with his Page*
    *bearing his sword and buckler.*
FALSTAFF  Sirrah, you giant, what says the doctor to my
2  water?
PAGE  He said, sir, the water itself was a good healthy
4  water; but, for the party that owed it, he might have
5  moe diseases than he knew for.
6  FALSTAFF  Men of all sorts take a pride to gird at me. The
brain of this foolish compounded clay-man is not able
to invent anything that intends to laughter more than I
invent or is invented on me. I am not only witty in myself, but the cause that wit is in other men. I do here walk
before thee like a sow that hath overwhelmed all her
litter but one. If the prince put thee into my service for
any other reason than to set me off, why then I have no
14  judgment. Thou whoreson mandrake, thou art fitter to
be worn in my cap than to wait at my heels. I was never
16  manned with an agate till now. But I will inset you
neither in gold nor silver, but in vile apparel, and send
18  you back again to your master, for a jewel – the juvenal,
19  the prince your master, whose chin is not yet fledged. I
will sooner have a beard grow in the palm of my hand
than he shall get one off his cheek, and yet he will not
22  stick to say his face is a face-royal. God may finish it
when he will, 'tis not a hair amiss yet. He may keep it
24  still at a face-royal, for a barber shall never earn sixpence
25  out of it; and yet he'll be crowing as if he had writ man
ever since his father was a bachelor. He may keep his
27  own grace, but he's almost out of mine, I can assure
him. What said Master Dombledon about the satin for
29  my short cloak and my slops?
PAGE  He said, sir, you should procure him better as-
31  surance than Bardolph. He would not take his band and
yours; he liked not the security.
33  FALSTAFF  Let him be damned, like the glutton! Pray

God his tongue be hotter! A whoreson Achitophel! A  34
rascally yea-forsooth knave! To bear a gentleman in  35
hand, and then stand upon security! The whoreson
smooth-pates do now wear nothing but high shoes, and  37
bunches of keys at their girdles; and if a man is through  38
with them in honest taking up, then they must stand
upon security. I had as lief they would put ratsbane in
my mouth as offer to stop it with security. I looked 'a  41
should have sent me two-and-twenty yards of satin, as I
am a true knight, and he sends me security. Well, he
may sleep in security, for he hath the horn of abundance,  44
and the lightness of his wife shines through it. And yet
cannot he see, though he have his own lanthorn to light  46
him. Where's Bardolph?
PAGE  He's gone into Smithfield to buy your worship a  47
horse.
FALSTAFF  I bought him in Paul's, and he'll buy me a  49
horse in Smithfield. An I could get me but a wife in the
stews, I were manned, horsed, and wived.  51
    *Enter Lord Chief Justice [and Servant].*
PAGE  Sir, here comes the nobleman that committed the  52
prince for striking him about Bardolph.
FALSTAFF  Wait close; I will not see him.  54
CHIEF JUSTICE  What's he that goes there?
SERVANT  Falstaff, an't please your lordship.
CHIEF JUSTICE  He that was in question for the robbery?  57
SERVANT  He, my lord. But he hath since done good ser-
vice at Shrewsbury, and, as I hear, is now going with
some charge to the Lord John of Lancaster.
CHIEF JUSTICE  What, to York? Call him back again.
SERVANT  Sir John Falstaff!
FALSTAFF  Boy, tell him I am deaf.
PAGE  You must speak louder; my master is deaf.
CHIEF JUSTICE  I am sure he is, to the hearing of any-
thing good. Go, pluck him by the elbow; I must speak
with him.
SERVANT  Sir John!
FALSTAFF  What! A young knave, and begging! Is there  69
not wars? Is there not employment? Doth not the king
lack subjects? Do not the rebels need soldiers? Though
it be a shame to be on any side but one, it is worse shame

192 *only . . . corpse* only the bodies of men whose hearts were not in the
fight  204 *enlarge his rising* extend the significance of his revolt  205
*Pomfret* Pomfret Castle, where Richard II was murdered  206 *Derives
from heaven* gives a religious significance to  208 *Bolingbroke* Henry IV
209 *more and less* high and low  214 *make* collect
I, ii A London street  2 *water* urine  4 *owed* owned  5 *moe* more  6 *gird*
jeer  14 *mandrake* a root popularly supposed to resemble a man  16
*manned . . . agate* served by a man as small as a carved agate stone  18
*juvenal* young man  19 *fledged* covered with down  22, 24 *face-royal* a pun
centering around a coin, the royal (worth 10s.), with the king's face stamped
on it  25 *writ man* attained manhood  27 *grace* (1) title of address ('your
grace'), (2) favor  29 *slops* wide breeches  31 *Bardolph* one of Falstaff's
cronies, not to be confused with Lord Bardolph; *band* bond  33 *glutton*
i.e. Dives, referred to in Luke xvi, 24  34 *Achitophel* the adviser of Absalom
(2 Samuel xv–xvii)  35–36 *bear . . . in hand* encourage  37 *smooth-pates*
city tradesmen, who wore their hair short  37–38 *high shoes . . . keys*
(tokens of prosperity and rank)  38–40 *if . . . security* if a man has ordered a
suit of clothes on promise of future payment, they demand security before
making delivery  41 *'a* he  44 *horn of abundance* the horn of the cuckold
46 *lanthorn* lantern (the pun is that the wife's lightness shines in the
cuckold's horn)  47 *Smithfield* a famous market  49 *Paul's* St Paul's
Cathedral (the nave of which was often used as a labor exchange)  51 *stews*
brothels; *manned . . . wived* (the sense is that a man who gets his horse at
Smithfield, his servant at Paul's, and his wife in the stews will get a poor
bargain in each case)  52 *committed* committed to prison (see V, ii, 7on.)
54 *close* close by  57 *in question* under judicial examination  69 *knave*
boy

to beg than to be on the worst side, were it worse than the name of rebellion can tell how to make it.

SERVANT You mistake me, sir.

FALSTAFF Why, sir, did I say you were an honest man? Setting my knighthood and my soldiership aside, I had lied in my throat if I had said so.

SERVANT I pray you, sir, then set your knighthood and your soldiership aside and give me leave to tell you you lie in your throat if you say I am any other than an honest man.

FALSTAFF I give thee leave to tell me so! I lay aside that which grows to me! If thou get'st any leave of me, hang me; if thou tak'st leave, thou wert better be hanged. You hunt counter. Hence! Avaunt!

SERVANT Sir, my lord would speak with you.

CHIEF JUSTICE Sir John Falstaff, a word with you.

FALSTAFF My good lord! God give your lordship good time of day. I am glad to see your lordship abroad. I heard say your lordship was sick. I hope your lordship goes abroad by advice. Your lordship, though not clean past your youth, have yet some smack of age in you, some relish of the saltness of time in you; and I most humbly beseech your lordship to have a reverent care of your health.

CHIEF JUSTICE Sir John, I sent for you before your expedition to Shrewsbury.

FALSTAFF An't please your lordship, I hear his majesty is returned with some discomfort from Wales.

CHIEF JUSTICE I talk not of his majesty. You would not come when I sent for you.

FALSTAFF And I hear, moreover, his highness is fallen into this same whoreson apoplexy.

CHIEF JUSTICE Well, God mend him! I pray you, let me speak with you.

FALSTAFF This apoplexy, as I take it, is a kind of lethargy, an't please your lordship, a kind of sleeping in the blood, a whoreson tingling.

CHIEF JUSTICE What tell you me of it? Be it as it is.

FALSTAFF It hath it original from much grief, from study and perturbation of the brain. I have read the cause of his effects in Galen. It is a kind of deafness.

CHIEF JUSTICE I think you are fallen into the disease, for you hear not what I say to you.

FALSTAFF Very well, my lord, very well. Rather, an't please you, it is the disease of not listening, the malady of not marking, that I am troubled withal.

CHIEF JUSTICE To punish you by the heels would amend the attention of your ears, and I care not if I do become your physician.

FALSTAFF I am as poor as Job, my lord, but not so patient. Your lordship may minister the potion of imprisonment to me in respect of poverty; but how I should be your patient to follow your prescriptions, the wise may make some dram of a scruple, or indeed a scruple itself.

CHIEF JUSTICE I sent for you, when there were matters against you for your life, to come speak with me.

FALSTAFF As I was then advised by my learned counsel in the laws of this land-service, I did not come.

CHIEF JUSTICE Well, the truth is, Sir John, you live in great infamy.

FALSTAFF He that buckles himself in my belt cannot live in less.

CHIEF JUSTICE Your means are very slender and your waste is great.

FALSTAFF I would it were otherwise. I would my means were greater and my waist slenderer.

CHIEF JUSTICE You have misled the youthful prince.

FALSTAFF The young prince hath misled me. I am the fellow with the great belly, and he my dog.

CHIEF JUSTICE Well, I am loath to gall a new-healed wound. Your day's service at Shrewsbury hath a little gilded over your night's exploit on Gad's Hill. You may thank the unquiet time for your quiet o'erposting that action.

FALSTAFF My lord?

CHIEF JUSTICE But since all is well, keep it so. Wake not a sleeping wolf.

FALSTAFF To wake a wolf is as bad as smell a fox.

CHIEF JUSTICE What! You are as a candle, the better part burnt out.

FALSTAFF A wassail candle, my lord, all tallow. If I did say of wax, my growth would approve the truth.

CHIEF JUSTICE There is not a white hair in your face but should have his effect of gravity.

FALSTAFF His effect of gravy, gravy, gravy.

CHIEF JUSTICE You follow the young prince up and down like his ill angel.

FALSTAFF Not so, my lord. Your ill angel is light, but I hope he that looks upon me will take me without weighing. And yet, in some respects, I grant, I cannot go. I cannot tell. Virtue is of so little regard in these costermongers' times that true valor is turned bearherd. Pregnancy is made a tapster, and hath his quick wit wasted in giving reckonings. All the other gifts appertinent to man, as the malice of this age shapes them, are not worth a gooseberry. You that are old consider not the capacities of us that are young; you do measure the heat of our livers with the bitterness of your galls. And we that are in the vaward of our youth, I must confess, are wags too.

CHIEF JUSTICE Do you set down your name in the scroll of youth, that are written down old with all the characters of age? Have you not a moist eye? A dry hand? A yellow cheek? A white beard? A decreasing leg? An increasing belly? Is not your voice broken? Your wind short? Your chin double? Your wit single? And every part about you blasted with antiquity? And will you yet call yourself young? Fie, fie, fie, Sir John!

FALSTAFF My lord, I was born about three of the clock in the afternoon, with a white head and something a

---

75 *mistake* misunderstand   82–83 *that . . . to me* i.e. my knighthood, which is an integral part of myself   85 *counter* in the wrong direction (with play upon 'the Counter,' a debtors' prison)   91 *by advice* i.e. with your physician's approval   109 *it original* its origin   111 *Galen* Greek medical writer of the second century A.D.   117 *by the heels* in the stocks (or in prison)   122 *in respect* by reason   124 *make . . . scruple* hesitate to admit ('dram' and 'scruple' are small weights used by apothecaries)   126 *for your life* for which your life might have been forfeit   128 *land-service* military service   140 *gall* irritate   142 *your . . . on Gad's Hill* (a robbing escapade of Falstaff and the prince; see *1 Henry IV*, II)   143 *o'erposting* escape from the consequences of   147 *smell a fox* be suspicious   150 *wassail candle* large candle used at feasts   151 *wax* a pun on (1) beeswax, (2) grow   153 *effect* outward sign   157 *ill angel* a clipped coin   159–60 *cannot go* cannot pass for currency   161 *costermongers' times* i.e. materialistic times (a costermonger is a huckster of apples and other fruits)   162 *Pregnancy* intellectual attainment   163 *reckonings* tavern bills   168 *vaward* vanguard   170 *characters* (1) characteristics, (2) letters   174 *single* poor, trivial

179 round belly. For my voice, I have lost it with halloing
and singing of anthems. To approve my youth further,
I will not. The truth is, I am only old in judgment and
182 understanding; and he that will caper with me for a
183 thousand marks, let him lend me the money, and have at
him! For the box of the ear that the prince gave you, he
gave it like a rude prince, and you took it like a sensible
lord. I have checked him for it, and the young lion
repents; marry, not in ashes and sackcloth, but in new
187 silk and old sack.

CHIEF JUSTICE Well, God send the prince a better
companion!

FALSTAFF God send the companion a better prince! I
cannot rid my hands of him.

CHIEF JUSTICE Well, the king hath severed you and
Prince Harry. I hear you are going with Lord John of
Lancaster against the archbishop and the Earl of
Northumberland.

194 FALSTAFF Yea, I thank your pretty sweet wit for it. But
195 look you pray, all you that kiss my lady Peace at home,
that our armies join not in a hot day, for, by the Lord, I
take but two shirts out with me, and I mean not to sweat
extraordinarily. If it be a hot day, and I brandish any-
199 thing but a bottle, I would I might never spit white
again. There is not a dangerous action can peep out his
head but I am thrust upon it. Well, I cannot last ever.
But it was alway yet the trick of our English nation, if
they have a good thing, to make it too common. If ye
will needs say I am an old man, you should give me rest.
I would to God my name were not so terrible to the
enemy as it is. I were better to be eaten to death with a
rust than to be scoured to nothing with perpetual
motion.

CHIEF JUSTICE Well, be honest, be honest, and God
bless your expedition!

FALSTAFF Will your lordship lend me a thousand
pound to furnish me forth?

CHIEF JUSTICE Not a penny, not a penny. You are too
213 impatient to bear crosses. Fare you well. Commend me
to my cousin Westmoreland.

*[Exeunt Chief Justice and Servant.]*

215 FALSTAFF If I do, fillip me with a three-man beetle. A
man can no more separate age and covetousness than 'a
can part young limbs and lechery. But the gout galls the
one and the pox pinches the other, and so both the
219 degrees prevent my curses. Boy!

PAGE Sir?

FALSTAFF What money is in my purse?

222 PAGE Seven groats and two pence.

FALSTAFF I can get no remedy against this consumption
of the purse. Borrowing only lingers and lingers it out,
but the disease is incurable. Go bear this letter to my
Lord of Lancaster, this to the prince, this to the Earl of
Westmoreland, and this to old Mistress Ursula, whom I
have weekly sworn to marry since I perceived the first
white hair of my chin. About it. You know where to find
me. *[Exit Page.]* A pox of this gout! Or a gout of this
pox! For the one or the other plays the rogue with my
232 great toe. 'Tis no matter if I do halt; I have the wars for
233 my color, and my pension shall seem the more reasonable. A good wit will make use of anything. I will turn
235 diseases to commodity.                          *[Exit.]*

*

*Enter the Archbishop, Thomas Mowbray [Earl
Marshal], the Lords Hastings and Bardolph.*

ARCHBISHOP
Thus have you heard our cause and known our means;
And, my most noble friends, I pray you all,
Speak plainly your opinions of our hopes.
And first, lord marshal, what say you to it?

MOWBRAY
I well allow the occasion of our arms,                       5
But gladly would be better satisfied
How in our means we should advance ourselves             7
To look with forehead bold and big enough
Upon the power and puissance of the king.                   9

HASTINGS
Our present musters grow upon the file                      10
To five-and-twenty thousand men of choice;
And our supplies live largely in the hope                   12
Of great Northumberland, whose bosom burns
With an incensèd fire of injuries.

LORD BARDOLPH
The question then, Lord Hastings, standeth thus:
Whether our present five-and-twenty thousand
May hold up head without Northumberland?

HASTINGS
With him, we may.

LORD BARDOLPH                Yea, marry, there's the point.
But if without him we be thought too feeble,
My judgment is, we should not step too far
[Till we had his assistance by the hand.
For in a theme so bloody-faced as this,                     20
Conjecture, expectation, and surmise
Of aids incertain should not be admitted.]

ARCHBISHOP
'Tis very true, Lord Bardolph, for indeed                   23
It was young Hotspur's case at Shrewsbury.

LORD BARDOLPH
It was, my lord, who lined himself with hope,               25
Eating the air on promise of supply,
Flattering himself in project of a power                    27
Much smaller than the smallest of his thoughts,
And so, with great imagination                              29
Proper to madmen, led his powers to death
And winking leaped into destruction.                        31

HASTINGS
But, by your leave, it never yet did hurt
To lay down likelihoods and forms of hope.

LORD BARDOLPH
[Yes, if this present quality of war,                       34
Indeed the instant action, a cause on foot,
Lives so in hope as in an early spring

---

179 *halloing* shouting to hounds    182 *caper* compete in a dance    183 *marks*
coins worth 13s. 6d. apiece    187 *sack* a Spanish wine    194 *wit* intellect
195 *look you pray* be sure to pray    199 *spit white* (meaning uncertain; in the
light of Falstaff's character, the general sense is probably: May I never take
another drink)    213 *crosses* (1) afflictions, (2) coins stamped with a cross
215 *fillip* strike; *three-man beetle* ram or pile driver requiring three men to
lift it    219 *prevent* anticipate    222 *groats* coins worth 4d. apiece    232
*halt* limp    233 *color* excuse    235 *commodity* profit
I, iii The palace of the Archbishop of York    5 *allow the occasion* admit the
justification    7 *in* with    9 *puissance* power    10 *file* roll    12 *supplies*
reinforcements    22 *theme* matter    26 *case* situation    27 *lined* reinforced
29–30 *in . . . thoughts* in the foolish notion that his army was much larger
than it was in fact    33 *winking* shutting his eyes    36–41 (an obscure
passage; the sense is: Yes, but in this instance there is harm in over-
optimism, just as there is harm in being overhopeful about the buds of
early spring and forgetting the possibility of a killing frost)

We see the appearing buds, which to prove fruit,
Hope gives not so much warrant as despair
That frosts will bite them. When we mean to build,
42 We first survey the plot, then draw the model.
43 And when we see the figure of the house,
Then must we rate the cost of the erection,
Which if we find outweighs ability,
What do we then but draw anew the model
47 In fewer offices, or at least desist
To build at all? Much more, in this great work,
Which is almost to pluck a kingdom down
And set another up, should we survey
The plot of situation and the model, ·
52 Consent upon a sure foundation,
53 Question surveyors, know our own estate,
How able such a work to undergo,
55 To weigh against his opposite. Or else]
56 We fortify in paper and in figures,
Using the names of men instead of men,
Like one that draws the model of a house
Beyond his power to build it, who, half through,
60 Gives o'er and leaves his part-created cost
A naked subject to the weeping clouds
62 And waste for churlish winter's tyranny.

HASTINGS
Grant that our hopes, yet likely of fair birth,
Should be still-born, and that we now possessed
The utmost man of expectation,
I think we are a body strong enough,
Even as we are, to equal with the king.

LORD BARDOLPH
What, is the king but five-and-twenty thousand?

HASTINGS
To us no more, nay, not so much, Lord Bardolph.
For his divisions, as the times do brawl,
Are in three heads: one power against the French,
And one against Glendower, perforce a third
Must take up us. So is the unfirm king
74 In three divided, and his coffers sound
With hollow poverty and emptiness.

ARCHBISHOP
76 That he should draw his several strengths together
And come against us in full puissance
Need not be dreaded.

HASTINGS                    If he should do so,
[He leaves his back unarmed, the French and Welsh]
Baying him at the heels. Never fear that.

LORD BARDOLPH
81 Who is it like should lead his forces hither?

HASTINGS
The Duke of Lancaster and Westmoreland.
Against the Welsh, himself and Harry Monmouth.
But who is substituted 'gainst the French,                84
I have no certain notice.
[ARCHBISHOP                    Let us on,
And publish the occasion of our arms.
The commonwealth is sick of their own choice;
Their overgreedy love hath surfeited.                        88
An habitation giddy and unsure
Hath he that buildeth on the vulgar heart.
O thou fond many, with what loud applause                91
Didst thou beat heaven with blessing Bolingbroke,        92
Before he was what thou wouldst have him be!
And being now trimmed in thine own desires,             94
Thou, beastly feeder, art so full of him
That thou provok'st thyself to cast him up.
So, so, thou common dog, didst thou disgorge
Thy glutton bosom of the royal Richard;
And now thou wouldst eat thy dead vomit up,
And howl'st to find it. What trust is in these times?
They that when Richard lived would have him die
Are now become enamored on his grave.
Thou that threw'st dust upon his goodly head            103
When through proud London he came sighing on
After the admired heels of Bolingbroke
Criest now, 'O earth, yield us that king again,
And take thou this!' O thoughts of men accursed!
Past and to come seems best, things present worst.]
[MOWBRAY]
Shall we go draw our numbers and set on?                  109
HASTINGS
We are time's subjects, and time bids be gone. [Exeunt.]

*

*Enter Hostess of the Tavern and an Officer or two*     II, i
*[Fang and another, followed by Snare].*
HOSTESS Master Fang, have you entered the action?        1
FANG It is entered.
HOSTESS Where's your yeoman? Is't a lusty yeoman?      3
Will 'a stand to't?
FANG [to Officer] Sirrah, where's Snare?
HOSTESS O Lord, ay! Good Master Snare.
SNARE Here, here.
FANG Snare, we must arrest Sir John Falstaff.
HOSTESS Yea, good Master Snare, I have entered him
and all.
SNARE It may chance cost some of us our lives, for he will
stab.
HOSTESS Alas the day! Take heed of him. He stabbed me
in mine own house, and that most beastly. In good
faith, he cares not what mischief he does, if his weapon
be out. He will foin like any devil; he will spare neither  16
man, woman, nor child.
FANG If I can close with him, I care not for his thrust.    18
HOSTESS No, nor I neither. I'll be at your elbow.
FANG An I but fist him once, an 'a come but within my    20
vice—                                                                        21
HOSTESS I am undone by his going. I warrant you, he's
an infinitive thing upon my score. Good Master Fang,    23
hold him sure. Good Master Snare, let him not 'scape.
'A comes continuantly to Pie Corner – saving your
manhoods – to buy a saddle; and he is indited to dinner  26
to the Lubber's Head in Lumbert Street, to Master        27

42 *model* plan  43 *figure* design  47 *offices* supplementary rooms for
services  52 *Consent* agree  53 *surveyors* architects  55 *his opposite*
the opposition  56 *We fortify in paper* our strength is all on paper
60 *part-created cost* building unfinished because there was insufficient
money to complete it  62 *churlish* violent  74 *sound* echo  76 *several*
separate  81 *Who . . . should* who is likely to  84 *substituted* delegated
88 *surfeited* overeaten  91 *fond many* foolish multitude  92 *beat heaven*
assail heaven with prayers  94 *trimmed* dressed  103 *Thou* i.e. the multitude  109 *draw our numbers* assemble our troops
II, i Before an Eastcheap tavern  1 *Master Fang* the sheriff's sergeant;
*entered the action* begun the lawsuit  3 *yeoman* the sergeant's man  16
*foin* thrust (with an indecent double meaning)  18 *close* grapple  20 *fist*
punch  21 *vice* grip  23 *infinitive* infinite (Mistress Quickly's spectacular misuse of words will be obvious throughout); *score* tavern account
26 *indited* i.e. invited  27 *Lubber's Head* Libbard's (Leopard's) Head
(a shop sign); *Lumbert* Lombard

28    Smooth's the silkman. I pray you, since my exion is
entered and my case so openly known to the world, let
him be brought in to his answer. A hundred mark is a
long one for a poor lone woman to bear, and I have
32    borne, and borne, and borne, and have been fubbed off,
and fubbed off, and fubbed off, from this day to that
day, that it is a shame to be thought on. There is no
honesty in such dealing, unless a woman should be
made an ass and a beast, to bear every knave's wrong.
37    Yonder he comes, and that arrant malmsey-nose knave,
Bardolph, with him. Do your offices, do your offices.
Master Fang and Master Snare, do me, do me, do me
your offices.

    *Enter Sir John [Falstaff] and Bardolph, and the Boy*
    *[Page].*

FALSTAFF How now! Whose mare 's dead? What's the
matter?

FANG Sir John, I arrest you at the suit of Mistress
Quickly.

FALSTAFF Away, varlets! Draw, Bardolph. Cut me off
44    the villain's head. Throw the quean in the channel.

HOSTESS Throw me in the channel! I'll throw thee in the
channel. Wilt thou? Wilt thou? Thou bastardly rogue!
47    Murder, murder! Ah, thou honeysuckle villain! Wilt
48    thou kill God's officers and the king's? Ah, thou honey-
49    seed rogue! Thou art a honeyseed, a man-queller, and a
woman-queller.

FALSTAFF Keep them off, Bardolph.

FANG A rescue! A rescue!

HOSTESS Good people, bring a rescue or two. Thou wo't,
wo't thou? Thou wo't, wo't ta? Do, do, thou rogue!
55    Do, thou hempseed!
56 PAGE Away, you scullion! You rampallian! You fustilar-
57    ian! I'll tickle your catastrophe.

    *Enter Lord Chief Justice and his Men.*

CHIEF JUSTICE
What is the matter? Keep the peace here, ho!

HOSTESS Good my lord, be good to me. I beseech you,
60    stand to me.

CHIEF JUSTICE
How now, Sir John! What are you brawling here?
Doth this become your place, your time and business?
You should have been well on your way to York.
Stand from him, fellow. Wherefore hang'st upon him?

HOSTESS O my most worshipful lord, an't please your
grace, I am a poor widow of Eastcheap, and he is
arrested at my suit.

CHIEF JUSTICE For what sum?

HOSTESS It is more than for some, my lord; it is for all,
all I have. He hath eaten me out of house and home; he
hath put all my substance into that fat belly of his. But I
will have some of it out again, or I will ride thee o' nights
73    like the mare.

FALSTAFF I think I am as like to ride the mare, if I have
any vantage of ground to get up.

CHIEF JUSTICE How comes this, Sir John? Fie! what
man of good temper would endure this tempest of
exclamation? Are you not ashamed to enforce a poor
widow to so rough a course to come by her own?

FALSTAFF What is the gross sum that I owe thee?

HOSTESS Marry, if thou wert an honest man, thyself and
82    the money too. Thou didst swear to me upon a parcel-
83    gilt goblet, sitting in my Dolphin chamber, at the round
84    table, by a sea-coal fire, upon Wednesday in Wheeson

week, when the prince broke thy head for liking his 85
father to a singing-man of Windsor, thou didst swear to
me then, as I was washing thy wound, to marry me and
make me my lady thy wife. Canst thou deny it? Did not
goodwife Keech, the butcher's wife, come in then and
call me gossip Quickly? Coming in to borrow a mess of 90
vinegar, telling us she had a good dish of prawns, where- 91
by thou didst desire to eat some, whereby I told thee
they were ill for a green wound? And didst thou not, 93
when she was gone down stairs, desire me to be no more
so familiarity with such poor people, saying that ere long
they should call me madam? And didst thou not kiss me
and bid me fetch thee thirty shillings? I put thee now to
thy book-oath. Deny it, if thou canst.

FALSTAFF My lord, this is a poor mad soul, and she says
up and down the town that her eldest son is like you. She
hath been in good case, and the truth is, poverty hath 10
distracted her. But for these foolish officers, I beseech 10
you I may have redress against them.

CHIEF JUSTICE Sir John, Sir John, I am well acquainted
with your manner of wrenching the true cause the false
way. It is not a confident brow, nor the throng of words
that come with such more than impudent sauciness
from you, can thrust me from a level consideration. You 10
have, as it appears to me, practiced upon the easy-
yielding spirit of this woman, and made her serve your
uses both in purse and in person.

HOSTESS Yea, in truth, my lord.

CHIEF JUSTICE Pray thee, peace. Pay her the debt you
owe her and unpay the villainy you have done with her.
The one you may do with sterling money, and the other
with current repentance. 11

FALSTAFF My lord, I will not undergo this sneap with- 11
out reply. You call honorable boldness impudent
sauciness. If a man will make curtsy and say nothing, he
is virtuous. No, my lord, my humble duty remembered,
I will not be your suitor. I say to you, I do desire deliverance from these officers, being upon hasty employment in the king's affairs.

CHIEF JUSTICE You speak as having power to do wrong.
But answer in the effect of your reputation, and satisfy 12
the poor woman.

FALSTAFF Come hither, hostess.

    *Enter a Messenger [Gower].*

CHIEF JUSTICE Now, Master Gower, what news?

GOWER
The king, my lord, and Harry Prince of Wales
Are near at hand. The rest the paper tells.

FALSTAFF As I am a gentleman.

HOSTESS Faith, you said so before.

FALSTAFF As I am a gentleman. Come, no more words of
it.

HOSTESS By this heavenly ground I tread on, I must be

28 *exion* action   32 *fubbed off* put off   37 *malmsey-nose* red-nosed from
drinking wine   44 *quean* slut; *channel* gutter   47 *honeysuckle* i.e. homi-
cidal   48 *honeyseed* i.e. homicide   49 *man-queller* i.e. man-killer   55
*hempseed* gallows-bird   56 *scullion* kitchen wench; *rampallian* scoundrel;
*fustilarian* frowsy fat woman   57 *catastrophe* backside   60 *stand to*
help   73 *mare* nightmare   82 *parcel-gilt* partly gilded   83 *Dolphin
chamber* (a room in her tavern)   84 *sea-coal* coal mined from sea-coast
veins; *Wheeson* Whitsun (Pentecost)   85 *liking* comparing   90 *gossip*
(a familiar term of address)   91 *prawns* shrimps   93 *green* raw   101
*in good case* prosperous   102 *distracted her* driven her mad   108 *level*
unbiased   116 *current* genuine   117 *sneap* rebuke   125 *in . . . reputation*
suitably for a man of your reputation

fain to pawn both my plate and the tapestry of my
dining-chambers.

37 FALSTAFF Glasses, glasses, is the only drinking. And for
38 thy walls, a pretty slight drollery, or the story of the
39 Prodigal, or the German hunting in water-work, is
worth a thousand of these bed-hangings and these fly-
bitten tapestries. Let it be ten pound, if thou canst.
42 Come, an 'twere not for thy humors, there's not a better
43 wench in England. Go, wash thy face, and draw the
action. Come, thou must not be in this humor with me.
Dost not know me? Come, come, I know thou wast set
on to this.

46 HOSTESS Pray thee, Sir John, let it be but twenty nobles.
I' faith, I am loath to pawn my plate, so God save me,
la!

FALSTAFF Let it alone; I'll make other shift. You'll be a
fool still.

HOSTESS Well, you shall have it, though I pawn my
gown. I hope you'll come to supper. You'll pay me all
together?

FALSTAFF Will I live? [to Bardolph] Go, with her, with
55 her. Hook on, hook on.

HOSTESS Will you have Doll Tearsheet meet you at
supper?

FALSTAFF No more words. Let's have her.
     Exeunt Hostess and Sergeant [Fang, Bardolph, and
       others].

CHIEF JUSTICE I have heard better news.

FALSTAFF What's the news, my lord?

CHIEF JUSTICE Where lay the king last night?

GOWER At Basingstoke, my lord.

FALSTAFF I hope, my lord, all's well. What is the news,
my lord?

CHIEF JUSTICE Come all his forces back?

GOWER
No. Fifteen hundred foot, five hundred horse,
Are marched up to my lord of Lancaster,
Against Northumberland and the archbishop.

FALSTAFF
Comes the king back from Wales, my noble lord?

CHIEF JUSTICE
You shall have letters of me presently.
70 Come, go along with me, good Master Gower.

FALSTAFF My lord!

CHIEF JUSTICE What's the matter?

FALSTAFF Master Gower, shall I entreat you with me to
dinner?

GOWER I must wait upon my good lord here, I thank you,
good Sir John.

CHIEF JUSTICE Sir John, you loiter here too long, being
you are to take soldiers up in counties as you go.    178

FALSTAFF Will you sup with me, Master Gower?

CHIEF JUSTICE What foolish master taught you these
manners, Sir John?

FALSTAFF Master Gower, if they become me not, he was
a fool that taught them me. This is the right fencing    183
grace, my lord – tap for tap, and so part fair.

CHIEF JUSTICE Now the Lord lighten thee! Thou art a    185
great fool.    [Exeunt.]

*

PRINCE Before God, I am exceeding weary.

POINS Is't come to that? I had thought weariness durst
not have attached one of so high blood.    3

PRINCE Faith, it does me, though it discolors the com-    4
plexion of my greatness to acknowledge it. Doth it not
show vilely in me to desire small beer?

POINS Why, a prince should not be so loosely studied as    7
to remember so weak a composition.    8

PRINCE Belike, then, my appetite was not princely got,    9
for, by my troth, I do now remember the poor creature,
small beer. But indeed these humble considerations
make me out of love with my greatness. What a disgrace
is it to me to remember thy name! Or to know thy face
to-morrow! Or to take note how many pair of silk
stockings thou hast, viz. these, and those that were thy
peach-colored ones! Or to bear the inventory of thy
shirts, as, one for superfluity, and another for use! But    17
that the tennis-court-keeper knows better than I; for it
is a low ebb of linen with thee when thou keepest not
racket there, as thou hast not done a great while, because the rest of thy low countries have made a shift to    21
eat up thy holland. And God knows whether those that    22
bawl out the ruins of thy linen shall inherit his kingdom.
But the midwives say the children are not in the fault,
whereupon the world increases, and kindreds are
mightily strengthened.

POINS How ill it follows, after you have labored so hard,
you should talk so idly! Tell me, how many good young
princes would do so, their fathers being so sick as yours
at this time is?

PRINCE Shall I tell thee one thing, Poins?

POINS Yes, faith, and let it be an excellent good thing.

PRINCE It shall serve among wits of no higher breeding
than thine.

POINS Go to. I stand the push of your one thing that you    34
will tell.

PRINCE Marry, I tell thee, it is not meet that I should be
sad, now my father is sick. Albeit I could tell to thee, as
to one it pleases me, for fault of a better, to call my
friend, I could be sad, and sad indeed too.

POINS Very hardly upon such a subject.    40

PRINCE By this hand, thou thinkest me as far in the
devil's book as thou and Falstaff for obduracy and    42
persistency. Let the end try the man. But I tell thee, my
heart bleeds inwardly that my father is so sick. And
keeping such vile company as thou art hath in reason
taken from me all ostentation of sorrow.    46

POINS The reason?

PRINCE What wouldst thou think of me if I should
weep?

---

137 Glasses . . . drinking glasses, not metal tankards, are now fashionable
138 drollery comic picture    139 water-work water color    142 humors
vagaries    143 draw withdraw    146 nobles coins worth 6s. 8d. each    155
Hook on stay with her and don't let her change    178 take soldiers up
recruit soldiers    183–84 right fencing grace correct form in fencing    185
lighten enlighten
II, ii The London dwelling of Prince Henry    3 attached seized    4 discolors the complexion makes me blush    7 so loosely studied such a careless
student    8 so weak a composition such small beer, i.e. trifles    9 got begotten
17 one for superfluity an extra one    17–20 But . . . while (the sense of the
passage is that a courtier needs to change his shirt after playing tennis;
Poins, with only one shirt, has not been seen recently on the tennis-courts)
21 thy low countries i.e. the brothels frequented by Poins; made a shift
contrived, with a play upon 'shift' meaning shirt    22 holland best linen
22–23 those . . . linen i.e. your bastards, who wear your shirts    34 push
thrust    40 Very hardly with great difficulty    42 obduracy unregeneracy
46 ostentation outward display

POINS I would think thee a most princely hypocrite.

PRINCE It would be every man's thought, and thou art a blessed fellow to think as every man thinks. Never a man's thought in the world keeps the roadway better than thine. Every man would think me an hypocrite
55 indeed. And what accites your most worshipful thought to think so?

57 POINS Why, because you have been so lewd and so much
58 engraffed to Falstaff.

PRINCE And to thee.

POINS By this light, I am well spoke on; I can hear it with mine own ears. The worst that they can say of me is that
62 I am a second brother and that I am a proper fellow of my hands, and those two things I confess I cannot help. By the mass, here comes Bardolph.

*Enter Bardolph and Boy [Page].*

PRINCE And the boy that I gave Falstaff. 'A had him from me Christian, and look if the fat villain have not transformed him ape.

BARDOLPH God save your grace!

PRINCE And yours, most noble Bardolph!

POINS Come, you virtuous ass, you bashful fool, must
71 you be blushing? Wherefore blush you now? What a maidenly man-at-arms are you become! Is't such a
73 matter to get a pottle-pot's maidenhead?

74 PAGE 'A calls me e'en now, my lord, through a red lattice, and I could discern no part of his face from the window. At last I spied his eyes, and methought he had made two holes in the ale-wife's new petticoat and so peeped through.

79 PRINCE Has not the boy profited?

BARDOLPH Away, you whoreson upright rabbit, away!

81 PAGE Away, you rascally Althaea's dream, away!

PRINCE Instruct us, boy. What dream, boy?

83 PAGE Marry, my lord, Althaea dreamed she was delivered of a firebrand, and therefore I call him her dream.

PRINCE A crown's worth of good interpretation. There 'tis, boy.

POINS O, that this good blossom could be kept from
88 cankers! Well, there is sixpence to preserve thee.

BARDOLPH An you do not make him hanged among you, the gallows shall have wrong.

PRINCE And how doth thy master, Bardolph?

BARDOLPH Well, my lord. He heard of your grace's coming to town. There's a letter for you.

94 POINS Delivered with good respect. And how doth the
95 martlemas, your master?

BARDOLPH In bodily health, sir.

POINS Marry, the immortal part needs a physician, but that moves not him. Though that be sick, it dies not.

99 PRINCE I do allow this wen to be as familiar with me as my dog, and he holds his place, for look you how he writes.

POINS [reads] 'John Falstaff, knight' – every man must know that, as oft as he has occasion to name himself. Even like those that are kin to the king, for they never prick their finger but they say, 'There's some of the king's blood spilt.' 'How comes that?' says he that takes upon him not to conceive. The answer is as ready as a borrower's cap, 'I am the king's poor cousin, sir.'

108 PRINCE Nay, they will be kin to us, or they will fetch it from Japhet. But to the letter. [reads] 'Sir John Falstaff, knight, to the son of the king, nearest his father, Harry Prince of Wales, greeting.'

POINS Why, this is a certificate.

PRINCE Peace! [reads] 'I will imitate the honorable Romans in brevity.'

POINS He sure means brevity in breath, short-winded.

[PRINCE reads] 'I commend me to thee, I commend thee, and I leave thee. Be not too familiar with Poins, for he misuses thy favors so much that he swears thou art to marry his sister Nell. Repent at idle times as thou mayest, and so farewell.

'Thine, by yea and no, which is as much as to say, as thou usest him, JACK FALSTAFF with my familiars, JOHN with my brothers and sisters, and SIR JOHN with all Europe.'

POINS My lord, I'll steep this letter in sack and make him eat it.

PRINCE That's to make him eat twenty of his words. But do you use me thus, Ned? Must I marry your sister?

POINS God send the wench no worse fortune! But I never said so.

PRINCE Well, thus we play the fools with the time, and the spirits of the wise sit in the clouds and mock us. Is your master here in London?

BARDOLPH Yea, my lord.

PRINCE Where sups he? Doth the old boar feed in the old frank?

BARDOLPH At the old place, my lord, in Eastcheap.

PRINCE What company?

PAGE Ephesians, my lord, of the old church.

PRINCE Sup any women with him?

PAGE None, my lord, but old Mistress Quickly and Mistress Doll Tearsheet.

PRINCE What pagan may that be?

PAGE A proper gentlewoman, sir, and a kinswoman of my master's.

PRINCE Even such kin as the parish heifers are to the town bull. Shall we steal upon them, Ned, at supper?

POINS I am your shadow, my lord; I'll follow you.

PRINCE Sirrah, you boy, and Bardolph, no word to your master that I am yet come to town. There's for your silence.

BARDOLPH I have no tongue, sir.

PAGE And for mine, sir, I will govern it.

PRINCE Fare you well; go. [Exeunt Bardolph and Page.] This Doll Tearsheet should be some road.

POINS I warrant you, as common as the way between Saint Alban's and London.

---

55 *accites* arouses   57 *lewd* base   58 *engraffed* attached   62 *second brother* younger son, without inheritance   62–63 *proper . . . hands* good fighter   71 *blushing* (Bardolph's red face calls forth this jibe and what follows)   73 *get . . . maidenhead* drink up a two-quart tankard of ale   74 *red lattice* (the lattices of the tavern windows were painted red)   79 *profited* become proficient   81 *Althaea's dream* (Althaea dreamed that her son would live only so long as a brand burned in the fire)   83–85 (the page, suffering from a little learning, describes Hecuba's dream, not Althaea's)   88 *cankers* canker worms   94 *good respect* proper ceremony (spoken ironically)   95 *martlemas* martlemas beef, i.e. beef fattened for slaughter on Martinmas Day (November 11)   99 *wen* tumor   108–09 *fetch . . . Japhet* trace their ancestry back to Noah's son Japhet (traditionally regarded as the progenitor of the peoples of Europe)   112 *certificate* legal document   121 *by yea and no* (a Puritan oath)   127 *twenty* (used loosely to mean a large number)   136 *frank* sty   139 *Ephesians . . . church* i.e. boon companions   143 *pagan* strumpet   150 *There's* there's money   155 *road* i.e. whore (who, like a highway, is common to all)

58 PRINCE How might we see Falstaff bestow himself to-
night in his true colors, and not ourselves be seen?

160 POINS Put on two leathern jerkins and aprons, and wait
161 upon him at his table as drawers.

PRINCE From a God to a bull? A heavy descension! It
163 was Jove's case. From a prince to a prentice? A low
transformation! That shall be mine, for in everything
165 the purpose must weigh with the folly. Follow me, Ned.
*Exeunt.*

\*

iii          *Enter Northumberland, his Wife [Lady*
*Northumberland], and the Wife to Harry Percy*
*[Lady Percy].*

NORTHUMBERLAND
1   I pray thee, loving wife, and gentle daughter,
2   Give even way unto my rough affairs.
Put not you on the visage of the times
And be like them to Percy troublesome.

LADY NORTHUMBERLAND
I have given over, I will speak no more.
Do what you will, your wisdom be your guide.

NORTHUMBERLAND
Alas, sweet wife, my honor is at pawn,
8   And, but my going, nothing can redeem it.

LADY PERCY
O yet, for God's sake, go not to these wars!
The time was, father, that you broke your word,
11  When you were more endeared to it than now,
12  When your own Percy, when my heart's dear Harry,
Threw many a northward look to see his father
Bring up his powers, but he did long in vain.
Who then persuaded you to stay at home?
There were two honors lost, yours and your son's.
17  For yours, the God of heaven brighten it!
For his, it stuck upon him as the sun
19  In the grey vault of heaven, and by his light
Did all the chivalry of England move
21  To do brave acts. He was indeed the glass
Wherein the noble youth did dress themselves.
[He had no legs that practiced not his gait;
24  And speaking thick, which nature made his blemish,
Became the accents of the valiant,
For those that could speak low and tardily
Would turn their own perfection to abuse,
To seem like him. So that in speech, in gait,
29  In diet, in affections of delight,
30  In military rules, humors of blood,
He was the mark and glass, copy and book,
That fashioned others. And him – O wondrous him!
O miracle of men! – him did you leave,

Second to none, unseconded by you,
To look upon the hideous god of war
In disadvantage, to abide a field          36
Where nothing but the sound of Hotspur's name
Did seem defensible. So you left him.          38
Never, O never, do his ghost the wrong
To hold your honor more precise and nice
With others than with him! Let them alone.
The marshal and the archbishop are strong.
Had my sweet Harry had but half their numbers,
To-day might I, hanging on Hotspur's neck,
Have talked of Monmouth's grave.]          45

NORTHUMBERLAND          Beshrew your heart,
Fair daughter, you do draw my spirits from me
With new lamenting ancient oversights.
But I must go and meet with danger there,
Or it will seek me in another place
And find me worse provided.

LADY NORTHUMBERLAND O, fly to Scotland,
Till that the nobles and the armèd commons
Have of their puissance made a little taste.

LADY PERCY
If they get ground and vantage of the king,
Then join you with them, like a rib of steel,
To make strength stronger. But, for all our loves,
First let them try themselves. So did your son;
He was so suffered. So came I a widow,          57
And never shall have length of life enough
To rain upon remembrance with mine eyes,          59
That it may grow and sprout as high as heaven,
For recordation to my noble husband.          61

NORTHUMBERLAND
Come, come, go in with me. 'Tis with my mind
As with the tide swelled up unto his height,
That makes a still-stand, running neither way.
Fain would I go to meet the archbishop,
But many thousand reasons hold me back.
I will resolve for Scotland. There am I,
Till time and vantage crave my company.          *Exeunt.*          68

\*

*Enter a Drawer or two [Francis and a second].*          II, iv
FRANCIS What the devil hast thou brought there? Apple-          1
johns? Thou knowest Sir John cannot endure an apple-
john.

2. DRAWER Mass, thou sayest true. The prince once set a
dish of apple-johns before him, and told him there were
five more Sir Johns, and, putting off his hat, said, 'I will
now take my leave of these six dry, round, old, withered
knights.' It angered him to the heart. But he hath forgot
that.

FRANCIS Why, then, cover, and set them down. And see          10
if thou canst find out Sneak's noise; Mistress Tear-          11
sheet would fain hear some music. Dispatch. The room
where they supped is too hot; they'll come in straight.
*Enter Will [a third Drawer].*

3. DRAWER Sirrah, here will be the prince and Master
Poins anon, and they will put on two of our jerkins and
aprons, and Sir John must not know of it. Bardolph
hath brought word.          *[Exit.]*

FRANCIS By the mass, here will be old Utis. It will be an          18
excellent stratagem.

2. DRAWER I'll see if I can find out Sneak.          *Exit.*

158 *bestow* behave   160 *jerkins* jackets   161 *drawers* servers of liquor   163
*Jove's case* (for love of Europa, Jove transformed himself into a bull)
165 *weigh with* be equal to
II, iii Northumberland's castle   1 *daughter* i.e. daughter-in-law   2 *even
way* free scope   8 *but* except for   11 *endeared* bound by duty   12–14 *When
. . . vain* (a reference to Northumberland's failure to come to his son's
support at Shrewsbury)   17 *For* as for   19 *grey* sky-blue   21 *glass* mirror
24 *thick* fast   29 *affections of delight* pleasures   30 *humors of blood* temperament   36 *abide a field* fight a battle   38 *defensible* able to defend   45
*Monmouth's* Prince Hal's; *Beshrew* plague on   57 *suffered* allowed to have his
own way   59 *rain* weep   61 *recordation* memorial   68 *vantage* superiority
II, iv Within an Eastcheap tavern   1–2 *Apple-johns* kind of apple that
looks withered when ripe   10 *cover* lay the cloth   11 *noise* band of
musicians   18 *old Utis* a noisy row

*Enter Mistress Quickly [the Hostess] and Doll Tearsheet.*

HOSTESS I' faith, sweetheart, methinks now you are in an
22 excellent good temperality. Your pulsidge beats as
23 extraordinarily as heart would desire, and your color, I
warrant you, is as red as any rose, in good truth, la! But,
25 i' faith, you have drunk too much canaries, and that's a
26 marvellous searching wine, and it perfumes the blood
ere one can say, 'What's this?' How do you now?

DOLL Better than I was. Hem!

HOSTESS Why, that's well said. A good heart 's worth
gold. Lo, here comes Sir John.

*Enter Sir John [Falstaff].*

31 FALSTAFF [sings] 'When Arthur first in court' – Empty
32 the jordan. [Exit Francis.] – [sings] 'And was a worthy
king.' – How now, Mistress Doll!

34 HOSTESS Sick of a calm, yea, good faith.

35 FALSTAFF So is all her sect. An they be once in a calm,
they are sick.

37 DOLL A pox damn you, you muddy rascal, is that all the
comfort you give me?

39 FALSTAFF You make fat rascals, Mistress Doll.

DOLL I make them! Gluttony and diseases make them; I
make them not.

FALSTAFF If the cook help to make the gluttony, you
help to make the diseases, Doll. We catch of you, Doll,
we catch of you. Grant that, my poor virtue, grant that.

DOLL Yea, joy, our chains and our jewels.

46 FALSTAFF 'Your brooches, pearls, and ouches.' For to
serve bravely is to come halting off, you know. To come
off the breach with his pike bent bravely, and to surgery
49 bravely; to venture upon the charged chambers
bravely –

50 DOLL Hang yourself, you muddy conger, hang yourself!

HOSTESS By my troth, this is the old fashion. You two
never meet but you fall to some discord. You are both, i'
53 good truth, as rheumatic as two dry toasts; you cannot
54 one bear with another's confirmities. What the good-
year! One must bear, and that must be you [to Doll].
You are the weaker vessel, as they say, the emptier
vessel.

DOLL Can a weak empty vessel bear such a huge full hogs-
58 head? There's a whole merchant's venture of Bordeaux
stuff in him; you have not seen a hulk better stuffed in
the hold. Come, I'll be friends with thee, Jack. Thou art
going to the wars, and whether I shall ever see thee
again or no, there is nobody cares.

*Enter Drawer [Francis].*

63 FRANCIS Sir, Ancient Pistol 's below and would speak
with you.

DOLL Hang him, swaggering rascal! Let him not come
hither. It is the foul-mouthed'st rogue in England.

HOSTESS If he swagger, let him not come here. No, by my
faith. I must live among my neighbors, I'll no swaggerers. I am in good name and fame with the very best.
Shut the door, there comes no swaggerers here. I have
not lived all this while to have swaggering now. Shut the
door, I pray you.

FALSTAFF Dost thou hear, hostess?

HOSTESS Pray ye, pacify yourself, Sir John. There comes
no swaggerers here.

FALSTAFF Dost thou hear? It is mine ancient.

77 HOSTESS Tilly-fally, Sir John, ne'er tell me. Your ancient
swaggerer comes not in my doors. I was before Master

Tisick, the debuty, t' other day, and, as he said to me, 79
'twas no longer ago than Wednesday last, 'I' good faith,
neighbor Quickly,' says he – Master Dumbe, our minister, was by then – 'neighbor Quickly,' says he, 'receive
those that are civil, for,' said he, 'you are in an ill name.'
Now 'a said so, I can tell whereupon. 'For,' says he, 'you
are an honest woman, and well thought on; therefore
take heed what guests you receive. Receive,' says he,
'no swaggering companions.' There comes none here. 87
You would bless you to hear what he said. No, I'll no
swaggerers.

FALSTAFF He's no swaggerer, hostess; a tame cheater, i' 90
faith; you may stroke him as gently as a puppy greyhound. He'll not swagger with a Barbary hen, if her 92
feathers turn back in any show of resistance. Call him
up, drawer.                                    [Exit Francis.]

HOSTESS Cheater, call you him? I will bar no honest man
my house, nor no cheater. But I do not love swaggering,
by my troth; I am the worse when one says swagger.
Feel, masters, how I shake, look you, I warrant you.

DOLL So you do, hostess.

HOSTESS Do I? Yea, in very truth, do I, an 'twere an
aspen leaf. I cannot abide swaggerers.

*Enter Ancient Pistol, [Bardolph,] and Bardolph's
Boy [Page].*

PISTOL God save you, Sir John!

FALSTAFF Welcome, Ancient Pistol. Here, Pistol, I
charge you with a cup of sack. Do you discharge upon 102
mine hostess.

PISTOL I will discharge upon her, Sir John, with two
bullets.                                                     105

FALSTAFF She is pistol-proof, sir; you shall hardly offend 106
her.

HOSTESS Come, I'll drink no proofs nor no bullets. I'll
drink no more than will do me good, for no man's
pleasure, I.

PISTOL Then to you, Mistress Dorothy; I will charge you.

DOLL Charge me! I scorn you, scurvy companion. What!
You poor, base, rascally, cheating, lack-linen mate! 111
Away, you mouldy rogue, away! I am meat for your
master.

PISTOL I know you, Mistress Dorothy.

DOLL Away, you cut-purse rascal! You filthy bung, 115
away! By this wine, I'll thrust my knife in your mouldy
chaps, an you play the saucy cuttle with me. Away, you 117
bottle-ale rascal! You basket-hilt stale juggler, you! 118
Since when, I pray you, sir? God's light, with two
points on your shoulder? Much!                          120

---

**22** *temperality* i.e. temper; *pulsidge* i.e. pulse   **23** *extraordinarily* i.e. ordi-
narily   **25** *canaries* a sweet wine   **26** *searching* potent   **31** *When . . . court*
(a snatch from the ballad *Sir Launcelot du Lake*)   **32** *jordan* chamber-pot
**34** *calm* i.e. qualm   **35** *sect* sex   **37** *muddy* dirty   **39** *rascals* (a pun on
'rascal' meaning lean deer)   **46** *Your . . . ouches* (a snatch from another
ballad); *ouches* gems   **49** *charged chambers* small cannon   **50** *conger*
conger eel   **53** *rheumatic* (perhaps she means 'splenetic'); *dry toasts* (which
grate upon each other)   **54** *confirmities* i.e. infirmities   **54-55** *What the
good-year* what the devil   **58-59** *merchant's . . . stuff* shipload of Bordeaux
wine   **63** *Ancient* ensign, lieutenant   **77** *Tilly-fally* nonsense   **79** *debuty*
deputy   **87** *companions* ruffians   **90** *cheater* come-on man in a team of
confidence men   **92** *Barbary hen* guinea hen   **102** *charge* toast (with a play
on the name Pistol)   **102-03** *discharge . . . hostess* toast the hostess   **105**
*bullets* (an indecency which the hostess fails to understand)   **106** *offend*
wound   **111** *mate* (a term of contempt)   **115** *bung* pickpocket   **117** *chaps*
cheeks; *cuttle* cut-throat   **118** *basket-hilt stale juggler* an impostor who
pretends to be a soldier by carrying a sword with a basketlike hand-guard
**120** *points* laces by which pieces of armor were tied to the shoulders

PISTOL God let me not live but I will murder your ruff for this.

FALSTAFF No more, Pistol; I would not have you go off here. Discharge yourself of our company, Pistol.

HOSTESS No, good Captain Pistol, not here, sweet captain.

DOLL Captain! Thou abominable damned cheater, art thou not ashamed to be called captain? An captains were of my mind, they would truncheon you out for taking their names upon you before you have earned them. You a captain! You slave, for what? For tearing a poor whore's ruff in a bawdy-house? He a captain! Hang him, rogue! He lives upon mouldy stewed prunes and dried cakes. A captain! God's light, these villains will make the word as odious as the word 'occupy,' which was an excellent good word before it was ill sorted. Therefore captains had need look to't.

BARDOLPH Pray thee, go down, good ancient.

FALSTAFF Hark thee hither, Mistress Doll.

PISTOL Not I. I tell thee what, Corporal Bardolph, I could tear her. I'll be revenged of her.

PAGE Pray thee, go down.

PISTOL I'll see her damned first, to Pluto's damned lake, by this hand, to the infernal deep, with Erebus and tortures vile also. Hold hook and line, say I. Down, down, dogs! Down, faitors! Have we not Hiren here?

HOSTESS Good Captain Peesel, be quiet; 'tis very late, i' faith. I beseek you now, aggravate your choler.

PISTOL
These be good humors, indeed! Shall pack-horses
And hollow pampered jades of Asia,
Which cannot go but thirty mile a-day,
Compare with Caesars, and with Cannibals,
And Trojan Greeks? Nay, rather damn them with
King Cerberus, and let the welkin roar.
Shall we fall foul for toys?

HOSTESS By my troth, captain, these are very bitter words.

BARDOLPH Be gone, good ancient. This will grow to a brawl anon.

PISTOL Die men like dogs! Give crowns like pins! Have we not Hiren here?

HOSTESS O' my word, captain, there's none such here. What the good-year! Do you think I would deny her? For God's sake, be quiet.

PISTOL
Then feed, and be fat, my fair Calipolis. 163
Come, give's some sack.
'Si fortune me tormente, sperato me contento.' 165
Fear we broadsides? No, let the fiend give fire.
Give me some sack. And, sweetheart, lie thou there.
[Lays down his sword.]
Come we to full points here, and are etceteras nothing? 168

FALSTAFF Pistol, I would be quiet.

PISTOL Sweet knight, I kiss thy neif. What! We have 170 seen the seven stars. 171

DOLL For God's sake, thrust him down stairs. I cannot endure such a fustian rascal. 173

PISTOL Thrust him down stairs! Know we not Galloway 174 nags?

FALSTAFF Quoit him down, Bardolph, like a shove- 176 groat shilling. Nay, an 'a do nothing but speak nothing, 'a shall be nothing here.

BARDOLPH Come, get you down stairs.

PISTOL
What! shall we have incision? Shall we imbrue? 180
[Snatches up his sword.]
Then death rock me asleep, abridge my doleful days!
Why, then, let grievous, ghastly, gaping wounds
Untwine the Sisters Three! Come, Atropos, I say! 183

HOSTESS Here's a goodly stuff toward!

FALSTAFF Give me my rapier, boy.

DOLL I pray thee, Jack, I pray thee, do not draw.

FALSTAFF Get you down stairs.
[Draws, and drives Pistol out.]

HOSTESS Here's a goodly tumult! I'll forswear keeping house afore I'll be in these tirrits and frights. So, 189 murder, I warrant now. Alas, alas! Put up your naked weapons, put up your naked weapons.
[Exeunt Pistol and Bardolph.]

DOLL I pray thee, Jack, be quiet; the rascal 's gone. Ah, you whoreson little valiant villain, you!

HOSTESS Are you not hurt i' the groin? Methought 'a made a shrewd thrust at your belly.
[Enter Bardolph.]

FALSTAFF Have you turned him out o' doors?

BARDOLPH Yea, sir. The rascal 's drunk. You have hurt him, sir, i' the shoulder.

FALSTAFF A rascal! to brave me!

DOLL Ah, you sweet little rogue, you! Alas, poor ape, how thou sweatest! Come, let me wipe thy face; come on, you whoreson chops. Ah, rogue! i' faith, I love thee. 202 Thou art as valorous as Hector of Troy, worth five of Agamemnon, and ten times better than the Nine Wor- 204 thies. Ah, villain!

FALSTAFF A rascally slave! I will toss the rogue in a blanket.

DOLL Do, an thou darest for thy heart. An thou dost, I'll canvass thee between a pair of sheets. 208
Enter Music.

PAGE The music is come, sir.

FALSTAFF Let them play. Play, sirs. Sit on my knee, Doll. A rascal bragging slave! The rogue fled from me like quicksilver.

DOLL I' faith, and thou followedst him like a church. Thou whoreson little tidy Bartholomew boar-pig, when 214 wilt thou leave fighting o' days and foining o' nights, 215 and begin to patch up thine old body for heaven?
Enter [behind] Prince [Henry] and Poins [disguised].

128 *truncheon* beat with a truncheon or staff 134 *occupy* fornicate 135 *ill sorted* misused 142 *Pluto's . . . lake* (Pistol confuses the river Styx with a lake) 143 *Erebus* the underworld 145 *faitors* impostors; *Have . . . here* (a quotation from a play by George Peele) 147 *aggravate* i.e. moderate 149–50 *And . . . day* (a garbled quotation from Marlowe's *Tamburlaine*, Part II) 151 *Cannibals* i.e. Hannibals 152 *Trojan Greeks* (Trojans and Greeks are all one to the excited Pistol) 153 *Cerberus* the three-headed dog who guarded the entrance to Hades 163 *Then . . . Calipolis* (a burlesque of a line in another play by Peele) 165 *Si . . . contento* (a multilingual misquotation of a proverb meaning 'If fortune torments me, hope contents me') 168 *full points* full stops, periods 170 *neif* fist 171 *seven stars* the Pleiades (the idea is that Falstaff and Pistol have often made a night of it) 173 *fustian* worthless 174–75 *Galloway nags* Irish horses of inferior breed 176 *Quoit* throw 176–77 *shove-groat shilling* a coin used in a game somewhat like shuffleboard played on a smooth table 180 *incision* bloodshed; *imbrue* shed blood 183 *Sisters Three* the Fates, of whom Atropos was one 189 *tirrits* fits of temper 202 *chops* fat-cheeked fellow 204 *Nine Worthies* Hector, Alexander, Julius Caesar, Joshua, David, Judas Maccabaeus, Arthur, Charlemagne, Godfrey of Bouillon 208 *canvass* toss in a canvas sheet (but Doll gives her own special meaning to the expression); s.d. *Music* musicians 214 *Bartholomew boar-pig* (roast pig was a favorite delicacy at Bartholomew Fair, held annually on August 24 at Smithfield) 215 *foining* thrusting

217 FALSTAFF Peace, good Doll! Do not speak like a death's-
head. Do not bid me remember mine end.

DOLL Sirrah, what humor 's the prince of?

FALSTAFF A good shallow young fellow. 'A would have
221 made a good pantler, 'a would ha' chipped bread well.

DOLL They say Poins has a good wit.

FALSTAFF He a good wit? Hang him, baboon! His wit 's
224 as thick as Tewkesbury mustard. There's no more
225 conceit in him than is in a mallet.

DOLL Why does the prince love him so, then?

FALSTAFF Because their legs are both of a bigness, and 'a
228 plays at quoits well, and eats conger and fennel, and
229 drinks off candles' ends for flap-dragons, and rides the
230 wild-mare with the boys, and jumps upon joined-stools,
and swears with a good grace, and wears his boots very
232 smooth, like unto the sign of the leg, and breeds no bate
with telling of discreet stories; and such other gambol
faculties 'a has, that show a weak mind and an able body,
for the which the prince admits him. For the prince
himself is such another; the weight of a hair will turn
the scales between their avoirdupois.

238 PRINCE Would not this nave of a wheel have his ears cut
off?

POINS Let's beat him before his whore.

240 PRINCE Look, whether the withered elder hath not his
poll clawed like a parrot.

POINS Is it not strange that desire should so many years
outlive performance?

FALSTAFF Kiss me, Doll.

245 PRINCE Saturn and Venus this year in conjunction!
What says the almanac to that?

247 POINS And look whether the fiery Trigon, his man, be
248 not lisping to his master's old tables, his note-book, his
counsel-keeper.

250 FALSTAFF Thou dost give me flattering busses.

DOLL By my troth, I kiss thee with a most constant
heart.

FALSTAFF I am old, I am old.

DOLL I love thee better than I love e'er a scurvy young
boy of them all.

255 FALSTAFF What stuff wilt have a kirtle of? I shall receive
money o' Thursday. Shalt have a cap to-morrow. A
merry song, come. It grows late; we'll to bed. Thou'lt
forget me when I am gone.

DOLL By my troth, thou'lt set me a-weeping, an thou
sayest so. Prove that ever I dress myself handsome till
261 thy return. Well, hearken a' th' end.

FALSTAFF Some sack, Francis.

PRINCE, POINS Anon, anon, sir.

[Come forward.]

FALSTAFF Ha! a bastard son of the king's? And art not
thou Poins his brother?

266 PRINCE Why, thou globe of sinful continents, what a life
dost thou lead!

FALSTAFF A better than thou. I am a gentleman, thou
art a drawer.

PRINCE Very true, sir, and I come to draw you out by the
ears.

HOSTESS O, the Lord preserve thy good grace! By my
troth, welcome to London. Now, the Lord bless that
sweet face of thine! O Jesu, are you come from Wales?

275 FALSTAFF Thou whoreson mad compound of majesty,
276 by this light flesh and corrupt blood, thou art welcome.

DOLL How, you fat fool! I scorn you.

POINS My lord, he will drive you out of your revenge and
turn all to a merriment, if you take not the heat.          27

PRINCE You whoreson candle-mine you, how vilely did     28
you speak of me even now before this honest, virtuous,
civil gentlewoman!

HOSTESS God's blessing of your good heart! And so she
is, by my troth.

FALSTAFF Didst thou hear me?

PRINCE Yea, and you knew me, as you did when you ran    28
away by Gad's Hill. You knew I was at your back, and
spoke it on purpose to try my patience.

FALSTAFF No, no, no; not so. I did not think thou wast
within hearing.

PRINCE I shall drive you then to confess the willful
abuse, and then I know how to handle you.

FALSTAFF No abuse, Hal, o' mine honor, no abuse.

PRINCE Not to dispraise me and call me pantler and
bread-chipper and I know not what?

FALSTAFF No abuse, Hal.

POINS No abuse?

FALSTAFF No abuse, Ned, i' the world. Honest Ned,
none. I dispraised him before the wicked, that the
wicked might not fall in love with him. In which doing,   30
I have done the part of a careful friend and a true subject, and thy father is to give me thanks for it. No abuse,
Hal. None, Ned, none. No, faith, boys, none.

PRINCE See now, whether pure fear and entire cowardice
doth not make thee wrong this virtuous gentlewoman to
close with us. Is she of the wicked? Is thine hostess here  30
of the wicked? Or is thy boy of the wicked? Or honest
Bardolph, whose zeal burns in his nose, of the wicked?

POINS Answer, thou dead elm, answer.

FALSTAFF The fiend hath pricked down Bardolph irre-    31
coverable, and his face is Lucifer's privy-kitchen,
where he doth nothing but roast malt-worms. For the   31
boy, there is a good angel about him, but the devil
blinds him too.

PRINCE For the women?

FALSTAFF For one of them, she is in hell already, and
burns poor souls. For the other, I owe her money, and   31
whether she be damned for that, I know not.

HOSTESS No, I warrant you.

FALSTAFF No, I think thou art not. I think thou art quit  31
for that. Marry, there is another indictment upon thee,

---

217-18 *death's-head* (the figure of a skull was used traditionally as a reminder of mortality)   221 *pantler* pantryman; *chipped bread* cut off the
crusts   224 *Tewkesbury mustard* (Tewkesbury mustard balls were famous)
225 *conceit* wit   228 *conger and fennel* the meat of conger eel highly seasoned
with fennel   229 *drinks . . . flap-dragons* (lighted candles were floated in a
glass of liquor, and the trick was either to drink the liquor without disturbing the candle, or, more daringly, to take the candle in the mouth and
extinguish the flame by closing the mouth)   230 *wild-mare* seesaw;
*joined-stools* stools expertly made by a joiner   232 *sign . . . leg* sign over the
door of a bootmaker's shop; *bate* quarrel   238 *nave* large hub of the wheel
of a country cart (with a play upon 'knave')   240-41 *elder . . . parrot* (Doll is
rumpling Falstaff's hair)   245 *Saturn* the planet believed to be especially
influential upon the aged   247 *fiery Trigon* the three fiery signs of the
Zodiac – Aries, Leo, and Sagittarius (alluding to Bardolph's red face)
248 *lisping . . . tables* making love to his master's old note-book, i.e. Mistress
Quickly   250 *busses* kisses   255 *kirtle* skirt   261 *hearken a' th' end* i.e. in
the end you will have proof of my fidelity   266 *continents* (with a play upon
'continence')   275 *compound* lump   276 *light . . . blood* i.e. Doll   279
*if . . . heat* if you do not strike while the iron is hot   280 *candle-mine* mine
of tallow   286-87 *as . . . Gad's Hill* (see *1 Henry IV*, II, ii; iv)   306
*close* come to terms   310 *pricked down* chosen   312 *malt-worms* topers
316 *burns* infects with venereal disease   319-20 *quit for that* acquitted of
that charge

321 for suffering flesh to be eaten in thy house, contrary to
the law, for the which I think thou wilt howl.

HOSTESS All victuallers do so. What's a joint of mutton or
two in a whole Lent?

PRINCE You, gentlewoman –

DOLL What says your grace?

FALSTAFF His grace says that which his flesh rebels
against.
    *Peto knocks at door.*

HOSTESS Who knocks so loud at door? Look to the door
there, Francis.
    *[Enter Peto.]*

PRINCE
Peto, how now! What news?

PETO
The king your father is at Westminster,
332 And there are twenty weak and wearied posts
Come from the north. And as I came along
I met and overtook a dozen captains,
Bareheaded, sweating, knocking at the taverns,
And asking every one for Sir John Falstaff.

PRINCE
By heaven, Poins, I feel me much to blame,
So idly to profane the precious time,
339 When tempest of commotion, like the south
340 Borne with black vapor, doth begin to melt
And drop upon our bare unarmèd heads.
Give me my sword and cloak. Falstaff, good night.
    *Exeunt Prince Henry, Poins [, Peto, and Bardolph].*

FALSTAFF Now comes in the sweetest morsel of the
night, and we must hence and leave it unpicked.
*[Knocking within.]* More knocking at the door!
    *[Enter Bardolph.]*
How now! What's the matter?

BARDOLPH
347 You must away to court, sir, presently.
A dozen captains stay at door for you.

FALSTAFF *[to the Page]* Pay the musicians, sirrah. Farewell, hostess. Farewell, Doll. You see, my good
wenches, how men of merit are sought after. The un-
deserver may sleep when the man of action is called on.
353 Farewell, good wenches. If I be not sent away post, I
will see you again ere I go.

DOLL I cannot speak. If my heart be not ready to burst –
well, sweet Jack, have a care of thyself.

FALSTAFF Farewell, farewell.
    *[Exeunt Falstaff and Bardolph.]*

HOSTESS Well, fare thee well. I have known thee these
359 twenty-nine years, come peascod-time, but an honester
and truer-hearted man – well, fare thee well.

BARDOLPH *[within]* Mistress Tearsheet!

HOSTESS What's the matter?

BARDOLPH *[within]* Bid Mistress Tearsheet come to my
master.

---

HOSTESS O, run, Doll, run. Run, good Doll. Come. *[to
Bardolph within]* She comes blubbered. Yea, will you 366
come, Doll?           *Exeunt.*

\*

    *Enter the King in his nightgown, alone [with a Page].*   III, i

KING
Go call the Earls of Surrey and of Warwick.
But, ere they come, bid them o'erread these letters
And well consider of them. Make good speed.
    *[Exit Page.]*
How many thousand of my poorest subjects
Are at this hour asleep! O sleep, O gentle sleep,
Nature's soft nurse, how have I frighted thee,
That thou no more wilt weigh my eyelids down
And steep my senses in forgetfulness?      8
Why rather, sleep, liest thou in smoky cribs,      9
Upon uneasy pallets stretching thee      10
And hushed with buzzing night-flies to thy slumber,
Than in the perfumed chambers of the great,
Under the canopies of costly state,      13
And lulled with sound of sweetest melody?
O thou dull god, why liest thou with the vile      15
In loathsome beds, and leavest the kingly couch
A watch-case or a common 'larum-bell?      17
Wilt thou upon the high and giddy mast
Seal up the ship-boy's eyes, and rock his brains
In cradle of the rude imperious surge
And in the visitation of the winds,
Who take the ruffian billows by the top,
Curling their monstrous heads and hanging them
With deafening clamor in the slippery clouds,
That, with the hurly, death itself awakes?      25
Canst thou, O partial sleep, give thy repose
To the wet sea-son in an hour so rude,
And in the calmest and most stillest night,
With all appliances and means to boot,      29
Deny it to a king? Then happy low, lie down!      30
Uneasy lies the head that wears a crown.
    *Enter Warwick, Surrey, and Sir John Blunt.*

WARWICK
Many good morrows to your majesty!

KING
Is it good morrow, lords?

WARWICK
'Tis one o'clock, and past.

KING
Why, then, good morrow to you all, my lords.
Have you read o'er the letters that I sent you?

WARWICK
We have, my liege.

KING
Then you perceive the body of our kingdom
How foul it is, what rank diseases grow,      39
And with what danger, near the heart of it.

WARWICK
It is but as a body yet distempered,      41
Which to his former strength may be restored
With good advice and little medicine.
My Lord Northumberland will soon be cooled.

KING
O God! that one might read the book of fate,
And see the revolution of the times

---

321–22 *suffering . . . law* permitting meat to be served at your inn during
Lent in defiance of the ordinance which forbade such sale   332 *posts*
messengers   339 *commotion* insurrection; *south* south wind   340 *Borne*
laden   347 *presently* immediately   353 *post* posthaste   359 *peascod-time*
early summer, when the peas are in blossom   366 *blubbered* weeping
III, i King Henry's palace (Westminster)   s.d. *nightgown* dressing gown
8 *steep* saturate   9 *cribs* hovels   10 *uneasy pallets* uncomfortable beds
13 *canopies . . . state* elaborate canopies over the beds of the wealthy   15
*dull god* Morpheus   17 *watch-case* sentry-box; *'larum-bell* alarm bell
25 *hurly* tumult   29 *to boot* in addition   30 *low* lowly folk   39 *rank*
festering   41 *distempered* sick

47 Make mountains level, and the continent,
Weary of solid firmness, melt itself
Into the sea! And other times to see
The beachy girdle of the ocean
Too wide for Neptune's hips, how chances mock,
And changes fill the cup of alteration
With divers liquors! O, if this were seen,
The happiest youth, viewing his progress through,
55 What perils past, what crosses to ensue,
Would shut the book, and sit him down and die.
'Tis not ten years gone
Since Richard and Northumberland, great friends,
Did feast together, and in two years after
Were they at wars. It is but eight years since
This Percy was the man nearest my soul,
Who like a brother toiled in my affairs
63 And laid his love and life under my foot,
Yea, for my sake, even to the eyes of Richard
Gave him defiance. But which of you was by –
    [To Warwick]
66 You, cousin Nevil, as I may remember –
When Richard, with his eye brimful of tears,
68 Then checked and rated by Northumberland,
Did speak these words, now proved a prophecy?
70 'Northumberland, thou ladder by the which
My cousin Bolingbroke ascends my throne' –
Though then, God knows, I had no such intent,
But that necessity so bowed the state
That I and greatness were compelled to kiss –
'The time shall come,' thus did he follow it,
76 'The time will come that foul sin, gathering head,
Shall break into corruption.' So went on,
Foretelling this same time's condition
And the division of our amity.
WARWICK
There is a history in all men's lives,
81 Figuring the nature of the times deceased,
The which observed, a man may prophesy,
83 With a near aim, of the main chance of things
As yet not come to life, which in their seeds
85 And weak beginnings lie intreasurèd.
Such things become the hatch and brood of time,
87 And by the necessary form of this
King Richard might create a perfect guess
That great Northumberland, then false to him,
Would of that seed grow to a greater falseness,
Which should not find a ground to root upon,
Unless on you.
KING     Are these things then necessities?
Then let us meet them like necessities.
And that same word even now cries out on us.
They say the bishop and Northumberland
Are fifty thousand strong.
WARWICK     It cannot be, my lord.
Rumor doth double, like the voice and echo,
The numbers of the feared. Please it your grace
To go to bed. Upon my soul, my lord,
The powers that you already have sent forth
Shall bring this prize in very easily.
To comfort you the more, I have received
103 A certain instance that Glendower is dead.
Your majesty hath been this fortnight ill,
105 And these unseasoned hours perforce must add
Unto your sickness.

KING     I will take your counsel.
And were these inward wars once out of hand,   107
We would, dear lords, unto the Holy Land.     Exeunt.

*

*Enter Justice Shallow and Justice Silence [with*   III
*Mouldy, Shadow, Wart, Feeble, Bullcalf].*

SHALLOW Come on, come on, come on, sir. Give me your
hand, sir, give me your hand, sir; an early stirrer, by the
rood! And how doth my good cousin Silence?   3
SILENCE Good morrow, good cousin Shallow.
SHALLOW And how doth my cousin, your bedfellow?
And your fairest daughter and mine, my god-daughter
Ellen?
SILENCE Alas, a black ousel, cousin Shallow!   7
SHALLOW By yea and no, sir, I dare say my cousin
William is become a good scholar. He is at Oxford still,
is he not?
SILENCE Indeed, sir, to my cost.
SHALLOW 'A must, then, to the Inns o' Court shortly. I   11
was once of Clement's Inn, where I think they will talk   12
of mad Shallow yet.
SILENCE You were called 'lusty Shallow' then, cousin.
SHALLOW By the mass, I was called anything. And I
would have done anything indeed too, and roundly too.   16
There was I, and little John Doit of Staffordshire, and
black George Barnes, and Francis Pickbone, and Will
Squele, a Cotswold man; you had not four such swinge-   19
bucklers in all the Inns o' Court again. And I may say to
you we knew where the bona-robas were and had the   21
best of them all at commandment. Then was Jack Fal-   22
staff, now Sir John, a boy, and page to Thomas Mowbray, Duke of Norfolk.
SILENCE This Sir John, cousin, that comes hither anon
about soldiers?
SHALLOW The same Sir John, the very same. I see him
break Skogan's head at the court-gate, when 'a was a
crack not thus high. And the very same day did I fight   29
with one Sampson Stockfish, a fruiterer, behind Gray's   30
Inn. Jesu, Jesu, the mad days that I have spent! And to
see how many of my old acquaintance are dead!
SILENCE We shall all follow, cousin.
SHALLOW Certain, 'tis certain, very sure, very sure.
Death, as the Psalmist saith, is certain to all, all shall die.
How a good yoke of bullocks at Stamford fair?   36
SILENCE By my troth, I was not there.
SHALLOW Death is certain. Is old Double of your town
living yet?
SILENCE Dead, sir.

47 *continent* dry land   55 *crosses* troubles   63 *under my foot* at my disposal   66 *Nevil* (actually the family name of the Earl of Warwick at this
period was not Nevil but Beauchamps)   68 *rated* berated   70–77 (the
lines in quotation marks are paraphrased from *Richard II*, V, i, 55–68)
76 *gathering head* coming to a head   81 *Figuring* revealing   83 *main
chance* general probability   85 *intreasurèd* stored up   87 *necessary . . . this*
logical application of this principle   103 *instance* proof   105 *unseasoned*
unseasonable   107 *inward* civil; *out of hand* done with
III, ii Before Shallow's house in Gloucestershire   3 *rood* cross   7 *ousel*
blackbird   11 *Inns o' Court* the law schools   12 *Clement's Inn* one of the
Inns of Chancery, which in Shallow's time were preparatory to the Inns
of Court   16 *roundly* thoroughly   19 *Cotswold* (the Cotswolds are a range
of hills in Gloucestershire); *swinge-bucklers* swashbucklers   21 *bona-
robas* wenches   22 *at commandment* at will   29 *crack* lively boy   30–31
*Gray's Inn* one of the Inns of Court   36 *How* how much

SHALLOW Jesu, Jesu, dead! 'A drew a good bow, and
dead! 'A shot a fine shoot. John a Gaunt loved him well
and betted much money on his head. Dead! 'A would
have clapped i' the clout at twelve score, and carried
you a forehand shaft a fourteen and fourteen and a half,
that it would have done a man's heart good to see. How
a score of ewes now?

SILENCE Thereafter as they be. A score of good ewes
may be worth ten pounds.

SHALLOW And is old Double dead?

SILENCE Here come two of Sir John Falstaff's men, as I
think.

*Enter Bardolph and one with him.*

[SHALLOW] Good morrow, honest gentlemen.

BARDOLPH I beseech you, which is Justice Shallow?

SHALLOW I am Robert Shallow, sir, a poor esquire of
this county, and one of the king's justices of the peace.
What is your good pleasure with me?

BARDOLPH My captain, sir, commends him to you, my
captain, Sir John Falstaff, a tall gentleman, by heaven,
and a most gallant leader.

SHALLOW He greets me well, sir. I knew him a good
backsword man. How doth the good knight? May I ask
how my lady his wife doth?

BARDOLPH Sir, pardon, a soldier is better accommodated than with a wife.

SHALLOW It is well said, in faith, sir, and it is well said
indeed too. Better accommodated! It is good, yea, indeed, is it. Good phrases are surely, and ever were, very
commendable. Accommodated! It comes of 'accom-
modo.' Very good, a good phrase.

BARDOLPH Pardon me, sir. I have heard the word.
Phrase call you it? By this good day, I know not the
phrase, but I will maintain the word with my sword to
be a soldierlike word, and a word of exceeding good
command, by heaven. Accommodated, that is, when a
man is, as they say, accommodated; or when a man is,
being, whereby 'a may be thought to be accommodated,
which is an excellent thing.

*Enter Sir John Falstaff.*

SHALLOW It is very just. Look, here comes good Sir
John. Give me your good hand, give me your worship's
good hand. By my troth, you like well and bear your
years very well. Welcome, good Sir John.

FALSTAFF I am glad to see you well, good Master Robert
Shallow. Master Surecard, as I think?

SHALLOW No, Sir John, it is my cousin Silence, in commission with me.

FALSTAFF Good Master Silence, it well befits you should
be of the peace.

---

42 *shot . . . shoot* (referring to archery); *John a Gaunt* father of Henry IV
44 *clapped . . . score* hit the mark at 240 yards   44–45 *carried . . . half* could
shoot a heavy arrow point blank (rather than in a curved trajectory) so that
it carried 280 or 290 yards   48 *Thereafter . . . be* the price varies according
to the quality   54 *esquire* gentleman, just below the rank of knight   58
*tall* valiant   61 *backsword* stick with a basket hilt used instead of a sword
in fencing   63 *accommodated* provided (in Shakespeare's time the word
was considered 'precious')   78 *It . . . just* that's very true   80 *like* thrive
84–85 *in . . . me* we both hold commissions as justices of the peace   90
*sufficient* able   94–95 *So . . . so* (Shallow goes through the business of
checking the men against the names on the muster roll)   100 *friends*
family   107 *Prick* choose   109 *dame* mother   110 *husbandry* farm work
131 *shadows* names of non-existent men for whom the commanding officer
received pay   140 *stands* depends   142 *you . . . it* you know how to do it
149 *pricked* attired   150 *battle* army

---

SILENCE Your good worship is welcome.

FALSTAFF Fie! This is hot weather, gentlemen. Have
you provided me here half a dozen sufficient men?

SHALLOW Marry, have we, sir. Will you sit?

FALSTAFF Let me see them, I beseech you.

SHALLOW Where's the roll? Where's the roll? Where's
the roll? Let me see, let me see, let me see. So, so, so, so,
so, so, so. Yea, marry, sir. Ralph Mouldy! Let them
appear as I call, let them do so, let them do so. Let me
see, where is Mouldy?

MOULDY Here, an't please you.

SHALLOW What think you, Sir John? A good-limbed
fellow, young, strong, and of good friends.

FALSTAFF Is thy name Mouldy?

MOULDY Yea, an't please you.

FALSTAFF 'Tis the more time thou wert used.

SHALLOW Ha, ha, ha! most excellent, i' faith! Things
that are mouldy lack use. Very singular good! In faith,
well said, Sir John, very well said.

[FALSTAFF Prick him.]

MOULDY I was pricked well enough before, an you could
have let me alone. My old dame will be undone now for
one to do her husbandry and her drudgery. You need not
to have pricked me. There are other men fitter to go out
than I.

FALSTAFF Go to. Peace, Mouldy, you shall go. Mouldy,
it is time you were spent.

MOULDY Spent!

SHALLOW Peace, fellow, peace. Stand aside. Know you
where you are? For the other, Sir John, let me see.
Simon Shadow!

FALSTAFF Yea, marry, let me have him to sit under. He's
like to be a cold soldier.

SHALLOW Where's Shadow?

SHADOW Here, sir.

FALSTAFF Shadow, whose son art thou?

SHADOW My mother's son, sir.

FALSTAFF Thy mother's son! Like enough, and thy
father's shadow. So the son of the female is the shadow
of the male. It is often so, indeed, but much of the
father's substance!

SHALLOW Do you like him, Sir John?

FALSTAFF Shadow will serve for summer. Prick him, for
we have a number of shadows to fill up the muster-book.

SHALLOW Thomas Wart!

FALSTAFF Where's he?

WART Here, sir.

FALSTAFF Is thy name Wart?

WART Yea, sir.

FALSTAFF Thou art a very ragged wart.

SHALLOW Shall I prick him down, Sir John?

FALSTAFF It were superfluous, for his apparel is built
upon his back and the whole frame stands upon pins.
Prick him no more.

SHALLOW Ha, ha, ha! you can do it, sir, you can do it. I
commend you well. Francis Feeble!

FEEBLE Here, sir.

SHALLOW What trade art thou, Feeble?

FEEBLE A woman's tailor, sir.

SHALLOW Shall I prick him, sir?

FALSTAFF You may. But if he had been a man's tailor,
he'd a' pricked you. Wilt thou make as many holes in an
enemy's battle as thou hast done in a woman's petticoat?

FEEBLE I will do my good will, sir. You can have no more.

FALSTAFF Well said, good woman's tailor! Well said, courageous Feeble! Thou wilt be as valiant as the
154 wrathful dove or most magnanimous mouse. Prick the woman's tailor well, Master Shallow, deep, Master Shallow.

FEEBLE I would Wart might have gone, sir.

FALSTAFF I would thou wert a man's tailor, that thou mightst mend him and make him fit to go. I cannot put him to a private soldier that is the leader of so many
159 thousands. Let that suffice, most forcible Feeble.

FEEBLE It shall suffice, sir.

FALSTAFF I am bound to thee, reverend Feeble. Who is next?

SHALLOW Peter Bullcalf o' the green!

FALSTAFF Yea, marry, let's see Bullcalf.

BULLCALF Here, sir.

FALSTAFF 'Fore God, a likely fellow! Come, prick Bullcalf till he roar again.

BULLCALF O Lord! good my lord captain –

FALSTAFF What, dost thou roar before thou art pricked?

BULLCALF O Lord, sir! I am a diseased man.

FALSTAFF What disease hast thou?

BULLCALF A whoreson cold, sir, a cough, sir, which I
173 caught with ringing in the king's affairs upon his coronation day, sir.

175 FALSTAFF Come, thou shalt go to the wars in a gown. We will have away thy cold, and I will take such order that thy friends shall ring for thee. Is here all?

SHALLOW Here is two more called than your number. You must have but four here, sir. And so, I pray you, go in with me to dinner.

FALSTAFF Come, I will go drink with you, but I cannot
182 tarry dinner. I am glad to see you, by my troth, Master Shallow.

184 SHALLOW O, Sir John, do you remember since we lay all
185 night in the Windmill in Saint George's Field?

FALSTAFF No more of that, good Master Shallow, no more of that.

SHALLOW Ha! 'Twas a merry night. And is Jane Nightwork alive?

FALSTAFF She lives, Master Shallow.

190 SHALLOW She never could away with me.

FALSTAFF Never, never, she would always say she could not abide Master Shallow.

SHALLOW By the mass, I could anger her to the heart. She was then a bona-roba. Doth she hold her own well?

FALSTAFF Old, old, Master Shallow.

SHALLOW Nay, she must be old. She cannot choose but be old. Certain she's old, and had Robin Nightwork by old Nightwork before I came to Clement's Inn.

SILENCE That's fifty-five year ago.

SHALLOW Ha, cousin Silence, that thou hadst seen that that this knight and I have seen! Ha, Sir John, said I well?

FALSTAFF We have heard the chimes at midnight, Master Shallow.

SHALLOW That we have, that we have, that we have, in
205 faith, Sir John, we have. Our watchword was 'Hem, boys!' Come, let's to dinner, come, let's to dinner. Jesus, the days that we have seen! Come, come.

*Exeunt [Falstaff and the Justices].*

208 BULLCALF Good Master Corporate Bardolph, stand my
209 friend, and here's four Harry ten shillings in French crowns for you. In very truth, sir, I had as lief be hanged,

sir, as go. And yet for mine own part, sir, I do not care, but rather, because I am unwilling, and, for mine own part, have a desire to stay with my friends. Else, sir, I did not care, for mine own part, so much.

BARDOLPH Go to, stand aside.

MOULDY And, good master corporal captain, for my old dame's sake, stand my friend. She has nobody to do anything about her when I am gone, and she is old, and can-
21 not help herself. You shall have forty, sir.

BARDOLPH Go to, stand aside.

FEEBLE By my troth, I care not. A man can die but once. We owe God a death. I'll ne'er bear a base mind. An't be 22 my destiny, so. An't be not, so. No man is too good to serve's prince. And let it go which way it will, he that 22 dies this year is quit for the next.

BARDOLPH Well said. Th'art a good fellow.

FEEBLE Faith, I'll bear no base mind.

*Enter Falstaff and the Justices.*

FALSTAFF Come, sir, which men shall I have?

SHALLOW Four of which you please.

BARDOLPH Sir, a word with you. I have three pound to free Mouldy and Bullcalf.

FALSTAFF Go to, well.

SHALLOW Come, Sir John, which four will you have?

FALSTAFF Do you choose for me.

SHALLOW Marry, then, Mouldy, Bullcalf, Feeble, and Shadow.

FALSTAFF Mouldy and Bullcalf. For you, Mouldy, stay at home till you are past service. And for your part, Bullcalf, grow till you come unto it. I will none of you.

SHALLOW Sir John, Sir John, do not yourself wrong. They are your likeliest men, and I would have you served with the best.

FALSTAFF Will you tell me, Master Shallow, how to choose a man? Care I for the limb, the thews, the stature, bulk, 24 and big assemblance of a man! Give me the spirit, Master 24 Shallow. Here's Wart. You see what a ragged appearance it is. 'A shall charge you and discharge you with the 24 motion of a pewterer's hammer, come off and on swifter 24 than he that gibbets on the brewer's bucket. And this 24 same half-faced fellow, Shadow. Give me this man. He presents no mark to the enemy; the foeman may with as great aim level at the edge of a penknife. And for a retreat, how swiftly will this Feeble the woman's tailor run off! O, give me the spare men, and spare me the great ones. Put me a caliver into Wart's hand, Bardolph. 25

BARDOLPH Hold, Wart, traverse. Thus, thus, thus. 25

FALSTAFF Come, manage me your caliver. So. Very well. Go to. Very good, exceeding good. O, give me always a little, lean, old, chopped, bald shot. Well said, i' faith, 25

154 *magnanimous* stout-hearted 159 *thousands* i.e. of lice 173–74 *ringing . . . day* ringing church bells in celebration of the anniversary of the king's coronation 175 *gown* dressing gown 182 *tarry* stay for 184 *since* when 185 *Windmill* a brothel; *Saint George's Field* a favorite Sunday resort of Londoners, on the Surrey side of the Thames 190 *away with* tolerate 205–06 *Hem, boys!* here's how! down the hatch! 208 *Corporate* i.e. corporal 209–10 *four . . . crowns* (an anachronism; the 'Harry ten shilling' piece was first coined in the reign of Henry VII. In Shakespeare's time one of these pieces was worth 5s.; a French crown was worth 4s. Bullcalf's 'present' was five French crowns, the equivalent of one pound.) 219 *forty* probably forty shillings, or two pounds 222 *bear* harbor 225 *quit* free 244 *thews* strength 245 *assemblance* appearance 247 *charge . . . discharge you* load and fire 248 *motion . . . hammer* i.e. swift, regular beat 249 *gibbets . . . bucket* hangs the pails of brew on the yoke of the carrier 255 *caliver* light musket 256 *traverse* take aim 259 *chopped* chapped; *shot* armed soldier

Wart. Th' art a good scab. Hold, there's a tester for thee.

SHALLOW He is not his craft's master, he doth not do it right. I remember at Mile-end Green, when I lay at Clement's Inn – I was then Sir Dagonet in Arthur's show – there was a little quiver fellow, and 'a would manage you his piece thus, and 'a would about and about, and come you in and come you in. 'Rah, tah, tah,' would 'a say, 'Bounce,' would 'a say, and away again would 'a go, and again would 'a come. I shall ne'er see such a fellow.

FALSTAFF These fellows will do well, Master Shallow. God keep you, Master Silence. I will not use many words with you. Fare you well, gentlemen both. I thank you. I must a dozen mile to-night. Bardolph, give the soldiers coats.

SHALLOW Sir John, the Lord bless you! God prosper your affairs! God send us peace! At your return visit our house, let our old acquaintance be renewed. Peradventure I will with ye to the court.

FALSTAFF 'Fore God, would you would, Master Shallow.

SHALLOW Go to, I have spoke at a word. God keep you.

FALSTAFF Fare you well, gentle gentlemen. *Exeunt [Justices]*. On, Bardolph, lead the men away. *[Exeunt all but Falstaff.]* As I return, I will fetch off these justices. I do see the bottom of Justice Shallow. Lord, Lord, how subject we old men are to this vice of lying! This same starved justice hath done nothing but prate to me of the wildness of his youth and the feats he hath done about Turnbull Street, and every third word a lie, duer paid to the hearer than the Turk's tribute. I do remember him at Clement's Inn like a man made after supper of a cheese-paring. When 'a was naked, he was, for all the world, like a forked radish, with a head fantastically carved upon it with a knife. 'A was so forlorn that his dimensions to any thick sight were invincible. 'A was the very genius of famine, yet lecherous as a monkey, and the whores called him mandrake. 'A came ever in the rearward of the fashion, and sung those tunes to the overscutched huswives that he heard the carmen whistle, and sware they were his fancies or his good-nights. And now is this Vice's dagger become a squire, and talks as familiarly of John a Gaunt as if he had been sworn brother to him, and I'll be sworn 'a ne'er saw him but once in the Tilt-yard, and then he burst his head for crowding among the marshal's men. I saw it, and told John a Gaunt he beat his own name, for you might have thrust him and all his apparel into an eel-skin, the case of a treble hautboy was a mansion for him, a court. And now has he land and beefs. Well, I'll be acquainted with him, if I return, and 't shall go hard but I will make him a philosopher's two stones to me. If the young dace be a bait for the old pike, I see no reason in the law of nature but I may snap at him. Let time shape, and there an end. *Exit.*

\*

*Enter the Archbishop [of York], Mowbray, Hastings [and others], within the Forest of Gaultree.*    IV, i

ARCHBISHOP
What is this forest called?

HASTINGS
'Tis Gaultree Forest, an't shall please your grace.

ARCHBISHOP
Here stand, my lords, and send discoverers forth    3
To know the numbers of our enemies.

HASTINGS
We have sent forth already.

ARCHBISHOP                              'Tis well done.
My friends and brethren in these great affairs,
I must acquaint you that I have received
New-dated letters from Northumberland,
Their cold intent, tenor, and substance, thus:
Here doth he wish his person, with such powers    10
As might hold sortance with his quality,    11
The which he could not levy. Whereupon
He is retired, to ripe his growing fortunes,    13
To Scotland, and concludes in hearty prayers
That your attempts may overlive the hazard    15
And fearful meeting of their opposite.    16

MOWBRAY
Thus do the hopes we have in him touch ground
And dash themselves to pieces.
*Enter a Messenger.*

HASTINGS                              Now, what news?

MESSENGER
West of this forest, scarcely off a mile,
In goodly form comes on the enemy,    20
And, by the ground they hide, I judge their number
Upon or near the rate of thirty thousand.    22

MOWBRAY
The just proportion that we gave them out.    23
Let us sway on and face them in the field.    24

ARCHBISHOP
What well-appointed leader fronts us here?    25
*Enter Westmoreland.*

MOWBRAY
I think it is my Lord of Westmoreland.

WESTMORELAND
Health and fair greeting from our general,
The prince, Lord John and Duke of Lancaster.

ARCHBISHOP
Say on, my Lord of Westmoreland, in peace.
What doth concern your coming?

WESTMORELAND                              Then, my lord,
Unto your grace do I in chief address    31
The substance of my speech. If that rebellion
Came like itself, in base and abject routs,    33
Led on by bloody youth, guarded with rags,    34
And countenanced by boys and beggary,    35

260 *scab* a pun on the name 'Wart'; *tester* sixpence  262 *Mile-end Green* a training ground for citizen soldiers  263 *Sir Dagonet* King Arthur's fool; *Arthur's show* a group who staged an annual archery exhibition, each member taking the name of a character from Arthurian legend  264 *quiver* nimble  278 *at a word* hastily  281 *fetch off* get the better of  285–86 *Turnbull Street* a resort of prostitutes  286 *duer* more promptly  287 *Turk's tribute* tribute-money exacted by the Turk  291 *thick* dull  292 *invincible* i.e. invisible  294 *mandrake* (the mandrake root resembles the figure of a man)  295 *overscutched huswives* worn-out hussies  296 *carmen* wagoners  297 *fancies* musical compositions; *good-nights* good-night songs; *Vice's dagger* thin wooden dagger carried by Vice, the comic character in the old morality plays  304 *hautboy* oboe  307 *philosopher's two stones* i.e. the elixir of life (which was believed to preserve health) and the philosopher's stone (which, it was believed, could transmute base metal into gold). Both were referred to as stones, although the *'elixir vitae'* was also regarded as a liquid  308 *dace* small fish used as live bait
IV, i *Within the forest of Gaultree* s.d. *Forest of Gaultree* a royal forest in Yorkshire  3 *discoverers* scouts  10 *powers* forces  11 *hold sortance* accord; *quality* rank  13 *ripe* make ripe  15 *overlive* outlive  16 *opposite* adversary  20 *form* formation  22 *rate* estimated number  23 *just ... out* exact number we estimated  24 *sway* move  25 *well-appointed* well-armed; *fronts* faces  31 *in chief* principally  33 *routs* mobs  34 *guarded* trimmed  35 *countenanced* supported; *beggary* beggars

36 I say, if damned commotion so appeared,
In his true, native and most proper shape,
You, reverend father, and these noble lords
Had not been here, to dress the ugly form
Of base and bloody insurrection
With your fair honors. You, lord archbishop,
42 Whose see is by a civil peace maintained,
Whose beard the silver hand of peace hath touched,
44 Whose learning and good letters peace hath tutored,
45 Whose white investments figure innocence,
The dove and very blessèd spirit of peace,
47 Wherefore do you so ill translate yourself
Out of the speech of peace that bears such grace,
Into the harsh and boisterous tongue of war,
Turning your books to graves, your ink to blood,
Your pens to lances, and your tongue divine
52 To a loud trumpet and a point of war?
  ARCHBISHOP
Wherefore do I this? So the question stands.
Briefly to this end: we are all diseased,
55 [And with our surfeiting and wanton hours
Have brought ourselves into a burning fever,
57 And we must bleed for it. Of which disease
Our late king, Richard, being infected, died.
But, my most noble Lord of Westmoreland,
60 I take not on me here as a physician,
Nor do I as an enemy to peace
Troop in the throngs of military men,
But rather show awhile like fearful war,
64 To diet rank minds sick of happiness
And purge the obstructions which begin to stop
Our very veins of life. Hear me more plainly.
67 I have in equal balance justly weighed
What wrongs our arms may do, what wrongs we suffer,
69 And find our griefs heavier than our offenses.
We see which way the stream of time doth run,
And are enforced from our most quiet there
72 By the rough torrent of occasion,
And have the summary of all our griefs,
74 When time shall serve, to show in articles;
Which long ere this we offered to the king,
And might by no suit gain our audience.
When we are wronged and would unfold our griefs,
We are denied access unto his person
Even by those men that most have done us wrong.]
The dangers of the days but newly gone,
Whose memory is written on the earth
With yet appearing blood, and the examples
83 Of every minute's instance, present now,
Hath put us in these ill-beseeming arms,
Not to break peace or any branch of it,
But to establish here a peace indeed,
87 Concurring both in name and quality.
  WESTMORELAND
When ever yet was your appeal denied?
89 Wherein have you been gallèd by the king?
90 What peer hath been suborned to grate on you,
That you should seal this lawless bloody book
Of forged rebellion with a seal divine
And consecrate commotion's bitter edge?
  ARCHBISHOP
94 My brother general, the commonwealth,
95 To brother born an household cruelty,
I make my quarrel in particular.

WESTMORELAND
There is no need of any such redress,
Or if there were, it not belongs to you.
MOWBRAY
Why not to him in part, and to us all
That feel the bruises of the days before,
And suffer the condition of these times
To lay a heavy and unequal hand    10
Upon our honors?
WESTMORELAND [O, my good Lord Mowbray,
Construe the times to their necessities,    10
And you shall say indeed, it is the time,
And not the king, that doth you injuries.
Yet for your part, it not appears to me
Either from the king or in the present time
That you should have an inch of any ground
To build a grief on. Were you not restored
To all the Duke of Norfolk's signories,    11
Your noble and right well remembered father's?
MOWBRAY
What thing, in honor, had my father lost,    11
That need to be revived and breathed in me?
The king that loved him, as the state stood then,
Was force perforce compelled to banish him.
And then that Henry Bolingbroke and he,
Being mounted and both rousèd in their seats,
Their neighing coursers daring of the spur,
Their armèd staves in charge, their beavers down,    12
Their eyes of fire sparkling through sights of steel,
And the loud trumpet blowing them together,
Then, then, when there was nothing could have stayed
My father from the breast of Bolingbroke,
O, when the king did throw his warder down,    12
His own life hung upon the staff he threw.
Then threw he down himself and all their lives
That by indictment and by dint of sword
Have since miscarried under Bolingbroke.    12
WESTMORELAND
You speak, Lord Mowbray, now you know not what.
The Earl of Hereford was reputed then    13
In England the most valiant gentleman.
Who knows on whom fortune would then have smiled?
But if your father had been victor there,
He ne'er had borne it out of Coventry.    13
For all the country in a general voice
Cried hate upon him, and all their prayers and love
Were set on Hereford, whom they doted on
And blessed and graced indeed, more than the king.]

36 *commotion* rebellion  42 *see* diocese  44 *good letters* study of correct authors  45 *investments* vestments  47 *translate* transform  52 *point of war* signal on the trumpet  55 *surfeiting* gluttony; *wanton* self-indulgent  57 *bleed* be bled, as a therapeutic measure  60 *take . . . as* do not assume the character of  64 *rank* obese  67 *equal* exact  69 *griefs* grievances  72 *occasion* circumstances  74 *articles* an itemized list  83 *Of . . . instance* occurring every minute  87 *Concurring . . . quality* which shall be peace in both name and fact  89 *gallèd* made sore  90 *suborned* bribed; *grate on* vex  94 *brother general* my brothers the people at large  95 (This line has never been explained satisfactorily. It was dropped from the folio, and, along with line 93, from some copies of the quarto. Without it, the archbishop's words are perfectly intelligible.)  102 *unequal* unjust  104 *to* according to  111 *signories* properties  113–29 (for the quarrel between Mowbray and Bolingbroke see *Richard II*, I, i; iii)  116 *force perforce* whether he wished it or not  120 *staves in charge* lances ready for action; *beavers* visors of their helmets  125 *warder* staff  129 *miscarried* perished  131 *Hereford* i.e. Bolingbroke  135 *borne it* carried the prize; *Coventry* (where the combat took place)

But this is mere digression from my purpose.
Here come I from our princely general
To know your griefs, to tell you from his grace
That he will give you audience, and wherein
It shall appear that your demands are just,
45 You shall enjoy them, everything set off
That might so much as think you enemies.

MOWBRAY
But he hath forced us to compel this offer,
And it proceeds from policy, not love.

WESTMORELAND
49 Mowbray, you overween to take it so.
This offer comes from mercy, not from fear.
51 For, lo! within a ken our army lies,
Upon mine honor, all too confident
To give admittance to a thought of fear.
54 Our battle is more full of names than yours,
Our men more perfect in the use of arms,
Our armor all as strong, our cause the best.
57 Then reason will our hearts should be as good.
Say you not then our offer is compelled.

MOWBRAY
Well, by my will we shall admit no parley.

WESTMORELAND
That argues but the shame of your offense.
61 A rotten case abides no handling.

HASTINGS
Hath the Prince John a full commission,
63 In very ample virtue of his father,
To hear and absolutely to determine
Of what conditions we shall stand upon?

WESTMORELAND
That is intended in the general's name.
67 I muse you make so slight a question.

ARCHBISHOP
Then take, my Lord of Westmoreland, this schedule,
For this contains our general grievances.
70 Each several article herein redressed,
All members of our cause, both here and hence,
72 That are insinewed to this action,
73 Acquitted by a true substantial form
And present execution of our wills
To us and to our purposes confined,
76 We come within our awful banks again
And knit our powers to the arm of peace.

WESTMORELAND
This will I show the general. Please you, lords,
In sight of both our battles we may meet,
80 And either end in peace – which God so frame –
81 Or to the place of difference call the swords

Which must decide it.

ARCHBISHOP     My lord, we will do so.
           *Exit Westmoreland.*

MOWBRAY
There is a thing within my bosom tells me
That no conditions of our peace can stand.

HASTINGS
Fear you not that. If we can make our peace
Upon such large terms and so absolute
As our conditions shall consist upon,
Our peace shall stand as firm as rocky mountains.

MOWBRAY
Yea, but our valuation shall be such     189
That every slight and false-derivèd cause,
Yea, every idle, nice, and wanton reason     191
Shall to the king taste of this action,
That, were our royal faiths martyrs in love,     193
We shall be winnowed with so rough a wind
That even our corn shall seem as light as chaff
And good from bad find no partition.     196

ARCHBISHOP
No, no, my lord. Note this. The king is weary
Of dainty and such picking grievances.     198
For he hath found to end one doubt by death     199
Revives two greater in the heirs of life,
And therefore will he wipe his tables clean     201
And keep no tell-tale to his memory
That may repeat and history his loss
To new remembrance. For full well he knows
He cannot so precisely weed this land     205
As his misdoubts present occasion.     206
His foes are so enrooted with his friends
That, plucking to unfix an enemy,
He doth unfasten so and shake a friend.
So that this land, like an offensive wife
That hath enraged him on to offer strokes,
As he is striking, holds his infant up
And hangs resolved correction in the arm     213
That was upreared to execution.

HASTINGS
Besides, the king hath wasted all his rods
On late offenders, that he now doth lack
The very instruments of chastisement.
So that his power, like to a fangless lion,
May offer, but not hold.     219

ARCHBISHOP     'Tis very true.
And therefore be assured, my good lord marshal,
If we do now make our atonement well,     221
Our peace will, like a broken limb united,
Grow stronger for the breaking.

MOWBRAY     Be it so.
Here is returned my Lord of Westmoreland.
           *Enter Westmoreland.*

WESTMORELAND
The prince is here at hand. Pleaseth your lordship
To meet his grace just distance 'tween our armies.     226

MOWBRAY
Your grace of York, in God's name then, set forward.

ARCHBISHOP
Before, and greet his grace, my lord; we come.     228

---

145 *set off* removed   149 *overween* are presumptuous   151 *ken* range of vision   154 *battle . . . names* army has more leaders with distinguished reputations   157 *reason will* it is reasonable that   161 *rotten* weak   163 *In . . . virtue* by full authority   167 *muse* am surprised   170 *several* separate   172 *insinewed* joined by strong sinews   173 *substantial form* formal agreement   176 *banks* i.e. as a stream which has been in flood subsides to the confines of its banks   180 *frame* bring to pass   181 *difference* battle   189 *our valuation* the king's valuation of us   191 *nice* petty; *wanton* frivolous   193 *That . . . love* so that even if we suffered martyrdom for our love of the king   196 *partition* distinction   198 *dainty* precise; *picking* trifling   199 *doubt* danger   201 *tables* note-book   205 *precisely* thoroughly   206 *misdoubts* suspicions   213–14 *hangs . . . execution* causes him to stay his arm and resolve upon correction rather than execution   219 *offer* threaten   221 *atonement* reconciliation   226 *just* exact   228 *Before* go before

*

IV, ii    *Enter Prince John [of Lancaster] and his army.*

LANCASTER
You are well encountered here, my cousin Mowbray.
Good day to you, gentle lord archbishop.
And so to you, Lord Hastings, and to all.
My Lord of York, it better showed with you
When that your flock, assembled by the bell,
Encircled you to hear with reverence
Your exposition on the holy text
8  Than now to see you here an iron man,
Cheering a rout of rebels with your drum,
10  Turning the word to sword and life to death.
That man that sits within a monarch's heart
And ripens in the sunshine of his favor,
Would he abuse the countenance of the king,
14  Alack, what mischiefs might he set abroach
In shadow of such greatness. With you, lord bishop,
It is even so. Who hath not heard it spoken
How deep you were within the books of God?
To us the speaker in His parliament,
To us the imagined voice of God himself,
20  The very opener and intelligencer
Between the grace, the sanctities of heaven
22  And our dull workings. O, who shall believe
But you misuse the reverence of your place,
Employ the countenance and grace of heaven,
As a false favorite doth his prince's name,
26  In deeds dishonorable? You have ta'en up,
Under the counterfeited zeal of God,
28  The subjects of His substitute, my father,
And both against the peace of heaven and him
Have here upswarmed them.

ARCHBISHOP    Good my Lord of Lancaster,
I am not here against your father's peace,
But, as I told my Lord of Westmoreland,
33  The time misordered doth, in common sense,
34  Crowd us and crush us to this monstrous form,
To hold our safety up. I sent your grace
36  The parcels and particulars of our grief,
The which hath been with scorn shoved from the court,
38  Whereon this Hydra son of war is born,
Whose dangerous eyes may well be charmed asleep
With grant of our most just and right desires,
And true obedience, of this madness cured,
Stoop tamely to the foot of majesty.

MOWBRAY
If not, we ready are to try our fortunes
To the last man.

HASTINGS    And though we here fall down,
45  We have supplies to second our attempt.
If they miscarry, theirs shall second them,
47  And so success of mischief shall be born
And heir from heir shall hold this quarrel up
49  Whiles England shall have generation.

LANCASTER
You are too shallow, Hastings, much too shallow,
To sound the bottom of the after-times.

WESTMORELAND
Pleaseth your grace to answer them directly
How far forth you do like their articles.

LANCASTER
I like them all, and do allow them well,
And swear here, by the honor of my blood,
My father's purposes have been mistook,

And some about him have too lavishly    57
Wrested his meaning and authority.    58
My lord, these griefs shall be with speed redressed,
Upon my soul, they shall. If this may please you,
Discharge your powers unto their several counties,
As we will ours. And here between the armies
Let's drink together friendly and embrace,
That all their eyes may bear those tokens home
Of our restorèd love and amity.

ARCHBISHOP
I take your princely word for these redresses.

[LANCASTER]
I give it you, and will maintain my word.
And thereupon I drink unto your grace.

[HASTINGS]
Go, captain, and deliver to the army
This news of peace. Let them have pay, and part.    70
I know it will well please them. Hie thee, captain.
*Exit [Officer].*

ARCHBISHOP
To you, my noble Lord of Westmoreland.

WESTMORELAND
I pledge your grace, and, if you knew what pains
I have bestowed to breed this present peace,
You would drink freely. But my love to ye
Shall show itself more openly hereafter.

ARCHBISHOP
I do not doubt you.

WESTMORELAND    I am glad of it.
Health to my lord and gentle cousin, Mowbray.

MOWBRAY
You wish me health in very happy season,
For I am, on the sudden, something ill.    80

ARCHBISHOP
Against ill chances men are ever merry,    81
But heaviness foreruns the good event.

WESTMORELAND
Therefore be merry, coz, since sudden sorrow
Serves to say thus, 'Some good thing comes to-morrow.'

ARCHBISHOP
Believe me, I am passing light in spirit.    85

MOWBRAY
So much the worse, if your own rule be true.
*Shouts [within].*

LANCASTER
The word of peace is rendered. Hark, how they shout!    87

MOWBRAY
This had been cheerful after victory.

ARCHBISHOP
A peace is of the nature of a conquest,
For then both parties nobly are subdued,
And neither party loser.

IV, ii (It is not certain that any change of scene was intended here. In the quarto the stage direction follows l. 226. The folio has instead 'Enter Prince John' following l. 228, which seems a better position. Neither stage direction indicates a change of scene; but the dialogue of ll. 227–28 seems to indicate that the stage was cleared after l. 228.)  8 *an iron man* clad in armor  10 *the word* the Scripture  14 *abroach* afoot  20 *opener* interpreter; *intelligencer* messenger  22 *workings* operations of the mind  26 *ta'en up* enlisted  28 *substitute* deputy  33 *common sense* the judgment of all the people  34 *monstrous* unnatural  36 *parcels* details  38 *Hydra* many-headed  45 *supplies* reinforcements; *second* take the place of  47 *success* succession  49 *generation* offspring  57 *lavishly* loosely  58 *Wrested* twisted  70 *part* depart  80 *something* somewhat  81 *Against* in expectation of  85 *passing* exceedingly  87 *rendered* declared

LANCASTER                    Go, my lord,
And let our army be dischargèd too.
                              *[Exit Westmoreland.]*

93  And, good my lord, so please you, let our trains
    March by us, that we may peruse the men
95  We should have coped withal.
ARCHBISHOP                    Go, good Lord Hastings,
And, ere they be dismissed, let them march by.
                              *[Exit Hastings.]*
LANCASTER
    I trust, lords, we shall lie to-night together.
    *Enter Westmoreland.*
    Now cousin, wherefore stands our army still?
WESTMORELAND
    The leaders, having charge from you to stand,
    Will not go off until they hear you speak.
LANCASTER
    They know their duties.
    *Enter Hastings.*
HASTINGS
    My lord, our army is dispersed already.
    Like youthful steers unyoked, they take their courses
    East, west, north, south, or, like a school broke up,
105 Each hurries toward his home and sporting-place.
WESTMORELAND
    Good tidings, my Lord Hastings, for the which
    I do arrest thee, traitor, of high treason.
    And you, lord archbishop, and you, Lord Mowbray,
109 Of capital treason I attach you both.
MOWBRAY
    Is this proceeding just and honorable?
WESTMORELAND
    Is your assembly so?
ARCHBISHOP
    Will you thus break your faith?
112 LANCASTER                    I pawned thee none.
    I promised you redress of these same grievances
    Whereof you did complain, which, by mine honor,
    I will perform with a most Christian care.
    But for you, rebels, look to taste the due
    Meet for rebellion and such acts as yours.
    Most shallowly did you these arms commence,
119 Fondly brought here and foolishly sent hence.
120 Strike up our drums, pursue the scattered stray.
    God, and not we, hath safely fought to-day.
    Some guard these traitors to the block of death,
    Treason's true bed and yielder up of breath.    *[Exeunt.]*
, iii    *Alarum. Excursions. Enter Falstaff [and Coleville,
         meeting].*
1  FALSTAFF What's your name, sir? Of what condition are
    you, and of what place, I pray?
COLEVILLE I am a knight, sir, and my name is Coleville
    of the dale.
FALSTAFF Well, then, Coleville is your name, a knight is
    your degree, and your place the dale. Coleville shall be

still your name, a traitor your degree, and the dungeon
your place, a place deep enough. So shall you be still
Coleville of the dale.
COLEVILLE Are not you Sir John Falstaff?
FALSTAFF As good a man as he, sir, whoe'er I am. Do ye
yield, sir, or shall I sweat for you? If I do sweat, they are
the drops of thy lovers, and they weep for thy death.    13
Therefore rouse up fear and trembling, and do observance to my mercy.
COLEVILLE I think you are Sir John Falstaff, and in that
thought yield me.
FALSTAFF I have a whole school of tongues in this belly of  18
mine, and not a tongue of them all speaks any other word
but my name. An I had but a belly of any indifferency, I   20
were simply the most active fellow in Europe. My
womb, my womb, my womb undoes me. Here comes       22
our general.
    *Enter [Prince] John [of Lancaster], Westmoreland,
    [Blunt,] and the rest. Retreat [sounded].*
LANCASTER
    The heat is past, follow no further now.                24
    Call in the powers, good cousin Westmoreland.
                              *[Exit Westmoreland.]*
    Now, Falstaff, where have you been all this while?
    When everything is ended, then you come.
    These tardy tricks of yours will, on my life,
    One time or other break some gallows' back.
FALSTAFF I would be sorry, my lord, but it should be
thus. I never knew yet but rebuke and check was the
reward of valor. Do you think me a swallow, an arrow, or
a bullet? Have I, in my poor and old motion, the expedition of thought? I have speeded hither with the very extremest inch of possibility. I have foundered nine score  35
and odd posts, and here, travel-tainted as I am, have, in   36
my pure and immaculate valor, taken Sir John Coleville
of the dale, a most furious knight and valorous enemy.
But what of that? He saw me, and yielded, that I may
justly say, with the hook-nosed fellow of Rome, their
Caesar, 'I came, saw, and overcame.'
LANCASTER It was more of his courtesy than your deserving.
FALSTAFF I know not. Here he is, and here I yield him.
And I beseech your grace, let it be booked with the rest
of this day's deeds, or, by the Lord, I will have it in a par-  45
ticular ballad else, with mine own picture on the top on't,
Coleville kissing my foot. To the which course if I be
enforced, if you do not all show like gilt twopences to     48
me, and I in the clear sky of fame o'ershine you as much
as the full moon doth the cinders of the element, which    50
show like pins' heads to her, believe not the word of the
noble. Therefore let me have right, and let desert
mount.
LANCASTER Thine's too heavy to mount.
FALSTAFF Let it shine, then.
LANCASTER Thine's too thick to shine.
FALSTAFF Let it do something, my good lord, that may
do me good, and call it what you will.
LANCASTER Is thy name Coleville?
COLEVILLE It is, my lord.
LANCASTER A famous rebel art thou, Coleville.
FALSTAFF And a famous true subject took him.
COLEVILLE
    I am, my lord, but as my betters are
    That led me hither. Had they been ruled by me,

---

93 *trains* armies  95 *coped withal* been matched with  105 *sporting-place*
playground  109 *capital* punishable by death  112 *pawned* pledged  119
*Fondly* foolishly  120 *stray* stragglers
IV, iii  1 *condition* rank  13 *drops* tear-drops; *lovers* friends  18–20 *I ...
name* i.e. my corpulency makes my identity unmistakable  18 *school*
crowd  20 *indifferency* moderate size  22 *womb* belly  24 *heat* height of
the action  35 *foundered* lamed  36 *posts* post-horses  45–46 *particular
ballad* broadside ballad celebrating my own exploits  48 *show* appear; *to*
in comparison with  50 *cinders ... element* stars

You should have won them dearer than you have.

FALSTAFF I know not how they sold themselves. But thou, like a kind fellow, gavest thyself away gratis, and I thank thee for thee.

*Enter Westmoreland.*

LANCASTER
Now, have you left pursuit?

WESTMORELAND

69 Retreat is made and execution stayed.

LANCASTER
Send Coleville with his confederates

71 To York, to present execution.
Blunt, lead him hence, and see you guard him sure.

*[Exeunt Blunt and others with Coleville.]*

73 And now dispatch we toward the court, my lords.
I hear the king my father is sore sick.
Our news shall go before us to his majesty,
Which, cousin, you shall bear to comfort him,
And we with sober speed will follow you.

FALSTAFF
My lord, I beseech you give me leave to go
Through Gloucestershire. And when you come to court,

80 Stand my good lord, pray, in your good report.

LANCASTER

81 Fare you well, Falstaff. I, in my condition,
Shall better speak of you than you deserve.

*[Exeunt all but Falstaff.]*

FALSTAFF I would you had but the wit. 'Twere better than your dukedom. Good faith, this same young sober-blooded boy doth not love me, nor a man cannot make him laugh. But that's no marvel, he drinks no wine.

87 There's never none of these demure boys come to any
88 proof, for thin drink doth so overcool their blood, and making many fish-meals, that they fall into a kind of

90 male green-sickness, and then, when they marry, they get wenches. They are generally fools and cowards, which

92 some of us should be too, but for inflammation. A good
93 sherris-sack hath a twofold operation in it. It ascends me into the brain, dries me there all the foolish and dull and

95 crudy vapors which environ it, makes it apprehensive,
96 quick, forgetive, full of nimble, fiery, and delectable shapes, which, delivered o'er to the voice, the tongue,

98 which is the birth, becomes excellent wit. The second property of your excellent sherris is the warming of the

100 blood, which, before cold and settled, left the liver white and pale, which is the badge of pusillanimity and coward-ice. But the sherris warms it and makes it course from the inwards to the parts extremes. It illumineth the face, which as a beacon gives warning to all the rest of this

105 little kingdom, man, to arm, and then the vital com-moners and inland petty spirits muster me all to their captain, the heart, who, great and puffed up with this retinue, doth any deed of courage, and this valor comes of sherris. So that skill in the weapon is nothing without sack, for that sets it a-work, and learning a mere hoard of gold kept by a devil, till sack commences it and sets it in

111 act and use. Hereof comes it that Prince Harry is valiant, for the cold blood he did naturally inherit of his father,

114 he hath, like lean, sterile, and bare land, manured, hus-banded, and tilled with excellent endeavor of drinking good and good store of fertile sherris, that he is become very hot and valiant. If I had a thousand sons, the first humane principle I would teach them should be to for-swear thin potations and to addict themselves to sack.

*Enter Bardolph.*
How now, Bardolph?

BARDOLPH The army is discharged all and gone.

FALSTAFF Let them go. I'll through Gloucestershire, and there will I visit Master Robert Shallow, esquire. I have 123 him already tempering between my finger and my thumb, and shortly will I seal with him. Come away. 125

*[Exeunt.]*

\*

*Enter the King, Warwick, Thomas Duke of Clarence,* IV
*Humphrey [Duke] of Gloucester [, and others].*

KING
Now, lords, if God doth give successful end
To this debate that bleedeth at our doors, 2
We will our youth lead on to higher fields 3
And draw no swords but what are sanctified.
Our navy is addressed, our power collected, 5
Our substitutes in absence well invested, 6
And everything lies level to our wish. 7
Only, we want a little personal strength,
And pause us, till these rebels, now afoot,
Come underneath the yoke of government.

WARWICK
Both which we doubt not but your majesty
Shall soon enjoy.

KING                    Humphrey, my son of Gloucester,
Where is the prince your brother?

GLOUCESTER
I think he's gone to hunt, my lord, at Windsor.

KING
And how accompanied?

GLOUCESTER          I do not know, my lord.

KING
Is not his brother, Thomas of Clarence, with him?

GLOUCESTER
No, my good lord, he is in presence here. 17

CLARENCE
What would my lord and father?

KING
Nothing but well to thee, Thomas of Clarence.
How chance thou art not with the prince thy brother?
He loves thee, and thou dost neglect him, Thomas;
Thou hast a better place in his affection
Than all thy brothers. Cherish it, my boy,
And noble offices thou mayst effect
Of mediation, after I am dead,
Between his greatness and thy other brethren.
Therefore omit him not, blunt not his love, 27

69 *Retreat is made* the order for retreat has been given; *stayed* stopped 71 *present* immediate  73 *dispatch we* let us hurry  80 *Stand . . . lord* be my patron  81 *in my condition* i.e. as commanding officer  87–88 *come . . . proof* stand up under testing  88 *thin drink* beer  90 *green-sickness* a form of anemia, usually associated with young girls; *get* beget  92 *inflammation* i.e. inflaming the mind with liquor  93 *sherris-sack* sherry  95 *crudy* curded; *apprehensive* discerning  96 *forgetive* inventive  98 *wit* understanding  100 *liver* (regarded as the seat of courage)  105–06 *vital . . . spirits* vital spirits which inhabit man's inward parts  111 *commences it* gives it license to act (as a university commencement gives the graduate authority to put his knowledge to use)  114 *manured* cultivated  123–25 *I . . . thumb* I am warming him, as sealing-wax is warmed between the fingers  125 *seal with* i.e. make use of
IV, iv Within King Henry's palace, Westminster  2 *debate* quarrel  3–4 (for the king's intention to go on crusade to the Holy Land, see *1 Henry IV*, I, i, 18–29)  5 *addressed* ready  6 *substitutes* deputies  7 *level to* in accordance with  17 *in presence* present at court  27 *omit* neglect

Nor lose the good advantage of his grace
By seeming cold or careless of his will.
30 For he is gracious, if he be observed.
He hath a tear for pity and a hand
32 Open as day for meting charity.
Yet notwithstanding, being incensed, he's flint,
34 As humorous as winter and as sudden
35 As flaws congealèd in the spring of day.
His temper, therefore, must be well observed.
Chide him for faults, and do it reverently,
When you perceive his blood inclined to mirth,
But, being moody, give him time and scope,
Till that his passions, like a whale on ground,
41 Confound themselves with working. Learn this,
    Thomas,
And thou shalt prove a shelter to thy friends,
A hoop of gold to bind thy brothers in,
That the united vessel of their blood,
45 Mingled with venom of suggestion –
As, force perforce, the age will pour it in –
Shall never leak, though it do work as strong
48 As aconitum or rash gunpowder.

CLARENCE
I shall observe him with all care and love.

KING
Why art thou not at Windsor with him, Thomas?

CLARENCE
He is not there to-day; he dines in London.

KING
And how accompanied? Canst thou tell that?

CLARENCE
With Poins and other his continual followers.

KING
54 Most subject is the fattest soil to weeds,
And he, the noble image of my youth,
Is overspread with them. Therefore my grief
Stretches itself beyond the hour of death.
The blood weeps from my heart when I do shape
In forms imaginary the unguided days
And rotten times that you shall look upon
When I am sleeping with my ancestors.
For when his headstrong riot hath no curb,
When rage and hot blood are his counsellors,
64 When means and lavish manners meet together,
O, with what wings shall his affections fly
66 Towards fronting peril and opposed decay!

WARWICK
67 My gracious lord, you look beyond him quite.
The prince but studies his companions
Like a strange tongue, wherein, to gain the language,
'Tis needful that the most immodest word
Be looked upon and learned, which once attained,
Your highness knows, comes to no further use

But to be known and hated. So, like gross terms, 73
The prince will in the perfectness of time 74
Cast off his followers, and their memory
Shall as a pattern or a measure live,
By which his grace must mete the lives of others, 77
Turning past evils to advantages.

KING
'Tis seldom when the bee doth leave her comb 79
In the dead carrion.
    *Enter Westmoreland.*
            Who's here? Westmoreland?

WESTMORELAND
Health to my sovereign, and new happiness
Added to that that I am to deliver.
Prince John your son doth kiss your grace's hand.
Mowbray, the Bishop Scroop, Hastings and all
Are brought to the correction of your law.
There is not now a rebel's sword unsheathed,
But Peace puts forth her olive everywhere.
The manner how this action hath been borne
Here at more leisure may your highness read,
With every course in his particular. 90

KING
O Westmoreland, thou art a summer bird,
Which ever in the haunch of winter sings 92
The lifting up of day.
    *Enter Harcourt.*
            Look, here's more news.

HARCOURT
From enemies heaven keep your majesty,
And, when they stand against you, may they fall
As those that I am come to tell you of!
The Earl Northumberland and the Lord Bardolph,
With a great power of English and of Scots,
Are by the shrieve of Yorkshire overthrown. 99
The manner and true order of the fight
This packet, please it you, contains at large.

KING
And wherefore should these good news make me sick?
Will Fortune never come with both hands full,
But write her fair words still in foulest letters? 104
She either gives a stomach and no food –
Such are the poor, in health – or else a feast
And takes away the stomach – such are the rich,
That have abundance and enjoy it not.
I should rejoice now at this happy news,
And now my sight fails, and my brain is giddy.
O me! Come near me. Now I am much ill.

GLOUCESTER
Comfort, your majesty!

CLARENCE          O my royal father!

WESTMORELAND
My sovereign lord, cheer up yourself, look up.

WARWICK
Be patient, princes. You do know these fits
Are with his highness very ordinary.
Stand from him, give him air, he'll straight be well. 116

CLARENCE
No, no, he cannot long hold out these pangs. 117
The incessant care and labor of his mind
Hath wrought the mure that should confine it in 119
So thin that life looks through and will break out.

GLOUCESTER
The people fear me, for they do observe 121

30 *observed* respected   32 *meting* distributing   34 *humorous* capricious
35 *flaws congealèd* snowflakes   41 *Confound* consume; *working* struggling
45 *suggestion* false insinuation   48 *aconitum* monkshood, a violent poison;
*rash* quick and strong   54 *fattest* richest   64 *lavish* licentious   66 *fronting*
opposing; *decay* ruin   67 *look beyond* misunderstand   73 *terms* expressions   74 *perfectness* perfection   77 *mete* appraise   79–80 *'Tis . . . carrion*
the bee which has placed her comb in a carcass seldom leaves her honey
90 *every . . . particular* every phase of the action set forth in detail   92
*haunch* hinder part, end   99 *shrieve* sheriff   104 *still* ever   116 *straight*
straightway   117 *hold out* endure   119 *wrought the mure* made the wall
121 *fear* frighten

122 Unfathered heirs and loathly births of nature.
The seasons change their manners, as the year
Had found some months asleep and leaped them over.

CLARENCE

125 The river hath thrice flowed, no ebb between,
And the old folk, time's doting chronicles,
Say it did so a little time before

128 That our great-grandsire, Edward, sicked and died.

WARWICK

Speak lower, princes, for the king recovers.

GLOUCESTER

This apoplexy will certain be his end.

KING

I pray you, take me up, and bear me hence

132 Into some other chamber. Softly, pray.
*[They bear him to another place.]*

IV, v    Let there be no noise made, my gentle friends,

2 Unless some dull and favorable hand
Will whisper music to my weary spirit.

WARWICK

Call for the music in the other room.

KING

Set me the crown upon my pillow here.

CLARENCE

6 His eye is hollow, and he changes much.

WARWICK

Less noise, less noise !
*Enter Prince Henry.*

PRINCE                Who saw the Duke of Clarence ?

CLARENCE

I am here, brother, full of heaviness.

PRINCE

9 How now ! Rain within doors, and none abroad !
How doth the king ?

GLOUCESTER

Exceeding ill.

PRINCE                Heard he the good news yet ?
Tell it him.

GLOUCESTER

He altered much upon the hearing it.

PRINCE

If he be sick with joy, he'll recover without physic.

WARWICK

Not so much noise, my lords. Sweet prince, speak low.
The king your father is disposed to sleep.

CLARENCE

Let us withdraw into the other room.

WARWICK

Will't please your grace to go along with us ?

PRINCE

No, I will sit and watch here by the king.
*[Exeunt all but the Prince.]*
Why doth the crown lie there upon his pillow,
Being so troublesome a bedfellow ?

22 O polished perturbation ! Golden care !

23 That keep'st the ports of slumber open wide
To many a watchful night ! Sleep with it now !
Yet not so sound and half so deeply sweet

26 As he whose brow with homely biggen bound
Snores out the watch of night. O majesty !
When thou dost pinch thy bearer, thou dost sit
Like a rich armor worn in heat of day,

30 That scald'st with safety. By his gates of breath
There lies a downy feather which stirs not.

Did he suspire, that light and weightless down    32

Perforce must move. My gracious lord ! my father !
This sleep is sound indeed. This is a sleep
That from this golden rigol hath divorced    35

So many English kings. Thy due from me
Is tears and heavy sorrows of the blood,
Which nature, love, and filial tenderness
Shall, O dear father, pay thee plenteously.
My due from thee is this imperial crown,
Which, as immediate from thy place and blood,    41

Derives itself to me. *[Puts on the crown.]* Lo, where it sits,    42

Which God shall guard. And put the world's whole
strength
Into one giant arm, it shall not force
This lineal honor from me. This from thee    45

Will I to mine leave, as 'tis left to me.    *[Exit.]*

KING

Warwick ! Gloucester ! Clarence !
*Enter Warwick, Gloucester, Clarence.*

CLARENCE

Doth the king call ?

WARWICK

What would your majesty ? How fares your grace ?

KING

Why did you leave me here alone, my lords ?

CLARENCE

We left the prince my brother here, my liege,
Who undertook to sit and watch by you.

KING

The Prince of Wales ! Where is he ? Let me see him.
He is not here.

WARWICK

The door is open ; he is gone this way.

GLOUCESTER

He came not through the chamber where we stayed.

KING

Where is the crown ? Who took it from my pillow ?

WARWICK

When we withdrew, my liege, we left it here.

KING

The prince hath ta'en it hence. Go, seek him out.
Is he so hasty that he doth suppose
My sleep my death ?
Find him, my Lord of Warwick, chide him hither.
*[Exit Warwick.]*
This part of his conjoins with my disease    6

And helps to end me. See, sons, what things you are !
How quickly nature falls into revolt
When gold becomes her object !
For this the foolish overcareful fathers
Have broke their sleep with thoughts, their brains with    68
care,
Their bones with industry.
For this they have engrossed and pilèd up    70

122 *Unfathered heirs* persons thought to be supernaturally conceived;
*loathly births* monstrous infants   125 *river* Thames   128 *Edward* Edward
III   132 *Into some other chamber* (the king remains in view, and so was
perhaps borne to a bed placed at some other point on the stage)
IV, v   2 *dull* soothing; *favorable* kindly   6 *changes* grows pale   9 *Rain*
i.e. tears   22 *perturbation* cause of perturbation   23 *ports* gates   26
*biggen* nightcap   30 *scald'st with safety* burns while it protects; *gates of
breath* lips   32 *suspire* breathe   35 *rigol* circle   41 *immediate from* nearest
to   42 *Derives* descends   45 *lineal* inherited   63 *part* conduct   68
*thoughts* anxieties   70 *engrossed* accumulated

71 The cankered heaps of strange-achievèd gold;
72 For this they have been thoughtful to invest
73 Their sons with arts and martial exercises.
74 When, like the bee, tolling from every flower
    [The virtuous sweets],
    Our thighs packed with wax, our mouths with honey,
    We bring it to the hive, and, like the bees,
78 Are murdered for our pains. This bitter taste
79 Yields his engrossments to the ending father.
      *Enter Warwick.*
    Now, where is he that will not stay so long
81 Till his friend sickness hath determined me?

WARWICK
    My lord, I found the prince in the next room,
83 Washing with kindly tears his gentle cheeks,
84 With such a deep demeanor in great sorrow
    That tyranny, which never quaffed but blood,
    Would, by beholding him, have washed his knife
    With gentle eye-drops. He is coming hither.

KING
    But wherefore did he take away the crown?
      *Enter [Prince] Henry.*
    Lo, where he comes. Come hither to me, Harry.
    Depart the chamber, leave us here alone.
      *Exeunt [Warwick and the rest].*

PRINCE
    I never thought to hear you speak again.

KING
    Thy wish was father, Harry, to that thought.
    I stay too long by thee, I weary thee.
    Dost thou so hunger for mine empty chair
    That thou wilt needs invest thee with my honors
    Before thy hour be ripe? O foolish youth!
    Thou seek'st the greatness that will overwhelm thee.
    Stay but a little, for my cloud of dignity
    Is held from falling with so weak a wind
    That it will quickly drop. My day is dim.
    Thou hast stolen that which after some few hours
    Were thine without offense, and at my death
103 Thou hast sealed up my expectation.
    Thy life did manifest thou lovedst me not,
    And thou wilt have me die assured of it.
    Thou hidest a thousand daggers in thy thoughts,
    Which thou hast whetted on thy stony heart,
    To stab at half an hour of my life.
    What! Canst thou not forbear me half an hour?
    Then get thee gone and dig my grave thyself,
    And bid the merry bells ring to thine ear
    That thou art crownèd, not that I am dead.
    Let all the tears that should bedew my hearse
114 Be drops of balm to sanctify thy head.
115 Only compound me with forgotten dust;
    Give that which gave thee life unto the worms.
    Pluck down my officers, break my decrees,
118 For now a time is come to mock at form.

Harry the Fifth is crowned. Up, vanity!     119
Down, royal state! All you sage counsellors, hence!
And to the English court assemble now,
From every region, apes of idleness!
Now, neighbor confines, purge you of your scum.     123
Have you a ruffian that will swear, drink, dance,
Revel the night, rob, murder, and commit
The oldest sins the newest kind of ways?
Be happy, he will trouble you no more.
England shall double gild his treble guilt,
England shall give him office, honor, might,
For the fifth Harry from curbed license plucks
The muzzle of restraint, and the wild dog
Shall flesh his tooth on every innocent.     132
O my poor kingdom, sick with civil blows!
When that my care could not withhold thy riots,     134
What wilt thou do when riot is thy care?     135
O, thou wilt be a wilderness again,
Peopled with wolves, thy old inhabitants.

PRINCE
    O, pardon me, my liege! But for my tears,
    The moist impediments unto my speech,
    I had forestalled this dear and deep rebuke     140
    Ere you with grief had spoke and I had heard
    The course of it so far. There is your crown,
    And He that wears the crown immortally
    Long guard it yours. If I affect it more     144
    Than as your honor and as your renown,
    Let me no more from this obedience rise,     146
    Which my most inward true and duteous spirit
    Teacheth, this prostrate and exterior bending.
    God witness with me, when I here came in,
    And found no course of breath within your majesty,
    How cold it struck my heart. If I do feign,
    O, let me in my present wildness die
    And never live to show the incredulous world
    The noble change that I have purposèd.
    Coming to look on you, thinking you dead,
    And dead almost, my liege, to think you were,
    I spake unto this crown as having sense,
    And thus upbraided it: 'The care on thee depending
    Hath fed upon the body of my father.
    Therefore, thou best of gold art worst of gold.
    Other, less fine in carat, is more precious,
    Preserving life in medicine potable,     162
    But thou, most fine, most honored, most renowned,
    Hast eat thy bearer up.' Thus, my most royal liege,
    Accusing it, I put it on my head,
    To try with it, as with an enemy
    That had before my face murdered my father,
    The quarrel of a true inheritor.
    But if it did infect my blood with joy,
    Or swell my thoughts to any strain of pride,     170
    If any rebel or vain spirit of mine
    Did with the least affection of a welcome
    Give entertainment to the might of it,
    Let God for ever keep it from my head
    And make me as the poorest vassal is
    That doth with awe and terror kneel to it.

KING
    [O my son,]
    God put it in thy mind to take it hence,
    That thou mightst win the more thy father's love,
    Pleading so wisely in excuse of it!

71 *cankered* tarnished  72 *thoughtful* careful  73 *arts* learning  74 *tolling* gathering  78–79 *This . . . engrossments* his accumulations leave this bitter taste  79 *ending* dying  81 *determined* put an end to  83 *kindly* natural  84 *deep* intense  103 *sealed up* confirmed  114 *balm* oil of consecration  115 *compound* mix  118 *form* ceremony  119 *vanity* folly  123 *confines* regions  132 *flesh* plunge into flesh  134 *care* carefulness  135 *care* occupation  140 *dear* severe  144 *affect* desire  146 *obedience* obeisance, low curtsy  162 *medicine potable* (gold in solution was often prescribed as a medicine)  170 *strain* feeling

Come hither, Harry, sit thou by my bed,
182  And hear, I think, the very latest counsel
That ever I shall breathe. God knows, my son,
By what bypaths and indirect crooked ways
I met this crown, and I myself know well
How troublesome it sat upon my head.
To thee it shall descend with better quiet,
188  Better opinion, better confirmation,
189  For all the soil of the achievement goes
With me into the earth. It seemed in me
But as an honor snatched with boisterous hand,
And I had many living to upbraid
My gain of it by their assistances,
Which daily grew to quarrel and to bloodshed
195  Wounding supposèd peace. All these bold fears
Thou seest with peril I have answerèd,
For all my reign hath been but as a scene
198  Acting that argument. And now my death
199  Changes the mode, for what in me was purchased
Falls upon thee in a more fairer sort,
201  So thou the garland wear'st successively.
Yet, though thou stand'st more sure than I could do,
203  Thou art not firm enough, since griefs are green.
And all my friends, which thou must make thy friends,
Have but their stings and teeth newly ta'en out,
206  By whose fell working I was first advanced
207  And by whose power I well might lodge a fear
To be again displaced. Which to avoid,
I cut them off, and had a purpose now
To lead out many to the Holy Land,
211  Lest rest and lying still might make them look
Too near unto my state. Therefore, my Harry,
Be it thy course to busy giddy minds
214  With foreign quarrels, that action, hence borne out,
May waste the memory of the former days.
More would I, but my lungs are wasted so
That strength of speech is utterly denied me.
How I came by the crown, O God forgive,
And grant it may with thee in true peace live!

PRINCE
[My gracious liege,]
You won it, wore it, kept it, gave it me.
Then plain and right must my possession be,
Which I with more than with a common pain
'Gainst all the world will rightfully maintain.
     Enter [Prince John of] Lancaster [and Warwick].

KING
Look, look, here comes my John of Lancaster.

LANCASTER
Health, peace, and happiness to my royal father!

KING
Thou bring'st me happiness and peace, son John,
But health, alack, with youthful wings is flown
From this bare withered trunk. Upon thy sight
My worldly business makes a period.
Where is my Lord of Warwick?

PRINCE                          My Lord of Warwick!
KING
Doth any name particular belong
Unto the lodging where I first did swoon?

WARWICK
234  'Tis called Jerusalem, my noble lord.

KING
Laud be to God! Even there my life must end.

It hath been prophesied to me many years
I should not die but in Jerusalem,
Which vainly I supposed the Holy Land.
But bear me to that chamber; there I'll lie.
In that Jerusalem shall Harry die.          [Exeunt.]

\*

*Enter Shallow, Falstaff, and Bardolph [and Page].*          V,

SHALLOW  By cock and pie, sir, you shall not away to-  1
night. What, Davy, I say!

FALSTAFF  You must excuse me, Master Robert Shallow.

SHALLOW  I will not excuse you, you shall not be excused,
excuses shall not be admitted, there is no excuse shall
serve, you shall not be excused. Why, Davy!
     *Enter Davy.*

DAVY  Here, sir.

SHALLOW  Davy, Davy, Davy, Davy, let me see, Davy.
Let me see, Davy, let me see. Yea, marry, William cook,
bid him come hither. Sir John, you shall not be excused.

DAVY  Marry, sir, thus, those precepts cannot be served.  11
And, again, sir, shall we sow the headland with wheat?  12

SHALLOW  With red wheat, Davy. But for William cook –
are there no young pigeons?

DAVY  Yes, sir. Here is now the smith's note for shoeing  15
and plough-irons.

SHALLOW  Let it be cast and paid. Sir John, you shall not  17
be excused.

DAVY  Now, sir, a new link to the bucket must needs be  19
had. And, sir, do you mean to stop any of William's
wages, about the sack he lost the other day at Hinckley
fair?

SHALLOW  'A shall answer it. Some pigeons, Davy, a  23
couple of short-legged hens, a joint of mutton, and any
pretty little tiny kickshaws, tell William cook.  25

DAVY  Doth the man of war stay all night, sir?

SHALLOW  Yea, Davy. I will use him well. A friend i' th'
court is better than a penny in purse. Use his men well,
Davy, for they are arrant knaves and will backbite.

DAVY  No worse than they are backbitten, sir, for they  30
have marvellous foul linen.

SHALLOW  Well conceited, Davy. About thy business,  32
Davy.

DAVY  I beseech you, sir, to countenance William Visor of  34
Woncot against Clement Perkes o' th' hill.  35

SHALLOW  There is many complaints, Davy, against that
Visor. That Visor is an arrant knave, on my knowledge.

DAVY  I grant your worship that he is a knave, sir, but yet,
God forbid, sir, but a knave should have some countenance at his friend's request. An honest man, sir, is able
to speak for himself, when a knave is not. I have served
your worship truly, sir, this eight years, and if I cannot

---

182 *latest* last  188 *opinion* reputation  189 *soil* stain  195 *bold fears*
grave dangers  198 *argument* theme  199 *mode* musical key, mood;
*purchased* acquired by my own act  201 *garland* crown; *successively* by
hereditary right  203 *griefs are green* grievances are fresh  206 *fell* fierce
207 *lodge* harbor  211–12 *look ... near* examine too closely  214 *action ...
out* military action waged abroad  223 *pain* effort  234 *Jerusalem* (actually
in Westminster Abbey rather than in the palace)
V, i Shallow's house in Gloucestershire  1 *By cock and pie* (a mild oath)
11 *precepts* orders  12 *headland* unploughed strip between two ploughed
fields  15 *note* bill  17 *cast* verified  19 *bucket* yoke  23 *answer* pay for
25 *kickshaws* delicacies  30 *backbitten* i.e. by vermin  32 *Well conceited*
wittily said  34 *countenance* favor  34, 35 *Visor, Perkes* familiar Gloucestershire names in Shakespeare's day

42 once or twice in a quarter bear out a knave against an
honest man, I have but a very little credit with your worship. The knave is mine honest friend, sir. Therefore, I
beseech you, let him be countenanced.

46 SHALLOW Go to, I say he shall have no wrong. Look
about, Davy. *[Exit Davy.]* Where are you, Sir John?
Come, come, come, off with your boots. Give me your
hand, Master Bardolph.

BARDOLPH I am glad to see your worship.

SHALLOW I thank thee with all my heart, kind Master
Bardolph. *[to the Page]* And welcome, my tall fellow.
Come, Sir John.

FALSTAFF I'll follow you, good Master Robert Shallow.
*[Exit Shallow.]* Bardolph, look to our horses. *[Exeunt*
56 *Bardolph and Page.]* If I were sawed into quantities, I
should make four dozen of such bearded hermits' staves
58 as Master Shallow. It is a wonderful thing to see the semblable coherence of his men's spirits and his. They, by
observing him, do bear themselves like foolish justices;
he, by conversing with them, is turned into a justice-like
serving-man. Their spirits are so married in conjunction
63 with the participation of society that they flock together
64 in consent, like so many wild geese. If I had a suit to
Master Shallow, I would humor his men with the imputation of being near their master. If to his men, I would
curry with Master Shallow that no man could better
command his servants. It is certain that either wise bearing or ignorant carriage is caught, as men take diseases,
one of another. Therefore let men take heed of their company. I will devise matter enough out of this Shallow to
keep Prince Harry in continual laughter the wearing out
73 of six fashions, which is four terms, or two actions, and
74 'a shall laugh without intervallums. O, it is much that a lie
75 with a slight oath and a jest with a sad brow will do with
a fellow that never had the ache in his shoulders! O, you
77 shall see him laugh till his face be like a wet cloak ill laid
up!

SHALLOW *[within]* Sir John!

FALSTAFF I come, Master Shallow, I come, Master
Shallow.               *[Exit.]*

*

ii       *Enter Warwick, [meeting the] Lord Chief Justice.*

WARWICK
How now, my lord chief justice! whither away?

CHIEF JUSTICE
How doth the king?

WARWICK
Exceeding well. His cares are now all ended.

CHIEF JUSTICE
I hope, not dead.

---

42 *quarter* i.e. of a year; *bear out* support  46–47 *Look about* on your toes!
56 *quantities* small pieces  58–59 *semblable coherence* similarity  63 *the*
*participation of society* close association  64 *consent* unanimity  73 *four*
*terms* i.e. a year, since there are four 'terms' in the legal year; *actions* suits
for the recovery of debt  74 *intervallums* interruptions (literally, intervals
between legal 'terms')  75 *sad* serious  77–78 *ill laid up* i.e. full of
wrinkles
V, ii Within King Henry's palace  7 *truly* faithfully  13 *fantasy* fancy
14 *heavy issue* sorrowing sons  18 *strike sail* i.e. submit themselves  23
*argument* situation  30 *grace to find* favor he will find  31 *coldest* gloomiest
34 *swims . . . stream* of goes against the grain of your  37–38 *beg . . . re-*
*mission* ask pardon, like a ragged beggar, for an offense I have not committed

WARWICK         He's walked the way of nature,
And to our purposes he lives no more.

CHIEF JUSTICE
I would his majesty had called me with him.
The service that I truly did his life          7
Hath left me open to all injuries.

WARWICK
Indeed I think the young king loves you not.

CHIEF JUSTICE
I know he doth not, and do arm myself
To welcome the condition of the time,
Which cannot look more hideously upon me
Than I have drawn it in my fantasy.      13
     *Enter [Prince] John [of Lancaster], Thomas*
     *[of Clarence], and Humphrey [of Gloucester,*
     *with Westmoreland].*

WARWICK
Here come the heavy issue of dead Harry.    14
O that the living Harry had the temper
Of him, the worst of these three gentlemen!
How many nobles then should hold their places
That must strike sail to spirits of vile sort!    18

CHIEF JUSTICE
O God, I fear all will be overturned!

LANCASTER
Good morrow, cousin Warwick, good morrow.

GLOUCESTER, CLARENCE
Good morrow, cousin.

LANCASTER
We meet like men that had forgot to speak.

WARWICK
We do remember, but our argument      23
Is all too heavy to admit much talk.

LANCASTER
Well, peace be with him that hath made us heavy.

CHIEF JUSTICE
Peace be with us, lest we be heavier.

GLOUCESTER
O, good my lord, you have lost a friend indeed,
And I dare swear you borrow not that face
Of seeming sorrow, it is sure your own.

LANCASTER
Though no man be assured what grace to find,  30
You stand in coldest expectation.        31
I am the sorrier. Would 'twere otherwise.

CLARENCE
Well, you must now speak Sir John Falstaff fair,
Which swims against your stream of quality.  34

CHIEF JUSTICE
Sweet princes, what I did, I did in honor,
Led by the impartial conduct of my soul,
And never shall you see that I will beg     37
A ragged and forestalled remission.
If truth and upright innocency fail me,
I'll to the king my master that is dead,
And tell him who hath sent me after him.

WARWICK
Here comes the prince.
     *Enter the Prince [as King Henry the Fifth] and Blunt.*

CHIEF JUSTICE
Good morrow, and God save your majesty!

KING
This new and gorgeous garment, majesty,
Sits not so easy on me as you think.

Brothers, you mix your sadness with some fear.
This is the English, not the Turkish court.
48 Not Amurath an Amurath succeeds,
But Harry Harry. Yet be sad, good brothers,
For, by my faith, it very well becomes you.
Sorrow so royally in you appears
52 That I will deeply put the fashion on
And wear it in my heart. Why then, be sad,
But entertain no more of it, good brothers,
Than a joint burden laid upon us all.
For me, by heaven, I bid you be assured,
I'll be your father and your brother too.
Let me but bear your love, I'll bear your cares.
Yet weep that Harry's dead, and so will I,
But Harry lives, that shall convert those tears
By number into hours of happiness.

PRINCES
We hope no other from your majesty.

KING
63 You all look strangely on me.
     *[To the Chief Justice]* And you most.
You are, I think, assured I love you not.

CHIEF JUSTICE
65 I am assured, if I be measured rightly,
Your majesty hath no just cause to hate me.

KING
No?
How might a prince of my great hopes forget
So great indignities you laid upon me?
70 What! Rate, rebuke, and roughly send to prison
71 The immediate heir of England! Was this easy?
May this be washed in Lethe, and forgotten?

CHIEF JUSTICE
73 I then did use the person of your father.
74 The image of his power lay then in me.
And, in the administration of his law,
Whiles I was busy for the commonwealth,
Your highness pleasèd to forget my place,
The majesty and power of law and justice,
79 The image of the king whom I presented,
And struck me in my very seat of judgement.
Whereon, as an offender to your father,
I gave bold way to my authority
83 And did commit you. If the deed were ill,
Be you contented, wearing now the garland,
To have a son set your decrees at nought,
86 To pluck down justice from your awful bench,
To trip the course of law and blunt the sword
That guards the peace and safety of your person,
Nay, more, to spurn at your most royal image
90 And mock your workings in a second body.
Question your royal thoughts, make the case yours.
92 Be now the father and propose a son,
Hear your own dignity so much profaned,
See your most dreadful laws so loosely slighted,
Behold yourself so by a son disdained,
And then imagine me taking your part
And in your power soft silencing your son.
98 After this cold considerance, sentence me,
99 And, as you are a king, speak in your state
What I have done that misbecame my place,
My person, or my liege's sovereignty.

KING
You are right, justice, and you weigh this well.

Therefore still bear the balance and the sword.
And I do wish your honors may increase,
Till you do live to see a son of mine
Offend you and obey you, as I did.
So shall I live to speak my father's words:
'Happy am I, that have a man so bold
That dares do justice on my proper son,
And not less happy, having such a son
That would deliver up his greatness so
Into the hands of justice.' You did commit me.
For which, I do commit into your hand
The unstained sword that you have used to bear,
With this remembrance, that you use the same    115
With the like bold, just, and impartial spirit
As you have done 'gainst me. There is my hand.
You shall be as a father to my youth.
My voice shall sound as you do prompt mine ear,    119
And I will stoop and humble my intents
To your well-practiced wise directions.
And, princes all, believe me, I beseech you,
My father is gone wild into his grave,    123
For in his tomb lie my affections,    124
And with his spirit sadly I survive,
To mock the expectation of the world,
To frustrate prophecies and to raze out
Rotten opinion, who hath writ me down
After my seeming. The tide of blood in me    129
Hath proudly flowed in vanity till now.
Now doth it turn and ebb back to the sea,
Where it shall mingle with the state of floods    132
And flow henceforth in formal majesty.
Now call we our high court of parliament.
And let us choose such limbs of noble counsel
That the great body of our state may go
In equal rank with the best-governed nation;
That war, or peace, or both at once, may be
As things acquainted and familiar to us,
In which you, father, shall have foremost hand.
Our coronation done, we will accite,    141
As I before remembered, all our state.    142
And, God consigning to my good intents,    143
No prince nor peer shall have just cause to say,
God shorten Harry's happy life one day!    *Exeunt.*

\*

*Enter Sir John [Falstaff], Shallow, Silence, Davy,*    V,
     *Bardolph, Page.*
SHALLOW Nay, you shall see my orchard, where, in an
arbor, we will eat a last year's pippin of my own graffing,   2

---

48 *Amurath* a Turkish sultan who, upon his accession, caused all his brothers to be strangled   52 *deeply* solemnly   63 *strangely* suspiciously   65 *measured* judged   70 *Rate* chide; *send to prison* (the story of Prince Hal's imprisonment for striking the Chief Justice was first told in Sir Thomas Elyot's *The Book Named the Governor*, 1531)   71 *easy* insignificant   73 *use the person* perform the function   74 *image* symbol   79 *presented* represented   83 *commit* commit to prison   86 *awful* awesome   90 *your . . . body* the actions of your deputy   92 *propose* imagine   98 *cold considerance* cool consideration   99 *state* royal capacity   115 *remembrance* reminder   119 *sound* speak   123 *My . . . grave* i.e. my wildness is buried with my father   124 *affections* wayward propensities   129 *seeming* outward appearance   132 *state of floods* majesty of the sea   141 *accite* summon   142 *remembered* mentioned; *state* nobles and great men of the realm   143 *consigning* agreeing

V, iii Within Shallow's orchard   2 *pippin* a variety of apple; *graffing* grafting

3 with a dish of caraways, and so forth. Come, cousin
Silence. And then to bed.

FALSTAFF 'Fore God, you have here a goodly dwelling
and a rich.

SHALLOW Barren, barren, barren. Beggars all, beggars
8 all, Sir John. Marry, good air. Spread, Davy, spread,
9 Davy. Well said, Davy.

FALSTAFF This Davy serves you for good uses. He is
11 your serving-man and your husband.

12 SHALLOW A good varlet, a good varlet, a very good varlet, Sir John. By the mass, I have drunk too much sack
at supper. A good varlet. Now sit down, now sit down.
Come, cousin.

16 SILENCE Ah, sirrah ! quoth-a, we shall
[Sings]
　　Do nothing but eat, and make good cheer,
　　And praise God for the merry year,
19　　When flesh is cheap and females dear,
　　And lusty lads roam here and there
　　　　So merrily,
　　And ever among so merrily.

FALSTAFF There's a merry heart ! Good Master Silence,
I'll give you a health for that anon.

SHALLOW Give Master Bardolph some wine, Davy.

DAVY Sweet sir, sit, I'll be with you anon. Most sweet sir,
27 sit. Master page, good master page, sit. Proface ! What
28 you want in meat, we'll have in drink. But you must
29 bear, the heart 's all. [Exit.]

SHALLOW Be merry, Master Bardolph, and, my little
soldier there, be merry.

SILENCE [sings]
　　Be merry, be merry, my wife has all,
　　For women are shrews, both short and tall.
　　'Tis merry in hall when beards wag all,
35　　And welcome merry Shrove-tide.
　　Be merry, be merry.

FALSTAFF I did not think Master Silence had been a man
of this mettle.

SILENCE Who, I ? I have been merry twice and once ere
now.
Enter Davy.

40 DAVY [to Bardolph] There's a dish of leather-coats for you.

SHALLOW Davy !

DAVY Your worship ! [to Bardolph] I'll be with you
straight. – A cup of wine, sir ?

SILENCE [sings]
　　A cup of wine that's brisk and fine,
45　　And drink unto the leman mine,
　　And a merry heart lives long-a.

FALSTAFF Well said, Master Silence.

SILENCE An we shall be merry, now comes in the sweet o'
the night.

FALSTAFF Health and long life to you, Master Silence.

SILENCE [sings]
　　Fill the cup, and let it come,
　　I'll pledge you a mile to the bottom.

SHALLOW Honest Bardolph, welcome. If thou want'st
anything, and wilt not call, beshrew thy heart. [to the 54
Page] Welcome, my little tiny thief, and welcome indeed too. I'll drink to Master Bardolph, and to all the
cabileros about London. 57

DAVY I hope to see London once ere I die.

BARDOLPH An I might see you there, Davy –

SHALLOW By the mass, you'll crack a quart together, ha !
Will you not, Master Bardolph ?

BARDOLPH Yea, sir, in a pottle-pot. 62

SHALLOW By God's liggens, I thank thee. The knave will 63
stick by thee, I can assure thee that. 'A will not out, he is 64
true bred.

BARDOLPH And I'll stick by him, sir.
One knocks at door.

SHALLOW Why, there spoke a king. Lack nothing. Be
merry. Look who's at door there, ho ! Who knocks ?
[Exit Davy.]

FALSTAFF [to Silence, seeing him drinking] Why, now you
have done me right. 70

SILENCE [sings]
　　Do me right,
　　And dub me knight.
　　　　Samingo. 73
Is't not so ?

FALSTAFF 'Tis so.

SILENCE Is't so ? Why then, say an old man can do somewhat.
[Enter Davy.]

DAVY An't please your worship, there's one Pistol come
from the court with news.

FALSTAFF From the court ! Let him come in.
Enter Pistol.
How now, Pistol !

PISTOL Sir John, God save you !

FALSTAFF What wind blew you hither, Pistol ?

PISTOL Not the ill wind which blows no man to good.
Sweet knight, thou art now one of the greatest men in
this realm.

SILENCE By'r lady, I think 'a be, but goodman Puff of 87
Barson.

PISTOL Puff !
Puff i' thy teeth, most recreant coward base !
Sir John, I am thy Pistol and thy friend,
And helter-skelter have I rode to thee,
And tidings do I bring and lucky joys
And golden times and happy news of price.

FALSTAFF I pray thee now, deliver them like a man of this
world.

PISTOL
A foutra for the world and worldlings base ! 97
I speak of Africa and golden joys.

FALSTAFF
O base Assyrian knight, what is thy news ? 99
Let King Cophetua know the truth thereof. 100

SILENCE [sings]
　　And Robin Hood, Scarlet, and John.

PISTOL
Shall dunghill curs confront the Helicons ? 102
And shall good news be baffled ? 103
Then, Pistol, lay thy head in Furies' lap.

3 caraways caraway seeds　8 Spread lay the table　9 said done　11
husband steward　12 varlet servant　16 quoth-a said he　19 flesh meat
27 Proface a form of welcome at dinner　28 want lack　29 bear be patient
35 Shrove-tide season of feasting before Lent　40 leather-coats russet
apples　45 leman sweetheart　54 beshrew the devil take　57 cabileros
gallants　62 pottle-pot two quart tankard　63 By God's liggens (this oath
has not been satisfactorily explained)　64 'A . . . out he won't pass out
70 done me right drunk even with me　73 Samingo Sir Mingo, the hero of
the song　87 but except; goodman yeoman　97 foutra an indecent term of
contempt　99 Assyrian i.e. heathen　100 Cophetua (an allusion to the
ballad of the king who married a beggar-maid)　102 Helicons poets　103
baffled disgraced

SHALLOW Honest gentleman, I know not your breeding.
106 PISTOL Why then, lament therefore.
SHALLOW Give me pardon, sir. If, sir, you come with
news from the court, I take it there's but two ways,
either to utter them, or to conceal them. I am, sir, under
the king, in some authority.
PISTOL
111 Under which king, Besonian? Speak, or die.
SHALLOW
Under King Harry.
PISTOL                    Harry the Fourth? or Fifth?
SHALLOW
Harry the Fourth.
PISTOL                    A foutra for thine office!
Sir John, thy tender lambkin now is king.
Harry the Fifth's the man. I speak the truth.
116 When Pistol lies, do this, and fig me, like
The bragging Spaniard.
FALSTAFF
What, is the old king dead?
PISTOL
As nail in door. The things I speak are just.
FALSTAFF Away, Bardolph! Saddle my horse. Master
Robert Shallow, choose what office thou wilt in the
122 land, 'tis thine. Pistol, I will double-charge thee with
dignities.
BARDOLPH
O joyful day!
I would not take a knighthood for my fortune.
PISTOL
What! I do bring good news.
FALSTAFF Carry Master Silence to bed. Master Shallow,
my Lord Shallow – be what thou wilt, I am fortune's
steward – get on thy boots. We'll ride all night. O sweet
Pistol! Away, Bardolph! [Exit Bardolph.] Come, Pistol,
utter more to me, and withal devise something to do
thyself good. Boot, boot, Master Shallow. I know the
young king is sick for me. Let us take any man's horses;
the laws of England are at my commandment. Blessed
are they that have been my friends, and woe to my lord
chief justice!
PISTOL
Let vultures vile seize on his lungs also!
137 'Where is the life that late I led?' say they.
Why, here it is. Welcome these pleasant days! Exeunt.

*

V, iv        Enter Beadle and three or four Officers [with Hostess
             Quickly and Doll Tearsheet].
HOSTESS No, thou arrant knave, I would to God that I
might die, that I might have thee hanged. Thou hast
drawn my shoulder out of joint.
BEADLE The constables have delivered her over to me,
5 and she shall have whipping-cheer enough, I warrant
6 her. There hath been a man or two lately killed about her.
7 DOLL Nut-hook, nut-hook, you lie. Come on, I'll tell thee
8 what, thou damned tripe-visaged rascal, an the child I
now go with do miscarry, thou wert better thou hadst
struck thy mother, thou paper-faced villain.
HOSTESS O the Lord, that Sir John were come! He would
make this a bloody day to somebody. But I pray God
the fruit of her womb miscarry!

BEADLE If it do, you shall have a dozen of cushions again.
You have but eleven now. Come, I charge you both go 15
with me, for the man is dead that you and Pistol beat
amongst you.                                              17
DOLL I'll tell you what, you thin man in a censer, I will 18
have you as soundly swinged for this – you blue-bottle 19
rogue, you filthy famished correctioner, if you be not
swinged, I'll forswear half-kirtles.                      21
BEADLE Come, come, you she knight-errant, come.
HOSTESS O God, that right should thus overcome might!
Well, of sufferance comes ease.                           24
DOLL Come, you rogue, come, bring me to a justice.
HOSTESS Ay, come, you starved bloodhound.
DOLL Goodman death, goodman bones!
HOSTESS Thou atomy, thou!                                 28
DOLL Come, you thin thing, come, you rascal.
BEADLE Very well.                          [Exeunt.]

*

Enter [Grooms as] strewers of rushes.                      V,
1. GROOM More rushes, more rushes.                          1
2. GROOM The trumpets have sounded twice.
3. GROOM 'Twill be two o'clock ere they come from the
coronation. Dispatch, dispatch.           [Exeunt.]
Trumpets sound, and the King and his Train pass over
the stage. After them enter Falstaff, Shallow, Pistol,
Bardolph, and the Boy [Page].
FALSTAFF Stand here by me, Master Robert Shallow, I
will make the king do you grace. I will leer upon him as 6
'a comes by, and do but mark the countenance that he
will give me.
PISTOL God bless thy lungs, good knight.
FALSTAFF Come here, Pistol, stand behind me. O, if I had
had time to have made new liveries, I would have be- 11
stowed the thousand pound I borrowed of you. But 'tis
no matter; this poor show doth better. This doth infer
the zeal I had to see him.
SHALLOW It doth so.
FALSTAFF It shows my earnestness of affection –
SHALLOW It doth so.
FALSTAFF My devotion –
SHALLOW It doth, it doth, it doth.
FALSTAFF As it were, to ride day and night, and not to de-
liberate, not to remember, not to have patience to shift 21
me –
SHALLOW It is best, certain.
FALSTAFF But to stand stained with travel, and sweating
with desire to see him, thinking of nothing else, putting
all affairs else in oblivion, as if there were nothing else to
be done but to see him.

106 *therefore* on that account  111 *Besonian* knave  116 *fig* insult by
putting the thumb between the index and third fingers  122 *double-charge*
(another play on Pistol's name)  137 'Where . . . led' (a snatch from an old
song)
V, iv A London street  5 *whipping-cheer* a whipping for supper  6 *about
her* on her account  7 *Nut-hook* a hooked stick used in nutting  8 *tripe-
visaged* flabby-faced  15 *eleven now* (Doll has used one of the cushions to
simulate pregnancy)  17 *amongst you* the two of you together  18 *thin . . .
censer* embossed figure on the lid of a censer, a pot for burning incense  19
*swinged* thrashed; *blue-bottle* (the beadles wore blue coats)  21 *half-
kirtles* skirts  24 *sufferance* suffering  28 *atomy* anatomy, skeleton
V, v Before Westminster Abbey  1 *rushes* (floors were strewn with rushes on
ceremonial occasions; in this case the streets seem to have been lined with
them)  6 *grace* honor; *leer* glance sidewise  11 *bestowed* spent  21–22
*shift me* change my clothes

8 PISTOL 'Tis 'semper idem,' for 'obsque hoc nihil est.'
     'Tis all in every part.
SHALLOW 'Tis so, indeed.
PISTOL
     My knight, I will inflame thy noble liver,
     And make thee rage.
     Thy Doll, and Helen of thy noble thoughts,
4   Is in base durance and contagious prison,
     Haled thither
6   By most mechanical and dirty hand.
7   Rouse up revenge from ebon den with fell Alecto's
          snake,
     For Doll is in. Pistol speaks nought but truth.
FALSTAFF
     I will deliver her.
PISTOL
     There roared the sea, and trumpet-clangor sounds.
          [The trumpets sound.] Enter the King and his Train
          [, the Lord Chief Justice among them].
FALSTAFF
     God save thy grace, King Hal, my royal Hal!
PISTOL
2   The heavens thee guard and keep, most royal imp of
          fame!
FALSTAFF
     God save thee, my sweet boy!
KING
     My lord chief justice, speak to that vain man.
CHIEF JUSTICE
     Have you your wits? Know you what 'tis you speak?
FALSTAFF
     My king! My Jove! I speak to thee, my heart!
KING
     I know thee not, old man. Fall to thy prayers.
     How ill white hairs become a fool and jester!
     I have long dreamed of such a kind of man,
     So surfeit-swelled, so old, and so profane,
     But, being awaked, I do despise my dream.
3   Make less thy body hence, and more thy grace.
     Leave gormandizing. Know the grave doth gape
     For thee thrice wider than for other men.
     Reply not to me with a fool-born jest.
     Presume not that I am the thing I was,
     For God doth know, so shall the world perceive,
     That I have turned away my former self.
     So will I those that kept me company.
     When thou dost hear I am as I have been,
     Approach me, and thou shalt be as thou wast,
     The tutor and the feeder of my riots.
     Till then, I banish thee, on pain of death,
     As I have done the rest of my misleaders,
     Not to come near our person by ten mile.
7   For competence of life I will allow you,
     That lack of means enforce you not to evils.
     And, as we hear you do reform yourselves,

We will, according to your strengths and qualities,
Give you advancement. Be it your charge, my lord,
To see performed the tenor of our word.                         72
Set on.                    [Exeunt the King and his Train.]
FALSTAFF Master Shallow, I owe you a thousand pound.
SHALLOW Yea, marry, Sir John, which I beseech you to
     let me have home with me.
FALSTAFF That can hardly be, Master Shallow. Do not
     you grieve at this. I shall be sent for in private to him.
     Look you, he must seem thus to the world. Fear not
     your advancements; I will be the man yet that shall
     make you great.
SHALLOW I cannot well perceive how, unless you should
     give me your doublet and stuff me out with straw. I
     beseech you, good Sir John, let me have five hundred of
     my thousand.
FALSTAFF Sir, I will be as good as my word. This that
     you heard was but a color.                                87
SHALLOW A color that I fear you will die in, Sir John.
FALSTAFF Fear no colors. Go with me to dinner. Come,   89
     Lieutenant Pistol, come, Bardolph. I shall be sent for
     soon at night.                                            91
          Enter [the Lord Chief] Justice and Prince John [of
          Lancaster, with Officers].
CHIEF JUSTICE
     Go, carry Sir John Falstaff to the Fleet.                 92
     Take all his company along with him.
FALSTAFF
     My lord, my lord –
CHIEF JUSTICE
     I cannot now speak. I will hear you soon.
     Take them away.
PISTOL
     'Si fortuna me tormenta, spero contenta.'                 97
                         Exeunt [all but Prince John and the
                                           Chief Justice].
LANCASTER
     I like this fair proceeding of the king's.
     He hath intent his wonted followers                       99
     Shall all be very well provided for,
     But all are banished till their conversations
     Appear more wise and modest to the world.
CHIEF JUSTICE
     And so they are.
LANCASTER
     The king hath called his parliament, my lord.
CHIEF JUSTICE
     He hath.
LANCASTER
     I will lay odds that, ere this year expire,
     We bear our civil swords and native fire                  107
     As far as France. I heard a bird so sing,
     Whose music, to my thinking, pleased the king.
     Come, will you hence?                       [Exeunt.]

---

28 *semper idem* always the same; *obsque . . . est* without this, nothing **34**
*contagious* noxious **36** *mechanical* workman's, base **37** *ebon* black;
*Alecto* one of the Furies **42** *royal imp* young son of the royal house
**53** *hence* henceforth **67** *competence of life* allowance for support **72**
*tenor* intention **87** *color* pretense **89** *colors* enemy **91** *soon at night*
early in the evening **92** *Fleet* a famous London prison **97** *Si . . . con-
tenta* if fortune torments me, hope contents me **99** *wonted* accustomed
**107** *civil swords* swords used in civil wars
**Epi.**   **4** *undo* ruin   **5** *doubt* fear

                    [Spoken by a Dancer]

First my fear, then my curtsy, last my speech. My fear is,
your displeasure; my curtsy, my duty; and my speech,
to beg your pardons. If you look for a good speech now, you
undo me, for what I have to say is of mine own making,   4
and what indeed I should say will, I doubt, prove mine own   5

marring. But to the purpose, and so to the venture. Be it known to you, as it is very well, I was lately here in the end
8 of a displeasing play, to pray your patience for it and to promise you a better. I meant indeed to pay you with this,
10 which, if like an ill venture it come unluckily home, I break, and you, my gentle creditors, lose. Here I promised you I would be and here I commit my body to your mercies.
13 Bate me some and I will pay you some and, as most debtors do, promise you infinitely.

If my tongue cannot entreat you to acquit me, will you command me to use my legs? And yet that were but light payment, to dance out of your debt. But a good conscience will make any possible satisfaction, and so would I. All the gentlewomen here have forgiven me. If the gentlemen will not, then the gentlemen do not agree with the gentlewomen, which was never seen before in such an assembly.

One word more, I beseech you. If you be not too much cloyed with fat meat, our humble author will continue the story, with Sir John in it, and make you merry with fair Katherine of France. Where, for anything I know, Falstaff shall die of a sweat, unless already 'a be killed with your hard opinions, for Oldcastle died a martyr, and this is not 27 the man. My tongue is weary. When my legs are too, I will bid you good night, and so kneel down before you, but, indeed, to pray for the queen.

---

8 *displeasing play* (this play has never been identified)  10 *break* am bankrupt  13 *Bate me some* relieve me of some of my debts  27–28 *Oldcastle . . . man* (In the Henry IV plays Falstaff was originally called Oldcastle. Objection was made to the use of this name since the historical Sir John Oldcastle, who was executed for treason in 1417, was in the sixteenth century honored as a martyr in the cause of Protestantism. Here Shakespeare is saying 'My character was not intended as the historical Oldcastle.')

# THE LIFE OF KING HENRY THE FIFTH

## INTRODUCTION

The Epilogue to *2 Henry IV* promises that "our humble author will continue the story, with Sir John in it, and make you merry with fair Katherine of France" – will provide, in other words, more light entertainment spun out of Harry of Monmouth's famous victories and rollicking pastimes. This jovial preview little prepares us for the opening of *Henry V*:

> O for a Muse of fire, that would ascend
> The brightest heaven of invention;
> A kingdom for a stage, princes to act
> And monarchs to behold the swelling scene!

Still, the original promise is substantially kept. No other play of the Lancastrian trilogy so persistently bids for laughter, even though Sir John is *not* "in it." If this play were referred to Polonius, he might accurately classify it as "comical heroical."

There are various reasons why *Henry V* assumed its present curious form – in part dramatic epic, in part comic pastiche. The dramatic adventures of Prince and King Hal had in a measure been pre-selected, with Shakespeare bound by a theatrical tradition. *The Famous Victories of Henry V*, an anonymous play registered for publication in 1594 and printed in 1598, is a visible token of this tradition, presenting in crude outline most of the episodes, historical and fictitious, which reappear in *1 & 2 Henry IV* and, even more conspicuously, in *Henry V*. There had been stage treatments of Henry's career at least since 1588, and although the precise relation to them of the extant *Famous Victories* and Shakespeare's trilogy must remain conjectural, it is clear that audiences had come to expect fun as well as fireworks whenever Hal appeared. After 1598 these audiences preferred Sir John Falstaff as the funster in chief, and if he were denied them, the playwright must be liberal in providing substitutes. It has been argued that Falstaff was at first included in *Henry V* according to plan, in the role assigned in the present version to Pistol, but was deleted by death in order to placate the Brooke family, which still resented the fact that he had originally been named for its revered Lollard ancestor Sir John Oldcastle. This may be so, but to most readers the explosive ensign sounds Pistol-pure, and it is hard to imagine him as Sir John transmogrified.

A reason at least equally plausible for the exclusion of Falstaff is that he was a character to whom Henry could scarcely have remained aloof, and aloofness, at least to scalawag knights, would seem to be the order of the day for the pious and patriotic hero of Agincourt. Shakespeare had special reasons for sounding the high heroic note when *Henry V* was written. Not only would it be the capstone of his series of histories ascending through *Richard II* and *1 & 2 Henry IV* and descending through *1, 2, & 3 Henry VI* and *Richard III*, but the audiences of the moment were athirst for glory. Within the memory of most living men, the English had been ruled by a woman, and although loyal at heart to their Elizabeth, they had come to find something slightly dispiriting about an elderly woman and pacifist as the available royal image. Henry's image was that of a man and a warrior, endowed with eternal youth by virtue of his early death; and to intensify the emotions which his memory stirred there was the figure of the Earl of Essex leading, during the summer and fall of 1599, an English army in Ireland to put down Tyrone's rebellion. Henry's triumphant return from Agincourt evokes a reference to Essex in the fifth chorus of Shakespeare's play:

> Were now the general of our gracious empress,
> As in good time he may, from Ireland coming,
> Bringing rebellion broachèd on his sword,
> How many would the peaceful city quit
> To welcome him!

These lines provide us with the date of composition of *Henry V*, and a hint of the warlike spirit in London just before Essex proceeded to demonstrate how inglorious an English expedition could sometimes be.

Although Shakespeare may have worked hastily upon his play, and resorted to considerable patching (cf. II, Cho., 41–42 and note), he took its serious portions seriously, and went beyond the existing theatrical versions of Henry's career for his materials. He read with more than usual attentiveness the account of the reign in Holinshed, and turned for details to Hall and perhaps older chroniclers as well as to non-dramatic poets.

Before considering the portrait of Henry which Shakespeare produced, we had best come to what terms we can with the comic interludes. An inventory proves revealing: we have the preparation of Sir John's "staff" to follow and exploit the French wars, with a quarrel between Pistol and Nym (II, i); Hostess Quickly's report of Falstaff's death before his survivors shog off to the port of embarkation (II, iii); their reluctant participation in the assault on Harfleur, followed by a dispute in assorted dialects between Fluellen, Macmorris, and Jamy (III, ii); the English lesson of Princess Katherine (III, iv); Fluellen's quarrel with Pistol (first episode of III, vi); the Dauphin's infatuation with his horse, and the contest in proverb-capping between Orleans and the Constable of France (III, vii); Pistol's threat against Fluellen made to Henry incognito (middle episode of IV, i); further display of the Dauphin's fatuousness (IV, ii); Pistol's conquest of a cowardly Frenchman (IV, iv); Fluellen's groping comparison of

Henry and King Alexander (first episode in IV, vii); Fluellen's expression of devotion to the leek and to Henry, and the latter's ruse in making him wear in his cap the glove offered by Williams as a gage (final episode in IV, vii); the averted conflict between Williams and Fluellen (first episode in IV, viii); Fluellen's forcing of Pistol to eat the leek worn in his cap, and Pistol's final deflation (V, i); Henry's bluff courtship of Katherine (middle episode, and bulk, of V, ii).

This implacably regular insertion of the comic episodes in alternate scenes would seem mechanical were it not for their diversity. Their diversity, on the other hand, and their fragmentary character, make the episodes seem gratuitous as compared with the comic matter in *1 & 2 Henry IV*. We may even mildly complain that either leeks or gloves, but not both, may be fittingly "worn" in the caps of a single play. Abundant enough already, the comedy of the play is often augmented in modern productions by making the Bishops of Ely and Canterbury senile (which they are not), the King of France a mental defective (which he may have been in fact, but is not in Shakespeare's portrayal), and the French lords ludicrously foppish as well as over-confident, although Shakespeare confers upon all except the Dauphin a fair degree of dignity. Although introduced adroitly enough, considering the unlikely setting in wartime courts and camps, the comic episodes cannot be considered neatly "thematic." The presence of the English, Welsh, Irish, and Scots captains in Henry's army has been taken as expressing an aspiration for British unity, but the portrait of Macmorris would scarcely propitiate the Irish, and that of Jamy is not favorable enough to offset the animadversions upon Scotland expressed by Henry and his counsellors early in the play. Gower and Fluellen, to be sure, are good and companionable men, but the union of the English and Welsh was more than an aspiration in 1599.

The contest for comic honors is between Pistol and Fluellen. We can understand why the former won the palm in contemporary esteem, as suggested by the title page of the first (and bad) quarto of 1600: *The Cronicle History of Henry the Fift. With his battell fought at Agin Court in France. Togither with Auntient Pistol.* While Bardolph's carbuncular face fails to project its pristine glow when there is only the Boy and not Falstaff to crack jests on it, and Nym's sullen "humors" lack variety, the dauntless fakery of Pistol and his on-beat rodomontade retains the true touch of Cheapside magic. Pistol's final passing drew a sigh from Dr Johnson. The Fluellen-funniness does not quite come off, at least in the reading, but it follows an interesting formula. Fluellen is an anti-Falstaff, not only in his unmasking of Pistol, who is serving as Falstaff's surrogate, but in his very character and personality. Fluellen is a ponderously dutiful non-wit, master of "the disciplines of the wars" but not of the English language, which issues from him like cold whey, whereas Falstaff had been a nimbly non-dutiful wit, master of nothing but brisk prose. Although Henry can safely associate with Fluellen, and we must give our moral approval to the substitution of good comic angel for bad comic angel, we cannot pretend that solemn respectability is as amusing as its reverse.

By common critical consent, the high moment in the comedy comes early and involves neither Pistol nor Fluellen, but the passing of Sir John Falstaff as reported by Hostess Nell. The wonder of the speech is that it hovers just this side of sacrilege (that side ribaldry) and yet is truly pathetic, with a touch of rough poetry. When this deplorable woman, who confuses Arthur and Abraham, and fails even to recognize the 23rd Psalm, speaks of having told the dying old sinner that he "should not think of God; I hoped there was no need to trouble himself with any such thoughts yet," we should recoil at the grim irony, but, strangely, we do not. She told him so "to comfort him." With every conceivable defect, moral as well as mental – except bad nature – the Hostess is still godly after her fashion.

No doubt Shakespeare considered fun its own excuse for being, and his dissatisfaction with *Henry V*, expressed in prologue, epilogue, and choruses, had nothing to do with its motley. He felt, or professed to feel, that the resources of his theatre, indeed the dramatic form itself, were inadequate for the presentation of an epic theme. In epic fashion his "plot" concentrates on one great action – the victory at Agincourt – and all else in Henry's three actual invasions of France, spread over a period of five years, is ignored or made to serve merely as prelude and postlude to that victory. The choral speeches do not really, as they purport to do, fill in the historical record, but merely link together the chosen episodes so as to contribute to the epic sweep of the play. The size of the action is made the measure of the size of Henry, the epic hero, with everything contributing to his aggrandizement.

It is noteworthy, under the circumstances, that Henry has failed to win from readers anything like uniform approval, in fact has provoked occasional cold hostility. Certainly Shakespeare did not intentionally "undercut" his hero, any more than he intentionally "undercut" the glory of the English feat of arms by displaying the martial failings of Pistol, Bardolph, and Nym. Bardolph's exhortation (from a stationary position) "On, on, on, on, on! to the breach, to the breach!" follows with travesty immediately upon Henry's famous battle speech at Harfleur; and Pistol's mulcting of his captive is the only military exploit on the glorious field of Agincourt which we actually *see*. The intention is not parodic. If the effect is so, it is a consequence of the comical-heroical blend to which the playwright had committed himself. So far as the character of his hero is concerned, he had committed himself to something even more dangerous, a kind of religio-comical-heroical blend.

*Henry V* is a hard play to analyze in respect to intentional and unintentional effects. Ely and Canterbury provoke Henry to war in order to sidetrack a movement to expropriate church lands. In the course of their private discussion, they mention what may appeal to us (and may have appealed to sixteenth-century Englishmen) as some very good economic and charitable results of such expropriation, and yet if we approve of Henry's conquest, we must presumably approve of their ruse. Why did Shakespeare choose to include this matter from his sources when there was so much else which he excluded? Was Henry to be shown as now so pious that he took suggestion from holy men without reflecting that they might act from somewhat less than holy motives? He sternly adjures them to speak the truth, so far as the legality of his claim to France is concerned, but he displays no curiosity about their present interest in it. Perhaps we are intended to conclude that if high churchmen approve of war, it would be too much to expect their royal parishioner to do otherwise.

The "faults" which critics have found in Henry are really the side-effects of Shakespeare's having tried to do too much for him – by conferring upon him incompatible virtues. He is the religious convert, the pattern of a Christian Prince – morally impeccable, careful of his subjects by whom he is beloved, and highly competent in his judicial and administrative capacity. But at the same time that he exemplifies Christian virtue, he also exemplifies non-Christian *virtu* – that of pagan conquerors like Alexander and Caesar, or medieval champions like Hotspur, by whose light "Did all the chivalry of England move / To do brave acts." As blatantly as Hotspur he confesses that he is as covetous of "honor" as the "most offending soul alive." He proclaims that

> In peace there's nothing so becomes a man
> As modest stillness and humility,
> But when the blast of war blows in our ears,
> Then imitate the action of the tiger.

Presumably the opposite types of virtue are adaptable to the opposite conditions of peace and war, but the fact stands that Henry chooses war. A man of peace cannot be a man of war unless his own nation is under attack. Henry is not the attacked but the attacker. It is the King of France who shows a disposition to negotiate, with the offer of his daughter's hand and, in Henry's view, some "petty and unprofitable dukedoms." Now it is quite true that the historical Henry and his nation considered his cause just, but it is difficult for us to grow excited about the illegality of the Salic law, or the eagerness of a litigant to recover family property. It is impossible for us to consider his cause religious. But Henry, the religious man and humane ruler, is obliged to think of his war as a crusade, and his assumption taints the air.

At the same time that he loves this war, he loathes war in general. The expression of loathing takes the form of listing its horrors and holding others responsible for them – the Archbishop of Canterbury if he wrongly "incites" him, the Dauphin for sending him a "mock," the citizens of Harfleur if they resist, and so on. It is impossible for the religious wielder of a secular sword to do anything quite to our satisfaction. Even Henry's modesty comes under question. He attributes the victory at Agincourt to God, but we might prefer a claim of personal prowess to a claim of special influence with God. Henry's incompatible virtues sometimes produce the effect of duplicity since his actions and words contend with each other, as when he preaches at the Dauphin and the French in general about provocations which are not the true cause of the war, or when he orders the slaying of the French prisoners (as a justifiable military measure) and then, retroactively (unless this is a defect in the text of the play), speaks of it as retaliation for the French attack on the camp-boys – "I was not angry since I came to France / Until this instant." The killing of the prisoners, though an historical fact, has caused Henry's admirers more concern than anything else. The true fault is that Henry is not permitted by the over-zealous playwright to wear his religio-moral and military haloes turn and turn about, but is forced to wear them both at once.

Finally, Henry is given a quality, intermittently displayed, which is compatible neither with the "modest stillness and humility" proper to peace, nor the "action of the tiger" proper to war. He must be shown as an informal, humorous "regular guy" – a self-styled "king of good fellows." He interrupts his reflections upon God's grace in visiting carnage upon the French in order to play a friendly practical joke on Fluellen, and he courts Princess Katherine with a manly bluntness which is ultimately a trial to our nerves. It contains amusing matter, but it does go on and on; never has anyone advertised his inarticulateness with such loquacity.

Henry is, in fact, the victim of Shakespeare's good will. It is somewhat naive to mistake defects in the playwright's conception for defects in Henry's personal character. More in the true spirit of the play is another kind of naiveté – the fervor of the patriotic Englishman as he contemplates Agincourt and Shakespeare's tribute to its hero. The nineteenth-century American was little inclined to grow analytical about the portrait of George Washington produced by Parson Weems, and Weems was something less than a literary genius. In its fine moments *Henry V* expresses perfectly the spirit (including perhaps the sense of divine call) of a little nation with a great history:

> O England! model to thy inward greatness,
> Like little body with a mighty heart....

The play is also able to achieve a foreign conquest of its own, and to stir non-English hearts. If Henry is the aggressor, he is also the underdog, and his devotion to his purpose confers a kind of purity upon him and his tattered host. The choruses, which show that Shakespeare might have succeeded where other Elizabethans failed – in writing an epic poem – dazzle with their descriptions of the youth of England selling "the pasture now to buy the horse," the brave fleet "on th' inconstant billows dancing," the remnant army with "lank-lean cheeks and war-worn coats" as "by their watchful fires" they "Sit patiently and inly ruminate."

The chorus and early scenes of Act IV are admirable. As Henry in disguise shares the watch of Bates, Court, and Williams, and utters his troubled defense of kingship, we are expected to reflect upon what a fine monarch he is. We must try to do so. But it requires no effort for us to reflect upon what fine subjects he has. There is something amazingly modern about Bates, Court, and Williams. Unique in their day as straight portraits of common soldiers, they have become the prototypes of such in a host of British war dramas and motion pictures. Grumpy, undemonstrative, unillusioned, they are still men of tenacious faith – resolved to trust their leaders and to do their duty well. Their character more than Henry's explains the victory at Agincourt. Henry himself grows in appeal as he accepts the loneliness of leadership and kneels in solitary prayer. For once he escapes self-righteousness.

Henry's address at Agincourt is in a class by itself as inspirational poetry. It is a different kind of thing from the battle oration before Harfleur, because it defines the moral value, perhaps the only moral value, which battle can develop. The *comitatus* is restored, and for a moment the high and the low, the leaders and the led, come together as a unit in mutual interdependence, trust, and admiration. The great day is seen prophetically as a point in history –

> Old men forget; yet all shall be forgot,
> But he'll remember, with advantages,
> What feats he did that day.

No one, English or non-English, can read the lines and fail to "rouse him at the name of Crispian" or escape a momentary pang of regret that he could not have been one of that "happy few" who on that day were able (Pistol excepted) to "gentle" their condition. The late John Kennedy was neither English nor recognizably kin to Macmorris, but when Shakespeare entered the White House in the brave new days of 1961, Henry's speech at Agincourt was the Shakespearean passage which this young leader was most eager once more to hear.

*Harvard University*                    ALFRED HARBAGE

## NOTE ON THE TEXT

*King Henry the Fifth* was first printed in a quarto of 1600 in "cut" and corrupted form, and this version was twice reprinted. A much-improved version was printed in the folio of 1623, evidently from pages of the later quartos corrected by reference to the author's draft. The present edition is based on the folio text on principles explained in the Appendix. The quarto text is not divided into acts and scenes. The folio text is divided, imperfectly, into acts; the relation of this division to the one supplied marginally in the present edition is indicated in the Appendix.

# THE LIFE OF KING HENRY THE FIFTH

[NAMES OF THE ACTORS

Chorus
King Henry the Fifth
Dukes of Gloucester and Bedford, brothers of the King
Duke of Exeter, uncle of the King
Duke of York, cousin of the King
Earls of Salisbury, Westmoreland, Warwick,
  and Cambridge
Archbishop of Canterbury
Bishop of Ely
Lord Scroop
Sir Thomas Grey
Sir Thomas Erpingham
Gower, Fluellen, Macmorris, Jamy, officers in the
  English army
John Bates, Alexander Court, Michael Williams,
  soldiers in the English army
Pistol, Nym, Bardolph

Boy
An English Herald
Charles the Sixth, King of France
Lewis, the Dauphin
Dukes of Burgundy, Orleans, Bourbon, and Britaine
The Constable of France
Rambures, Grandpré, French lords
Governor of Harfleur
Montjoy, a French herald
Ambassadors to King Henry
Isabel, Queen of France
Katherine, daughter of the French King and Queen
Alice, an attendant to Katherine
Hostess Quickly of an Eastcheap tavern,
  wedded to Pistol
Lords, Ladies, Officers, Soldiers, Citizens,
  Messengers, and Attendants

Scene : *England and France*]

*

**Enter Prologue.**

*ro.*
1 O for a Muse of fire, that would ascend
2 The brightest heaven of invention ;
  A kingdom for a stage, princes to act
4 And monarchs to behold the swelling scene !
5 Then should the warlike Harry, like himself,
6 Assume the port of Mars, and at his heels,
  Leashed in like hounds, should famine, sword, and fire
  Crouch for employment. But pardon, gentles all,
9 The flat unraisèd spirits that hath dared
10 On this unworthy scaffold to bring forth
  So great an object. Can this cockpit hold
  The vasty fields of France ? Or may we cram
13 Within this wooden O the very casques
  That did affright the air at Agincourt ?
15 O, pardon ! since a crooked figure may
  Attest in little place a million ;

And let us, ciphers to this great accompt,            17
On your imaginary forces work.
Suppose within the girdle of these walls
Are now confined two mighty monarchies,
Whose high-uprearèd and abutting fronts          21
The perilous narrow ocean parts asunder.          22
Piece out our imperfections with your thoughts :
Into a thousand parts divide one man
And make imaginary puissance.                        25
Think, when we talk of horses, that you see them
Printing their proud hoofs i' th' receiving earth ;
For 'tis your thoughts that now must deck our kings,   28
Carry them here and there, jumping o'er times,
Turning th' accomplishment of many years
Into an hourglass – for the which supply,            31
Admit me Chorus to this history,
Who, Prologue-like, your humble patience pray,
Gently to hear, kindly to judge, our play.     *Exit.*

**Pro.** 1 *fire* (most buoyant of the four elements : earth, water, air, fire ; the one which ascended to the empyrean) 2 *invention* creative imagination 4 *swelling* increasing in grandeur 5 *like* in a manner worthy of 6 *port* bearing 9 *unraisèd* unleavened 10 *scaffold* stage 13 *wooden O* circular theatre (depreciatory, like *cockpit* at l. 11) ; *the very casques* i.e. even the helmets 15 *crooked figure* cipher (which can raise 100,000 to 1,000,000) 17 *accompt* (1) story, (2) reckoning (continuing the word-play on 'cipher' initiated by *wooden O*) 21 *abutting fronts* frontiers 22 *perilous . . . ocean* i.e. English Channel 25 *puissance* armed forces 28 *deck* array 31 *hourglass* i.e. short measure of time ; *for . . . supply* in aid whereof
**I, i** Within the palace of the King of England 1 *self* selfsame 4 *scambling* snatching, predatory 5 *question* discussion

**Enter the two Bishops, [the Archbishop] of**      I, i
**Canterbury and [the Bishop of] Ely.**
CANTERBURY
My lord, I'll tell you, that self bill is urged        1
Which in th' eleventh year of the last king's reign
Was like, and had indeed against us passed
But that the scambling and unquiet time               4
Did push it out of farther question.                  5

319

**ELY**
But how, my lord, shall we resist it now?

**CANTERBURY**
It must be thought on. If it pass against us,
We lose the better half of our possession;
9　For all the temporal lands which men devout
By testament have given to the Church
Would they strip from us; being valued thus—
As much as would maintain, to the king's honor,
Full fifteen earls and fifteen hundred knights,
Six thousand and two hundred good esquires,
15　And to relief of lazars, and weak age
Of indigent faint souls past corporal toil,
A hundred almshouses right well supplied;
And to the coffers of the king beside
A thousand pounds by th' year. Thus runs the bill.

**ELY**
This would drink deep.

**CANTERBURY**　　　　　'Twould drink the cup and all.

**ELY**
But what prevention?

**CANTERBURY**
The king is full of grace and fair regard.

**ELY**
And a true lover of the holy Church.

**CANTERBURY**
The courses of his youth promised it not.
The breath no sooner left his father's body
26　But that his wildness, mortified in him,
Seemed to die too. Yea, at that very moment
28　Consideration like an angel came
And whipped th' offending Adam out of him,
Leaving his body as a paradise
T' envelop and contain celestial spirits.
32　Never was such a sudden scholar made;
Never came reformation in a flood
34　With such a heady currance scouring faults;
35　Nor never Hydra-headed willfulness
36　So soon did lose his seat—and all at once—
As in this king.

**ELY**　　　　　We are blessèd in the change.

**CANTERBURY**
Hear him but reason in divinity,
And, all-admiring, with an inward wish
You would desire the king were made a prelate;
Hear him debate of commonwealth affairs,
You would say it hath been all in all his study;
List his discourse of war, and you shall hear
A fearful battle rend'red you in music;
45　Turn him to any cause of policy,
46　The Gordian knot of it he will unloose,
47　Familiar as his garter; that when he speaks,
48　The air, a chartered libertine, is still,
49　And the mute wonder lurketh in men's ears
To steal his sweet and honeyed sentences;
51　So that the art and practic part of life
Must be the mistress to this theoric;
Which is a wonder how his grace should glean it,
Since his addiction was to courses vain,
His companies unlettered, rude, and shallow,
His hours filled up with riots, banquets, sports;
And never noted in him any study,
Any retirement, any sequestration
59　From open haunts and popularity.

**ELY**
The strawberry grows underneath the nettle,
And wholesome berries thrive and ripen best
Neighbored by fruit of baser quality;
And so the prince obscured his contemplation
Under the veil of wildness, which, no doubt,
Grew like the summer grass, fastest by night,
Unseen, yet crescive in his faculty.　　　　　66

**CANTERBURY**
It must be so, for miracles are ceased
And therefore we must needs admit the means　　　68
How things are perfected.

**ELY**　　　　　But, my good lord,
How now for mitigation of this bill
Urged by the commons? Doth his majesty
Incline to it or no?

**CANTERBURY**　　　　　He seems indifferent,
Or rather swaying more upon our part
Than cherishing th' exhibiters against us;　　　74
For I have made an offer to his majesty,
Upon our spiritual Convocation　　　　　76
And in regard of causes now in hand
Which I have opened to his grace at large
As touching France, to give a greater sum
Than ever at one time the clergy yet
Did to his predecessors part withal.

**ELY**
How did this offer seem received, my lord?

**CANTERBURY**
With good acceptance of his majesty,
Save that there was not time enough to hear,
As I perceived his grace would fain have done,
The severals and unhidden passages　　　　　86
Of his true titles to some certain dukedoms,
And generally to the crown and seat of France
Derived from Edward his great-grandfather.　　89

**ELY**
What was th' impediment that broke this off?

**CANTERBURY**
The French ambassador upon that instant
Craved audience; and the hour I think is come
To give him hearing. Is it four o'clock?

**ELY**
It is.

**CANTERBURY**
Then go we in to know his embassy,
Which I could with a ready guess declare
Before the Frenchman speak a word of it.

**ELY**
I'll wait upon you, and I long to hear it.　　　*Exeunt.*

*

9 *temporal* in secular use　15 *lazars* lepers　26 *mortified* struck dead　28 *Consideration* penitent reflection　32 *scholar* i.e. man of disciplined mind　34 *heady currance* headlong current　35 *Hydra* the monster with proliferating heads slain by Hercules at Lerna　36 *his seat* its throne　45 *cause of policy* political issue　46 *Gordian knot* intricate knot cut by Alexander in asserting his destiny to rule over Asia　47 *Familiar* offhandedly, mechanically　48 *chartered* licensed; *libertine* one free from bondage or restraint　49 *mute wonder* silent wonderer　51–52 *the art . . . theoric* i.e. study and practise must be the teacher of this mastery of theory　59 *open haunts* places of public resort; *popularity* low company　66 *crescive . . . faculty* i.e. given to growth　68 *means* i.e. natural means　74 *exhibiters* introducers of the bill　76 *Upon* on behalf of　86 *severals* particulars; *unhidden passages* open transmission　89 *Edward* i.e. King Edward III

ii

*Enter the King, Humphrey [Duke of Gloucester],*
*Bedford, Clarence, Warwick, Westmoreland, and*
*Exeter [with Attendants].*

KING
  Where is my gracious Lord of Canterbury?
EXETER
  Not here in presence.
KING                                    Send for him, good uncle.
WESTMORELAND
  Shall we call in th' ambassador, my liege?
KING
4  Not yet, my cousin. We would be resolved,
   Before we hear him, of some things of weight
6  That task our thoughts concerning us and France.
     *Enter two Bishops [the Archbishop of Canterbury*
     *and the Bishop of Ely].*
CANTERBURY
  God and his angels guard your sacred throne
  And make you long become it!
KING                              Sure we thank you.
  My learnèd lord, we pray you to proceed
  And justly and religiously unfold
  Why the Law Salic, that they have in France,
2  Or should or should not bar us in our claim.
  And God forbid, my dear and faithful lord,
  That you should fashion, wrest, or bow your reading,
5  Or nicely charge your understanding soul
6  With opening titles miscreate, whose right
  Suits not in native colors with the truth;
  For God doth know how many now in health
9  Shall drop their blood in approbation
  Of what your reverence shall incite us to.
1  Therefore take heed how you impawn our person,
  How you awake our sleeping sword of war.
  We charge you in the name of God take heed;
  For never two such kingdoms did contend
  Without much fall of blood, whose guiltless drops
6  Are every one a woe, a sore complaint
7  'Gainst him whose wrongs gives edge unto the swords
  That makes such waste in brief mortality.
  Under this conjuration speak, my lord;
  For we will hear, note, and believe in heart
  That what you speak is in your conscience washed
2  As pure as sin with baptism.
CANTERBURY
  Then hear me, gracious sovereign, and you peers,
  That owe yourselves, your lives, and services
  To this imperial throne. There is no bar
  To make against your highness' claim to France
7  But this which they produce from Pharamond:
  'In terram Salicam mulieres ne succedant';
  'No woman shall succeed in Salic land.'
  Which Salic land the French unjustly gloze

I, ii The presence chamber of the palace   s.d. *Clarence* (a 'ghost' character,
mute and appearing only in this single stage direction)   4 *resolved* freed
from doubt   6 *task* burden   12 *Or* either   15 *nicely . . . soul* subtly
impugn your rational faculty; i.e. rationalize   16–17 *opening . . . colors*
advancing illegitimate claims, the validity of which fails to harmonize
19 *approbation* support   21 *impawn* engage   26 *woe* grievance   27
*wrongs* wrongdoing   32 *sin* original sin   37 *Pharamond* legendary Frankish
king   46 *Charles the Great* Charlemagne   49 *dishonest* unchaste   58 *de-*
*function* death   72 *find* furnish   75, 77 *Charlemain, Lewis the Tenth* (actually Charles the Bald and Louis IX; errors repeated from the chronicles)
88 *his satisfaction* i.e. King Lewis's conviction   93 *net* i.e. web of sophistry
94 *imbar* bar claim to, impeach   98 *Numbers* (see Numbers xxvii, 8)

  To be the realm of France, and Pharamond
  The founder of this law and female bar.
  Yet their own authors faithfully affirm
  That the land Salic is in Germany,
  Between the floods of Sala and of Elbe;
  Where Charles the Great, having subdued the Saxons,   46
  There left behind and settled certain French;
  Who, holding in disdain the German women
  For some dishonest manners of their life,              49
  Established then this law: to wit, no female
  Should be inheritrix in Salic land;
  Which Salic, as I said, 'twixt Elbe and Sala
  Is at this day in Germany called Meisen.
  Then doth it well appear the Salic Law
  Was not devisèd for the realm of France;
  Nor did the French possess the Salic land
  Until four hundred one and twenty years
  After defunction of King Pharamond,                    58
  Idly supposed the founder of this law,
  Who died within the year of our redemption
  Four hundred twenty-six; and Charles the Great
  Subdued the Saxons, and did seat the French
  Beyond the river Sala, in the year
  Eight hundred five. Besides, their writers say,
  King Pepin, which deposèd Childeric,
  Did, as heir general, being descended
  Of Blithild, which was daughter to King Clothair,
  Make claim and title to the crown of France.
  Hugh Capet also, who usurped the crown
  Of Charles the Duke of Lorraine, sole heir male
  Of the true line and stock of Charles the Great,
  To find his title with some shows of truth,           72
  Though in pure truth it was corrupt and naught,
  Conveyed himself as th' heir to th' Lady Lingard,
  Daughter to Charlemain, who was the son             75
  To Lewis the Emperor, and Lewis the son
  Of Charles the Great. Also King Lewis the Tenth,     77
  Who was sole heir to the usurper Capet,
  Could not keep quiet in his conscience,
  Wearing the crown of France, till satisfied
  That fair Queen Isabel, his grandmother,
  Was lineal of the Lady Ermengard,
  Daughter to Charles the foresaid Duke of Lorraine;
  By the which marriage the line of Charles the Great
  Was reunited to the crown of France.
  So that, as clear as is the summer's sun,
  King Pepin's title and Hugh Capet's claim,
  King Lewis his satisfaction, all appear               88
  To hold in right and title of the female:
  So do the kings of France unto this day.
  Howbeit they would hold up this Salic Law
  To bar your highness claiming from the female,
  And rather choose to hide them in a net               93
  Than amply to imbar their crooked titles              94
  Usurped from you and your progenitors.
KING
  May I with right and conscience make this claim?
CANTERBURY
  The sin upon my head, dread sovereign!
  For in the Book of Numbers is it writ:                98
  When the man dies, let the inheritance
  Descend unto the daughter. Gracious lord,
  Stand for your own, unwind your bloody flag,
  Look back into your mighty ancestors;

Go, my dread lord, to your great-grandsire's tomb,
From whom you claim; invoke his warlike spirit,
And your great-uncle's, Edward the Black Prince,
106 Who on the French ground played a tragedy,
Making defeat on the full power of France,
Whiles his most mighty father on a hill
Stood smiling to behold his lion's whelp
110 Forage in blood of French nobility.
111 O noble English, that could entertain
With half their forces the full pride of France
And let another half stand laughing by,
114 All out of work and cold for action!

ELY
Awake remembrance of these valiant dead,
116 And with your puissant arm renew their feats.
You are their heir; you sit upon their throne;
118 The blood and courage that renownèd them
Runs in your veins; and my thrice-puissant liege
Is in the very May-morn of his youth,
Ripe for exploits and mighty enterprises.

EXETER
Your brother kings and monarchs of the earth
Do all expect that you should rouse yourself
As did the former lions of your blood.

WESTMORELAND
They know your grace hath cause, and means, and
    might –
126 So hath your highness! Never king of England
Had nobles richer and more loyal subjects,
Whose hearts have left their bodies here in England
129 And lie pavilioned in the fields of France.

CANTERBURY
O, let their bodies follow, my dear liege,
With blood, and sword, and fire to win your right!
132 In aid whereof we of the spiritualty
Will raise your highness such a mighty sum
As never did the clergy at one time
Bring in to any of your ancestors.

KING
We must not only arm t' invade the French,
137 But lay down our proportions to defend
138 Against the Scot, who will make road upon us
139 With all advantages.

CANTERBURY
140 They of those marches, gracious sovereign,
Shall be a wall sufficient to defend
Our inland from the pilfering borderers.

KING
143 We do not mean the coursing snatchers only,
144 But fear the main intendment of the Scot,
145 Who hath been still a giddy neighbor to us
For you shall read that my great-grandfather
Never went with his forces into France
148 But that the Scot on his unfurnished kingdom
Came pouring like the tide into a breach,
With ample and brim fullness of his force,
151 Galling the gleanèd land with hot assays,
Girding with grievous siege castles and towns;
That England, being empty of defense,
154 Hath shook and trembled at th' ill neighborhood.

CANTERBURY
155 She hath been then more feared than harmed, my liege;
For hear her but exampled by herself;
When all her chivalry hath been in France

And she a mourning widow of her nobles,
She hath herself not only well defended
But taken and impounded as a stray
The King of Scots; whom she did send to France
To fill King Edward's fame with prisoner kings,
And make her chronicle as rich with praise
As is the ooze and bottom of the sea
With sunken wrack and sumless treasuries.

ELY
But there's a saying very old and true:
    'If that you will France win,
        Then with Scotland first begin.'
For once the eagle England being in prey,
To her unguarded nest the weasel Scot
Comes sneaking, and so sucks her princely eggs,
Playing the mouse in absence of the cat,
To 'tame and havoc more than she can eat.

EXETER
It follows then, the cat must stay at home;
Yet that is but a crushed necessity,
Since we have locks to safeguard necessaries
And pretty traps to catch the petty thieves.
While that the armèd hand doth fight abroad,
Th' advisèd head defends itself at home;
For government, though high, and low, and lower,
Put into parts, doth keep in one consent,
Congreeing in a full and natural close
Like music.

CANTERBURY  Therefore doth heaven divide
The state of man in divers functions,
Setting endeavor in continual motion;
To which is fixèd as an aim or butt
Obedience; for so work the honeybees,
Creatures that by a rule in nature teach
The act of order to a peopled kingdom.
They have a king, and officers of sorts,
Where some like magistrates correct at home,
Others like merchants venture trade abroad,
Others like soldiers armèd in their stings
Make boot upon the summer's velvet buds,
Which pillage they with merry march bring home
To the tent-royal of their emperor,
Who, busied in his majesties, surveys
The singing masons building roofs of gold,
The civil citizens kneading up the honey,
The poor mechanic porters crowding in
Their heavy burdens at his narrow gate,
The sad-eyed justice with his surly hum
Delivering o'er to executors pale

---

106 *tragedy* i.e. Battle of Crécy, 1346   110 *Forage* in prey on   111 *entertain* engage   114 *action* i.e. inaction   116 *puissant* powerful   118 *renownèd* brought renown to   126 *So* so indeed   129 *pavilioned* in tents of war   132 *spiritualty* clergy   137 *lay . . . proportions* estimate our forces   138 *road* inroads   139 *all advantages* every opportunity   140 *marches* i.e. northern borderlands   143 *coursing snatchers* mounted raiders   144 *intendment* intent, design   145 *still* always; *giddy* unstable   148 *unfurnished* unprepared   151 *gleanèd* stripped (of manpower)   154 *neighborhood* neighborliness   155 *feared* frightened   160 *as a stray* like a stray beast   164 *ooze and bottom* oozy bottom   165 *sumless* inestimable   173 *'tame* attame, broach   175 *crushed* voided   177 *pretty* neat   179 *advisèd* prudent   180–81 *though . . . parts* i.e. though made up of three estates   181 *one* mutual   182 *Congreeing* agreeing; *close* cadence   186 *fixèd as* attached like; *aim or butt* i.e. target   191 *correct* maintain discipline   194 *Make boot* prey   197 *majesties* royal functions   202 *sad-eyed* solemneyed   203 *executors* executioners

The lazy yawning drone. I this infer,
That many things having full reference
To one consent may work contrariously,
As many arrows loosèd several ways
Come to one mark ;
As many several ways meet in one town,
As many fresh streams meet in one salt sea,
As many lines close in the dial's centre ;
So may a thousand actions, once afoot,
End in one purpose, and be all well borne
Without defeat. Therefore to France, my liege !
Divide your happy England into four,
Whereof take you one quarter into France,
And you withal shall make all Gallia shake.
If we, with thrice such powers left at home,
Cannot defend our own doors from the dog,
Let us be worried, and our nation lose
The name of hardiness and policy.

KING
Call in the messengers sent from the Dauphin.
                    [Exeunt some Attendants.]
Now are we well resolved, and by God's help
And yours, the noble sinews of our power,
France being ours, we'll bend it to our awe
Or break it all to pieces. Or there we'll sit,
Ruling in large and ample empery
O'er France and all her almost kingly dukedoms,
Or lay these bones in an unworthy urn,
Tombless, with no remembrance over them.
Either our history shall with full mouth
Speak freely of our acts, or else our grave,
Like Turkish mute, shall have a tongueless mouth,
Not worshipped with a waxen epitaph.
                    Enter Ambassadors of France [attended].
Now are we well prepared to know the pleasure
Of our fair cousin Dauphin ; for we hear
Your greeting is from him, not from the king.

AMBASSADOR
May't please your majesty to give us leave
Freely to render what we have in charge,
Or shall we sparingly show you far off
The Dauphin's meaning and our embassy ?

KING
We are no tyrant, but a Christian king,
Unto whose grace our passion is as subject
As is our wretches fett'red in our prisons.
Therefore with frank and with uncurbèd plainness
Tell us the Dauphin's mind.

AMBASSADOR                    Thus then, in few :
Your highness, lately sending into France,
Did claim some certain dukedoms in the right
Of your great predecessor, King Edward the Third.

In answer of which claim, the prince our master
Says that you savor too much of your youth,
And bids you be advised : There's naught in France       252
That can be with a nimble galliard won ;                 253
You cannot revel into dukedoms there.
He therefore sends you, meeter for your spirit,
This tun of treasure ; and in lieu of this,
Desires you let the dukedoms that you claim
Hear no more of you. This the Dauphin speaks.

KING
What treasure, uncle ?

EXETER                    Tennis balls, my liege.

KING
We are glad the Dauphin is so pleasant with us.
His present and your pains we thank you for.
When we have matched our rackets to these balls,
We will in France, by God's grace, play a set
Shall strike his father's crown into the hazard.         264
Tell him he hath made a match with such a wrangler       265
That all the courts of France will be disturbed          266
With chases. And we understand him well,                 267
How he comes o'er us with our wilder days,               268
Not measuring what use we made of them.
We never valued this poor seat of England,
And therefore, living hence, did give ourself            271
To barbarous license ; as 'tis ever common
That men are merriest when they are from home.
But tell the Dauphin I will keep my state,               274
Be like a king, and show my sail of greatness
When I do rouse me in my throne of France.               276
For that I have laid by my majesty
And plodded like a man for working days,
But I will rise there with so full a glory
That I will dazzle all the eyes of France,
Yea, strike the Dauphin blind to look on us.
And tell the pleasant prince this mock of his
Hath turned his balls to gunstones, and his soul         283
Shall stand sore chargèd for the wasteful vengeance      284
That shall fly with them ; for many a thousand widows
Shall this his mock mock out of their dear husbands,
Mock mothers from their sons, mock castles down ;
And some are yet ungotten and unborn
That shall have cause to curse the Dauphin's scorn.
But this lies all within the will of God,                290
To whom I do appeal, and in whose name,
Tell you the Dauphin, I am coming on
To venge me as I may, and to put forth
My rightful hand in a well-hallowed cause.
So get you hence in peace. And tell the Dauphin
His jest will savor but of shallow wit
When thousands weep more than did laugh at it.
Convey them with safe conduct. Fare you well.
                    Exeunt Ambassadors.

EXETER
This was a merry message.

KING
We hope to make the sender blush at it.
Therefore, my lords, omit no happy hour
That may give furth'rance to our expedition ;
For we have now no thought in us but France,
Save those to God, that run before our business.
Therefore let our proportions for these wars             305
Be soon collected, and all things thought upon
That may with reasonable swiftness add

205–06 reference . . . consent i.e. relationship to a single agreement   206
contrariously diversely   207 loosèd . . . ways i.e. shot from different angles
217 Gallia France   221 policy statesmanship   225 our awe awe of us
227 empery sovereignty   234 with . . . epitaph i.e. with even so much as
a wax (as opposed to durable bronze) epitaph   252 be advised take counsel
253 galliard merry dance   264 crown (1) symbol of majesty, (2) wager-
money ; hazard (1) an aperture functioning like a goal in an Elizabethan
type of tennis court, (2) jeopardy   265 wrangler opponent   266 courts
(1) tennis courts, (2) royal courts   267 chases (1) unsuccessful attempts
to return tennis ball on first bounce, (2) pursuits   268 comes o'er taunts
271 hence i.e. out of our proper realm (France)   274 state kingly decorum
276 rouse me in mount   283 gunstones cannon balls   284 sore chargèd
grievously accused   305 proportions required forces

308 More feathers to our wings; for, God before,
      We'll chide this Dauphin at his father's door.
310 Therefore let every man now task his thought
      That this fair action may on foot be brought.    *Exeunt.*

                 *

II, Cho.      *Flourish. Enter Chorus.*
      Now all the youth of England are on fire,
2 And silken dalliance in the wardrobe lies.
   Now thrive the armorers, and honor's thought
   Reigns solely in the breast of every man.
   They sell the pasture now to buy the horse,
6 Following the mirror of all Christian kings
7 With wingèd heels, as English Mercuries.
   For now sits Expectation in the air
9 And hides a sword, from hilts unto the point,
   With crowns imperial, crowns, and coronets
   Promised to Harry and his followers.
   The French, advised by good intelligence
   Of this most dreadful preparation,
14 Shake in their fear, and with pale policy
   Seek to divert the English purposes.
16 O England! model to thy inward greatness,
   Like little body with a mighty heart,
   What mightst thou do that honor would thee do,
19 Were all thy children kind and natural!
   But see, thy fault France hath in thee found out,
21 A nest of hollow bosoms, which he fills
   With treacherous crowns; and three corrupted men –
   One, Richard Earl of Cambridge, and the second,
   Henry Lord Scroop of Masham, and the third,
   Sir Thomas Grey, knight, of Northumberland –
26 Have, for the gilt of France (O guilt indeed!),
   Confirmed conspiracy with fearful France,
   And by their hands this grace of kings must die,
   If hell and treason hold their promises,
   Ere he take ship for France, and in Southampton.
31 Linger your patience on, and we'll digest
   Th' abuse of distance, force a play.
   The sum is paid, the traitors are agreed,
   The king is set from London, and the scene
   Is now transported, gentles, to Southampton.
   There is the playhouse now, there must you sit,
   And thence to France shall we convey you safe
   And bring you back, charming the narrow seas
39 To give you gentle pass; for, if we may,
40 We'll not offend one stomach with our play.
41 But, till the king come forth, and not till then,
   Unto Southampton do we shift our scene.    *Exit.*

II, i      *Enter Corporal Nym and Lieutenant Bardolph.*
   BARDOLPH Well met, Corporal Nym.
   NYM Good morrow, Lieutenant Bardolph.
3 BARDOLPH What, are Ancient Pistol and you friends yet?
   NYM For my part, I care not. I say little; but when time
shall serve, there shall be smiles – but that shall be as it
may. I dare not fight, but I will wink and hold out mine
iron. It is a simple one, but what though? It will toast
cheese, and it will endure cold as another man's sword
will – and there's an end.

BARDOLPH I will bestow a breakfast to make you friends,
and we'll be all three sworn brothers to France. Let 't be
so, good Corporal Nym.
NYM Faith, I will live so long as I may, that's the certain
of it; and when I cannot live any longer, I will do as I
may. That is my rest, that is the rendezvous of it.    15
BARDOLPH It is certain, corporal, that he is married to
Nell Quickly, and certainly she did you wrong, for you
were troth-plight to her.    18
NYM I cannot tell. Things must be as they may. Men may
sleep, and they may have their throats about them at
that time, and some say knives have edges. It must be as
it may. Though patience be a tired mare, yet she will
plod. There must be conclusions. Well, I cannot tell.    23
    *Enter Pistol and [Hostess] Quickly.*
BARDOLPH Here comes Ancient Pistol and his wife.
Good corporal, be patient here.
NYM How now, mine host Pistol?
PISTOL
  Base tyke, call'st thou me host?
  Now by this hand I swear I scorn the term;
  Nor shall my Nell keep lodgers!
HOSTESS No, by my troth, not long; for we cannot lodge
and board a dozen or fourteen gentlewomen that live
honestly by the prick of their needles but it will be
thought we keep a bawdy house straight. *[Nym and Pistol*
*draw.]* O well-a-day, Lady, if he be not hewn now, we   34
shall see willful adultery and murder committed.   35
BARDOLPH Good lieutenant – good corporal – offer   36
nothing here.
NYM Pish!
PISTOL Pish for thee, Iceland dog, thou prick-eared cur   39
of Iceland!
HOSTESS Good Corporal Nym, show thy valor, and put
up your sword.
NYM Will you shog off? I would have you solus.   43
PISTOL
  'Solus,' egregious dog? O viper vile!
  The 'solus' in thy most mervailous face!   45
  The 'solus' in thy teeth, and in thy throat,
  And in thy hateful lungs, yea, in thy maw, perdy!   47
  And, which is worse, within thy nasty mouth!   48
  I do retort the 'solus' in thy bowels;
  For I can take, and Pistol's cock is up.   50
  And flashing fire will follow.

---

308 *God before* i.e. God leading   310 *task* exercise
II, Cho. 2 *silken dalliance* pleasure garments of silk   6 *mirror* image,
pattern   7 *Mercuries* (Mercury, messenger of the gods, was usually
pictured wearing winged sandals)   9 *hides a sword* i.e. completely impaled
with captured crowns   14 *pale policy* timorous intrigue   16 *model to* i.e.
small visible replica of ·  19 *kind* loyal to kindred   21 *hollow bosoms* (1)
hypocrites, (2) empty receptacles for money   26 *gilt* i.e. gold crowns
31–32 *digest . . . play* i.e. render intelligible the shifting scene and compress
the action   39 *pass* passage   40 *offend . . . stomach* (1) make seasick, (2)
displease   41 *But, till* i.e. only when (ll. 41–42 were apparently added to
the original speech – cf. ll. 35–36 – when the following comic episode, still
set in London, was interpolated)
II, i A London street   3 *Ancient* ensign, standardbearer   15 *rest* last
stake (in the game of primero); *rendezvous* resort   18 *troth-plight* betrothed   23 *conclusions* i.e. an end to everything   34 *if . . . hewn* i.e. if
Nym is not cut down (?)   35 *adultery* (malapropism, for 'battery'?)
36–37 *offer nothing* i.e. do not offer to fight   39 *Iceland dog* (a breed with
long hair and pointed ears)   43 *shog off* move along; *solus* alone (taken by
Pistol as an insult)   45 *mervailous* marvellous (?)   47 *maw* belly; *perdy*
(mild oath, from '*par dieu*')   48 *nasty* foul-speaking   50 *take* strike;
*cock is up* i.e. anger is aroused (with play on 'cocked Pistol')

NYM I am not Barbason; you cannot conjure me. I have an
humor to knock you indifferently well. If you grow foul
with me, Pistol, I will scour you with my rapier, as I may,
in fair terms. If you would walk off, I would prick your
guts a little in good terms, as I may, and that's the humor
of it.

PISTOL
O braggard vile, and damnèd furious wight,
The grave doth gape, and doting death is near.
Therefore exhale!

BARDOLPH Hear me, hear me what I say! He that strikes
the first stroke, I'll run him up to the hilts, as I am a
soldier.     [Draws.]

PISTOL
An oath of mickle might, and fury shall abate.
    [Pistol and Nym sheathe their swords.]
Give me thy fist, thy forefoot to me give.
Thy spirits are most tall.

NYM I will cut thy throat one time or other in fair terms.
That is the humor of it.

PISTOL
Coupe la gorge!
That is the word. I thee defy again.
O hound of Crete, think'st thou my spouse to get?
No; to the spital go,
And from the powd'ring tub of infamy
Fetch forth the lazar kite of Cressid's kind,
Doll Tearsheet, she by name, and her espouse.
I have, and I will hold, the quondam Quickly
For the only she; and, pauca! there's enough.
Go to!
    Enter the Boy.

BOY Mine host Pistol, you must come to my master – and
you, hostess. He is very sick and would to bed. Good
Bardolph, put thy face between his sheets and do the
office of a warming pan. Faith, he's very ill.

BARDOLPH Away, you rogue!

HOSTESS By my troth, he'll yield the crow a pudding one
of these days. The king has killed his heart. Good husband, come home presently.     Exit.

BARDOLPH Come, shall I make you two friends? We
must to France together: why the devil should we keep
knives to cut one another's throats?

PISTOL
Let floods o'erswell and fiends for food howl on!

NYM You'll pay me the eight shillings I won of you at
betting?

PISTOL
Base is the slave that pays.

NYM That now I will have. That's the humor of it.

PISTOL
As manhood shall compound. Push home.     94
    [They] draw.

BARDOLPH By this sword, he that makes the first thrust,
I'll kill him! By this sword, I will.
    [Draws.]

PISTOL
'Sword' is an oath, and oaths must have their course.
    [Sheathes his sword.]

BARDOLPH Corporal Nym, an thou wilt be friends, be
friends; an thou wilt not, why then be enemies with me
too. Prithee put up.

[NYM I shall have my eight shillings I won of you at betting?]

PISTOL
A noble shalt thou have, and present pay;     103
And liquor likewise will I give to thee,
And friendship shall combine, and brotherhood.
I'll live by Nym, and Nym shall live by me.
Is not this just? For I shall sutler be
Unto the camp, and profits will accrue.
Give me thy hand.
    [Nym sheathes his sword.]

NYM I shall have my noble?

PISTOL
In cash, most justly paid.

NYM Well then, that's the humor of't.
    Enter Hostess.

HOSTESS As ever you come of women, come in quickly to     113
Sir John. Ah, poor heart! he is so shaked of a burning
quotidian tertian that it is most lamentable to behold.     115
Sweet men, come to him.

NYM The king hath run bad humors on the knight; that's
the even of it.     118

PISTOL
Nym, thou hast spoke the right.
His heart is fracted and corroborate.     120

NYM The king is a good king, but it must be as it may:
he passes some humors and careers.     122

PISTOL
Let us condole the knight; for, lambkins, we will live.
    [Exeunt.]

\*

    Enter Exeter, Bedford, and Westmoreland.     II, ii

BEDFORD
'Fore God, his grace is bold to trust these traitors.

EXETER
They shall be apprehended by and by.

WESTMORELAND
How smooth and even they do bear themselves,
As if allegiance in their bosoms sat
Crownèd with faith and constant loyalty!

BEDFORD
The king hath note of all that they intend
By interception which they dream not of.

EXETER
Nay, but the man that was his bedfellow,     8
Whom he hath dulled and cloyed with gracious favors –     9
That he should, for a foreign purse, so sell
His sovereign's life to death and treachery!

---

52 *Barbason* (name of a devil, Pistol's preceding speech having resembled
a formula for exorcising devils) 53 *foul* (from firing) 54 *rapier* (serving
as a scouring-rod) 56–57 *that's . . . it* i.e. that's my mood (an all-purpose
tag, glancing at popular abuse of the terms of 'humoral' psychology)
60 *exhale* expire 68 *Coupe la gorge* cut the throat 70 *hound of Crete*
(a shaggy breed) 71 *spital* hospital 72 *powd'ring tub* sweating tub
(used as cure for venereal disease) 73 *lazar kite* leprous bird of prey;
*Cressid's kind* i.e. prostitute (a popular epithet, derived from Cressida's
fate in Henryson's *Testament*) 76 *pauca* i.e. in few words 83 *yield
. . . pudding* i.e. become carrion food 85 *presently* at once 94 *compound*
settle it 103 *noble* 6s. 8d. (in cash) 113 *come* are born 115 *quotidian
tertian* (a confusion of the 'tertian' fever, which occurs on alternate
days, and the 'quotidian,' which occurs daily) 118 *the even of it* i.e.
on the level 120 *fracted* broken; *corroborate* pieced together by grace,
reconciled (probably a malapropism) 122 *passes* indulges in; *careers*
capers
II, ii The King's quarters at Southampton 8 *bedfellow* favorite (Scroop)
9 *cloyed* surfeited

*Sound trumpets. Enter the King, Scroop, Cambridge,
and Grey [, Lords, and Attendants].*

KING

Now sits the wind fair, and we will aboard.
My Lord of Cambridge, and my kind Lord of Masham,
And you, my gentle knight, give me your thoughts.
Think you not that the pow'rs we bear with us
Will cut their passage through the force of France,
Doing the execution and the act
18   For which we have in head assembled them?

SCROOP

No doubt, my liege, if each man do his best.

KING

I doubt not that, since we are well persuaded
We carry not a heart with us from hence
That grows not in a fair consent with ours,
Nor leave not one behind that doth not wish
Success and conquest to attend on us.

CAMBRIDGE

Never was monarch better feared and loved
Than is your majesty. There's not, I think, a subject
That sits in heart-grief and uneasiness
Under the sweet shade of your government.

GREY

True. Those that were your father's enemies
30   Have steepèd their galls in honey and do serve you
With hearts create of duty and of zeal.

KING

We therefore have great cause of thankfulness,
33   And shall forget the office of our hand
34   Sooner than quittance of desert and merit
According to the weight and worthiness.

SCROOP

So service shall with steelèd sinews toil,
And labor shall refresh itself with hope,
To do your grace incessant services.

KING

We judge no less. Uncle of Exeter,
40   Enlarge the man committed yesterday
That railed against our person. We consider
It was excess of wine that set him on,
43   And on his more advice, we pardon him.

SCROOP

44   That's mercy, but too much security:
Let him be punished, sovereign, lest example
46   Breed by his sufferance more of such a kind.

KING

O, let us yet be merciful.

CAMBRIDGE

So may your highness, and yet punish too.

GREY

Sir,
You show great mercy if you give him life
After the taste of much correction.

KING

Alas, your too much love and care of me
53   Are heavy orisons 'gainst this poor wretch.
54   If little faults proceeding on distemper
Shall not be winked at, how shall we stretch our eye
56   When capital crimes, chewed, swallowed, and digested,
Appear before us? We'll yet enlarge that man,
Though Cambridge, Scroop, and Grey, in their dear care
And tender preservation of our person,

Would have him punished. And now to our French
causes.
Who are the late commissioners?    6

CAMBRIDGE

I one, my lord.
Your highness bade me ask for it to-day.    6

SCROOP

So did you me, my liege.

GREY

And I, my royal sovereign.

KING

Then, Richard Earl of Cambridge, there is yours;
There yours, Lord Scroop of Masham; and, sir knight,
Grey of Northumberland, this same is yours.
Read them, and know I know your worthiness.
My Lord of Westmoreland, and uncle Exeter,
We will aboard to-night. – Why, how now, gentlemen?
What see you in those papers that you lose
So much complexion? – Look ye, how they change!
Their cheeks are paper. – Why, what read you there
That hath so cowarded and chased your blood    7
Out of appearance?    7

CAMBRIDGE      I do confess my fault,
And do submit me to your highness' mercy.

GREY, SCROOP

To which we all appeal.

KING

The mercy that was quick in us but late,    7
By your own counsel is suppressed and killed.
You must not dare for shame to talk of mercy;
For your own reasons turn into your bosoms    8
As dogs upon their masters, worrying you.
See you, my princes and my noble peers,
These English monsters! My Lord of Cambridge here –   8
You know how apt our love was to accord    8
To furnish him with all appertinents    8
Belonging to his honor; and this man
Hath, for a few light crowns, lightly conspired
And sworn unto the practices of France    9
To kill us here in Hampton; to the which
This knight, no less for bounty bound to us
Than Cambridge is, hath likewise sworn. But O,
What shall I say to thee, Lord Scroop, thou cruel,
Ingrateful, savage, and inhuman creature?
Thou that didst bear the key of all my counsels,
That knew'st the very bottom of my soul,
That almost mightst have coined me into gold,
Wouldst thou have practiced on me for thy use?
May it be possible that foreign hire
Could out of thee extract one spark of evil
That might annoy my finger? 'Tis so strange    1
That, though the truth of it stands off as gross
As black and white, my eye will scarcely see it.
Treason and murder ever kept together,

---

18 *head* an army   30 *galls* sources of bitterness · 33 *office* use   34 *quittance*
requital   40 *Enlarge* set free   43 *more advice* i.e. recovered judgment
44 *security* overconfidence   46 *his sufferance* toleration of him   53 *Are
heavy orisons* i.e. beget weighty pleas   54 *proceeding on distemper* following
drunkenness   56 *chewed . . . digested* i.e. premeditated   61 *late* lately
appointed   63 *it* i.e. the commission   75 *cowarded* frightened   76 *appearance* sight   79 *quick* living   82 *turn* return   85 *English monsters* (as distinct
from exotic freaks imported for exhibition)   86 *accord* consent   87
*appertinents* appurtenances   90 *practices* plots   102 *annoy* injure

As two yoke-devils sworn to either's purpose,
107 Working so grossly in a natural cause
That admiration did not whoop at them;
109 But thou, 'gainst all proportion, didst bring in
110 Wonder to wait on treason and on murder;
And whatsoever cunning fiend it was
112 That wrought upon thee so preposterously
113 Hath got the voice in hell for excellence.
114 All other devils that suggest by treasons
115 Do botch and bungle up damnation
With patches, colors, and with forms being fetched
From glist'ring semblances of piety;
118 But he that tempered thee bade thee stand up,
Gave thee no instance why thou shouldst do treason,
120 Unless to dub thee with the name of traitor.
If that same demon that hath gulled thee thus
Should with his lion gait walk the whole world,
123 He might return to vasty Tartar back
And tell the legions, 'I can never win
A soul so easy as that Englishman's.'
126 O, how hast thou with jealousy infected
127 The sweetness of affiance! Show men dutiful?
Why, so didst thou. Seem they grave and learnèd?
Why, so didst thou. Come they of noble family?
Why, so didst thou. Seem they religious?
Why, so didst thou. Or are they spare in diet,
Free from gross passion or of mirth or anger,
133 Constant in spirit, not swerving with the blood,
134 Garnished and decked in modest complement,
135 Not working with the eye without the ear,
And but in purgèd judgment trusting neither?
137 Such and so finely bolted didst thou seem;
And thus thy fall hath left a kind of blot
139 To mark the full-fraught man and best indued
With some suspicion. I will weep for thee;
For this revolt of thine, methinks, is like
Another fall of man. Their faults are open.
Arrest them to the answer of the law;
And God acquit them of their practices!

EXETER I arrest thee of high treason by the name of
Richard Earl of Cambridge.
I arrest thee of high treason by the name of Henry
Lord Scroop of Masham.
I arrest thee of high treason by the name of Thomas
Grey, knight, of Northumberland.

SCROOP
Our purposes God justly hath discovered,

And I repent my faults more than my death,
Which I beseech your highness to forgive,
Although my body pay the price of it.

CAMBRIDGE
For me, the gold of France did not seduce,
Although I did admit it as a motive    156
The sooner to effect what I intended.
But God be thankèd for prevention,
Which I in sufferance heartily will rejoice,    159
Beseeching God, and you, to pardon me.

GREY
Never did faithful subject more rejoice
At the discovery of most dangerous treason
Than I do at this hour joy o'er myself,
Prevented from a damnèd enterprise.
My fault, but not my body, pardon, sovereign.

KING
God quit you in his mercy! Hear your sentence.    166
You have conspired against our royal person,
Joined with an enemy proclaimed, and from his coffers
Received the golden earnest of our death;    169
Wherein you would have sold your king to slaughter,
His princes and his peers to servitude,
His subjects to oppression and contempt,
And his whole kingdom into desolation,
Touching our person, seek we no revenge,
But we our kingdom's safety must so tender,    175
Whose ruin you have sought, that to her laws
We do deliver you. Get you therefore hence,
Poor miserable wretches, to your death;
The taste whereof God of his mercy give
You patience to endure and true repentance
Of all your dear offenses! Bear them hence.    181
    *Exit [Guard, with Cambridge, Scroop, and Grey].*
Now, lords, for France; the enterprise whereof
Shall be to you as us, like glorious.    183
We doubt not of a fair and lucky war,
Since God so graciously hath brought to light
This dangerous treason, lurking in our way
To hinder our beginnings. We doubt not now
But every rub is smoothèd on our way.    188
Then forth, dear countrymen. Let us deliver
Our puissance into the hand of God,
Putting it straight in expedition.    191
Cheerly to sea the signs of war advance.    192
No king of England, if not King of France!
    *Flourish. [Exeunt.]*

\*

107–08 *Working . . . them* i.e. cooperating with such obvious fitness as to provoke no cry of wonder  109 *proportion* fitness  110 *wait on* attend  112 *preposterously* abnormally  113 *voice* vote; *excellence* supreme achievement  114 *suggest* tempt  115–17 *Do botch . . . piety* i.e. trick out sin with disguises of shining virtue  118 *tempered* moulded; *stand up* volunteer  120 *dub . . . name* acquire the title  123 *Tartar* Tartarus (deepest Hades)  126 *jealousy* suspicion  127 *affiance* trust  133 *blood* passions  134 *decked . . . complement* i.e. wearing the look of modesty  135–36 *Not . . . neither* i.e. judiciously trusting neither eye nor ear alone  137 *bolted* sifted, refined  139 *full-fraught* most richly endowed  156 *did admit allowed to stand* (the actual 'motive' of Cambridge, here scarcely glanced at, was to further Mortimer's claim to the crown)  159 *sufferance* suffering  166 *quit* acquit, forgive  169 *earnest* advance payment  175 *tender* hold dear  181 *dear* rare  183 *like* alike  188 *But* but that; *rub* obstacle (bowling term)  191 *expedition* motion  192 *signs* ensigns
II, iii A London street  2 *Staines* place on the road to Southampton  3, 6 *earn* grieve  9 *Arthur* (confused with Abraham)  11 *christom* newly baptized

*Enter Pistol, Nym, Bardolph, Boy, and Hostess.*    II, iii

HOSTESS Prithee, honey-sweet husband, let me bring
thee to Staines.    2

PISTOL
No; for my manly heart doth earn.    3
Bardolph, be blithe; Nym, rouse thy vaunting veins;
Boy, bristle thy courage up; for Falstaff he is dead,
And we must earn therefore.    6

BARDOLPH Would I were with him, wheresome'er he is,
either in heaven or in hell!

HOSTESS Nay sure, he's not in hell! He's in Arthur's    9
bosom, if ever man went to Arthur's bosom. 'A made a
finer end, and went away an it had been any christom    11

child. 'A parted ev'n just between twelve and one, ev'n
at the turning o' th' tide. For after I saw him fumble with
the sheets, and play with flowers, and smile upon his
finger's end, I knew there was but one way ; for his nose
16 was as sharp as a pen, and 'a babbled of green fields.
'How now, Sir John ?' quoth I. 'What, man ? be o' good
cheer.' So 'a cried out 'God, God, God !' three or four
times. Now I, to comfort him, bid him 'a should not
think of God ; I hoped there was no need to trouble himself with any such thoughts yet. So 'a bade me lay more
clothes on his feet. I put my hand into the bed and felt
them, and they were as cold as any stone. Then I felt to
his knees, and so upward and upward, and all was as
cold as any stone.

25 NYM  They say he cried out of sack.

HOSTESS  Ay, that 'a did.

BARDOLPH  And of women.

HOSTESS  Nay, that 'a did not.

BOY  Yes, that 'a did, and said they were devils incarnate.

HOSTESS  'A could never abide carnation ; 'twas a color he
never liked.

BOY  'A said once the devil would have him about women.

HOSTESS  'A did in some sort, indeed, handle women ; but
34 then he was rheumatic, and talked of the Whore of
Babylon.

BOY  Do you not remember 'a saw a flea stick upon Bardolph's nose, and 'a said it was a black soul burning in
hell ?

38 BARDOLPH  Well, the fuel is gone that maintained that
fire. That's all the riches I got in his service.

40 NYM  Shall we shog ? The king will be gone from Southampton.

PISTOL
Come, let's away. My love, give me thy lips.
Look to my chattels and my moveables.
44 Let senses rule. The word is 'Pitch and pay.'
Trust none ;
46 For oaths are straws, men's faiths are wafer-cakes,
47 And Hold-fast is the only dog, my duck.
48 Therefore Caveto be thy counsellor.
49 Go, clear thy crystals. Yoke-fellows in arms,
Let us to France, like horse-leeches, my boys,
To suck, to suck, the very blood to suck !

BOY  And that's but unwholesome food, they say.

PISTOL
Touch her soft mouth, and march.

BARDOLPH  Farewell, hostess.
   [Kisses her.]

NYM  I cannot kiss, that is the humor of it ; but adieu !

PISTOL
56 Let housewifery appear. Keep close, I thee command.

HOSTESS  Farewell, adieu !        *Exeunt.*

\*

II, iv     *Flourish. Enter the French King, the Dauphin,*
*the Dukes of Berri and Britaine [, the Constable,*
*and others].*

KING
Thus comes the English with full power upon us,
And more than carefully it us concerns
To answer royally in our defenses.
Therefore the Dukes of Berri and Britaine,
Of Brabant and of Orleans, shall make forth,

And you, Prince Dauphin, with all swift dispatch,
To line and new repair our towns of war     7
With men of courage and with means defendant ;
For England his approaches makes as fierce
As waters to the sucking of a gulf.     10
It fits us then to be as provident
As fear may teach us out of late examples     12
Left by the fatal and neglected English     13
Upon our fields.

DAUPHIN        My most redoubted father,
It is most meet we arm us 'gainst the foe ;     15
For peace itself should not so dull a kingdom
Though war nor no known quarrel were in question
But that defenses, musters, preparations
Should be maintained, assembled, and collected,
As were a war in expectation.
Therefore I say 'tis meet we all go forth
To view the sick and feeble parts of France ;
And let us do it with no show of fear –
No, with no more than if we heard that England
Were busied with a Whitsun morris dance ;     25
For, my good liege, she is so idly kinged,     26
Her sceptre so fantastically borne,
By a vain, giddy, shallow, humorous youth,
That fear attends her not.     29

CONSTABLE        O peace, Prince Dauphin !
You are too much mistaken in this king.
Question your grace the late ambassadors,
With what great state he heard their embassy,
How well supplied with noble counsellors,
How modest in exception, and withal     34
How terrible in constant resolution,
Were but the outside of the Roman Brutus,     36
Covering discretion with a coat of folly ;     37
As gardeners do with ordure hide those roots
That shall first spring and be most delicate.

DAUPHIN
Well, 'tis not so, my Lord High Constable !
But though we think it so, it is no matter.
In cases of defense 'tis best to weigh
The enemy more mighty than he seems.
So the proportions of defense are filled ;     45
Which of a weak and niggardly projection     46
Doth, like a miser, spoil his coat with scanting
A little cloth.

16 *'a . . . fields* (authenticating this famous emendation is the likelihood that
the Hostess, whose religious education is defective – cf. *Arthur's bosom* –
has been puzzled by 'green pastures' as Falstaff repeated the 23rd Psalm)
25 *cried . . . sack* exclaimed against wine  34 *rheumatic* i.e. feverish (with
pronunciation 'rom-atic' triggering the allusion to 'Whore of Babylon',
i.e the Roman Church)  38 *fuel* i.e. liquor supplied by Falstaff  40 *shog*
move along  44 *Let . . . rule* i.e. use your eyes and ears ; *Pitch and pay*
i.e. cash down  46 *wafer-cakes* i.e. easily broken (proverbial)  47 *Hold-*
*fast . . . dog* (from proverb, 'Brag is a good dog, but Hold-fast is a better')
48 *Caveto* beware  49 *clear thy crystals* i.e. wipe your eyes  56 *Let . . .*
*appear* i.e. be a good housekeeper ; *close* i.e. indoors
II, iv Within the palace of the French King  7 *line* reinforce  10 *sucking*
i.e. whirlpool  12 *examples* i.e. of military defeats  13 *fatal and neglected*
fatally disregarded  15 *meet* fitting  25 *Whitsun* festal week beginning
the seventh Sunday after Easter ; *morris* folk dance in antic costumes
26 *idly* worthlessly  29 *attends* accompanies  34 *exception* taking issue
36 *forespent* now done with  37 *Brutus* Lucius Junius Brutus, who disguised his acumen from the tyrant Tarquin Superbus until ready to join
in revolt  45 *proportions* adequate forces  46–47 *Which . . . Doth* (gram-
matically incoherent, possibly owing to a missing line, but clear in sense)
46 *weak . . . projection* small and miserly scale

KING        Think we King Harry strong;
And, princes, look you strongly arm to meet him.
The kindred of him hath been fleshed upon us;
And he is bred out of that bloody strain
That haunted us in our familiar paths.
Witness our too much memorable shame
When Crécy battle fatally was struck,
And all our princes captived, by the hand
Of that black name, Edward, Black Prince of Wales;
Whiles that his mountain sire – on mountain standing,
Up in the air, crowned with the golden sun –
Saw his heroical seed, and smiled to see him
Mangle the work of nature, and deface
The patterns that by God and by French fathers
Had twenty years been made. This is a stem
Of that victorious stock; and let us fear
The native mightiness and fate of him.
    *Enter a Messenger.*

MESSENGER
Ambassadors from Harry King of England
Do crave admittance to your majesty.

KING
We'll give them present audience. Go, and bring them.
    *[Exeunt Messenger and certain Lords.]*
You see this chase is hotly followed, friends.

DAUPHIN
Turn head, and stop pursuit; for coward dogs
Most spend their mouths when what they seem to
    threaten
Runs far before them. Good my sovereign,
Take up the English short and let them know
Of what a monarchy you are the head.
Self-love, my liege, is not so vile a sin
As self-neglecting.
    *Enter [Lords, with] Exeter [and Train].*

KING        From our brother of England?

EXETER
From him, and thus he greets your majesty:
He wills you, in the name of God Almighty,
That you divest yourself, and lay apart
The borrowed glories that by gift of heaven,
By law of nature and of nations, 'longs
To him and to his heirs – namely, the crown
And all wide-stretchèd honors that pertain
By custom, and the ordinance of times,
Unto the crown of France. That you may know
'Tis no sinister nor no awkward claim,
Picked from the wormholes of long-vanished days,
Nor from the dust of old oblivion raked,
He sends you this most memorable line,
    *[Gives a paper.]*
In every branch truly demonstrative;

Willing you overlook this pedigree;
And when you find him evenly derived  91
From his most famed of famous ancestors,
Edward the Third, he bids you then resign
Your crown and kingdom, indirectly held  94
From him, the native and true challenger.  95

KING
Or else what follows?

EXETER
Bloody constraint; for if you hide the crown  97
Even in your hearts, there will he rake for it.
Therefore in fierce tempest is he coming,
In thunder and in earthquake, like a Jove;
That if requiring fail, he will compel;  101
And bids you, in the bowels of the Lord,  102
Deliver up the crown, and to take mercy
On the poor souls for whom this hungry war
Opens his vasty jaws; and on your head
Turning the widows' tears, the orphans' cries,  106
The dead men's blood, the privèd maidens' groans,  107
For husbands, fathers, and betrothèd lovers
That shall be swallowed in this controversy.
This is his claim, his threat'ning, and my message;
Unless the Dauphin be in presence here,
To whom expressly I bring greeting too.

KING
For us, we will consider of this further.
To-morrow shall you bear our full intent
Back to our brother of England.

DAUPHIN        For the Dauphin,
I stand here for him. What to him from England?

EXETER
Scorn and defiance, slight regard, contempt,
And anything that may not misbecome
The mighty sender, doth he prize you at.
Thus says my king: and if your father's highness
Do not, in grant of all demands at large,
Sweeten the bitter mock you sent his majesty,
He'll call you to so hot an answer of it
That caves and womby vaultages of France  124
Shall chide your trespass, and return your mock
In second accent of his ordinance.  126

DAUPHIN
Say, if my father render fair return,
It is against my will; for I desire
Nothing but odds with England. To that end,
As matching to his youth and vanity,
I did present him with the Paris balls.  131

EXETER
He'll make your Paris Louvre shake for it,  132
Were it the mistress court of mighty Europe;
And be assured you'll find a difference,
As we his subjects have in wonder found,
Between the promise of his greener days
And these he masters now. Now he weighs time  137
Even to the utmost grain. That you shall read
In your own losses, if he stay in France.

KING
To-morrow shall you know our mind at full.
    *Flourish.*

EXETER
Dispatch us with all speed, lest that our king
Come here himself to question our delay;
For he is footed in this land already.

---

50 *fleshed* initiated in blood shedding  54 *struck* waged  57 *mountain* i.e. towering (?)  64 *fate* fortune, luck  69 *Turn head* stand at bay; *stop* i.e. put an end to  80 *By law . . . nations* i.e. morally and legally; *'longs* belongs  82 *all wide-stretched* i.e. the whole range of  83 *ordinance of times* decree of tradition  85 *sinister* illegitimate; *awkward* shambling  88 *line* line of descent  91 *evenly* directly  94 *indirectly* wrongfully  95 *challenger* claimant  97 *constraint* force  101 *requiring* demanding  102 *in the bowels* i.e. in the very being (Biblical metaphor)  106 *Turning* retorting, flinging back  107 *privèd* deprived (i.e. of their *betrothèd lovers*)  124 *womby vaultages* hollow caverns  126 *second accent* i.e. echo; *ordinance* cannon  131 *Paris balls* tennis balls  132 *Louvre* (pronounced 'lover' with play on *mistress* in next line)  137 *masters* governs

KING
You shall be soon dispatched with fair conditions.
A night is but small breath and little pause
To answer matters of this consequence.          *Exeunt.*

\*

III, Cho.          *Enter Chorus.*
1      Thus with imagined wing our swift scene flies,
       In motion of no less celerity
       Than that of thought. Suppose that you have seen
       The well-appointed king at Hampton pier
       Embark his royalty; and his brave fleet
6      With silken streamers the young Phoebus fanning.
       Play with your fancies, and in them behold
       Upon the hempen tackle shipboys climbing;
       Hear the shrill whistle which doth order give
10     To sounds confused; behold the threaden sails,
       Borne with th' invisible and creeping wind,
12     Draw the huge bottoms through the furrowed sea,
       Breasting the lofty surge. O, do but think
14     You stand upon the rivage and behold
       A city on th' inconstant billows dancing;
       For so appears this fleet majestical,
       Holding due course to Harfleur. Follow, follow!
18     Grapple your minds to sternage of this navy,
       And leave your England as dead midnight still,
       Guarded with grandsires, babies, and old women,
21     Either past or not arrived to pith and puissance;
       For who is he whose chin is but enriched
       With one appearing hair that will not follow
       These culled and choice-drawn cavaliers to France?
       Work, work your thoughts, and therein see a siege:
       Behold the ordinance on their carriages,
27     With fatal mouths gaping on girded Harfleur.
       Suppose th' ambassador from the French comes back;
       Tells Harry that the king doth offer him
       Katherine his daughter, and with her to dowry
       Some petty and unprofitable dukedoms.
32     The offer likes not; and the nimble gunner
33     With linstock now the devilish cannon touches,
             *Alarum, and chambers go off.*
       And down goes all before them. Still be kind,
       And eke out our performance with your mind.          *Exit.*

III, i          *Enter the King, Exeter, Bedford, and Gloucester.*
                *Alarum: [with Soldiers carrying] scaling ladders at*
                *Harfleur.*
          KING
       Once more unto the breach, dear friends, once more,
       Or close the wall up with our English dead!
       In peace there's nothing so becomes a man
       As modest stillness and humility,
       But when the blast of war blows in our ears,
       Then imitate the action of the tiger:
       Stiffen the sinews, summon up the blood,
       Disguise fair nature with hard-favored rage;
       Then lend the eye a terrible aspect:
10     Let it pry through the portage of the head
       Like the brass cannon; let the brow o'erwhelm it
12     As fearfully as doth a gallèd rock
13     O'erhang and jutty his confounded base,

Swilled with the wild and wasteful ocean.
Now set the teeth and stretch the nostril wide,
Hold hard the breath and bend up every spirit
To his full height! On, on, you noble English,
Whose blood is fet from fathers of war-proof,
Fathers that like so many Alexanders
Have in these parts from morn till even fought
And sheathed their swords for lack of argument.
Dishonor not your mothers; now attest
That those whom you called fathers did beget you!
Be copy now to men of grosser blood
And teach them how to war! And you, good yeomen,
Whose limbs were made in England, show us here
The mettle of your pasture. Let us swear
That you are worth your breeding; which I doubt not,
For there is none of you so mean and base
That hath not noble lustre in your eyes.
I see you stand like greyhounds in the slips,
Straining upon the start. The game's afoot!
Follow your spirit; and upon this charge
Cry 'God for Harry! England and Saint George!'
          *[Exeunt.] Alarum, and chambers go off.*
     *Enter Nym, Bardolph, Pistol, and Boy.*
BARDOLPH On, on, on, on, on! to the breach, to the
breach!
NYM Pray thee, corporal, stay. The knocks are too hot;
and, for mine own part, I have not a case of lives. The
humor of it is too hot; that is the very plain-song of it.
PISTOL
The plain-song is most just; for humors do abound.
Knocks go and come; God's vassals drop and die;
          And sword and shield
          In bloody field
          Doth win immortal fame.
BOY Would I were in an alehouse in London! I would
give all my fame for a pot of ale and safety.
PISTOL And I:
          If wishes would prevail with me,
          My purpose should not fail with me,
          But thither would I hie.
BOY          As duly, but not as truly,
          As bird doth sing on bough.
     *Enter Fluellen.*
FLUELLEN Up to the preach, you dogs! Avaunt, you cul-
lions!
     *[Drives them in.]*
PISTOL
Be merciful, great duke, to men of mould!
Abate thy rage, abate thy manly rage,
Abate thy rage, great duke!
Good bawcock, bate thy rage! Use lenity, sweet chuck!

III, Cho.  1 *imagined wing* wing of imagination  6 *the . . . fanning* i.e.
waving in the dawn  10 *threaden* woven of thread  12 *bottoms* hulls
14 *rivage* shore  18 *Grapple* fasten; *sternage* the wake  21 *pith* muscle,
strength  27 *girded* surrounded, besieged  32 *likes* pleases  33 *linstock*
lighting-stick
III, i  Before the walls of Harfleur  10 *portage* portholes  12 *gallèd* eroded
(at base)  13 *jutty his confounded* jut over its ruined  14 *Swilled* consumed  18 *fet* fetched, derived  21 *argument* opposition  24 *copy* examples  27 *mettle . . . pasture* quality of your rearing  31 *slips* leashes
34 *Saint George* (England's patron saint)
III, ii  2 *corporal* (at II, i, 2 Bardolph was a lieutenant)  3 *case* set  4
*plain-song* unelaborated melody, i.e. unadorned truth  18 *Avaunt* be
gone; *cullions* base fellows  19 *men of mould* mere mortals  22 *bawcock*
fine fellow (from 'beau coq')

NYM These be good humors. Your honor wins bad humors.                                    *Exit [with all but Boy].*

BOY As young as I am, I have observed these three swashers. I am boy to them all three; but all they three, though they would serve me, could not be man to me; for indeed three such antics do not amount to a man. For Bardolph, he is white-livered and red-faced; by the means whereof 'a faces it out, but fights not. For Pistol, he hath a killing tongue and a quiet sword; by the means whereof 'a breaks words and keeps whole weapons. For Nym, he hath heard that men of few words are the best men, and therefore he scorns to say his prayers, lest 'a should be thought a coward; but his few bad words are matched with as few good deeds, for 'a never broke any man's head but his own, and that was against a post when he was drunk. They will steal anything, and call it purchase. Bardolph stole a lute-case, bore it twelve leagues, and sold it for three halfpence. Nym and Bardolph are sworn brothers in filching, and in Calais they stole a fire-shovel. I knew by that piece of service the men would carry coals. They would have me as familiar with men's pockets as their gloves or their handkerchers; which makes much against my manhood, if I should take from another's pocket to put into mine; for it is plain pocketing up of wrongs. I must leave them and seek some better service. Their villainy goes against my weak stomach, and therefore I must cast it up.                              *Exit.*

*Enter Gower [and Fluellen].*

GOWER Captain Fluellen, you must come presently to the mines. The Duke of Gloucester would speak with you.

FLUELLEN To the mines? Tell you the duke, it is not so good to come to the mines; for look you, the mines is not according to the disciplines of the war. The concavities of it is not sufficient; for look you, th' athversary, you may discuss unto the duke, look you, is digt himself four yard under the countermines. By Cheshu, I think 'a will plow up all, if there is not petter directions.

GOWER The Duke of Gloucester, to whom the order of the siege is given, is altogether directed by an Irishman, a very valiant gentleman, i' faith.

FLUELLEN It is Captain Macmorris, is it not?

GOWER I think it be.

FLUELLEN By Cheshu, he is an ass as in the orld! I will verify as much in his peard. He has no more directions in the true disciplines of the wars, look you, of the Roman disciplines, than is a puppy-dog.

*Enter Macmorris and Captain Jamy.*

GOWER Here 'a comes, and the Scots captain, Captain Jamy, with him.

FLUELLEN Captain Jamy is a marvellous falorous gentleman, that is certain, and of great expedition and knowledge in th' aunchient wars, upon my particular knowledge of his directions. By Cheshu, he will maintain his argument as well as any military man in the orld in the disciplines of the pristine wars of the Romans.

JAMY I say gud day, Captain Fluellen.

FLUELLEN God-den to your worship, good Captain James.

GOWER How now, Captain Macmorris? Have you quit the mines? Have the pioners given o'er?                79

MACMORRIS By Chrish, law, tish ill done! The work ish give over, the trompet sound the retreat. By my hand I swear, and my father's soul, the work ish ill done! It ish give over. I would have blowed up the town, so Chrish save me, law, in an hour. O, tish ill done! tish ill done! By my hand, tish ill done!

FLUELLEN Captain Macmorris, I beseech you now, will you voutsafe me, look you, a few disputations with you, as partly touching or concerning the disciplines of the war, the Roman wars? In the way of argument, look you, and friendly communication; partly to satisfy my   90 opinion, and partly for the satisfaction, look you, of my mind, as touching the direction of the military discipline, that is the point.

JAMY It sall be vary gud, gud feith, gud captens bath, and I sall quit you with gud leve, as I may pick occasion.  95 That sall I, mary.

MACMORRIS It is no time to discourse, so Chrish save me! The day is hot, and the weather, and the wars, and the king, and the dukes. It is no time to discourse. The town is beseeched, and the trompet call us to the breach, and we talk, and, be Chrish, do nothing. 'Tis shame for us all. So God sa' me, 'tis shame to stand still, it is shame, by my hand! and there is throats to be cut, and works to be done, and there ish nothing done, so Chrish sa' me, law!

JAMY By the mess, ere theise eyes of mine take themselves 105 to slomber, ay'll de gud service, or ay'll lig i' th' grund for it! ay, or go to death! And ay'll pay't as valorously as I may, that sall I suerly do, that is the breff and the long. Mary, I wad full fain heard some question 'tween you 109 tway.

FLUELLEN Captain Macmorris, I think, look you, under your correction, there is not many of your nation –

MACMORRIS Of my nation? What ish my nation? Ish a 113 villain and a bastard, and a knave, and a rascal! What ish my nation? Who talks of my nation?

FLUELLEN Look you, if you take the matter otherwise than is meant, Captain Macmorris, peradventure I shall think you do not use me with that affability as in discretion you ought to use me, look you, being as good a man as yourself, poth in the disciplines of war, and in the derivation of my pirth, and in other particularities.

MACMORRIS I do not know you so good a man as myself. So Chrish save me, I will cut off your head!

GOWER Gentlemen both, you will mistake each other.   124

JAMY A', that's a foul fault!                          125

*A parley [sounded].*

GOWER The town sounds a parley.

FLUELLEN Captain Macmorris, when there is more petter opportunity to be required, look you, I will be so pold as to tell you I know the disciplines of war; and there is an end.                         *Exit [with others].*

23–24 *These . . . humors* (a cryptic utterance, even for Nym)  25 *swashers* swashbucklers  28 *antics* fantastics, zanies  32 *breaks* i.e. fails to keep his  42 *carry coals* i.e. put up with abuse  44 *makes* i.e. offends  53 *mines* undermining operations  54 *disciplines* i.e. correct procedure; *concavities* i.e. slope, downward pitch  56 *discuss* explain  57 *Cheshu* Jesu  58 *plow* blow  65 *in his peard* in his beard, i.e. to his face; *directions* instruction  71 *expedition* readiness  79 *pioners* sappers  90 *communication* consultation  95 *quit* answer  105 *mess* i.e. Mass  109 *question* discussion  113 *What ish* i.e. what about; *Ish* i.e. someone, not exclusively Fluellen, is (Macmorris' sensitivity about his nationality makes him discharge at a general target the insulting epithets which follow)  124 *will mistake* persist in misjudging  125 *A'* (equivalent to 'Ach')

III, iii  *Enter the King [Henry] and all his Train before the gates.*

KING

How yet resolves the governor of the town?
2  This is the latest parle we will admit:
Therefore to our best mercy give yourselves,
4  Or, like to men proud of destruction,
Defy us to our worst; for, as I am a soldier,
A name that in my thoughts becomes me best,
If I begin the batt'ry once again,
I will not leave the half-achievèd Harfleur
Till in her ashes she lie burièd.
The gates of mercy shall be all shut up,
11  And the fleshed soldier, rough and hard of heart,
In liberty of bloody hand shall range
13  With conscience wide as hell, mowing like grass
Your fresh fair virgins and your flow'ring infants.
What is it then to me if impious war,
Arrayed in flames to the prince of fiends,
17  Do with his smirched complexion all fell feats
Enlinked to waste and desolation?
What is't to me, when you yourselves are cause,
If your pure maidens fall into the hand
Of hot and forcing violation?
What rein can hold licentious wickedness
23  When down the hill he holds his fierce career?
24  We may as bootless spend our vain command
Upon th' enragèd soldiers in their spoil
26  As send precepts to the leviathan
To come ashore. Therefore, you men of Harfleur,
Take pity of your town and of your people
Whiles yet my soldiers are in my command,
30  Whiles yet the cool and temperate wind of grace
31  O'erblows the filthy and contagious clouds
32  Of heady murder, spoil, and villainy.
If not – why, in a moment look to see
The blind and bloody soldier with foul hand
Defile the locks of your shrill-shrieking daughters;
Your fathers taken by the silver beards,
And their most reverend heads dashed to the walls;
Your naked infants spitted upon pikes,
Whiles the mad mothers with their howls confused
Do break the clouds, as did the wives of Jewry
41  At Herod's bloody-hunting slaughtermen.
What say you? Will you yield, and this avoid?
43  Or, guilty in defense, be thus destroyed?
*Enter Governor [on the wall].*

GOVERNOR

Our expectation hath this day an end.
The Dauphin, whom of succors we entreated,
46  Returns us that his powers are not yet ready
To raise so great a siege. Therefore, great king,
We yield our town and lives to thy soft mercy.
Enter our gates, dispose of us and ours,
For we no longer are defensible.

KING

Open your gates. Come, uncle Exeter,
Go you and enter Harfleur; there remain
And fortify it strongly 'gainst the French.
Use mercy to them all. For us, dear uncle,
The winter coming on, and sickness growing
Upon our soldiers, we will retire to Calais.
To-night in Harfleur will we be your guest;
58  To-morrow for the march are we addrest.
*Flourish, and enter the town.*

*Enter Katherine and [Alice,] an old Gentlewoman.*

KATHERINE  Alice, tu as esté en Angleterre, et tu bien parles le langage.
ALICE  Un peu, madame.
KATHERINE  Je te prie m'enseigner; il faut que j'apprends à parler. Comment appelez-vous le main en Anglois?
ALICE  Le main? Il est appelé de hand.
KATHERINE  De hand. Et les doigts?
ALICE  Les doigts? Ma foi, j'oublie les doigts; mais je me souviendrai. Les doigts? Je pense qu'ils'ont appelé de fingres; oui, de fingres.
KATHERINE  Le main, de hand; les doigts, de fingres. Je pense que je suis le bon escolier; j'ai gagné deux mots d'Anglois vistement. Comment appelez-vous les ongles?
ALICE  Les ongles, les appelons de nailès.
KATHERINE  De nailès. Escoute; dites-moi si je parle bien: de hand, de fingres, et de nailès.
ALICE  C'est bien dict, madame; il est fort bon Anglois.
KATHERINE  Dites-moi l'Anglois pour le bras.
ALICE  De arm, madame.
KATHERINE  Et le coude.
ALICE  D'elbow.
KATHERINE  D'elbow. Je me'en fais le répétition de tous les mots que vous m'avez apprins dès à présent.
ALICE  Il est trop difficile, madame, comme je pense.
KATHERINE  Excuse moi, Alice; escoute: d' hand, de fingre, de nailès, d' arma, de bilbow.
ALICE  D'elbow, madame.
KATHERINE  O Seigneur Dieu, je m'en oublie d' elbow! Comment appelez-vous le col?
ALICE  De nick, madame.
KATHERINE  De nick. Et le menton?
ALICE  De chin.
KATHERINE  De sin. Le col, de nick; le menton, de sin.
ALICE  Oui. Sauf vostre honneur, en vérité, vous prononcez les mots aussi droict que les natifs d'Angleterre.
KATHERINE  Je ne doute point d'apprendre, par la grace de Dieu, et en peu de temps.
ALICE  N'avez-vous pas déjà oublié ce que je vous ai enseigné?

---

III, iii Before the walls of Harfleur at the gates  2 *parle* parley  4 *proud of* who glory in  11 *fleshed* hardened with killing  13 *wide* permissive  17 *smirched* sooty  23 *holds . . . career* maintains his fierce gallop  24 *bootless* uselessly  26 *precepts* written summons  30 *grace* mercy  31 *O'erblows* outblows  32 *heady* headstrong  41 *Herod's . . . slaughtermen* (cf. Matthew ii, 16–18)  43 *in defense* i.e. of reckless defense  46 *Returns us* replies  58 *addrest* prepared

III, iv Within the palace of the French King  1–58 KATH. Alice, you have been in England, and you speak the language well. AL. A little, my lady. KATH. I beg you teach me; I must learn to speak it. What do you call *le main* in English? AL. *Le main?* It is called *de hand.* KATH. *De hand.* And *les doigts?* AL. *Les doigts?* My faith, I forget *les doigts;* but I will remember. *Les doigts?* I think they are called *de fingres;* yes, *de fingres.* KATH. *Le main, de hand; les doigts, de fingres.* I think I am a good scholar; I have learned two words of English quickly. What do you call *les ongles?* AL. *Les ongles* we call *de nailès.* KATH. *De nailès.* Listen; tell me if I speak well: *de hand, de fingres,* and *de nailès.* AL. Well spoken, my lady; it is very good English. KATH. Tell me the English for *le bras.* AL. *De arm,* my lady. KATH. And *le coude.* AL. *D'elbow.* KATH. *D'elbow.* I am going to repeat all the words you have taught me so far. AL. It is too hard, my lady, so I think. KATH. Excuse me, Alice; listen: *d'hand, de fingre, de nailès, d'arma, de bilbow.* AL. *D'elbow,* my lady. KATH. O Lord God, I can't remember *d'elbow.* What do you call *le col?* AL. *De nick,* my lady. KATH. *De nick.* And *le menton?* AL. *De chin.* KATH. *De sin. Le col, de nick; le menton, de sin.* AL. Yes. Save your honor, indeed you pronounce the words as well as the native English. KATH. I trust to learn, by the grace of God, and in short time. AL. You have not already forgotten what I have taught you?

40 KATHERINE Non, je réciterai à vous promptement: d'
    hand, de fingre, de mailès –

ALICE De nailès, madame.

KATHERINE De nailès, de arm, de ilbow –

ALICE Sauf vostre honneur, d'elbow.

KATHERINE Ainsi dis-je; d'elbow, de nick, et de sin.
    Comment appelez-vous le pied et la robe?

ALICE De foot, madame; et de count.

KATHERINE De foot et de count! O Seigneur Dieu! ils'ont
    les mots de son mauvais, corruptible, gros, et impudi-

50 que, et non pour les dames d'honneur d'user: je ne
    voudrais prononcer ces mots devant les seigneurs de
    France pour tout le monde. Foh! de foot et de count!
    Néantmoins, je réciterai une autre fois ma leçon en-
    semble: d'hand, de fingre, de nailès, d'arm, d'elbow,
    de nick, de sin, de foot, de count.

ALICE Excellent, madame!

KATHERINE C'est assez pour une fois: allons-nous à
    diner.                           *Exit [with Alice]*.

*

v      *Enter the King of France, the Dauphin [, Britaine],*
         *the Constable of France, and others.*

KING

1  'Tis certain he hath passed the river Somme.

CONSTABLE

    And if he be not fought withal, my lord.
    Let us not live in France; let us quit all
    And give our vineyards to a barbarous people.

DAUPHIN

5  O Dieu vivant! Shall a few sprays of us,
6  The emptying of our fathers' luxury,
7  Our scions, put in wild and savage stock,
    Spurt up so suddenly into the clouds
    And overlook their grafters?

BRITAINE

    Normans, but bastard Normans, Norman bastards!
11  Mort de ma vie! if they march along
    Unfought withal, but I will sell my dukedom
13  To buy a slobb'ry and a dirty farm
14  In that nook-shotten isle of Albion.

CONSTABLE

15  Dieu de batailles! where have they this mettle?
    Is not their climate foggy, raw, and dull,
    On whom, as in despite, the sun looks pale,

KATH. No, I shall recite for you promptly: *d'hand, de fingre, de mailès* – AL.
*De nailès,* my lady. KATH. *De nailès, de arm, de ilbow* – AL. Save your honor,
*d'elbow.* KATH. So I said – *d'elbow, de nick, and de sin.* What do you call *le
pied* and *la robe?* AL. *De foot,* my lady; and *de count* [i.e. gown]. KATH.
*De foot* [which she mistakes for indecent '*foutre*'] and *de count* ! O Lord
God! they are bad words, wicked, coarse, and immodest, and not for ladies
of honor to use: I would not speak those words before the gentlemen of
France for all the world. Foh! *de foot* and *de count* ! Nevertheless, I will
recite once more my entire lesson: *d'hand, de fingre, de nailès, d'arm,
d'elbow, de nick, de sin, de foot, de count.* AL. Excellent, my lady! KATH.
That's enough for one time; let's go to dinner.
III, v The French King's quarters at Rouen   1 *passed . . . Somme* (in the
withdrawal to Calais)   5 *sprays* offshoots   6 *fathers' luxury* i.e. forefathers' lust   7 *scions* grafts   11 *Mort . . . vie* death of my life   13 *slobb'ry*
slovenly   14 *nook-shotten* full of nooks, i.e. with a ragged coastline   15
*batailles* battles   18 *sodden* boiled   19 *drench . . . jades* draught for exhausted horses; *barley broth* ale (sometimes used as a drench)   20 *Decoct*
infuse   23 *roping* spun out by dripping   26 '*Poor*' *. . . lords* i.e. but not
rich in their possessors   33 *And* i.e. to; *lavoltas* dance characterized by
leaps; *corantos* dance characterized by running steps   34 *in our heels* (1)
as dancers, (2) as those who 'take to their heels'   47 *quit* acquit   59 *sink*
pit   60 *for achievement* i.e. instead of conquering
III, vi The English camp in Picardy

    Killing their fruit with frowns? Can sodden water,     18
    A drench for sur-reined jades, their barley broth,     19
    Decoct their cold blood to such valiant heat?     20
    And shall our quick blood, spirited with wine,
    Seem frosty? O, for honor of our land,
    Let us not hang like roping icicles     23
    Upon our houses' thatch, whiles a more frosty people
    Sweat drops of gallant youth in our rich fields –
    'Poor' we call them in their native lords!     26

DAUPHIN

    By faith and honor,
    Our madams mock at us and plainly say
    Our mettle is bred out, and they will give
    Their bodies to the lust of English youth
    To new-store France with bastard warriors.

BRITAINE

    They bid us to the English dancing schools
    And teach lavoltas high, and swift corantos,     33
    Saying our grace is only in our heels     34
    And that we are most lofty runaways.

KING

    Where is Montjoy the herald? Speed him hence;
    Let him greet England with our sharp defiance.
    Up, princes! and with spirit of honor edged
    More sharper than your swords, hie to the field.
    Charles Delabreth, High Constable of France,
    You Dukes of Orleans, Bourbon, and of Berri,
    Alençon, Brabant, Bar, and Burgundy;
    Jacques Chatillon, Rambures, Vaudemont,
    Beaumont, Grandpré, Roussi, and Faulconbridge,
    Foix, Lestrale, Bouciqualt, and Charolois,
    High dukes, great princes, barons, lords, and knights,
    For your great seats now quit you of great shames.     47
    Bar Harry England, that sweeps through our land
    With pennons painted in the blood of Harfleur.
    Rush on his host as doth the melted snow
    Upon the valleys whose low vassal seat
    The Alps doth spit and void his rheum upon.
    Go down upon him – you have power enough –
    And in a captive chariot into Rouen
    Bring him our prisoner.

CONSTABLE              This becomes the great.
    Sorry am I his numbers are so few,
    His soldiers sick and famished in their march;
    For I am sure, when he shall see our army,
    He'll drop his heart into the sink of fear     59
    And, for achievement, offer us his ransom.     60

KING

    Therefore, Lord Constable, haste on Montjoy,
    And let him say to England that we send
    To know what willing ransom he will give.
    Prince Dauphin, you shall stay with us in Rouen.

DAUPHIN

    Not so, I do beseech your majesty.

KING

    Be patient, for you shall remain with us.
    Now forth, Lord Constable and princes all,
    And quickly bring us word of England's fall.     *Exeunt*.

*

    *Enter Captains, English and Welsh – Gower and*     III, vi
    *Fluellen.*

GOWER How now, Captain Fluellen? Come you from the
    bridge?

FLUELLEN I assure you there is very excellent services committed at the pridge.

GOWER Is the Duke of Exeter safe?

FLUELLEN The Duke of Exeter is as magnanimous as Agamemnon, and a man that I love and honor with my
8 soul, and my heart, and my duty, and my live, and my living, and my uttermost power. He is not – God be praised and plessed! – any hurt in the orld, but keeps the pridge most valiantly, with excellent discipline.
12 There is an aunchient lieutenant there at the pridge, I think in my very conscience he is as valiant a man as
14 Mark Anthony, and he is a man of no estimation in the
15 orld, but I did see him do as gallant service.

GOWER What do you call him?

FLUELLEN He is called Aunchient Pistol.

GOWER I know him not.

*Enter Pistol.*

FLUELLEN Here is the man.

PISTOL
Captain, I thee beseech to do me favors.
The Duke of Exeter doth love thee well.

FLUELLEN Ay, I praise God; and I have merited some love at his hands.

PISTOL
Bardolph, a soldier firm and sound of heart,
And of buxom valor, hath by cruel fate,
And giddy Fortune's furious fickle wheel –
That goddess blind,
That stands upon the rolling restless stone –

FLUELLEN By your patience, Aunchient Pistol. Fortune
30 is painted plind, with a muffler afore her eyes, to signify to you that Fortune is plind; and she is painted also with a wheel, to signify to you, which is the moral of it, that she is turning and inconstant, and mutability, and variation; and her foot, look you, is fixed upon a spherical stone, which rolls, and rolls, and rolls. In good truth, the poet makes a most excellent description of it.
37 Fortune is an excellent moral.

PISTOL
38 Fortune is Bardolph's foe, and frowns on him;
39 For he hath stol'n a pax, and hangèd must 'a be –
A damnèd death!
Let gallows gape for dog; let man go free,
And let not hemp his windpipe suffocate.
43 But Exeter hath given the doom of death
For pax of little price.
Therefore, go speak – the duke will hear thy voice;
And let not Bardolph's vital thread be cut
With edge of penny cord and vile reproach.
Speak, captain, for his life, and I will thee requite.

FLUELLEN Aunchient Pistol, I do partly understand your meaning.

PISTOL
Why then, rejoice therefore!

FLUELLEN Certainly, Aunchient, it is not a thing to rejoice at; for if, look you, he were my prother, I would desire the duke to use his good pleasure and put him to execution; for discipline ought to be used.

PISTOL
56 Die and be damned! and figo for thy friendship!

FLUELLEN It is well.

PISTOL
The fig of Spain!                                        *Exit.*

FLUELLEN Very good.

GOWER Why, this is an arrant counterfeit rascal! I remember him now – a bawd, a cutpurse.

FLUELLEN I'll assure you, 'a uttered as prave words at the pridge as you shall see in a summer's day. But it is very well. What he has spoke to me, that is well, I warrant you, when time is serve.

GOWER Why, 'tis a gull, a fool, a rogue, that now and then goes to the wars to grace himself, at his return into London, under the form of a soldier. And such fellows are
69 perfit in the great commanders' names, and they will learn you by rote where services were done: at such
71 and such a sconce, at such a breach, at such a convoy; who came off bravely, who was shot, who disgraced, what terms the enemy stood on; and this they con perfitly in the phrase of war, which they trick up with new-tuned
75 oaths; and what a beard of the general's cut and a horrid suit of the camp will do among foaming bottles and ale-washed wits is wonderful to be thought on. But you
78 must learn to know such slanders of the age, or else you may be marvellously mistook.

FLUELLEN I tell you what, Captain Gower, I do perceive he is not the man that he would gladly make show to the
82 orld he is. If I find a hole in his coat, I will tell him my mind. *[Drum within.]* Hark you, the king is coming, and I must speak with him from the pridge.

*Drum and Colors. Enter the King and his poor
Soldiers [and Gloucester].*

God pless your majesty!

KING
How now, Fluellen? Cam'st thou from the bridge?

FLUELLEN Ay, so please your majesty. The Duke of Exeter has very gallantly maintained the pridge; the French is gone off, look you, and there is gallant and
90 most prave passages. Marry, th' athversary was have possession of the pridge, but he is enforced to retire, and the Duke of Exeter is master of the pridge. I can tell your majesty, the duke is a prave man.

KING What men have you lost, Fluellen?

FLUELLEN The perdition of th' athversary hath been very
95 great, reasonable great. Marry, for my part, I think the duke hath lost never a man but one that is like to be executed for robbing a church – one Pardolph, if your majesty know the man. His face is all bubukles and whelks,
99 and knobs, and flames o' fire, and his lips plows at his nose, and it is like a coal of fire, sometimes plue and sometimes red; but his nose is executed, and his fire's out.

KING We would have all such offenders so cut off. And we give express charge that in our marches through the country there be nothing compelled from the villages, nothing taken but paid for; none of the French upbraided or abused in disdainful language; for when

---

8 *live* i.e. life   12 *aunchient lieutenant* (Pistol is elsewhere ranked simply as 'ancient,' i.e. ensign)   14 *estimation* fame   15 *gallant service* i.e. with words (cf. ll. 62–63)   37 *moral* i.e. emblem of instruction (the goddess Fortune figured prominently in literary and pictorial admonitions about the mutability of life)   38 *foe . . . frowns* (reminiscent of popular ballad, 'Fortune, my foe, why dost thou frown on me?')   39 *pax* metal disk engraved with crucifix, kissed during celebration of Mass   43 *doom* sentence   56 *figo* i.e. Spanish for fig (epithet and gesture of contempt)   69 *perfit* word-perfect   71 *sconce* earthwork; *convoy* transport of troops   75–76 *horrid suit* fierce attire   78 *slanders* disgraces   82 *a hole . . . coat* i.e. a means of exposing him   90 *passages* (of arms)   95 *perdition* loss, casualties   99 *bubukles and whelks* carbuncles and pimples

lenity and cruelty play for a kingdom, the gentler
gamester is the soonest winner.
  *Tucket. Enter Montjoy.*
MONTJOY You know me by my habit.
KING Well then, I know thee. What shall I know of thee?
MONTJOY My master's mind.
KING Unfold it.
MONTJOY Thus says my king: Say thou to Harry of England: Though we seemed dead, we did but sleep. Advantage is a better soldier than rashness. Tell him we
could have rebuked him at Harfleur, but that we thought
not good to bruise an injury till it were full ripe. Now we
speak upon our cue, and our voice is imperial. England
shall repent his folly, see his weakness, and admire our
sufferance. Bid him therefore consider of his ransom,
which must proportion the losses we have borne, the subjects we have lost, the disgrace we have digested; which
in weight to re-answer, his pettiness would bow under.
For our losses, his exchequer is too poor; for th' effusion
of our blood, the muster of his kingdom too faint a number; and for our disgrace, his own person kneeling at
our feet but a weak and worthless satisfaction. To this
add defiance; and tell him for conclusion he hath be-
trayed his followers, whose condemnation is pronoun-
ced. So far my king and master; so much my office.
KING
 What is thy name? I know thy quality.
MONTJOY Montjoy.
KING
 Thou dost thy office fairly. Turn thee back,
 And tell thy king I do not seek him now,
 But could be willing to march on to Calais
 Without impeachment: for, to say the sooth,
 Though 'tis no wisdom to confess so much
 Unto an enemy of craft and vantage,
 My people are with sickness much enfeebled,
 My numbers lessened, and those few I have
 Almost no better than so many French,
 Who when they were in health, I tell thee, herald,
 I thought upon one pair of English legs
 Did march three Frenchmen. Yet forgive me, God,
 That I do brag thus! This your air of France
 Hath blown that vice in me. I must repent.
 Go therefore tell thy master here I am;
 My ransom is this frail and worthless trunk;
 My army but a weak and sickly guard;
 Yet, God before, tell him we will come on,
 Though France himself and such another neighbor
 Stand in our way. There's for thy labor, Montjoy.
  *[Gives a purse.]*
 Go bid thy master well advise himself:

If we may pass, we will; if we be hind'red,
We shall your tawny ground with your red blood
Discolor; and so, Montjoy, fare you well.
The sum of all our answer is but this:
We would not seek a battle as we are,
Nor, as we are, we say we will not shun it.
So tell your master.
MONTJOY
 I shall deliver so. Thanks to your highness.  *[Exit.]*
GLOUCESTER
 I hope they will not come upon us now.
KING
 We are in God's hand, brother, not in theirs.
 March to the bridge. It now draws toward night.
 Beyond the river we'll encamp ourselves,
 And on to-morrow bid them march away.  *Exeunt.*

*

*Enter the Constable of France, the Lord Rambures,* III, vii
*Orleans, Dauphin, with others.*
CONSTABLE Tut! I have the best armor of the world.
Would it were day!
ORLEANS You have an excellent armor; but let my horse
have his due.
CONSTABLE It is the best horse of Europe.
ORLEANS Will it never be morning?
DAUPHIN My Lord of Orleans, and my Lord High Con-
stable, you talk of horse and armor?
ORLEANS You are well provided of both as any prince in
the world.
DAUPHIN What a long night is this! I will not change my
horse with any that treads but on four pasterns. Ça, ha!
he bounds from the earth, as if his entrails were hairs;
le cheval volant, the Pegasus, chez les narines de feu!
When I bestride him, I soar, I am a hawk. He trots the
air. The earth sings when he touches it. The basest horn
of his hoof is more musical than the pipe of Hermes.
ORLEANS He's of the color of the nutmeg.
DAUPHIN And of the heat of the ginger. It is a beast for
Perseus: he is pure air and fire; and the dull elements of
earth and water never appear in him, but only in patient
stillness while his rider mounts him. He is indeed a
horse, and all other jades you may call beasts.
CONSTABLE Indeed, my lord, it is a most absolute and
excellent horse.
DAUPHIN It is the prince of palfreys. His neigh is like the
bidding of a monarch, and his countenance enforces
homage.
ORLEANS No more, cousin.
DAUPHIN Nay, the man hath no wit that cannot, from the
rising of the lark to the lodging of the lamb, vary deserved praise on my palfrey. It is a theme as fluent as the
sea. Turn the sands into eloquent tongues, and my horse
is argument for them all. 'Tis a subject for a sovereign to
reason on, and for a sovereign's sovereign to ride on;
and for the world, familiar to us and unknown, to lay
apart their particular functions and wonder at him. I
once writ a sonnet in his praise and began thus, 'Wonder
of nature!'
ORLEANS I have heard a sonnet begin so to one's mistress.
DAUPHIN Then did they imitate that which I composed
to my courser, for my horse is my mistress.
ORLEANS Your mistress bears well.

109 s.d. *Tucket* trumpet call 110 *habit* attire 115 *Advantage* circumspection 118 *bruise* squeeze (as in treating a boil) 120–21 *admire . . .
sufferance* wonder at our patience 123–24 *which . . . under* i.e. to com-
pensate for which his means are too small 132 *quality* rank 137
*impeachment* challenge 139 *vantage* superiority in numbers 147 *blown*
brought to bloom 154 *advise himself* consider
III, vii The French camp near Agincourt 13 *hairs* (like the stuffing of a
tennis ball) 14 *le cheval . . . feu* the flying horse, Pegasus, with nostrils of
fire 16 *basest horn* i.e. hoofbeat (with pun on the musical instrument)
17 *pipe* (the musical instrument with which Hermes, i.e. Mercury, lulled
to sleep the monster Argus) 20 *Perseus* (in Ovid, the rider of Pegasus
while rescuing Andromeda from a dragon) 24 *absolute* perfect 26 *palfreys*
saddle-horses 31 *lodging* i.e. going to bed 35 *reason on* discourse upon
36–37 *to lay . . . functions* i.e. to combine

44 DAUPHIN  Me well, which is the prescript praise and perfection of a good and particular mistress.

CONSTABLE  Nay, for methought yesterday your mistress
47  shrewdly shook your back.

DAUPHIN  So perhaps did yours.

CONSTABLE  Mine was not bridled.

DAUPHIN  O, then belike she was old and gentle, and you
51  rode like a kern of Ireland, your French hose off, and in
52  your strait strossers.

CONSTABLE  You have good judgment in horsemanship.

DAUPHIN  Be warned by me then. They that ride so, and
ride not warily, fall into foul bogs. I had rather have my
56  horse to my mistress.

CONSTABLE  I had as lief have my mistress a jade.

DAUPHIN  I tell thee, Constable, my mistress wears his
own hair.

CONSTABLE  I could make as true a boast as that, if I had a
sow to my mistress.

62 DAUPHIN  'Le chien est retourné à son propre vomissement, et la truie lavée au bourbier.' Thou mak'st use of
anything.

CONSTABLE  Yet do I not use my horse for my mistress,
or any such proverb so little kin to the purpose.

RAMBURES  My Lord Constable, the armor that I saw in
your tent to-night – are those stars or suns upon it?

CONSTABLE  Stars, my lord.

DAUPHIN  Some of them will fall to-morrow, I hope.

71 CONSTABLE  And yet my sky shall not want.

DAUPHIN  That may be, for you bear a many superfluously, and 'twere more honor some were away.

CONSTABLE  Ev'n as your horse bears your praises, who
would trot as well, were some of your brags dismounted.

DAUPHIN  Would I were able to load him with his desert!
Will it never be day? I will trot to-morrow a mile, and
my way shall be paved with English faces.

79 CONSTABLE  I will not say so, for fear I should be faced
out of my way: but I would it were morning, for I
would fain be about the ears of the English.

82 RAMBURES  Who will go to hazard with me for twenty
prisoners?

CONSTABLE  You must first go yourself to hazard ere you
have them.

DAUPHIN  'Tis midnight; I'll go arm myself.     Exit.

ORLEANS  The Dauphin longs for morning.

RAMBURES  He longs to eat the English.

CONSTABLE  I think he will eat all he kills.

ORLEANS  By the white hand of my lady, he's a gallant
prince.

CONSTABLE  Swear by her foot, that she may tread out
the oath.

ORLEANS  He is simply the most active gentleman of
France.

95 CONSTABLE  Doing is activity, and he will still be doing.

ORLEANS  He never did harm, that I heard of.

CONSTABLE  Nor will do none to-morrow. He will keep
that good name still.

ORLEANS  I know him to be valiant.

CONSTABLE  I was told that by one that knows him better
than you.

ORLEANS  What's he?

CONSTABLE  Marry, he told me so himself, and he said he
cared not who knew it.

ORLEANS  He needs not; it is no hidden virtue in him.

106 CONSTABLE  By my faith, sir, but it is! Never anybody

saw it but his lackey. 'Tis a hooded valor; and when it
appears, it will bate.

ORLEANS  Ill will never said well.

CONSTABLE  I will cap that proverb with 'There is flattery in friendship.'

ORLEANS  And I will take up that with 'Give the devil his
due.'

CONSTABLE  Well placed! There stands your friend for
the devil. Have at the very eye of that proverb with 'A
pox of the devil!'

ORLEANS  You are the better at proverbs, by how much 'a
fool's bolt is soon shot.'

CONSTABLE  You have shot over.

ORLEANS  'Tis not the first time you were overshot.

        *Enter a Messenger.*

MESSENGER  My Lord High Constable, the English lie
within fifteen hundred paces of your tents.

CONSTABLE  Who hath measured the ground?

MESSENGER  The Lord Grandpré.

CONSTABLE  A valiant and most expert gentleman. Would
it were day! Alas, poor Harry of England! He longs not
for the dawning, as we do.

ORLEANS  What a wretched and peevish fellow is this king
of England, to mope with his fat-brained followers so
far out of his knowledge!

CONSTABLE  If the English had any apprehension, they
would run away.

ORLEANS  That they lack; for if their heads had any intellectual armor, they could never wear such heavy headpieces.

RAMBURES  That island of England breeds very valiant
creatures. Their mastiffs are of unmatchable courage.

ORLEANS  Foolish curs, that run winking into the mouth
of a Russian bear and have their heads crushed like
rotten apples! You may as well say that's a valiant flea
that dare eat his breakfast on the lip of a lion.

CONSTABLE  Just, just! and the men do sympathize with
the mastiffs in robustious and rough coming on, leaving
their wits with their wives; and then give them great
meals of beef and iron and steel, they will eat like wolves
and fight like devils.

ORLEANS  Ay, but these English are shrewdly out of beef.

CONSTABLE  Then shall we find to-morrow they have
only stomachs to eat and none to fight. Now is it time to
arm. Come, shall we about it?

ORLEANS
It is now two o'clock; but let me see – by ten
We shall have each a hundred Englishmen.     *Exeunt.*

        *

44 *prescript* appropriate  47 *shrewdly* grievously  51 *kern* Irish bushfighter; *French hose* breeches  52 *strait strossers* tight trousers, i.e. barelegged  56 *to* as  62–63 *Le chien . . . bourbier* the dog is returned to his own vomit and the washed sow to the mire (2 Peter ii, 22)  71 *want* be lacking (in stars, i.e. honors)  79 *faced* braved  82 *go to hazard* play at dice  95 *Doing* i.e. acting, pretending  106–07 *Never . . . lackey* i.e. he is valiant only with his lackey  107 *hooded* with head covered, i.e. like a quiescent hawk  108 *bate* flutter, i.e. like a hawk when unhooded (with pun on 'bate' in sense of 'diminish')  114 *Well placed* well played, i.e. appropriate  115 *Have . . . eye* i.e. right on the mark (another sporting term evoked by this contest in proverb-capping)  119 *shot over* i.e. over the mark  120 *overshot* i.e. defeated  128 *peevish* silly  129 *mope* grope about  130 *out . . . knowledge* i.e. over his head  131 *apprehension* understanding  138 *winking* with eyes shut  142 *sympathize* i.e. have fellow-feeling  147 *shrewdly* grievously

Cho.        *Chorus.*
1   Now entertain conjecture of a time
2   When creeping murmur and the poring dark
    Fills the wide vessel of the universe.
    From camp to camp, through the foul womb of night,
5   The hum of either army stilly sounds,
6   That the fixed sentinels almost receive
    The secret whispers of each other's watch.
8   Fire answers fire, and through their paly flames
9   Each battle sees the other's umbered face.
    Steed threatens steed, in high and boastful neighs
    Piercing the night's dull ear ; and from the tents
12  The armorers accomplishing the knights,
    With busy hammers closing rivets up,
    Give dreadful note of preparation.
    The country cocks do crow, the clocks do toll
    And the third hour of drowsy morning name.
17  Proud of their numbers and secure in soul,
18  The confident and over-lusty French
19  Do the low-rated English play at dice ;
    And chide the cripple tardy-gaited night
    Who like a foul and ugly witch doth limp
    So tediously away. The poor condemnèd English,
    Like sacrifices, by their watchful fires
    Sit patiently and inly ruminate
    The morning's danger ; and their gesture sad,
    Investing lank-lean cheeks and war-worn coats,
    Presenteth them unto the gazing moon
28  So many horrid ghosts. O, now, who will behold
    The royal captain of this ruined band
    Walking from watch to watch, from tent to tent,
    Let him cry, 'Praise and glory on his head !'
    For forth he goes and visits all his host,
    Bids them good morrow with a modest smile
    And calls them brothers, friends, and countrymen.
    Upon his royal face there is no note
36  How dread an army hath enrounded him ;
37  Nor doth he dedicate one jot of color
    Unto the weary and all-watchèd night,
39  But freshly looks, and overbears attaint
    With cheerful semblance and sweet majesty ;
    That every wretch, pining and pale before,
    Beholding him, plucks comfort from his looks.
    A largess universal, like the sun.
    His liberal eye doth give to every one,
    Thawing cold fear, that mean and gentle all
46  Behold, as may unworthiness define,
47  A little touch of Harry in the night.
    And so our scene must to the battle fly ;

Where (O for pity !) we shall much disgrace
With four or five most vile and ragged foils,
Right ill-disposed in brawl ridiculous,
The name of Agincourt. Yet sit and see,
Minding true things by what their mock'ries be.   *Exit.* 53

*Enter the King, Bedford, and Gloucester.*          IV, i

KING
    Gloucester, 'tis true that we are in great danger ;
    The greater therefore should our courage be.
    Good morrow, brother Bedford. God Almighty !
    There is some soul of goodness in things evil,
    Would men observingly distill it out ;
    For our bad neighbor makes us early stirrers,
    Which is both healthful, and good husbandry.      7
    Besides, they are our outward consciences,
    And preachers to us all, admonishing
    That we should dress us fairly for our end.        10
    Thus may we gather honey from the weed
    And make a moral of the devil himself.
        *Enter Erpingham.*
    Good morrow, old Sir Thomas Erpingham.
    A good soft pillow for that good white head
    Were better than a churlish turf of France.
ERPINGHAM
    Not so, my liege. This lodging likes me better,
    Since I may say, 'Now lie I like a king.'
KING
    'Tis good for men to love their present pains
    Upon example : so the spirit is eased ;            19
    And when the mind is quick'ned, out of doubt       20
    The organs, though defunct and dead before,
    Break up their drowsy grave and newly move         22
    With casted slough and fresh legerity.             23
    Lend me thy cloak, Sir Thomas. Brothers both,
    Commend me to the princes in our camp ;
    Do my good morrow to them, and anon
    Desire them all to my pavilion.
GLOUCESTER
    We shall, my liege.
ERPINGHAM
    Shall I attend your grace ?
KING                            No, my good knight.
    Go with my brothers to my lords of England.
    I and my bosom must debate awhile,                 31
    And then I would no other company.
ERPINGHAM
    The Lord in heaven bless thee, noble Harry !
                    *Exeunt [all but the King].*
KING
    God-a-mercy, old heart ! thou speak'st cheerfully.
        *Enter Pistol.*
PISTOL  Che vous la ?                                  35
KING  A friend.
PISTOL
    Discuss unto me, art thou officer ;
    Or art thou base, common, and popular ?            38
KING  I am a gentleman of a company.
PISTOL
    Trail'st thou the puissant pike ?                  40
KING  Even so. What are you ?
PISTOL
    As good a gentleman as the emperor.

IV, Cho.  1 *entertain conjecture of* imagine  2 *poring* peering  5 *stilly*
quietly  6 *That* so that  8 *paly* pale (with play on heraldic meaning of
alternately tinctured vertical lines ?)  9 *battle* army ; *umbered* shadowed
(with play on 'umbred,' i.e. visored ?, or on heraldic 'umbrated,' i.e. out-
lined, here silhouetted ?)  12 *accomplishing* equipping  17 *secure in soul*
confident in spirit  18 *over-lusty* over-lively  19 *play* i.e. play for  28
*horrid* fearful  36 *enrounded* surrounded  37 *dedicate* yield up  39 *overbears attaint* masters fatigue  46 *as . . . define* as it may be roughly expressed
47 *touch* i.e. essence  53 *Minding* bearing in mind ; *mock'ries* absurd
imitations
IV, i The English camp near Agincourt  7 *husbandry* good management
10 *dress us* prepare ourselves  19 *Upon example* in exemplary fashion  20
*quick'ned* enlivened  22 *Break . . . grave* break out of their grave of lethargy
23 *casted slough* discarded old skin ; *legerity* briskness  31 *bosom* i.e.
inner self, soul  35 *Che vous la* (Pistol's version of '*Qui va là*,' i.e. who
goes there)  38 *popular* plebeian  40 *Trail'st . . . pike* i.e. are you an
infantryman

KING Then you are a better than the king.

PISTOL

44 The king's a bawcock, and a heart of gold,
45 A lad of life, an imp of fame,
Of parents good, of fist most valiant.
47 I kiss his dirty shoe, and from heartstring
I love the lovely bully. What is thy name?

KING Harry le Roy.

PISTOL

Le Roy? A Cornish name. Art thou of Cornish crew?

51 KING No, I am a Welshman.

PISTOL

Know'st thou Fluellen?

KING Yes.

PISTOL

Tell him I'll knock his leek about his pate
55 Upon Saint Davy's day.

KING Do not you wear your dagger in your cap that day,
lest he knock that about yours.

PISTOL

Art thou his friend?

KING And his kinsman too.

PISTOL

60 The figo for thee then!

KING I thank you. God be with you!

PISTOL

My name is Pistol called.

63 KING It sorts well with your fierceness.

*Exit [Pistol]. Manet King [aside].*
*Enter Fluellen and Gower.*

GOWER Captain Fluellen!

FLUELLEN So! in the name of Cheshu Christ, speak
66 fewer. It is the greatest admiration in the universal orld,
when the true and aunchient prerogatifes and laws of
the wars is not kept. If you would take the pains but to
examine the wars of Pompey the Great, you shall find, I
70 warrant you, that there is no tiddle taddle nor pibble
pabble in Pompey's camp. I warrant you, you shall find
the ceremonies of the wars, and the cares of it, and the
forms of it, and the sobriety of it, and the modesty of it,
to be otherwise.

GOWER Why, the enemy is loud; you hear him all night.

FLUELLEN If the enemy is an ass and a fool and a prating
coxcomb, is it meet, think you, that we should also, look
77 you, be an ass and a fool and a prating coxcomb? In your
own conscience now?

GOWER I will speak lower.

FLUELLEN I pray you and beseech you that you will.

*Exit [with Gower].*

KING

Though it appear a little out of fashion,
There is much care and valor in this Welshman.

*Enter three Soldiers, John Bates, Alexander Court,*
*and Michael Williams.*

COURT Brother John Bates, is not that the morning which
breaks yonder?

BATES I think it be; but we have no great cause to desire
the approach of day.

WILLIAMS We see yonder the beginning of the day, but I
think we shall never see the end of it. Who goes there?

KING A friend.

WILLIAMS Under what captain serve you?

KING Under Sir Thomas Erpingham.

WILLIAMS A good old commander and a most kind
gentleman. I pray you, what thinks he of our estate?   93

KING Even as men wracked upon a sand, that look to be
washed off the next tide.

BATES He hath not told his thought to the king?

KING No; nor it is not meet he should. For though I speak
it to you, I think the king is but a man, as I am. The violet
smells to him as it doth to me; the element shows to him   99
as it doth to me; all his senses have but human condi-   100
tions. His ceremonies laid by, in his nakedness he ap-   101
pears but a man; and though his affections are higher   102
mounted than ours, yet when they stoop, they stoop   103
with the like wing. Therefore, when he sees reason of
fears, as we do, his fears, out of doubt, be of the same
relish as ours are. Yet, in reason, no man should possess   106
him with any appearance of fear, lest he, by showing it,
should dishearten his army.

BATES He may show what outward courage he will; but I
believe, as cold a night as 'tis, he could wish himself in
Thames up to the neck; and so I would he were, and I
by him, at all adventures, so we were quit here.   111

KING By my troth, I will speak my conscience of the
king: I think he would not wish himself anywhere but
where he is.

BATES Then I would he were here alone. So should he be
sure to be ransomed, and a many poor men's lives saved.

KING I dare say you love him not so ill to wish him here
alone, howsoever you speak this to feel other men's
minds. Methinks I could not die anywhere so contented
as in the king's company, his cause being just and his
quarrel honorable.

WILLIAMS That's more than we know.

BATES Ay, or more than we should seek after, for we know
enough if we know we are the king's subjects. If his
cause be wrong, our obedience to the king wipes the
crime of it out of us.

WILLIAMS But if the cause be not good, the king himself
hath a heavy reckoning to make when all those legs and
arms and heads, chopped off in a battle, shall join together at the latter day and cry all, 'We died at such a   130
place,' some swearing, some crying for a surgeon, some
upon their wives left poor behind them, some upon the
debts they owe, some upon their children rawly left. I   133
am afeard there are few die well that die in a battle; for
how can they charitably dispose of anything when blood   135
is their argument? Now, if these men do not die well, it
will be a black matter for the king that led them to it;
who to disobey were against all proportion of subjection.   138

KING So, if a son that is by his father sent about merchan-
dise do sinfully miscarry upon the sea, the imputation of
his wickedness, by your rule, should be imposed upon
his father that sent him; or if a servant, under his master's
command transporting a sum of money, be assailed by

44 *bawcock* fine fellow (cf. III, ii, 22)   45 *imp* child   47 *heartstring* i.e. the very cords of my heart   51 *a Welshman* (technically true, like his reply 'Harry le Roy'; cf. IV, vii, 100)   55 *Saint Davy's day* March 1, the Welsh national holiday   60 *figo* (cf. III, vi, 56)   63 *sorts* suits   66 *admiration* wonder   70–71 *pibble pabble* bibble babble, chatter   77 *In* on   93 *estate* state   99 *element* shows sky appears   100 *conditions* i.e. limitations   101 *ceremonies* observances due royalty   102 *affections* emotions   103 *stoop* swoop downward (hawking term)   106 *relish* taste   106–07 *possess him with* induce in him   111 *at all adventures* by all means   130 *latter* last   133 *rawly* unprepared   135 *charitably* in Christian love   138 *proportion of subjection* due obedience

144 robbers and die in many irreconciled iniquities, you may
call the business of the master the author of the servant's
damnation. But this is not so. The king is not bound to
answer the particular endings of his soldiers, the father of
his son, nor the master of his servant; for they purpose
not their death when they purpose their services. Besides, there is no king, be his cause never so spotless, if it
come to the arbitrement of swords, can try it out with all
unspotted soldiers. Some peradventure have on them
the guilt of premeditated and contrived murder; some,
of beguiling virgins with the broken seals of perjury;
some, making the wars their bulwark, that have before
gored the gentle bosom of peace with pillage and rob-
157 bery. Now, if these men have defeated the law and out-
158 run native punishment, though they can outstrip men,
they have no wings to fly from God. War is his beadle,
war is his vengeance; so that here men are punished for
before-breach of the king's laws in now the king's quarrel. Where they feared the death, they have borne life
away; and where they would be safe, they perish. Then
164 if they die unprovided, no more is the king guilty of
their damnation than he was before guilty of those im-
pieties for the which they are now visited. Every subject's duty is the king's, but every subject's soul is his
own. Therefore should every soldier in the wars do as
169 every sick man in his bed – wash every mote out of his
170 conscience; and dying so, death is to him advantage; or
not dying, the time was blessedly lost wherein such
preparation was gained; and in him that escapes, it
were not sin to think that, making God so free an offer,
he let him outlive that day to see his greatness and to
teach others how they should prepare.

WILLIAMS 'Tis certain, every man that dies ill, the ill
upon his own head – the king is not to answer it.

BATES I do not desire he should answer for me, and yet I
determine to fight lustily for him.

KING I myself heard the king say he would not be ransomed.

WILLIAMS Ay, he said so, to make us fight cheerfully;
but when our throats are cut, he may be ransomed, and
we ne'er the wiser.

KING If I live to see it, I will never trust his word after.

WILLIAMS You pay him then! That's a perilous shot out
187 of an elder-gun that a poor and a private displeasure can
do against a monarch! You may as well go about to turn
the sun to ice with fanning in his face with a peacock's
feather. You'll never trust his word after! Come, 'tis a
foolish saying.

192 KING Your reproof is something too round. I should be
angry with you if the time were convenient.

WILLIAMS Let it be a quarrel between us if you live.

KING I embrace it.

---

144 *irreconciled* unabsolved   157 *defeated* broken   158 *native* in their own
country   164 *unprovided* unprepared   169 *mote* small impurity   170
*advantage* a gain (in that he dies prepared)   187 *elder-gun* pop-gun   192
*round* unsparing   197 *gage* token of challenge   211 *enow* enough   212
*crowns* gold pieces (with play on 'heads' since the English are outnumbered)
214 *cut* i.e. clip edges of (a crime against the monarch's coinage classified as
treason)   217 *careful* careworn   222 *wringing* suffering   225 *ceremony*
royal pomp   231 *soul of adoration* i.e. true essence of, or reason for,
worship   241 *flexure* bowing   245 *find thee* find thee out, expose   246
*balm* consecrated oil used in coronation   249 *farcèd* stuffed, padded;
*the king* i.e. the king's name   251 *high shore* i.e. sea cliffs (impervious to
tides)   256 *distressful* i.e. hard-earned (?)

WILLIAMS How shall I know thee again?

KING Give me any gage of thine, and I will wear it in my   197
bonnet. Then, if ever thou dar'st acknowledge it, I will
make it my quarrel.

WILLIAMS Here's my glove. Give me another of thine.

KING There.

WILLIAMS This will I also wear in my cap. If ever thou
come to me and say, after to-morrow, 'This is my glove,'
by this hand, I will take thee a box on the ear.

KING If ever I live to see it, I will challenge it.

WILLIAMS Thou dar'st as well be hanged.

KING Well, I will do it, though I take thee in the king's
company.

WILLIAMS Keep thy word. Fare thee well.

BATES Be friends, you English fools, be friends! We have
French quarrels enow, if you could tell how to reckon.   211

KING Indeed the French may lay twenty French crowns to   212
one they will beat us, for they bear them on their shoulders; but it is no English treason to cut French crowns,   214
and to-morrow the king himself will be a clipper.
                          *Exit [Bates with other] Soldiers.*

Upon the king! Let us our lives, our souls,
Our debts, our careful wives,                             217
Our children, and our sins, lay on the king!
We must bear all. O hard condition,
Twin-born with greatness, subject to the breath
Of every fool, whose sense no more can feel
But his own wringing! What infinite heart's-ease         222
Must kings neglect that private men enjoy!
And what have kings that privates have not too,
Save ceremony, save general ceremony?                    225
And what art thou, thou idol Ceremony?
What kind of god art thou, that suffer'st more
Of mortal griefs than do thy worshippers?
What are thy rents? What are thy comings-in?
O Ceremony, show me but thy worth!
What is thy soul of adoration?                           231
Art thou aught else but place, degree, and form,
Creating awe and fear in other men?
Wherein thou art less happy being feared
Than they in fearing.
What drink'st thou oft, instead of homage sweet,
But poisoned flattery? O, be sick, great greatness,
And bid thy ceremony give thee cure!
Think'st thou the fiery fever will go out
With titles blown from adulation?
Will it give place to flexure and low bending?           241
Canst thou, when thou command'st the beggar's knee,
Command the health of it? No, thou proud dream,
That play'st so subtilly with a king's repose.
I am a king that find thee; and I know                   245
'Tis not the balm, the sceptre, and the ball,            246
The sword, the mace, the crown imperial,
The intertissued robe of gold and pearl,
The farcèd title running 'fore the king,                 249
The throne he sits on, nor the tide of pomp
That beats upon the high shore of this world –           251
No, not all these, thrice-gorgeous ceremony,
Not all these, laid in bed majestical,
Can sleep so soundly as the wretched slave,
Who, with a body filled, and vacant mind,
Gets him to rest, crammed with distressful bread;        256
Never sees horrid night, the child of hell;

258 But like a lackey, from the rise to set,
259 Sweats in the eye of Phoebus, and all night
    Sleeps in Elysium; next day after dawn,
261 Doth rise and help Hyperion to his horse;
    And follows so the ever-running year
    With profitable labor to his grave;
    And but for ceremony, such a wretch,
    Winding up days with toil and nights with sleep,
    Had the forehand and vantage of a king.
267 The slave, a member of the country's peace,
    Enjoys it; but in gross brain little wots
269 What watch the king keeps to maintain the peace,
270 Whose hours the peasant best advantages.
        *Enter Erpingham.*

ERPINGHAM
271 My lord, your nobles, jealous of your absence,
    Seek through your camp to find you.
KING                                    Good old knight,
    Collect them all together at my tent.
    I'll be before thee.
ERPINGHAM        I shall do't, my lord.        *Exit.*
KING
    O God of battles, steel my soldiers' hearts,
    Possess them not with fear! Take from them now
277 The sense of reck'ning, if th' opposèd numbers
    Pluck their hearts from them. Not to-day, O Lord,
    O, not to-day, think not upon the fault
280 My father made in compassing the crown!
281 I Richard's body have interrèd new;
    And on it have bestowed more contrite tears
    Than from it issued forcèd drops of blood.
    Five hundred poor I have in yearly pay,
    Who twice a day their withered hands hold up
286 Toward heaven to pardon blood;
287 And I have built two chantries,
288 Where the sad and solemn priests sing still
    For Richard's soul. More will I do:
    Though all that I can do is nothing worth,
291 Since that my penitence comes after all,
    Imploring pardon.
        *Enter Gloucester.*
GLOUCESTER
    My liege!
KING
    My brother Gloucester's voice. Ay.
    I know thy errand; I will go with thee.
    The day, my friends, and all things stay for me. *Exeunt.*

\*

IV, ii        *Enter the Dauphin, Orleans, Rambures, and
             Beaumont.*
ORLEANS
    The sun doth gild our armor. Up, my lords!
2 DAUPHIN Monte, cheval! My horse, varlet lacquais! Ha!
ORLEANS O brave spirit!
4 DAUPHIN Via les eaux et terre!
5 ORLEANS Rien puis les air et feu?
6 DAUPHIN Cieux! cousin Orleans.
        *Enter Constable.*
    Now, my Lord Constable?
CONSTABLE
    Hark how our steeds for present service neigh!

DAUPHIN
    Mount them and make incision in their hides,
    That their hot blood may spin in English eyes
    And dout them with superfluous courage, ha!        11
RAMBURES
    What, will you have them weep our horses' blood?
    How shall we then behold their natural tears?
        *Enter Messenger.*
MESSENGER
    The English are embattled, you French peers.
CONSTABLE
    To horse, you gallant princes! straight to horse!
    Do but behold yond poor and starvèd band,
    And your fair show shall suck away their souls,
    Leaving them but the shales and husks of men.       18
    There is not work enough for all our hands,
    Scarce blood enough in all their sickly veins
    To give each naked curtle-axe a stain              21
    That our French gallants shall to-day draw out
    And sheathe for lack of sport. Let us but blow on them,
    The vapor of our valor will o'erturn them.
    'Tis positive 'gainst all exceptions, lords,        25
    That our superfluous lackeys and our peasants,
    Who in unnecessary action swarm
    About our squares of battle, were enow
    To purge this field of such a hilding foe,          29
    Though we upon this mountain's basis by            30
    Took stand for idle speculation:                   31
    But that our honors must not. What's to say?
    A very little little let us do,
    And all is done. Then let the trumpets sound
    The tucket sonance and the note to mount;          35
    For our approach shall so much dare the field      36
    That England shall couch down in fear and yield.
        *Enter Grandpré.*
GRANDPRÉ
    Why do you stay so long, my lords of France?
    Yond island carrions, desperate of their bones,    39
    Ill-favoredly become the morning field.
    Their ragged curtains poorly are let loose,        41
    And our air shakes them passing scornfully.
    Big Mars seems bankrout in their beggared host     43
    And faintly through a rusty beaver peeps.          44
    The horsemen sit like fixèd candlesticks

258 *lackey* constant attendant  259 *Sweats . . . Phoebus* i.e. works in sight of the sun  261 *Hyperion* charioteer of the sun  267 *member* sharer  269 *watch* wakeful guard  270 *advantages* profits  271 *jealous of* concerned about  277 *sense of reck'ning* ability to count  280 *compassing* obtaining  281 *new* anew  286 *blood* sinful flesh (?), the spilling of blood (?)  287 *chantries* chapels where masses are celebrated for the souls of the dead  288 *still* continuously  291 *Since that* i.e. as shown by the fact that
IV, ii The French camp  s.d. *Beaumont* (a 'ghost' character, mute and appearing only in this one stage direction)  2 *Monte, cheval* soar, horse (cf. III, vii, 11–16); *varlet lacquais* rascal groom  4 *Via . . . terre* away waters and earth (i.e. streams and solid ground)  5 *Rien . . . feu?* not also air and fire? (Orleans jestingly takes the Dauphin's '*eaux*' and '*terre*' to refer to two of the four elements over which his horse will soar; and asks if it will not also soar above the realms of air and fire)  6 *Cieux* the heavens (to which, in the old cosmology, the realm of fire extended; the Dauphin has converted the joke into serious hyperbole)  11 *dout* extinguish; *superfluous courage* i.e. blood we can spare  18 *shales* shells  21 *curtle-axe* cutlass  25 *exceptions* objections  29 *hilding* worthless  30 *mountain's basis* by i.e. nearby foothill  31 *speculation* viewing  35 *tucket sonance* trumpet call  36 *dare* daze (as the hawk terrifies its prey)  39 *carrions* cadavers; *desperate* despairing  41 *curtains* flags  43 *bankrout* bankrupt  44 *beaver* visor

46 With torch-staves in their hand ; and their poor jades
47 Lob down their heads, dropping the hides and hips,
48 The gum down roping from their pale-dead eyes,
49 And in their pale dull mouths the gimmaled bit
   Lies foul with chawed grass, still and motionless ;
51 And their executors, the knavish crows,
   Fly o'er them all, impatient for their hour.
   Description cannot suit itself in words
   To demonstrate the life of such a battle
55 In life so lifeless as it shows itself.

CONSTABLE
56 They have said their prayers, and they stay for death.

DAUPHIN
   Shall we go send them dinners and fresh suits
   And give their fasting horses provender,
   And after fight with them ?

CONSTABLE
60 I stay but for my guard. On to the field !
61 I will the banner from a trumpet take
   And use it for my haste. Come, come away !
63 The sun is high, and we outwear the day.          *Exeunt.*

                              *

, iii      *Enter Gloucester, Bedford, Exeter, Erpingham with*
          *all his Host, Salisbury, and Westmoreland.*

GLOUCESTER
   Where is the king ?

BEDFORD
2  The king himself is rode to view their battle.

WESTMORELAND
   Of fighting men they have full three-score thousand.

EXETER
   There's five to one ; besides, they all are fresh.

SALISBURY
   God's arm strike with us ! 'Tis a fearful odds.
   God bye you, princes all ; I'll to my charge.
   If we no more meet till we meet in heaven,
   Then joyfully, my noble Lord of Bedford,
   My dear Lord Gloucester, and my good Lord Exeter,
   And my kind kinsman, warriors all, adieu !

BEDFORD
   Farewell, good Salisbury, and good luck go with thee !

EXETER
   Farewell, kind lord : fight valiantly to-day ;
   And yet I do thee wrong to mind thee of it,
14 For thou art framed of the firm truth of valor.
                                   *[Exit Salisbury.]*

BEDFORD
   He is as full of valor as of kindness,
   Princely in both.
          *Enter the King.*

WESTMORELAND   O that we now had here
   But one ten thousand of those men in England
   That do no work to-day !

KING                    What's he that wishes so ?
   My cousin Westmoreland ? No, my fair cousin.
   If we are marked to die, we are enow          20
   To do our country loss ; and if to live,
   The fewer men, the greater share of honor.
   God's will ! I pray thee wish not one man more.
   By Jove, I am not covetous for gold,
   Nor care I who doth feed upon my cost ;
   It yearns me not if men my garments wear ;     26
   Such outward things dwell not in my desires :
   But if it be a sin to covet honor,
   I am the most offending soul alive.
   No, faith, my coz, wish not a man from England.  30
   God's peace ! I would not lose so great an honor
   As one man more methinks would share from me
   For the best hope I have. O, do not wish one more !
   Rather proclaim it, Westmoreland, through my host,
   That he which hath no stomach to this fight,
   Let him depart ; his passport shall be made,
   And crowns for convoy put into his purse.       37
   We would not die in that man's company
   That fears his fellowship to die with us.        39
   This day is called the Feast of Crispian.        40
   He that outlives this day, and comes safe home,
   Will stand a-tiptoe when this day is namèd
   And rouse him at the name of Crispian.
   He that shall see this day, and live old age,
   Will yearly on the vigil feast his neighbors
   And say, 'To-morrow is Saint Crispian.'
   Then will he strip his sleeve and show his scars,
   [And say, 'These wounds I had on Crispin's day.']
   Old men forget ; yet all shall be forgot,
   But he'll remember, with advantages,             50
   What feats he did that day. Then shall our names,
   Familiar in his mouth as household words –
   Harry the King, Bedford and Exeter,
   Warwick and Talbot, Salisbury and Gloucester –
   Be in their flowing cups freshly rememb'red.
   This story shall the good man teach his son ;
   And Crispin Crispian shall ne'er go by,
   From this day to the ending of the world,
   But we in it shall be rememberèd –
   We few, we happy few, we band of brothers ;
   For he to-day that sheds his blood with me
   Shall be my brother. Be he ne'er so vile,        62
   This day shall gentle his condition ;            63
   And gentlemen in England now abed
   Shall think themselves accursed they were not here,
   And hold their manhoods cheap whiles any speaks
   That fought with us upon Saint Crispin's day.
          *Enter Salisbury.*

SALISBURY
   My sovereign lord, bestow yourself with speed.
   The French are bravely in their battles set
   And will with all expedience charge on us.       70

KING
   All things are ready, if our minds be so.

WESTMORELAND
   Perish the man whose mind is backward now !

KING
   Thou dost not wish more help from England, coz ?

WESTMORELAND
   God's will, my liege ! would you and I alone,
   Without more help, could fight this royal battle !

---

46 *torch-staves* tapers  47 *Lob* droop  48 *roping* (cf. III, v, 23)  49
*gimmaled* jointed  51 *executors* disposers of the remains  55 *In life* in
actuality  56 *stay* wait  60 *guard* (including color-bearer)  61 *trumpet*
trumpeter  63 *outwear* waste
IV, iii The English camp  2 *battle* army  14 *framed . . . truth* i.e. made of
the authentic stuff  20–21 *enow To do* enough to cause  26 *yearns* moves,
grieves  30 *coz* cousin, kinsman  37 *convoy* transport  39 *fellowship* i.e.
fraternal right  40 *Feast of Crispian* October 25 (the brothers Crispianus
and Crispinus were martyred A.D. 487 ; they became the patron saints of
shoemakers)  50 *advantages* i.e. embellishments  62 *vile* low-born  63
*gentle his condition* i.e. achieve gentility  70 *expedience* expedition

KING
Why, now thou hast unwished five thousand men !
Which likes me better than to wish us one.
You know your places. God be with you all !
*Tucket. Enter Montjoy.*

MONTJOY
Once more I come to know of thee, King Harry,
80 If for thy ransom thou wilt now compound,
Before thy most assurèd overthrow ;
83 For certainly thou art so near the gulf
84 Thou needs must be englutted. Besides, in mercy,
The Constable desires thee thou wilt mind
Thy followers of repentance, that their souls
May make a peaceful and a sweet retire
From all these fields, where (wretches !) their poor bodies
Must lie and fester.

KING                    Who hath sent thee now ?

MONTJOY
The Constable of France.

KING
I pray thee bear my former answer back :
91 Bid them achieve me, and then sell my bones.
Good God ! why should they mock poor fellows thus ?
The man that once did sell the lion's skin
While the beast lived, was killed with hunting him.
A many of our bodies shall no doubt
96 Find native graves ; upon the which, I trust,
Shall witness live in brass of this day's work ;
And those that leave their valiant bones in France,
Dying like men, though buried in your dunghills,
They shall be famed ; for there the sun shall greet them
101 And draw their honors reeking up to heaven,
Leaving their earthly parts to choke your clime,
The smell whereof shall breed a plague in France.
Mark then abounding valor in our English,
105 That, being dead, like to the bullet's crasing,
Break out into a second course of mischief,
107 Killing in relapse of mortality.
Let me speak proudly. Tell the Constable
109 We are but warriors for the working day.
Our gayness and our gilt are all besmirched
111 With rainy marching in the painful field.
112 There's not a piece of feather in our host –
Good argument, I hope, we will not fly –
And time hath worn us into slovenry.
But, by the mass, our hearts are in the trim ;
And my poor soldiers tell me, yet ere night
117 They'll be in fresher robes, or they will pluck
The gay new coats o'er the French soldiers' heads
119 And turn them out of service. If they do this,
As, if God please, they shall, my ransom then
121 Will soon be levied. Herald, save thou thy labor.
Come thou no more for ransom, gentle herald.
They shall have none, I swear, but these my joints ;
Which if they have as I will leave 'em them
Shall yield them little, tell the Constable.

MONTJOY
I shall, King Harry. And so fare thee well.
Thou never shalt hear herald any more.          *Exit.*

KING
128 I fear thou wilt once more come again for a ransom.
*Enter York.*

YORK
My lord, most humbly on my knee I beg

The leading of the vaward.                    130

KING
Take it, brave York. Now, soldiers, march away ;
And how thou pleasest, God, dispose the day !    *Exeunt.*

\*

*Alarum. Excursions. Enter Pistol, French Soldier,*  IV,
*Boy.*

PISTOL Yield, cur !

FRENCH SOLDIER Je pense que vous estes le gentil-   2
homme de bon qualité.

PISTOL Qualtitie calmie custure me ! Art thou a gentle-  4
man ? What is thy name ? Discuss.                     5

FRENCH SOLDIER O Seigneur Dieu !

PISTOL
O Signieur Dew should be a gentleman.
Perpend my words, O Signieur Dew, and mark.          8
O Signieur Dew, thou diest on point of fox,          9
Except, O signieur, thou do give to me
Egregious ransom.                                    11

FRENCH SOLDIER O, prenez miséricorde ! ayez pitié de  12
moi !

PISTOL
Moy shall not serve. I will have forty moys,
Or I will fetch thy rim out at thy throat            14
In drops of crimson blood.

FRENCH SOLDIER Est-il impossible d'eschapper le force  16
de ton bras ?

PISTOL Brass, cur ?
Thou damnèd and luxurious mountain goat,             19
Offer'st me brass ?

FRENCH SOLDIER O, pardonnez-moi !

PISTOL
Say'st thou me so ? Is that a ton of moys ?
Come hither, boy ; ask me this slave in French
What is his name.

BOY Escoute. Comment estes-vous appelé ?              25

FRENCH SOLDIER Monsieur le Fer.

BOY He says his name is Master Fer.

PISTOL Master Fer ? I'll fer him, and firk him, and ferret  28
him ! Discuss the same in French unto him.

BOY I do not know the French for 'fer,' and 'ferret,' and
'firk.'

PISTOL
Bid him prepare, for I will cut his throat.

80 *compound* come to terms   83 *englutted* swallowed up   84 *mind* remind
91 *achieve* win, capture   96 *native* i.e. English   96–97 *upon . . . work*
i.e. bearing bronze tablets commemorating their deeds at Agincourt
101 *reeking* breathing   105 *crasing* grazing, rebounding   107 *in . . .
mortality* i.e. while in the process of decaying   109 *warriors . . . day* i.e.
workaday or commonplace soldiers   111 *painful* arduous   112 *piece of
feather* decorative plume   117 *in fresher robes* i.e. new-garbed in heaven
119 *turn . . . service* i.e. dismiss them stripped of their livery   121 *levied*
collected (from the French themselves)   128 *again* (perhaps an intrusion
in the text)   130 *vaward* vanguard
IV, iv The battlefield of Agincourt   2–3 *Je . . . qualité* I think you are a
gentleman of rank   4 *Qualtitie . . . me* (gibberish, echoing *qualité* in l. 3,
together with refrain of a popular ballad, 'Callen o custare me'; the
refrain itself derives from an Irish line '*Cailin ó chois tSúire me*, meaning
'I am a girl from beside the Suir')   5 *Discuss* declare   8 *Perpend* consider   9 *fox* sword (derived from trademark of a famous swordmaker)
11 *Egregious* extraordinary   12–13 *O . . . moi* O, have mercy ! take pity on
me   14 *rim* belly-lining   16–17 *Est-il . . . bras* is it impossible to escape the
strength of your arm   19 *luxurious* lecherous   25 *Escoute . . . appelé* listen,
what is your name   28 *firk* beat ; *ferret* worry

33 FRENCH SOLDIER Que dit-il, monsieur?

34 BOY Il me commande de vous dire que vous faites vous

35 prest; car ce soldat ici est disposé tout asture de couper vostre gorge.

PISTOL

Owy, cuppe le gorge, permafoy,

Peasant, unless thou give me crowns, brave crowns,

O'er-mangled shalt thou be by this my sword.

FRENCH SOLDIER O, je vous supplie, pour l'amour de Dieu, me pardonner! Je suis le gentilhomme de bon maison. Gardez ma vie, et je vous donnerai deux cents escus.

PISTOL

What are his words?

BOY He prays you to save his life. He is a gentleman of a good house, and for his ransom he will give you two hundred crowns.

PISTOL

Tell him my fury shall abate, and I

The crowns will take.

49 FRENCH SOLDIER Petit monsieur, que dit-il?

50 BOY Encore qu'il est contre son jurement de pardonner aucun prisonnier; néantmoins, pour les escus que vous l'avez promis, il est content de vous donner le liberté, le franchisement.

FRENCH SOLDIER Sur mes genoux je vous donne mille remercîmens; et je m'estime heureux que j'ai tombé entre les mains d'un chevalier, je pense, le plus brave, vaillant, et très-distingué seigneur d'Angleterre.

PISTOL

Expound unto me, boy.

BOY He gives you, upon his knees, a thousand thanks; and he esteems himself happy that he hath fall'n into the hands of one, as he thinks, the most brave, valorous, and thrice-worthy signieur of England.

PISTOL

63 As I suck blood, I will some mercy show!

Follow me.                                   [Exit.]

BOY Suivez-vous le grand capitaine. [Exit French Soldier.] I did never know so full a voice issue from so empty a heart; but the saying is true, 'The empty vessel makes the greatest sound.' Bardolph and Nym had ten times

69 more valor than this roaring devil i' th' old play that every one may pare his nails with a wooden dagger; and they are both hanged; and so would this be, if he durst steal anything adventurously. I must stay with the lackeys with the luggage of our camp. The French might have a good prey of us, if he knew of it; for there is none to guard it but boys.                      Exit.

IV, v     Enter Constable, Orleans, Bourbon, Dauphin, and Rambures.

CONSTABLE O diable!

---

33 Que . . . monsieur what does he say, sir  34–36 Il . . . gorge he bids me tell you to prepare, for this soldier is disposed to cut your throat at once 35 asture i.e. 'à cette heure,' at once  49 Petit . . . dit-il small sir, what says he  50–53 Encore . . . franchisement although it is against his oath to pardon any prisoner, still for the crowns you have promised he is willing to give you liberty, freedom  63 suck blood (cf. II, iii, 50–51)  69 roaring devil i.e. the devil or Vice in the old morality plays, sometimes subjected to the indignity of having his claws pared
IV, v  2 O . . . perdu O Lord! the day is lost, all is lost  3 Mort . . . vie death of my life; confounded ruined  6 O . . . fortune O tainted Fortune 8 perdurable enduring  18 spoiled despoiled, ruined
IV, vi  8 Larding fattening, fertilizing  11 haggled hacked  21 raught reached

---

ORLEANS O Seigneur! le jour est perdu, tout est perdu!   2

DAUPHIN

Mort de ma vie! all is confounded, all!           3

Reproach and everlasting shame

Sits mocking in our plumes.

        A short alarum.

O meschante fortune! Do not run away.             6

CONSTABLE

Why, all our ranks are broke.

DAUPHIN

O perdurable shame! Let's stab ourselves.         8

Be these the wretches that we played at dice for?

ORLEANS

Is this the king we sent to for his ransom?

BOURBON

Shame, and eternal shame! nothing but shame!

Let us die in honor. Once more back again!

And he that will not follow Bourbon now,

Let him go hence, and with his cap in hand

Like a base pander hold the chamber door

Whilst by a slave, no gentler than my dog,

His fairest daughter is contaminated.

CONSTABLE

Disorder, that hath spoiled us, friend us now!     18

Let us on heaps go offer up our lives.

ORLEANS

We are enow yet living in the field

To smother up the English in our throngs,

If any order might be thought upon.

BOURBON

The devil take order now! I'll to the throng.

Let life be short; else shame will be too long.   Exeunt.

    Alarum. Enter the King and his Train, [Exeter, and   IV, vi
    others,] with Prisoners.

KING

Well have we done, thrice-valiant countrymen;

But all's not done, yet keep the French the field.

EXETER

The Duke of York commends him to your majesty.

KING

Lives he, good uncle? Thrice within this hour

I saw him down; thrice up again and fighting.

From helmet to the spur all blood he was.

EXETER

In which array, brave soldier, doth he lie,

Larding the plain; and by his bloody side,         8

Yoke-fellow to his honor-owing wounds,

The noble Earl of Suffolk also lies.

Suffolk first died; and York, all haggled over,    11

Comes to him, where in gore he lay insteepèd,

And takes him by the beard, kisses the gashes

That bloodily did yawn upon his face,

And cries aloud, 'Tarry, my cousin Suffolk!

My soul shall thine keep company to heaven.

Tarry, sweet soul, for mine, then fly abreast;

As in this glorious and well-foughten field

We kept together in our chivalry!'

Upon these words I came and cheered him up.

He smiled me in the face, raught me his hand,      21

And with a feeble gripe, says, 'Dear my lord,

Commend my service to my sovereign.'

So did he turn, and over Suffolk's neck

He threw his wounded arm and kissed his lips;

And so, espoused to death, with blood he sealed

A testament of noble-ending love.
The pretty and sweet manner of it forced
Those waters from me which I would have stopped;
But I had not so much of man in me,
31 And all my mother came into mine eyes
And gave me up to tears.
  KING                I blame you not;
33 For hearing this, I must perforce compound
34 With mistful eyes, or they will issue too.      *Alarum.*
But hark! what new alarum is this same?
The French have reinforced their scattered men.
Then every soldier kill his prisoners!
Give the word through.          *Exit [with others].*

\*

IV, vii       *Enter Fluellen and Gower.*
  FLUELLEN Kill the poys and the luggage? 'Tis expressly
against the law of arms. 'Tis as arrant a piece of knavery,
mark you now, as can be offert. In your conscience, now,
is it not?
  GOWER 'Tis certain there's not a boy left alive; and the
cowardly rascals that ran from the battle ha' done this
slaughter. Besides, they have burned and carried away
all that was in the king's tent; wherefore the king most
worthily hath caused every soldier to cut his prisoner's
throat. O, 'tis a gallant king!
11 FLUELLEN Ay, he was porn at Monmouth, Captain
Gower. What call you the town's name where Alexander the Pig was born.
  GOWER Alexander the Great.
  FLUELLEN Why, I pray you, is not 'pig' great? The pig,
or the great, or the mighty, or the huge, or the magnanimous are all one reckonings, save the phrase is a
17 little variations.
  GOWER I think Alexander the Great was born in Macedon.
His father was called Philip of Macedon, as I take it.
  FLUELLEN I think it is in Macedon where Alexander is
porn. I tell you, captain, if you look in the maps of the
orld, I warrant you sall find, in the comparisons between Macedon and Monmouth, that the situations,
24 look you, is poth alike. There is a river in Macedon, and
there is also moreover a river at Monmouth. It is called
Wye at Monmouth; but it is out of my prains what is the
name of the other river. But 'tis all one; 'tis alike as my
fingers is to my fingers, and there is salmons in poth. If
you mark Alexander's life well, Harry of Monmouth's
30 life is come after it indifferent well; for there is figures
in all things. Alexander, God knows and you know, in
his rages, and his furies, and his wraths, and his cholers,
and his moods, and his displeasures, and his indigna-
tions, and also being a little intoxicates in his prains, did,
in his ales and his angers, look you, kill his best friend,
35 Cleitus.
  GOWER Our king is not like him in that. He never killed
any of his friends.
  FLUELLEN It is not well done, mark you now, to take the
tales out of my mouth ere it is made and finished. I speak
but in the figures and comparisons of it. As Alexander
killed his friend Cleitus, being in his ales and his cups,
so also Harry Monmouth, being in his right wits and his
good judgments, turned away the fat knight with the
44 great pelly doublet. He was full of jests, and gipes, and
knaveries, and mocks. I have forgot his name.
  GOWER Sir John Falstaff.

FLUELLEN That is he. I'll tell you there is good men porn
at Monmouth.
  GOWER Here comes his majesty.
       *Alarum. Enter King Harry and Bourbon, [Warwick,*
       *Gloucester, Exeter, and Herald,] with Prisoners.*
       *Flourish.*
  KING
I was not angry since I came to France
Until this instant. Take a trumpet, herald;       51
Ride thou unto the horsemen on yond hill.
If they will fight with us, bid them come down
Or void the field. They do offend our sight.       54
If they'll do neither, we will come to them
And make them skirr away as swift as stones      56
Enforcèd from the old Assyrian slings.       57
Besides, we'll cut the throats of those we have;
And not a man of them that we shall take
Shall taste our mercy. Go and tell them so.
              *[Exeunt Herald and Gower.]*
       *Enter Montjoy.*
  EXETER
Here comes the herald of the French, my liege.
  GLOUCESTER
His eyes are humbler than they used to be.
  KING
How now? What means this, herald? Know'st thou not
That I have fined these bones of mine for ransom?    64
Com'st thou again for ransom?
  HERALD              No, great king.
I come to thee for charitable license
That we may wander o'er this bloody field
To book our dead, and then to bury them;       68
To sort our nobles from our common men.
For many of our princes, woe the while!
Lie drowned and soaked in mercenary blood.      71
So do our vulgar drench their peasant limbs
In blood of princes, and the wounded steeds
Fret fetlock-deep in gore and with wild rage
Yerk out their armèd heels at their dead masters,    75
Killing them twice. O, give us leave, great king,
To view the field in safety and dispose
Of their dead bodies!
  KING            I tell thee truly, herald,
I know not if the day be ours or no;
For yet a many of your horsemen peer       80
And gallop o'er the field.
  HERALD            The day is yours.
  KING
Praisèd be God and not our strength for it!
What is this castle called that stands hard by?
  HERALD
They call it Agincourt.
  KING
Then call we this the field of Agincourt,
Fought on the day of Crispin Crispianus.

31 *mother* i.e. womanly tenderness   33 *compound* come to terms   34
*mistful* tearful; *issue* run (tears)
IV, vii The battlefield of Agincourt   11 *Monmouth* i.e. in Wales   17 *variations* i.e. altered   24 *river* (there follows a parody of rhetorical 'comparisons')   30 *is come after* i.e. resembles; *figures* comparisons   35
*Cleitus* friend of Alexander, slain in drunken rage for praising Philip
44 *great pelly* stuffed belly; *gipes* japes   51 *trumpet* trumpeter   54 *void*
leave, depart from   56 *skirr* scurry   57 *Enforcèd* driven   64 *fined* pledged
68 *book* register   71 *mercenary blood* blood of hired soldiers   75 *Yerk*
kick   80 *peer* appear

FLUELLEN Your grandfather of famous memory, an't please your majesty, and your great-uncle Edward the Plack Prince of Wales, as I have read in the chronicles, fought a most prave pattle here in France.

KING They did, Fluellen.

FLUELLEN Your majesty says very true. If your majesties is rememb'red of it, the Welshmen did good service in a garden where leeks did grow, wearing leeks in their Monmouth caps; which your majesty know to this hour is an honorable padge of the service; and I do believe your majesty takes no scorn to wear the leek upon Saint Tavy's day.

KING

I wear it for a memorable honor;
For I am Welsh, you know, good countryman.

FLUELLEN All the water in Wye cannot wash your majesty's Welsh plood out of your pody, I can tell you that. God pless it and preserve it, as long as it pleases his grace, and his majesty too!

KING Thanks, good my countryman.

FLUELLEN By Cheshu, I am your majesty's countryman, I care not who know it! I will confess it to all the orld. I need not to be ashamed of your majesty, praised be God, so long as your majesty is an honest man.

KING

God keep me so! Our heralds go with him.
*Enter Williams.*
Bring me just notice of the numbers dead
On both our parts.    *[Exeunt Heralds with Montjoy.]*
Call yonder fellow hither.

EXETER Soldier, you must come to the king.

KING Soldier, why wear'st thou that glove in thy cap?

WILLIAMS An't please your majesty, 'tis the gage of one that I should fight withal, if he be alive.

KING An Englishman?

WILLIAMS An't please your majesty, a rascal that swaggered with me last night; who, if 'a live and ever dare to challenge this glove, I have sworn to take him a box o' th' ear; or if I can see my glove in his cap, which he swore, as he was a soldier, he would wear if alive, I will strike it out soundly.

KING What think you, Captain Fluellen? Is it fit this soldier keep his oath?

FLUELLEN He is a craven and a villain else, an't please your majesty, in my conscience.

KING It may be his enemy is a gentleman of great sort, quite from the answer of his degree.

FLUELLEN Though he be as good a gentleman as the devil is, as Lucifer and Belzebub himself, it is necessary, look your grace, that he keep his vow and his oath. If he be perjured, see you now, his reputation is as arrant a villain and a jack sauce as ever his plack shoe trod upon God's ground and his earth, in my conscience, law!

KING Then keep thy vow, sirrah, when thou meet'st the fellow.

WILLIAMS So I will, my liege, as I live.

KING Who serv'st thou under?

WILLIAMS Under Captain Gower, my liege.

FLUELLEN Gower is a good captain and is good knowledge and literatured in the wars.    142

KING Call him hither to me, soldier.

WILLIAMS I will, my liege.    *Exit.*

KING Here, Fluellen; wear thou this favor for me and stick it in thy cap. When Alençon and myself were down together, I plucked this glove from his helm. If any man challenge this, he is a friend to Alençon and an enemy to our person. If thou encounter any such, apprehend him, an thou dost me love.

FLUELLEN Your grace doo's me as great honors as can be desired in the hearts of his subjects. I would fain see the man, that has but two legs, that shall find himself aggriefed at this glove, that is all. But I would fain see it once, an please God of his grace that I might see.    153

KING Know'st thou Gower?

FLUELLEN He is my dear friend, an please you.

KING Pray thee go seek him and bring him to my tent.

FLUELLEN I will fetch him.    *Exit.*

KING

My Lord of Warwick, and my brother Gloucester,
Follow Fluellen closely at the heels.
The glove which I have given him for a favor    162
May haply purchase him a box o' th' ear;
It is the soldier's. I by bargain should
Wear it myself. Follow, good cousin Warwick.
If that the soldier strike him—as I judge
By his blunt bearing, he will keep his word—
Some sudden mischief may arise of it;
For I do know Fluellen valiant,
And, touched with choler, hot as gunpowder,    170
And quickly will return an injury.
Follow, and see there be no harm between them.
Go you with me, uncle of Exeter.    *Exeunt.*

*

*Enter Gower and Williams.*    IV, viii

WILLIAMS I warrant it is to knight you, captain.
*Enter Fluellen.*

FLUELLEN God's will and his pleasure, captain, I beseech you now, come apace to the king. There is more good toward you peradventure than is in your knowledge to dream of.

WILLIAMS Sir, know you this glove?

FLUELLEN Know the glove? I know the glove is a glove.

WILLIAMS I know this; and thus I challenge it.
*Strikes him.*

FLUELLEN 'Sblood! an arrant traitor as any's in the universal orld, or in France, or in England!

GOWER How now, sir? You villain!

WILLIAMS Do you think I'll be forsworn?

FLUELLEN Stand away, Captain Gower. I will give treason his payment into plows, I warrant you.    12

WILLIAMS I am no traitor.

FLUELLEN That's a lie in thy throat. I charge you in his majesty's name apprehend him. He's a friend of the Duke Alençon's.
*Enter Warwick and Gloucester.*

WARWICK How now, how now? What's the matter?

FLUELLEN My Lord of Warwick, here is, praised be God for it, a most contagious treason come to light, look you,    20
as you shall desire in a summer's day. Here is his majesty.
*Enter King and Exeter.*

95 *Monmouth caps* tall tapering hats without brims    129 *from . . . degree* above responding to a challenge from one of his rank    134 *as ever* as sure as    142 *literatured* well-read, learned    153 *aggriefed* aggrieved, incensed    162 *favor* token    170 *touched . . . choler* i.e. quick-tempered
IV, viii The English camp    12 *his* its    20 *contagious* noxious

KING  How now? What's the matter?

FLUELLEN  My liege, here is a villain and a traitor that, look your grace, has struck the glove which your majesty is take out of the helmet of Alençon.

26 WILLIAMS  My liege, this was my glove, here is the fellow
27 of it; and he that I gave it to in change promised to wear it in his cap. I promised to strike him if he did. I met this man with my glove in his cap, and I have been as good as my word.

FLUELLEN  Your majesty hear now, saving your majesty's manhood, what an arrant, rascally, peggarly, lousy knave it is! I hope your majesty is pear me testimony and wit-
34 ness, and will avouchment, that this is the glove of Alençon that your majesty is give me, in your conscience, now.

KING
Give me thy glove, soldier. Look, here is the fellow of it.
'Twas I indeed thou promisèd'st to strike;
And thou hast given me most bitter terms.

FLUELLEN  An please your majesty, let his neck answer for it, if there is any martial law in the orld.

KING  How canst thou make me satisfaction?

WILLIAMS  All offenses, my lord, come from the heart. Never came any from mine that might offend your majesty.

KING  It was ourself thou didst abuse.

WILLIAMS  Your majesty came not like yourself. You ap-peared to me but as a common man; witness the night,
48 your garments, your lowliness. And what your highness suffered under that shape, I beseech you take it for your own fault, and not mine; for had you been as I took you for, I made no offense. Therefore I beseech your high-ness pardon me.

KING
Here, uncle Exeter, fill this glove with crowns
And give it to this fellow. Keep it, fellow,
And wear it for an honor in thy cap
Till I do challenge it. Give him the crowns;
And captain, you must needs be friends with him.

FLUELLEN  By this day and this light, the fellow has
58 mettle enough in his pelly. Hold, there is twelve pence for you; and I pray you to serve God, and keep you out of prawls, and prabbles, and quarrels, and dissensions, and, I warrant you, it is the petter for you.

WILLIAMS  I will none of your money.

FLUELLEN  It is with a good will. I can tell you it will serve you to mend your shoes. Come, wherefore should you be so pashful? Your shoes is not so good. 'Tis a good silling, I warrant you, or I will change it.
*Enter [an English] Herald.*

KING
Now, herald, are the dead numb'red?

HERALD
Here is the number of the slaught'red French.
*[Gives a paper.]*

KING
70 What prisoners of good sort are taken, uncle?

EXETER
Charles Duke of Orleans, nephew to the king;
John Duke of Bourbon and Lord Bouciqualt:
Of other lords and barons, knights and squires,
Full fifteen hundred, besides common men.

KING
This note doth tell me of ten thousand French

That in the field lie slain. Of princes, in this number,
And nobles bearing banners, there lie dead
One hundred twenty-six; added to these,
Of knights, esquires, and gallant gentlemen,
Eight thousand and four hundred; of the which,
Five hundred were but yesterday dubbed knights;
So that in these ten thousand they have lost
There are but sixteen hundred mercenaries;
The rest are princes, barons, lords, knights, squires,
And gentlemen of blood and quality.
The names of those their nobles that lie dead:
Charles Delabreth, High Constable of France;
Jacques of Chatillon, Admiral of France;
The master of the crossbows, Lord Rambures;
Great Master of France, the brave Sir Guichard Dauphin;
John Duke of Alençon; Anthony Duke of Brabant,
The brother to the Duke of Burgundy;
And Edward Duke of Bar; of lusty earls,
Grandpré and Roussi, Faulconbridge and Foix,
Beaumont and Marle, Vaudemont and Lestrale.
Here was a royal fellowship of death!
Where is the number of our English dead?
*[Herald gives another paper.]*
Edward the Duke of York, the Earl of Suffolk,
Sir Richard Ketly, Davy Gam, esquire;
None else of name; and of all other men
But five-and-twenty. O God, thy arm was here!
And not to us, but to thy arm alone,
Ascribe we all! When, without stratagem,
But in plain shock and even play of battle,
Was ever known so great and little loss
On one part and on th' other? Take it, God,
For it is none but thine!

EXETER                        'Tis wonderful!

KING
Come, go we in procession to the village;
And be it death proclaimèd through our host
To boast of this, or take that praise from God
Which is his only.

FLUELLEN  Is it not lawful, an please your majesty, to tell how many is killed?

KING
Yes, captain; but with this acknowledgment,
That God fought for us.

FLUELLEN  Yes, my conscience, he did us great good.

KING
Do we all holy rites.
Let there be sung 'Non nobis' and 'Te Deum,'
The dead with charity enclosed in clay,
And then to Calais; and to England then;
Where ne'er from France arrived more happy men.
                                        *Exeunt.*

*

26 *fellow* mate  27 *change* exchange  34 *avouchment* i.e. avouch  48 *lowliness* i.e. humble bearing  58 *mettle* i.e. courage  70 *good sort* high rank  77 *bearing banners* (cf. IV, ii, 61–62)  82 *ten thousand* (the mortality figures are from Hall and Holinshed; the modern estimate is about 7000)  99 *Davy Gam* David ap Llewellyn  101 *five-and-twenty* (the figure given by Hall; the modern estimate is about 450)  106 *Take it* i.e. take the credit  118 *Non nobis* i.e. Psalm cxv, beginning in English 'Not unto us, O Lord, not unto us, but unto thy name give glory'; *Te Deum* song of thanksgiving beginning in English 'We praise thee, O God'  121 *happy* fortunate

*Enter Chorus.*

Vouchsafe to those that have not read the story
That I may prompt them ; and of such as have,
3  I humbly pray them to admit th' excuse
Of time, of numbers, and due course of things
Which cannot in their huge and proper life
Be here presented. Now we bear the king
Toward Calais. Grant him there. There seen,
Heave him away upon your wingèd thoughts
Athwart the sea. Behold, the English beach
10  Pales in the flood with men, wives, and boys,
Whose shouts and claps outvoice the deep-mouthed sea,
12  Which, like a mighty whiffler 'fore the king,
Seems to prepare his way. So let him land,
And solemnly see him set on to London.
So swift a pace hath thought that even now
You may imagine him upon Blackheath ;
Where that his lords desire him to have borne
His bruisèd helmet and his bended sword
Before him through the city. He forbids it,
Being free from vainness and self-glorious pride ;
21  Giving full trophy, signal, and ostent
Quite from himself to God. But now behold,
23  In the quick forge and working-house of thought,
How London doth pour out her citizens !
The mayor and all his brethren in best sort,
Like to the senators of th' antique Rome,
With the plebeians swarming at their heels,
Go forth and fetch their conqu'ring Caesar in ;
29  As, by a lower but by loving likelihood,
30  Were now the general of our gracious empress,
As in good time he may, from Ireland coming,
32  Bringing rebellion broachèd on his sword,
How many would the peaceful city quit
To welcome him ! Much more, and much more cause,
Did they this Harry. Now in London place him ;
36  As yet the lamentation of the French
Invites the King of England's stay at home ;
38  The emperor's coming in behalf of France
To order peace between them ; and omit
All the occurrences, whatever chanced,
Till Harry's back-return again to France.
42  There must we bring him ; and myself have played
43  The interim, by rememb'ring you 'tis past.
44  Then brook abridgment ; and your eyes advance,
After your thoughts, straight back again to France.

*Exit.*

V, Cho.  3 *admit th'excuse* i.e. tolerate the treatment  10 *Pales* hems
12 *whiffler* member of an armed escort clearing the way for a procession
21 *signal, and ostent* token and show (of victory)  23 *quick . . . thought*
i.e. nimble creative imagination  29 *lower . . . likelihood* i.e. less exalted
but no less longed-for possibility  30 *general* i.e. Robert Devereux, Earl
of Essex, whose inglorious campaign in Ireland ended in September, 1599
32 *broachèd* impaled  36 *As . . . lamentation* while the continuing state of
dejection  38 *emperor's coming* i.e. the Holy Roman Emperor Sigismund's
mission to England in May, 1416  42–43 *played The interim* filled up the
interval  43 *rememb'ring* reminding  44 *brook* put up with
V, i The English camp  5 *scald* scurvy  7 *fellow* i.e. groom  10 *preed* i.e.
breed, foment  17 *bedlam* mad ; *Trojan* roisterer  18 *fold . . . web* i.e. complete the design of the Parcae (Fates) by ending your life  25 *Cadwallader*
(last of the British kings) ; *goats* (associated with Welsh poverty)  35
*astonished* dazed  38 *green* raw ; *coxcomb* fool's scalp  52 *groat* fourpenny
piece

*Enter Fluellen and Gower.*  V, i

GOWER  Nay, that's right. But why wear you your leek to-
day ? Saint Davy's day is past.
FLUELLEN  There is occasions and causes why and wherefore in all things. I will tell you ass my friend, Captain
Gower. The rascally, scald, peggarly, lousy, pragging  5
knave, Pistol, which you and yourself and all the orld
know to be no petter than a fellow, look you now, of no  7
merits, he is come to me and prings me pread and salt
yesterday, look you, and pid me eat my leek. It was in a
place where I could not preed no contention with him ;  10
but I will be so pold as to wear it in my cap till I see him
once again, and then I will tell him a little piece of my
desires.
*Enter Pistol.*
GOWER  Why, here he comes, swelling like a turkey cock.
FLUELLEN  'Tis no matter for his swellings nor his turkey
cocks. God pless you, Aunchient Pistol ! you scurvy,
lousy knave, God pless you !
PISTOL
Ha ! art thou bedlam ? Dost thou thirst, base Trojan,  17
To have me fold up Parca's fatal web ?  18
Hence ! I am qualmish at the smell of leek.
FLUELLEN  I beseech you heartily, scurvy, lousy knave, at
my desires, and my requests, and my petitions, to eat,
look you, this leek. Because, look you, you do not love it,
nor your affections and your appetites and your disges-
tions doo's not agree with it, I would desire you to eat it.
PISTOL
Not for Cadwallader and all his goats.  25
FLUELLEN  There is one goat for you. (*Strikes him.*) Will
you be so good, scald knave, as eat it ?
PISTOL
Base Trojan, thou shalt die !
FLUELLEN  You say very true, scald knave, when God's
will is. I will desire you to live in the meantime, and eat
your victuals. Come, there is sauce for it. *[Strikes him.]*
You called me yesterday mountain-squire ; but I will
make you to-day a squire of low degree. I pray you fall
to. If you can mock a leek, you can eat a leek.
GOWER  Enough, captain. You have astonished him.  35
FLUELLEN  I say I will make him eat some part of my leek,
or I will peat his pate four days. – Pite, I pray you. It is
good for your green wound and your ploody coxcomb.  38
PISTOL  Must I bite ?
FLUELLEN  Yes, certainly, and out of doubt, and out of
question too, and ambiguities.
PISTOL  By this leek, I will most horribly revenge. I eat
and eat, I swear.
FLUELLEN  Eat, I pray you. Will you have some more
sauce to your leek ? There is not enough leek to swear by.
PISTOL  Quiet thy cudgel, thou dost see I eat.
FLUELLEN  Much good do you, scald knave, heartily.
Nay, pray you throw none away, the skin is good for
your proken coxcomb. When you take occasions to see
leeks hereafter, I pray you mock at 'em ; that is all.
PISTOL  Good.
FLUELLEN  Ay, leeks is good. Hold you, there is a groat to  52
heal your pate.
PISTOL  Me a groat ?
FLUELLEN  Yes verily, and in truth you shall take it, or I
have another leek in my pocket which you shall eat.
PISTOL
I take thy groat in earnest of revenge.

FLUELLEN If I owe you anything, I will pay you in cudgels. You shall be a woodmonger and buy nothing of me but cudgels. God bye you, and keep you, and heal your pate.                                                        *Exit*.

PISTOL
All hell shall stir for this!

GOWER Go, go. You are a counterfeit cowardly knave. Will you mock at an ancient tradition, begun upon an
64 honorable respect and won as a memorable trophy of predeceased valor, and dare not avouch in your deeds any
66 of your words? I have seen you gleeking and galling at this gentleman twice or thrice. You thought, because he could not speak English in the native garb, he could not therefore handle an English cudgel. You find it otherwise, and henceforth let a Welsh correction teach you a good English condition. Fare ye well.                 *Exit*.

PISTOL
72 Doth Fortune play the huswife with me now?
73 News have I, that my Doll is dead i' th' spital
74 Of a malady of France;
And there my rendezvous is quite cut off.
Old I do wax, and from my weary limbs
Honor is cudgelled. Well, bawd I'll turn,
78 And something lean to cutpurse of quick hand.
To England will I steal, and there I'll steal;
And patches will I get unto these cudgelled scars
81 And swear I got them in the Gallia wars.              *Exit*.

*

V, ii        *Enter, at one door, King Henry, Exeter, Bedford,*
             *[Gloucester,] Warwick, [Westmoreland,] and other*
             *Lords; at another, Queen Isabel, the [French] King,*
             *the Duke of Burgundy, [the Princess Katherine,*
             *Alice,] and other French.*

KING HENRY
Peace to this meeting, wherefore we are met.
Unto our brother France and to our sister
Health and fair time of day. Joy and good wishes
To our most fair and princely cousin Katherine.
5 And as a branch and member of this royalty,
By whom this great assembly is contrived,
We do salute you, Duke of Burgundy.
And, princes French, and peers, health to you all.

FRANCE
Right joyous are we to behold your face,
Most worthy brother England. Fairly met.
So are you, princes English, every one.

QUEEN
So happy be the issue, brother England,
Of this good day and of this gracious meeting
As we are now glad to behold your eyes –
Your eyes which hitherto have borne in them,
Against the French that met them in their bent,
17 The fatal balls of murdering basilisks.
The venom of such looks, we fairly hope,
Have lost their quality, and that this day
Shall change all griefs and quarrels into love.

KING HENRY
To cry amen to that, thus we appear.

QUEEN
You English princes all, I do salute you.

BURGUNDY
My duty to you both, on equal love,

Great Kings of France and England! That I have labored
With all my wits, my pains, and strong endeavors
To bring your most imperial majesties
Unto this bar and royal interview,                      27
Your mightiness on both parts best can witness.
Since, then, my office hath so far prevailed
That, face to face and royal eye to eye,
You have congreeted, let it not disgrace me          31
If I demand before this royal view,
What rub or what impediment there is                  33
Why that the naked, poor, and mangled Peace,
Dear nurse of arts, plenties, and joyful births,
Should not, in this best garden of the world,
Our fertile France, put up her lovely visage.
Alas, she hath from France too long been chased,
And all her husbandry doth lie on heaps,
Corrupting in it own fertility.                       40
Her vine, the merry cheerer of the heart,
Unprunèd dies; her hedges even-pleached,            42
Like prisoners wildly overgrown with hair,
Put forth disordered twigs; her fallow leas           44
The darnel, hemlock, and rank fumitory
Doth root upon, while that the coulter rusts          46
That should deracinate such savagery.
The even mead, that erst brought sweetly forth        48
The freckled cowslip, burnet, and green clover,
Wanting the scythe, all uncorrected, rank,
Conceives by idleness, and nothing teems
But hateful docks, rough thistles, kecksies, burrs,   52
Losing both beauty and utility.
And all our vineyards, fallows, meads, and hedges,
Defective in their natures, grow to wildness.         55
Even so our houses and ourselves and children
Have lost, or do not learn for want of time,
The sciences that should become our country;
But grow like savages, as soldiers will,
That nothing do but meditate on blood,
To swearing and stern looks, diffused attire,         61
And everything that seems unnatural.
Which to reduce into our former favor                 63
You are assembled; and my speech entreats
That I may know the let why gentle Peace              65
Should not expel these inconveniences
And bless us with her former qualities.

KING HENRY
If, Duke of Burgundy, you would the peace
Whose want gives growth to th' imperfections
Which you have cited, you must buy that peace
With full accord to all our just demands;
Whose tenures and particular effects                  72
You have, enscheduled briefly, in your hands.

BURGUNDY
The king hath heard them; to the which as yet

64 *respect* consideration  66 *gleeking and galling* gibing and scoffing
72 *huswife* hussy  73 *Doll* (error for Nell); *spital* hospital  74 *malady of France* venereal disease  78 *something . . . hand* i.e. lean to quick-handed purse-cutting  81 *Gallia* French
V, ii Within the palace of the French king at Troyes  5 *royalty* royal family  17 *basilisks* monsters which killed with a look; here, cannons  27 *bar* court of justice  31 *congreeted* greeted each other; *disgrace* ill become  33 *rub* obstacle  40 *it* its  42 *even-pleached* evenly pleated  44 *leas* arable fields  46 *coulter* cutting wheel or blade in front of plough-share  48 *erst* formerly  52 *kecksies* kexes, dry stems  55 *Defective* i.e. fallen, blighted by original sin  61 *diffused* disordered  63 *reduce* lead back; *favor* appearance  65 *let* hindrance  72 *tenures* gist

There is no answer made.

KING HENRY     Well then, the peace,
Which you before so urged, lies in his answer.

FRANCE

77 I have but with a cursitory eye
O'erglanced the articles. Pleaseth your grace
To appoint some of your Council presently
To sit with us once more, with better heed
To resurvey them, we will suddenly
82 Pass our accept and peremptory answer.

KING HENRY

Brother, we shall. Go, uncle Exeter,
And brother Clarence, and you, brother Gloucester,
Warwick, and Huntingdon, go with the king;
And take with you free power to ratify,
Augment, or alter, as your wisdoms best
Shall see advantageable for our dignity,
Anything in or out of our demands,
90 And we'll consign thereto. Will you, fair sister,
Go with the princes or stay here with us?

QUEEN

Our gracious brother, I will go with them.
93 Happily a woman's voice may do some good
94 When articles too nicely urged be stood on.

KING HENRY

Yet leave our cousin Katherine here with us.
96 She is our capital demand, comprised
Within the fore-rank of our articles.

QUEEN

She hath good leave.

    *Exeunt omnes. Manent King [Henry] and
    Katherine [with the Gentlewoman Alice].*

KING HENRY     Fair Katherine, and most fair,
Will you vouchsafe to teach a soldier terms
Such as will enter at a lady's ear
And plead his love suit to her gentle heart?

KATHERINE Your majesty shall mock at me. I cannot
speak your England.

KING HENRY O fair Katherine, if you will love me
soundly with your French heart, I will be glad to hear
you confess it brokenly with your English tongue. Do
you like me, Kate?

KATHERINE Pardonnez-moi, I cannot tell wat is 'like
me.'

KING HENRY An angel is like you, Kate, and you are like
an angel.

111 KATHERINE Que dit-il? Que je suis semblable à les
anges?

113 ALICE Oui, vraiment, sauf vostre grace, ainsi dit-il.

KING HENRY I said so, dear Katherine, and I must not
blush to affirm it.

KATHERINE O bon Dieu! les langues des hommes sont
pleine de tromperies.

KING HENRY What says she, fair one? that the tongues
of men are full of deceits? ·

ALICE Oui, dat de tongues of de mans is be full of deceits.
Dat is de princesse.

121 KING HENRY The princess is the better Englishwoman.
I' faith, Kate, my wooing is fit for thy understanding. I
am glad thou canst speak no better English; for if thou
couldst, thou wouldst find me such a plain king that
thou wouldst think I had sold my farm to buy my crown.
I know no ways to mince it in love but directly to say, 'I
love you.' Then, if you urge me farther than to say, 'Do
you in faith?' I wear out my suit. Give me your answer, 128
i' faith, do: and so clap hands and a bargain. How say
you, lady?

KATHERINE Sauf vostre honneur, me understand well.

KING HENRY Marry, if you would put me to verses or to
dance for your sake, Kate, why, you undid me. For the
one I have neither words nor measure; and for the other
I have no strength in measure, yet a reasonable measure
in strength. If I could win a lady at leapfrog, or by vaulting into my saddle with my armor on my back, under the 137
correction of bragging be it spoken, I should quickly leap
into a wife. Or if I might buffet for my love, or bound
my horse for her favors, I could lay on like a butcher and
sit like a jackanapes, never off. But, before God, Kate, I 141
cannot look greenly, not gasp out my eloquence, nor I 142
have no cunning in protestation, only downright oaths
which I never use till urged, nor never break for urging.
If thou canst love a fellow of this temper, Kate, whose
face is not worth sunburning, that never looks in his
glass for love of anything he sees there, let thine eye be
thy cook. I speak to thee plain soldier. If thou canst love 148
me for this, take me; if not, to say to thee that I shall die,
is true; but for thy love, by the Lord, no; yet I love thee
too. And while thou liv'st, dear Kate, take a fellow of
plain and uncoined constancy, for he perforce must do 152
thee right, because he hath not the gift to woo in other
places. For these fellows of infinite tongue that can
rhyme themselves into ladies' favors, they do always
reason themselves out again. What! A speaker is but a
prater; a rhyme is but a ballad. A good leg will fall, a 157
straight back will stoop, a black beard will turn white, a
curled pate will grow bald, a fair face will wither, a full
eye will wax hollow; but a good heart, Kate, is the sun
and the moon; or rather, the sun, and not the moon, for
it shines bright and never changes, but keeps his course
truly. If thou would have such a one, take me; and take
me, take a soldier; take a soldier, take a king. And what
say'st thou then to my love? Speak, my fair, and fairly, I
pray thee.

KATHERINE Is it possible dat I sould love de ennemie of
France?

KING HENRY No, it is not possible you should love the
enemy of France, Kate; but in loving me you should
love the friend of France, for I love France so well that I 170
will not part with a village of it – I will have it all mine.
And, Kate, when France is mine and I am yours, then
yours is France and you are mine.

KATHERINE I cannot tell wat is dat.

KING HENRY No, Kate? I will tell thee in French, which
I am sure will hang upon my tongue like a new-married
wife about her husband's neck, hardly to be shook off.
Je quand sur le possession de France, et quand vous avez 178
le possession de moi (let me see, what then? Saint Denis
be my speed!), donc vostre est France et vous estes
mienne. It is as easy for me, Kate, to conquer the king-

dom as to speak so much more French. I shall never move thee in French, unless it be to laugh at me.

184 KATHERINE Sauf vostre honneur, le François que vous parlez, il est meilleur que l'Anglois lequel je parle.

KING HENRY No, faith, is't not, Kate. But thy speaking of my tongue, and I thine, most truly-falsely, must needs be granted to be much at one. But, Kate, dost thou understand thus much English? Canst thou love me?

KATHERINE I cannot tell.

KING HENRY Can any of your neighbors tell, Kate? I'll ask them. Come, I know thou lovest me; and at night
193 when you come into your closet, you'll question this gentlewoman about me, and I know, Kate, you will to her dispraise those parts in me that you love with your heart; but, good Kate, mock me mercifully, the rather, gentle princess, because I love thee cruelly. If ever thou beest mine, Kate, as I have a saving faith within me tells
199 me thou shalt, I get thee with scambling, and thou must therefore needs prove a good soldier-breeder. Shall not thou and I, between Saint Denis and Saint George, compound a boy, half French, half English, that shall go to Constantinople and take the Turk by the beard? Shall we not? What say'st thou, my fair flower-de-luce?

KATHERINE I do not know dat.

KING HENRY No; 'tis hereafter to know, but now to promise. Do but now promise, Kate, you will endeavor for your French part of such a boy, and for my English
209 moiety take the word of a king and a bachelor. How
210 answer you, la plus belle Katherine du monde, mon trèscher et devin déesse?

KATHERINE Your majestee ave fausse French enough to deceive de most sage demoiselle dat is en France.

KING HENRY Now, fie upon my false French! By mine honor in true English, I love thee, Kate; by which honor I dare not swear thou lovest me; yet my blood begins to flatter me that thou dost, notwithstanding the poor and
218 untempering effect of my visage. Now beshrew my father's ambition! He was thinking of civil wars when he got me; therefore was I created with a stubborn outside, with an aspect of iron, that when I come to woo ladies, I fright them. But in faith, Kate, the elder I wax the better I shall appear. My comfort is that old age, that ill layer-up of beauty, can do no more spoil upon my face. Thou hast me, if thou hast me, at the worst; and thou shalt wear me, if thou wear me, better and better; and therefore tell me, most fair Katherine, will you have me? Put off your maiden blushes; avouch the thoughts of your heart with the looks of an empress; take me by the hand, and say, 'Harry of England, I am thine!' which word thou shalt no sooner bless mine ear withal but I will tell thee aloud, 'England is thine, Ireland is thine, France is thine, and Henry Plantagenet is thine';
234 who, though I speak it before his face, if he be not fellow with the best king, thou shalt find the best king of good fellows. Come, your answer in broken music! for thy voice is music and thy English broken; therefore, queen of all, Katherine, break thy mind to me in broken English. Wilt thou have me?

239 KATHERINE Dat is as it sall please de roi mon père.

KING HENRY Nay, it will please him well, Kate; it shall please him, Kate.

KATHERINE Den it sall also content me.

KING HENRY Upon that I kiss your hand and I call you my queen.

KATHERINE Laissez, mon seigneur, laissez, laissez! Ma 24 foi, je ne veux point que vous abaissiez vostre grandeur en baisant le main d'une de vostre seigneurie indigne serviteur. Excusez-moi, je vous supplie, mon très-puissant seigneur.

KING HENRY Then I will kiss your lips, Kate.

KATHERINE Les dames et demoiselles pour estre baisée devant leur nopces, il n'est pas la coutume de France.

KING HENRY Madam my interpreter, what says she?

ALICE Dat it is not be de fashon pour le ladies of France – I cannot tell wat is 'baiser' en Anglish.

KING HENRY To kiss.

ALICE Your majestee entendre bettre que moi. 25

KING HENRY It is not a fashion for the maids in France to kiss before they are married, would she say?

ALICE Oui, vraiment.

KING HENRY O Kate, nice customs curtsy to great kings. Dear Kate, you and I cannot be confined within the weak list of a country's fashion. We are the makers of 26 manners, Kate; and the liberty that follows our places 26 stops the mouth of all findfaults, as I will do yours for upholding the nice fashion of your country in denying 26 me a kiss. Therefore patiently, and yielding. [Kisses her.] You have witchcraft in your lips, Kate. There is more eloquence in a sugar touch of them than in the tongues of the French Council, and they should sooner persuade Harry of England than a general petition of monarchs. Here comes your father.

*Enter the French Power and the English Lords.*

BURGUNDY God save your majesty! My royal cousin, teach you our princess English?

KING HENRY I would have her learn, my fair cousin, how perfectly I love her, and that is good English.

BURGUNDY Is she not apt?

KING HENRY Our tongue is rough, coz, and my condi- 27 tion is not smooth; so that, having neither the voice nor the heart of flattery about me, I cannot so conjure up the spirit of love in her that he will appear in his true likeness.

BURGUNDY Pardon the frankness of my mirth if I answer you for that. If you would conjure in her, you must make a circle; if conjure up love in her in his true likeness, he must appear naked and blind. Can you blame her then, 28 being a maid yet rosed over with the virgin crimson of modesty, if she deny the appearance of a naked blind boy in her naked seeing self? It were, my lord, a hard condition for a maid to consign to. 28

KING HENRY Yet they do wink and yield, as love is blind 28 and enforces.

BURGUNDY They are then excused, my lord, when they see not what they do.

184-85 *Sauf ... parle* save your honor, the French you speak is better than the English I speak   193 *closet* private room   199 *scambling* scrambling for possessions, snatching   209 *moiety* half   210-11 *la ... déesse* the most beautiful Katherine of the world, my very dear and divine goddess   218 *untempering* unpropitiating   234-35 *fellow with* equal to   239 *de ... père* the king my father   245-49 *Laissez ... seigneur* desist, my lord, desist, desist! My faith, I do not wish you to lower your dignity by kissing the hand of your lordship's unworthy servant. Excuse me, I pray you, my all-powerful lord   256 *entendre* understands   262 *list* barrier   263 *follows our places* attends our rank   265 *nice* fastidious   277 *condition* personality   284 *blind* (1) sightless, (2) reckless, brutal   288 *consign* consent   289 *wink* shut eyes

KING HENRY  Then, good my lord, teach your cousin to
consent winking.
BURGUNDY  I will wink on her to consent, my lord, if you
will teach her to know my meaning; for maids well summered and warm kept are like flies at Bartholomew-tide,
blind, though they have their eyes; and then they will
endure handling which before would not abide looking
on.
KING HENRY  This moral ties me over to time and a hot
summer; and so I shall catch the fly, your cousin, in the
latter end, and she must be blind too.
BURGUNDY  As love is, my lord, before it loves.
KING HENRY  It is so; and you may, some of you, thank
love for my blindness, who cannot see many a fair
French city for one fair French maid that stands in my
way.
FRANCE  Yes, my lord, you see them perspectively, the
cities turned into a maid; for they are all girdled with
maiden walls that war hath never entered.
KING HENRY  Shall Kate be my wife?
FRANCE  So please you.
KING HENRY  I am content, so the maiden cities you talk
of may wait on her. So the maid that stood in the way for
my wish shall show me the way to my will.
FRANCE
  We have consented to all terms of reason.
KING HENRY
  Is't so, my lords of England?
WESTMORELAND
  The king hath granted every article:
  His daughter first; and in sequel all,
  According to their firm proposèd natures.
EXETER  Only he hath not yet subscribèd this: Where
your majesty demands that the King of France, having
any occasion to write for matter of grant, shall name
your highness in this form and with this addition, in
French, 'Nostre très-cher fils Henri, Roi d'Angleterre,
Héritier de France'; and thus in Latin, 'Praeclarissi-
mus filius noster Henricus, Rex Angliae et Haeres
Franciae.'
FRANCE
  Nor this I have not, brother, so denied
  But your request shall make me let it pass.

KING HENRY
  I pray you then, in love and dear alliance,
  Let that one article rank with the rest,
  And thereupon give me your daughter.
FRANCE
  Take her, fair son, and from her blood raise up
  Issue to me, that the contending kingdoms
  Of France and England, whose very shores look pale    334
  With envy of each other's happiness,
  May cease their hatred, and this dear conjunction
  Plant neighborhood and Christian-like accord
  In their sweet bosoms, that never war advance
  His bleeding sword 'twixt England and fair France.
LORDS  Amen!
KING HENRY
  Now, welcome, Kate; and bear me witness all
  That here I kiss her as my sovereign queen.
      *Flourish.*
QUEEN
  God, the best maker of all marriages,
  Combine your hearts in one, your realms in one!
  As man and wife, being two, are one in love,
  So be there 'twixt your kingdoms such a spousal
  That never may ill office, or fell jealousy,           347
  Which troubles oft the bed of blessèd marriage,
  Thrust in between the paction of these kingdoms        349
  To make divorce of their incorporate league;
  That English may as French, French Englishmen,
  Receive each other! God speak this Amen!
ALL  Amen!
KING HENRY
  Prepare we for our marriage; on which day,
  My Lord of Burgundy, we'll take your oath,
  And all the peers', for surety of our leagues.
  Then shall I swear to Kate, and you to me,
  And may our oaths well kept and prosp'rous be!
                        *Sennet. Exeunt.*

---

*Enter Chorus [as Epilogue].*                            Epi.
Thus far, with rough and all-unable pen,
    Our bending author hath pursued the story,           2
In little room confining mighty men,
    Mangling by starts the full course of their glory.   4
Small time; but in that small most greatly lived
    This Star of England. Fortune made his sword,
By which the world's best garden he achieved,            7
    And of it left his son imperial lord.
Henry the Sixth, in infant bands crowned King            9
    Of France and England, did this king succeed;
Whose state so many had the managing
    That they lost France and made his England bleed:
Which oft our stage hath shown; and for their sake,      13
In your fair minds let this acceptance take.             14

---

296 *well summered* i.e. carefully nurtured  297 *like . . . Bartholomew-tide*
i.e. sluggish in the heat of summer  307 *perspectively* i.e. through an
optic glass (which multiplies images)  313 *wait on her* i.e. come with
her as a dowry  319 *firm . . . natures* strict stipulations  323–26 *Nostre . . .
France*; . . . *Praeclarissimus . . . Franciae* our dear son Henry, King of
England and heir of France  334 *look pale* i.e. with their chalk cliffs  347
*ill office* evil dealing  349 *paction* pact
Epi.  2 *bending* bowing, humble  4 *Mangling by starts* misrepresenting in
fragments  7 *best garden* i.e. France (cf. V, ii, 36)  9 *infant bands* swaddling
clothes  13 *for their sake* i.e. inasmuch as they have pleased you  14 *this*
this play

The 1600 quarto of *Henry V*, although twice reprinted, presents a curtailed and corrupt version of the play, probably obtained by memorial reconstruction of the original. It is sometimes maintained that the actors playing the parts of Exeter and Gower were the chief agents in this reconstruction, since the portions of the play where they are on stage are somewhat more accurately preserved than the rest. The quarto is useful in supplying an occasional line or reading in instances where the folio text is clearly defective. The folio text, although reliable in the main, is marred by a number of misprints and a somewhat capricious division into acts. The first act corresponds to acts I and II in modern editions, the second to III, the third to the first six scenes of IV, the fourth to the remainder of IV, and the fifth to V. The modern division is based on the position of the four internal speeches by the Chorus. The logic of this solution may be more apparent than real, since it substitutes for the inordinately long first "act" of the folio the inordinately long fourth "act" of modern editions. It is possible that the choruses were originally no more than a narrative convenience, their number formally insignificant.

In the present edition, there is a minimum of departure from the folio text except for the usual modernization of spelling and punctuation, the normalization of speech-prefixes, and occasional relineation. (In the folio, Pistol's speeches are printed in prose, apparently because his thumping iambics appear in the midst of the prose dialogue of his comic associates.) Such proper names as "Dauphin," "Burgundy," "Calais," "Harfleur," etc. have been consistently substituted for the original "Dolphin," "Burgonie" (or "Burgogne"), "Callice," "Harflew," etc. Fluellen's Welsh dialect has been normalized by the consistent use of "orld" for "world," "Cheshu" for "Jesu," and "p" for initial "b" in stressed syllables. However, Macmorris' "sh" for "s" is allowed to remain intermittent.

Contrary to general practice in modern editions of this play, the passages in French are no more extensively modified than the passages in English. Archaic and familiar grammatical forms, as well as errors in grammar and idiom, have been retained. The advantage of this kind of fidelity to the copy-text is that more of the original quality and flavour of Shakespeare's French is preserved than is possible when modern copybook correctness is substituted, and, in one instance (IV, ii, 2–6), an original meaning is restored. After expending much effort upon my attempt to restore Princess Katherine's English lesson (III, iv) to its Shakespearean form, I found that I had been anticipated in most details by Nikolaus Delius.

The following is a complete list of all substantive departures from the text of the folio of 1623 (F). The adopted readings in italics from the quarto of 1600 (Q) and from the later folios and the editors are followed by the folio readings in roman.

I, ii, 38 *succedant* (F2) succedaul  45, 52 *Elbe* (Capell) Elue  74 *Lingard* (Sisson) Lingare  82 *Ermengard* (Sisson) Ermengare  94 *imbar* (F3) imbarre  131 *blood* (F3) Bloods  163 *her* (Capell) their  209 *many several* (Q) many  213 *End* (Q) And

II, i, 22 *mare* (Q) name  26 *How . . . Pistol* (joined in F to preceding speech by Bardolph; assigned in Q to Nym)  39, 40 *Iceland* (Steevens) Island  68 *Coupe la* (Dyce) Couple a  69 *thee defy* (Q) defie thee  76 *enough.* (Pope) enough to  79 *you,* (Hanmer) your  101–02 *I . . . betting* (Q) Omitted  112 *that's* (Q) that  114 *Ah* (Pope) A

II, ii, 75 *hath* (Q) have  87 *furnish him* (F2) furnish  108 *whoop* (Theobald) hoope  114 *All* (Hanmer) And  122 *lion gait* (Capell) Lyon-gate  139 *mark the* (Malone) make thee  147 *Henry* (Q) Thomas  148 *Masham* (Rowe) Marsham  159 *Which I* (F2) which  176 *have sought* (Q) sought

II, iii, 3, 6 *earn* (Camb.) erne  16 *'a babbled* (Theobald) a Table  24 *upward and upward* (Q) vp-peer'd and vpward  44 *word* (Q) world

II, iv, 68 *followed* (Pope) followèd  79 *borrowed* (Pope) borrowèd  107 *privèd* (Walter) privy  109 *swallowed* (Pope) swallowèd  134 *difference* (Camb.) diff'rence

III, Cho., 4 *Hampton* (Theobald) Dover  6 *fanning* (Rowe) fayning  12 *furrowed* (Rowe) furrowèd

III, i, 7 *summon* (Rowe) commune  17 *noble* (Malone) noblish  24 *men* (F4) me  32 *Straining* (Rowe) Straying

III, ii, 15 *hie* (Q) high  18 *preach* (Hanmer, as also for some similar normalizations of Welsh accent following) breach  58, 127 *petter* better  64, 74 *orld* world  65 *peard* beard  100 *trompet* trumpet  106 *ay'll lig* (Camb.) Ile ligge  107 *ay'll* (Camb.) Ile  120 *poth* both  121 *pirth* birth  129 *pold* bold

III, iii, 16 *Arrayed* (Pope) Arrayèd  32 *heady* (F2) headly  35 *Defile* (Rowe) Desire

III, iv, 2 *parles* (Warburton) parlas  4 *enseigner* (F2) ensigniez  *j'apprends* (This ed.) ie apprend  6, 17, 24 *est* (F2) &  7 *Et les doigts* (misplaced in a separate speech given to *Alice* in F; corrected by Theobald) *Et les* (Capell) E le  8 *Alice* (Theobald) Kat  *Les* (Capell) Le  *les* (Capell) e  9 *souviendrai* (F2) souemeray  11 *Katherine* (Theobald) Alice (F, with proper assignment to Katherine restored at *j'ai gagné*)  *de fingres* (Capell) le Fingres  11, 13 *les* (Capell) le  14 *Les* (F2) Le  20 *Et le* (F2) E de  36 *la* (F2) de  38 *N'avez-vous pas* (F2) N'ave vos y  *déjà* (Warburton) desia  40 *Non* (Warburton) Nome  44 *Sauf* (Rowe) Sans  45 *dis-je* (F2) de ie  46 *le* (Capell) les  *la* (Capell) de  *robe* (Rowe) roba  47, 48 *De . . . de* (Capell) Le . . . le  50 *les* (F2) le  51 *ces* (F2) ce  *les* (F2) le  52 *Foh!* (Camb.) fo  *de* (Capell) le  53 *Néantmoins* (F2) neant moys  55 *de count* (Warburton) le count

III, v, 7 *scions* (Var., 1803) Syens  11 *de* (F2) du  43 *Vaudemont* (F2) Vandemont  45 *Foix* (Capell) Loys  46 *knights* (Theobald conj.; Pope) Kings

III, vi, 4, 11 *pridge* Bridge  10 *plessed* blessed  10, 15, 82 *orld* world  30, 31 *plind* blind  30 *her* (Q) his  53 *prother* Brother  98 *Pardolph* Bardolph  100 *plows* blows  108 *lenity* (Q) Leuitie

III, vii, 12 *pasterns* (F2) postures  *Ça* (Theobald) ch'  57 *lief* (Capell) liue  62 *vomissement* (F2) vemissement  63 *et la truie* (Rowe) est la leuye

IV, Cho., 16 *name* (Tyrwhitt conj.; Steevens) nam'd  20 *cripple* (Theobald) creeple –  27 *Presenteth* (Hanmer) Presented

IV, i, 3 *Good* (F3) God  65 *Cheshu* Jesu  66 *orld* world  71 *pabble* babble  91 *Thomas* (Theobald) John  231 *What is* (Knight) What? is  *adoration* (F2) Odoration  239 *Think'st* (Rowe) Thinks  261 *Hyperion* (F2) Hiperio  277 *if* (Tyrwhitt conj.; Steevens) of  282 *bestowed* (Pope) bestowèd

IV, ii, 4 *eaux* (Theobald) ewes  5 *les* (This ed.) le  6 *Cieux* (Munro, as 'cieu') Cien  11 *dout* (Rowe) doubt  25 *'gainst* (F2) against  49 *gimmaled* (Delius) Iymold

IV, iii, 13–14 *And . . . valor* (after l. 11 in F; correction by Theobald supported by Q)  48 *And . . . day* (Q) Omitted  59 *rememberèd* (Rowe) rememb'red  99 *buried* (Eds.) buryèd

IV, iv, 12 *pitié* (F2) pitez  14 *Or* (Hanmer) For  34 *de* (F2) a  *faites* (Malone) faite  37 *cuppe le* (This ed.) cuppele  39 *O'er-* (This ed.) Or  51 *néantmoins* (F2) neant-mons  52 *l'avez promis* (Malone) layt a promets  55 *remercîmens* (F2) remercious  *j'ai tombé* (This ed.) Je intombe  57 *distingué* (Capell) distinie  65 *Suivez* (Rowe) Saaue

IV, v, 2 *perdu . . . est perdu* (Rowe) perdia . . . et perdie  3 *Mort de* (Rowe) Mor Dieu  12 *honor* (Q) Omitted  16 *by a slave* (Q) a base slave  24 *Exeunt* (Eds.) Exit

IV, vi, 15 *And* (Q) He  34 *mistful* (Theobald) mixtful

IV, vii, 24, 28 *poth* both   44 *pelly* belly   73 *the* (Capell) with   96 *padge* badge   106 *Cheshu* Jeshu   110 *God* (F3) Good   119 '*a live* (Capell) aliue   134 *plack* blacke

IV, viii, 10, 41 *orld* world   32 *peggarly* beggarly   58 *pelly* belly   61 *petter* better   94 *Foix* (Capell) Foyes   108 *we* (F2) me

V, i, 5 *peggarly* beggarly   6 *orld* world   9 *pid* bid   10 *preed* breed   11 *pold* bold   20 *beseech* peseech   37 *Pite* Bite   49 *proken* broken   81 *swear* (F3) swore

V, ii, 12 *England* (F2) Ireland   45 *fumitory* (F4) Femetary   50 *all* (Rowe) withall   77 *cursitory* (Wilson) curselarie   185 *est* (Pope) & *meilleur* (Hanmer) melius   246 *abaissiez* (Johnson) abbaise *grandeur* (F2) grandeus   247 *de vostre* (Camb.) nostre *seigneurie* (Camb.) Seigneur   252 *coutume* (Rowe) costume   255 *baiser* (Hanmer) buisse   259 *vraiment* (Hanmer) verayment   309 *never* (Rowe) Omitted   324 *Héritier* (Rowe) Heretere   349 *paction* (Theobald) Pation

# THE LIFE OF KING HENRY THE EIGHTH

## INTRODUCTION

There can be few serious students of Shakespeare who have not sometimes felt that possibly the hardest problem involved in their study is that which requires for its solution some reasonable and acceptable theory as to the play of *King Henry VIII*. None such has ever yet been offered....

If the situation can be said to have changed since Swinburne wrote these words over eighty years ago, it is only because it has become still more common than in his day for scholars to express their disappointment, or even to condemn the play outright. "Less interesting than any other in the Folio" and "Shakespeare has lost the impulse which gave his final stories their mellow power" are typical judgments by contemporary Shakespeareans. Those who have attempted a defense of the play as worthy of Shakespeare have but a small following.

At first thought this might seem curious considering that the play has fared quite well on the stage. Producers of almost every generation have been attracted by its color and pageantry, of which indeed *Henry VIII* has more to offer than many of Shakespeare's plays. Betterton's productions at the end of the seventeenth century were applauded for their "magnificence." In a mid-eighteenth-century staging, over 130 figures participated in the procession of IV, i. In the nineteenth century Kean employed a moving panorama of London, and a real barge in which Buckingham made his exit in II, i. Even more lavish was the coronation scene in Henry Irving's production near the end of the century; and if in modern productions there is greater reluctance to spend vast sums of money on merely pictorial or spectacular effects, one nevertheless remembers them, especially Tyrone Guthrie's, for their handling of large numbers of people on the stage and their ceremonial color.

The actors have likewise been tempted by the play's great roles. Readers may be disappointed with the character of Henry, but actors have liked impersonating a living Holbein portrait of the King, who seems as cheerful and healthy and young at the play's end as he was at the beginning, whatever has happened to Buckingham, Katherine, Wolsey, or his own troubled conscience. We all know that he will continue to tread over corpses, but mind little because it is all past history. Buckingham's role is hardly more than that of prologue, but he becomes sufficiently attractive in the opening scene for the audience to remain hushed during his farewell speech in II, i: the young, frank, congenial nobleman has been slandered, it is all so unjust, and how manly, how noble his forgiving spirit! But it is naturally the richer parts of Wolsey and Katherine that have drawn actors and actresses, from Kemble and Mrs Siddons to Irving and Ellen Terry and, in more recent times, Lewis Casson and Sibyl Thorndike. Owing

largely to the influence of these and other actors, certain set speeches and passages of dialogue from *Henry VIII* were, until recently at least, among the most widely quoted of Shakespeare's. Fifty years ago, one could hardly imagine a Shakespearean recital which did not include Wolsey's leave-taking from Cromwell in III, ii. "Scenes from Shakespeare" presented by some pair of travelling actors would inevitably include Katherine's trial, II, iv.

Why then such disenchantment with the play? Here are some of the criticisms frequently made: the play may lend itself to impressive pageantry but it is not great drama; it may contain famous speeches but most of the verse is smoothly languid rather than breathtakingly Shakespearean; we are gripped intensely by only a few scenes: dramatic tension is aroused only episodically; after the fall of the most developed and interesting characters, Katherine and Wolsey, there is only sentimentality and anticlimax; the quarrel between Cranmer and Gardiner in the final act fails to excite us because our interest in these characters has not been aroused before, and they are pale shadows after Katherine and Wolsey. The play, as one critic put it, "falls utterly away, and leaves us in the last act among persons we scarcely know, and events for which we do not care." So the complaints run. Some readers even feel morally outraged that a play which dwells so long on the tribulations of Katherine should end in a celebration of events which were only made possible by the injustice done to her. And some do not hesitate to state that they would have preferred a tragedy ending on the execution of Anne, or a historical treatment showing how Henry's personal difficulties with Katherine led to England's adopting the Protestant cause. But if the events dramatized in the play bear any relation to the Reformation, Shakespeare did his best to avoid saying so.

Against such strictures only one kind of defense of the play is possible, other than insistence upon its appeal in a good performance – namely, in terms of a purpose and dramatic form that are usually misunderstood or overlooked. But let us first deal with some facts and fancies: when it was written and when first staged, how it fits into the Shakespeare canon, and whether indeed Shakespeare should be held totally responsible for the play as we have it.

Scholars are agreed that *Henry VIII* was composed very late in Shakespeare's career and first produced in 1613. It was probably written last of all the plays included in the first folio. Originally, Shakespeare and his company may well have planned to present the play first at Whitehall during the wedding ceremonies of the Elector Palatine and Princess Elizabeth in February, 1613. The Princess often made people think of her great namesake of recent memory

– Queen Elizabeth had died only ten years before. Several passages of the play's fifth act would have fitted the occasion admirably. But the list of plays we actually know to have been presented then does not include *Henry VIII*, and it appears more probable that it was first produced at the Globe on the fateful day of June 29, 1613, when the discharge of the chambers in I, iv set the thatch of the roof on fire. Within an hour the stately building had burnt to the ground. The event was sufficient news to be given a paragraph in more than one letter of state. There was no loss of life; "nothing did perish, but a few forsaken Cloaks," according to one correspondent; presumably he did not enquire about the prompt-books or other manuscripts of the King's Men.

Is *Henry VIII* then Shakespeare's last play? If the answer were a simple yes, the implications would be challenging. But there is a rub, a complication at both ends. There is a stubborn tradition that Prospero's Epilogue in *The Tempest* represents Shakespeare's final leavetaking of his art. And in at least two recent books on Shakespeare's last plays, *Henry VIII* is virtually ignored. On the other hand we know that Shakespeare had a share, with Fletcher as the other author, in a play probably written later than *Henry VIII*, *The Two Noble Kinsmen*, and perhaps also in the lost *Cardenio*. If we primarily link *Henry VIII* to *The Winter's Tale* and *The Tempest*, plays of Shakespeare's sole authorship, then we must regard it as his last major work. But perhaps, like *The Two Noble Kinsmen*, *Henry VIII* is of divided authorship?

This has indeed been a widely held view for over a hundred years. We may place the ultimate blame – or credit – for it on the poet Tennyson, about whose sensitivity to style and rhythm, and training in the technicalities of metre, there can be little question. Tennyson intimated to his friends that the verse of large parts of *Henry VIII* seemed to him much more like Fletcher's than like Shakespeare's. James Spedding, the famous editor of Bacon, took the hint, and in 1850 published a paper which has become a classic. In an eloquent scene-by-scene examination of the style, he argued the view that only certain scenes, namely I, i-ii, II, iii-iv, III, ii (up to line 203), and V, i are by Shakespeare, and the rest by Fletcher. In the "Shakespearean" scenes, Spedding found a style similar to that of Shakespeare's other late work, thick with imagery, highly involved, remarkably free in metre, and almost careless in syntax, while the other scenes show a small "proportion of thought and fancy to words and images." He further found that in the "Fletcherian" scenes the frequency of end-stopped lines and of weak endings or redundant syllables at the end of lines – lines of 11 or even 12 syllables are indeed frequent in this play – is similar to that of *Valentinian* and other Fletcher plays, while in the "Shakespearean" scenes the proportion is quite different. To cap the whole matter, Samuel Hickson independently arrived in the same year at essentially the same conclusions. Consternation was great, especially since, according to the division, all the great speeches for which the play has become famous, except for Katherine's defense in II, iv, were here attributed to Fletcher. Yet one lonely voice apart, Swinburne's, the position remained practically unchallenged until 1930, and the voices echoing Spedding are still numerous and strong.

Spedding's thesis has since been supported with a great wealth of statistical analysis of several aspects of the play's language. Here there is room only to tell those who are skeptical in principle of the value of such statistics that the cumulative detail of the assembled evidence is more impressive than similar evidence for perhaps any other Elizabethan or Jacobean drama of doubtful authorship; that the best of the scholars participating in the debate have been impelled, as was Spedding, by a general sense of incongruity of style; and that any careful reader of the play who is sensitive to style will be bound to notice this incongruity, even if he does not necessarily wish to draw Spedding's conclusions. Let him read only the first two scenes and then continue with the third, or read II, ii after I, ii – scenes which provide a better standard of comparison, for they both include Wolsey and the King. In style the play's opening scenes remind one much of *Cymbeline* or of the first acts of *The Winter's Tale*, in their knottiness, their involutions, and, as not always acknowledged, their sometimes downright carelessness in syntax (dangling clauses beginning with *that*) and in development of imagery (see I, i, 224–26): it is as if a brilliant artist had dashed the lines down. In the "Fletcherian" scenes, on the other hand, the style is consistently clear and never careless; it also seems very competent rather than brilliant, lacking in the spark of Shakespeare.

Yet scholarly caution is in order. It seems all too convenient to place the blame for the play's weaknesses on Fletcher's shoulders, or those of a presumed imperfect partnership of the two dramatists. One needs to remember that *Henry VIII* is in the first folio, while *The Two Noble Kinsmen* is not, and that there are no other external data; that hardly anyone thought of Fletcher in connection with *Henry VIII* before the middle of the last century; that stylistic comparison with Fletcher's other plays may not be wholly trustworthy because Fletcher wrote no other history play in the least like *Henry VIII*; that Fletcher's plays provide us with plenty of evidence of the enormous influence on him of Shakespeare, while, from 1608 on at least, Shakespeare was probably somewhat influenced by his able junior. Further, one may ask whether two collaborating playwrights would be likely to divide up their share of work in the manner Spedding's division of scenes suggests. We know that the collaboration between Lady Gregory and Yeats operated in a quite different manner, and however Jonson, Marston, and Chapman divided up their labors for *Eastward Ho!*, it can hardly have been by scene. Finally, some readers well acquainted with Fletcher's work have asked themselves whether he indeed could have written the speech of Buckingham's farewell, which has all the superficial characteristics of Fletcher's style; to quote Swinburne:

Here is the same smooth and fluent declamation, the same prolonged and persistent melody, which if not monotonous is certainly not various; the same pure, lucid, perspicuous flow of simple rather than strong and elegant rather than exquisite English; and yet . . . I cannot but think that we shall perceive in it a comparative severity and elevation which will be missed when we turn back from it to the text of Fletcher. There is an aptness of phrase, an abstinence from excess, a "plentiful lack" of mere flowery and superfluous beauties, which we may rather wish than hope to find in the most famous of Shakespeare's successors.

One will either agree with this comment or not: there is no basis for argument. A better case against Fletcher's authorship can perhaps be made for the death-scene of Katherine, IV, ii, upon which Dr Johnson bestowed the highest praise, and which has been called "the glory of the play." One thinks especially of the Queen's last moment of resurgence when she firmly rebukes the Messenger : "You are a saucy fellow ; / Deserve we no more reverence ?" That even in her great weakness, near death, and in her humility, Katherine should so insist on her queenly dignity and its proper due, is indeed a very Shakespearean touch. One recalls Imogen's "But clay and clay differs in dignity, / Whose dust is both alike." And, no less important, the development of the entire scene seems natural, without the least sense of the artificially contrived which, in Fletcher's plays, is so rarely absent.

But let us leave this debate and boldly assume that Shakespeare at least thought of *Henry VIII* as his concluding work – he did at least write those scenes which introduce the major characters – and then ask whether we can discern significant relations to his other work. And of course two groups are bound to spring to mind : his earlier English history plays and the Romances. Like the former, *Henry VIII* is an English chronicle play, and if one considers the period of history which Shakespeare dramatized in his two historical tetralogies, from *Henry VI* to *Richard III*, and from *Richard II* to *Henry V*, then indeed *Henry VIII* looks like the completion of a pattern. It brings relevant modern English history up to the birth of England's golden Queen, and in Cranmer's final prophecy includes even a clear allusion to James I, the contemporary Stuart king. We are not exactly saying that Shakespeare thought of *Henry VIII* as in a sense completing his dramatic *epic* on English history – in that case he might indeed be blamed for making his last play too undramatic – but are implying that the play's final act may have been extremely important to him, and that Shakespeare perhaps did not mind if the play's chronicle structure was as loose as that of his earliest history plays. Indeed there are signs in Shakespeare's late work that his mind sometimes wandered back to his earliest artistic preoccupations – from *The Tempest*, for instance, to *The Comedy of Errors*.

The other significant connection is with the Romances. We have already pointed to similarities of style, at least in the "Shakespearean" scenes. Another characteristic feature of *Henry VIII*, the use of narrative rather than dramatic technique in several scenes, also reminds one of the Romances. Several times in *Henry VIII*, noblemen or gentlemen recall events which have taken place off stage, for the audience's benefit, somewhat in the manner of the last scene but one of *The Winter's Tale*. The large time-span in the Romances, *Henry VIII*, and some other chronicle plays encourages the use of narrative techniques. Striking also is the dramatist's greater than customary readiness to employ spectacular stage devices, supernatural and other colorful effects, of which the most pertinent examples are the theophanies in the Romances and Katherine's vision in IV, ii (cf. Posthumus' vision in *Cymbeline* and the appearance of Diana in *Pericles*). The scene of Katherine's trial does not merely remind one generally of Hermione's trial in *The Winter's Tale* but resembles that earlier scene in much detail. But perhaps the most significant similarity may be seen in the general pattern of the action of the Romances and *Henry VIII*, which moves from a series of misfortunes and tragic events to a conclusion of joy and promise.

If indeed there is a meaningful relation in *Henry VIII* between the sufferings of Buckingham, Katherine, and Wolsey in the early acts, and the joyful ending, one of the most common interpretations of the play must be wrong : that the first three or four acts are like a morality play in which three noble and proud characters undergo a sudden fall from fortune, become conscious of the "Vain pomp and glory of this world" (III, ii, 365), and learn how to endure their tribulations with patience and how to forgive their enemies, with the final act merely tagged on. But we will misunderstand the play if we concentrate only on Buckingham, Katherine, and Wolsey, even if the play's Prologue may encourage us to do just that. Granted that Anne Bullen's role is remarkably undeveloped, the three scenes in which she is given a part perform a function in the play's developing design. Of these the first, I, iv, the banquet at Wolsey's house where the masked Henry is attracted by Anne's youthful beauty, is certainly gay in mood. What is striking is that here the dramatist consciously departed from his sources – mainly Holinshed – for he placed an episode which occurred only in 1527 immediately before the scene of Buckingham's (reported) trial and execution, events which had occurred five years earlier. The contrast in mood between the two scenes was surely designed. When next we encounter Anne with the Old Lady in II, iii, she appears attractive in the sympathy she voices for Katherine, though it must dawn on her that she herself is on the way to becoming queen. The banter with the Old Lady on "queen" and "quean" is interrupted by the announcement of her elevation to Marchioness of Pembroke. This scene precedes that of the trial which leads to the unqueening of Katherine. Anne's next scene, IV, i, is that of her coronation. There she does not speak a single word but unquestionably becomes the centre of interest. The Third Gentleman reports how she sat down

> In a rich chair of state, opposing freely
> The beauty of her person to the people.
> Believe me, sir, she is the goodliest woman
> That every lay by man ; which when the people
> Had the full view of, such a noise arose
> As the shrouds make at sea in a stiff tempest,
> As loud, and to as many tunes. Hats, cloaks
> (Doublets, I think) flew up ; and had their faces
> Been loose, this day they had been lost. Such joy
> I never saw before.          (IV, i, 67–76)

Such a scene has no place in the fourth act of a morality play. A little before, the other two Gentlemen had lamented the fate of Katherine Dowager – "she was removed to Kimbolton, / Where she remains now sick" – but were interrupted in their musings by the hautboys and flourish of trumpets announcing the "order" of the coronation, which then passed in all its royal color over the stage. Katherine is momentarily forgotten. But in the next scene we meet her once more, for the last time, and hear of Wolsey's death. Again Shakespeare changed the order of history : for Holinshed and other historians had written that Wolsey died three years before the divorce and Anne's coronation. And again the change was made for the sake of an evolving dramatic pattern.

The famous Anne Bullen of history appears surprisingly little on the stage in *Henry VIII*, but the scenes in which she does enter, strategically placed as they are, and with the facts of history adjusted as we have noted, afford a hint of the mood of the play's ending. In the final act she herself does not appear; we need only the birth of her daughter Elizabeth and Cranmer's prophecy. And naturally we are given no intimation of what was to follow soon after in history : a stillborn male child and Anne's execution.

The presentation of Cranmer is perhaps less satisfactory. But we must remember that Shakespeare's contemporaries looked upon Cranmer as the founder of their own church, the Church of England. For his role in the final scenes we are prepared, though insufficiently, by the King's remarks at the very moment when Wolsey begins to fall out of favor (II, iv, 233–38). The quarrel between Gardiner and Cranmer drives home the contrast between the new archbishop and the old, and also shows the King for the first time actively exercising justice – early in the play he had leaned on the Cardinal's shoulders. Again, the change befits the mood of the play's ending, even if it does not quite fit the facts of history. The earlier acts showed Henry as a singularly neutral figure, developed in such a way as hardly to encourage us to blame him for the events. Absorbed as we were by Buckingham first, and then by Katherine and Wolsey, we neither sympathized with nor were very critical of Henry. But now in the fifth act he takes active command of his kingdom, and on the side of justice ; and then he becomes the father of Elizabeth – the Elizabeth of England's golden age.

A Christian note sounds more strongly through *Henry VIII* than in any other of Shakespeare's plays – at least it receives more overt expression. It is heard first in the forgiving words of Buckingham's farewell, then very clearly in Wolsey's conversion after his fall :

> I feel within me
> A peace above all earthly dignities,
> A still and quiet conscience.  (III, ii, 378–80)

The recollection of his "virtue" strengthens Katherine in her mood of patient forgiveness and acceptance in IV, ii, but even more striking in this scene is Katherine's vision, which assures us that she will find happiness and peace in heaven. In the last act we are first made to see Cranmer's Christian humility, and then listen to his prophecy. There, of course, we are meant to feel that God is speaking through Cranmer ; and we may not be wrong to remember those prophecies of Shakespeare's earlier history plays which brought upon England the series of tribulations that furnish the main material of these plays, and of which there are still some in *Henry VIII* ; only that at the end we are shown justice and reconciliation, and hear the promise of a great queen followed by a peaceful reign under James.

If this was the intent of the play, Shakespeare, or Shakespeare with Fletcher, may not have completely succeeded, as indeed the reaction of so many of its readers would appear to suggest. But one can then see the work as a final bold experiment in writing a new kind of English history

play in which some of the themes and devices and even the symbolism of the Romances would be put to new use. The play would also conclude the pattern begun in the early histories by extending the view to the birth of Queen Elizabeth, in a sense even to 1613.

*Victoria College*                    F. David Hoeniger
*University of Toronto*

## NOTE ON THE TEXT

*Henry VIII* was first printed in the folio of 1623, in a good text set up from what modern textual scholars believe to have been a fair scribal copy of the author's manuscript. The general nature and elaboration of the stage directions and the considerable variation in speech-prefixes suggest author's manuscript rather than theatrical prompt-copy, but the relative absence in the folio text of known unusual Shakespearean spellings suggests scribal copy rather than direct original. The folio text is divided into acts and scenes, and this division was followed by later editors except that the folio V, ii, was divided into ii and iii and the remaining scenes were renumbered as in the division provided marginally for reference in the present edition. The folio is least trustworthy in matters of punctuation. In general its errors, relatively few, appear to have derived from either the scribe or the compositors. The present edition follows the folio text closely. All substantive departures from it are listed below, with the adopted reading in italics followed by the folio reading in roman :

I, i, 42–47 *All . . . together* (assigned to Buckingham in F)  63 *web, 'a* Web. O  69–70 *that? | . . . hell the* that, | . . . Hell? The  79–80 *council out, | . . . in he* Councell, out | . . . in, he  96 *Bordeaux* Burdeux  120 *venom-mouthed* venom'd–mouth'd  123 *chafed* chaff'd  200 *Hereford* Hertford  219 *Perk* Pecke *chancellor* Councellour  221 *Nicholas* Michaell

I, ii, 67 *business* basenesse  156 *feared* feare  164 *confession's* Commissions  170 *To win the* To the ('win' appearing in source)  180 *To* For this to  190 *Bulmer* Blumer  191 *time.* Being time, being

I, iii, 59 *wherewithal. In him* wherewithall in him ;

II, i, 18 *have* him  20 *Perk* Pecke  86 *mark* make

II, iii, 14 *quarrel, fortune, do* quarrel. Fortune, do  32 *cheveril* Chiverell  59 *note's* notes  61 *of you, and* of you, to you ; and

II, iv, 131 *Exeunt* Exit  172 *A* And  197 *throe* throw  217 *summons. Unsolicited* Summons unsolicited

III, i, 23 s.d. *Campeius* Campian  61 *your* our  83 *profit. Can profit* can  124 *accursed* a curse

III, ii, 142 *glad* gald  233 *commissions, lords?* Commission? Lords,  292 *Who* Whom  343 *Chattels* Castels

IV, i, 20 2. *Gentleman* 1  34 *Kimbolton* Kymmalton  36 s.d. *Choristers* Quirristers  54–56 2. *Gentleman. Their . . . | 1. Gentleman. And . . . 2. Gentleman. No . . . | 1. Gentleman. God . . .* 2 Their . . . | And . . . 2 No . . . | 1 God . . .  78 *press* prease  101 *Stokesly* Stokeley

IV, ii, 7 *think* thank  82 s.d. *reverent* reverend

V, i, 37 *time* Lime  55 *Exeunt* Exit  139 *precipice* Precepit

V, ii, 8 *piece* Peere

V, iii, 85, 87 *Chancellor* Cham.  172 *brother-love* Brother ; loue

V, iv, 79 *press* praesse

V, v, 37 *ways* way

# THE LIFE OF KING HENRY THE EIGHTH

[NAMES OF THE ACTORS

| | |
|---|---|
| King Henry the Eighth | Cromwell, servant to Wolsey |
| Cardinal Wolsey | Griffith, gentleman usher to Queen Katherine |
| Cardinal Campeius | Three Gentlemen |
| Capuchius, ambassador from the Emperor Charles V | Dr Butts, physician to the King |
| Cranmer, Archbishop of Canterbury | Garter King-at-Arms |
| Duke of Norfolk | Surveyor to the Duke of Buckingham |
| Duke of Buckingham | Doorkeeper of the Council Chamber |
| Duke of Suffolk | Sergeant-at-Arms |
| Earl of Surrey | Porter, and his Man |
| Lord Chamberlain | Page to Gardiner |
| Lord Chancellor | Secretaries to Wolsey |
| Gardiner, King's Secretary, afterwards | A Crier |
|    Bishop of Winchester | Queen Katherine, wife to King Henry, afterwards divorced |
| Bishop of Lincoln | Anne Bullen, her Maid of Honor, afterwards Queen |
| Lord Abergavenny | An Old Lady, friend to Anne Bullen |
| Lord Sandys (also styled Sir Walter Sandys) | Patience, woman to Queen Katherine |
| Sir Henry Guilford | Spirits |
| Sir Thomas Lovell | Lords, Ladies, Bishops, Judges, Gentlemen, and Priests ; |
| Sir Anthony Denny |    Lord Mayor of London and Aldermen ; Vergers, |
| Sir Nicholas Vaux |    Scribes, Guards, Attendants, Servants, and Common |
| Brandon |    People ; Women attending upon Queen Katherine |

Scene : *London ; Kimbolton*]

\*

## THE PROLOGUE

Pro.

I come no more to make you laugh. Things now
That bear a weighty and a serious brow,
3 Sad, high, and working, full of state and woe,
Such noble scenes as draw the eye to flow
We now present. Those that can pity, here
May (if they think it well) let fall a tear :
The subject will deserve it. Such as give
Their money out of hope they may believe,
May here find truth too. Those that come to see'
Only a show or two and so agree
The play may pass – if they be still and willing,
12 I'll undertake may see away their shilling
13 Richly in two short hours. Only they
14 That come to hear a merry bawdy play,
15 A noise of targets, or to see a fellow
16 In a long motley coat guarded with yellow,
17 Will be deceived. For, gentle hearers, know
To rank our chosen truth with such a show
19 As fool and fight is, beside forfeiting
20 Our own brains and the opinion that we bring
21 To make that only true we now intend,

Will leave us never an understanding friend.
22
Therefore, for goodness' sake, and as you are known
The first and happiest hearers of the town,
24
Be sad, as we would make ye. Think ye see
25
The very persons of our noble story
As they were living. Think you see them great,
And followed with the general throng and sweat
Of thousand friends. Then, in a moment, see
How soon this mightiness meets misery.
And if you can be merry then, I'll say
A man may weep upon his wedding day.

**Names of the Actors** *Brandon* (perhaps identical with the Duke of Suffolk above, whose name was Charles Brandon)

**Pro.** 3 *Sad . . . working* serious, lofty, and effective  12 *shilling* (for the 'twelve-penny room' next to the stage)  13 *two . . . hours* (a round number ; i.e. 2–3 hours)  14–19 *merry . . . fight is* (probably an allusion to Rowley's play on Henry VIII, *When You See Me,* 1605, which has two fools and a sword-and-buckler fight)  15 *targets* shields  16 *motley coat* coat in pied colors, worn by the fool ; *guarded* trimmed  17 *deceived* disappointed  19–20 *forfeiting . . . brains* abandoning all claims to intelligence  20 *opinion* reputation  21 *make . . . intend* i.e. make the play we have in view truthful to fact  22 *understanding* (with quibble on 'understanders' or groundlings)  24 *happiest* most favored  25 *sad* serious

358

, i    *Enter the Duke of Norfolk at one door ; at the other,*
       *the Duke of Buckingham and the Lord Abergavenny.*

BUCKINGHAM
   Good morrow and well met. How have ye done
   Since last we saw in France ?

NORFOLK                             I thank your grace,
3  Healthful, and ever since a fresh admirer
   Of what I saw there.

BUCKINGHAM              An untimely ague
   Stayed me a prisoner in my chamber when
6  Those suns of glory, those two lights of men,
   Met in the vale of Andren.

7  NORFOLK                 'Twixt Guynes and Arde.
   I was then present, saw them salute on horseback,
9  Beheld them when they lighted, how they clung
10 In their embracement, as they grew together ;
11 Which had they, what four throned ones could have
       weighed
   Such a compounded one ?

12 BUCKINGHAM             All the whole time
   I was my chamber's prisoner.

NORFOLK                     Then you lost
   The view of earthly glory. Men might say
15 Till this time pomp was single, but now married
   To one above itself. Each following day
17 Became the next day's master, till the last
18 Made former wonders, its. To-day the French,
19 All clinquant, all in gold, like heathen gods
   Shone down the English ; and to-morrow they
21 Made Britain India – every man that stood
   Showed like a mine. Their dwarfish pages were
23 As cherubins, all gilt. The madams too,
   Not used to toil, did almost sweat to bear
25 The pride upon them, that their very labor
26 Was to them as a painting. Now this masque
27 Was cried incomparable ; and th' ensuing night
   Made it a fool and beggar. The two kings,
   Equal in lustre, were now best, now worst,
30 As presence did present them : him in eye
   Still him in praise ; and being present both,
32 'Twas said they saw but one, and no discerner
33 Durst wag his tongue in censure. When these suns

(For so they phrase 'em) by their heralds challenged    34
The noble spirits to arms, they did perform
Beyond thought's compass, that former fabulous story,   36
Being now seen possible enough, got credit,
That Bevis was believed.                                38

BUCKINGHAM                 O you go far.
NORFOLK
   As I belong to worship and affect                    39
   In honor honesty, the tract of ev'ry thing            40
   Would by a good discourser lose some life
   Which action's self was tongue to. All was royal.
   To the disposing of it naught rebelled ;
   Order gave each thing view. The office did            44
   Distinctly his full function.

BUCKINGHAM                 Who did guide,
   I mean who set the body and the limbs
   Of this great sport together ?                        47

NORFOLK                     As you guess :
   One certes, that promises no element                 48
   In such a business.

BUCKINGHAM         I pray you who, my lord ?
NORFOLK
   All this was ord'red by the good discretion
   Of the right reverend Cardinal of York.

BUCKINGHAM
   The devil speed him ! No man's pie is freed
   From his ambitious finger. What had he
   To do in these fierce vanities ? I wonder            54
   That such a keech can with his very bulk             55
   Take up the ray o' th' beneficial sun                56
   And keep it from the earth.

NORFOLK                     Surely, sir,
   There's in him stuff that puts him to these ends ;
   For, being not propped by ancestry, whose grace
   Chalks successors their way, nor called upon
   For high feats done to th' crown, neither allied     61
   To eminent assistants, but spiderlike                62
   Out of his self-drawing web, 'a gives us note,       63
   The force of his own merit makes his way,            64
   A gift that heaven gives for him, which buys         65
   A place next to the king.

ABERGAVENNY             I cannot tell
   What heaven hath given him. Let some graver eye
   Pierce into that ; but I can see his pride
   Peep through each part of him. Whence has he that ?
   If not from hell the devil is a niggard,
   Or has given all before, and he begins
   A new hell in himself.

BUCKINGHAM             Why the devil,
   Upon this French going out, took he upon him         73
   (Without the privity o' th' king) t' appoint          74
   Who should attend on him ? He makes up the file      75
   Of all the gentry, for the most part such
   To whom as great a charge as little honor            77
   He meant to lay upon ; and his own letter,           78
   The honorable board of council out,
   Must fetch him in he papers.

ABERGAVENNY             I do know
   Kinsmen of mine, three at the least, that have
   By this so sickened their estates that never         82
   They shall abound as formerly.

BUCKINGHAM             O many
   Have broke their backs with laying manors on 'em     84
   For this great journey. What did this vanity

I, i The royal palace in London   3 *fresh* strong, unimpaired   6 *two . . . men* i.e. Henry VIII and Francis I   3 *Arde* Ardres (in Picardy)   9 *lighted* alighted   10 *as* as if   11 *weighed* equalled in weight   12–13 *All . . . prisoner* (in fact Buckingham was present in France)   15 *single* i.e. unmarried and therefore less   17 *master* teacher   18 *Made . . . its* united in itself all the wonders of previous days   19 *clinquant* glittering   21 *India* i.e. the West Indies   23 *madams* ladies of rank   25 *that* so that   26 *Was . . . painting* had the same effect on them as cosmetics   27 *cried* proclaimed   30–31 *him . . . praise* the one in view was ever the one praised   32 *discerner* beholder   33 *censure* judgment   34 *phrase* describe   36–38 *that . . . That* so that the . . . namely that (loose syntax)   38 *Bevis* Bevis of Southampton (a legendary hero of ballads and romances)   39 *worship* nobility   39–40 *affect . . . honesty* i.e. love truth honorably   40 *tract* course   44–45 *The office . . . function* each official performed his role perfectly   47 *sport* entertainment   48 *certes* certainly ; *that . . . element* whom you would not expect to take a part   54 *fierce* extravagant   55 *keech* lump of fat (Wolsey was a butcher's son)   56 *sun* i.e. king   61 *to th' crown* for king and country   61–62 *allied To* associated with   62 *assistants* public functionaries   63 *self-drawing* self-spun ; *'a . . . note* he informs us that   64 *makes his way* wins advancement   65 *for him* i.e. on Wolsey's behalf   73 *going out* expedition   74 *privity* joint knowledge of something private   75 *file* list   77–78 *To . . . upon* (the prepositions are redundant)   78–80 *his . . . papers* i.e. his mere letter is sufficient to compel those whose names are cited to enlist, without reference to council   82 *sickened* made poor   84 *Have . . . 'em* i.e. have ruined themselves by spending whole manors' worth on their wardrobe

86 But minister communication of
A most poor issue?

NORFOLK      Grievingly I think
88 The peace between the French and us not values
The cost that did conclude it.

BUCKINGHAM      Every man,
90 After the hideous storm that followed, was
91 A thing inspired, and not consulting broke
Into a general prophecy – that this tempest,
93 Dashing the garment of this peace, aboded
94 The sudden breach on't.

NORFOLK      Which is budded out;
95 For France hath flawed the league and hath attached
Our merchants' goods at Bordeaux.

ABERGAVENNY      Is it therefore
97 Th' ambassador is silenced?

NORFOLK      Marry is't!

ABERGAVENNY
98 A proper title of a peace, and purchased
99 At a superfluous rate!

BUCKINGHAM      Why, all this business
Our reverend cardinal carried.

100 NORFOLK      Like it your grace,
101 The state takes notice of the private difference
Betwixt you and the cardinal. I advise you
(And take it from a heart that wishes towards you
104 Honor and plenteous safety) that you read
The cardinal's malice and his potency
Together; to consider further, that
107 What his high hatred would effect wants not
A minister in his power. You know his nature,
That he's revengeful; and I know his sword
Hath a sharp edge; it's long, and 't may be said
It reaches far, and where 'twill not extend
112 Thither he darts it. Bosom up my counsel;
You'll find it wholesome. Lo where comes that rock
114 That I advise your shunning.

    *Enter Cardinal Wolsey, the purse borne before him,*
    *certain of the Guard, and two Secretaries with*
    *papers. The Cardinal in his passage fixeth his eye on*
    *Buckingham, and Buckingham on him, both full*
    *of disdain.*

WOLSEY
115 The Duke of Buckingham's surveyor? Ha!
116 Where's his examination?

FIRST SECRETARY      Here, so please you.

WOLSEY
Is he in person ready?

FIRST SECRETARY      Ay, please your grace.

WOLSEY
Well, we shall then know more, and Buckingham
Shall lessen this big look.

    *Exeunt Cardinal and his train.*

BUCKINGHAM
120 This butcher's cur is venom-mouthed, and I
Have not the power to muzzle him; therefore best
122 Not wake him in his slumber. A beggar's book
Outworths a noble's blood.

123 NORFOLK      What, are you chafed?
124 Ask God for temp'rance. That's th' appliance only
Which your disease requires.

BUCKINGHAM      I read in's looks
Matter against me, and his eye reviled
127 Me as his abject object. At this instant

He bores me with some trick. He's gone to th' king.    128
I'll follow and outstare him.

NORFOLK      Stay, my lord,
And let your reason with your choler question
What 'tis you go about. To climb steep hills
Requires slow pace at first. Anger is like
A full hot horse, who being allowed his way,
Self-mettle tires him. Not a man in England    134
Can advise me like you. Be to yourself
As you would to your friend.

BUCKINGHAM      I'll to the king
And from a mouth of honor quite cry down
This Ipswich fellow's insolence, or proclaim
There's difference in no persons.    139

NORFOLK      Be advised.
Heat not a furnace for your foe so hot
That it do singe yourself. We may outrun
By violent swiftness that which we run at,
And lose by overrunning. Know you not
The fire that mounts the liquor till't run o'er    144
In seeming to augment it wastes it? be advised.
I say again there is no English soul
More stronger to direct you than yourself,
If with the sap of reason you would quench,
Or but allay the fire of passion.

BUCKINGHAM      Sir,
I am thankful to you, and I'll go along
By your prescription. But this top-proud fellow –
Whom from the flow of gall I name not, but    152
From sincere motions – by intelligence,    153
And proofs as clear as founts in July when
We see each grain of gravel, I do know
To be corrupt and treasonous.

NORFOLK      Say not treasonous.

BUCKINGHAM
To th' king I'll say't and make my vouch as strong    157
As shore of rock. Attend. This holy fox,
Or wolf, or both (for he is equal rav'nous    159
As he is subtile, and as prone to mischief
As able to perform't), his mind and place
Infecting one another, yea reciprocally,
Only to show his pomp as well in France
As here at home, suggests the king our master    164
To this last costly treaty; th' interview
That swallowed so much treasure and like a glass
Did break i' th' wrenching.

86 *minister communication* furnish occasion for talk 86–87 *of . . . issue* i.e. of little consequence 88 *not values* is not worth 90 *hideous storm* (on June 18, interrupting the tournament) 91 *not consulting* without taking counsel together 93 *aboded* boded, foreshadowed (with following quibble in *budded*, l. 94) 94 *sudden* immediate; *on't* of it 95 *flawed* broken; *attached* seized 97 *silenced* (Ed. Hall reports that he was 'commaunded to kepe his house in silence') 98 *A proper . . . peace* a fine thing to call a peace 99 *a superfluous rate* too high a price 100 *Like it* if it please 101 *difference* quarrel 104 *read* consider 107–08 *wants . . . minister* does not lack an agent 112 *Bosom up* hide in your bosom 114 s.d. *purse* the bag containing the great seal, emblem of the Lord High Chancellor's office 115 *surveyor* steward, overseer of estates (Charles Knyvet, Buckingham's cousin) 116 *examination* paper containing the witness's deposition 120 *butcher's cur* (see note to l. 55) 122 *book* learning 123 *chafed* heated, angry 124 *appliance* remedy 127 *abject* spurned 128 *bores* cheats 134 *Self-mettle* his own ardor 139 *difference* distinction of rank or quality; *Be advised* take care 144 *mounts* causes to rise 152–53 *Whom . . . motions* whom I mention not out of anger but from sincere motives 153 *intelligence* secret information 157 *vouch* attestation 159 *equal* equally, as 164 *suggests* incites, tempts

NORFOLK            Faith, and so it did.
BUCKINGHAM
    Pray give me favor, sir. This cunning cardinal
    The articles o' th' combination drew
    As himself pleased; and they were ratified
    As he cried 'Thus let be,' to as much end
    As give a crutch to th' dead. But our count-cardinal
    Has done this, and 'tis well; for worthy Wolsey
    (Who cannot err) he did it. Now this follows
    (Which, as I take it, is a kind of puppy
    To th' old dam, treason), Charles the emperor,
    Under pretense to see the queen his aunt
    (For 'twas indeed his color, but he came
    To whisper Wolsey), here makes visitation.
    His fears were that the interview betwixt
    England and France might through their amity
    Breed him some prejudice, for from this league
    Peeped harms that menaced him: privily
    Deals with our cardinal, and, as I trow,
    Which I do well; for I am sure the emperor
    Paid ere he promised, whereby his suit was granted
    Ere it was asked; but when the way was made,
    And paved with gold, the emperor thus desired,
    That he would please to alter the king's course
    And break the foresaid peace. Let the king know
    (As soon he shall by me) that thus the cardinal
    Does buy and sell his honor as he pleases,
    And for his own advantage.
NORFOLK            I am sorry
    To hear this of him, and could wish he were
    Something mistaken in't.
BUCKINGHAM         No, not a syllable.
    I do pronounce him in that very shape
    He shall appear in proof.
       *Enter Brandon, a Sergeant-at-arms before him,*
       *and two or three of the Guard.*
BRANDON
    Your office, sergeant; execute it.
SERGEANT            Sir,
    My lord the Duke of Buckingham, and Earl
    Of Hereford, Stafford, and Northampton, I
    Arrest thee of high treason, in the name
    Of our most sovereign king.
BUCKINGHAM        Lo you, my lord,
    The net has fall'n upon me! I shall perish
    Under device and practice.
BRANDON            I am sorry
    To see you ta'en from liberty, to look on
    The business present. 'Tis his highness' pleasure
    You shall to th' Tower.
BUCKINGHAM        It will help me nothing
    To plead mine innocence, for that dye is on me

Which makes my whit'st part black. The will of heav'n
Be done in this and all things! I obey.
O my Lord Aberga'ny, fare you well!
BRANDON
    Nay, he must bear you company.
       *[To Abergavenny]*        The king
    Is pleased you shall to th' Tower till you know
    How he determines further.
ABERGAVENNY        As the duke said,
    The will of heaven be done, and the king's pleasure
    By me obeyed!
BRANDON        Here is a warrant from
    The king t' attach Lord Montacute and the bodies    217
    Of the duke's confessor, John de la Car,
    One Gilbert Perk, his chancellor –
BUCKINGHAM        So, so!
    These are the limbs o' th' plot. No more, I hope.
BRANDON
    A monk o' th' Chartreux.
BUCKINGHAM        O, Nicholas Hopkins?
BRANDON            He.
BUCKINGHAM
    My surveyor is false. The o'er-great cardinal
    Hath showed him gold; my life is spanned already.    223
    I am the shadow of poor Buckingham,            224
    Whose figure even this instant cloud puts on
    By dark'ning my clear sun. My lord, farewell.    *Exeunt.*

                     *

       *Cornets. Enter King Henry, leaning on the*      I, ii
       *Cardinal's shoulder, the Nobles, [the Cardinal's*
       *Secretary,] and Sir Thomas Lovell. The Cardinal*
       *places himself under the King's feet on his right side.*
KING
    My life itself, and the best heart of it,            1
    Thanks you for this great care. I stood i' th' level    2
    Of a full-charged confederacy, and give thanks      3
    To you that choked it. Let be called before us
    That gentleman of Buckingham's; in person
    I'll hear him his confessions justify,           6
    And point by point the treasons of his master
    He shall again relate.                    8
       *A noise within, crying 'Room for the Queen!' Enter*
       *the Queen, ushered by the Duke of Norfolk, and*
       *Suffolk. She kneels. [The] King riseth from his*
       *state, takes her up, kisses and placeth her by him.*
KATHERINE
    Nay, we must longer kneel. I am a suitor.
KING
    Arise and take place by us. Half your suit
    Never name to us; you have half our power.
    The other moiety ere you ask is given.         12
    Repeat your will, and take it.              13
KATHERINE        Thank your majesty.
    That you would love yourself, and in that love
    Not unconsidered leave your honor nor
    The dignity of your office, is the point
    Of my petition.
KING            Lady mine, proceed.
KATHERINE
    I am solicited, not by a few,
    And those of true condition, that your subjects    19

20 Are in great grievance. There have been commissions
21 Sent down among 'em, which hath flawed the heart
Of all their loyalties; wherein, although,
My good lord cardinal, they vent reproaches
Most bitterly on you as putter-on
Of these exactions, yet the king our master,
26 Whose honor heaven shield from soil! – even he escapes
     not
27 Language unmannerly; yea such which breaks
The sides of loyalty and almost appears
In loud rebellion.
     NORFOLK      Not almost appears –
It doth appear; for upon these taxations,
The clothiers all not able to maintain
32 The many to them longing, have put off
33 The spinsters, carders, fullers, weavers, who,
Unfit for other life, compelled by hunger
And lack of other means, in desperate manner
36 Daring th' event to th' teeth, are all in uproar,
37 And danger serves among them.
     KING      Taxation?
Wherein? and what taxation? My lord cardinal,
You that are blamed for it alike with us,
Know you of this taxation?
     WOLSEY      Please you, sir,
41 I know but of a single part in aught
42 Pertains to th' state, and front but in that file
43 Where others tell steps with me.
     KATHERINE      No, my lord?
44 You know no more than others? but you frame
Things that are known alike, which are not wholesome
To those which would not know them and yet must
Perforce be their acquaintance. These exactions
48 (Whereof my sovereign would have note) – they are
Most pestilent to th' hearing; and, to bear 'em,
50 The back is sacrifice to th' load. They say
They are devised by you, or else you suffer
52 Too hard an exclamation.
     KING      Still exaction!
53 The nature of it? In what kind, let's know,
Is this exaction?
     KATHERINE      I am much too venturous
In tempting of your patience, but am bold'ned
56 Under your promised pardon. The subject's grief
Comes through commissions, which compels from each
The sixth part of his substance, to be levied
Without delay; and the pretense for this
Is named, your wars in France. This makes bold mouths.
Tongues spit their duties out, and cold hearts freeze
Allegiance in them. Their curses now
Live where their prayers did; and it's come to pass
64 This tractable obedience is a slave
65 To each incensèd will. I would your highness
Would give it quick consideration, for
67 There is no primer business.
     KING      By my life,
This is against our pleasure.
     WOLSEY      And for me,
I have no further gone in this than by
70 A single voice, and that not passed me but
By learned approbation of the judges. If I am
Traduced by ignorant tongues, which neither know
73 My faculties nor person yet will be
The chronicles of my doing, let me say

'Tis but the fate of place and the rough brake
That virtue must go through. We must not stint
Our necessary actions in the fear
To cope malicious censurers, which ever,
As rav'nous fishes, do a vessel follow
That is new-trimmed, but benefit no further
Than vainly longing. What we oft do best,
By sick interpreters (once weak ones) is
Not ours, or not allowed; what worst, as oft
Hitting a grosser quality, is cried up
For our best act. If we shall stand still,
In fear our motion will be mocked or carped at,
We should take root here where we sit,
Or sit state-statues only.
     KING      Things done well
And with a care exempt themselves from fear;
Things done without example, in their issue
Are to be feared. Have you a precedent
Of this commission? I believe, not any.
We must not rend our subjects from our laws
And stick them in our will. Sixth part of each?
A trembling contribution! Why, we take
From every tree lop, bark, and part o' th' timber;
And though we leave it with a root, thus hacked,
The air will drink the sap. To every county
Where this is questioned, send our letters with
Free pardon to each man that has denied
The force of this commission. Pray look to 't.
I put it to your care.
WOLSEY [aside to the Secretary] A word with you.
Let there be letters writ to every shire
Of the king's grace and pardon. The grievèd commons
Hardly conceive of me. Let it be noised
That through our intercession this revokement
And pardon comes. I shall anon advise you
Further in the proceeding.      Exit Secretary.
     Enter Surveyor.
KATHERINE
I am sorry that the Duke of Buckingham
Is run in your displeasure.
     KING      It grieves many.
The gentleman is learned and a most rare speaker,
To nature none more bound; his training such

20 grievance distress; commissions writs of authority (for collecting taxes)
21 flawed broken 26 soil moral stain 27–28 breaks The sides i.e. bursts
the bounds 32 longing belonging, i.e. working for them; put off dismissed
from employment 33 spinsters spinners; carders those who comb out
impurities from wool; fullers those who 'full,' i.e. clean cloth by beating
36 Daring . . . teeth defiantly challenging the outcome 37 danger . . .
them i.e. they almost welcome danger 41 a single part one person's share
42 front march in the front rank 43 tell steps march in step 44–47 You
. . . acquaintance i.e. in a sense you do not know more than others, but
rather are the instigator of measures familiar to all which those (of the
council) who regard them as undesirable and would therefore wish to reject
them are nevertheless forced to accept 48 note knowledge 50 is sacrifice
becomes a sacrifice 52 exclamation outcry, reproach 53 In what kind of
what form 56 grief grievance 64 tractable docile (in the negative sense;
one should obey reason and one's king) 65 each incensèd will each individual's aroused passion 67 primer more important 70 single voice
unanimous vote 73 faculties qualities 75 place office, rank; brake
thicket 76 stint cease to do 78 cope encounter; censurers judges 82
sick envious 83 allowed approved 84 Hitting . . . quality catching favor
with lower-class (and ignorant) people 86 motion move 90 issue outcome 94 stick . . . will i.e. deal with them according to our pleasure 95
trembling fearful 101 force power 104 grace mercy 105 Hardly conceive think harshly; noised rumored 110 Is run in has incurred 112
bound indebted

That he may furnish and instruct great teachers
114 And never seek for aid out of himself. Yet see,
When these so noble benefits shall prove
116 Not well disposed, the mind growing once corrupt,
117 They turn to vicious forms, ten times more ugly
118 Than ever they were fair. This man so complete,
Who was enrolled 'mongst wonders, and when we,
Almost with ravished list'ning, could not find
His hour of speech a minute – he, my lady,
122 Hath into monstrous habits put the graces
That once were his, and is become as black
As if besmeared in hell. Sit by us ; you shall hear
(This was his gentleman in trust) of him
Things to strike honor sad. Bid him recount
127 The fore-recited practices, whereof
We cannot feel too little, hear too much.

WOLSEY
Stand forth, and with bold spirit relate what you
130 Most like a careful subject have collected
Out of the Duke of Buckingham.

KING                                    Speak freely.

SURVEYOR
First, it was usual with him – every day
It would infect his speech – that if the king
134 Should without issue die, he'll carry it so
To make the sceptre his. These very words
I've heard him utter to his son-in-law,
Lord Aberga'ny, to whom by oath he menaced
Revenge upon the cardinal.

WOLSEY                           Please your highness note
This dangerous conception in this point :
140 Not friended by his wish to your high person,
His will is most malignant, and it stretches
Beyond you to your friends.

KATHERINE                    My learned lord cardinal,
143 Deliver all with charity.

KING                                    Speak on.
How grounded he his title to the crown
145 Upon our fail ? To this point hast thou heard him
At any time speak aught ?

SURVEYOR                    He was brought to this
147 By a vain prophecy of Nicholas Henton.

KING
What was that Henton ?

SURVEYOR                    Sir, a Chartreux friar,
His confessor, who fed him every minute
With words of sovereignty.

KING                                    How know'st thou this ?

SURVEYOR
Not long before your highness sped to France,
152 The duke being at the Rose, within the parish
Saint Lawrence Poultney, did of me demand
What was the speech among the Londoners

Concerning the French journey. I replied,
Men feared the French would prove perfidious,
To the king's danger. Presently the duke          157
Said 'twas the fear indeed, and that he doubted
'Twould prove the verity of certain words
Spoke by a holy monk 'that oft,' says he,
'Hath sent to me, wishing me to permit
John de la Car, my chaplain, a choice hour
To hear from him a matter of some moment ;        163
Whom after under the confession's seal
He solemnly had sworn that what he spoke
My chaplain to no creature living but
To me should utter, with demure confidence        167
This pausingly ensued : Neither the king nor 's heirs   168
(Tell you the duke) shall prosper. Bid him strive
To win the love o' th' commonalty. The duke       170
Shall govern England.'

KATHERINE                    If I know you well,
You were the duke's surveyor and lost your office
On the complaint o' th' tenants. Take good heed
You charge not in your spleen a noble person      174
And spoil your nobler soul. I say, take heed ;      175
Yes, heartily beseech you.

KING                                    Let him on.
Go forward.

SURVEYOR          On my soul, I'll speak but truth.
I told my lord the duke, by th' devil's illusions    178
The monk might be deceived ; and that 'twas dangerous
To ruminate on this so far until
It forged him some design, which, being believed,   181
It was much like to do. He answered 'Tush,
It can do me no damage !' adding further
That, had the king in his last sickness failed,      184
The cardinal's and Sir Thomas Lovell's heads
Should have gone off.

KING                    Ha ! What, so rank ? Ah, ha !   186
There's mischief in this man. Canst thou say further ?

SURVEYOR
I can, my liege.

KING                    Proceed.

SURVEYOR                    Being at Greenwich,
After your highness had reproved the duke
About Sir William Bulmer –

KING                    I remember
Of such a time. Being my sworn servant,
The duke retained him his. But on : what hence ?

SURVEYOR
'If,' quoth he, 'I for this had been committed,
As to the Tower I thought, I would have played
The part my father meant to act upon
Th' usurper Richard, who, being at Salisbury,
Made suit to come in 's presence, which if granted,
As he made semblance of his duty, would            198
Have put his knife into him.'

KING                    A giant traitor !

WOLSEY
Now, madam, may his highness live in freedom,
And this man out of prison ?

KATHERINE                    God mend all.

KING
There's something more would out of thee. What say'st ?

SURVEYOR
After 'the duke his father,' with the 'knife,'
He stretched him, and, with one hand on his dagger,  204

114 *out of* beyond   116 *disposed* directed   117 *vicious* evil   118 *complete*
accomplished   122 *habits* shapes (from the sense 'dresses, garments')
127 *practices* intrigues   130 *collected* gathered   134 *carry it so* manage it
in such a way as   140 *friended by* successful in   143 *Deliver* tell   145
*fail* (1) death, (2) failure to have issue   147 *Henton* (otherwise *Hopkins*,
cf. I, i, 221)   152 *Rose* i.e. manor of the Red Rose, belonging to Buckingham
157 *Presently* at once   163 *moment* importance   167 *demure* grave   168
*pausingly* with pauses between words   170 *commonalty* common people
174 *spleen* malice   175 *spoil* ruin   178 *illusions* deceptions   181–82 *being
. . . do* once believed in, was very likely to do him harm   184 *failed* died
186 *rank* haughtily rebellious (*O.E.D.*, A, I, 1)   198 *semblance . . . duty*
pretense of homage   204 *stretched him* straightened himself

205 Another spread on's breast, mounting his eyes,
    He did discharge a horrible oath, whose tenor
207 Was, were he evil used, he would outgo
    His father by as much as a performance
    Does an irresolute purpose.
209 KING                   There's his period,
210 To sheathe his knife in us. He is attached;
211 Call him to present trial. If he may
    Find mercy in the law, 'tis his: if none,
    Let him not seek't of us. By day and night,
214 He's traitor to th' height!          *Exeunt.*

\*

**I, iii**     *Enter Lord Chamberlain and Lord Sandys.*

CHAMBERLAIN
1 Is't possible the spells of France should juggle
2 Men into such strange mysteries?
    SANDYS              New customs,
    Thou they be never so ridiculous
    (Nay, let 'em be unmanly), yet are followed.
CHAMBERLAIN
    As far as I see, all the good our English
    Have got by the late voyage is but merely
7 A fit or two o' th' face; but they are shrewd ones,
8 For when they hold 'em, you would swear directly
    Their very noses had been counsellors
10 To Pepin or Clotharius, they keep state so.
SANDYS
    They have all new legs, and lame ones. One would take it,
12 That never see 'em pace before, the spavin,
13 A springhalt reigned among 'em.
CHAMBERLAIN           Death my lord,
14 Their clothes are after such a pagan cut to't
    That sure th' have worn out Christendom.
    *Enter Sir Thomas Lovell.*       How now?
    What news, Sir Thomas Lovell?
LOVELL             Faith, my lord,
    I hear of none but the new proclamation
    That's clapped upon the court-gate.
CHAMBERLAIN          What is't for?
LOVELL
    The reformation of our travelled gallants
    That fill the court with quarrels, talk and tailors.
CHAMBERLAIN
    I'm glad 'tis there. Now I would pray our monsieurs
    To think an English courtier may be wise
    And never see the Louvre.
LOVELL             They must either
    (For so run the conditions) leave those remnants
    Of fool and feather that they got in France,
26 With all their honorable points of ignorance
27 Pertaining thereunto – as fights and fireworks;
    Abusing better men than they can be,
    Out of a foreign wisdom – renouncing clean
    The faith they have in tennis and tall stockings,
31 Short blist'red breeches, and those types of travel,
32 And understand again like honest men,
33 Or pack to their old playfellows. There, I take it,
34 They may cum privilegio 'wee' away
35 The lag-end of their lewdness and be laughed at.
SANDYS
    'Tis time to give 'em physic, their diseases
    Are grown so catching.

CHAMBERLAIN         What a loss our ladies
    Will have of these trim vanities!
LOVELL             Ay, marry,
    There will be woe indeed, lords. The sly whoresons
    Have got a speeding trick to lay down ladies.     40
    A French song and a fiddle has no fellow.
SANDYS
    The devil fiddle 'em! I am glad they are going,
    For sure there's no converting of 'em. Now
    An honest country lord, as I am, beaten
    A long time out of play, may bring his plain-song     45
    And have an hour of hearing, and, by'r Lady,
    Held current music too.     47
CHAMBERLAIN         Well said, Lord Sandys.
    Your colt's tooth is not cast yet?     48
SANDYS             No, my lord,
    Nor shall not while I have a stump.     49
CHAMBERLAIN             Sir Thomas,
    Whither were you a-going?
LOVELL           To the cardinal's.
    Your lordship is a guest too.
CHAMBERLAIN         O, 'tis true;
    This night he makes a supper, and a great one,     52
    To many lords and ladies. There will be
    The beauty of this kingdom, I'll assure you.
LOVELL
    That churchman bears a bounteous mind indeed,
    A hand as fruitful as the land that feeds us;
    His dews fall everywhere.
CHAMBERLAIN         No doubt he's noble.
    He had a black mouth that said other of him.     58
SANDYS
    He may, my lord; has wherewithal. In him
    Sparing would show a worse sin than ill doctrine.
    Men of his way should be most liberal;     61
    They are set here for examples.
CHAMBERLAIN         True, they are so;
    But few now give so great ones. My barge stays;
    Your lordship shall along. Come, good Sir Thomas,
    We shall be late else; which I would not be,
    For I was spoke to, with Sir Henry Guilford     66
    This night to be comptrollers.     67
SANDYS            I am your lordship's.
            *Exeunt.*

\*

205 *mounting* raising  207 *evil* badly; *outgo* surpass  209 *period* end and goal  210 *attached* arrested  211 *present* immediate  214 *to th' height* in the highest degree

I, iii The royal palace  s.d. *Sandys* (pronounced 'Sands')  1 *juggle* trick  2 *mysteries* i.e. artificial fashions (comically 'mysterious')  7 *A fit . . . o'* a way of screwing up; *shrewd* artful (O.E.D., 13)  8 *hold 'em* i.e. keep their grimaces  10 *Pepin, Clotharius* early kings of the Franks  12 *see* saw (an old form of the past tense); *pace* walk, strut; *spavin* tumor on a horse's leg  13 *A* even a, what's more a (but often emended to 'And' or 'Or' by editors); *springhalt* disease causing spasmodic contractions in the leg muscles  14 *to't* in addition, moreover  26 *With . . . ignorance* with what they ignorantly regard as honorable  27 *fights and fireworks* (probably) duelling and whoring (with additional allusion to the mock-battles and fireworks staged at Princess Elizabeth's wedding in 1613)  31 *blist'red* garnished with puffs; *types* marks, badges  32 *understand* (see note to Prologue, l. 22)  33 *pack* depart, clear off  34 *cum privilegio* with immunity; *'wee'* (the Englishman's aping of French *'oui'*)  35 *lag-end* remainder  40 *speeding* effective, successful  45 *play* (with sexual allusion); *plain-song* simple melody (see *French song*, l. 41)  47 *current* good, of full value  48 *colt's tooth* (proverbial for wantonness)  49 *stump* i.e. of a tooth (with bawdy quibble)  52 *makes* gives  58 *black* evil  61 *way* way of life  66 *spoke to* asked  67 *comptrollers* stewards

v  *Hautboys. A small table under a state for the*
   *Cardinal, a longer table for the guests. Then enter*
   *Anne Bullen and divers other Ladies and*
   *Gentlemen, as guests at one door ; at another door*
   *enter Sir Henry Guilford.*

GUILFORD
Ladies, a general welcome from his grace
Salutes ye all. This night he dedicates
To fair content and you. None here, he hopes,
4   In all this noble bevy, has brought with her
One care abroad. He would have all as merry
6   As first, good company, good wine, good welcome
Can make good people.
            *Enter Lord Chamberlain, Lord Sandys, and Lovell.*
                        O my lord, y' are tardy !
The very thought of this fair company
Clapped wings to me.

CHAMBERLAIN            You are young, Sir Harry Guilford.

SANDYS
Sir Thomas Lovell, had the cardinal
11  But half my lay thoughts in him, some of these
12  Should find a running banquet ere they rested,
I think would better please 'em. By my life,
They are a sweet society of fair ones.

LOVELL
O that your lordship were but now confessor
To one or two of these !

SANDYS                    I would I were.
They should find easy penance.

LOVELL                    Faith, how easy ?

SANDYS
As easy as a down-bed would afford it.

CHAMBERLAIN
Sweet ladies, will it please you sit ? Sir Harry,
20  Place you that side ; I'll take the charge of this.
His grace is ent'ring. Nay, you must not freeze !
Two women placed together makes cold weather.
23  My Lord Sandys, you are one will keep 'em waking.
Pray sit between these ladies.

SANDYS                    By my faith,
And thank your lordship. By your leave, sweet ladies,
   *[Seats himself between Anne Bullen and another*
   *lady.]*
If I chance to talk a little wild, forgive me ;
I had it from my father.

ANNE                    Was he mad, sir ?

SANDYS
O very mad, exceeding mad, in love too.
But he would bite none. Just as I do now,
He would kiss you twenty with a breath.
   *[Kisses her.]*

30  CHAMBERLAIN                    Well said, my lord.
So now y' are fairly seated. Gentlemen,
The penance lies on you if these fair ladies
Pass away frowning.

33  SANDYS                    For my little cure,
Let me alone.

I, iv York Place  4 *bevy* company  6 *first* i.e. first . . . then . . . then  11 *lay*
secular  12 *running banquet* (with bawdy quibble)  20 *Place* assign places
23 *waking* i.e. lively  30 *said* done  33 *cure* remedy  34 s.d. *state* chair of
state  41 *beholding* beholden  45 *gamester* pleasant fellow (with bawdy
innuendo)  46 *make my play* win  49 s.d. *Chambers* small cannons used
in salutes (which probably caused the fire at the Globe in 1613)  61 *broken*
intercepted  66 *fame* report  70 *conduct* guidance

*Hautboys. Enter Cardinal Wolsey, [attended,] and*   34
*takes his state.*

WOLSEY
Y' are welcome, my fair guests. That noble lady
Or gentleman that is not freely merry
Is not my friend. This to confirm my welcome ;
And to you all, good health.
   *[Drinks.]*

SANDYS                    Your grace is noble.
Let me have such a bowl may hold my thanks
And save me so much talking.

WOLSEY                    My Lord Sandys,
I am beholding to you : cheer your neighbors :   41
Ladies, you are not merry ; gentlemen,
Whose fault is this ?

SANDYS                    The red wine first must rise
In their fair cheeks, my lord ; then we shall have 'em
Talk us to silence.

ANNE                    You are a merry gamester,   45
My Lord Sandys.

SANDYS                    Yes, if I make my play.   46
Here's to your ladyship ; and pledge it, madam,
For 'tis to such a thing –

ANNE                    You cannot show me.

SANDYS
I told your grace they would talk anon.   49
   *Drum and trumpet. Chambers discharged.*

WOLSEY                    What's that ?

CHAMBERLAIN
Look out there, some of ye.            *[Exit a Servant.]*

WOLSEY                    What warlike voice,
And to what end is this ? Nay ladies, fear not.
By all the laws of war y' are privileged.
   *Enter a Servant.*

CHAMBERLAIN
How now, what is't ?

SERVANT                    A noble troop of strangers
For so they seem. Th' have left their barge and landed,
And hither make, as great ambassadors
From foreign princes.

WOLSEY                    Good lord chamberlain,
Go, give 'em welcome ; you can speak the French
   tongue ;
And pray receive 'em nobly and conduct 'em
Into our presence, where this heaven of beauty
Shall shine at full upon them. Some attend him !
                        *[Exit Chamberlain, attended.]*
                        *All rise, and tables removed.*
You have now a broken banquet, but we'll mend it.   61
A good digestion to you all ! and once more
I show'r a welcome on ye : welcome all.
   *Hautboys. Enter King and others, as maskers,*
   *habited like shepherds, ushered by the Lord*
   *Chamberlain. They pass directly before the*
   *Cardinal and gracefully salute him.*
A noble company ! What are their pleasures ?

CHAMBERLAIN
Because they speak no English, thus they prayed
To tell your grace : that having heard by fame   66
Of this so noble and so fair assembly
This night to meet here, they could do no less
(Out of the great respect they bear to beauty)
But leave their flocks and, under your fair conduct,   70
Crave leave to view these ladies and entreat

72   An hour of revels with 'em.

WOLSEY                    Say, lord chamberlain,
They have done my poor house grace; for which I pay
'em
A thousand thanks and pray 'em take their pleasures.
       *Choose ladies. King and Anne Bullen.*

KING
The fairest hand I ever touched: O beauty,
Till now I never knew thee!
       *Music. Dance.*

WOLSEY
My lord!

CHAMBERLAIN   Your grace?

WOLSEY                 Pray tell 'em thus much from me:
There should be one amongst 'em, by his person,
79   More worthy this place than myself; to whom,
If I but knew him, with my love and duty
I would surrender it.

CHAMBERLAIN          I will, my lord.
       *Whisper [with the Maskers].*

WOLSEY
What say they?

CHAMBERLAIN   Such a one they all confess
There is indeed, which they would have your grace
84   Find out, and he will take it.

WOLSEY                    Let me see then;
By all your good leaves, gentlemen; here I'll make
My royal choice.

KING *[unmasks]*  Ye have found him, cardinal.
You hold a fair assembly. You do well, lord.
You are a churchman, or I'll tell you, cardinal,
89   I should judge now unhappily.

WOLSEY                   I am glad
90   Your grace is grown so pleasant.

KING                       My lord chamberlain,
Prithee come hither. What fair lady's that?

CHAMBERLAIN
An't please your grace, Sir Thomas Bullen's daughter,
The Viscount Rochford, one of her highness' women.

KING
By heaven she is a dainty one. Sweetheart,
95   I were unmannerly to take you out
And not to kiss you. *[Kisses her.]* A health, gentlemen!
97   Let it go round.

WOLSEY
Sir Thomas Lovell, is the banquet ready
I' th' privy chamber?

LOVELL          Yes, my lord.

WOLSEY                       Your grace,
I fear, with dancing is a little heated.

KING
I fear, too much.

WOLSEY          There's fresher air, my lord,
In the next chamber.

KING
Lead in your ladies ev'ry one. Sweet partner,
I must not yet forsake you. Let's be merry,
Good my lord cardinal; I have half a dozen healths
106  To drink to these fair ladies, and a measure
To lead 'em once again; and then let's dream
108  Who's best in favor. Let the music knock it.
       *Exeunt with Trumpets.*

*

*Enter two Gentlemen at several doors.*          I

1. GENTLEMAN
Whither away so fast?

2. GENTLEMAN          O, God save ye!
Ev'n to the Hall, to hear what shall become      2
Of the great Duke of Buckingham.

1. GENTLEMAN                    I'll save you
That labor, sir. All's now done but the ceremony
Of bringing back the prisoner.

2. GENTLEMAN               Were you there?

1. GENTLEMAN
Yes indeed was I.

2. GENTLEMAN    Pray speak what has happened.

1. GENTLEMAN
You may guess quickly what.

2. GENTLEMAN              Is he found guilty?

1. GENTLEMAN
Yes truly is he, and condemned upon't.

2. GENTLEMAN
I am sorry for't.

1. GENTLEMAN  So are a number more.

2. GENTLEMAN
But pray how passed it?                           10

1. GENTLEMAN
I'll tell you in a little. The great duke          11
Came to the bar; where to his accusations
He pleaded still not guilty, and allegèd           13
Many sharp reasons to defeat the law.             14
The king's attorney, on the contrary,
Urged on the examinations, proofs, confessions     16
Of divers witnesses, which the duke desired
To have brought viva voce to his face;             18
At which appeared against him his surveyor,
Sir Gilbert Perk his chancellor, and John Car,
Confessor to him, with that devil monk,
Hopkins, that made this mischief.

2. GENTLEMAN                    That was he
That fed him with his prophecies.

1. GENTLEMAN                    The same.
All these accused him strongly, which he fain      24
Would have flung from him, but indeed he could not;
And so his peers upon this evidence
Have found him guilty of high treason. Much
He spoke, and learnedly for life; but all
Was either pitied in him or forgotten.

2. GENTLEMAN
After all this how did he bear himself?

1. GENTLEMAN
When he was brought again to th' bar, to hear
His knell rung out, his judgment, he was stirred   32
With such an agony he sweat extremely
And something spoke in choler, ill and hasty;      34
But he fell to himself again, and sweetly          35
In all the rest showed a most noble patience.

72 *revels* dancing  79 *this place* i.e. place of honor  84 *it* (refers to *place* in
l. 79)  89 *unhappily* unfavorably  90 *pleasant* merry  95 *take you out* lead
you out to a dance  97 *it* i.e. the cup  106 *measure* stately dance  108 *in
favor* i.e. with the ladies; *knock it* strike up
II, i A street  s.d. *several* different  2 *Hall* Westminster Hall  10 *passed it*
did the trial proceed  11 *in a little* briefly  13 *alleged* put forward  14
*sharp reasons* acute arguments; *defeat* make void, frustrate  16 *Urged on*
pressed as evidence; *proofs* written statements or evidence  18 *viva voce*
(literally) with a living voice  24 *which* i.e. which accusations  32 *judgment*
sentence  34 *ill* offensive  35 *fell . . . again* regained self-control

2 . GENTLEMAN
I do not think he fears death.

1 . GENTLEMAN                    Sure he does not ;
He never was so womanish. The cause
He may a little grieve at.

2 . GENTLEMAN          Certainly
40 The cardinal is the end of this.

1 . GENTLEMAN          'Tis likely
41 By all conjectures : first Kildare's attendure,
42 Then Deputy of Ireland, who removed,
Earl Surrey was sent thither, and in haste too,
44 Lest he should help his father.

2 . GENTLEMAN          That trick of state
45 Was a deep envious one.

1 . GENTLEMAN          At his return
No doubt he will requite it. This is noted
47 (And generally), whoever the king favors,
48 The card'nal instantly will find employment,
And far enough from court too.

2 . GENTLEMAN          All the commons
50 Hate him perniciously, and o' my conscience
Wish him ten fathom deep. This duke as much
They love and dote on, call him bounteous Buckingham
53 The mirror of all courtesy –

*Enter Buckingham from his arraignment ; Tipstaves*
*before him ; [Officer bearing] the [executioner's] axe*
*with the edge towards him ; Halberds on each side ;*
*accompanied with Sir Thomas Lovell, Sir Nicholas*
*Vaux, Sir Walter Sandys, and common people, etc.*

1 . GENTLEMAN          Stay there, sir,
And see the noble ruined man you speak of.

2 . GENTLEMAN
Let's stand close and behold him.

BUCKINGHAM          All good people,
You that thus far have come to pity me,
57 Hear what I say and then go home and lose me.
58 I have this day received a traitor's judgment
And by that name must die. Yet heaven bear witness,
60 And if I have a conscience, let it sink me
Even as the axe falls, if I be not faithful !
The law I bear no malice for my death,
63 'T has done upon the premises but justice :
But those that sought it I could wish more Christians.
Be what they will, I heartily forgive 'em.
66 Yet let 'em look they glory not in mischief,
67 Nor build their evils on the graves of great men ;
For then my guiltless blood must cry against 'em.
For further life in this world I ne'er hope,

Nor will I sue, although the king have mercies
More than I dare make faults. You few that loved me     71
And dare be bold to weep for Buckingham,
His noble friends and fellows, whom to leave
Is only bitter to him, only dying,     74
Go with me like good angels to my end ;
And, as the long divorce of steel falls on me,
Make of your prayers one sweet sacrifice     77
And lift my soul to heaven. Lead on a God's name.     78

LOVELL
I do beseech your grace, for charity,     79
If ever any malice in your heart
Were hid against me, now to forgive me frankly.

BUCKINGHAM
Sir Thomas Lovell, I as free forgive you
As I would be forgiven : I forgive all.
There cannot be those numberless offenses
'Gainst me that I cannot take peace with : no black envy     85
Shall mark my grave. Commend me to his grace ;
And if he speak of Buckingham, pray tell him
You met him half in heaven. My vows and prayers
Yet are the king's, and till my soul forsake     89
Shall cry for blessings on him. May he live
Longer than I have time to tell his years ;     91
Ever beloved and loving may his rule be ;
And when old time shall lead him to his end,     93
Goodness and he fill up one monument !     94

LOVELL
To th' waterside I must conduct your grace ;
Then give my charge up to Sir Nicholas Vaux,
Who undertakes you to your end.     97

VAUX          Prepare there,
The duke is coming. See the barge be ready
And fit it with such furniture as suits     99
The greatness of his person.

BUCKINGHAM          Nay, Sir Nicholas,
Let it alone ; my state now will but mock me.
When I came hither I was Lord High Constable
And Duke of Buckingham ; now poor Edward Bohun.
Yet I am richer than my base accusers,
That never knew what truth meant : I now seal it ;     105
And with that blood will make 'em one day groan for't.
My noble father, Henry of Buckingham,
Who first raised head against usurping Richard,     108
Flying for succor to his servant Banister,
Being distressed, was by that wretch betrayed,
And without trial fell ; God's peace be with him !
Henry the Seventh succeeding, truly pitying
My father's loss, like a most royal prince
Restored me to my honors ; and out of ruins
Made my name once more noble. Now his son,
Henry the Eighth, life, honor, name, and all
That made me happy, at one stroke has taken
For ever from the world. I had my trial,
And must needs say a noble one ; which makes me
A little happier than my wretched father.
Yet thus far we are one in fortunes : both
Fell by our servants, by those men we loved most –
A most unnatural and faithless service.
Heaven has an end in all ; yet you that hear me,     124
This from a dying man receive as certain :     125
Where you are liberal of your loves and counsels
Be sure you be not loose ; for those you make friends     127
And give your hearts to, when they once perceive

40 *the end of* responsible for, at the bottom of   41 *attendure* attainder (the
confiscation of the Earl of Kildare's estate, upon the death sentence)   42
*Deputy* i.e. viceroy   44 *father* (Surrey was Buckingham's son-in-law)
45 *deep, envious* profoundly malicious   47 *generally* by everybody   48 *employment* employment for   50 *perniciously* to the death   53 *mirror* model ;
*courtesy* courtly behavior ; **s.d.** *Tipstaves* officers who take the accused from
the court into custody (so called because they carried staves tipped with
silver) ; *Halberds* halberdiers (carrying long-handled battle-axes with
spearpoints)   57 *lose* forget   58 *judgment* sentence   60 *sink* destroy   63
*premises* evidence   66 *look* take care   67 *build . . . graves* i.e. thrive in their
evil designs on the downfalls   71 *make faults* commit offenses   74 *Is only
. . . only* alone is . . . alone is   77 *sacrifice* offering   78 *a* in   79–81 *I . . .
frankly* (see I, ii, 185–86)   85 *envy* malice   89 *forsake* leave the body   91
*tell* count   93 *old time* old age   94 *monument* tomb   97 *undertakes you*
takes charge of you   99 *furniture* equipment   105 *seal* ratify   108 *raised
head* gathered a force   124 *end* purpose   125 *receive as certain* accept as
truth   127 *loose* unrestrained

129 The least rub in your fortunes, fall away
Like water from ye, never found again
131 But where they mean to sink ye. All good people,
Pray for me! I must now forsake ye; the last hour
Of my long weary life is come upon me.
Farewell!
And when you would say something that is sad,
Speak how I fell. I have done, and God forgive me!
*Exeunt Duke and train.*

1. GENTLEMAN
137 O this is full of pity! Sir, it calls,
I fear, too many curses on their heads
That were the authors.
2. GENTLEMAN          If the duke be guiltless,
'Tis full of woe. Yet I can give you inkling
Of an ensuing evil, if it fall,
Greater than this.
1. GENTLEMAN          Good angels keep it from us!
143 What may it be? you do not doubt my faith, sir?
2. GENTLEMAN
This secret is so weighty 'twill require
A strong faith to conceal it.
1. GENTLEMAN          Let me have it;
I do not talk much.
146 2. GENTLEMAN          I am confident.
You shall, sir. Did you not of late days hear
148 A buzzing of a separation
Between the king and Katherine?
149 1. GENTLEMAN          Yes, but it held not;
For when the king once heard it, out of anger
151 He sent command to the lord mayor straight
152 To stop the rumor and allay those tongues
That durst disperse it.
2. GENTLEMAN          But that slander, sir,
Is found a truth now; for it grows again
155 Fresher than e'er it was, and held for certain
The king will venture at it. Either the cardinal,
157 Or some about him near, have out of malice
158 To the good queen possessed him with a scruple
That will undo her. To confirm this too,
Cardinal Campeius is arrived, and lately,
As all think, for this business.
1. GENTLEMAN          'Tis the cardinal;
162 And merely to revenge him on the emperor
For not bestowing on him at his asking
The archbishopric of Toledo, this is purposed.
2. GENTLEMAN
I think you have hit the mark. But is't not cruel
That she should feel the smart of this? The cardinal
Will have his will, and she must fall.
1. GENTLEMAN          'Tis woeful.
168 We are too open here to argue this;
Let's think in private more.          *Exeunt.*

\*

II, ii          *Enter Lord Chamberlain, reading this letter.*
[CHAMBERLAIN] 'My lord – The horses your lordship
2 sent for, with all the care I had, I saw well chosen, rid-
3 den, and furnished. They were young and handsome
and of the best breed in the north. When they were
ready to set out for London, a man of my lord cardinal's
6 by commission and main power took 'em from me, with
this reason: his master would be served before a subject,

if not before the king; which stopped our mouths, sir.'
I fear he will indeed. Well, let him have them.
He will have all, I think.
          *Enter to the Lord Chamberlain the Dukes of Norfolk
          and Suffolk.*
NORFOLK
Well met, my lord chamberlain.
CHAMBERLAIN
Good day to both your graces.
SUFFOLK
How is the king employed?
CHAMBERLAIN          I left him private,
Full of sad thoughts and troubles.          14
NORFOLK          What's the cause?
CHAMBERLAIN
It seems the marriage with his brother's wife
Has crept too near his conscience.
SUFFOLK *[aside]*          No, his conscience
Has crept too near another lady.
NORFOLK          'Tis so.
This is the cardinal's doing: the king-cardinal,
That blind priest, like the eldest son of Fortune,          19
Turns what he list. The king will know him one day.
SUFFOLK
Pray God he do, he'll never know himself else.
NORFOLK
How holily he works in all his business
And with what zeal! for, now he has cracked the league          23
Between us and the emperor, the queen's great nephew,
He dives into the king's soul, and there scatters
Dangers, doubts, wringing of the conscience,          26
Fears, and despairs, and all these for his marriage.
And out of all these, to restore the king,
He counsels a divorce, a loss of her
That like a jewel has hung twenty years          30
About his neck, yet never lost her lustre;
Of her that loves him with that excellence          32
That angels love good men with; even of her
That, when the greatest stroke of fortune falls,
Will bless the king. And is not this course pious?
CHAMBERLAIN
Heaven keep me from such counsel! 'Tis most true
These news are everywhere, every tongue speaks 'em,
And every true heart weeps for't. All that dare
Look into these affairs see this main end –          39
The French king's sister. Heaven will one day open
The king's eyes that so long have slept upon          41
This bold bad man.
SUFFOLK          And free us from his slavery.
NORFOLK
We had need pray,
And heartily, for our deliverance,
Or this imperious man will work us all

129 *rub* check, impediment  131 *sink* ruin  137 *calls* summons  143 *faith*
trustworthiness  146 *am confident* trust you  148 *buzzing* rumor  149
*held not* did not continue  151 *straight* at once  152 *allay* restrain  155
*held* is thought  157 *about him near* intimate with him  158 *possessed*
imbued  162 *emperor* Charles V (Holy Roman Emperor, and nephew of
Queen Katherine)  168 *open* public, exposed to view; *argue* discuss
II, ii The royal palace  2 *ridden* broken in  3 *furnished* equipped  6 *main
power* superior force  14 *sad* serious  19–20 *blind . . . list* (an allusion to
Fortune, conceived in the Middle Ages as blind, and her wheel which she
turns arbitrarily)  23 *cracked* broken  26 *wringing* torture  30 *jewel* costly
gold chain (worn by gentlemen)  32 *excellence* surpassing virtue  39 *end*
object  41 *slept upon* been blind to

From princes into pages. All men's honors
47 Lie like one lump before him, to be fashioned
48 Into what pitch he please.
SUFFOLK                              For me, my lords,
I love him not, nor fear him; there's my creed:
50 As I am made without him, so I'll stand,
If the king please. His curses and his blessings
Touch me alike; th' are breath I not believe in.
I knew him, and I know him: so I leave him
To him that made him proud, the pope.
NORFOLK                              Let's in,
And with some other business put the king
From these sad thoughts that work too much upon him.
My lord, you'll bear us company?
CHAMBERLAIN                         Excuse me.
The king has sent me otherwhere. Besides,
You'll find a most unfit time to disturb him.
Health to your lordships!
NORFOLK                    Thanks, my good lord chamberlain.
        *Exit Lord Chamberlain; and the King draws
            the curtain and sits reading pensively.*
SUFFOLK
61 How sad he looks; sure he is much afflicted.
KING
Who's there, ha?
NORFOLK                    Pray God he be not angry.
KING
Who's there, I say? How dare you thrust yourselves
Into my private meditations?
Who am I? ha?
NORFOLK
A gracious king that pardons all offenses
67 Malice ne'er meant. Our breach of duty this way
68 Is business of estate; in which we come
To know your royal pleasure.
KING                              Ye are too bold:
Go to! I'll make ye know your times of business.
Is this an hour for temporal affairs? ha?
        *Enter Wolsey and Campeius with a commission.*
Who's there? My good lord cardinal? O my Wolsey,
The quiet of my wounded conscience;
Thou art a cure fit for a king. *[to Campeius]* You're wel-
        come,
Most learned reverend sir, into our kingdom.
Use us and it. *[to Wolsey]* My good lord, have great care
77 I be not found a talker.
WOLSEY                    Sir, you cannot;
I would your grace would give us but an hour
Of private conference.
KING *[to Norfolk and Suffolk]* We are busy: go.
NORFOLK *[aside to Suffolk]*
This priest has no pride in him!
SUFFOLK *[aside to Norfolk]*          Not to speak of.
81 I would not be so sick though for his place.
But this cannot continue.

NORFOLK *[aside to Suffolk]* If it do,
I'll venture one; have at him!                          83
SUFFOLK *[aside to Norfolk]*          I another.
                    *Exeunt Norfolk and Suffolk.*
WOLSEY
Your grace has given a precedent of wisdom
Above all princes in committing freely
Your scruple to the voice of Christendom.              86
Who can be angry now? what envy reach you?            87
The Spaniard, tied by blood and favor to her,
Must now confess, if they have any goodness,
The trial just and noble. All the clerks               90
(I mean the learned ones in Christian kingdoms)
Have their free voices. Rome, the nurse of judgment,   92
Invited by your noble self, hath sent
One general tongue unto us, this good man,             94
This just and learned priest, Cardinal Campeius,
Whom once more I present unto your highness.
KING
And once more in mine arms I bid him welcome
And thank the holy conclave for their loves.           98
They have sent me such a man I would have wished for.
CAMPEIUS
Your grace must needs deserve all strangers' loves,   100
You are so noble. To your highness' hand
I tender my commission; by whose virtue,
The court of Rome commanding, you, my Lord
Cardinal of York, are joined with me their servant
In the unpartial judging of this business.
KING
Two equal men. The queen shall be acquainted          106
Forthwith for what you come. Where's Gardiner?
WOLSEY
I know your majesty has always loved her
So dear in heart, not to deny her that
A woman of less place might ask by law –               110
Scholars allowed freely to argue for her.
KING
Ay, and the best she shall have; and my favor
To him that does best, God forbid else. Cardinal,
Prithee call Gardiner to me, my new secretary.
I find him a fit fellow.                    *[Exit Wolsey.]*
        *Enter [Wolsey, with] Gardiner.*
WOLSEY *[aside to Gardiner]*
Give me your hand. Much joy and favor to you;
You are the king's now.
GARDINER *[aside to Wolsey]* But to be commanded
For ever by your grace, whose hand has raised me.
KING
Come hither, Gardiner.
        *Walks and whispers.*
CAMPEIUS
My Lord of York, was not one Doctor Pace
In this man's place before him?
WOLSEY                              Yes, he was.
CAMPEIUS
Was he not held a learned man?
WOLSEY                              Yes, surely.
CAMPEIUS
Believe me, there's an ill opinion spread then,
Even of yourself, lord cardinal.
WOLSEY                              How? of me?
CAMPEIUS
They will not stick to say you envied him,              125

47 *lump* i.e. lump of clay   48 *pitch* level, status   50 *stand* stand firm   61 *afflicted* troubled   67 *this way* in this respect   68 *estate* state   77 *I . . . talker* i.e. that this be not found mere empty talk   81 *sick . . . place* sick with pride even to gain his position   83 *have at him* (a challenge)   86 *voice* vote   87 *envy* malice   90 *clerks* scholars   92 *voices* votes   94 *One general tongue* one to speak for all   98 *conclave* assembly of cardinals   100 *strangers'* foreigners'   106 *equal* impartial   110 *less place* lower rank   125 *stick* scruple

And fearing he would rise (he was so virtuous),
127    Kept him a foreign man still, which so grieved him
That he ran mad and died.
WOLSEY        Heav'n's peace be with him!
129    That's Christian care enough. For living murmurers
There's places of rebuke. He was a fool,
For he would needs be virtuous. That good fellow,
132    If I command him, follows my appointment;
133    I will have none so near else. Learn this, brother,
134    We live not to be griped by meaner persons.
KING
135    Deliver this with modesty to th' Queen.   *Exit Gardiner.*
The most convenient place that I can think of
137    For such receipt of learning is Blackfriars.
There ye shall meet about this weighty business.
My Wolsey, see it furnished. O my lord,
Would it not grieve an able man to leave
So sweet a bedfellow? But conscience, conscience!
O 'tis a tender place, and I must leave her.   *Exeunt.*

*

II, iii    *Enter Anne Bullen and an Old Lady.*
ANNE
1    Not for that neither; here's the pang that pinches:
His highness having lived so long with her, and she
So good a lady that no tongue could ever
4    Pronounce dishonor of her – by my life,
She never knew harm-doing – O, now after
6    So many courses of the sun enthronèd,
7    Still growing in a majesty and pomp, the which
To leave a thousandfold more bitter than
9    'Tis sweet at first t' acquire – after this process
10    To give her the avaunt, it is a pity
Would move a monster.
11  OLD LADY        Hearts of most hard temper
Melt and lament for her.
ANNE        O God's will much better
13    She ne'er had known pomp. Though't be temporal,
14    Yet if that quarrel, fortune, do divorce
15    It from the bearer, 'tis a sufferance panging
As soul and body's severing.
OLD LADY        Alas, poor lady,
17    She's a stranger now again.
ANNE        So much the more
Must pity drop upon her. Verily
I swear 'tis better to be lowly born
20    And range with humble livers in content
21    Than to be perked up in a glist'ring grief
And wear a golden sorrow.
OLD LADY        Our content
Is our best having.
ANNE        By my troth and maidenhead,
I would not be a queen.
24  OLD LADY        Beshrew me, I would,
And venture maidenhead for't; and so would you,
26    For all this spice of your hypocrisy.
27    You that have so fair parts of women on you
Have, too, a woman's heart, which ever yet
29    Affected eminence, wealth, sovereignty;
30    Which, to say sooth, are blessings; and which gifts
31    (Saving your mincing) the capacity
32    Of your soft cheveril conscience would receive,
If you might please to stretch it.

ANNE        Nay, good troth.   33
OLD LADY
Yes troth, and troth; you would not be a queen?   34
ANNE
No, not for all the riches under heaven.
OLD LADY
'Tis strange; a threepence bowed would hire me,   36
Old as I am, to queen it. But I pray you,   37
What think you of a duchess? Have you limbs
To bear that load of title?
ANNE        No, in truth.
OLD LADY
Then you are weakly made. Pluck off a little;   40
I would not be a young count in your way   41
For more than blushing comes to. If your back   42
Cannot vouchsafe this burden, 'tis too weak
Ever to get a boy.
ANNE        How you do talk!
I swear again, I would not be a queen
For all the world.
OLD LADY        In faith, for little England   46
You'ld venture an emballing. I myself   47
Would for Carnarvonshire, although there longed   48
No more to th' crown but that. Lo, who comes here?
*Enter Lord Chamberlain.*
CHAMBERLAIN
Good morrow, ladies. What were't worth to know
The secret of your conference?   51
ANNE        My good lord,
Not your demand; it values not your asking:   52
Our mistress' sorrows we were pitying.
CHAMBERLAIN
It was a gentle business and becoming
The action of good women. There is hope
All will be well.
ANNE        Now I pray God, amen.
CHAMBERLAIN
You bear a gentle mind, and heav'nly blessings
Follow such creatures. That you may, fair lady,
Perceive I speak sincerely, and high note 's
Ta'en of your many virtues, the king's majesty
Commends his good opinion of you, and   61

127 *a foreign man still* continually employed in other countries  129 *murmurers* grumblers  132 *appointment* bidding  133 *near* familiar  134 *griped* grasped by the hand  135 *Deliver . . . modesty* i.e. inform her of this without making too much of it  137 *such . . . learning* hearing such learned discourses (?), the reception of such learned men (?)
II, iii The Queen's apartments  1 *pinches* hurts, torments  4 *Pronounce* make known  6 *courses . . . enthronèd* years  7–8 *the which To leave* which to leave is  9 *process* proceeding  10 *avaunt* order to leave; *pity* cause for pity  11 *temper* disposition  13 *temporal* i.e. merely worldly, not eternal  14 *quarrel* quarreller (use of abstract noun for agent; the emendation 'quarr'lous' is plausible)  15 *sufferance panging* suffering painful  17 *stranger* foreigner  20 *range . . . livers* rank with humble people  21 *perked up* perched up, made smart  24 *Beshrew me* woe befall me (a mild oath)  26 *spice* dash  27 *fair parts* attractive qualities  29 *Affected* aspired to  30 *to say sooth* truly, indeed  31 *Saving your mincing* with all respect to your affectation  32 *cheveril* flexible, stretching (like kid-leather)  33, 34 *troth* faith (with pun on 'trot': old hag)  36 *bowed* bent (and thus worthless) (with further quibble on 'bawd')  37 *queen* (punning on 'quean')  40 *Pluck off* come lower  41 *count* i.e. one rank lower than a duke; *way* path (with sexual innuendo)  42 *For . . . to* i.e. with (no) more fuss than a mere blush  46 *little England* (possibly) Pembrokeshire (see l. 63)  47 *emballing* investing with the ball as the emblem of royalty (but with sexual innuendo?)  48 *Carnarvonshire* a barren county in Wales (with quibble on its shape and on 'carnal'?); *longed* belonged  51 *conference* conversation  52 *values not* is not worth  61 *Commends . . . you* presents his compliments

Does purpose honor to you no less flowing
Than Marchioness of Pembroke ; to which title
A thousand pound a year, annual support,
Out of his grace he adds.

ANNE                         I do not know
What kind of my obedience I should tender.
67  More than my all is nothing ; nor my prayers
Are not words duly hallowed, nor my wishes
More worth than empty vanities ; yet prayers and wishes
Are all I can return. Beseech your lordship,
71  Vouchsafe to speak my thanks and my obedience,
As from a blushing handmaid, to his highness ;
Whose health and royalty I pray for.

CHAMBERLAIN                         Lady,
74  I shall not fail t' approve the fair conceit
The king hath of you. [aside] I have perused her well.
Beauty and honor in her are so mingled
That they have caught the king ; and who knows yet
But from this lady may proceed a gem
79  To lighten all this isle. – I'll to the king
And say I spoke with you.

ANNE                         My honored lord.
                         Exit Lord Chamberlain.

OLD LADY
81  Why, this it is ! See, see,
I have been begging sixteen years in court
83  (Am yet a courtier beggarly) nor could
Come pat betwixt too early and too late
85  For any suit of pounds ; and you (O fate !),
A very fresh fish here – fie, fie, fie upon
87  This compelled fortune ! – have your mouth filled up
Before you open it.

ANNE                         This is strange to me.

OLD LADY
89  How tastes it ? Is it bitter ? Forty pence, no.
There was a lady once ('tis an old story)
That would not be a queen, that would she not,
92  For all the mud in Egypt ; have you heard it ?

ANNE
Come, you are pleasant.

OLD LADY                         With your theme I could
O'ermount the lark. The Marchioness of Pembroke ?
A thousand pounds a year, for pure respect ?
No other obligation ? By my life,
97  That promises moe thousands ! Honor's train
Is longer than his foreskirt. By this time
I know your back will bear a duchess. Say,
Are you not stronger than you were ?

ANNE                         Good lady,
Make yourself mirth with your particular fancy        101
And leave me out on't. Would I had no being
If this salute my blood a jot ! It faints me        103
To think what follows.
The queen is comfortless, and we forgetful
In our long absence. Pray do not deliver        106
What here y' have heard to her.

OLD LADY                         What do you think me ?
                         Exeunt.

                         *

                         Trumpets, sennet, and cornets.        II, iv
                         Enter two Vergers, with short silver wands ; next
                         them, two Scribes, in the habit of doctors ; after
                         them, the [Arch-]bishop of Canterbury alone ; after
                         him, the Bishops of Lincoln, Ely, Rochester, and
                         Saint Asaph ; next them, with some small distance,
                         follows a Gentleman bearing the purse, with the great
                         seal and a cardinal's hat ; then two Priests, bearing
                         each a silver cross ; then [Griffith,] a Gentleman
                         Usher, bareheaded, accompanied with a Sergeant-
                         at-arms bearing a silver mace ; then two Gentlemen
                         bearing two great silver pillars ; after them, side by
                         side, the two Cardinals, two Noblemen with the
                         sword and mace. The King takes place under the cloth
                         of state ; the two Cardinals sit under him as Judges.
                         The Queen takes place some distance from the King.
                         The Bishops place themselves on each side the court,
                         in manner of a consistory ; below them, the Scribes.
                         The Lords sit next the Bishops. The rest of the
                         Attendants stand in convenient order about the stage.

WOLSEY
Whilst our commission from Rome is read,
Let silence be commanded.

KING                         What's the need ?
It hath already publicly been read,
And on all sides th' authority allowed.
You may then spare that time.

WOLSEY                         Be't so. Proceed.

SCRIBE
Say, 'Henry King of England, come into the court.'

CRIER
Henry King of England, etc.

KING
Here.

SCRIBE
Say, 'Katherine Queen of England, come into the court.'

CRIER
Katherine Queen of England, etc.
                         The Queen makes no answer, rises out of her chair,
                         goes about the court, comes to the King, and kneels
                         at his feet ; then speaks.

[KATHERINE]
Sir, I desire you do me right and justice,
And to bestow your pity on me ; for
I am a most poor woman and a stranger,        13
Born out of your dominions : having here
No judge indifferent, nor no more assurance        15
Of equal friendship and proceeding. Alas, sir,        16
In what have I offended you ? What cause
Hath my behavior given to your displeasure
That thus you should proceed to put me off        19
And take your good grace from me ? Heaven witness,        20

67–68 nor . . . not (double negative for emphasis)  71 Vouchsafe be so
kind as  74 approve corroborate ; fair conceit good opinion  79 lighten
give light to (gems were thought to emit light)  81 this i.e. thus  83
beggarly poor  85 suit of pounds petition that would bring in money
('pounds') (with possible allusion to 'ponds' – see next line)  87 compelled i.e. forced upon her  89 Forty pence 3s. 4d., ten groats or half a noble
(the usual fee for an attorney)  92 mud in Egypt i.e. its wealth  97 moe
more  101 particular private  103 salute . . . jot arouses the least kind
of physical response in me ; faints me makes me faint  106 deliver make
known
II, iv The court at Blackfriars  s.d. sennet a fanfare played on trumpets,
at the approach or departure of a procession ; habit of doctors i.e. furred
black gowns and flat caps of Doctors of Law ; silver pillars (cardinals had
the right to a silver mace, but only Wolsey employed silver pillars) ; takes
place sits down  13 stranger foreigner  15 indifferent impartial  16 equal
fair ; proceeding legal process  19 put me off discard me  20 your good grace
your favor and your person

I have been to you a true and humble wife,
At all times to your will conformable,
Ever in fear to kindle your dislike,
Yea, subject to your countenance – glad or sorry
As I saw it inclined. When was the hour
I ever contradicted your desire
Or made it not mine too? Or which of your friends
Have I not strove to love, although I knew
He were mine enemy? What friend of mine
30 That had to him derived your anger, did I
Continue in my liking? nay, gave notice
He was from thence discharged? Sir, call to mind
That I have been your wife in this obedience
Upward of twenty years, and have been blest
With many children by you. If in the course
And process of this time you can report,
And prove it too, against mine honor aught,
My bond to wedlock, or my love and duty
39 Against your sacred person, in God's name
Turn me away, and let the foul'st contempt
Shut door upon me, and so give me up
To the sharp'st kind of justice. Please you, sir,
The king your father was reputed for
A prince most prudent, of an excellent
45 And unmatched wit and judgment. Ferdinand,
46 My father, King of Spain, was reckoned one
The wisest prince that there had reigned by many
A year before. It is not to be questioned
That they had gathered a wise council to them
Of every realm, that did debate this business,
Who deemed our marriage lawful. Wherefore I humbly
Beseech you, sir, to spare me till I may
Be by my friends in Spain advised, whose counsel
I will implore. If not, i' th' name of God,
Your pleasure be fulfilled!
WOLSEY             You have here, lady
(And of your choice), these reverend fathers, men
Of singular integrity and learning:
Yea, the elect o' th' land, who are assembled
59 To plead your cause. It shall be therefore bootless
60 That longer you desire the court, as well
For your own quiet as to rectify
What is unsettled in the king.
CAMPEIUS            His grace
Hath spoken well and justly. Therefore, madam,
It's fit this royal session do proceed
And that without delay their arguments
66 Be now produced and heard.
KATHERINE          Lord cardinal,
To you I speak.
WOLSEY      Your pleasure, madam.
67 KATHERINE              Sir,
I am about to weep; but, thinking that
69 We are a queen (or long have dreamed so), certain
The daughter of a king, my drops of tears
I'll turn to sparks of fire.
WOLSEY         Be patient yet.
KATHERINE
I will, when you are humble; nay before,
Or God will punish me. I do believe
74 (Induced by potent circumstances) that
75 You are mine enemy; and make my challenge
You shall not be my judge. For it is you
77 Have blown this coal betwixt my lord and me –

Which God's dew quench! Therefore I say again
I utterly abhor, yea, from my soul     79
Refuse you for my judge, whom yet once more
I hold my most malicious foe and think not
At all a friend to truth.
WOLSEY        I do profess     82
You speak not like yourself, who ever yet
Have stood to charity and displayed th' effects     84
Of disposition gentle, and of wisdom
O'ertopping woman's pow'r. Madam, you do me wrong.
I have no spleen against you, nor injustice     87
For you or any. How far I have proceeded,
Or how far further shall, is warranted
By a commission from the consistory,     90
Yea, the whole consistory of Rome. You charge me
That I have blown this coal: I do deny it.
The king is present. If it be known to him
That I gainsay my deed, how may he wound,     94
And worthily, my falsehood, yea, as much     95
As you have done my truth. If he know
That I am free of your report, he knows     97
I am not of your wrong. Therefore in him     98
It lies to cure me, and the cure is to
Remove these thoughts from you; the which before
His highness shall speak in, I do beseech     101
You, gracious madam, to unthink your speaking
And to say so no more.
KATHERINE        My lord, my lord,
I am a simple woman, much too weak
T' oppose your cunning. Y' are meek and humble-
   mouthed;
You sign your place and calling, in full seeming,     106
With meekness and humility; but your heart
Is crammed with arrogancy, spleen, and pride.
You have, by fortune and his highness' favors,
Gone slightly o'er low steps, and now are mounted     110
Where pow'rs are your retainers, and your words     111
(Domestics to you) serve your will as't please
Yourself pronounce their office. I must tell you
You tender more your person's honor than     114
Your high profession spiritual; that again
I do refuse you for my judge and here,
Before you all, appeal unto the pope,
To bring my whole cause 'fore his holiness
And to be judged by him.
      *She curtsies to the King and offers to depart.*
CAMPEIUS        The queen is obstinate,
Stubborn to justice, apt to accuse it, and     120
Disdainful to be tried by't. 'Tis not well.
She's going away.
KING
Call her again.

30 *derived* drawn   39 *Against* towards   45 *wit* wisdom   46–47 *one The wisest* the very wisest   59 *bootless* profitless   60 *desire* i.e. to protract the business of   66 *produced* brought forward   67 ff. *Sir* . . . (cf. Hermione in *The Winter's Tale*, III, ii)   69 *certain* certainly   74 *Induced* persuaded   75 *challenge* (legal term) objection to a person, raised during a trial   77 *blown this coal* i.e. stirred up strife   79 *abhor* (legal term) protest against   82 *profess* affirm   84 *stood to* upheld   87 *spleen* strong hatred or anger   90 *consistory* assembly of cardinals   94 *gainsay my deed* deny what I have done   95 *worthily* deservedly   97 *report* (mild) accusation   98 *I . . . wrong* i.e. I have done nothing to injure you   101 *in* in reference to   106 *sign your place* mark your office   110 *slightly* easily   111 *pow'rs* i.e. powerful men   111–13 *words . . . office* i.e. his words are immediately acted upon, as if they were his 'domestics'   114 *tender* hold tenderly, cherish   120 *accuse* find fault with

CRIER

    Katherine Queen of England, come into the court.

GRIFFITH

    Madam, you are called back.

KATHERINE

26  What need you note it? pray you keep your way;
    When you are called, return. Now the Lord help,
    They vex me past my patience. Pray you pass on.
    I will not tarry; no, nor ever more
    Upon this business my appearance make
    In any of their courts. *Exeunt Queen and her Attendants.*

KING           Go thy ways, Kate.
    That man i' th' world who shall report he has
    A better wife, let him in naught be trusted
    For speaking false in that. Thou art alone
35  (If thy rare qualities, sweet gentleness,
    Thy meekness saint-like, wife-like government,
37  Obeying in commanding, and thy parts
38  Sovereign and pious else, could speak thee out)
    The queen of earthly queens. She's noble born,
    And like her true nobility she has
41  Carried herself towards me.

WOLSEY          Most gracious sir,
42  In humblest manner I require your highness
    That it shall please you to declare in hearing
    Of all these ears (for where I am robbed and bound,
    There must I be unloosed, although not there
46  At once and fully satisfied) whether ever I
    Did broach this business to your highness, or
    Laid any scruple in your way which might
49  Induce you to the question on't; or ever
    Have to you, but with thanks to God for such
51  A royal lady, spake one the least word that might
52  Be to the prejudice of her present state
53  Or touch of her good person.

KING           My lord cardinal,
54  I do excuse you; yea, upon mine honor,
    I free you from't. You are not to be taught
    That you have many enemies that know not
    Why they are so, but like to village curs
    Bark when their fellows do. By some of these
    The queen is put in anger. Y' are excused:
    But will you be more justified? you ever
    Have wished the sleeping of this business; never desired
    It to be stirred, but oft have hind'red, oft
63  The passages made toward it. On my honor,
    I speak my good lord card'nal to this point,
    And thus far clear him. Now what moved me to't,

I will be bold with time and your attention:
Then mark th' inducement. Thus it came; give heed to't:  167
My conscience first received a tenderness,
Scruple and prick, on certain speeches uttered
By th' Bishop of Bayonne, then French ambassador,
Who had been hither sent on the debating
A marriage 'twixt the Duke of Orleans and
Our daughter Mary. I' th' progress of this business,
Ere a determinate resolution, he  174
(I mean the bishop) did require a respite,  175
Wherein he might the king his lord advertise  176
Whether our daughter were legitimate,
Respecting this our marriage with the dowager,
Sometimes our brother's wife. This respite shook  179
The bosom of my conscience, entered me,  180
Yea, with a spitting power, and made to tremble  181
The region of my breast, which forced such way
That many mazed considerings did throng  183
And pressed in with this caution. First, methought
I stood not in the smile of heaven, who had  185
Commanded nature that my lady's womb,
If it conceived a male child by me, should
Do no more offices of life to't than  188
The grave does to th' dead; for her male issue
Or died where they were made or shortly after
This world had aired them. Hence I took a thought
This was a judgment on me, that my kingdom
(Well worthy the best heir o' th' world) should not
Be gladded in't by me. Then follows that
I weighed the danger which my realms stood in
By this my issue's fail, and that gave to me  196
Many a groaning throe. Thus hulling in  197
The wild sea of my conscience, I did steer
Toward this remedy whereupon we are
Now present here together; that's to say
I mean to rectify my conscience, which  201
I then did feel full sick, and yet not well,  202
By all the reverend fathers of the land
And doctors learned. First I began in private  204
With you, my Lord of Lincoln. You remember
How under my oppression I did reek  206
When I first moved you.  207

LINCOLN          Very well, my liege.

KING

I have spoke long. Be pleased yourself to say
How far you satisfied me.

LINCOLN          So please your highness,
The question did at first so stagger me,
Bearing a state of mighty moment in't  211
And consequence of dread, that I committed  212
The daring'st counsel which I had to doubt
And did entreat your highness to this course
Which you are running here.

KING          I then moved you,
My Lord of Canterbury, and got your leave
To make this present summons. Unsolicited
I left no reverend person in this court,
But by particular consent proceeded
Under your hands and seals. Therefore go on,  220
For no dislike i' th' world against the person
Of the good queen, but the sharp thorny points
Of my allegèd reasons, drives this forward.  223
Prove but our marriage lawful, by my life
And kingly dignity, we are contented

126 *keep your way* keep going  135 *rare* excelling  137 *parts* qualities 138 *Sovereign* excellent, supreme; *speak thee out* describe you  141 *Carried herself* behaved  142 *require* request  146 *satisfied* given satisfaction  149 *on't* of it  151 *one the least* the very least  152 *prejudice* detriment  153 *touch* taint, sullying  154 *excuse* i.e. free from imputation 163 *passages* proceedings  163–65 *On . . . him* (the king now addresses the whole court)  167 *inducement* incentive  174 *determinate resolution* final settlement  175 *require* request  176 *advertise* inform  179 *Sometimes* formerly  180 *bosom* i.e. seat (cf. *The Tempest*, II, i, 271–72)  181 *spitting* piercing, and thereby transfixing  183 *mazed* perplexed  185 *smile* favor  188 *offices* functions  196 *issue's fail* lack of issue  197 *throe* pang; *hulling* drifting  201 *rectify* set right  202 *yet* which is still  204 *doctors learned* learned lawyers  206 *oppression* distress; *reek* sweat  207 *moved* appealed to  211 *Bearing . . . moment* concerning a state of affairs of great importance  212 *consequence of dread* fearful outcome  212–13 *committed . . . to doubt* i.e. distrusted . . .  220 *Under your hands* with your written consent  223 *allegèd* put forward (cf. II, i, 13–14)

226 To wear our mortal state to come with her,
Katherine our queen, before the primest creature
228 That's paragoned o' th' world.
   CAMPEIUS            So please your highness,
The queen being absent, 'tis a needful fitness
230 That we adjourn this court till further day.
231 Meanwhile must be an earnest motion
Made to the queen to call back her appeal
She intends unto his holiness.
   KING [aside]            I may perceive
These cardinals trifle with me. I abhor
This dilatory sloth and tricks of Rome.
My learnèd and well-belovèd servant Cranmer,
Prithee return. With thy approach I know
My comfort comes along. – Break up the court;
I say set on.       *Exeunt, in manner as they entered.*

\*

III, i      *Enter the Queen and her Women, as at work.*
   KATHERINE
Take thy lute, wench, my soul grows sad with troubles;
2 Sing, and disperse 'em if thou canst: leave working.

              *Song.*

Orpheus with his lute made trees,
And the mountain tops that freeze,
    Bow themselves when he did sing.
To his music plants and flowers
7 Ever sprung, as sun and showers
    There had made a lasting spring.

Every thing that heard him play,
10 Even the billows of the sea,
11     Hung their heads, and then lay by.
In sweet music is such art,
Killing care and grief of heart
    Fall asleep, or hearing die.

      *Enter a Gentleman.*
   KATHERINE
How now?
   GENTLEMAN
16 An't please your grace, the two great cardinals
17 Wait in the presence.
   KATHERINE       Would they speak with me?
   GENTLEMAN
18 They willed me say so, madam.
   KATHERINE            Pray their graces
To come near.           *[Exit Gentleman.]*
      What can be their business
With me, a poor weak woman, fall'n from favor?
I do not like their coming. Now I think on't,
22 They should be good men, their affairs as righteous;
But all hoods make not monks.
      *Enter the two Cardinals, Wolsey and Campeius.*
   WOLSEY            Peace to your highness.
   KATHERINE
Your graces find me here part of a housewife
25 (I would be all) against the worst may happen.
What are your pleasures with me, reverend lords?
   WOLSEY
May it please you, noble madam, to withdraw
Into your private chamber, we shall give you
The full cause of our coming.

   KATHERINE            Speak it here.
There's nothing I have done yet, o' my conscience,
Deserves a corner. Would all other women    31
Could speak this with as free a soul as I do!    32
My lords, I care not (so much I am happy
Above a number) if my actions    34
Were tried by ev'ry tongue, ev'ry eye saw 'em,
Envy and base opinion set against 'em,    36
I know my life so even. If your business    37
Seek me out, and that way I am wife in,    38
Out with it boldly: truth loves open dealing.
   WOLSEY Tanta est erga te mentis integritas, regina    40
serenissima –
   KATHERINE
O, good my lord, no Latin!
I am not such a truant since my coming    43
As not to know the language I have lived in.
A strange tongue makes my cause more strange, sus-    45
picious.
Pray speak in English. Here are some will thank you,
If you speak truth, for their poor mistress' sake.
Believe me, she has had much wrong. Lord cardinal,
The willing'st sin I ever yet committed    49
May be absolved in English.
   WOLSEY            Noble lady,
I am sorry my integrity should breed
(And service to his majesty and you)
So deep suspicion where all faith was meant.    53
We come not by the way of accusation    54
To taint that honor every good tongue blesses,
Nor to betray you any way to sorrow –    56
You have too much, good lady – but to know
How you stand minded in the weighty difference
Between the king and you, and to deliver    59
(Like free and honest men) our just opinions    60
And comforts to your cause.
   CAMPEIUS        Most honored madam,
My Lord of York, out of his noble nature,
Zeal and obedience he still bore your grace,    63
Forgetting (like a good man) your late censure
Both of his truth and him (which was too far),    65
Offers, as I do, in a sign of peace,    66
His service and his counsel.
   KATHERINE [aside]       To betray me. –
My lords, I thank you both for your good wills,
Ye speak like honest men (pray God ye prove so).
But how to make ye suddenly an answer    70
In such a point of weight, so near mine honor    71
(More near my life, I fear), with my weak wit,    72
And to such men of gravity and learning,

---

226 *our mortal state* everything that pertains to my being and majesty on earth   228 *paragoned o'* put forward as a model of excellence by   230 *further* a future   231 *motion* appeal
III, i The Queen's apartments   2 *leave* cease   7 *as* as if   10 *sea* (in Shakespeare's time pronounced 'say')   11 *lay by* rested   16 *An't* if it   17 *presence* presence-chamber   18 *willed* desired   22 *affairs* business   25 *against* in preparation for   31 *a corner* i.e. secrecy   32 *free* innocent   34 *a number* many   36 *Envy* malice; *opinion* gossip, rumor   37 *even* constant (in its uprightness)   38 *Seek . . . in* concerns me in my capacity as a wife   40–41 *Tanta . . . serenissima* such is the integrity of mind towards you, O most serene queen   43 *truant* idler   45 *strange . . . strange, suspicious* foreign . . . unfamiliar, and thus suspicious   49 *willing'st* most deliberate   53 *faith* loyalty   54 *by . . . accusation* in order to accuse you   56 *any way* in any manner   59 *deliver* declare   60 *honest* honorable   63 *still* always   65 *was* went   66 *in a sign* as a token   70 *suddenly* extempore   71, 72 *near* intimately affecting   72 *wit* understanding

74 In truth I know not. I was set at work
Among my maids, full little (God knows) looking
Either for such men or such business.
For her sake that I have been – for I feel
The last fit of my greatness – good your graces,
Let me have time and counsel for my cause.
Alas, I am a woman friendless, hopeless.

WOLSEY
Madam, you wrong the king's love with these fears ;
Your hopes and friends are infinite.

KATHERINE         In England
But little for my profit. Can you think, lords,
That any Englishman dare give me counsel ?
Or be a known friend 'gainst his highness' pleasure
86 (Though he be grown so desperate to be honest)
And live a subject ? Nay forsooth, my friends,
88 They that must weigh out my afflictions,
They that my trust must grow to, live not here.
They are (as all my other comforts) far hence
In mine own country, lords.

CAMPEIUS        I would your grace
Would leave your griefs and take my counsel.

KATHERINE         How, sir ?

CAMPEIUS
Put your main cause into the king's protection,
He's loving and most gracious. 'Twill be much
Both for your honor better and your cause ;
For if the trial of the law o'ertake ye,
97 You'll part away disgraced. .

WOLSEY        He tells you rightly.

KATHERINE
Ye tell me what ye wish for both – my ruin.
Is this your Christian counsel ? Out upon ye !
Heaven is above all yet ; there sits a judge
That no king can corrupt.

101 CAMPEIUS       Your rage mistakes us.

KATHERINE
The more shame for ye ! Holy men I thought ye,
103 Upon my soul, two reverend cardinal virtues ;
But cardinal sins and hollow hearts I fear ye :
Mend 'em for shame, my lords ! Is this your comfort ?
The cordial that ye bring a wretched lady ?
107 A woman lost among ye, laughed at, scorned ?
I will not wish ye half my miseries,
I have more charity. But say I warned ye.
110 Take heed, for heaven's sake take heed, lest at once
The burthen of my sorrows fall upon ye.

WOLSEY
112 Madam, this is a mere distraction.
113 You turn the good we offer into envy.

KATHERINE
Ye turn me into nothing. Woe upon ye

And all such false professors ! Would you have me   115
(If you have any justice, any pity,
If ye be anything but churchmen's habits)   117
Put my sick cause into his hands that hates me ?
Alas, has banished me his bed already,   119
His love, too long ago. I am old, my lords,
And all the fellowship I hold now with him
Is only my obedience. What can happen
To me above this wretchedness ? All your studies   123
Make me accursed like this.   124

CAMPEIUS         Your fears are worse.

KATHERINE
Have I lived thus long (let me speak myself,
Since virtue finds no friends) a wife, a true one ?
A woman ( I dare say without vainglory)
Never yet branded with suspicion ?
Have I with all my full affections   129
Still met the king ? loved him next heav'n ? obeyed him ?   130
Been (out of fondness) superstitious to him ?   131
Almost forgot my prayers to content him ?
And am I thus rewarded ? 'tis not well, lords.
Bring me a constant woman to her husband,   134
One that ne'er dreamed a joy beyond his pleasure,
And to that woman (when she has done most)
Yet will I add an honor – a great patience.

WOLSEY
Madam, you wander from the good we aim at.

KATHERINE
My lord, I dare not make myself so guilty
To give up willingly that noble title   140
Your master wed me to. Nothing but death
Shall e'er divorce my dignities.

WOLSEY        Pray hear me.

KATHERINE
Would I had never trod this English earth
Or felt the flatteries that grow upon it !
Ye have angels' faces, but heaven knows your hearts.
What will become of me now, wretched lady ?
I am the most unhappy woman living.
    [To her Women]
Alas, poor wenches, where are now your fortunes ?
Shipwracked upon a kingdom where no pity,
No friends, no hope, no kindred weep for me, ·
Almost no grave allowed me. Like the lily
That once was mistress of the field and flourished,
I'll hang my head and perish.

WOLSEY         If your grace
Could but be brought to know our ends are honest,   154
You'ld feel more comfort. Why should we, good lady,
Upon what cause, wrong you ? Alas, our places,   156
The way of our profession is against it.
We are to cure such sorrows, not to sow 'em.
For goodness' sake, consider what you do ;
How you may hurt yourself, ay, utterly
Grow from the king's acquaintance by this carriage.   161
The hearts of princes kiss obedience,
So much they love it ; but to stubborn spirits
They swell and grow as terrible as storms.
I know you have a gentle, noble temper,   165
A soul as even as a calm. Pray think us
Those we profess, peacemakers, friends, and servants.

CAMPEIUS
Madam, you'll find it so. You wrong your virtues
With these weak women's fears. A noble spirit,

170   As yours was put into you, ever casts
Such doubts as false coin from it. The king loves you :
Beware you lose it not. For us, if you please
To trust us in your business, we are ready
174   To use our utmost studies in your service.

KATHERINE
Do what ye will, my lords ; and pray forgive me ;
176   If I have used myself unmannerly,
177   You know I am a woman, lacking wit
To make a seemly answer to such persons.
179   Pray do my service to his majesty,
He has my heart yet, and shall have my prayers
While I shall have my life. Come, reverend fathers,
Bestow your counsels on me. She now begs
That little thought, when she set footing here,
She should have bought her dignities so dear.    *Exeunt.*

\*

III, ii     *Enter the Duke of Norfolk, Duke of Suffolk, Lord
Surrey, and Lord Chamberlain.*

NORFOLK
If you will now unite in your complaints
2   And force them with a constancy, the cardinal
3   Cannot stand under them. If you omit
The offer of this time, I cannot promise
5   But that you shall sustain moe new disgraces
With these your bear already.

SURREY          I am joyful
To meet the least occasion that may give me
8   Remembrance of my father-in-law, the duke,
To be revenged on him.

SUFFOLK        Which of the peers
10   Have uncontemned gone by him, or at least
Strangely neglected ? When did he regard
The stamp of nobleness in any person
13   Out of himself ?

CHAMBERLAIN   My lords, you speak your pleasures.
What he deserves of you and me I know.
What we can do to him (though now the time
16   Gives way to us) I much fear. If you cannot
17   Bar his access to th' king, never attempt
Anything on him ; for he hath a witchcraft
Over the king in's tongue.

NORFOLK        O fear him not,
20   His spell in that is out. The king hath found
Matter against him that for ever mars
22   The honey of his language. No, he's settled
23   (Not to come off) in his displeasure.

SURREY          Sir,
I should be glad to hear such news as this
Once every hour.

NORFOLK       Believe it, this is true.
26   In the divorce his contrary proceedings
27   Are all unfolded ; wherein he appears
As I would wish mine enemy.

SURREY          How came
29   His practices to light ?

SUFFOLK       Most strangely.
SURREY          O how ? how ?
SUFFOLK
30   The cardinal's letters to the pope miscarried
And came to th' eye o' th' king, wherein was read
How that the cardinal did entreat his holiness

To stay the judgment o' th' divorce ; for if
It did take place, 'I do,' quoth he, 'perceive
My king is tangled in affection to
A creature of the queen's, Lady Anne Bullen.'    36

SURREY
Has the king this ?
SUFFOLK       Believe it.
SURREY          Will this work ?
CHAMBERLAIN
The king in this perceives him, how he coasts    38
And hedges his own way. But in this point    39
All his tricks founder and he brings his physic    40
After his patient's death : the king already
Hath married the fair lady.

SURREY          Would he had !
SUFFOLK
May you be happy in your wish, my lord,
For I profess you have it.    44

SURREY        Now all my joy
Trace the conjunction !    45
SUFFOLK       My amen to't !
NORFOLK         All men's !
SUFFOLK
There's order given for her coronation.
Marry this is yet but young, and may be left    47
To some ears unrecounted. But, my lords,
She is a gallant creature and complete    49
In mind and feature. I persuade me, from her
Will fall some blessing to this land, which shall
In it be memorized.    52

SURREY        But will the king
Digest this letter of the cardinal's ?    53
The Lord forbid !
NORFOLK       Marry amen.
SUFFOLK        No, no ;
There be moe wasps that buzz about his nose
Will make this sting the sooner. Cardinal Campeius
Is stol'n away to Rome, hath ta'en no leave,
Has left the cause o' th' king unhandled, and
Is posted as the agent of our cardinal    59
To second all his plot. I do assure you
The king cried 'Ha' at this.    61

CHAMBERLAIN       Now God incense him
And let him cry 'Ha' louder !
NORFOLK       But, my lord,
When returns Cranmer ?
SUFFOLK
He is returned in his opinions, which    64

170 *As . . . you* i.e. such as that you are endowed with   174 *studies* efforts
176 *used myself* behaved   177 *wit* understanding   179 *do my service* pay
my respects
III, ii *The King's* apartments   2 *force* press home ; *constancy* persistence
3 *omit* neglect   5 *moe* more   8 *duke* i.e. of Buckingham   10 *uncontemned*
not despised   13 *Out of* except ; *speak your pleasures* say freely what you
will   16 *Gives way to* favors   17–18 *attempt Anything* make any attack
20 *out* finished   22 *he* (probably Wolsey)   23 *come off* escape ; *his* i.e. the
King's   26 *contrary* contradictory (see ll. 32–36)   27 *unfolded* disclosed
29 *practices* intrigues   30 *miscarried* went astray   36 *creature* servant, anyone employed or favored by her   38 *coasts* (the metaphor is carried on in
*founder,* l. 40)   39 *his own way* i.e. towards his own ends   40 *physic*
medicine   44 *profess* declare   45 *conjunction* marriage, union   47 *Marry*
to be sure (derived from 'by Mary') ; *young* new   49 *gallant* splendid ;
*complete* perfect   52 *memorized* made memorable   53 *Digest* i.e. put up
with   59 *posted* gone with haste   61 *Ha* (the king's favorite exclamation)
64 *is . . . opinions* has returned with his views confirmed (?), has sent in
advance the opinions he gathered before returning in person (?)

Have satisfied the king for his divorce,
Together with all famous colleges
Almost in Christendom. Shortly, I believe,
His second marriage shall be published and
Her coronation. Katherine no more
Shall be called queen, but princess dowager,
And widow to Prince Arthur.

NORFOLK          This same Cranmer's
A worthy fellow, and hath ta'en much pain
In the king's business.

SUFFOLK        He has, and we shall see him
For it an archbishop.

NORFOLK        So I hear.

SUFFOLK        'Tis so.
     *Enter Wolsey and Cromwell.*
The cardinal!

NORFOLK      Observe, observe, he's moody.

WOLSEY
The packet, Cromwell,
Gave't you the king?

CROMWELL        To his own hand, in's bedchamber.

WOLSEY
Looked he o' th' inside of the paper?

CROMWELL          Presently
He did unseal them, and the first he viewed,
He did it with a serious mind; a heed
Was in his countenance. You he bade
Attend him here this morning.

WOLSEY          Is he ready
To come abroad?

CROMWELL      I think by this he is.

WOLSEY
Leave me awhile.          *Exit Cromwell.*
     [*Aside*]
It shall be to the Duchess of Alençon,
The French king's sister; he shall marry her.
Anne Bullen? no! I'll no Anne Bullens for him;
There's more in't than fair visage. Bullen?
No, we'll no Bullens! Speedily I wish
To hear from Rome. The Marchioness of Pembroke?

NORFOLK
He's discontented.

SUFFOLK        May be he hears the king
Does whet his anger to him.

SURREY          Sharp enough,
Lord, for thy justice!

WOLSEY [*aside*]
The late queen's gentlewoman? a knight's daughter
To be her mistress' mistress? the queen's queen?
This candle burns not clear, 'tis I must snuff it;
Then out it goes. What though I know her virtuous

---

68 *published* proclaimed   72 *pain* pains   78 *paper* wrapper with contents inside; *Presently* immediately   99 *spleeny* passionate; *wholesome* suitable, beneficial   100 *lie . . . bosom of* (1) marry, (2) share the secrets of   101 *hard-ruled* managed with difficulty   102 *arch one* chief   103 *Hath* who has   104 *oracle* i.e. trusted adviser   **s.d.** *schedule* scroll of paper   105 *fret* corrode (with play on the 'fret' of a stringed instrument, a bar to regulate fingering)   106 *master-cord* (not merely a metaphor; the Elizabethan believed in heart-strings); *on's* of his   108 *portion* allotted share   112 *commotion* rebellion, perturbation   122 *wot* know   124 *importing* signifying   125 *several parcels* various items   127 *rate* value   127–28 *outspeaks . . . subject* describes more than what is fitting for a subject to possess   130 *withal* therewith   134 *below the moon* worldly   137 *stuff* (cf. l. 126)   140 *spiritual leisure* i.e. time devoted to religious duties   142 *ill husband* bad manager

---

And well-deserving? yet I know her for
A spleeny Lutheran, and not wholesome to    99
Our cause that she should lie i' th' bosom of    100
Our hard-ruled king. Again there is sprung up    101
An heretic, an arch one – Cranmer, one    102
Hath crawled into the favor of the king    103
And is his oracle.    104

NORFOLK      He is vexed at something.
     *Enter King, reading of a schedule [, and Lovell].*

SURREY
I would 'twere something that would fret the string,    105
The master-cord on's heart.    106

SUFFOLK        The king, the king!

KING
What piles of wealth hath he accumulated
To his own portion! and what expense by th' hour    108
Seems to flow from him! How i' th' name of thrift
Does he rake this together? – Now, my lords,
Saw you the cardinal?

NORFOLK        My lord, we have
Stood here observing him. Some strange commotion    112
Is in his brain. He bites his lip, and starts,
Stops on a sudden, looks upon the ground,
Then lays his finger on his temple; straight
Springs out into fast gait, then stops again,
Strikes his breast hard, and anon he casts
His eye against the moon: in most strange postures
We have seen him set himself.

KING          It may well be,
There is a mutiny in's mind. This morning
Papers of state he sent me to peruse
As I required; and wot you what I found    122
There, on my conscience, put unwittingly?
Forsooth an inventory, thus importing    124
The several parcels of his plate, his treasure,    125
Rich stuffs and ornaments of household; which
I find at such proud rate that it outspeaks    127
Possession of a subject.

NORFOLK        It's heaven's will;
Some spirit put this paper in the packet
To bless your eye withal.    130

KING        If we did think
His contemplation were above the earth
And fixed on spiritual object, he should still
Dwell in his musings; but I am afraid
His thinkings are below the moon, not worth    134
His serious considering.
     *King takes his seat; whispers Lovell, who goes to*
     *the Cardinal.*

WOLSEY        Heaven forgive me;
Even God bless your highness!

KING        Good my lord,
You are full of heavenly stuff, and bear the inventory    137
Of your best graces in your mind; the which
You were now running o'er. You have scarce time
To steal from spiritual leisure a brief span    140
To keep your earthly audit; sure in that
I deem you an ill husband, and am glad    142
To have you therein my companion.

WOLSEY        Sir,
For holy offices I have a time; a time
To think upon the part of business which
I bear i' th' state; and nature does require
Her times of preservation, which perforce

    I, her frail son, amongst my brethren mortal,
149 Must give my tendance to.
KING            You have said well.
WOLSEY
    And ever may your highness yoke together
    (As I will lend you cause) my doing well
    With my well saying !
KING           'Tis well said again,
    And 'tis a kind of good deed to say well ;
    And yet words are no deeds. My father loved you ;
155 He said he did, and with his deed did crown
    His word upon you. Since I had my office,
    I have kept you next my heart ; have not alone
    Employed you where high profits might come home,
159 But pared my present havings to bestow
    My bounties upon you.
WOLSEY *[aside]*        What should this mean ?
SURREY *[aside]*
    The Lord increase this business !
KING            Have I not made you
162 The prime man of the state ? I pray you tell me
163 If what I now pronounce you have found true ;
164 And if you may confess it, say withal
    If you are bound to us or no. What say you ?
WOLSEY
    My sovereign, I confess your royal graces,
    Showered on me daily, have been more than could
168 My studied purposes requite, which went
    Beyond all man's endeavors. My endeavors
    Have ever come too short of my desires,
171 Yet filled with my abilities. Mine own ends
172 Have been mine so, that evermore they pointed
    To th' good of your most sacred person and
    The profit of the state. For your great graces
    Heaped upon me (poor undeserver) I
    Can nothing render but allegiant thanks,
    My prayers to heaven for you, my loyalty,
    Which ever has and ever shall be growing,
    Till death (that winter) kill it.
KING            Fairly answered :
    A loyal and obedient subject is
181 Therein illustrated. The honor of it
    Does pay the act of it, as i' th' contrary
183 The foulness is the punishment. I presume
184 That, as my hand has opened bounty to you,
    My heart dropped love, my pow'r rained honor, more
    On you than any, so your hand and heart,
    Your brain and every function of your power
188 Should, notwithstanding that your bond of duty,
189 As 'twere in love's particular, be more
    To me, your friend, than any.
WOLSEY           I do profess
    That for your highness' good I ever labored
192 More than mine own ; that am, have, and will be –
    Though all the world should crack their duty to you
    And throw it from their soul ; though perils did
    Abound as thick as thought could make 'em and
    Appear in forms more horrid – yet my duty,
197 As doth a rock against the chiding flood,
    Should the approach of this wild river break,
    And stand unshaken yours.
KING           'Tis nobly spoken.
    Take notice, lords, he has a loyal breast,
    For you have seen him open't. Read o'er this,

*[Gives him papers.]*
    And after, this, and then to breakfast with
    What appetite you have.
            *Exit King frowning upon the Cardinal.*
            *The Nobles throng after him,*
            *smiling and whispering.*
WOLSEY           What should this mean ?
    What sudden anger 's this ? How have I reaped it ?
    He parted frowning from me, as if ruin
    Leaped from his eyes. So looks the chafèd lion     206
    Upon the daring huntsman that has galled him ;     207
    Then makes him nothing. I must read this paper ;     208
    I fear, the story of his anger. 'Tis so ;
    This paper has undone me. 'Tis th' accompt
    Of all that world of wealth I have drawn together
    For mine own ends – indeed to gain the popedom
    And fee my friends in Rome. O negligence
    Fit for a fool to fall by ! What cross devil     214
    Made me put this main secret in the packet     215
    I sent the king ? Is there no way to cure this ?
    No new device to beat this from his brains ?
    I know 'twill stir him strongly ; yet I know
    A way, if it take right, in spite of fortune,     219
    Will bring me off again. What's this ? 'To th' pope' ?     220
    The letter (as I live) with all the business
    I writ to 's holiness. Nay then, farewell !     222
    I have touched the highest point of all my greatness,
    And from that full meridian of my glory     224
    I haste now to my setting. I shall fall
    Like a bright exhalation in the evening,     226
    And no man see me more.
        *Enter to Wolsey the Dukes of Norfolk and Suffolk,*
        *the Earl of Surrey, and the Lord Chamberlain.*
NORFOLK
    Hear the king's pleasure, cardinal, who commands you
    To render up the great seal presently     229
    Into our hands and to confine yourself
    To Asher House, my Lord of Winchester's,
    Till you hear further from his highness.
WOLSEY           Stay :
    Where's your commission, lords ? Words cannot carry
    Authority so weighty.
SUFFOLK          Who dare cross 'em,     234
    Bearing the king's will from his mouth expressly ?
WOLSEY
    Till I find more than will or words to do it     236
    (I mean your malice) know, officious lords,
    I dare and must deny it. Now I feel
    Of what coarse metal ye are moulded – envy ;     239
    How eagerly ye follow my disgraces
    As if it fed ye, and how sleek and wanton     241

---

149 *tendance* attention   155 *crown* perfect, complete nobly   159 *havings* possessions   162 *prime* principal   163 *pronounce* declare   164 *withal* also, in addition   168 *studied purposes* efforts   171 *filled with* fulfilled to the best of ; *ends* aims   172 *so* in such a way   181–82 *The honor . . . it* the honor of being loyal is the reward of loyalty   183 *foulness* moral impurity   184 *opened* generously made available   188 *that . . . duty* i.e. his commitment to the pope   189 *particular* special intimacy   192 *have* have been   197 *chiding* noisily scolding   206 *chafèd* angry, raging   207 *galled* wounded   208 *makes him nothing* annihilates him   214 *cross* thwarting   215 *main* chief, very important   219 *take right* succeed   220 *bring me off* rescue me, acquit me   222 *writ* wrote   224 *meridian* prime, splendor, point of highest altitude of a star   226 *exhalation* meteor   229 *presently* at once   234 *cross* oppose   236 *do it* i.e. render up the seal   239 *envy* malice   241 *wanton* reckless and willful

Ye appear in everything may bring my ruin!
Follow your envious courses, men of malice.
4   You have Christian warrant for 'em, and no doubt
5   In time will find their fit rewards. That seal
    You ask with such a violence, the king
    (Mine and your master) with his own hand gave me;
8   Bade me enjoy it, with the place and honors,
    During my life; and to confirm his goodness
0   Ties it by letters patents. Now who'll take it?

SURREY
    The king that gave it.

WOLSEY                    It must be himself then.

SURREY
    Thou art a proud traitor, priest.

WOLSEY                    Proud lord, thou liest!
3   Within these forty hours Surrey durst better
    Have burnt that tongue than said so.

SURREY                        Thy ambition
5   (Thou scarlet sin) robbed this bewailing land
    Of noble Buckingham, my father-in-law.
    The heads of all thy brother cardinals
8   (With thee and all thy best parts bound together)
9   Weighed not a hair of his. Plague of your policy!
    You sent me Deputy for Ireland,
    Far from his succor, from the king, from all
2   That might have mercy on the fault thou gav'st him;
    Whilst your great goodness, out of holy pity,
    Absolved him with an axe.

WOLSEY                    This, and all else
5   This talking lord can lay upon my credit,
    I answer is most false. The duke by law
    Found his deserts. How innocent I was
8   From any private malice in his end,
    His noble jury and foul cause can witness.
    If I loved many words, lord, I should tell you
    You have as little honesty as honor,
2   That in the way of loyalty and truth
    Toward the king, my ever royal master,
4   Dare mate a sounder man than Surrey can be
    And all that love his follies.

SURREY                    By my soul,
    Your long coat, priest, protects you; thou shouldst feel
    My sword i' th' lifeblood of thee else. My lords,
    Can ye endure to hear this arrogance?
9   And from this fellow? If we live thus tamely,
0   To be thus jaded by a piece of scarlet,

Farewell nobility! let his grace go forward
And dare us with his cap, like larks.                    282

WOLSEY                    All goodness
Is poison to thy stomach.

SURREY                    Yes, that goodness
Of gleaning all the land's wealth into one,
Into your own hands, cardinal, by extortion;
The goodness of your intercepted packets
You writ to th' pope against the king. Your goodness,
Since you provoke me, shall be most notorious.
My Lord of Norfolk, as you are truly noble,
As you respect the common good, the state
Of our despised nobility, our issues                    291
(Who, if he live, will scarce be gentlemen),
Produce the grand sum of his sins, the articles         293
Collected from his life. I'll startle you
Worse than the sacring bell when the brown wench        295
Lay kissing in your arms, lord cardinal.

WOLSEY
How much, methinks, I could despise this man
But that I am bound in charity against it.

NORFOLK
Those articles, my lord, are in the king's hand;
But thus much – they are foul ones.                     300

WOLSEY                        So much fairer
And spotless shall mine innocence arise
When the king knows my truth.

SURREY                        This cannot save you.
I thank my memory, I yet remember
Some of these articles, and out they shall!
Now if you can blush and cry guilty, cardinal
You'll show a little honesty.

WOLSEY                    Speak on, sir,
I dare your worst objections. If I blush,                307
It is to see a nobleman want manners.

SURREY
I had rather want those than my head. Have at you!      309
First, that without the king's assent or knowledge
You wrought to be a legate, by which power              311
You maimed the jurisdiction of all bishops.

NORFOLK
Then, that all you writ to Rome, or else
To foreign princes, 'Ego et Rex meus'                   314
Was still inscribed; in which you brought the king      315
To be your servant.                                     316

SUFFOLK                    Then, that without the knowledge
Either of king or council, when you went
Ambassador to the emperor, you made bold                318
To carry into Flanders the great seal.

SURREY
Item, you sent a large commission
To Gregory de Cassado to conclude,
Without the king's will or the state's allowance,       322
A league between his highness and Ferrara.

SUFFOLK
That out of mere ambition you have caused               324
Your holy hat to be stamped on the king's coin.         325

SURREY
Then, that you have sent innumerable substance          326
(By what means got, I leave to your own conscience)
To furnish Rome and to prepare the ways                 328
You have for dignities, to the mere undoing             329
Of all the kingdom. Many more there are,
Which, since they are of you, and odious,

---

244 *Christian warrant* (ironical)  245 *find* meet with  248 *place and honors* i.e. of the office of Lord Chancellor  250 *letters patents* open documents conferring certain rights (from French, '*lettres patentes*')  253 *forty* (used as a round number)  255 *scarlet* (alluding both to Isaiah i, 18 and to the cardinal's robes)  258 *parts* qualities  259 *Weighed not* was not worth; *Plague of* plague upon  262 *fault* offense  265 *credit* good name  268 *From of*  272 *That . . . way of* I that in  274 *mate* match  279 *fellow* (gross insult, for the term was usually used towards servants)  280 *jaded* cowed  282 *dare* dazzle (and thus render helpless; alludes to the method of catching larks with the help of a mirror and a red cloth)  291 *issues* sons  293 *articles* counts of indictment  295 *sacring* consecrating  300 *thus much* i.e. I can say this much  307 *objections* accusations  309 *Have at you* (a phrase announcing the attack)  311 *legate* pope's official representative  314 *Ego . . . meus* I and my king  315 *still* always  316 *servant* (a mistaken idea, not original in this play; the Latin phrase suggests equality)  318 *emperor* i.e. Charles V  322 *allowance* permission  324 *mere* sheer  325 *Your . . . coin* (Wolsey had the right to coin half-groats, but not groats, with his initials and the cardinal's hat upon them)  326 *innumerable substance* countless wealth  328 *furnish* supply  329 *mere undoing* complete ruin

I will not taint my mouth with.

CHAMBERLAIN                                    O my lord,
Press not a falling man too far ! 'Tis virtue.
His faults lie open to the laws ; let them,
Not you, correct him. My heart weeps to see him
So little of his great self.

SURREY                          I forgive him.

SUFFOLK
Lord cardinal, the king's further pleasure is –
Because all those things you have done of late
339    By your power legative within this kingdom
340    Fall into th' compass of a praemunire –
341    That therefore such a writ be sued against you,
To forfeit all your goods, lands, tenements,
Chattels, and whatsoever, and to be
344    Out of the king's protection. This is my charge.

NORFOLK
And so we'll leave you to your meditations
How to live better. For your stubborn answer
About the giving back the great seal to us,
The king shall know it, and (no doubt) shall thank you.
349    So fare you well, my little good lord cardinal.
                          *Exeunt all but Wolsey.*

WOLSEY
So farewell to the little good you bear me.
351    Farewell ? a long farewell to all my greatness !
This is the state of man : to-day he puts forth
The tender leaves of hopes ; to-morrow blossoms
354    And bears his blushing honors thick upon him ;
The third day comes a frost, a killing frost,
356    And when he thinks, good easy man, full surely
His greatness is a-ripening, nips his root,
And then he falls as I do. I have ventured,
Like little wanton boys that swim on bladders,
This many summers in a sea of glory,
But far beyond my depth. My high-blown pride
At length broke under me, and now has left me,
Weary and old with service, to the mercy
364    Of a rude stream that must for ever hide me.
365    Vain pomp and glory of this world, I hate ye !
I feel my heart new opened. O, how wretched
Is that poor man that hangs on princes' favors !
There is betwixt that smile we would aspire to,
369    That sweet aspect of princes, and their ruin,
More pangs and fears than wars or women have ;
And when he falls, he falls like Lucifer,
Never to hope again.
          *Enter Cromwell, standing amazed.*
                          Why how now, Cromwell ?

CROMWELL
I have no power to speak, sir.

WOLSEY                          What, amazed
At my misfortunes ? Can thy spirit wonder
375    A great man should decline ? Nay, an you weep,
I am fall'n indeed.

CROMWELL          How does your grace ?

WOLSEY                                    Why well ;
Never so truly happy, my good Cromwell.
I know myself now, and I feel within me
A peace above all earthly dignities,
A still and quiet conscience. The king has cured me –
I humbly thank his grace – and from these shoulders,
These ruined pillars, out of pity taken
A load would sink a navy – too much honor.

O 'tis a burden, Cromwell, 'tis a burden
Too heavy for a man that hopes for heaven.

CROMWELL
I am glad your grace has made that right use of it.

WOLSEY
I hope I have. I am able now, methinks,
Out of a fortitude of soul I feel,
To endure more miseries and greater far
Than my weak-hearted enemies dare offer.
What news abroad ?

CROMWELL          The heaviest and the worst
Is your displeasure with the king.                3o

WOLSEY                          God bless him !

CROMWELL
The next is that Sir Thomas More is chosen
Lord Chancellor in your place.

WOLSEY                          That's somewhat sudden.
But he's a learnèd man. May he continue
Long in his highness' favor, and do justice
For truth's sake and his conscience ; that his bones,
When he has run his course and sleeps in blessings,
May have a tomb of orphans' tears wept on him.     3o
What more ?

CROMWELL    That Cranmer is returned with welcome ;
Installed Lord Archbishop of Canterbury.

WOLSEY
That's news indeed.

CROMWELL          Last, that the Lady Anne,
Whom the king hath in secrecy long married,
This day was viewed in open as his queen,
Going to chapel ; and the voice is now             4o
Only about her coronation.

WOLSEY
There was the weight that pulled me down. O Cromwell,
The king has gone beyond me : all my glories        4c
In that one woman I have lost for ever.
No sun shall ever usher forth mine honors
Or gild again the noble troops that waited          4
Upon my smiles. Go get thee from me, Cromwell !
I am a poor fall'n man, unworthy now
To be thy lord and master. Seek the king
(That sun, I pray, may never set). I have told him
What and how true thou art. He will advance thee :
Some little memory of me will stir him
(I know his noble nature) not to let
Thy hopeful service perish too. Good Cromwell,
Neglect him not ; make use now, and provide        42
For thine own future safety.

CROMWELL                          O my lord,
Must I then leave you ? Must I needs forgo
So good, so noble, and so true a master ?
Bear witness, all that have not hearts of iron,

---

339 *legative* as a legate   340 *praemunire* a writ by which a person could be summoned on a charge of asserting papal jurisdiction in England   341 *sued* applied for   344 *Out . . . protection* i.e. without legal protection   349 *little good* little-good (?)   351 *Farewell?* (so in the folio ; Wolsey suddenly realizes the appropriateness of the word to his whole career ; but editors often replace the query mark by a comma)   354 *blushing* glowing   356 *easy* easygoing   364 *rude* rough   365 *Vain . . . world* (an intentional allusion to the Anglican baptismal service)   369 *their ruin* the ruin they cause   375 *decline* fall from prosperity ; *an* if   392 *your . . . king* the king's displeasure towards you   399 *tomb . . . him* (for the Lord Chancellor is the general guardian, or legal protector, of children)   405 *voice* general talk   408 *gone beyond* overreached   411 *troops* retainers   420 *make use* take advantage

With what a sorrow Cromwell leaves his lord.
The king shall have my service, but my pray'rs
For ever and for ever shall be yours.

WOLSEY
Cromwell, I did not think to shed a tear
In all my miseries ; but thou hast forced me
(Out of thy honest truth) to play the woman.
Let's dry our eyes : and thus far hear me, Cromwell,
And when I am forgotten, as I shall be,
And sleep in dull cold marble, where no mention
Of me more must be heard of, say I taught thee ;
Say, Wolsey, that once trod the ways of glory
And sounded all the depths and shoals of honor,
Found thee a way (out of his wrack) to rise in,
A sure and safe one, though thy master missed it.
Mark but my fall and that that ruined me.
Cromwell, I charge thee, fling away ambition !
By that sin fell the angels ; how can man then
(The image of his Maker) hope to win by it ?
Love thyself last, cherish those hearts that hate thee ;
Corruption wins not more than honesty.
Still in thy right hand carry gentle peace
To silence envious tongues. Be just, and fear not.
Let all the ends thou aim'st at be thy country's,
Thy God's and truth's : then if thou fall'st, O Cromwell,
Thou fall'st a blessed martyr.
Serve the king. And prithee lead me in :
There take an inventory of all I have
To the last penny : 'tis the king's. My robe,
And my integrity to heaven, is all
I dare now call mine own. O Cromwell, Cromwell,
Had I but served my God with half the zeal
I served my king, he would not in mine age
Have left me naked to mine enemies.

CROMWELL
Good sir, have patience.

WOLSEY            So I have. Farewell
The hopes of court ; my hopes in heaven do dwell.

*Exeunt.*

\*

i      *Enter two Gentlemen, meeting one another.*

1 . GENTLEMAN
Y' are well met once again.

2 . GENTLEMAN        So are you.

1 . GENTLEMAN
You come to take your stand here, and behold
The Lady Anne pass from her coronation ?

2 . GENTLEMAN
'Tis all my business. At our last encounter

The Duke of Buckingham came from his trial.

1 . GENTLEMAN
'Tis very true ; but that time offered sorrow,
This, general joy.

2 . GENTLEMAN     'Tis well. The citizens
I am sure have shown at full their royal minds –    8
As let 'em have their rights, they are ever forward –    9
In celebration of this day with shows,
Pageants, and sights of honor.

1 . GENTLEMAN          Never greater,
Nor, I'll assure you, better taken, sir.       12

2 . GENTLEMAN
May I be bold to ask what that contains,
That paper in your hand ?

1 . GENTLEMAN        Yes, 'tis the list
Of those that claim their offices this day,
By custom of the coronation.
The Duke of Suffolk is the first, and claims
To be high steward ; next, the Duke of Norfolk,
He to be earl marshal. You may read the rest.

2 . GENTLEMAN
I thank you, sir. Had I not known those customs,
I should have been beholding to your paper.     21
But, I beseech you, what's become of Katherine,
The princess dowager ? how goes her business ?

1 . GENTLEMAN
That I can tell you too. The Archbishop
Of Canterbury, accompanied with other
Learnèd and reverend fathers of his order,
Held a late court at Dunstable, six miles off    27
From Ampthill, where the princess lay, to which    28
She was often cited by them, but appeared not ;    29
And to be short, for not-appearance and
The king's late scruple, by the main assent     31
Of all these learned men she was divorced
And the late marriage made of none effect ;     33
Since which she was removed to Kimbolton,     34
Where she remains now sick.

2 . GENTLEMAN         Alas good lady.
[*Trumpets.*]
The trumpets sound. Stand close, the queen is coming.   36
*Hautboys.*

### THE ORDER OF THE CORONATION

*1. A lively flourish of trumpets.*

*2. Then two Judges.*

*3. Lord Chancellor, with purse and mace before him.*

*4. Choristers singing. Music.*

*5. Mayor of London, bearing the mace. Then Garter, in his coat of arms, and on his head he wore a gilt copper crown.*

*6. Marquess Dorset, bearing a sceptre of gold, on his head a demi-coronal of gold. With him the Earl of Surrey, bearing the rod of silver with the dove, crowned with an earl's coronet. Collars of Esses.*

*7. Duke of Suffolk, in his robe of estate, his coronet on his head, bearing a long white wand, as high steward. With him the Duke of Norfolk, with the rod of marshalship, a coronet on his head. Collars of Esses.*

*8. A canopy borne by four of the Cinque-Ports ; under it the Queen in her robe ; in her hair, richly adorned with pearl, crowned. On each side her the Bishops of London and Winchester.*

---

**430** *play the woman* shed tears   **436** *sounded* fathomed   **442** *win* profit
**443** *Love . . . thee* (a paraphrase of Matthew v, 44)   **445** *Still* constantly
**446** *envious* malicious   **448-49** *if . . . martyr* (a prediction of Cromwell's
fate)   **457** *naked* i.e. defenseless
**IV, i** A street in Westminster   **8** *royal minds* devotion to royalty   **9** *As
. . . rights* give them their due ('As' merely introduces the parenthesis) ;
*forward* eager   **12** *taken* received   **21** *beholding* indebted   **27** *late* recent
**28** *lay* resided   **29** *cited* summoned   **31** *late* former ; *main assent* general
agreement   **33** *of none effect* null   **34** *Kimbolton* (in Huntingdonshire ; the
'b' is not pronounced)   **36** *close* out of sight   **s.d.** *item 3 Lord Chancellor*
i.e. Sir Thomas More   *item 5 Garter* the chief herald, Garter King-at-
Arms   *item 6 demi-coronal* small crown-like circlet   *items 6, 7 Collars of
Esses* ornamental chains made of a series of joined letters 'S'   *item 7 estate*
state   *item 8 Cinque-Ports* barons of the five Channel ports of Hastings,
Sandwich, Dover, Romney, and Hythe ; *in her hair* with her hair loosely
hanging (as customary for brides)

    9. *The old Duchess of Norfolk, in a coronal of gold,*
       *wrought with flowers, bearing the Queen's train.*
   10. *Certain ladies or countesses, with plain circlets of*
       *gold without flowers.*

           *Exeunt, first passing over the stage*
            *in order and state, and then a*
             *great flourish of trumpets.*

2. GENTLEMAN

37  A royal train, believe me. These I know.
    Who's that that bears the sceptre?

1. GENTLEMAN         Marquess Dorset,
    And that the Earl of Surrey with the rod.

2. GENTLEMAN
    A bold brave gentleman. That should be
    The Duke of Suffolk.

1. GENTLEMAN        'Tis the same: high steward.

2. GENTLEMAN
    And that my Lord of Norfolk?

1. GENTLEMAN         Yes.

2. GENTLEMAN *[looks on the Queen]* Heaven bless thee,
    Thou hast the sweetest face I ever looked on.
    Sir, as I have a soul, she is an angel;

45  Our king has all the Indies in his arms,
46  And more, and richer, when he strains that lady.
    I cannot blame his conscience.

1. GENTLEMAN       They that bear
48  The cloth of honor over her are four barons
    Of the Cinque-Ports.

2. GENTLEMAN
50  Those men are happy, and so are all near her.
51  I take it, she that carries up the train
    Is that old noble lady, Duchess of Norfolk.

1. GENTLEMAN
    It is, and all the rest are countesses.

2. GENTLEMAN
54  Their coronets say so. These are stars indeed –

1. GENTLEMAN
55  And sometimes falling ones.

2. GENTLEMAN        No more of that.
                  *[Exit procession.]*
    *Enter a third Gentleman.*

1. GENTLEMAN
    God save you, sir. Where have you been broiling?

3. GENTLEMAN
57  Among the crowd i' th' Abbey, where a finger
    Could not be wedged in more. I am stifled
59  With the mere rankness of their joy.

2. GENTLEMAN         You saw
    The ceremony?

3. GENTLEMAN  That I did.

1. GENTLEMAN        How was it?

3. GENTLEMAN
    Well worth the seeing.

61 2. GENTLEMAN       Good sir, speak it to us.

3. GENTLEMAN
    As well as I am able. The rich stream
    Of lords and ladies, having brought the queen
64  To a prepared place in the choir, fell off
    A distance from her; while her grace sat down
    To rest awhile, some half an hour or so,
67  In a rich chair of state, opposing freely
    The beauty of her person to the people.
69  Believe me, sir, she is the goodliest woman

That ever lay by man; which when the people
Had the full view of, such a noise arose
As the shrouds make at sea in a stiff tempest,    72
As loud, and to as many tunes. Hats, cloaks
(Doublets, I think) flew up; and had their faces
Been loose, this day they had been lost. Such joy
I never saw before. Great-bellied women
That had not half a week to go, like rams    77
In the old time of war, would shake the press    78
And make 'em reel before 'em. No man living
Could say 'This is my wife' there, all were woven
So strangely in one piece.    81

2. GENTLEMAN        But what followed?

3. GENTLEMAN
At length her grace rose and with modest paces    82
Came to the altar, where she kneeled, and saint-like
Cast her fair eyes to heaven and prayed devoutly;
Then rose again and bowed her to the people;
When by the Archbishop of Canterbury
She had all the royal makings of a queen,    87
As holy oil, Edward Confessor's crown,    88
The rod, and bird of peace, and all such emblems
Laid nobly on her; which performed, the choir
With all the choicest music of the kingdom    91
Together sung 'Te Deum.' So she parted,    92
And with the same full state packed back again    93
To York Place, where the feast is held.

1. GENTLEMAN           Sir,
You must no more call it York Place. That's past;
For since the cardinal fell that title's lost;
'Tis now the king's, and called Whitehall.

3. GENTLEMAN         I know it;
But 'tis so lately altered that the old name
Is fresh about me.

2. GENTLEMAN    What two reverend bishops
Were those that went on each side of the queen?

3. GENTLEMAN
Stokesly and Gardiner; the one of Winchester,
Newly preferred from the king's secretary;    10
The other, London.

2. GENTLEMAN    He of Winchester
Is held no great good lover of the archbishop's,
The virtuous Cranmer.

3. GENTLEMAN        All the land knows that.
However, yet there is no great breach. When it comes,
Cranmer will find a friend will not shrink from him.

2. GENTLEMAN
Who may that be, I pray you?

3. GENTLEMAN          Thomas Cromwell,
A man in much esteem with th' king, and truly
A worthy friend. The king has made him
Master o' th' Jewel House,    11
And one, already, of the Privy Council.

37 *train* retinue   45 *Indies* i.e. abundant riches (both East and West Indies were sources of wealth)   46 *strains* embraces   48 *cloth of honor* canopy   50 *all* all who   51 *carries . . . train* bears the robes   54 *stars* (a common image for nobles)   55 *falling* (with sexual quibble)   57 *Abbey* Westminster Abbey   59 *mere rankness* sheer exuberance   61 *speak* describe   64 *fell off* withdrew   67 *opposing* exposing   69 *goodliest* most attractive   72 *shrouds* sail-ropes   77 *rams* battering-rams   78 *press* crowd   81 *piece* i.e. of cloth   82 *modest* moderate (and therefore decorous)   87 *makings* i.e. ceremonial tokens and symbolic attributes   88 *As* namely   91 *music* musicians   92 *parted* departed   93 *state* pomp   102 *Newly . . . secretary* (cf. II, ii, 114)   111 *Master . . . Jewel House* keeper of the crown jewels, the king's silver, etc.

**2. GENTLEMAN**
He will deserve more.

**3. GENTLEMAN**     Yes, without all doubt.
Come, gentlemen, ye shall go my way,
Which is to th' court, and there ye shall be my guests.
Something I can command. As I walk thither,
I'll yell ye more.

**BOTH**     You may command us, sir.     *Exeunt.*

\*

*Enter Katherine Dowager, sick; led between Griffith,*
*her gentleman usher, and Patience, her woman.*

**GRIFFITH**
How does your grace?

**KATHERINE**     O Griffith, sick to death.
My legs like loaden branches bow to th' earth,
Willing to leave their burden. Reach a chair.
So now, methinks, I feel a little ease.
Didst thou not tell me, Griffith, as thou led'st me,
That the great child of honor, Cardinal Wolsey,
Was dead?

**GRIFFITH**     Yes, madam; but I think your grace,
Out of the pain you suffered, gave no ear to't.

**KATHERINE**
Prithee, good Griffith, tell me how he died.
If well, he stepped before me happily
For my example.

**GRIFFITH**     Well, the voice goes, madam;
For after the stout Earl Northumberland
Arrested him at York and brought him forward
As a man sorely tainted, to his answer,
He fell sick suddenly, and grew so ill
He could not sit his mule.

**KATHERINE**     Alas, poor man.

**GRIFFITH**
At last, with easy roads, he came to Leicester,
Lodged in the abbey; where the reverend abbot
With all his covent honorably received him;
To whom he gave these words: 'O father abbot,
An old man, broken with the storms of state,
Is come to lay his weary bones among ye:
Give him a little earth for charity!'
So went to bed, where eagerly his sickness
Pursued him still; and three nights after this,

After the hour of eight, which he himself
Foretold should be his last, full of repentance,
Continual meditations, tears and sorrows,
He gave his honors to the world again,
His blessèd part to heaven, and slept in peace.

**KATHERINE**
So may he rest, his faults lie gently on him!
Yet thus far, Griffith, give me leave to speak him,
And yet with charity. He was a man
Of an unbounded stomach, ever ranking
Himself with princes; one that by suggestion
Tied all the kingdom. Simony was fair play;
His own opinion was his law. I' th' presence
He would say untruths, and be ever double
Both in his words and meaning. He was never
(But where he meant to ruin) pitiful.
His promises were, as he then was, mighty;
But his performance, as he is now, nothing.
Of his own body he was ill, and gave
The clergy ill example.

**GRIFFITH**     Noble madam,
Men's evil manners live in brass; their virtues
We write in water. May it please your highness
To hear me speak his good now?

**KATHERINE**     Yes, good Griffith,
I were malicious else.

**GRIFFITH**     This cardinal,
Though from an humble stock, undoubtedly
Was fashioned to much honor. From his cradle
He was a scholar, and a ripe and good one,
Exceeding wise, fair-spoken, and persuading;
Lofty and sour to them that loved him not,
But to those men that sought him, sweet as summer.
And though he were unsatisfied in getting
(Which was a sin), yet in bestowing, madam,
He was most princely. Ever witness for him
Those twins of learning that he raised in you,
Ipswich and Oxford; one of which fell with him,
Unwilling to outlive the good that did it;
The other, though unfinished, yet so famous,
So excellent in art, and still so rising,
That Christendom shall ever speak his virtue.
His overthrow heaped happiness upon him;
For then, and not till then, he felt himself,
And found the blessedness of being little.
And, to add greater honors to his age
Than man could give him, he died fearing God.

**KATHERINE**
After my death I wish no other herald,
No other speaker of my living actions
To keep mine honor from corruption,
But such an honest chronicler as Griffith.
Whom I most hated living, thou hast made me,
With thy religious truth and modesty,
Now, in his ashes, honor: peace be with him!
Patience, be near me still, and set me lower;
I have not long to trouble thee. Good Griffith,
Cause the musicians play me that sad note
I named my knell, whilst I sit meditating
On that celestial harmony I go to.
    *Sad and solemn music.*

**GRIFFITH**
She is asleep. Good wench, let's sit down quiet
For fear we wake her. Softly, gentle Patience.

---

116 *Something . . . command* i.e. the cupboard is not bare
**IV, ii** Katherine's apartments (at Kimbolton)   6 *child* youth of noble birth (a chivalric title; here applied though Wolsey was not of noble birth) 7 *dead* (actually Wolsey died five years before Katherine)   10 *happily* haply, perhaps (?), fortunately (?)   11 *voice* common talk   14 *sorely tainted* severely discredited; *to his answer* to answer the charges against him   17 *roads* stages of a journey   19 *covent* convent   28 *sorrows* sighs, expressions of sorrow   30 *blessèd part* soul   32 *speak* describe   34 *stomach* ambition   35 *suggestion* evil seduction (?), underhand practice (?) (Holinshed's term is 'craftie suggestion')   36 *Tied* fettered, enslaved; *Simony* trafficking in ecclesiastical preferments   37 *presence* presence-chamber   38 *double* deceitfully ambiguous   39 *meaning* i.e. matter, content (mere words, the ornaments of style, are contrasted with substance or matter) 43 *ill* depraved   45–46 *Men's . . . water* i.e. men's vices are remembered, their virtues forgotten   50–51 *From . . . one* (Wolsey was reputed to have been extraordinarily learned as a child)   53 *Lofty* haughty   58 *raised* built   59 *Ipswich and Oxford* (Wolsey founded a college at Ipswich, his birthplace, and also Christ Church College, Oxford)   60 *good good man;* *did* created   62 *art* learning; *rising* (as a structure and in influence)   65 *felt himself* knew himself (cf. III, ii, 377–80)   70 *living* while alive   74 *religious* scrupulous; *modesty* moderation   78 *note* melody   80 *celestial harmony* the music of the spheres (believed to be too rarefied for mortal ears)

82

THE VISION

*Enter, solemnly tripping one after another, six*
*personages clad in white robes, wearing on their heads*
*garlands of bays, and golden vizards on their faces,*
*branches of bays or palm in their hands. They first*
*congee unto her, then dance ; and, at certain changes,*
*the first two hold a spare garland over her head ; at*
*which the other four make reverent curtsies. Then the*
*two that held the garland deliver the same to the other*
*next two, who observe the same order in their changes,*
*and holding the garland over her head ; which done,*
*they deliver the same garland to the last two, who*
*likewise observe the same order ; at which ( as it were*
*by inspiration) she makes (in her sleep) signs of*
*rejoicing and holdeth up her hands to heaven. And so*
*in their dancing vanish, carrying the garland with*
*them. The music continues.*

KATHERINE
Spirit of peace, where are ye ? Are ye all gone
And leave me here in wretchedness behind ye ?

GRIFFITH
Madam, we are here.

KATHERINE       It is not you I call for.
Saw ye none enter since I slept ?

GRIFFITH              None, madam.

KATHERINE
No ? Saw you not even now a blessed troop
Invite me to a banquet, whose bright faces
Cast thousand beams upon me like the sun ?
They promised me eternal happiness
And brought me garlands, Griffith, which I feel
I am not worthy yet to wear ; I shall assuredly.

GRIFFITH
I am most joyful, madam, such good dreams
94   Possess your fancy.

KATHERINE       Bid the music leave.
95   They are harsh and heavy to me.
*Music ceases.*

PATIENCE         Do you note
How much her grace is altered on the sudden ?
How long her face is drawn ? how pale she looks,
98   And of an earthly cold ? Mark her eyes !

GRIFFITH
She is going, wench. Pray, pray !

PATIENCE         Heaven comfort her !
*Enter a Messenger.*

MESSENGER
An't like your grace –

KATHERINE       You are a saucy fellow ;
Deserve we no more reverence ?

GRIFFITH         You are to blame,
102   Knowing she will not lose her wonted greatness,
To use so rude behavior. Go to, kneel !

MESSENGER
I humbly do entreat your highness' pardon ;
105   My haste made me unmannerly. There is staying
A gentleman sent from the king, to see you.

KATHERINE
107   Admit him entrance, Griffith. But this fellow
Let me ne'er see again.       [Exit Messenger].
*Enter Lord Capuchius.*
        If my sight fail not,
You should be lord ambassador from the emperor,
My royal nephew, and your name Capuchius.

CAPUCHIUS
Madam, the same – your servant.

KATHERINE         O my lord,
The times and titles now are altered strangely
With me since first you knew me. But I pray you,
What is your pleasure with me ?

CAPUCHIUS       Noble lady,
First mine own service to your grace ; the next,
The king's request that I would visit you,
Who grieves much for your weakness, and by me
Sends you his princely commendations,      118
And heartily entreats you take good comfort.

KATHERINE
O my good lord, that comfort comes too late,
'Tis like a pardon after execution.
That gentle physic, given in time, had cured me ;
But now I am past all comforts here but prayers.
How does his highness ?

CAPUCHIUS       Madam, in good health.

KATHERINE
So may he ever do, and ever flourish,
When I shall dwell with worms, and my poor name
Banished the kingdom. Patience, is that letter
I caused you write yet sent away ?

PATIENCE         No madam.
*[Gives it to Katherine.]*

KATHERINE
Sir, I most humbly pray you to deliver
This to my lord the king.

CAPUCHIUS       Most willing, madam.    130

KATHERINE
In which I have commended to his goodness
The model of our chaste loves, his young daughter –   132
The dews of heaven fall thick in blessings on her ! –
Beseeching him to give her virtuous breeding –    134
She is young and of a noble modest nature ;
I hope she will deserve well – and a little
To love her for her mother's sake, that loved him,
Heaven knows how dearly. My next poor petition
Is that his noble grace would have some pity
Upon my wretched women, that so long
Have followed both my fortunes faithfully ;     14
Of which there is not one, I dare avow
(And now I should not lie), but will deserve    14
For virtue and true beauty of the soul,
For honesty and decent carriage,      14
A right good husband : let him be a noble ;
And sure those men are happy that shall have 'em.
The last is for my men – they are the poorest
(But poverty could never draw 'em from me) –
That they may have their wages duly paid 'em,
And something over to remember me by.
If heaven had pleased to have given me longer life
And able means, we had not parted thus.      15

82 s.d. *white robes* (symbolic of purity) ; *bays* bay leaves (in token of joy or triumph) ; *golden vizards* (to indicate spirits ?) ; *congee* bow ; *changes* figures in the dance   94 *Possess* occupy ; *music* musicians ; *leave* cease playing   95 *heavy* oppressive   98 *cold* coldness (a sign of death ; often emended to 'color')   102 *lose* forgo   105 *staying* waiting   107 *Admit* allow   118 *commendations* compliments   130 *willing* willingly   132 *model* image, symbol   134 *virtuous breeding* a good education   141 *both my fortunes* my good and bad fortunes   143 *now . . . lie* (it was believed that people close to death spoke truth)   145 *honesty* integrity ; *decent carriage* proper demeanor   153 *able* sufficient, generously adequate

These are the whole contents; and, good my lord,
By that you love the dearest in this world,
As you wish Christian peace to souls departed,
Stand these poor people's friend, and urge the king
To do me this last right.
CAPUCHIUS      By heaven I will,
Or let me lose the fashion of a man!
KATHERINE
I thank you, honest lord. Remember me
In all humility unto his highness.
Say his long trouble now is passing
Out of this world. Tell him in death I blessed him,
For so I will. Mine eyes grow dim. Farewell,
My lord. Griffith, farewell. Nay, Patience,
You must not leave me yet. I must to bed;
Call in more women. When I am dead, good wench,
Let me be used with honor. Strew me over
With maiden flowers, that all the world may know
I was a chaste wife to my grave. Embalm me,
Then lay me forth. Although unqueened, yet like
A queen, and daughter to a king, inter me.
I can no more.      *Exeunt, leading Katherine.*

\*

Enter Gardiner, Bishop of Winchester, a Page with
a torch before him, met by Sir Thomas Lovell.
GARDINER
It's one o'clock, boy is't not?
BOY      It hath struck.
GARDINER
These should be hours for necessities,
Not for delights; times to repair our nature
With comforting repose, and not for us
To waste these times. Good hour of night, Sir Thomas:
Whither so late?
LOVELL      Came you from the king, my lord?
GARDINER
I did, Sir Thomas, and left him at primero
With the Duke of Suffolk.
LOVELL      I must to him too
Before he go to bed. I'll take my leave.
GARDINER
Not yet, Sir Thomas Lovell. What's the matter?
It seems you are in haste. An if there be
No great offense belongs to't, give your friend
Some touch of your late business. Affairs that walk
(As they say spirits do) at midnight have
In them a wilder nature than the business
That seeks dispatch by day.
LOVELL      My lord, I love you,

And durst commend a secret to your ear
Much weightier than this work. The queen's in labor,
They say in great extremity, and feared
She'll with the labor end.
GARDINER      The fruit she goes with
I pray for heartily, that it may find
Good time, and live; but for the stock, Sir Thomas,
I wish it grubbed up now.
LOVELL      Methinks I could
Cry the amen, and yet my conscience says
She's a good creature and sweet lady, does
Deserve our better wishes.
GARDINER      But, sir, sir,
Hear me, Sir Thomas! Y' are a gentleman
Of mine own way. I know you wise, religious;
And let me tell you it will ne'er be well —
'Twill not, Sir Thomas Lovell, take't of me —
Till Cranmer, Cromwell, her two hands, and she
Sleep in their graves.
LOVELL      Now, sir, you speak of two
The most remarked i' th' kingdom. As for Cromwell,
Beside that of the Jewel House, is made Master
O' th' Rolls and the king's secretary; further, sir,
Stands in the gap and trade of moe preferments,
With which the time will load him. Th' archbishop
Is the king's hand and tongue, and who dare speak
One syllable against him?
GARDINER      Yes, yes, Sir Thomas,
There are that dare, and I myself have ventured
To speak my mind of him; and indeed this day,
Sir (I may tell it you), I think I have
Incensed the lords o' th' council that he is
(For so I know he is, they know he is)
A most arch-heretic, a pestilence
That does infect the land; with which they moved
Have broken with the king, who hath so far
Given ear to our complaint — of his great grace
And princely care, foreseeing those fell mischiefs
Our reasons laid before him — hath commanded
To-morrow morning to the council board
He be convented. He's a rank weed, Sir Thomas,
And we must root him out. From your affairs
I hinder you too long, good night, Sir Thomas.
LOVELL
Many good nights, my lord; I rest your servant.
     *Exeunt Gardiner and Page.*
Enter King and Suffolk.
KING
Charles, I will play no more to-night,
My mind's not on't, you are too hard for me.
SUFFOLK
Sir, I did never win of you before.
KING
But little, Charles,
Nor shall not when my fancy's on my play.
Now, Lovell, from the queen what is the news?
LOVELL
I could not personally deliver to her
What you commanded me, but by her woman
I sent your message, who returned her thanks
In the great'st humbleness, and desired your highness
Most heartily to pray for her.
KING      What say'st thou? Ha?
To pray for her? what, is she crying out?

157 *Stand* be   159 *fashion* nature (literally, shape)   160 *honest* good
169 *maiden flowers* (befitting chastity; cf. *Hamlet*, V, i, 220)   171 *lay
me forth* lay me out for burial   173 *I . . . more* i.e. I am too weak to say
more
V, i The royal palace   3 *repair* restore   7 *primero* a gambling card game
fashionable at court   11 *An if* if truly   13 *touch* hint; *walk* (this term suggests the spirits of the following line)   17 *commend* entrust   18 *this work* i.e.
what I am about   19 *feared* i.e. it is feared that   22 *Good time* good fortune
23 *grubbed up* rooted out   24 *Cry the amen* assent   28 *way* i.e. religious
thinking (they are both anti-protestant)   33 *remarked* noted   34–35
*Master . . . Rolls* judge of the court of appeal   36 *gap and trade* opening and
beaten path   37 *time* course of events   43 *Incensed* set on, roused (or perhaps 'insensed,' i.e. informed)   45 *most* extreme   46 *moved* aroused   47
*broken with* revealed their views to   49 *fell* terrible   50 *hath* that he has
52 *convented* summoned   55 *rest* remain   62 *deliver* make known

LOVELL
68 So said her woman, and that her suff'rance made
Almost each pang a death.

KING                 Alas good lady.

SUFFOLK
70 God safely quit her of her burden, and
71 With gentle travail, to the gladding of
Your highness with an heir.

KING                'Tis midnight, Charles.
Prithee to bed, and in thy pray'rs remember
74 Th' estate of my poor queen. Leave me alone,
For I must think of that which company
Would not be friendly to.

SUFFOLK             I wish your highness
A quiet night, and my good mistress will
Remember in my prayers.

KING                Charles, good night.
                         *Exit Suffolk.*
*Enter Sir Anthony Denny.*
Well, sir, what follows?

DENNY
Sir, I have brought my lord the archbishop
As you commanded me.

KING             Ha? Canterbury?

DENNY
Ay, my good lord.

KING          'Tis true: where is he, Denny?

DENNY
He attends your highness' pleasure.

KING             Bring him to us.
                         *Exit Denny.*

LOVELL *[aside]*
This is about that which the bishop spake.
85 I am happily come hither.
      *Enter Cranmer and Denny.*

KING
86 Avoid the gallery.
    *[Lovell seems to stay.]* Ha! I have said. Be gone.
What!            *Exeunt Lovell and Denny.*

CRANMER *[aside]*
87       I am fearful. Wherefore frowns he thus?
88 'Tis his aspect of terror. All's not well.

KING
How now, my lord? You do desire to know
Wherefore I sent for you?

CRANMER *[kneels]*        It is my duty
T' attend your highness' pleasure.

KING              Pray you arise,
My good and gracious Lord of Canterbury.
Come, you and I must walk a turn together;
I have news to tell you. Come, come give me your hand.
Ah, my good lord, I grieve at what I speak
And am right sorry to repeat what follows.
I have, and most unwillingly, of late
Heard many grievous – I do say, my lord,
Grievous complaints of you; which being considered,
100 Have moved us and our council, that you shall
This morning come before us; where I know
102 You cannot with such freedom purge yourself
But that, till further trial in those charges
104 Which will require your answer, you must take
Your patience to you, and be well contented
106 To make your house our Tower. You, a brother of us,
107 It fits we thus proceed, or else no witness

Would come against you.

CRANMER *[kneels]*     I humbly thank your highness,
And am right glad to catch this good occasion
Most throughly to be winnowed, where my chaff
And corn shall fly asunder. For I know
There's none stands under more calumnious tongues
Than I myself, poor man.

KING          Stand up, good Canterbury,
Thy truth and thy integrity is rooted
In us, thy friend. Give me thy hand, stand up;
    *[Cranmer rises.]*
Prithee let's walk. Now by my holidame,
What manner of man are you? My lord, I looked
You would have given me your petition, that
I should have ta'en some pains to bring together
Yourself and your accusers, and to have heard you
Without indurance further.

CRANMER         Most dread liege,
The good I stand on is my truth and honesty:
If they shall fail, I with mine enemies
Will triumph o'er my person, which I weigh not,
Being of those virtues vacant. I fear nothing
What can be said against me.

KING            Know you not
How your state stands i' th' world, with the whole world?
Your enemies are many and not small; their practices
Must bear the same proportion, and not ever
The justice and the truth o' th' question carries
The due o' th' verdict with it. At what ease
Might corrupt minds procure knaves as corrupt
To swear against you! such things have been done.
You are potently opposed, and with a malice
Of as great size. Ween you of better luck,
I mean in perjured witness, than your Master,
Whose minister you are, whiles here he lived
Upon this naughty earth? Go to, go to,
You take a precipice for no leap of danger,
And woo your own destruction.

CRANMER        God and your majesty
Protect mine innocence, or I fall into
The trap is laid for me!

KING            Be of good cheer,
They shall no more prevail than we give way to.
Keep comfort to you, and this morning see
You do appear before them. If they shall chance
In charging you with matters to commit you,
The best persuasions to the contrary
Fail not to use, and with what vehemency
Th' occasion shall instruct you. If entreaties
Will render you no remedy, this ring

68 *suff'rance* suffering   70 *quit* release   71 *gladding* making happy   74 *estate* state, condition   85 *happily* by good fortune   86 *Avoid* leave; *gallery* (not necessarily the upper stage; this word is taken over from Foxe's *Acts and Monuments*)   87 *fearful* afraid   88 *aspect* expression   100 *moved* prompted   102 *freedom* ease (and therefore completeness); *purge* clear of guilt   104–05 *take . . . you* (cf. the same phrase in *The Winter's Tale*, III, ii, 229)   106 *You . . . us* i.e. you, being a fellow councillor   107 *fits* is fitting   110 *throughly* thoroughly   112 *stands under* is subject to   116 *by my holidame* i.e. by our Lady   117 *looked* expected   121 *indurance further* further hardship   122 *good* virtue   124 *weigh not* do not value   125 *vacant* devoid (of); *nothing* not at all   128 *practices* intrigues, plots   129 *bear . . . proportion* be correspondingly great; *ever* always   130 *question* cause   130–31 *carries . . . it* make for the fitting verdict   131 *At what ease* how easily   135 *Ween you of* do you imagine   136 *witness* evidence   138 *naughty* wicked   143 *give way to* give them scope   146 *commit* i.e. to the prison of the Tower

Deliver them, and your appeal to us
There make before them. Look, the good man weeps :
He's honest on mine honor ! God's blest mother,
I swear he is true-hearted, and a soul
None better in my kingdom. Get you gone
And do as I have bid you.        *[Exit Cranmer.]*
              He has strangled
His language in his tears.
      *Enter Old Lady.*
GENTLEMAN *[within]*     Come back : what mean you ?
OLD LADY
I'll not come back. The tidings that I bring
Will make my boldness manners. Now good angels
60   Fly o'er thy royal head and shade thy person
Under their blessed wings !
KING           Now by thy looks
I guess thy message. Is the queen delivered ?
Say ay, and of a boy.
OLD LADY        Ay, ay, my liege,
And of a lovely boy. The God of heaven
Both now and ever bless her : 'tis a girl
Promises boys hereafter. Sir, your queen
67   Desires your visitation, and to be
Acquainted with this stranger. 'Tis as like you
As cherry is to cherry.
KING        Lovell !
    *[Enter Lovell.]*
LOVELL             Sir ?
KING
70   Give her an hundred marks. I'll to the queen. *Exit King.*
OLD LADY
An hundred marks ? By this light, I'll ha' more !
An ordinary groom is for such payment.
I will have more or scold it out of him.
Said I for this the girl was like to him ?
I'll have more or else unsay't ; and now, while 'tis hot,
76   I'll put it to the issue.      *Exit Lady [with Lovell].*

                    *

, ii       *Enter Cranmer, Archbishop of Canterbury*
        *[ ; Pursuivants, Pages, and Footboys at the door].*
CRANMER
I hope I am not too late, and yet the gentleman
That was sent to me from the council prayed me
3   To make great haste. All fast ? What means this ? Ho !
Who waits there ? Sure you know me ?
      *Enter Keeper.*
KEEPER            Yes, my lord.
But yet I cannot help you.
CRANMER
Why ?

167 *visitation* visit   170 *an hundred marks* about £65 (by no means a small gift)   176 *put . . . issue* bring it to a head
V, ii Outside the council chamber   s.d. *Pursuivants* junior officers ; *at the door* i.e. outside the door of the council chamber (but of course just inside one of the main 'doors' of the stage)   3 *fast* shut   9 *happily* fortunately   10 *presently* at once   13 *sound* make known   14 *laid* prepared as a trap   19 s.d. *above* (note use of upper stage ; perhaps the only time in this play)   22 *Body a me* (a mild oath ; *a* : of)   24 *holds his state* maintains his dignity   27 *one above* God (?), Henry (?), both (?)   28 *parted* shared ; *honesty* honorable conduct, decency   30 *place* office, rank   32 *post* courier ; *packets* mail   34 *curtain* i.e. the upper-stage curtain (after l. 35 the action returns to the main stage)
V, iii The council chamber   s.d. *state* chair of state   4 *had knowledge* been informed   5 *Without* outside

KEEPER
Your grace must wait till you be called for.
      *Enter Doctor Butts.*
CRANMER                So.
BUTTS *[aside]*
This is a piece of malice. I am glad
I came this way so happily. The king          9
Shall understand it presently.      *Exit.* 10
CRANMER           'Tis Butts,
The king's physician. As he passed along,
How earnestly he cast his eyes upon me :
Pray heaven he sound not my disgrace ; for certain    13
This is of purpose laid by some that hate me       14
(God turn their hearts, I never sought their malice)
To quench mine honor. They would shame to make me
Wait else at door, a fellow councillor,
'Mong boys, grooms, and lackeys. But their pleasures
Must be fulfilled, and I attend with patience.      19
      *Enter the King and Butts at a window above.*
BUTTS
I'll show your grace the strangest sight –
KING              What's that, Butts ?
BUTTS
I think your highness saw this many a day.
KING
Body a me ; where is it ?              22
BUTTS          There, my lord :
The high promotion of his grace of Canterbury,
Who holds his state at door 'mongst pursuivants,    24
Pages, and footboys.
KING        Ha ? 'Tis he indeed.
Is this the honor they do one another ?
'Tis well there's one above 'em yet. I had thought    27
They had parted so much honesty among 'em –    28
At least good manners – as not thus to suffer
A man of his place and so near our favor        30
To dance attendance on their lordships' pleasures,
And at the door too, like a post with packets.      32
By holy Mary, Butts, there's knavery !
Let 'em alone, and draw the curtain close :      34
We shall hear more anon.
      *A council table brought in with chairs and stools, and*   V, iii
      *placed under the state. Enter Lord Chancellor, places*
      *himself at the upper end of the table on the left hand,*
      *a seat being left void above him, as for Canterbury's*
      *seat. Duke of Suffolk, Duke of Norfolk, Surrey,*
      *Lord Chamberlain, Gardiner seat themselves in order*
      *on each side. Cromwell at lower end, as secretary.*
CHANCELLOR
Speak to the business, master secretary ;
Why are we met in council ?
CROMWELL         Please your honors,
The chief cause concerns his grace of Canterbury.
GARDINER
Has he had knowledge of it ?             4
CROMWELL       Yes.
NORFOLK              Who waits there ?
KEEPER
Without, my noble lords ?              5
GARDINER       Yes.
KEEPER           My lord archbishop,
And has done half an hour to know your pleasures.
CHANCELLOR
Let him come in.

KEEPER          Your grace may enter now.
*Cranmer approaches the council table.*
CHANCELLOR
My good lord archbishop, I'm very sorry
9    To sit here at this present and behold
That chair stand empty; but we all are men
11   In our own natures frail, and capable
Of our flesh; few are angels; out of which frailty
And want of wisdom, you, that best should teach us,
Have misdemeaned yourself, and not a little:
Toward the king first, then his laws, in filling
The whole realm by your teaching and your chaplains'
(For so we are informed) with new opinions,
18   Divers and dangerous; which are heresies,
19   And not reformed, may prove pernicious.
GARDINER
Which reformation must be sudden too,
My noble lords; for those that tame wild horses
Pace 'em not in their hands to make 'em gentle,
23   But stop their mouths with stubborn bits and spur 'em
24   Till they obey the manage. If we suffer,
25   Out of our easiness and childish pity
To one man's honor, this contagious sickness,
Farewell all physic! And what follows then?
28   Commotions, uproars, with a general taint
Of the whole state, as of late days our neighbors,
30   The upper Germany, can dearly witness,
Yet freshly pitied in our memories.
CRANMER
My good lords, hitherto, in all the progress
Both of my life and office, I have labored,
34   And with no little study, that my teaching
And the strong course of my authority
Might go one way, and safely; and the end
Was ever to do well; nor is there living
38   (I speak it with a single heart, my lords)
39   A man that more detests, more stirs against,
40   Both in his private conscience and his place,
41   Defacers of a public peace than I do.
Pray heaven the king may never find a heart
With less allegiance in it! Men that make
Envy and crookèd malice nourishment
Dare bite the best. I do beseech your lordships
That in this case of justice, my accusers,
47   Be what they will, may stand forth face to face
48   And freely urge against me.
SUFFOLK                    Nay, my lord,
That cannot be. You are a councillor,
50   And by that virtue no man dare accuse you.
GARDINER
51   My lord, because we have business of more moment,
We will be short with you. 'Tis his highness' pleasure
And our consent, for better trial of you,
From hence you be committed to the Tower
Where, being but a private man again,
You shall know many dare accuse you boldly,
More than, I fear, you are provided for.
CRANMER
Ah, my good Lord of Winchester, I thank you;
You are always my good friend; if your will pass,
I shall both find your lordship judge and juror,
You are so merciful. I see your end —
62   'Tis my undoing. Love and meekness, lord,
Become a churchman better than ambition;

Win straying souls with modesty again,                        64
Cast none away. That I shall clear myself,
Lay all the weight ye can upon my patience,                   66
I make as little doubt as you do conscience                   67
In doing daily wrongs. I could say more,
But reverence to your calling makes me modest.
GARDINER
My lord, my lord, you are a sectary,                          70
That's the plain truth. Your painted gloss discovers,        71
To men that understand you, words and weakness.              72
CROMWELL
My lord of Winchester, y' are a little,
By your good favor, too sharp. Men so noble,
However faulty, yet should find respect                       75
For what they have been: 'tis a cruelty
To load a falling man.
GARDINER                    Good master secretary,
I cry your honor mercy. You may worst                         78
Of all this table say so.
CROMWELL                    Why, my lord?
GARDINER
Do not I know you for a favorer
Of this new sect? Ye are not sound.                           81
CROMWELL                    Not sound?
GARDINER
Not sound, I say.
CROMWELL          Would you were half so honest!
Men's prayers then would seek you, not their fears.
GARDINER
I shall remember this bold language.
CROMWELL                    Do.
Remember your bold life too.
CHANCELLOR                    That is too much;
Forbear for shame, my lords.
GARDINER                    I have done.
CROMWELL                    And I.
CHANCELLOR
Then thus for you, my lord: it stands agreed,
I take it, by all voices, that forthwith                      88
You be conveyed to th' Tower a prisoner,                      89
There to remain till the king's further pleasure
Be known unto us. Are you all agreed, lords?
ALL
We are.
CRANMER Is there no other way of mercy
But I must needs to th' Tower, my lords?
GARDINER                    What other
Would you expect? You are strangely troublesome:             94
Let some o' th' guard be ready there!
*Enter the Guard.*
CRANMER                    For me?
Must I go like a traitor thither?

9 *present* very time   11-12 *capable . . . flesh* prone to the weaknesses of the
flesh   18 *Divers* various, perverse (?)   19 *pernicious* disastrous   23 *stubborn* hard   24 *manage* handling   25 *easiness* indulgence   28 *taint* corruption   30 *upper* i.e. interior   34 *study* effort   38 *single* single-minded (cf.
'singleness of heart,' Acts ii, 46)   39 *stirs* is active   40 *place* office   41
*Defacers* destroyers   47 *Be . . . will* whoever they are   48 *urge* press their
case   50 *by that virtue* by virtue of that   51 *moment* importance   62 *undoing* ruin   64 *modesty* moderation   66 *Lay . . . weight* put all the pressure
67 *do conscience* have scruples   70 *sectary* follower of an heretical sect
71 *painted gloss* specious language and behavior; *discovers* reveals   72
*words* mere words   75 *find* meet with   78 *cry . . . mercy* beg your honor's
pardon; *worst* with least cause   81 *sound* loyal   88 *voices* votes   89
*conveyed* escorted   94 *strangely* extraordinarily

96 GARDINER        Receive him
And see him safe i' th' Tower.
    CRANMER       Stay, good my lords,
I have a little yet so say. Look there, my lords.
By virtue of that ring I take my cause
00    Out of the gripes of cruel men and give it
To a most noble judge, the king my master.
    CHAMBERLAIN
This is the king's ring.
    SURREY         'Tis no counterfeit.
    SUFFOLK
'Tis the right ring, by heav'n! I told ye all,
04    When we first put this dangerous stone a-rolling,
'Twould fall upon ourselves.
    NORFOLK       Do you think, my lords,
The king will suffer but the little finger
Of this man to be vexed?
    CHAMBERLAIN      'Tis now too certain,
08    How much more is his life in value with him.
Would I were fairly out on 't!
09 CROMWELL       My mind gave me,
10    In seeking tales and informations
Against this man, whose honesty the devil
And his disciples only envy at,
13    Ye blew the fire that burns ye: now have at ye!
        *Enter King, frowning on them; takes his seat.*
    GARDINER
Dread sovereign, how much are we bound to heaven
In daily thanks, that gave us such a prince,
Not only good and wise but most religious;
One that in all obedience makes the church
The chief aim of his honor, and to strengthen
19    That holy duty out of dear respect,
His royal self in judgment comes to hear
The cause betwixt her and this great offender.
    KING
22    You were ever good at sudden commendations,
Bishop of Winchester. But know I come not
To hear such flattery now, and in my presence
They are too thin and base to hide offenses;
To me you cannot reach. You play the spaniel,
And think with wagging of your tongue to win me.
But whatsoe'er thou tak'st me for, I'm sure
Thou hast a cruel nature and a bloody.
      *[To Cranmer]*
Good man, sit down. Now let me see the proudest
31    He, that dares most, but wag his finger at thee:
32    By all that's holy, he had better starve
Than but once think his place becomes thee not.
    SURREY
May it please your grace –

96 *Receive* take   100 *gripes* clutches   104–05 *stone . . . ourselves* (cf. Proverbs xxvi, 27)   108 *in value with* esteemed by   109 *My . . . me* I had a misgiving   110 *tales and informations* malicious and incriminating hearsay   113 *have at ye* prepare   119 *dear* heartfelt, zealous   122 *sudden commendations* impromptu compliments   131 *He* man, he-man   132 *starve* die   141 *shame* infliction of dishonor   146 *try* (1) put on trial, (2) afflict; *mean* means   148 *like* please   152 *purgation* clearing of himself (a law term)   156 *beholding* indebted   166 *spare your spoons* i.e. wish to be that niggardly (a gently mocking comment, alluding to the custom of giving christening or apostle spoons to god-children)   167 *partners* i.e. godparents   172 *brother-love* brotherly love   175 *voice* judgment   177 *shrewd* malicious, bad
V, iv The palace court   2 *Parish Garden* Paris Garden (great centre of bear- and bull-baiting in London)   3 *gaping* shouting, bawling   4 *belong to* i.e. am employed in

    KING        No, sir, it does not please me.
I had thought I had had men of some understanding
And wisdom of my council; but I find none.
Was it discretion, lords, to let this man,
This good man (few of you deserve that title),
This honest man, wait like a lousy footboy
At chamber door? and one as great as you are?
Why, what a shame was this? Did my commission    141
Bid ye so far forget yourselves? I gave ye
Power as he was a councillor to try him,
Not as a groom. There's some of ye, I see,
More out of malice than integrity,
Would try him to the utmost, had ye mean,       146
Which ye shall never have while I live.
    CHANCELLOR       Thus far,
My most dread sovereign, may it like your grace   148
To let my tongue excuse all. What was purposed
Concerning his imprisonment was rather
(If there be faith in men) meant for his trial
And fair purgation to the world than malice,     152
I'm sure, in me.
    KING       Well, well, my lords, respect him.
Take him, and use him well; he's worthy of it.
I will say thus much for him: if a prince
May be beholding to a subject, I           156
Am for his love and service so to him.
Make me no more ado, but all embrace him.
Be friends for shame, my lords. My Lord of Canterbury,
I have a suit which you must not deny me;
That is, a fair young maid that yet wants baptism,
You must be godfather and answer for her.
    CRANMER
The greatest monarch now alive may glory
In such an honor: how may I deserve it
That am a poor and humble subject to you?
    KING Come, come, my lord, you'ld spare your spoons! 166
you shall have two noble partners with you, the old 167
Duchess of Norfolk and Lady Marquess Dorset. Will
these please you?
Once more, my Lord of Winchester, I charge you
Embrace and love this man.
    GARDINER        With a true heart
And brother-love I do it.            172
    CRANMER       And let heaven
Witness how dear I hold this confirmation
    KING
Good man, those joyful tears show thy true heart.
The common voice I see is verified       175
Of thee, which says thus: 'Do my Lord of Canterbury
A shrewd turn, and he's your friend for ever.'   177
Come, lords, we trifle time away: I long
To have this young one made a Christian.
As I have made ye one, lords, one remain;
So I grow stronger, you more honor gain.     *Exeunt.*

                        *

      *Noise and tumult within. Enter Porter and his Man.* V, iv
PORTER You'll leave your noise anon, ye rascals! Do you
take the court for Parish Garden? Ye rude slaves, leave 2
your gaping!                               3
[ONE] *within* Good master porter, I belong to th' larder. 4
PORTER Belong to th' gallows and be hanged, ye rogue!
Is this a place to roar in? Fetch me a dozen crabtree

7 staves, and strong ones; these are but switches to 'em:
 I'll scratch your heads. You must be seeing christenings?
9 Do you look for ale and cakes here, you rude rascals?

MAN
 Pray, sir, be patient; 'tis as much impossible,
 Unless we sweep 'em from the door with cannons,
 To scatter 'em as 'tis to make 'em sleep
13 On May-day morning, which will never be.
14 We may as well push against Paul's as stir 'em.

PORTER How got they in, and be hanged?

MAN
 Alas I know not, how gets the tide in?
 As much as one sound cudgel of four foot
 (You see the poor remainder) could distribute,
 I made no spare, sir.

PORTER    You did nothing, sir.

MAN
20 I am not Samson, nor Sir Guy, nor Colebrand,
 To mow 'em down before me; but if I spared any
 That had a head to hit, either young or old,
 He or she, cuckold or cuckold-maker,
24 Let me ne'er hope to see a chine again;
25 And that I would not for a cow, God save her.

[ONE] *within* Do you hear, master porter?

PORTER I shall be with you presently, good master puppy;
 keep the door close, sirrah.

MAN What would you have me do?

PORTER What should you do but knock 'em down by th'
31 dozens? Is this Moorfields to muster in? Or have we
32 some strange Indian with the great tool come to court,
33 the women so besiege us? Bless me, what a fry of fornication is at door! On my Christian conscience this one
 christening will beget a thousand; here will be father,
 godfather, and all together.

37 MAN The spoons will be the bigger, sir. There is a fellow
38 somewhat near the door, he should be a brazier by his
39 face, for o' my conscience twenty of the dog-days now
 reign in's nose. All that stand about him are under the
41 line; they need no other penance. That fire-drake did I
 hit three times on the head, and three times was his nose
43 discharged against me; he stands there like a mortar-
44 piece to blow us. There was a haberdasher's wife of small
45 wit near him, that railed upon me till her pinked porringer fell off her head, for kindling such a combustion in the
47 state. I missed the meteor once and hit that woman, who
48 cried out 'Clubs,' when I might see from far some forty
49 truncheoners draw to her succor, which were the hope
50 o' th' Strond, where she was quartered. They fell on, I
51 made good my place. At length they came to th' broom-
 staff to me, I defied 'em still; when suddenly a file of
53 boys behind 'em, loose shot, delivered such a shower of
54 pebbles that I was fain to draw mine honor in and let
55 'em win the work. The devil was amongst 'em I think
 surely.

PORTER These are the youths that thunder at a playhouse
58 and fight for bitten apples; that no audience but the tri-
59 bulation of Tower Hill or the limbs of Limehouse, their
 dear brothers, are able to endure. I have some of 'em in
61 Limbo Patrum, and there they are like to dance these
62 three days, besides the running banquet of two beadles
 that is to come.

 *Enter Lord Chamberlain.*

CHAMBERLAIN
 Mercy o' me, what a multitude are here!

They grow still too; from all parts they are coming
As if we kept a fair here. Where are these porters,
These lazy knaves? Y' have made a fine hand, fellows! 65
There's a trim rabble let in; are all these 66
Your faithful friends o' th' suburbs? We shall have 67
Great store of room, no doubt, left for the ladies
When they pass back from the christening.

PORTER    An't please your honor, 69
We are but men; and what so many may do,
Not being torn a-pieces, we have done:
An army cannot rule 'em. 72

CHAMBERLAIN    As I live,
If the king blame me for't, I'll lay ye all 73
By th' heels, and suddenly; and on your heads 74
Clap round fines for neglect. Y' are lazy knaves, 75
And here ye lie baiting of bombards when 76
Ye should do service. Hark, the trumpets sound!
Th' are come already from the christening.
Go break among the press, and find a way out 79
To let the troop pass fairly, or I'll find 80
A Marshalsea shall hold ye play these two months. 81

PORTER
Make way there for the princess!

MAN    You great fellow,
Stand close up, or I'll make your head ache!

PORTER
You i' th' chamblet, get up o' th' rail, 84
I'll peck you o'er the pales else!   *Exeunt.* 85

\*

7 *switches* thin shoots 9 *ale and cakes* (traditional festival fare) 13 *May-day* May 1 (a day of great festivity) 14 *Paul's* St Paul's Cathedral 20 *Samson . . . Colebrand* (all noted for their strength; Guy, Earl of Warwick, slays Colebrand, a giant, in a well-known story) 24 *chine* joint of beef 25 *not . . . cow* (a common phrase of no special meaning; here used by association with *chine*) 31 *Moorfields* a park (seems also to have been used as a training ground for the London militia) 32 *strange Indian* North American Indian (Virginia was much in the news in 1612–13); *tool* (with bawdy significance) 33 *fry of fornication* swarm of would-be fornicators 37 *spoons* christening spoons (see note on V, iii, 166) 38 *brazier* brass-maker 39 *dog-days* hottest season (July 13–August 15, when Sirius, the dog-star, rises about the same time as the sun) 41 *line* equator; *fire-drake* i.e. meteor (still referring to the red-nosed brazier) 43 *like a mortar-piece* i.e. gaping upwards 44 *blow* blast 45 *pinked porringer* round cap ornamented with perforations, and resembling a porridge dish 47 *meteor* (still the brazier) 48 *'Clubs'* the call which summoned apprentices to start or stop a fight 49 *truncheoners* cudgel-bearers 50 *Strond* Strand, a main shopping street in London, then a fashionable residential area; *fell on* attacked 51 *broom-staff* i.e. close quarters (fighting with staves) 53 *loose shot* marksmen not attached to a company (the term fits the humor of the whole speech) 54 *fain* glad, obliged 55 *work* fort 58–59 *tribulation . . . Hill* a local gang of ruffians (?) 59 *limbs* young lads (also a gang?); *Limehouse* a dockyard town just east of what was then London 61 *Limbo Patrum* prison (literally, a region near hell; with quibble on *limbs* and *Limehouse*) 62 *running banquet* of public whipping by (running offenders through the street; this punishment being the 'dessert' to the 'feast' of being in *Limbo Patrum*) 65 *a find hand* a fine success of things (ironic) 66 *trim* fine (ironic) 67 *suburbs* (suggests lawlessness, because outside the jurisdiction of the city) 69 *An't* if it 72 *rule* control 73–74 *lay . . . heels* put you in the stocks 74 *suddenly* immediately 75 *Clap* impose; *round* heavy 76 *baiting of bombards* drinking deep (out of leathern bottles) 79 *press* crowd 80 *fairly* properly 81 *Marshalsea* a prison in Southwark 84 *chamblet* camlet, a rich fabric made of goat's hair 85 *peck . . . else* pitch you over the rails if you don't

v    *Enter Trumpets, sounding ; then two Aldermen, Lord*
     *Mayor, Garter, Cranmer, Duke of Norfolk with his*
     *marshal's staff, Duke of Suffolk, two Noblemen*
     *bearing great standing bowls for the christening gifts ;*
     *then four Noblemen bearing a canopy, under which*
     *the Duchess of Norfolk, godmother, bearing the child*
     *richly habited in a mantle, etc., train borne by a*
     *Lady ; then follows the Marchioness Dorset, the other*
     *godmother, and Ladies. The troop pass once about*
     *the stage, and Garter speaks.*

1    GARTER Heaven, from thy endless goodness, send pros-
     perous life, long and ever happy, to the high and mighty
     princess of England, Elizabeth.
          *Flourish. Enter King and Guard.*
     CRANMER *[kneels]*
     And to your royal grace and the good queen,
5    My noble partners and myself thus pray
     All comfort, joy in this most gracious lady,
     Heaven ever laid up to make parents happy,
     May hourly fall upon ye !
     KING                    Thank you, good lord archbishop :
     What is her name ?
     CRANMER        Elizabeth.
     KING                          Stand up, lord.
          *[Cranmer rises. The King kisses the child.]*
     With this kiss take my blessing. God protect thee,
     Into whose hand I give thy life.
     CRANMER                   Amen.
     KING
2    My noble gossips, y' have been too prodigal ;
     I thank ye heartily. So shall this lady,
     When she has so much English.
     CRANMER            Let me speak, sir,
     For heaven now bids me ; and the words I utter
     Let none think flattery, for they'll find 'em truth.
7    This royal infant – heaven still move about her ! –
     Though in her cradle, yet now promises
     Upon this land a thousand thousand blessings,
     Which time shall bring to ripeness. She shall be
     (But few now living can behold that goodness)
     A pattern to all princes living with her
3    And all that shall succeed. Saba was never
     More covetous of wisdom and fair virtue
     Than this pure soul shall be. All princely graces
26   That mould up such a mighty piece as this is,
     With all the virtues that attend the good,
     Shall still be doubled on her. Truth shall nurse her,
29   Holy and heavenly thoughts still counsel her ;
30   She shall be loved and feared ; her own shall bless her ;
     Her foes shake like a field of beaten corn
     And hang their heads with sorrow. Good grows with her ;

In her days every man shall eat in safety
Under his own vine what he plants, and sing
The merry songs of peace to all his neighbors.
God shall be truly known, and those about her
From her shall read the perfect ways of honor,              37
And by those claim their greatness, not by blood.
Nor shall this peace sleep with her ; but as when
The bird of wonder dies, the maiden phoenix,              40
Her ashes new create another heir                        41
As great in admiration as herself,                       42
So shall she leave her blessedness to one
(When heaven shall call her from this cloud of darkness)  44
Who from the sacred ashes of her honor
Shall starlike rise, as great in fame as she was,
And so stand fixed. Peace, plenty, love, truth, terror,
That were the servants to this chosen infant,
Shall then be his, and like a vine grow to him.
Wherever the bright sun of heaven shall shine,           50
His honor and the greatness of his name
Shall be, and make new nations. He shall flourish        52
And like a mountain cedar reach his branches
To all the plains about him. Our children's children
Shall see this, and bless heaven.
KING                    Thou speakest wonders.
CRANMER
She shall be, to the happiness of England,
An aged princess ; many days shall see her,
And yet no day without a deed to crown it.
Would I had known no more ! but she must die,
She must, the saints must have her : yet a virgin,
A most unspotted lily shall she pass                     61
To th' ground, and all the world shall mourn her.
KING
O lord archbishop,
Thou hast made me now a man ; never before              64
This happy child did I get anything.                    65
This oracle of comfort has so pleased me
That when I am in heaven I shall desire
To see what this child does, and praise my Maker.
I thank ye all. To you, my good lord mayor,
And you good brethren I am much beholding.              70
I have received much honor by your presence,
And ye shall find me thankful. Lead the way, lords,
Ye must all see the queen, and she must thank ye ;
She will be sick else. This day, no man think           74
'Has business at his house ; for all shall stay :
This little one shall make it Holy-day.        *Exeunt.*


THE EPILOGUE                            Epi.

'Tis ten to one this play can never please
All that are here. Some come to take their ease
And sleep an act or two ; but those we fear
W' have frighted with our trumpets ; so 'tis clear
They'll say 'tis naught ; others to hear the city        5
Abused extremely, and to cry 'That's witty,'
Which we have not done neither ; that I fear             7
All the expected good w' are like to hear
For this play at this time, is only in
The merciful construction of good women,                10
For such a one we showed 'em. If they smile
And say 'twill do, I know within a while
All the best men are ours ; for 'tis ill hap,
If they hold when their ladies bid 'em clap.            14

V, v The palace  s.d. *Garter* (see note on IV, i, 36 s.d. item 5); *marshal's*
Earl Marshal's ; *standing bowls* bowls with legs; *habited* clothed  1–3 *Heaven
. . . Elizabeth* (the usual formula on such occasions)  5 *partners* fellow godparents  12 *gossips* godparents  17 *heaven . . . her* God be always near her
23 *Saba* Queen of Sheba  26 *mould . . . piece* inform such a great person  29
*still* always  30 *own* own people  37 *read* learn  40 *maiden phoenix* (comparisons between Queen Elizabeth and the phoenix, a mythical unique bird,
were common)  41 *heir* i.e. James I  42 *admiration* arousing wonder  44
*cloud of darkness* i.e. earth  50–54 *Wherever . . . him* (cf. Genesis xvii, 4–6
and Romans iv, 17 ; the passage compliments both James I and Princess
Elizabeth, his daughter)  52 *new nations* (a probable reference to Virginia)
61 *pass* pass away  64 *a man* i.e. a successful, prospering man  65 *get*
achieve (quibbling on 'beget')  70 *beholding* indebted  74 *sick* unhappy
Epi.  5 *naught* nothing, worthless  7 *that* so that  10 *construction* interpretation  14 *hold* keep back

# THE NON-DRAMATIC POETRY

# FOREWORD

The sonnets and narrative poems bring us back to the earlier years of Shakespeare's creative career. Sonnets, in translation and in imitation of Petrarch's, had been introduced to English readers by Wyatt and Surrey in *Tottel's Miscellany*, 1557. The Italian two-part form, with octave rhyming *abbaabba* and sestet working variations upon two or three additional rhymes, was abandoned by most English poets, including Shakespeare, who substituted the more supple three-quatrain-couplet form: *abab cdcd efef gg*. The earliest full sonnet sequence was Thomas Watson's *Hecatompathia or The Passionate Century of Love* (1582). It was followed by Sidney's *Astrophel and Stella*, written before 1586 though not published until 1591, and this by Daniel's *Delia*, Drayton's *Idea's Mirror*, Spenser's *Amoretti*, and others. The period of greatest vogue was 1590 to 1595. Although all sonnets must presumably be personal, only Spenser's are unequivocally autobiographical, and, curiously, his are by no means the least conventional. Sidney was more successful than most in conveying a sense of genuine emotional involvement, and Shakespeare, not unexpectedly, was still more successful than Sidney. Still he was writing in an established tradition, and although the best of his sonnets transcend the tradition, the majority must be read with the nature of the shared idiom and conventions in mind; otherwise one may be only dimly aware of what the poet was actually saying. A naive and anachronistic reading of the sonnets is responsible for a number of theories, solemnly clumsy when not ridiculous, about disturbances in Shakespeare's psyche, and about his sexual and social behavior; however, recent commentary indicates an increasing prevalence of sanity.

An older tradition, Ovidian and erotic, supplies the context of *Venus and Adonis* and *Lucrece*, although the latter is affiliated with "lament" narratives and is more anti-erotic than otherwise. Marlowe's *Hero and Leander* is the most distinguished of the contemporary narratives of amorous adventure, and its excellence prevents us from saying that, in this genre, Shakespeare "transcended" the tradition; however, either one of his poems would have established the reputation of a lesser poet. As a matter of fact, *Venus and Adonis* did much to establish that of Shakespeare.

A. H.

# THE NARRATIVE POEMS

## INTRODUCTION

And Shakespeare, thou whose honey-flowing vein,
Pleasing the world, thy praises doth obtain;
Whose *Venus* and whose *Lucrece*, sweet and chaste,
Thy name in fame's immortal book have placed:
Live ever you, at least in fame live ever;
Well may the body die, but fame dies never.
Richard Barnfield, 1598

Some poetic genera have survived in our practise, understanding, or both, and some have not. The sonnet, and even the sonnet-sequence, are still being written, and the earliest English sonnets (Shakespeare's among them) are still being read. We have, in consequence, a going sense of what the sonnet can accomplish, and also of what subjects and attitudes traditionally belong to it. But of the masque, for instance, we have no corresponding natural awareness; only the specialist in Stuart literature could say whether Robert Frost's *A Masque of Reason* is in any way a revival of the art-form, and most readers have enjoyed Milton's *Comus* without much notion of its relation to the norms of courtly entertainment. We can, of course, find an antique work good without knowing precisely how it is "good of its kind"; but much depends, in such cases, on the simplicity of the convention and on the persistence of analogous forms of poetry. The two long poems which, in Barnfield's judgment, were to assure Shakespeare's immortality are complex and confusing in relation to a number of conventions, literary and pictorial, and those conventions are dead; poems of the kind are no longer written, and few of them are still read. Since one cannot cheer without knowing what the game is, the reader of these poems today is likely to find himself wishing for some historical guidance.

The literature on the poems is extensive, but that vast machinery of mediation does not answer one's questions with the sure brevity of a computer. Some things are clear, however. The *Venus*, of which I shall speak first and most, is an Ovidian narrative poem which derives the greater part of its material from passages of the *Metamorphoses*: those on Venus and Adonis, on Narcissus, and on Salmacis and Hermaphroditus. The epigraph, moreover, is taken from Ovid's *Amores*. Shakespeare was thus promising in some measure to emulate a witty, charming, and delicately sensual Latin poet. He was also choosing to retell a tale which every literate person knew in the original, and which had already been variously treated by English poets: by Golding in his moralized translation of Ovid, by Spenser, by Lodge, and by several others.

The dedicatee of Shakespeare's poem was the Earl of Southampton, a young courtier who employed John Florio as his tutor in Italian and was presumably a sophisticate. Given such a first reader, Shakespeare would doubtless be inclined to make his poem not a moral allegory (as medieval Ovidian tradition would have urged) but lightly erotic and fashionably artificial, in the manner of Marlowe's *Hero and Leander*. If these were Shakespeare's desiderata, he cannot be said to have consistently achieved them; but that he aimed well enough at the tastes of Southampton and his like is indicated both by Gabriel Harvey's reference to *Venus'* rage among the "younger sort" and by the greater assurance of Shakespeare's dedication of *Lucrece* to Southampton one year later.

The poem has been praised for its quick, decisive beginning, and it is true that the first stanza provides the time, some sense of place, the persons, their motives, and the beginning of the action: Adonis is off to hunt, and the enamored Venus comes running to intercept him. But this sort of narrative urgency does not continue; indeed, it stops right there, and we see at once that Shakespeare is not plunging into his narrative but getting some part of it over with. As Venus begins her leisured and mannered importunities in stanza 2, it is clear that her much-told story will not be told here for story's sake. There is no question, of course, of any incapacity for narrative writing, as one may tell by this later stanza in which Venus, seeking Adonis, encounters his wounded and complaining hounds:

> When he hath ceased his ill-resounding noise,
> Another flap-mouthed mourner, black and grim,
> Against the welkin volleys out his voice.
> Another and another answer him,
>     Clapping their proud tails to the ground below,
>     Shaking their scratched ears, bleeding as they go.
> (919 ff.)

That is cleanly written, it is vivid for eye and ear, and it does not hover too much, but keeps the story in motion; the pack goes bleeding by, and Venus moves on with increased anxiety toward the discovery of Adonis. But when she does find him, when she "unfortunately spies / The foul boar's conquest on her fair delight," the event is almost parenthetical, and the poem characteristically swerves from direct narrative into a cascade of similes, in which Venus' afflicted eyes are likened to fading stars, retracting snail-horns, and the unnerved intelligence-officers of a court.

Not only are the few happenings of the plot minimized in favor of such embroidery, but no depth or intelligible development can be found in the characters or relationship of Venus and Adonis. Adonis is a boy who likes hunting and is prodigiously insusceptible to love; sullenly, and on the whole mutely, he resists Venus' pleas and caresses

397

from beginning to end. The one other thing we know about this rudimentary person is that he does have the decency to resuscitate a woman who has fainted. Venus, for her part, is at one moment moved by pity, but everything else she does and says – her wrestlings, her sophistries, her tricks, her reproaches – is traceable to her one allotted motive : a sometimes etherealized sensual passion. The death of Adonis saddens but does not chasten her, and though we leave her "immured" in Paphos she has not conceivably become a conventual type.

The poem differs from Ovidian poetry generally in containing a very high proportion of dialogue, but its many speeches do not serve, by characteristic cadence and lexicon, or by the betrayal of emotional pattern or conflict, to give the speakers any individual savor, or psychic volume. Their attitudes have been assigned in stanza 1, and whenever they sound unlike themselves we are dealing not with the emergence or revelation of a new quality but with inconsistency on the part of the author. For example, in her prophecy that sorrow shall hereafter attend on love (1135 ff.) Venus takes high moral ground and deplores jealousy, deceit, and unrestraint in a manner which is foreign to her but convenient for the poet's local purposes. Adonis asserts (409 ff.) that he knows not love and does not care to know it, but in the next stanza argues from a quite different and more knowing position that one may be spoilt for sexual love if one experiences it too early. The fine homily on Love and Lust (like the love-persuasions of Marlowe's Leander) comes oddly from one so innocent, and the inconsistency is not removed by the fact that Adonis admits it (806).

In addition to such distortions of character, which Shakespeare seems to have permitted himself for the sake of immediate effects, the reader must cope with apparent shifts in the poet's attitude toward his material. It will be granted, I am sure, that comedy enters the poem at the end of stanza 5, where Venus pulls Adonis from his horse and lugs him off under her arm, blushing and pouting. We are amused because a female is manhandling a male, and because the goddess of Love (though later she will stress her weightlessness) here seems not merely Rubenesque but grotesquely muscular. The occurrence is a sexual assault which, if described in a different key, might invite prurience and encourage perverse or passive fantasy. But there is no Swinburnian heavy breathing here; it is vaudeville, and it is vaudeville when Venus later falls flat not once but twice (463, 593).

If the presence of broad comedy forbids a prurient response to the early stanzas, the element of slapstick is in turn refined by the graceful artifice of Venus' entreaties, by her persistent high idealization of Adonis' beauty, by Shakespeare's stress on the loveliness of Adonis' "pretty ear" or Venus' "fair immortal hand," and by the benign ambience of summer dawn. We cannot take the word "lust" very seriously in an atmosphere of violets and dive-dappers; and when Venus "devours" Adonis as an eagle its prey, we are less likely to think of *Vénus tout entière à sa proie attachée* than of the amorous commonplace "I could eat you alive." The reader, in short, feels himself to be in that special literary preserve where the erotic may freely be enjoyed because taste and humor attend and control it. This is the domain of much of Herrick's poetry, and here as there it is understood that moral objections would be churlish.

A critic of 1823 described *Venus and Adonis* as "deficient in that delicacy which has happily been introduced by modern refinement." The eroticism of the poem, however, is never culpably gross. Venus' celebrated "deer park" speech (229 ff.) is far too clever for pornographic purposes, and such lines as the following have a Marlovian coolness and suavity :

> Who sees his true-love in her naked bed,
> Teaching the sheets a whiter hue than white,
> But, when his glutton eye so full hath fed,
> His other agents aim at like delight ?
>
> (397–400)

There are also (in addition to the other alleviations I have mentioned) occasional maxims of this sort :

> Were beauty under twenty locks kept fast,
> Yet love breaks through and picks them all at last.
>
> (575–76)

This lacks the irony of Marlowe, but like his maxims in *Hero and Leander* it distances the action by amused generalization.

Nevertheless, Shakespeare's poem breaks its own contract with the reader. By line 551 Venus' eagle has become a vulture, her face "doth reek and smoke," and her "lust" is being denounced by the poet for its shamelessness and its subversion of reason. This passage endorses in advance Adonis' tirade (769 ff.) against "sweating Lust," in which that sweat which first seemed earthily matter-of-fact (25) and later erotically attractive (143–44) becomes wholly distasteful. Is the reader expected, at this point, to make such judgments retroactive, and to see the first part of the poem in a radically altered light ? If so, it is too much to ask. One could no more do it than one could reconceive *Macbeth* as comedy. Shakespeare's (and Adonis') distinctions between Love and Lust are in themselves eloquent and sound, but they have no place in such a poem as *Venus* started out to be, and one is forced to consider two possible explanations : either Shakespeare thought that he could jump, with aesthetic safety, from one Ovidian tradition to another; or the poet who was soon to write Sonnet 129 ("Th' expense of spirit in a waste of shame / Is lust in action") could not temperamentally sustain a blithe and amoral approach to sexual love.

Some critics, unwilling that Shakespeare should seem imperfect even in "the first heir of" his invention, have tried to read *Venus* as a coherent moral allegory. It is not hard to guess what sort of thing such attempts would entail : the identification of Adonis with reason and ideal beauty, Venus with lust; the assumption that hunting is here, as in *A Midsummer Night's Dream*, a metaphor for the conquest of the irrational; the interpretation of Adonis' horse as ungoverned appetite running mad; the placing of special emphasis on all passages (such as 889 ff.) having to do with the hierarchy of the faculties; and so on. The poem would thus become a myth (rather like Marlowe's digression, in *Hero and Leander*, on the enmity of Love and the Fates) of the flight of true Love and Beauty to heaven – a myth in which the imperfection of love on earth is explained as the result of passion's incapacity to defer to reason. Having come so far, an allegorical interpreter might dare to construe, in accordance with his view of the poem, that dense complex of repeated images or symbols which we encounter from the first stanza onward :

suns and moons and faces red or pale, hot or cold; eye-beams or sunbeams commercing with the several elements, and with earth or heaven. By the time one finds the fatal boar being condemned for a "downward eye" imperceptive of beauty (1105 ff.) one is aware that these recurrent motifs may indeed be driving at something; but the present writer is unable, thus far, to resolve them into any structure, and finds that the chief result of so many burning faces, eyes, tears, and exhalations is an impression of close-up photography.

We are all, I hope, ambitious for Shakespeare, and would be pleased if the discovery of consistent moral allegory in his poem could be made in better conscience – with less suppression and inflation of evidence, and less disregard of tone. The moral and allegorical elements are really there; unfortunately, they are fitful and vague. It would please us, too, if the poem could be shown to have a clear pattern of attitudes embodied in its prevalent symbols; we might then hope to discover deep and powerful focal passages, as in the plays. The suns, moons, heads, and coins of *1 Henry IV*, and their attendant political conceptions, have such cumulative effect upon the reader's imagination that when, in Act IV, the Prince's troops are seen approaching Shrewsbury, "Glittering in golden coats like images . . . / And gorgeous as the sun at midsummer," those few words render the whole play simultaneous, and reverberate through all its architecture. But *Venus* is not architectural; there are no moments in which the entire work is many-dimensionally presented to the mind through a concentrative use of symbol or idea. The poem is additive, linear, spasmodic, opportunistic; it resembles a medieval episodic painting, or a series of tapestry panels deriving from one story but only tenuously related to each other. Or, to use a comparison nearer to our experience, it is like those musical comedies of the 1920's in which the "book" was a series of casual excuses for songs and dances, and the least mention of Chicago was sufficient to motivate a massive Chicago Number.

In order to enjoy *Venus and Adonis*, one must accept it as a lesser and looser thing than the more familiar plays, and not waste too much time in clucking one's tongue over its "frigid artificiality," its "remoteness from life," its deficiencies in story, character, and idea. The pleasures of the poem may be found anywhere at random, as in these lines from Venus' three-stanza vaunt about her conquest of Mars:

> Over my altars hath he hung his lance,
> His batt'red shield, his uncontrollèd crest,
> And for my sake hath learned to sport and dance,
> To toy, to wanton, dally, smile, and jest,
> Scorning his churlish drum and ensign red,
> Making my arms his field, his tent my bed.
>
> (103–8)

That is part of an eighteen-line development of the paradox that the god of war should surrender. Both in *Venus* and in *Lucrece* Shakespeare sometimes employs brisk and arresting paradoxes ("O modest wantons, wanton modesty!"), but the relish of this passage lies in an eloquent expansion of the paradox, and a continually varied attack upon it. Wit is not always brief; Venus offers Adonis "Ten kisses short as one, one long as twenty," and Shakespeare knows that in witty verse one must similarly divert by unexpected proportion and duration. In the

early poems, where subtlety is chiefly of the surface, he inclines to surprise more by excess than by concision, and we respond not with a jarred delight but with that growing wonder we feel when the still-strong miler lets himself out in the stretch, or the jazz trumpeter sails on into yet another chorus. We enjoy the display of resources, the prodigality, the abundance. In the stanza above, there is a fairly full inventory of Martial properties – lance, shield, helmet, drum, ensign, field, and tent; but these things are so variously tucked into the grammar as to give no impression of padding or of tiresome catalogue. And it is precisely this handling of one enumeration which permits another (the rather redundant infinitives of lines 105 and 106) to be contrastingly presented in bald sequence.

No reader with an ear can fail to note that the vowel-progressions of the stanza are melodious, and that the line, though end-stopped, is highly versatile in pace and rhythm; the movement of the whole is nervously fluent, as suits an extended poem so decoratively aloof from action and drama. It will be noticed here, as in the poem generally, that Shakespeare's lines tend to contain words, or groups of words, which balance upon some principle or other: very often, as in a line I have quoted ("The foul boar's conquest on her fair delight"), the balance involves antithesis. Line 104 above represents "balancing" at its most obvious, but in line 107 we have something subtler: a strong initial verb defers the seesaw effect, and the balanced words are inversely arranged as adjective-noun and noun-adjective. Line 108 then cleverly repeats the pattern with other grammatical elements.

Such talk is exceedingly dry, but it does bear upon the main and steadiest sources of pleasure in the poem – for us as for the artifice-loving Elizabethans: its elaborate inventiveness, its rhetorical dexterity, its technical *éclat*. There are numerous moments at which the poem creates a response to its subject, as in the beautiful stanza of the hands (361 ff.), but mostly one is reacting to an ostentatious poetic performance the artful variety of which I have scarcely begun to describe. Shakespeare has used an Ovidian story as the basis, not of a narrative, dramatic, or philosophic poem, but of a concatenation of virtuoso descriptions, comparisons, apostrophes, essays, pleas, reproaches, digressions, laments, and what have you. The same is true of *Lucrece*, that "graver labor" which Shakespeare promised in his dedication of *Venus*, and which he published a year later, in 1594.

In this case the Ovidian source is the *Fasti*, and again Shakespeare was working with a story which English writers (among them Chaucer) had helped to make familiar. A prose "argument," and a first stanza which starts the action well along in the plot, serve to curtail the narrative, and the 1855-line poem will really tell or show us only this: the inner struggles of Tarquin as he approaches Lucrece's bed; his threatening proposal, and her pleas and refusals; her lamentations, once she has been dishonored; her revelation of Tarquin's guilt to Collatine and others; her suicide, and the banishment of the Tarquins. A very large part of the poem consists of solitary lamentation by Lucrece, and it is undoubtedly true that Shakespeare was here creating a hybrid genre by combining a species of Ovidian narrative with the "complaint": it was probably from Daniel's *Complaint of Rosamond* (1593), in which the ghost of Henry II's unfortunate mistress asks our prayers and pity, that Shakespeare borrowed the stately 7-line stanza of *Lucrece*. At the same time, *Lucrece* greatly differs from *Rosamond*, the latter being a first-person account which offers neither scene nor dialogue until the poem is two-thirds done. Like *Venus*, *Lucrece* is narrated by the poet; it has access to the thoughts of its two principals, and consists in great part of rhetorical speeches which may at times suggest declamatory or Senecan drama, but seldom suggest that the poet has a future in the theatre. Critics agree that among the few moments of dramatic potentiality are those in which Lucrece countermands her agitated orders to her maid (1289 ff.) and misunderstands the blushes of her groom (1338 ff.). One also feels that the reunion of Lucrece and her husband might be touching on the stage:

> Both stood, like old acquaintance in a trance,
> Met far from home, wond'ring each other's chance.
> (1595–96)

Action in *Lucrece* is smothered in poetry, as when the concrete effect of Tarquin's lifted sword (505) is instantly blunted by a comparison; moreover, the action is given us in disjunct and unresolved tableaux. The sword is never lowered, and the hand remains indefinitely on the breast. Our mind's eye beholds not a cinematic continuity, but slides or tapestries which description may explore (as Lucrece explores her painting of Troy) or rhetoric at once forsake. Ideas are unimportant; the poet is not out to demonstrate the nature of chastity, or to confront the problem of evil in the world; his thought is conventional and can often be rendered by proverbs. Character in *Lucrece* is shallow, fixed, yet inconsistent, as in *Venus and Adonis*, and for the same reason: it is brilliance of the surface which has priority. Thus Tarquin is at first the "devil" to Lucrece's "saint" (85), but once alone and pondering he is provided with a better nature, so that he may be torn between conscience and lust; and this is done not for the sake of psychological revelation but for the provision of antithesis and rhetorical opportunity. Lucrece, when contemplating suicide, takes temporarily the Christian view of self-slaughter (1156 ff.) in order to divide herself for three stanzas. Divisions, vacillations, inward debates, anatomies of stimulus and response (426 ff.) and of psychic politics (288 ff.) – the poem is full of these things, and their main *raison d'être* is stylistic: they break down the characters and their thoughts into elements which can be balanced and elaborated.

The verse of *Lucrece* is even more obtrusively artificial than that of *Venus*, and its trickiness is somehow more difficult to like. Our first view of the heroine consists of a 28-line description of the "war of lilies and of roses" in her complexion (50–77), and its length and difficulty are exasperatingly disproportionate to the content. Perhaps the subject and initial tone of *Venus* make its extravagances – the egregious dimples of 241–48, for example – seem forgivably playful, while in a grave poem about rape and suicide such fiddling with red and white seems Neronian. There are, however, passages to admire, especially in the linked lamentations of Lucrece, which flow into each other with a smoothness worthy of Ovid. In contrast to Ovid and the Ovidians, Shakespeare makes little use, either in *Venus* or in *Lucrece*, of mythological reference, but when Lucrece invites Philomel to a duet (1128 ff.) a most obvious comparison of fates is made with the utmost freshness. And – to praise one passage more – Lucrece's contemplation of

the painting of Troy is far more than a standard Elizabethan descriptive exercise, written to occupy the interval between the sending of the scroll and Collatine's return. It is, for one thing, full of explicit and implicit relationships between Troy and Lucrece's Rome. We are to liken Ardea's siege to Troy's; Helen in her "rape" resembles Lucrece, but in her infidelity contrasts with her; Paris, like Tarquin, is a king's son who puts his "private pleasure" before the public good; Sinon, like Tarquin, is a dissimulator, and the entry of the Greek horse into Troy is like Tarquin's ill-intentioned entry into Collatine's house. The description is also relevant to Tarquin's moral collapse, in its several contrasts between displays of passion (such as anger or cowardice) and examples of "government" or control. Finally, the passage dwells considerably on the clear depiction and ready perception of character or emotion in physiognomy, and so builds throughout toward Lucrece's bitter reflection that such a face as Tarquin's can yet "bear a wicked mind."

I have left myself scarcely any space in which to speak of that strange and masterly metaphysical poem, "The Phoenix and Turtle." Published in 1601, the poem is a celebration of ideal love between two people, its perfect lovers being presented as symbolic birds, the phoenix and the turtledove. Poets have often made *ad hoc* revisions of mythology or conventional symbolism, and Shakespeare has done so here: while the turtledove keeps its accepted meaning of Constancy, the phoenix is assigned the feminine gender and is made to stand not for Immortality, as would be traditional, but for Love. These initial attributions, however, are in no way limiting, for since the two birds accomplish a total fusion of their natures, they have at last the one joint meaning of pure and imperishable love. The poem is undoubtedly indebted to other literary bird-assemblies, such as Chaucer's *Parliament of Fowls*, but given the chaste and world-forsaking character of the love whereby they are translated "In a mutual flame from hence," I think that the lovers must owe something of their wingedness to the *Phaedrus*. There Plato describes the highest love as an absolute spiritual union through which the lovers' souls recover their lost wings, and "when the end comes . . . are light and winged for flight."

The first part of the poem, in which the phoenix and turtle go unmentioned, is a summons to the celebrants and worthy witnesses of their funeral rite. The second part, which begins at the sixth stanza, is an anthem of praise in which those assembled "chaste wings" approach the transcendent truth of ideal love by demonstrating the powerlessness of reason to describe it: that two souls should be one is an idea which defeats mathematics and logic, and forces language into violent paradox. The collective reason of the mourners, convinced by self-defeat that "Love hath reason, reason none," proceeds then to compose a "threne" or dirge which is the poem's third movement. In it, reason affirms that the lovers have embodied a truth which lies beyond reason, and which with their death is lost to the world; at the same time, in response to the spirit of renewal which concludes all obsequies, and to the phoenix's association with the idea of rebirth, the "true or fair" are quietly made heirs of the lovers' example.

The language of this poem is intellectually strict and dry; the rhythm is abrupt and rugged in the tetrameter quatrains, like that of a nursery rhyme, and just a shade more serene in the triplets of the *Threnos*. The product of this precise abstract language and these spirited trochaic lines is, for one reader at least, an impression of complete vitality. We need not ask, in this poem, what and how much is meant by predatory birds or by burning eyes; the meanings are strong and ultimately plain. The Platonic conception of love, which in *Venus and Adonis* was inchoate and momentary, is here sharply realized, and the gift of paradox, which in *Venus* and *Lucrece* was exercised for its own sake, here serves a theme which cannot be expressed without it.

*Wesleyan University*          RICHARD WILBUR

### NOTE ON THE TEXTS

*Venus and Adonis* was first printed in quarto in 1593, and was often reprinted; *Lucrece* (with the head title *The Rape of Lucrece*) was first printed in quarto in 1594, and was reprinted a number of times, although less often than its predecessor. Both poems bear dedications to the Earl of Southampton subscribed "William Shakespeare," and both are well printed, probably from the author's fair copies. It is generally agreed that the later editions lack independent authority. "The Phoenix and Turtle" was first printed in a quarto of 1601: Robert Chester's *Love's Martyr,*

*or Rosaline's Complaint*, a volume containing, besides the quaint verses of Chester himself, variations upon the theme of the Phoenix and Turtle "by the best and chiefest of our modern writers, with their names subscribed to their particular works, never before extant. And now first consecrated by them all generally to the love and merit of the true-noble knight, Sir John Salisbury." Of the cluster of poems thus described, two are signed "Vatum Chorus," one "Ignoto," one "William Shake-speare," one "John Marston," one "George Chapman," and two "Ben Jonson." Although reprinted, the original quarto of 1601 is the sole authority for the text. The present edition of the three poems is based on the text of the original quartos, with the following material emendations. The adopted reading in italics is followed by the quarto reading in roman.

VENUS AND ADONIS   19 *satiety* saciety   147 *dishevelled* dishevellèd   358 *wooed* wooèd   366 *Showed* Showèd   432 *Ear's* Eares   616 *javelin's* iavelings   644 *Saw'st* Sawest   680 *overshoot* ouer-shut   754 *sons* suns   873 *twind* twin'd   940 *dost* doest   1003 *fault* fault,   1031 *as* are   1054 *was* had

THE RAPE OF LUCRECE (press-corrected Q)   23 *decayed* decayèd   50 *Collatium* (uncorrected Q) Colatia (corrected Q)   111 *heaved-up* heauèd-up   192, 392, 552 *unhallowed* vnhallowèd   395 *Showed* showèd   573, 1549 *borrowed* borrowèd   883 *mak'st* makest   884 *blow'st* blowest   1159 *swallowed* swallowèd   1416 *shadowed* shadowèd   1662 *wreathèd* wretchèd   1680 *one woe* on woe   1713 *in it* it in

The text and glossarial notes have been prepared by the general editor.

# VENUS AND ADONIS

*Vilia miretur vulgus : mihi flavus Apollo*
*Pocula Castalia plena ministret aqua.*

TO THE RIGHT HONORABLE
## HENRY WRIOTHESLEY
EARL OF SOUTHAMPTON, AND BARON OF TITCHFIELD

RIGHT HONORABLE,

I know not how I shall offend in dedicating my unpolished lines to your Lordship, nor how the world will censure me for choosing so strong a prop to support so weak a burden ; only, if your Honor seem but pleased, I account myself highly praised, and vow to take advantage of all idle hours, till I have honored you with some graver labor. But if the first heir of my invention prove deformed, I shall be sorry it had so noble a godfather, and never after ear so barren a land, for fear it yield me still so bad a harvest. I leave it to your honorable survey, and your Honor to your heart's content ; which I wish may always answer your own wish and the world's hopeful expectation.

Your Honor's in all duty,
WILLIAM SHAKESPEARE

1 Even as the sun with purple-colored face
Had ta'en his last leave of the weeping morn,
Rose-cheeked Adonis hied him to the chase.
Hunting he loved, but love he laughed to scorn..
5   Sick-thoughted Venus makes amain unto him
  And like a bold-faced suitor 'gins to woo him.

'Thrice fairer than myself,' thus she began,
'The field's chief flower, sweet above compare,
9 Stain to all nymphs, more lovely than a man,
More white and red than doves or roses are,
11   Nature that made thee, with herself at strife,
  Saith that the world hath ending with thy life.

'Vouchsafe, thou wonder, to alight thy steed,
And rein his proud head to the saddlebow.
If thou wilt deign this favor, for thy meed
A thousand honey secrets shalt thou know.
  Here come and sit, where never serpent hisses
  And being set, I'll smother thee with kisses.

'And yet not cloy thy lips with loathed satiety,
But rather famish them amid their plenty,
21 Making them red and pale with fresh variety —
Ten kisses short as one, one long as twenty.
  A summer's day will seem an hour but short,
24   Being wasted in such time-beguiling sport.'

25 With this she seizeth on his sweating palm,
26 The precedent of pith and livelihood,
And trembling in her passion, calls it balm,
Earth's sovereign salve to do a goddess good.
29   Being so enraged, desire doth lend her force
  Courageously to pluck him from his horse.

Over one arm the lusty courser's rein,
Under her other was the tender boy,
Who blushed and pouted in a dull disdain,
With leaden appetite, unapt to toy ;
  She red and hot as coals of glowing fire,
  He red for shame, but frosty in desire.

The studded bridle on a ragged bough
Nimbly she fastens. O, how quick is love !
The steed is stallèd up, and even now
To tie the rider she begins to prove.   40
  Backward she pushed him, as she would be thrust,
  And governed him in strength, though not in lust.

So soon was she along as he was down,   43
Each leaning on their elbows and their hips.
Now doth she stroke his cheek, now doth he frown
And 'gins to chide ; but soon she stops his lips
  And kissing speaks, with lustful language broken,
  'If thou wilt chide, thy lips shall never open.'

*Vilia . . . aqua* (from Ovid's *Amores*, I, xv, 35–36: Let the cheap dazzle the crowd; for me, may golden Apollo minister full cups from the Castalian spring) **Ded.**, **2** *Henry Wriothesley* third Earl of Southampton, 1573–1624, a favorite at the court of Elizabeth until imprisoned, 1601–03, for complicity in the Essex Rebellion **9** *first . . . invention* i.e. first work of literary pretensions? (since a number of plays had already been written) **10** *ear* cultivate, till

**1** *purple-colored* i.e. crimson ('purple' being used for a considerable range of colors) **5** *Sick-thoughted* i.e. suffering from love-melancholy **9** *Stain . . . nymphs* i.e. making all nymphs suffer by comparison **11** *with . . . strife* i.e. striving to outdo herself **21** *Making . . . pale* i.e. alternately suffused with and drained of blood **24** *wasted* spent **25** *sweating* i.e. not parched, youthful **26** *precedent* promise, sign; *pith and livelihood* strength and vitality **29** *enraged* aroused **40** *prove* try **43** *along* beside him

He burns with bashful shame; she with her tears
Doth quench the maiden burning of his cheeks.
Then with her windy sighs and golden hairs
To fan and blow them dry again she seeks.
53    He saith she is immodest, blames her miss;
What follows more she murders with a kiss.

55  Even as an empty eagle, sharp by fast,
56  Tires with her beak on feathers, flesh, and bone,
Shaking her wings, devouring all in haste,
Till either gorge be stuffed or prey be gone –
Even so she kissed his brow, his cheek, his chin,
And where she ends she doth anew begin.

61  Forced to content, but never to obey,
Panting he lies and breatheth in her face.
She feedeth on the steam as on a prey
And calls it heavenly moisture, air of grace,
Wishing her cheeks were gardens full of flowers,
So they were dewed with such distilling showers.

Look how a bird lies tangled in a net,
So fast'ned in her arms Adonis lies.
69  Pure shame and awed resistance made him fret,
Which bred more beauty in his angry eyes.
71    Rain added to a river that is rank
Perforce will force it overflow the bank.

Still she entreats, and prettily entreats,
74  For to a pretty ear she tunes her tale.
Still is he sullen, still he low'rs and frets,
'Twixt crimson shame and anger ashy-pale.
Being red, she loves him best; and being white,
78    Her best is bettered with a more delight.

Look how he can, she cannot choose but love;
And by her fair immortal hand she swears
From his soft bosom never to remove
82  Till he take truce with her contending tears,
Which long have rained, making her cheeks all wet;
84    And one sweet kiss shall pay this comptless debt.

Upon this promise did he raise his chin,
86  Like a divedapper peering through a wave,
Who, being looked on, ducks as quickly in.
So offers he to give what she did crave;
But when her lips were ready for his pay,
90  He winks and turns his lips another way.

Never did passenger in summer's heat                    91
More thirst for drink than she for this good turn.
Her help she sees, but help she cannot get;
She bathes in water, yet her fire must burn.
'O, pity,' 'gan she cry, 'flint-hearted boy!
'Tis but a kiss I beg – why are thou coy?

'I have been wooed, as I entreat thee now,
Even by the stern and direful god of war,
Whose sinewy neck in battle ne'er did bow,
Who conquers where he comes in every jar;          100
Yet hath he been my captive and my slave,
And begged for that which thou unasked shalt have.

'Over my altars hath he hung his lance,
His batt'red shield, his uncontrollèd crest,            104
And for my sake hath learned to sport and dance,
To toy, to wanton, dally, smile, and jest,
Scorning his churlish drum and ensign red,
Making my arms his field, his tent my bed.

'Thus he that overruled I overswayèd,
Leading him prisoner in a red-rose chain.
Strong-tempered steel his stronger strength obeyèd;
Yet was he servile to my coy disdain.
O, be not proud, nor brag not of thy might,
For mast'ring her that foiled the god of fight!

'Touch but my lips with those fair lips of thine –
Though mine be not so fair, yet are they red –
The kiss shall be thine own as well as mine.
What seest thou in the ground? Hold up thy head.
Look in mine eyeballs, there thy beauty lies,
Then why not lips on lips, since eyes in eyes?

'Art thou ashamed to kiss? Then wink again,          121
And I will wink – so shall the day seem night.         122
Love keeps his revels where there are but twain.
Be bold to play; our sport is not in sight.              124
These blue-veined violets whereon we lean
Never can blab, nor know not what we mean.          126

'The tender spring upon thy tempting lip               127
Shows thee unripe; yet mayst thou well be tasted.
Make use of time, let not advantage slip;             129
Beauty within itself should not be wasted.             130
Fair flowers that are not gath'red in their prime
Rot and consume themselves in little time.

'Were I hard-favored, foul, or wrinkled old,          133
Ill-nurtured, crooked, churlish, harsh in voice,
O'erworn, despisèd, rheumatic, and cold,             135
Thick-sighted, barren, lean and lacking juice          136
Then mightst thou pause, for then I were not for thee;
But having no defects, why dost abhor me?

'Thou canst not see one wrinkle in my brow;
Mine eyes are grey and bright and quick in turning;   140
My beauty as the spring doth yearly grow,
My flesh is soft and plump, my marrow ourning;
My smooth moist hand, were it with thy hand felt,
Would in thy palm dissolve or seem to melt.

53 *miss* misbehavior  55 *sharp by fast* hungry from fasting  56 *Tires*
preys hungrily  61 *content* i.e. put up with it  69 *awed* overborne  71 *rank*
teeming  74 *ear* (punning on 'air')  78 *more* greater  82 *take truce* make
peace  84 *comptless* countless  86 *divedapper* dabchick, little grebe  90
*winks* shuts his eyes  91 *passenger* wayfarer  100 *jar* fight  104 *uncontrollèd crest* unbowed helmet  121, 122 *wink* shut eyes  124 *not in
sight* i.e. unseen  126 *blab* tell tales; *nor know not* i.e. or know; *mean*
intend to do  127 *tender spring* i.e. light down  129 *advantage* opportunity
130 *within itself* i.e. buried in itself  133 *foul* ugly  135 *O'erworn* jaded
136 *Thick-sighted* dull of sight  140 *grey* (used of a range of iris-coloring
which included blue)

'Bid me discourse, I will enchant thine ear,
Or, like a fairy, trip upon the green,
Or, like a nymph, with long dishevelled hair,
148 Dance on the sands, and yet no footing seen.
149   Love is a spirit all compact of fire,
    Not gross to sink, but light, and will aspire.

'Witness this primrose bank whereon I lie;
152 These forceless flowers like sturdy trees support me.
Two strengthless doves will draw me through the sky
From morn till night, even where I list to sport me.
  Is love so light, sweet boy, and may it be
    That thou should think it heavy unto thee?

157 'Is thine own heart to thine own face affected?
158 Can thy right hand seize love upon thy left?
Then woo thyself, be of thyself rejected;
Steal thine own freedom, and complain on theft.
161   Narcissus so himself himself forsook.
    And died to kiss his shadow in the brook.

'Torches are made to light, jewels to wear,
Dainties to taste, fresh beauty for the use,
Herbs for their smell, and sappy plants to bear.
166 Things growing to themselves are growth's abuse.
  Seeds spring from seeds, and beauty breedeth beauty.
    Thou wast begot; to get it is thy duty.

169 'Upon the earth's increase why shouldst thou feed
Unless the earth with thy increase be fed?
By law of nature thou art bound to breed,
That thine may live when thou thyself art dead;
  And so, in spite of death, thou dost survive,
    In that thy likeness still is left alive.'

By this, the lovesick queen began to sweat,
For where they lay the shadow had forsook them,
177 And Titan, tirèd in the midday heat,
With burning eye did hotly over-look them,
  Wishing Adonis had his team to guide,
180   So he were like him, and by Venus' side.

181 And now Adonis, with a lazy sprite,
And with a heavy, dark, disliking eye,
His low'ring brows o'erwhelming his fair sight,
Like misty vapors when they blot the sky,
  Souring his cheeks, cries, 'Fie, no more of love!
    The sun doth burn my face – I must remove.'

'Ay me,' quoth Venus, 'young, and so unkind?
What bare excuses mak'st thou to be gone!
I'll sigh celestial breath, whose gentle wind
Shall cool the heat of this descending sun.
  I'll make a shadow for thee of my hairs;
    If they burn too, I'll quench them with my tears.

'The sun that shines from heaven shines but warm;
And, lo, I lie between that sun and thee.
The heat I have from thence doth little harm;
Thine eye darts forth the fire that burneth me,
  And were I not immortal, life were done
    Between this heavenly and earthly sun.

'Art thou obdurate, flinty, hard as steel?
Nay, more than flint, for stone at rain relenteth.   200
Art thou a woman's son, and canst not feel
What 'tis to love? how want of love tormenteth?
  O, had thy mother borne so hard a mind,
    She had not brought forth thee, but died unkind.

'What am I that thou shouldst contemn me this?   205
Or what great danger dwells upon my suit?   206
What were thy lips the worse for one poor kiss?
Speak, fair, but speak fair words or else be mute.
  Give me one kiss, I'll give it thee again,
    And one for int'rest, if thou wilt have twain.

'Fie, liveless picture, cold and senseless stone,
Well-painted idol, image dull and dead,
Statue contenting but the eye alone,
Thing like a man, but of no woman bred!
  Thou art no man, though of a man's complexion,
    For men will kiss even by their own direction.'   216

This said, impatience chokes her pleading tongue,
And swelling passion doth provoke a pause;
Red cheeks and fiery eyes blaze forth her wrong:
Being judge in love, she cannot right her cause,   220
  And now she weeps, and now she fain would speak,
    And now her sobs do her intendments break.   222

Sometime she shakes her head, and then his hand;
Now gazeth she on him, now on the ground;
Sometime her arms infold him like a band –
She would, he will not in her arms be bound;
  And when from thence he struggles to be gone,
    She locks her lily fingers one in one.

'Fondling,' she saith, 'since I have hemmed thee here   229
Within the circuit of this ivory pale,   230
I'll be a park, and thou shalt be my deer:   231
Feed where thou wilt, on mountain or in dale;
  Graze on my lips; and if those hills be dry,
    Stray lower, where the pleasant fountains lie.

'Within this limit is relief enough,   235
Sweet bottom-grass, and high delightful plain,   236
Round rising hillocks, brakes obscure and rough,   237
To shelter thee from tempest and from rain.
  Then be my deer, since I am such a park.
    No dog shall rouse thee, though a thousand bark.'   240

148 *footing* footprint 149 *compact* composed 152 *forceless* without strength 157 *affected* devoted 158 *upon thy left* i.e. by clasping your left hand 161 *Narcissus* in classical myth, the youth in love with his own image and transformed into the narcissus 166 *to* for (i.e. with no other purpose but growth) 169 *increase* harvest 177 *Titan* the sun-god; *tirèd* attired 180 *he* i.e. Titan 181 *lazy sprite* dull spirit 200 *relenteth* yields, is worn away 205 *this* thus (old form) 206 *dwells upon* attends 216 *by . . . direction* i.e. without prompting 220 *Being . . . cause* i.e. Venus, although presiding over the court of love, cannot obtain a favorable verdict in her own case 222 *do . . . break* frustrate her intentions 229 *Fondling* fondled one, darling (?), cause of infatuation (?) 230 *pale* fence 231 *park* deer-preserve 235 *limit* boundary 236 *bottom-grass* valley-grass 237 *brakes* thickets 240 *rouse* start

At this Adonis smiles as in disdain,
242 That in each cheek appears a pretty dimple.
243 Love made those hollows, if himself were slain,
244 He might be buried in a tomb so simple,
Foreknowing well, if there he came to lie,
Why, there Love lived, and there he could not die.

These lovely caves, these round enchanting pits,
Opened their mouths to swallow Venus' liking.
249 Being mad before, how doth she now for wits?
Struck dead at first, what needs a second striking?
251 Poor queen of love, in thine own law forlorn,
To love a cheek that smiles at thee in scorn!

Now which way shall she turn? what shall she say?
Her words are done, her woes the more increasing;
The time is spent, her object will away,
And from her twining arms doth urge releasing.
257 'Pity!' she cries, 'Some favor, some remorse!'
Away he springs and hasteth to his horse.

But, lo, from forth a copse that neighbors by
260 A breeding jennet, lusty, young, and proud,
Adonis' trampling courser doth espy,
And forth she rushes, snorts, and neighs aloud.
The strong-necked steed, being tied unto a tree,
Breaketh his rein, and to her straight goes he.

Imperiously he leaps, he neighs, he bounds,
And now his woven girths he breaks asunder;
267 The bearing earth with his hard hoof he wounds,
Whose hollow womb resounds like heaven's thunder;
The iron bit he crusheth 'tween his teeth,
Controlling what he was controllèd with.

His ears up-pricked; his braided hanging mane
272 Upon his compassed crest now stand on end;
His nostrils drink the air, and forth again,
As from a furnace, vapors doth he send;
275 His eye, which scornfully glisters like fire,
276 Shows his hot courage and his high desire.

277 Sometime he trots, as if he told the steps,
With gentle majesty and modest pride;
Anon he rears upright, curvets, and leaps,
As who should say, 'Lo, thus my strength is tried,
And this I do to captivate the eye
Of the fair breeder that is standing by.'

What recketh he his rider's angry stir, 283
His flattering 'Holla' or his 'Stand, I say'? 284
What cares he now for curb or pricking spur?
For rich caparisons or trappings gay?
He sees his love, and nothing else he sees,
For nothing else with his proud sight agrees.

Look when a painter would surpass the life 289
In limning out a well-proportionèd steed, 290
His art with nature's workmanship at strife,
As if the dead the living should exceed – 292
So did this horse excel a common one
In shape, in courage, color, pace, and bone. 294

Round-hoofed, short-jointed, fetlocks shag and long, 295
Broad breast, full eye, small head, and nostril wide,
High crest, short ears, straight legs and passing strong, 297
Thin mane, thick tail, broad buttock, tender hide:
Look what a horse should have he did not lack, 299
Save a proud rider on so proud a back.

Sometimes he scuds far off, and there he stares;
Anon he starts at stirring of a feather;
To bid the wind a base he now prepares, 303
And where he run or fly they know not whether, 304
For through his mane and tail the high wind sings,
Fanning the hairs, who wave like feath'red wings.

He looks upon his love and neighs unto her;
She answers him, as if she knew his mind.
Being proud, as females are, to see him woo her,
She puts on outward strangeness, seems unkind, 310
Spurns at his love and scorns the heat he feels,
Beating his kind embracements with her heels.

Then, like a melancholy malcontent,
He vails his tail, that, like a falling plume, 314
Cool shadow to his melting buttock lent;
He stamps, and bites the poor flies in his fume. 316
His love, perceiving how he is enraged,
Grew kinder, and his fury was assuaged.

His testy master goeth about to take him,
When, lo, the unbacked breeder, full of fear, 320
Jealous of catching, swiftly doth forsake him, 321
With her the horse, and left Adonis there. 322
As they were mad, unto the woods they hie them,
Outstripping crows that strive to overfly them. 324

All swol'n with chafing, down Adonis sits,
Banning his boist'rous and unruly beast; 326
And now the happy season once more fits
That lovesick Love by pleading may be blest; 328
For lovers say the heart hath treble wrong
When it is barred the aidance of the tongue.

An oven that is stopped, or river stayed, 331
Burneth more hotly, swelleth with more rage;
So of concealèd sorrow may be said:
Free vent of words love's fire doth assuage;
But when the heart's attorney once is mute, 335
The client breaks, as desperate in his suit. 336

242 *That* so that   243 *if* so that if   244 *tomb* i.e. grave   249 *how . . . wits* i.e. how keep her sanity now   251 *in . . . forlorn* wretched under your own rule (of love)   257 *remorse* pity   260 *jennet* small Spanish horse   267 *bearing* receiving   272 *compassed* arched   275 *scornfully glisters* (perhaps transposed by printer)   276 *courage* passion   277 *told* counted   283 *stir* bustle   284 *flattering* soothing   289 *Look when* as when   290 *limning out* portraying   292 *dead* i.e. lifeless image   294 *bone* frame   295 *shag* bushy   297 *crest* ridge of the neck   299 *Look what* whatever   303 *bid . . . base* i.e. challenge the wind to outrun him or be taken prisoner (as in game of prisoner's base)   304 *where* whether   310 *outward strangeness* show of coyness   314 *vails* lowers   316 *fume* rage   320 *unbacked* unridden, unbroken   321 *Jealous of catching* fearful of being caught   322 *horse* i.e. stallion   324 *overfly them* i.e. remain over them in flight   326 *Banning* cursing   328 *Love* i.e. Venus   331 *stopped* i.e. with door closed; *stayed* i.e. dammed   335 *attorney* pleader   336 *breaks* goes bankrupt

He sees her coming and begins to glow,
Even as a dying coal revives with wind,
And with his bonnet hides his angry brow,
Looks on the dull earth with disturbèd mind,
　Taking no notice that she is so nigh,
　For all askance he holds her in his eye.

343 O, what a sight it was, wistly to view
How she came stealing to the wayward boy!
To note the fighting conflict of her hue,
How white and red each other did destroy!
　But now her cheek was pale, and by and by
　It flashed forth fire, as lightning from the sky.

Now was she just before him as he sat,
And like a lowly lover down she kneels;
With one fair hand she heaveth up his hat,
Her other tender hand his fair cheek feels.
　His tend'rer cheek receives her soft hand's print
354 As apt as new-fall'n snow takes any dint.

O, what a war of looks was then between them,
Her eyes petitioners to his eyes suing!
357 His eyes saw her eyes as they had not seen them;
Her eyes wooed still, his eyes disdained the wooing;
359 And all this dumb play had his acts made plain
360 With tears which chorus-like her eyes did rain.

Full gently now she takes him by the hand,
A lily prisoned in a jail of snow,
363 Or ivory in an alablaster band –
So white a friend engirts so white a foe.
　This beauteous combat, willful and unwilling,
　Showed like two silver doves that sit a-billing.

367 Once more the engine of her thoughts began:
368 'O fairest mover on this mortal round,
Would thou wert as I am, and I a man,
370 My heart all whole as thine, thy heart my wound!
　For one sweet look thy help I would assure thee,
372 　Though nothing but my body's bane would cure thee.'

'Give me my hand,' saith he. 'Why dost thou feel it?'
'Give me my heart,' saith she, 'and thou shalt have it.
375 O, give it me, lest thy hard heart do steel it,
376 And being steeled, soft sighs can never grave it.
　Then love's deep groans I never shall regard,
　Because Adonis' heart hath made mine hard.'

'For shame!' he cries. 'Let go, and let me go:
My day's delight is past, my horse is gone,
And 'tis your fault I am bereft him so.
I pray you hence, and leave me here alone;
　For all my mind, my thought, my busy care
　Is how to get my palfrey from the mare.'

Thus she replies: 'Thy palfrey, as he should,
Welcomes the warm approach of sweet desire.
387 Affection is a coal that must be cooled;
388 Else, suffered, it will set the heart on fire.
　The sea hath bounds, but deep desire hath none;
　Therefore no marvel though thy horse be gone.

'How like a jade he stood, tied to the tree,
Servilely mastered with a leathern rein;
But when he saw his love, his youth's fair fee,　393
He held such petty bondage in disdain,
　Throwing the base thong from his bending crest,
　Enfranchising his mouth, his back, his breast.　396

'Who sees his true-love in her naked bed,
Teaching the sheets a whiter hue than white,
But, when his glutton eye so full hath fed,
His other agents aim at like delight?　400
　Who is so faint that dares not be so bold
　To touch the fire, the weather being cold?

'Let me excuse thy courser, gentle boy;
And learn of him, I heartily beseech thee,
To take advantage on presented joy.
Though I were dumb, yet his proceedings teach thee.
　O, learn to love! The lesson is but plain,
　And once made perfect, never lost again.'

'I know not love,' quoth he, 'nor will not know it,
Unless it be a boar, and then I chase it.
'Tis much to borrow, and I will not owe it.　411
My love to love is love but to disgrace it;　412
　For I have heard it is a life in death,
　That laughs, and weeps, and all but with a breath.　414

'Who wears a garment shapeless and unfinished?
Who plucks the bud before one leaf put forth?
If springing things be any jot diminished,　417
They wither in their prime, prove nothing worth.
　The colt that's backed and burdened being young　419
　Loseth his pride and never waxeth strong.

'You hurt my hand with wringing. Let us part,
And leave this idle theme, this bootless chat.　422
Remove your siege from my unyielding heart;
To love's alarms it will not ope the gate.　424
　Dismiss your vows, your feignèd tears, your flatt'ry;
　For where a heart is hard they make no batt'ry.'　426

'What! canst thou talk?' quoth she. 'Hast thou a tongue?
O, would thou hadst not, or I had no hearing!
Thy mermaid's voice hath done me double wrong;　429
I had my load before, now pressed with bearing:　430
　Melodious discord, heavenly tune harsh sounding,
　Ear's deep-sweet music, and heart's deep-sore wounding.

343 *wistly* intently　354 *dint* impression　357 *as* as if　359 *dumb play* dumbshow, wordless drama; *his* its　360 *chorus-like* i.e. as a commentary　363 *band* bond　367 *engine* instrument, i.e. tongue　368 *mortal round* i.e. earth　370 *my wound* i.e. wounded like mine　372 *bane* death by poison　375 *steel* turn to steel　376 *grave* engrave　387 *Affection* passion　388 *suffered* disregarded　393 *fair fee* due reward　396 *Enfranchising* setting free　400 *agents* organs　411 *borrow* take on as an obligation; *owe* own, have　412 *My . . . it* i.e. my only feeling about love is the desire to belittle it　414 *all but with a* all but in one　417 *springing* sprouting　419 *backed* ridden　422 *bootless* profitless　424 *alarms* attacks　426 *batt'ry* forced entrance　429 *mermaid's* siren's　430 *pressed* oppressed, weighted down

'Had I no eyes but ears, my ears would love
That inward beauty and invisible;
Or were I deaf, thy outward parts would move
436 Each part in me that were but sensible.
    Though neither eyes nor ears, to hear nor see,
    Yet should I be in love by touching thee.

'Say that the sense of feeling were bereft me,
And that I could not see, nor hear, nor touch,
And nothing but the very smell were left me,
Yet would my love to thee be still as much;
443     For from the stillitory of thy face excelling
    Comes breath perfumed that breedeth love by smelling.

'But, O, what banquet wert thou to the taste,
Being nurse and feeder of the other four!
Would they not wish the feast might ever last
448 And bid Suspicion double-lock the door,
    Lest Jealousy, that sour unwelcome guest,
    Should by his stealing in disturb the feast?'

Once more the ruby-colored portal opened
452 Which to his speech did honey passage yield;
Like a red morn, that ever yet betokened
Wrack to the seaman, tempest to the field,
    Sorrow to shepherds, woe unto the birds,
456     Gusts and foul flaws to herdmen and to herds.

This ill presage advisedly she marketh.
Even as the wind is hushed before it raineth,
459 Or as the wolf doth grin before he barketh,
Or as the berry breaks before it staineth,
    Or like the deadly bullet of a gun,
    His meaning struck her ere his words begun.

And at his look she flatly falleth down,
For looks kill love, and love by looks reviveth;
465 A smile recures the wounding of a frown.
466 But blessèd bankrout that by loss so thriveth!
467     The silly boy, believing she is dead,
    Claps her pale cheek till clapping makes it red,

And all amazed brake off his late intent,
For sharply he did think to reprehend her,
471 Which cunning love did wittily prevent.
472 Fair fall the wit that can so well defend her!
    For on the grass she lies as she were slain
    Till his breath breatheth life in her again.

He wrings her nose, he strikes her on the cheeks,
He bends her finger, holds her pulses hard,
He chafes her lips; a thousand ways he seeks
To mend the hurt that his unkindness marred.          478
    He kisses her; and she, by her good will,
    Will never rise, so he will kiss her still.

The night of sorrow now is turned to day:
Her two blue windows faintly she upheaveth,
Like the fair sun when in his fresh array                482
He cheers the morn and all the earth relieveth;
    And as the bright sun glorifies the sky,
    So is her face illumined with her eye;

Whose beams upon his hairless face are fixed,
As if from thence they borrowèd all their shine.
Were never four such lamps together mixed,
Had not his clouded with his brow's repine;            490
    But hers, which through the crystal tears gave light,
    Shone like the moon in water seen by night.

'O, where am I?' quoth she, 'in earth or heaven,
Or in the ocean drenched, or in the fire?
What hour is this? or morn or weary even?               494
Do I delight to die, or life desire?
    But now I lived, and life was death's annoy;        497
    But now I died, and death was lively joy.

'O, thou didst kill me, kill me once again!
Thy eyes' shrewd tutor, that hard heart of thine,       500
Hath taught them scornful tricks, and such disdain
That they have murd'red this poor heart of mine;
    And these mine eyes, true leaders to their queen,   503
    But for thy piteous lips no more had seen.

'Long may they kiss each other, for this cure!
O, never let their crimson liveries wear;               506
And as they last, their verdure still endure,           507
To drive infection from the dangerous year;
    That the stargazers, having writ on death,           509
    May say the plague is banished by thy breath.

'Pure lips, sweet seals in my soft lips imprinted,
What bargains may I make, still to be sealing?          512
To sell myself I can be well contented,
So thou wilt buy, and pay, and use good dealing;
    Which purchase if thou make, for fear of slips       515
    Set thy seal manual on my wax-red lips.

'A thousand kisses buys my heart from me;
And pay them at thy leisure, one by one.
What is ten hundred touches unto thee?                   519
Are they not quickly told and quickly gone?             520
    Say for nonpayment that the debt should double,
    Is twenty hundred kisses such a trouble?'

'Fair queen,' quoth he, 'if any love you owe me,         523
Measure my strangeness with my unripe years.            524
Before I know myself, seek not to know me.
No fisher but the ungrown fry forbears.                  526
    The mellow plum doth fall, the green sticks fast,
    Or being early plucked is sour to taste.

436 *sensible* sensitive to impressions   443 *stillitory* still   448 *Suspicion* caution   452 *honey* honeyed, sweet   456 *flaws* squalls   459 *grin* bare its teeth   465 *recures* cures   466 *bankrout* bankrupt   467 *silly* unsophisticated   471 *wittily* cleverly   472 *Fair fall* fair fortune befall   478 *marred* i.e. inflicted (in a forced antithesis with 'mended')   482 *blue windows* i.e. eyelids   490 *repine* repining, dissatisfaction   494 *drenched* immersed   497 *annoy* harm   500 *shrewd* sharp   503 *queen* i.e. the heart   506 *liveries* vestments; *wear* wear out   507 *verdure* fresh foliage (such as was brought indoors as a fumigant)   509 *stargazers . . . death* i.e. astrologers having predicted an epidemic   512 *still* so as always   515 *slips* errors   519 *touches* i.e. kisses   520 *told* counted   523 *owe* bear   524 *Measure . . . with* i.e. account for my reserve by   526 *fry* fish

529 'Look, the world's comforter, with weary gait,
His day's hot task hath ended in the west;
The owl, night's herald, shrieks; 'tis very late;
The sheep are gone to fold, birds to their nest,
    And coal-black clouds that shadow heaven's light
    Do summon us to part and bid good night.

'Now let me say "Good night," and so say you.
If you will say so, you shall have a kiss.'
'Good night,' quoth she; and, ere he says 'Adieu,'
The honey fee of parting tend'red is:
    Her arms do lend his neck a sweet embrace;
540     Incorporate then they seem; face grows to face;

541 Till breathless he disjoined, and backward drew
The heavenly moisture, that sweet coral mouth,
Whose precious taste her thirsty lips well knew,
Whereon they surfeit, yet complain on drouth.
545     He with her plenty pressed, she faint with dearth,
    Their lips together glued, fall to the earth.

Now quick desire hath caught the yielding prey,
And glutton-like she feeds, yet never filleth.
Her lips are conquerors, his lips obey,
550 Paying what ransom the insulter willeth;
551     Whose vulture thought doth pitch the price so high
    That she will draw his lips' rich treasure dry.

And having felt the sweetness of the spoil,
With blindfold fury she begins to forage.
555 Her face doth reek and smoke, her blood doth boil,
And careless lust stirs up a desperate courage,
557     Planting oblivion, beating reason back,
558     Forgetting shame's pure blush and honor's wrack.

Hot, faint, and weary with her hard embracing,
Like a wild bird being tamed with too much handling,
Or as the fleet-foot roe that's tired with chasing,
562 Or like the froward infant stilled with dandling,
    He now obeys and now no more resisteth,
564     While she takes all she can, not all she listeth.

565 What wax so frozen but dissolves with temp'ring
And yields at last to every light impression?
567 Things out of hope are compassed oft with vent'ring,
568 Chiefly in love, whose leave exceeds commission.
569     Affection faints not like a pale-faced coward,
570     But then woos best when most his choice is froward.

When he did frown, O, had she then gave over,
Such nectar from his lips she had not sucked.
573 Foul words and frowns must not repel a lover.
What though the rose have prickles, yet 'tis plucked.
    Were beauty under twenty locks kept fast,
    Yet love breaks through and picks them all at last.

For pity now she can no more detain him;
578 The poor fool prays her that he may depart.
She is resolved no longer to restrain him;
Bids him farewell, and look well to her heart,
    The which, by Cupid's bow she doth protest,
    He carries thence incagèd in his breast.

'Sweet boy,' she says, 'this night I'll waste in sorrow, 583
For my sick heart commands mine eyes to watch. 584
Tell me, love's master, shall we meet to-morrow?
Say, shall we? shall we? wilt thou make the match?'
    He tells her no; to-morrow he intends
    To hunt the boar with certain of his friends.

'The boar!' quoth she; whereat a sudden pale, 589
Like lawn being spread upon the blushing rose,
Usurps her cheek; she trembles at his tale,
And on his neck her yoking arms she throws;
    She sinketh down, still hanging by his neck,
    He on her belly falls, she on her back.

Now is she in the very lists of love, 595
Her champion mounted for the hot encounter.
All is imaginary she doth prove, 597
He will not manage her, although he mount her; 598
    That worse than Tantalus' is her annoy, 599
    To clip Elysium and to lack her joy. 600

Even so poor birds, deceived with painted grapes,
Do surfeit by the eye and pine the maw; 602
Even so she languisheth in her mishaps
As those poor birds that helpless berries saw.
    The warm effects which she in him finds missing 605
    She seeks to kindle with continual kissing.

But all in vain. Good Queen, it will not be!
She hath assayed as much as may be proved. 608
Her pleading hath deserved a greater fee:
She's Love, she loves, and yet she is not loved.
    'Fie, fie!' he says. 'You crush me; let me go!
    You have no reason to withhold me so.'

'Thou hadst been gone,' quoth she, 'sweet boy, ere this,
But that thou told'st me thou wouldst hunt the boar.
O, be advised, thou know'st not what it is
With javelin's point a churlish swine to gore,
    Whose tushes never sheathed he whetteth still, 617
    Like to a mortal butcher bent to kill. 618

'On his bow-back he hath a battle set
Of bristly pikes that ever threat his foes;
His eyes like glowworms shine when he doth fret;
His snout digs sepulchres where'er he goes;
    Being moved, he strikes whate'er is in his way, 623
    And whom he strikes his crooked tushes slay.

529 *world's comforter* i.e. the sun  540 *Incorporate* joined in a single body 541 *disjoined* i.e. ended the incorporate state  545 *pressed* oppressed  550 *insulter* i.e. triumphant winner  551 *vulture* i.e. ravenous  555 *reek* i.e. steam  557 *Planting oblivion* i.e. implanting blind disregard of consequences  558 *wrack* wreck  562 *froward* fretful  564 *listeth* wishes  565 *temp'ring* heating  567 *out of* beyond; *compassed* accomplished; *vent'ring* venturing  568 *leave . . . commission* i.e. liberties exceed permission 569 *Affection* passion  570 *when . . . froward* i.e. when the object of his desire is most stubborn  573 *Foul* hostile  578 *fool* plaything  583 *waste* spend  584 *watch* remain open  589 *pale* pallor  595 *lists* field of combat  597 *prove* experience  598 *manage* ride  599 *That . . . annoy* i.e. so that her torment exceeds that of Tantalus (punished in Hades by sight of unobtainable food and drink)  600 *clip* embrace; *Elysium* pagan paradise (here Adonis)  602 *pine the maw* starve the stomach  605 *effects* symptoms  608 *assayed* tried; *proved* tried  617 *tushes* tusks  618 *mortal* deadly  623 *moved* angered

'His brawny sides, with hairy bristles armèd,
26  Are better proof than thy spear's point can enter;
His short thick neck cannot be easily harmèd;
28  Being ireful, on the lion he will venter.
 The thorny brambles and embracing bushes,
 As fearful of him, part; through whom he rushes.

'Alas, he naught esteems that face of thine,
To which Love's eyes pays tributary gazes;
33  Nor thy soft hands, sweet lips, and crystal eyne,
Whose full perfection all the world amazes;
35   But having thee at vantage (wondrous dread!)
36   Would root these beauties as he roots the mead.

37  'O, let him keep his loathsome cabin still:
38  Beauty hath naught to do with such foul fiends.
39  Come not within his danger by thy will:
They that thrive well take counsel of their friends.
 When thou didst name the boar, not to dissemble,
 I feared thy fortune, and my joints did tremble.

'Didst thou not mark my face? Was it not white?
Saw'st thou not signs of fear lurk in mine eye?
45  Grew I not faint? and fell I not downright?
Within my bosom, whereon thou dost lie,
47   My boding heart pants, beats, and takes no rest,
 But, like an earthquake, shakes thee on my breast.

49  'For where Love reigns, disturbing Jealousy
Doth call himself Affection's sentinel,
51  Gives false alarms, suggesteth mutiny,
And in a peaceful hour doth cry "Kill, kill!"
53   Distemp'ring gentle Love in his desire,
 As air and water do abate the fire.

55  'This sour informer, this bate-breeding spy,
56  This canker that eats up Love's tender spring,
This carry-tale, dissentious Jealousy,
That sometime true news, sometime false doth bring,
 Knocks at my heart, and whispers in mine ear
 That if I love thee, I thy death should fear;

'And more than so, presenteth to mine eye
The picture of an angry-chafing boar,
Under whose sharp fangs on his back doth lie
An image like thyself, all stained with gore;
 Whose blood upon the fresh flowers being shed
 Doth make them droop with grief and hang the head.

'What should I do, seeing thee so indeed,
That tremble at th' imagination?
The thought of it doth make my faint heart bleed,
And fear doth teach it divination.   670
 I prophesy thy death, my living sorrow,
 If thou encounter with the boar to-morrow.

'But if thou needs wilt hunt, be ruled by me;
Uncouple at the timorous flying hare,   674
Or at the fox which lives by subtlety,
Or at the roe which no encounter dare.
 Pursue these fearful creatures o'er the downs, 677
 And on thy well-breathed horse keep with thy hounds. 678

'And when thou hast on foot the purblind hare, 679
Mark the poor wretch, to overshoot his troubles, 680
How he outruns the wind, and with what care
He cranks and crosses with a thousand doubles. 682
 The many musits through the which he goes 683
 Are like a labyrinth to amaze his foes. 684

'Sometime he runs among a flock of sheep,
To make the cunning hounds mistake their smell,
And sometime where earth-delving conies keep, 687
To stop the loud pursuers in their yell;  688
 And sometime sorteth with a herd of deer. 689
 Danger deviseth shifts, wit waits on fear; 690

'For there his smell with others being mingled,
The hot scent-snuffing hounds are driven to doubt,
Ceasing their clamorous cry till they have singled
With much ado the cold fault cleanly out.  694
 Then do they spend their mouths; echo replies,
 As if another chase were in the skies.

'By this, poor Wat, far off upon a hill,  697
Stands on his hinder legs with list'ning ear,
To hearken if his foes pursue him still.
Anon their loud alarums he doth hear,
 And now his grief may be comparèd well
 To one sore sick that hears the passing bell. 702

'Then shalt thou see the dew-bedabbled wretch
Turn and return, indenting with the way.  704
Each envious brier his weary legs do scratch; 705
Each shadow makes him stop, each murmur stay;
 For misery is trodden on by many
 And, being low, never relieved by any.

'Lie quietly and hear a little more.
Nay, do not struggle, for thou shalt not rise.
To make thee hate the hunting of the boar,
Unlike myself thou hear'st me moralize,
 Applying this to that, and so to so;
 For love can comment upon every woe.

'Where did I leave?' 'No matter where,' quoth he;
'Leave me, and then the story aptly ends.
The night is spent.' 'Why, what of that?' quoth she.
'I am,' quoth he, 'expected of my friends;
 And now 'tis dark, and going I shall fall.'
 'In night,' quoth she, 'desire sees best of all.

**626** *better proof* stronger armor **628** *venter* venture **633** *eyne* eyes
**635** *vantage* an advantage **636** *root* root up **637** *cabin* i.e. natural sty
**638** *fiends* destroyers **639** *danger* i.e. zone of danger **645** *downright* without pause **647** *boding* foreboding **649** *Jealousy* apprehension **651** *suggesteth mutiny* incites violence **653** *Distemp'ring* reducing **655** *bate-breeding* strife-breeding **656** *canker* rose-worm; *spring* shoot **670** *divination* power to prophesy **674** *Uncouple at* loose your hound upon **677** *fearful* timid **678** *well-breathed* sound-winded; *keep* keep up **679** *on foot* in chase; *purblind* dimsighted **680** *overshoot* run beyond **682** *cranks* turns **683** *musits* gaps in a hedge or fence **684** *amaze* confuse **687** *conies* rabbits **688** *yell* full cry **689** *sorteth* mingles **690** *shifts* ruses; *waits on* goes with **694** *cold fault* lost scent **697** *Wat* hare (popular term) **702** *passing* funeral **704** *indenting* zigzagging **705** *envious* malicious

'But if thou fall, O, then imagine this:
The earth, in love with thee, thy footing trips,
And all is but to rob thee of a kiss.
724 Rich preys make true men thieves. So do thy lips
725    Make modest Dian cloudy and forlorn,
726    Lest she should steal a kiss and die forsworn.

727 'Now of this dark night I perceive the reason:
728 Cynthia for shame obscures her silver shine,
729 Till forging Nature be condemned of treason
For stealing moulds from heaven that were divine;
   Wherein she framed thee, in high heaven's despite,
732    To shame the sun by day, and her by night.

'And therefore hath she bribed the Destinies
734 To cross the curious workmanship of Nature,
To mingle beauty with infirmities
736 And pure perfection with impure defeature,
   Making it subject to the tyranny
   Of mad mischances and much misery;

'As burning fevers, agues pale and faint,
740 Life-poisoning pestilence, and frenzies wood,
741 The marrow-eating sickness whose attaint
Disorder breeds by heating of the blood,
743    Surfeits, imposthumes, grief, and damned despair
   Swear Nature's death for framing thee so fair.

745 'And not the least of all these maladies
But in one minute's fight brings beauty under.
747 Both favor, savor, hue, and qualities,
748 Whereat th' impartial gazer late did wonder,
   Are on the sudden wasted, thawed, and done,
   As mountain snow melts with the midday sun.

751 'Therefore, despite of fruitless chastity,
752 Love-lacking vestals, and self-loving nuns,
That on the earth would breed a scarcity
And barren dearth of daughters and of sons,
755    Be prodigal. The lamp that burns by night
   Dries up his oil to lend the world his light.

'What is thy body but a swallowing grave,
Seeming to bury that posterity
759 Which by the rights of time thou needs must have
If thou destroy them not in dark obscurity?
   If so, the world will hold thee in disdain,
762    Sith in thy pride so fair a hope is slain.

'So in thyself thyself art made away,
A mischief worse than civil home-bred strife,
Or theirs whose desperate hands themselves do slay,
766 Or butcher sire that reaves his son of life.
767    Foul cank'ring rust the hidden treasure frets,
   But gold that's put to use more gold begets.'

'Nay, then,' quoth Adon, 'you will fall again
770 Into your idle over-handled theme.
The kiss I gave you is bestowed in vain,
And all in vain you strive against the stream;
   For, by this black-faced night, desire's foul nurse,
774    Your treatise makes me like you worse and worse.

'If love have lent you twenty thousand tongues,
And every tongue more moving than your own,
Bewitching like the wanton mermaid's songs,
Yet from mine ear the tempting tune is blown;
   For know, my heart stands armèd in mine ear 77
   And will not let a false sound enter there,

'Lest the deceiving harmony should run
Into the quiet closure of my breast; 78
And then my little heart were quite undone,
In his bedchamber to be barred of rest.
   No, lady, no; my heart longs not to groan,
   But soundly sleeps while now it sleeps alone.

'What have you urged that I cannot reprove? 78
The path is smooth that leadeth on to danger.
I hate not love, but your device in love, 78
That lends embracements unto every stranger.
   You do it for increase. O strange excuse,
   When reason is the bawd to lust's abuse!

'Call it not love, for Love to heaven is fled
Since sweating Lust on earth unsurped his name;
Under whose simple semblance he hath fed 79
Upon fresh beauty, blotting it with blame;
   Which the hot tyrant stains and soon bereaves, 79
   As caterpillars do the tender leaves.

'Love comforteth like sunshine after rain,
But Lust's effect is tempest after sun.
Love's gentle spring doth always fresh remain;
Lust's winter comes ere summer half be done.
   Love surfeits not, Lust like a glutton dies;
   Love is all truth, Lust full of forgèd lies.

'More I could tell, but more I dare not say:
The text is old, the orator too green. 80
Therefore in sadness now I will away. 80
My face is full of shame, my heart of teen; 80
   Mine ears, that to your wanton talk attended,
   Do burn themselves for having so offended.'

With this he breaketh from the sweet embrace
Of those fair arms which bound him to her breast
And homeward through the dark laund runs apace; 81
Leaves Love upon her back, deeply distressed.
   Look how a bright star shooteth from the sky,
   So glides he in the night from Venus' eye;

724 *preys* spoils  725 *Dian* Diana (chaste goddess of the moon)  726 *forsworn* i.e. violating the oath of chastity  727 *of* for  728 *Cynthia* i.e. Diana  729 *forging* counterfeiting  732 *her* i.e. the moon  734 *cross* thwart; *curious* ingenious  736 *defeature* defect  740 *wood* mad  741 *attaint* infection  743 *imposthumes* abscesses  745–46 *And . . . under* i.e. the least of these maladies subdues beauty in a minute  747 *favor* features  748 *impartial* just  751 *fruitless* sterile  752 *self-loving* i.e. intent upon their own salvation (?)  755 *prodigal* i.e. outgiving  759 *rights* claims  762 *Sith* since  766 *reaves* deprives  767 *cank'ring* eating (as does the cankerworm); *frets* erodes  770 *over-handled* threadbare  774 *treatise* discourse  779 *heart* i.e. inner resolution  782 *closure* enclosure  787 *reprove* refute  789 *device* i.e. sleights  795 *simple semblance* guileless aspect  797 *hot tyrant* i.e. lust; *bereaves* impairs, spoils  806 *green* unripe, inexperienced  807 *in sadness* in all seriousness  808 *teen* grief  813 *laund* i.e. grassy fields

Which after him she darts, as one on shore
Gazing upon a late-embarkèd friend
Till the wild waves will have him seen no more,
Whose ridges with the meeting clouds contend.
    So did the merciless and pitchy night
    Fold in the object that did feed her sight.

3 Whereat amazed, as one that unaware
Hath dropped a precious jewel in the flood,
5 Or stonished as night-wand'rers often are,
6 Their light blown out in some mistrustful wood,
    Even so confounded in the dark she lay,
    Having lost the fair discovery of her way.

And now she beats her heart, whereat it groans,
That all the neighbor caves, as seeming troubled,
Make verbal repetition of her moans.
2 Passion on passion deeply is redoubled :
    'Ay me!' she cries, and twenty times, 'Woe, woe!'
    And twenty echoes twenty times cry so.

She, marking them, begins a wailing note
And sings extemporally a woeful ditty –
7 How love makes young men thrall, and old men dote ;
How love is wise in folly, foolish-witty.
    Her heavy anthem still concludes in woe,
    And still the choir of echoes answer so.

Her song was tedious and outwore the night,
For lovers' hours are long, though seeming short.
If pleased themselves, others, they think, delight
In such-like circumstance, with such-like sport.
    Their copious stories, oftentimes begun,
    End without audience and are never done.

For who hath she to spend the night withal
8 But idle sounds resembling parasits,
Like shrill-tongued tapsters answering every call,
Soothing the humor of fantastic wits ?
    She says ' 'Tis so.' They answer all, ' 'Tis so,'
    And would say after her if she said 'No.'

Lo, here the gentle lark, weary of rest,
4 From his moist cabinet mounts up on high
And wakes the morning, from whose silver breast
The sun ariseth in his majesty ;
    Who doth the world so gloriously behold
    That cedar tops and hills seem burnished gold.

**823** *amazed* confused, at a loss  **825** *stonished* dismayed  **826** *mistrustful* mistrusted, feared  **832** *Passion* lamentation; *redoubled* re-echoed  **837** *thrall* captive  **848** *parasits* parasites, attendants  **854** *moist cabinet* dewy cottage  **870** *coasteth to* runs to head off  **873** *twind* wind  **874** *strict* tight **877** *at a bay* i.e. confronted by their quarry  **884** *blunt* crude  **887** *curst* fierce-tempered  **888** *strain court'sy* i.e. are over-polite in yielding precedence; *cope* cope with  **890** *surprise* attack  **892** *feeling part* organ of sense  **895** *ecstasy* fit  **897** *causeless fantasy* baseless fancy  **907** *spleens* emotional starts  **909** *mated* overcome  **911** *respects* designs  **912** *In hand with* busy about

Venus salutes him with this fair good-morrow :
'O thou clear god, and patron of all light,
From whom each lamp and shining star doth borrow
The beauteous influence that makes him bright,
    There lives a son that sucked an earthly mother
    May lend thee light, as thou dost lend to other.'

This said, she hasteth to a myrtle grove,
Musing the morning is so much o'erworn
And yet she hears no tidings of her love.
She hearkens for his hounds and for his horn.
    Anon she hears them chant it lustily,
    And all in haste she coasteth to the cry ;    870

And as she runs, the bushes in the way
Some catch her by the neck, some kiss her face,
Some twind about her thigh to make her stay.    873
She wildly breaketh from their strict embrace,    874
    Like a milch doe whose swelling dugs do ache
    Hasting to feed her fawn hid in some brake.

By this, she hears the hounds are at a bay ;    877
Whereat she starts, like one that spies an adder
Wreathed up in fatal folds just in his way,
The fear whereof doth make him shake and shudder.
    Even so the timorous yelping of the hounds
    Appals her senses and her spirit confounds.

For now she knows it is no gentle chase,
But the blunt boar, rough bear, or lion proud,    884
Because the cry remaineth in one place,
Where fearfully the dogs exclaim aloud.
    Finding their enemy to be so curst,    887
    They all strain court'sy who shall cope him first.    888

This dismal cry rings sadly in her ear,
Through which it enters to surprise her heart,    890
Who, overcome by doubt and bloodless fear,
With cold-pale weakness numbs each feeling part :    892
    Like soldiers when their captain once doth yield,
    They basely fly and dare not stay the field.

Thus stands she in a trembling ecstasy ;    895
Till, cheering up her senses all dismayed,
She tells them 'tis a causeless fantasy,    897
And childish error that they are afraid ;
    Bids them leave quaking, bids them fear no more ;
    And with that word she spied the hunted boar,

Whose frothy mouth, bepainted all with red,
Like milk and blood being mingled both togither,
A second fear through all her sinews spread,
Which madly hurries her she knows not whither.
    This way she runs, and now she will no further,
    But back retires to rate the boar for murther.

A thousand spleens bear her a thousand ways ;    907
She treads the path that she untreads again ;
Her more than haste is mated with delays,    909
Like the proceedings of a drunken brain,
    Full of respects, yet naught at all respecting,    911
    In hand with all things, naught at all effecting.    912

Here kennelled in a brake she finds a hound
914 And asks the weary caitiff for his master;
And there another licking of his wound,
916 'Gainst venomed sores the only sovereign plaster;
    And here she meets another, sadly scowling,
    To whom she speaks, and he replies with howling.

When he hath ceased his ill-resounding noise,
920 Another flap-mouthed mourner, black and grim,
Against the welkin volleys out his voice.
Another and another answer him,
    Clapping their proud tails to the ground below,
    Shaking their scratched ears, bleeding as they go.

925 Look how the world's poor people are amazèd
At apparitions, signs, and prodigies,
Whereon with fearful eyes they long have gazèd,
928 Infusing them with dreadful prophecies:
    So she at these sad signs draws up her breath
930    And, sighing it again, exclaims on Death.

'Hard-favored tyrant, ugly, meagre, lean,
932 Hateful divorce of love!' – thus chides she Death –
933 'Grim-grinning ghost, earth's worm, what dost thou mean
To stifle beauty and to steal his breath
    Who, when he lived, his breath and beauty set
    Gloss on the rose, smell to the violet?

'If he be dead – O no, it cannot be,
Seeing his beauty, thou shouldst strike at it!
O yes, it may! Thou hast no eyes to see,
940 But hatefully at randon dost thou hit.
    Thy mark is feeble age; but thy false dart
    Mistakes that aim and cleaves an infant's heart.

'Hadst thou but bid beware, then he had spoke,
944 And, hearing him, thy power had lost his power.
The Destinies will curse thee for this stroke.
They bid thee crop a weed; thou pluck'st a flower.
    Love's golden arrow at him should have fled,
948    And not Death's ebon dart to strike him dead.

'Dost thou drink tears, that thou provok'st such weeping?
950 What may a heavy groan advantage thee?
Why hast thou cast into eternal sleeping
Those eyes that taught all other eyes to see?
953    Now Nature cares not for thy mortal vigor,
    Since her best work is ruined with thy rigor.'

Here overcome, as one full of despair,
956 She vailed her eyelids, who, like sluices, stopped
The crystal tide that from her two cheeks fair
In the sweet channel of her bosom dropped;
    But through the floodgates breaks the silver rain
    And with his strong course opens them again.

961 O, how her eyes and tears did lend and borrow,
Her eye seen in the tears, tears in her eye,
963 Both crystals, where they viewed each other's sorrow –
Sorrow that friendly sighs sought still to dry;
    But like a stormy day, now wind, now rain,
    Sighs dry her cheeks, tears make them wet again.

Variable passions throng her constant woe,
As striving who should best become her grief. 96
All entertained, each passion labors so 96
That every present sorrow seemeth chief,
    But none is best; then join they all together
    Like many clouds consulting for foul weather. 97

By this, far off she hears some huntsman halloa.
A nurse's song ne'er pleased her babe so well.
The dire imagination she did follow
This sound of hope doth labor to expel;
    For now reviving joy bids her rejoice
    And flatters her it is Adonis' voice.

Whereat her tears began to turn their tide, 97
Being prisoned in her eye like pearls in glass; 98
Yet sometimes falls an orient drop beside,
Which her cheek melts, as scorning it should pass 98
    To wash the foul face of the sluttish ground,
    Who is but drunken when she seemeth drowned.

O hard-believing love, how strange it seems 9
Not to believe, and yet too credulous!
Thy weal and woe are both of them extremes; 98
Despair and hope makes thee ridiculous:
    The one doth flatter thee in thoughts unlikely, 9
    In likely thoughts the other kills thee quickly. 9

Now she unweaves the web that she hath wrought:
Adonis lives, and Death is not to blame;
It was not she that called him all to naught. 9
Now she adds honors to his hateful name:
    She clepes him king of graves, and grave for kings, 9
    Imperious supreme of all mortal things. 9

'No, no,' quoth she, 'sweet Death, I did but jest;
Yet pardon me I felt a kind of fear
When as I met the boar, that bloody beast
Which knows no pity but is still severe.
    Then, gentle shadow (truth I must confess), 1
    I railed on thee, fearing my love's decesse. 1

''Tis not my fault the boar provoked my tongue.
Be wreaked on him, invisible commander; 1
'Tis he, foul creature, that hath done thee wrong.
I did but act; he's author of thy slander.
    Grief hath two tongues, and never woman yet
    Could rule them both without ten women's wit.'

914 *caitiff* base wretch  916 *plaster* dressing  920 *flap-mouthed* i.e. with dangling lips of a hound  925 *amazèd* perplexed  928 *Infusing . . . prophecies* i.e. converting them into dreadful omens  930 *exclaims on* inveighs against  932 *divorce* terminator  933 *worm* i.e. canker, begetter of rot  940 *randon* random  944 *his* its  948 *ebon* ebony, black  950 *advantage* profit  953 *mortal vigor* deadly strength  956 *vailed* lowered; *who . . . stopped* which, like floodgates, dammed  961 *lend and borrow* i.e. reflect each other  963 *crystals* i.e. mirrors  968 *striving who* contending which  969 *entertained* admitted  972 *consulting for* i.e. planning to produce  979 *turn their tide* ebb, subside  980 *like . . . glass* i.e. with the fixed quality of a pearl-shaped glass-bubble (?)  982 *melts* i.e. reduces to mere moisture  985 *hard-believing* i.e. stubborn, wrongheaded  987 *weal* gladness  989 *The one* i.e. hope; *thoughts unlikely* i.e. cheerful fancies  990 *likely thoughts* i.e. ominous probabilities  993 *all to naught* evil  995 *clepes* names  996 *Imperious supreme* imperial ruler  1001 *shadow* shade, spectre  1002 *decesse* decease  1004 *wreaked* revenged

Thus hoping that Adonis is alive,
Her rash suspect she doth extenuate;
And that his beauty may the better thrive,
With Death she humbly doth insinuate;
    Tells him of trophies, statues, tombs; and stories
    His victories, his triumphs, and his glories.

'O Jove,' quoth she, 'how much a fool was I
To be of such a weak and silly mind
To wail his death who lives, and must not die
Till mutual overthrow of mortal kind!
    For he being dead, with him is beauty slain,
    And, beauty dead, black chaos comes again.

'Fie, fie, fond love, thou art as full of fear
As one with treasure laden hemmed with thieves.
Trifles, unwitnessèd with eye or ear,
Thy coward heart with false bethinking grieves.'
    Even at this word she hears a merry horn,
    Whereat she leaps that was but late forlorn.

As falcons to the lure, away she flies.
The grass stoops not, she treads on it so light;
And in her haste unfortunately spies
The foul boar's conquest on her fair delight;
    Which seen, her eyes, as murd'red with the view,
    Like stars ashamed of day, themselves withdrew;

Or as the snail, whose tender horns being hit,
Shrinks backward in his shelly cave with pain,
And there, all smooth'red up, in shade doth sit,
Long after fearing to creep forth again;
    So at his bloody view her eyes are fled
    Into the deep-dark cabins of her head;

Where they resign their office and their light
To the disposing of her troubled brain;
Who bids them still consort with ugly night
And never wound the heart with looks again;
    Who, like a king perplexèd in his throne,
    By their suggestion gives a deadly groan,

Whereat each tributary subject quakes,
As when the wind, imprisoned in the ground,
Struggling for passage, earth's foundation shakes,
Which with cold terror doth men's minds confound.
    This mutiny each part doth so surprise
    That from their dark beds once more leap her eyes,

And, being opened, threw unwilling light
Upon the wide wound that the boar had trenched   1052
In his soft flank; whose wonted lily white
With purple tears that his wound wept was drenched.
    No flow'r was nigh, no grass, herb, leaf, or weed,
    But stole his blood and seemed with him to bleed.

This solemn sympathy poor Venus noteth.
Over one shoulder doth she hang her head.
Dumbly she passions, franticly she doteth:   1059
She thinks he could not die, he is not dead;
    Her voice is stopped, her joints forget to bow;
    Her eyes are mad that they have wept till now.   1062

Upon his hurt she looks so steadfastly
That her sight dazzling makes the wound seem three;   1064
And then she reprehends her mangling eye,
That makes more gashes where no breach should be.
    His face seems twain, each several limb is doubled;
    For oft the eye mistakes, the brain being troubled.

'My tongue cannot express my grief for one,
And yet,' quoth she, 'behold two Adons dead!
My sighs are blown away, my salt tears gone,
Mine eyes are turned to fire, my heart to lead.
    Heavy heart's lead, melt at mine eyes' red fire!
    So shall I die by drops of hot desire.

'Alas, poor world, what treasure hast thou lost!
What face remains alive that's worth the viewing?
Whose tongue is music now? What canst thou boast
Of things long since, or any thing ensuing?   1078
    The flowers are sweet, their colors fresh and trim;
    But true-sweet beauty lived and died with him.

'Bonnet nor veil henceforth no creature wear!
Nor sun nor wind will ever strive to kiss you.
Having no fair to lose, you need not fear.   1083
The sun doth scorn you, and the wind doth hiss you;
    But when Adonis lived, sun and sharp air
    Lurked like two thieves, to rob him of his fair;

'And therefore would he put his bonnet on,
Under whose brim the gaudy sun would peep;
The wind would blow it off, and, being gone,
Play with his locks, then would Adonis weep;
    And straight, in pity of his tender years,
    They both would strive who first should dry his tears.

'To see his face the lion walked along
Behind some hedge, because he would not fear him.   1094
To recreate himself when he hath song,
The tiger would be tame, and gently hear him.
    If he had spoke, the wolf would leave his prey
    And never fright the silly lamb that day.

'When he beheld his shadow in the brook,
The fishes spread on it their golden gills.
When he was by, the birds such pleasure took
That some would sing, some other in their bills
    Would bring him mulberries and ripe-red cherries:
    He fed them with his sight, they him with berries.

1010 *suspect* suspicion  1012 *insinuate* ingratiate herself  1013 *stories* narrates  1023 *unwitnessèd with* not perceived by  1032 *ashamed of* put to shame by  1041 *still consort* always dwell  1042 *looks* i.e. looking  1043 *Who* i.e. which; *perplexèd* tormented  1044 *suggestion* incitement  1049 *mutiny* attack  1052 *trenched* ripped  1059 *passions* grieves, displays emotion  1062 *mad* frenzied; *till* i.e. before  1064 *dazzling* i.e. losing distinctness of vision  1078 *long since* i.e. far in the past  1083 *fair* beauty  1094 *fear* frighten

1105 'But this foul, grim, and urchin-snouted boar,
Whose downward eye still looketh for a grave,
1107 Ne'er saw the beauteous livery that he wore:
1108 Witness the entertainment that he gave.
    If he did see his face, why then I know
    He thought to kiss him, and hath killed him so.

' 'Tis true, 'tis true! thus was Adonis slain:
He ran upon the boar with his sharp spear,
Who did not whet his teeth at him again,
But by a kiss thought to persuade him there;
    And nuzzling in his flank, the loving swine
    Sheathed unaware the tusk in his soft groin.

'Had I been toothed like him, I must confess,
With kissing him I should have killed him first;
But he is dead, and never did he bless
1120 My youth with his – the more am I accurst.'
    With this, she falleth in the place she stood
    And stains her face with his congealèd blood.

She looks upon his lips, and they are pale;
She takes him by the hand, and that is cold;
She whispers in his ears a heavy tale,
As if they heard the woeful words she told;
    She lifts the coffer-lids that close his eyes,
    Where, lo, two lamps burnt out in darkness lies;

Two glasses, where herself herself beheld
A thousand times, and now no more reflect,
Their virtue lost wherein they late excelled,
And every beauty robbed of his effect.
1133   'Wonder of time,' quoth she, 'this is my spite,
    That, thou being dead, the day should yet be light.

'Since thou art dead, lo, here I prophesy
Sorrow on love hereafter shall attend.
1137 It shall be waited on with jealousy,
Find sweet beginning, but unsavory end,
    Ne'er settled equally, but high or low,
    That all love's pleasure shall not match his woe.

'It shall be fickle, false, and full of fraud,
1142 Bud and be blasted in a breathing while,
1143 The bottom poison, and the top o'erstrawed
With sweets that shall the truest sight beguile.
    The strongest body shall it make most weak,
    Strike the wise dumb, and teach the fool to speak.

'It shall be sparing, and too full of riot,
Teaching decrepit age to tread the measures;
1149 The staring ruffian shall it keep in quiet,
Pluck down the rich, enrich the poor with treasures;
    It shall be raging mad and silly mild,
    Make the young old, the old become a child.

'It shall suspect where is no cause of fear;
It shall not fear where it should most mistrust;
It shall be merciful, and too severe,
And most deceiving when it seems most just;
1157   Perverse it shall be where it shows most toward,
    Put fear to valor, courage to the coward.

'It shall be cause of war and dire events
And set dissension 'twixt the son and sire,
Subject and servile to all discontents,
As dry combustious matter is to fire.
    Sith in his prime death doth my love destroy,
    They that love best their loves shall not enjoy.'

By this, the boy that by her side lay killed
Was melted like a vapor from her sight,
And in his blood, that on the ground lay spilled,
A purple flower sprung up, check'red with white,
    Resembling well his pale cheeks and the blood
    Which in round drops upon their whiteness stood.

She bows her head the new-sprung flower to smell,
Comparing it to her Adonis' breath,
And says within her bosom it shall dwell,
Since he himself is reft from her by death;
    She crops the stalk, and in the breach appears
    Green-dropping sap, which she compares to tears.

'Poor flow'r,' quoth she, 'this was thy father's guise –
Sweet issue of a more sweet-smelling sire –
For every little grief to wet his eyes.
To grow unto himself was his desire,
    And so 'tis thine; but know, it is as good
    To wither in my breast as in his blood.

'Here was thy father's bed, here in my breast;
Thou art the next of blood, and 'tis thy right.
Lo, in this hollow cradle take thy rest;
My throbbing heart shall rock thee day and night.
    There shall not be one minute in an hour
    Wherein I will not kiss my sweet love's flow'r.'

Thus weary of the world, away she hies
And yokes her silver doves, by whose swift aid
Their mistress, mounted, through the empty skies
In her light chariot quickly is conveyed,
    Holding their course to Paphos, where their queen
    Means to immure herself and not be seen.

FINIS

1105 *urchin-snouted* hedgehog-snouted, i.e. rooting   1107 *livery* i.e. outsides, appearance   1108 *entertainment* treatment   1133 *spite* torment   1137 *jealousy* apprehension of evil   1142 *breathing while* space of a breath   1143 *o'erstrawed* overstrewn   1149 *staring* glaring, threatening   1157 *toward* tractable   1168 *purple flower* i.e. the anemone (cf. Ovid, *Metamorphoses*, x, 731–39)   1177 *guise* i.e. way, manner   1193 *Paphos* (the abode of Venus in Cyprus)

# THE RAPE OF LUCRECE

TO THE RIGHT HONORABLE

## HENRY WRIOTHESLEY

### EARL OF SOUTHAMPTON, AND BARON OF TITCHFIELD

4
5

The love I dedicate to your Lordship is without end; whereof this pamphlet without beginning is but a superfluous moiety. The warrant I have of your honorable disposition, not the worth of my untutored lines, makes it assured of acceptance. What I have done is yours; what I have to do is yours; being part in all I have, devoted yours. Were my worth greater, my duty would show greater; meantime, as it is, it is bound to your Lordship, to whom I wish long life still lengthened with all happiness.

Your Lordship's in all duty,
WILLIAM SHAKESPEARE

## THE ARGUMENT

Lucius Tarquinius (for his excessive pride surnamed Superbus), after he had caused his own father-in-law Servius Tullius to be cruelly murdered, and, contrary to the Roman laws and customs, not requiring or staying for the people's suffrages, had possessed himself of the kingdom, went, accompanied with his sons and other noblemen of Rome, to besiege Ardea; during which siege the principal men of the army meeting one evening at the tent of Sextus Tarquinius, the King's son, in their discourses after supper every one commended the virtues of his own wife; among whom Collatinus extolled the incomparable chastity of his wife Lucretia. In that pleasant humor they all posted to Rome; and intending by their secret and sudden arrival to make trial of that which every one had before avouched, only Collatinus finds his wife (though it were late in the night) spinning amongst her maids; the other ladies were all found dancing and revelling, or in several disports. Whereupon the noblemen yielded Collatinus the victory, and his wife the fame. At that time
20 Sextus Tarquinius being inflamed with Lucrece' beauty, yet smothering his passions for the present, departed with the rest back to the camp; from whence he shortly after privily withdrew himself, and was (according to his estate) royally entertained and lodged by Lucrece at Collatium. The same night he treacherously stealeth into her chamber, violently ravished her, and early in the morning speedeth away. Lucrece, in this lamentable plight, hastily dispatcheth messengers, one to Rome for

her father, another to the camp for Collatine. They came, the one accompanied with Junius Brutus, the other with Publius Valerius; and finding Lucrece attired in mourning habit, demanded the cause of her sorrow. She, first taking an oath of them for her revenge, revealed the actor and whole manner of his dealing, and withal suddenly stabbed herself. Which done, with one consent they all vowed to root out the whole hated family of the Tarquins; and bearing the dead body to Rome, Brutus acquainted the people with the doer and manner of the vile deed, with a bitter invective against the tyranny of the King; wherewith the people were so moved that with one 40 consent and a general acclamation the Tarquins were all exiled, and the state government changed from kings to consuls.

From the besiegèd Ardea all in post, 1
Borne by the trustless wings of false desire, 2
Lust-breathèd Tarquin leaves the Roman host
And to Collatium bears the lightless fire 4
Which, in pale embers hid, lurks to aspire
 And girdle with embracing flames the waist
 Of Collatine's fair love, Lucrece the chaste.

Haply that name of 'chaste' unhap'ly set 8
This bateless edge on his keen appetite; 9
When Collatine unwisely did not let 10
To praise the clear unmatchèd red and white
Which triumphed in that sky of his delight, 12
 Where mortal stars, as bright as heaven's beauties, 13
 With pure aspects did him peculiar duties. 14

For he the night before, in Tarquin's tent,
Unlocked the treasure of his happy state:
What priceless wealth the heavens had him lent
In the possession of his beauteous mate;
Reck'ning his fortune at such high proud rate
 That kings might be espousèd to more fame,
 But king nor peer to such a peerless dame.

Ded., 4–5 *without beginning* (often explained as signifying that the story begins *in medias res*, but perhaps only a vague term of deprecation, i.e. 'maimed,' 'imperfect') 5 *superfluous moiety* i.e. uncontained portion, spillover; *warrant* assurance
1 *all in post* post-haste 2 *trustless* treacherous 4 *lightless* i.e. smouldering 8 *Haply* perchance 9 *bateless* unabated, sharp 10 *let* forbear 12 *sky* i.e. the face of Lucrece 13 *mortal stars* i.e. the eyes of Lucrece 14 *aspects* (1) gazes, (2) astrological portents; *peculiar duties* i.e. duties reserved for him

22 O happiness enjoyed but of a few,
23 And, if possessed, as soon decayed and done
   As is the morning's silver-melting dew
25 Against the golden splendor of the sun !
26 An expired date, cancelled ere well begun.
     Honor and beauty, in the owner's arms,
     Are weakly fortressed from a world of harms.

29 Beauty itself doth of itself persuade
30 The eyes of men without an orator.
31 What needeth then apologies be made
32 To set forth that which is so singular ?
33 Or why is Collatine the publisher
   Of that rich jewel he should keep unknown
   From thievish ears, because it is his own ?

   Perchance his boast of Lucrece' sov'reignty
37 Suggested this proud issue of a king ;
   For by our ears our hearts oft tainted be.
   Perchance that envy of so rich a thing
40 Braving compare, disdainfully did sting
     His high-pitched thoughts that meaner men should vaunt
42    That golden hap which their superiors want.

   But some untimely thought did instigate
44 His all too timeless speed, if none of those.
45 His honor, his affairs, his friends, his state,
   Neglected all, with swift intent he goes
47 To quench the coal which in his liver glows.
48    O rash false heat, wrapped in repentant cold,
49    Thy hasty spring still blasts and ne'er grows old !

   When at Collatium this false lord arrivèd,
   Well was he welcomed by the Roman dame,
   Within whose face Beauty and Virtue strivèd
53 Which of them both should underprop her fame.
   When Virtue bragged, Beauty would blush for shame ;
     When Beauty boasted blushes, in despite
     Virtue would stain that o'er with silver white.

57 But Beauty, in that white entitulèd,
58 From Venus' doves doth challenge that fair field,
   Then Virtue claims from Beauty Beauty's red,
60 Which Virtue gave the Golden Age to gild
   Their silver cheeks, and called it then their shield,
     Teaching them thus to use it in the fight,
63    When shame assailed, the red should fence the white.

   This heraldry in Lucrece' face was seen,
65 Argued by Beauty's red and Virtue's white.
   Of either's color was the other queen,
67 Proving from world's minority their right.
   Yet their ambition makes them still to fight,
69    The sovereignty of either being so great
     That oft they interchange each other's seat.

   This silent war of lilies and of roses
   Which Tarquin viewed in her fair face's field,
73 In their pure ranks his traitor eye encloses ;
   Where, lest between them both it should be killed,
   The coward captive vanquishèd doth yield
     To those two armies that would let him go
     Rather than triumph in so false a foe.

Now thinks he that her husband's shallow tongue,
The niggard prodigal that praised her so,
In that high task hath done her beauty wrong,
Which far exceeds his barren skill to show.    81
Therefore that praise which Collatine doth owe
   Enchanted Tarquin answers with surmise,    83
   In silent wonder of still-gazing eyes.

This earthly saint, adorèd by this devil,
Little suspecteth the false worshipper ;
For unstained thoughts do seldom dream on evil ;
Birds never limed no secret bushes fear.    88
So guiltless she securely gives good cheer    89
   And reverend welcome to her princely guest,
   Whose inward ill no outward harm expressed ;

For that he colored with his high estate,    92
Hiding base sin in pleats of majesty ;
That nothing in him seemed inordinate,    94
Save something too much wonder of his eye,
Which, having all, all could not satisfy ;
   But, poorly rich, so wanteth in his store    97
   That, cloyed with much, he pineth still for more.

But she, that never coped with stranger eyes,    99
Could pick no meaning from their parling looks,    10
Nor read the subtle-shining secrecies
Writ in the glassy margents of such books.    10
She touched no unknown baits, nor feared no hooks ;
   Nor could she moralize his wanton sight,    10
   More than his eyes were opened to the light.    10

He stories to her ears her husband's fame,
Won in the fields of fruitful Italy ;
And decks with praises Collatine's high name,
Made glorious by his manly chivalry,
With bruisèd arms and wreaths of victory.    11
   Her joy with heaved-up hand she doth express,    11
   And wordless so greets heaven for his success.

Far from the purpose of his coming thither
He makes excuses for his being there.
No cloudy show of stormy blust'ring weather
Doth yet in his fair welkin once appear,    11
Till sable Night, mother of dread and fear,
   Upon the world dim darkness doth display
   And in her vaulty prison stows the day.

22 *of* by   23 *done* done with   25 *Against* i.e. in face of   26 *date* term   29 *of* by   30 *orator* pleader   31 *apologies* justifications   32 *singular* unique   33 *publisher* advertiser   37 *Suggested* prompted ; *issue* offspring   40 *Braving compare* defying comparisons   42 *hap* luck   44 *timeless* untimely   45 *state* i.e. royal status   47 *liver* (supposed seat of sexual desire)   48 *wrapped* in i.e. attended by   49 *blasts* is blasted   53 *underprop* bear up   57 *entitulèd* having a claim   58 *field* (1) field of combat, (2) armorial ground   60 *gild* i.e. cover with a blush of modesty   63 *fence* shield   65 *Argued* disputed   67 *minority* youth, i.e. the Golden Age   69 *sovereignty* natural superiority   73 *encloses* overwhelms   81 *show* i.e. do justice to   83 *surmise* i.e. mounting speculation   88 *limed* snared with birdlime   89 *securely* overconfidently   92 *that he colored* i.e. the harmfulness he disguised   94 *That* so that   97 *store* abundance   99 *stranger eyes* eyes of a stranger   100 *parling* speaking   102 *glassy margents* mirroring margins   104 *moralize* interpret ; *sight* glance   105 *than* than that   110 *bruisèd arms* battered armor   111 *heaved-up* upreared   116 *welkin* sky

For then is Tarquin brought unto his bed,
Intending weariness with heavy sprite;
For, after supper, long he questionèd
With modest Lucrece, and wore out the night.
Now leaden slumber with live's strength doth fight,
    And every one to rest themselves betake,
    Save thieves, and cares, and troubled minds that wake.

As one of which doth Tarquin lie revolving
The sundry dangers of his will's obtaining;
Yet ever to obtain his will resolving,
Though weak-built hopes persuade him to abstaining.
Despair to gain doth traffic oft for gaining;
    And when great treasure is the meed proposèd,
    Though death be adjunct, there's no death supposèd.

Those that much covet are with gain so fond
That what they have not, that which they possess,
They scatter and unloose it from their bond,
And so, by hoping more, they have but less;
Or, gaining more, the profit of excess
    Is but to surfeit, and such griefs sustain
    That they prove bankrout in this poor rich gain.

The aim of all is but to nurse the life
With honor, wealth, and ease in waning age;
And in this aim there is such thwarting strife
That one for all, or all for one we gage:
As life for honor in fell battle's rage;
    Honor for wealth; and oft that wealth doth cost
    The death of all, and all together lost;

So that in vent'ring ill we leave to be
The things we are for that which we expect;
And this ambitious foul infirmity,
In having much, torments us with defect
Of that we have: so then we do neglect
    The thing we have; and, all for want of wit,
    Make something nothing by augmenting it.

Such hazard now must doting Tarquin make,
Pawning his honor to obtain his lust;
And for himself himself he must forsake.
Then where is truth, if there be no self-trust?
When shall he think to find a stranger just
    When he himself himself confounds, betrays
    To sland'rous tongues and wretched hateful days?

Now stole upon the time the dead of night,
When heavy sleep had closed up mortal eyes.
No comfortable star did lend his light, 164
No noise but owls' and wolves' death-boding cries.
Now serves the season that they may surprise
    The silly lambs. Pure thoughts are dead and still,
    While lust and murder wakes to stain and kill.

And now this lustful lord leapt from his bed,
Throwing his mantle rudely o'er his arm;
Is madly tossed between desire and dread;
Th' one sweetly flatters, th' other feareth harm;
But honest fear, bewitched with lust's foul charm,
    Doth too too oft betake him to retire,
    Beaten away by brainsick rude desire.

His falchion on a flint he softly smiteth, 176
That from the cold stone sparks of fire do fly;
Whereat a waxen torch forthwith he lighteth,
Which must be lodestar to his lustful eye;
And to the flame thus speaks advisedly: 180
    'As from this cold flint I enforced this fire,
    So Lucrece must I force to my desire.'

Here pale with fear he doth premeditate
The dangers of his loathsome enterprise,
And in his inward mind he doth debate
What following sorrow may on this arise;
Then looking scornfully, he doth despise
    His naked armor of still-slaughterèd lust 188
    And justly thus controls his thoughts unjust:

'Fair torch, burn out thy light, and lend it not
To darken her whose light excelleth thine;
And die, unhallowed thoughts, before you blot
With your uncleanness that which is divine.
Offer pure incense to so pure a shrine.
    Let fair humanity abhor the deed
    That spots and stains love's modest snow-white weed. 196

'O shame to knighthood and to shining arms!
O foul dishonor to my household's grave! 198
O impious act including all foul harms!
A martial man to be soft fancy's slave!
True valor still a true respect should have; 201
    Then my digression is so vile, so base,
    That it will live engraven in my face.

'Yea, though I die, the scandal will survive
And be an eyesore in my golden coat. 205
Some loathsome dash the herald will contrive 206
To cipher me how fondly I did dote; 207
That my posterity, shamed with the note,
    Shall curse my bones, and hold it for no sin
    To wish that I their father had not been.

'What win I if I gain the thing I seek?
A dream, a breath, a froth of fleeting joy.
Who buys a minute's mirth to wail a week?
Or sells eternity to get a toy? 214
For one sweet grape who will the vine destroy?
    Or what fond beggar, but to touch the crown,
    Would with the sceptre straight be stroken down?

121 *Intending* pretending; *sprite* spirit  122 *questionèd* discoursed  124 *live's* life's  126 *wake* keep watch  130 *weak-built hopes* i.e. small hope of true felicity  131 *traffic* barter  132 *meed proposed* i.e. reward in view  133 *supposed* i.e. taken into consideration  134 *fond* infatuated  135 *what* for what  136 *bond* i.e. possession  140 *bankrout* bankrupt  143 *And* but  144 *gage* stake  149 *expect* i.e. hope to be  151 *defect* i.e. the inadequacy  152 *neglect* disregard  157 *himself himself* i.e. his physical self his true self  160 *confounds* ruins  164 *comfortable* comforting, propitious  176 *falchion* curved sword  180 *advisedly* deliberately  188 *His . . . lust* i.e. his transient physical potency  196 *weed* garment  198 *grave* memorial tomb  201 *respect* veneration  205 *coat* coat of arms  206 *dash* bar, armorial abatement  207 *cipher* signal  214 *toy* trifle

'If Collatinus dream of my intent,
Will he not wake, and in a desp'rate rage
Post hither this vile purpose to prevent?
221 This siege that hath engirt his marriage,
This blur to youth, this sorrow to the sage,
   This dying virtue, this surviving shame,
224    Whose crime will bear an ever-during blame?

'O, what excuse can my invention make
When thou shalt charge me with so black a deed?
Will not my tongue be mute, my frail joints shake,
Mine eyes forgo their light, my false heart bleed?
The guilt being great, the fear doth still exceed;
   And extreme fear can neither fight nor fly,
   But coward-like with trembling terror die.

'Had Collatinus killed my son or sire,
Or lain in ambush to betray my life,
Or were he not my dear friend, this desire
Might have excuse to work upon his wife,
236 As in revenge or quittal of such strife;
   But as he is my kinsman, my dear friend,
   The shame and fault finds no excuse nor end.

'Shameful it is. Ay, if the fact be known.
Hateful it is. There is no hate in loving.
I'll beg her love. But she is not her own.
The worst is but denial and reproving.
243 My will is strong, past reason's weak removing.
244    Who fears a sentence or an old man's saw
245    Shall by a painted cloth be kept in awe.'

Thus graceless holds he disputation
'Tween frozen conscience and hot-burning will,
248 And with good thoughts makes dispensation,
249 Urging the worser sense for vantage still;
Which in a moment doth confound and kill
251    All pure effects, and doth so far proceed
   That what is vile shows like a virtuous deed.

Quoth he, 'She took me kindly by the hand
And gazed for tidings in my eager eyes,
Fearing some hard news from the warlike band
Where her belovèd Collatinus lies.
O, how her fear did make her color rise!
   First red as roses that on lawn we lay,
   Then white as lawn, the roses took away.

'And how her hand, in my hand being locked,
Forced it to tremble with her loyal fear!
Which struck her sad, and then it faster rocked
Until her husband's welfare she did hear;
Whereat she smilèd with so sweet a cheer
265    That, had Narcissus seen her as she stood,
   Self-love had never drowned him in the flood.

267 'Why hunt I then for color or excuses?
All orators are dumb when beauty pleadeth;
269 Poor wretches have remorse in poor abuses;
270 Love thrives not in the heart that shadows dreadeth.
271 Affection is my captain, and he leadeth;
   And when his gaudy banner is displayed,
273    The coward fights and will not be dismayed.

'Then childish fear avaunt, debating die!
Respect and reason wait on wrinkled age!
My heart shall never countermand mine eye.
Sad pause and deep regard beseems the sage;
My part is youth, and beats these from the stage.
   Desire my pilot is, beauty my prize;
   Then who fears sinking where such treasure lies?'

As corn o'ergrown by weeds, so heedful fear
Is almost choked by unresisted lust.
Away he steals with open list'ning ear,
Full of foul hope and full of fond mistrust;
Both which, as servitors to the unjust,
   So cross him with their opposite persuasion
   That now he vows a league, and now invasion.

Within his thought her heavenly image sits,
And in the selfsame seat sits Collatine.
That eye which looks on her confounds his wits;
That eye which him beholds, as more divine,
Unto a view so false will not incline;
   But with a pure appeal seeks to the heart,
   Which once corrupted takes the worser part;

And therein heartens up his servile powers,
Who, flatt'red by their leader's jocund show,
Stuff up his lust, as minutes fill up hours;
And as their captain, so their pride doth grow,
Paying more slavish tribute than they owe.
   By reprobate desire thus madly led,
   The Roman lord marcheth to Lucrece' bed.

The locks between her chamber and his will,
Each one by him enforced retires his ward;
But, as they open, they all rate his ill,
Which drives the creeping thief to some regard.
The threshold grates the door to have him heard;
   Night-wand'ring weasels shriek to see him there;
   They fright him, yet he still pursues his fear.

As each unwilling portal yields him way,
Through little vents and crannies of the place
The wind wars with his torch to make him stay,
And blows the smoke of it into his face,
Extinguishing his conduct in this case;
   But his hot heart, which fond desire doth scorch,
   Puffs forth another wind that fires the torch;

221 *engirt* encroached upon   224 *ever-during* ever-enduring   236 *quittal* requital   243 *removing* dissuasion   244 *sentence* moral maxim   245 *painted cloth* hanging painted with biblical or moral texts and illustrations   248 *makes dispensation* dispenses   249 *vantage* advantage   251 *effects* impulses   265 *Narcissus* in classical myth, the youth who fell in love with his own image reflected in water, and was transformed into the narcissus   267 *color* disguising appearance   269 *Poor . . . abuses* i.e. only the petty in their petty transgressions feel compunction   270 *shadows* i.e. the immaterial obstacles of conscience   271 *Affection* passion   273 *The coward* i.e. even the coward   275 *Respect* circumspection; *wait on* go with, attend   276 *countermand* run counter to   277 *Sad* serious   278 *stage* platform of action or disputation   281 *corn* grain   286 *cross* thwart   287 *league* i.e. treaty of non-aggression   293 *seeks to* seeks out, applies to   295 *servile powers* i.e. physical capacities   296 *Who* which   298 *as their captain* i.e. like their captain's (the heart's)   303 *his ward* (1) its locking bolt, (2) its posture of defense   304 *rate his ill* scold his wickedness   305 *regard* caution   307 *weasels* i.e. domestic rat-catchers (themselves furtive but startled by the furtive Tarquin)   313 *conduct* conductor, i.e. the torch

316 And being lighted, by the light he spies
Lucretia's glove, wherein her needle sticks.
He takes it from the rushes where it lies,
And griping it, the needle his finger pricks,
As who should say, 'This glove to wanton tricks
321 Is not inured. Return again in haste –
Thou seest our mistress' ornaments are chaste.'

323 But all these poor forbiddings could not stay him;
324 He in the worst sense consters their denial:
The doors, the wind, the glove, that did delay him,
326 He takes for accidental things of trial;
327 Or as those bars which stop the hourly dial,
328 Who with a ling'ring stay his course doth let
Till every minute pays the hour his debt.

'So, so,' quoth he, 'these lets attend the time,
Like little frosts that sometime threat the spring
To add a more rejoicing to the prime
333 And give the sneapèd birds more cause to sing.
334 Pain pays the income of each precious thing:
Huge rocks, high winds, strong pirates, shelves and sands,
The merchant fears ere rich at home he lands.'

Now is he come unto the chamber door
That shuts him from the heaven of his thought,
Which with a yielding latch, and with no more,
Hath barred him from the blessèd thing he sought.
341 So from himself impiety hath wrought
That for his prey to pray he doth begin,
As if the heavens should countenance his sin.

But in the midst of his unfruitful prayer,
Having solicited th' eternal power
346 That his foul thoughts might compass his fair fair,
And they would stand auspicious to the hour,
Even there he starts. Quoth he, 'I must deflow'r.
The powers to whom I pray abhor this fact;
How can they then assist me in the act?

'Then Love and Fortune be my gods, my guide:
My will is backed with resolution.
Thoughts are but dreams till their effects be tried;
The blackest sin is cleared with absolution;
Against love's fire fear's frost hath dissolution.
The eye of heaven is out, and misty night
Covers the shame that follows sweet delight.'

This said, his guilty hand plucked up the latch,
And with his knee the door he opens wide.
The dove sleeps fast that this night owl will catch. 360
Thus treason works ere traitors be espied.
Who sees the lurking serpent steps aside;
But she, sound sleeping, fearing no such thing,
Lies at the mercy of his mortal sting.

Into the chamber wickedly he stalks
And gazeth on her yet unstainèd bed.
The curtains being close, about he walks,
Rolling his greedy eyeballs in his head.
By their high treason is his heart misled,
Which gives the watchword to his hand full soon
To draw the cloud that hides the silver moon.

Look, as the fair and fiery-pointed sun,
Rushing from forth a cloud, bereaves our sight, 373
Even so, the curtain drawn, his eyes begun
To wink, being blinded with a greater light;
Whether it is that she reflects so bright
That dazzleth them, or else some shame supposèd; 377
But blind they are, and keep themselves enclosèd.

O, had they in that darksome prison died,
Then had they seen the period of their ill; 380
Then Collatine again, by Lucrece' side,
In his clear bed might have reposèd still. 382
But they must ope, this blessèd league to kill,
And holy-thoughted Lucrece to their sight
Must sell her joy, her life, her world's delight.

Her lily hand her rosy cheek lies under,
Coz'ning the pillow of a lawful kiss; 387
Who, therefore angry, seems to part in sunder,
Swelling on either side to want his bliss; 389
Between whose hills her head entombèd is;
Where like a virtuous monument she lies,
To be admired of lewd unhallowed eyes.

Without the bed her other fair hand was,
On the green coverlet; whose perfect white
Showed like an April daisy on the grass,
With pearly sweat resembling dew of night.
Her eyes, like marigolds, had sheathed their light,
And canopied in darkness sweetly lay
Till they might open to adorn the day.

Her hair like golden threads played with her breath –
O modest wantons, wanton modesty!
Showing life's triumph in the map of death, 402
And death's dim look in life's mortality. 403
Each in her sleep themselves so beautify
As if between them twain there were no strife,
But that life lived in death, and death in life.

Her breasts like ivory globes circled with blue,
A pair of maiden worlds unconquerèd,
Save of their lord no bearing yoke they knew,
And him by oath they truly honorèd. 410
These worlds in Tarquin new ambition bred,
Who like a foul usurper went about
From this fair throne to heave the owner out.

316 *lighted* i.e. relighted  321 *inured* brazened  323 *stay* restrain  324 *consters* construes  326 *accidental . . . trial* i.e. morally insignificant tests of resolution  327 *bars . . . dial* the sixty check-points on the face of a clock  328 *Who* which; *his* its; *let* stop  333 *sneapèd* frost-nipped  334 *income* gain  341 *wrought* i.e. wrought him  346 *compass his fair fair* possess his virtuous fair one  373 *bereaves* takes away  377 *supposèd* felt, apprehended  380 *period* end; *ill* evil  382 *clear* innocent  387 *Coz'ning* cheating  389 *want* lack  402 *map* image  403 *life's mortality* i.e. sleep  410 *by oath* i.e. in accordance with the marriage vow

What could he see but mightily he noted?
What did he note but strongly he desirèd?
What he beheld, on that he firmly doted,
417 And in his will his willful eye he tirèd.
 With more than admiration he admirèd
  Her azure veins, her alablaster skin,
  Her coral lips, her snow-white dimpled chin.

As the grim lion fawneth o'er his prey,
Sharp hunger by the conquest satisfied,
So o'er this sleeping soul doth Tarquin stay,
His rage of lust by gazing qualified;
Slacked, not suppressed; for, standing by her side,
426  His eye, which late this mutiny restrains,
  Unto a greater uproar tempts his veins;

428 And they, like straggling slaves for pillage fighting,
Obdurate vassals fell exploits effecting,
In bloody death and ravishment delighting,
Nor children's tears nor mothers' groans respecting,
432 Swell in their pride, the onset still expecting.
 Anon his beating heart, alarum striking,
  Gives the hot charge and bids them do their liking.

His drumming heart cheers up his burning eye,
His eye commends the leading to his hand;
His hand, as proud of such a dignity,
Smoking with pride, marched on to make his stand
On her bare breast, the heart of all her land;
440  Whose ranks of blue veins, as his hand did scale,
  Left their round turrets destitute and pale.

442 They, must'ring to the quiet cabinet
Where their dear governess and lady lies,
Do tell her she is dreadfully beset
And fright her with confusion of their cries.
She, much amazed, breaks ope her locked-up eyes,
 Who, peeping forth this tumult to behold,
448  Are by his flaming torch dimmed and controlled.

Imagine her as one in dead of night,
From forth dull sleep by dreadful fancy waking,
That thinks she hath beheld some ghastly sprite,
Whose grim aspect sets every joint a-shaking.
453 What terror 'tis! but she, in worser taking,
 From sleep disturbèd, heedfully doth view
  The sight which makes supposèd terror true.

Wrapped and confounded in a thousand fears,
Like to a new-killed bird she trembling lies.
She dares not look; yet, winking, there appears
459 Quick-shifting antics ugly in her eyes.
460 Such shadows are the weak brain's forgeries,
461  Who, angry that the eyes fly from their lights,
  In darkness daunts them with more dreadful sights.

His hand, that yet remains upon her breast
464 (Rude ram, to batter such an ivory wall!)
May feel her heart (poor citizen) distressed,
Wounding itself to death, rise up and fall,
467 Beating her bulk, that his hand shakes withal.
 This moves in him more rage and lesser pity,
  To make the breach and enter this sweet city.

First like a trumpet doth his tongue begin
To sound a parley to his heartless foe;  471
Who o'er the white sheet peers her whiter chin,
The reason of this rash alarm to know,
Which he by dumb demeanor seeks to show; 474
 But she with vehement prayers urgeth still
  Under what color he commits this ill. 476

Thus he replies: 'The color in thy face,
That even for anger makes the lily pale
And the red rose blush at her own disgrace,
Shall plead for me and tell my loving tale.
Under that color am I come to scale 48●
 Thy never-conquerèd fort. The fault is thine,
  For those thine eyes betray thee unto mine.

'Thus I forestall thee, if thou mean to chide:
Thy beauty hath ensnared thee to this night, 485
Where thou with patience must my will abide, 486
My will that marks thee for my earth's delight,
Which I to conquer sought with all my might;
 But as reproof and reason beat it dead,
  By thy bright beauty was it newly bred.

'I see what crosses my attempt will bring, 49●
I know what thorns the growing rose defends,
I think the honey guarded with a sting;
All this beforehand counsel comprehends,
But Will is deaf and hears no heedful friends:
 Only he hath an eye to gaze on Beauty,
  And dotes on what he looks, 'gainst law or duty.

'I have debated even in my soul
What wrong, what shame, what sorrow I shall breed;
But nothing can affection's course control 500
Or stop the headlong fury of his speed.
I know repentant tears ensue the deed, 502
 Reproach, disdain, and deadly enmity;
  Yet strive I to embrace mine infamy.'

This said, he shakes aloft his Roman blade,
Which, like a falcon tow'ring in the skies,
Coucheth the fowl below with his wings' shade, 507
Whose crooked beak threats if he mount he dies.
So under his insulting falchion lies
 Harmless Lucretia, marking what he tells
  With trembling fear, as fowl hear falcons' bells.

417 *will* lust 426 *late* i.e. a moment before; *mutiny* i.e. rebellion of the blood, lust 428 *straggling* i.e. not in military order 432 *pride* lust 440 *scale* successfully mount (continuing the military imagery) 442 *must'ring* gathering; *cabinet* the heart, where veins presumably would muster (?), or the brain, where consciousness resides (?) 448 *controlled* overpowered 453 *taking* fright 459 *antics* grotesques 460 *shadows* shapes 461 *lights* i.e. sight 464 *ram* battering-ram 467 *bulk* body 471 *heartless* timorous 474 *dumb demeanor* dumbshow 476 *color* pretext 481 *color* banner 485 *to this night* i.e. into this night's meeting 486 *will* sexual desire 491 *crosses* troubles 500 *affection's* passion's 502 *ensue* follow upon 507 *Coucheth* makes cower

'Lucrece,' quoth he, 'this night I must enjoy thee.
If thou deny, then force must work my way;
For in thy bed I purpose to destroy thee.
That done, some worthless slave of thine I'll slay,
To kill thine honor with thy live's decay;
    And in thy dead arms do I mean to place him,
    Swearing I slew him, seeing thee embrace him.

'So thy surviving husband shall remain
The scornful mark of every open eye;
Thy kinsmen hang their heads at this disdain,
Thy issue blurred with nameless bastardy;
And thou, the author of their obloquy,
    Shalt have thy trespass cited up in rhymes
    And sung by children in succeeding times.

'But if thou yield, I rest thy secret friend;
The fault unknown is as a thought unacted.
A little harm done to a great good end
For lawful policy remains enacted.
The poisonous simple sometime is compacted
    In a pure compound; being so applied,
    His venom in effect is purified.

'Then, for thy husband and thy children's sake,
Tender my suit. Bequeath not to their lot
The shame that from them no device can take,
The blemish that will never be forgot;
Worse than a slavish wipe or birth-hour's blot;
    For marks descried in men's nativity
    Are nature's faults, not their own infamy.'

Here with a cockatrice' dead-killing eye
He rouseth up himself and makes a pause;
While she, the picture of pure piety,
Like a white hind under the gripe's sharp claws,
Pleads, in a wilderness where are no laws,
    To the rough beast that knows no gentle right
    Nor aught obeys but his foul appetite.

But when a black-faced cloud the world doth threat,
In his dim mist th' aspiring mountains hiding,
From earth's dark womb some gentle gust doth get,
Which blows these pitchy vapors from their biding,
Hind'ring their present fall by this dividing,
    So his unhallowed haste her words delays,
    And moody Pluto winks while Orpheus plays.

Yet, foul night-waking cat, he doth but dally,
While in his hold-fast foot the weak mouse panteth.
Her sad behavior feeds his vulture folly,
A swallowing gulf that even in plenty wanteth.
His ear her prayers admits, but his heart granteth
    No penetrable entrance to her plaining.
    Tears harden lust, though marble wear with raining.

Her pity-pleading eyes are sadly fixèd
In the remorseless wrinkles of his face.
Her modest eloquence with sighs is mixèd,
Which to her oratory adds more grace.
She puts the period often from his place,
    And midst the sentence so her accent breaks
    That twice she doth begin ere once she speaks.

She conjures him by high almighty Jove,
By knighthood, gentry, and sweet friendship's oath,
By her untimely tears, her husband's love,
By holy human law and common troth,
By heaven and earth, and all the power of both,
    That to his borrowed bed he make retire
    And stoop to honor, not to foul desire.

Quoth she, 'Reward not hospitality
With such black payment as thou hast pretended;
Mud not the fountain that gave drink to thee;
Mar not the thing that cannot be amended.
End thy ill aim before thy shoot be ended.
    He is no woodman that doth bend his bow
    To strike a poor unseasonable doe.

'My husband is thy friend: for his sake spare me;
Thyself art mighty: for thine own sake leave me;
Myself a weakling: do not then ensnare me;
Thou look'st not like deceit: do not deceive me.
My sighs like whirlwinds labor hence to heave thee.
    If ever man were moved with woman's moans,
    Be movèd with my tears, my sighs, my groans;

'All which together, like a troubled ocean,
Beat at thy rocky and wrack-threat'ning heart,
To soften it with their continual motion;
For stones dissolved to water do convert.
O, if no harder than a stone thou art,
    Melt at my tears and be compassionate!
    Soft pity enters at an iron gate.

'In Tarquin's likeness I did entertain thee.
Hast thou put on his shape to do him shame?
To all the host of heaven I complain me.
Thou wrong'st his honor, wound'st his princely name.
Thou art not what thou seem'st; and if the same,
    Thou seem'st not what thou art, a god, a king;
    For kings like gods should govern everything.

'How will thy shame be seeded in thine age
When thus thy vices bud before thy spring?
If in thy hope thou dar'st do such outrage,
What dar'st thou not when once thou art a king?
O, be rememb'red, no outrageous thing
    From vassal actors can be wiped away;
    Then kings' misdeeds cannot be hid in clay.

**516** *live's* life's   **521** *disdain* stain, disgrace   **530** *simple* herb; *compacted* compounded   **534** *Tender* regard   **535** *device* armorial figure   **537** *wipe* brand-mark; *birth-hour's blot* birthmark   **540** *cockatrice*' basilisk's (legendary serpent which killed with a look)   **543** *gripe's* griffin's (?)   **549** *doth get* is begot   **551** *dividing* dispersal   **553** *Pluto* ruler of the underworld, who was charmed by the lyre of Orpheus, husband of Eurydice; *winks* sleeps   **556** *sad* grave; *vulture* ravenous   **557** *gulf* belly   **559** *plaining* complaining, lament   **562** *remorseless* pitiless   **564** *oratory* pleading   **565** *his place* i.e. its proper place (in broken utterance)   **574** *stoop* bow, defer   **576** *pretended* proposed   **579** *shoot* act of shooting (perhaps with pun on homonymic 'suit')   **580** *woodman* huntsman   **586** *heave* move   **592** *convert* change   **603** *be seeded* i.e. come to fruition   **608** *vassal actors* i.e. subjects who do it   **609** *in clay* i.e. even in death

'This deed will make thee only loved for fear;
But happy monarchs still are feared for love.
With foul offenders thou perforce must bear
When they in thee the like offenses prove.
614 If but for fear of this, thy will remove;
    For princes are the glass, the school, the book,
    Where subjects' eyes do learn, do read, do look.

'And wilt thou be the school where Lust shall learn?
Must he in thee read lectures of such shame?
Wilt thou be glass wherein it shall discern
Authority for sin, warrant for blame,
To privilege dishonor in thy name?
622     Thou back'st reproach against long-living laud
    And mak'st fair reputation but a bawd.

'Hast thou command? By him that gave it thee,
From a pure heart command thy rebel will!
Draw not thy sword to guard iniquity,
For it was lent thee all that brood to kill.
Thy princely office how canst thou fulfill
    When, patterned by thy fault, foul Sin may say,
    He learned to sin, and thou didst teach the way?

'Think but how vile a spectacle it were
To view thy present trespass in another.
Men's faults do seldom to themselves appear;
Their own transgressions partially they smother.
This guilt would seem death-worthy in thy brother.
    O, how are they wrapped in with infamies
637     That from their own misdeeds askaunce their eyes!

'To thee, to thee, my heaved-up hands appeal,
639 Not to seducing lust, thy rash relier.
640 I sue for exiled majesty's repeal;
    Let him return, and flatt'ring thoughts retire.
642 His true respect will prison false desire
    And wipe the dim mist from thy doting eyne,
    That thou shalt see thy state, and pity mine.'

'Have done,' quoth he. 'My uncontrollèd tide
646 Turns not, but swells the higher by this let.
Small lights are soon blown out; huge fires abide
And with the wind in greater fury fret.
The petty streams that pay a daily debt
650     To their salt sovereign with their fresh falls' haste,
    Add to his flow, but alter not his taste.'

'Thou art,' quoth she, 'a sea, a sovereign king;
And, lo, there falls into thy boundless flood
Black lust, dishonor, shame, misgoverning,
Who seek to stain the ocean of thy blood.
If all these petty ills shall change thy good,
657     Thy sea within a puddle's womb is hearsèd,
    And not the puddle in thy sea dispersèd.

'So shall these slaves be king, and thou their slave;
Thou nobly base, they basely dignified;
Thou their fair life, and they thy fouler grave;
Thou loathèd in their shame, they in thy pride.
The lesser thing should not the greater hide.
    The cedar stoops not to the base shrub's foot,
    But low shrubs wither at the cedar's root.

'So let thy thoughts, low vassals to thy state.'
'No more,' quoth he. 'By heaven, I will not hear thee!
Yield to my love; if not, enforcèd hate,
Instead of love's coy touch, shall rudely tear thee.
That done, despitefully I mean to bear thee    670
    Unto the base bed of some rascal groom,
    To be thy partner in this shameful doom.'

This said, he sets his foot upon the light,
For light and lust are deadly enemies;
Shame folded up in blind concealing night,
When most unseen, then most doth tyrannize.
The wolf hath seized his prey; the poor lamb cries,
    Till with her own white fleece her voice controlled    678
    Entombs her outcry in her lips' sweet fold;

For with the nightly linen that she wears
He pens her piteous clamors in her head,
Cooling his hot face in the chastest tears
That ever modest eyes with sorrow shed.
O, that prone lust should stain so pure a bed,
    The spots whereof, could weeping purify,
    Her tears should drop on them perpetually!

But she hath lost a dearer thing than life,
And he hath won what he would lose again.
This forcèd league doth force a further strife;
This momentary joy breeds months of pain;
This hot desire converts to cold disdain;
    Pure Chastity is rifled of her store,
    And Lust, the thief, far poorer than before.

Look, as the full-fed hound or gorgèd hawk,
Unapt for tender smell or speedy flight,    695
Make slow pursuit, or altogether balk    696
The prey wherein by nature they delight,
So surfeit-taking Tarquin fares this night:
    His taste delicious, in digestion souring,
    Devours his will, that lived by foul devouring.

O, deeper sin than bottomless conceit    701
Can comprehend in still imagination!
Drunken Desire must vomit his receipt    703
Ere he can see his own abomination.
While Lust is in his pride, no exclamation    705
    Can curb his heat or rein his rash desire
    Till, like a jade, Self-will himself doth tire.

And then with lank and lean discolored cheek,
With heavy eye, knit brow, and strengthless pace,
Feeble Desire, all recreant, poor, and meek,    710
Like to a bankrout beggar wails his case.    711
The flesh being proud, Desire doth fight with Grace,
    For there it revels; and when that decays,    713
    The guilty rebel for remission prays.

---

614 *thy will remove* dissuade your lust  622 *back'st* support; *laud* praise  637 *askaunce* avert  639 *relier* thing relied upon (?)  640 *repeal* return from exile  642 *respect* sense of decorum; *prison* imprison  646 *let* hindrance  650 *salt sovereign* i.e. the ocean; *falls'* flows'  657 *hearsèd* entombed  678 *controlled* overpowered  695 *tender smell* weak scent  696 *balk* turn from  701 *bottomless conceit* unlimited fancy  703 *his receipt* what he has received  705 *exclamation* protest  710 *recreant* beaten, cowed  711 *bankrout* bankrupt  713 *that* i.e. pride, lust

So fares it with this fault-full lord of Rome,
Who this accomplishment so hotly chasèd;
For now against himself he sounds this doom,
That through the length of times he stands disgracèd.
Besides, his soul's fair temple is defacèd;
    To whose weak ruins muster troops of cares,
721    To ask the spotted princess how she fares.

22 She says her subjects with foul insurrection
Have battered down her consecrated wall,
24 And by their mortal fault brought in subjection
Her immortality and made her thrall
To living death and pain perpetual;
27    Which in her prescience she controllèd still,
    But her foresight could not forestall their will.

Ev'n in this thought through the dark night he stealeth,
A captive victor that hath lost in gain;
Bearing away the wound that nothing healeth,
The scar that will despite of cure remain;
Leaving his spoil perplexed in greater pain.
    She bears the load of lust he left behind,
    And he the burden of a guilty mind.

He like a thievish dog creeps sadly thence;
She like a wearied lamb lies panting there.
He scowls, and hates himself for his offense;
She desperate with her nails her flesh doth tear.
He faintly flies, sweating with guilty fear;
    She stays, exclaiming on the direful night;
    He runs, and chides his vanished loathed delight.

743 He thence departs a heavy convertite;
744 She there remains a hopeless castaway.
He in his speed looks for the morning light;
She prays she never may behold the day,
747 'For day,' quoth she, 'night's scapes doth open lay,
    And my true eyes have never practiced how
    To cloak offenses with a cunning brow.

'They think not but that every eye can see
The same disgrace which they themselves behold;
And therefore would they still in darkness be,
To have their unseen sin remain untold;
For they their guilt with weeping will unfold;
755    And grave, like water that doth eat in steel,
    Upon my cheeks what helpless shame I feel.'

Here she exclaims against repose and rest,
And bids her eyes hereafter still be blind.
She wakes her heart by beating on her breast,
And bids it leap from thence, where it may find
761 Some purer chest to close so pure a mind.
    Frantic with grief thus breathes she forth her spite
    Against the unseen secrecy of night:

'O comfort-killing Night, image of hell,
Dim register and notary of shame,    765
Black stage for tragedies and murders fell,
Vast sin-concealing chaos, nurse of blame,
Blind muffled bawd, dark harbor for defame!
    Grim cave of death, whisp'ring conspirator
    With close-tongued treason and the ravisher!    770

'O hateful, vaporous, and foggy Night,
Since thou art guilty of my cureless crime,
Muster thy mists to meet the eastern light,
Make war against proportioned course of time;    774
Or if thou wilt permit the sun to climb
    His wonted height, yet ere he go to bed,
    Knit poisonous clouds about his golden head.

'With rotten damps ravish the morning air;
Let their exhaled unwholesome breaths make sick
The life of purity, the supreme fair,    780
Ere he arrive his weary noontide prick;    781
And let thy musty vapors march so thick
    That in their smoky ranks his smoth'red light
    May set at noon and make perpetual night.

'Were Tarquin Night, as he is but Night's child,
The silver-shining queen he would distain;    786
Her twinkling handmaids too, by him defiled,
Through Night's black bosom should not peep again.
So should I have co-partners in my pain;
    And fellowship in woe doth woe assuage,
    As palmers' chat makes short their pilgrimage;    791

'Where now I have no one to blush with me,
To cross their arms and hang their heads with mine,
To mask their brows and hide their infamy;
But I alone, alone must sit and pine,
Seasoning the earth with show'rs of silver brine,
    Mingling my talk with tears, my grief with groans,
    Poor wasting monuments of lasting moans.

'O Night, thou furnace of foul reeking smoke,
Let not the jealous Day behold that face    800
Which underneath thy black all-hiding cloak
Immodestly lies martyred with disgrace!
Keep still possession of thy gloomy place,
    That all the faults which in thy reign are made
    May likewise be sepulchered in thy shade!

'Make me not object to the telltale Day.    806
The light will show, charactered in my brow,
The story of sweet chastity's decay,
The impious breach of holy wedlock vow.
Yea, the illiterate, that know not how
    To cipher what is writ in learnèd books,
    Will quote my loathsome trespass in my looks.    812

'The nurse, to still her child, will tell my story
And fright her crying babe with Tarquin's name.
The orator, to deck his oratory,
Will couple my reproach to Tarquin's shame.
Feast-finding minstrels, tuning my defame,    817
    Will tie the hearers to attend each line,
    How Tarquin wrongèd me, I Collatine.

820 'Let my good name, that senseless reputation,
  For Collatine's dear love be kept unspotted.
  If that be made a theme for disputation,
  The branches of another root are rotted,
  And undeserved reproach to him allotted
    That is as clear from this attaint of mine
    As I ere this was pure to Collatine.

  'O unseen shame, invisible disgrace!
828 O unfelt sore, crest-wounding private scar!
  Reproach is stamped in Collatinus' face,
830 And Tarquin's eye may read the mot afar,
  How he in peace is wounded, not in war.
    Alas, how many bear such shameful blows
    Which not themselves, but he that gives them knows!

  'If, Collatine, thine honor lay in me,
  From me by strong assault it is bereft;
  My honey lost, and I, a drone-like bee,
  Have no perfection of my summer left,
  But robbed and ransacked by injurious theft.
    In thy weak hive a wand'ring wasp hath crept
    And sucked the honey which thy chaste bee kept.

  'Yet am I guilty of thy honor's wrack;
  Yet for thy honor did I entertain him.
843 Coming from thee, I could not put him back,
  For it had been dishonor to disdain him.
  Besides, of weariness he did complain him
    And talked of virtue – O unlooked-for evil
    When virtue is profaned in such a devil!

  'Why should the worm intrude the maiden bud?
  Or hateful cuckoos hatch in sparrow's nests?
  Or toads infect fair founts with venom mud?
  Or tyrant folly lurk in gentle breasts?
852 Or kings be breakers of their own behests?
    But no perfection is so absolute
    That some impurity doth not pollute.

  'The agèd man that coffers up his gold
  Is plagued with cramps and gouts and painful fits,
  And scarce hath eyes his treasure to behold,
  But like still-pining Tantalus he sits
859 And useless barns the harvest of his wits,
    Having no other pleasure of his gain
    But torment that it cannot cure his pain.

  'So then he hath it when he cannot use it,
  And leaves it to be mast'red by his young,
  Who in their pride do presently abuse it.
  Their father was too weak, and they too strong,
  To hold their cursèd-blessèd fortune long.
    The sweets we wish for turn to loathèd sours
    Even in the moment that we call them ours.

  'Unruly blasts wait on the tender spring;
  Unwholesome weeds take root with precious flow'rs;
  The adder hisses where the sweet birds sing;
  What Virtue breeds Iniquity devours.
  We have no good that we can say is ours,
874   But ill-annexèd Opportunity
875   Or kills his life or else his quality.

  'O Opportunity, thy guilt is great!
  'Tis thou that execut'st the traitor's treason;
  Thou sets the wolf where he the lamb may get;
  Whoever plots the sin, thou point'st the season.
  'Tis thou that spurn'st at right, at law, at reason;
    And in thy shady cell, where none may spy him,
    Sits Sin, to seize the souls that wander by him.

  'Thou mak'st the vestal violate her oath;
  Thou blow'st the fire when temperance is thawed;
  Thou smother'st honesty, thou murd'rest troth.
  Thou foul abettor, thou notorious bawd,
  Thou plantest scandal and displacest laud.          88
    Thou ravisher, thou traitor, thou false thief,
    Thy honey turns to gall, thy joy to grief.

  'Thy secret pleasure turns to open shame,
  Thy private feasting to a public fast,
  Thy smoothing titles to a ragged name,              89
  Thy sug'red tongue to bitter wormwood taste:
  Thy violent vanities can never last.
    How comes it then, vile Opportunity,
    Being so bad, such numbers seek for thee?

  'When wilt thou be the humble suppliant's friend
  And bring him where his suit may be obtainèd?
  When wilt thou sort an hour great strifes to end?   89
  Or free that soul which wretchedness hath chainèd?
  Give physic to the sick, ease to the painèd?
    The poor, lame, blind, halt, creep, cry out for thee;
    But they ne'er meet with Opportunity.

  'The patient dies while the physician sleeps;
  The orphan pines while the oppressor feeds;
  Justice is feasting while the widow weeps;
  Advice is sporting while infection breeds.          9c
  Thou grant'st no time for charitable deeds:
    Wrath, envy, treason, rape, and murder's rages,
    Thy heinous hours wait on them as their pages.

  'When Truth and-Virtue have to do with thee,
  A thousand crosses keep them from thy aid.          91
  They buy thy help; but Sin ne'er gives a fee,
  He gratis comes; and thou art well apaid
  As well to hear as grant what he hath said.
    My Collatine would else have come to me
    When Tarquin did, but he was stayed by thee.

820 *senseless* impalpable, spiritual (?)   828 *crest-wounding* i.e. that which
blots the escutcheon   830 *mot* motto   843 *put him back* repel him   852
*behests* commands, laws   859 *useless . . . wits* i.e. keeps uselessly in storage
the product of his acumen   874 *ill-annexèd* evilly coupled   875 *Or* either;
*his* its (i.e. good's)   887 *displacest laud* displant praise   892 *smoothing*
flattering; *ragged* worn away, disgraced   899 *sort* appoint   907 *Advice is
sporting* i.e. medical advice (or adviser) is engaged in amusement   912
*crosses* hindrances

'Guilty thou art of murder and of theft,
Guilty of perjury and subornation,
20 Guilty of treason, forgery, and shift,
Guilty of incest, that abomination –
An accessary by thine inclination
    To all sins past and all that are to come,
    From the creation to the general doom.

25 'Misshapen Time, copesmate of ugly Night,
26 Swift subtle post, carrier of grisly care,
Eater of youth, false slave to false delight,
28 Base watch of woes, sin's packhorse, virtue's snare !
Thou nursest all, and murd'rest all that are.
    O, hear me then, injurious shifting Time ;
    Be guilty of my death, since of my crime.

'Why hath thy servant Opportunity
Betrayed the hours thou gav'st me to repose ?
Cancelled my fortunes, and enchainèd me
To endless date of never-ending woes ?
36 Time's office is to fine the hate of foes,
    To eat up errors by opinion bred,
38     Not spend the dowry of a lawful bed.

'Time's glory is to calm contending kings,
To unmask falsehood and bring truth to light,
To stamp the seal of time in agèd things,
42 To wake the morn and sentinel the night,
To wrong the wronger till he render right,
44     To ruinate proud buildings with thy hours,
    And smear with dust their glitt'ring golden tow'rs ;

'To fill with wormholes stately monuments,
To feed oblivion with decay of things,
To blot old books and alter their contents,
49 To pluck the quills from ancient ravens' wings,
50 To dry the old oak's sap and cherish springs,
    To spoil antiquities of hammered steel
    And turn the giddy round of Fortune's wheel ;

'To show the beldame daughters of her daughter,
To make the child a man, the man a child,
To slay the tiger that doth live by slaughter,
To tame the unicorn and lion wild,
57 To mock the subtle in themselves beguiled,
    To cheer the ploughman with increaseful crops
59     And waste huge stones with little water-drops.

'Why work'st thou mischief in thy pilgrimage,
Unless thou couldst return to make amends ?
One poor retiring minute in an age       962
Would purchase thee a thousand thousand friends,
Lending him wit that to bad debtors lends.
    O this dread night, wouldst thou one hour come back,
    I could prevent this storm and shun thy wrack !

'Thou ceaseless lackey to Eternity,       967
With some mischance cross Tarquin in his flight.
Devise extremes beyond extremity       969
To make him curse this cursèd crimeful night.
Let ghastly shadows his lewd eyes affright,
    And the dire thought of his committed evil
    Shape every bush a hideous shapeless devil.

'Disturb his hours of rest with restless trances ;   974
Afflict him in his bed with bedrid groans ;
Let there bechance him pitiful mischances
To make him moan, but pity not his moans.
Stone him with hard'ned hearts harder than stones,
    And let mild women to him lose their mildness,
    Wilder to him than tigers in their wildness.

'Let him have time to tear his curlèd hair,
Let him have time against himself to rave,
Let him have time of Time's help to despair,
Let him have time to live a loathèd slave,
Let him have time a beggar's orts to crave,    985
    And time to see one that by alms doth live
    Disdain to him disdainèd scraps to give.

'Let him have time to see his friends his foes
And merry fools to mock at him resort ;
Let him have time to mark how slow time goes
In time of sorrow, and how swift and short
His time of folly and his time of sport ;
    And ever let his unrecalling crime    993
    Have time to wail th' abusing of his time.

'O Time, thou tutor both to good and bad,
Teach me to curse him that thou taught'st this ill.
At his own shadow let the thief run mad,
Himself himself seek every hour to kill.
Such wretched hands such wretched blood should spill,
    For who so base would such an office have
    As sland'rous deathsman to so base a slave ?    1001

'The baser is he, coming from a king,
To shame his hope with deeds degenerate.
The mightier man, the mightier is the thing
That makes him honored or begets him hate ;
For greatest scandal waits on greatest state.
    The moon being clouded presently is missed,
    But little stars may hide them when they list.

'The crow may bathe his coal-black wings in mire
And unperceived fly with the filth away ;
But if the like the snow-white swan desire,
The stain upon his silver down will stay.
Poor grooms are sightless night, kings glorious day ;   1013
    Gnats are unnoted wheresoe'er they fly,
    But eagles gazed upon with every eye.

920 *shift* fraud 925 *copesmate* boon companion 926 *subtle post* sly
messenger 928 *watch* crier 936 *fine* end 938 *spend* waste, dissipate
942 *sentinel* keep watch over, tell the hours of 944 *ruinate* i.e. reduce to
ruins (and thus teach humility) 949 *pluck . . . wings* i.e. end the life even
of the long-lived raven 950 *springs* saplings, new growth 957 *subtle*
crafty 959 *waste* wear away 962 *retiring minute* moment of respite
(allowing opportunity for a different choice) 967 *ceaseless lackey* ever-
present attendant 969 *extremes beyond extremity* i.e. inconceivably extreme occasions 974 *trances* transports, fits 985 *orts* scraps 993 *un-
recalling* irrevocable 1001 *sland'rous* disgraced 1013 *sightless* unseen

'Out, idle words, servants to shallow fools,
1017 Unprofitable sounds, weak arbitrators!
1018 Busy yourselves in skill-contending schools;
Debate where leisure serves with full debaters;
To trembling clients be you mediators:
1021    For me, I force not argument a straw,
Since that my case is past the help of law.

'In vain I rail at Opportunity,
At Time, at Tarquin, and uncheerful Night;
In vain I cavil with mine infamy;
1026 In vain I spurn at my confirmed despite:
This helpless smoke of words doth me no right.
   The remedy indeed to do me good
   Is to let forth my foul defilèd blood.

'Poor hand, why quiver'st thou at this decree?
Honor thyself to rid me of this shame;
For if I die, my honor lives in thee;
But if I live, thou liv'st in my defame.
Since thou couldst not defend thy loyal dame
   And wast afeard to scratch her wicked foe,
   Kill both thyself and her for yielding so.'

This said, from her betumbled couch she starteth
To find some desp'rate instrument of death;
1039 But this no slaughterhouse no tool imparteth
To make more vent for passage of her breath;
Which, thronging through her lips, so vanisheth
   As smoke from Aetna that in air consumes
   Or that which from dischargèd cannon fumes.

'In vain,' quoth she, 'I live, and seek in vain
Some happy mean to end a hapless life.
1046 I feared by Tarquin's falchion to be slain,
Yet for the selfsame purpose seek a knife;
But when I feared I was a loyal wife.
   So am I now. – O no, that cannot be:
1050   Of that true type hath Tarquin rifled me.

'O, that is gone for which I sought to live,
And therefore now I need not fear to die.
To clear this spot by death, at least I give
1054 A badge of fame to slander's livery,
A dying life to living infamy.
   Poor helpless help, the treasure stol'n away,
   To burn the guiltless casket where it lay!

'Well, well, dear Collatine, thou shalt not know
The stainèd taste of violated troth.
I will not wrong thy true affection so,
To flatter thee with an infringèd oath.
1062 This bastard graff shall never come to growth:
   He shall not boast who did thy stock pollute
   That thou art doting father of his fruit.

'Nor shall he smile at thee in secret thought,
Nor laugh with his companions at thy state;
1067 But thou shalt know thy int'rest was not bought
Basely with gold, but stol'n from forth thy gate.
For me, I am the mistress of my fate,
1070   And with my trespass never will dispense
1071   Till life to death acquit my forced offense.

'I will not poison thee with my attaint
Nor fold my fault in cleanly coined excuses;
My sable ground of sin I will not paint
To hide the truth of this false night's abuses.
My tongue shall utter all; mine eyes, like sluices,
   As from a mountain spring that feeds a dale,
   Shall gush pure streams to purge my impure tale.'

By this, lamenting Philomele had ended
The well-tuned warble of her nightly sorrow,
And solemn night with slow sad gait descended
To ugly hell; when, lo, the blushing morrow
Lends light to all fair eyes that light will borrow;
   But cloudy Lucrece shames herself to see
   And therefore still in night would cloist'red be.

Revealing day through every cranny spies
And seems to point her out where she sits weeping;
To whom she sobbing speaks: 'O eye of eyes
Why pry'st thou through my window? Leave thy peeping.
Mock with thy tickling beams eyes that are sleeping.
   Brand not my forehead with thy piercing light
   For day hath naught to do what's done by night.'

Thus cavils she with everything she sees.
True grief is fond and testy as a child,
Who wayward once, his mood with naught agrees.
Old woes, not infant sorrows, bear them mild:
Continuance tames the one; the other wild,
   Like an unpracticed swimmer plunging still,
   With too much labor drowns for want of skill.

So she, deep drenchèd in a sea of care,
Holds disputation with each thing she views
And to herself all sorrow doth compare;
No object but her passion's strength renews;
And as one shifts, another straight ensues.
   Sometime her grief is dumb and hath no words;
   Sometime 'tis mad and too much talk affords.

The little birds that tune their morning's joy
Make her moans mad with their sweet melody:
For mirth doth search the bottom of annoy;
Sad souls are slain in merry company;
Grief best is pleased with grief's society;
   True sorrow then is feelingly sufficed
   When with like semblance it is sympathized.

1017 *arbitrators* i.e. compromisers  1018 *skill-contending schools* i.e. schoolmen's contests of skill · 1021 *force . . . straw* i.e. place not the value of a straw upon argument  1026 *despite* wrong  1039 *imparteth* provides  1046 *falchion* curved sword  1050 *type* stamp  1054 *livery* garment, uniform (with *badge* of household worn on sleeve)  1062 *graff* graft  1067 *int'rest* claim, right  1070 *dispense* i.e. be reconciled  1071 *to death acquit* i.e. cancel by death  1073 *cleanly coined* brightly counterfeited  1094 *fond* foolish; *testy* fretful  1095 *wayward once* i.e. once out of temper  1096 *them* themselves  1104 *shifts* yields place; *ensues* follows  1107 *tune* sing  1109 *search* plumb; *annoy* sorrow  1112 *sufficed* satisfied  1113 *sympathized* matched

1114 'Tis double death to drown in ken of shore;
He ten times pines that pines beholding food;
To see the salve doth make the wound ache more;
Great grief grieves most at that would do it good;
Deep woes roll forward like a gentle flood,
 Who, being stopped, the bounding banks o'erflows;
1120 Grief dallied with nor law nor limit knows.

'You mocking birds,' quoth she, 'your tunes entomb
Within your hollow-swelling featherèd breasts,
And in my hearing be you mute and dumb;
1124 My restless discord loves no stops nor rests:
A woeful hostess brooks not merry guests.
1126 Relish your nimble notes to pleasing ears;
1127 Distress likes dumps when time is kept with tears.

1128 'Come, Philomele, that sing'st of ravishment,
Make thy sad grove in my dishevelled hair.
As the dank earth weeps at thy languishment,
So I at each sad strain will strain a tear
1132 And with deep groans the diapason bear;
 For burden-wise I'll hum on Tarquin still,
1134 While thou on Tereus descants better skill;

1135 'And whiles against a thorn thou bear'st thy part
To keep thy sharp woes waking, wretched I,
To imitate thee well, against my heart
Will fix a sharp knife to affright mine eye;
1139 Who, if it wink, shall thereon fall and die.
 These means, as frets upon an instrument,
 Shall tune our heartstrings to true languishment.

'And for, poor bird, thou sing'st not in the day,
As shaming any eye should thee behold,
1144 Some dark deep desert, seated from the way,
That knows not parching heat nor freezing cold,
Will we find out; and there we will unfold
1147 To creatures stern sad tunes, to change their kinds.
 Since men prove beasts, let beasts bear gentle minds.'

1149 As the poor frighted deer that stands at gaze,
Wildly determining which way to fly,
Or one encompassed with a winding maze
That cannot tread the way out readily,
So with herself is she in mutiny,
 To live or die which of the twain were better
1155 When life is shamed and death reproach's debtor.

'To kill myself,' quoth she, 'alack, what were it
But with my body my poor soul's pollution?
They that lose half with greater patience bear it
Than they whose whole is swallowed in confusion. 1159
That mother tries a merciless conclusion 1160
 Who, having two sweet babes, when death takes one,
 Will slay the other and be nurse to none.

'My body or my soul, which was the dearer
When the one, pure, the other made divine?
Whose love of either to myself was nearer
When both were kept for heaven and Collatine?
Ay me! the bark pilled from the lofty pine, 1167
 His leaves will wither and his sap decay:
 So must my soul, her bark being pilled away.

'Her house is sacked, her quiet interrupted,
Her mansion battered by the enemy;
Her sacred temple spotted, spoiled, corrupted,
Grossly engirt with daring infamy. 1173
Then let it not be called impiety
 If in this blemished fort I make some hole 1175
 Through which I may convey this troubled soul.

'Yet die I will not till my Collatine
Have heard the cause of my untimely death;
That he may vow, in that sad hour of mine,
Revenge on him that made me stop my breath.
My stainèd blood to Tarquin I'll bequeath,
 Which, by him tainted, shall for him be spent
 And as his due writ in my testament.

'My honor I'll bequeath unto the knife
That wounds my body so dishonorèd.
'Tis honor to deprive dishonored life:
The one will live, the other being dead.
So of shame's ashes shall my fame be bred,
 For in my death I murder shameful scorn;
 My shame so dead, mine honor is new born. *1190*

'Dear lord of that dear jewel I have lost,
What legacy shall I bequeath to thee?
My resolution, love, shall be thy boast,
By whose example thou revenged mayst be.
How Tarquin must be used, read it in me:
 Myself thy friend will kill myself thy foe,
 And for my sake serve thou false Tarquin so.

'This brief abridgment of my will I make:
My soul and body to the skies and ground;
My resolution, husband, do thou take;
Mine honor be the knife's that makes my wound;
My shame be his that did my fame confound; 1202
 And all my fame that lives disbursèd be
 To those that live and think no shame of me.

'Thou, Collatine, shalt oversee this will. 1205
(How was I overseen that thou shalt see it!) 1206
My blood shall wash the slander of mine ill; 1207
My live's foul deed, my life's fair end shall free it.
Faint not, faint heart, but stoutly say, "So be it."
 Yield to my hand; my hand shall conquer thee:
 Thou dead, both die, and both shall victors be.'

1114 *ken* sight 1120 *dallied with* teased 1124 *stops, rests* (1) musical
pauses, (2) cessation 1126 *Relish* warble; *pleasing* i.e. capable of being
pleased 1127 *dumps* mournful airs 1128 *Philomele* (in classical myth,
ravished by Tereus and transformed into the nightingale) 1132 *diapason*
bass accompaniment 1134 *descants better skill* i.e. sings more skillfully
(?), sings the intricate melody (?) 1135 *bear'st* sing'st 1139 *Who* which
(i.e. her heart); *it wink* i.e. her eye close 1144 *seated from* situated out of
1147 *kinds* species 1149 *at gaze* transfixed (hunting term) 1155 *death . . .
debtor* i.e. suicide incurs reproach 1159 *confusion* destruction 1160 *conclusion* experiment 1167 *pilled* peeled 1173 *engirt* besieged; *daring* i.e.
brazen 1175 *fort* i.e. body 1202 *confound* destroy 1205 *oversee* execute, deal with 1206 *overseen* i.e. dealt with 1207 *wash* wash away;
*ill* sin

This plot of death when sadly she had laid
And wiped the brinish pearl from her bright eyes,
1214 With untuned tongue she hoarsely calls her maid,
Whose swift obedience to her mistress hies;
For swift-winged duty with thought's feathers flies.
    Poor Lucrece' cheeks unto her maid seem so
    As winter meads when sun doth melt their snow.

1219 Her mistress she doth give demure good-morrow
With soft-slow tongue, true mark of modesty,
1221 And sorts a sad look to her lady's sorrow,
1222 For why her face wore sorrow's livery;
But durst not ask of her audaciously
    Why her two suns were cloud-eclipsèd so,
    Nor why her fair cheeks overwashed with woe.

But as the earth doth weep, the sun being set,
Each flower moist'nèd like a melting eye,
Even so the maid with swelling drops gan wet
1229 Her circled eyne, enforced by sympathy
Of those fair suns set in her mistress' sky,
    Who in a salt-waved ocean quench their light,
    Which makes the maid weep like the dewy night.

A pretty while these pretty creatures stand,
1234 Like ivory conduits coral cisterns filling.
1235 One justly weeps, the other takes in hand
No cause, but company, of her drops spilling.
Their gentle sex to weep are often willing,
1238     Grieving themselves to guess at others' smarts,
    And then they drown their eyes or break their hearts.

1240 For men have marble, women waxen minds,
1241 And therefore are they formed as marble will.
The weak oppressed, th' impression of strange kinds
Is formed in them by force, by fraud, or skill.
Then call them not the authors of their ill,
    No more than wax shall be accounted evil
    Wherein is stamped the semblance of a devil.

1247 Their smoothness, like a goodly champain plain,
1248 Lays open all the little worms that creep;
In men, as in a rough-grown grove, remain
1250 Cave-keeping evils that obscurely sleep.
1251 Through crystal walls each little mote will peep.
    Though men can cover crimes with bold stern looks,
    Poor women's faces are their own faults' books.

No man inveigh against the witherèd flow'r,
But chide rough winter that the flow'r hath killed.
Not that devoured, but that which doth devour,
1257 Is worthy blame. O, let it not be hild
1258 Poor women's faults that they are so fulfilled
1259     With men's abuses: those proud lords to blame
    Make weak-made women tenants to their shame.

1261 The precedent whereof in Lucrece view,
1262 Assailed by night with circumstances strong
Of present death, and shame that might ensue
By that her death, to do her husband wrong.
Such danger to resistance did belong
1266     That dying fear through all her body spread;
1267     And who cannot abuse a body dead?

By this, mild patience bid fair Lucrece speak 1268
To the poor counterfeit of her complaining. 1269
'My girl,' quoth she, 'on what occasion break
Those tears from thee that down thy cheeks are raining?
If thou dost weep for grief of my sustaining, 1272
    Know, gentle wench, it small avails my mood.
    If tears could help, mine own would do me good.

'But tell me, girl, when went' (and there she stayed
Till after a deep groan) 'Tarquin from hence?'
'Madam, ere I was up,' replied the maid,
'The more to blame my sluggard negligence.
Yet with the fault I thus far can dispense –
    Myself was stirring ere the break of day,
    And ere I rose was Tarquin gone away.

'But, lady, if your maid may be so bold,
She would request to know your heaviness.' 1283
'O, peace,' quoth Lucrece. 'If it should be told,
The repetition cannot make it less;
For more it is than I can well express,
    And that deep torture may be called a hell
    When more is felt than one hath power to tell.

'Go get me hither paper, ink, and pen.
Yet save that labor, for I have them here.
What should I say? One of my husband's men
Bid thou be ready, by and by, to bear
A letter to my lord, my love, my dear.
    Bid him with speed prepare to carry it;
    The cause craves haste, and it will soon be writ.'

Her maid is gone, and she prepares to write,
First hovering o'er the paper with her quill.
Conceit and grief an eager combat fight; 1298
What wit sets down is blotted straight with will. 1299
This is too curious good, this blunt and ill. 1300
    Much like a press of people at a door,
    Throng her inventions, which shall go before.

At last she thus begins: 'Thou worthy lord
Of that unworthy wife that greeteth thee,
Health to thy person. Next vouchsafe t' afford
(If ever, love, thy Lucrece thou wilt see)
Some present speed to come and visit me.
    So I commend me, from our house in grief.
    My woes are tedious, though my words are brief.' 1309

1214 *untuned* discordant 1219 *demure* meek 1221 *sorts* matches 1222 *For why* because 1229 *circled* dark-circled (?), rounded (?); *eyne* eyes 1234 *coral cisterns* i.e. their reddened eyes (?) 1235 *takes in hand* acknowledges 1238 *to guess at* i.e. in mere conjecture of 1240 *waxen* i.e. yielding to impressions 1241 *will* i.e. will have them formed 1247 *champain* level and fertile 1248 *Lays open* reveals; *worms* reptiles 1250 *Cavekeeping* inhabiting caves 1251 *mote* speck 1257 *hild* held 1258 *fulfilled* filled 1259 *abuses* misdemeanors 1261 *precedent* example 1262 *with . . . strong* i.e. under threat 1266 *dying* i.e. paralyzing 1267 *abuse* misuse 1268 *this* i.e. this time 1269 *counterfeit* copy, mirror 1272 *of my sustaining* i.e. which I sustain 1283 *know* i.e. learn the reason for 1298 *Conceit* i.e. the conception of what she will write 1299 *wit* i.e. the intellectual faculty; *blotted* cancelled 1300 *curious* ingeniously 1309 *tedious* prolonged

Here folds she up the tenure of her woe,      *0*
Her certain sorrow writ uncertainly.
By this short schedule Collatine may know      *2*
Her grief, but not her grief's true quality.
She dares not thereof make discovery,      *5*
    Lest he should hold it her own gross abuse
    Ere she with blood had stained her stained excuse.      *6*

Besides, the life and feeling of her passion
She hoards, to spend when he is by to hear her,
When sighs and groans and tears may grace the fashion
Of her disgrace, the better so to clear her
From that suspicion which the world might bear her.
    To shun this blot, she would not blot the letter      *22*
    With words till action might become them better.

To see sad sights moves more than hear them told,
For then the eye interprets to the ear
The heavy motion that it doth behold      *26*
When every part a part of woe doth bear.
'Tis but a part of sorrow that we hear.
    Deep sounds make lesser noise than shallow fords,      *29*
    And sorrow ebbs, being blown with wind of words.

Her letter now is sealed, and on it writ,
'At Ardea to my lord with more than haste.'
The post attends, and she delivers it,
Charging the sour-faced groom to hie as fast
As lagging fowls before the Northern blast.      *5*
    Speed more than speed but dull and slow she deems :
    Extremity still urgeth such extremes.

The homely villain cursies to her low ;      *8*
And, blushing on her, with a steadfast eye,      *9*
Receives the scroll without or yea or no
And forth with bashful innocence doth hie.
But they whose guilt within their bosoms lie
    Imagine every eye beholds their blame ;
    For Lucrece thought he blushed to see her shame,

When, seely groom, God wot it was defect      *5*
Of spirit, life, and bold audacity.      *6*
Such harmless creatures have a true respect      *7*
To talk in deeds, while others saucily
Promise more speed, but do it leisurely.
    Even so this pattern of the worn-out age      *0*
    Pawned honest looks, but laid no words to gage.      *1*

1310 *tenure* brief statement 1312 *schedule* summary 1315 *gross abuse* i.e. willful wrongdoing 1316 *stained excuse* i.e. explanation of her stain 1322 *blot . . . blot* disgrace 1326 *heavy motion* sad action 1329 *sounds* soundings, levels of water 1335 *lagging* i.e. those tardy in their migratory flight 1338 *villain* serf; *cursies* genuflects 1339 *on her* i.e. in awe of her 1345 *seely* simple 1346 *life* liveliness 1347 *respect* care 1350 *worn-out age* i.e. the good old days (of faithful service) 1351 *Pawned* offered as security; *gage* guaranty 1355 *wistly* meaningfully 1359 *long* i.e. it is a long time 1364 *entertain* occupy 1364 *stay* restrain 1367 *made for* depicting 1368 *power* army 1370 *cloud-kissing Ilion* i.e. high-towered Troy; *annoy* injury 1371 *conceited* inventive 1374 *In scorn of* i.e. in defiant rivalry with; *liveless* inanimate 1377 *strife* effort 1380 *pioner* engineer, sapper 1384 *lust* liking 1385 *sweet observance* i.e. loving attention to detail 1389 *quick bearing* lively deportment 1392 *heartless* uncourageous 1396 *ciphered* expressed 1400 *deep regard* i.e. profundity; *smiling government* i.e. diplomatic skill 1403 *action* gesture 1406 *Wagged* waved (non-humorous) 1407 *purled* curled

His kindled duty kindled her mistrust,
That two red fires in both their faces blazèd.
She thought he blushed as knowing Tarquin's lust,
And, blushing with him, wistly on him gazèd ;      1355
Her earnest eye did make him more amazèd.
    The more she saw the blood his cheeks replenish,
    The more she thought he spied in her some blemish.

But long she thinks till he return again,      1359
And yet the duteous vassal scarce is gone.
The weary time she cannot entertain,      1361
For now 'tis stale to sigh, to weep and groan.
So woe hath wearied woe, moan tirèd moan,
    That she her plaints a little while doth stay,      1364
    Pausing for means to mourn some newer way.

At last she calls to mind where hangs a piece
Of skillful painting, made for Priam's Troy,      1367
Before the which is drawn the power of Greece,      1368
For Helen's rape the city to destroy,
Threat'ning cloud-kissing Ilion with annoy ;      1370
    Which the conceited painter drew so proud      1371
    As heaven, it seemed, to kiss the turrets bowed.

A thousand lamentable objects there,
In scorn of nature, art gave liveless life.      1374
Many a dry drop seemed a weeping tear
Shed for the slaught'red husband by the wife.
The red blood reeked, to show the painter's strife ;      1377
    And dying eyes gleamed forth their ashy lights,
    Like dying coals burnt out in tedious nights.

There might you see the laboring pioner      1380
Begrimed with sweat, and smearèd all with dust ;
And from the tow'rs of Troy there would appear
The very eyes of men through loopholes thrust,
Gazing upon the Greeks with little lust.      1384
    Such sweet observance in this work was had      1385
    That one might see those far-off eyes look sad.

In great commanders grace and majesty
You might behold triumphing in their faces ;
In youth, quick bearing and dexterity ;      1389
And here and there the painter interlaces
Pale cowards marching on with trembling paces,
    Which heartless peasants did so well resemble      1392
    That one would swear he saw them quake and tremble.

In Ajax and Ulysses, O, what art
Of physiognomy might one behold !
The face of either ciphered either's heart ;      1396
Their face their manners most expressly told :
In Ajax' eyes blunt rage and rigor rolled ;
    But the mild glance that sly Ulysses lent
    Showed deep regard and smiling government.      1400

There pleading might you see grave Nestor stand,
As 'twere encouraging the Greeks to fight,
Making such sober action with his hand      1403
That it beguiled attention, charmed the sight.
In speech it seemed, his beard, all silver white,
    Wagged up and down, and from his lips did fly      1406
    Thin winding breath, which purled up to the sky.      1407

About him were a press of gaping faces
Which seemed to swallow up his sound advice,
All jointly list'ning, but with several graces,
1411 As if some mermaid did their ears entice,
1412 Some high, some low – the painter was so nice.
    The scalps of many, almost hid behind,
1414   To jump up higher seemed, to mock the mind.

Here one man's hand leaned on another's head,
His nose being shadowed by his neighbor's ear;
1417 Here one, being thronged, bears back, all boll'n and red;
1418 Another, smothered, seems to pelt and swear;
And in their rage such signs of rage they bear
    As, but for loss of Nestor's golden words,
    It seemed they would debate with angry swords.

For much imaginary work was there;
1423 Conceit deceitful, so compact, so kind,
That for Achilles' image stood his spear,
Griped in an armèd hand; himself behind
Was left unseen, save to the eye of mind:
    A hand, a foot, a face, a leg, a head
    Stood for the whole to be imaginèd.

And from the walls of strong-besiegèd Troy
When their brave hope, bold Hector, marched to field,
Stood many Troyan mothers, sharing joy
To see their youthful sons bright weapons wield;
1433 And to their hope they such odd action yield
    That through their light joy seemèd to appear
    (Like bright things stained) a kind of heavy fear:

1436 And from the strond of Dardan, where they fought,
1437 To Simois' reedy banks the red blood ran,
Whose waves to imitate the battle sought
With swelling ridges; and their ranks began
1440 To break upon the gallèd shore, and than
    Retire again, till, meeting greater ranks,
    They join, and shoot their foam at Simois' banks.

To this well-painted piece is Lucrece come,
1444 To find a face where all distress is stelled.
Many she sees where cares have carvèd some,
But none where all distress and dolor dwelled
Till she despairing Hecuba beheld,
    Staring on Priam's wounds with her old eyes,
    Which bleeding under Pyrrhus' proud foot lies.

1450 In her the painter had anatomized
Time's ruin, beauty's wrack, and grim care's reign;
1452 Her cheeks with chops and wrinkles were disguised;
Of what she was no semblance did remain.
Her blue blood, changed to black in every vein,
    Wanting the spring that those shrunk pipes had fed,
    Showed life imprisoned in a body dead.

On this sad shadow Lucrece spends her eyes
1458 And shapes her sorrow to the beldame's woes,
Who nothing wants to answer her but cries
1460 And bitter words to ban her cruel foes.
The painter was no god to lend her those;
    And therefore Lucrece swears he did her wrong
    To give her so much grief and not a tongue.

'Poor instrument,' quoth she, 'without a sound:
I'll tune thy woes with my lamenting tongue,    14
And drop sweet balm in Priam's painted wound,
And rail on Pyrrhus that hath done him wrong,
And with my tears quench Troy that burns so long,
    And with my knife scratch out the angry eyes
    Of all the Greeks that are thine enemies.

'Show me the strumpet that began this stir,    14
That with my nails her beauty I may tear.
Thy heat of lust, fond Paris, did incur    14
This load of wrath that burning Troy doth bear.
Thy eye kindled the fire that burneth here,
    And here in Troy, for trespass of thine eye,
    The sire, the son, the dame and daughter die.

'Why should the private pleasure of some one
Become the public plague of many moe?    14
Let sin, alone committed, light alone
Upon his head that hath transgressèd so;
Let guiltless souls be freed from guilty woe.
    For one's offense why should so many fall,
    To plague a private sin in general?    14

'Lo, here weeps Hecuba, here Priam dies,
Here manly Hector faints, here Troilus sounds,    14
Here friend by friend in bloody channel lies,
And friend to friend gives unadvisèd wounds,    14
And one man's lust these many lives confounds.
    Had doting Priam checked his son's desire,
    Troy had been bright with fame, and not with fire.'

Here feelingly she weeps Troy's painted woes,
For sorrow, like a heavy hanging bell,
Once set on ringing, with his own weight goes;
Then little strength rings out the doleful knell.
So Lucrece, set awork, sad tales doth tell
    To pencilled pensiveness and colored sorrow:    14
    She lends them words, and she their looks doth borrow.

She throws her eyes about the painting round,    14
And who she finds forlorn she doth lament.
At last she sees a wretched image bound    15
That piteous looks to Phrygian shepherds lent.    15
His face, though full of cares, yet showed content;
    Onward to Troy with the blunt swains he goes,    15
    So mild that patience seemed to scorn his woes.    15

1411 *mermaid* i.e. siren  1412 *Some . . . low* some tall and some short;
*nice* precise  1414 *mock* vainly tempt (so the spectator of the picture might
see those hidden in the rear)  1417 *thronged* crowded; *boll'n* swollen
1418 *pelt* scold  1423 *Conceit* contrivance; *compact* economical; *kind*
natural  1433 *odd action* contrary gestures; *yield* lend  1436 *strond of
Dardan* shore of Troas  1437 *Simois* river flowing from Mt Ida  1440
*gallèd* eroded; *than* then  1444 *stelled* engraved  1450 *anatomized* laid
open  1452 *chops* chapping; *disguised* disfigured  1458 *beldame's* aged
woman's  1460 *ban* curse  1465 *tune* voice  1471 *stir* war  1473 *fond*
foolish  1479 *moe* more  1484 *plague* i.e. punish; *in general* i.e. on the
general public  1486 *sounds* swoons  1488 *unadvisèd* unintentional  1497
*pencilled, colored* painted  1499 *round* all around  1501 *wretched image*
i.e. of the traitor Sinon  1502 *piteous . . . lent* i.e. drew looks of pity from
Phrygian shepherds  1504 *blunt* rude  1505 *patience . . . scorn* i.e. his
patience seemed to make light of

In him the painter labored with his skill
1507 To hide deceit, and give the harmless show
An humble gait, calm looks, eyes wailing still,
1509 A brow unbent that seemed to welcome woe,
Cheeks neither red nor pale, but mingled so
That blushing red no guilty instance gave
Nor ashy pale the fear that false hearts have;

But, like a constant and confirmèd devil,
1514 He entertained a show so seeming just,
And therein so ensconced his secret evil,
1516 That jealousy itself could not mistrust
False creeping craft and perjury should thrust
Into so bright a day such black-faced storms
Or blot with hell-born sin such saintlike forms.

The well-skilled workman this mild image drew
1521 For perjured Sinon, whose enchanting story
The credulous old Priam after slew;
Whose words like wildfire burnt the shining glory
Of rich-built Ilion, that the skies were sorry,
And little stars shot from their fixèd places
1526 When their glass fell wherein they viewed their faces.

1527 This picture she advisedly perused
And chid the painter for his wondrous skill,
1529 Saying, some shape in Sinon's was abused;
So fair a form lodged not a mind so ill.
And still on him she gazed, and gazing still,
Such signs of truth in his plain face she spied
1533 That she concludes the picture was belied.

'It cannot be,' quoth she, 'that so much guile' –
She would have said 'can lurk in such a look';
But Tarquin's shape came in her mind the while
And from her tongue 'can lurk' from 'cannot' took.
1538 'It cannot be' she in that sense forsook
And turned it thus: 'It cannot be, I find,
But such a face should bear a wicked mind;

'For even as subtile Sinon here is painted,
So sober-sad, so weary, and so mild
(As if with grief or travail he had fainted),
1544 To me came Tarquin armèd, to beguiled
With outward honesty, but yet defiled
With inward vice. As Priam him did cherish,
So did I Tarquin; so my Troy did perish.

'Look, look how list'ning Priam wets his eyes
To see those borrowed tears that Sinon sheeds!     1549
Priam, why art thou old, and yet not wise?
For every tear he falls a Troyan bleeds.
His eye drops fire, no water thence proceeds.
Those round clear pearls of his that move thy pity
Are balls of quenchless fire to burn thy city.

'Such devils steal effects from lightless hell,
For Sinon in his fire doth quake with cold
And in that cold hot burning fire doth dwell.
These contraries such unity do hold              1558
Only to flatter fools and make them bold.        1559
So Priam's trust false Sinon's tears doth flatter
That he finds means to burn his Troy with water.'

Here, all enraged, such passion her assails
That patience is quite beaten from her breast.
She tears the senseless Sinon with her nails,
Comparing him to that unhappy guest              1565
Whose deed hath made herself herself detest.
At last she smilingly with this gives o'er:
'Fool, fool!' quoth she, 'his wounds will not be sore.'

Thus ebbs and flows the current of her sorrow,
And time doth weary time with her complaining.
She looks for night, and then she longs for morrow,
And both she thinks too long with her remaining.
Short time seems long in sorrow's sharp sustaining;    1573
Though woe be heavy, yet it seldom sleeps,        1574
And they that watch see time how slow it creeps;

Which all this time hath overslipped her thought   1576
That she with painted images hath spent,
Being from the feeling of her own grief brought
By deep surmise of others' detriment,             1579
Losing her woes in shows of discontent.           1580
It easeth some, though none it ever curèd,
To think their dolor others have endurèd.

But now the mindful messenger, come back,
Brings home his lord and other company;
Who finds his Lucrece clad in mourning black,
And round about her tear-distainèd eye            1586
Blue circles streamed, like rainbows in the sky.
These water-galls in her dim element             1588
Foretell new storms to those already spent.

Which when her sad-beholding husband saw,
Amazedly in her sad face he stares.
Her eyes, though sod in tears, looked red and raw,   1592
Her lively color killed with deadly cares.
He hath no power to ask her how she fares;
Both stood, like old acquaintance in a trance,
Met far from home, wond'ring each other's chance.    1596

At last he takes her by the bloodless hand
And thus begins: 'What uncouth ill event           1598
Hath thee befall'n, that thou dost trembling stand?
Sweet love, what spite hath thy fair color spent?    1600
Why art thou thus attired in discontent?
Unmask, dear dear, this moody heaviness            1602
And tell thy grief, that we may give redress.'

1507 *show* appearance (affected by Sinon) 1509 *unbent* unfrowning 1514
*entertained a show* i.e. adopted an appearance 1516 *jealousy* suspicion
1521 *enchanting story* i.e. seductive lie 1526 *glass* mirror (i.e. glittering
Troy) 1527 *advisedly* thoughtfully 1529 *some shape* i.e. the figure of
someone else; *abused* traduced 1533 *belied* proved false. 1538 *that sense*
i.e. the sense originally intended 1544 *armèd* equipped; *beguiled* beguile
(with the superfluous 'd' providing a rhyme) 1549 *borrowed* i.e. false,
not truly his; *sheeds* sheds 1558 *hold* maintain 1559 *flatter . . . bold* i.e.
deceive fools and give them confidence 1565 *unhappy* unlucky, fatal
1573 *in . . . sustaining* in the sharp sorrow sustained 1574 *heavy* (1) burdensome, (2) sleepy 1576 *overslipped her thought* passed unnoticed 1579
*surmise* contemplation 1580 *shows* representations (i.e. of the woes of
Troy) 1586 *tear-distainèd* tear-stained 1588 *water-galls* fragmentary
rainbows (presaging stormy weather); *element* sky 1592 *sod* sodden
1596 *wond'ring . . . chance* i.e. wondering at each other's fortune 1598
*uncouth* strange 1600 *spent* dispersed 1602 *Unmask* disclose

1604 Three times with sighs she gives her sorrow fire
Ere once she can discharge one word of woe.
At length addressed to answer his desire,
She modestly prepares to let them know
Her honor is ta'en prisoner by the foe,
1609   While Collatine and his consorted lords
With sad attention long to hear her words.

And now this pale swan in her wat'ry nest
1612 Begins the sad dirge of her certain ending :
'Few words,' quoth she, 'shall fit the trespass best
Where no excuse can give the fault amending.
1615 In me moe woes than words are now depending,
And my laments would be drawn out too long
To tell them all with one poor tirèd tongue.

'Then be this all the task it hath to say :
1619 Dear husband, in the interest of thy bed
A stranger came and on that pillow lay
Where thou wast wont to rest thy weary head ;
And what wrong else may be imaginèd
By foul enforcement might be done to me,
From that, alas, thy Lucrece is not free.

'For in the dreadful dead of dark midnight
With shining falchion in my chamber came
A creeping creature with a flaming light
And softly cried, "Awake, thou Roman dame,
And entertain my love ; else lasting shame
On thee and thine this night I will inflict,
1631   If thou my love's desire do contradict.

' "For some hard-favored groom of thine," quoth he,
"Unless thou yoke thy liking to my will,
I'll murder straight, and then I'll slaughter thee
And swear I found you where you did fulfill
The loathsome act of lust, and so did kill
The lechers in their deed. This act will be
My fame and thy perpetual infamy."

'With this I did begin to start and cry ;
And then against my heart he set his sword,
Swearing, unless I took all patiently,
I should not live to speak another word.
So should my shame still rest upon record,
And never be forgot in mighty Rome
Th' adulterate death of Lucrece and her groom.

'Mine enemy was strong, my poor self weak
And far the weaker with so strong a fear.
1648 My bloody judge forbod my tongue to speak ;
No rightful plea might plead for justice there.
His scarlet lust came evidence to swear
That my poor beauty had purloined his eyes ;
And when the judge is robbed, the prisoner dies.

'O, teach me how to make mine own excuse,
Or at the least this refuge let me find :
Though my gross blood be stained with this abuse,
Immaculate and spotless is my mind ;
That was not forced ; that never was inclined
To accessary yieldings, but still pure
Doth in her poisoned closet yet endure.'

Lo, here, the hopeless merchant of this loss,     1660
With head declined and voice dammed up with woe,
With sad-set eyes and wreathèd arms across,
From lips new waxen pale begins to blow
The grief away that stops his answer so.
But, wretched as he is, he strives in vain ;
What he breathes out his breath drinks up again.

As through an arch the violent roaring tide     1667
Outruns the eye that doth behold his haste,
Yet in the eddy boundeth in his pride
Back to the strait that forced him on so fast ;
In rage sent out, recalled in rage being past :
Even so his sighs, his sorrows, make a saw,     1672
To push grief on, and back the same grief draw.

Which speechless woe of his poor she attendeth
And his untimely frenzy thus awaketh :     1675
'Dear lord, thy sorrow to my sorrow lendeth
Another power, no flood by raining slaketh ;
My woe too sensible thy passion maketh     1678
More feeling-painful. Let it then suffice
To drown one woe, one pair of weeping eyes.

'And for my sake when I might charm thee so,     1681
For she that was thy Lucrece (now attend me)
Be suddenly revengèd on my foe,
Thine, mine, his own : suppose thou dost defend me
From what is past – the help that thou shalt lend me
Comes all too late, yet let the traitor die ;
For sparing justice feeds iniquity.

'But ere I name him, you fair lords,' quoth she,
Speaking to those that came with Collatine,
'Shall plight your honorable faiths to me
With swift pursuit to venge this wrong of mine ;
For 'tis a meritorious fair design
To chase injustice with revengeful arms.
Knights by their oaths should right poor ladies' harms.'

At this request, with noble disposition
Each present lord began to promise aid,
As bound in knighthood to her imposition,
Longing to hear the hateful foe bewrayed.     1695
But she, that yet her sad task hath not said,     1696
The protestation stops. 'O, speak !' quoth she,
'How may this forcèd stain be wiped from me ?     1701

1604 *fire* i.e. the ignition needed to discharge ancient firearms   1609 *consorted* associated   1612 *certain ending* impending death   1615 *moe* more ; *depending* impending   1619 *interest* possession   1631 *contradict* i.e. deny, counter   1648 *forbod* forbade   1660 *merchant . . . loss* i.e. Collatine, seen as a merchant whose ship has been wrecked   1667 *arch* (such as those of London Bridge, which provide the following image of current and back-current swirls)   1672 *saw* i.e. back-and-forth or sawlike motion   1675 *his . . . awaketh* i.e. breaks into his untimely trance   1678 *too sensible* i.e. already too sensitive   1681 *so* as such (i.e. as her former self implied in *my sake*)   1698 *bewrayed* discovered   1699 *yet . . . said* i.e. had not yet finished this sad task of saying   1701 *forcèd* imposed by force

02 'What is the quality of my offense,
Being constrained with dreadful circumstance?
04 May my pure mind with the foul act dispense,
05 My low-declinèd honor to advance?
May any terms acquit me from this chance?
   The poisonèd fountain clears itself again;
   And why not I from this compellèd stain?'

With this they all at once began to say,
Her body's stain her mind untainted clears;
While with a joyless smile she turns away
The face, that map which deep impression bears
Of hard misfortune, carved in it with tears.
   'No, no!' quoth she, 'no dame hereafter living
   By my excuse shall claim excuse's giving.'

Here with a sigh as if her heart would break
She throws forth Tarquin's name: 'He, he!' she says,
But more than 'he' her poor tongue could not speak,
19 Till after many accents and delays,
20 Untimely breathings, sick and short assays,
   She utters this: 'He, he! fair lords, 'tis he
   That guides this hand to give this wound to me.'

Even here she sheathèd in her harmless breast
A harmful knife, that thence her soul unsheathèd.
25 That blow did bail it from the deep unrest
Of that polluted prison where it breathèd.
Her contrite sighs unto the clouds bequeathèd
28    Her wingèd sprite, and through her wounds doth fly
29    Live's lasting date from cancelled destiny.

Stone-still, astonished with this deadly deed,
Stood Collatine and all his lordly crew,
Till Lucrece' father, that beholds her bleed,
Himself on her self-slaught'red body threw,
And from the purple fountain Brutus drew
   The murd'rous knife, and, as it left the place,
   Her blood, in poor revenge, held it in chase;

And bubbling from her breast, it doth divide
In two slow rivers, that the crimson blood
Circles her body in on every side,
40 Who, like a late-sacked island, vastly stood
Bare and unpeopled in this fearful flood.
   Some of her blood still pure and red remained,
   And some looked black, and that false Tarquin stained.

About the mourning and congealèd face
Of that black blood a wat'ry rigoll goes,    1745
Which seems to weep upon the tainted place;
And ever since, as pitying Lucrece' woes,
Corrupted blood some watery token shows,
   And blood untainted still doth red abide,
   Blushing at that which is so putrefied.

'Daughter, dear daughter!' old Lucretius cries,
'That life was mine which thou hast here deprivèd.
If in the child the father's image lies,
Where shall I live now Lucrece is unlivèd?
Thou wast not to this end from me derivèd.
   If children predecease progenitors,
   We are their offspring, and they none of ours.

'Poor broken glass, I often did behold    1758
In thy sweet semblance my old age new born;
But now that fresh fair mirror, dim and old,
Shows me a bare-boned death by time outworn.    1761
O, from thy cheeks my image thou hast torn
   And shivered all the beauty of my glass,
   That I no more can see what once I was.

'O time, cease thou thy course, and last no longer,
If they surcease to be that should survive.
Shall rotten death make conquest of the stronger
And leave the falt'ring feeble souls alive?
The old bees die, the young possess their hive.
   Then live, sweet Lucrece, live again and see
   Thy father die, and not thy father thee.'

By this, starts Collatine as from a dream
And bids Lucretius give his sorrow place;
And then in key-cold Lucrece' bleeding stream    1774
He falls, and bathes the pale fear in his face,    1775
And counterfeits to die with her a space;
   Till manly shame bids him possess his breath
   And live to be revengèd on her death.

The deep vexation of his inward soul
Hath served a dumb arrest upon his tongue;    1780
Who, mad that sorrow should his use control,
Or keep him from heart-easing words so long,
Begins to talk; but through his lips do throng
   Weak words, so thick come in his poor heart's aid    1784
   That no man could distinguish what he said.

Yet sometime 'Tarquin' was pronouncèd plain,
But through his teeth, as if the name he tore.
This windy tempest, till it blow up rain,
Held back his sorrow's tide, to make it more.
At last it rains, and busy winds give o'er;
   Then son and father weep with equal strife
   Who should weep most, for daughter or for wife.

The one doth call her his, the other his;
Yet neither may possess the claim they lay.
The father says, 'She's mine.' 'O, mine she is!'
Replies her husband. 'Do not take away
My sorrow's interest. Let no mourner say    1797
   He weeps for her; for she was only mine,
   And only must be wailed by Collatine.'

1702 *quality* nature  1704 *dispense* be reconciled  1705 *advance* raise
1719 *accents* utterances  1720 *assays* attempts  1725 *bail* release  1728
*sprite* spirit  1729 *Live's . . . date* i.e. eternal life; *cancelled destiny* i.e. the
termination of earthly life  1740 *late-sacked* recently pillaged; *vastly
stood* i.e. rose high above  1745 *wat'ry rigoll* i.e. the rim of serum which
separates from coagulated blood  1758 *glass* mirror  1761 *death* i.e.
death's-head, skull  1774 *key-cold* i.e. cold as steel  1775 *pale fear* fearful
pallor  1780 *dumb arrest* i.e. injunction of silence  1784 *so thick* so rapidly
1797 *sorrow's interest* claim to sorrow

'O,' quoth Lucretius, 'I did give that life
1801 Which she too early and too late hath spilled.'
'Woe, woe!' quoth Collatine. 'She was my wife,
1803 I owed her, and 'tis mine that she hath killed.'
'My daughter' and 'my wife' with clamors filled
1805     The dispersed air, who, holding Lucrece' life,
    Answered their cries, 'my daughter' and 'my wife.'

Brutus, who plucked the knife from Lucrece' side,
Seeing such emulation in their woe,
1809 Began to clothe his wit in state and pride,
1810 Burying in Lucrece' wound his folly's show.
He with the Romans was esteemèd so
1812     As seely jeering idiots are with kings,
    For sportive words and utt'ring foolish things;

1814 But now he throws that shallow habit by
Wherein deep policy did him disguise,
And armed his long-hid wits advisedly
To check the tears in Collatinus' eyes.
'Thou wrongèd lord of Rome,' quoth he, 'arise!
1819     Let my unsounded self, supposed a fool,
    Now set thy long-experienced wit to school.

'Why, Collatine, is woe the cure for woe?
Do wounds help wounds, or grief help grievous deeds?
Is it revenge to give thyself a blow
For his foul act by whom thy fair wife bleeds?
Such childish humor from weak minds proceeds.
    Thy wretched wife mistook the matter so,
    To slay herself that should have slain her foe.

'Courageous Roman, do not steep thy heart
In such relenting dew of lamentations;
But kneel with me, and help to bear thy part
To rouse our Roman gods with invocations
1832 That they will suffer these abominations
    (Since Rome herself in them doth stand disgracèd)
1834     By our strong arms from forth her fair streets chasèd.

'Now, by the Capitol that we adore,
And by this chaste blood so unjustly stainèd,
By heaven's fair sun that breeds the fat earth's store,   18
By all our country rights in Rome maintainèd,
And by chaste Lucrece' soul that late complainèd
    Her wrongs to us, and by this bloody knife,
    We will revenge the death of this true wife.'

This said, he struck his hand upon his breast
And kissed the fatal knife to end his vow;
And to his protestation urged the rest,   18
Who, wond'ring at him, did his words allow.   18
Then jointly to the ground their knees they bow;
    And that deep vow which Brutus made before
    He doth again repeat, and that they swore.

When they had sworn to this advisèd doom,   18
They did conclude to bear dead Lucrece thence,   18
To show her bleeding body thorough Rome,
And so to publish Tarquin's foul offense;
Which being done with speedy diligence,
    The Romans plausibly did give consent   18
    To Tarquin's everlasting banishment.

FINIS

1801 *late* recently   1803 *owed* owned   1805 *dispersed air* i.e. circumambient air (into which Lucrece's *life* has passed)   1809 *state and pride* i.e. dignified statesmanship   1810 *folly's show* pretense of folly   1812 *seely . . . idiots* i.e. kings' jesters; *seely* simple   1814 *habit* cloak   1819 *unsounded* unplumbed   1832 *suffer* allow   1834 *chasèd* i.e. to be chased   1837 *fat* rich, fertile   1844 *to his protestation* i.e. to take a similar vow   1845 *allow* accept   1849 *advisèd doom* deliberate judgment   1850 *to bear* by bearing   1854 *plausibly* i.e. plausively, with a *general acclamation* (see Argument, line 41)

# THE PHOENIX AND TURTLE

1 Let the bird of loudest lay
2 On the sole Arabian tree
3 Herald sad and trumpet be,
4 To whose sound chaste wings obey,

5 But thou shrieking harbinger,
6 Foul precurrer of the fiend,
7 Augur of the fever's end,
To this troop come thou not near.

From this session interdict
10 Every fowl of tyrant wing,
Save the eagle, feath'red king :
Keep the obsequy so strict.

Let the priest in surplice white,
14 That defunctive music can,
15 Be the death-divining swan,
16 Lest the requiem lack his right.

17 And thou treble-dated crow,
18 That thy sable gender mak'st
19 With the breath thou giv'st and tak'st,
'Mongst our mourners shalt thou go.

Here the anthem doth commence :
Love and constancy is dead,
Phoenix and the turtle fled
In a mutual flame from hence.

25 So they loved as love in twain
Had the essence but in one ;
27 Two distincts, division none :
28 Number there in love was slain.

Hearts remote, yet not asunder ; 29
Distance, and no space was seen
'Twixt this turtle and his queen ;
But in them it were a wonder. 32

So between them love did shine
That the turtle saw his right 34
Flaming in the phoenix' sight :
Either was the other's mine. 36

Property was thus appallèd, 37
That the self was not the same ;
Single nature's double name 39
Neither two nor one was callèd.

Reason, in itself confounded, 41
Saw division grow together,
To themselves yet either neither,
Simple were so well compounded ; 44

That it cried, 'How true a twain 45
Seemeth this concordant one !
Love hath reason, reason none,
If what parts can so remain.' 48

Whereupon it made this threne 49
To the phoenix and the dove,
Co-supremes and stars of love,
As chorus to their tragic scene.

## THRENOS

Beauty, truth, and rarity,
Grace in all simplicity,
Here enclosed, in cinders lie. 55

Death is now the phoenix' nest ;
And the turtle's loyal breast
To eternity doth rest,

Leaving no posterity :
'Twas not their infirmity, 60
It was married chastity. 61

Truth may seem, but cannot be ; 62
Beauty brag, but 'tis not she : 63
Truth and Beauty buried be.

To this urn let those repair
That are either true or fair ;
For these dead birds sigh a prayer.

Title : *Phoenix* mythical bird which expires in flame and is reborn in its own ashes, thus symbolizing immortality ; *Turtle* turtledove (symbol of true love)  1 *bird . . . lay* i.e. the bird (unidentified) having the loudest song  2 *sole Arabian tree* i.e. the only one of its kind (unidentified) in which the phoenix nests  3 *trumpet* trumpeter  4 *To whose* whose  5 *shrieking harbinger* i.e. the owl  6 *precurrer* precursor  7 *Augur . . . end* i.e. prophet of death  10 *fowl . . . wing* i.e. bird of prey  14 *defunctive music can* i.e. can provide funeral music  15 *death-divining* (in its legendary 'swan-song' occurring only before its death)  16 *his* its  17 *treble-dated* i.e. long-lived, the length of three ordinary lives  18 *thy . . . mak'st* i.e. re-produce your own black species  19 *breath* (the crow, or at least the raven, was popularly believed to engender by billing)  25 *So . . . as* i.e. they so loved that  27 *distincts* i.e. distinct persons  28 *slain* i.e. obliterated  29 *remote* i.e. separated in space  32 *But* except (i.e. in them it was simply natural)  34 *right* i.e. due of love  36 *mine* i.e. very own  37–38 *Property . . . same* i.e. the very idea of private possession was thrown into confusion by the obliteration of the distinct or individual possessor  39–40 *Single . . . callèd* i.e. the single nature composed of two persons could be called neither two nor one  41 *in itself confounded* i.e. baffled by its own logical process  44 *Simple* i.e. simples (the individual ingredients in a compound)  45 *it* i.e. Reason  48 *If . . . remain* i.e. if what divides into two can remain one  49 *threne* funeral song (*Threnos*)  55 *Here enclosed* i.e. in the *urn* (cf. line 65) enclosing the *cinders* or ashes  60 *infirmity* i.e. sterility (?)  61 *married chastity* i.e. abstinence in marriage (?)  62 *seem* i.e. appear to exist  63 *she* i.e. true Beauty

*A Lover's Complaint* "By William Shake-speare" was first printed in 1609 in *Shakespeare's Sonnets,* the famous quarto issued by Thomas Thorpe. The poem begins at signature K1ᵛ and concludes the volume. Although critical opinion is divided, it tends, perhaps mistakenly, to deny Shakespeare's authorship of the poem, which is often assigned to some unidentified imitator of Shakespeare, Spenser, Sidney, and Daniel. The present text is based upon the 1609 quarto, and admits only the following material emendations: 7 *sorrow's wind* sorrowes, wind 14 *lattice* lettice 18 *seasoned* seasonèd 68 *aught* ought 80 *Of* O 103 *breathe* breath 112 *manage* mannad'g 118 *Came* Can 208 *the* th' 228 *Hallowed* Hollowèd 241 *Paling* Playing 242 *unconstrainèd* unconstraind 252 *procured* procure 260 *nun* Sunne 265 *stint* sting 284 *flowed* flowèd 293 *O* Or 326 *bestowed* bestowèd 327 *borrowed* borrowèd *owed* owèd 328 *betrayed* betrayèd.

*The Passionate Pilgrim* "By W. Shakespeare" was printed by William Jaggard in an octavo of 1599. At C3ᵛ, preceding the poem numbered in modern editions XV, the volume has a second title page, *Sonnets to Sundry Notes of Music.* A fragment of another and probably earlier octavo is in the Folger collection, in leaves containing the poems numbered in modern editions I, II, III, IV, V, XVI, XVII, XVIII. Jaggard's volume is an unscrupulously assembled miscellany, containing (a) poems by Shakespeare available elsewhere, (b) poems known to be by writers other than he, and (c) poems of doubtful authorship, some of them reappearing in another miscellany, *England's Helicon,* 1600, or in dubious compilations associated with specific poets.

Omitted from the present edition are the following poems in *The Passionate Pilgrim,* since they are printed from better texts elsewhere in the *Pelican Shakespeare*: I, Sonnet 138; II, Sonnet 144; III, *Love's Labor's Lost,* IV, iii, 55–68; V, *ibid.,* IV, ii, 101–14; XVI, *ibid.,* IV, iii, 96–115. Omitted also is XIX, a version of Marlowe's "The Passionate Shepherd to His Love."

Included are the remaining poems in the miscellany, although some of these can be assigned, with varying degrees of confidence, to particular poets. Numbers IV, VI, IX, and XI are on the Venus and Adonis theme, but they are more likely to have been the work of Bartholomew Griffin than of Shakespeare, Number XI having already appeared in Griffin's *Fidessa,* 1596. Numbers VIII and XX had appeared in Barnfield's *Poems: In Divers Humors,* 1598. Number XII was to reappear in Thomas Deloney's *Garden of Goodwill,* 1631; and Number XVII (as well as XVI, XIX, and, in part, XX) in *England's Helicon,* 1600. Numbers VII, X, XII, XIII, XIV, XV, XVII, XVIII cannot be proved "non-Shakespearean" on the basis of external evidence, but the majority obviously are. Several have merit, but only Number XII is worth the effort to establish a Shakespearean claim.

The present edition is based upon Jaggard's octavo of 1599, with the following material emendations or readings from alternative texts: IV, 5 *ear* eares 10 *figured* figurèd VII, 11 *midst* mids X, 5 *plum* plumbe 8, 9 *left'st* lefts XIII, 9 *with'red* witherèd XIV, 24 *sighed* sight 27 *a moon an hour* XV, 3 *fair'st* fairest XVII, 5 *Love's denying* Love is dying 7 *Heart's renying* Harts nenying 19 *mourn* morn 43 *back* blacke 49 *lass* love 51 *moan* woe XVIII, 4 *fancy (partial) might* fancy (partyall might) 12 *thy* her *sell* sale 14, 17 *ere* yer 45 *be* by 51 *ear* are XX, 22 *beasts* Beares 27–28 (omitted from *The Passionate Pilgrim* and supplied from *England's Helicon*).

## A LOVER'S COMPLAINT

1 From off a hill whose concave womb re-worded
2 A plaintful story from a sist'ring vale,
3 My spirits t' attend this double voice accorded,
  And down I laid to list the sad-tuned tale;
5 Ere long espied a fickle maid full pale,
6 Tearing of papers, breaking rings a-twain,
  Storming her world with sorrow's wind and rain.

8 Upon her head a platted hive of straw,
  Which fortified her visage from the sun,
10 Whereon the thought might think sometime it saw
11 The carcass of a beauty spent and done.
12 Time had not scythèd all that youth begun,
13 Nor youth all quit; but, spite of heaven's fell rage,
  Some beauty peeped through lattice of seared age.

Oft did she heave her napkin to her eyne, 15
Which on it had conceited characters, 16
Laund'ring the silken figures in the brine
That seasoned woe had pelleted in tears, 18
And often reading what contents it bears;
As often shrieking undistinguished woe 20
In clamors of all size, both high and low.

1 *womb re-worded* i.e. valley re-echoed 2 *sist'ring* i.e. matching (one similar and nearby) 3 *accorded* inclined 5 *fickle* changeable, perturbed 6 *papers* i.e. love-letters 8 *platted hive* i.e. woven hat 10 *thought* i.e. mind 11 *carcass* remnant 12 *scythèd* cropped, cut down 13 *all quit* i.e. left everything; *fell* deadly 15 *heave* lift; *napkin* handkerchief 16 *conceited* ingenious 18 *seasoned* (1) matured, (2) salted (punning on *brine*); *pelleted* (1) rounded, (2) prepared as seasoners (punning on 'pellet' as culinary term) 20 *undistinguished* incoherent

22 Sometime her levelled eyes their carriage ride,
23 As they did batt'ry to the spheres intend;
Sometimes diverted their poor balls are tied
To th' orbèd earth; sometimes they do extend
Their view right on; anon their gazes lend
To every place at once, and, nowhere fixed,
The mind and sight distractedly commixed.

Her hair, nor loose nor tied in formal plat,
Proclaimed in her a careless hand of pride;
31 For some, untucked, descended her sheaved hat,
Hanging her pale and pinèd cheek beside;
33 Some in her threaden fillet still did bide
And, true to bondage, would not break from thence,
Though slackly braided in loose negligence.

36 A thousand favors from a maund she drew,
37 Of amber, crystal, and of bedded jet,
Which one by one she in a river threw,
39 Upon whose weeping margent she was set,
Like usury, applying wet to wet,
Or monarch's hands that lets not bounty fall
Where want cries some but where excess begs all.

43 Of folded schedules had she many a one
Which she perused, sighed, tore, and gave the flood;
45 Cracked many a ring of posied gold and bone,
Bidding them find their sepulchres in mud;
47 Found yet moe letters sadly penned in blood,
48 With sleided silk feat and affectedly
49 Enswathed and sealed to curious secrecy.

50 These often bathed she in her fluxive eyes,
51 And often kissed, and often gave to tear;
Cried, 'O false blood, thou register of lies,
53 What unapprovèd witness dost thou bear!
Ink would have seemed more black and damnèd here!'
This said, in top of rage the lines she rents,
Big discontent so breaking their contents.

A reverend man that grazed his cattle nigh, 57
Sometime a blusterer that the ruffle knew 58
Of court, of city, and had let go by 59
The swiftest hours, observèd as they flew,
Towards this afflicted fancy fastly drew, 61
And, privileged by age, desires to know
In brief the grounds and motives of her woe.

So slides he down upon his grainèd bat, 64
And comely-distant sits he by her side; 65
When he again desires her, being sat,
Her grievance with his hearing to divide: 67
If that from him there may be aught applied
Which may her suffering ecstasy assuage, 69
'Tis promised in the charity of age.

'Father,' she says, 'though in me you behold
The injury of many a blasting hour,
Let it not tell your judgment I am old;
Not age, but sorrow, over me hath power:
I might as yet have been a spreading flower,
Fresh to myself, if I had self-applied
Love to myself and to no love beside.

'But, woe is me, too early I attended 78
A youthful suit – it was to gain my grace –
Of one by nature's outwards so commended
That maidens' eyes stuck over all his face;
Love lacked a dwelling, and made him her place;
And when in his fair parts she did abide,
She was new lodged and newly deified.

'His browny locks did hang in crooked curls,
And every light occasion of the wind 86
Upon his lips their silken parcels hurls.
What's sweet to do, to do will aptly find: 88
Each eye that saw him did enchant the mind,
For on his visage was in little drawn
What largeness thinks in Paradise was sawn. 91

'Small show of man was yet upon his chin;
His phoenix down began but to appear, 93
Like unshorn velvet, on that termless skin 94
Whose bare out-bragged the web it seemed to wear. 95
Yet showed his visage by that cost more dear; 96
And nice affections wavering stood in doubt 97
If best were as it was, or best without.

'His qualities were beauteous as his form,
For maiden-tongued he was, and thereof free; 100
Yet, if men moved him, was he such a storm
As oft 'twixt May and April is to see,
When winds breathe sweet, unruly though they be.
His rudeness so with his authorized youth 104
Did livery falseness in a pride of truth. 105

'Well could he ride, and often men would say,
"That horse his mettle from his rider takes.
Proud of subjection, noble by the sway,
What rounds, what bounds, what course, what stop he
And controversy hence a question takes, [makes!" 110
Whether the horse by him became his deed, 111
Or he his manage by th' well-doing steed. 112

22 *levelled* (1) directed, (2) aimed; *carriage ride* move (punning on gun-carriage) 23 *As* as if; *batt'ry . . . spheres* i.e. to direct fire against the heavenly bodies (continuing the artillery metaphor) 31 *sheaved* straw 33 *threaden fillet* i.e. ribbon circling the head 36 *favors* love-tokens; *maund* basket 37 *bedded* inlaid 39 *weeping margent* wet bank 43 *schedules* missives 45 *posied* i.e. inscribed with love-mottoes 47 *moe* more 48 *sleided* ravelled; *feat and affectedly* neatly and lovingly 49 *curious* fastidious 50 *fluxive* flowing 51 *gave* i.e. shared an impulse 53 *unapproved* unconfirmed 57 *reverend* aged 58 *ruffle* pretentious bustle 59–60 *had . . . flew* i.e. had gained knowledge through observation during the brief time of youth 61 *fancy* i.e. lady in her love-sick mood; *fastly* closely (?), quickly (?) 64 *grainèd bat* shepherd's staff (so worn as to show the grain) 65 *comely-distant* i.e. at appropriate distance 67 *divide* share 69 *ecstasy* fit 78 *attended* gave attention to 86 *occasion* occurrence, i.e. movement 88 *What's . . . find* i.e. what's pleasant to do is readily done 91 *largeness* i.e. in large (in opposition to *in little*); *thinks* i.e. one thinks; *sawn* seen 93 *phoenix down* i.e. incipient beard signalling the inevitable birth of man from boy (?) 94 *termless* i.e. young 95 *out-bragged* out-braved 96 *by that cost* i.e. by that expense, for that very reason 97 *nice affections* fastidious taste 100 *maiden-tongued* modest-spoken; *free* innocent 104 *His rudeness so* his turbulent behavior then; *authorized* privileged 105 *livery falseness* i.e. cloak or conceal indecorousness; *truth* decorum 110 *takes* takes up, becomes involved in 111 *by . . . deed* i.e. was exalted because of him 112 *his . . . steed* i.e. excelled in horsemanship because of the skill of the steed

113 'But quickly on this side the verdict went :
114 His real habitude gave life and grace
115 To appertainings and to ornament,
116 Accomplished in himself, not in his case.
All aids, themselves made fairer by their place,
118 Came for additions ; yet their purposed trim
119 Pieced not his grace but were all graced by him.

'So on the tip of his subduing tongue
All kinds of arguments and question deep,
122 All replication prompt and reason strong,
123 For his advantage still did wake and sleep.
To make the weeper laugh, the laugher weep,
125 He had the dialect and different skill,
126 Catching all passions in his craft of will ;

127 'That he did in the general bosom reign
128 Of young, of old, and sexes both enchanted
To dwell with him in thoughts, or to remain
130 In personal duty, following where he haunted.
Consents bewitched, ere he desire, have granted,
132 And dialogued for him what he would say,
133 Asked their own wills and made their wills obey.

'Many there were that did his picture get,
135 To serve their eyes, and in it put their mind ;
Like fools that in th' imagination set
The goodly objects which abroad they find
Of lands and mansions, theirs in thought assigned,
139 And laboring in moe pleasures to bestow them
140 Than the true gouty landlord which doth owe them.

'So many have, that never touched his hand,
Sweetly supposed them mistress of his heart.
My woeful self, that did in freedom stand
144 And was my own fee-simple, not in part,
What with his art in youth and youth in art,
Threw my affections in his charmèd power,
Reserved the stalk and gave him all my flower.

148 'Yet did I not, as some my equals did,
149 Demand of him, nor being desirèd yielded.
Finding myself in honor so forbid,
With safest distance I mine honor shielded.
152 Experience for me many bulwarks builded
153 Of proofs new-bleeding, which remained the foil
Of this false jewel, and his amorous spoil.

'But, ah, who ever shunned by precedent
The destined ill she must herself assay ?
157 Or forced examples, 'gainst her own content,
158 To put the by-past perils in her way ?
159 Counsel may stop awhile what will not stay ;
160 For when we rage, advice is often seen
161 By blunting us to make our wits more keen.

162 'Nor gives it satisfaction to our blood
163 That we must curb it upon others' proof,
164 To be forbod the sweets that seems so good
165 For fear of harms that preach in our behoof.
166 O appetite, from judgment stand aloof !
The one a palate hath that needs will taste,
Though Reason weep and cry, "It is thy last."

'For further I could say this man's untrue,          169
And knew the patterns of his foul beguiling ;
Heard where his plants in others' orchards grew ;     171
Saw how deceits were gilded in his smiling ;
Knew vows were ever brokers to defiling ;             173
Thought characters and words merely but art,          174
And bastards of his foul adulterate heart.            175

'And long upon these terms I held my city,            176
Till thus he 'gan besiege me : "Gentle maid,
Have of my suffering youth some feeling pity
And be not of my holy vows afraid.
That's to ye sworn to none was ever said ;            180
For feasts of love I have been called unto,           181
Till now did ne'er invite nor never woo.

'"All my offenses that abroad you see
Are errors of the blood, none of the mind.
Love made them not. With acture they may be,          185
Where neither party is nor true nor kind.
They sought their shame that so their shame did find ;
And so much less of shame in me remains
By how much of me their reproach contains.            189

'"Among the many that mine eyes have seen,
Not one whose flame my heart so much as warmèd,
Or my affection put to th' smallest teen,             192
Or any of my leisures ever charmèd.
Harm have I done to them, but ne'er was harmèd ;
Kept hearts in liveries, but mine own was free        195
And reigned commanding in his monarchy.

'"Look here what tributes wounded fancies sent me
Of pallid pearls and rubies red as blood,
Figuring that they their passions likewise lent me
Of grief and blushes, aptly understood
In bloodless white and the encrimsoned mood –         201
Effects of terror and dear modesty,
Encamped in hearts, but fighting outwardly.

113 *this* i.e. the following   114 *real habitude* i.e. inborn characteristics
115 *appertainings* things associated with him   116 *case* outsides   118 *Came
for additions* came in for advantages ; *yet . . . trim* i.e. always their intended
improvement   119 *Pieced* mended   122 *replication prompt* quick rejoin-
ders   123 *wake and sleep* i.e. flow and ebb   125 *dialect* discourse ; *different*
varying   126 *craft of will* power of persuasion   127 *That* so that   128
*enchanted* charmed, i.e. influenced   130 *haunted* frequented   132 *dialogued . . . say* spoke his part as well as their own   133 *Asked* made demands
upon   135 *put their mind* i.e. used their imaginations   139 *laboring . . .
them* i.e. laboring to extract more pleasure from them   140 *gouty* rheumatic, i.e. old ; *owe* own   144 *my . . . part* i.e. wholly, not partly, at my own
disposal (like land in freehold)   148 *my equals* i.e. those like me, my kind
149 *Demand . . . yielded* i.e. yield to my own desires or his   152 *Experience*
knowledge, awareness ; *bulwarks* i.e. restraints   153 *proofs new-bleeding*
i.e. persons recently victimized ; *foil* i.e. dark ground against which he
shone   157 *forced* gave weight to ; *content* presumed satisfaction   158
*To . . . way* i.e. to raise as obstacles the past perils (of others)   159 *stop
awhile* i.e. only check   160 *rage* i.e. are aroused   161 *By . . . keen* i.e. to
sharpen our wits by opposition (with *blunting us* used in a forced antithesis)   162 *blood* passion   163 *proof* example   164 *forbod* forbidden   165
*harms . . . behoof* i.e. dangers which give good counsel   166 *stand aloof*
i.e. remain ever unreconciled   169 *say . . . untrue* i.e. tell of this man's
untruth   171 *plants* i.e. adulterate offspring ; *orchards* gardens   173
*brokers* panders   174 *characters and words* i.e. written and spoken words
175 *bastards* i.e. base offspring   176 *city* i.e. citadel of chastity   180
*That's* what's   181 *called unto* invited, solicited   185 *acture* i.e. mechanical action   189 *By . . . contains* i.e. the more they reproach me   192
*teen* stress   195 *liveries* garments of service   201 *mood* mode

204 ' "And, lo, behold these talents of their hair,
205 With twisted metal amorously empleached,
206 I have received from many a several fair,
Their kind acceptance weepingly beseeched,
208 With the annexions of fair gems enriched,
209 And deep-brained sonnets that did amplify
Each stone's dear nature, worth, and quality.

' "The diamond – why, 'twas beautiful and hard,
212 Whereto his invised properties did tend ;
213 The deep-green em'rald, in whose fresh regard
214 Weak sights their sickly radiance do amend ;
215 The heaven-hued sapphire, and the opal blend
With objects manifold : each several stone,
217 With wit well blazoned, smiled or made some moan.

218 ' "Lo, all these trophies of affections hot,
219 Of pensived and subdued desires the tender,
Nature hath charged me that I hoard them not,
But yield them up where I myself must render :
222 That is, to you, my origin and ender ;
For these of force must your oblations be,
224 Since I their altar, you enpatron me.

225 ' "O, then, advance of yours that phraseless hand
Whose white weighs down the airy scale of praise !
227 Take all these similes to your own command,
Hallowed with sighs that burning lungs did raise.
229 What me, your minister, for you obeys,
230 Works under you ; and to your audit comes
231 Their distract parcels in combinèd sums.

' "Lo, this device was sent me from a nun,
Or sister sanctified, of holiest note,
Which late her noble suit in court did shun, 234
Whose rarest havings made the blossoms dote ; 235
For she was sought by spirits of richest coat, 236
But kept cold distance, and did thence remove
To spend her living in eternal love. 238

' "But, O my sweet, what labor is't to leave 239
The thing we have not, mast'ring what not strives,
Paling the place which did no form receive, 241
Playing patient sports in unconstrainèd gyves ? 242
She that her fame so to herself contrives, 243
The scars of battle 'scapeth by the flight 244
And makes her absence valiant, not her might. 245

' "O, pardon me, in that my boast is true :
The accident which brought me to her eye
Upon the moment did her force subdue,
And now she would the cagèd cloister fly.
Religious love put out religion's eye. 250
Not to be tempted, would she be inured, 251
And now, to tempt all, liberty procured. 252

' "How mighty then you are, O hear me tell :
The broken bosoms that to me belong 254
Have emptied all their fountains in my well,
And mine I pour your ocean all among.
I strong o'er them, and you o'er me being strong, 257
Must for your victory us all congest, 258
As compound love to physic your cold breast. 259

' "My parts had pow'r to charm a sacred nun,
Who, disciplined, ay, dieted in grace,
Believed her eyes when they t' assail begun, 262
All vows and consecrations giving place.
O most potential love ! vow, bond, nor space 264
In thee hath neither stint, knot, nor confine, 265
For thou art all, and all things else are thine.

' "When thou impressest, what are precepts worth 267
Of stale example ? When thou wilt inflame,
How coldly those impediments stand forth 269
Of wealth, of filial fear, law, kindred, fame !
Love's arms are peace, 'gainst rule, 'gainst sense, 271
['gainst shame ;
And sweetens, in the suff'ring pangs it bears, .
The aloes of all forces, shocks, and fears. 273

' "Now all these hearts that do on mine depend,
Feeling it break, with bleeding groans they pine ;
And supplicant their sighs to you extend, 276
To leave the batt'ry that you make 'gainst mine,
Lending soft audience to my sweet design,
And credent soul to that strong-bonded oath 279
That shall prefer and undertake my troth." 280

'This said, his wat'ry eyes he did dismount, 281
Whose sights till then were levelled on my face ;
Each cheek a river running from a fount
With brinish current downward flowed apace.
O, how the channel to the stream gave grace !
Who glazed with crystal gate the glowing roses 286
That flame through water which their hue encloses.

204 *talents* i.e. golden riches  205 *empleached* entwined  206 *many* . . . *fair* many different fair ones  208 *annexions* additions (to the gold settings of the locks of hair)  209 *deep-brained* learned ; *amplify* expatiate upon  212 *his invised* i.e. seen within it (?)  213 *regard* aspect  214 *radiance* power of vision  215–16 *blend* . . . *manifold* with the blended colors of many objects (?)  217 *blazoned* proclaimed (in the accompanying sonnets)  218 *affections* passions  219 *pensived* saddened ; *tender* offering  222 *my* . . . *ender* i.e. beginning and end, my all  224 *Since* . . . *enpatron me* i.e. since you are the patron or founder of me (the altar at which they are offered)  225 *phraseless* indescribable  227 *similes* love-tokens and accompanying sonnets  229 *What* . . . *obeys* i.e. whatever pays homage to me as minister to you  230 *audit* accounting  231 *distract* separate  234 *suit* attendance  235 *havings* personal gifts ; *blossoms* i.e. flower of the nobility  236 *coat* i.e. heraldry, descent  238 *eternal love* i.e. love of the divine  239 *leave* i.e. renounce (ironic comment upon nun retreating from love which she did not feel)  241 *Paling* . . . *receive* i.e. fencing an undefined area  242 *Playing* . . . *gyves* i.e. pretending patiently to endure bonds which do not exist  243 *her* . . . *contrives* i.e. creates for herself the reputation for renouncing love  244 *scars* . . . *flight* i.e. avoids the wounds of a true encounter  245 *her absence* i.e. fictitious reputation because of absence ; *might* true power (to resist love)  250 *Religious* . . . *eye* i.e. worshipful love (of the speaker) cancelled her love of the divine  251 *inured* steeled  252 *tempt* venture  254 *bosoms* i.e. hearts  257 *strong* victorious  258 *congest* gather together  259 *physic* . . . *breast* i.e. cure the existing 'congestion'  262 *Believed* . . . *begun* i.e. put her faith in her eyes when assailed by what they saw  264 *space* i.e. place (of confinement)  265 *knot* binding force  267 *impressest* conscript  269 *stand forth* appear  271 *are peace* effect victory  273 *aloes* i.e. bitters  276 *supplicant* i.e. as supplicant  279 *credent* believing, trusting  280 *prefer* advance ; *undertake* support  281 *dismount* lower  286 *Who* which

'O father, what a hell of witchcraft lies
In the small orb of one particular tear!
But with the inundation of the eyes
What rocky heart to water will not wear!
What breast so cold that is not warmèd here,
293 O cleft effect! cold modesty, hot wrath,
294 Both fire from hence and chill extincture hath.

'For, lo, his passion, but an art of craft,
296 Even there resolved my reason into tears;
297 There my white stole of chastity I daffed,
Shook off my sober guards and civil fears;
299 Appear to him as he to me appears,
300 All melting; though our drops this diff'rence bore:
His poisoned me, and mine did him restore.

'In him a plenitude of subtle matter,
303 Applied to cautels, all strange forms receives,
Of burning blushes, or of weeping water,
305 Or sounding paleness; and he takes and leaves,
306 In either's aptness, as it best deceives,
To blush at speeches rank, to weep at woes,
308 Or to turn white and sound at tragic shows;

'That not a heart which in his level came                    309
Could 'scape the hail of his all-hurting aim,               310
Showing fair nature is both kind and tame;                  311
And, veiled in them, did win whom he would maim.            312
Against the thing he sought he would exclaim:
When he most burned in heart-wished luxury,                 314
He preached pure maid and praised cold chastity.

'Thus merely with the garment of a Grace
The naked and concealèd fiend he covered;
That th' unexperient gave the tempter place,                318
Which, like a cherubin, above them hovered;                 319
Who, young and simple, would not be so lovered?
Ay me! I fell, and yet do question make
What I should do again for such a sake.

'O, that infected moisture of his eye,                       323
O, that false fire which in his cheek so glowed,
O, that forced thunder from his heart did fly,
O, that sad breath his spongy lungs bestowed,               326
O, all that borrowed motion seeming owed,                   327
Would yet again betray the fore-betrayed
And new pervert a reconcilèd maid!'                          329

FINIS

# THE PASSIONATE PILGRIM

### IV

1 Sweet Cytherea, sitting by a brook
2 With young Adonis, lovely, fresh, and green,
3 Did court the lad with many a lovely look,
Such looks as none could look but beauty's queen.
She told him stories to delight his ear;
6 She showed him favors to allure his eye;
To win his heart she touched him here and there—
Touches so soft still conquer chastity.
9 But whether unripe years did want conceit,
10 Or he refused to take her figured proffer,
The tender nibbler would not touch the bait,
But smile and jest at every gentle offer.
13　　Then fell she on her back, fair queen, and toward.
14　　He rose and ran away. Ah, fool too froward!

### VI

Scarce had the sun dried up the dewy morn,
And scarce the herd gone to the hedge for shade,
When Cytherea, all in love forlorn,
4 A longing tarriance for Adonis made
5 Under an osier growing by a brook,
6 A brook where Adon used to cool his spleen.
Hot was the day; she hotter that did look
For his approach that often there had been.
9 Anon he comes, and throws his mantle by,
And stood stark naked on the brook's green brim.
The sun looked on the world with glorious eye,
12 Yet not so wistly as this queen on him.
13　　He, spying her, bounced in whereas he stood.
　　'O Jove,' quoth she, 'why was not I a flood!'

### VII

Fair is my love, but not so fair as fickle;
Mild as a dove, but neither true nor trusty;

Brighter than glass, and yet as glass is, brittle;
Softer than wax, and yet as iron rusty:
　A lily pale, with damask dye, to grace her;                 5
　None fairer, nor none falser, to deface her.                6

Her lips to mine how often hath she joinèd,
Between each kiss her oaths of true love swearing!
How many tales to please me hath she coinèd,                 9
Dreading my love, the loss whereof still fearing!
　Yet, in the midst of all her pure protestings,
　Her faith, her oaths, her tears, and all were jestings.

She burnt with love, as straw with fire flameth;
She burnt out love, as soon as straw outburneth;
She framed the love, and yet she foiled the framing;        15
She bade love last, and yet she fell a-turning.             16
　Was this a lover, or a lecher whether?                      17
　Bad in the best, though excellent in neither.

293 *cleft* divided, double　294 *extincture* extinguishing　296 *resolved* dissolved　297 *daffed* doffed　299 *Appear* I appear　300 *drops* medicinal drops　303 *cautels* trickeries, deceits　305 *sounding* swooning; *takes and leaves* i.e. alternately employs　306 *In . . . aptness* i.e. each thing's immediate usefulness　308 *sound* swoon　309 *level* i.e. sights　310 *hail* i.e. bullets　311 *Showing . . . is* i.e. appearing to be in his nature　312 *them* i.e. kindness and tameness　314 *luxury* lechery　318 *th' unexperient . . . place* i.e. the inexperienced admitted the tempter　319 *Which . . . cherubin* i.e. who, like an angel　323 *infected* infectious　326 *spongy* i.e. diseased　327 *borrowed . . . owed* i.e. assumed behavior seemingly his own　329 *reconcilèd* penitent

IV　1 *Cytherea* Venus　2 *green* i.e. new-grown　3 *lovely* loving　6 *favors* charms, gracious appearances　9 *conceit* understanding　10 *figured* signalled　13 *toward* tractable, willing　14 *froward* recalcitrant

VI　4 *tarriance* period of waiting　5 *osier* willow　6 *spleen* heat　9 *Anon* presently　12 *wistly* eagerly　13 *whereas* whereat

VII　5 *damask* mingled red and white (of the damask rose); *to . . . her* i.e. to her credit　6 *to deface her* i.e. to her discredit　9 *coinèd* counterfeited　15 *framed* formed, created; *foiled* countered　16 *fell a-turning* i.e. proved fickle　17 *whether* i.e. which of the two

### VIII

If music and sweet poetry agree,
As they must needs (the sister and the brother),
Then must the love be great 'twixt thee and me,
Because thou lov'st the one, and I the other.
5 Dowland to thee is dear, whose heavenly touch
Upon the lute doth ravish human sense;
7 Spenser to me, whose deep conceit is such
8 As, passing all conceit, needs no defense.
Thou lov'st to hear the sweet melodious sound
10 That Phoebus' lute (the queen of music) makes;
And I in deep delight am chiefly drowned
When as himself to singing he betakes.
13     One god is god of both, as poets feign;
14     One knight loves both, and both in thee remain.

### IX

Fair was the morn when the fair queen of love,
2 *   *   *   *   *   *   *
Paler for sorrow than her milk-white dove,
For Adon's sake, a youngster proud and wild,
5 Her stand she takes upon a steep-up hill.
Anon Adonis comes with horn and hounds.
She, silly queen, with more than love's good will,
Forbade the boy he should not pass those grounds.
'Once,' quoth she, 'did I see a fair sweet youth
Here in these brakes deep-wounded with a boar,
11 Deep in the thigh, a spectacle of ruth!
See, in my thigh,' quoth she, 'here was the sore.'
    She showèd hers; he saw more wounds than one,
    And blushing fled and left her all alone.

### X

1 Sweet rose, fair flower, untimely plucked, soon vaded,
Plucked in the bud, and vaded in the spring!
3 Bright orient pearl, alack, too timely shaded!
Fair creature, killed too soon by death's sharp sting!
    Like a green plum that hangs upon a tree,
    And falls, through wind, before the fall should be.

I weep for thee, and yet no cause I have;
8 For why, thou left'st me nothing in thy will:
And yet thou left'st me more than I did crave;
For why, I cravèd nothing of thee still.
    O yes, dear friend, I pardon crave of thee:
    Thy discontent thou didst bequeath to me.

### XI

Venus, with young Adonis sitting by her
Under a myrtle shade, began to woo him.
3 She told the youngling how god Mars did try her,
4 And as he fell to her, she fell to him.
'Even thus,' quoth she, 'the warlike god embraced me,'
And then she clipped Adonis in her arms.
7 'Even thus,' quoth she, 'the warlike god unlaced me,'
As if the boy should use like loving charms.
'Even thus,' quoth she, 'he seizèd on my lips,'
And with her lips on his did act the seizure;
And as she fetchèd breath, away he skips,
12 And would not take her meaning nor her pleasure.
13     Ah, that I had my lady at this bay,
14     To kiss and clip me till I run away!

### XII

Crabbed age and youth cannot live together:
2 Youth is full of pleasance, age is full of care;
Youth like summer morn, age like winter weather;
Youth like summer brave, age like winter bare.
Youth is full of sport, age's breath is short;
Youth is nimble, age is lame;
Youth is hot and bold, age is weak and cold;
Youth is wild, and age is tame.
Age, I do abhor thee; youth, I do adore thee.
O, my love, my love is young!
11 Age, I do defy thee. O sweet shepherd, hie thee,
12 For methinks thou stays too long.

### XIII

Beauty is but a vain and doubtful good;
2 A shining gloss that vadeth suddenly;
A flower that dies when first it 'gins to bud;
4 A brittle glass that's broken presently;
    A doubtful good, a gloss, a glass, a flower,
    Lost, vaded, broken, dead within an hour.

And as goods lost are seld or never found,
7 As vaded gloss no rubbing will refresh,
As flowers dead lie with'red on the ground,
As broken glass no cement can redress:
10     So beauty blemished once, for ever lost,
    In spite of physic, painting, pain, and cost.
12

VIII   5 *Dowland* John Dowland, lutenist and composer   7 *Spenser* Edmund Spenser, author of *The Faerie Queene*; *deep conceit* resourceful creativeness   8 *passing all conceit* surpassing all imagination   10 *Phoebus* Apollo, musician of the gods   13 *feign* i.e. say in their creations   14 *One knight* (conjectured to be Sir George Carey, to whom was dedicated Dowland's first book of airs, 1597, and to whose wife was dedicated Spenser's *Muiopotmos*, 1590)
IX   2 (the line rhyming with *wild* is missing)   5 *steep-up* sharply rising   11 *ruth* pity
X   1 *vaded* faded   3 *timely* soon   8 *For why* because
XI   3 *try* attempt   4 *he . . . her* i.e. he fell to her lot (with ribald pun on second *fell*   7 *unlaced* i.e. undressed   12 *pleasure* proffered gratification   13 *bay* stand   14 *clip* embrace
XII   2 *pleasance* cheer   11 *hie thee* hasten   12 *stays* delayest
XIII   2 *vadeth* fades   4 *presently* at once   7 *seld* seldom   10 *redress* repair   12 *physic* medicine; *cost* expenditures
XIV   3 *daffed* doffed, sent off; *hanged* furnished   4 *descant* enlarge, expatiate; *doubts* fears   8 *nill . . . whether* I know not which   12 *pelf* reward, booty

### XIV

Good night, good rest. Ah, neither be my share!
She bade good night that kept my rest away,
And daffed me to a cabin hanged with care
3
To descant on the doubts of my decay.
4
    'Farewell,' quoth she, 'and come again to-morrow.'
    Fare well I could not, for I supped with sorrow.

Yet at my parting sweetly did she smile,
In scorn or friendship, nill I conster whether.
8
'T may be she joyed to jest at my exile;
'T may be, again to make me wander thither:
    'Wander'—a word for shadows like myself
    As take the pain but cannot pluck the pelf.
12

Lord, how mine eyes throw gazes to the east!
14 My heart doth charge the watch; the morning rise
15 Doth cite each moving sense from idle rest,
Not daring trust the office of mine eyes,
17    While Philomela sits and sings, I sit and mark,
18    And wish her lays were tunèd like the lark;

For she doth welcome daylight with her ditty
And drives away dark dreaming night.
21 The night so packed, I post unto my pretty;
Heart hath his hope, and eyes their wishèd sight;
Sorrow changed to solace and solace mixed with sorrow;
For why, she sighed and bade me come to-morrow.

25 Were I with her, the night would post too soon,
26 But now are minutes added to the hours;
27 To spite me now, each minute seems a moon;
Yet not for me, shine sun to succor flowers!
Pack night, peep day! Good day, of night now borrow:
30    Short, night, to-night, and length thyself to-morrow.

### XV

1 It was a lording's daughter, the fairest one of three,
2 That likèd of her master as well as well might be,
Till looking on an Englishman, the fair'st that eye could see,
Her fancy fell a-turning.
Long was the combat doubtful that love with love did fight,
To leave the master loveless, or kill the gallant knight:
7 To put in practice either, alas, it was a spite
Unto the silly damsel!
9 But one must be refusèd; more mickle was the pain
That nothing could be usèd to turn them both to gain,
For of the two the trusty knight was wounded with disdain:
Alas, she could not help it!
13 Thus art with arms contending was victor of the day,
Which by a gift of learning did bear the maid away:
15 Then, lullaby, the learned man hath got the lady gay;
For now my song is ended.

### XVII

My flocks feed not,
My ewes breed not,
My rams speed not,
    All is amiss:
Love's denying,
6 Faith's defying,
7 Heart's renying,
    Causer of this.
All my merry jigs are quite forgot,
All my lady's love is lost, God wot.
Where her faith was firmly fixed in love,
There a nay is placed without remove.
13 One silly cross
Wrought all my loss.
    O frowning Fortune, cursèd fickle dame!
For now I see
Inconstancy
More in women than in men remain.

In black mourn I,
All fears scorn I,
21 Love hath forlorn me,
    Living in thrall.

Heart is bleeding,
All help needing –
O cruel speeding,                                         25
    Fraughted with gall!                                  26
My shepherd's pipe can sound no deal;                     27
My wether's bell rings doleful knell;
My curtail dog, that wont to have played,                 29
Plays not at all, but seems afraid;
With sighs so deep
Procures to weep,
    In howling wise, to see my doleful plight.
How sighs resound
Through heartless ground,                                 35
    Like a thousand vanquished men in bloody fight!

Clear wells spring not,
Sweet birds sing not,
Green plants bring not
Forth their dye.
Herds stand weeping,
Flocks all sleeping,
Nymphs back peeping
    Fearfully.
All our pleasure known to us poor swains,
All our merry meetings on the plains,
All our evening sport from us is fled,
All our love is lost, for love is dead.
Farewell, sweet lass!
Thy like ne'er was
    For a sweet content, the cause of all my moan.
Poor Corydon
Must live alone.
    Other help for him I see that there is none.

### XVIII

When as thine eye hath chose the dame
And stalled the deer that thou shouldst strike,       2
Let reason rule things worthy blame,
As well as fancy (partial) might;                     4
    Take counsel of some wiser head,
    Neither too young, nor yet unwed.

And when thou com'st thy tale to tell,
Smooth not thy tongue with filèd talk,                8
Lest she some subtile practice smell –                9
A cripple soon can find a halt;                       10
    But plainly say thou lov'st her well,
    And set thy person forth to sell.

14 *charge* i.e. keep watch over   15 *cite* incite   17 *Philomela* the nightingale
18 *tunèd ... lark* i.e. attuned to the morn   21 *packed* disposed of   25 *post*
hasten on   26 *added to* i.e. made to resemble   27 *moon* month   30 *Short
... length* shorten ... lengthen
XV   1 *lording's* lord's   2 *master* teacher, tutor   7 *put in practice* i.e. act
upon, come to a decision about   9 *mickle* great   13 *art* learning   15
*lullaby* good night
XVII   6 *defying* rejection   7 *renying* forswearing, disowning   13 *cross*
misfortune   21 *forlorn me* rendered me forlorn   25 *speeding* progress,
journey   26 *Fraughted* laden   27 *no deal* not at all   29 *curtail* dock-tailed
35 *heartless* desolate (?), pitiless (?)
XVIII   2 *stalled* brought to a stand   4 *fancy (partial) might* (so punctuated
the words suggest that 'partial' affection should share rule with impartial
reason; but the passage remains obscure)   8 *filèd* polished   9 *practice*
plot   10 *A cripple ... halt* (proverb resembling 'Set a thief to catch a
thief'); *halt* limp

What though her frowning brows be bent,
Her cloudy looks will calm ere night;
And then too late she will repent
That thus dissembled her delight,
   And twice desire, ere it be day,
   That which with scorn she put away.

20 What though she strive to try her strength,
And ban and brawl and say thee nay,
Her feeble force will yield at length,
When craft hath taught her thus to say:
   'Had women been so strong as men,
   In faith, you had not had it then.'

And to her will frame all thy ways.
Spare not to spend, and chiefly there
Where thy desert may merit praise
By ringing in thy lady's ear.
   The strongest castle, tower, and town,
   The golden bullet beats it down.

Serve always with assurèd trust
And in thy suit be humble-true.
33 Unless thy lady prove unjust,
Press never thou to choose a new.
   When time shall serve, be thou not slack
   To proffer, though she put thee back.

The wiles and guiles that women work,
Dissembled with an outward show,
The tricks and toys that in them lurk,
The cock that treads them shall not know.
   Have you not heard it said full oft,
   A woman's nay doth stand for naught?

43 Think women still to strive with men
44 To sin, and never for to saint.
45 There is no heaven: be holy then
When time with age shall them attaint.
   Were kisses all the joys in bed,
   One woman would another wed.

But soft, enough! too much, I fear;
Lest that my mistress hear my song.
51 She will not stick to round me on th' ear,
To teach my tongue to be so long.
   Yet will she blush, here be it said,
54    To hear her secrets so bewrayed.

XX

As it fell upon a day
In the merry month of May,
Sitting in a pleasant shade
Which a grove of myrtles made,
Beasts did leap and birds did sing,
Trees did grow and plants did spring;
Everything did banish moan,
Save the nightingale alone.
She, poor bird, as all forlorn,
Leaned her breast up-till a thorn   *10*
And there sung the dolefull'st ditty,
That to hear it was great pity.
'Fie, fie, fie!' now would she cry;
'Tereu, tereu!' by and by;
That to hear her so complain
Scarce I could from tears refrain;
For her griefs, so lively shown,
Made me think upon mine own.
'Ah,' thought I, 'thou mourn'st in vain;
None takes pity on thy pain.
Senseless trees they cannot hear thee;
Ruthless beasts they will not cheer thee.
King Pandion, he is dead;   *23*
All thy friends are lapped in lead;
All thy fellow birds do sing,
Careless of thy sorrowing.
[Even so, poor bird, like thee,
None alive will pity me.]
Whilst as fickle Fortune smiled,
Thou and I were both beguiled.'
Every one that flatters thee
Is no friend in misery.
Words are easy, like the wind;
Faithful friends are hard to find.
Every man will be thy friend
Whilst thou hast wherewith to spend;
But if store of crowns be scant,
No man will supply thy want.
If that one be prodigal,
Bountiful they will him call,
And with such-like flattering,
'Pity but he were a king.'   *42*
If he be addict to vice,
Quickly him they will entice.
If to women he be bent,
They have at commandement.
But if fortune once do frown,
Then farewell his great renown!
They that fawned on him before
Use his company no more.
He that is thy friend indeed,
He will help thee in thy need.
If thou sorrow, he will weep;
If thou wake, he cannot sleep.
Thus of every grief in heart
He with thee doth bear a part.
These are certain signs to know
Faithful friend from flatt'ring foe.

20 *ban* curse  33 *unjust* untrue, faithless  43 *Think* believe  44 *to saint* i.e. to be saintly  45 *There* i.e. in women  51 *stick . . . ear* i.e. hesitate to scold  54 *bewrayed* revealed
XX  23 *Pandion* a king of Athens, father of the ravished Philomela, who was transformed into the nightingale; cf. Ovid, *Metamorphoses*, VI, 424–676
42 *but he* that he was not

443

# SHAKESPEARE'S SONNETS

## INTRODUCTION

Shakespeare's sonnets are an island of poetry surrounded by a barrier of icebergs and dense fog; or, in the metaphor of Sir Walter Raleigh (the modern Oxford scholar, not the poet's contemporary), they have been used like wedding cake, not to eat but to dream upon. In more prosaic terms, the sonnets, as poems, have been obscured by the huge mass of speculation, much of it uncritical or crackpot, that has grown up around the "problems" presented by the dedication and the "story" adumbrated in the text. These few pages will be concerned largely with the character of the poetry, but enough must be said to justify dismissal of the speculations as immaterial and irrelevant.

The chief external facts are these: in 1598 Francis Meres, in a roll-call of contemporary authors in his *Palladis Tamia*, mentioned a number of Shakespeare's earlier plays and also "his sugred Sonnets among his private friends"; in 1599 the piratical William Jaggard printed two of the sonnets (138 and 144) in *The Passionate Pilgrim*; and in 1609 the publisher Thomas Thorpe issued 154 sonnets entitled *Shake-speares Sonnets: Never before Imprinted*, with a dedication signed "T.T." and addressed "To the onlie begetter of these insuing sonnets Mr. W. H. . . ." Although in this period an attractive name on a title page was not a guarantee of authenticity, we have no grounds for doubting that sonnets 1–152 are Shakespeare's (the apparently alien and unrelated 153 and 154 may be a spurious appendage). But we know nothing about some other important matters.

By 1609 – when Shakespeare was near the end of his dramatic career – the main vogue of sonneteering had long passed. Sir Philip Sidney's *Astrophel and Stella* (published posthumously in 1591) had inaugurated the fashion of sonnet sequences among the Elizabethan poets, Daniel, Lodge, Drayton, Spenser, and others. None of Shakespeare's sonnets can be, or at any rate has been, dated. There has been quite unconvincing argument that all or most of them were written in or by 1589. More persuasive arguments – parallels in idea and diction (some of them rare items in the poet's vocabulary) with the narrative poems and plays – would spread the sonnets over 1593–1609 but would assign the large majority to 1593–1596.

In this period books were often published without the author's knowledge or consent, since manuscript copies circulated and multiplied and one might readily fall into a publisher's hands. Evidently the publication of the sonnets was not authorized by Shakespeare but was managed by Thomas Thorpe; and he may have followed a manuscript of the whole sequence or assembled it piecemeal from fragmentary copies. Some modern scholars have rearranged the sonnets, on either mechanical or subjective principles; these rearrangements have seldom pleased anyone except the contriver. The 1609 arrangement is unsatisfactory and strongly suspect but is the only authority we have.

General opinion divides the sonnets into two main groups, though these do not form consecutive or coherent wholes. The first comprises 1–126, which may be addressed to one young man, the poet's much loved and admired friend, his junior in years and superior in social station. Obviously the first seventeen poems – commonly if rather quaintly known as "the procreation sonnets" – are appeals to a young man to marry and circumvent mortality by perpetuating his beauty and virtue in children. This plea is perhaps not in complete harmony with sonnets 18–126, in which the poet further celebrates the young man (if it is the same one, and if the subject is always a man) and his own complete love, with more or less related themes. In sonnets 127–52, the second group, he makes a radical switch to tell of his mingled passion and loathing for a dark woman (most Elizabethan heroines were golden blondes), a forsworn wife – if one woman only is involved – who, having already had the poet as a lover, has beguiled the young man into an affair, so that the poet has encountered a double disloyalty. This brief outline passes by a number of apparent discrepancies: for example, sonnets 40–42, which reproach the young man (forgivingly, to be sure) for his as yet unexplained liaison, are followed by sonnets which carry on the earlier vein of whole-hearted eulogy, as if nothing had happened. (We do not of course know the order in which the sonnets were written – or whether we have them all.) Another element in the dramatic situation is that in sonnets 79–86 the poet is displaced in the young friend's favor by a rival poet. In general, whether the cause is fidelity to real or imagined fact or dramatic art or accidental arrangement, the sonnets have the air of being day-to-day reflections, as if the poet were living in the moment, not looking back over a closed chapter, and knowing no more than the reader of what is to come.

In contrast with the relative conventionality of the other Elizabethan sequences, this dramatic "plot" – the poet, his young friend, the rival poet, and "the dark lady" – has seemed to many critics to carry special marks of actuality, and there has been much throwing about of brains (the phrase is something of a euphemism) in the effort to identify the *dramatis personae* as figures in Shakespeare's world. One source of misguided guesswork, based on a misreading of Thorpe's dedication, was the attempt to identify Mr W. H. with the poet's friend. The leading candidates for this role were Henry Wriothesley, Earl of Southampton, to whom Shakespeare dedicated *Venus and Adonis* and *Lucrece* in 1593 and 1594, and William Herbert, third Earl of Pembroke. It is now considered probable that in his dedication Thorpe was speaking, not about the contents and "story" of the sonnets, but about the manner of their procurement; that he was – with a touch of mystification calculated to excite interest in the volume – thanking a friend, Mr W. H., for having got hold of the material. However, while the dedication drops out of the case, the two young noblemen remain candidates, Herbert apparently the favorite. But the one fact is that we know nothing, and the wise reader will ignore the whole business. The same agnostic answer must be given in regard to the dark lady and her supposed originals and to the rival poet, who has been identified with a variety of Elizabethan writers. So much for "monsters and things indigest."

But agnosticism needs to go further. We do not know if the several characters (the poet included) and their relations with one another had some basis in fact or were entirely imaginary. To say that these poems, as distinguished from most other Elizabethan sequences, have a special note of actuality and intensity is only to say that Shakespeare was a greater poet – and no one would suggest that the actuality and intensity of his major plays came from personal experience of the situations and emotions there set forth. Apart from the particular and non-poetical puzzles touched on above, there have been two main approaches to the sonnets: they have been seen as only another, and superior, literary exercise in a conventional mode, and, from the opposite pole, as an intimately confessional and profound self-revelation. To cite two names no editor can overlook, Wordsworth, writing of the sonnet form, declared "With this key Shakespeare unlocked his heart"; "If so," affirmed Browning, "the less Shakespeare he." It is best to recognize that, for poets and their readers alike, the difference between actual and imaginative experience is indefinable and meaningless, and also that Shakespeare's sonnets are, like all great poetry, at once exercises in literary form and – in a broad general sense – self-revelation. They are, to be sure, very uneven, and many are far from great.

The Italian sonnet had been inaugurated in English poetry by Sir Thomas Wyatt, whose poems, with the Earl of Surrey's, were printed in *Tottel's Miscellany* (1557). But whereas the normal Italian sonnet had two divisions, an octave and a sestet, Wyatt introduced, and Surrey developed, what is called the English or Shakespearean form (*abab cdcd efef gg*), the one used, with variations, by the Elizabethan poets generally. This form, with its three quatrains and a concluding couplet (a pattern more congenial to English because of its fuller range of rhymes), fostered a manipulation of idea and imagery different from that of the Italian. In Shakespeare's sonnets the argument normally proceeds by quatrains, each one constituting a definite step, and the summarizing couplet acquires an epigrammatic or aphoristic quality (which can be weak). Thus in the famous "When, in disgrace with Fortune and men's eyes" (29), the poet in the first quatrain bewails his own lot; in the second, contrasts that lot with other men's; in the third, thinking of his beloved friend, he rises like the lark that "sings hymns at heaven's gate"; and in the couplet his felicity is generalized in a final contrast. The same formal and logical division and progression are not quite lost even in the most explosively emotional utterances, such as "What potions have I drunk of Siren tears" (119), "Th' expense of spirit in a waste of shame" (129), or "Poor soul, the center of my sinful

earth" (146). If to the reader of more freewheeling modern poetry such logical formalism suggests artifice and insincerity, he forgets the rigorous training in rhetoric, given to every Elizabethan schoolboy, which made such processes of thought and feeling instinctive. The same schoolroom training, the handbooks of rhetoric, and mature poetic practise ensured the systematic knowledge and use of all kinds of verbal figures, patterns of both phrase and sound. Renaissance poets (and their readers) preferred, to borrow Robert Frost's phrase, to play tennis with a net.

Shakespeare, even more than most Elizabethan writers, thinks and feels in images, and his imagery is no less notable for control than for fecundity. The material of his images, like that of his plays and Elizabethan poetry in general, is drawn chiefly from nature and everyday life, from business and law and the fine arts. A sonnet may work out a single metaphor (from business in 4, the seasons in 5, the sun in 7, music in 8), or, sometimes, may use a separate metaphor in each quatrain (as in 73 decay is treated in terms of summer and winter, day and night, fire and ashes), or (as in 1 and 19) may employ a new image in almost every line. A number of sonnets elaborate one metaphor – such as the art of the painter in 24 – with the most finespun ingenuity. This control of images, like that of the divisions of progressive argument with which it is bound up, is seldom relaxed or disrupted even in what appear to be the most deeply disturbed utterances. We are not surprised when, say, the serene exaltation of "Shall I compare thee to a summer's day?" (18) receives logical development; but 147, a violent revulsion from sensual love for the dark lady, is a no less ordered exposition of a ravaging fever incurable by reason.

The structure and texture of the sonnets combine a disciplined, orthodox formalism with the passionate ratiocination that we associate with the "metaphysical" poets – a strain that was emerging in the early 1590's, notably in Donne and Chapman. On the one hand, Shakespeare's style and rhythm, "the proud full sail of his great verse" (to quote his phrase about the rival poet), are mainly in the grand manner and have a smooth Italianate amplitude and flow, the rhetorical rotundity that we find in the earlier plays. One element in that effect is the abundant but discriminating use of alliteration and assonance – "the sessions of sweet silent thought" and "the surly sullen bell," to cite two simple examples. On the other hand, Shakespeare's diction (often monosyllabic) and images can be colloquial and homely, even when his argumentative conceits are most intricate – and to say that is to recall Coleridge's comment on Donne's and other old poets' expressing fantastic ideas in pure English. But, though active cerebration is always going on (and, like Donne's, does not always make poetry), the results are seldom intellectualized through recondite allusion; annotation of the sonnets requires the explaining, not of erudition, but of obsolete words and idioms or complex density of thought. And, while Donne's forceful language does its work in its local context but carries little or no aura of suggestion, Shakespeare's sets up rich reverberations – as lines quoted in these pages remind us.

The characters and situations of Shakespeare's sonnets, in diverging widely from the restricted Petrarchan tradition, freed him from many stereotyped themes, attitudes, and images (sonnet 130 satirizes the conventional catalogue of feminine beauties). That is not to say that those themes and attitudes – of which the most central was of course the persuasive adoration of a reluctant or disdainful mistress – did not evoke many fine sonnets from other Elizabethan poets. Moreover, Shakespeare's young man, like a Petrarchan mistress, is more loved than loving, and ten dozen sonnets in praise of him and friendship can, with all their fertile and graceful invention, fall at times into a semi-Petrarchan monotony. Since modern readers are unused to such ardor in masculine friendship and are likely to leap at the notion of homosexuality (a notion sufficiently refuted by the sonnets themselves), we may remember that such an ideal – often exalted above the love of women – could exist in real life, from Montaigne to Sir Thomas Browne, and was conspicuous in Renaissance literature (*Euphues*, Sidney's *Arcadia*, the fourth book of *The Faerie Queene*, some of Shakespeare's plays), whether on the merely human level or linked with cosmic concord. The poet's young friend, though alive, familiarly known, and sometimes charged with vices, becomes a kind of equivalent of Donne's Elizabeth Drury, a symbol of living perfection. It may be further remarked that one often could not say, and does not need to ask, whether an individual sonnet is concerned with love for a man or a woman; one supreme example is "Let me not to the marriage of true minds / Admit impediments" (116).

Indeed the "story" has value only in the poet's distillation of universal emotions and values. (The few indecent sonnets, by the way, may be regretted, not because obscenity cannot be functional, as it often is in the plays, but because here the tone is brittle and jarring.) Most of the great sonnets are at once self-sufficient units and notes in a complex symphony. While the eternizing power of poetry is an especially Renaissance theme, the modern reader, even if he does not recall the proud claims of Ovid and Horace, must be stirred by the forward-looking

> Not marble nor the gilded monuments
> Of princes shall outlive this pow'rful rime,

or by the backward-looking

> When in the chronicle of wasted time
> I see descriptions of the fairest wights,
> And beauty making beautiful old rime
> In praise of ladies dead and lovely knights....

But such passages are more than themselves; they are partial expressions of the pervasive, all-embracing theme of "Devouring Time" – a theme which inspired much of the greatest poetry and prose of the English Renaissance. Even writers, from Spenser and Raleigh to Browne and Taylor, whose most earnest vision was fixed on heaven, were poignantly conscious of the much-loved earth and time and mutability. Shakespeare's voice – heard also through Hamlet in the graveyard and elsewhere – is in the sonnets mainly the outcry of the natural man against the decay and extinction of beauty and vitality and love:

> Since brass, nor stone, nor earth, nor boundless sea,
> But sad mortality o'ersways their power,
> How with this rage shall beauty hold a plea,
> Whose action is no stronger than a flower?

Moments of unclouded happiness are moments only. The objects of love – like the lover – are subject to time, from "the darling buds of May" to "precious friends hid in death's dateless night." The young friend, in his spring-time of life and pleasure, awakens thoughts of the poet's autumnal age, of leafless boughs, "Bare ruined choirs where late the sweet birds sang." Yet perhaps the greatest of all the sonnets is a defiant affirmation, the affirmation of a man who has no Platonic supports but only his human hold on the particular:

> Love's not Time's fool, though rosy lips and cheeks
> Within his bending sickle's compass come.

But the man sustained by love is still, like all human creatures, subject not only to destructive time but to inward evil. The main contrast in the sonnets, C. S. Lewis remarks, "is between the two loves, that 'of comfort' and that 'of despair'" (Sonnet 144). No conception was more deeply rooted in the Renaissance mind than the unceasing conflict in man between the bestial and the angelic elements in his nature; and, of course, the finer the individual nature the more agonizing the conflict. What was said a while ago about the voice of "the natural man" in Shakespeare's sonnets must be qualified. It seems nowadays to be agreed that Shakespeare the dramatist shared the religious beliefs of his fellow citizens, however far his imagination might transcend popular orthodoxy; the appeals in the greater plays to Christian faith and Christian values are too numerous and too significant to be brushed off. If Elizabethan sonnets, like plays, were an essentially secular and naturalistic genre, none the less religion was too much an enveloping fact of life to be kept out. One incidental and unexpected – and, if not quite certain, strongly probable – reference at the end of Shakespeare's 110th sonnet ranks the poet's love for the young man next to the Christian heaven. But there are clearer and more important things.

In *Astrophel and Stella* Sidney had felt acute conflict between the claims of illicit but ennobling love and the claims of Christian virtue, and the last group of Shakespeare's sonnets depict an illicit, intense, and far from ennobling passion for an unworthy woman. If the praises given to her charms are mostly conventional, the savage denunciations of her falsity go well beyond the considerable license permitted to sonneteers. While both attraction and repulsion are commonly painted in naturalistic terms, there are some appeals to the moral and the religious conscience. The most often-quoted testimony is "Th' expense of spirit in a waste of shame" (129), which is at once a naturalistic and rational and impassioned analysis of "lust in action"; and the sensual lover's "heaven" and "hell" are grimly ironic reminders of their religious counterparts. The religious consciousness is present likewise in 142, 144, and above all in 146 ("Poor soul, the center of my sinful earth"), a Shakespearean parallel to that detached sonnet of Sidney's, "Leave me, O love which reachest but to dust"; both combine the despair and the comfort of *contemptus mundi*. These sonnets, few in relation to the rest, still add a major dimension to the world of experience created in the series (as, to recall a very different context, a few lines add a similar dimension to the fleshly Wife of Bath). Shakespeare's world is composed of universal elements, beauty and decay, time and death, permanence and flux, truth and falsehood, and love in all its forms, from lust to "charity"; and the changes are rung on these timeless themes by an artist of supreme sensitivity to feeling and thought and word and rhythm.

*Harvard University*                    DOUGLAS BUSH

## NOTE ON THE TEXT

The only authority for the text of the sonnets other than 138 and 144, versions of which appeared in *The Passionate Pilgrim* (1599), is the quarto volume issued by Thomas Thorpe in 1609. Although this volume contains, in addition to the 154 sonnets, a poem of doubtful authenticity (*A Lover's Complaint*. "By William Shakespeare"), and although it is unlikely that it was printed from a manuscript in the author's own hand and certain that it was not proofread by him, it provides nevertheless a text which seems reliable in the main. A rearrangement of the sonnets pirated from Thorpe's quarto by John Benson in 1640 lacks independent authority. The present edition follows the text of the quarto of 1609 and retains its order of the sonnets. The following list of emendations is complete except for corrections of obvious misprints; the adopted reading is given in italics followed by the quarto reading in roman: 12 : 4 *all* or 13 : 7 *Yourself* You selfe

25 : 9 *fight* worth 26 : 12 *thy* their 27 : 10 *thy* their 28 : 14 *strength* length 31 : 8 *thee* there. 34 : 12 *cross* losse 35 : 8 *thy . . . thy* their . . . their 37 : 7 *thy* their 39 : 12 *doth* dost 41 : 8 *she* he 43 : 11 *thy* their 45 : 12 *thy* their 46 : 3, 8, 13, 14 *thy* their 47 : 11 *not* nor 50 : 6 *dully* duly 51 : 11 *weigh* naigh 55 : 1 *monuments* monument 56 : 13 *Or* As 65 : 12 *of* or 69 : 3 *due* end 69 : 5 *Thy* Their 70 : 1 *art* are 70 : 6 *Thy* Their 74 : 12 *rememberèd* remembred 76 : 7 *tell* fel 77 : 10 *blanks* blacks 99 : 9 *One* Our 102 : 8 *her* his 112 : 14 *are* y'are 113 : 6 *latch* lack 113 : 14 *mine eye* mine 127 : 9 *brows* eyes 128 : 11 *thy* their 129 : 11 *proved, a* proud and 132 : 2 *torments* torment 132 : 6 *of the* of th' 132 : 9 *mourning* morning 144 : 6 *side* sight 146 : 2 *Fooled by* My sinfull earth 153 : 14 *eyes* eye. The spelling and punctuation have been modernized as in the other works in the present edition. The glossarial notes, supplied by the general editor, are greatly indebted to the *New Variorum Edition* by Hyder Rollins (2 vols, 1944), a superb example of modern scholarship.

# SHAKESPEARE'S SONNETS

**1**

From fairest creatures we desire increase,
That thereby beauty's rose might never die,
But as the riper should by time decease,
His tender heir might bear his memory ;
But thou, contracted to thine own bright eyes,
Feed'st thy light's flame with self-substantial fuel,
Making a famine where abundance lies,
Thyself thy foe, to thy sweet self too cruel.
Thou that art now the world's fresh ornament
And only herald to the gaudy spring,
Within thine own bud buriest thy content
And, tender churl, mak'st waste in niggarding.
  Pity the world, or else this glutton be,
  To eat the world's due, by the grave and thee.

**3**

Look in thy glass, and tell the face thou viewest
Now is the time that face should form another,
Whose fresh repair if now thou not renewest,
Thou dost beguile the world, unbless some mother.
For where is she so fair whose uneared womb
Disdains the tillage of thy husbandry ?
Or who is he so fond will be the tomb
Of his self-love, to stop posterity ?
Thou art thy mother's glass, and she in thee
Calls back the lovely April of her prime ;
So thou through windows of thine age shalt see,
Despite of wrinkles, this thy golden time.
  But if thou live rememb'red not to be,
  Die single, and thine image dies with thee.

**2**

When forty winters shall besiege thy brow
And dig deep trenches in thy beauty's field,
Thy youth's proud livery, so gazed on now,
Will be a tottered weed of small worth held :
Then being asked where all thy beauty lies,
Where all the treasure of thy lusty days,
To say within thine own deep-sunken eyes
Were an all-eating shame and thriftless praise.
How much more praise deserved thy beauty's use
If thou couldst answer, 'This fair child of mine
Shall sum my count and make my old excuse,'
Proving his beauty by succession thine.
  This were to be new made when thou art old
  And see thy blood warm when thou feel'st it cold.

**4**

Unthrifty loveliness, why dost thou spend
Upon thyself thy beauty's legacy ?
Nature's bequest gives nothing but doth lend,
And, being frank, she lends to those are free.
Then, beauteous niggard, why dost thou abuse
The bounteous largess given thee to give ?
Profitless usurer, why dost thou use
So great a sum of sums, yet canst not live ?
For, having traffic with thyself alone,
Thou of thyself thy sweet self dost deceive :
Then how, when Nature calls thee to be gone,
What acceptable audit canst thou leave ?
  Thy unused beauty must be tombed with thee,
  Which, usèd, lives th' executor to be.

---

3 : 3 *fresh repair* youthful state   4 *unbless some mother* fail to bless some woman with motherhood   5 *uneared* untilled   7 *fond* foolish; *tomb* monument   8 *to stop posterity* thus bringing an end to his line   11 *windows . . . age* apertures in the enclosure of old age   13 *rememb'red . . . be* to be forgotten

1 : 2 *rose* (capitalized and italicized in Q)   5 *contracted* betrothed   6 *self-substantial* of your own substance   10 *only* principal   11 *thy content* what you contain (i.e. potentiality for parenthood; with play on 'self-satisfaction'?)   12 *niggarding* hoarding   14 *by . . . thee* i.e. by wilfully dying without issue

4 : 2 *beauty's legacy* inheritance of beauty   3–4 *Nature's . . . free* (cf. parable of the talents, Matthew xxv, 14–30, and *Measure for Measure*, I, i, 36–40)   4 *frank* generous; *free* generous   5 *niggard* miser   7 *use* invest   8 *live* (1) make a living, (2) survive through posterity   9 *traffic* commerce   10 *deceive* cheat   14 *lives* i.e. in the person of a son

2 : 2 *trenches* furrows, wrinkles   3 *livery* marks, fittings   4 *tottered weed* tattered garment   8 *thriftless* unprofitable   9 *use* investment   11 *sum . . . excuse* i.e. even my account and make amends for growing old

5 Those hours that with gentle work did frame
  The lovely gaze where every eye doth dwell
  Will play the tyrants to the very same
4 And that unfair which fairly doth excel;
  For never-resting time leads summer on
  To hideous winter and confounds him there,
  Sap checked with frost and lusty leaves quite gone,
8 Beauty o'ersnowed and bareness everywhere.
  Then, were not summer's distillation left
  A liquid prisoner pent in walls of glass,
  Beauty's effect with beauty were bereft,
12 Nor it nor no remembrance what it was:
    But flowers distilled, though they with winter meet,
    Leese but their show; their substance still lives sweet.

Is it for fear to wet a widow's eye
That thou consum'st thyself in single life?
Ah, if thou issueless shalt hap to die,
The world will wail thee like a makeless wife;
The world will be thy widow, and still weep
That thou no form of thee hast left behind,
When every private widow well may keep,
By children's eyes, her husband's shape in mind.
Look what an unthrift in the world doth spend
Shifts but his place, for still the world enjoys it;
But beauty's waste hath in the world an end,
And, kept unused, the user so destroys it:
  No love toward others in that bosom sits
  That on himself such murd'rous shame commits.

6 Then let not winter's ragged hand deface
  In thee thy summer ere thou be distilled:
  Make sweet some vial; treasure thou some place
4 With beauty's treasure ere it be self-killed.
  That use is not forbidden usury
  Which happies those that pay the willing loan;
  That's for thyself to breed another thee,
8 Or ten times happier be it ten for one.
  Ten times thyself were happier than thou art,
  If ten of thine ten times refigured thee:
  Then what could death do if thou shouldst depart,
12 Leaving thee living in posterity?
    Be not self-willed, for thou art much too fair
    To be death's conquest and make worms thine heir.

For shame, deny that thou bear'st love to any
Who for thyself art so unprovident:
Grant, if thou wilt, thou art beloved of many,
But that thou none lov'st is most evident;
For thou art so possessed with murd'rous hate
That 'gainst thyself thou stick'st not to conspire,
Seeking that beauteous roof to ruinate
Which to repair should be thy chief desire.
O, change thy thought, that I may change my mind;
Shall hate be fairer lodged than gentle love?
Be as thy presence is, gracious and kind,
Or to thyself at least kind-hearted prove:
  Make thee another self for love of me,
  That beauty still may live in thine or thee.

7 Lo, in the orient when the gracious light
  Lifts up his burning head, each under eye
  Doth homage to his new-appearing sight,
4 Serving with looks his sacred majesty;
  And having climbed the steep-up heavenly hill,
  Resembling strong youth in his middle age,
  Yet mortal looks adore his beauty still,
8 Attending on his golden pilgrimage;
  But when from highmost pitch, with weary car,
  Like feeble age he reeleth from the day,
  The eyes, fore duteous, now converted are
12 From his low tract and look another way:
    So thou, thyself outgoing in thy noon,
    Unlooked on diest unless thou get a son.

8 Music to hear, why hear'st thou music sadly?
  Sweets with sweets war not, joy delights in joy:
  Why lov'st thou that which thou receiv'st not gladly,
4 Or else receiv'st with pleasure thine annoy?
  If the true concord of well-tunèd sounds,
  By unions married, do offend thine ear,
  They do but sweetly chide thee, who confounds
8 In singleness the parts that thou shouldst bear.
  Mark how one string, sweet husband to another,
  Strikes each in each by mutual ordering;
  Resembling sire and child and happy mother,
12 Who, all in one, one pleasing note do sing;
    Whose speechless song, being many, seeming one,
    Sings this to thee, 'Thou single wilt prove none.'

5: 2 *gaze* object of gazes, cynosure  4 *unfair* deface; *fairly* in beauty  6 *confounds* destroys  9 *summer's distillation* essence of flowers, perfumes  11 *were bereft* would be taken away  12 *Nor it* (leaving behind) neither itself  14 *Leese* lose

6: 1 *ragged* rough  3 *treasure* enrich  5 *forbidden usury* (lending money at interest – 'use' – had formerly been illegal)  6 *happies . . . loan* makes happy those who willingly pay for the loan  9 *happier* better, luckier  10 *refigured* duplicated

7: 1 *orient* east; *light* sun  2 *each under eye* each eye on earth below  5 *steep-up* precipitous  9 *highmost pitch* apex; *car* Phoebus' chariot  11 *fore* before; *converted* turned away  12 *tract* course  13 *outgoing . . . noon* i.e. passing your prime

8: 1 *Music to hear* you whom it is music to hear (a vocative); *sadly* soberly, without joy  3–4 *Why . . . annoy* i.e. you must either love what gives you no pleasure, or else take pleasure in what annoys you  7–8 *confounds . . . bear* i.e. spoils the harmony (of marriage) by performing singly instead of in concert  14 *none* no one, nothing

9: 3 *issueless* childless  4 *makeless* mateless  7 *private* particular  9 *Look what* whatever; *unthrift* prodigal  10 *his* its  14 *murd'rous shame* shameful murder

10: 6 *thou stick'st* you scruple  7 *roof* structure (your person); *ruinate* ruin  9 *change my mind* think otherwise  11 *presence* appearance  14 *still* always

11 As fast as thou shalt wane, so fast thou grow'st
In one of thine, from that which thou departest;
And that fresh blood which youngly thou bestow'st
4 Thou mayst call thine when thou from youth convertest.
Herein lives wisdom, beauty, and increase;
Without this, folly, age, and cold decay.
If all were minded so, the times should cease,
8 And threescore year would make the world away.
Let those whom Nature hath not made for store,
Harsh, featureless, and rude, barrenly perish:
Look whom she best endowed she gave the more,
12 Which bounteous gift thou shouldst in bounty cherish.
She carved thee for her seal, and meant thereby
Thou shouldst print more, not let that copy die.

12 When I do count the clock that tells the time
And see the brave day sunk in hideous night,
When I behold the violet past prime
4 And sable curls all silvered o'er with white,
When lofty trees I see barren of leaves,
Which erst from heat did canopy the herd,
And summer's green all girded up in sheaves
8 Borne on the bier with white and bristly beard;
Then of thy beauty do I question make
That thou among the wastes of time must go,
Since sweets and beauties do themselves forsake
12 And die as fast as they see others grow;
And nothing 'gainst Time's scythe can make defense
Save breed, to brave him when he takes thee hence.

O, that you were yourself, but, love, you are 13
No longer yours than you yourself here live:
Against this coming end you should prepare,
And your sweet semblance to some other give. 4
So should that beauty which you hold in lease
Find no determination; then you were
Yourself again after yourself's decease
When your sweet issue your sweet form should bear. 8
Who lets so fair a house fall to decay,
Which husbandry in honor might uphold
Against the stormy gusts of winter's day
And barren rage of death's eternal cold? 12
O, none but unthrifts! Dear my love, you know
You had a father – let your son say so.

Not from the stars do I my judgment pluck,
And yet methinks I have astronomy; 14
But not to tell of good or evil luck,
Of plagues, of dearths, or seasons' quality;
Nor can I fortune to brief minutes tell, 4
Pointing to each his thunder, rain, and wind,
Or say with princes if it shall go well
By oft predict that I in heaven find; 8
But from thine eyes my knowledge I derive,
And, constant stars, in them I read such art
As truth and beauty shall together thrive
If from thyself to store thou wouldst convert: 12
Or else of thee this I prognosticate,
Thy end is truth's and beauty's doom and date.

When I consider everything that grows 15
Holds in perfection but a little moment,
That this huge stage presenteth nought but shows
Whereon the stars in secret influence comment; 4
When I perceive that men as plants increase,
Cheerèd and checked even by the selfsame sky,
Vaunt in their youthful sap, at height decrease,
And wear their brave state out of memory: 8
Then the conceit of this inconstant stay
Sets you most rich in youth before my sight,
Where wasteful Time debateth with Decay
To change your day of youth to sullied night; 12
And, all in war with Time for love of you,
As he takes from you, I ingraft you new.

11: 1–2 *thou grow'st ... departest* i.e. you become, in one of your children,
what you cease to be in yourself  3 *youngly* in youth  4 *thou ... convertest*
you ... turn away  7 *times* generations of man  9 *store* replenishment
10 *featureless* ill-featured  11 *Look whom* whomever  13 *seal* stamp from
which impressions are made

12: 2 *brave* splendid  4 *sable* black  6 *erst* formerly  7 *summer's green*
i.e. wheat  8 *bier* i.e. the harvest cart  9 *question make* speculate  14
*breed* offspring; *brave* defy

13: 1 *O ... yourself* i.e. O, that your eternal self and present self were one
5 *in lease* i.e. for a term  6 *determination* end  8 *issue* offspring  10 *husbandry* thrifty management (with pun on 'marriage')  13 *unthrifts* prodigals

14: 1 *judgment* opinion; *pluck* derive  2 *astronomy* astrology  5 *fortune
... tell* i.e. foretell the events of every moment  6 *Pointing* appointing;
*his* its  8 *oft predict that* frequent prediction of what  10 *read such art*
gather such lore  11 *As* as that  12 *store* replenishment; *convert* turn
14 *doom and date* prescribed end

15: 3 *stage* the world  4 *in secret ... comment* i.e. provide a silent commentary by influencing the action  6 *Cheerèd and checked* (1) applauded and
hissed, (2) nourished and starved  7 *Vaunt* boast; *sap* i.e. vigor  8 *brave*
splendid; *out of memory* i.e. until forgotten  9 *conceit* idea; *stay* duration
11 *wasteful* destructive; *debateth* joins forces, fights  14 *ingraft* graft,
infuse new life into (with poetry)

16: 5 *on the top* at the peak  6 *unset* unplanted  7 *wish* i.e. willingness  8
*counterfeit* portrait  9 *lines of life* living lineaments (of children)  10 *this
time's pencil* contemporary portraiture; *pupil* inexpert  11 *fair* beauty  13
*give away yourself* i.e. transfer yourself into children

But wherefore do not you a mightier way 16
Make war upon this bloody tyrant, Time?
And fortify yourself in your decay
With means more blessèd than my barren rime? 4
Now stand you on the top of happy hours,
And many maiden gardens, yet unset,
With virtuous wish would bear your living flowers,
Much liker than your painted counterfeit: 8
So should the lines of life that life repair
Which this time's pencil or my pupil pen,
Neither in inward worth nor outward fair
Can make you live yourself in eyes of men. 12
To give away yourself keeps yourself still,
And you must live, drawn by your own sweet skill.

17 Who will believe my verse in time to come
If it were filled with your most high deserts?
Though yet, heaven knows, it is but as a tomb
4 Which hides your life and shows not half your parts.
If I could write the beauty of your eyes
And in fresh numbers number all your graces,
The age to come would say, 'This poet lies –
8 Such heavenly touches ne'er touched earthly faces.'
So should my papers, yellowed with their age,
Be scorned, like old men of less truth than tongue,
And your true rights be termed a poet's rage
12 And stretchèd metre of an antique song.
　　But were some child of yours alive that time,
　　You should live twice – in it and in my rime.

18 Shall I compare thee to a summer's day?
Thou art more lovely and more temperate.
Rough winds do shake the darling buds of May,
4 And summer's lease hath all too short a date.
Sometime too hot the eye of heaven shines,
And often is his gold complexion dimmed;
And every fair from fair sometime declines,
8 By chance, or nature's changing course, untrimmed:
But thy eternal summer shall not fade
Nor lose possession of that fair thou ow'st,
Nor shall Death brag thou wand'rest in his shade
12 When in eternal lines to time thou grow'st.
　　So long as men can breathe or eyes can see,
　　So long lives this, and this gives life to thee.

19 Devouring Time, blunt thou the lion's paws,
And make the earth devour her own sweet brood;
Pluck the keen teeth from the fierce tiger's jaws,
4 And burn the long-lived phoenix in her blood;
Make glad and sorry seasons as thou fleet'st,
And do whate'er thou wilt, swift-footed Time,
To the wide world and all her fading sweets,
8 But I forbid thee one most heinous crime:
O, carve not with thy hours my love's fair brow,
Nor draw no lines there with thine antique pen;
Him in thy course untainted do allow
12 For beauty's pattern to succeeding men.
　　Yet do thy worst, old Time: despite thy wrong,
　　My love shall in my verse ever live young.

20 A woman's face, with Nature's own hand painted,
Hast thou, the master-mistress of my passion;
A woman's gentle heart, but not acquainted
4 With shifting change, as is false women's fashion;
An eye more bright than theirs, less false in rolling,
Gilding the object whereupon it gazeth;
A man in hue all hues in his controlling,
8 Which steals men's eyes and women's souls amazeth.
And for a woman wert thou first created,
Till Nature as she wrought thee fell a-doting,
And by addition me of thee defeated
12 By adding one thing to my purpose nothing.
　　But since she pricked thee out for women's pleasure,
　　Mine be thy love, and thy love's use their treasure.

21 So is it not with me as with that Muse
Stirred by a painted beauty to his verse,
Who heaven itself for ornament doth use
4 And every fair with his fair doth rehearse;
Making a couplement of proud compare
With sun and moon, with earth and sea's rich gems,
With April's first-born flowers, and all things rare
8 That heaven's air in this huge rondure hems.
O let me, true in love, but truly write,
And then believe me, my love is as fair
As any mother's child, though not so bright
12 As those gold candles fixed in heaven's air:
　　Let them say more that like of hearsay well;
　　I will not praise that purpose not to sell.

22 My glass shall not persuade me I am old
So long as youth and thou are of one date;
But when in thee time's furrows I behold,
4 Then look I death my days should expiate.
For all that beauty that doth cover thee
Is but the seemly raiment of my heart,
Which in thy breast doth live, as thine in me:
8 How can I then be elder than thou art?
O therefore, love, be of thyself so wary
As I, not for myself, but for thee will,
Bearing thy heart, which I will keep so chary
12 As tender nurse her babe from faring ill.
　　Presume not on thy heart when mine is slain;
　　Thou gav'st me thine not to give back again.

17: 2 *deserts* merits   4 *parts* qualities   6 *numbers* verses   8 *touches* strokes
of artistry   11 *true rights* due praise   12 *stretchèd metre* poetic hyperbole
13 *that time* in that future time

18: 4 *lease* allotted time; *date* duration   5 *eye* sun   6 *dimmed* clouded
over   7 *fair from fair* beautiful thing from beauty   8 *untrimmed* stripped
of adornment   10 *thou ow'st* you own   11 *shade* i.e. oblivion   12 *lines*
poetry; *thou grow'st* you are grafted

19: 2 *brood* i.e. the children of earth   4 *phoenix* a legendary bird which
lives for hundreds of years and then propagates itself from its own ashes
(symbol of immortality); *in her blood* alive   10 *antique* (1) antic, capricious,
(2) old   11 *untainted* unspoiled

20: 1 *with . . . hand* i.e. naturally, without cosmetics   2 *master-mistress*
master and mistress; *passion* love   5 *rolling* i.e. passing from one to another   6 *Gilding* brightening (as do the rays of the sun)   7 *A man . . .
controlling* i.e. a man in complexion with all complexions – 'humors' – under
his control (the line may be corrupt or, as glossed thus, may contrast male
constancy with feminine inconstancy); *hues* (capitalized and italicized in Q)
11 *defeated* cheated, deprived   12 *one thing* i.e. a penis

21: 1 *Muse* poet   2 *Stirred . . . beauty* inspired by artificial beauty   4
*every . . . rehearse* i.e. mentions everything beautiful in relation to his mistress   5 *couplement* combination; *compare* comparison   8 *rondure* sphere;
*hems* encircles   12 *gold candles* i.e. stars   13 *that . . . well* i.e. that are fond
of large and specious comparisons   14 *that* who, i.e. since I am not a
huckster

22: 2 *of one date* of an age; i.e. so long as you are young   4 *expiate* wind up
5–8 *For . . . art* i.e. the friend's beautiful body encloses the poet's heart,
and this transfer of hearts makes friend and poet of one age   11 *chary*
carefully   13 *Presume not on* do not expect to regain

**3** As an unperfect actor on the stage,
Who with his fear is put besides his part,
Or some fierce thing replete with too much rage,
4 Whose strength's abundance weakens his own heart;
So I, for fear of trust, forget to say
The perfect ceremony of love's rite,
And in mine own love's strength seem to decay,
8 O'ercharged with burden of mine own love's might.
O, let my books be then the eloquence
And dumb presagers of my speaking breast,
Who plead for love, and look for recompense,
12 More than that tongue that more hath more expressed.
O, learn to read what silent love hath writ:
To hear with eyes belongs to love's fine wit.

**4** Mine eye hath played the painter and hath stelled
Thy beauty's form in table of my heart;
My body is the frame wherein 'tis held,
4 And perspective it is best painter's art.
For through the painter must you see his skill
To find where your true image pictured lies,
Which in my bosom's shop is hanging still,
8 That hath his windows glazèd with thine eyes.
Now see what good turns eyes for eyes have done:
Mine eyes have drawn thy shape, and thine for me
Are windows to my breast, wherethrough the sun
12 Delights to peep, to gaze therein on thee.
Yet eyes this cunning want to grace their art;
They draw but what they see, know not the heart.

Let those who are in favor with their stars **25**
Of public honor and proud titles boast,
Whilst I, whom fortune of such triumph bars,
Unlooked for joy in that I honor most. 4
Great princes' favorites their fair leaves spread
But as the marigold at the sun's eye;
And in themselves their pride lies burièd,
For at a frown they in their glory die. 8
The painful warrior famousèd for fight,
After a thousand victories once foiled,
Is from the book of honor rasèd quite,
And all the rest forgot for which he toiled. 12
Then happy I, that love and am beloved
Where I may not remove nor be removed.

Lord of my love, to whom in vassalage **26**
Thy merit hath my duty strongly knit,
To thee I send this written ambassage
To witness duty, not to show my wit; 4
Duty so great, which wit so poor as mine
May make seem bare, in wanting words to show it,
But that I hope some good conceit of thine
In thy soul's thought, all naked, will bestow it; 8
Till whatsoever star that guides my moving
Points on me graciously with fair aspect,
And puts apparel on my tottered loving
To show me worthy of thy sweet respect: 12
Then may I dare to boast how I do love thee;
Till then not show my head where thou mayst prove me.

Weary with toil, I haste me to my bed, **27**
The dear repose for limbs with travel tired,
But then begins a journey in my head
To work my mind when body's work's expired; 4
For then my thoughts, from far where I abide,
Intend a zealous pilgrimage to thee,
And keep my drooping eyelids open wide,
Looking on darkness which the blind do see; 8
Save that my soul's imaginary sight
Presents thy shadow to my sightless view,
Which, like a jewel hung in ghastly night,
Makes black night beauteous and her old face new. 12
Lo, thus, by day my limbs, by night my mind,
For thee and for myself no quiet find.

How can I then return in happy plight **28**
That am debarred the benefit of rest,
When day's oppression is not eased by night,
But day by night and night by day oppressed, 4
And each, though enemies to either's reign,
Do in consent shake hands to torture me,
The one by toil, the other to complain
How far I toil, still farther off from thee? 8
I tell the day, to please him, thou art bright
And dost him grace when clouds do blot the heaven;
So flatter I the swart-complexioned night,
When sparkling stars twire not, thou gild'st the even. 12
But day doth daily draw my sorrows longer,
And night doth nightly make grief's strength seem stronger.

23: 1 *unperfect actor* i.e. imperfect in his craft or in his part   2 *besides* out of   4 *heart* i.e. capacity for performance   5 *for . . . trust* in self-distrust   5–6 *forget . . . rite* i.e. am not word-perfect in love's ritual   7 *decay* i.e. falter   10 *dumb presagers* silent messengers   12 *more expressed* more often expressed   14 *wit* intelligence

24: 1 *stelled* portrayed   2 *table* tablet (?), picture (?)   4 *perspective it is* i.e. given perspective, which is (?)   8 *his* its; *glazèd* paned   13 *cunning* skill; *want* lack; *grace* enhance

25: 1 *who . . . stars* i.e. whose stars are propitious   4 *Unlooked for* unexpectedly; *that* what   6 *But* only   7 *lies burièd* i.e. is already in its grave   9 *painful* striving; *fight* (an emendation for 'worth'; some editors retain 'worth' and emend *quite* in l. 11 to 'forth')   11 *rasèd* erased

26: 3 *ambassage* overture, message (probably the present sonnet)   4 *wit* poetic powers   7 *conceit* conception   8 *all . . . bestow it* i.e. will give it lodging despite its nakedness   9 *moving* i.e. life and actions   10 *aspect* influence (astrological term)   11 *tottered* tattered   14 *prove* test

27: 2 *travel* (1) journeying, (2) travail   4 *To work* to set to work   6 *pilgrimage* journey of devotion   8 *which* such as   9 *imaginary* imagining   10 *shadow* image

28: 6 *shake hands* unite   7 *the other to complain* i.e. the night making me complain   9 *I tell . . . bright* i.e. I please the day by telling him you are bright   10 *And . . . heaven* and can shine in his place when it is cloudy   11 *swart* dark   12 *twire* peek; *thou . . . even* you make the evening bright

29 When, in disgrace with Fortune and men's eyes,
   I all alone beweep my outcast state,
   And trouble deaf heaven with my bootless cries,
4 And look upon myself and curse my fate,
   Wishing me like to one more rich in hope,
   Featured like him, like him with friends possessed,
   Desiring this man's art, and that man's scope,
8 With what I most enjoy contented least;
   Yet in these thoughts myself almost despising,
   Haply I think on thee, and then my state,
   Like to the lark at break of day arising
12 From sullen earth, sings hymns at heaven's gate;
    For thy sweet love rememb'red such wealth brings
    That then I scorn to change my state with kings.

30 When to the sessions of sweet silent thought
   I summon up remembrance of things past,
   I sigh the lack of many a thing I sought,
4 And with old woes new wail my dear time's waste:
   Then can I drown an eye, unused to flow,
   For precious friends hid in death's dateless night,
   And weep afresh love's long since cancelled woe,
8 And moan th' expense of many a vanished sight.
   Then can I grieve at grievances foregone,
   And heavily from woe to woe tell o'er
   The sad account of fore-bemoanèd moan,
12 Which I new pay as if not paid before.
    But if the while I think on thee, dear friend,
    All losses are restored and sorrows end.

31 Thy bosom is endearèd with all hearts
   Which I by lacking have supposèd dead;
   And there reigns love, and all love's loving parts,
4 And all those friends which I thought burièd.
   How many a holy and obsequious tear
   Hath dear religious love stol'n from mine eye,
   As interest of the dead, which now appear
8 But things removed that hidden in thee lie!
   Thou art the grave where buried love doth live,
   Hung with the trophies of my lovers gone,
   Who all their parts of me to thee did give;
12 That due of many now is thine alone.
    Their images I loved I view in thee,
    And thou, all they, hast all the all of me.

32 If thou survive my well-contented day
   When that churl Death my bones with dust shall cover,
   And shalt by fortune once more resurvey
4 These poor rude lines of thy deceasèd lover,
   Compare them with the bett'ring of the time,
   And though they be outstripped by every pen,
   Reserve them for my love, not for their rime,
8 Exceeded by the height of happier men.
   O, then vouchsafe me but this loving thought:
   'Had my friend's Muse grown with this growing age,
   A dearer birth than this his love had brought
12 To march in ranks of better equipage;
    But since he died, and poets better prove,
    Theirs for their style I'll read, his for his love.'

Full many a glorious morning have I seen   3.
Flatter the mountain tops with sovereign eye,
Kissing with golden face the meadows green,
Gilding pale streams with heavenly alchemy;   4
Anon permit the basest clouds to ride
With ugly rack on his celestial face,
And from the forlorn world his visage hide,
Stealing unseen to west with this disgrace:   8
Even so my sun one early morn did shine
With all-triumphant splendor on my brow;
But, out alack, he was but one hour mine,
The region cloud hath masked him from me now.   12
   Yet him for this my love no whit disdaineth;
   Suns of the world may stain when heaven's sun staineth.

Why didst thou promise such a beauteous day   3.
And make me travel forth without my cloak,
To let base clouds o'ertake me in my way,
Hiding thy brav'ry in their rotten smoke?   4
'Tis not enough that through the cloud thou break
To dry the rain on my storm-beaten face,
For no man well of such a salve can speak
That heals the wound, and cures not the disgrace:   8
Nor can thy shame give physic to my grief;
Though thou repent, yet I have still the loss:
Th' offender's sorrow lends but weak relief
To him that bears the strong offense's cross.   12
   Ah, but those tears are pearl which thy love sheeds,
   And they are rich and ransom all ill deeds.

29: 1 *disgrace* disfavor; *eyes* regard  3 *bootless* useless  6 *like him, like him* i.e. like another, like still another  7 *art* literary skill; *scope* intellectual power  10 *Haply* perchance; *state* i.e. mood, state of mind  12 *sullen* gloomy  14 *state* lot

30: 1 *sessions* sittings, as of a court  3 *sigh* lament  4 *new wail* newly bewail; *dear time's waste* time's destruction of precious things (?), the wasteful passing of precious time (?)  6 *dateless* endless  7 *cancelled* fully paid  8 *expense* loss  9 *foregone* former  10 *tell* count

31: 1 *endearèd* enriched  5 *obsequious* mourning  6 *religious* venerating  7 *interest* rightful due; *which* who  8 *removed* absent  10 *trophies* memorials; *lovers* loved ones  11 *parts* shares  12 *That . . . many* what was due to many  14 *all they* who are all of them combined

32: 1 *my well-contented day* i.e. the ripe day of my death  5 *bett'ring* improved writing  7 *Reserve* preserve; *rime* poetic skill  8 *height* superiority; *happier* more gifted  11 *dearer* more precious  12 *of better equipage* more finely equipped

33: 2 *Flatter . . . eye* i.e. honor with a royal glance of the sun  5 *Anon* soon; *basest* darkest  6 *rack* cloud streamers  7 *forlorn* sadly forsaken  11 *out alack* alas  12 *region cloud* clouds of the upper air

34: 3 *base* dark  4 *brav'ry* splendor; *rotten smoke* unwholesome vapors  8 *disgrace* shame  9 *shame* regret; *physic* remedy  13 *sheeds* sheds  14 *ransom* atone for

35 No more be grieved at that which thou hast done :
   Roses have thorns, and silver fountains mud ;
   Clouds and eclipses stain both moon and sun,
4  And loathsome canker lives in sweetest bud.
   All men make faults, and even I in this,
   Authorizing thy trespass with compare,
   Myself corrupting, salving thy amiss,
8  Excusing thy sins more than thy sins are ;
   For to thy sensual fault I bring in sense
   (Thy adverse party is thy advocate)
   And 'gainst myself a lawful plea commence ;
12 Such civil war is in my love and hate
      That I an accessary needs must be
      To that sweet thief which sourly robs from me.

36 Let me confess that we two must be twain
   Although our undivided loves are one :
   So shall those blots that do with me remain,
4  Without thy help by me be borne alone.
   In our two loves there is but one respect,
   Though in our lives a separable spite,
   Which though it alter not love's sole effect,
8  Yet doth it steal sweet hours from love's delight.
   I may not evermore acknowledge thee,
   Lest my bewailèd guilt should do thee shame ;
   Nor thou with public kindness honor me
12 Unless thou take that honor from thy name :
      But do not so ; I love thee in such sort
      As, thou being mine, mine is thy good report.

37 As a decrepit father takes delight
   To see his active child do deeds of youth,
   So I, made lame by Fortune's dearest spite,
4  Take all my comfort of thy worth and truth.
   For whether beauty, birth, or wealth, or wit,
   Or any of these all, or all, or more,
   Intitled in thy parts do crownèd sit,
8  I make my love ingrafted to this store.
   So then I am not lame, poor, nor despised
   Whilst that this shadow doth such substance give
   That I in thy abundance am sufficed
12 And by a part of all thy glory live.
      Look what is best, that best I wish in thee.
      This wish I have ; then ten times happy me !

38 How can my Muse want subject to invent
   While thou dost breathe, that pour'st into my verse
   Thine own sweet argument, too excellent
4  For every vulgar paper to rehearse ?
   O, give thyself the thanks if aught in me
   Worthy perusal stand against thy sight,
   For who's so dumb that cannot write to thee
8  When thou thyself dost give invention light ?
   Be thou the tenth Muse, ten times more in worth
   Than those old nine which rimers invocate ;
   And he that calls on thee, let him bring forth
12 Eternal numbers to outlive long date.
      If my slight Muse do please these curious days,
      The pain be mine, but thine shall be the praise.

39 O, how thy worth with manners may I sing
   When thou art all the better part of me ?
   What can mine own praise to mine own self bring,
4  And what is't but mine own when I praise thee ?
   Even for this let us divided live
   And our dear love lose name of single one,
   That by this separation I may give
8  That due to thee which thou deserv'st alone.
   O absence, what a torment wouldst thou prove
   Were it not thy sour leisure gave sweet leave
   To entertain the time with thoughts of love,
12 Which time and thoughts so sweetly doth deceive,
      And that thou teachest how to make one twain
      By praising him here who doth hence remain !

40 Take all my loves, my love, yea, take them all :
   What hast thou then more than thou hadst before ?
   No love, my love, that thou mayst true love call ;
4  All mine was thine before thou hadst this more.
   Then, if for my love thou my love receivest,
   I cannot blame thee for my love thou usest ;
   But yet be blamed if thou this self deceivest
8  By wilful taste of what thyself refusest.
   I do forgive thy robb'ry, gentle thief,
   Although thou steal thee all my poverty ;
   And yet love knows it is a greater grief
12 To bear love's wrong than hate's known injury.
      Lascivious grace, in whom all ill well shows,
      Kill me with spites ; yet we must not be foes.

35 : 3 *stain* darken   4 *canker* destroying worm   5 *make faults* are faulty
6 *Authorizing* justifying ; *with compare* by comparison   7 *salving thy amiss*
palliating your offense   8 *Excusing . . . are* i.e. going further in excusing
your sins than you in sinning   9 *to . . . sense* i.e. to your physical fault I add
my intellectual fault (perhaps with a pun on 'incense')   13 *accessary*
fellow sinner

36 : 3 *blots* defects   5 *but one respect* a singleness of attitude   6 *separable
spite* spiteful separation   7 *sole* singleness of   10 *bewailèd* lamented   14
*report* reputation

37 : 3 *made lame* i.e. handicapped (in a general sense) ; *dearest* most grievous
4 *of* in   5 *wit* intelligence   7 *Intitled . . . sit* sit enthroned among your
qualities   8 *ingrafted . . . store* i.e. fastened to and drawing upon this
abundance   10 *shadow* the idea ; *substance* the actuality   13 *Look what*
whatever

38 : 1 *want . . . invent* lack subject matter   3 *argument* theme   4 *vulgar
paper* common composition   5 *in me* of mine   6 *stand . . . sight* meet your
eye   8 *invention* power of creation   10 *invocate* invoke   12 *numbers* verses ; *long* a distant   13 *curious* critical   14 *pain* painstaking

39 : 1 *manners* modesty   5 *for* because of   6 *name* report   8 *That due*
what is owing   11 *entertain* pass   12 *thoughts* melancholy ; *deceive* beguile
away   13 *And . . . twain* i.e. and were it not that you teach how to divide one
into two

40 : 1 *Take . . . loves* (read in the context of later sonnets, the allusion seems
to be to the poet's mistress whom the friend has taken)   6 *for* because ; *thou
usest* you enjoy   7 *this self* i.e. this one of your selves, the poet (often
emended to 'thyself' without marked improvement of the sense)   8 *wilful
taste of* i.e. capricious dalliance with (?) ; *thyself* i.e. your true self (?)   10 *my
poverty* my little   12 *known* open, intended   13 *Lascivious grace* you who
are gracious even in your amours

41   Those pretty wrongs that liberty commits
     When I am sometime absent from thy heart,
     Thy beauty and thy years full well befits,
4   For still temptation follows where thou art.
     Gentle thou art, and therefore to be won;
     Beauteous thou art, therefore to be assailed;
     And when a woman woos, what woman's son
8   Will sourly leave her till she have prevailed?
     Ay me, but yet thou mightst my seat forbear,
     And chide thy beauty and thy straying youth,
     Who lead thee in their riot even there
12   Where thou art forced to break a twofold truth:
      Hers, by thy beauty tempting her to thee,
      Thine, by thy beauty being false to me.

42   That thou hast her, it is not all my grief,
     And yet it may be said I loved her dearly;
     That she hath thee is of my wailing chief,
4   A loss in love that touches me more nearly.
     Loving offenders, thus I will excuse ye:
     Thou dost love her because thou know'st I love her,
     And for my sake even so doth she abuse me,
8   Suff'ring my friend for my sake to approve her.
     If I lose thee, my loss is my love's gain,
     And losing her, my friend hath found that loss:
     Both find each other, and I lose both twain,
12   And both for my sake lay on me this cross.
      But here's the joy: my friend and I are one;
      Sweet flattery! then she loves but me alone.

43   When most I wink, then do mine eyes best see,
     For all the day they view things unrespected;
     But when I sleep, in dreams they look on thee
4   And, darkly bright, are bright in dark directed.
     Then thou, whose shadow shadows doth make bright,
     How would thy shadow's form form happy show
     To the clear day with thy much clearer light
8   When to unseeing eyes thy shade shines so!
     How would, I say, mine eyes be blessèd made
     By looking on thee in the living day,
     When in dead night thy fair imperfect shade
12   Through heavy sleep on sightless eyes doth stay!
      All days are nights to see till I see thee,
      And nights bright days when dreams do show thee me.

44   If the dull substance of my flesh were thought,
     Injurious distance should not stop my way;
     For then, despite of space, I would be brought,
4   From limits far remote, where thou dost stay.
     No matter then although my foot did stand
     Upon the farthest earth removed from thee;
     For nimble thought can jump both sea and land
8   As soon as think the place where he would be.
     But, ah, thought kills me that I am not thought,
     To leap large lengths of miles when thou art gone,
     But that, so much of earth and water wrought,
12   I must attend time's leisure with my moan,
      Receiving naught by elements so slow
      But heavy tears, badges of either's woe.

     The other two, slight air and purging fire,
     Are both with thee, wherever I abide;
     The first my thought, the other my desire,
4   These present-absent with swift motion slide.
     For when these quicker elements are gone
     In tender embassy of love to thee,
     My life, being made of four, with two alone
8   Sinks down to death, oppressed with melancholy;
     Until life's composition be recured
     By those swift messengers returned from thee,
     Who even but now come back again, assured
12   Of thy fair health, recounting it to me.
      This told, I joy; but then no longer glad,
      I send them back again and straight grow sad.

     Mine eye and heart are at a mortal war
     How to divide the conquest of thy sight;
     Mine eye my heart thy picture's sight would bar,
4   My heart mine eye the freedom of that right.
     My heart doth plead that thou in him dost lie,
     A closet never pierced with crystal eyes,
     But the defendant doth that plea deny
8   And says in him thy fair appearance lies.
     To 'cide this title is impanellèd
     A quest of thoughts, all tenants to the heart,
     And by their verdict is determinèd
12   The clear eye's moiety and the dear heart's part:
      As thus: mine eye's due is thy outward part,
      And my heart's right thy inward love of heart.

41: 1 *pretty wrongs* peccadilloes; *liberty* license  3 *befits* makes inevitable  4 *still* always  9 *my seat forbear* forgo the place belonging to me  11 *Who* which; *riot* revels

42: 3 *of my wailing chief* my chief lament  7 *abuse* betray  8 *approve* prove, try  9 *love's* mistress's  12 *cross* affliction

43: 1 *wink* shut my eyes in sleep  2 *unrespected* unnoticed  4 *darkly . . . directed* i.e. mysteriously lighted, see clearly in the dark  5 *shadow shadows* image darkness  6 *shadow's form* actual body  14 *show thee me* show you to me

44: 1 *dull substance* i.e. earth and water (dull as compared with the other elements, fire and air)  2 *Injurious* spiteful  4 *limits* bounds; *where* to where  6 *farthest earth* earth farthest  9 *ah, thought* ah, the thought  11 *wrought* fashioned  12 *attend* await  14 *either's woe* (i.e. the earth supplies the weight, the water the moisture of the 'heavy tears')

45: 1 *two* i.e. elements; *slight* insubstantial  4 *present-absent* now here, now there  7 *life* living body  8 *melancholy* (induced by an excess of particular elements or 'humors,' in this case earth and water)  9 *composition* proper balance; *recured* restored  10 *messengers* i.e. fire and air

46: 2 *conquest . . . sight* i.e. spoils, consisting of the sight of you  3 *bar* deny  4 *freedom* free exercise  9 *'cide* decide  10 *quest* jury; *tenants to* i.e. from the holdings of  12 *moiety* share

7 Betwixt mine eye and heart a league is took,
And each doth good turns now unto the other:
When that mine eye is famished for a look,
4 Or heart in love with sighs himself doth smother,
With my love's picture then my eye doth feast
And to the painted banquet bids my heart;
Another time mine eye is my heart's guest
8 And in his thoughts of love doth share a part.
So, either by thy picture or my love,
Thyself away are present still with me;
For thou not farther than my thoughts canst move,
12 And I am still with them, and they with thee;
    Or, if they sleep, thy picture in my sight
    Awakes my heart to heart's and eye's delight.

8 How careful was I, when I took my way,
Each trifle under truest bars to thrust,
That to my use it might unusèd stay
4 From hands of falsehood, in sure wards of trust!
But thou, to whom my jewels trifles are,
Most worthy comfort, now my greatest grief,
Thou best of dearest, and mine only care,
8 Art left the prey of every vulgar thief.
Thee have I not locked up in any chest,
Save where thou art not, though I feel thou art,
Within the gentle closure of my breast,
12 From whence at pleasure thou mayst come and part;
    And even thence thou wilt be stol'n, I fear,
    For truth proves thievish for a prize so dear.

Against that time, if ever that time come, 49
When I shall see thee frown on my defects,
Whenas thy love hath cast his utmost sum,
Called to that audit by advisèd respects; 4
Against that time when thou shalt strangely pass
And scarcely greet me with that sun, thine eye,
When love, converted from the thing it was,
Shall reasons find of settled gravity: 8
Against that time do I ensconce me here
Within the knowledge of mine own desert,
And this my hand against myself uprear
To guard the lawful reasons on thy part. 12
    To leave poor me thou hast the strength of laws,
    Since why to love I can allege no cause.

How heavy do I journey on the way 50
When what I seek (my weary travel's end)
Doth teach that ease and that repose to say,
'Thus far the miles are measured from thy friend.' 4
The beast that bears me, tired with my woe,
Plods dully on, to bear that weight in me,
As if by some instinct the wretch did know
His rider loved not speed, being made from thee. 8
The bloody spur cannot provoke him on
That sometimes anger thrusts into his hide,
Which heavily he answers with a groan,
More sharp to me than spurring to his side; 12
    For that same groan doth put this in my mind:
    My grief lies onward and my joy behind.

Thus can my love excuse the slow offense 51
Of my dull bearer when from thee I speed:
From where thou art why should I haste me thence?
Till I return, of posting is no need. 4
O, what excuse will my poor beast then find
When swift extremity can seem but slow?
Then should I spur, though mounted on the wind,
In wingèd speed no motion shall I know. 8
Then can no horse with my desire keep pace;
Therefore desire, of perfect'st love being made,
Shall weigh no dull flesh in his fiery race;
But love, for love, thus shall excuse my jade: 12
    Since from thee going he went wilful slow,
    Towards thee I'll run and give him leave to go.

So am I as the rich whose blessèd key 52
Can bring him to his sweet up-lockèd treasure,
The which he will not ev'ry hour survey,
For blunting the fine point of seldom pleasure. 4
Therefore are feasts so solemn and so rare,
Since, seldom coming, in the long year set,
Like stones of worth they thinly placèd are,
Or captain jewels in the carcanet. 8
So is the time that keeps you as my chest,
Or as the wardrobe which the robe doth hide,
To make some special instant special blest
By new unfolding his imprisoned pride. 12
    Blessèd are you, whose worthiness gives scope,
    Being had, to triumph, being lacked, to hope.

47: 1 *a league is took* an agreement is reached   6 *painted banquet* i.e. visual feast   12 *still* always

48: 1 *took my way* set out on my journey   4 *hands of falsehood* thieves   5 *to* in comparison with; *jewels* prized material possessions   7 *only care* only thing valued   8 *vulgar* common   11 *closure* enclosure   14 *truth* i.e. truth (honesty) itself

49: 1 *Against* in provision for   3 *Whenas* when; *cast . . . sum* made its final reckoning   4 *advised respects* considered reasons   5 *strangely* like a stranger   8 *of settled gravity* for continued coldness (?), of sufficient weight (?)   9 *ensconce* fortify   11–12 *this . . . part* i.e. swear, to my own disadvantage, that your actions are lawful   14 *cause* i.e. lawful obligation

50: 1 *heavy* sadly   2–3 *When . . . say* i.e. when the longed-for journey's end will bring, along with its ease and repose, the reminder that   12 *sharp* painful

51: 1 *slow offense* tardiness   4 *posting* riding in haste   6 *swift extremity* extreme swiftness   8 *know* recognize   11 *weigh* consider (?), bear (?) (emendation of 'naigh' in Q)   12 *for love* for love's sake (?)   14 *go* walk

52: 4 *For* for fear of; *seldom pleasure* pleasure seldom enjoyed   8 *captain* chief; *carcanet* jewelled collar   9 *as* like   12 *his* its

53 What is your substance, whereof are you made,
   That millions of strange shadows on you tend?
   Since every one hath, every one, one shade,
4  And you, but one, can every shadow lend.
   Describe Adonis, and the counterfeit
   Is poorly imitated after you.
   On Helen's cheek all art of beauty set,
8  And you in Grecian tires are painted new.
   Speak of the spring and foison of the year:
   The one doth shadow of your beauty show,
   The other as your bounty doth appear,
12 And you in every blessèd shape we know.
      In all external grace you have some part,
      But you like none, none you, for constant heart.

54 O, how much more doth beauty beauteous seem
   By that sweet ornament which truth doth give:
   The rose looks fair, but fairer we it deem
4  For that sweet odor which doth in it live.
   The canker blooms have full as deep a dye
   As the perfumèd tincture of the roses,
   Hang on such thorns, and play as wantonly
8  When summer's breath their maskèd buds discloses;
   But, for their virtue only is their show,
   They live unwooed and unrespected fade,
   Die to themselves. Sweet roses do not so:
12 Of their sweet deaths are sweetest odors made.
      And so of you, beauteous and lovely youth,
      When that shall vade, my verse distills your truth.

55 Not marble nor the gilded monuments
   Of princes shall outlive this pow'rful rime,
   But you shall shine more bright in these contents
4  Than unswept stone, besmeared with sluttish time.
   When wasteful war shall statues overturn,
   And broils root out the work of masonry,
   Nor Mars his sword nor war's quick fire shall burn
8  The living record of your memory.
   'Gainst death and all oblivious enmity
   Shall you pace forth; your praise shall still find room
   Even in the eyes of all posterity
12 That wear this world out to the ending doom.
      So, till the judgment that yourself arise,
      You live in this, and dwell in lovers' eyes.

56 Sweet love, renew thy force; be it not said
   Thy edge should blunter be than appetite,
   Which but to-day by feeding is allayed,
4  To-morrow sharp'ned in his former might.
   So, love, be thou: although to-day thou fill
   Thy hungry eyes even till they wink with fulness,
   To-morrow see again, and do not kill
8  The spirit of love with a perpetual dulness.
   Let this sad int'rim like the ocean be
   Which parts the shore where two contracted new
   Come daily to the banks, that, when they see
12 Return of love, more blest may be the view;
      Or call it winter, which, being full of care,
      Makes summer's welcome thrice more wished, more rare.

57 Being your slave, what should I do but tend
   Upon the hours and times of your desire?
   I have no precious time at all to spend,
4  Nor services to do till you require.
   Nor dare I chide the world-without-end hour
   Whilst I, my sovereign, watch the clock for you,
   Nor think the bitterness of absence sour
8  When you have bid your servant once adieu.
   Nor dare I question with my jealous thought
   Where you may be, or your affairs suppose,
   But, like a sad slave, stay and think of nought
   Save where you are how happy you make those.
      So true a fool is love that in your will,
      Though you do anything, he thinks no ill.

58 That god forbid that made me first your slave
   I should in thought control your times of pleasure,
   Or at your hand th' account of hours to crave,
4  Being your vassal bound to stay your leisure.
   O, let me suffer, being at your beck,
   Th' imprisoned absence of your liberty;
   And patience, tame to sufferance, bide each check
8  Without accusing you of injury.
   Be where you list; your charter is so strong
   That you yourself may privilege your time
   To what you will; to you it doth belong
12 Yourself to pardon of self-doing crime.
      I am to wait, though waiting so be hell,
      Not blame your pleasure, be it ill or well.

53: 2 *strange shadows* foreign shades (Venus, Adonis, etc.); *tend* attend 4 *And . . . lend* i.e. each *shadow* can reflect but one of your excellencies (with *you* the object of *lend*) 5 *counterfeit* picture 8 *tires* attire 9 *foison* harvest

54: 2 *By* by means of 5 *canker blooms* dog-roses 6 *tincture* color 7 *wantonly* sportively 8 *maskèd* hidden 9 *for* since 14 *vade* depart; *distills your truth* i.e. preserves your essence as a distillation

55: 2 *rime* poem 3 *these contents* what is here contained 4 *Than* than in; *stone* memorial tablet; *sluttish* untidy 6 *broils* battles 7 *Nor* neither; *Mars his sword* i.e. the sword of Mars shall destroy 9 *all oblivious enmity* i.e. oblivion the enemy of all 12 *That wear* who last 13 *judgment that* judgment day when

56: 1 *love* spirit of love 2 *appetite* lust 4 *sharp'ned in* sharpened to 6 *wink* shut 9 *sad int'rim* lamentable interval 10 *parts the shore* divides the shores; *contracted new* newly betrothed 12 *love* the loved one

57: 5 *world-without-end* tedious, everlasting 9 *question* dispute; *jealous* jealous 10 *suppose* speculate about 11 *sad* sober

58: 3 *th' account of* an accounting for; *to crave* should crave 4 *stay* await 6 *Th' . . . liberty* i.e. the imprisonment that your freedom-to-be-absent brings 7 *tame to sufferance* trained to accept suffering; *bide each check* put up with each rebuke 9 *list* wish; *charter* privilege 10 *privilege* dispose of, assign 12 *self-doing* done by yourself

59
If there be nothing new, but that which is
Hath been before, how are our brains beguiled,
Which, laboring for invention, bear amiss
4 The second burden of a former child !
O that record could with a backward look,
Even of five hundred courses of the sun,
Show me your image in some antique book,
8 Since mind at first in character was done :
That I might see what the old world could say
To this composèd wonder of your frame ;
Whether we are mended, or whe'r better they,
12 Or whether revolution be the same.
   O, sure I am the wits of former days
   To subjects worse have given admiring praise.

60
Like as the waves make towards the pebbled shore,
So do our minutes hasten to their end ;
Each changing place with that which goes before,
4 In sequent toil all forwards do contend.
Nativity, once in the main of light,
Crawls to maturity, wherewith being crowned,
Crooked eclipses 'gainst his glory fight,
8 And Time that gave doth now his gift confound.
Time doth transfix the flourish set on youth
And delves the parallels in beauty's brow,
Feeds on the rarities of nature's truth,
12 And nothing stands but for his scythe to mow :
   And yet to times in hope my verse shall stand,
   Praising thy worth, despite his cruel hand.

Is it thy will thy image should keep open 61
My heavy eyelids to the weary night ?
Dost thou desire my slumbers should be broken
While shadows like to thee do mock my sight ? 4
Is it thy spirit that thou send'st from thee
So far from home into my deeds to pry,
To find out shames and idle hours in me,
The scope and tenure of thy jealousy ? 8
O no, thy love, though much, is not so great ;
It is my love that keeps mine eye awake,
Mine own true love that doth my rest defeat
To play the watchman ever for thy sake. 12
   For thee watch I whilst thou dost wake elsewhere,
   From me far off, with others all too near.

Sin of self-love possesseth all mine eye 62
And all my soul and all my every part ;
And for this sin there is no remedy,
It is so grounded inward in my heart. 4
Methinks no face so gracious is as mine,
No shape so true, no truth of such account,
And for myself mine own worth do define
As I all other in all worths surmount. 8
But when my glass shows me myself indeed,
Beated and chopped with tanned antiquity,
Mine own self-love quite contrary I read ;
Self so self-loving were iniquity : 12
   'Tis thee (myself) that for myself I praise,
   Painting my age with beauty of thy days.

Against my love shall be as I am now, 63
With Time's injurious hand crushed and o'erworn ;
When hours have drained his blood and filled his brow
With lines and wrinkles, when his youthful morn 4
Hath travelled on to age's steepy night,
And all those beauties whereof now he's king
Are vanishing, or vanished out of sight,
Stealing away the treasure of his spring – 8
For such a time do I now fortify
Against confounding age's cruel knife,
That he shall never cut from memory
My sweet love's beauty, though my lover's life. 12
   His beauty shall in these black lines be seen,
   And they shall live, and he in them still green.

When I have seen by Time's fell hand defaced 64
The rich proud cost of outworn buried age,
When sometime lofty towers I see down-rased
And brass eternal slave to mortal rage ; 4
When I have seen the hungry ocean gain
Advantage on the kingdom of the shore,
And the firm soil win of the wat'ry main,
Increasing store with loss and loss with store ; 8
When I have seen such interchange of state,
Or state itself confounded to decay,
Ruin hath taught me thus to ruminate,
That Time will come and take my love away. 12
   This thought is as a death, which cannot choose
   But weep to have that which it fears to lose.

59 : 1 *that* everything  3 *invention* novelty  3–4 *bear . . . of* i.e. merely
miscarry  5 *record* memory  6 *courses . . . sun* years  8 *Since . . . done*
since thought was first expressed in writing  10 *composèd wonder* wonderful
composition  11 *mended* improved ; *whe'r* whether  12 *revolution . . . same*
one cycle repeats another

60 : 4 *sequent* successive ; *contend* struggle  5 *Nativity* the new-born ; *the
. . . light* orbit  7 *Crooked* adverse, malignant  8 *confound* destroy  10
*delves the parallels* digs the lines  13 *times in hope* hoped-for times ; *stand*
endure

61 : 7 *shames* faults  8 *scope and tenure* aim and purport  11 *defeat*
destroy

62 : 5 *gracious* pleasing  8 *As* as if ; *other* others  10 *chopped* seamed ;
*tanned antiquity* i.e. leathery old age  11 *contrary* in a different way  13
*'Tis . . . praise* i.e. I am praising you whom I identify with myself

63 : 1 *Against* in expectation of the time when  5 *steepy* deep, precipitous
9 *fortify* build defenses  10 *confounding* destroying  12 *though* i.e. though
he cuts

64 : 2 *cost* outlay  3 *sometime* formerly  4 *brass eternal* everlasting brass ;
*mortal rage* ravages of mortality  6 *Advantage* inroads  8 *Increasing . . .
store* i.e. one gaining by the other's loss, one losing by the other's gain  10
*confounded* reduced  14 *to have* for having

65 Since brass, nor stone, nor earth, nor boundless sea,
But sad mortality o'ersways their power,
How with this rage shall beauty hold a plea,
4 Whose action is no stronger than a flower?
O, how shall summer's honey breath hold out
Against the wrackful siege of batt'ring days,
When rocks impregnable are not so stout,
8 Nor gates of steel so strong but Time decays?
O fearful meditation: where, alack,
Shall Time's best jewel from Time's chest lie hid?
Or what strong hand can hold his swift foot back,
12 Or who his spoil of beauty can forbid?
     O, none, unless this miracle have might,
     That in black ink my love may still shine bright.

66 Tired with all these, for restful death I cry:
As, to behold desert a beggar born,
And needy nothing trimmed in jollity,
4 And purest faith unhappily forsworn,
And gilded honor shamefully misplaced,
And maiden virtue rudely strumpeted,
And right perfection wrongfully disgraced,
8 And strength by limping sway disablèd,
And art made tongue-tied by authority,
And folly (doctor-like) controlling skill,
And simple truth miscalled simplicity,
12 And captive good attending captain ill.
     Tired with all these, from these would I be gone,
     Save that, to die, I leave my love alone.

67 Ah, wherefore with infection should he live
And with his presence grace impiety,
That sin by him advantage should achieve
4 And lace itself with his society?
Why should false painting imitate his cheek
And steal dead seeing of his living hue?
Why should poor beauty indirectly seek
8 Roses of shadow, since his rose is true?
Why should he live, now Nature bankrout is,
Beggared of blood to blush through lively veins,
For she hath no exchequer now but his,
12 And, proud of many, lives upon his gains?
     O, him she stores, to show what wealth she had
     In days long since, before these last so bad.

68 Thus is his cheek the map of days outworn
When beauty lived and died as flowers do now,
Before these bastard signs of fair were born
4 Or durst inhabit on a living brow;
Before the golden tresses of the dead,
The right of sepulchers, were shorn away
To live a second life on second head,
8 Ere beauty's dead fleece made another gay:
In him those holy antique hours are seen,
Without all ornament, itself and true,
Making no summer of another's green,
12 Robbing no old to dress his beauty new;
     And him as for a map doth Nature store,
     To show false Art what beauty was of yore.

Those parts of thee that the world's eye doth view    66
Want nothing that the thought of hearts can mend;
All tongues, the voice of souls, give thee that due,
Utt'ring bare truth, even so as foes commend.    4
Thy outward thus with outward praise is crowned,
But those same tongues that give thee so thine own
In other accents do this praise confound
By seeing farther than the eye hath shown.    8
They look into the beauty of thy mind,
And that in guess they measure by thy deeds;
Then, churls, their thoughts, although their eyes were kind,
To thy fair flower add the rank smell of weeds:    12
     But why thy odor matcheth not thy show,
     The soil is this, that thou dost common grow.

That thou art blamed shall not be thy defect,    70
For slander's mark was ever yet the fair;
The ornament of beauty is suspect,
A crow that flies in heaven's sweetest air.    4
So thou be good, slander doth but approve
Thy worth the greater, being wooed of time;
For canker vice the sweetest buds doth love,
And thou present'st a pure unstainèd prime.    8
Thou hast passed by the ambush of young days,
Either not assailed, or victor being charged;
Yet this thy praise cannot be so thy praise
To tie up envy, evermore enlarged:    12
     If some suspect of ill masked not thy show,
     Then thou alone kingdoms of hearts shouldst owe.

65: 1 *Since* since there is neither    3 *rage* destructive power; *hold* maintain
4 *action* case    6 *wrackful* wrecking    10 *from Time's chest* i.e. from being
coffered up by Time    12 *spoil* spoliation

66: 2 *As* such as, for instance    3 *needy . . . jollity* i.e. the lack-all nobody
festively attired    4 *unhappily forsworn* evilly betrayed    7 *disgraced* banished from favor    8 *by . . . disablèd* i.e. weakened by incompetent leadership    9 *art . . . . authority* (possibly an allusion to state censorship of
literature)    10 *doctor-like* i.e. owlishly    11 *simplicity* stupidity

67: 1 *wherefore* why; *infection* corruption    3 *advantage* profit    4 *lace* i.e.
ornament    6 *dead seeing* the lifeless appearance    7 *poor* inferior; *indirectly*
by imitation    8 *Roses of shadow* i.e. pictured roses    9 *bankrout* bankrupt
10 *Beggared . . . veins* i.e. lacking the blood to blush naturally instead of by
the use of cosmetics    11 *exchequer* i.e. treasury of natural beauty    12
*proud* falsely proud (?)    13 *stores* preserves

68: 1 *map* representation; *outworn* outlived    3 *bastard signs* i.e. cosmetics; *fair* beauty    4 *inhabit* dwell    6 *The right of* belonging properly to
9 *antique hours* ancient times    13 *as . . . map* i.e. as if for a guide; *store*
preserve

69: 1 *parts* outward parts    4 *as foes commend* i.e. forced to the admission
6 *thine own* what is due you    7 *confound* destroy    10 *in guess* at a guess
13 *odor matcheth not* (cf. Sonnet 54)    14 *soil* (1) ground, (2) soilure;
*common* (1) uncultivated, like weeds, (2) overfamiliar

70: 1 *defect* fault    3 *ornament* (like a 'beauty mark'); *suspect* suspicion    5
*approve* prove    6 *wooed of time* solicited to evil by the times (?)    7 *canker*
destructive worm    9 *ambush* i.e. dangerous lure, trap    10 *charged* assailed
12 *tie up envy* i.e. silence malice    13 *If . . . show* i.e. if some suspicion did
not obscure your fine appearance    14 *owe* own

71  No longer mourn for me when I am dead
    Than you shall hear the surly sullen bell
    Give warning to the world that I am fled
4   From this vile world, with vilest worms to dwell.
    Nay, if you read this line, remember not
    The hand that writ it, for I love you so
    That I in your sweet thoughts would be forgot
8   If thinking on me then should make you woe.
    O, if, I say, you look upon this verse
    When I, perhaps, compounded am with clay,
    Do not so much as my poor name rehearse,
12  But let your love even with my life decay,
        Lest the wise world should look into your moan
        And mock you with me after I am gone.

72  O, lest the world should task you to recite
    What merit lived in me that you should love
    After my death, dear love, forget me quite,
4   For you in me can nothing worthy prove ;
    Unless you would devise some virtuous lie,
    To do more for me than mine own desert
    And hang more praise upon deceasèd I
8   Than niggard truth would willingly impart.
    O, lest your true love may seem false in this,
    That you for love speak well of me untrue,
    My name be buried where my body is,
12  And live no more to shame nor me nor you ;
        For I am shamed by that which I bring forth,
        And so should you, to love things nothing worth.

73  That time of year thou mayst in me behold
    When yellow leaves, or none, or few, do hang
    Upon those boughs which shake against the cold,
4   Bare ruined choirs where late the sweet birds sang.
    In me thou seest the twilight of such day
    As after sunset fadeth in the west,
    Which by and by black night doth take away,
8   Death's second self that seals up all in rest.
    In me thou seest the glowing of such fire
    That on the ashes of his youth doth lie,
    As the deathbed whereon it must expire,
12  Consumed with that which it was nourished by.
        This thou perceiv'st, which makes thy love more strong,
        To love that well which thou must leave ere long.

74  But be contented : when that fell arrest
    Without all bail shall carry me away,
    My life hath in this line some interest
4   Which for memorial still with thee shall stay.
    When thou reviewest this, thou dost review
    The very part was consecrate to thee :
    The earth can have but earth, which is his due ;
8   My spirit is thine, the better part of me.
    So then thou hast but lost the dregs of life,
    The prey of worms, my body being dead,
    The coward conquest of a wretch's knife,
12  Too base of thee to be rememberèd.
        The worth of that is that which it contains,
        And that is this, and this with thee remains.

75  So are you to my thoughts as food to life,
    Or as sweet-seasoned showers are to the ground ;
    And for the peace of you I hold such strife
4   As 'twixt a miser and his wealth is found :
    Now proud as an enjoyer, and anon
    Doubting the filching age will steal his treasure ;
    Now counting best to be with you alone,
8   Then bettered that the world may see my pleasure ;
    Sometime all full with feasting on your sight,
    And by and by clean starvèd for a look,
    Possessing or pursuing no delight
12  Save what is had or must from you be took.
        Thus do I pine and surfeit day by day,
        Or gluttoning on all, or all away.

76  Why is my verse so barren of new pride ?
    So far from variation or quick change ?
    Why, with the time, do I not glance aside
4   To new-found methods and to compounds strange ?
    Why write I still all one, ever the same,
    And keep invention in a noted weed,
    That every word doth almost tell my name,
8   Showing their birth, and where they did proceed ?
    O, know, sweet love, I always write of you,
    And you and love are still my argument ;
    So all my best is dressing old words new,
12  Spending again what is already spent :
        For as the sun is daily new and old,
        So is my love still telling what is told.

71 : 8 *make you woe* make woe for you  10 *compounded* blended  13 *wise* i.e. disdainful of foolish sentiment  14 *with* because of

72 : 1 *task . . . recite* put you to the task of telling  5 *virtuous lie* noble lie (?), false attribution of virtue (?)  8 *niggard* miserly  10 *untrue* untruly  12 *nor . . . nor* either . . . or  13 *which . . . forth* (probably a deprecatory allusion to the sonnets)

73 : 4 *choirs* i.e. the part of a church or monastery where services were sung  7 *by and by* shortly  8 *seals up* encloses  10 *That* as  12 *with . . . by* i.e. by life

74 : 1 *fell* fatal  2 *Without all bail* i.e. irrievably  3 *line* poem ; *interest* share  4 *still* always  7 *his due* its due (i.e. 'dust to dust')  11 *The . . . knife* i.e. easily cut down by the bravo Death (?)  13–14 *The worth . . . is this* i.e. the only value of the body is as a container of the soul, and the soul is in this poem

75 : 2 *sweet-seasoned* of the sweet season, spring  3 *peace of you* i.e. peace you bring me ; *hold such strife* i.e. exist on such uneasy terms  5 *anon* soon  6 *Doubting* fearing  8 *bettered* better pleased  14 *Or . . . away* i.e. either feeding on the full feast of your presence or having nothing in your absence

76 : 1 *pride* adornment  2 *quick change* modishness  3 *the time* the times, i.e. the current styles  4 *compounds strange* i.e. literary concoctions (?), neologisms, like those being introduced by Marston (?)  5 *one* one way  6 *invention* poetic creation ; *noted weed* familiar garb  10 *argument* theme  11 *So . . . best* i.e. so that the best I am capable of

77  Thy glass will show thee how thy beauties wear,
    Thy dial how thy precious minutes waste;
    The vacant leaves thy mind's imprint will bear,
 4  And of this book this learning mayst thou taste.
    The wrinkles which thy glass will truly show,
    Of mouthèd graves will give thee memory.
    Thou by thy dial's shady stealth mayst know
 8  Time's thievish progress to eternity.
    Look what thy memory cannot contain,
    Commit to these waste blanks, and thou shalt find
    Those children nursed, delivered from thy brain,
12  To take a new acquaintance of thy mind.
       These offices, so oft as thou wilt look,
       Shall profit thee and much enrich thy book.

   Or I shall live your epitaph to make,             8
   Or you survive when I in earth am rotten.
   From hence your memory death cannot take,
   Although in me each part will be forgotten.        4
   Your name from hence immortal life shall have,
   Though I, once gone, to all the world must die.
   The earth can yield me but a common grave
   When you entombèd in men's eyes shall lie.         8
   Your monument shall be my gentle verse,
   Which eyes not yet created shall o'erread;
   And tongues to be your being shall rehearse
   When all the breathers of this world are dead.    12
      You still shall live (such virtue hath my pen)
      Where breath most breathes, even in the mouths of men.

78  So oft have I invoked thee for my Muse
    And found such fair assistance in my verse
    As every alien pen hath got my use
 4  And under thee their poesy disperse.
    Thine eyes, that taught the dumb on high to sing
    And heavy ignorance aloft to fly,
    Have added feathers to the learnèd's wing
 8  And given grace a double majesty.
    Yet be most proud of that which I compile,
    Whose influence is thine and born of thee.
    In others' works thou dost but mend the style,
12  And arts with thy sweet graces gracèd be;
       But thou art all my art and dost advance
       As high as learning my rude ignorance.

   I grant thou wert not married to my Muse           8
   And therefore mayst without attaint o'erlook
   The dedicated words which writers use
   Of their fair subject, blessing every book.        4
   Thou art as fair in knowledge as in hue,
   Finding thy worth a limit past my praise;
   And therefore art enforced to seek anew
   Some fresher stamp of the time-bettering days.     8
   And do so, love; yet when they have devised
   What strainèd touches rhetoric can lend,
   Thou, truly fair, wert truly sympathized
   In true plain words by thy true-telling friend:   12
      And their gross painting might be better used
      Where cheeks need blood; in thee it is abused.

79  Whilst I alone did call upon thy aid,
    My verse alone had all thy gentle grace;
    But now my gracious numbers are decayed,
 4  And my sick Muse doth give another place.
    I grant, sweet love, thy lovely argument
    Deserves the travail of a worthier pen;
    Yet what of thee thy poet doth invent
 8  He robs thee of, and pays it thee again.
    He lends thee virtue, and he stole that word
    From thy behavior; beauty doth he give,
    And found it in thy cheek: he can afford
12  No praise to thee but what in thee doth live.
       Then thank him not for that which he doth say,
       Since what he owes thee thou thyself dost pay.

77: 1 *glass* mirror; *wear* wear out  2 *dial* sun-dial  3 *vacant leaves* i.e. the blank leaves of a tablet (?) (cf. Sonnet 122); *mind's imprint* i.e. the reflections to be written in the tablet  4 *this learning* i.e. the wisdom brought by his own reflections  6 *mouthèd* devouring; *memory* reminder  8 *thievish* stealthy  9 *Look what* whatever  10 *waste blanks* blank pages  11 *nursed* preserved  13 *offices* regular duties; *look* i.e. at the glass, the dial, and what has been previously written in the book

78: 3 *As* that; *alien* i.e. belonging to outsiders; *got my use* followed my practise  4 *under thee* i.e. with you as their Muse  5 *on high* in exultation (like the lark)  7 *added feathers* i.e. imped their wings for still higher flights  8 *grace* (an attribute of majesty)  10 *Whose . . . thine* i.e. wholly inspired by you  11 *mend* i.e. merely improve

79: 4 *give another place* yield place to another  5 *thy lovely argument* the theme of your loveliness  11 *afford* offer  14 *owes* is obliged to give

80  O, how I faint when I of you do write,
    Knowing a better spirit doth use your name
    And in the praise thereof spends all his might
 4  To make me tongue-tied, speaking of your fame.
    But since your worth (wide as the ocean is)
    The humble as the proudest sail doth bear,
    My saucy bark, inferior far to his,
 8  On your broad main doth wilfully appear.
    Your shallowest help will hold me up afloat
    Whilst he upon your soundless deep doth ride;
    Or, being wracked, I am a worthless boat,
12  He of tall building and of goodly pride.
       Then if he thrive, and I be cast away,
       The worst was this: my love was my decay.

80: 1 *faint* falter  2 *better spirit* i.e. more richly gifted poet  4 *tongue-tied* i.e. in comparison with the other  6 *as* as well as  8 *wilfully* i.e. boldly, in spite of all  10 *soundless* unfathomable  11 *wracked* wrecked; *boat* (any vessel less considerable than a ship)  12 *tall* sturdy; *pride* splendor  14 *decay* destruction

81: 1 *Or* either  3, 5 *hence* the present poems  4 *in . . . part* every part of me  8 *entombèd . . . lie* i.e. kept always before their eyes  11 *rehearse* recite  13 *virtue* power  14 *breath* speech (?), soul (?)

82: 2 *attaint* dishonor; *o'erlook* peruse  3 *dedicated* devoted; *writers* i.e. other writers  5 *hue* complexion  6 *Finding . . . past* i.e. knowing your worth to extend beyond  8 *stamp* imprint; *time-bettering* improving. progressing with the times  10 *strainèd* excessive  11 *sympathized* represented  14 *abused* i.e. an abuse

**83**
I never saw that you did painting need,
And therefore to your fair no painting set;
I found, or thought I found, you did exceed
4  The barren tender of a poet's debt:
And therefore have I slept in your report,
That you yourself, being extant, well might show
How far a modern quill doth come too short,
8  Speaking of worth, what worth in you doth grow.
This silence for my sin you did impute,
Which shall be most my glory, being dumb,
For I impair not beauty, being mute,
12  When others would give life and bring a tomb.
  There lives more life in one of your fair eyes
  Than both your poets can in praise devise.

**84**
Who is it that says most, which can say more
Than this rich praise, that you alone are you,
In whose confine immurèd is the store
4  Which should example where your equal grew?
Lean penury within that pen doth dwell
That to his subject lends not some small glory,
But he that writes of you, if he can tell
8  That you are you, so dignifies his story.
Let him but copy what in you is writ,
Not making worse what nature made so clear,
And such a counterpart shall fame his wit,
12  Making his style admirèd everywhere.
  You to your beauteous blessings add a curse,
  Being fond on praise, which makes your praises worse.

**85**
My tongue-tied Muse in manners holds her still
While comments of your praise, richly compiled,
Reserve their character with golden quill
4  And precious phrase by all the Muses filed.
I think good thoughts whilst other write good words,
And, like unlettered clerk, still cry 'Amen'
To every hymn that able spirit affords
8  In polished form of well-refinèd pen.
Hearing you praised, I say, ''Tis so, 'tis true,'
And to the most of praise add something more;
But that is in my thought, whose love to you,
12  Though words come hindmost, holds his rank before.
  Then others for the breath of words respect;
  Me for my dumb thoughts, speaking in effect.

**86**
Was it the proud full sail of his great verse,
Bound for the prize of all-too-precious you,
That did my ripe thoughts in my brain inhearse,
4  Making their tomb the womb wherein they grew?
Was it his spirit, by spirits taught to write
Above a mortal pitch, that struck me dead?
No, neither he, nor his compeers by night
8  Giving him aid, my verse astonishèd.
He, nor that affable familiar ghost
Which nightly gulls him with intelligence,
As victors, of my silence cannot boast;
12  I was not sick of any fear from thence:
  But when your countenance filled up his line,
  Then lacked I matter; that enfeebled mine.

**87**
Farewell: thou art too dear for my possessing,
And like enough thou know'st thy estimate.
The charter of thy worth gives thee releasing;
4  My bonds in thee are all determinate.
For how do I hold thee but by thy granting,
And for that riches where is my deserving?
The cause of this fair gift in me is wanting,
8  And so my patent back again is swerving.
Thyself thou gav'st, thy own worth then not knowing,
Or me, to whom thou gav'st it, else mistaking;
So thy great gift, upon misprision growing,
12  Comes home again, on better judgment making.
  Thus have I had thee as a dream doth flatter,
  In sleep a king, but waking no such matter.

83: **2** *fair* beauty; *set* applied  **4** *barren tender* worthless offering; *debt* payment  **5** *slept ... report* been inactive in writing of you  **7** *modern* trite  **8** *Speaking in speaking*; *what worth* i.e. to speak of such worth as  **12** *bring a tomb* bring death (i.e. by reducing your living features to a dead image)

84: **1** *Who ... more* i.e. who that says the utmost can say more  **3–4** *In ... grew* in whom are locked up all the qualities needed to provide an equal example  **6** *his* its  **8** *so* i.e. sufficiently  **11** *counterpart* copy; *fame* bring fame to  **14** *fond on* (probably a corruption: the *curse* would appear to be on poets, who fail because he is beyond their praise)

85: **1** *in ... still* i.e. politely remains silent  **2–3** *While ... character* (an obscure passage. possibly corrupt)  **2** *comments* expositions (?); *compiled* composed (?)  **3** *Reserve* preserve (?); *character* writing (?)  **4** *filed* polished  **5** *other* others  **6** *unlettered clerk* illiterate parish clerk; *still* always  **6–7** *cry ... affords* i.e. give approval to every poem offered by an able poet  **10** *most* utmost  **13** *the ... words* i.e. actual speech  **14** *speaking in effect* i.e. virtually speaking

86: **1** *his* i.e. an unidentified rival poet's  **2** *Bound ... of* i.e. designed to capture  **3** *inhearse* coffin up  **5** *spirits* divine inspirers  **6** *dead* dead silent  **7** *compeers by night* collaborators, spirit aids  **8** *astonishèd* dumbfounded  **10** *gulls ... intelligence* tricks him with spying reports (allusion obscure)  **13** *countenance filled up* approval repaired any defect in

87: **1** *dear* precious. costly  **2** *estimate* value  **3** *charter* privilege; *releasing* i.e. release from obligation  **4** *bonds* claims; *determinate* ended  **7** *cause* justification; *wanting* lacking  **8** *patent* right; *swerving* turning away  **10** *mistaking* i.e. overestimating  **11** *upon misprision growing* based on error  **12** *on ... making* on your coming to a better judgment  **13** *as ... flatter* as in a flattering dream

88: **1** *set me light* make light of me  **7** *attainted* dishonored  **8** *losing* getting rid of  **10** *bending* turning  **12** *vantage* advantage

**88**
When thou shalt be disposed to set me light
And place my merit in the eye of scorn,
Upon thy side against myself I'll fight
4  And prove thee virtuous, though thou art forsworn.
With mine own weakness being best acquainted,
Upon thy part I can set down a story
Of faults concealed wherein I am attainted,
8  That thou, in losing me, shall win much glory:
And I by this will be a gainer too;
For, bending all my loving thoughts on thee,
The injuries that to myself I do,
12  Doing thee vantage, double-vantage me.
  Such is my love, to thee I so belong,
  That for thy right myself will bear all wrong.

89 Say that thou didst forsake me for some fault,
And I will comment upon that offense;
Speak of my lameness, and I straight will halt,
4 Against thy reasons making no defense.
Thou canst not, love, disgrace me half so ill,
To set a form upon desirèd change,
As I'll myself disgrace; knowing thy will,
8 I will acquaintance strangle and look strange,
Be absent from thy walks, and in my tongue
Thy sweet belovèd name no more shall dwell,
Lest I, too much profane, should do it wrong
12 And haply of our old acquaintance tell.
   For thee, against myself I'll vow debate,
   For I must ne'er love him whom thou dost hate.

90 Then hate me when thou wilt; if ever, now;
Now, while the world is bent my deeds to cross,
Join with the spite of fortune, make me bow,
4 And do not drop in for an after-loss.
Ah, do not, when my heart hath scaped this sorrow,
Come in the rearward of a conquered woe;
Give not a windy night a rainy morrow,
8 To linger out a purposed overthrow.
If thou wilt leave me, do not leave me last,
When other petty griefs have done their spite,
But in the onset come: so shall I taste
12 At first the very worst of fortune's might;
   And other strains of woe, which now seem woe,
   Compared with loss of thee will not seem so.

91 Some glory in their birth, some in their skill,
Some in their wealth, some in their body's force,
Some in their garments, though newfangled ill;
4 Some in their hawks and hounds, some in their horse;
And every humor hath his adjunct pleasure,
Wherein it finds a joy above the rest,
But these particulars are not my measure;
8 All these I better in one general best.
Thy love is better than high birth to me,
Richer than wealth, prouder than garments' cost,
Of more delight than hawks or horses be;
12 And having thee, of all men's pride I boast:
   Wretched in this alone, that thou mayst take
   All this away and me most wretched make.

92 But do thy worst to steal thyself away,
For term of life thou art assurèd mine,
And life no longer than thy love will stay,
4 For it depends upon that love of thine.
Then need I not to fear the worst of wrongs
When in the least of them my life hath end;
I see a better state to me belongs
8 Than that which on thy humor doth depend.
Thou canst not vex me with inconstant mind,
Since that my life on thy revolt doth lie.
O, what a happy title do I find,
12 Happy to have thy love, happy to die!
   But what's so blessèd-fair that fears no blot?
   Thou mayst be false, and yet I know it not.

So shall I live, supposing thou art true, 93
Like a deceivèd husband; so love's face
May still seem love to me though altered new,
Thy looks with me, thy heart in other place. 4
For there can live no hatred in thine eye;
Therefore in that I cannot know thy change;
In many's looks the false heart's history
Is writ in moods and frowns and wrinkles strange: 8
But heaven in thy creation did decree
That in thy face sweet love should ever dwell;
Whate'er thy thoughts or thy heart's workings be,
Thy looks should nothing thence but sweetness tell. 12
   How like Eve's apple doth thy beauty grow
   If thy sweet virtue answer not thy show!

They that have pow'r to hurt and will do none, 94
That do not do the thing they most do show,
Who, moving others, are themselves as stone,
Unmovèd, cold, and to temptation slow; 4
They rightly do inherit heaven's graces
And husband nature's riches from expense;
They are the lords and owners of their faces,
Others but stewards of their excellence. 8
The summer's flow'r is to the summer sweet,
Though to itself it only live and die;
But if that flow'r with base infection meet,
The basest weed outbraves his dignity: 12
   For sweetest things turn sourest by their deeds;
   Lilies that fester smell far worse than weeds.

89: 2 *comment* expatiate 3 *lameness* i.e. defect (metaphorical); *halt* limp 4 *reasons* charges 6 *To . . . change* i.e. to seem to justify the change you wish to make in our relationship 7 *disgrace* depreciate 8 *acquaintance* i.e. the fact of my being acquainted with you; *strange* as a stranger 12 *haply* accidentally 13 *vow debate* declare war

90: 2 *bent* determined; *cross* thwart 4 *drop . . . after-loss* i.e. casually add to my griefs later on 5 *scaped* escaped 6 *Come . . . woe* i.e. attack after I have overcome my sorrow 8 *linger out* protract; *purposed* predestined 13 *strains* kinds

91: 2 *force* strength 3 *newfangled ill* modishly ugly 4 *horse* horses 5 *humor* disposition; *his* its; *adjunct* corresponding 7 *particulars* i.e. various possessions; *measure* standard of happiness 8 *better* improve upon 12 *all men's pride* i.e. all the things that men take pride in

92: 2 *term of life* my lifetime 5–6 *Then . . . end* i.e. there is no distinction in misfortunes since there is really only one – the loss of friendship, which ends life 8 *humor* whim 10 *on thy . . . lie* i.e. ends with your turning away from me 11 *happy title* title to happiness 14 *Thou . . . not* i.e. I may be denied the releasing death which certainty of your falsehood would bring

93: 2 *face* appearance 8 *moods* looks of moodiness; *strange* unaccustomed 12 *thence* i.e. by themselves 13 *Eve's apple* i.e. fair only in appearance; *grow* become

94: 1 *and . . . none* i.e. without actively trying to hurt 2 *show* i.e. seem to do, or seem capable of doing 5 *rightly* as a right, veritably 6 *expense* expenditure 7 *owners . . . faces* permanent possessors of the qualities that show in them 8 *stewards* dispensers 12 *outbraves his* outglories its 14 *Lilies . . . weeds* (this line also appears in the anonymous play *Edward III*, pub. 1596, ed. 1897, II, i, 451, in one of the scenes frequently attributed to Shakespeare)

95 How sweet and lovely dost thou make the shame
   Which, like a canker in the fragrant rose,
   Doth spot the beauty of thy budding name !
4  O, in what sweets dost thou thy sins enclose !
   That tongue that tells the story of thy days,
   Making lascivious comments on thy sport,
   Cannot dispraise but in a kind of praise ;
8  Naming thy name blesses an ill report.
   O, what a mansion have those vices got
   Which for their habitation chose out thee,
   Where beauty's veil doth cover every blot
12 And all things turns to fair that eyes can see !
      Take heed, dear heart, of this large privilege ;
      The hardest knife ill used doth lose his edge.

96 Some say thy fault is youth, some wantonness ;
   Some say thy grace is youth and gentle sport ;
   Both grace and faults are loved of more and less :
4  Thou mak'st faults graces that to thee resort.
   As on the finger of a thronèd queen
   The basest jewel will be well esteemed,
   So are those errors that in thee are seen
8  To truths translated and for true things deemed.
   How many lambs might the stern wolf betray
   If like a lamb he could his looks translate !
   How many gazers mightst thou lead away
12 If thou wouldst use the strength of all thy state !
      But do not so ; I love thee in such sort
      As, thou being mine, mine is thy good report.

How like a winter hath my absence been    97
From thee, the pleasure of the fleeting year !
What freezings have I felt, what dark days seen !
What old December's bareness everywhere !    4
And yet this time removed was summer's time,
The teeming autumn, big with rich increase,
Bearing the wanton burden of the prime,
Like widowed wombs after their lords' decease :    8
Yet this abundant issue seemed to me
But hope of orphans and unfathered fruit ;
For summer and his pleasures wait on thee,
And, thou away, the very birds are mute ;    12
   Or, if they sing, 'tis with so dull a cheer
   That leaves look pale, dreading the winter's near.

From you have I been absent in the spring,    98
When proud-pied April, dressed in all his trim,
Hath put a spirit of youth in everything,
That heavy Saturn laughed and leapt with him ;    4
Yet nor the lays of birds, nor the sweet smell
Of different flowers in odor and in hue,
Could make me any summer's story tell,
Or from their proud lap pluck them where they grew :    8
Nor did I wonder at the lily's white,
Nor praise the deep vermilion in the rose ;
They were but sweet, but figures of delight,
Drawn after you, you pattern of all those.    12
   Yet seemed it winter still, and you away,
   As with your shadow I with these did play.

The forward violet thus did I chide :    99
Sweet thief, whence didst thou steal thy sweet that smells,
If not from my love's breath ? The purple pride
Which on thy soft cheek for complexion dwells    4
In my love's veins thou hast too grossly dyed.
The lily I condemnèd for thy hand ;
And buds of marjoram had stol'n thy hair ;
The roses fearfully on thorns did stand,    8
One blushing shame, another white despair ;
A third, nor red nor white, had stol'n of both,
And to his robb'ry had annexed thy breath ;
But, for his theft, in pride of all his growth    12
A vengeful canker eat him up to death.
   More flowers I noted, yet I none could see
   But sweet or color it had stol'n from thee.

Where art thou, Muse, that thou forget'st so long    100
To speak of that which gives thee all thy might ?
Spend'st thou thy fury on some worthless song,
Dark'ning thy pow'r to lend base subjects light ?    4
Return, forgetful Muse, and straight redeem
In gentle numbers time so idly spent ;
Sing to the ear that doth thy lays esteem
And gives thy pen both skill and argument.    8
Rise, resty Muse, my love's sweet face survey,
If Time have any wrinkle graven there ;
If any, be a satire to decay
And make Time's spoils despisèd everywhere.    12
   Give my love fame faster than Time wastes life ;
   So thou prevent'st his scythe and crooked knife.

95 : 2 *canker* worm   3 *name* reputation   5 *thy days* i.e. how you spend
your days   6 *sport* amours   9 *mansion* dwelling   14 *his* its

96 : 1 *wantonness* amorous dalliance (the *gentle sport* of l. 2)   3 *of more and
less* by great and small   8 *translated* transformed   9 *stern* cruel   12 *state*
power   13–14 *But . . . report* (the same couplet ends Sonnet 36)

97 : 2 *pleasure* i.e. pleasant portion   5 *removed* i.e. when I was absent   6
*teeming* fertile ; *increase* harvest   7 *wanton burden* i.e. fruit of wantonness ;
*prime* spring   9 *issue* progeny   10 *hope of orphans* orphaned hope   11
*his* its

98 : 2 *proud-pied* gloriously dappled ; *trim* ornament   4 *heavy Saturn* (the
melancholy planet)   5 *nor . . . nor* neither . . . nor ; *lays* songs   6 *different*
*flowers* flowers different   7 *summer's* summery, gay   8 *proud lap* i.e.
mother earth   11 *figures* emblems   14 *shadow* portrait

99 : 1 *forward* early   3 *pride* splendor   5 *grossly* obviously   6 *condemnèd*
*for* i.e. found guilty of stealing the color of   11 *annexed* compounded the
theft of   13 *canker eat* worm ate   15 *sweet* scent

100 : 3 *fury* poetic frenzy   4 *Dark'ning* diminishing   6 *gentle numbers*
noble verses   9 *resty* lazy   11 *be a satire to* satirize   14 *thou prevent'st*
you thwart

101 O truant Muse, what shall be thy amends
    For thy neglect of truth in beauty dyed?
    Both truth and beauty on my love depends;
4 So dost thou too, and therein dignified.
    Make answer, Muse : wilt thou not haply say,
    'Truth needs no color with his color fixed,
    Beauty no pencil, beauty's truth to lay;
8 But best is best, if never intermixed.'
    Because he needs no praise, wilt thou be dumb?
    Excuse not silence so, for 't lies in thee
    To make him much outlive a gilded tomb
12 And to be praised of ages yet to be.
      Then do thy office, Muse; I teach thee how
      To make him seem, long hence, as he shows now.

Let not my love be called idolatry,    I
    Nor my belovèd as an idol show,
    Since all alike my songs and praises be
To one, of one, still such, and ever so.    4
    Kind is my love to-day, to-morrow kind,
    Still constant in a wondrous excellence;
    Therefore my verse, to constancy confined,
One thing expressing, leaves out difference.    8
    'Fair, kind, and true' is all my argument,
    'Fair, kind, and true,' varying to other words;
    And in this change is my invention spent,
Three themes in one, which wondrous scope affords.    12
      Fair, kind, and true have often lived alone,
      Which three till now never kept seat in one.

102 My love is strength'ned, though more weak in seeming;
    I love not less, though less the show appear:
    That love is merchandized whose rich esteeming
4 The owner's tongue doth publish everywhere.
    Our love was new, and then but in the spring,
    When I was wont to greet it with my lays,
    As Philomel in summer's front doth sing
8 And stops her pipe in growth of riper days;
    Not that the summer is less pleasant now
    Than when her mournful hymns did hush the night,
    But that wild music burdens every bough,
12 And sweets grown common lose their dear delight.
      Therefore, like her, I sometime hold my tongue,
      Because I would not dull you with my song.

When in the chronicle of wasted time    I
    I see descriptions of the fairest wights,
    And beauty making beautiful old rime
In praise of ladies dead and lovely knights;    4
    Then, in the blazon of sweet beauty's best,
    Of hand, of foot, of lip, of eye, of brow,
    I see their antique pen would have expressed
Even such a beauty as you master now.    8
    So all their praises are but prophecies
    Of this our time, all you prefiguring;
    And, for they looked but with divining eyes,
They had not skill enough your worth to sing:    1
      For we, which now behold these present days,
      Have eyes to wonder, but lack tongues to praise.

103 Alack, what poverty my Muse brings forth,
    That, having such a scope to show her pride,
    The argument all bare is of more worth
4 Than when it hath my added praise beside.
    O, blame me not if I no more can write!
    Look in your glass, and there appears a face
    That overgoes my blunt invention quite,
8 Dulling my lines and doing me disgrace.
    Were it not sinful then, striving to mend,
    To mar the subject that before was well?
    For to no other pass my verses tend
12 Than of your graces and your gifts to tell;
      And more, much more, than in my verse can sit
      Your own glass shows you when you look in it.

101: 2 *dyed* stamped  4 *thou* i.e. his Muse; *dignified* you are dignified  5 *haply* perchance  6 *no color* no artificial coloring; *his color fixed* its natural and permanent color  7 *lay* lay on  8 *intermixed* i.e. with true and false intermingled  13 *do thy office* perform your function

102: 1 *seeming* outward appearance  3 *merchandized* bartered; *esteeming* valuation  7 *Philomel* the nightingale; *front* forefront, beginning  8 *riper* later, more mature  11 *But . . . music* but because a wealth of bird-song  14 *dull* cloy, surfeit

103: 1 *poverty* inferior stuff  2 *pride* splendor  3 *argument* theme  7 *overgoes* outdoes; *blunt invention* crude creation  8 *Dulling* i.e. by comparison  11 *pass* purpose  13 *sit* reside

104 To me, fair friend, you never can be old,
    For as you were when first your eye I eyed,
    Such seems your beauty still. Three winters cold
4 Have from the forests shook three summers' pride,
    Three beauteous springs to yellow autumn turned
    In process of the seasons have I seen,
    Three April perfumes in three hot Junes burned,
8 Since first I saw you fresh, which yet are green.
    Ah, yet doth beauty, like a dial hand,
    Steal from his figure, and no pace perceived;
    So your sweet hue, which methinks still doth stand,
12 Hath motion, and mine eye may be deceived;
      For fear of which, hear this, thou age unbred:
      Ere you were born was beauty's summer dead.

104: 6 *process* the progress  7 *burned* (as incense)  9 *dial* watch  10 *his figure* (1) the dial's numeral, (2) the friend's form; *and . . . perceived* i.e. with invisible movement  11 *sweet hue* fair aspect; *still* (1) motionless, unchanged, (2) always; *stand* remain constant  13 *unbred* unborn  14 *summer* i.e. peak (the friend)

105: 4 *one* (in contrast to the 'many' of idolatrous worship); *still* always  6 *Still constant* always the same  8 *difference* variety  9 *argument* theme  11 *in this change* i.e. in ringing these changes  14 *kept seat* lodged

106: 1 *wasted* past  2 *wights* persons  5 *blazon* commemorative record  8 *master* command  10 *prefiguring* picturing in advance  11 *for* because; *divining* guessing  13 *we* i.e. even we

**107**

Not mine own fears, nor the prophetic soul
Of the wide world, dreaming on things to come,
Can yet the lease of my true love control,
Supposed as forfeit to a confined doom.
The mortal moon hath her eclipse endured,
And the sad augurs mock their own presage ;
Incertainties now crown themselves assured,
And peace proclaims olives of endless age.
Now with the drops of this most balmy time
My love looks fresh, and Death to me subscribes,
Since, spite of him, I'll live in this poor rime,
While he insults o'er dull and speechless tribes :
   And thou in this shalt find thy monument
   When tyrants' crests and tombs of brass are spent.

**108**

What's in the brain that ink may character
Which hath not figured to thee my true spirit ?
What's new to speak, what now to register,
That may express my love or thy dear merit ?
Nothing, sweet boy ; but yet, like prayers divine,
I must each day say o'er the very same ;
Counting no old thing old, thou mine, I thine,
Even as when first I hallowed thy fair name.
So that eternal love in love's fresh case
Weighs not the dust and injury of age,
Nor gives to necessary wrinkles place,
But makes antiquity for aye his page,
   Finding the first conceit of love there bred
   Where time and outward form would show it dead.

**109**

O, never say that I was false of heart,
Though absence seemed my flame to qualify ;
As easy might I from myself depart
As from my soul, which in thy breast doth lie.
That is my home of love : if I have ranged,
Like him that travels I return again,
Just to the time, not with the time exchanged,
So that myself bring water for my stain.
Never believe, though in my nature reigned
All frailties that besiege all kinds of blood,
That it could so preposterously be stained
To leave for nothing all thy sum of good ;
   For nothing this wide universe I call
   Save thou, my rose ; in it thou art my all.

**110**

Alas, 'tis true I have gone here and there
And made myself a motley to the view,
Gored mine own thoughts, sold cheap what is most dear,
Made old offenses of affections new.
Most true it is that I have looked on truth
Askance and strangely ; but, by all above,
These blenches gave my heart another youth,
And worse essays proved thee my best of love.
Now all is done, have what shall have no end :
Mine appetite I never more will grind
On newer proof, to try an older friend,
A god in love, to whom I am confined.
   Then give me welcome, next my heaven the best,
   Even to thy pure and most most loving breast.

**111**

O, for my sake do you with Fortune chide,
The guilty goddess of my harmful deeds,
That did not better for my life provide
Than public means which public manners breeds ;
Thence comes it that my name receives a brand ;
And almost thence my nature is subdued
To what it works in, like the dyer's hand :
Pity me then, and wish I were renewed,
Whilst, like a willing patient, I will drink
Potions of eisell 'gainst my strong infection ;
No bitterness that I will bitter think,
Nor double penance, to correct correction.
   Pity me then, dear friend, and I assure ye
   Even that your pity is enough to cure me.

**112**

Your love and pity doth th' impression fill
Which vulgar scandal stamped upon my brow ;
For what care I who calls me well or ill,
So you o'ergreen my bad, my good allow ?
You are my all the world, and I must strive
To know my shames and praises from your tongue ;
None else to me, nor I to none alive,
That my steeled sense or changes right or wrong.
In so profound abysm I throw all care
Of others' voices that my adder's sense
To critic and to flatterer stoppèd are ;
Mark how with my neglect I do dispense :
   You are so strongly in my purpose bred
   That all the world besides methinks are dead.

107 : 3 *lease* term   4 *Supposed . . . doom* i.e. presumed to be subject to a limited duration   5 *mortal . . . endured* (an allusion variously interpreted, most plausibly related to the death in 1603 of Queen Elizabeth, 'Cynthia')   6 *sad augurs* foreboding prognosticators ; *presage* predictions   7 *Incertainties . . . assured* i.e. uncertainty has triumphed as certainty   8 *olives . . . age* i.e. an eternal continuance of peace   10 *subscribes* surrenders   12 *insults* triumphs ; *tribes* multitudes   14 *spent* wasted away

108 : 1 *character* inscribe   2 *figured* revealed   3 *register* record   8 *hallowed* made sacred   9 *fresh case* youthful exterior   10 *Weighs not* cares not for   12 *page* i.e. to wait upon him   13 *conceit* conception

109 : 2 *qualify* abate, cool   5 *ranged* wandered   7 *Just* punctual ; *exchanged* changed   10 *blood* i.e. flesh   12 *for* in exchange for

110 : 2 *motley* jester   3 *Gored* wounded   4 *offenses* trespasses ; *affections* passions   6 *Askance and strangely* i.e. obliquely and at a distance   7 *blenches* turnings aside   8 *worse essays* trials of worse relationships   9 *shall . . . end* i.e. is eternal   10 *grind* whet   11 *proof* test   13 *my heaven* i.e. the Christian heaven

111 : 1 *chide* quarrel   2 *guilty goddess* i.e. goddess responsible for   3 *life* livelihood   4 *public means* (probably an allusion to activity in the popular playhouses)   5 *brand* stigma   6–7 *subdued To* reduced to, made one with   8 *renewed* cleansed   10 *eisell* vinegar (used against the plague)   12 *Nor . . . correction* i.e. I will not consider the cure worse than the disease

112 : 1 *th' impression fill* i.e. efface the scar   2 *vulgar scandal* i.e. notoriety (as a public performer ?)   4 *o'ergreen* conceal with verdure ; *allow* approve   6 *shames* faults   7–8 *None . . . wrong* (the sense of this obscure passage seems to be that no other human relationship affects his fixed sense of what is right and wrong)   9 *profound* deep   10 *adder's sense* i.e. deaf ears   12 *how . . . dispense* how I disregard public opinion   13 *so . . . bred* i.e. of such strong influence on my motives

113 Since I left you, mine eye is in my mind,
   And that which governs me to go about
   Doth part his function and is partly blind,
4  Seems seeing, but effectually is out ;
   For it no form delivers to the heart
   Of bird, of flow'r, or shape which it doth latch ;
   Of his quick objects hath the mind no part,
8  Nor his own vision holds what it doth catch ;
   For if it see the rud'st or gentlest sight,
   The most sweet favor or deformèd'st creature,
   The mountain or the sea, the day or night,
12 The crow or dove, it shapes them to your feature.
      Incapable of more, replete with you,
      My most true mind thus maketh mine eye untrue.

Accuse me thus, that I have scanted all                          11
   Wherein I should your great deserts repay ;
   Forgot upon your dearest love to call,
4  Whereto all bonds do tie me day by day ;
   That I have frequent been with unknown minds
   And given to time your own dear-purchased right ;
   That I have hoisted sail to all the winds
8  Which should transport me farthest from your sight.          8
   Book both my wilfulness and errors down,
   And on just proof surmise accumulate ;
   Bring me within the level of your frown,
12 But shoot not at me in your wakened hate :                   12
      Since my appeal says I did strive to prove
      The constancy and virtue of your love.

114 Or whether doth my mind, being crowned with you,
   Drink up the monarch's plague, this flattery ?
   Or whether shall I say mine eye saith true,
4  And that your love taught it this alchemy,
   To make of monsters and things indigest
   Such cherubins as your sweet self resemble,
   Creating every bad a perfect best
8  As fast as objects to his beams assemble ?
   O, 'tis the first ; 'tis flatt'ry in my seeing,
   And my great mind most kingly drinks it up :
   Mine eye well knows what with his gust is 'greeing,
12 And to his palate doth prepare the cup.
      If it be poisoned, 'tis the lesser sin
      That mine eye loves it and doth first begin.

115 Those lines that I before have writ do lie,
   Even those that said I could not love you dearer ;
   Yet then my judgment knew no reason why
4  My most full flame should afterwards burn clearer.
   But reckoning Time, whose millioned accidents
   Creep in 'twixt vows and change decrees of kings,
   Tan sacred beauty, blunt the sharp'st intents,
8  Divert strong minds to th' course of alt'ring things !
   Alas, why, fearing of Time's tyranny,
   Might I not then say, 'Now I love you best'
   When I was certain o'er incertainty,
12 Crowning the present, doubting of the rest ?
      Love is a babe ; then might I not say so,
      To give full growth to that which still doth grow.

116 Let me not to the marriage of true minds
   Admit impediments ; love is not love
   Which alters when it alteration finds
4  Or bends with the remover to remove.
   O, no, it is an ever-fixèd mark
   That looks on tempests and is never shaken ;
   It is the star to every wand'ring bark,
8  Whose worth 's unknown, although his height be taken.
   Love 's not Time's fool, though rosy lips and cheeks
   Within his bending sickle's compass come ;
   Love alters not with his brief hours and weeks,
12 But bears it out even to the edge of doom.
      If this be error, and upon me proved,
      I never writ, nor no man ever loved.

113: 1 *mine . . . mind* i.e. I am directed by inner sight  2 *governs . . . about* i.e. directs my steps  3 *part* divide  3, 7, 8 *his* its (i.e. the physical eye's)  4 *effectually* in effect  6 *latch* catch sight of  7 *quick* fleeting  8 *Nor . . . holds* i.e. nor does the eye itself retain  10 *favor* face  12 *feature* likeness  13 *replete* filled

114: 1, 3 *Or whether* (indicating alternative possibilities)  1 *being . . . you* i.e. by being crowned by you  4 *alchemy* i.e. power to transform substances  5 *indigest* shapeless  6 *cherubins* angelic forms  8 *to . . . assemble* i.e. are presented to the eye's gaze  11 *with . . . 'greeing* is agreeable to the mind's taste  14 *That* since

115: 2 *dearer* more dearly  5 *reckoning . . . accidents* i.e. time whose casual events are reckoned in the millions  7 *Tan* coarsen ; *intents* intentions  8 *Divert* accommodate ; *alt'ring things* things as they change  12 *Crowning* glorifying  13 *then* therefore ; *so* i.e. 'Now I love you best'

116: 2 *impediments* (an echo of the marriage service)  4 *bends . . . remove* i.e. agrees with the withdrawer to withdraw  5 *mark* sea-mark  8 *worth's unknown* i.e. value is incalculable ; *his height* the star's altitude  9 *fool* plaything  10 *Within . . . compass* i.e. within the range of Time's curving sickle  11 *his* Time's  12 *bears it out* persists  13 *upon* against

117: 1 *scanted* come short of  3 *Forgot . . . call* have forgotten to invoke your most precious love  4 *bonds* obligations  5 *frequent* familiar ; *unknown minds* i.e. negligible spirits  6 *given to time* i.e. wasted away  9 *Book . . . down* i.e. record both my intentional and unintentional trespasses  10 *on . . . accumulate* i.e. take account of valid circumstantial evidence  11 *level* range  13 *appeal* plea ; *strive to prove* i.e. thus try to test

18 Like as to make our appetites more keen,
　With eager compounds we our palate urge;
　As to prevent our maladies unseen,
4 We sicken to shun sickness when we purge:
　Even so, being full of your ne'er-cloying sweetness,
　To bitter sauces did I frame my feeding;
　And, sick of welfare, found a kind of meetness
8 To be diseased ere that there was true needing.
　Thus policy in love, t' anticipate
　The ills that were not, grew to faults assured,
　And brought to medicine a healthful state
12 Which, rank of goodness, would by ill be cured.
　　But thence I learn, and find the lesson true,
　　Drugs poison him that so fell sick of you.

What potions have I drunk of Siren tears　119
Distilled from limbecks foul as hell within,
Applying fears to hopes and hopes to fears,
Still losing when I saw myself to win!　4
What wretched errors hath my heart committed
Whilst it hath thought itself so blessèd never!
How have mine eyes out of their spheres been fitted
In the distraction of this madding fever!　8
O benefit of ill: now I find true
That better is by evil still made better;
And ruined love, when it is built anew,
Grows fairer than at first, more strong, far greater.　12
　So I return rebuked to my content,
　And gain by ills thrice more than I have spent.

That you were once unkind befriends me now,　120
And for that sorrow which I then did feel
Needs must I under my transgression bow,
Unless my nerves were brass or hammered steel.　4
For if you were by my unkindness shaken,
As I by yours, you've passed a hell of time,
And I, a tyrant, have no leisure taken
To weigh how once I suffered in your crime.　8
O that our night of woe might have rememb'red
My deepest sense how hard true sorrow hits,
And soon to you, as you to me then, tend'red
The humble salve which wounded bosoms fits!　12
　But that your trespass now becomes a fee;
　Mine ransoms yours, and yours must ransom me.

'Tis better to be vile than vile esteemed　121
When not to be receives reproach of being,
And the just pleasure lost, which is so deemed
Not by our feeling but by others' seeing.　4
For why should others' false adulterate eyes
Give salutation to my sportive blood?
Or on my frailties why are frailer spies,
Which in their wills count bad what I think good?　8
No, I am that I am; and they that level
At my abuses reckon up their own:
I may be straight though they themselves be bevel;
By their rank thoughts my deeds must not be shown,　12
　Unless this general evil they maintain:
　All men are bad and in their badness reign.

Thy gift, thy tables, are within my brain　122
Full charactered with lasting memory,
Which shall above that idle rank remain
Beyond all date, even to eternity;　4
Or, at the least, so long as brain and heart
Have faculty by nature to subsist,
Till each to rased oblivion yield his part
Of thee, thy record never can be missed.　8
That poor retention could not so much hold,
Nor need I tallies thy dear love to score;
Therefore to give them from me was I bold,
To trust those tables that receive thee more.　12
　To keep an adjunct to remember thee
　Were to import forgetfulness in me.

118: 1 *Like as* just as　2 *eager compounds* sharp condiments; *urge* stimulate　3 *As* just as; *prevent* ward off, forestall　6 *bitter sauces* i.e. unsavory persons; *frame* direct　7 *meetness* appropriateness　9 *anticipate* forestall　10 *faults assured* actual faults　11 *medicine* i.e. medical treatment　12 *rank* too full　14 *so* thus

119: 1 *Siren tears* i.e. appeals of the temptress　2 *limbecks* alembics, stills (i.e. the person of the temptress)　3 *Applying* i.e. as a salve　4 *Still* always; *saw myself* expected　6 *so blessèd never* never so blessed　7 *spheres* sockets (?), orbits (?); *fitted* forced by fits　8 *madding* maddening, producing delirium

120: 2 *for* because of　3 *my transgression* i.e. my present unkindness to you　4 *nerves* sinews　7 *tyrant* oppressor; *no leisure taken* i.e. failed to take the time　8 *weigh* consider; *crime* i.e. unkindness to me　9 *night of woe* i.e. estrangement, for which you were responsible; *rememb'red* reminded　11 *tend'red* offered　12 *salve* apology; *fits* suits　13 *fee* payment　14 *ransoms* redeems, excuses

121: 1 *esteemed* considered　2 *not to be* i.e. not to be vile; *being* i.e. being vile　3 *just* right, proper; *so* i.e. vile　4 *Not . . . seeing* i.e. not in our own mind but in the view of others　5 *false adulterate* prurient　6 *Give salutation to* greet, i.e. meet more than halfway; *sportive* wanton　7 *frailties* faults; *frailer* faultier　8 *in their wills* i.e. wishfully　9 *that* what; *level* aim　10 *abuses* transgressions　11 *bevel* i.e. crooked

122: 1 *tables* writing-tablet　2 *charactered* inscribed　3 *that idle rank* the leaves of the tablet (?); *remain* endure　6 *faculty . . . subsist* natural power to survive　7 *rased* blank; *his* its　8 *missed* lost　9 *retention* retainer (i.e. the tablet)　10 *tallies* anything on which scores were kept　11 *to . . . from me* i.e. to give away that tablet　12 *those tables* i.e. the tablet of the memory　13 *adjunct* aid, implement　14 *import* imply

123 No, Time, thou shalt not boast that I do change :
     Thy pyramids built up with newer might
     To me are nothing novel, nothing strange ;
  4  They are but dressings of a former sight.
     Our dates are brief, and therefore we admire
     What thou dost foist upon us that is old,
     And rather make them born to our desire
  8  Than think that we before have heard them told.
     Thy registers and thee I both defy,
     Not wond'ring at the present nor the past ;
     For thy records and what we see doth lie,
 12  Made more or less by thy continual haste.
         This I do vow, and this shall ever be :
         I will be true, despite thy scythe and thee.

In the old age black was not counted fair,                       127
Or, if it were, it bore not beauty's name ;
But now is black beauty's successive heir,
And beauty slandered with a bastard shame ;                    4
For since each hand hath put on nature's power,
Fairing the foul with art's false borrowed face,
Sweet beauty hath no name, no holy bower,
But is profaned, if not lives in disgrace.                      8
Therefore my mistress' brows are raven black,
Her eyes so suited, and they mourners seem
At such who, not born fair, no beauty lack,
Sland'ring creation with a false esteem :                      12
    Yet so they mourn, becoming of their woe,
    That every tongue says beauty should look so.

124 If my dear love were but the child of state,
     It might for Fortune's bastard be unfathered,
     As subject to Time's love or to Time's hate,
  4  Weeds among weeds, or flowers with flowers gathered.
     No, it was builded far from accident ;
     It suffers not in smiling pomp, nor falls
     Under the blow of thrallèd discontent,
  8  Whereto th' inviting time our fashion calls :
     It fears not Policy, that heretic
     Which works on leases of short-numb'red hours,
     But all alone stands hugely politic,
 12  That it nor grows with heat nor drowns with show'rs.
         To this I witness call the fools of Time,
         Which die for goodness, who have lived for crime.

125 Were't aught to me I bore the canopy,
     With my extern the outward honoring,
     Or laid great basès for eternity,
  4  Which proves more short than waste or ruining ?
     Have I not seen dwellers on form and favor
     Lose all and more by paying too much rent,
     For compound sweet forgoing simple savor,
  8  Pitiful thrivers, in their gazing spent ?
     No, let me be obsequious in thy heart,
     And take thou my oblation, poor but free,
     Which is not mixed with seconds, knows no art
 12  But mutual render, only me for thee.
         Hence, thou suborned informer ; a true soul
         When most impeached stands least in thy control.

123 : 2 *pyramids . . . might* (perhaps a topical allusion, possibly to the pyramids erected on London streets as part of the pageant welcoming King James in 1603 ; cf. Sonnet 107) 4 *dressings* i.e. imitations 5 *dates* lifespans 7 *born . . . desire* i.e. created newly to our taste 8 *told* reckoned 9 *registers* records of time 11 *records . . . see* i.e. both past and present ; *lie* misrepresent

124 : 1 *love* love of you ; *but* only ; *child of state* i.e. product of material circumstances 2 *for . . . unfathered* i.e. go unclaimed, as Fortune's bastard 5 *accident* chance occurrence 7 *thrallèd* oppressed 8 *Whereto . . . calls* to which condition our times invite us (?) 9 *Policy, that heretic* i.e. false practicality 10 *on . . . hours* i.e. on short-term leases 11 *all . . . politic* i.e. only love is truly practical 12 *That it nor* since it neither 13 *fools* playthings 14 *Which . . . crime* i.e. eleventh-hour repenters (often dubiously associated with various Catholic or other martyrs of the time)

125 : 1 *Were't aught* would it be anything ; *canopy* i.e. the covering with which the persons of the great are honored 2 *With . . . honoring* i.e. externally honoring the external 3 *bases* foundations (of monuments) 5 *dwellers on* i.e. those who dwell upon or overvalue (with pun on 'tenants') 8 *Pitiful thrivers* i.e. those who thrive pitifully since their gains are empty ; *in . . . spent* i.e. starved by mere looking 9 *be obsequious* have my devotion recognized 10 *oblation* offering 11 *seconds* i.e. second-best, inferior ; *art* artifice 12 *mutual . . . thee* i.e. surrender of my true self for your true self 13 *suborned informer* false witness 14 *impeached* accused

126 : 2 *glass* mirror ; *hour* hourglass 3 *by waning grown* i.e. increased in loveliness with the passing of time ; *show'st* i.e. show in contrast 5 *wrack* wreckage, ruin 9 *minion* darling 11 *audit* final reckoning ; *answered* paid 12 *quietus* settlement ; *render* surrender

Number 126 is exceptional among the sonnets, since it is a poem of twelve lines rhyming in pairs.

127 : 1 *old* former ; *black* i.e. brunette (equated with ugliness) ; *fair* beautiful (with play on 'blonde') 3 *successive heir* heir in line of succession 4 *slandered . . . shame* i.e. declared illegitimate 5 *put* taken 6 *Fairing* beautifying ; *art's . . . face* i.e. cosmetics 7 *Sweet beauty* i.e. natural blonde beauty ; *holy bower* i.e. shrine 8 *if . . . disgrace* (the sense seems to be that blonde beauty is so habitually enhanced or simulated with cosmetics that it is discredited in its natural form) 10 *so suited* i.e. also black 11 *At* for ; *no beauty lack* i.e. nevertheless possess the appearance of beauty 12 *Sland'ring . . . esteem* i.e. misrepresenting the natural process with counterfeit value 13 *becoming of* gracing

126 O thou, my lovely boy, who in thy power
     Dost hold Time's fickle glass, his sickle hour ;
     Who hast by waning grown, and therein show'st
  4  Thy lovers withering as thy sweet self grow'st ;
     If Nature, sovereign mistress over wrack,
     As thou goest onwards, still will pluck thee back,
     She keeps thee to this purpose, that her skill
  8  May Time disgrace and wretched minutes kill.
     Yet fear her, O thou minion of her pleasure !
     She may detain, but not still keep, her treasure ;
     Her audit, though delayed, answered must be,
 12  And her quietus is to render thee.

28 How oft, when thou, my music, music play'st
    Upon that blessèd wood whose motion sounds
    With thy sweet fingers when thou gently sway'st
4 The wiry concord that mine ear confounds,
    Do I envy those jacks that nimble leap
    To kiss the tender inward of thy hand,
    Whilst my poor lips, which should that harvest reap,
8 At the wood's boldness by thee blushing stand.
    To be so tickled they would change their state
    And situation with those dancing chips
    O'er whom thy fingers walk with gentle gait,
12 Making dead wood more blest than living lips.
      Since saucy jacks so happy are in this,
      Give them thy fingers, me thy lips to kiss.

Th' expense of spirit in a waste of shame    129
Is lust in action; and, till action, lust
Is perjured, murd'rous, bloody, full of blame,
Savage, extreme, rude, cruel, not to trust;    4
Enjoyed no sooner but despisèd straight;
Past reason hunted, and no sooner had,
Past reason hated as a swallowed bait
On purpose laid to make the taker mad:    8
Mad in pursuit, and in possession so;
Had, having, and in quest to have, extreme;
A bliss in proof, and proved, a very woe;
Before, a joy proposed; behind, a dream.    12
    All this the world well knows; yet none knows well
    To shun the heaven that leads men to this hell.

My mistress' eyes are nothing like the sun;    130
Coral is far more red than her lips' red;
If snow be white, why then her breasts are dun;
If hairs be wires, black wires grow on her head.    4
I have seen roses damasked, red and white,
But no such roses see I in her cheeks;
And in some perfumes is there more delight
Than in the breath that from my mistress reeks.    8
I love to hear her speak; yet well I know
That music hath a far more pleasing sound:
I grant I never saw a goddess go;
My mistress, when she walks, treads on the ground.    12
    And yet, by heaven, I think my love as rare
    As any she belied with false compare.

Thou art as tyrannous, so as thou art,    131
As those whose beauties proudly make them cruel;
For well thou know'st to my dear, doting heart
Thou art the fairest and most precious jewel.    4
Yet, in good faith, some say that thee behold,
Thy face hath not the power to make love groan;
To say they err I dare not be so bold,
Although I swear it to myself alone.    8
And, to be sure that is not false I swear,
A thousand groans, but thinking on thy face,
One on another's neck, do witness bear
Thy black is fairest in my judgment's place.    12
    In nothing art thou black save in thy deeds,
    And thence this slander, as I think, proceeds.

128: 2 *wood* keys of the spinet or virginal; *motion* mechanism  3 *thou . . . sway'st* you . . . control  4 *wiry concord* harmony of strings; *confounds* i.e. makes swoon  5 *jacks* (not the keys proper, which would be touched by the finger-tips, but the levers which on some virginals touched the *tender inward* of the hand when the instrument was played or tuned)  9 *they* i.e. the lips

129: 1 *Th' expense . . . shame* i.e. the expenditure of vital power in shameful waste  2 *action* consummation  4 *rude* brutal; *to trust* to be trusted  6 *Past reason hunted* i.e. madly sought  10 *quest* pursuit; *extreme* excessive, given to extremes  11 *in proof* in testing; *proved* tested  12 *dream* delusion  14 *heaven* i.e. promise of bliss

130: 5 *damasked* mingled red and white  8 *reeks* breathes forth  11 *go* walk  14 *compare* comparison (with sun, coral, snow, etc.)

131: 1 *so . . . art* even as you are (i.e. not a recognized beauty)  3 *dear* fond  8 *Although* (1) even providing that, (2) however (humorously ambiguous: it is not made certain whether the poet does or does not agree privately with her critics)  9 *to be sure* i.e. for proof  10 *but thinking* when I only think of  11 *One . . . neck* i.e. in quick succession  12 *in . . . place* where my judgment is  13 *black* i.e. not fair, foul

132: 4 *ruth* pity  6 *becomes . . . cheeks* i.e. adorns the early-morning sky  7 *even* evening  8 *Doth* i.e. renders  9 *mourning* (1) mourning, (2) morning  10 *beseem* i.e. be seemly to  12 *suit . . . like* dress your pity alike; *every part* i.e. *heart* as well as *eyes*

Thine eyes I love, and they, as pitying me,    132
Knowing thy heart torments me with disdain,
Have put on black and loving mourners be,
Looking with pretty ruth upon my pain.    4
And truly not the morning sun of heaven
Better becomes the gray cheeks of the east,
Nor that full star that ushers in the even
Doth half that glory to the sober west,    8
As those two mourning eyes become thy face.
O, let it then as well beseem thy heart
To mourn for me, since mourning doth thee grace,
And suit thy pity like in every part.    12
    Then will I swear beauty herself is black,
    And all they foul that thy complexion lack.

133 Beshrew that heart that makes my heart to groan
For that deep wound it gives my friend and me :
Is't not enough to torture me alone,
4 But slave to slavery my sweet'st friend must be ?
Me from myself thy cruel eye hath taken,
And my next self thou harder hast engrossed ;
Of him, myself, and thee I am forsaken,
8 A torment thrice threefold thus to be crossed.
Prison my heart in thy steel bosom's ward,
But then my friend's heart let my poor heart bail ;
Whoe'er keeps me, let my heart be his guard :
12 Thou canst not then use rigor in my jail.
    And yet thou wilt ; for I, being pent in thee,
    Perforce am thine, and all that is in me.

134 So, now I have confessed that he is thine
And I myself am mortgaged to thy will,
Myself I'll forfeit, so that other mine
4 Thou wilt restore to be my comfort still :
But thou wilt not, nor he will not be free,
For thou art covetous, and he is kind ;
He learned but surety-like to write for me
8 Under that bond that him as fast doth bind.
The statute of thy beauty thou wilt take,
Thou usurer that put'st forth all to use,
And sue a friend came debtor for my sake ;
12 So him I lose through my unkind abuse.
    Him have I lost, thou hast both him and me ;
    He pays the whole, and yet am I not free.

135 Whoever hath her wish, thou hast thy Will,
And Will to boot, and Will in overplus.
More than enough am I that vex thee still,
4 To thy sweet will making addition thus.
Wilt thou, whose will is large and spacious,
Not once vouchsafe to hide my will in thine ?
Shall will in others seem right gracious,
8 And in my will no fair acceptance shine ?
The sea, all water, yet receives rain still
And in abundance addeth to his store ;
So thou, being rich in Will, add to thy Will
12 One will of mine to make thy large Will more.
    Let no unkind, no fair beseechers kill ;
    Think all but one, and me in that one Will.

136 If thy soul check thee that I come so near,
Swear to thy blind soul that I was thy Will,
And will, thy soul knows, is admitted there :
4 Thus far for love my love-suit, sweet, fulfil.
Will will fulfil the treasure of thy love
Ay, fill it full with wills, and my will one.
In things of great receipt with ease we prove
8 Among a number one is reckoned none.
Then in the number let me pass untold,
Though in thy store's account I one must be ;
For nothing hold me, so it please thee hold
12 That nothing me, a something, sweet, to thee.
    Make but my name thy love, and love that still,
    And then thou lovest me, for my name is Will.

Thou blind fool, Love, what dost thou to mine eyes    13
That they behold and see not what they see ?
They know what beauty is, see where it lies,
Yet what the best is take the worst to be.    4
If eyes, corrupt by over-partial looks,
Be anchored in the bay where all men ride,
Why of eyes' falsehood hast thou forgèd hooks,
Whereto the judgment of my heart is tied ?    8
Why should my heart think that a several plot
Which my heart knows the wide world's common place ?
Or mine eyes seeing this, say this is not,
To put fair truth upon so foul a face ?    12
    In things right true my heart and eyes have erred,
    And to this false plague are they now transferred.

133: 1 *Beshrew* curse (mild in connotation)  2 *For* because of  4 *slave to slavery* i.e. sharer of my enslavement  5 *myself* i.e. my true self  6 *my . . . engrossed* i.e. you have placed my friend under even greater bondage  8 *crossed* afflicted  9 *ward* bondage  10 *bail* i.e. free by serving as substitute  11 *keeps* imprisons; *his guard* my friend's guardhouse  12 *rigor* cruelty; *jail* i.e. heart which holds the friend  13 *pent* pent up

134: 2 *mortgaged* held as security; *will* (1) purpose, (2) carnal desire  3 *other mine* i.e. alter ego  4 *restore* return; *still* always, in the future  5 *will not* (1) will not, (2) wills not to  6 *kind* compliant  7–8 *He . . . bind* i.e. it was as if to serve as security for me that he signed the bond that now binds us both (with a play on *learned . . . to write for me* in the sense of 'took my place with my mistress')  9 *take* invoke  10 *use* usury  11 *came* who became  12 *my unkind abuse* i.e. your deceiving me

135: 1 *Will* (1) one of various persons named 'Will,' including the poet and perhaps the friend and the husband, (2) carnal desire ('Will' is both capitalized and italicized in Q wherever capitalized here, in the present sonnet and Sonnet 136)  2 *to boot* i.e. in addition  3 *still* always  4 *will* (where so printed, here and in Q, the word seems usually to have the more neutral meaning of 'wish,' but it incorporates an indeterminable number of puns); *making addition thus* i.e. by adding myself  6 *vouchsafe* consent; *hide* shelter  8 *acceptance* acceptability  10 *his* its  13 *no unkind* i.e. no unkind word, no refusal; *no fair beseechers* i.e. no applicants for your favors (as punctuated, here and in Q, the line contains a double negative ; some editors omit the comma and place the 'no' in quotation marks)  14 *and me* i.e. including me

136: 1 *check* rebuke; *come so near* (1) am so candid, (2) have access to you  2 *blind* obtuse  4 *fulfil* grant  5 *fulfil the treasure* fill the treasury  6 *one* among them  7 *receipt* capacity  8 *reckoned* none not counted (cf. an adage of the time, 'one is no number')  9 *untold* uncounted  10 *thy store's account* i.e. the inventory of your numerous lovers  13 *my name* i.e. 'will,' in the sense of 'carnal desire'

137: 3 *lies* resides  5 *corrupt* corrupted  6 *Be . . . ride* i.e. have brought me to anchor in a common roadway (with *double entendre* in 'ride')  7 *falsehood* deception; *forgèd* fashioned  9 *that . . . plot* i.e. that plot a private one  10 *knows* knows to be  11 *not* not so  13 *erred* gone astray  14 *false plague* (1) plague of falseness, (2) plaguey mistress

472

8 When my love swears that she is made of truth
  I do believe her, though I know she lies,
  That she might think me some untutored youth,
4 Unlearnèd in the world's false subtilties.
  Thus vainly thinking that she thinks me young,
  Although she knows my days are past the best,
  Simply I credit her false-speaking tongue;
8 On both sides thus is simple truth suppressed.
  But wherefore says she not she is unjust?
  And wherefore say not I that I am old?
  O, love's best habit is in seeming trust,
12 And age in love loves not to have years told.
     Therefore I lie with her and she with me,
     And in our faults by lies we flattered be.

O, call not me to justify the wrong                          139
That thy unkindness lays upon my heart;
Wound me not with thine eye but with thy tongue;
Use power with power, and slay me not by art.               4
Tell me thou lov'st elsewhere; but in my sight,
Dear heart, forbear to glance thine eye aside;
What need'st thou wound with cunning when thy might
Is more than my o'erpressed defense can bide?               8
Let me excuse thee: ah, my love well knows
Her pretty looks have been mine enemies;
And therefore from my face she turns my foes,
That they elsewhere might dart their injuries:              12
   Yet do not so; but since I am near slain,
   Kill me outright with looks and rid my pain.

Be wise as thou art cruel: do not press                     140
My tongue-tied patience with too much disdain,
Lest sorrow lend me words, and words express
The manner of my pity-wanting pain.                         4
If I might teach thee wit, better it were,
Though not to love, yet, love, to tell me so;
As testy sick men, when their deaths be near,
No news but health from their physicians know.              8
For if I should despair, I should grow mad,
And in my madness might speak ill of thee:
Now this ill-wresting world is grown so bad
Mad slanderers by mad ears believèd be.                     12
   That I may not be so, nor thou belied,
   Bear thine eyes straight, though thy proud heart go wide.

138: 1 *truth* fidelity  2 *believe* seem to believe  5 *vainly thinking* i.e. acting as if I thought  7 *Simply* pretending to be simple; *credit* give credence to  9 *unjust* unfaithful  11 *habit* dress, guise; *seeming trust* apparent fidelity  12 *told* counted  13 *lie with* i.e. lie to (with *double entendre*)

In the version of the above sonnet printed in *The Passionate Pilgrim* (1st ed. 1599) the following variants appear:  4 *Unlearnèd* Unskillful *subtilties* forgeries  6 *she knows my days are* I know my years be  7 *Simply I* I smiling  8 *On both sides thus is simple truth suppressed* Outfacing faults in love, with love's ill rest  9 *not she is unjust* my love that she is young  11 *habit is in seeming trust* habit's in a soothing tongue  12 *t'* to (the reading here adopted)  13 *I . . . her . . . she* I'll . . . love . . . love  14 *And in our faults by lies we flattered be* Since that our faults in love thus smothered be

139: 1 *call* call on, ask  2 *unkindness* i.e. infidelity  3 *not . . . tongue* i.e. not with roving looks but with actual words  4 *Use . . . power* i.e. use your power directly; *art* artifice  5 *but* but while  8 *o'erpressed* i.e. attacked beyond its power to withstand; *bide* stand  9 *excuse thee* i.e. excuse you thus  11 *foes* i.e. the *pretty looks*  14 *rid* dispatch

140: 1 *press* oppress  4 *manner* nature; *pity-wanting* unpitied  5 *wit* wisdom  6 *so* i.e. that you do love me  7 *testy* peevish  8 *know* i.e. hear  11 *ill-wresting* i.e. that wrests things to an evil sense  13 *so* i.e. a 'mad slanderer'  14 *wide* astray

141: 4 *Who . . . view* i.e. which in spite of what is seen  6 *Nor . . . prone* i.e. nor does the delicate sense of feeling incline toward contact with you  8 *sensual feast* feast of the senses  9 *But* but neither; *five wits* (the mental faculties, such as intelligence, imagination, memory, etc.)  11 *Who . . . man* i.e. which leaves ungoverned the outer man (i.e. the heart, which should be monarch of the body, has abdicated to become another's heart's slave)  13 *Only . . . gain* i.e. one thing certain, my suffering is to my advantage to the following extent  14 *That . . . pain* i.e. the sin is its own punishment

142: 2 *Hate . . . loving* i.e. hate of the adulterous character of my love  4 *it* i.e. my state  6 *scarlet ornaments* i.e. the lips (here equated with the seals of red wax authenticating documents)  7 *mine* i.e. mine have  8 *Robbed . . . rents* i.e. and stolen from wives the due of the marriage bed  9 *Be it lawful* i.e. consider it lawful that  12 *Thy . . . be* i.e. your pity will make you deserving of pity  13 *hide* withhold

In faith, I do not love thee with mine eyes,                141
For they in thee a thousand errors note;
But 'tis my heart that loves what they despise,
Who in despite of view is pleased to dote.                  4
Nor are mine ears with thy tongue's tune delighted,
Nor tender feeling to base touches prone,
Nor taste, nor smell, desire to be invited
To any sensual feast with thee alone;                       8
But my five wits nor my five senses can
Dissuade one foolish heart from serving thee,
Who leaves unswayed the likeness of a man,
Thy proud heart's slave and vassal wretch to be:           12
   Only my plague thus far I count my gain,
   That she that makes me sin awards me pain.

Love is my sin, and thy dear virtue hate,                   142
Hate of my sin, grounded on sinful loving.
O, but with mine compare thou thine own state,
And thou shalt find it merits not reproving;               4
Or if it do, not from those lips of thine,
That have profaned their scarlet ornaments
And sealed false bonds of love as oft as mine,
Robbed others' beds' revenues of their rents.              8
Be it lawful I love thee as thou lov'st those
Whom thine eyes woo as mine importune thee:
Root pity in thy heart, that, when it grows,
Thy pity may deserve to pitied be.                          12
   If thou dost seek to have what thou dost hide,
   By self-example mayst thou be denied.

143 Lo, as a careful housewife runs to catch
    One of her feathered creatures broke away,
    Sets down her babe, and makes all swift dispatch
4 In pursuit of the thing she would have stay;
    Whilst her neglected child holds her in chase,
    Cries to catch her whose busy care is bent
    To follow that which flies before her face,
8 Not prizing her poor infant's discontent :
    So runn'st thou after that which flies from thee,
    Whilst I, thy babe, chase thee afar behind ;
    But if thou catch thy hope, turn back to me
12 And play the mother's part, kiss me, be kind.
      So will I pray that thou mayst have thy Will,
      If thou turn back and my loud crying still.

My love is as a fever, longing still     1.
For that which longer nurseth the disease,
Feeding on that which doth preserve the ill,
Th' uncertain sickly appetite to please.    4
My reason, the physician to my love,
Angry that his prescriptions are not kept,
Hath left me, and I desperate now approve
Desire is death, which physic did except.    8
Past cure I am, now reason is past care,
And frantic-mad with evermore unrest ;
My thoughts and my discourse as madmen's are,
At randon from the truth vainly expressed :  12
    For I have sworn thee fair, and thought thee bright,
    Who art as black as hell, as dark as night.

144 Two loves I have, of comfort and despair,
    Which like two spirits do suggest me still :
    The better angel is a man right fair,
4 The worser spirit a woman colored ill.
    To win me soon to hell, my female evil
    Tempteth my better angel from my side,
    And would corrupt my saint to be a devil,
8 Wooing his purity with her foul pride.
    And whether that my angel be turned fiend
    Suspect I may, yet not directly tell ;
    But being both from me, both to each friend,
12 I guess one angel in another's hell.
      Yet this shall I ne'er know, but live in doubt,
      Till my bad angel fire my good one out.

O me, what eyes hath Love put in my head,  1.
Which have no correspondence with true sight ;
Or, if they have, where is my judgment fled,
That censures falsely what they see aright ?  4
If that be fair whereon my false eyes dote,
What means the world to say it is not so ?
If it be not, then love doth well denote
Love's eye is not so true as all men's no.  8
How can it ? O, how can Love's eye be true,
That is so vexed with watching and with tears ?
No marvel then though I mistake my view :
The sun itself sees not till heaven clears.  12
    O cunning Love, with tears thou keep'st me blind,
    Lest eyes well-seeing thy foul faults should find.

145 Those lips that Love's own hand did make
    Breathed forth the sound that said 'I hate'
    To me that languished for her sake ;
4 But when she saw my woeful state,
    Straight in her heart did mercy come,
    Chiding that tongue that ever sweet
    Was used in giving gentle doom,
8 And taught it thus anew to greet :
    'I hate' she altered with an end
    That followed it as gentle day
    Doth follow night, who, like a fiend,
12 From heaven to hell is flown away.
      'I hate' from hate away she threw,
      And saved my life, saying 'not you.'

**143**: 3 *dispatch* haste  5 *holds . . . chase* i.e. chases her in turn  8 *prizing* considering important  11 *hope* hoped-for object  13 *Will* (capitalized and italicized in Q; cf. Sonnets 135 and 136)

**144**: 1 *comfort and despair* i.e. mercy and despair (in Christian theology instrumental respectively in bringing the soul to salvation and damnation)  2 *suggest me still* always prompt me  4 *colored ill* i.e. dark  5 *evil* evil angel  8 *pride* sexual heat  11 *each* each other  12 *in another's hell* (a double entendre)  14 *fire . . . out* i.e. infect with venereal disease

In the version of the above sonnet printed in *The Passionate Pilgrim* (1st ed. 1599) the following variants appear : 2 *Which* That  3 *The* My  4 *The* My  6 *sight* side (the reading here adopted)  8 *foul* fair  9 *find* fiend (the reading here adopted)  11 *But . . . from* For . . . to  13 *Yet this shall I ne'er* The truth I shall not

**145**: 7 *doom* sentence, judgment  8 *greet* i.e. accost me

The authenticity of this sonnet, in tetrameters and rudimentary diction, has been questioned, with considerable show of reason ; in any case, it is not in context with the adjacent sonnets.

146 Poor soul, the center of my sinful earth,
    [Fooled by] these rebel pow'rs that thee array,
    Why dost thou pine within and suffer dearth,
4 Painting thy outward walls so costly gay ?
    Why so large cost, having so short a lease,
    Dost thou upon thy fading mansion spend ?
    Shall worms, inheritors of this excess,
8 Eat up thy charge ? Is this thy body's end ?
    Then, soul, live thou upon thy servant's loss,
    And let that pine to aggravate thy store ;
    Buy terms divine in selling hours of dross ;
12 Within be fed, without be rich no more :
      So shalt thou feed on Death, that feeds on men,
      And Death once dead, there's no more dying then.

**146**: 1 *earth* i.e. body  2 *Fooled by* (Malone's conjecture ; Q repeats 'My sinful earth') ; *rebel pow'rs* rebellious flesh ; *array* dress, enclose  4 *Painting* i.e. while ornamenting  5 *cost* sums  8 *charge* i.e. the costly body  9 *servant's* body's  10 *aggravate* increase  11 *terms divine* immortality in heaven ; *hours of dross* wasteful hours

**147**: 1 *still* always  2 *longer nurseth* prolongs  4 *uncertain* fickle  6 *kept* followed  7 *approve* i.e. prove by my experience that  8 *Desire . . . except* i.e. desire, which rejected reason's medicine, proves fatal  12 *At randon* at random, in deviation

**148**: 4 *censures* judges  7 *denote* indicate  8 *Love's eye* i.e. Love's 'ay' (punning with *men's no*)  10 *vexed* afflicted ; *watching* lying awake  11 *my view* i.e. what I see  14 *find* discover

9 Canst thou, O cruel, say I love thee not
 When I against myself with thee partake?
 Do I not think on thee when I forgot
4 Am of myself, all tyrant for thy sake?
 Who hateth thee that I do call my friend?
 On whom frown'st thou that I do fawn upon?
 Nay, if thou lour'st on me, do I not spend
8 Revenge upon myself with present moan?
 What merit do I in myself respect
 That is so proud thy service to despise,
 When all my best doth worship thy defect,
12 Commanded by the motion of thine eyes?
  But, love, hate on, for now I know thy mind;
  Those that can see thou lov'st, and I am blind.

0 O, from what pow'r hast thou this pow'rful might
 With insufficiency my heart to sway?
 To make me give the lie to my true sight
4 And swear that brightness doth not grace the day?
 Whence hast thou this becoming of things ill,
 That in the very refuse of thy deeds
 There is such strength and warrantise of skill
8 That in my mind thy worst all best exceeds?
 Who taught thee how to make me love thee more,
 The more I hear and see just cause of hate?
 O, though I love what others do abhor,
12 With others thou shouldst not abhor my state:
  If thy unworthiness raised love in me,
  More worthy I to be beloved of thee.

149: 2 *partake* join 3–4 *I forgot . . . myself* i.e. I forget myself 4 *all tyrant* complete self-oppressor 7 *thou lour'st* you frown 8 *present moan* immediate suffering 10 *thy . . . despise* i.e. as to despise serving you 11 *defect* insufficiency (cf. Sonnet 150, l. 2) 14 *Those . . . lov'st* i.e. you love those who can see

150: 2 *sway* rule 4 *that . . . day* (the opposite, that darkness graces the day, is implied) 5 *becoming . . . ill* i.e. power to lend grace to evil things 6 *very . . . deeds* most worthless of your actions 7 *warrantise of skill* warranty of competence 12 *state* i.e. bemused condition

151: 1 *conscience* consciousness, awareness 3 *cheater* betrayer; *urge . . . amiss* i.e. do not press charges against me 8 *stays* awaits; *reason* reasoning 9 *rising* revolting (with *double entendre*) 10 *pride* i.e. heat 13 *want of conscience* lack of awareness

152: 1 *am forsworn* i.e. have violated my marriage vows 3 *bed-vow* marriage vows; *new faith torn* i.e. a new contract of fidelity torn up 4 *bearing* i.e. professing 7 *but to misuse* i.e. merely to misrepresent 11 *enlighten* brighten; *gave . . . blindness* i.e. made the eyes swear to things they did not see 12 *swear against* i.e. falsely deny 13 *eye* eyes (with a pun on *I*, cf. ll. 11–12)

153: 1 *brand* torch 2 *Dian* Diana, goddess of chastity; *advantage* opportunity 4 *of that ground* i.e. nearby 6 *dateless* eternal; *still* always 7 *grew* became; *yet* to this day 10 *for . . . would* as an experiment had to 11 *withal* therefrom 12 *distempered* diseased

154: 5 *votary* votaress (nymph of Diana) 7 *general* commander (Cupid) 9 *by* nearby 12 *thrall* slave

The parts of Sonnets 153 and 154 having to do with the creation of a hot bath by means of the quenching of Cupid's torch are variations upon a theme treated in various earlier epigrams, including one in fifth-century Greek by Marianus Scholasticus. These sonnets seem detached from the rest of the sequence, and their authenticity has been questioned.

Love is too young to know what conscience is;  151
Yet who knows not conscience is born of love?
Then, gentle cheater, urge not my amiss,
Lest guilty of my faults thy sweet self prove.  4
For, thou betraying me, I do betray
My nobler part to my gross body's treason;
My soul doth tell my body that he may
Triumph in love; flesh stays no farther reason,  8
But, rising at thy name, doth point out thee
As his triumphant prize. Proud of this pride,
He is contented thy poor drudge to be,
To stand in thy affairs, fall by thy side.  12
 No want of conscience hold it that I call
 Her 'love' for whose dear love I rise and fall.

In loving thee thou know'st I am forsworn,  152
But thou art twice forsworn, to me love swearing;
In act thy bed-vow broke, and new faith torn
In vowing new hate after new love bearing.  4
But why of two oaths' breach do I accuse thee
When I break twenty? I am perjured most,
For all my vows are oaths but to misuse thee,
And all my honest faith in thee is lost;  8
For I have sworn deep oaths of thy deep kindness,
Oaths of thy love, thy truth, thy constancy;
And, to enlighten thee, gave eyes to blindness,
Or made them swear against the thing they see;  12
 For I have sworn thee fair: more perjured eye,
 To swear against the truth so foul a lie.

Cupid laid by his brand and fell asleep:  153
A maid of Dian's this advantage found
And his love-kindling fire did quickly steep
In a cold valley-fountain of that ground;  4
Which borrowed from this holy fire of Love
A dateless lively heat, still to endure,
And grew a seething bath, which yet men prove
Against strange maladies a sovereign cure.  8
But at my mistress' eye Love's brand new-fired,
The boy for trial needs would touch my breast;
I, sick withal, the help of bath desired
And thither hied, a sad distempered guest,  12
 But found no cure: the bath for my help lies
 Where Cupid got new fire, my mistress' eyes.

The little Love-god, lying once asleep,  154
Laid by his side his heart-inflaming brand,
Whilst many nymphs that vowed chaste life to keep
Came tripping by; but in her maiden hand  4
The fairest votary took up that fire
Which many legions of true hearts had warmed;
And so the general of hot desire
Was, sleeping, by a virgin hand disarmed.  8
This brand she quenchèd in a cool well by,
Which from Love's fire took heat perpetual,
Growing a bath and healthful remedy
For men diseased; but I, my mistress' thrall,  12
 Came there for cure, and this by that I prove:
 Love's fire heats water, water cools not love.

# INDEX OF FIRST LINES

# INDEX OF FIRST LINES